COLLINS MILESTONES IN AUSTRALIAN HISTORY

1788 to the Present

COMPILED BY ROBIN BROWN
EDITED BY RICHARD APPLETON
FOREWORD BY MANNING CLARK

G.K().HALL &CO.
70 LINCOLN STREET, BOSTON, MASS.

© Robin Brown 1986

First published in the United States of America by G.K. Hall and Co.,
70 Lincoln Street, Boston, MA 02111 U.S.A.
Published simultaneously in Australia by William Collins Pty Ltd, GPO Box 476, Sydney, Australia, NSW 2001.

Typeset by Asco Trade Typesetting Ltd, Hong Kong
Printed and bound by Dai Nippon Printing Co., Hong Kong

Library of Congress Cataloguing-in-Publication Data

Brown, Robin
   COLLINS: MILESTONES IN AUSTRALIAN HISTORY

   1. Australia—History—Chronology. I. Appleton, Richard. II. Title.
DU110.B76   1986   994'002'02   86-4664
ISBN 0-8161-8820-3

All rights reserved. No part of this publication may be reproduced, stored in a retrieval system, or transmitted, in any form, or by any means, electronic, mechanical, photocopying, recording or otherwise, without the prior permission of the publishers.

Acknowledgements

I am deeply grateful to a number of people for their assistance in the preparation of this work. For their relentless support in all aspects of the work I thank Colin H. Brown and Robert A. Swan. The time they spent meticulously unravelling problems and offering advice is deeply appreciated. I also thank Richard K. Netzel and the late Dr. Robert G. Wyllie for their part in examining the manuscript.

Throughout the lengthy preparation of this work I am indebted to my wife Mary for her constant support and encouragement in all manner of ways.

My sincere thanks go to the Aldersey family of Penola, South Australia, Philip J. Browne, Diana Brown, Mary Joan Cain, Roslyn A. Cain, Francis M. Elliott, and Ronald and Louise Levy for their much valued help at various stages of the work.

I would have been lost without the dedicated effort afforded by Lynette F. Archibald in typing the manuscript and most of the index and would like to thank Anne M. Cafferty for her assistance in typing the index. I also acknowledge with thanks the many organizations and institutions throughout Australia which have offered valuable assistance.

Finally, I would like to thank Dick Appleton for his professional expertise in dealing with the many complexities associated with a vast work of this kind.

Robin Brown

Foreword

The compiler of this work has described in the Preface the reasons for making this collection of historical information. I welcome this work as another aid and guide for that ever-increasing number of people taking an interest in Australian history. All of us need not only books which tell us the story but books which give us the facts. We are all presumably anxious to increase in wisdom and understanding. We are all also driven by curiosity to find out more and more about the world in which we live. But we need to get our facts straight. We all need books of information to guide us through the labyrinth of the past. That is why I recommend this book to that army of workers burrowing around in the past. It can take a place on the desk or on the bookshelf beside the dictionary, the Thesaurus, the encyclopaedia and other books of reference. Like a good dictionary it is an expander of the mind. It is at once a source of entertainment and a store of knowledge. Robin Brown has performed a useful service.

Manning Clark

Preface

Most of us are interested in our past and at least some of the many influences which have made Australia the nation it is today. It is surprising that so far few serious attempts have been made to produce, in one handy volume, a comprehensive chronological record of the major events, ideas, influences and personalities which have shaped our heritage. Anyone with an interest in the past is at times uncertain as to exactly what important happenings have influenced various parts of the Australian experience. In the absence of such a precise record, our past often appears as a blurred series of events, with no point or purpose, but which somehow make up the overall picture of our history.

Milestones in Australian History endeavours to remove that confusion by drawing together a huge quantity of important and interesting factual material from widely scattered sources, and presenting it simply and logically so that anyone may locate basic facts easily. It is a guide to the significant events and achievements in every walk of Australian life over the period 1788 to the present, a kind of 'ready reckoner' of Australian heritage, carefully arranged to provide quick accurate answers to those 'who', 'what', 'when' and 'where' questions we all ask at times.

The book is not just a useful reference for students, professionals, offices and libraries. It is also designed for use in the busy household where questions about our past arise repeatedly but where there is insufficient time to find the answers. *Milestones* has the unique advantage of being set out in such a way as to put *all* information concerning a particular year together, thus enabling any event to be viewed within the framework of the general state of Australia at that time.

Because of the diversity of information included, each entry is pertinent but necessarily brief. The book is not designed to provide the depth of guidance found in encyclopaedic works, but rather, to present a concise factual statement which can be used as a guide to further exploration of a subject.

The research process used required an in-depth examination of a wide range of Australian archives. Although the final selection of material was not always an easy task, an attempt has been made to maintain a proper balance. Any number of authors undertaking the same task would have included most of the same information but in a work of this nature there will always be some differences of opinion over the inclusion of certain entries. In the final selection and after consultation with the editor the responsibility of inclusion or omission has rested with the author. The number of common errors located in existing published works has at times been alarming, and every effort has been made to prevent their repetition in this work. This has often meant going to primary sources to verify facts and resolve inconsistencies. But in a work of this magnitude it is inevitable that some mistakes will occur. Readers are invited to inform the publisher of any entries which they can show to be misleading or inaccurate, and to suggest any new entries which they feel should be included in future editions.

In some cases items might well have appeared in sections other than the ones in which they have been placed. Any problems raised by the choice of sections and any remaining doubts can be easily resolved by use of the index.

Entries are presented under six subject headings:

A **History, Politics, Economics, Law** Where relevant this section begins with a subsection titled 'Government', which includes Governors General, Prime Ministers, Premiers and Colonial Administrators, their offices and dates of office.

B **Science, Technology, Transport, Discovery**

C **Arts** This section is subdivided into Literature; Music, Dance; Drama, Theatre, Film; Fine Arts; and Architecture.

D **Religion, Learning**

E **Sport** This section contains a comprehensive record of all Australian sport.

F **Historia Dignum** (Memorable Events) This section contains a wide range of subject matter which must be included, but which does not fit comfortably into any of the other sections. It also includes a subsection titled 'Communities' which lists when most Australian towns were established as communities, that is when a group of people began living as a community, out of which grew a town. Unless indicated, care has been taken not to confuse such 'communities' with the pioneering or opening up of areas by isolated farmers, prospectors and the like, or with towns when officially gazetted, proclaimed, planned or named. In many cases, a community was established under a different name to that which is now used. In this work, towns are generally listed under their current names even though they may have been established as communities with different names.

Where applicable each section contains a Births & Deaths list. This list provides the full name, and any other if appropriate, the person's status, and birth (represented by b.) and/or death (represented by d.) information. Where births (b.) are given, the date of the death usually follows in parenthesis but is not listed separately under the actual year of death.

The body of information presented in this volume is supported by a detailed index. Entries for persons, places, subjects, titles of works and so on are listed in alphabetical sequence. All index entries refer readers to a year and a section, rather than to a page number. This comprehensive, cross-referenced index is designed to guide users quickly and easily, to the textual matter. For maximum immediate benefit users are advised to look up both individual and subject entries.

Please note that *Milestones in Australian History* begins in 1788 with the arrival of the First Fleet. No attempt has been made to list in this book, the major events of our history prior to this time.

The nomadic existence of Aboriginal communities and absence of written records makes it difficult to locate reliable and specific dates, and since *Milestones in Australian History* is a book of facts as they have been recorded, it is inappropriate to venture into the inconclusive and uncertain eras preceding first white settlement.

Similarly, no attempt has been made to examine the history of white man in the country prior to 1788. The chronicles of early explorers and even Captain Cook's proclamation of the land in 1770 have been omitted. Any selection of these entries without mention of Aboriginal history would have presented a one-eyed viewpoint and detracted from the overall value and intention of this book.

Tasmania (Tas.) is referred to in the text as Van Diemens Land (VDL) until 1855, when it was officially proclaimed Tasmania. There are certain exceptions, as in the case of Communities listed in Section F. These are listed as Tas., on the grounds that they still exist in what is now Tasmania. Also, in the Births & Deaths sections, where a person was born before 1855 but the main event or activity for which they are known took place after 1855, then their State is listed as Tas.

Robin Brown

Collins Milestones in Australian History

1788 to the Present

A

History, Politics, Economics, Law

1788

Government

26 Jan. 1788–10 Dec. 1792, Arthur Phillip Captain-General and Governor-in-Chief NSW Colony.

18 Jan. HMS *Supply*, first ship of First Fleet to arrive, reaches Botany Bay. Capt Arthur Phillip finds Botany Bay area unsuitable for settlement. Expedition moves to Port Jackson 26 Jan. First Fleet lands 736 convicts.

26 Jan. Formal possession taken of Colony of NSW. Phillip becomes Governor of Colony, having jurisdiction over area bounded by lat. 10°37′ to lat. 43°49′S and inland to long. 135°E.

28 Jan. French ships *Astrolabe* and *Boussole*, under Jean-François de la Pérouse, enter Botany Bay. French ships are on exploratory expedition. Depart 10 Mar.

During Jan. James Smith first settler to receive govt assistance for passage to Colony.

7 Feb. Judge-Advocate David Collins officially proclaims Colony of NSW, establishing formal govt.

11 Feb. Governor Phillip convenes first Court of Criminal Judicature. (Civil Court first sits in Jul.)

15 Feb. Philip Gidley King, Superintendent and Commandant of Norfolk I., sails to settle the island to forestall occupation by any other European power. Estb. penal colony 2–8 Mar.

17 Feb. Lieut Henry Lidgbird Ball discovers Lord Howe I.

23 Apr. Governor Phillip selects site of Parramatta. Estb. Rose Hill settlement 2 Nov. (Renamed Parramatta 1791.)

29 May. Aborigines kill two convicts at Rushcutters Bay, marking first conflict with First Fleet Europeans.

During May. Richard Johnson plants first orange trees in Sydney (from Brazilian seeds).

17 Jun. First occasion on which settlement at Sydney Cove was officially called Sydney (named after Thomas Townshend, 1st Viscount Sydney).

Aug. Botanists on William Bligh's ship plant first apple trees and potatoes at Adventure Bay, VDL during stop on way to Tahiti.

2 Oct. HMS *Sirius* sets out from Port Jackson to Cape Town for provisions.

During 1788
Period of Free Grants land settlement begins.
Eucalyptus oil among first products exported.

Births & Deaths

Charles Hervey Bagot, SA settler, b. (d. 1880)
Osmond Gilles, SA pioneer, b. (d. 1866)
Frederick Goulburn, first NSW Colonial Secretary, b. (d. 1837)
Hannibal Hawkins Macarthur, NSW pioneer pastoralist, b. (d. 1861)
George Augustus Robinson, Aboriginal Protector, 'Apostle of the Blacks', b. (d. 1866)
Edward Buckley Wynyard, military officer, b. (d. 1864)

1788

B
Science, Technology, Transport, Discovery

Mar. First bricks made, at Brickfield Hill, Sydney Cove.
Oct. Colony's first bridge built, over Tank Stream at Sydney Cove.
Nov. *Government Rules* issued. First example of printing in Colony.

During 1788
William Dawes, first Colonial Astronomer, begins building observatory at Port Jackson.
William Balmain and John White conduct first post-mortems and amputations.
First hospital estb., on western side of Sydney Cove.
Disease resembling smallpox begins to break out among Aborigines.
Track cleared between Dawes Point and Government House, Sydney Cove (1 mile); first road in Colony.
Augustus Theodore Henry Alt, Surveyor-General, plans Sydney streets (200 feet wide).

Births & Deaths

William Crowther, pioneer surgeon VDL, b. (d. 1839)
Charles Frazer (or Frazier), first NSW Govt Botanist, probably b. (d. 1831)
David Lennox, bridge engineer, master mason responsible for many early colonial bridges, b. (d. 1873)
John Ovens, engineer, bridge builder, b. (d. 1825)
Henry Willey Reveley, pioneer engineer, architect WA, b. (d. 1875)
Christian Carl Ludwig Rümker, astronomer, b. (d. 1862)

C
Arts

Music, Dance

9 Feb. *The Rogue's March* becomes first named piece of music known to have been performed in Colony, at Sydney Cove.

Fine Arts

During 1788
Early colonial period of art begins, scientific recording of flora and fauna, Aborigines, growth of settlement and colonial life. (Period ends *c.* 1850.)
Unidentified 'Port Jackson Painter' arrives with First Fleet.

Births & Deaths

Henry Curzon Allport, watercolourist, probably b. (d. 1854)
Edward Hodges Baily, sculptor, b. (d. 1867)
Thomas Evans Chapman, artist, b. (d. 1864)

Architecture

15 May. James Bloodsworth designs and supervises construction of first Government House, Sydney.
During 1788
Primitive period of Colonial architecture begins. (Ends *c.* 1809.)

D
Religion, Learning

3 Feb. Rev. Richard Johnson conducts first church service in Colony, Church of England. (Conducts first Holy Communion 17 Feb.)
10 Feb. First currency lads and lasses, Aust.-born children John Matthew, Joseph Bellamy and Elizabeth Bacon, baptized.
During 1788
About eight children of school age (between 3½ and 12 yrs) in Colony.
Tory–Anglican tradition of elementary teaching established. (Dominates education until *c.* 1831.)

Births & Deaths

William Grant Broughton, first Anglican bishop of Aust., 1836, b. (d. 1853)
Lancelot Edward Threlkeld, Congregational missionary, among first to study Aboriginal language, b. (d. 1859)
John Burdett Wittenoom, first WA chaplain, probably b. (d. 1855)

F
Historia Dignum

Population
Estimated total white, 1024.
Estimated Aboriginal, 250,000–300,000.

6 Mar. James Barrett, 17 years old, first person in Colony executed (for robbery conviction).
During Jul. First earthquake shock recorded in NSW.
During 1788
Andrew White becomes first Aboriginal adopted by white settler.
Samuel Barsby receives first flogging in Colony, 150 lashes for striking a guard.
First burial ground estb., on ridge west of Lower George St, Sydney.
Governor Phillip restricts felling of trees around Tank Stream, Sydney: first conservation measure.

Communities
Kingston, Norfolk I., NSW, estb.
Sydney, NSW, estb.
Parramatta, NSW, estb. as Rose Hill

1789

A
History, Politics, Economics, Law

28 Apr. Crew of HMS *Bounty* mutiny near Tonga against Capt William Bligh.
8 May. Supply ship HMS *Sirius* returns Sydney from Cape Colony with provisions.
8 Jun. Francis Grose appointed officer in charge NSW Corps in England.
During Jun. Governor Phillip discovers mouth of Hawkesbury R., NSW.
Watkin Tench leads expedition to Hawkesbury R., NSW. Discovers Nepean R., Blue Mts, 26 Jun., opening way to fertile alluvial flats for settlement.
8 Aug. First police force in Colony; named Nightwatch and consisting of 12 men selected from well-behaved convicts, estb. to protect public property.
21 Nov. James Ruse begins rural experiment farm at Rose Hill (Parramatta). Edward Dodd supervises farm. (First successful wheat harvest in Dec.)
25 Nov. Aborigines Bennelong, and later Yemmerrawannie, captured to provide information on Aboriginal customs and on surrounding districts.
During Nov. Food rations reduced to cope with severe shortages.
23 Dec. *Guardian*, storeship bringing rations from England, founders on iceberg near Cape of Good Hope, losing most of cargo.
During Dec. William Dawes begins first, but unsuccessful, attempt to cross Blue Mts, NSW.
Governor Phillip instructed to make land grants to free settlers and marines.
During 1789
Governor Phillip introduces Assignment System, allocating convicts to private employers to promote agriculture.
Capt Dillon and J. H. Cox survey south coast of VDL.
John Hayes explores Derwent R., VDL.

Birth & Deaths

George Fife Angas, SA founder, philanthropist, b. (d. 1879)
John Beaumont, first VDL postmaster, b. (d. 1872)
William Bland, NSW emancipist politician, medical practitioner, b. (d. 1868)
Anthony Hordern, drapery businessman, b. (d. 1869)
Sir Edward Macarthur, Vic. Lieut-Governor, b. (d. 1872)
Charles Swanston, merchant, pioneer banker, b. (d. 1850)

B
Science, Technology, Transport, Discovery

6 Oct. *Rose Hill Packet*, first boat built in Colony on mainland, launched in Sydney.
During 1789
James Underwood opens first privately owned shipyard in Colony.

C
Arts

Literature

During 1789
Watkin Tench's *Narrative of the Expedition to Botany Bay* published in London.

Drama, Theatre

4 Jun. First theatrical performance, *The Recruiting Officer* by George Farquhar, performed by convicts in honour of King George III's birthday.

Fine Arts

Births & Deaths
Pietro Tenerani, sculptor, b. (d. 1869)

D
Religion, Learning

During 1789
Isabella Rosson conducts first school in Sydney, probably Colony's first teacher.

1789

E
Sport

During 1789
First handball played in Sydney.

F
Historia Dignum

8 Jan. First child born on Norfolk I.; named Norfolk.
Mar. Six marines hanged Sydney for stealing food.
Apr. Epidemic resembling smallpox spreads widely, claiming many Aboriginal lives.
During 1789
Drought begins in NSW. (Ends 1791.)

A

History, Politics, Economics, Law

28 Feb. John Irving becomes first male convict emancipated.
19 Mar. Supply ship HMS *Sirius* wrecked on Norfolk I. reef while en route to pick up supplies. In Apr. HMS *Supply* repaired and sent to Batavia (Indonesia) for supplies. (Returns Sydney 19 Oct.)
During Mar. Robert Ross, NSW Lieut-Governor, takes 280 convicts and marines to Norfolk I.
Philip Gidley King sent to London to report on difficulties of settlement.
3 Jun. *Lady Juliana*, first ship of Second Fleet, arrives Port Jackson. Fleet carries 980 convicts, supplies and first detachment of NSW Corps (Rum Corps).
During Jun. First shop opens in Sydney. (First brick-built shop opens Jul.)
Sep. Aborigine, Willemering, spears Governor Phillip in shoulder near Manly, Sydney.
17 Dec. Dutch trading vessel *Waaksamheydt* arrives in Sydney with food supplies.
During 1790
Governor Phillip introduces ticket of leave system, enabling some convicts to work for wages and choose masters.
William Dawes plans Parramatta township, second settlement in Aust.
Henry Lidgbird Ball becomes first man to circumnavigate continent, in storeship *Supply*.
Serious famine threatens Colony.

Births & Deaths

Joseph Anderson, military officer, b. (d. 1877)
Saxe Bannister, first NSW Attorney-General, b. (d. 1877)
Andrew Bent, convict, pioneer printer, b. (d. 1851)
Jules d'Urville Dumont, French explorer, b. (d. 1842)
James Hurtle Fisher, SA politician, lawyer, b. (d. 1875)
Foster Fyans, commandant Moreton Bay settlement (Brisbane), b. (d. 1870)
William Henry Hamilton, pioneer bank manager, probably b. (d. 1870)
Henry Hellyer, VDL surveyor, b. (d. 1832)
John Knatchbull, naval officer convict, probably b. (d. 1844)
Joshua John Moore, pioneer Canberra district, b. (d. 1864)
Sir William Edward Parry, Australian Agricultural Co. Commissioner, b. (d. 1855)

B

Science, Technology, Transport, Discovery

May. First salt in Colony made, from seawater at Dawe's Battery, Sydney.

Births & Deaths

Henry Grattan Douglass, NSW surgeon, magistrate, b. (d. 1865)
James Scott, pioneer physician, b. (d. 1837)

1790

1790

C

Arts

Literature

During 1790. John White's *Journal of a Voyage to New South Wales* published in London.

Music, Dance

During 1790
First piano arrives in Sydney.

Births & Deaths
Isaac Nathan, music pioneer, father of Aust. music, b. (d. 1864)

Fine Arts

Births & Deaths
Jacques Estienne Arago, French maritime artist, b. (d. 1855)
Thomas Bock, engraver, photographer, first portrait painter to work professionally in VDL, b. (d. 1857)
John McArthur, amateur painter, commandant first settlement Port Essington, NT, 1838, b. (d. 1862)

Architecture

During 1790
Old Government House, Parramatta built. First recorded public building in Colony.

D

Religion, Learning

Births & Deaths
James Clow, Presbyterian minister, b. (d. 1861)
John Joseph Therry, pioneer Catholic priest, b. (d. 1864)

F
Historia Dignum

1790

Jun. Philip Schaeffer arrives in Sydney as first free immigrant in Colony.
During 1790
NSW drought.
St John's Cemetery, Parramatta, estb. Now among oldest undisturbed cemeteries in Aust.

1791

A
History, Politics, Economics, Law

22 Feb. James Ruse receives first official land grant, becoming first self-supporting farmer in Colony.

28 Mar. Mary Bryant and eight male convicts escape from Colony in open boat. (Bryant becomes first convict to return to England.)

14 June. Rose Hill, NSW, renamed Parramatta.

7 Jul. *Mary Anne*, first ship of Third Fleet, arrives Sydney. Fleet carries 1,695 male and 68 female convicts.

Aug. Richard Bowen charts and names Jervis Bay, NSW (later ACT).

26 Sep. Philip Gidley King returns to Colony with official Territorial seal. This empowered governors to remit the term for which convicts were transported to the Colony. Henceforth governors could issue pardons.

28 Sep. George Vancouver discovers King George Sound (later Albany) and Chatham I., WA.

10 Nov. Samuel Enderby returns to Sydney from successful whaling expedition in Aust. waters, beginning whaling and sealing industry.

15 Nov. First grape vine in Colony planted, at Parramatta, NSW.

During 1791
Watkin Tench and William Dawes locate junction of Nepean and Hawkesbury rivers, NSW.

Births & Deaths

Allan Cunningham, explorer, botanist, b. (d. 1839)
Henry Edward Dodd, Governor Phillip's servant, agricultural superintendent, d.
Charles Fitzgerald, WA Governor, b. (d. 1887)
Lady Jane Franklin, publicist and wife of Sir John Franklin, b. (d. 1875)
Sir George Gipps, NSW Governor, probably b. (d. 1847)
James Kelly, explorer, seafarer, b. (d. 1859)
Phillip Parker King, explorer, among first white children b. on Norfolk I. (d. 1856)
Patrick Logan, explorer, commandant Moreton Bay settlement (Brisbane), b. (d. 1830)
Sir James Stirling, first WA Governor, b. (d. 1865)

B
Science, Technology, Transport, Discovery

Mar. Mary Bryant convict escapee party discover bituminous coal at Port Stephens, Newcastle area of Colony north of Sydney. (Other first bituminous coal discoveries: VDL 1824, Vic. 1825, Qld 1827, WA 1846, SA 1889.)

Births & Deaths

John Lee Archer, engineer, architect noted for use of neo-Gothic style, b. (d. 1852)

C
Arts

Literature

Births & Deaths

Henry Savery, convict author, b. (d. 1842)

D
Religion, Learning

During 1791
Mary Johnson conducts school at Parramatta, NSW.

Births & Deaths

John Ramsden Wollaston, first WA Church of England archdeacon, b. (d. 1856)

1791

1791

Historia Dignum

Population
Estimated total white, 2,887.

29 Aug. HMS *Pandora* wrecked on Torres Strait reef; 39 lives lost.
21 Nov. Twenty convicts escape from Sydney and attempt to reach China by land.

A

History, Politics, Economics, Law

Government
11 Dec. 1792–12 Dec. 1794, Francis Grose administered NSW Colony.

24 Feb. Second detachment NSW Corps arrives Sydney.
Apr. Joseph-Antoine D'Entrecasteaux, French explorer, surveys east coast VDL. Discovers Riviere du Nord (Derwent R.) 25 Apr.
Jul. NSW Corps charters whaling boat to South Africa for merchandise, initiating first private trading venture.
1 Nov. American vessel *Philadelphia*, first foreign trading vessel to reach Colony, arrives.
11 Dec. Governor Phillip, in broken health, leaves Colony for England with Aborigines Bennelong and Yemmerrawannie.
During Dec. Francis Grose suspends powers of civil magistrates, transferring their functions to NSW Corps. (Until 1796.)

During 1792
Three convict ships bring 610 male and 123 female convicts to Colony.
British East India Co. receives sole rights to bring convicts and supplies to Colony. (Monopoly revoked *c.* 1812.)
Elizabeth Ruse becomes first female convict in Colony to be emancipated.
Governor Phillip estb. convict-worked govt farm at Toongabbie, near Parramatta.
British Govt opens NSW to free settlers. By Dec. there are about 67 free settlers holding land grants around Port Jackson, NSW.
First land grants made to officers of NSW Corps.
William Bligh and Nathaniel Portlock chart south-east coast VDL, planting fruit and vegetables there.

Births & Deaths
Fletcher Christian, *Bounty* mutineers leader, d. (b. 1763)
Henry Dumaresq, NSW colonial official, b. (d. 1838)
John Pascoe Fawkner, Melbourne pioneer, b. (d. 1869)
Richard Hamilton, vigneron, b. (d. 1852)
Thomas Livingstone Mitchell, explorer, NSW Surveyor-General, b. (d. 1855)
John Helder Wedge, surveyor, explorer, artist, b. (d. 1872)

B

Science, Technology, Transport, Discovery

May. Marine pilots begin to guide ships from Sydney Heads into Cove.

Births & Deaths
George Barney, engineer, b. (d. 1862)
William Sharp Macleay, naturalist, b. (d. 1865)
James Mitchell, physician, industrialist, b. (d. 1869)

1792

1792

C
Arts

Literature

Births & Deaths
William Howitt, writer, b. (d. 1879)

Drama, Theatre

24 Nov. *Les Emigres aux Terres Australes*, first play about Aust., performed in Paris.

Fine Arts

During 1792
Thomas Watling, convict artist, arrives in Sydney.

D
Religion, Learning

During 1792
Rev. Richard Johnson estb. first official schools in Sydney, Parramatta and Norfolk I. NSW. (To open 1793.)

Births & Deaths
Ralph Drummond, Presbyterian clergyman, b. (d. 1872)
William Hutchins, first Anglican archdeacon VDL, 1836, b. (d. 1841)

F
Historia Dignum

1792

Population
Estimated total white, 3,120.

1793

A
History, Politics, Economics, Law

12 Feb. John Macarthur receives land grant of 100 acres near Parramatta, on which he estb. Elizabeth Farm for sheep-breeding experiments.
16 Feb. Free immigrant settlers from England arrive Sydney in *Bellona*.
Apr. John Hayes begins exploring Derwent estuary, VDL.
Sep. Officers of NSW Corps attempt unsuccessfully to cross Blue Mts, NSW.
Nov. Govt purchases and issues first wheat produced in the Colony by settlers.
During 1793
Three convict ships bring 233 male and 87 female convicts to Colony.
NSW develops strong trading links with India.

Births & Deaths
Andrew Clarke, WA Governor b. (d. 1847)
Alexander Collie, WA explorer, b. (d. 1835)
Prosper de Mestre, first American merchant in Sydney, 1818, b. (d. 1844)
Joseph-Antoine Raymond de Bruni D'Entrecasteaux, French navigator, explorer, d. (b. 1739)
William John Dumaresq, NSW official, engineer, b. (d. 1868)
William Hobson, first NZ Governor, 1839, b. (d. 1842)
David Jones, businessman, b. (d. 1873)
Henry O'Brien, NSW squatter, b. (d. 1866)
Sir John Lewes Pedder, first VDL Chief Justice, 1823, b. (d. 1859)
Thomas Peel, WA pioneer settler and Swan R. settlement promoter, b. (d. 1865)
William Charles Wentworth, explorer, NSW statesman, 'the Aust. Patriot', probably b. (d. 1872)

B
Science, Technology, Transport, Discovery

Mar. Spanish ships *Descubierta* and *Atrevida* visit Sydney during scientific expedition, depart 12 Apr.
24 Jul. Colonial vessel *Francis*, brought from England in frame, launched in Sydney.

Births & Deaths
Richard Cunningham, botanist, b. (d. 1835)
James Dunlop, astronomer, b. (d. 1848)

C

Arts

Literature

During 1793
Watkin Tench's *A Complete Account of the Settlement at Port Jackson* published in London.

Architecture

During 1793
John Macarthur builds Elizabeth Farm House, now oldest extant dwelling in Aust.

Births & Deaths

Augustus Earle, colonial portrait painter, topographical artist, b. (d. 1838)
John Alexander Gilfillan, painter, b. (d. 1864)

D

Religion, Learning

1793

18 Feb. Rev. Richard Johnson opens first official Church school in Colony. William Richardson, W. Webster and Susannah Hunt among first teachers. Stephen Barnes first headmaster.

25 Aug. Rev. Richard Johnson completes first church in Colony, a cruciform wattle and plaster structure on corner of Hunter and Castlereagh streets, Sydney. First service 25 Aug. (Destroyed by fire 1798.)

1793

F
Historia Dignum

Population
Estimated total white, 3,016.

A
History, Politics, Economics, Law

Government
12 Dec. 1794–11 Sep. 1795, William Paterson administered NSW Colony.

1 Apr. John Macarthur receives second 100-acre land grant as reward for clearing and cultivating 50 acres.

25 Oct. First Scottish Martyrs (Scottish political prisoners transported for making and publishing seditious speeches during agitation for political reform) arrive Sydney.

During 1794
George Shaw among first writers to use name 'Australia' for whole continent.

First settlements estb. on Hawkesbury R., NSW. John Hayes names Derwent R., VDL.

Henry Waterhouse buys merino sheep in South Africa for Aust.

Births & Deaths
Robert Hoddle, Vic. surveyor, b. (d. 1881)
William Lee, NSW pioneer pastoralist, probably b. (d. 1870)
Solomon Levey, emancipist financier, b. (d. 1833)
Thomas Raine, seaman, adventurer, pastoralist, probably b. (d. 1860)
Sir George Stephen, Vic. barrister, b. (d. 1879)
Robert Towns, Qld pioneer merchant, ship owner, b. (d. 1873)
Robert Wardell, barrister, editor, probably b. (d. 1834)
Aborigine, Yemmerrawannie, who sailed to England with Governor Phillip, 1792, d. England

B
Science, Technology, Transport, Discovery

During 1794
Francis Grose builds first road from Sydney to banks of Hawkesbury R., NSW.

Sydney to Parramatta road estb. First road connecting Sydney with another settlement.

1794

1794

C
Arts

Fine Arts

During 1794
Thomas Watling, emancipist artist, paints first oil painting of Sydney, *A View of Sydney Cove*.

Births & Deaths
Thomas Griffiths Wainewright, convict artist, writer, b. (d. 1847)

D
Religion, Learning

10 Mar. Rev. Samuel Marsden arrives in Sydney; opens first Parramatta church in Sep.

Births & Deaths
James Backhouse, Quaker missionary, artist, b. (d. 1869)
Thomas Hassall, pioneer Church of England minister, b. (d. 1868)
John McEncroe, Roman Catholic archdeacon, b. (d. 1868)
John Bede Polding, first Roman Catholic bishop in Aust., 1842, b. (d. 1877)
Robert William Willson, Roman Catholic prelate, b. (d. 1866)

F
Historia Dignum

1794

Communities
Windsor, NSW, first settled.

1795

A
History, Politics, Economics, Law

Government
11 Sep. 1795–27 Sep. 1800, John Hunter Governor NSW Colony.

Feb. Charles Grimes surveys Port Stephens, NSW.
Jul. James Squire estb. first brewery in Colony, near Parramatta, NSW.
7 Sep. Aboriginal Bennelong returns Sydney from England.
Oct. Matthew Flinders and George Bass explore Botany Bay and Georges R., NSW, in 8-ft long boat *Tom Thumb*.
Nov. Descendants of strayed cattle discovered at Cowpastures, Nepean R., NSW. Locality becomes dairying centre.

During 1795
Henry Waterhouse departs S. Africa with Spanish merino sheep.
John Macarthur develops grazing land at Cowpastures, Camden, NSW, and is first in Colony to use bullocks for ploughing.
NSW becomes self-sufficient in grain.
First cedar exported to India.
First civil legal action in Colony comes to trial. Concerns squabble regarding a pig belonging to a Mr Bolton.

Births & Deaths
James Atkinson, NSW pioneer settler, b. (d. 1834)
George Gawler, SA Governor, b. (d. 1869)
Samuel Hoffman, pioneer vigneron, b. (d. 1878)
John Hutt, WA Governor, b. (d. 1880)
George Imlay, NSW pioneer, b. (d. 1846)
John Irving, convict, d.
Henry John Rous, explorer, horse and racing authority, b. (d. 1877)
Charles Sturt, explorer, b. (d. 1869)

B
Science, Technology, Transport, Discovery

During 1795
First windmill in Colony used to grind flour erected, at Observatory Hill, Sydney.

Births & Deaths
John Lhotsky, naturalist, doctor, explorer, probably b. (probably d. 1866)

C
Arts

Music, Dance

Births & Deaths
John Woodcock Graves, composer, b. (d. 1886)

Drama, Theatre

During 1795
Edward Young's play, *The Revenge*, performed in Sydney.

D
Religion, Learning

During 1795
Rev. Samuel Marsden estb. first mission in Aust.

Births & Deaths
Francis Murphy, Catholic bishop, b. (d. 1858)
Joseph Rennard Orton, Methodist missionary, b. (d. 1842)
William Waterfield, Congregational minister, b. (d. 1868)

1795

F

Historia Dignum

Population
Estimated total white, 3,388.

Dec. Severe storm damages NSW crops.

Births & Deaths
Robert Howe, pioneer magazine publisher, b. (d. 1829)

A
History, Politics, Economics, Law

Mar. Matthew Flinders explores Illawarra coast, NSW, traces Georges R. (Examines Port Hacking, Wattamolla and Lake Illawarra in Apr.)

During 1796
Wages fixed for all types of farm work.
There are 81 free settlers in NSW.
Governor John Hunter divides Sydney into areas to be covered by Watchmen, the early constabulary.
John Boston brews first beer in Colony.

Births & Deaths
John Caesar, probably a West Indian, and known as 'Black Caesar', Colony's first bushranger, shot near Strathfield, NSW
Sir Charles Augustus Fitz Roy, NSW Governor, b. (d. 1858)
Edward Gibbon Wakefield, colonization theorist, b. (d. 1862)
James Williams, convict, pioneer sugar-cane grower, b. (d. 1828)
Henry Dangar, NSW surveyor, pastoralist, probably b. (d. 1861)

B
Science, Technology, Transport, Discovery

Jun. Convict fishermen discover coal at Coal R. (Newcastle), NSW.
16 Nov. Colony's first hand-operated screw printing press begins operating. Convict George Hughes prints *Instructions for the Constables of Country Districts*.

During 1796
Building of Duck R. Bridge between Sydney and Parramatta begins.
Naval dockyard estb. at Sydney Cove.

1796

C
Arts

Music, Dance

During 1796
John O'Keefe and William Shield's opera, *The Poor Soldier*, performed in Sydney. Among first performed in Colony.

Births & Deaths
John Philip Deane, musician, b. (d. 1849)

Drama, Theatre

16 Jan. Robert Sidaway opens Colony's first full-time theatre playhouse, in Bligh Street, Sydney. (Closes 1798.)

Fine Arts

Births & Deaths
Henry Brewer, topographical artist, d. (probably b. 1743)
Thomas James Lempriere, painter, b. (d. 1852)

Architecture

Births & Deaths
Mortimer William Lewis, first colonial architect to use neo-Gothic and Classical revival forms, b. (d. 1879)

D
Religion, Learning

During 1796
London Missionary Society introduced to Colony. Rev. Samuel Marsden accepts office of Civil Magistrate in Sydney.

F
Historia Dignum

1796

Population
Estimated total white, 4,016.
During 1796
Illicit distilling of spirits widely practised.

1797

A
History, Politics Economics, Law

8 Feb. Ship *Sydney Cove* wrecked in Bass Strait. Seventeen of crew set off from Point Hicks (now in Vic.) to walk to Sydney. Three survived, becoming first Europeans to make such an overland journey in Aust.
Jun. Henry Waterhouse lands first merino sheep from Cape of Good Hope, S. Africa. Progeny purchased by John Macarthur, William Cox, Alexander Riley, Samuel Marsden, beginning sheep-breeding which eventually becomes important Aust. industry.
Aug. George Bass explores coal seams south of Sydney. On 3 Dec. leaves Sydney in whaleboat expedition to Westernport, Vic. Discovers Shoalhaven R., NSW, 7 Dec.
9 Sep. John Shortland, explorer and navigator, discovers estuary of Hunter R., NSW.
Dec. Philip Schaeffer receives first land lease in Sydney Town.
During 1797
Convict ships bring 324 male and 43 female convicts to Colony.

Births & Deaths
Richard Bowen, naval officer, d. (b. 1761)
Hamilton Hume, explorer, b. (d. 1873)
Thomas Icely, NSW pioneer pastoralist, shorthorn cattle breeder, b. (d. 1874)
John Montagu, VDL colonial official 1824–42, b. (d. 1853)
Thomas Shuldham O'Halloran, pioneer, SA Police Commissioner, b. (d. 1870)
John Septimus Roe, explorer, first WA Surveyor-General, b. (d. 1878)
Sir Paul Edmund de Strzelecki, geologist and explorer, b. (d. 1873)

B
Science, Technology, Transport, Discovery

Jan. Granary with winding machine completed in Sydney.
Aug. George Bass discovers coal south of Botany Bay, in Illawarra region, NSW.
Sep. John Shortland discovers coal, Hunter R. area, NSW.
During 1797
Survivors of *Sydney Cove* wreck report coal south of Cape Solander, Botany Bay, NSW.

C
Arts

Fine Arts

Births & Deaths
Daniel Herbert, sculptor, b. (d. 1868)
George Raper, maritime bird painter, d. (probably b. 1768)
George Rowe, goldfields painter, b. (d. 1864)

D
Religion, Learning

During 1797
There are six schools in NSW, all subsidized by the Society for the Propagation of the Gospel.

1797

1797

Historia Dignum

8 Feb. *Sydney Cove* wrecked on Preservation I., VDL.

27 Mar. First public pound to enclose stray animals estb. Sydney.

1 Aug. Crew of *Lady Shore*, convict ship carrying 66 female convicts, mutiny and sail to South America. First and only successful mutiny in convict ship (although mutineers later imprisoned).

During Aug. Colonial vessel *Cumberland* captured by prisoners.

During 1797
First recorded discovery of platypus by Europeans, Hawkesbury R., NSW.

A
History, Politics, Economics, Law

Jan. John Wilson guides exploratory expedition in district south-west of Sydney. Penetrates as far as Wingecarribee R.
24 Feb. George Bass returns to Sydney after discovering Wilsons Promontory, most southerly point of continent (2 Jan.) and Westernport, Vic. (5 Jan.).
May. Richard Dore, first trained lawyer to be appointed Deputy Judge-Advocate, arrives in Sydney.
Half Moon battery fort erected eastern end Sydney Cove.
Jun. British House of Commons Select Committee on Finance expresses concern at high cost of convict transportation.
7 Oct. Matthew Flinders and George Bass begin journey to circumnavigate VDL. Confirm existence of strait between mainland and VDL, proving VDL island (Dec.).

During 1798
Convict ships bring 492 male and 94 female convicts to Colony.
John Harris' Experiment Farm at Parramatta, NSW, produces substantial quantities of grain.
Spanish alliance with France forces English whalers out of S. American waters to Aust. and NZ waters.

Births & Deaths
Edward Curr, VDL pioneer settler, 'Father of Vic. Separation', b. (d. 1850)
Sir Dominick Daly, SA Governor, b. (d. 1868)
John Gardiner, Vic. pioneer overlander, b. (d. 1878)
Thomas George Gregson, painter, Tas. Premier, b. (d. 1874)
August Ludwig Christian Kavel, SA pioneer settler, Lutheran minister, b. (d. 1860)
James Macarthur, NSW pastoralist, politician, b. (d. 1867)
George Fletcher Moore, WA pioneer, Advocate-General, b. (d. 1886)
Andrew Petrie, Qld pioneer, explorer, b. (d. 1872)
John Fitzgerald Uniacke, NSW govt official, b. (d. 1825)
John Clements Wickham, explorer, first Govt Resident, Moreton Bay (Brisbane), b. (d. 1864)

B
Science, Technology, Transport, Discovery

Births & Deaths
William Bramwhite Clarke, geologist, and Church of England clergyman who made first assessment of probable gold-bearing rocks in Aust., b. (d. 1878)
Johann Reinhold Forster, naturalist, d. (b. 1729)

1798

C
Arts

Literature

During 1798
David Collins publishes *An Account of the English Colony in NSW* in London.

Drama, Theatre

During 1798
Governor Hunter closes Robert Sidaway's Sydney theatre.

Births & Deaths
Barnett Levey, theatre entrepreneur, founder, b. (d. 1837)

Fine Arts

During 1798
Henry Webber and William Hackwood make medallion, *Hope, Art, Labour and Peace*, encouraging art and labour under influence of peace, earliest work of sculpture associated with Colony.

D
Religion, Learning

Apr. Ministers from London Missionary Society with strong Congregational and Methodist affinities arrive in Sydney from Tahiti.
May. James Fleet Cover becomes first Congregational Church minister in Colony.
During 1798
Rev. Richard Johnson amalgamates three Sydney schools. William Richardson, Isaac Nelson and Thomas Taber become joint teachers.
Matthew Hughes founds school at Kissing Point, Sydney. (Church and school erected in Jul. 1800.)

F

Historia Dignum

1798

Population
Estimated total white, 5,000.

14 May. Severe hail-storm damages Sydney.
19 Sep. Isaac Nichols receives first recorded licence in Colony. Opens 'Jolly Sailor' hotel, Sydney's first.

1799

A
History, Politics, Economics, Law

12 Jan. Matthew Flinders and George Bass return to Sydney after circumnavigating VDL, confirming separation from mainland.
8 Jul. Matthew Flinders begins exploring north-east coast of continent.

During 1799
Whalers arrive in Sydney with *Lady Shore*, convict ship captured off Uruguay. Proceeds from cargo sold and presented to captors as 'Spanish Prize'.
First whaling-ship base estb. in Sydney.
M. de la Clampe, French Royalist refugee, attempts unsuccessfully to cultivate cotton and cocoa near Sydney.
Coal from Newcastle, NSW, sent to Bengal. Among first colonial exports.
Aborigines begin to resist white settlement in Parramatta and Hawkesbury areas, NSW.
First English-bred stallion to be imported to Aust. arrives in Sydney.
Legislation in England prohibits NSW workers from forming unions or taking strike action. (Act repealed 1824.)

Births & Deaths
Matthew Brady, VDL bushranger, b. (d. 1826)
Wilbraham Frederick Evelyn Liardet, Melbourne pioneer, amateur topographic artist, b. (d. 1878)
Archibald Mosman, NSW merchant, pastoralist, b. (d. 1863)
Lionel Samson, WA pioneer merchant, b. (d. 1878)

B
Science, Technology, Transport, Discovery

Births & Deaths
Samuel Waterman Viveash, WA pioneer doctor and magistrate, b. (d. 1880)

C

Arts

Literature

Births & Deaths

Richard Howitt, poet, b. (probably d. 1870)

Drama, Theatre

Births & Deaths

Edmund David Burn, playwright, probably b. (d. 1875)

D

Religion, Learning

During 1799

London Missionary School opens at Toongabbie, NSW.

Births & Deaths

John Dunmore Lang, Presbyterian minister, NSW politician who encouraged skilled artisans to migrate to Aust., b. (d. 1878)

William Longbottom, SA Wesleyan missionary, b. (d. 1849)

Hussey Burgh Macartney, Anglican dean Melbourne, b. (d. 1894)

Ralph Mansfield, radical Methodist clergyman, journalist, b. (d. 1880)

1799

F
Historia Dignum

Population
Estimated total white (Jun.) 4,746.

3–19 Mar. Hawkesbury R. floods destroy wheat granary, crops and livestock.
17 Jun. First public meeting held in Colony. To raise funds to build jail in Sydney.
Jul. Sydney soldiers murder missionary from London Missionary Society.

Births & Deaths

George Stevenson, first SA newspaper editor, b. (d. 1856)

A
History, Politics, Economics, Law

1800

Government

28 Sep. 1800–12 Aug. 1806, Philip Gidley King Governor NSW Colony.

Feb. Robert Campbell becomes first merchant from outside Colony to estb. import–export trading business in NSW. Boosts sealing industry to provide return cargo for his trading vessels.

16 Apr. Philip Gidley King arrives in Sydney with instructions to end the NSW Corps monopoly in trade.

31 Oct. General Order regularizes the assigned convict system.

19 Nov. Governor King fixes local currency values in pound, shillings and pence for all forms of currency circulating. First copper coins arrive from England.

16 Dec. James Grant arrives in Sydney from England in *Lady Nelson*. During voyage Grant surveyed coastal features from Cape Northumberland, SA, to Wilsons Promontory, Vic. *Lady Nelson* first vessel to sail eastward through Bass Strait.

18 Dec. Richard Atkins re-appointed Judge-Advocate of NSW.

During 1800

First Customs house in Colony estb., Sydney.

Administration imposes customs and excise duties on spirits, wine and beer imports. First taxes in Colony weaken officers' control of imports.

First wool fleece samples prepared for transport to England.

William Kent imports first pure-bred dairy stock to NSW.

George Suttor plants first citrus orchard in Colony, near Parramatta, NSW.

Rapid development of Bass Strait sealing industry increases American activity in colonial waters.

System of registering deeds and land titles in Judge-Advocate's office estb.

Births & Deaths

George Allen, first lawyer to receive legal training in NSW, b. (d. 1877)

Charles O'Hara Booth, commandant convict establishments VDL, b. (d. 1851)

Benjamin Boyd, adventurer, entrepreneur, probably b. (d. 1851)

William Bradley, NSW pioneer pastoralist, b. (d. 1868)

Sir Charles Howe Fremantle, admiral, b. (d. 1869)

James Henty, explorer, Vic. pioneer, pastoralist, merchant, b. (d. 1882)

Archibald Clunes Innes, pioneer, policeman, b. (d. 1857)

James King, pioneer merchant, vigneron, b. (d. 1857)

William Lonsdale, first Administrator Port Phillip District (Vic.), probably b. (d. 1864)

Henry Melville, newspaper proprietor, probably b. (d. 1873)

George Hall Peppin, sheep breeder, b. (d. 1872)

Maria Ann 'Granny' Smith, originator Granny Smith Apple, probably b. (d. 1870)

Sir Roger Therry, Supreme Court Judge, b. (d. 1874)

Sir Edward Deas Thomson, NSW Colonial Secretary 1837–56, b. (d. 1879)

1800

B

Science, Technology, Transport, Discovery

Apr. George Caley, botanist and naturalist, arrives in Sydney. Among first to study Aust. marsupials.

During 1800
Hunter R. coalmines worked.

Births & Deaths
John Bailey, SA botanist, b. (d. 1864)
Godfrey Howitt, naturalist, doctor of medicine, b. (d. 1873)
Sir William Macarthur, horticulturist, first Aust.-born amateur photographer, b. (d. 1882)
Sir Robert Officer, colonial surgeon, Vic. politician, b. (d. 1879)

C

Arts

Drama, Theatre

During 1800
Robert Sidaway opens second theatre in Sydney (short-lived).

Fine Arts

11 Jan. John William Lewin arrives in Sydney, becomes first professional painter in Colony.

During 1800
French artists Petit, Milbert, Lebrun and Garnier attached to Nicolas Baudin's exploratory expedition in colonial waters.

Births & Deaths
James Colbeck, sculptor, b.

D
Religion, Learning

10 Oct. Governor King estb. education fund, beginning State aid to education.
During 1800
John Tull opens first private school in Colony for middle-class pupils, at Parramatta, NSW.

Births & Deaths
John Brady, WA Roman Catholic bishop, probably b. (d. 1871)
George Washington Walker, missionary, merchant, b. (d. 1859)
William Walker, Methodist missionary, b. (d. 1855)

F
Historia Dignum

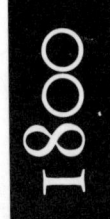

Population
Estimated total white, 4,958.

17 Jan. Earthquake shock recorded in Sydney.
7 Oct. Irish convicts flogged for planning insurrection.
During 1800
Playbill for performance of *The Recruiting Officer* printed. Now among oldest advertisements in Aust.

1801

A
History, Politics, Economics, Law

8 Mar. James Grant leaves Sydney to explore Westernport, Vic. Plants first wheat to be grown in Vic., at Churchill I.
18 Jul. Matthew Flinders begins journey to circumnavigate and map whole continent. Expedition lasts two years.
23 Nov. John Murray leaves Sydney to explore Westernport, Vic.
During Nov. First Hunter R., NSW, coal exported, to S. Africa.
During 1801
Convict settlement estb. Newcastle, NSW.
Augustus Alt appointed first Surveyor-General in NSW.
Ship named *Cumberland* launched. First armed vessel built and owned by Colony.
John Macarthur takes samples of merino fleeces to England.
First woollen and linen products manufactured in Colony produced, at Parramatta jail. (Wool manufacturing begins: Vic. 1868, SA 1870, Tas. 1874, Qld 1875, WA 1925.)
To reduce colonial expenses, Governor King raises price of goods, resulting in market glut.
Nicolas Baudin surveys west coast of New Holland.

Births & Deaths

John Batman, Melbourne pioneer, founder, b. (d. 1839)
John Cotton, Vic. pioneer, naturalist, probably b. (d. 1849)
Edward Denny Day, NSW Police Magistrate, b. (d. 1876)
Alexander Imlay, NSW pioneer, b. (d. 1847)
Charles Joseph La Trobe, first Vic. Lieut-Governor, b. (d. 1875)

B
Science, Technology, Transport, Discovery

During 1801
First cargo of Hunter R., NSW, coal reaches Sydney for export to Calcutta and S. Africa.

Births & Deaths

James Busby, viticulturist and administrator, founding father of wine industry, b. (d. 1871)

C
Arts

Drama, Theatre

Births & Deaths

Evan Henry Thomas, playwright, journalist, probably b. (d. 1837)

Fine Arts

During 1801

William Westall, topographical artist, appointed to Matthew Flinders' expedition.

Births & Deaths

William Buelow Gould, convict artist, b. (d. 1853)
Henricus Leonardus van der Houten, painter, b. (d. 1879)
Conrad Martens, watercolourist noted for use of light effect in interpretation of urban topography, b. (d. 1878)

D
Religion, Learning

8 Aug. Samuel Marsden opens female orphan school in Sydney.
Oct. Governor King opens female orphan school in Parramatta.

Births & Deaths

Thomas Quinton Stow, pioneer Congregational minister, b. (d. 1862)

1801

F

Historia Dignum

Population

Estimated total white, 5,515.

14 Sep. First duel in Colony. John Macarthur wounds Commanding Officer of NSW Corps, Col. William Paterson.

Communities

Newcastle, NSW, estb.

A
History, Politics, Economics, Law

5 Jan. John Murray names Port Phillip Bay, Vic., Port King after Governor. On 15 Feb. enters Port Phillip Bay in *Lady Nelson*. On 8 Mar. party lands. On 9 Mar. Murray takes formal possession of Port Phillip area. On 11 Mar., sets sail for Sydney.
8 Jan. Matthew Flinders enters King George Sound, WA. On 8 Apr. meets Nicolas Baudin at Encounter Bay, SA; discovers Spencer and St Vincents gulfs. On 26 Apr. enters Port Phillip Bay, Vic. On 9 May arrives Sydney. On 22 July begins journey north of Sydney, discovers Port Curtis and Port Bowen, Qld; surveys and charts Great Barrier Reef.
During Jan. Nicolas Baudin anchors at D'Entrecasteaux Channel, VDL. Expedition anchors at Botany Bay 20 Jun.
13 Jul. James Mein arrives in Sydney with first significant group of Presbyterian settlers.
Oct. Governor King grows 12,000 cuttings from vines carried in First Fleet.
Nov. Charles Grimes leaves Sydney to examine King I. and Port Phillip Bay, Vic. Warns Baudin expedition against forming French settlement in Colony.
Dec. John Murray reaps first Vic. wheat harvest (sown by James Grant in 1801).
During 1802
Governor King sends Charles Robbins to proclaim VDL, forestalling French in area. Robbins lands troops King I., hoists flag (upside down in haste) fires 3 volleys and proclaims island a British possession.
Francis Luis Barrallier attempts unsuccessfully to cross Blue Mts, NSW.
Govt store meat rations reduced. Meat shortage crisis avoided with arrival of American merchant ship *General Boyd* carrying salted beef.
Privy Council in England examines John Macarthur on prosperity of NSW wool industry. British Govt approves grant of 10,000 acres and provides rams and ewes from King George III's flocks.
Governor King imposes a 5 per cent duty on goods arriving from east of Cape of Good Hope, to protect British trade interests.

Births & Deaths
Robert Venour Dulhunty, NSW pioneer grazier, b. (d. 1853)
Robert Gouger, first SA Colonial Secretary, b. (d. 1846)
John Harrison, Vic. goldfields reformer, b. (d. 1869)
John Hubert Plunkett, NSW Attorney-General 1836–56, b. (d. 1869)
Frederick Holt Robe, SA Lieut-Governor, b. (d. 1871)
Sir Alfred Stephen, Tas. Attorney-General, b. (d. 1894)

B
Science, Technology, Transport, Discovery

During 1802
Robert Brown, naturalist, becomes first European to note and collect plants in Port Phillip Bay area, Vic.

Births & Deaths
Sir Joseph Banks, botanist, d. England (b. 1743)
Edward Dumaresq, engineer, Tas. public servant, b. (d. 1906)
James Stuart, surgeon, naturalist, artist, b. (d. 1842)

1802

1802

C
Arts

Literature

During 1802
George Howe issues first book published in Colony, *New South Wales General Standing Orders: Selected from the General Orders Issued by Former Governors.*

Fine Arts

Births & Deaths
Edward Charles Frome, painter, b. (d. 1890)
Charles Rodius, convict artist, b. (d. 1860)

D
Religion, Learning

23 Jul. NSW divided into two parishes, St Phillip, named in honour of Governor Arthur Phillip, and St John, named in honour of Governor John Hunter.
During 1802
Presbyterian Church begins in Aust.
J. Harris opens London Missionary School, at Windsor, NSW.

Births & Deaths
Thomas Fyshe Palmer, Unitarian minister, political reformer, d. (b. 1747)
Augustus Short, first Anglican bishop of Adelaide, 1847, b. (d. 1883)

F
Historia Dignum

1802

Population
Estimated total white, 5,975.

1803

A
History, Politics, Economics, Law

2 Feb. Charles Grimes discovers Yarra R., Port Phillip Bay, Vic. Surveys Melbourne–Geelong area.
25 Mar. Role of NSW Corps changed to include peacetime activities, including non-military police duties.
9 Jun. Matthew Flinders returns to Sydney after completely circumnavigating continent. On 10 Aug. sails for England, but wrecked on Great Barrier Reef, 17 Aug. (During later attempt to reach England, Flinders reaches Mauritius 17 Dec. There arrested by French and held until 14 Jun. 1810.)
12 Sep. John Bowen estb. first settlement in VDL, at Risdon Cove on Derwent R.
9 Oct. David Collins attempts to establish penal settlement at Sullivans Cove, near Sorrento, Port Phillip Bay, Vic. (Transferred to VDL 1804.)
27 Dec. William Buckley, convict, escapes from attempted penal settlement at Sorrento, Vic.

During 1803
Matthew Flinders first suggests using name 'Australia', meaning Southland (*Terra Australis*).
Robert Campbell opens wharf and warehouses in Sydney, developing maritime trade.
First whaling station built in VDL, beginning whaling industry in area.
Sealing base estb. Kangaroo I., SA.
Public brewery estb. at Parramatta. Woollen and flax mills and a salt factory open in Sydney.
James Meehan begins first field survey of VDL.

Births & Deaths
George Bass, maritime explorer, disappears en route to England
Nicolas Thomas Baudin, French explorer, d. (b. 1754)
George Meares Countess Bowen, soldier, b. (d. 1889)
Benjamin Boyd, entrepreneur, probably b. (d. 1851)
John Harris, among first policemen in Colony, d.
Sir Walter Watson Hughes, SA pastoralist, pioneer, b. (d. 1887)
John Shortland, explorer, naval officer, d. (b. 1739)
Truganini Lalla Rookh, last full-blooded female Aboriginal to live in Tas., b. (d. 1876)

B
Science, Technology, Transport, Discovery

May. William Bowen appointed first official shipping pilot at Port Jackson.

Births & Deaths
William Balmain, First Fleet surgeon, d. (b. 1762)
James Blackburn, emancipist engineer, VDL architect, b. (d. 1854)

C
Arts

Literature

Apr. David Collins completes second volume of *An Account of the English Colony in New South Wales*.

Births & Deaths

Richard Henry 'Orion' Horne, poet, probably b. (d. 1884). Known in Australia as Richard Hengist Horne.
James Rosenberg Tucker, convict and probably author, probably b. (d. 1866)

Architecture

During 1803
Henry Browne Hayes builds Vaucluse House, Sydney. First private stone dwelling in Colony built, in Sydney.

Births & Deaths

David Lambe, first VDL Colonial Architect, b. (d. 1843)

D
Religion, Learning

10 Apr. Rev. Samuel Marsden opens St John's Church of England stone church at Parramatta, NSW.
15 May. Rev. James Dixon, emancipist, begins Colony's first regular Roman Catholic mission in Sydney; marks first official recognition of Catholic Church.
23 Oct. Rev. Robert Knopwood holds first Church of England church service in southern NSW Colony (now Vic.), at Port Phillip Bay.
During 1803
Isaac Nelson opens Academy, secondary school for middle-class students, in Sydney.

Births & Deaths

Francis Russel Nixon, first Church of England bishop Tas., 1842, painter, b. (d. 1879)

1803

47

1803

E
Sport

During 1803
First recorded game of cricket in Colony played, in Sydney.
Trotting race at Parramatta; among earliest recorded in Colony.

F
Historia Dignum

Population
Estimated total white, 7,176.

5 Mar. George Howe publishes Colony's first newspaper, *The Sydney Gazette and New South Wales Advertiser*. (Terminates 1842.)
14 May. Sgt Whittle forms Freemason Lodge, leading to movement being banned.
17 Aug. *Porpoise* and *Cato*, vessels, wrecked outside Great Barrier Reef.
26 Aug. Joseph Luker, Sydney constable, murdered while on duty.
10 Oct. John Silkhorne becomes first white man to die in Vic.
25 Nov. William James Hobart Thorne is first white child born in Vic.
28 Nov. First marriage in Vic., between Harvey Garatt, convict, and Hannah Harvey, free woman.
During 1803
Joseph Samuels sentenced to hang for stealing desk containing money. Reprieved after three attempts to hang him, because of rope breaking in each case.
First suicide in Colony. Committed by prisoner at Sydney jail.
Severe drought in NSW.
Sir Henry Browne Hayes holds Freemason meeting in Sydney against Governor's orders, sentenced to hard labour.

Communities
Sorrento, Vic., estb. (re-estb. 1839)
St Marys, NSW, first settled

A
History, Politics, Economics, Law

1804

Government
16 Feb. 1804–24 Mar. 1810, David Collins Lieut-Governor VDL.

10 Feb. First govt instruction for ticket of leave holders issued.
15 Feb. David Collins founds penal settlement Risdon Cove, VDL, founds Hobart. (Called Hobart Town until 1881.)
5 Mar. Martial law proclaimed in NSW as George Johnston leads NSW Corps in quelling Irish convict rebellion, the Castle Hill Rising, at Castle Hill near Parramatta (claimed 15 lives).
Apr. Charles Grimes appointed second Surveyor-General of NSW.
25 Sep. Limits of some counties in VDL defined.
Nov. William Paterson forms settlement at George Town on Tamar R., VDL.
George Caley leads unsuccessful expedition to cross Blue Mts, NSW.
English whaling ship *Policy* takes 20,000 Spanish dollars from Dutch ship *Swift* off Sydney Heads after naval engagement.

During 1804
Name Coal R. officially changes to Newcastle, which becomes penal settlement for rebellious and twice-convicted convicts.
American sealers barred from colonial coastal waters, marking first entry of colonial govt into foreign relations.
John Macarthur sells in London first bale of colonial wool.
Colony first exports coal to England.
Charles Robbins and John Oxley examine Westernport, Vic.
Settlers at Risdon Cove, VDL, authorized to shoot Aborigines.

Births & Deaths
Archibald Bell, NSW explorer, pastoralist, b. (d. 1883)
John Boston, settler, brewer, d.
Sir William Thomas Denison, Tas. Lieut-Governor, b. (d. 1871)
John Fairfax, newspaper proprietor, b. (d. 1877)
Arthur Pooley Onslow, founder of Onslow family in Aust., b. (d. 1889)
William Salter, pioneer vigneron, b. (d. 1871)
Thomas Walker, Port Phillip District (Vic.) representative in NSW Legislative Council, public benefactor, b. (d. 1886)
William Pritchard Weston, Tas. Premier, b. (d. 1888)

B
Science, Technology, Transport, Discovery

May. First successful inoculation against smallpox in Sydney.
14 Oct. Thomas Jamison publishes first medical treatise, *General Observations of the Smallpox*.

Births & Deaths
George Bennett, naturalist, b. (d. 1893)
John Wrathall Bull, agriculturist, crop harvesting innovator, b. (d. 1886)
Edward Swarbreck Hall, sanitarian, probably b. (d. 1881)
William Sherwin, pioneer medical practitioner, b. (d. 1874)
William Wyatt, surgeon, SA pioneer, b. (d. 1886)

49

1804

C
Arts

Literature

4 Mar. C. S. publishes *The Vision of Melancholy, A Fragment*, among first poems published in Colony.

Births & Deaths

Georgiana Huntly McCrae, diarist, artist, b. (d. 1890)

Drama, Theatre

Births & Deaths

George Waldron or Barrington, convict actor, emancipist constable, d. (probably b. 1755)

Fine Arts

During 1804
William Westall completes sketches of Matthew Flinders' explorations in the *Investigator*.

Births & Deaths

Elizabeth Gould, illustrator, natural history artist, b. (d. 1841)
John Gould, ornithologist, b. (d. 1881)
Henry Gilbert Jones, artist, engineer, b. (d. 1887)

Architecture

During 1804
Prefabricated houses manufactured and their timber frames assembled at Parramatta for shipment to Hobart and Newcastle.

Births & Deaths

James Bloodsworth, first architect with practical building experience in NSW, d.

D
Religion, Learning

Feb. Rev. R. Knopwood becomes first Church of England chaplain in VDL.
Sep. D. Parnell opens Secondary School Academy, for middle-class students, in Sydney.
During 1804
Elementary School opens at Hawkesbury R., NSW, among first country schools in Colony.
W. P. Cook, Congregationalist, opens Colony's first boarding school, at Parramatta, NSW.

F
Historia Dignum

1804

Population
Estimated total white, 7,468.
Estimated Aborigines in VDL, *c.* 4,000.

26 Jan. First celebration of 26 Jan. 1788 as foundation date of Colony.
5 Feb. First colonial church-yard cemetery estb., on what was later site of Sydney Town Hall. (First used 1792, closed 1820.)
24 Apr. St David's cemetery estb., first in VDL.
During 1804
Thomas Williams first cabinet-maker to advertise his craft.

Communities
Franklin, Tas., estb.
George Town, Tas., estb.
Hobart, Tas., estb.
Kingston, Tas., first settled

1805

A
History, Politics, Economics, Law

30 Apr. *King George*, first deep-sea whaling ship built in Colony, launched in Sydney.

During 1805

John Macarthur occupies part of Camden Park Estate, near Sydney. Estb. first extensive sheep farm after bringing Spanish merino sheep from Royal Stud in England to Colony.

First woolclasser, Edward Wood, arrives in Sydney from England.

Norfolk I. penal settlement abandoned; free settlers transferred to VDL.

Hobart Government House opens. (Others, Perth 1829, Melbourne 1836, Adelaide 1837, Brisbane 1859.)

Robert Campbell defies East India Co.'s trade monopoly by sending shipment of sea elephant oil and sealskins to England.

Births & Deaths

Robert Cribb, Qld politician, b. (d. 1893)
Isabella Dalgarno, temperance reformer, b. (d. 1878)
John Barton Hack, pioneer farmer, merchant, b. (d. 1884)
Sir Richard Davies Hanson, SA Premier and Chief Justice, b. (d. 1876)
Ulrich Hubbe, legal scholar, b. (d. 1892)
William Henry Suttor, pastoralist, NSW politician, b. (d. 1877)

B
Science, Technology, Transport, Discovery

Births & Deaths

Georgiana Molloy, botanist, pioneer settler, b. (d. 1843)

C
Arts

Literature

Births & Deaths
Alexander Harris, novelist, b. (d. 1874)

Music, Dance

Births & Deaths
Stephen Hale Alonzo Marsh, musician, b. (d. 1888)

Fine Arts

During 1805
Earliest colonial engravings appear, in William Lewin's *Prodromus Entymology: Natural History of Lepidopterous Insects of NSW*.

D
Religion, Learning

During 1805
Susannah Hunt, convict, among first teachers in VDL.
Roman Catholic school for boys opens in Sydney, among first. (Lasts two years.)
First technical and vocational training for boys in Sydney begins.
John Mitchell and James MacConnell open Secondary School Academy for middle-class students in Sydney.

Births & Deaths
Patrick Bonaventure Geoghegan, Catholic bishop, b. (d. 1864)

E
Sport

Aug. Large crowd gathers near Sydney to gamble on a cockfight.

F
Historia Dignum

Population
Estimated total white, 7,830.

20–21 Mar. Colonial Schooner *Francis*, first vessel launched in Aust., wrecked near Newcastle.

A

History, Politics, Economics, Law

Government
13 Aug. 1806–26 Jan. 1808, William Bligh Governor NSW.

Oct. Drought conditions in NSW cause rise in price of wheat.
During 1806
William Bligh outlaws use of rum for purchase of commodities, weakening Rum Corps market control.
There are *c.* 646 landowners in NSW.
Whaling station estb. at Derwent estuary, VDL; among first in area.

Births & Deaths
Sir William à Beckett, first Vic. Chief Justice, 1851, b. (d. 1869)
John Henry Challis, merchant, benefactor, b. (d. 1880)
James Chisholm, NSW pioneer, b. (d. 1888)
John Nodes Dickinson, NSW judge, b. (d. 1882)
William Pitt Faithfull, NSW pastoralist, sheep breeder, b. (d. 1896)
Sir Charles Hotham, Vic. Governor, b. (d. 1855)
James Maria Matra, influential in advising British Govt on suitability of Aust. for penal settlement, d. (probably b. 1745)
Henry Reed, merchant, shipowner, b. (d. 1880)
Charles James Tyers, surveyor, b. (d. 1870)
Richard Windeyer, jurist, parliamentary reporter, journalist, b. (d. 1847)

B

Science, Technology, Transport, Discovery

Births & Deaths
Edward Davey, electric telegraph inventor, b. (d. 1885)
John Ridley, engineer, inventor of stripper-harvester, b. (d. 1887)

1806

C
Arts

Literature

Births & Deaths

John Stephens, writer, SA pioneer, b. (d. 1850)

Fine Arts

Births & Deaths

Mary Morton Allport, miniaturist painter, among first professional women artists in Tas., b. (d. 1895)
Frederick Garling, watercolourist, among first marine artists, b. (d. 1873)
John Skinner Prout, landscape painter, early settlement portraits, b. (d. 1876)

Architecture

Births and Deaths

Samuel Jackson, among first Vic. pioneer architects, b. (d. 1876)

D
Religion, Learning

c. 1806. Jane Noel opens school in Hobart.
During 1806
Mrs Williams opens first all-girls school in Sydney.

Births & Deaths

William Timothy Cape, educationist, b. (d. 1863)
John Saunders, Baptist minister, b. (d. 1859)
Nicol Drysdale Stenhouse, educationist, lawyer, 'The Maecenas of Australian Literature', b. (d. 1873)
William Bernard Ullathorne, pioneer Roman Catholic priest, b. (d. 1889)

Historia Dignum

1806

Population
Estimated total white, 7,686.

5 Jan. Amelia Rixon gives birth to first triplets in Colony.
20 Mar. Hawkesbury R., NSW, floods, destroying crops. Leads to reduction of weekly govt food ration, and increases costs.
17 Jun. Colonial brig *Venus*, carrying salted provisions and grains to Colony, is seized by crew and convicts off Port Dalrymple, VDL, and taken to NZ.
24 Sep. Strong earthquake felt at Richmond Hill, NSW.
During 1806
Sydney Gazette newspaper first uses term 'bushranger'.

Births & Deaths
George Terry Howe, newspaper pioneer, b. (d. 1863)

Communities
Launceston, Tas., estb.

1807

A
History, Politics, Economics, Law

Feb. Thomas Laycock makes first journey from south to north VDL, pioneering Hobart to Launceston land route.
28 Nov. First Norfolk I. deportees arrive in VDL.
During 1807
Edward Abbott and John Macarthur import two rum stills. Governor Bligh prohibits use.
James Meehan prepares map of Sydney. (This has been preserved and is now important historical document.)
American traders place trade embargo on NSW, causing economic crisis.
First big shipment of saleable wool (245 pounds) shipped to England, beginning wool export trade.

Births & Deaths

Sir Charles Cowper, 'Slippery Charlie', five times NSW Premier, b. (d. 1875)
Benjamin Cribb, Qld businessman and politician, b. (d. 1874)
John Donahoo, 'Bold Jack', NSW bushranger, probably b. (d. 1830)
Boyle Travers Finniss, first SA Premier, b. (d. 1893)
William Romaine Govett, surveyor, b. (d. 1848)
Charles Shum Henty, Tas. politician and banker, b. (d. 1864)
John Jardine, Qld magistrate, pioneer, b. (d. 1874)
Frederick Walker, expedition leader, probably b. (d. 1866)
Sir John Young, NSW Governor, b. (d. 1876)

B
Science, Technology, Transport, Discovery

During 1807
First VDL road built, two-mile section from Hobart to New Town.

C
Arts

Literature

Births & Deaths

Charles Tompson, poet, b. (d. 1883)

Fine Arts

Births & Deaths

Charles Bruce, convict engraver, b. (d. 1851)
Henry Burn, impressionist painter, probably b. (d. 1884)
Benjamin Law, sculptor, b. (probably d. 1890)
Frederick Strange, convict portrait painter, b. (d. 1854)
Teresa Snell Walker, first woman sculptor to work in Colony, b. (d. 1876)
William Pitt Wiltshire, portrait painter, among first artists born in Colony, b.

D
Religion, Learning

1807

29 May. First peal of bells in Colony rung, at St Phillip's church in Sydney.
Rev. Samuel Marsden builds Church of England church in Sydney.
Thomas Fitzgerald opens first private school in Hobart.

Births & Deaths

Charles Perry, first Church of England bishop of Melbourne, 1848, b. (d. 1891)
William Tyrrell, first Church of England bishop of Newcastle, NSW, b. (d. 1879)

1807

F
Historia Dignum

Population
Estimated total white, 8,327.

25 Jul. 'Whale Fishery' hotel opens; among first in VDL.

Births & Deaths
William Francis King, 'Flying Pieman', showman, noted for bizarre walking feats, probably b. (d. 1874)

Communities
New Norfolk, Tas., first settled

A

History, Politics, Economics, Law

Government
26 Jan. 1808–28 Jul. 1808, George Johnston administers NSW.
29 Jul. 1808–8 Jan 1809, Joseph Foveaux administers NSW.

26 Jan. George Johnston leads NSW Corps to arrest Governor Bligh for tyranny, beginning the 'Rum Rebellion'. Governor Bligh deposed, held prisoner in Sydney until Feb. 1809, when he agreed to return to England aboard HMS *Porpoise*. (On board he argued agreement extracted by force not binding. Sailed for Derwent R., VDL, on 17 Mar.)
During Jan. Charles Grimes acts as Judge-Advocate in John Macarthur trial, Sydney.
During 1808
Local farmers produce fresh beef and mutton for public consumption.

Births & Deaths
Thomas Turner à Beckett, Vic. politician, b. (d. 1892)
Richard Birnie, lawyer, author, b. (d. 1888)
Martin Cash, Tas. bushranger, probably b. (d. 1877)
William Thomas Napier Champ, first Tas. Premier, b. (d. 1892)
Caroline Chisholm, pioneer social worker devoted to welfare and employment of immigrants, b. (d. 1877)
William Henty, solicitor, b. (d. 1881)
Philip Gidley King, NSW Governor, d. (b. 1758)
Sir Charles Nicholson, politician, antiquities collector, b. (d. 1903)
Sir Henry Watson Parker, NSW Premier, probably b. (d. 1881)
John Giles Price, Norfolk I. prison official, VDL magistrate, b. (d. 1857)
Sir Henry Edward Fox Young, SA and Tas. Governor, b. (d. 1870)

B

Science, Technology, Transport, Discovery

During 1808
John William Lewin, naturalist, publishes first volume of an ornithological work prepared in Colony.
William Redfern, first medical teacher in Colony, is examined to test authenticity of credentials.

Births & Deaths
Ludwig Becker, naturalist on Burke and Wills expedition, probably b. (d. 1861)
Alexander Dalrymple, geographer, hydrographer, d. (b. 1737)
Ronald Campbell Gunn, Tas. botanist, b. (d. 1881)
William Horatio Sholl, WA colonial surgeon, b. (d. 1876)

1808

1808

C
Arts

Fine Arts

Births & Deaths

James Erskine Calder, surveyor and painter, b. (d. 1882)

Architecture

Births & Deaths

Robert Russell, architect, painter, Melbourne surveyor, b. (d. 1900)

D
Religion, Learning

During 1808

Rowland Hassall, lay Congregational missionary, raises funds for a Dissenting chapel in Hawkesbury district, NSW, first of kind in Colony.

Births & Deaths

Frederic Barker, Church of England bishop in Sydney, 1855, b. (d. 1882)

Thomas Frederick Elliot, public servant, b. (d. 1880)

F

Historia Dignum

1808

15 May. Fifty convicts seize brig *Harrington* while she is anchored in Sydney Harbour. They escape.
24 May. Hawkesbury R. floods, causing much damage to stock and crops. (Floods again 29 Jul.)
During 1808
First deer imported to Colony arrive Sydney.

Births & Deaths
George Mealmaker, convict weaver, d. (b. 1768)

1809

A
History, Politics, Economics, Law

Government

9 Jan. 1809–31 Dec. 1809, William Paterson administers NSW.

29 Mar. John Macarthur sails for England to support George Johnston in defence of role in Rum Rebellion. (Arrives 9 Oct. 1810; Johnston court-martialled Jun. 1811.)
25 Apr. General Order issued estb. official post office in Sydney. Isaac Nichols becomes first postmaster in Colony. (Post offices estb. VDL 1812, WA 1829, SA and Vic. 1837, Qld 1859.)
28 Dec. First battalion of 73rd Regiment arrives in Sydney with Major-General Lachlan Macquarie.
30 Dec. Ellis Bent arrives in Sydney as Judge-Advocate of NSW. (Recalled 1814.)
During 1809
Joseph Foveaux, colonial administrator, forms police fund in NSW, first Colonial Revenue Fund.
NSW Corps renamed 102nd Regiment. Imperial Regiments in Colony become responsible for land defence.

Births & Deaths

Francis Price Blackwood, maritime explorer, b. (d. 1854)
William Adams Brodribb, NSW squatter, b. (d. 1886)
Charles Coxen, Qld pioneer and politician, b. (d. 1876)
Sir Charles Henry Darling, Vic. Governor, b. (d. 1870)
John Stephen Hampton, WA Governor, probably b. (d. 1869)
John Hart, SA Premier, b. (d. 1873)
George Macleay, explorer accompanying Charles Sturt, 1829, b. (d. 1891)
Thomas Manifold, Vic. pioneer settler, b. (d. 1875)
Henry Miller, Vic. merchant, financier, b. (d. 1888)
Sir John Morphett, SA pioneer, b. (d. 1892)
John Reynell, vigneron, b. (d. 1873)
Samuel Stephens, SA pioneer, company manager, probably b. (d. 1840)
John Bligh Suttor, NSW politician, b. (d. 1886)
Jonathan Binns Were, financier, first director of Melbourne stock exchange, 1865, b. (d. 1885)

C
Arts

Drama, Theatre

Births & Deaths
Francis Nesbitt McCrone, actor, probably b. (d. 1853)
Robert Sidaway, theatre pioneer, d. (probably b. 1757)

Fine Arts

During 1809
Colonial period of art begins, focuses on topographical art, Macquarie's urbanism and Georgian architecture.

Births & Deaths
William Nicholas, engraver, lithographer, b. (d. 1854)

D

Religion, Learning

Jan. John Hosking, one of first free, non-convict qualified school teachers, arrives in Sydney.
18 Aug. William Cowper arrives in Sydney as Assistant Colonial Chaplain.
During 1809
First Presbyterian church in Colony built, at Ebenezer on Hawkesbury R., NSW. (Becomes oldest extant church in Aust.)

Births & Deaths

John West, Congregational clergyman, writer, b. (d. 1873)

F

Historia Dignum

1809

Population
Estimated total white, 11,952.

Jun. Hawkesbury R., NSW, floods, destroying stock and crops. (Floods again Aug.)
During 1809
NSW drought begins. (Ends 1811.)
Derwent R. floods; first major flood recorded in VDL.

Communities
Ebenezer, NSW, estb.
Evandale, Tas., estb.

1810

A
History, Politics, Economics, Law

Government
1 Jan. 1810–1 Dec. 1821, Lachlan Macquarie Governor NSW.
24 Mar. 1810–20 Feb. 1812, Edward Lord and John Murray Commandant Administrators VDL.

12 May. Governor Bligh sails for England in *Hindustan*. (Arrives 25 Oct.)
10 Jun. Military night patrol estb. Sydney.
13 Jun. Matthew Flinders liberated at Mauritius. Sails for England.
23 Jun. Isaac Nichols' house in Sydney becomes regular post office.
6 Oct. Sydney divided into five separate police districts. Streets given permanent names and signposts.
20 Oct. First public market in Colony opens, in George Street, Sydney.
Nov. Alexander Riley, Garnham Blaxcell, D'Arcy Wentworth receive monopoly over import of spirits.

During 1810
NSW Corps (102nd Regiment) recalled. Remainder of 73rd Highland Regiment arrives, implementing policy of stationing regular troops in Colony.
Rev. Samuel Marsden introduces European bees to Colony.
Macquarie I. sealing base estb. (Lasts *c.* 19 years.)
James Wishart estb. harbour for sealers at Port Fairy, Vic.

Births & Deaths
Sir Terence Aubrey, NSW pioneer pastoralist and politician, b. (d. 1873)
James Austin, Vic. pioneer settler, b. (d. 1896)
David Collins, first VDL Lieut-Governor, d. (b. 1756)
William Clark Haines, first Vic. Premier, b. (d. 1866)
Edward Henty, Vic. pioneer settler b. (d. 1878)
Sir Arthur Edward Kennedy, WA and Qld Governor, b. (d. 1883)
Alfred Kennerley, Tas. Premier, probably b. (d. 1897)
Alfred James Peter Lutwyche, judge, b. (d. 1880)
David Charteris McArthur, Melbourne banker, b. (d. 1887)
Lachlan McLachlan, Vic. Police Magistrate, b. (d. 1885)
Angus McMillan, Vic. pioneer and explorer, b. (d. 1865)
William Paterson, NSW Lieut-Governor, d. (b. 1755)
François Péron, French explorer, naturalist, d. (b. 1775)
John Shortland, naval commander, d. (b. 1769)
Andrew Thompson, emancipist, NSW pioneer settler, d. (b. 1773)
Sir James Arndell Youl, Tas. pastoralist, probably b. (d. 1904)

B
Science, Technology, Transport, Discovery

1 Jan. Sydney to Parramatta turnpike road completed.

Births & Deaths
John Gilbert, naturalist, explorer, probably b. (d. 1845)
John Frederick Hilly, engineer, architect, b. (d. 1883)

C
Arts

Literature

Jun. Michael Massey Robinson publishes poems, 'Royal Birthday Odes' in *Sydney Gazette*; among first poems published in Colony. (*Sydney Gazette* published until 1821.)

During 1810
Robert Brown publishes first part of *Prodromus Florae Novae Hollandiae et Insulae Van-Diemen*, botanical work.

Music, Dance

Births & Deaths
Carl Linger, musician, composer, b. (d. 1862)

Drama, Theatre

Births & Deaths
John Gordon Griffiths, Shakespearian actor, b. (d. 1857)

Fine Arts

Births & Deaths
Thomas Tyrwhitt Balcombe, painter, illustrator, b. (d. 1861)
George Prideaux Robert Harris, watercolourist, d. (b. 1775)
Charles Pechell, naval officer and painter, b.

Architecture

15 Dec. Governor Macquarie issues first building regulations, requiring houses to be made of brick or weatherboard, to have brick chimneys and shingled roofs, and to be no less than nine feet high.

Births & Deaths
Richard Roach Jewel, WA architect, b. (d. 1891)

D
Religion, Learning

1810

24 Feb. Governor Macquarie announces estb. of Free Public Charity School in Parramatta, with John Eyre as schoolmaster. (Opens 22 Mar.)
16 Apr. Governor Macquarie opens Free School in Sydney.
19 May. Servants of the Crown directed to attend church on Sundays.

During 1810
Congregational Church movement begins in Sydney. (VDL 1822, SA 1837, Vic. 1838, WA 1845, Qld 1849).
Rev. Samuel Marsden appointed chief Church of England chaplain of Colony. Consecrates first St Phillip's church in Sydney 25 Dec.

Births & Deaths
William Macquarie Cowper, Church of England dean, Sydney, b. (d. 1902)
Daniel James Draper, Methodist minister, pioneer church builder, b. (d. 1866)

1810

E
Sport

30 Apr. Earliest recorded horseracing in Colony, at Parramatta, NSW. 15–19 Oct. at Hyde Park, Sydney. First organized trotting race in Colony held at Parramatta 30 Apr.

During 1810
John Fisher becomes first professional jockey in Colony.
Dick Dowling, carrying 9 stone over 50 yards at Hyde Park, Sydney, estb. first recorded pedestrian match.
Hunting as a sport begins in Colony.

F
Historia Dignum

Population
Estimated total white, 11,773.

8 Jan. First VDL newspaper published, *The Derwent Star and Van Diemen's Land Intelligencer*.
24 Mar. First toll house in Colony erected, on South Head Road, Sydney, to raise money for road improvement. (Other first tolls estb. Tas. 1826, SA 1844, Vic. 1854.)
Sep. Caterpillar plague destroys crops in Hawkesbury area, NSW. (Again in 1812, 1814 and 1819.)

During 1810
Hyde Park in Sydney dedicated as citizens exercise ground.

Communities
Campbelltown, NSW, estb.
Governor Macquarie proclaims Windsor, Richmond, Liverpool, Pitt Town, Wilberforce and Castlereagh in NSW
Port Fairy, Vic., named after the cutter *Fairy*, driven into the port by bad weather

A

History, Politics, Economics, Law

Apr.–Jun. John Macarthur reprimanded at Johnston's court-martial, in England for his part in the Rum Rebellion.
2 Jul. George Johnston cashiered for his actions in deposing Bligh.
Aug. Robert Watson appointed Sydney's first senior pilot. (Harbourmaster in 1814.)
23 Nov. Governor Macquarie arrives in Hobart to inspect VDL. Lays out Hobart Town and names main streets.
2 Dec. Samuel Marsden sends large consignment of wool to England.
During 1811
Governor Macquarie introduces system of semi-civilian constables under direction of superintendent.
Development of trade ties with India results in oversupply of goods, leading to decline in prices.

Births & Deaths

James Chambers, SA pastoralist, b. (d. 1862)
William Dutton, whaler, Vic. settler, b. (d. 1878)
Charles Hotson Ebden, Vic. squatter, politician, businessman, b. (d. 1867)
William Forlong, wool pioneer, b. (d. 1890)
Stephen George Henty, Vic. merchant and politician, b. (d. 1872)
Thomas Holt, NSW politician, benefactor, b. (d. 1888)
Henry John Lindeman, vigneron, b. (d. 1881)
Robert Lowe, Viscount Sherbrooke, NSW and British politician, b. (d. 1892)
Sir Robert Ramsay Mackenzie, Qld Premier, b. (d. 1873)
Sir William Montagu Manning, NSW politician and judge, b. (d. 1895)
Sir William Henry Fancourt Mitchell, Vic. politician, landowner, b. (d. 1884)
Christopher Rawson Penfold, vigneron, b. (d. 1870)
Thomas Reibey, merchant, d. (b. 1769)
Owen Stanley, marine surveyor, b. (d. 1850)
Edward Stephens, SA pioneer banking accountant, b. (d. 1861)
Horatio Spencer Howe Wills, pioneer pastoralist, b. (d. 1861)

B

Science, Technology, Transport, Discovery

May. John O'Hearne completes stone arch bridge over Tank Stream, connecting eastern and western sections of Sydney.
30 Oct. Foundation stone of Sydney Rum Hospital laid. (Completed in 1816.)
During 1811
Governor Macquarie estb. first mental asylum, at Castle Hill, NSW. (Closes 1825.)

Births & Deaths

Richard Moritz Schomburgk, botanist, b. (d. 1891)

1811

1811

C
Arts

Fine Arts

Births & Deaths

Knut Geelmuyden Bull, painter, b. (d. 1889)
Marshall Claxton, painter, probably b. (d. 1881)
Johann Joseph Eugen Von Guérard, landscape painter, probably b. (d. 1901)
Matthew Willis, sculptor, b. (d. 1890)

D
Religion, Learning

During 1811
William Pascoe Crook introduces Lancastrian monitorial teaching system to Sydney. Caters for large numbers of students, all in one room, but graded into classes of uniform attainment.

Births & Deaths
Mathew Blagden Hale, first Anglican bishop, Perth, 1856, b. (d. 1895)

E
Sport

During 1811
Sydney Hunt Club estb.

F
Historia Dignum

Population
Estimated total white, 11,679.

Mar. Hawkesbury R. floods, destroying maize crop.
May. Burial grounds officially consecrated in various townships.
24 Aug. Pounds and poundkeepers estb. in various districts of NSW.

1812

A
History, Politics, Economics, Law

Government
20 Feb. 1812–4 Feb. 1813, Andrew Geils Commandant Administrator VDL.

Jan. John Oxley appointed Surveyor-General of NSW.
Mar. George W. Evans attempts to cross Blue Mts, NSW; explores and opens Illawarra District.
18 Jun. America declares war on Britain and her colonies.
10 Jul. British Parlt publishes report of Select Committee inquiry into state of Colony and transportation.
19 Oct. Convict ship *Indefatigable* lands 200 convicts in Hobart; first ship to sail there direct from England.
Nov. John Beaumont becomes first VDL postmaster.
22 Dec. Phillip Parker King and Allan Cunningham round Cape Leeuwin, WA, surveying west coast of continent.
During 1812
British Govt appoints Henry Bathurst as Secretary of State for the Colonies. (Holds position for 15 years.)
British Govt opens NSW to 'essential' trade.
Commerical crisis in Britain leads overseas suppliers to withdraw credit from Colony. First liquidity crisis in Aust.

Births & Deaths
Henry William St Pierre Bunbury, soldier, explorer, b. (d. 1875)
Sir Stuart Alexander Donaldson, first NSW Premier, b. (d. 1867)
Frederick Hansborough Dutton, SA pioneer pastoralist, b. (d. 1890)
Sir George Grey, explorer and SA Governor, b. (d. 1898)
George Hamilton, among first to overland stock from Vic. to SA, painter, b. (d. 1883)
William Kent, naval officer, d. (b. 1751)
John Lynch, NSW bushranger, b. (d. 1841)
Sir Maurice Charles O'Connell, colonial administrator, b. (d. 1879)
George Russell, Clyde Co. pastoral manager, b. (d. 1888)
Samuel Smith, vigneron, b. (d. 1889)
George Milner Stephen, lawyer, acting SA Governor, b. (d. 1894)
John Lort Stokes, maritime surveyor, b. (d. 1885)
Henry Waterhouse, who introduced merino sheep to Colony, d. (b. 1770)
Sir James Milne Wilson, Tas. Premier, b. (d. 1880)

C
Arts

Literature

Births & Deaths
Louisa Ann Meredith, author and artist, b. (d. 1895)

Music, Dance

Births & Deaths
William Vincent Wallace, 'The Paganini of Australia', composer, whose stay in Colony 1834–38 improved standards of musical performances, b. (d. 1865)

Fine Arts

During 1812
John William Lewin opens painting academy in Sydney.
Walter Preston, convict engraver, arrives in Sydney.

Births & Deaths
W. H. Fernyhough, painter, illustrator, architect, b. (d. 1849)
Robert Vaughan Hood, proprietor of first picture gallery in Colony (estb. in Hobart, 1846), b. (d. 1888)

D
Religion, Learning

7 Feb. First Wesleyan Methodist meeting held in Sydney; begins Methodist Church in Colony. (First Methodist meetings in Hobart 1820; Fremantle, WA, 1830; Perth 1834; Adelaide 1836; Melbourne 1837; Brisbane 1847.)

During 1812
Thomas Bowden uses Lancastrian education system at public school in Sydney.

Births & Deaths
James Alipius Goold, Catholic prelate, b. (d. 1886)

E
Sport

8 Oct. First recorded hunt using hounds, NSW.

1812

1812

F
Historia Dignum

Population
Estimated total white, 12,175.

10 Jun. Ship *Campbell Macquarie* wrecked on Macquarie I., claiming five lives.

Births & Deaths
Edward William Andrews, SA journalist, b. (d. 1877)

Communities
Ross, Tas., estb.

A
History, Politics, Economics, Law

Government
4 Feb. 1813–9 Apr. 1817, Thomas Davey Lieut-Governor VDL.

Jan. Parramatta becomes commercial centre for Colony's major agricultural and pastoral districts. Weekly market estb. 7 Jan.
11 May. Gregory Blaxland, William Wentworth and William Lawson lead first expedition to successfully find route across Blue Mts, NSW.
6 Jul. John Macarthur ships 36 bales of wool to England.
30 Sep. To alleviate currency shortages, Governor Macquarie circulates 'holey dollar' and 'dump'. Until c. 1824 both remained in use—the holey dollar valued at 5 shillings, and the dump at 15 pence.
20 Nov. George William Evans begins expedition across new Blue Mts track, becomes first to cross the Great Dividing Range; discovers Bathurst Plains, NSW, and is first to speculate on possibility of an inland sea.
During Nov. George William Evans discovers Macquarie R., NSW. First inland stream to be named by a European.
During 1813
Govt abolishes regulations prohibiting non-govt shipping enterprises from being established in Hobart, enabling whaling and ship-building industries to expand.

Births & Deaths
Charles Archer, Qld pioneer, b. (d. 1862)
Sir Redmond Barry, Vic. judge who presided over Eureka and Ned Kelly trials, b. (d. 1880)
Bennelong, one of Aborigines cultivated by Governor Phillip, d. (probably b. 1764)
Charles Bonney, SA overlander and politician, b. (d. 1897)
John Davies, emancipist, pioneer, b. (d. 1872)
Henry Fyshe Gisborne, NSW Commissioner of Crown Lands, b. (d. 1841)
Joseph Hawdon, Vic. pioneer settler, b. (d. 1871)
Henry Hopwood, pioneer 'King of Echuca', Vic., b. (d. 1869)
Henry Herman Kater, NSW stock breeder, b. (d. 1881)
Friedrich Wilhelm Ludwig Leichhardt, explorer, b. (probably d. 1848)
Joseph Ernst Seppelt, vigneron, b. (d. 1868)
William Howard Smith, shipowner, b. (d. 1890)
Peter Egerton Warburton, desert explorer b. (d. 1889)

B
Science, Technology, Transport, Discovery

Mar. King's Wharf, Sydney, completed. First public wharf in Colony.
10 Nov. Howe Bridge across South Creek, Windsor, NSW, completed.
During 1813
First steam engine imported, to drive flour mill in Sydney.
Simeon Lord opens first glass bottle-blowing shop, in Sydney. (Glass industry estb. 1872.)

Births & Deaths
Daniel Bunce, botanist, b. (d. 1872)
David John Thomas, surgeon, b. (d. 1871)

1813

1813

C
Arts

Literature

During 1813
John William Lewin's *Birds of New Holland with their Natural History* published; first illustrated book printed in Colony.

Births & Deaths
Charles Harpur, 'forefather of Aust. poets', b. (d. 1868)

Fine Arts

During 1813
Richard Read, convict artist, portrait painter, arrives in Sydney (probably b. 1765).

Births & Deaths
Martha S. Berkeley, SA landscape painter and miniaturist, b.
John Rae, painter of early Sydney street scenes, public servant, b. (d. 1900)

Architecture

During 1813
Daniel Dering Mathew, among first skilled architects in NSW, arrives in Sydney.

D
Religion, Learning

May. In effort to raise moral standards, Governor Macquarie orders that part of Sunday be reserved for religious duties.
During 1813
William Pascoe Crook opens first Sunday School in Colony, in Sydney.

Births & Deaths
Charles Badham, classical scholar, b. (d. 1884)
James Forbes, Presbyterian clergyman, b. (d. 1851)

Historia Dignum

1813

Population
Estimated total white, 13,827.

11 Mar. First fair in Colony held, in Sydney.
23 Apr. Convicts escape from Derwent R., VDL, in ship *Unity*, never heard of again.
8 May. Benevolent Society of NSW estb. First voluntary charitable organization in Colony. (Officially named on 4 June 1818.)
15 May. Regulations prohibit shops from opening on Sundays and require transport carriages to be registered.
During May. Passenger boats between Sydney and Parramatta prohibited from running on Sundays; watermen appointed to apply regulations.
During 1813
Severe drought prevails in NSW. (Ends 1815.)
Bushranger Michael Howe active in VDL.

Births & Deaths
Charles Kemp, journalist, b. (d. 1864)
Edward Wilson, journalist, philanthropist, b. (d. 1878)

1814

A
History, Politics, Economics, Law

7 Feb. Jeffery Hart Bent appointed first Judge of NSW Supreme Court.
11 Feb. 73rd Highland Regiment replaced by 46th Regiment.
18 Jul. Matthew Flinders publishes *A Voyage to Terra Australis*, in which he suggests that name 'Australia' for Colony be officially adopted. (Flinders dies next day.)
18 Jul. William Cox appointed supervisor for construction of road across Blue Mts, NSW.
12 Aug. Governor's Court and Supreme Court replace military-style civil and criminal courts in NSW.
25 Dec. Samuel Marsden estb. first mission and permanent white settlement in NZ.

During 1814
Norfolk I. finally abandoned as convict station.
American ships cease trading with Aust. while at war with Britain.
East India Co.'s trade monopoly in Aust. region ends. (Monopoly officially revoked in 1813.)
Hamilton Hume explores country near Berrima, NSW.
Aboriginal Boongaree placed in charge of farm for Aborigines near Sydney.

Births & Deaths
John Archer, Qld pioneer, b. (d. 1857)
Matthew Flinders, explorer, d. (b. 1774)
Francis Grose, NSW Lieut Governor, d. (probably b. 1754)
Sir Richard Graves MacDonnell, SA Governor, b. (d. 1881)
Sir John Henry Thomas Manners-Sutton, Vic. Governor, b. (d. 1877)
Arthur Phillip, NSW Governor, d. (b. 1738)
Sir Robert Richard Torrens, SA Premier, b. (d. 1884)
John Whitehead, VDL bushranger d.

B
Science, Technology, Transport, Discovery

22 Mar. Road from Sydney to Liverpool via Parramatta, built by William Roberts, opens.
1 Oct. Sydney–Parramatta coach service opens. William Highland begins weekly Sydney to Richmond, NSW, stage-cart service. First public road conveyances in Colony.

During 1814
Convicts cutting road to Bathurst, NSW, report gold in region. First report that gold exists in Colony.

Births & Deaths
William Thomas Haskell, better known as Horace Dean, medical practitioner, b. (d. 1887)
William Woolls, botanist, b. (d. 1893)

C
Arts

Fine Arts

Nov. Richard Read, first noted portrait painter in Colony, opens art school in Sydney.

Births & Deaths

Abram-Louis Buvelot, landscape painter, the 'grandfather' of Aust. landscape painting, b. (d. 1888)
Thomas Clark, painter, probably b. (d. 1883)
Alexander Schramm, painter, probably b. (d. 1864)
Thomas Watling, artist, probably d. (b. 1762)

D
Religion, Learning

1814

Jul. Henry Fulton opens Fulton's Classical Academy, for middle-upper-class students, in Sydney.

Births & Deaths

Charles Henry Bromby, Church of England bishop, Tas., 1864, b. (d. 1907)
Rosendo Salvado, WA pioneer Catholic bishop, b. (d. 1900)
Edward Wyndham Tufnell, first Church of England bishop, Brisbane, 1859, b. (d. 1896)

1814

E
Sport

7 Jan. First recorded bare-knuckle boxing contest in Colony, between John Berringer and Charles Lifton, in Sydney. Berringer wins in 56 rounds.
During 1814
First VDL horseraces held.

F
Historia Dignum

Population
Estimated total white, 15,014.

7 May. The *Van Diemen's Land Gazette and General Advertiser*, newspaper, published.
20 May. Ship *Three Bees*, carrying gunpowder, explodes and burns while moored in Sydney Harbour.
During 1814
Officers of 46th Regiment estb. first regular Freemasonry lodge, which they name Social and Military Virtues no. 227.

Communities
Appin, NSW, estb.

A
History, Politics, Economics, Law

11 May. William Henry Moore becomes first solicitor formally admitted to practice in any court in NSW.
25 May. George William Evans discovers Lachlan R., NSW.
12 Dec. James Kelly sets out in whaleboat on voyage on which he circumnavigates VDL. Takes 49 days.
During 1815
First VDL free settlers arrive.
Simeon Lord opens Botany Bay Woollen Mills, NSW.
Governor Macquarie appoints Aboriginal Boongaree as chief of Broken Bay Aboriginal tribe, NSW.

Births & Deaths
Sir James Willson Agnew, Tas. Premier, b. (d. 1901)
Augustus Theodore Henry Alt, NSW pioneer surveyor, d. (b. 1731)
Thomas Austin, Vic. pioneer settler, b. (d. 1871)
Sir Henry Barkly, Vic. Governor, b. (d. 1898)
Ellis Bent, NSW Judge-Advocate, d. (b. 1783)
Thomas Daniel Chapman, Tas. Premier, b. (d. 1884)
Thomas Chirnside, overlander, Vic. pioneer, b. (d. 1887)
Robert Barrington Dawson, NSW pioneer pastoralist, b. (d. 1891)
Sir Adye Douglas, Tas. Premier, b. (d. 1906)
Sir Richard Dry, Tas. Premier, b. (d. 1869)
Edward John Eyre, explorer, b. (d. 1901)
William Learmonth, pioneer pastoralist, b. (d. 1889)
Patrick Leslie, Qld pioneer settler, b. (d. 1881)
Maurice Margarot, 'Scottish Martyr' and witness at transportation inquiry held by British Parliamentary Committee, d. (b. 1745)
John Mitchel, Irish nationalist convict, b. (d. 1875)
Sir Henry Parkes, federationist and NSW Premier, b. (d. 1896)
Frank Potts, pioneer vigneron, b. (d. 1890)
Peter Frederick Shortland, naval officer, b. (d. 1888)
Sir William Foster Stawell, Vic. Chief Justice, b. (d. 1889)
John McDouall Stuart, explorer, b. (d. 1866)
Alexander Tolmer, SA Police Commissioner, b. (d. 1890)
William Westgarth, merchant and historian, b. (d. 1889)

B
Science, Technology, Transport, Discovery

21 Jan. 100-mile road from Sydney to Bathurst, NSW, over Blue Mts completed; took 28 men under William Cox 6 months to build.
29 May. John Dixon begins operating first steam engine in Colony, driving flour mill.
Dr William Bland estb. first private medical practice in Colony, in Sydney.
John Watts builds military hospital at Observatory Hill.

Births & Deaths
Benjamin Herschel Babbage, engineer, explorer, b. (d. 1878)
David Elliot Wilkie, Vic. pioneer medical practitioner, b. (d. 1885)

1815

C Arts

Literature

Births & Deaths
Mary Theresa Vidal, fiction writer, b. (d. 1869)

Music, Dance

Song 'Botany Bay' begins as broadsheet called 'A Farewell to Judges and Juries'.

Fine Arts

During 1815
Frederick Garling, among first Aust. marine painters, arrives in Sydney.

Births & Deaths
Joseph Backler, portrait painter, b. (d. 1897)
John Michael Skipper, painter, b. (d. 1883)

Architecture

During 1815
Verandas and wide roof overhang become dominant features of colonial architecture.
Francis Greenway first suggests creation of a Sydney Harbour bridge.

D Religion, Learning

18 Jan. Governor Macquarie estb. school for Aboriginal children at Parramatta, NSW.
15 Aug. Rev. Samuel Leigh becomes first Methodist minister in Colony.
During 1815
Church of England attempts to dominate education; successful until *c.* 1831.
NSW Sunday School Institution founded as a non-denominational association.
Isaac Wood opens Sydney Academy.

Births & Deaths
Samuel Bennett, historian, b. (d. 1878)
Charles Henry Davis, Catholic bishop, b. (d. 1854)

F
Historia Dignum

1815

Population
Total estimated white, 14,844.

27 Jan. James Oatley, convict and first professional clock-maker in Colony, arrives in Sydney.
29 Oct. Sealing ship *Betsey* wrecked in Tasman Sea; 11 lives lost.
During 1815
'Bush Inn' (hotel) estb. at New Norfolk, VDL; among first hotels in Aust.

Communities
Bargo, NSW, estb.
Bathurst, NSW, estb. First settlement west of Great Dividing Range
Springwood, NSW, estb.

1816

A
History, Politics, Economics, Law

4 May. Proclamation of annual friendly meeting of Aborigines in Sydney area; first to be held on 28 Dec.
5 Oct. John Wylde, Deputy Judge-Advocate NSW, arrives in Sydney.
During 1816
Macarthur Estate begins grape vine cultivation at Camden Park, NSW.
Hamilton Hume explores Berrima area, NSW.
VDL begins large-scale shipments of beef, grain and vegetables to NSW.

Births & Deaths

David Archer, Qld pioneer, b. (d. 1900)
James Brown, colliery proprietor, b. (d. 1894)
Edward Davis, NSW bushranger, 'the Jewboy', b. (d. 1841)
John Nicol Drummond, police inspector, Aboriginal controller, b. (d. 1906)
Sir Charles Gavan Duffy, Vic. Premier, b. (d. 1903)
Francis Stacker Dutton, SA Premier, probably b. (d. 1877)
George Fairbairn, Vic. pioneer pastoralist, b. (d. 1895)
Edward Hammond Hargraves, pioneer gold prospector, b. (d. 1891)
Frederick Maitland Innes, Tas. Premier, b. (d. 1882)
Anthony O'Grady Lefroy, WA pioneer, b. (d. 1897)
Thomas Sutcliffe Mort, pioneer merchant, b. (d. 1878)
Alexander Borthwick Murray, Vic. pastoralist, b. (d. 1903)
Sir John Robertson, NSW Premier, 'Free Selection Jack', b. (d. 1891)
Sir Charles Sladen, Vic. Premier, b. (d. 1884)
James Hingston Tuckey, naval officer, author, d. (b. 1776)

B
Science, Technology, Transport, Discovery

Jun. NSW Botanical Gardens estb. as the 'Middle Garden', in Sydney; first in Colony. Charles Frazer appointed Superintendent.
During 1816
Sydney Rum Hospital opens. (Used for 63 years.)
Hobart's first ferry service across Derwent R. begins.

Births & Deaths

James Harrison, inventor of meat freezing process, b. (d. 1893)
Sir Peter Nicol Russell, engineer, benefactor, first to produce cast iron locally (in 1840s), b. (d. 1905)
Thomas Christie Smart, colonial doctor, Tas., who encouraged nursing profession, b. (d. 1896)

C
Arts

Literature

Births & Deaths

John George Lang, author, probably first Aust.-born novelist, b. (d. 1864)

Architecture

Mar. Francis Greenway appointed Civil Architect and Assistant Engineer to NSW Govt.

Cadman's Cottage first occupied. (Named after John Cadman; now Sydney's oldest building.)

During 1816

John Watts, architect, enlarges Old Government House at Parramatta. (Originally built in 1800.)

D
Religion, Learning

1816

During 1816

Rev. Samuel Leigh holds first Methodist Church service in Colony; in private Sydney house for congregation of 44.

Henry Wrensford appointed headmaster of Newcastle East Public School for convict children.

Births & Deaths

John Woolley, Sydney educationist, first principal of Sydney University, b. (d. 1866)

1816

F

Historia Dignum

Population
Estimated total white, 17,090.

18 Jan. News of Napoleon Bonaparte's defeat at Waterloo reaches Sydney; much jubilation; relief fund for Waterloo veterans launched.
1 Jun. Andrew Bent founds newspaper *Hobart Town Gazette and Southern Reporter*.
12 Sep. Convicts seize brig *Trial* and escape; later wrecked.
Oct. Govt messenger begins Hobart to Launceston mail service, on foot.
During 1816
By end of year 14,236 convicts have been transported to Colony.
Irish Grand Lodge grants Freemasonry charter to 46th Regiment in NSW.

Communities
Wollongong, NSW, estb.

A
History, Politics, Economics, Law

Government
9 Apr. 1817–14 May 1824, William Sorell Lieut-Governor VDL.

24 Feb. Judge Barron Field arrives in Sydney to replace Jeffery Bent as Judge of Supreme Court.
8 Apr. Bank of NSW opens for business in Sydney; first trading bank and public co. in Aust. (Branches open in Brisbane 1850, Melbourne 1851.)
28 Apr. John Oxley begins expedition west of Bathurst, NSW, exploring inland plains and tracing course of Lachlan R.
9 Aug. 48th Regiment, commanded by Lieut-Col. Erskine, arrives in Sydney to relieve 46th Regiment.
Aug. Charles Throsby and Hamilton Hume explore Illawarra and Moss Vale districts, NSW.
Sep. John Macarthur returns to Sydney.
21 Dec. Governor Macquarie formally adopts name 'Australia' for Colony in official correspondence.
22 Dec. Phillip Parker King commissioned to complete Matthew Flinders' work of charting Aust. north coast, begins first of four voyages lasting $4\frac{1}{2}$ years. Begins surveying North-West Cape, WA, via King George Sound.

During 1817
George Johnston introduces clover seed to Illawarra district, NSW.
Jeffery Bent returns to England after being debarred from serving as judge.

Births & Deaths
William Bligh, NSW Governor, d. (b. 1754)
Frederick Gonnerman Dalgety, financier, b. (d. 1894)
Louis Hope, pioneer of sugar-cane industry, b. (d. 1894)
Lauchlan Mackinnon, pioneer pastoralist, newspaper proprietor, b. (d. 1888)
John Madden, Melbourne solicitor, b. (d. 1902)
John Ross, explorer, pastoralist, b. (d. 1903)

B
Science, Technology, Transport, Discovery

Births & Deaths
Sir Anthony Colling Brownless, physician, university chancellor, b. (d. 1897)
William Lodewyk Crowther, Tas. medical practitioner, b. (d. 1885)
Sir Joseph Dalton Hooker, botanist, b. (d. 1911)
Sir Frederick McCoy, geologist, naturalist, b. (d. 1899)

1817

1817

C Arts

Literature

Births & Deaths
Raffaello Carboni, author, poet, b. (d. 1875)

Fine Arts

During 1817
James Wallis paints *Corroboree at Newcastle*, among first portrayals of Aboriginal Corroboree.

Births & Deaths
Sir Oswald Walters Brierly, marine painter, topographer, b. (d. 1894)
Silvester Diggles, bird painter, scientist, b. (d. 1880)
Samuel Elyard, painter, b. (d. 1910)
Mary Hindmarsh, painter, b. (d. 1887)
John Carter Northcote, goldfields artist, b. (d. 1883)

Architecture

Dec. Francis Greenway completes construction of Tower Lighthouse, South Head, Sydney. (Replaced 1883.)
During 1817
Sydney Govt House stables completed.

Births & Deaths
Edmund Thomas Blacket, pioneer of Aust. Gothic architecture, b. (d. 1883)
Henry Ginn, Gothic revival architect, b. (d. 1892)

D Religion, Learning

19 Feb. Foundation stone of St David's church in Hobart laid; first permanent church in Hobart.
3 Mar. First branch of British and Foreign Bible Society forms in Sydney as Auxiliary Bible Society of NSW; aims to spread Scriptures.
9 Oct. Rev. Jeremiah O'Flynn, Catholic priest, arrives in Sydney without credentials. Governor Macquarie forbids him to preach.
11 Oct. Governor Macquarie lays foundation stone of St Matthew's church, Windsor, NSW.
During 1817
John Lees builds first Methodist chapel in southern hemisphere, at Castlereagh near Sydney.

Births & Deaths
James Bonwick, pioneer educationist, historian, pioneer Aust. documentary history, b. (d. 1906)
Richard Deodatus Poulett Harris, Tas. educationist, b. (d. 1899)

F
Historia Dignum

1817

Population
Estimated total white, 20,379.

Nov. Since Mar. 1815 Parramatta magistrates have sentenced 200 convicts to 11,321 cat-o-nine-tail lashes.
New Territorial Seal empowering governors to grant pardons (absolutely or conditionally) to convicts, arrives in Sydney.
Jewish convicts estb. Cherra Kadisha burial society, first Jewish organization in Aust.

1818

A
History, Politics, Economics, Law

Mar. James Meehan and Hamilton Hume lead expedition which discovers Lake Bathurst, and also Goulburn Plains, NSW.
Mar.-Apr. Charles Throsby pioneers overland route from Sydney to Jervis Bay, NSW (Later ACT).
28 May. John Oxley leads second expedition to trace destinations of west-flowing rivers. Expedition crosses and names Castlereagh R., NSW, Liverpool Plains, Peel R., Hastings R. and Manning R., NSW.
26 Jul. Phillip Parker King returns to Sydney after surveying northern coasts of Qld and NT.
21 Nov. Govt proclamation empowers justices of the peace to hear complaints from both employers and workmen and to direct payment of wages.

During 1818
Tobacco growing begins at Emu Plains, NSW.
First Aust. papermill estb., in Sydney.
Adolarius William Henry Humphrey appointed coroner, police superintendent and chief magistrate in Hobart.
Thomas Raine estb. first shore-based whaling station on Aust. mainland, at Twofold Bay, NSW.

Births & Deaths
William Archer, Qld pioneer, b. (d. 1896)
Andrew Spencer Chirnside, overlander, Vic. pioneer, b. (d. 1890)
Sir Thomas Elder, pastoralist, benefactor, b. (d. 1897)
William Forster, NSW Premier, b. (d. 1882)
John Fitzgerald Leslie Foster, Vic. politician, b. (d. 1900)
George Charles Hawker, SA pioneer and politician, sheep breeder, b. (d. 1895)
John Ainsworth Horrocks, among first explorers to use camels, b. (d. 1846)
Michael Howe, VDL bushranger, 'King of the Rangers', d. (b. 1787)
Edmund Besley Court Kennedy, explorer, b. (d. 1848)
Thomas Livingston Learmonth, Vic. pioneer pastoralist, b. (d. 1903)
Henry Maxwell Lefroy, WA explorer, b. (d. 1879)
Arthur Macalister, Qld Premier, b. (d. 1883)
David Cannon McConnel, cattle breeder and founder of Cressbrook beef cattle stud, b. (d. 1885)
Sir John O'Shanassy, Vic. Premier, b. (d. 1883)
Mary Penfold, vigneron, b. (d. 1895)
Thomas Reynolds, SA Premier, b. (d. 1875)
Henry Stuart Russell, pastoralist and historian, b. (d. 1889)
John Dickson Wyselaskie, grazier and benefactor, b. (d. 1883)

B
Science, Technology, Transport, Discovery

Jan. The Great Western Road links Blue Mts, NSW, to Sydney and Parramatta; first of main arterial roads in NSW.
30 May. Simon Lear and George White among first dentists practising in Colony.

During 1818
First lighthouse in Colony built, at South Head near Sydney.
Hobart to Launceston road completed.

C

Arts

Literature

During 1818
Andrew Bent publishes pamphlet by Thomas Wells based on convict Michael Howe, *The Last and Worst of the Bushrangers of Van Diemen's Land*. (Now among rarest publications, and first biography printed in Aust.)

Drama, Theatre

Births & Deaths
Gustavus Vaughan Brooke, Shakespearian actor, b. (d. 1866)
Maria Dolores Eliza Gilbert, better known as Lola Montez, actress and Vic. goldfields entertainer, b. (d. 1861)
Eliza Winstanley, actress, b. (d. 1882)

Fine Arts

Births & Deaths
William Dexter, still-life painter, b. (d. 1860)
Samuel Thomas Gill, goldfields artist, producer of lithographs depicting life on goldfields and watercolours depicting colonial life, b. (d. 1880)
Henry C. Gritten, painter, b. (d. 1873)

D

Religion, Learning

20 May. Governor Macquarie deports Catholic priest Jeremiah O'Flynn for being active among Irish convicts and soldiers.
30 Jun. Female orphans removed to new Orphan School near Parramatta.
William Cowper, Church of England minister, tightens Anglican control of education by introducing *Rules for the Management of Public Schools in Sydney*.

1818

E
Sport

16 May. First recorded rowing race in Aust. held. From Bradleys Head to Sydney Cove.

F
Historia Dignum

Population
Estimated total white, 20,822.

During 1818
Public flogging of convicts ends. Henceforth all flogging administered in barracks yard at regular flogging times.

A

History, Politics, Economics, Law

1819

19 Jan. General meeting of 'Landholders, Merchants and other respectable Inhabitants of the Colony' passes resolutions drawing attention to economic and social grievances; petition drawn up.
During Jan. Barron Field presides over first sitting of Supreme Court of Civil Judicature in VDL. Returns to Sydney on 14 Feb.
15 Feb. British Parlt passes Act empowering Governor Macquarie to make taxing proclamations.
Apr. Charles Throsby explores country from Moss Vale to Bathurst, NSW, opening alternative route west from Sydney.
During May. Phillip Parker King leaves Sydney to continue systematic investigation of north-west coastline, including Torres Strait, Gulf of Carpentaria, and south-west coast from Albany to Swan R., WA, filling most gaps in Matthew Flinders' charts. (Completes exploration 1822.)
4 Jun. Convict Barracks opened at Hyde Park, Sydney. Able to accommodate 600 convicts.
17 Jul. Robert Campbell opens NSW Savings Bank for business in Sydney. First Savings bank in Aust. (First Savings bank facilities estb. Tas. 1835, Vic. 1841, SA 1848, Qld 1854, WA 1863.)
25 Sep. John Thomas Bigge, appointed Commissioner to examine colonial affairs, arrives in Sydney. Thomas Hobbes arrives as Bigge's secretary.
26 Oct. John Howe begins expedition which finds overland route from Windsor to Hunter R., NSW.
1 Nov. French explorer Freycinet arrives at Port Jackson in ship *Uranie*. (Departs 25 Dec.)
15 Nov. George Paton replaces Isaac Nichols as postmaster in Sydney.
During 1819
Governor Macquarie estb. Emu Plains farm west of Sydney to absorb increasing numbers of convicts.
British import duty on Aust. wool lowered from 6 pence to 3 pence a pound.

Births & Deaths

Margaret Catchpole, convict, pioneer, d. (b. 1762)
Sir James Cockle, Qld Chief Justice, mathematician, b. (d. 1895)
Caroline Dexter, feminist, b. (d. 1884)
John Durack, NSW pioneer pastoralist, b. (d. 1873)
James Goodall Francis, Vic. Premier, b. (d. 1884)
Johann Gramp, vigneron, b. (d. 1903)
Sir Augustus Charles Gregory, explorer, b. (d. 1905)
Anthony Hordern, businessman, retailer, b. (d. 1876)
Sir Edward Knox, company director, b. (d. 1901)
Somerville Learmonth, Vic. pioneer pastoralist, b. (d. 1878)
Gerald de Courcy Lefroy, WA pioneer, b. (d. 1878)
Hugh McColl, irrigation pioneer, Vic. politician, b. (d. 1885)
Sir James McCulloch, Vic. Premier, b. (d. 1893)
John McKinlay, explorer, b. (d. 1872)
Thomas Lodge Murray-Prior, NSW pastoralist, first Qld postmaster, b. (d. 1892)
Isaac Nichols, pioneer postmaster, Sydney, d. (b. 1770)
Sir Arthur Hunter Palmer, Qld Premier, b. (d. 1898)
Robert John Sholl, WA pioneer, b. (d. 1886)
Sir Francis Villeneuve Smith, Tas. Premier, b. (d. 1909)
James Tyson, pastoralist millionaire, b. (d. 1898)
Robert Watson, first Sydney harbourmaster, d. (b. 1756)

1819

B

Science, Technology, Transport, Discovery

25 Oct. James Bowman replaces D'Arcy Wentworth as principal colonial surgeon.

During 1819
William Bland among first to perform lithotomy and treat cataracts in Aust. Improved medical instruments used to remove cataracts, gallstones and blood-clots.
Shipbuilding yards open in Newcastle, NSW.
Thomas Kent invents process of extracting tanning materials from wattle bark.

Births & Deaths
William Thomson, surgeon, b. (d. 1883)
John Whitton, first NSW chief railways engineer, probably b. (d. 1898)

C

Arts

Literature

During 1819
James Hardy Vaux, convict, publishes first Aust. slang dictionary, *Vocabulary of the Flash Language*, as part of his *Memoirs*.
George Howe publishes first volume of verse in Aust. in book form, *First Fruits of Australian Poetry*, by Barron Field.
William Charles Wentworth publishes, *A Statistical, Historical and Political Description of the Colony of New South Wales...*

Drama, Theatre

Births & Deaths
George Selth Coppin, actor and Vic. politician, 'Father of Australian Theatre', b. (d. 1906)
Charles Horace Frederick Frisby Young, comic actor, b. (d. 1874)

Fine Arts

Births & Deaths
Robert Proctor Beauchamp, artist, b. (d. 1889)
J. H. Carse, painter, probably b. (d. 1900)
John Gully, watercolourist, b. (d. 1888)
John William Lewin, naturalist, artist and engraver; among first to succeed in portraying Aust. bush scenery without European romantic sentiment, d. (b. 1770)
John Frederick Mann, artist, explorer, b. (d. 1907)
Frederick C. Smith, artist, explorer, b. (d. 1837)

Architecture

During 1819
Francis Greenway designs new Female Factory, with three storeys and able to house 300 women convicts.

D
Religion, Learning

1 Jan. First Orphan School for boys opens in Sydney.
7 Oct. Governor Macquarie lays foundation stone of St James church in Sydney.

Births & Deaths

John Harris, missionary schoolmaster, d. (b. 1754)
Thomas McCombie, historian, author, b. (d. 1869)
James Quinn, first Roman Catholic bishop, Brisbane, 1859, b. (d. 1881)
William Ridley, Presbyterian missionary, author, b. (d. 1878)
George William Rusden, educationist, historian, b. (d. 1903)

F
Historia Dignum

Population
Estimated total white, 30,296.

During 1819
Ship *Frederick* wrecked near western head of Bathurst Bay, Qld; 22 lives lost.

Births & Deaths
Edmund Finn, Melb. journalist who also wrote as Garryowen, b. (d. 1898)

Communities
Bong Bong, NSW, first settled
Sorell, Tas. estb.

1820

A
History, Politics, Economics, Law

20 Mar. & Apr. Four Russian ships visit Sydney on scientific expedition. Russians erect temporary observatory on Kirribilli Point, Sydney, which they name Russian Cape.
19 Aug. Joseph Wild discovers Lake George, NSW.
25 Nov. Governor Macquarie officially opens up south-western NSW to graziers.

During 1820
Commercial leather industry begins in Sydney.
William Sorell ships rams from Macarthur's flocks to VDL, beginning wool industry there.
Rapid pastoral expansion financed by overseas capital results in financial boom in NSW.
VDL becomes Aust.'s major wheat producer. (Until 1850.)
c. 1820. Pedigreed pigs and Devon cattle imported to Colony.
Aust. dairy industry founded in Illawarra district, NSW.

Births & Deaths

Archibald Archer, Qld politician, b. (d. 1902)
George Arden, newspaper proprietor, publisher, probably b. (d. 1854)
Richard Atkins, Rum Rebellion Judge-Advocate, d. (b. 1745)
Henry Edward Pulteney Dana, police superintendent, b. (d. 1852)
Thomas Fisher, Sydney merchant, b. (d. 1884)
Sir James Martin, NSW Premier and Chief Justice, b. (d. 1886)
Augustus Morris, NSW pastoralist, politician, probably b. (d. 1895)
Harry Power, Vic. bushranger, b. (d. 1891)
Hector Norman Simson, Vic. pioneer pastoralist, b. (d. 1880)
William Westwood, also known as 'Jackey Jackey', NSW bushranger, b. (d. 1846)
James Whyte, Tas. Premier, b. (d. 1882)

B
Science, Technology, Transport, Discovery

During 1820
First Aust. coal gas manufactured, in Sydney.
John Tawell opens first pharmaceutical shop in Sydney.

Births & Deaths

William Archer, botanist, architect, b. (d. 1874)
Sir Joseph Banks, botanist, d. (b. 1743)
Edward Micklethwaite Curr, pioneer, noted for work on reducing scab in sheep, and also author and authority on Aborigines, b. (d. 1889)
Sir William John Macleay, NSW scientist and politician, b. (d. 1891)
Charles Moore, botanist, b. (d. 1905)

Arts

Fine Arts

Births & Deaths
J. C. Armytage, illustrator, b. (d. 1897)
Samuel Prout Hill, seascape painter, probably b. (d. 1861)
Eliezer Levi Montefiore, painter, etcher, b. (d. 1894)
James Smith, art and drama critic, b. (d. 1910)
Edward Winstanley, horse painter, b. (d. 1849)
Frederick Woodhouse, horse painter, b. (d. 1909)

Architecture

During 1820
Francis Greenway completes Lancer Military Barracks at Parramatta. (Becomes oldest continuously used barracks in Aust.)
c. 1820. Pisé building becomes popular.

Births & Deaths
Robert George Thomas, SA Govt Architect, b. (d. 1883)

Religion, Learning

Jan. Laurence Hynes Halloran opens academy in Sydney for 'classical, mathematical and commercial education'. (Closes 1825.)
Apr. Dionysii celebrates first Russian Orthodox religious service in Aust., at Kirribilli Point, Sydney.
3 May. John Joseph Therry and Philip Conolly, first officially recognized Roman Catholic priests to arrive in Sydney, estb. Roman Catholic Church in Aust.
Aug. Rev. Benjamin Carvosso holds first Methodist Church service in VDL. (Methodist Society formed May.)
Sep. Rev. Thomas Reddall arrives in Sydney to implement modern educational methods based on the Bell system.

During 1820
St James Church of England church in Sydney completed.
There are 18 established schools in Aust.
Joseph Marcus conducts first Jewish worship services.

Births & Deaths
Rowland Hassall, preacher, landholder, d. (b. 1768)
John Watsford, Methodist minister, b. (d. 1907)

1820

1820

E
Sport

During 1820
First reported game of golf in Aust. played, in VDL.

F
Historia Dignum

Population
Estimated total white, 29,407.

6 Jan. Samuel Clayton founds first Australian Masonic Lodge in Sydney.
27 Jan. New burial ground opens near Sydney.
15 Aug. Left-hand driving regulations enforced for horse traffic in NSW.
During Aug. Catarrh epidemic in Colony.
During 1820
The newspaper *Sydney Gazette* printed on Aust.-made paper.

Communities

Falmouth, Tas., first settled
Hadspen, Tas., settled
Singleton, NSW, first settled
Ulladulla, NSW, estb.

A
History, Politics, Economics, Law

1821

Government
1 Dec. 1821–1 Dec. 1825, Sir Thomas Makdougall Brisbane Governor NSW.

23 Jan. Emancipated colonists petition the King over disadvantages incurred because of legal disqualifications imposed by British Govt.
29 Jan. First criminal court session in VDL held.
Charles Throsby becomes first white man to explore Canberra area; names it Limestone Plains.
14 Feb. Thomas Bigge concludes inquiry into Colony; returns to England.
21 Mar. Francis Allman leads party to estb. penal settlement for difficult convicts at Port Macquarie, NSW.
17 Aug. Macarthur wool sells for high prices at first large-scale auction of Aust. wool in London.
7 Nov. Sir Thomas Brisbane arrives in Sydney.
12 Nov. William Lawson explores Mudgee area, NSW.
Dec. Robert Johnston discovers Clyde R., Batemans Bay, NSW.

During 1821
Frederick Goulburn appointed first official NSW Colonial-Secretary.
Self-contained Female Factory to house female convicts opens at Parramatta, NSW.
Francis Allman among first to grow sugar-cane, at Port Macquarie, NSW.

Births & Deaths
Sir Henry Ayers, SA Premier, b. (d. 1897)
Sir George Ferguson Bowen, first Qld Governor, b. (d. 1899)
Robert O'Hara Burke, explorer, b. (d. 1861)
Richard Goldsbrough, Vic. pioneer, woolbroker, b. (d. 1886)
Francis Thomas Gregory, explorer, surveyor, b. (d. 1888)
John Hunter, NSW Governor, d. (b. 1737)
Sir William Francis Drummond Jervois, SA Governor, b. (d. 1897)
Alfred Joyce, Vic. pioneer settler, b. (d. 1901)
Peter Learmonth, Vic. pioneer, b. (d. 1893)
Alexander McGregor, Tas. shipowner, merchant, b. (d. 1896)
Thomas Reibey, Tas. Premier, b. (d. 1912)
William Kyffin Thomas, SA publisher, b. (d. 1878)

B
Science, Technology, Transport, Discovery

27 Jun. Philosophical Society of Australasia forms to study science. (Becomes Royal Society of NSW.—12 Dec. 1866)

Births & Deaths
Thomas Arndell, First Fleet surgeon, d. (probably b. 1752)
William Carron, botanist, b. (d. 1876)
Amalie Dietrich, naturalist, b. (d. 1891)
Henry Heylyn Hayter, Vic. statistician, b. (d. 1895)
John Smith, scientist, educationist, pioneer photographer, b. (d. 1885)

1821

C Arts

Literature

Births & Deaths
George Howe, poet, editor, publisher, d. (b. 1769)

Drama, Theatre

During 1821
J. Amherst's play *Michael Howe, The Terror of Van Diemen's Land* produced in London.

Fine Arts

During 1821
Aust. lithography begins. Presses used at Parramatta Observatory.

Births & Deaths
Ellen Burgess, watercolourist, b. (d. 1908)
George O'Brien, artist, b. (d. 1888)

D Religion, Learning

14 Apr. Rev. Philip Conolly becomes first Roman Catholic priest in VDL.
Jun. Peter Archer Mulgrave, educationist, appointed Superintendent of Schools in VDL, arrives in Hobart.
1 Jul. Methodist chapel opens in Sydney.
29 Oct. Governor Macquarie lays foundation stone for St Mary's Cathedral in Sydney. First Roman Catholic church in Aust.

During 1821
Samuel Leigh opens a Methodist mission in Hobart, with Rev. William Horton as first minister. Sunday School begins in May.
John Joseph Therry estb. Catholic school which later becomes the Parramatta Marist High School.

F
Historia Dignum

1821

Population
Estimated total white, 36,968.

May. First periodical in Aust., the *Australian Magazine*, begins (13 issues only).
Aug. Of 26 prisoners capitally convicted in Colony, 19 are executed.
17 Nov. Freak high tide, Sydney.
30 Dec. NSW Govt first permits private distillation from grapes, sugar and grain.
During Dec. Barnett Levey arrives in Sydney; first free Jewish settler in Colony.
Newcastle district opens for settlement.

Communities
Bothwell, Tas., first settled
Cranbrook, Tas., estb.
Port Macquarie, NSW, estb.

1822

A
History, Politics, Economics, Law

15 Feb. Governor Macquarie and family leave for England after 12 years in Colony.
Apr. Phillip Parker King returns to Sydney, after completing four voyages since 1819.
Jun. In London John Thomas Bigge completes report on the Colony; first report published 19 Jun.
24 Jul. George Allen admitted to practise as a solicitor; first solicitor to complete legal training in Colony, and founder of oldest legal firm in Aust.
8 Aug. First sale of Aust.-grown tobacco.
Oct. Bushranging becomes a serious problem. In Sydney 34 prisoners are condemned to hang for bushranging offences.
7 Nov. General govt order regularizes issue of tickets of leave.

During 1822
William Sorell opens penal settlement, 'The Gates of Hell', Macquarie Harbour, VDL.
First recorded strike in Aust. occurs when James Straiter, convict, incites his master's servants to combine for higher wages and better rations. Straiter severely punished.
NSW develops system of free immigration.
John Macarthur wins two gold medals for wool from British Society of Arts.
Cedar from Illawarra district, NSW, first exported.
James Williams among first to grow sugar-cane, near Port Macquarie, NSW.
Capt Wallis imports first commercially successful honey-producing bees to NSW.
Civil courts replace the courts-martial in VDL.
Alexander Berry and Edward Wollstonecraft pioneer settlement of South Coast, NSW.

Births & Deaths
Sir Graham Berry, Vic. Premier, b. (d. 1904)
Francis Cadell, pioneer Murray R. navigator, b. (d. 1879)
James 'Civil Jim' Edmond, among first Vic. gold diggers, b. (d. 1890)
James Macpherson Grant, Vic. lawyer, b. (d. 1885)
Richard Heales, Vic. Premier, probably b. (d. 1864)
'Captain Melville' Vic. bushranger b., probably Francis McNeiss McNiel McCallum, (d. 1857)
James Squire, pioneer brewer, d. (probably b. 1754)

B
Science, Technology, Transport, Discovery

Apr. James Dunlop estb. astronomical observatory a Parramatta, NSW.
22 Jun. Christian Carl Ludwig Rümker observes Pons' (Encke's) comet. Only reported sighting of Pons' comet on this orbit.

C
Arts

Music, Dance

19 Jun. John Philip Deane, influential musician, arrives in Hobart.
During 1822
First early Aust. chamber music group performs, at St David's church, Hobart.

Births & Deaths
Charles Edward Horsley, musician, composer, b. (d. 1876)

Fine Arts

Births & Deaths
George French Angas, painter, naturalist, b. (d. 1886)
Thomas Baines, artist and explorer, b. (d. 1875)
Frank Dunnett, painter, engraver, b. (d. 1891)
Chester Earles, portrait painter, probably b. (d. 1890)

D
Religion, Learning

27 Sep. Rev. William Walker, Wesleyan minister, baptizes Aboriginal, Thomas Walker Coke, Bennelong's son; among first Aborigines baptized.
During 1822
First Presbyterian Church minister from United Secession Church of Scotland, Rev. A. McArthur, arrives in Hobart. (United Secession Church later part of Presbyterian Church.)
First Roman Catholic school estb. in Sydney.
First library in Aust., a reading and newspaper room, estb. in Hobart.

1822

1822

E
Sport

Births & Deaths
Robert S. Still, cricketer, b. (d. 1907)

F
Historia Dignum

Population
Estimated total white, 38,395.

Jan. Hand-drawn pumps first used to fight a fire in Sydney.
19 Mar. Philosophical Society of NSW places memorial to James Cook (b. 1728 d. 1779) and Joseph Banks at S. Headland, Botany Bay, NSW.
5 Jul. Royal Agricultural Society of NSW forms, to encourage better farming methods.
5 Aug. Sydney Bethel Union (a non-conformist seamen's chapel) forms.
20 Sep. Eight convicts escape from Macquarie Harbour penal settlement; Alexander Pearce only one to survive.
22 Sep. Garden Palace in Sydney burns down.
During 1822
Treadmill system of convict punishment introduced to Carter's Barracks in Sydney.

Communities
Berry, NSW, first settled
Strahan, Tas., estb.

A

History, Politics, Economics, Law

1823

5 Mar. Droving road opens from Richmond to Newcastle, NSW; opens lower Hunter R. district to cultivation.

During Mar. Lieut Percy Simpson estb. agricultural depot at Wellington, central western NSW, as a penal settlement for twice-convicted convicts.

22 May. John Ovens and Mark Currie begin expedition. Discover Monaro Plains, NSW, in Jun.

Jun. Allan Cunningham discovers route, Pandora's Pass, leading to Liverpool Plains, NSW.

Thomas Raine and David Ramsay found Raine and Ramsay, company of shipowners, agents and general merchants.

19 Jul. British Govt passes New South Wales Judicature Act, providing for first Legislative Council in NSW. Primarily to remove legal disabilities, to provide for better relations between masters and servants and to carry out Bigge Report recommendations. Consists of five to seven nominated members to advise governor. First tentative step towards representative govt in Aust. (Effective 1824.)

1–5 Aug. Archibald Bell (junior) pioneers Bell's line of road across treacherous section of Blue Mts, NSW.

During Aug. 3rd Regiment replaces 48th Regiment.

13 Oct. A new Supreme Court of NSW constituted, with both civil and criminal jurisdiction and replacing both former Criminal Court and former Supreme Court of Civil Judicature, with Sir Francis Forbes as first Chief Justice. (Court opens 17 May 1824.)

23 Oct. John Oxley leaves Sydney in search of good site for penal settlement north of Sydney; discovers Brisbane R., Qld, and recommends site for settlement at Moreton Bay, in Nov.

During 1823

Gregory Blaxland awarded silver medal for first Aust. wine exported in bulk to London.

Hordern pioneer business and pastoral family arrive in Sydney.

First stockmen arrive Canberra area. J. J. Moore first grazier in area.

Colonial Secretary assumes responsibility for allocating convict labour. (Formerly exercised by Superintendent of Convicts.)

Births & Deaths

John Howard Angas, pioneer and philanthropist, b. (d. 1904)
Thomas Archer, Qld pioneer, b. (d. 1905)
Sir Arthur Blyth, SA Premier, b. (d. 1891)
Sir John Colton, SA Premier, b. (d. 1902)
Henry William Coxen, Qld pastoralist, b. (d. 1915)
George Crossley, convict lawyer, adviser to Governor Bligh, d. (b. 1749)
Thomas Davey, VDL Lieut-Governor, d. (b. 1758)
Hovenden Hely, explorer, b. (d. 1872)
George Johnston, soldier and pioneer, d. (b. 1764)
George Lansell, mining magnate, Bendigo, Vic., 'Australia's Quartz King', b. (d. 1906)
Francis Rossi, eccentric landowner, b. (d. 1903)
James Service, Vic. Premier, b. (d. 1899)
Sir Frederick Aloysius Weld, WA and Tas. Governor, b. (d. 1891)

1823

B
Science, Technology, Transport, Discovery

15 Feb. James McBrien makes first discovery of alluvial gold in Aust., on Fish R. between Bathurst and Rydal, NSW.
Dec. Thomas Alison Scott conducts sugar manufacturing experiments at Port Macquarie, NSW.
During 1823
Dr William Sherwin becomes first Aust. member of Royal College of Physicians in London.
Henry Cowper first uses quinine to treat fever in Qld; first Aust.-born medical practitioner to become member of Royal College of Surgeons, London.
Regular shipping service between Sydney and Newcastle estb.

Births & Deaths

Townsend Duryea, SA photographer, b. (d. 1888)
Eugene Dominique Nicolle, engineer, b. (d. 1909)
Sir Alfred Roberts, surgeon who contributed to starting nursing profession in Aust., b. (d. 1898)

C
Arts

Literature

During 1823
W. C. Wentworth among first Aust.-born poets to publish; acclaimed for poem 'Australasia'.
Gregory Blaxland publishes *A Journal of a Tour of Discovery Across the Blue Mountains in New South Wales.*

Music, Dance

During 1823
Barron Field publishes one of first transcriptions of an Aboriginal song tune.

Births & Deaths

Eliza Wallace Bushelle, musician, b. (d. 1878)

Architecture

During 1823
Construction of Richmond Bridge, VDL, begins, Thomas Bell architect. (Now among oldest bridges in Aust.)

Births & Deaths

William Wilkinson Wardell, architect, b. (d. 1899)
Joseph Reed, architect, probably b. (d. 1890s)

D
Religion, Learning

5 Jan. Archibald Macarthur conducts first Presbyterian service in Hobart.
During Jan. Rev. William Bedford arrives as Church of England chaplain in Hobart.
Feb. Samuel Marsden consecrates church of St David in Hobart.
23 May. John Dunmore Lang, first Presbyterian minister in NSW, arrives in Sydney, conducts first Presbyterian service in Sydney on 8 Jun.
Sep. The Australian Religious Tract Society forms to promote evangelical sentiments.
During 1823
George Erskine, Methodist educationist, arrives in Sydney.

Births & Deaths
Moses Rintel, Jewish rabbi, b. (d. 1880)

F
Historia Dignum

1823

Population
Estimated total white, 39,792.

28 Nov. Earthquake felt at Launceston.

Communities
Canberra, ACT, area first settled
Oatlands, Tas., estb.
Wellington, NSW, estb.
Wyong, NSW, area first settled

1824

A History, Politics, Economics, Law

Government

14 May 1824–30 Oct. 1836, George Arthur Lieut-Governor VDL.

5 Mar. William Balcombe, Colonial Treasurer, arrives in Sydney.
During Mar. Joseph Tice Gellibrand arrives in VDL as Attorney-General.
10 May. Sir John Lewes Pedder takes office as Chief Justice VDL; opens new Supreme Court.
17 May. Sir Francis Forbes takes office as first Chief Justice of NSW, inaugurates NSW Charter of Justice. On 10 Jun. opens Criminal Court in Sydney. On 14–15 Oct. introduces limited trial by jury for civil proceedings at Court of Quarter Sessions in Sydney. On 2 Nov. first civil jury empanelled.
21 Jun. Aust. Agricultural Co. founded in London to develop pastoral activities in NSW. Granted one million acres in NSW; Robert Dawson appointed first manager.
Jul. Commissioner Thomas Bigge's recommendation that Crown land be purchased at five shillings per acre payable over three years adopted. First step in freeing land from govt control.
5 Aug. Martial law proclaimed in Bathurst district, NSW, over conflicts with Aborigines. (Until Dec.)
11 Aug. NSW constituted a Crown Colony. Legislative Council proclaimed in *Sydney Gazette*. First meeting takes place on 25 Aug. (Executive Council appointed 20 Dec. 1825.)
1 Sep. Lieut Henry Miller of 40th Regiment, with John Oxley, leads advance party to estb. penal settlement at Moreton Bay. Selects temporary site at Redcliffe Point.
26 Sep. James Bremer founds Fort Dundas settlement at Melville I., NT. First attempt to colonize the north. (Abandoned 31 Mar. 1829.)
28 Sep. Legislative Council passes first Aust. enactment, a Currency Bill making promissory notes and bills payable in Spanish holey dollars or sterling pounds.
1 Oct. T. H. James and Co. import tobacco manufacturing machinery.
17 Oct. Hamilton Hume and William Hovell overland from Lake George district, NSW, to Port Phillip, Vic. Cross Murrumbidgee R. On 8 Nov. expedition names the Australian Alps. On 17 Nov. discovers Hume (Murray) R. On 16 Dec. reaches Corio Bay, Port Phillip Bay, Vic.
27 Oct. 40th Regiment arrives to relieve 3rd Regiment.
9 Nov.–5 Dec. Sir Thomas Makdougall Brisbane and party visit Moreton Bay and approve penal settlement. Chief Justice Sir Francis Forbes suggests naming it Edenglassie, but by 1825 the name Brisbane prevails.

During 1824
Name 'Australia' officially adopted.
First barristers and attorneys admitted to practise, include John Stephen, Dr Robert Wardell, W. C. Wentworth and Saxe Bannister, who arrives on 5 Apr. as first NSW Attorney-General.
First recorded request for separation of VDL from NSW; request signed by 103 settlers.
Bank of Van Diemen's Land estb.
First sugar manufactured, in mill built at Rolland Plains near Port Macquarie, NSW.
Buffalo first shipped from Timor to Melville I., NT.
Baron de Bougainville, French explorer, visits VDL.

Births & Deaths

Sir George Wigram Allen, NSW politician, b. (d. 1885)
William Frederick Buchanan, NSW pioneer pastoralist, b. (d. 1911)
Sir Andrew Clarke, Vic. politician, b. (d. 1902)
George Henry Cox, sheep breeder, b. (d. 1901)
Thomas Henry Fitzgerald, Qld politician, sugar pioneer, b. (d. 1888)
Lachlan Macquarie, NSW Governor, d. (b. 1762)
William Richard Randell, Murray R. steam navigator, pioneer, b. (d. 1911)
Sir Hercules George Robert Robinson, NSW Governor, b. (d. 1897)
Robert Barr Smith, businessman, philanthropist, b. (d. 1915)
Sir Alexander Stuart, NSW Premier, b. (d. 1886)
George Marsden Waterhouse, SA Premier, b. (d. 1906)
Wylie, WA Aboriginal partner to Edward Eyre, probably b.

B

Science, Technology, Transport, Discovery

During 1824
Coal discovered at South Cape Bay, VDL

Births & Deaths

Joseph Bosisto, chemist, b. (d. 1898)
George Britton Halford, surgeon, snake bite and heart pioneer, b. (d. 1910)
Edmund William Wright, SA civil engineer, architect, b. (d. 1888)

C

Arts

Literature

During 1824
Joseph Lycett's *Views in Australia* begins to be published; in 1825 becomes first important book of picturesque Aust. views.

Music, Dance

During 1824
Robert Campbell opens first music shop in Aust., in Sydney.

Fine Arts

Births & Deaths

Charles Hill, painter, engraver, b. (d. 1916)
James Oddie, pioneer, benefactor and painter, b. (d. 1911)

Architecture

3 Jun. David Lambe appointed first Colonial Architect VDL.

1824

1824

D
Religion, Learning

11 Feb. Samuel Marsden consecrates St James Anglican church in Sydney.
1 Jul. Foundation stone of Scots Presbyterian church, Sydney, laid.
18 Aug. Rev. Thomas Reddall appointed NSW Director-General of Public Schools.
2 Oct. Thomas Hobbes Scott becomes first Church of England archdeacon of NSW.
John Dunmore Lang estb. regular Presbyterian communion services at Ebenezer, NSW.
St Thomas' Church of England church built at Port Macquarie, NSW.
Church of England Church and School Corporation estb. NSW.
First infants' school in Aust. estb., in Sydney.

Births & Deaths

John Gibson Paton, Presbyterian missionary, b. (d. 1907)

E
Sport

20 Feb. First heavyweight bare-knuckle boxing championship; won by Jack Kable against Bill Clarke in five rounds.

F
Historia Dignum

1824

Population
Estimated total white, 42,426.

14 Oct. Robert Wardell and William Charles Wentworth begin Aust.'s first privately owned daily newspaper, the *Australian*.
15 Oct. Rigid censorship of press abolished.
During 1824
Aust.-manufactured tobacco first advertised.
NSW drought affects crops.

Births & Deaths
Jules François de Sales Joubert, showman, b. (d. 1907)

Communities
Brisbane, Qld, estb.
Gundaroo, NSW, settled
Gunning, NSW, estb.
Maitland, NSW, estb.
Redcliffe, Qld, estb.
Richmond, Tas., town site chosen
Tumut, NSW, estb.
Wallerawang, NSW, first settled

1825

A History, Politics, Economics, Law

Government
1 Dec. 1825–18 Dec. 1825, William Stewart administered NSW.
19 Dec. 1825–21 Oct. 1831, Ralph Darling Governor NSW.

12 Feb. First Supreme Court of NSW jury empanelled in Sydney. (Emancipists excluded from jury service until 1828.)
17 Feb. Capt Mitchell of HMS *Slaney* seizes ship *Almorah* carrying supplies from Batavia (now Jakarta, in Indonesia) for violating East India Company's charter.
First civil case, King *v.* Cooper, heard in Supreme Court of NSW.
Mar.–Jun. Allan Cunningham explores Liverpool Plains, NSW.
7 Apr. Two ships chartered by Thomas Potter Macqueen, absentee investor, arrive in Sydney carrying farm equipment, livestock and employees. Establish Segenhoe property on 10,000-acre grant in Hunter Valley. First direct shipment of free immigrants to NSW.
19 May. Francis N. Rossi takes up duties as first NSW Superintendent of Police.
7 Jun. Sydney Chamber of Commerce estb.
During Jun. Norfolk I. re-settled as penal settlement.
1 Sep.–16 Oct. Edmund Lockyer explores Brisbane R.
10 Sep. Moreton Bay settlement formally called Brisbane after being moved to northern bank of Brisbane R. in Feb.
21 Oct. William Charles Wentworth addresses public meeting; becomes popular leader in struggle against autocracy.
9 Nov. Van Diemen's Land Co. formed in London.
22 Nov. First Postal Act passed. Begins organized development of postal services.
1 Dec. Governor Brisbane leaves Aust. with petition for self-govt from colonists.
3 Dec. VDL declared a Colony independent of NSW. Executive authority vested in Lieut-Governor assisted by nominated Legislative and Executive Councils based on NSW pattern.
20 Dec. First Executive Council of NSW appointed.
During 1825
NSW boundaries extended west to long. 129°E. (Thus including all mainland Aust. other than the area now occupied by State of WA.)
NSW police first use black trackers and a horse patrol to hunt escaped convicts and bushrangers.
Timothy Goodwin Pitman, from the US, is among first persons legally naturalized in Aust.
Policy of encouraging men of wealth to settle on Aust. land begins.
NSW Govt passes first Aust. liquor-licensing statute.
Robert Campbell secures land grant at Duntroon, in Canberra area.
Workers given rights to form unions to improve wages and conditions.

Births & Deaths
James Snowden Calvert, explorer, botanist, b. (d. 1884)
Sir Charles Du Cane, Tas. Governor b. (d. 1889)
Sir Charles Squire Farnell, first native-born NSW Premier, b. (d. 1888)
Andrew Garran, NSW politician, journalist, b. (d. 1901)
William Landsborough, pastoralist, explorer, b. (d. 1886)
James Litchfield, sheep breeder, b. (d. 1905)
George Robertson, Melbourne publisher, b. (d. 1898)

B

Science, Technology, Transport, Discovery

During 1825
Edmund Lockyer discovers coal near Ipswich, Qld.

Births & Deaths
Thomas Henry Huxley, English biologist, painter, b. (d. 1895)
Baron Sir Ferdinand Jakob Heinrich von Mueller, botanist, explorer, b. (d. 1896)

C

Arts

Literature

Births & Deaths
Catherine Helen Spence, first Aust. woman novelist, b. (d. 1910)

Music, Dance

During 1825
First organ in Aust. installed, at St David's church in Hobart. John Philip Deane first organist.

Births & Deaths
William Henry Paling, musician, businessman, b. (d. 1895)

Fine Arts

18 Jan. Augustus Earle, topographical and portrait artist, arrives in VDL.
During 1825
Richmond Bridge, VDL, completed. (Now among oldest bridges in Aust.)

Births & Deaths
J. Haughton Forrest, marine painter, b. (d. 1925)
William Strutt, painter, draughtsman, b. (d. 1915)
Frederick Casemero Terry, watercolourist probably b. (d. 1869)
Thomas Woolner, sculptor, b. (d. 1892)

Architecture

Births & Deaths
Leonard Terry, architect, b. (d. 1884)

1825

1825

D
Religion, Learning

Jul. Thomas Hobbes Scott, first archdeacon of NSW, begins first teacher-training classes in Sydney. (Arrived in Sydney on 7 May.)
19 Nov. Laurence Hynes Halloran opens Sydney Free Public Grammar School. (Closes Oct. 1826.)
During 1825
London Missionary Society estb. mission at Lake Macquarie, NSW.

Births & Deaths

George Fairfowl Macarthur, Church of England clergyman, schoolmaster, b. (d. 1890)
Thomas Magarey, Church of Christ layman, pastoralist, b. (d. 1902)

E
Sport

18 Mar. Sydney Turf Club founded. First Aust. racing club. Holds first handicap race in Apr.

Historia Dignum

1825

Population
Estimated total white, 45,528. Only 20 per cent of population are immigrants.

5 Jan. First country newspaper in Aust., the *Tasmanian*, founded, in Launceston.
25 Feb. Aboriginal known as Mosquito executed in VDL.
19 Aug. Andrew Bent changes title of his VDL newspaper from *Hobart Town Gazette* to *Colonial Times*.
'Bush Hotel' in New Norfolk, VDL, licensed.

Communities
Belmont, NSW, estb.
Jerrys Plains, NSW, probably estb.
Swansea, NSW, estb.
Taralga, NSW, probably settled
Triabunna, Tas., estb.

1826

A History, Politics, Economics, Law

9 Jan. First Executive Council for VDL appointed. First meets on 12 Apr.

During Jan. Alexander Macleay takes office as NSW Colonial Secretary. (Until 1837.)

12 Jul. British Govt rules that English sterling currency should be used in Aust.

During Jul. Military station estb. at Five Islands in Illawarra district, NSW, to cope with fears of possible French invasion.

Bank of Australia opens in Sydney. (Closes 1848.)

15 Aug. Moreton Bay formally proclaimed penal settlement. Patrick Logan Commandant, responsible for laying foundations of settlement.

Sep. Governor Darling attempts to confine squatters to specific areas by replacing tickets of occupation with grazing licences.

Nov. Governor Darling sentences soldiers Joseph Sudds and Patrick Thompson for stealing; begins controversial Sudds-Thompson Case.

11 Dec. Samuel Wright estb. convict settlement at Corinella, Westernport, Vic. (abandoned in Jan. 1828.)

25 Dec. Edmund Lockyer founds convict settlement at Frederickstown (name changed to Albany in 1832), on King George Sound, WA, to forestall possible French colonization. First WA settlement. (Garrison withdrawn 1831.)

During 1826

Cressy Co. formed in NSW to breed sheep.

Hereford cattle imported to NSW.

Governor Darling estb. assignment board to allot convicts' labour and separate newly arrived convicts from old lags.

Van Diemen's Land Co. begins operating under management of Edward Curr at Circular Head, VDL. Granted 250,000 acres.

John Batman captures VDL bushranger, Matthew Brady.

Peter Dillon prepares to sail along south coast of Aust. in search of evidence of fate of Jean-François de Galaup, Comte de La Pérouse.

Dumont D'Urville, French navigator, sails through Bass Strait in the *Astrolabe*.

Edward Smith Hall, 'The Colonial Cobbett', becomes exponent of settlers' cause.

Alexander Riley imports 200 Saxon merino sheep into NSW.

Births & Deaths

Nathaniel Buchanan, overlander explorer, NSW pastoralist, b. (d. 1901)

George Augustus Frederick Elphinstone Dalrymple, explorer, pastoralist, b. (d. 1876)

George Woodroffe Goyder, surveyor, explorer, b. (d. 1898)

William Edward Hearn, economist, b. (d. 1888)

George Higinbotham, Vic. Chief Justice, b. (d. 1892)

Joseph Holt, Irish rebel, Castle Hill Rising, d. (b. 1756)

James Meehan, emancipist surveyor and explorer, d. (b. 1774)

Ebenezer Syme, journalist and newspaper proprietor, b. (d. 1860)

B

Science, Technology, Transport, Discovery

8 Apr. First street oil lamp in Aust. lit, at Macquarie Place, Sydney.
24 May. Construction of Sydney to Singleton road begins.
19 Jul. First recorded Aust. use of gaslight, in a Sydney shop.
Aug. William Bland founds Sydney dispensary to distribute medical aid; provides outpatients department and home treatment for the poor.

Births & Deaths

Georg Balthasar von Neumayer, scientist, b. (d. 1909)
Sir Charles Heavitree Todd, SA astronomer and Postmaster-General, b. (d. 1910)

C

Arts

Literature

During 1826
Charles Tompson publishes first book of poems by an Aust.-born poet, *Wild Notes from the Lyre of a Native Minstrel.*

Births & Deaths

Thomas Alexander Browne, best known by his pseudonym 'Ralph Boldrewood', author, b. (d. 1915)
Michael Massey Robinson, poet noted for odes written for Royal receptions and military occasions, d. (b. 1744)

Music, Dance

7 Jun. Sydney amateur concerts launched; included vocal and instrumental items.
Sep. John Philip Deane organizes first public concert in VDL.

Births & Deaths

Marie Carandini, contralto prima donna, b. (d. 1894)
Cesare Salvatore Fortunato Cutolo, musician, b. (d. 1867)

Fine Arts

Births & Deaths

Ferdinand Lukas Bauer, botanic artist, d. (b. 1760)
Andrew McCormac, portrait painter, b. (d. 1918)
Henry Webber, sculptor, d. (b. 1754)

Architecture

Births & Deaths

John George Knight, architect, b. (d. 1892)

1826

1826

D
Religion, Learning

9 Jan. District Committee of the Society for Promoting Christian Knowledge forms in Parramatta, NSW.
26 Feb. Aust. Subscription Library estb. in Sydney.
Apr. Sydney Female School of Industry estb. to educate female servants.
During 1826
Church of England Church and School Corporation granted one-seventh of Crown land in each county of NSW for maintenance and support of its education system. (Body suspended 1829, dissolved 1833.)
Hobart Town Book Society formed.
Philip Conolly estb. first Catholic school in VDL.

E
Sport

During 1826
Military and Aust. Cricket Clubs estb. in Sydney.

F
Historia Dignum

1826

Population
Estimated total white, 46,328.

19 May. Edward Smith Hall and Arthur Hill begin the *Monitor* newspaper in Sydney. (Lasts 15 years.)
18 Oct. Robert Wardell, journalist, attacks Saxe Bannister, NSW Attorney-General, in the *Australian* newspaper, duel follows on 21 Oct.
Nov. Influenza epidemic claims 37 lives in two days in Sydney.
Dec. *En route* to Norfolk I., 66 convicts take possession of brig *Wellington* and escape to NZ. Most re-captured; 23 sentenced to death but only 5 executed.

During 1826
Greatest number in any one year hanged in VDL, 53 persons.
John Dunmore Lang, in his first book *Aurora Australis*, offers an Aust. anthem.
Severe drought begins in NSW. (Lasts until 1829.)

Communities
Albany, WA, estb.
Blacktown, NSW, estb.
Koorda, WA, estb.
Port Kembla, NSW, first settled
Port Stephens, NSW, estb.
Stanley, Tas., estb.
Stroud, NSW, estb.
Westernport, Vic., estb. (Abandoned 1828)

1827

A
History, Politics, Economics, Law

Jan. Joseph Tice Gellibrand and John Batman unsuccessfully apply for land grant to estb. pastoral settlement at Westernport, Vic.
15 Feb. British Govt appoints Select Committee to examine immigration into Aust.
30 Apr. Allan Cunningham begins expedition through inland country west of Great Dividing Range between Hunter R., NSW and Moreton Bay. On 5 Jun. he discovers Darling Downs, Qld, and Cunninghams Gap through Great Dividing Range, thus opening Darling Downs for settlement.
During Apr. John Thomas Campbell appointed Collector of Customs in NSW.
During 1827
Eliza Walsh first single woman to receive land grant in NSW.
John Macarthur produces 90,000 litres of wine per year at Camden Park, NSW.
James Stirling explores Swan R., WA.
Melville I. settlement, NT, transferred to Raffles Bay on Cobourg Peninsula. Fort Wellington settlement estb. 17 Jun. to trade with Malays. (Abandoned 1829.)
Henry Hellyer, VDL Co. surveyor, explores and maps north-west VDL.
John Clunies-Ross settles in Cocos (Keeling) Islands, Indian Ocean. (Alexander Hare had settled there 1826.)
Chief Justice Forbes prevents Governor Darling from enacting law to stifle press criticism of his administration.
Reduction in flow of overseas capital, fall of wool prices, drop in prices of imported goods and drought are primarily responsible for liquidity crisis in Aust.

Births & Deaths
William Arnott, founder Arnott's Biscuits, b. (d. 1901)
Alexander Brown, colliery proprietor, b. (d. 1877)
John Bowen, naval officer, founder of Hobart, d. (b. 1780)
Joseph Bolitho Johns, 'Moondyne Joe', NSW bushranger, probably b. (d. 1900)
Thomas Kelly (alias Noon or Hannon) VDL bushranger, b. (d. 1866)
Peter Lalor, miners' leader at Eureka Stockade, b. (d. 1889)
James Mein, settler, d. (b. 1761)
Charles Myles Officer, Vic. politician, b. (d. 1904)
James Rutherford, coach owner, businessman, b. (d. 1911)
James Smith, known as 'Philosopher Smith', mineral prospector, b. (d. 1897)
David Syme, newspaper proprietor, 'Father of Protection', b. (d. 1908)
Ebenezer Vickery, businessman, philanthropist, b. (d. 1906)

B
Science, Technology, Transport, Discovery

20 Apr. Convict discovers copper at Macquarie Harbour, VDL.
21 Dec. Charles Luis Rümker appointed first NSW Govt Astronomer.
During 1827
Further coal discovered at Ipswich, Qld. (Colliery estb. 1846.)
Construction of cart track between Launceston and Emu Bay near Burnie, VDL, begins.

Births & Deaths
Frederick Manson Bailey, Qld botanist, b. (d. 1915)
D'Arcy Wentworth, surgeon, d. (probably b. 1762)

C
Arts

Literature

Births & Deaths

Matilda Jane Evans, who wrote as 'Maud Jeanne Franc', author, b. (d. 1886)
Caroline Woolmer Leakey, who also used the pseudonym Oliné Keese, poet and novelist, b. (d. 1881)

Fine Arts

Births & Deaths

Robert Hawker Dowling, Tas. painter, b. (d. 1886)
Nicholas François Habbe, painter, b. (d. 1889)
John Black Henderson, goldfields artist, b. (d. 1918)
Charles Summers, sculptor, b. (d. 1878)
Edmund Thomas, topographical artist, b. (d. 1867)

Architecture

Aug. John Lee Archer, architect, arrives in Hobart.
Dec. Building regulations issued in Sydney, estb. perpetual leases.

Births & Deaths

James Johnstone Barnet, colonial architect, b. (d. 1904)

D
Religion, Learning

1827

During 1827
Hobart Mechanics' Institute, including School of Design, estb. (Others estb. Sydney 1833, Newcastle 1835, Adelaide 1838, Melbourne 1839, Brisbane 1849, Perth 1851.)
Aust. Museum founded, as the Colonial Museum, in Sydney. (Name changed in 1834.)

Births & Deaths

Hugh Culling Eardley Childers, educationist and politician, b. (d. 1896)
Richard Johnson, first Church of England minister in NSW, 'The Bishop of Botany Bay', d. (probably b. 1753)
Robert Steel, Presbyterian minister, b. (d. 1893)
William Wilkins, teacher, educationist, b. (d. 1892)

1827

E
Sport

5 Jan. First recorded sailing and rowing regatta held on Derwent R., Hobart.
28 Apr. Henry John Rous organizes sailing regatta at Port Jackson.

Births & Deaths

Robert Cooper Bagot, 'Father of Melbourne Cup', probably b. (d. 1881)

F
Historia Dignum

Population
Estimated total white, 48,149.

During 1827
First Hobart fire brigade estb.

Communities
Cobbity, NSW, estb.
Huskisson, NSW, named
Ipswich, Qld, estb.
Longford, Tas., estb.
Muswellbrook, NSW, estb.
Narellan, NSW, estb.
Swansea, Tas., estb.

A

History, Politics, Economics, Law

1828

Government

30 Dec. 1828–5 Feb. 1832, James Stirling Lieut-Governor WA.

During Mar. James Stirling surveys WA coast from King George Sound to Swan R.
25 Jul. British Act of Parlt adds private members to NSW Legislative Council, enlarging it from 7 to 12 nominated members, and sets up nominated Legislative Council in VDL with powers to make laws and raise revenue.
25 Jul. The Australian Courts Act makes British statutes applicable in NSW and VDL.
Aug. Henry John Rous discovers Richmond River, NSW, and gives name Clarence to river now known as Tweed.
10 Nov. Charles Sturt leaves Sydney to begin his first attempt to trace inland rivers of NSW. Expedition traces Macquarie, Bogan and Castlereagh rivers and discovers Darling R.

During 1828
Second Judicature Act gives NSW Supreme Court right to refuse or to award a trial by jury in civil disputes on application of only one of parties. Civilian juries permitted in civil cases. Dual system operates in criminal cases, allowing the accused a choice of being tried by a jury of seven officers or twelve civilians. (First case tried in Jun. 1830.)
Emancipists admitted to exercise jury right.
Copy of Royal Charter formally constituting Legislative and Executive Councils arrives in Sydney from England.
First land sale in Hobart.
Sir Thomas Mitchell appointed NSW Surveyor-General. (Holds position for 27 years.)
Charles Frazer grows cotton at Sydney in area which becomes Botanic Gardens.
First Aust. fruit exported; apples from VDL, exported to Edinburgh.
Hawkesbury R., NSW, water used in first Aust. irrigation project.
John Thomas Bigge's recommendation to reduce rate of English import duty on Aust. goods adopted.
George Wyndham begins Dalwood vineyards in Hunter Valley, NSW.
Penal settlement at Westernport, Vic., abandoned.

Births & Deaths

John Douglas, Qld Premier, b. (d. 1904)
John Dulhunty, naval surgeon, NSW pioneer, d.
John McIlwraith, shipowner, manufacturer, b. (d. 1902)
Sir William Morgan, SA Premier, b. (d. 1883)
Sir Bryan O'Loghlen, Vic. Premier, b. (d. 1905)
John Joseph William Molesworth Oxley, explorer and surveyor, d. (probably b. 1785)
Sir Matthew Henry Stephen, first barrister admitted on colonial qualification (1850), Supreme Court Judge, b. (d. 1920)
Charles Throsby, NSW pastoralist, explorer, d. (b. 1777)
James White, NSW pastoralist, racehorse breeder, b. (d. 1890)

1828

B
Science, Technology, Transport, Discovery

During 1828
Mt Wingen, NSW, 'Burning Mountain', first sighted.

Births & Deaths
James George Beaney, surgeon, b. (d. 1891)
Jacob Mountgarrett, first VDL doctor, d. (probably b. 1773)

C
Arts

Literature

Births & Deaths
Daniel Henry Deniehy, poet, essayist, satirist, 'The Chatterton of the South', NSW politician, b. (d. 1865)

Music, Dance

Births & Deaths
William Saurin Lyster, opera producer, b. (d. 1880)

Fine Arts

Births & Deaths
Nicholas Chevalier, painter, lithographer, cartoonist, b. (d. 1902)
George Frederick Folingsby, oil portrait painter, b. (d. 1891)

Architecture

27 Dec. John Verge, architect, arrives in Sydney; noted for a rural architectural style.

D
Religion, Learning

E
Sport

18 Sep. John Vincent appointed chaplain (Church of England) of Moreton Bay penal settlement.
Methodist church estb. in WA.
Phillip Joseph Cohen conducts Jewish marriages and worship in Sydney.

During 1828
The King's Orphan Schools estb. in New Town, VDL.

Births & Deaths
Alexander Barnard Davis, Jewish minister, b. (d. 1913)
Roderick Flanagan, historian, b. (d. 1862)

23 Apr. Aust. Racing and Jockey Club founded in Sydney.
Aug. First recorded plough match in Aust. held, at Bogong Bogong, NSW.

1828

F
Historia Dignum

Population
Estimated total white, 55,006.

Mar. Because of press Licensing Act, Andrew Bent suspends publication of his VDL newspaper *Colonial Times* and begins publishing *Colonial Advocate*.
During Mar. Twice weekly postal service between principal NSW towns estb. Also regular sea postal deliveries begin.
Whooping cough epidemic spreads in NSW.
Jun. First English warrant for a Freemasonry lodge granted in NSW.
13 Sep. Bank of Australia robbed of £20,000; earliest bank robbery in Colony.
Nov. First full-scale official census of NSW estb. white population at 36,598.
During 1828
Severe drought persists in NSW, particularly in Hunter R. district.

Communities
Westbury, Tas., estb.

A
History, Politics, Economics, Law

1829

30 Jan. Executive Council in VDL increased to 15 members.
2 Feb. Charles Sturt discovers Darling R., NSW, traces Castlereagh R. showing main structure of western river system. On 23 Nov. begins second expedition, to trace Lachlan-Murrumbidgee river system.
2 May. Charles Fremantle arrives at entrance of Swan R., WA, formally claiming New Holland for British Crown. (Settlement estb. 1 Jun.)
14 May. British Govt passes first WA Constitution Act for govt of settlements in WA.
During May. James Raymond becomes principal postmaster in NSW. (Title changed to Postmaster-General 1835.)
1 Jun. First group of colonists land on Garden I., WA.
18 Jun. Governor James Stirling proclaims colony at Swan R., WA, formally making entire continent British territory. Territory west of 129th meridian constituted a colony with the name Western Australia.
Jul. William Dutton builds house at Portland Bay, Vic. Lives there from time to time until at least 1832.
12 Aug. Perth founded.
17 Aug. Justice James Dowling opens first circuit court, in Maitland, NSW.
17 Oct. The Nineteen Counties defines limits of NSW land settlement, to regulate occupation of Crown lands.
17 Nov. Alexander Collie and Lieut Preston set out to explore south-west coast of WA, opening land to agricultural and pastoral settlement.
Nov.–Dec. Newspaper compositors in Sydney strike against wage reductions; among first significant strikes in Aust.
4 Dec. M. J. Currie becomes first WA postmaster.
23 Dec. Sir William Edward Parry arrives from England to reorganize the Aust. Agricultural Co.
During Dec. Edward Gibbon Wakefield publishes *A Letter from Sydney* (though Wakefield had never visited Aust.), in which he suggests selling Crown land to stable skilled settlers to estb. industrious and well-structured society.

During 1829
Thomas Peel promotes settlement of Swan R. Colony, WA.
Governor Stirling appoints first WA constables.
Lionel Samson and family, pioneer settlers, purchase first town lots in Perth.
WA whaling industry begins.
John Blaxland appointed to NSW Legislative Council.
NSW Postal Act, establishing postal system, becomes fully effective.
Arrival of large quantity of British coinage begins to unify currency in Aust.
Aust. Agricultural Co. given rights to mine Hunter R. coal in NSW.
Fort Wellington at Raffles Bay, NT, abandoned.

Births & Deaths
John Adams, prominent mutineer of *Bounty*, d.
William Balcombe, NSW Treasurer, d. (b. 1779)
Peter Beveridge, squatter, author, b. (d. 1885)
Sir Edward Nicholas Coventry Braddon, Tas. Premier, b. (d. 1904)
John Speechly Gotch, publisher, b. (d. 1901)
Adolarius William Henry Humphrey, VDL magistrate, d. (probably b. 1782)
George Bain Johnston, steamboat capt, 'The Murray River Spaniel', b. (d. 1882)
Francis Ormond, Vic. settler and philanthopist, b. (d. 1889)
George Francis Train, pioneer Melbourne businessman, b. (d. 1904)

B

Science, Technology, Transport, Discovery

Jan. First copper discovered in NSW.
Sep. Robert Cooper first manufactures gunpowder in Sydney.
First regular horse coach service in VDL begins, in Hobart.
During 1829
VDL Philosophical Society forms as Scientific Society. (Lasts 2 years.)

Births & Deaths

George Caley, explorer and first botanist to study the Eucalyptus, d. (b. 1770)
Samuel Walker McGowan, telegraph pioneer, b. (d. 1887)

C

Arts

Literature

During 1829
Henry Savery, under the pseudonym Simon Stukeley, publishes *The Hermit of Van Diemen's Land* (previously published in *The Colonial Times*) in volume form, first volume of essays printed in Aust.

Music, Dance

20 Aug. Band of 57th Regiment gives first concert in Barnett Levey's Royal Hotel Theatre in Sydney.

Drama, Theatre

During 1829
David Burns' play, *The Bushrangers*, performed in Edinburgh.
Barnett Levey begins first professional, but temporary, theatre in Sydney.

Births & Deaths

John Turnbull Tait, founder of theatrical family, b. (d. 1902)

Fine Arts

Births & Deaths

David Murray, SA arts patron, b. (d. 1907)
George Podmore, fish painter, b. (d. 1916)
James Taylor, military artist, topographer, d.

Architecture

5 Mar. First surveying regulations applied to issue of land blocks in urban settings.
During 1829
The Observatory or Old Mill built in Brisbane, becomes oldest and only complete building constructed by convicts in Brisbane.

Births & Deaths

Benjamin Backhouse, architect, b. (d. 1904)
David Mitchell, Melbourne builder and contractor, b. (d. 1916)
Thomas Rowe, architect, b. (d. 1899)

D
Religion, Learning

16 Sep. William Grant Broughton becomes Church of England archdeacon of NSW.
During 1829
Construction of St Mary's, first Roman Catholic Cathedral in Aust., begins in Sydney.
VDL Museum estb. in Hobart. (Transferred to govt authority in 1835.)

E
Sport

Jul. First Rugby Union football in Aust. played, in Sydney.

1829

F
1829
Historia Dignum

Population
Estimated total white, 61,702.

9 Feb. John Pascoe Fawkner releases the *Launceston Advertiser*, VDL.
14 Aug. Eighteen convicts escape from Macquarie Harbour, VDL in brig *Cyprus*.
15 Sep. Edward Smith Hall of *Monitor* newspaper jailed for two counts of libel, one against Governor Darling.

During 1829
Fremantle Journal and General Advertiser begins as WA's first newspaper.
Royal Agricultural Society of WA estb.
First WA cemetery estb., in east Perth.

Communities
Boolaroo, NSW, estb.
Burnie, Tas., estb.
Fremantle, WA, estb.
Orange, NSW, estb.
Perth, WA, estb.
Speers Point, NSW, estb.

A

History, Politics, Economics, Law

1830

14 Jan. Charles Sturt expedition re-names Hume R. (named by Hamilton Hume in 1824) Murray R. On 23 Jan. discovers junction of Murray and Darling rivers. On 9 Feb. expedition reaches Encounter Bay, SA, after rowing down Murray R. and crossing Lake Alexandrina, SA. Expedition indicates that west-flowing rivers in NSW empty into Murray R. and not into an inland sea.

9 Feb. Public meeting in Sydney to agitate for responsible govt; considers petition prepared by Sir John Jamison requesting unlimited trial by jury and no taxation without representation.

By Mar. About 2,000 immigrants have landed in WA.

Apr. William Henry Hamilton becomes first full-time salaried bank manager in Aust., in Hobart.

May. Perth–Fremantle mail service estb.

13 Jul. Port Macquarie, NSW, penal colony declared closed.

4 Oct. Governor Arthur's 'Black Line' begins. About 5,000 men form combined civil, police and military dragnet in VDL designed to move across island from north to south-east shepherding Aboriginals into Tasman Peninsula. (Concludes 26 Nov.)

During Oct. Robert Dale discovers Avon Valley, WA.

1 Nov. British Govt officially authorizes formation of a nominated Legislative Council in WA.

During 1830

Governor Arthur estb. Port Arthur penal settlement in VDL. (Functions until 1877.)

About 50 bushrangers attack police and troops near Bathurst, NSW. Troops from Sydney used to quell riot. Governor Darling passes Bushranging Act, enabling any citizen to arrest suspected escapees or bushrangers without a warrant.

The Shipwrights' United Friendly Society, among first trade unions in Aust., forms in Sydney.

One thousand convicts guarded by a hundred soldiers sent to Moreton Bay, Qld, penal settlement.

Aust. dispatches first shipment of horses to India.

James Busby plants vines near Hunter R., NSW.

John Roe begins WA exploratory expeditions.

Aboriginal Truganini assists George Robinson transfer VDL Aboriginals to Flinders I.

Archibald Mosman and John Bell begin estb. whaling depots in Sydney. Fishery products dominate Aust. exports.

Births & Deaths

Walter Adams, sugar planter, businessman, b. (d. 1892)

Bungaree, Aboriginal interpreter who circumnavigated Aust. with Matthew Flinders 1801–1802, d.

John Thomas Campbell, secretary to Governor Macquarie, d. (probably b. 1770)

James Kinghorne Chisholm, NSW pastoralist, b. (d. 1912)

Frank Christie, known as 'Frank Gardiner', NSW bushranger, b. (probably d. 1903)

Henry Cary Dangar, NSW politician, b. (d. 1917)

Mark Foy, draper, b. (d. 1884)

Sir Edmund Frederick Du Cane, WA military officer and prison administrator, b. (d. 1903)

William Henry Gaunt, Vic. goldfields warden, judge, b. (d. 1905)

Thomas Hardy, pioneer viticulturist, 'Father of South Australian Wine Industry', b. (d. 1912)

Alfred William Howitt, explorer, anthropologist, b. (d. 1908)

Sir James George Lee-Steere, WA pioneer politician, b. (d. 1903)

Sir Charles Lilley, Qld Premier, b. (d. 1897)

John Moresby, northern coastal explorer, b. (d. 1922)

Daniel Morgan, NSW bushranger, b. (d. 1865)

Suetonius Henry Officer, pioneer farmer, b. (d. 1883)

1830

B
Science, Technology, Transport, Discovery

15 Nov. Mr Hart begins first hackney coach service in Sydney.

During 1830
James Busby publishes *A Manual of Plain Directions for Planting and Cultivating Vineyards and for Making Wine in NSW*.
Billy Blue runs first regular ferry service from city to northern shore, Sydney. (Other first ferry services estb. Hobart Harbour 1816; Swan R., WA, 1830; Port Phillip, Vic., 1838; Brisbane R., 1843.)
Henry Jeanneret publishes *Hints for the Preservation of the Teeth*, first published dental work in Aust.

Births & Deaths

Morton Allport, photographer who took earliest pictures of Tas. scenery, b. (d. 1878)
Freeman Cobb, coach contractor, b. (d. 1878)
Robert David FitzGerald, botanist, b. (d. 1892)
Henry Beaufoy Merlin, documentary photographer, b. (d. 1873)
J. Hubert Newman, photographer, b.
John Murray Peck, partner in Cobb & Co. coaching firm, b. (d. 1903)
Louis Lawrence Smith, doctor noted for consulting by post, b. (d. 1910)

C
Arts

Literature

During 1830
Henry Savery's *Quintus Servinton*, volume 1, becomes first novel to be written, printed and published in Aust.

Births & Deaths
Henry Kingsley, novelist, b. (d. 1876)

Fine Arts

Births & Deaths
Henry Grant Lloyd, painter, b. (d. 1904)
Cyrus Mason, illustrator, draughtsman, b. (d. 1915)
Thomas Wright, goldfields artist, b. (d. 1886)

Architecture

During 1830
John Verge introduces Colonial Regency style of architecture to Aust.
Mortimer Lewis first uses Classical style of architecture in Aust.
Toilets begin to be constructed inside upper-class houses.

D
Religion, Learning

26 Jan. Francis Forbes lays foundation stone for Sydney College. (Later becomes Sydney Grammar School.)
During Jan. John Burdett Wittenoom arrives in Perth as Church of England chaplain in WA.
July. Govt School opens in Perth. (Lasts 4 months.)
Oct. Rev. Frederick Miller holds first Congregational Church service in VDL to be conducted by minister. First resident Church of England clergyman stationed Port Phillip, Vic.
During 1830
First Jewish congregation in Aust. forms in Sydney about this time. Synagogue estb. 1831. (Other first Jewish congregations form in Vic. 1841, VDL 1842, SA 1848, Qld 1886, WA 1887.)

Births & Deaths

Robert Dunne, first Catholic archbishop of Brisbane, b. (d. 1917)
William McIntyre, school inspector, b. (d. 1911)
Patrick Francis Moran, Catholic prelate, b. (d. 1911)
Charles Henry Pearson, historian, Vic. politician, b. (d. 1894)

E
Sport

During 1830
Organized steeplechasing begins in Sydney.
Many cricket games played in Sydney.
Charles Smith begins Bungarribee racehorse stud farm near Sydney; first stud farm to make impact on Aust. horse-breeding.

1830

F
Historia Dignum

1830

Population
Estimated total white, 72,280.

May. First recorded flood in Perth.
During 1830
First Sydney hotel licence taken out: 'Barley Mow Hotel'. On 1 Jan. first Perth hotel opens.
Fremantle Observer, Perth Gazette and West Australian Journal newspaper published. (Becomes *West Australian Times* in 1863.)

Births & Deaths
Harriet Jemima Winifred Clisby, journalist and physician, b. (d. 1931)
James Joseph Crouch, eccentric imposter clergyman, probably b. (d. 1891)

Communities
Augusta, WA, settled
Cardiff, NSW, estb.
Guildford, WA, estb.
Kincumber, NSW, estb.
Manildra, NSW, first settled
Northam, WA, founded
Port Arthur, Tas., estb.
Rockingham, WA, estb.

A
History, Politics, Economics, Law

1831

Government

22 Oct. 1831–2 Dec. 1831, Patrick Lindesay administers NSW.
3 Dec. 1831–5 Dec. 1837, Sir Richard Bourke Governor NSW.

Jan. Eliza Forlonge and family arrive in Launceston; begin work on improving quality of Aust. sheep.
4 Feb. Thomas Bannister opens overland route between Fremantle and King George Sound, WA.
Aug. Ripon Regulations published. New Crown land regulations abolish land grants in all colonies and fix price for Crown land at 5 shillings per acre. (Price raised to 12 shillings per acre in 1838 and to 1 pound per acre in 1842.) Land sale by auction introduced on 2 Aug.
24 Nov. Thomas Mitchell begins expedition to explore country between Castlereagh and Gwydir rivers, NSW, in search of rivers flowing north-west. (Returns Sydney 1832.)

During 1831
Decision made that revenue from land fund be used for loans to migrants. Emigration Commissioners appointed in London to promote emigration to the colonies. NSW begins assisted immigration scheme.
Landowners petition NSW Govt for prohibition of sugar in brewing and imposition of import duty on corn as a means of increasing demand for grain. First application for protection.
E. G. Wakefield's theories on systematic colonization, which later influence the colonization of SA, attract much attention in London.
Aust. Agricultural Co. ships coal from Newcastle, NSW.
Charles Swanston estb. import agency for firms in India and China; introduces cash credit system into Aust.
English sealer John Biscoe explores Antarctica.
John Hart explores Gulf St Vincent and other SA waters.
Henry Reed estb. whaling station at Portland Bay, Vic.

Births & Deaths

Collet Barker, explorer, discoverer of mouth of Murray R., SA, d. (b. 1786)
Lewis Adolphus Bernays, Qld public servant, b. (d. 1908)
Sir James Penn Boucaut, SA Premier and judge, b. (d. 1916)
Sir William John Clarke, Vic. pioneer pastoralist, philanthropist, b. (d. 1897)
William Bede Dalley, 'Dilley Dalley', NSW lawyer and politician, b. (d. 1888)
John Darling, grain exporter, b. (d. 1905)
Alfred Felton, druggist, merchant, arts patron, b. (d. 1904)
Henry Hacking, seaman and explorer, d. (probably b. 1750)
Walter Russell Hall, businessman, benefactor, b. (d. 1911)
Sir John Hayes, VDL explorer, d. (b. 1768)
Sir Robert George Wyndham Herbert, first Qld Premier, b. (d. 1905)
Sir Patrick Alfred Jennings, NSW Premier, b. (d. 1897)
George Briscoe Kerferd, Vic. Premier, b. (d. 1889)
Duncan McIntyre, explorer, b. (d. 1866)
Thomas Petrie, Qld pioneer, b. (d. 1910)
Sir Frederick William Pottinger, NSW police inspector, b. (d. 1865)
David Thompson Seymour, Qld Police Commissioner, b. (d. 1916)
Henry Gyles Turner, banker, historian, b. (d. 1920)

1831

B

Science, Technology, Transport, Discovery

31 Mar. SS *Surprise*, first steam-powered vessel built in Aust., launched in Sydney.

16 May. Regular Sydney to Parramatta steamer service begins with arrival of *Sophia Jane*, steamer, from England.

During 1831
James Dunlop appointed Govt Astronomer at Parramatta, NSW.
Great North road linking Sydney to Hunter R. district, NSW, completed.
Sir Thomas Mitchell discovers osseous remains of early marsupials, in Wellington Caves, NSW.

C

Arts

Music, Dance

Births & Deaths
Charles Robert Thatcher, minstrel singer, 'The Colonial Minstrel', goldfields entertainer, b. (d. 1878)

Fine Arts

1 Apr. John Glover arrives in Hobart.
During 1831
Daniel Herbert carves two heads on church entrance at Bothwell, VDL; among first sculptures in Aust.
Thomas Bock, first professional portrait painter in VDL, opens studio in Hobart.

Births & Deaths
Adelaide Ironside, religious painter, among first note Aust. women painters, b. (d. 1867)

Architecture

During 1831
Henry Reveley completes the Round House jail at Fremantle, WA; among first buildings in WA.

D
Religion, Learning

24 Apr. Rev. John McKaeg holds first Baptist Church meeting in Sydney. (First Baptist church built in 1836.)

15 Nov. Rev. John Dunmore Lang, Presbyterian, opens Australian College in Sydney; among first collegiate schools in Aust. (Closes 1854.)

Liberal utilitarian traditional period of education begins. (Lasts until c. 1848.) Education dominated by liberal spirit, equal rights to Churches, useful commercial subjects in curriculum, denominational rivalry.

Births & Deaths

Laurence Hynes Halloran, rogue chaplain, forger, schoolmaster, d. (b. 1765)

Martin Howy Irving, educationist, b. (d. 1912)

E
Sport

8 Oct. First recorded pigeon shooting match in Aust., at Parramatta, NSW.

1831

F

Historia Dignum

Population
Estimated total white, 79,445.

18 Apr. Ward Stephens, Frederick Michael Stokes and William McGarvie start the *Sydney Herald* as a weekly newspaper; becomes daily in 1840. (Purchased by John Fairfax and Charles Kemp in 1841. Becomes *Sydney Morning Herald* in 1842; now oldest extant newspaper in S. Hemisphere.)
1 Aug. Convicts aboard convict ship *Eleanor* mutiny.
2 Dec. Sydney illuminated with bonfires in honour of Governor Bourke's arrival.
During 1831
Govt officials become aware of a human head trade between Aust. and NZ. Importation of preserved heads of New Zealanders prohibited 19 Apr.

Communities
Berrima, NSW, estb.
Beverley, WA, estb.
Deloraine, Tas., estb.
York, WA, estb.

A
History, Politics, Economics, Law

1832

Government
6 Feb. 1832–11 Aug. 1832, James Stirling Governor WA.
12 Aug. 1832–13 Sep. 1833. Frederick Chidley Irwin administers WA.

7 Feb. First Executive and nominated Legislative Council convened in WA. Estb. Civil Court which opens in Mar.
6 Mar. James Busby appointed first British Resident in NZ. (Arrives 1833.)
7 Mar. NSW *Government Gazette* first printed in Sydney.
18 Aug. Savings Bank of NSW opens for deposits.
During Aug. Governor Stirling leaves WA for England to discuss development of Colony.
Oct.–Nov. James Busby plants vines from French and Spanish vineyards at Kirkton, in Hunter Valley, NSW.

During 1832
James Backhouse advises NSW Govt on improving convict conditions.
Less restricted trial by jury made available in cases involving certain crimes and misdemeanours.
NSW Legislative Council votes £3,600 for immigration. First shipload of assisted female emigrants departs England.
Commercial Bank of Tas., Federal Bank and Mercantile Bank of Aust. founded.
First Angora goats imported from France.
Peter Degraves begins building Cascade brewery in Hobart.
Fremantle, WA, jetty opens, facilitating maritime trade.
Settlement of New England district, NSW, begins.
First shipment of WA wool sent to Hobart for shipment to England.
NSW Govt passes first Quarantine Act.
James King plants vineyard near Raymond Terrace, NSW. (Makes wine from its grapes in 1836.)

Births & Deaths
Edward Abbott, NSW Corps Capt., d. (b. 1766)
Colin Archer, Qld pioneer, b. (d. 1921)
James George Baillieu, Vic. pioneer, b. (d. 1897)
Jeremy Bentham, radical English philosopher whose writing influenced framing of SA Constitution, d. (b. 1748)
Henry Majoribanks Chester, Qld police magistrate, b. (d. 1914)
Edward William Cole, Melbourne bookseller, publisher, b. (d. 1918)
Sir James Robert Dickson, Qld Premier, b. (d. 1901)
Sir William Farmer, draper, businessman, b. (d. 1908)
Sir James Fergusson, SA Governor, b. (d. 1907)
John Murtagh Macrossan, Qld politician, probably b. (d. 1891)
James Munro, Vic. Premier, b. (d. 1908)
Henry Bull Templar Strangways, SA Premier, b. (d. 1920)
Sir George Tryon, admiral, b. (d. 1893)
Sir Samuel Wilson, grazier, benefactor, b. (d. 1895)
Edward Wollstonecraft, NSW pioneer merchant and landowner, d. (b. 1783)

1832

B
Science, Technology, Transport, Discovery

Jun. A Hobart auctioneer, James E. Cox, using horse tandem, begins first regular Hobart to Launceston coach service.

5 Oct. *Experiment*, paddle-wheel vessel, makes first (unsuccessful) run using four horses on a treadmill.

During 1832
NSW Govt passes first Act to control an animal disease, sheep scab.
Havilah merino stud of pure Saxon blood estb. in NSW.
Sir Thomas Mitchell builds road down Victoria Pass in Blue Mts, NSW (Great Western Highway route) and completes survey of Sydney to Goulburn road.
In his work on marsupial reproduction, George Bennett proves that kangaroo foetuses develop in the womb before being transferred to the pouch.

Births & Deaths
Richard Daintree, Qld photographer, geologist, b. (d. 1878)
Thomas Kent, inventor, settler, d.
John White, First Fleet surgeon, NSW Surgeon-General, d. (probably b. 1756)
Julian Edmund Tenison-Woods, scientist, Catholic priest, b. (d. 1889)

C
Arts

Literature

During 1832
Charles Sturt publishes influential book, *Two Expeditions into the Interior of Southern Australia During the Years 1828, 1829, 1830 and 1831*, in London.
Mary Leman Grimstone's *Woman's Love* is among first novels written in Aust. by a woman.

Drama, Theatre

26 Dec. New temporary Theatre Royal, the Sydney Theatre, opens.

Fine Arts

Births & Deaths
Ecclestone Frederick Du Faur, art organizer, philanthropist, b. (d. 1915)
James Clarke Waite, portrait and landscape painter, b. (d. 1920)

Architecture

During 1832
John Bibb, architect, arrives in Australia.
John Verge, architect, builds Elizabeth Bay House in Sydney.
David Lennox, architect, designs Lennox Bridge in Blue Mts, NSW, first stone arch bridge of significant size and oldest extant on mainland. (Completed Jul. 1833.)
Second lighthouse in Aust. built, on Derwent R., VDL.

Births & Deaths
Henry Hunter, architect, b. (d. 1892)

D
Religion, Learning

2 Jan. King's School in Sydney opens. (Closes 1848.)
8 Feb. James Backhouse and George Washington Walker hold first meeting of the Religious Society of Friends (Quakers), in Hobart. (First Sydney meeting 19 Dec. 1834, Melbourne and Mt Barker, SA 1843, Brisbane 1866.)
13 Feb. King's School at Parramatta opens.
Jun. John Hubert Plunkett becomes first Catholic appointed to high civil office when appointed NSW Solicitor-General.
Nov. Proprietary or subscribers' school opens in Perth.
14 Dec. The Presbytery of NSW, comprising all eastern Aust., estb.
During 1832
John McEncroe arrives in Aust. as Roman Catholic chaplain.
Infant School Societies founded in Sydney and Hobart.
NSW Govt gives aid to Church of England and Roman Catholic elementary schools. (Until 1843.) VDL Govt gives aid to Church of England elementary schools only. (Until 1839.) WA Govt gives aid to colonial elementary schools. (Until 1839.)

Births & Deaths

Lorimer Fison, Methodist clergyman, anthropologist, b. (d. 1907)

E
Sport

19 Oct. Bare-knuckle boxing fight between John Kable and Henry Chalker in Sydney attracts much betting interest.
During 1832
Hobart Town Cricket Club estb. (Launceston Cricket Club formed 1843.)
Round-arm cricket bowling first replaces underarm bowling in Sydney; cricket pads and gloves first used.
Amateur or Mary-le-bone Cricket Club estb. in NSW.
Hawkesbury Horse Race Club estb., NSW.
First races at Randwick racecourse in Sydney. (First official meeting held in 1833.)

1832

1832

F
Historia Dignum

Population
Estimated total white, 86,533.

6 Apr. Thomas Brennan, soldier, executed for discharging firearm at a sergeant.
25 Aug. Sydney journal *Currency Lad* founded.
During 1832
First recorded Jewish marriage in Aust. unites Moses Joseph and Miss Nathan.

Births & Deaths
Thomas John Augustus Griffin, police magistrate, murderer, b. (d. 1868)
Sir Henry Browne Hayes, adventurer, d. (b. 1762)

Communities
Busselton, WA, first settled
Mt Victoria, NSW, first settled

A
History, Politics, Economics, Law

Government

14 Sep. 1833–10 May 1834, Richard Daniell administers WA.

26 Jan. Large public meeting in Sydney demonstrates for granting of responsible govt. Patriotic Association later formed to direct the popular movement.
Mar. Charles O'Hara Booth appointed commandant of Port Arthur penal settlement, VDL.
Aug. Capital punishment for forgery and stealing of livestock abolished in NSW.
Nov. Lieut-Governor George Arthur moves main body of penal settlement from Macquarie Harbour to Port Arthur, VDL.
Dec. Robert Gouger forms the South Australian Association in London for the purpose of colonizing SA.

During 1833
Governor Bourke re-organizes police force, abolishes legislative function of police chief and introduces the beat system, uniforms and badges.
Sir Richard Spencer appointed Govt Resident for Albany settlement, WA; arrives in Sep.
Governor Bourke extends trial by jury in NSW to criminal cases.
About 50 per cent of NSW export trade comes from whaling industry, but wool begins to replace whaling as most important primary industry in Aust.
British Govt removes East India Co.'s trade monopoly in Aust.
The Cabinet Makers' Society and The Society of Emigrant Mechanics form in Sydney; among first unions.

Births & Deaths

William Bradley, painter, draughtsman, naval officer, d. (b. 1757)
Francis Boardman Clapp, entrepreneur, b. (d. 1920)
Edward Devine, known as 'Cabbage Tree Ned', coach driver, probably b. (d. 1908)
Franc Sadlier Falkiner, NSW pioneer pastoralist, b. (d. 1909)
James Grant, navigator, d. (b. 1772)
William Holyman, Tas. pioneer, shipowner, b. (d. 1919)
John Alexander MacPherson, Vic. Premier, b. (d. 1894)
Arthur Alexander Walton Onslow, naval officer, NSW politician, b. (d. 1882)
John Palmer, early Commissary of NSW, d. (b. 1760)
Sir James Brown Patterson, Vic. Premier, b. (d. 1895)
Alexander Riley, NSW pastoralist and merchant, d. (probably b. 1778)
John Ross, co-operative radical free thinker, b. (d. 1920)
John Stephen, pioneer judge, d. (b. 1771)
Joseph Underwood, Sydney merchant and shipowner, d. (b. 1779)
Thomas Wells, landowner and author, d. (probably b. 1781)

B

Science, Technology, Transport, Discovery

12 Apr. Aust. Steam Conveyance Co. formed to develop steamship services.
During 1833
Iron ore discovered near Mittagong, NSW.

Births & Deaths

William Redfern, pioneer surgeon transported to NSW for mutiny, d. (probably b. 1774)

C

Arts

Literature

During 1833
E. G. Wakefield publishes (anonymously) *England and America*.

Births & Deaths

Adam Lindsay Gordon, poet, among first notable literary balladists, b. (d. 1870)
George Gordon McCrae, poet, artist, b. (d. 1927)
Watkin Tench, marine official and author, d. (probably b. 1758)

Music, Dance

May. First Aust. Philharmonic Society founded, in Sydney.
During 1833
Cavendish de Castell opens school of dancing in Sydney.
Frederic White opens academy of dancing in Sydney, among first in Aust.
c. 1833. Vincent Wallace, musician arrives in Sydney.

Drama, Theatre

Mar. First recorded public theatre performances in Perth, Aboriginal corroborees.
5 Oct. Barnett Levey opens Theatre Royal in Sydney, first permanent professional theatre. (Marks the beginning of continuous stage history in Aust.)
17 Dec. Samson Cameron presents first VDL professional theatre production, at the Freemasons' tavern in Hobart.

D
Religion, Learning

19 Jan. First Aust. School of Arts estb., in Sydney.
During Jan. Rev. William Jarrett opens first lasting Congregational church in Sydney.
4 Feb. Church and School Corporation dissolves, ending Church of England monopoly of education.
During Feb. William Bernard Ullathorne arrives in Aust. as Catholic Vicar-General. By this time a Catholic tradition exists in Aust.
22 Mar. Sydney Mechanics' School of Arts founded.

Births & Deaths
James Jefferis, Congregational minister, b. (d. 1917)

E
Sport

2 Oct. First horseraces in WA, at Fremantle.

F
Historia Dignum

Population
Estimated total white, 96,744.

5 Jan. The *West Australian* newspaper first issued as *Perth Gazette and Western Australian Journal*.
5 Feb. Ship *Hibernia* burns while *en route* to NSW; loss of 152 lives.
Mar. The *Hobart Town Monthly Magazine*, first literary periodical in Aust., published in Hobart. (Until Aug. 1834.)
30 Aug. Ship *Amphitrite*, carrying 131 female convicts, wrecked at Boulogne, France; loss of 128 lives.
Sep. In NSW 247 convicts receive 9,909 lashes between them.
11 Oct. Ship *Lady Munro*, bound from Calcutta to Sydney, wrecked in Indian Ocean; loss of 75 lives.
30 Nov. Brig *Ann Jamieson* explodes while moored at King's Wharf, Sydney; loss of 8 lives.
During 1833
NSW Govt passes Act prohibiting bathing at Sydney Cove between hours of 6.00 am and 8.00 pm.

Communities
Goulburn, NSW, estb.
Hartley, NSW, estb.

A
History, Politics, Economics, Law

1834

Government

11 May 1834–23 May 1834, Picton Beete administers WA.
24 May 1834–18 Aug. 1834, Richard Daniell administers WA.
19 Aug. 1834–2 Jan. 1839, Sir James Stirling Governor WA.

Apr. Aust. Trade Union Benefit Society formed in Sydney to unite worker groups.
15 Aug. British Parlt passes South Australian Act to begin Colony of SA as non-convict, planned settlement.
During Aug. NSW Legislative Council passes the so-called Forbes Act, preventing British money-lending laws from applying in NSW.
24 Oct. Governor James Stirling personally leads 25 mounted police on punitive expedition against Aborigines because of their attacks on WA settlers. At least 14 Aborigines are shot dead in the 'Battle of Pinjarra'.
1 Nov. Commercial Banking Co. of Sydney opens for business. (Incorporated 1848.)
18 Nov. Edward Henty forms settlement at Portland, Vic. Plants first apple and potato crops in Colony. Joined by his father Thomas Henty in Dec.
17 Dec. Workers in VDL oppose assignment of convict workers to master tradesmen.

During 1834
NSW Legislative Council passes Bushranging Act, empowering constables to arrest any person unable to produce an official document or convincing proof that he or she is a free person.
Tolpuddle Martyrs, six men from Dorsetshire in England transported for administering unlawful oaths to members of an agricultural workers union, arrive in Aust.
First WA wool exported to England.
European bees introduced to VDL.
Lord Howe I. first occupied.
VDL tailors strike for better wages.
A Commissioner of Assignment replaces the Assignment Board to allocate convict labour.
Slaughterhouses licensed; inspectors appointed.
John Lhotsky explores Snowy Mts, Vic. and NSW, and names the Snowy R.
Charles Swanston introduces overdraft system into Aust. banking.

Births & Deaths

Sir George Richard Dibbs, NSW Premier, b. (d. 1904)
Patrick Durack, overlander and NSW and Qld pastoralist, b. (d. 1898)
Joseph Ravenscroft Elsey, explorer, naturalist, b. (d. 1857)
Sir James Reading Fairfax, newspaper proprietor, b. (d. 1919)
Duncan Gillies, Vic. Premier, b. (d. 1903)
George Lee, NSW pioneer pastoralist, b. (d. 1912)
John Macarthur, wool industry pioneer, d. (b. 1767)
Alfred Henry Massina, publisher, b. (d. 1917)
Sir William Owen, NSW Chief Judge, b. (d. 1912)
James Richmond, sheep breeder, b. (d. 1923)
William Henry Suttor, NSW overlander and politician, b. (d. 1905)
Peter Waite, SA pastoralist who first suggested paddocking sheep instead of shepherding, b. (d. 1922)
William John Wills, explorer, b. (d. 1861)
Sir William Charles Windeyer, NSW lawyer and politician, b. (d. 1897)

1834

B
Science, Technology, Transport, Discovery

During 1834
Charles O'Hara Booth begins work on first tramway in Aust., a vehicle on wooden rails in VDL.

Births & Deaths
Billy Blue, known as 'the Old Commodore', pioneer Sydney Harbour ferryman, d. (b. 1737)
James Charles Cox, scientist, medical practitioner, b. (d. 1912)
John Tebbutt, astronomer, b. (d. 1916)

C
Arts

Literature

During 1834
SA Literary Society estb.

Births & Deaths
Caroline Louisa Waring Calvert, novelist and geologist, b. (d. 1872)

Music, Dance

31 Oct. Sir Henry Bishop's opera *Clari* performed in Sydney; among first opera performances in Aust.
During 1834
John Lhotsky publishes 'The Song of the Women of the Menero Tribe', first specimen of Aust. music.
John Philip Deane gives first concert of sacred music in Aust., in Hobart.

Drama, Theatre

4 Nov. Building of Theatre Royal in Hobart commences. (Completed 1836; now among oldest extant theatres in Aust.)
During 1834
Henry Melville's 'The Bushranger; or, Norwood Vale' staged in Hobart; first play with Aust. theme

Fine Arts

Births & Deaths
Alfred Bock, Tas. engraver, b. (d. 1920)
John Simpson Mackennal, sculptor, b. (d. 1901)
William Short, painter, b. (d. 1917)

Architecture

During 1834
John Verge among first to include roof overhangs and verandas in Aust. buildings.
Old Farm, stone building, constructed at Strawberry Hill, WA.

Births & Deaths
George Allen Mansfield, architect, b. (d. 1908)

D
Religion, Learning

14 Jun. John Bede Polding appointed as first Roman Catholic Bishop, with jurisdiction which includes all Aust.
Dec. Rev. John Saunders arrives as first official Baptist minister in Aust.
During 1834
Prison school, the Point Puer experiment, estb. at Port Arthur, VDL.
Rev. J. J. Therry estb. Roman Catholic Orphanage in NSW.
Illawarra district, NSW, is first to vote in favour of system of national schools.
Rev. Henry Carmichael estb. 'Normal Institution' to train teachers for a proposed system of national schools in NSW.

Births & Deaths
Thomas Bowden, schoolmaster, pioneer Methodist, d. (b. 1778)
James Fleet Cover, Congregational minister, d. (b. 1762)
Christopher Augustine Reynolds, first Roman Catholic archbishop of Adelaide, 1873, b. (d. 1893)
Roger William Bede Vaughan, Roman Catholic prelate, b. (d. 1883)

F
Historia Dignum

Population
Estimated total white, 105,627.

14 Jan. Convicts unsuccessfully attempt to overpower guards on Norfolk I.; 9 convicts executed.
5 May. NSW Temperance Society formed in Sydney.
15 Aug. *Sydney Times* first published.
25 Aug. Ship *Edward Lombe* wrecked at Middle Head, Sydney; loss of 12 lives.
Aug. Ship *Charles Eaton* wrecked on Great Barrier Reef; loss of 25 lives.
During 1834
VDL Aborigines reduced in number to *c.* 200.
'The Surveyor General Inn' opens at Berrima, NSW.

Births & Deaths
Arthur Orton, Tichborne heir impostor, b. (d. 1898)
John Watson, journalist and editor of the SA newspaper, *Border Watch*, for 63 years 11 months, b. (probably d. 1924)

Communities
Eugowra, NSW, first settled
Jugiong, NSW, estb.
Lord Howe I., NSW, estb.
Portland, Vic., estb.
Port Lincoln, SA, estb.
Port Sorell, Tas., estb.
St Helens, Tas., first settled

1835

A
History, Politics, Economics, Law

Jan. Last VDL Aborigine captured and deported to Flinders I. in Bass Strait.

9 Mar. Thomas Mitchell sets out to trace Darling R., NSW, to its supposed junction with the Murray R., as assumed by Charles Sturt.

15 May. Names of the 10 Commissioners for SA, including Robert Richard Torrens and George Fife Angas, gazetted.

29 May. John Batman arrives at Port Phillip Bay (Vic.) from Launceston, VDL; explores country around Geelong before anchoring at mouth of Yarra R. On 6 Jun. Batman makes treaty with Aborigines in which they give him 600,000 acres of land in exchange for sundry hardware and merchandise articles. (Governor Bourke disallows treaty.)

10 Jun. William Wentworth founds the Australian Patriotic Association to campaign for liberal reform and representative govt. John Jamison foundation president. (First political party in Aust.)

13 Jun. 'Batmania' suggested as name for proposed settlement which later becomes Melbourne.

29 Jun. John Batman registers The Port Phillip Association for private colonization of Port Phillip district.

28 Aug. Convict escapee William Buckley granted free pardon after living with Vic. Aborigines for 32 years.

c. 10 Oct. John Pascoe Fawkner arrives at Port Phillip Bay (Vic.) from VDL; estb. camp on Yarra R., in area which is to become Melbourne. Site chosen by party organized by Fawkner in Aug.

26 Oct. At Williamstown, Port Phillip, 500 sheep and 50 Hereford cattle landed.

During Oct. George Robinson appointed Protector of Aborigines at Flinders I. in Bass Strait to supervise 300 remaining VDL Aborigines.

Governor Bourke introduces bounty immigrants scheme to encourage sponsorship of immigrant employees from Britain. Scheme pays a per capita bounty equal to expenses of passage for each free immigrant landed in NSW.

22 Nov. Edward Henty supervises first sheep shearing in Vic.

During 1835
John Helder Wedge surveys and names Yarra R. (Melbourne.)

Aborigine, Derrimut, befriends Port Phillip settlers.

Governor Arthur opens juvenile penal settlement at Point Puer, VDL.

The SA Association reforms to become the SA Land and Colonization Co. Acquires all lands in Colony from British Govt on certain conditions, one of which stipulates that land be sold for no less than 12 shillings per acre. (Subsequently increased to one pound.)

Tailors, bakers and compositors form workers' group in Sydney.

Wool replaces for first time fishery products as main export.

Anti-Transportation League founded in NSW.

Governor Bourke issues grazing rights to squatters, imposes licences.

First consumer protection measures introduced in NSW, quality and weight of bread regulated and product labelling estb.

Aust. and NZ Bank Ltd founded. Bank of Australasia opens in Sydney on 14 Dec. Launceston Savings Bank estb.

Foreign capital first enters Aust. banking transactions.

First Tooths Brewery estb. in Sydney.

c. 1835. First WA vineyards planted.

Births & Deaths

Sir Philip Oakley Fysh, Tas. Premier, b. (d. 1919)
William Ernest Powell Giles, desert explorer, b. (d. 1897)
William Oswald Hodgkinson, explorer, Qld politician, b. (d. 1900)
Elizabeth Henrietta Macquarie, wife of Governor Lachlan Macquarie, d. (b. 1778)
Sir Samuel McCaughey, NSW pastoralist noted for work on Murrumbidgee R. irrigation, b. (d. 1919)
Sir Thomas McIlwraith, Qld Premier, b. (d. 1900)
James Mitchell, pastoralist, b. (d. 1914)
Molly Morgan, convict, NSW pioneer settler, d. (b. 1760)
Sir Hugh Muir Nelson, Qld Premier, b. (d. 1906)
Frederick Ward, 'Captain Thunderbolt', NSW bushranger, b. (d. 1870)

B

Science, Technology, Transport, Discovery

During 1835
First railway in Aust. built, between Taranna, near Hobart, and Oakwood, VDL, just over 4 miles.
Sydney to Port Phillip (Melbourne) road opens, beginning road building in Vic.

Births & Deaths
Sir (Henry) Normand MacLaurin, physician, b. (d. 1914)
Thomas Mathewson, Qld photographer, b. (d. 1929)
Lucy Osburn, pioneer nurse, b. (d. 1891)
Sir Peter Henry Scratchley, military engineer, b. (d. 1885)
Samuel White, ornithologist, b. (d. 1880)

C

Arts

Literature

Births & Deaths
James Brunton Stephens, poet, b. (d. 1902)

Music, Dance

17 Jan. *The Fair Maid of Perth*, first recorded ballet produced in Aust., performed, at Theatre Royal in Sydney.

Drama, Theatre

Oct. Evan Henry Thomas publishes and produces play, *Bandit of the Rhine*, among earliest Aust. plays.
Charles Harpur publishes play, *The Tragedy of Donohoe*, in a Sydney newspaper.

Fine Arts

17 Apr. Conrad Martens, painter, arrives in Sydney.
During 1835
Colonial Romantic period of Aust. art, influenced by English Romanticism, begins.
Daniel Herbert and James Colbeck carve first large-scale sculpture, on bridge near Hobart.

Births & Deaths
John Barr Clarke Hoyte, art organizer, b. (d. 1913)
Henry James Johnstone, painter, photographer, b. (d. 1907)

Architecture

During 1835
Mortimer William Lewis appointed NSW Govt Architect. (Holds position 15 years.)

1835

D Religion, Learning

19 Jan. William T. Cape opens Sydney College.
6 Aug. John Bede Polding arrives in Hobart. (Sydney on 13 Sep.)
28 Nov. First Baptist church, founded by John Saunders, opens in Sydney.
During 1835
Rabbi Rose arrives in Aust.
Thomas Brooker Sherratt builds Octagon non-denominational church at Albany, WA. First in WA. (Demolished 1894.)
Australia College in Sydney fails, owing to lack of funds.
Primary schools established in VDL.
Australian Elementary School Society formed in NSW. Opens school based on the British and Foreign School's system, where administration is vested in Board of Education, and schools provide non-sectarian religious instruction.

Births & Deaths

George Brown, Methodist minister, b. (d. 1917)
George Henry Stanton, Anglican bishop, b. (d. 1905)

E Sport

May. First recorded inter-schools sporting competitions held, in Hobart.
During 1835
Cricket played in WA, but first games officially recorded in 1846.

Births & Deaths

Thomas Wentworth Wills, an originator of Aust. Rules football, b.

F

Historia Dignum

1835

Population
Estimated total white, 113,545.

1 Jan. John Dunmore Lang publishes weekly newspaper, the *Colonist*.
12 Apr. Convict ship *George III* wrecked in D'Entrecasteaux Channel, VDL, claiming 134 lives.
14 May. Convict ship *Neva* wrecked in Bass Strait, claiming 225 lives.
Jun. Registered mail deliveries introduced.
17 Jul. Barque *Enchantress* wrecked in D'Entrecasteaux Channel, claiming 50 lives.
17 Nov. First house erected on site which becomes Melbourne. 'Fawkner Inn', Melbourne's first hotel, opens on same site.
During 1835
In NSW, 7,103 convict lashings are officially ordered.

Communities
Cohuna, Vic., first settled
Cygnet, Tas., estb.
Gisborne, Vic., estb.
McLaren Flat, SA, probably estb.
Melbourne, Vic., founded
Omeo, Vic., estb.
Port Fairy, Vic., settled
Shellharbour, NSW, estb.
Swan Reach, SA, first settled
Tarcutta, NSW, estb.
Wollombi, NSW, estb.

A
History, Politics, Economics, Law

Government
31 Oct. 1836–5 Jan. 1837, Kenneth Snodgrass administers VDL.
28 Dec. 1836–16 July 1838, John Hindmarsh Governor SA.

26 Jan. George Fife Angas estb. the South Australian Co. with capital to invest in settlement of SA.
Feb. John Hubert Plunkett appointed NSW Attorney-General. (Holds position for 20 years.)
Mar.–Nov. Thomas Mitchell expedition discovers pattern of inland river system in south-east Aust. Mitchell explores rich grazing lands of inland Vic., which he calls 'Australia Felix'. Journey takes expedition from Sydney to Portland through Western District of Vic.
Apr. Fire and Life Assurance Co. estb. in Sydney; first of kind in Aust.
May. John Aitken, Port Phillip settler, becomes a 'City Father' of the settlement which is to be Melbourne.
14 Jul. James Hurtle Fisher appointed SA Resident Colonization Commissioner. (Arrives 28 Dec.) Robert Gouger appointed first SA Colonial Secretary. (Arrives 28 Dec.) Osmond Gilles becomes first SA Treasurer. (Appointed May 1835.)
27 Jul. First SA colonists arrive at Kangaroo I.
During Jul. NSW Legislative Council passes Act instituting annual licence fee of 10 pounds for squatting and also instituting grazing licences; ends concentration of settlement and controls unauthorized occupation of Crown land.
9 Sep. Governor Bourke ratifies John Batman's and John Fawkner's settlements at Port Phillip. Issues Proclamation formally declaring Port Phillip district open for settlement.
29 Sep. William Lonsdale arrives in Port Phillip district as first Administrator and registered magistrate. First constables arrive on 5 Oct.
27 Dec. William Light surveys Adelaide area and chooses site for city.
28 Dec. Governor John Hindmarsh proclaims Colony of SA between long. 141°E and long. 132°E, extending north to lat. 26°S. Colony controlled by Governor and Commissioners.
28 Dec. First immigrants arrive in Adelaide area under Wakefield scheme.
During 1836
John Fawkner estb. his Port Phillip settlement. Names it 'Beargrass'.
Grape vines planted in Melbourne area.
John Warren estb. first SA brewery and J. Stokes estb. first WA brewery.

Clyde Co. estb. in Scotland to stock Port Phillip district with sheep. (Dissolved 1858.)
Thomas Raine builds first commercial flour mill, at Bathurst, NSW.
First sheep landed in SA; merino sheep from Saxony.
Edward John Eyre begins series of droving trips from NSW to Port Phillip district.
Henry William St Pierre Bunbury begins exploring south-western districts of WA.
c. 1836. Olive industry founded in SA.

Births & Deaths
Sir Thomas à Beckett, judge, b. (d. 1919)
Sir Robert George Crookshank Hamilton, Tas. Governor, b. (d. 1895)
Richard Sholl, WA pioneer, d. (b. 1786)
Sir Samuel James Way, SA Chief Justice, b. (d. 1916)

B
Science, Technology, Transport, Discovery

Jan.–Mar. Charles Robert Darwin, naturalist in HMS *Beagle*, visits Aust.
c. 13 Apr. Aust. Gas Light Co. estb. in Sydney. First gas co. in Aust.
During 1836
SA printing begins with publication of Proclamation issued by Governor Hindmarsh.

Births & Deaths
Joseph Bancroft, surgeon, scientist, b. (d. 1894)
William Dawes, engineer, astronomer, d. (b. 1762)
Henry Richard Hancock, mining engineer, b. (d. 1919)
John Baillie Henderson, hydraulic engineer, b. (d. 1921)
Henry Hudson, engineer, b. (d. 1907)
Sir Philip Sydney Jones, tuberculosis researcher, b. (d. 1918)
Henry Chamberlain Russell, astronomer, meteorologist, b. (d. 1907)

C
Arts

Music, Dance
During 1836
William Vincent Wallace arrives Sydney (Jan.); opens first School of Music.
Thomas Stubbs publishes *The Minstrel Waltz*, one of first works by an Aust.-born composer.

Fine Arts
Oct. Robert Russell draws first sketches of Melbourne.
During 1836
Benjamin Law, sculptor, carves bust of Aboriginal Chief, Woureddy.

Births & Deaths
James A. C. Dickson, rural life painter, b.
Isaac Walter Jenner, marine painter, b. (d. 1901)
William Charles Piguenit, first Aust.-born oil painter to achieve fame as an Aust. landscape painter, b. (d. 1914)

Architecture
During 1836
W. Turner completes stone-sculptured bridge at Ross, VDL.

1836

D
Religion, Learning

1 Jan. Charles Beaumont, first Church of England chaplain in SA, conducts first service in Adelaide.
14 Feb. William Grant Broughton ordained first Aust. Church of England bishop, arrives back in Sydney on 2 Jun.
24 Apr. Joseph Rennard Orton conducts first religious service (Methodist) by a clergyman at Port Phillip.
29 Jul. NSW Legislative Council passes Act providing State financial aid to Church of England, Catholic, Presbyterian and, later, Methodist Churches on a pound-for-pound basis, for building churches. Estb. religious equality.

During 1836
John Bede Polding lays foundation stone for St John's Catholic church in Richmond, VDL. (Now among oldest extant churches in Aust.) On 29 Jun. Polding consecrates St Mary's Catholic Cathedral in Sydney.
Rev. William Horton and Rev. George Langhorne hold Methodist church services in Port Phillip district.
First school estb. at Port Phillip settlement for Aborigines.
SA School Society founded.
Governor Bourke abandons plans to introduce the Irish national system of education into Aust. following extreme Protestant opposition.
Alexander Macleay becomes first president of the Aust. Museum, in Sydney.
John C. White and Jacob Abbott hold first Methodist church services in Adelaide.

Births & Deaths
David Scott Mitchell, founder of Mitchell Library, b. (d. 1907)
William Saumarez Smith, first Anglican archbishop of Sydney, 1890, b. (d. 1909)

E
Sport

During 1836
Frances Macarthur popularizes hunting, with formation of hound packs in Goulburn district, NSW.
First billiard games in Aust. played, in Sydney.

Births & Deaths
Henry (Harry) Colden Antill Harrison, 'Father of Australian Rules Football', b. (d. 1929)

F
Historia Dignum

1836

Population
Estimated total white, 123,310.

24 Feb. Independent Order of Oddfellows Friendly Society estb. in Sydney. (Estb. Melbourne and Hobart 1840, Brisbane 1846 and Adelaide 1848.)
9 Mar. In support of Temperance Movement, John Tawell orders 600 gallons of rum to be emptied into Sydney Cove.
21 May. Brig *Stirling Castle* wrecked on reef near Bowen, Qld, claiming lives of most on board.
18 Jun. *The South Australian Gazette and Colonial Register*, London-printed newspaper, issued in Adelaide. (Printed in Adelaide 1837.)
28 Jun. Snowfalls reported in Sydney neighbourhood.
Jul. John Batman elected first unofficial postmaster at Port Phillip settlement.
6 Oct. *Swan River Guardian* newspaper begins publication in WA.
During 1836
First Vic. cemetery estb., on Flagstaff Hill in Melbourne.

Communities
Adelaide, SA, estb.
Harrow, Vic., estb.
Kempsey, NSW, estb.
Kingscote, SA, estb.
Kyneton, Vic., estb.
Mudgee, NSW, estb.
Narembeen, WA, named
Penola, SA, estb.
Perth, Tas., estb.
The Entrance, NSW, first settled

1837

A History, Politics, Economics, Law

Government

6 Jan. 1837–21 Aug. 1843, Sir John Franklin Lieut-Governor VDL.

6 Dec. 1837–23 Feb. 1838, Kenneth Snodgrass administers NSW.

1 Jan. Edward Deas Thomson becomes NSW Colonial Secretary. (Holds post for 19 years.)

11 Jan.–10 Mar. William Light surveys Adelaide, lays out grid system bounded by four terraces. First land sales in Adelaide conducted on 27 Mar.

4 Mar. Governor Bourke makes official visit to Beargrass; changes name to Melbourne on 8 May. On 1 Jun. Bourke arranges first sale of town allotments in Melbourne.

Mar.–Apr. Robert Hoddle lays out and names Melbourne streets; town plan approved 8 Mar.

21 Apr. Sir John Jeffcott arrives in Adelaide as first SA Chief Justice of Supreme Court.

1 Jun. Bank of WA opens for business.

During Jun. Governor Bourke declares John Batman's treaty with Port Phillip Aborigines invalid.

30 Aug. Sir James Dowling appointed NSW Chief Justice.

5 Dec. Governor Sir Richard Bourke leaves NSW.

During Dec. George Grey begins exploring north-western WA to examine possibility of estb. an Irish colony there.

During 1837

Samuel Stephens appointed manager of SA Co.

In London a Select Committee on Aborigines in Aust. reports one of the most serious cases of genocide in the nineteenth century.

Molesworth Select Committee on Transportation appointed in London.

Union Bank of Aust. founded.

John B. Hack introduces vines to SA.

First Chinese labourers arrive in Aust.

John Lort Stokes begins charting north-west coast of Aust. in the *Beagle*, to eliminate gaps in Matthew Flinders' chart. Arrives at Swan R. WA on 25 Nov.

Thomas Gilbert appointed first SA postmaster. E. J. Foster appointed first official postmaster in Port Phillip district on 13 Apr. First Sydney–Melbourne overland mail service estb.

Charles H. Ebden overlands first sheep from NSW to Melbourne, crossing the Murray R. at Albury, NSW.

John Gardiner, Joseph Hawdon, John Hepburn and George Hitchcock overland first cattle from NSW to Port Phillip district.

Joseph Tice Gellibrand killed by Aborigines while exploring country between Winchelsea and Birregurra, Vic.

George Hamilton overlands stock from Sydney to Melbourne.

Births & Deaths

John Atherton, pastoralist, pioneer settler, b. (d. 1913).

James Chisholm, NSW pioneer, d. (b. 1772).

Robert Christison, Qld pioneer, pastoralist who was among first to adopt water conservation methods, b. (d. 1915).

William Cox, pioneer road builder, d. (b. 1764).

Joseph Tice Gellibrand, lawyer who drew up John Batman's treaty with Aborigines, d. (b. 1786).

Benjamin Hall, NSW bushranger, probably b. (d. 1865).

William Hann, pioneer explorer, pastoralist, b. (d. 1889).

Ernest Henry, Qld explorer, prospector, pastoralist, b (d. 1919).

Alexander Kennedy, Qld pioneer pastoralist, b. (d. 1936).

William Mitchell, Vic. pioneer pastoralist, d. (b. 1786).

James Venture Mulligan, explorer, prospector, b. (d. 1907).

Thomas Playford, SA Premier, b. (d. 1915).

James Ruse, pioneer farmer, d. (b. 1760).

Thomas Sawtell, Sydney developer, businessman, b. (d. 1928).

B

Science, Technology, Transport, Discovery

Nov. The Tasmanian Society of Natural History estb., in Hobart.
During 1837
John Busby completes Busby's Bore, Sydney's first augmented water supply.
Stephen Spurling, photographer, arrives in VDL.
VDL Govt passes Pharmacy and Poisons Act, requiring pharmaceutical vendors to be qualified. (Similar legislation passed in NSW and Vic. 1876, Qld 1884, SA 1891, and WA 1892; legislation revised in Tas. 1908.)
George Barney designs Sydney's Circular Quay.
John Barton Hack builds first road bridge in SA, over Torrens R., Adelaide.
John Bagshaw manufactures chaff-cutters in Adelaide.

Births & Deaths
Gracius Jospeh Broinowski, ornithologist, painter, b. (d. 1913)
John Nicholas Caire, photographer, b. (d. 1918)
Sir Arthur Renwick, medical practitioner, NSW politician, b. (d. 1908)
Frederick York Wolseley, inventor of sheep shearing machine, b. (d. 1899)

C

Arts

1837

Literature

During 1837
James Mudie's *The Felonry of New South Wales* published in London.
Eliza Darling's *Simple Rules for the Guidance of Persons in Humble Life* published in Sydney.

Music, Dance

During 1837
Beauty and the Beast, ballet, opens at Royal Victoria Theatre in Hobart.
William Wallace and John Deane form first Aust. professional string quartet, in Sydney.

Drama, Theatre

6 Feb. Theatre at Sydney School of Arts opens.
6 Mar. Royal Victoria Theatre opens in Hobart (Hobart's first theatre).
18 May. John Lazar makes first appearance on colonial stage.

Births & Deaths
William Moore, drama and art critic, b.

Fine Arts

During 1837
George Edward Peacock, convict artist, arrives in Aust.
George Grey discovers Aboriginal rock paintings in Kimberley area, WA.

Births & Deaths
Charles Atkinson, lithograph artist, architect, d.
George Clewett, sculptor, d.
William Stanford, sculptor, b. (d. 1880)
William Tibbits, watercolourist, lithograph artist, b. (d. 1906)

Architecture

8 Sep. NSW Govt passes Building Act, embodying a comprehensive set of building regulations; ends early Colonial style of architecture. (Similar Acts passed Hobart 1840, Adelaide and Melbourne 1849, Brisbane 1852.)
During 1837
Construction of Circular Quay in Sydney begins.

1837

D
Religion, Learning

John Verge, architect, completes Elizabeth Bay House, in Sydney.

Births & Deaths

Francis Howard Greenway, first experienced architect employed on govt works, noted for blending Georgian style with individualism to give an Aust. identity, d. (b. 1777)

16 May. Construction of St Andrew's Cathedral in Sydney begins; first Church of England Cathedral in Aust. (Opens 1868.)

Oct. Rev. James Clow conducts first (unofficial) Presbyterian Church services in Melbourne.

11 Dec. Presbyterian minister John Dunmore Lang separates his new Synod of NSW from the Church of Scotland Presbytery of NSW.

During 1837

John Bede Polding opens St Mary's Seminary School in Sydney; first Catholic Secondary School in Aust.

First Church of England school opens in Melbourne.

Rev. Thomas Quinton Stow becomes first Congregational Church minister in SA.

Aust. Institute of Librarians founded.

SA Literary Society brings first public library into Aust. from England.

Births & Deaths

Joseph Coles Kirby, Congregational minister, b. (d. 1924)

Historia Dignum

1837

Population
Estimated total white, 132,819.

31 May. 'Guthrie's Hotel', first hotel in Adelaide, opens.
May–Dec. First floods around Adelaide recorded.
3 Jun. *South Australian Register* newspaper begins publication in Adelaide (hitherto published in London).
12 Aug. James Tegg publishes *Literary News: A Review and Magazine of Fact and Fiction, the Arts, Sciences and Belles Lettres*, in Sydney. First magazine in NSW with advertisements.
8 Oct. News of King William IV's death reaches Sydney.
18 Dec. Schooner *Schaw* wrecked near Ram Head, Vic., claiming six lives.

During 1837
First SA cemetery estb., at Kingscote, Kangaroo I.
Aust. Fire and Life Assurance Co. estb. First fire-fighting organization in Aust.
Coachmakers Friendly Society estb. in Sydney.
Sydney Herald newspaper issued as a tri-weekly.
In Hobart a judge orders that a man convicted of highway robbery be executed and then immediately gibbeted on site of offence.
Severe NSW drought begins. (Ends 1839.)

Communities
Balranald, NSW, first settled
Braidwood, NSW, estb.
Kilmore, Vic., estb.
Koroit, Vic., estb.
Raymond Terrace, NSW, estb.
Sandford, Vic., first settled
Scone, NSW, estb.
Victor Harbor, SA, estb.
Wauchope, NSW, area first settled

A History, Politics, Economics, Law

Government

24 Feb. 1838–11 Jul. 1846, Sir George Gipps Governor NSW.
16 Jul. 1838–17 Oct. 1838, George Milner Stephen administers SA.
17 Oct. 1838–15 May 1841, George Gawler Resident Commissioner SA.

24 Feb. Henry Parkes arrives in Sydney.
Mar. George Grey discovers Glenelg R., WA.
11 Apr. Faithfull Party Massacre. About 300 Aborigines attack 17 members of the George Faithfull party killing *c.* 10 south of the Murray R., in Vic. Some 28 Aborigines killed as retribution.
9–10 Jun. Myall Creek Massacre. About 12 white stockmen and assigned convicts indiscriminately shoot and burn 28 Aborigines at Myall Creek near Inverell, NSW. (On 18 Dec. 7 offenders hanged in Sydney.)
17 Jul. First Court of Petty Sessions held in Melbourne.
Sep. Caroline Chisholm arrives in Sydney to begin philanthropic work with immigrants.
12 Oct. Augustus Kavel arrives SA with 537 German Lutherans, migrating because of religious repression in Prussia.
26 Oct. James John Gordon Bremer forms settlement at Port Essington, NT, naming townsite Port Victoria. (Abandoned Dec. 1849.)
Dec. Henry Watts appointed Postmaster-General SA.
During 1838
Molesworth Select Committee on Transportation recommends abolition of convict assignment system. Assignment of convict labour abolished in NSW (effective 1839).
German Lutheran missionaries settle at Brisbane as first free colonists in area.
SA Police Force estb.
Robert Hoddle surveys and lays out Geelong, Vic.
Adelaide jetty opens, facilitating maritime trade.
David Jones opens first David Jones & Co. shop in Sydney.
Sheep first boiled down for tallow as commercial enterprise.
A Mr Moss estb. first commercial brewery in Melbourne.
William Ryrie plants first Vic. commercial vineyard, near Lilydale, Melbourne.
George Stevenson among first to bring wine to SA.
Charles Bonney and Joseph Hawdon overland first cattle to Adelaide, along Murray R., becoming first overlanders to traverse 'Australia Felix'. Arrive Adelaide 3 Apr.
Charles Whalan discovers the 'Devil's Coach House' in the Jenolan Caves, NSW.
c. 1838. The name Canberra first used to describe present locality of national capital.

Births & Deaths

Sir Thomas Bent, Vic. Premier, b. (d. 1909)
Sir James Elphinstone Erskine, naval officer, b. (d. 1911)
Bernhardt Otto Holtermann, goldminer, photographer sponsor, politician, b. (d. 1885)
Samuel Terry, NSW land speculator, 'The Botany Bay Rothschild', d. (probably b. 1776)
George Thorn, Qld Premier, b. (d. 1905)
Solomon Wiseman, NSW pioneer, d. (b. 1778)

B

Science, Technology, Transport, Discovery

Apr. 30. Sydney Botanical Gardens open; first in Aust.
Dec. John Dobie appointed first public health officer in NSW.

During 1838
William Faithfull begins experimenting with selective merino sheep breeding.
John Gould, ornithologist, visits Aust. to recommence work on *Birds of Australia* (published in 7 volumes 1841–1848).
First mental asylum in Aust. built, at Gladesville, NSW.
Two French-trained nuns become first trained nurses in Aust.
William Watts begins ferry service across Melbourne's Yarra R.
Buffalo fly introduced to Aust.
NSW Govt passes Act regulating medical practice in Colony.
T. L. Mitchell publishes first Aust. geological map (Wellington Valley).

Births & Deaths
Barcroft Chapel Boake, photographer, b.
Sir Thomas Naghten FitzGerald, surgeon, b. (d. 1908)
John Harris, NSW colonial surgeon, d. (b. 1754)
Robert Bower Smith, inventor stumpjump plough, b. (d. 1919)

C

Arts

Literature

During 1838
Anna Maria Bunn's *The Guardian* published. (Among first novels published in Sydney.)

Births & Deaths
John Henry Nicholson, author, b. (d. 1923)

Music, Dance

31 Jan. First music festival in Aust. held, at St Mary's Cathedral in Sydney.
14 Feb. Vincent Wallace, popular musician, secretly leaves Sydney in debt.

Drama, Theatre

26 Mar. Joseph Wyatt opens Royal Victoria Theatre, in Sydney.
28 May. Adelaide Theatre Royal, in ballroom of Adelaide Tower, opens with play *The Mountaineers or Love and Madness*, beginning theatre in SA.
27 Nov. Samson Cameron opens Royal Victoria Theatre, in Adelaide.

Fine Arts

During 1838
VDL Museum and Art Gallery founded.

Births & Deaths
George Tobin, maritime artist, d. (b. 1768)

Architecture

During 1838
NSW Govt implements building regulations in Sydney. The regulations insist on parapeted roofing and ban verandas or any timber closer than 4 inches to the outside face of the wall.
Unknown architect completes Clarendon House in VDL, acclaimed as fine example of domestic architecture in the age of Classical proportions.
Convicts build Franklin House in VDL, late Georgian architecture.

Births & Deaths
John James Clark, architect, b. (d. 1915)
John Horbury Hunt, architect, b. (d. 1904)

D
Religion, Learning

28 May. SA School Society opens its first school.
May. Rev. William Waterfield becomes first Congregational Church minister in Vic.
Jul. First SA Baptist church estb. in Adelaide. (Melbourne 1839.)
Oct. Pastor Augustus Kavel introduces Lutheran Church to Aust.
Oct. Rev. James Grylls appointed Church of England Bishop Surrogate in Melbourne.
31 Dec. Rev. William Ullathorne returns to Sydney with contingent of Catholic priests, school teachers and nuns.
During 1838
William Grant Broughton consecrates St Luke's Church of England church in Richmond, VDL.
VDL becomes a Church of England Archdeaconry.
Rev. James Forbes conducts first official Presbyterian Church services in Melbourne.
Presbyterians open Scots School in Melbourne.
Adelaide Mechanics' Institute estb.
Thomas Frederick Elliot appointed Agent-General for Emigration in British Colonial Office.

Births & Deaths

Robert Knopwood, Church of England chaplain, d. (probably b. 1763)
Samuel Marsden, pioneer Church of England clergyman, sheep breeder and magistrate noted for harsh sentences, d. (probably b. 1765)

E
Sport

1 Jan. First SA horserace meeting held, in Adelaide.
During Jan. Melbourne Horse Racing Club founded.
6–7 Mar. First horserace meeting in Vic. held, in Melbourne.
During 1838
Melbourne Cricket Club founded.

Births & Deaths

Joe Thompson, punter, bookmaker, 'King of the Ring', b. (d. 1909)

Historia Dignum

1838

Population
Estimated total white, 155,197.

1 Jan. John Pascoe Fawkner founds first Vic. newspaper, the *Melbourne Advertiser*.
2 Jan. Joseph Hawdon begins Sydney to Melbourne overland coach mail service.
23 Jan. Emigrant ship *Minerva* arrives with 235 passengers, many with typhoid fever. (Ship quarantined until 6 Apr.; 30 died of typhoid.)
10 May. Sydney Floral and Horticultural Society estb.; holds first show on 19 Sep.
6 Jun. NSW newspaper reporters are allowed in Sydney Council Chambers.
27 Oct. Thomas Strode and George Arden launch the newspaper *Port Phillip Gazette* in Melbourne. (Runs until Apr. 1845.)
1 Nov. James Raymond introduces Penny Post, special stamp covers, folded sheets of note paper with embossed seal, sold at 1 shilling 3 pence per dozen, first pre-paid postage scheme in British Empire.

During 1838
Annual Midlands Agricultural Show estb. at Campbell Town, VDL. (Now oldest continuous show in British Commonwealth.)
The Australia Club estb. in Sydney to promote social and literary intercourse.
Melbourne Club founded.
First cemetery in Qld estb., at Nundah.
Influenza epidemic spreads through eastern Aust., claiming thousands of lives.
Michael Magee first man hanged in SA (attempted murder).
'Hero of Waterloo Hotel' licensed in NSW.
Mary Anne Rutledge first Aust. postmistress, at Cassilis, NSW.
Drought in WA.

Communities
Aberdeen, NSW, estb.
Bacchus Marsh, Vic., estb.
Ballan, Vic., first settled
Dungog, NSW, estb.
Geelong, Vic., estb.
Grafton, NSW, estb.
Gundagai, NSW, estb.
Hamilton, Vic., estb.
Kiama, NSW, estb.
Lyndoch, SA, estb.
Mangalore, Vic., area first settled
Meadows, SA, area first settled
Mortlake, Vic., estb.
Mulgoa, NSW, estb.
Queanbeyan, NSW, estb.
Violet Town, Vic., estb.

A
History, Politics, Economics, Law

1839

Government

3 Jan. 1839–26 Jan. 1846, John Hutt Governor WA.
30 Sep. 1839–15 Jul. 1851, Charles Joseph La Trobe Superintendent Port Phillip District.

1 Jan. Assignment of male convicts ends. (Assignment of male domestic servants ends in Aug.)
7 Jan. British Govt raises price of Crown land sold at auction from 5 shillings an acre to 12 shillings an acre in NSW, and one pound an acre in Port Phillip District.
25 Feb. Edward John Eyre becomes first to overland sheep across 'Australia Felix' to Adelaide.
During Feb. Governor Gipps decides squatters should pay, in addition to fixed licence fees, a variable tax based on number of stock being raised. Revenue from tax to be used for a special border police force.
May. Angus McMillan begins expedition opening new route from NSW to Port Phillip District, down Snowy and Tambo rivers in Vic. (McMillan begins first expedition to Gippsland in Port Phillip District 26 Dec. Calls area 'Caledonia Australis'.
5 Sep. John Lort Stokes in HMS *Beagle* discovers and names Port Darwin, NT. (Discovers and names Fitzroy R. in Dec.)
During Sep. NSW Govt abolishes military juries. All crimes and offences to be tried before a jury of 12 citizens.
27 Oct. First shipment of immigrants arrives at Port Phillip, from Scotland.
Nov. American naval scientific expedition arrives in Sydney without notice, causing defence scare.
Dec. Paul Strzelecki begins exploring Aust. Alps to make geological map.
During 1839
First SA Supreme Court hearing held in Adelaide.
James Croke appointed first Crown law officer at Port Phillip. Court of Quarter Sessions estb.
Charles James Tyers, surveyor, locates 141°E meridian of long., marking SA and Port Phillip District border.
Jurisdiction of NSW extended to include any territory acquired in NZ for Britain.
Western Australia Co. launched, largely to implement E. G. Wakefield's colonization scheme; and to settle Australind area near Bunbury, WA.
The SA Co. transfers headquarters from Kangaroo I. to Adelaide.
Convict era in Brisbane ends.
Cockatoo I. in Sydney Harbour becomes penal settlement. (Until 1872.)
Canadian exiles transported to NSW and VDL for rising against British rule in Canada; 149 sent to Australian colonies.
VDL first Colony to introduce provisions for the civil registration of births, deaths and marriages.
NSW landowners petition for protection to stimulate local growth by imposing increased import duties on tobacco.
John Reynell plants vines in SA near Adelaide.
The Aust. Sugar Co., estb. in NSW.
Adelaide Chamber of Commerce estb.
Thomas and Alexander Elder estb. Elder Smith and Co. Ltd, agricultural company.
Edward John Eyre discovers Lake Torrens, SA.
George Grey explores south-western Aust.; discovers land north of Perth up to Murchison R.

Births & Deaths

George Adams, businessman, b. (d. 1904)
Thomas Henty, pioneer pastoralist, d. (b. 1775)
William Light, surveyor, 'Founder of Adelaide', d. (b. 1786)
Sir Patrick Lindesay, Acting NSW Governor, d. (b. 1778)
Sir Richard Spencer, WA Government Resident, d. (b. 1779)
Sir Francis Bathurst Suttor, NSW sheep breeder and politician, b. (d. 1915)

B

Science, Technology, Transport, Discovery

During 1839
Prickly pear, *Opuntia stricta*, first introduced to Aust. as pot plant at Scone, NSW.
First Adelaide botanical gardens estb.
Hunter River Steam Navigation Co. formed in NSW; first coastal steamship company in Aust.
Adelaide to Port Adelaide road, first properly constructed road in SA, begun. (Completed 14 Oct. 1840.)
Silver and lead first discovered at Glen Osmond, SA. (Not mined until 1851.)
Paul Strzelecki discovers gold at Vale of Clwydd, in Lithgow district, NSW. Fearing convict outbreak Governor Gipps keeps discovery secret.
Govt hospitals introduce fees; convicts and military personnel exempted.
First continuous Aust. rainfall records begin, in Adelaide.

Births & Deaths
James Oatley, clockmaker, d. (b. 1770)
Norman Selfe, civil engineer, b. (d. 1911)

C

Arts

Literature

Births & Deaths
(Thomas) Henry Kendall, lyrical poet, b. (d. 1882)

Drama, Theatre

9 Jul. First recorded theatre performance in WA held, in Perth.

Births & Deaths
George Richard Rignold, theatre manager and Shakespearian actor, b. (d. 1912)

Fine Arts

During 1839
Melbourne Cultural Centre opens as part of Melbourne Mechanics' Institute and School of Arts. (Becomes Melbourne Athenaeum in 1872; art gallery opens 1910.)
John Lhotsky, scientist, writes first recorded critical evaluation of Aust. art potential.

Architecture

During 1839
G. K. Strickland begins building Govt House in Adelaide, Regency style.

Births & Deaths
James Waltham Curtis, painter, b. (d. 1901)
Tomaso Sani, sculptor, b. (d. 1915)

1839

D
Religion, Learning

19 May. Patrick Geoghegan begins Roman Catholic Church in Melbourne.
14 Jul. Ralph Drummond begins Presbyterian Church services in Adelaide.
Sep. VDL adopts British and Foreign School Society system of education.
9 Nov. Foundation stone of old St Paul's Cathedral laid in Melbourne. (Opens 2 Oct. 1842.)
During 1839
Peter Virtue and James Wilson begin Baptist Church in Melbourne.(First Baptist church opens in 1842.)
Mechanics' Institutes open in Melbourne, and Maitland, NSW.
WA gives aid to private elementary schools only. (Until 1846.)
First full-time ethnic schools in Aust. estb., by German settlers in SA.

Births & Deaths

Thomas Joseph Carr, Catholic prelate, b. (d. 1876)
Philip Conolly, Roman Catholic chaplain, VDL, d. (b. 1786)
William George Lawes, missionary, b. (d. 1907)

E
Sport

During 1839
Royal Victoria Cricket Club formed in Melbourne.
Cricket officially played in Adelaide.

Births & Deaths

Frederick Cavill, swimmer, b. (d. 1927)

F
Historia Dignum

1839

Population
Estimated total white, 176,473.

15 Jan. Barque *Children* wrecked east of Portland Bay, Vic., claiming 16 lives.
During Jan. Barque *Thomas Laurie* leaves Melbourne carrying first mail direct to England.
6 Feb. *Melbourne Advertiser* newspaper becomes *Port Phillip Patriot and Melbourne Advertiser*. (Later named the *Daily News*.)
During Feb. First SA Fire Brigade estb., in Adelaide.
28 May. Sailors' Home estb. in Sydney.
Nov. Brig *Pelorus* wrecked at Port Essington, NT, claiming 12 lives.
Dec. Yarra R. floods; one of first recorded floods in Vic.

During 1839
First reported drought in SA.
Drought in eastern Aust. raises price of food.
Royal Agricultural and Horticultural Society of SA founded.
The Manchester Unity Independent Order of Oddfellows Friendly Society estb. in Sydney.
Edward Davis, 'The Jewboy', forms gang of bushrangers in northern NSW.
NSW Market Act provides for appointment of food inspectors.

Births & Deaths
Howard Willoughby, journalist, b. (d. 1908)

Communities
Albury, NSW, estb.
Armidale, NSW, estb.
Bega, NSW, estb.
Coleraine, Vic., estb.
Crafers, SA, estb.
Gawler, SA, estb.
Gosford, NSW, estb.
Hahndorf, SA, estb.
Kyogle, NSW, first settled
Murrurundi, NSW, estb.
Seymour, Vic., estb.
Strathalbyn, SA, estb.
Streaky Bay, SA, estb.
Tamworth, NSW, estb.
Tanunda, SA, estb.
Toodyay, WA, estb.

1840

A
History, Politics, Economics, Law

29 Jan. William Hobson signs Treaty of Waitangi, whereby 50 chiefs of the North Island of NZ cede their territory to Queen Victoria.

During Jan. Paul Strzelecki, James Macarthur and James Ridley explore country between Westernport and Gippsland, Port Phillip District. On 15 Feb. Paul Strzelecki discovers, ascends and names highest mountain in Aust., Mt Kosciusko, NSW.

John Campbell droves cattle from NSW to Dumaresq R., Qld; among first Qld settlers.

24 Feb. Aust. Steam Navigation Co. formed as a joint stock company.

25 Feb. First of 206 political prisoners from Canada arrive in Aust.

During Feb. Two compositors in Sydney sentenced to two months on the treadmill for not working on a Saturday.

10 Mar. Patrick Leslie begins overlanding first cattle to Darling Downs, Qld; estb. first settlement there.

During Mar. Alexander Maconochie appointed administrator of Norfolk I. penitentiary.

21 May. William Hobson proclaims British sovereignty over all islands of NZ.

22 May. Order of Council ends transportation of convicts from England to NSW; effective from 1 Aug. (Between 1788 and 1840 111,500 convicts transported to NSW and VDL.)

18 Jun. Edward John Eyre begins overland journey into Aust. interior, from Adelaide to King George Sound, WA.

During Jun. Thomas O'Halloran appointed first SA Police Commissioner.

Jul. Tailors strike in Sydney for improved working conditions.

Aug. Adelaide Municipal Corporation estb. First local govt body in Aust. James Hurtle Fisher appointed first Mayor.

Oct. First camels to be introduced into Aust. arrive in Hobart.

18 Nov. Convict ship *Eden* last convict transport to arrive in NSW.

5 Dec. Lord John Russell remodels land policy by dividing NSW into three districts. Districts are: Northern or Moreton Bay District, Southern or Port Phillip District (estb. northern border of future Colony of Vic.) and Middle NSW.

During Dec. Three members of Shipwrights' Society are prosecuted for refusing to work with a non-member.

During 1840

Carpenters, joiners and plumbers, painters form respective workers' groups in Sydney.

First shorter-hour movement begins in Sydney.

Colonial Land and Emigration Commissioners replace SA Commissioners in England.

Moreton Bay District begins to open up for general settlement as penal settlement closes.

First petition from Port Phillip District for separation from NSW.

Joseph and Caroline Farmer estb. drapery business which becomes leading NSW department store, Farmer & Co. Ltd. (Myer Emporium takes over in 1961; Myers taken over by Coles 1985.)

Anthony Hordern founds Hordern Bros department store in Sydney.

Sydney recognized as second-largest British manufacturing centre in Far East. (Calcutta largest.)

Scottish Aust. Holdings Ltd Investment Co. founded as Scottish Australia Co.

Henry Hamilton plants vines in SA.

Melbourne jetty opens, facilitating maritime trade.

Benjamin Boyd organizes Royal Bank of Aust.

Protective tariffs estb. on goods traded between Aust. colonies.

Cessation of Imperial expenditure on transportation, withdrawal of govt funds from banks, and decline in value of livestock begins severe six-year economic depression.

Births & Deaths

Albert Augustus Dangar, NSW stockbreeder and businessman, b. (d. 1921)

William Robert Giblin, Tas. Premier, b. (d. 1887)

Simeon Lord, pioneer merchant, among first to estb. manufacture of essential products, d. (b. 1771)

Allan McLean, Vic. Premier, b. (d. 1911)

Thomas Moore, pioneer settler, benefactor, d. (b. 1762)

John Coghill Campbell Simson, Vic. pioneer pastoralist, b. (d. 1915)

George Throssell, WA Premier, b. (d. 1910)

Tommy Windich, Aboriginal tracker, b. (d. 1876)

B
Science, Technology, Transport, Discovery

During 1840
Mechanically powered hoists introduced to Sydney flour mills.
Hobart Observatory estb.
First properly constructed road in Moreton Bay District estb.
Continuous rainfall records begin in Sydney.
c. 1840. Bathurst burr, *Xanthium spinosum* reaches NSW from Valparaiso.

Births & Deaths
William Robert Guilfoyle, botanist, landscape gardener, b. (d. 1912)
Maurice Waldemar Holtze, SA botanist, b. (d. 1923)
William Vincent Legge, ornithologist, b. (d. 1918)
William Sandford, industrialist, first in Aust. to manufacuture steel from open-hearth furnace, b. (d. 1932)
R. Tate, SA botanist, b. (d. 1901)

C
Arts

Literature

During 1840
Fidelia S. T. Hill's *Poems and Recollections of the Past* published. Among first books of verse written by women in Aust.
George Arden's *Latest Information with Regard to Australia Felix* becomes first book published in Melbourne.
Robert Porter Welch's *A Familiar Treatise on the Diseases of the Eye* is first medical text book published in Aust.

Music, Dance

During 1840
Madame Veilburn, ballet dancer, teaches dance at Royal Victoria Theatre in Sydney.

Drama, Theatre

18 Mar. Theatre Royal in Sydney destroyed by fire.

Fine Arts

Mar. Samuel Thomas Gill, first professional artist in Adelaide, opens studio.

Births & Deaths
William Andrews, landscape artist, b. (d. 1887)
Joseph August Clarke, painter, etcher, b. (d. 1890)
Achille Simonetti, sculptor, probably b.
Margaret Thomas, first woman sculptor in Vic., b. (d. 1929)

Architecture

c. 1840. Terrace houses become popular in cities.

1840

D
Religion, Learning

During 1840
Primitive Methodist Church group estb. in SA. (Estb. in NSW 1846, Vic. 1848, Tas. 1858, Qld 1863.)
WA begins State aid to all Christian denominations.
NSW introduces Denominational School system.
The Moore Theological College estb. in Sydney.

Births & Deaths
James Dixon, Catholic priest, d. (b. 1758)
Henry Fulton, pioneer Church of England clergyman, d. (b. 1761)
Albert Bythesea Weigall, educationist, b. (d. 1912)

E
Sport

Mar. First horseraces at Flemington racecourse in Melbourne.
During 1840
Wilbraham Frederick Evelyn Liardet introduces archery to Aust., in Melbourne.
Prince Albert Cricket Club formed in Melbourne.
First recorded hunt in SA.

F
Historia Dignum

1840

Population
Estimated total white, 202,195.

3 Jan. *Port Phillip Herald* first published in Melbourne. (Becomes *Melbourne Morning Herald* in 1849.)
During Jan. The ship *Britomart* disappears in mysterious circumstances while *en route* from Hobart to Sydney; no survivors.
May. Geelong Post Office estb.
Jun. Brig *Maria* wrecked off SA coast; 27 survivors massacred by Aborigines.
2 Sep. *Sydney Herald* becomes daily newspaper.
21 Nov. Newspaper *Geelong Advertiser* estb. in Vic.
During 1840
Aust. Chess Club estb. in Sydney, beginning chess in Aust. (First Aust. chess championships held in 1885.)
Snowfalls reported in Melbourne.

Births & Deaths
Henry Louis Bertrand, Sydney murderer, b. (d. 1903)

Communities
Albion Park, NSW, estb.
Beaufort, Vic., estb.
Bingara, NSW, estb.
Casterton, Vic., estb.
Delegate, NSW, estb.
Jamberoo, NSW, estb.
Kojonup, WA, estb.
Noarlunga, SA, estb.
Penshurst, Vic., estb.

1841

A History, Politics, Economics, Law

Government

15 May 1841–25 Oct. 1845, George Grey Governor SA.

Jan. Caroline Chisholm estb. Female Immigrants Home in Sydney.
5 Feb. John Walpole Willis appointed first resident judge in Melbourne.
16 Mar. 'Jewboy's Mob' of bushrangers executed in Sydney after terrorizing Hunter R. district, NSW.
During Mar. First settlers arrive in Australind, near Bunbury, WA, as part of WA Co.'s settlement scheme. District found unsuitable for settlement. (Project abandoned by 1845.)
Sir Roger Therry appointed NSW Attorney-General.
12 Apr. First Supreme Court hearing held in Melbourne.
3 May. NZ proclaimed a colony independent of NSW. William Hobson appointed Governor.
7 Jul. Edward John Eyre arrives in Albany, WA, becoming first European to make overland crossing to WA and to reach Albany other than by ship.
12 Aug. First Melbourne post office opens.
1 Sep. Port Phillip Savings Bank estb.
During 1841
British Govt suspends all forms of assisted emigration to Aust.
Engineers and bootmakers estb. workers' groups in Sydney.
WA introduces provisions for the registration of births, deaths and marriages.
John Kitchen becomes first Government Printer in Sydney.
First trout imported to VDL.
John Orr, W. A. Brodribb, Edward Baxter and Edward Hobson continue exploring Gippsland in Port Phillip District.
Hobart becomes one of biggest whaling ports in British Empire.

Births & Deaths

John Ewan Davidson, pioneer sugar grower, b. (d. 1924)
Sir Hugh Dixson, businessman, philanthropist, b. (d. 1926)
Henry Dobson, Tas. Premier, b. (d. 1918)
Sir Francis Forbes, first NSW Chief Justice, 1824, d. (b. 1784)
William Austin Horn, mining magnate, philanthropist, b. (d. 1922)
Francis (Frank) Lascelles Jardine, Qld explorer, b. (d. 1919)
Jorgen Jorgensen, marine explorer, convict adventurer, among first philosophers and economic theorists, d. (b. 1780)
Henry Edward Kater, NSW sheep breeder, b. (d. 1924)
John King, sole survivor of Burke and Wills expedition, b. (d. 1872)
Alpin McPherson, 'the Wild Scotsman', Qld's only notable bushranger, probably b. (d. 1895)

B

Science, Technology, Transport, Discovery

24 May. Aust. Gas Light Co. inaugurates first gas-lighting scheme in Aust., in Sydney.

During 1841
First silver-lead mine estb., near Adelaide.
William Clarke discovers gold in Macquarie Valley, Lithgow district, NSW.
Gold discovered near Hartley, NSW.
Hunter R. Steam Navigation Co. begins regular steamship service to Brisbane.
Irregular rainfall records estb. in Hobart.

Births & Deaths
Robert Hamilton Mathews, ethnologist, b. (d. 1918)
John Moffat, Qld mining pioneer, 'Father of Engineering in the North', b. (d. 1918)

C

Arts

Literature

During 1841
Lady Gordon Bremer's *A Mother's Offering to her Children* published. Earliest recorded book written especially for children in NSW.
John Gould publishes first volume of *Birds of Australia*. (Published in seven volumes between 1841 and 1848.)

Music, Dance

7 Apr. Isaac Nathan, musician, arrives in Sydney; elevates status of music in NSW.

During 1841
M. Charrière, Jerome Carandini, F. Howson, ballet dancers, arrive in Sydney and Hobart.

Drama, Theatre

11 Jan. John Lazar opens Queen's Theatre, first building designed as a theatre in Adelaide.
12 Apr. Thomas Hodge's Royal Pavilion Saloon opens in Melbourne. (Becomes Victoria Theatre.)

Fine Arts

During 1841
Edward Hodges Baly's *Sir Richard Bourke* completed. First large bronze statue made in Aust.

1841

1841

D
Religion, Learning

11 May. Foundation stone of Church of England St John's church laid at Camden, Sydney. Gothic Revival style designed by Mortimer Lewis. (Completed in 1845.)

4 Oct. Foundation stone of St Francis' Catholic church in Melbourne laid. (Opened 23 Oct. 1845.)

During 1841
Church of England Christ's College estb. in Hobart.
Christian Israelites, religious movement, begins in Melbourne. (First sanctuary built in Sydney in 1853.)

Births & Deaths

James Chalmers, Congregational minister, PNG explorer, b. (d. 1901)
James Egan Moulton, Wesleyan missionary, b. (d. 1909)

E
Sport

During 1841
First VDL hunting club estb.

F
Historia Dignum

1841

Population
Estimated total white, 220,415.

Jan. Brisbane R. floods.
May. French visitor takes first known photograph in Aust., of a Sydney scene.
Jul. *South Australian Magazine* first published.
11 Dec. Newspaper *Hunter River Gazette* published in Maitland, NSW; among first country newspapers published. (Closes Jun. 1842.)
During 1841
Scarlet fever epidemic sweeps Sydney.
Asiatic cholera epidemic spreads in Melbourne.

Communities
Angaston, SA, estb.
Jervis Bay, NSW (later ACT), estb.
Jimbour, Qld, estb.
Leigh Creek, SA, first settled
Mallacoota, Vic., estb.
Mittagong, NSW, estb.
Mount Barker, SA, estb.
Wynyard, Tas., estb.

1842

A
History, Politics, Economics, Law

10 Feb. Governor Gipps officially declares Moreton Bay open to free settlers.

24 Feb. Henry Dana forms Port Phillip Native Police.

During Feb. Speculative market in Sydney begins to collapse. By Dec. 600 people declared bankrupt.

14 Jul. First building allotments sold in Brisbane.

30 Jul. British Act of Parlt reforming govt of NSW and VDL estb. system of representative govt in NSW. NSW Legislative Council expanded to 36 members, 12 nominated and 24 elected on property franchise. First recognition of elective principle in Aust. Marks beginning of transition to self-govt.

British Act of Parlt authorizes estb. of nominated legislative body in SA.

8 Oct. Robert Lowe, lawyer and politician, arrives in Sydney.

1 Nov. First councillors elected to municipal corporation in Sydney. First popular election in NSW and second in Aust. history. (On 1 Dec. Melbourne Council elections held.)

During Nov. John Hosking appointed first Mayor of Sydney, and Charles H. Chambers first Town Clerk.

Dec. Henry Condell appointed first Mayor of Melbourne.

During 1842

SA falls into financial crisis. Legislative and administrative functions revert to Crown, thus delaying effectiveness of Legislative Council.

NSW Legislative Council passes Bill for incorporation of Sydney and Melbourne. Sydney incorporated a city on 20 Jul. Melbourne incorporated a town on 12 Aug.

Sale of Crown land in all colonies regulated to a fixed price of 1 pound per acre, with at least half of proceeds from sales to be spent on assisting immigration from Britain to Aust.

SA introduces provisions for the registration of births, deaths and marriages.

Association for the introduction of labourers from India forms, but Govt refuses application to import Indian labour.

VDL Aboriginal population reduced to c. 44. (From an original 5,000.)

Gilbert White becomes first non-military postmaster in Brisbane.

Tobacco first manufactured in NSW.

John Nodes Dickinson appointed Judge of the Supreme Court of NSW.

Robert Towns estb. R. Towns and Co., mercantile and shipping agents, to trade in the Pacific Islands.

The holey dollar ceases to be legal tender.

Births & Deaths

Sir Joseph Palmer Abbott, NSW pastoralist and politician, b. (d. 1901)

John McGill Biraban, translator and interpreter of Aboriginal Languages, d.

Sir John Cox Bray, first Aust.-born SA Premier, b. (d. 1894)

Sir Frederick Napier Broome, WA Governor, b. (d. 1896)

John Ellis (Yankee Jack), Vic. bushranger, d.

Louis Claude de Saulces de Freycinet, French navigator, cartographer, d. (b. 1779)

Johnny Gilbert, NSW bushranger, b. (d. 1865)

William Christie Gosse, explorer, SA surveyor, b. (d. 1881)

Patrick Hannan, gold prospector, b. (d. 1925)

John Lewis, explorer, SA pastoralist, b. (d. 1923)

Alexander Miller, businessman and benefactor, b. (d. 1914)

Sir Alexander Campbell Onslow, WA Chief Justice, b. (d. 1908)

Andrew George Scott (Captain Moonlite) bushranger, b. (d. 1880)

David Dalgetty Simson, Vic. pioneer pastoralist, b. (d. 1907)

Emma Mary Withnell, WA pioneer settler, b. (d. 1928).

B

Science, Technology, Transport, Discovery

Dec. George B. Goodman, first professional Aust. photographer, opens studio in Sydney.
During 1842
North Shore Sydney ferry service inaugurated.
First vehicular ferry, a double-ended paddle punt, begins running on Sydney Harbour.
Charles Samuel Bagot discovers first significant copper deposit in Aust., at Kapunda, SA.
Marble discovered in NSW.
Tas. Society of Natural History publishes *Tasmanian Journal of Natural Science*; probably first scholarly journal of Aust. science.

Births & Deaths
John William Brazier, conchologist, b. (d. 1930)
John Daniel Custance, agriculture professor, b. (d. 1923)
Charles French, entomologist, b. (d. 1933)
Robert Rowan Purdon Hickson, harbour engineer, b. (d. 1923)
Edward Pearson Ramsay, zoologist, b. (d. 1916)

C

Arts

Music, Dance

Births & Deaths
Julia Matthews, singer, actress, b. (d. 1876)

Drama, Theatre

26 Jan. Signor Dalle Case opens Olympic Theatre in Sydney.
21 Feb. George Buckingham begins theatre in Melbourne with performance of *The Widow's Victim*.
During 1842
David Burn's *Plays and Fugitive Pieces in Verse* published. First collection of dramatic works published in Aust.
John Griffiths first appears on stage in Sydney.
G. H. Rogers, popular actor, is acclaimed for portrayal of old men.

Fine Arts

18 Jul. Sir Oswald Walters Brierly, marine painter, topographer, arrives in Sydney. (Leaves 1851.)

Births & Deaths
Catherine Elizabeth Streeter, painter, b. (d. 1930)

Architecture

During 1842
Edmund Thomas Blacket, early exponent of Gothic style in Aust., arrives in Sydney.

1842

D
Religion, Learning

22 Feb. Presbyterians in Sydney formally renounce connection with the Synod of Aust. (estb. 1840) and all State support.
29 Jul. John Bede Polding appointed Roman Catholic Archbishop of Sydney and Aust.
18 Aug. Church of England See in Aust. first divided, with VDL becoming separate diocese.
21 Aug. Name 'Tasmania' instead of Van Diemen's Land used in title of Church of England bishopric.
During 1842
Francis Russell Nixon appointed first Church of England Bishop of Tas. (Arrives Jul. 1843.)
Queen's Church of England School opens in Hobart.
John Mouritz forms first Baptist Church in Melbourne.
John Brady appointed first Roman Catholic bishop of Perth. (Arrives 13 Dec. 1843.)

Births & Deaths

Llewelyn David Bevan, Congregational clergyman, b. (d. 1918)
Abraham Tobias Boas, Jewish rabbi, b. (d. 1923)
George Judah Cohen, Jewish layman and benefactor, b. (d. 1937)
William Henry Fitchett, clergyman and author, b. (d. 1928)
Hugh Gilmore, Methodist minister, b. (d. 1891)
Mary Helen McKillop, 'Mother Mary of the Cross', b. (d. 1909)

E
Sport

Apr. Aust. Jockey Club (AJC) estb. in NSW.
During 1842
AJC makes jockeys' silks compulsory.
Moreton Bay Horse Racing Club estb. (First Qld races held on 17 Jul. 1843.)
Sydney Rifle Club estb.; first civilian rifle club in Aust
William Francis King, 'Flying Pieman', carries 6 stone weight over $14\frac{1}{2}$ miles in 3 hours 20 minutes in pedestrian event.

F
Historia Dignum

1842

Population
Estimated total white, 259,762.

12 Mar. The newspaper *Examiner* estb. as weekly in Launceston. (Becomes daily in 1877.)
11 Apr. Sir Richard Bourke statue unveiled in Sydney, first statue erected in Aust.
Between 7,000 and 10,000 people assemble in Sydney to honour ex-Governor Sir Richard Bourke. First occasion of this kind.
22 Apr. John Lynch executed at Berrima, NSW, for nine murders.
24 May. Schooner *Eliza* capsizes in Sydney Harbour, claiming seven lives.
1 Aug. The *Sydney Herald* renamed *Sydney Morning Herald*.
20 Oct. *Sydney Gazette and NSW Advertiser* ceases publication.
8 Nov. Four prisoners executed on Norfolk I. for piracy and murder.
During 1842
Charles Gavan Duffy founds the *Nation*, weekly paper dedicated to fostering Irish national unity.
First hotel opens in Brisbane.

Communities
Bairnsdale, Vic., first settled
Bethany, SA, settled
Clare, SA, estb.
Dalby, Qld, estb.
Donnybrook, WA, first settled
Eden, NSW, estb.
Greta, NSW, estb.
Heywood, Vic., estb.
Kapunda, SA, estb.
Lobethal, SA, estb.
Mount Pleasant, SA, estb.
Portsea, Vic., estb.
St Albans, NSW, estb.
St Arnaud, Vic., estb.
Texas, Qld, estb.
Yellingbo, Vic., probably estb.

1843

A
History, Politics, Economics, Law

Government

21 Aug. 1843–13 Oct. 1846, Sir John Eardley-Wilmot Lieut-Governor VDL.

5 Jan. New Constitution granting representative govt in NSW proclaimed. On 15 Jun. first election for representative Legislative Council held in Sydney. Squatters win control in first Parlt elections in Aust. Council meets for first time on 1 Aug.
During Jan. Henry O'Brien, NSW sheep farmer, boils down sheep for tallow during economic depression, setting trend which saves many farmers from financial ruin.
Mar. Bank of Aust., Sydney Banking Co. and Port Phillip Bank crash in financial crisis known as 'the Monetary Confusion'.
5 Apr. Mutual Protection Society forms in Sydney to express liberal and radical opinion and to unite worker groups.
Aug. Alexander Macleay appointed Speaker of first representative NSW Legislative Council.
15 Sep. NSW Govt passes insolvency legislation and Lien-on-Wool Act to fight depression. Act abolishes imprisonment for debt and allows graziers to borrow money on the security of a future wool clip.
10 Oct. First meeting of SA Legislative Council, in Adelaide.
Moreton Bay granted representation in NSW Legislative Council.

During 1843
SA Act of Parlt forbids admission of convicts into Colony.
British Govt reintroduces assistance to emigrants bound for Aust.
Schooner *Eliza* built in Hobart; among first war vessels built in Aust.
Aust. Sugar Co. estb. in Sydney.
Thomas Mort estb. first wool auctioneers and brokers in Aust., Mort & Co., in Sydney. Introduces auction method of selling wool. (Melbourne auctions begin in 1848.)
Benjamin Boyd estb. large whaling stations in NSW.
Benjamin Boyd estb. Sydney Office Royal Bank of Australia. (Crashes in 1849 leaving shareholders 80,000 pounds in debt.)
Henry Lindeman plants vines at Cawarra, Hunter Valley, NSW.
John Reynell produces wine in SA.
George Anstey becomes large-scale vigneron in SA.
Henry Lefroy leaves York in WA to search for an inland sea.

Births & Deaths

John Thomas Bigge, King's Commissioner, d. (b. 1780)
Robert Collins, Qld pastoralist, b. (d. 1913)
James Patrick Garvan, insurance entrepreneur, b. (d. 1896)
Alexander W. Jardine, Qld explorer, b. (d. 1920)
Robert Arthur Johnstone, Qld explorer, police inspector, b. (d. 1905)
Boyd Dunlop Morehead, Qld Premier, b. (d. 1905)
Hugh Mosman, Qld pastoralist, b. (d. 1909)
Sir Harry Holdsworth Rawson, NSW Governor, b. (d. 1910)
Charles Robert Wynn-Carrington, NSW Governor, b (d. 1928)

B

Science, Technology, Transport, Discovery

11 Mar. Tin discovered near Beechworth, Vic.
24 May. Causeway Bridge over Swan R. opens as toll bridge.
Oct. Botanical and Horticultural Society of VDL estb. In 1844 becomes Royal Society of VDL for Horticulture, Botany and Advancement of Science; first Royal Society outside United Kingdom. (Name changes to Royal Society of Tas. in 1911. Other Royal Societies founded in Vic. 1859, NSW 1866, SA 1880, Qld 1884, WA 1913, ACT 1930.)
Nov. John Ridley constructs first workable stripper-harvester.

During 1843
Brisbane's first cross-river ferries begin operating.
Irrigation used to grow hops on Derwent R., VDL.
F. H. Faulding begins commercial distilling of eucalyptus oil and magnesia, in Adelaide.
First VDL coal mined, at Colebrook.
NSW introduces first mental health legislation.

Births & Deaths
Edward Lodewyk Crowther, Tas. medical practitioner, b. (d. 1931)
Charles Yelverton O'Connor, marine engineer, designer of WA Goldfields Water Supply Scheme, b. (d. 1902)

C

Arts

Literature

During 1843
Charles Rowcroft's *Tales of the Colonies* published.

Births & Deaths
Joseph Furphy (pseudonym Tom Collins), novelist, b. (d. 1912)
John Stanley James (pseudonym Julian Thomas), author, journalist, b. (d. 1896)
Garnet Walch, author and dramatist, b. (d. 1913)

Music, Dance

During 1843
Barber of Seville is first classical opera performed in Aust.
Joseph Chambers, ballet dancer, makes début at Royal Victoria Theatre in Sydney at age of six years.
Charles Young, ballet dancer, arrives in Hobart.

Drama, Theatre

18 Mar. George Selth Coppin first performs at Royal Victoria Theatre, in Sydney.
***c*. 1843.** Launceston Theatre opens.

Fine Arts

During 1843
T. Bluett, lithographer, arrives in Hobart.

Births & Deaths
Thomas Carrington, cartoonist, b. (d. 1918)
Alfred Clint, black-and-white artist, scenic painter, b. (d. 1924)

1843

1843

D
Religion, Learning

14 Feb. Foundation stone laid for new Aust. Subcription Library building in Sydney.

9 Mar. John Bede Polding returns to Sydney with 18 Catholic priests, brothers and students, largest ecclesiastical party yet to land in Aust. Large public welcome alarms Protestants.

Dec. First Catholic priests arrive in Brisbane.

During 1843
St Mary's Benedictine monastery estb. in Sydney.
NSW gives aid to Church of England, Catholic, Presbyterian and Methodist elementary schools.
SA gives aid to private schools only. (Until 1847.)
First private school opens in Brisbane.
James Walker appointed headmaster of King's School at Parramatta.

Births & Deaths
Nathaniel Dawes, Church of England bishop, b. (d. 1910)
Edward Ellis Morris, lexicographer, b. (d. 1902)

E
Sport

Mar. Robert S. Still credited with introducing round-arm bowling into cricket.

During 1843
Launceston Cricket Club estb.

Births & Deaths
Johnny Mullagh, Aboriginal cricketer, first internationally known Aboriginal sportsman, b. (d. 1891)

Historia Dignum

1843

Population
Estimated total white, 269,178.

7 Jan. The *Maitland Mercury*, NSW country newspaper, first published.
During Jan. The *Port Phillip Magazine* published, first magazine in Vic.
Jul. John Stephens estb. the *Adelaide Observer* newspaper. (Closes down 1931.)
Oct. The *Western Australian Monthly Magazine* first published. (Closes down 1844.)
Nov. Brig *Brigand* clashes with people of Maré, Loyalty Group, 17 crew killed.
First Scottish warrant for Freemasons' Lodge granted.
During 1843
Severe drought in Hobart.

Communities
Barham, NSW, first settled
Blayney, NSW, estb.
Boydtown, NSW, estb.
Bunbury, WA, estb.
Huonville, Tas., estb.
McCrae, Vic., estb.
Shepparton, Vic., estb.
Wingham, NSW, estb.

1844

A
History, Politics, Economics, Law

Apr. Export of Aust. horses to India estb. on regular basis.
13 Aug. Ludwig Leichhardt leaves Brisbane to explore unknown country between Darling Downs, Qld, and Port Essington, NT.
15 Aug. Charles Sturt and John McDouall Stuart begin journey from junction of Darling and Murray rivers to Cooper Creek, SA. This journey demolishes theory of an inland sea.
29 Sep. Norfolk I. annexed to VDL. (Returns to NSW jurisdiction in 1856.)
16 Nov. First Exiles arrive from England. 'Exiles' name given to convicted men landed in Aust. with conditional pardons after serving periods of imprisonment in Britain.

During 1844
Squatters estb. the Pastoral Association of NSW to protest against squatting regulations introduced by NSW Govt. Aims are to procure security of land tenure.
Financial crisis to this year has resulted in 1,638 insolvencies with collective debts amounting to about 3,500,000 pounds.
SA begins to recover from economic depression.
Christopher Rawson Penfold and wife begin Penfolds wineries in SA.
Francis Price Blackwood makes detailed surveys and charts the Great Barrier Reef.
SA first to accept Aboriginal evidence in courts of law. (Vic. 1854, NSW 1876, Qld 1884.)

Births & Deaths
William Edward Abbott, pastoralist leader, b. (d. 1924)
Sir James Dowling, judge, d. (b. 1787)
Sir John William Downer, SA Premier, b. (d. 1915)
John Gavan Duffy, Vic. politician, b. (d. 1917)
Sir John Jamison, NSW pioneer settler, d. (b. 1776)
Sir William John Lyne, NSW Premier, b. (d. 1913)
Sir John Madden, Vic. Chief Justice, b. (d. 1918)
Sir John See, NSW Premier, b. (d. 1907)
Lionel Henry Sholl, SA public servant, statistician, b. (d. 1930)
William Henry Tietkins, explorer, b. (d. 1933)
James Underwood, NSW merchant, shipbuilder, d. (probably b. 1772)
Watkin Wynne, newspaper proprietor, b. (d. 1921)

B
Science, Technology, Transport, Discovery

9 Apr. William Branwhite Clarke reveals his gold discoveries to NSW Legislature.

During 1844
Opening of copper mine at Kapunda, SA, begins copper-mining industry in Aust. and boosts SA economy.
Surveyor Smyth discovers gold near Ovens R., Vic.
George Peat estb. first regular ferry service across Hawkesbury R., NSW.
James Smith Norvie appointed first govt chemist in Aust.

Births & Deaths
Henry Yorke Lyell Brown, geologist, b. (d. 1928)
Sir Charles Kinnaird Mackellar, physician, sociologist, b. (d. 1926)
John McGarvie Smith, bacteriologist, metallurgist, b. (d. 1918)

C
Arts

Literature

During 1844
Louisa Anne Meredith publishes *Notes and Sketches of New South Wales*, in London.

Births & Deaths
Ada Cambridge, novelist, poet, b. (d. 1926)
Henry Ebenezer Clay, poet, b. (d. 1896)
John Boyle O'Reilly, convict novelist and Irish patriot, b. (d. 1890)

Music, Dance

27 May. Edward Geoghegan's musical comedy opera, *The Currency Lass*, first produced.
During 1844
Madame Marie Carandini, singer, makes début in Hobart.
William Vincent Wallace composes greater part of opera *Maritana*, in Sydney.

Fine Arts

Births & Deaths
Edward à Beckett, portrait painter, b. (d. 1932)
Percival Ball, sculptor, b. (d. 1900)
E. Wake Cook, painter, engraver, b. (d. 1926)
Alfred James Daplyn, watercolourist, b. (d. 1926)

D
Religion, Learning

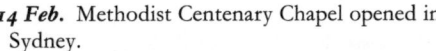

14 Feb. Methodist Centenary Chapel opened in Sydney.
2 Apr. First Synagogue in Aust. opens, in Sydney. (First Synagogues open in Adelaide Mar. 1871, Melbourne 20 Mar. 1877.)
11 May. Robert William Willson, first Catholic bishop of VDL, arrives in Hobart.
Aug. Robert Lowe's report on NSW education recommends introduction of Irish national education system.
8 Sep. Francis Murphy is first bishop consecrated in Aust. (in Sydney). Becomes first Catholic bishop of Adelaide.
During 1844
First Garrison church in Aust. estb., in Sydney.
SA Subscription Library founded.
John Brady estb. first Catholic school in Perth.

Births & Deaths
Francis Bertie Boyce, Church of England clergyman, social reformer, b. (d. 1931)
Sir Henry Briggs, educationist, politician, b. (d. 1919)
Andrew Harper, scholar, teacher, b. (d. 1936)
Charles Strong, Presbyterian minister, b. (d. 1942)

1844

E
Sport

During 1844
First full-size lawn bowls green made in Hobart. (First bowling greens made in NSW 1845, Vic. 1860, Qld 1870s, SA 1876, WA 1895, ACT 1925.)

F
Historia Dignum

Population
Estimated total white, 284,963.

13 Feb. John Knatchbull's execution for murder draws reported crowd of up to 10,000 outside Darlinghurst Jail, NSW.
During Feb. Melbourne to Mt Macedon mail service begins.
21 Aug. Mayor of Sydney holds first recorded fancy-dress ball in Aust., at Victoria Theatre.
1 Oct. Pastoral Society of Australia Felix founded.
13 Oct. Sydney Fire Insurance Co. estb.
During Oct. More than 70 inches of rain reported to have fallen in one day at South Head, near Sydney.
30 Nov. Robert Lowe founds the *Atlas*, weekly newspaper magazine, in Sydney. (Published until Dec. 1848.)
During 1844
United Waterman's Benefit Society estb.
First monthly contract mail arrives from England.
Since end of transportation to eastern colonies crime rate in Sydney has escalated. Govt appoints Select Committee to look into the insecurity of life and property.
First mail-receiving boxes erected in Melbourne.
The Printers' Benefit Society estb. in Melbourne to aid the unemployed printers.

Births & Deaths
William Henry Traill, journalist, editor, b. (d. 1902)

Communities
Girgarre, Vic., estb.

A
History, Politics, Economics, Law

1845

Government
25 Oct. 1845–2 Aug. 1848, Frederick Holt Robe Lieut-Governor SA.

During Jan. Charles Sturt expedition explores centre of continent, entering the Simpson Desert in Sep. and discovering main stream of Cooper Creek on 13 Oct.

31 Oct. 'Patriotic Six' political crisis in VDL; 6 of 8 non-official members of Legislative Council simultaneously resign, ending proceedings and preventing Governor Eardley-Wilmot from enacting NSW legislation compelling Colony, instead of Imperial Govt, to carry costs of police and judicial establishments.

Dec. Sir Thomas Mitchell begins expedition, with Edmund Kennedy as second-in-command, from near Orange, NSW, to north-western districts as far as central Qld.

17 Dec. Ludwig Leichhardt arrives Port Essington, NT, completing overland trip from Brisbane. Success of expedition owes much to skill of Aboriginal guides Harry Brown and Charley Fisher.

During 1845
Port Phillip members of NSW Legislative Council petition for separation of district and estb. of independent colony.
First NSW Constitutional crisis begins in the Great Seal Case over rights to the John Tawell estate.
Public discussion on lack of Aust. defences begins.
First Australians prepare to engage in Maori wars in NZ. (Continues over next 27 years.)
Assistance to emigrants resumed as economy improves.
Cotton planted at Moreton Bay, Qld.
Whaling industry declines with near extinction of whales.

Births & Deaths
Maybanke Susannah Anderson, social worker, b. (d. 1927)
John Blaxland, pioneer settler, merchant, produced first salt for preserving meat in NSW, d. (b. 1769)
Thomas Bridson Cribb, Qld politician, b. (d. 1913)
Michael Durack, Qld pioneer pastoralist, b. (d. 1895)
Ernest Favenc, explorer, journalist, b. (d. 1908)
William Gore, pioneer official, d. (b. 1765)
Sir Samuel Walker Griffith, Qld Premier, b. (d. 1920)
Victor Albert George Child-Villiers, Earl of Jersey, NSW Governor, b. (d. 1915)
Sir George Houston Reid, NSW Premier and Free Trade-Protectionist Coalition Prime Minister, b. (d. 1918)
D'Arcy Wentworth Uhr, overlander, b. (d. 1907)

B
Science, Technology, Transport, Discovery

Mar. General Hospital in Sydney incorporated with Sydney Dispensary to form the Sydney Infirmary and Dispensary.

19 May. Shepherd named Pickitt discovers copper at Burra, SA. Mining operations begin on 29 Sep., saving SA from virtual bankruptcy.

During 1845
First recorded meteorite in Aust. discovered, near Deniliquin, NSW.
Ludwig Leichhardt discovers a giant saw-fish in Lynd R., Qld.
Charles La Trobe estb. Melbourne Botanical Gardens.
T. S. Mort opens major shipbuilding and repair business in Sydney.

Births & Deaths
William James Farrer, wheat propagator, b. (d. 1906)
Walker Howchin, geologist, b. (d. 1937)
Robert Logan Jack, geologist, explorer, b. (d. 1921)
William Charles Kernot, engineer, b. (d. 1909)
John William Lindt, photographer, b. (d. 1926)

C

Arts

Literature

During 1845
Giacomo di Rosenberg (probably pseudonym of James Tucker) begins *Ralph Rashleigh ...*, convict story in autobiographical form.
Charles Harpur's *Thoughts: A Series of Sonnets* published in Sydney.

Music, Dance

25 Sep. *Les Sylphides*, ballet, produced in Melbourne; first major international work produced in Aust.
10 Nov. Jerome Carandini stages *La Muette de Portici* in Sydney.
During 1845
First civilian brass band in Aust. forms, in Launceston, VDL.
Sacred Concerto performed in St George's church, Perth; probably first public performance in WA.

Drama, Theatre

21 Apr. George Coppin opens Queen's Theatre in Melbourne.
During 1845
Giacomo d; Rosenberg (probably pseudonym of James Tucker) writes comedy script *Jemmy Green in Australia* about this time.

Births & Deaths

Henry Benjamin Leete, better known by stage name of Harry Rickards, theatrical entrepreneur, comedian, probably b. (d. 1911)
Howard Vernon, actor, b. (d. 1921)
James Cassius Williamson, theatrical entrepreneur, 'King of Melbourne Show Business', b. (d. 1913)

Fine Arts

6 Jan. J. S. Prout holds first exhibition of paintings in Aust., at Hobart.
Feb. Charles Abrahams holds first exhibition of Aust. sculpture, at Royal Hotel in Sydney.
During 1845
Charles Meryon, French etcher, among first major European artists to make contact with Aust.

Births & Deaths

Mary Augusta Greig, painter, b. (d. 1917)

Architecture

Jun. NSW Government House completed in Sydney. (Government Houses completed Hobart 1805, Melbourne and Adelaide 1837, Brisbane 1862, Perth 1829 and 1859.)
During 1845
First locally made cast-iron for building produced, at Richard Dawson's foundry in Sydney.

D
Religion, Learning

4 May. St Patrick's Catholic church opens in Sydney.
4 Oct. St Francis' Catholic church opens in Melbourne.
During 1845
First Roman Catholic schools open in Brisbane.
James Forbes founds Presbyterian Female Visiting Society.
First Catholic school built in Adelaide.

E
Sport

Jan. First recorded lawn bowls match in Aust. played, at Sandy Bay, Hobart.

1845

F
Historia Dignum

Population
Estimated total white, 303,134.

Apr. Cutter *America* wrecked in Torres Strait; 5 lives lost.

24 May. Ship *Mary* wrecked in Bass Strait; 17 lives lost.

20 Jun. Grand Teetotal Festival held in Victoria Theatre, Sydney, attracts 1,000 people.

4 Aug. Migrant ship *Cataraqui* wrecked on coast off King I.; more than 400 lives lost. (One of worst maritime disasters in Aust.)

During 1845
First Orange Lodge estb., in Melbourne.
Melbourne Fire Prevention Society estb. Melbourne's first Fire Brigade.
Brickmakers Friendly Society estb.
Friendly Society, Holy Catholic Guild, estb. in Sydney as Guild of St Mary and St Joseph.
Foxes first imported to Aust.
James·Maiden estb. 'Junction Inn' and river punt at Echuca, on Murray R., Vic.

Births & Deaths
James Munro, 'King of Bass Strait', d. (b. 1763)
John Tawell, criminal, merchant, d. (b. 1784)

Communities
Ashbourne, SA, probably first settled
Beaconsfield, Vic., estb.
Birdwood, SA, probably estb.
Bordertown, SA, estb.
Burra, SA, estb.
Denmark, WA, estb.
Dunolly, Vic., estb.
Macclesfield, SA, probably estb.
Melton, Vic., probably estb.
Moama, NSW, estb.
Molong, NSW, estb.
Murtoa, Vic., area probably first settled
Nanango, Qld, estb.
Naracoorte, SA, estb.
Picton, NSW, estb.
Pyramid Hill, Vic., estb.
Sale, Vic., estb.
Seven Hill, SA, probably estb.
Traralgon, Vic., probably estb.
Truro, SA, probably estb.
Wangaratta, Vic., estb.

A
History, Politics, Economics, Law

1846

Government

27 Jan. 1846–11 Feb. 1847, Andrew Clarke Governor WA.
12 Jul. 1846–2 Aug. 1846, Sir Maurice Charles Philip O'Connell administered NSW.
3 Aug. 1846–1 Jan. 1851, Sir Charles Augustus Fitz Roy Governor NSW.
13 Oct. 1846–25 Jan. 1847, Charles Joseph La Trobe administered VDL.

19 Jan. Charles Sturt returns to Adelaide, completing 18-month expedition into middle of continent.
29 Mar. Ludwig Leichhardt returns to Sydney, completing expedition to Port Essington, NT.
30 Sep. Governor Fitz Roy makes first official suggestions of a central authority for the whole of Aust. (in dispatch to British Govt).
Convict transportation to VDL suspended for two years.
22 Oct. Public meeting in Sydney held to protest against official proposals to resume transportation. Petition of nearly 7,000 signatures collected over four days.

During 1846
In London, Secretary of State for Colonies proposes that all NSW north of lat. 26°S and east of WA be constituted a separate colony to enable reinstatement of convict transportation. In Nov. George Barney becomes Superintendent of the Colony of North Australia, or Gladstone Colony; chooses Port Curtis (Qld) as capital of Colony on 28 Nov. (Colony abandoned in 1847.)
Name 'Tasmania' becomes widely used for Van Diemen's Land.
Since 1838 Caroline Chisholm has helped 11,000 immigrants settle in NSW.
Frederick Gonnerman Dalgety founds Dalgety and Co., agricultural agents, in Melbourne.
WA Mining Co. estb. following discovery of coal in WA.
Aust.-cut sandalwood first exported from WA.
Brisbane jetty opens, facilitating maritime trade.
Sir Thomas Mitchell's expedition travels north to Belyando R. and west to discover Barcoo R. in Sep.
Sir Augustus Charles Gregory and party begin exploring area north and east of Perth.
War steamer *The Driver* acquired for Aust. defence.

Births & Deaths
Sir James Burns, businessman, b. (d. 1923)
Robert Campbell, NSW pioneer merchant, pastoralist, d. (b. 1769)
Richard Gardiner Casey, pastoralist, company director, b. (d. 1919)
Johnny Dunn, NSW bushranger, b. (d. 1866)
Barron Field, judge, writer, d. (b. 1786)
Joseph Foveaux, Lieut-Governor Norfolk I. 1800–1804, d. (b. 1765)
Frank Hugh Hann, pioneer explorer, b. (d. 1921)
Henry Kable, emancipist, businessman, merchant, shipowner, d. (b. 1763)
Sir William MacGregor, explorer, New Guinea administrator, Qld Governor, b. (d. 1919)
Henry Stafford Northcote, Aust. Governor-General, b. (d. 1911)
Timothy O'Hea, explorer, b. (d. 1874)
Edward William O'Sullivan, NSW politician, journalist, b. (d. 1910)
Sir Stephen Henry Parker, WA Chief Justice, b. (d. 1927)
Charles Rasp, boundary rider, b. (d. 1907)
William Guthrie Spence, labor leader, Federal politician, b. (d. 1926)
Sir Josiah Henry Symon, SA lawyer and politician, b. (d. 1934)

1846

B

Science, Technology, Transport, Discovery

30 Jan. First proposal, at public meetings, for construction of railway from Sydney to Goulburn, NSW.
1 Mar. John Arthur appointed first Superintendent of Melbourne Botanical Gardens.
11 Sep. Sydney Tramroad and Railway Co. estb.
18 Dec. Copper first discovered in WA.

During 1846
Brisbane Observatory estb.
Sizar Elliott is first to experiment with preserving meat; demonstrates production of tinned food in substantial quantities.
First bicycle seen on Melbourne streets.
Francis Gregory discovers coal on Irwin R., WA.
First gold in SA mined, east of Adelaide.
J. Wiseman horse-bus service begins in Adelaide.
Frederick H. Dutton discovers first tin in SA.
Port Phillip Medical Association estb.; first Aust. medical society.

Births & Deaths

James Bowman, colonial surgeon, hospital administrator, d. (b. 1784)
Robert Etheridge, palaeontologist, b. (d. 1920)
Nikolai Nikolaievich Mikluho-Maklai, scientist, New Guinea explorer, b. (d. 1888)

C

Arts

Literature

During 1846
Charles Rowcroft's *The Bushranger of Van Diemen's Land* published.
Charles Harpur's 'The Temple of Infamy' published.
John Stokes' *Discoveries in Australia* published.

Births & Deaths
Marcus Andrew Hislop Clarke, novelist, journalist, b. (d. 1881)
Mary Hannay Foott, poet, b. (d. 1918)
George Herbert Gibson, bush balladist who used pseudonym Ironbark, b. (d. 1921)

Music, Dance

During 1846
Isaac Nathan publishes *The First, Second and Third of a Series of Lectures on the Theory and Practice of Music*.

Drama, Theatre

During 1846
Royal Adelaide Theatre opens.

Fine Arts

During 1846
R. V. Hind, fine arts dealer, estb. private gallery in Hobart.

Births & Deaths
Guiseppe Ferrarini, mural painter, b.
Livingstone Hopkins, cartoonist, b. (d. 1927)
Charles Alexander Lesueur, French artist attached to Baudin's expedition, d. (b. 1778)

Architecture

During 1846
David Lennox begins building first Prince's Bridge over Yarra R. in Melbourne. (First of three such bridges.)
Samuel Jackson designs Melbourne Hospital.
Patrick Leslie builds Newstead House in Brisbane. (Now among oldest buildings in Brisbane.)

D
Religion, Learning

May. Launceston Grammar School opens.
3 Aug. Hutchins Grammar School in Hobart opens.
During 1846
Angelo Confalonieri is first Catholic missionary in north Aust.
Joseph Benedict Serra and Rosenda Salvado, Spanish Benedictines, found New Norcia mission and education centre at Batgi Batgi, WA.
Thomas Magarey estb. Church of Christ in Adelaide. (Begins in Sydney 1852, Melbourne 1853, Hobart 1871, Brisbane 1882, Perth 1891.)
State aid to Christian denominations begins in SA.
First WA Catholic boys' school opens in Perth.

Births & Deaths
William Pascoe Crook, missionary, schoolmaster, d. (b. 1775)
John Gore, Salvation Army officer, b. (d. 1931)
John Laurence Rentoul, Presbyterian clergyman, b. (d. 1926)

E
Sport

14 Feb. First organized swimming championships in Aust. held, at Robinson's Baths in Sydney.
During 1846
First recorded cricket games played in WA.

Births & Deaths
William Miller, all-round athlete, b. (d. 1939)

1846

1846

F
Historia Dignum

Population
Estimated total white, 323,689.

Feb. Bushfires near Liverpool, NSW, destroy much property.
2 Jun. Melbourne newspaper *Argus* first issued. (Runs until 1956.)
20 Jun. A. S. Lyon and James Swan estb. the newspaper *Moreton Bay Courier* in Brisbane.
1 Jul. Convicts riot on Norfolk I., killing four guards. (Oct. 14 convicts executed.)
11 Jul. Group of Irish Catholics attack 'Pastoral Hotel' during Battle of Boyne celebrations in Melbourne.
31 Aug. Public meeting in Sydney estb. committee to organize a relief appeal for Irish famine; first time NSW offers pecuniary assistance to Mother country.
17 Oct. Mr Moreau publicly advertises as an 'Astrologer and Fortune-Teller' in Sydney.
During 1846
Aust. Clerks' Provident Friendly Society estb.

Communities
Aireys Inlet, Vic., estb.
Benalla, Vic., estb.
Cowra, NSW, estb.
Dirranbandi, Qld, estb.
Queenscliff, Vic. estb.
Robe, SA, estb.
St George, Qld, estb.
Swan Hill, Vic. estb.

A
History, Politics, Economics, Law

1847

Government

26 Jan. 1847–8 Jan. 1855, Sir William Thomas Denison Lieut-Governor VDL.
12 Feb. 1847–11 Aug. 1848, Frederick Chidley Irwin Governor WA.

30 Jan. Officials and soldiers arrive in Port Curtis, capital of the new Gladstone Colony. Civilians arrive in Mar. News of British Govt decision to abandon settlement arrives on 15 Apr. Settlement abandoned by Jul.
9 Mar. Order-in-Council approves land expansion beyond the Nineteen Counties in NSW, giving squatters security of tenure of their Crown land leases.
22 Mar. The Patriotic Six accept reappointment to Legislative Council in Hobart.
During Mar. Edmund Kennedy begins expedition investigating Mitchell's theories on western river systems in Qld. (Returns to Sydney Jan. 1848.)
22 Sep. The Savings Bank of SA estb. The Bank of WA founded during year.
During Sep. Edward Buckley Wynyard appointed commander of all troops in NSW, VDL, and NZ.
Oct. Ludwig Leichhardt prepares for expedition into Qld.
During 1847
Of the 2,000 Aborigines originally placed on Flinders I., only about 47 still survive.
British Govt renews assisted emigration schemes, but abandons bounty scheme.
Hobart Free Labour Union forms to unite worker groups.
Cadman's cottage in Sydney becomes water-police headquarters.
Cooked canned meat successfully exported.
Johann Gramp plants first vines in Barossa Valley, at Jacob Creek, SA. (Major wine families estb. from 1851.)
Melbourne declared a city.
Thomas Henry Huxley, English biologist, travels to Aust. in HMS *Rattlesnake*. (Reaches Sydney in Jul.)
Intense opposition throughout Aust. to renewal of transportation.
British Govt warns colonies that British garrison will soon be withdrawn.

Births & Deaths

Angus Cameron, trade unionist and politician, b. (d. 1896)
Sir John Eardley Eardley-Wilmot, Lieut-Governor VDL, d. (b. 1783)
Benjamin Josman Fink, Vic. businessman and land speculator, b. (d. 1909)
Sir John Forrest, WA explorer, first WA Premier, b. (d. 1918)
Sir John Franklin, Arctic explorer, Lieut-Governor VDL, d. (b. 1786)
James Huddart, shipowner, b. (d. 1901)
Edward Harewood Lascelles, pastoralist, businessman, b. (d. 1917)
Sir Frank Madden, Melbourne lawyer, b. (d. 1921)
Rose Scott, social reformer, women's rights advocate, b. (d. 1925)
William Arthur Trenwith, Vic. politician, b. (d. 1925)
Joseph Wild, NSW emancipist, explorer d. (probably b. 1773)

1847

B
Science, Technology, Transport, Discovery

Jun.–Nov. Ether first used as general anaesthetic in Aust. William Pugh develops its use as an anaesthetic in Launceston, VDL.

During 1847
Henry and William Dangar estb. first commercial meat-canning works, near Newcastle, NSW.
Parramatta Observatory closes.
Peter Russell's gold quartz crushing machine and retort first used for refining gold.
Iron smelting begins near Berrima, NSW.
Douglas Kilburn becomes Melbourne's first estb. photographer.
Peter Jackson drives first hackney horse carriage in Melbourne; hackney horse cab service estb.
Minor gold discoveries in Port Phillip District, Vic.
 c. 1847. Anthrax sheep and cattle disease begins near Sydney.

Births & Deaths
Archibald Liversidge, chemist, geologist, b. (d. 1927)

C
Arts

Literature

During 1847
Alexander Harris publishes *Settlers and Convicts*, novel.

Music, Dance

May. Isaac Nathan's *Don John of Austria* is among first operas written, composed and performed in Aust.
26 Jul. *La Somnambule*, ballet, performed in Hobart.

Drama, Theatre

Nov. Supreme Court rules in Smith–Hambleton Case on inapplicability of Masters and Servants Act for actors breaking agreements.

Fine Arts

3 Feb. S. T. Gill holds *An Artist's Exhibition* in Adelaide.
During 1847
Society for the Promotion of the Fine Arts estb. in Sydney; among first art organizations in Aust.

Births & Deaths
Robert Camm, painter, b.
George Alphonse de Tourcey Collingridge, draughtsman, engraver, b. (d. 1929)
William Howitt, woodcarver, sculptor, b. (d. 1929)
Bernard H. Woodward, WA art organizer, b. (d. 1916)

D
Religion, Learning

11 May. NSW Colonial Secretary announces introduction of national system of schools.
9 Jul. James A. Goold appointed first Catholic bishop of Melbourne.
During Jul. SA estb. a Board of Education; gives aid to denominational elementary schools.
Church of England Collegiate School opens in Adelaide. (Becomes St Peter's in 1849.)
Sep. Perth Colonial Boys' School opens.
During 1847
New Norcia Benedictine monastery built at Batgi Batgi, WA.
Charles Perry appointed Church of England bishop in Melbourne, Augustus Short in Adelaide, William Tyrrell in Newcastle, NSW, and William Grant Broughton Metropolitan Bishop for all Aust. Consecrated in Westminster Abbey on 29 Jun.
VDL gives aid to Church of England and Roman Catholic elementary schools.

Births & Deaths

William Cape, educationist and NSW settler, d. (d. 1773)
Henry Hutchison Montgomery, Tas. Church of England bishop, b. (d. 1932)
Peter Archer Mulgrave, public service educationist, d. (probably b. 1778)
Edward Augustus Petherick, book collector, b. (d. 1917)

E
Sport

During 1847
James Graham lays out first significant golf course in Aust., at Flagstaff Hill in Melbourne.

1847

F
Historia Dignum

Population
Estimated total white, 353,115.

1 Jan. Overland mail services estb. between Melbourne and Adelaide and Sydney and Adelaide.
4 Mar. Paddle-steamer *Sovereign* wrecked at Amity Point, Qld; 46 lives lost.
9 Dec. Sydney closes down to allow population to attend Lady Mary Fitz Roy's funeral. (Wife of Governor Fitz Roy who was killed in carriage accident.)

During 1847
Sydney Millwrights' and Engineers' Provident Society, friendly society estb.
Series of droughts begin in NSW. (Until 1859.)

Births & Deaths
Maurice Brodzky, journalist, b. (d. 1919).
Henri Louis Grin (or Grien, better known as Louis De Rougemont), Swiss-born eccentric adventurer recorded as 'The Greatest Liar on Earth', who travelled in outback Aust. for 28 years, probably b. (d. 1921)
Frederick William Ward, journalist, b. (d. 1934)

Communities
Balaklava, SA, first settled
Bateman's Bay, NSW, estb.
Boort, Vic., estb.
Broadford, Vic., probably estb.
Callington, SA, estb.
Echuca, Vic., estb.
Gladstone, Qld, estb.
Horsham, Vic., estb.
Maryborough, Qld, estb.
Monarto, SA, estb.
Mount Gambier, SA estb.
Warrnambool, Vic., estb.

A
History, Politics, Economics, Law

1848

Government

2 Aug. 1848–20 Dec. 1854, Sir Henry Edward Fox Young Lieut-Governor SA.

12 Aug. 1848–22 Jul. 1855, Charles Fitzgerald Governor WA.

Mar. Ludwig Leichhardt leaves Darling Downs, Qld, and disappears, while attempting to cross Aust. from E to W. Last communication dated 3 Apr. received from Cogoon Station, Qld.

30 May. Edmund Kennedy begins expedition from Rockingham Bay, WA, to Cape York Peninsula, where he is speared by Aborigines on 1 Dec.

During May. Owen Stanley surveys inner passage between Qld coast and the Great Barrier Reef.

Jul. Agitation in Melbourne for an independent Port Phillip District reaches climax when electors refuse to elect their five allotted representatives to the NSW Legislative Council.

31 Aug. Preliminary meeting leading to the foundation of Aust. Mutual Provident Society held. Society first meets on 15 Dec.

Sep. Employees at Burra copper mine in SA strike over wage reductions.

13 Dec. First Brisbane-bound immigrant ship, *Artemesia*, carrying 240, arrives in Brisbane.

During 1848

Constitution Association estb. in Sydney and Melbourne. Advocates radical political reforms.

Order-in-Council abolishing transportation of convicts to NSW revoked.

First Chinese brought to Sydney from Hong Kong, for hire to private settlers as shepherds.

Qld Native Police Corps estb.

Richard Goldsbrough estb. Melbourne's first wool business.

Silk first cultivated in Aust.

John Septimus Roe explores south-western WA, opening up good grazing lands.

Augustus Charles Gregory leads settlers' expedition to explore Gascoyne R., WA.

Births & Deaths

Sir John Langdon Bonython, SA newspaper proprietor, Federal politician, b. (d. 1939)

Sir Thomas Buckland, NSW financier and pastoralist, b. (d. 1947)

John Cadman, NSW Superintendent of Govt Boats, d. (b. 1772)

Andrew Inglis Clark, constitutional lawyer, politician, b. (d. 1907)

Frederick Garling, NSW pioneer, solicitor, d. (b. 1775)

Sir John Winthrop Hackett, lawyer, editor, politician, probably b. (d. 1916)

Sir John Henniker Heaton, postal reformer, b. (d. 1914)

Sir Edward Thomas Henry Hutton, military commander, b. (d. 1923)

Louisa Lawson, social reformer, journalist, b. (d. 1920)

Sir Lauchlan Charles Mackinnon, newspaper proprietor, b. (d. 1925)

Alexander Macleay, NSW Colonial Secretary, horticulturist, d. (b. 1767)

Walter Madden, Vic. politician, b. (d. 1925)

Sir Edward Miller, businessman, b. (d. 1932)

Sir Maurice Charles Philip O'Connell, NSW Lieut-Governor, d. (b. 1768)

William Shiels, Vic. Premier, b. (d. 1904)

William Sorell, VDL Governor, d. (b. 1775)

1848

B
Science, Technology, Transport, Discovery

Oct. A. C. Gregory discovers lead in bed of Murchison R. in Northampton district, WA.

During 1848
Iron works estb. near Mittagong, NSW; first Aust. iron and steel industry.
First Aust. Zoo estb. Menagerie in Hyde Park Sydney.
Henry Gratton Douglass becomes first clinical teacher at Sydney Hospital.
William G. Freeman estb. first permanent photographic studio in Sydney.
NSW accepts British standard railway gauge of 4 feet 8½ inches.
Military medical service in NSW ends.

Births & Deaths
George Chaffey, pioneer irrigationist, b. (d. 1932)
Amos William Howard, agricultural pioneer, b. (d. 1930)
Sir Edward Charles Stirling, physiologist, anthropologist, b. (d. 1919)
John Ashburton Thompson, public health pioneer, leprosy and plague expert, b. (d. 1915)

C
Arts

Literature

Births & Deaths
Madame Couvreur, née Jessie Catherine Huybers, 'Tasma', author, b. (d. 1897)
Lady Anne Wilson, poet, novelist, b. (d. 1930)

Drama, Theatre

Births & Deaths
Alfred Dampier, actor, pioneer producer, probably b. (d. 1908)

Fine Arts

Births & Deaths
Charles Edward Hern, watercolourist, b. (d. 1894)
John Mather, painter, etcher, b. (d. 1916)
Ebenezer Murray, black-and-white artist, b. (d. 1913)
Marian Ellis Rowan, botanical and flower painter, b. (d. 1922)
Thomas Symmonds, engraver, landscape painter, b. (d. 1928)

Architecture

During 1848
Edmund William Wright, architect, arrives in Adelaide.

D
Religion, Learning

Jan. NSW estb. National and Denominational School Boards to fund elementary education. National Board to run State or Public schools and Denominational Board to run Church schools.
17 Jun. WA opens schools to children of different classes and of all religious denominations.
During 1848
St John's Church of England church in Albany, WA, consecrated. (Now oldest extant church in WA.)
United Methodist Free Churches Group begins in Vic. (NSW 1870.)
Period of shared power in education begins; State elementary schools develop alongside of State-aided Church schools.
There are about 222 schools in NSW, including Port Phillip District, enrolling 15,426 students.
Pulteney Grammar School estb. in Adelaide.

Births & Deaths
Alexander Leeper, educationist, b. (d. 1934)

E
Sport

Oct. The *New South Wales Sporting Magazine* first published, in Sydney.
c. 1848. Fox hounds introduced for hunting.

Births & Deaths
Laurence (Larry) Foley, boxer known as 'Pride of the Fancy', probably b. (d. 1917)

F

1848

Historia Dignum

Population
Estimated total white, 389,893.

6 Jan. Carl Kornhardt publishes *Die Deutsche Post fuer die Australischen Kolonien*, first foreign-language newspaper in Adelaide.
28 Sep. The *Australian* newspaper ceases publication.
2 Oct. Charles St Julian estb. first evening daily newspaper in Sydney, the *Daily News and Evening Chronicle*.
30 Dec. Weekly newspaper magazine *Atlas* ceases publication.

During 1848
Agricultural Society of Berwick, in Vic., founded. (Now among oldest farmers' societies in Vic.)
Port Phillip Farmers Society estb. (Becomes Royal Agricultural Society of Vic. in 1890.)
SA Destitute Board estb. to look after immigrants.

Communities
Branxton, NSW, estb.
Charlton, Vic., area settled
Culcairn, NSW, first settled
Deniliquin, NSW, estb.
Echunga, SA, estb.
Gayndah, Qld, estb.
Mendooran, NSW, estb.
Port Pirie, SA, estb.
Ravensthorpe, WA, estb.
Tara, Qld, first settled
Tenterfield, NSW, estb.
Warwick, Qld, estb.

A

History, Politics, Economics, Law

1 Jan. Aust. Mutual Provident Society opens for insurance business in Sydney.
During Jan. First vessels sail from Sydney to Californian goldrushes in America.
24 Feb. Public meeting requests that WA be converted into regular penal settlement.
1 May. Transportation of convicts to WA begins.
11 Jun. Convict ship *Hashemy* arrives in Sydney. Colonists protest. Some convicts sent to squatters on Darling Downs, Qld.
Aug. Convict ship *Randolph* prevented from landing at Port Phillip.
Dec. Flinders I. Aboriginal protectorate abandoned, most Aborigines having died from disease.
During 1849
British Govt rejects Earl Grey's suggestion of forming a Federal Assembly in Aust.
Benjamin Boyd brings Kanakas to NSW to work on sheep properties.
Tradesmen's tokens for currency begin circulating. First issued by Melbourne grocers Annand, Smith and Co.
Caroline Chisholm founds Family Colonization Loan Society in London.
Britain loses trade monopoly with colonies when Navigation Act is repealed.
Privy Council recommends more extensive powers of self-government for Aust. colonies.

Births & Deaths

Sir Edmund Barton, Aust.'s first Prime Minister, 'Australia's Noblest Son', b. (d. 1920)
Alexander Forrest, explorer, financier, b. (d. 1901)
William Kidston, Qld Premier, b. (d. 1919)

B

Science, Technology, Transport, Discovery

1849

Jan. Thomas Chapman discovers gold in Maryborough district, Vic.
Aug. William Branwhite Clarke discovers tin along Murrumbidgee R. in Aust. Alps.
10 Oct. Construction by private company of NSW railway linking Sydney to Goulburn, NSW, begins. Company fails, and in 1855 NSW Govt acquires its assets.
During 1849
Corrugated sheet-iron widely used.
Mingaye, German geologist discovers first Aust. opals, near Angaston, SA.
c. 1849. Melbourne's first hansom cab appears.

Births & Deaths

Sir Horace Lamb, mathematician, b. (d. 1934)
Archibald A. Watson, anatomist, physician, b. (d. 1940)

1849

C
Arts

Literature

During 1849
Alexander Harris publishes *The Emigrant Family*.

Music, Dance

During 1849
Vincent Wallace's opera *Maritana* staged in Sydney.

Drama, Theatre

During 1849
Francis Nesbitt McCrone, a leading Aust. actor since 1842, leaves for California.

Fine Arts

During 1849
Society for the Promotion of the Fine Arts holds its first exhibition in Sydney.
Qld School of Arts founded.

Births & Deaths

John Glover, founder of Aust. landscape painting, d. (b. 1767)
Hume Nisbet, painter, b. (probably d. 1921)
James Lawrence Watts, sculptor, b. (d. 1925)

Architecture

During 1849
Edmund T. Blacket appointed NSW Colonial Architect.

Births & Deaths

Sir John Sulman, architect, town planner, educationist, b. (d. 1934)

D
Religion, Learning

2 Feb. Benedictine Order of nuns estb. Subiaco convent near Parramatta, NSW.
Jul. George Rusden begins horse-back journey from Brisbane to Portland, Vic., to estb. National Schools
During 1849
Presbyterian and Baptist Churches estb. in Brisbane.
One of first National Schools opens at Kempsey, NSW.
WA gives aid to Roman Catholic elementary schools.
VDL applies regulations placing all schools, Public or Denominational, under same financial system.
VDL public library estb. in Hobart.

Births & Deaths

William Marcus Dill Macky, Presbyterian minister, b. (d. 1913)

E
Sport

During 1849
The *Australian Sportsman*, among first sporting papers, published.
Horseracing now an established business in Aust.

F
Historia Dignum

Population
Estimated total white, 418,961.

28 Nov. Serious flooding in Melbourne.
During 1849
Significant exodus of population from Aust. to Californian goldfields.
NSW Govt introduces uniform two penny postal rate, reducing rates for inland postage. Sir Rowland Hill introduces postage stamps.
Railway crash at Redfern, Sydney, claims 11 lives.
George Morphesis, one of first Greeks to settle in Aust., arrives in Melbourne.

Communities
Bicheno, Tas., first settled
Canowindra, NSW, estb.
Cooma, NSW, estb.
Dubbo, NSW, estb.
Geeveston, Tas., estb.
Littlehampton, SA, estb.
Normanville, SA, estb.
Surat, Qld, estb.
Toowoomba, Qld, estb.
Wagga Wagga, NSW, estb.
Warialda, NSW, estb.

1850

A
History, Politics, Economics, Law

13 Apr. The Aust. Agricultural Co.'s 20-year monopoly on coalmining in NSW ends.
13 May. Circuit courts begin in Brisbane.
1 Jun. First convict ship, carrying 75 male convicts, arrives in WA.
5 Aug. Queen Victoria assents to the Australian Colonies Government Act, foreshadowing introduction of fully elected legislatures in place of partly elected, and transfer of legislative and executive authority from London to Aust.
Australian Colonies Government Act authorizes separation of Port Phillip District from NSW (11 Nov.) and estb. partly elected legislative bodies in Vic., Tas., WA, and SA.
16 Sep. About 16,000 people meet in Sydney to protest against renewal of transportation of convicts to eastern colonies.
Nov. First Vic. Stonemasons' Society estb.
During 1850
Australasian Anti-transportation League estb.
First Red Poll cattle arrive in Aust.
NSW first exports coal to South America.

Births & Deaths

Sir George Brookman, financier, benefactor, b. (d. 1927)
John Brown, NSW coal-mine owner and industrialist, b. (d. 1930)
Sir Richard Butler, SA Premier, b. (d. 1925)
Sir John Alexander Cockburn, SA Premier, b. (d. 1929)
Sir Matthew Henry Davies, solicitor, land speculator, b. (d. 1912)
Sir Frederick William Holder, SA Premier, b. (d. 1909)
Charles Cameron Kingston, SA Premier, b. (d. 1908)
William Lawson, explorer and pioneer official, d. (b. 1774)
Elizabeth Macarthur, pioneer settler and wife of John Macarthur, d. (b. 1766)
Christie Palmerston, explorer adventurer, probably b. (d. 1897)
Mei Quong Tart, businessman, authority on Scottish literature, history and folk lore, b. (d. 1903)
Yuranigh, Aborigine on Mitchell's 1845 expedition, d.

B
Science, Technology, Transport, Discovery

Mar. William Campbell discovers gold at Clunes, Vic.
3 Jul. Construction of Sydney to Parramatta railway line, part of Sydney-Goulburn line, begins.
Dec. Messrs Beaumont and Waller found zoo at Botany Bay, NSW.
During 1850
James Harrison begins experimenting with refrigeration techniques.
William Bland invents an 'atmotic ship', a gas filled balloon airship. (Releases plans in Sydney on 10 Mar. 1851.)
J. B. Jukes prepares first geological map of the Aust. continent.
Iron ore mined in NSW for Mittagong smelting works.
Lieut Helpman discovers pearlshell at Saturday I. Shoal, WA.
Construction of first properly built road in WA begins.
Charles Nicholson and Henry G. Douglass found the Aust. Philosophical Society.
W. Menz and Co. manufacture first biscuits in Aust., in Adelaide.
NSW Govt appoints Samuel Stutchbury first official geological surveyor. (Similar appointments in Vic. 1852, Tas. 1859, Qld 1868.)
c. 1850. Walter Bently Woodbury, photographer, arrives in Aust. (Stays for 10 years.)

Births & Deaths

Charles Bayliss, photographer, b. (d. 1897)
Joseph James Fletcher, biologist, probably b. (d. 1926)
Lawrence Hargrave, aeronautical pioneer, b. (d. 1915)
Thomas Whitelegge, naturalist, b. (d. 1927)

C
Arts

Music, Dance

24 May. *Gustavus III* is first opera staged at Queen's Theatre in Melbourne.

Births & Deaths

Octavius Charles Beale, piano manufacturer, b. (d. 1930)

Fine Arts

Sep. Marshall Claxton, painter, arrives in Aust. (Leaves in 1854.)

Births & Deaths

Guilio Anivitti, portrait painter, b. (d. 1881)
Arthur Esam, painter, b.
Charles Gregory, marine painter, b.
Lucien Felix Henry, painter and sculptor, b. (d. 1896)
William MacLeod, artist, newspaper proprietor, b. (d. 1929)
John A. Upton, portrait painter, b.
William Westall, landscape painter, topographer, d. (b. 1781)

Architecture

15 Nov. David Lennox's Prince's Bridge in Melbourne officially opens.
During 1850
Peter Beveridge builds first brick veneer structure, near Swan Hill, Vic. Possibly first in world.

D
Religion, Learning

May. First National School in Vic. opens at Bacchus Marsh.
30 Jun. First Unitarian Church in Aust. founded, in Sydney. (Melbourne in 1852, Adelaide in 1855.)
1 Oct. First Church of England conference, of six bishops, held in Sydney to discuss future of Church.
13 Nov. James Way, Bible Christian Methodist minister, arrives in Adelaide to estb. Christian Societies. (Estb. in Melbourne 1853, in Brisbane 1866.)
During Nov. Aust. Board of Missions estb. to spread Gospel in Pacific Is.
During 1850
Foundation stone of St Patrick's Cathedral laid in Melbourne.
Young Men's Christian Association (YMCA) estb. in Aust., in Adelaide. (Sydney and Melbourne 1853, Hobart 1854.)
National elementary education system well estb. in NSW.
Hobart High School opens.
Teacher training in Aust. begins with opening of Fort Street Model School in Sydney. (Other teacher training model schools open in Melbourne 1854, Brisbane 1862, Adelaide 1876.)
Barzillai Quaife presents philosophy lectures, *The Intellectual Sciences*, in Sydney. (Published in book form 1872.)

Births & Deaths

Henry Lowther Clarke, Church of England Archbishop of Melbourne in 1902, b. (d. 1926)
Alexander Robert Edgar, Methodist missionary, b. (d. 1914)
Michael Kelly, Roman Catholic Archbishop of Sydney in 1901, b. (d. 1940)

1850

E
Sport

During 1850
Professional athletic footracing begins in Aust.
Cockfighting officially banned.

Births & Deaths
William Beach, sculler, b. (d. 1935)

F
Historia Dignum

Population
Estimated total white, 484,728.

1 Jan. NSW issues first adhesive postage stamps, 'Sydney Views'. On 3 Jan. Vic. issues 'Half-Length' series showing half-length portrait of Queen Victoria holding the orb and sceptre.
28 Dec. Henry Parkes founds *Empire* newspaper. (First published Jan. 1851.)
During 1850
John Malcolm's Royal Aust. Equestrian Circus opens in Sydney.
Eastern Aust. suffers drought.
c. 1850. The billy or billycan replaces the quart pot.

Births & Deaths
Robert William Felton Lathrop Murray, VDL pioneer journalist, d. (b. 1777)

Communities
Boorowa, NSW, estb.
Camperdown, Vic., estb.
Cleveland, Qld, estb.
Esk, Qld, first settled
Euroa, Vic., estb.
Geraldton, WA, estb.
Lakes Entrance, Vic., first settled
Latrobe, Tas., estb.
Murringo, NSW, estb.
Port Elliot, SA, estb.
Port Wakefield, SA, estb.
Terang, Vic., estb.
Tweed Heads, NSW, estb.
Urunga, NSW, estb.
Williams, WA, estb.
Woodside, SA, estb.

A
History, Politics, Economics, Law

1851

Government

2 Jan. 1851–17 Jan. 1855, Sir Charles Augustus Fitz Roy Captain-General of NSW, Vic., VDL and SA, and Governor-General of all these colonies plus WA.

15 Jul. 1851–5 May 1854, Charles Joseph La Trobe Lieut-Governor Vic.

1 Feb. Anti-transportation Leagues meet in Melbourne to lobby for permanent cessation of convict transportation to eastern colonies. British Govt suspends transportation to NSW and Moreton Bay District but not prepared to promise abolition to all eastern Aust.

28 Feb. John West, Henry Hopkins and others estb. an anti-transportation league in Hobart.

During Feb. The United Operative Masons' Society forms; first trade union in Vic. (Estb. in Sydney on 7 May 1853.)

13 Mar. Act empowering WA to estb. Legislative Council proclaimed.

During Mar. Sydney merchants estb. Sydney Exchange Co.

21 May. Goldmining on Crown lands prohibited.

23 May. NSW Govt introduces compulsory goldmining licence costing 30 shillings.

24 May. First licence to dig for gold in NSW issued to Richard Roe. (First miner's licence in Vic. issued on 21 Sep.)

30 Jun. Aust. Steam Navigation Co. takes over Hunter R. Steam Navigation Co. to become leader in Aust. coastal trade.

1 Jul. Port Phillip District of NSW becomes separate Colony with the name of Victoria. Separated from NSW by Murray R. and from SA by long. 141°E.

2–12 Jul. Legislative Council elections in SA. (First meets on 20 Aug.)

8 Jul. First public meeting to consider constituting Moreton Bay District a separate colony held in Brisbane.

21 Sep. Vic. estb. compulsory goldmining licences.

24 Oct. First Legislative Council elections in VDL. (First meets on 2 Jan. 1852.)

During 1851
Partly elected (two-thirds) representative govt estb. in Vic., SA and VDL.

Goldrushes to Bathurst district, NSW, in early May; to banks of Turon R., NSW, in Jun.; to Ballarat, Vic., in Sep.; to Mt Alexander, Vic., in Oct.; and Bendigo, Vic., in Nov.

Sir Redmond Barry appointed Vic. Solicitor-General. (Until Jan. 1852.)

Buckley & Nunn trading stores founded in Melbourne.

Joseph Ernst Seppelt founds vineyards at Seppeltsfield, SA.

James and Alexander Brown further break coal trade monopoly held by Aust. Agricultural Co., enabling a more extensive development of mineral wealth in Newcastle area.

G. W. Francis produces Aust. olive oil.

Discovery of gold brings industry to a halt as workers join goldrushes. Labour shortages cause wages and prices to rise.

Births & Deaths

Thomas Edward Anstey, VDL pioneer settler, d. (b. 1777)

James Ebenezer Bicheno, public servant and botanist, d. (b. 1785)

Henry Bournes Higgins, judge, 'Father of the Basic Wage', Federal politician, b. (d. 1929)

William Manifold, VDL pioneer, d. (probably b. 1767)

Archibald Meston, administrator and explorer, b. (d. 1924)

John Murray, Vic. Premier, b. (d. 1916)

Richard Edward O'Connor, judge, Federal politician, b. (d. 1912)

Sir Robert Philp, Qld Premier and merchant, b. (d. 1922)

John Piper, Collector of Customs, d. (b. 1773)

James Raymond, NSW Postmaster-General, d. (b. 1786)

Francis Nicholas Rossi, police superintendent, d. (b. 1776)

Donald Campbell Simson, Vic. pioneer pastoralist, d.

Sir George Turner, Vic. Premier, and first Federal Treasurer, b. (d. 1916)

1851

B

Science, Technology, Transport, Discovery

12 Feb. Edward Hammond Hargraves discovers first Aust. diamond, near Guyong, NSW.

Gold discoveries

12 Feb. Edward Hammond Hargraves and John Lister discover specks of gold in Lewis Ponds Creek near Bathurst, NSW. Payable gold (probably first in Australia) discovered by Lister and William and James Tom in Ophir district on 7 Apr.
10 Jun. William Campbell discovers specks of gold in quartz in Clunes district, Vic. (Publishes finds 8 Jul.)
28 Jun. James 'Civil Jim' Esmond discovers gold in Clunes district, Vic.
13 Jul. Louis Michel discovers gold in Yarra Ranges near Melbourne.
8 Aug. Thomas Hiscock discovers gold in Buninyong Ranges near Ballarat, Vic.
25 Aug.–Sep. John Dunlop discovers payable gold in Ballarat area.
8 Sep. Significant gold discoveries at Ballarat, Vic.
10 Sep. Gold discovered at Mount Alexander, Vic.
29 Sep. Gold discovered at Broken R., Vic.
Oct. Margaret Kennedy locates gold at Bednego (Bendigo) Creek, Vic.
Nov. Henry Frenchham discovers gold at Bendigo, Vic.
During 1851
William Bland exhibits a model of his 'atmotic ship' invention in London, elongated balloon to be powered by steam-engine.
Tin discovered in NSW, but no major mining until 1872.

Births & Deaths

Charles Henry Hoskins, iron and steel pioneer, b. (d. 1926)
Sir Joseph Coote Verco, medical researcher, hydatids specialist, b. (d. 1933)

C

Arts

Literature

Births & Deaths

James Lister Cuthbertson, poet and teacher, b. (d. 1910)
John Farrell, author, b. (d. 1904)
Rosa Caroline Praed, novelist who wrote as Mrs Campbell Praed, b. (d. 1935)

Music, Dance

18 Dec. *Jocko, the Brazilian Ape*, dance, produced in Adelaide.
During 1851
Samuel Prout, bandmaster, tours Vic. goldfields.

Births & Deaths

Maggie Moore, musical comedy actress, b. (d. 1926)

Drama, Theatre

Births & Deaths

Barry Dan, actor, showman, b. (d. 1908)
George Darrell, playwright, probably b. (d. 1921)

Fine Arts

7 Oct. First Brisbane School of Arts opens.
During 1851
Late Colonial period or Early Aust. period of art begins. First serious attempt to depict history and life of Aust. colonies, characterized by gold discoveries. Rapid population increase accelerates development of graphic arts, lithography, cartooning and newspaper illustrations. (Period lasts until *c.* 1884.)

Births & Deaths

Julian Rossi Ashton, painter, illustrator, b. (d. 1942)
Benjamin Duterrau, engraver, portrait painter, etcher, sculptor, d. (b. 1767)
John Ford Paterson, landscape painter, b. (d. 1912)
William Brookes Spong, painter, theatre designer, b. (d. 1929)

Architecture

12 May. First professional group of architects forms in Melbourne, Vic. Architects Association.

D
Religion, Learning

1851

During 1851
Early Victorian period of architecture begins. (Ends c. 1860.)
Thomas English, architect, designs Scots Church in Adelaide.

28 Jan. William Wilkins takes charge of teacher training Model School in Sydney and develops formal system of pupil-teacher education, which begins in Nov.

During Jan. Hugh Culling Eardley Childers appointed to investigate state of education in Vic. On 9 Feb. estb. the Board of National Education to control National Schools in Vic.

30 Oct. John Murdoch and Charles Wandell, American missionaries, introduce Mormon Church to Aust.

During 1851
Enactment of Constitution Act enables each Colony to fix the amount to be voted for religious purposes.
SA Govt aid to religion abolished. A Central Board estb, later becoming Central Education Authority. (SA becomes first part of British Empire to separate Church and State.)
Scotch College, independent school, founded as Melbourne Academy.
First Melbourne Catholic and Presbyterian schools open.

Births & Deaths
Sir John Henry Macfarland, educationist, b. (d. 1935)

1851

E
Sport

Feb. VDL and Vic. cricket matches among first intercolonial played.
During 1851
First Aust. champion racehorse, Jorrocks, wins its last race, at Bathurst, NSW.

Births & Deaths
Charles Bannerman, cricketer, noted batsman, b. (d. 1930)
Henry John Pearce, always known as Harry, oarsman, b. (d. 1920)

F
Historia Dignum

Population
Estimated total white, 437,665.

1 Jan. *Empire* newspaper first published.
6 Feb. Known as Black Thursday because of devastating bushfires from Melbourne to SA.
Jul. 'Kerr Hundredweight', gold-bearing mass weighing 2,400 ounces, of which 1,272 ounces were gold, discovered near Turon R., NSW.
27 Sep. Sir Thomas Mitchell fights one of last recorded duels in NSW, with Stuart Donaldson.
During 1851
Sydney Typographical Society estb.
Aust. goods exhibited at Great Exhibition in London
Of 50 policemen in Vic. police force, 40 resign to join goldrushes.
The NSW Society for the Relief of Destitute Children estb. in Sydney.
Drought in eastern SA.
Serious bushfires in VDL.

Communities
Ballarat, Vic., estb.
Bendigo, Vic., estb.
Castlemaine, Vic., estb.
Clunes, Vic., estb.
Dunkeld, Vic., estb.
Ebenezer, SA, estb.
Gerringong, NSW, estb.
Glen Innes, NSW, estb.
Hill End, NSW, estb.
Lucknow, NSW, estb.
Moree, NSW, estb.
Moruya, NSW, estb.
Saddleworth, SA, estb.
Sunbury, Vic., estb.

A

History, Politics, Economics, Law

1852

2 Jan. Meeting of first elected council in VDL protests against transportation of convicts. Large anti-transportation meeting in Sydney in Apr. results in final cessation of transportation to all eastern colonies.

6 Jan. Supreme Court of Vic. estb., with civil and criminal jurisdiction. William à Beckett becomes Vic.'s first Chief Justice on 24 Jan.

28 Jan. SA Legislative Council passes Bullion Act, empowering it to assay gold into stamped ingots for use as legal tender. (In Nov. 1 pound gold tokens, called Adelaide sovereigns, replace ingots.)

During Jan. Hovenden Hely begins journey from Darling Downs, Qld, to Peak Downs, Qld, in search of Ludwig Leichhardt.

10 Feb. Alexander Tolmer conducts first successful gold escort services between Vic. and SA; attempts to bring gold to Adelaide to save SA from economic crisis. (First gold escort arrives in Adelaide on 19 Mar.)

Sep. Vic. Legislative Council passes Convict Prevention Act, allowing only free persons to enter Colony.

Oct. Amalgamated Engineering Union estb. in Sydney.

During 1852

British Govt surrenders control of land policy in Aust.

John Dunmore Lang draws up principles of land subdivision for development of Aust.

Melbourne Metropolitan Police Force estb. under Samuel Freeman. Sydney Police Force upgraded.

'D Notice' (defence), system of voluntary censorship, introduced into Aust.

Chinese gold diggers arrive in Aust.

Exodus from SA to Vic. goldfields threatens Colony with insolvency.

National Bank of Vic. estb., Bank of Vic. estb., English Scottish and Australian Chartered Bank estb.

William Barton, among first Aust. stockbrokers, begins work in Sydney.

Francis Cadell begins rowing down Murray R. from Echuca, Vic., to Lake Alexandrina, SA, to determine navigability of river for steamers.

NSW Goldfields Management Act increases monthly goldmining fee to 60 shillings for non-British miners.

George Robertson, first regular book publisher in Aust., arrives in Melbourne. (Opens Melbourne bookshop Mar. 1853.)

Births & Deaths

Henry Colden Anthill, soldier, pastoralist, d. (b. 1779)
Jeffery Hart Bent, NSW judge, d. (probably b. 1780)
Sir William Rooke Creswell, naval commander, 'Father of Australian Navy', b. (d. 1933)
John Darling, SA politician, industrialist, b. (d. 1914)
Sir Frank Gavan Duffy, Aust. Chief Justice, b. (d. 1936)
George William Evans, surveyor and explorer, d. (b. 1780)
Maximilian Hirsch, economist, probably b. (d. 1909)
John Howe, explorer, NSW pioneer, d. (b. 1774)
Richard 'China' Jones, pioneer merchant and marine insurance agent, d. (probably b. 1787)
Sir Algernon Hawkins Thomond Keith-Falconer, Earl of Kintore, SA Governor, b. (d. 1930)
Sir Malcolm McEacharn, shipowner, Federal politician, b. (d. 1910)
James Thomas Morisset, military officer, d. (probably b. 1780)
James Mudie, NSW pioneer, d. (b. 1779)
Thomas Price, SA Premier, b. (d. 1909)
Sir John Quick, Federal politician, author, b. (d. 1932)
Richard Rouse, NSW pioneer settler, Superintendent of Public Works, d. (b. 1774)
Joseph Cowan Syme, newspaper proprietor, b. (d. 1916)
Hallam Tennyson, Baron Tennyson, Governor-General, b. (d. 1928)

1852

B
Science, Technology, Transport, Discovery

3 Aug. First steamship to arrive in Sydney, SS *Chusan*, berths after 80-day voyage from England; beginning of regular steamship communication.
11 Nov. Six-masted iron screw-steamer *Great Britain*, weighing 3,500 tons, arrives in Melbourne.
James Harrison begins work on inventing and building first ice works at Rocky Point in Vic.
During 1852
Payable gold discovered at the Nook, near Fingal, and 9 Mile Springs, in VDL.
Gold discovered at Bingera, near Burnett R., Qld.
NSW plans to adopt Irish railway gauge standard of 5 feet 3 inches. Vic. agrees in Jan. 1853 to follow. In Aug. 1853 NSW changes plans and adopts English standard gauge of 4 feet 8½ inches, by which time it was too late for Vic. to change.

Births & Deaths
Louis Brennan, inventor of guided torpedo, b. (d. 1932)
Peter Degraves, engineer, d. (b. 1778)
Edward Henry Rennie, scientist, b. (d. 1927)
Walter Henry Warren, engineer, b. (d. 1926)
Clement Lindley Wragge, meteorologist who began giving female names to cyclones, b. (d. 1922)

C
Arts

Literature

During 1852
John West publishes *The History of Tasmania*.

Births & Deaths
Edmund James Banfield, journalist and author, b. (d. 1923)
Alexander Sutherland, writer, philosopher, b. (d. 1902)

Music, Dance

During 1852
Opera *Norma* performed in Melbourne.

Fine Arts

Aug. S. T. Gill publishes 24 drawings of Vic. goldfields.
During 1852
William Austin, engraver, produces coloured lithograph, *Arrival of the First Gold Escort Melbourne, June, 1852*.

Births & Deaths
Louis Abrahams, watercolourist, etcher, b. (d. 1903)
Edward Gouldsmith, painter, b. (d. 1932)
Henri Tebbit, painter, b. (d. 1926)

D
Religion, Learning

2 Jan. South Australia Education Act introduces secular primary education system and officially abolishes State aid to Church schools.
11 Oct. University of Sydney opens.
During 1852
St Mary's Roman Catholic College opens at Lyndhurst, NSW.

Births & Deaths
William Bedford, known as 'Holy Willie', Church of England chaplain in Hobart, d. (probably b. 1781)
John Ferguson, Presbyterian minister, b. (d. 1925)
Samuel Leigh, Methodist minister, d. (b. 1785)

E
Sport

Oct. WA Turf Club estb.
Wallabadah Horse Racing Club, NSW, estb. Among first country racing clubs.

1852

F

Historia Dignum

Population
Estimated total white, 513,796.

2 Apr. Twenty-two robbers steal 8,000 ounces of gold from barque *Nelson*, anchored off Williamstown, Vic.

24–25 Jun. Floods wash away Gundagai township, NSW, claiming 77 lives out of a total population of 250; among worst flood disasters in Aust. history.

31 Aug. SS *Chusan* leaves Sydney with first mail for Singapore, via Melbourne, Adelaide and Perth.

During 1852

The *Birkenhead* wrecked off Point Danger, NSW, claiming 438 lives.

Sailing vessel *Ticonderoga* arrives Portsea, Vic., from England carrying 400 cases of typhoid fever, 100 died on journey.

NSW Govt makes use of adhesive postage stamps compulsory. Among first in world to do so.

Births & Deaths
James Hull, who lived longest recorded male life in Aust., 109 years 139 days, b. (d. 1961)

Communities
Avoca, Vic., estb.
Barraba, NSW, estb.
Beechworth, Vic., estb.
Biloela, Qld, first settled
Cranbourne, Vic., estb.
Creswick, Vic., estb.
Daylesford, Vic., estb.
Dongara, WA, estb.
Goolwa, SA, estb.
Heathcote, Vic., estb.
Pakenham, Vic., estb.
Port Augusta, SA, estb.
Skipton, Vic., estb.
Uralla, NSW, estb.
Walcha, NSW, estb.
Wodonga, Vic., estb.

A
History, Politics, Economics, Law

1853

Jan. William Carter becomes first Mayor of Hobart.
19 Mar. Charles Sturt leaves Aust.
29 Mar. Lachlan McLachlan appointed Bendigo police magistrate; noted for handing down severe sentences.
26 May. Last convict arrives in Hobart; transportation ends. In 50 years of transportation to VDL 56,042 males and 11,613 females were landed.
During May. Samuel Freeman and staff from London police arrive in Melbourne to assist in development of Aust. police forces.
6 Jun. An Anti-Gold Licence Association estb. in Vic. Grievances over price of goldmining licences intensify.
10 Aug. Public opposition to proposed NSW Constitution providing for hereditary nobility, or aristocratic order, as suggested by W. C. Wentworth. Daniel Deniehy describes proposed system of Aust. titles as 'bunyip aristocracy'.
15 Aug.–mid Oct. William Randell navigates steamboat up Murray R., pioneering way for Murray R. boat trade.
26 Aug.–17 Sep. Francis Cadell in the *Lady Augusta* navigates the Murray R. from Goolwa, SA, to Swan Hill, Vic.
24 Sep. France takes possession of New Caledonia.
During 1853
Imperial Govt authorizes Aust. colonies to draft separate constitutions.
NSW Constitutional Bill provides for two chambers; the Assembly (elected), and the Council (nominated).
Revenue from Crown lands placed under control of local legislatures.
Riots over disputes between Chinese and European miners at Bendigo, Vic.
Charles La Trobe estb. Vic. Public Service.
Vic. introduces provision for registration of births, deaths and marriages.
Peel River Land and Mineral Co. Ltd formed to acquire and develop Peel R. estate on Liverpool Plains, NSW.
First vineyards planted at Great Western, in Vic.
Thomas Hardy plants vines at Bankside, SA.
Bushrangers become serious problem on goldfields roads.
Gold overtakes wool as premier Aust. export.
Order-in-Council officially terminates Norfolk I. penal settlement.
Kiama Steam Navigation Co. estb. to trade on NSW coast. (Becomes Illawarra Steam Navigation Co. in 1904.)

Births & Deaths

Francis Luis Barrallier, explorer, ensign in NSW Corps, d. (b. 1773)
Gregory Blaxland, explorer, pioneer pastoralist, d. (b. 1778)
William Pitt Cobbett, lawyer, professor, b. (d. 1919)
Daniel Cooper, emancipist, merchant, d. (b. 1785)
Richard Hipkiss, social and political reformer, d. (probably b. 1772)
William Jamieson, mining magnate, b. (d. 1926)
Kenneth Snodgrass, administrator, colonial military commander, d. (probably b. 1784)
John Street, NSW politician, businessman, d. (b. 1781)

1853

B

Science, Technology, Transport, Discovery

20 Apr. Maitland Railway Co. begins work on Newcastle–Maitland railway line in NSW.
Jul. Freeman Cobb, John Peck, James Swanton and John Lamber estb. Cobb & Co. coach services in Melbourne; first service runs from Melbourne to Port Melbourne.
30 Sep. *Sydney Morning Herald* becomes first newspaper in Aust. printed by a steam press.
During 1853
Ballarat, first iron-hulled vessel built in Aust., launched in Sydney.
George Collins Levey first uses quartz-crushing machinery to extract gold at Forest Creek, Vic.
Williamstown Observatory opens near Melbourne.
James Ellis begins Vic.'s first private zoo.
Ferdinand J. H. von Mueller becomes Vic. Govt Botanist.
Royal Society of SA estb., as Adelaide Philosophical Society.
NSW reverts to English standard railway gauge, by which time Vic. and SA have ordered rolling stock for Irish gauge.
Paddle-steamers operate on Murray and Darling rivers. On 19 Feb. *Mary Ann* launched at Mannum, SA; first steamer to travel on Murray R.

Births & Deaths

Archibald James Campbell, ornithologist, b. (d. 1929)
Thomas Henry Fiaschi, surgeon, b. (d. 1927)
Leonard Rodway, Tas. botanist, b. (d. 1936)
Sir Charles Snodgrass Ryan, surgeon, ornithologist, b. (d. 1926)

C

Arts

Literature

Nov. Adam Lindsay Gordon arrives in Adelaide.
During 1853
John Lang's *The Wetherbys* and *Too Clever by Half* serialized in India. Among first Aust.-born writers to publish fiction.

Music, Dance

May. Therese Ferdinand-Strebinger, dancer, makes début in Melbourne.
During 1853
Melbourne Philharmonic Society estb. Among first choral groups in Aust.
J. Winterbottom begins promenade concerts in Melbourne.

Drama, Theatre

During 1853
Charles Harpur publishes *The Bushrangers, a Play in Five Acts and other Poems*. This was the first play published in book form in Aust.
American 'Tragedians', Mr and Mrs Stark, perform in Melbourne.

Births & Deaths

Joseph Bland Holt, comedian, producer, theatrical entrepreneur, b. (d. 1942)

Fine Arts

Sep. Fine Arts Society of the Melbourne Mechanics' Institute opens fine arts exhibition building to exhibit 400 paintings by local artists.
During 1853
Vic. Fine Arts Society estb. (Becomes Vic. Society of Fine Arts in 1856.)

Births & Deaths

Joseph Arthur Bennett, watercolourist, b. (d. 1929)
George Thomas William Boyes, watercolourist, d. (b. 1787)
R. W. Bugg, painter, b. (d. 1937)
Neville Henry Peniston Cayley, bird painter, b. (d. 1903)
Arthur de Tourcey Collingridge, painter, illustrator, b. (d. 1907)
Archibald Collins, painter, b. (d. 1922)
H. Edward Davies, artist, architect, b. (d. 1927)
John Baxter Mather, etcher, critic, b. (d. 1940)

D
Religion, Learning

1853

J. A. Panton, painter, probably b. (d. 1913)
Charles Douglas Richardson, sculptor, painter, b. (d. 1932)
Frederic S. Sheldon, English animal painter, sculptor, active in Aust. c. 1890, b.

Architecture

During 1853
Charles Summers, sculptor, arrives in Aust.
First pre-fabricated iron cottages arrive from England.

3 Jul. Vic. State Library founded in Melbourne. First govt-estb. public library in Aust.
30 Oct. Rev. G. H. Stanley holds regular Unitarian Church services in Sydney. Rev. Maxwell Davidson appointed first Unitarian Church minister in Melbourne.
Nov. VDL ends State aid to Church schools. Creates central Board of Education, introducing modified version of Irish National System.

During 1853
Act of Parlt incorporates the Aust. Museum; board of trustees appointed.

1853

E
Sport

During 1853
Melbourne Cricket Ground estb.
Henry Upton Alcock opens billiard factory in Melbourne; estb. billiards in Aust.

Births & Deaths
John Blackman, cricket pioneer, b. (d. 1932)
Frederick Robert 'Demon' Spofforth, cricketer, first Aust. fast bowler, b. (d. 1926)

F
Historia Dignum

Population
Estimated total white, 600,992.

15 May. American steamer *Monumental City* wrecked; 30 lives lost.
24 Oct. Paddle-steamer *Juno* wrecked near Manning R., NSW; 6 lives lost.
9 Dec. The *Bendigo Advertiser* newspaper estb., Vic.

During 1853
First VDL postage stamps, of Queen Victoria's portrait, issued.
Ship *Dalhousie* wrecked while *en route* from England; 60 lives lost.

Births & Deaths
Cheok Hong Cheong, Chinese anti-opium campaigner, probably b. (d. 1928)
Frederick Deeming, Melbourne murderer, b. (d. 1892)
James Hardy Vaux, adventurer, probably d. (b. 1782)

Communities
Cessnock, NSW, estb.
Great Western, Vic., estb.
Inverell, NSW, estb.
Lismore, Vic., estb.
Maldon, Vic., estb.
Manilla, NSW, estb.
Moss Vale, NSW, estb.
Railton, Tas., estb.
Rushworth, Vic., estb.
Stawell, Vic., estb.

A

History, Politics, Economics, Law

1854

Government

6 May 1854–22 Jun. 1854, John Vesey Fitzgerald administers Vic.
22 Jun. 1854–21 May 1855, Sir Charles Hotham Lieut-Governor Vic.
20 Dec. 1854–8 Jun. 1855, Boyle Travers Finniss administers SA.

29 Jan. First Aust. cotton exported to England.
May. Coalminers in Newcastle, NSW, strike for higher wages.
Robert William Rede becomes goldfields Commissioner at Ballarat, Vic.
Nov. Ferdinand von Mueller begins exploration of Great Dividing Range in Vic.
4 Dec. Vic. Master Printers' Association estb.

Eureka Stockade

3 Sep. Lieut-Governor Hotham orders Gold Commissioners to increase goldmining licence checks on Vic. goldfields from once a month to twice a week. Increased licence hunts begin 17 Sep.
6 Oct. Young miner, James Scobie, kicked to death after attempting to enter James Bentley's Eureka Hotel in early hours of morning. Bentley and three others charged with murder.
12 Oct. Court dismisses charges of murder against James Bentley and alleged accomplices.
17 Oct. Miners retaliate against perceived injustice by burning down the Eureka Hotel.
11 Nov. Miners meet and demand reforms to remove goldfield grievances. Ballarat Reform League estb. As well as abolition of licence system, demands include universal suffrage, voting by ballot and annual parliaments. Govt re-inforcements arrive.
23 Nov. James Bentley re-arrested and convicted of manslaughter.
29 Nov. Miners meet to discuss grievances. Decide to make bonfire of licences and to protect anyone arrested for being without licence. Southern Cross flag raised.
30 Nov. Gold Commissioner initiates another licence hunt. Peter Lalor elected diggers' leader.
1 Dec. Armed diggers prepare for confrontation with troops. Stockade built on Eureka Hill.
3 Dec. About 300 troops attack c. 150 miners on Eureka Hill: 6 soldiers and 22 miners killed; 13 miners taken prisoner and sent for trial.
6 Dec. Martial law proclaimed in Ballarat district.
8 Dec. Ballarat police court commits 13 diggers for trial on charges of high treason. Charges against one later dropped. Remaining 12 acquitted Feb. 1855.
14 Dec. Colonial Secretary William Clark Haines promises goldfields reform.

During 1854

Crimean War heightens. Aust. fears Russian invasion; batteries estb. at Sydney Harbour. (On 28 Mar. Britain and France declare war on Russia.)
Hunter Coal Miners' Union estb.
VDL Aboriginal population reduced to about 16.
Chinese arrive on Vic. goldfields in large numbers.
Metropolitan Permanent Building Society registered in Melbourne.
Melbourne becomes principal commercial port in Aust.
Tin first produced in Ovens district, Vic.
Robert Austin explores Murchison R. area, WA, in search of pastoral land, discovers Mt Garnet on 25 Aug.
Moreton Bay Savings Bank estb.
Headquarters of Imperial Forces transferred from Sydney to Melbourne.

Births & Deaths

Sir George Arthur, VDL Governor, d. (b. 1784)
Jacky Jacky Galmarra, Aboriginal hero in Kennedy's 1848 expedition to Cape York Peninsula, Qld, d.
Sir Henry Bruce Lefroy, WA Premier, b. (d. 1930)
William Robert Nuttall Maloney, Labor politician, 'The Little Doctor', b. (d. 1940)
George Michael Prendergast, Vic. Premier, b. (d. 1937)
Thomas Waddell, NSW Premier, b. (d. 1940)
Sir Edward Horne Wittenoom, WA pioneer pastoralist, politician, b. (d. 1936)

1854

B
Science, Technology, Transport, Discovery

13 Jan. Freeman Cobb begins Melbourne to Castlemaine, Vic., Cobb & Co coach service.

3 Mar. Samuel Walker McGowan erects and opens first electric telegraph line in Southern Hemisphere, between Melbourne and Williamstown, Vic. Completes Melbourne to Geelong line on 5 Dec. (Electric telegraph lines open in SA 1856, Tas. 1857, NSW 1858 and WA 1859.)

18 May. Horse-drawn tramway service from Port Elliot to Goolwa, SA, opens. First line of rail opened for public traffic in Aust.

12 Sep. First public steam railway in Aust. opens, from Flinders Street, Melbourne, to Port Melbourne.

During 1854
Robertson, Martin and Smith manufacture first locomotive made in Aust.
Vic. Institute for the Advancement of Science, and Philosophical Society of Vic. estb. (Amalgamate in 1855 to form the Philosophical Institute of Vic.)
Joseph Bosisto estb. first eucalyptus oil still for commercial production in Vic.
Morts Dock and Engineering Co. Ltd estb. in Sydney; first major Aust. engineering firm.
Steam ferry services across Swan R. begin in Perth.
John Tebbutt begins astronomical observations which bring prestige to Aust. astronomy.
Ronald Gunn and William Archer from Tas. elected Fellows of the Royal Society for services to botany.

Births & Deaths
Sir Harry Brookes Allen, pathologist, b. (d. 1926)
Richard Thomas Baker, botanist, b. (d. 1941)
Sir Charles Percy Barlee Clubbe, surgeon, pioneer of baby health centres in NSW, b. (d. 1932)
William Aitcheson Haswell, biologist, b. (d. 1925)
James Park Thomson, geographer, b. (d. 1941)
James Walker, botanist, educationist, d.

C
Arts

Literature

During 1854
Catherine Helen Spence publishes *Clara Morison* in London.

Births & Deaths
Sir Mungo William MacCallum, author, scholar, b. (d. 1942)

Music, Dance

Oct. Catherine Hayes among first opera singers to visit Aust.

During 1854
Charles Thatcher becomes popular as goldfields minstrel singer.
Sydney Philharmonic Society founded.

Drama, Theatre

11 Oct. Edwin Booth among first actors of international repute to visit Aust.

During 1854
Theatre Royal opens in Bendigo, Vic.
Thomas Mooney builds Astley's Amphitheatre in Melbourne. (Becomes Princess Theatre in 1857.)

Births & Deaths
George Musgrove, theatrical manager, b. (d. 1916)

Fine Arts

During 1854
Emil Todt's sculpture *The Diggers* among earliest Aust. sculptures.

Births & Deaths
Samuel Begg, black-and-white artist, b.
Alfred Scott Broad, black-and-white artist, b. (d. 1929)
Rosa Catherine Fiveash, wildflower painter, b. (d. 1938)
Arthur José de Souza Loureiro, painter, b. (d. 1932)
John White, painter, b. (d. 1943)
Walter Herbert Withers, landscape painter noted for portrayal of atmospheric conditions, b. (d. 1914)

D
Religion, Learning

Architecture

During 1854
Edmund Thomas Blacket designs neo-Gothic Great Hall at Sydney University.
Louis Hope builds Ormiston House in Brisbane, notable example of Qld Colonial architecture.
Construction of Victoria Barracks in Melbourne begins.
Joseph Reed begins building in Melbourne. Designs Public Library.
John Simpson Mackennal, sculptor, arrives in Aust.

3 Jul. Foundation stone of Melbourne Public Library laid.

During 1854
William Stawell assists Charles Perry, Bishop of Melbourne, draft a constitution for Church of England diocese, first successful attempt to achieve religious independence by Church of England in Aust.
National Museum of Vic. estb.
St Patrick's Catholic College opens in Melbourne.
Two Queen's orphan schools estb. in VDL.
Mechanics' Institute in Melbourne estb. (Becomes Prahran College of Advanced Education in 1974.)

Births & Deaths

Charles Owen Leaver Riley, first Anglican Archbishop of Perth, 1914, b. (d. 1929)
Albert Rivett, Congregational minister, b. (d. 1934)
Edward Holdsworth Sugden, educationist, b. (d. 1935)

1854

E
Sport

During 1854
Melbourne Hunt Club estb.

F
Historia Dignum

Population
Estimated total white, 694,917.

13 Jan. Fire in Elizabeth Street, Melbourne destroys several houses and stores.
5 Jul. *Mercury* newspaper (renamed in 1860) estb. as *Hobarton Mercury* in Hobart.
Aug. First WA stamp, 1d Black, issued, showing black swan.
10 Oct. First volunteer fire co. estb. in Sydney.
17 Oct. Henry Cook, Walter Powell and other merchants found *The Age*, morning broadsheet, in Melbourne, running it as a printers' co-operative.
Melbourne Exhibition opens.
Melbourne Town Hall opens, first in Aust.
Sir Charles Fitz Roy opens NSW Exhibition for preview in Sydney before exposure in Paris.
Ship *Madagascar* wrecked *en route* from Melbourne to London; 130 lives lost.
There are about 2,300 adult male Chinese on Vic. goldfields.
First recorded drought in Vic. affects Maryborough district.

Communities

Ararat, Vic., estb.
Fingal, Tas., first settled
Mannum, SA, estb.
Maryborough, Vic., estb.
Nannup, WA, estb.
Nuriootpa, SA, estb.
Pittsworth, Qld, first settled
Reynella, SA, estb.
Rochester, Vic., estb.
Sandstone, WA, estb.
Taree, NSW, estb.
Wee Waa, NSW, estb.

A
History, Politics, Economics, Law

1855

Government

8 Jan. 1855–10 Dec. 1861, Sir Henry Edward Fox Young Governor Tas.
20 Jan. 1855–19 Dec. 1855, Sir William Thomas Denison Governor-General of all five Aust. colonies.
22 May 1855–31 Dec. 1855, Sir Charles Hotham Governor Vic.
8 Jun. 1855–4 Mar. 1862, Sir Richard Graves MacDonnell Governor SA.
23 Jul. 1855–19 Feb. 1862, Arthur Edward Kennedy Governor WA.
28 Nov. 1855–Mar. 1857, William Clark Haines Premier Vic.
19 Dec. 1855–22 Jan. 1861, Sir William Thomas Denison Governor NSW.

1 Jan. Robert Knox forms Colonial Sugar Refining Co., which takes over the liquidated Aust. Sugar Co.
Feb.–Mar. Juries at Eureka trials acquit all charged.
4 Apr. Gunboat *Spitfire* launched in Sydney.
14 May. Royal Mint opens in Sydney.
May–Jul. NSW coalminers strike for higher wages at Newcastle, NSW. First significant strike involving non-craft labour.
Jun. Vic. passes first anti-Chinese restrictive legislation with imposition of a £10 poll tax on all Chinese arriving at Vic. ports. (Anti-Chinese restrictive legislation passed in SA 1857, NSW 1861, Qld 1871, again in NSW 1881 and all colonies 1888.)
Tipperary riots between miners on Maryborough goldfields, Vic., result in formation of Maryborough Mutual Protection Society to protect miners against lawless elements on the goldfields.
16 Jul. Imperial Govt assents to responsible govt in NSW. Assents to same in Vic. 21 Jul. and Tas. 24 Oct. NSW and Vic. constitutions effective from Nov. 1855. Tas. Constitution effective from Oct. 1856.
Aug. Augustus C. Gregory and Sir Ferdinand J. H. von Mueller begin North Aust. expedition from NT overland to E coast of Qld.
Sep. Sydney stonemasons are first in Aust. to be granted an 8-hour working day.
26 Nov. The name 'Van Diemen's Land' officially changed by proclamation to 'Tasmania'.
28 Nov. First Vic. Govt ministry under self-govt appointed.

During 1855
Convention to reform methods of disposing lands held in Melbourne. James Grant becomes leading spokesman for the 'unlock the lands' movement.
The Early Closing Movement and Eight-Hour Movement form to improve working conditions.

Commissioners on goldfields replaced by wardens; local courts estb. The Miners Right, costing £1 per year and entitling holder to vote, replaces Miners' Licences.
NSW Govt railways take over Sydney Railway Co., beginning Govt control of railways. NSW first in British Empire to nationalize railways.
Phillip Parker King becomes first colonial-born Australian to attain Rear Admiral's rank in the Royal Navy.
George Bain Johnston becomes first to take steamer up Murray R. as far as Albury, NSW.

Births & Deaths

Sir Richard Bourke, NSW Governor, d. (b. 1777)
Sir William Portus Cullen, NSW Chief Justice from 1910 to 1935, b. (d. 1935)
Charles Gavan Duffy, Federal public servant, b. (d. 1932)
Sir George Fairbairn, Vic. politician, b. (d. 1943)
Sir Isaac Alfred Isaacs, first Aust.-born Governor-General, b. (d. 1948)
G. Edward 'Ned' Kelly, bushranger, b. (d. 1880).
James Sinclair Taylor McGowan, NSW Premier, b. (d. 1922)
Sir Edward Fancourt Mitchell, Melbourne barrister, b. (d. 1941)
Mary Reibey, emancipist, merchant, pastoralist, d. (b. 1777).
Sir James John Joynton Smith, businessman, b. (d. 1943)
Charles Windeyer, law and parliamentary reporter, first recognized reporter in House of Lords, London, d. (b. 1780)

1855

B
Science, Technology, Transport, Discovery

10 Mar. Planning of Adelaide Botanical Gardens begins.
During Mar. Thomas Sutcliffe Mort invests in construction of a dry dock at Balmain, Sydney.
26 Sep. First govt-owned steam railway in British Empire and first steam railway in NSW opens, from Sydney to Parramatta.
Oct. Francis Cadell receives grant from NSW Govt to remove snags from Murray R. to improve river transport.
During 1855
Sir William Denison estb. Aust. Philosophical Society. (Becomes Philosophical Society of NSW.)
First passenger lifts (non-mechanical) estb. in Sydney.
Botanical Gardens estb. in Brisbane.
First amateur Photographic Society estb., in Sydney.
John Kitchen begins making soap in Melbourne.
Vic. Govt passes first Public Health Act in Aust.
John McIlwraith, engineer, produces first extruded lead pipes in Aust.

Births & Deaths
John McConnell Black, SA botanist, b. (d. 1951)
Francis James Gillen, anthropologist who carried out one of first important studies of Aborigines, b. (d. 1912)
Alfred John North, ornithologist, b. (d. 1917)
Henry Ling Roth, anthropologist, b. (d. 1925)
John William Springthorpe, physician, b. (d. 1933)

C
Arts

Literature

During 1855
John Lang publishes *The Forger's Wife*, first Aust. mystery detective novel.

Births & Deaths
William Astley, short story writer and journalist who used pseudonym Price Warung, b. (d. 1911)
George Lewis Becke, novelist, short story writer, b. (d. 1913)
Catherine Somerville Stow, author who usually wrote as K. Langloh Parker, probably b. (d. 1940)

Music, Dance

18 Aug. Aurelia Dimier, dancer, performs in Sydney.
24 Aug. Julia Matthews makes operatic début at Victoria Theatre in Sydney.
Dec. Anna Bishop, opera singer, visits Aust.
During 1855
Accelerated development of choral music.
First recorded Eisteddfod competition for music and elocution held, in Ballarat, Vic.

Births & Deaths
Amy Sherwin, 'The Tasmanian Nightingale', one of first dramatic sopranos known overseas probably b. (d. 1935)

Drama, Theatre

26 Feb. Gustavus Vaughan Brooke, Irish Tragedian, performs in Melbourne.
12 Mar. Joseph Wyatt's Princess of Wales Theatre opens in Sydney.
16 Jul. John Black opens Theatre Royal in Melbourne.
30 Jul. George Selth Coppin opens Olympic Theatre known as 'the Iron Pot', in Melbourne.

Fine Arts

During 1855
First recorded representation of Aust. art to go abroad sent to International Exhibition in Paris.
William Dexter founds Gallery of Art and School of Design in Sydney. (Closes 1856.)
Nicholas Chevalier becomes first staff cartoonist on *Melbourne Punch*. Introduces chromolithography.

D

Religion, Learning

1855

Births & Deaths
Donald George Commons, marine painter, b. (d. 1942)
Harry Pelling Gill, landscape painter, b. (d. 1916)
Frederick McCubbin, impressionist painter, b. (d. 1917)
Tom Midwood, cartoonist, b. (d. 1912)
Jane Sutherland, oil painter, b. (d. 1928)

Architecture

During 1855
Como House in Melbourne completed.
Corio Villa arrives at Geelong pier unassembled.
Curved corrugated iron becomes readily available.

18 Jan. First conference of the Wesleyan Methodist Connexion in Aust. held in Sydney to consider autonomy of Methodist Church.
13 Apr. Melbourne University officially opens.
During 1855
J. C. Wood estb. first Unitarian church in Adelaide.
First Qld Baptist church estb. in Brisbane.
Horton College opens in Hobart.
W. McIntyre opens West Maitland High School, NSW.
Ragged School for deprived children estb. in Hobart.
SA Museum estb. in Adelaide.
Qld Museum opens in Brisbane.
Charles Southwell brings Rationalist Movement to Aust. Advocates application of reason to solving human problems. (Rationalist Associations form in NSW 1910, Qld 1914, WA, Vic., and SA in 1918.)
Hugh Darling estb. first United Presbyterian Congregation in Sydney.

Births & Deaths
Theodore Fink, educationist, Vic. politician, b. (d. 1942)

1855

E
Sport

During 1855
Longest bare-knuckle boxing fight recorded in Vic. Lasts 6 hours 15 minutes.

Births & Deaths
William Lloyd Murdoch, cricketer, noted batsman, b. (d. 1911)

F
Historia Dignum

Population
Estimated total white, 793,260.

Jan. First SA stamps, 'Queen with diadem', showing profile design of Queen Victoria, issued.
2 Aug. *Melbourne Punch* begins publication, founded by James Smith. (Lasts until 1924.)
8 Oct. *Illawarra Mercury* newspaper first published, at Wollongong, NSW, by Thomas Garrett.
During 1855
There are about 17,000 Chinese on Vic. goldfields.
Geelong (Vic.) Town Hall built. (Now oldest continuously used town hall in Aust.)

Communities
Blanchetown, SA, estb.
Casino, NSW, estb.
Coonamble, NSW, estb.
Gatton, Qld, estb.
Gumeracha, SA, probably estb.
Lismore, NSW, estb.
Lithgow, NSW, estb.
Mansfield, Vic., probably estb.
Merimbula, NSW, estb.
Myrtleford, Vic., probably estb.
Rockhampton, Qld, estb.
Scottsdale, Tas., estb.
Smithton, Tas., probably first settled
Spalding, SA, probably estb.
Steiglitz, Vic., probably estb.
St Marys, Tas., estb.
Tallangatta, Vic., probably estb.
Toronto, NSW, estb.
Uraidla, SA, probably estb.
Woodend, Vic., probably estb.
Yea, Vic., estb.

A

History, Politics, Economics, Law

1856

Government

1 Jan. 1856–26 Dec. 1856, Edward Macarthur administers Vic.
6 Jun. 1856–Aug. 1856, S. A. Donaldson Premier NSW.
26 Aug. 1856–Oct. 1856, C. Cowper Premier NSW.
3 Oct. 1856–Sep. 1857, H. W. Parker Premier NSW.
24 Oct. 1856–Aug. 1857, B. T. Finniss Premier SA.
1 Nov. 1856–Feb. 1857, W. T. N. Champ Premier Tas.
26 Dec. 1856–10 Sep. 1863, Sir Henry Barkly Governor Vic.

4 Jan. Act to estb. Constitution for SA passed; assented to on 24 Jun. Responsible govt proclaimed; comes into force in Oct. SA Act provides for triennial parlts, first full male suffrage without property qualification for Lower House members.

19 Mar. Vic. introduces voting by secret ballot. (SA on 2 Apr.)

21 Apr. First 8-hour working day procession in Melbourne.

25 Apr. Eight-Hour Labour League forms in Melbourne. John Sinclair president.

30 Apr. First Assembly elections held in NSW. (Tas. 17 Oct., Vic. 6 Nov.)

22 May. First meeting of both Houses of Parlt held in NSW. (Vic. 21 Nov., Tas. 2 Dec.)

31 May. First Vic. warship sloop, *Victoria*, arrives in Melbourne from England, beginning Vic. navy.

6 Jun. Ebenezer Syme buys the Melbourne *Age* from printers' co-operative. His brother David joins enterprise 27 Sep.

8 Jun. Descendants of the *Bounty* mutineers removed from Pitcairn to Norfolk I., which is declared a separate settlement under NSW jurisdiction. Last convicts leave.

21 Jul. Secretary of State in London announces intention of British Govt to create new colony of Qld.

During 1856

Govt ministers under responsible govt appointed in NSW on 8 Jun., SA 24 Oct., Tas. 1 Nov.
NSW introduces provisions for the registration of births, deaths and marriages.
Vic. first to introduce *Hansard* to record Parlt proceedings. (*Hansard* introduced SA 1857, Qld 1864, NSW 1879, WA 1890, NT 1948, Tas. 1979.)
Colonial Naval Defence Act empowers colonies to estb. their own warships and manpower.
National Trades Hall and Literary Institute forms in Melbourne to agitate for an eight-hour working day.
Friendly Society of Operative Stonemasons of NSW strike for an 8-hour working day. Request granted on 12 May, at a loss of 2 shillings and 6 pence per day in wages.
Name 'Diggers Parliament' given to Vic. Legislative Assembly.
Cotton grown in Hunter Valley, NSW.
Benjamin Herschel Babbage begins exploring around Lake Torrens, SA.

Births & Deaths

Sir John Bowser, Vic. Premier, b. (d. 1936)
William Buckley, convict escapee who lived with Aborigines for 32 years, d. (b. 1780)
Dame Alice Isabel Chisholm, welfare worker, founder of canteen services for World War I servicemen, b. (d. 1954)
James Clarke Cribb, Qld businessman, b. (d. 1926)
Sir Alfred Deakin, Protectionist Prime Minister, b. (d. 1919)
Harold Heneage Finch-Hatton, Imperial Federationist, b. (d. 1904)
Henry Goulburn, administrator, NSW politician, d. (b. 1784)
Sir John Charles Hoad, military commander, b. (d. 1911)
George Leake, WA Premier, b. (d. 1902)
David Lindsay, NT explorer, b. (d. 1922)
George Meredith, Tas. pioneer settler, d. (b. 1778)
Peter Stuckey Mitchell, grazier and philanthropist, b. (d. 1921)
Sir Arthur Morgan, Qld Premier and Lieut-Governor, b. (d. 1916)
John Verran, SA Premier, b. (d. 1932)

1856

B
Science, Technology, Transport, Discovery

1 Jan. First bridge over Nepean R., at Penrith, NSW, opens.
18 Feb. Electric telegraph first used in SA, between Adelaide and Port Adelaide.
26 Apr. SA's first steam railway, between Adelaide and Port Adelaide, opens.
14 Dec. Geelong–Ballarat telegraph line opens.

During 1856
Melbourne Observatory estb., on Flagstaff Hill.
James Harrison develops world's first system of commercial refrigeration.
First permanent weather bureaus estb. in Adelaide and Sydney, officially beginning weather observation. (Weather bureaus estb. in Vic. 1858, Qld 1860, Tas. 1882, and WA 1896.)
Frederick Dutton produces robust wool at Anlaby stud by crossing Rambouillet rams with Saxon ewes.
Scott, Clow and Prebble open Melbourne's first cast-iron foundry.
Philosophical Society of NSW founded.
First iron post boxes estb. in Sydney. (Melbourne 1858.)

Births & Deaths
Sir Thomas Peter Anderson, physiologist, b. (d. 1920)
Auguste Joseph François de Bavay, scientist, b. (d. 1944)
William Benjamin Chaffey, pioneer irrigationist, b. (d. 1926)
Sir Timothy Augustine Coghlan, statistician, b. (d. 1926)
Guillaume Daniel Delprat, engineer, b. (d. 1937)
Henry Joseph Grayson, scientist, b. (d. 1918)
Robert Carl Sticht, metallurgist, b. (d. 1922)
Emma Constance Stone, Aust.'s first woman physician, b. (d. 1902)
Henry Sutton, inventor, b. (d. 1912)
Henry Tryon, naturalist, scientist b. (d. 1943)

C
Arts

Literature

Births & Deaths
Douglas Brook Wheelton Sladen, critic, editor, b. (d. 1947)

Music, Dance

During 1856
Walter Sherwin and Rose Wallach promote English opera in Aust.
Feb.–Mar. Lola Montez, entertainer, dancer, tours Vic. goldfields. On 17 Feb. sparks public controversy by performing provocative 'Spider dance'.

Fine Arts

15 Oct. Royal SA Society of Arts founded. (Now oldest extant art society in Aust.)
During Oct. Vic. Society of Fine Arts founded in Melbourne.

Births & Deaths
Thomas William Roberts, painter, pioneer of impressionism in Aust., b. (d. 1931)

Architecture

11 Sep. Vic. Institute of Architects founded.
During 1856
Corio House built in Geelong, Vic.
Kerr and Knight, architects, design Parliament House in Melbourne. First section completed in Nov., opens 25 Nov.
Domestic Gothic house, Roslyndale, built at Woollahra, NSW.

D
Religion, Learning

E
Sport

12 Feb. Melbourne Public Library opens.
May. Frederic Barker estb. Church of England Church Society in Sydney.
25 Jul. Matthew Blagden Hale appointed first Church of England Bishop of Perth.
Dec. NSW National Education Board estb. 'Table of minimum requirements' for school classes.
During 1856
Construction of St Francis Xavier's Cathedral in Adelaide begins.
Agitation against State aid to Churches spreads.
SA Library merges with SA Mechanics' Institute to form SA Institute.
University of Melbourne Library opens.

Births & Deaths

Robert Cartwright, Church of England clergyman who advocated British citizenship for Aborigines, d. (b. 1771)
John Edward Mercer, Tas. Church of England bishop, b. (d. 1922)
James Murdoch, Oriental language teacher, b. (d. 1921)

24 Jan. SA Jockey Club estb.
26–27 Mar. First acknowledged representative intercolonial cricket match played, between NSW and Vic. in Melbourne. NSW wins.
During 1856
Royal Vic. Yacht Club formed as Vic. Yacht Club. First major yacht club in Aust.
American goldminers first play baseball in Aust.
c. 1856. Sydney Archery Club estb.

1856

F

Historia Dignum

Population
Estimated total white, 876,729.

5 Jan. The Melbourne *Age* begins weekly magazine, the *Leader*.
Mar. Crimean War ends. Aust. contributes to relief fund for English widows and orphans.
5 Apr. The newspaper *Armidale Express* estb. in NSW.
Jul. Illustrated Journal of Australasia first published.
During 1856
Newsletter of Australasia first published.
Sydney and Melbourne *Punch* magazines issued.
First registration postage stamps issued.
Vic. becomes first to adopt a flag. (Flags adopted in NSW, Qld, Tas. in 1876, SA 1904, NT 1978. WA date uncertain.)
Drought conditions in WA.

Births & Deaths
John Feltham Archibald, better known as Jules François Archibald, journalist and benefactor, b. (d. 1919)

Communities
Adelong, NSW, estb.
Ballina, NSW, estb.
Bodalla, NSW, estb.
Canoona, Qld, first settled
Gunnedah, NSW, estb.
Kerang, Vic., estb.
Quirindi, NSW, estb.
Ulverstone, Tas., estb.

A
History, Politics, Economics, Law

1857

Government
26 Feb. 1857–Apr. 1857, T. G. Gregson Premier Tas.
11 Mar. 1857–Apr. 1857, J. O'Shanassy Premier Vic.
25 Apr. 1857–May 1857, W. P. Weston Premier Tas.
29 Apr. 1857–Mar. 1858, W. C. Haines Premier Vic.
12 May 1857–Nov. 1860, F. Smith Premier Tas.
21 Aug. 1857–Sep. 1857, J. Baker Premier SA.
1 Sep. 1857–Sep. 1857, R. R. Torrens Premier SA.
7 Sep. 1857–Oct. 1859, C. Cowper Premier NSW.
30 Sep. 1857–May 1860, R. D. Hanson Premier SA.

Jan.–Jun. About 15,000 Chinese diggers land in Robe, SA, and then proceed overland to Vic. goldfields to avoid paying £10 tax imposed by Vic. Govt.
10 Mar. First SA State Assembly elections held under responsible govt.
14 Apr. Robert Richard Torrens introduces the Torrens System of registering land titles in SA.
22 Apr. First meeting of both SA Houses of Parlt.
May. Border duties agreement signed between SA, Vic. and NSW, whereby SA collected customs duties at NSW rates and shared proceeds equally between NSW and Vic.
Racial friction between European and Chinese diggers, at Ararat in May, Daylesford in Jun., and Buckland R. in Jul., leads to Vic. Govt enforcing anti-Chinese legislation, imposing heavy fees on all adult Chinese.
15 Jul.–6 Aug. National convention meets in Melbourne to consider land question. 'Unlock the Land' movement.
27 Aug. Vic. provides for abolition of property qualifications for members of Legislative Assemblies.
27 Oct. Aborigines massacre 11 whites on Hornet Bank station in Qld.
24 Nov. Vic. introduces male suffrage.
30 Dec. Sydney Stock Exchange opens for public business. (Becomes the Royal Exchange in 1875.)
During 1857
NSW and Vic. estb. Select Committee to examine Federal Union of Aust. colonies; marks first step towards Federation.
Trade union movement estb. Labour Electoral League in NSW to contest parlt seats; forerunner of Aust. Labor Party.
Trades Hall Committee formed in Melbourne.
There are about 28,000 Chinese on Vic. goldfields.
First Brisbane Supreme Court hearing held.
Construction of Fort Denison to defend Sydney completed.
Henry Hopwood lays a pontoon bridge across the Murray R. near Echuca, Vic.
Grafton Steam Navigation Co. estb. in NSW. (Becomes North Coast Steam Navigation Co. in 1891.)
Thomas Hardy exports wine to England in hogsheads.

Births & Deaths
Sir Joseph Hector McNeil Carruthers, NSW Premier, b. (d. 1932)
Robert Cooper, NSW businessman, d. (b. 1776)
Alice Henry, trade union movement pioneer, b. (d. 1943)
Sir Sidney Kidman, SA pastoralist, 'The Cattle King', b. (d. 1935)
Samuel Mauger, Vic. social worker, Federal politician, b. (d. 1936)
Janet Templeton, NSW and Vic. pastoralist, d. (b. 1785)

1857

B
Science, Technology, Transport, Discovery

Jan. Ferdinand von Mueller founds the National Herbarium of Vic. in Melbourne. Imports Monterey pine from California.
12 Mar. Gas lighting first used in Hobart. Melbourne on 10 Aug.
30 May. NSW Great Northern Railway, from Honeysuckle Point, Newcastle, to E Maitland, opens.
25 Jun. Melbourne to Geelong railway opens. Adelaide to Gawler, SA, railway opens on 5 Oct.
2 Aug. Hobart and Launceston linked by electric telegraph. Sydney and Liverpool linked on 30 Dec.
During 1857
Sulphuric acid plant in Geelong, Vic., begins Aust. chemical industry.
Yan Yean dam north of Melbourne completed. First sizeable dam built in Aust. and first storage for Melbourne water supply.
Pharmaceutical Society of Vic. founded; first pharmaceutical organization in Aust. (Others founded in NSW 1876, Qld 1880, SA 1884, Tas. 1891, WA 1892.)
Edward Wilson founds Acclimatization Society of Vic. for zoological interests.
Hawk and Co. Pty Ltd, engineering firm, estb. Among first in Aust.
Aust. eucalyptus tree plantations estb. in France. (Spain 1863, Algeria 1862, Italy 1877.)
Timber bridge built at Glebe I., Sydney.
Brown coal first discovered in Vic., at Lal Lal, near Ballarat.
Construction of new Sydney Observatory begins.

Births & Deaths
John Busby, civil engineer, d. (b. 1765)
William Henry Dudley Le Souef, zoologist, b. (d. 1923)

C
Arts

Literature

During 1857
Caroline Louisa Waring Calvert (née Atkinson), first Aust.-born woman novelist, publishes *Gertrude the Emigrant*.

Music, Dance

Jul. Edouin dancers make Aust. début.
26 Dec. Leopold ballet dancers make début in Melbourne.
During 1857
Robert Thatcher publishes musical ballads, *Colonial Songster*, in book form.

Fine Arts

During 1857
Pottery works estb. at Bendigo, Vic.
Vic. Society of Fine Arts holds first and only exhibition.

Births & Deaths
George Rossi Ashton, painter, illustrator, b.
Helen Hambridge, watercolourist, b. (d. 1937)
Emily Leysalle, sculptor, probably b.
William P. McIntosh, sculptor, b. (d. 1930)

Architecture

During 1857
Edmund T. Blacket designs buildings at Sydney University.
J. J. Clark supervises construction of old Treasury Building in Melbourne.
Fort Denison, designed by George Barney, completed in Sydney.

D
Religion, Learning

24 Jun. Geelong Church of England Grammar School opens near Geelong, Vic.
3 Aug. Sydney Grammar, autonomous non-denominational school, opens.
Oct. The Gawler Institute of SA estb. to provide literary and other facilities for intellectual pursuits.
During 1857
Benedictine Institute of the Good Samaritan founded in Sydney.

Births & Deaths

Arthur Vincent Green, Church of England bishop, b. (d. 1944)

E
Sport

During 1857
Vic. Jockey Club founded.
Vic. Archery Club founded.

1857

Historia Dignum

Population
Estimated total white, 970,287.

19 Feb. NSW Alliance for the Suppression of Intemperance estb. in Sydney.
26 Mar. Prisoners at Williamstown, Vic., murder John Price, Inspector-General of Vic. penal establishment. Seven prisoners hanged for the murder.
30 Jun. Dutch barque *Koenig Willem II* wrecked at Guichen Bay, SA; 16 lives lost.
10 Jul. First fatal train derailment, at Haslem Creek near Lidcombe, NSW, claims 2 lives.
Jul. *The Month: A Literary and Critical Journal* first published in Sydney.
20 Aug. *Dunbar* wrecked at S Head, Sydney; 121 lives lost.
24 Aug. *Lady Bird* collides with another ship off Cape Otway, Vic.; 31 lives lost.
24 Oct. *Catherine Adamson* wrecked at Sydney Heads; 21 lives lost.

During 1857
SE Aust. suffers severe drought.
Miranda swindle fraud case. Francis Miranda successfully swindles £19,000 in gold from Bank of Australasia.
Blanch Barkly gold nugget, weighing 1,743 ounces, discovered at Kingower, Vic.
Highland Society of Maryborough, Vic., estb. (Now oldest continuing Scottish society in Aust.)
Outbreak of leprosy at Castlemaine, Vic.

Births & Deaths
Donald Alistair Macdonald, journalist, naturalist, b. (d. 1932)

Communities
Nowra, NSW, estb.
Pinjarra, WA, estb.

A

History, Politics, Economics, Law

1858

Government

10 Mar. 1858–Oct. 1859, J. O'Shanassy Premier Vic.

12 Jan. A. C. Gregory begins second journey, leaving Sydney in search of Leichhardt. Explores Cooper and Barcoo creeks, SA. Traces Thomson R. and reaches Adelaide in Jul.

18 Jan. Stonemasons' Union estb. in Qld. First Qld union.

27 Jan. SA Parlt passes the Torrens Real Property Act. This began what is known as Torrens Title, a statutory system registering ownership of land, designed to simplify and facilitate transfer of land. (Torrens Title introduced to Qld in Jan. 1862, Tas. Jul. 1862, Vic. Oct. 1862, NSW Jan. 1863, WA Jul. 1875.)

25 Feb. Tas. enacts vote by secret ballot.

During Feb. Benjamin Babbage, Stuart Davenport and Peter Warburton explore country NW of Port Augusta, SA, providing a physiography of the area.

Apr.–Jun. F. T. Gregory explores overland from Geraldton, WA, to Adelaide, SA, discovering pastoral country and several rivers in NW Aust.

May. John McDouall Stuart begins expedition into country W of Torrens Basin, SA, to Streaky Bay, arriving in Aug.

24 Nov. NSW Govt enacts male suffrage, vote by secret ballot and abolition of property qualifications for members of Legislative Assembly.

During 1858

Tas. Govt passes first Selection Act for agricultural settlement.

SA Govt passes first Divorce Act.

SA Govt passes anti-Chinese legislation.

Sir Richard Dry, Tas. politician is first Tasmanian and among first Australians to be knighted.

NSW creates system of District Courts.

Camels purchased from India.

Vic. Association for the Protection of Native Industry estb.

National Bank of Australasia founded in Melbourne.

Goldrush to Canoona, Qld.

Births & Deaths

Sir Ralph Darling, NSW Governor, d. (b. 1775)
Charles Edward Grimes, NSW Surveyor-General, d. (b. 1772)
William Hamilton, Qld politician, probably b. (d. 1920)
Sir William Hill Irvine, Vic. Premier and Chief Justice, b. (d. 1943)
Sir George Handley Knibbs, first Commonwealth Statistician, b. (d. 1929)
Sir Neil Elliott Lewis, Tas. Premier, b. (d. 1935)
Hugh Mahon, Federal politician, WA journalist, b. (d. 1931)
King O'Malley, Federal politician noted for estb. Canberra, probably b. (d. 1953)
Sir Cornthwaite Hector Rason, WA Premier, b. (d. 1927)
Sir William John Sowden, newspaper proprietor, b. (d. 1943)
Frederic Charles Urquhart, Qld police officer, administrator, b. (d. 1935)

1858

B
Science, Technology, Transport, Discovery

1 Feb. William Dean pilots first balloon ascent in Aust. in Melbourne. First balloon flight in Sydney on 30 Dec.
21 Jul. Melbourne and Adelaide linked by electric telegraph.
During Jul. W. C. Chapel discovers gold at Canoona, near Rockhampton, Qld.
29 Oct. Sydney linked to Adelaide by electric telegraph via Melbourne. (Electric telegraph linked to Hobart in 1859, Brisbane 1861 and Perth 1877.)
During 1858
First public exhibition of Aust. photography held in Sydney.
Andrew Brown mines first coal at Lithgow, NSW.
The Peppin flock estb. from Aust. sheep.
Pleuropneumonia in cattle introduced in Aust.

Births & Deaths

Robert Brown, pioneer botanist, d. (b. 1773)
Herbert James Carter, entomologist, b. (d. 1940)
Sir Tannatt William Edgeworth David, geologist, Antarctic explorer, b. (d. 1934)
Walter Wilson Froggatt, entomologist, b. (d. 1937)
Thomas Sergeant Hall, geologist, b. (d. 1915)
Sir David Orme Masson, scientist, b. (d. 1937)
Henry Teesdale Smith, railway contractor, b. (d. 1921)

C
Arts

Literature

Births & Deaths

Victor James William Patrick Daley, poet and journalist, b. (d. 1905)

Music, Dance

During 1858
The Bianchi troupe introduces Italian opera to Aust.
Joseph Chambers writes his first choreographic essay.

Births & Deaths

Nellie Stewart, singer, actress, b. (d. 1931)

Fine Arts

Births & Deaths

George Henry Male Addison, painter, architect, b. (d. 1922)
Thomas Humphrey, painter, b. (d. 1922)
Annie Watson Laughton, painter, b. (d. 1903)
Charles Francis Summers, sculptor, b. (d. 1945)
John Robertson Tranthim-Fryer, sculptor, b. (d. 1928)
Ada Whiting, miniaturist, b.

Architecture

During 1858
Leonard Terry, architect, designs the Melbourne Club building.
William Wardell designs and supervises construction of St Patrick's Cathedral in Melbourne.
William Ponden Kay's Govt House in Hobart completed.

D
Religion, Learning

E
Sport

Mar. Asylum for destitute children opens in Sydney; among first of kind.
28 Jun. Matthew Hale opens first secondary school in WA.
During 1858
Melbourne Church of England Grammar School founded.
St James' Church of England Teacher Training School opens in Sydney.
Good Samaritan Sisters, Catholic teaching order, estb. to help the poor in Sydney.

Births & Deaths

Sir Francis Anderson, educationist, philosopher, b. (d. 1941)
Peter Board, educationist, b. (d. 1945)
William Cowper, Church of England archdeacon, d. (probably b. 1778)
Louisa Macdonald, educationist, b. (d. 1949)

During 1858
Thomas W. Wills founds Australian Rules Football in Melbourne. First reported game, between Scotch College and Melbourne Grammar School, on 7 Aug.
H. C. A. Harrison and Thomas W. Wills form Melbourne Australian Rules Football Club. First in Aust.
Mat Higgins becomes leading athlete in Aust.

F
Historia Dignum

1858

Population
Estimated total white, 1,050,828.

12 Jul. J. H. Barrow estb. the newspaper *Advertiser* as the *South Australian Advertiser* in Adelaide.

During 1858
The *Newcastle Morning Herald and Miners' Advocate* published in Newcastle, NSW.
'Welcome Nugget', gold nugget found near Ballarat, Vic., weighs 2,217 ounces.
Melbourne Club facilities estb.
Diphtheria first recorded in Aust.
First recorded drought in Qld, in the Richmond and Barcoo areas.
Severe drought begins in SA. (Ends in 1860.)

Communities
Chiltern, Vic., estb.
Corowa, NSW, estb.
Hay, NSW, estb.
Heyfield, NSW, estb.
Holbrook, NSW, estb.
Jerilderie, NSW, estb.
Kingston, SA, estb.
Penguin, Tas., estb.

A
History, Politics, Economics, Law

Government
27 Oct. 1859–Mar. 1860, W. Forster Premier NSW.
27 Oct. 1859–Nov. 1860, W. Nicholson Premier Vic.
10 Dec. 1859–4 Jan. 1868, Sir George Ferguson Bowen Governor Qld.
10 Dec. 1859–Feb. 1866, R. G. W. Herbert Premier Qld.

27 Jan. The paddle-steamer *Albury* pioneers Darling R., NSW.
During Jan. Tariff League of Vic. estb. to oppose free trade and to petition for protection of Aust. labour against cheaper overseas labour.
21 Feb. Alfred J. P. Lutwyche appointed resident Judge of Supreme Court at Moreton Bay. Court opens on 9 Mar.
26 Mar. The Aust. Station of Imperial Naval Command is constituted an independent naval command under Capt. William Loring.
24 May. Melbourne Trades Hall opens to facilitate Trades Hall Committee meetings. Trades delegates estb. Political and Social Labour League of Vic. to agitate for an eight-hour working day.
6 Jun. British Act of Parliament authorizes separation of Qld from NSW.
16 Aug. George Dalrymple explores Bowen and Burdekin river areas, Qld.
During Aug. Charles Jardine Don elected to represent Collingwood in Vic. Legislative Assembly, becoming first member of any Aust. Parlt to represent organized labour.
6 Sep. Brisbane incorporated Qld capital. John Petrie becomes first Mayor.
10 Dec. Governor Bowen proclaims northern NSW area a separate colony, bounded by long. 141°E and lat. 29°S, with the name Queensland. Responsible govt granted.
12 Dec. First Qld Govt ministry appointed.
20 Dec. Qld Govt enacts male suffrage, vote by secret ballot and abolition of property qualifications for Members of the Legislative Assembly.

During 1859
Vic. Govt introduces triennial parliaments.
Houghton vineyards estb. on Swan R., WA.
Melbourne Brokers' Association estb.
Mark Foy arrives in Melbourne to begin Foy and Gibson's business.
First sugar produced in Brisbane from locally grown cane.
Rigby retail booksellers estb. (Begin publishing in 1950.)
W. R. Randell navigates the Darling R. north of Bourke, NSW.

Law Institute of Vic. estb. (Becomes oldest surviving legal body in Aust.)

Births & Deaths
William Lawrence Baillieu, financier, b. (d. 1936)
Digby Francis Denham, Qld Premier, b. (d. 1944)
Arthur Lovekin, newspaper proprietor, WA politician, b. (d. 1931)
George Arnot Maxwell, barrister, Federal politician, b. (d. 1935)
Archibald Henry Peake, SA Premier, b. (d. 1920)
George Suttor, NSW pioneer orchardist, d. (b. 1774)
John Herbert Syme, newspaper proprietor, b. (d. 1939)
Sir William Vicars, wool manufacturer, b. (d. 1940)
Frank Wilson, WA Premier, b. (d. 1918)
Sir John Wylde, NSW Deputy Judge-Advocate, constitutionalist, d. (b. 1781)

243

1859

B
Science, Technology, Transport, Discovery

Jan. Richard Daintree pioneers use of photography in field work.
30 Sep. First submarine cable linking Tas. and Vic., via Circular Head and King I. to Cape Otway, Vic., opens.
25 Dec. Thomas Austin receives rabbits, and liberates them for sporting purposes near Winchelsea, Vic. Rabbit becomes pest in three years.
During Dec. John and David Pollock discover gold at Kiandra, NSW.
During 1859
Philosophical Institute of Vic. becomes Royal Society of Vic.
Philosophical Society of Qld founded.
William Bland becomes first president of the Aust. Medical Association (later known as the British Medical Assn in Aust., unitl 1962.)
Shepherd discovers copper on Yorke Peninsula, SA.
Rivers are now main routes for transport of wool.

Births & Deaths
John Watt Beattie, photographer, b. (d. 1930)
Richard Hind Cambage, botanist, b. (d. 1928)
John Jacob Cohen, mathematician, engineer, politician, judge, b. (d. 1939)
Joseph Henry Maiden, botanist specializing in *Eucalyptus* and *Acacia* genera, b. (d. 1925)
Sir Henry Carr Maudsley, physician, b. (d. 1944)
Robert Scot Skirving, medical practitioner, b. (d. 1956)
William Ramsay Smith, anthropologist, b. (d. 1937)
William Sutherland, physicist, b. (d. 1911)
Sir George Adlington Syme, surgeon, b. (d. 1929)

C
Arts

Literature

During 1859
John Lang publishes *Botany Bay; or, True Tales of Early Australia*.
Caroline Leakey publishes *The Broad Arrow*.
Henry Kingsley publishes *The Recollections of Geoffry Hamlyn*.
James George Beaney publishes *Original Contributions to the Practice of Conservative Surgery*, one of first medical books published in Aust.

Births & Deaths
James Edmond, writer, journalist, b. (d. 1933)
Fergusson Wright Hume, novelist who published as Fergus Hume, b. (d. 1932)
Alice Werner, poet, b. (d. 1935)

Music, Dance

During 1859
Sydney Harmonic Vocal Society estb.
Carl Linger wins first prize for writing music for *Song of Australia*, with words by Caroline Carleton.
Signor Bianchi brings first regular opera company to Aust.
Brisbane Choral Society founded.
Charles Parker's *The Second Advent* performed in Melbourne.
Charles Robert Thatcher publishes book of musical ballads, *Colonial Minstrel*. (Republished 1864 with many additional songs.)

Births & Deaths
Johan Secundus Kruse, violinist, b. (d. 1927)
Ernest Henry Charles Wunderlich, composer, b. (d. 1945)

Drama, Theatre

During 1859
Royal Theatre opens in Ballarat, Vic.

Fine Arts

24 May. Queen's Room picture gallery in Melbourne opens as public art gallery. (Among first.)
During 1859
National Art School founded in Sydney as Sydney Mechanics' School of Arts.

D

Religion, Learning

1859

Births & Deaths

Amandus Julius Fisher, black-and-white artist, b.
Lindsay Bernard Hall, oil portrait painter, b. (d. 1935)
William Lister Lister, seascape painter, b. (d. 1943)
Mortimer Menpes, painter etcher, b. (d. 1938)
Richard Godfrey Rivers, painter, b. (d. 1925)
John Peter Russell, impressionist, among first Australians known abroad, b. (d. 1930)

Architecture

During 1859

Joseph Curet patents design for terracotta roof tiles in Melbourne.
Charles Tiffen builds Ipswich Court House, Qld.
Richard Roach Jewel begins work on Govt House in Perth.

14 Jun. Rev. Edward Wyndham Tufnell appointed first Church of England bishop in Brisbane.

During 1859

First travelling libraries in world estb., in Vic. and SA.
Frederic Barker estb. Church of England Teachers' Association in Sydney.

Births & Deaths

Samuel Alexander, philosopher, b. (d. 1938)
Henry Howard, Methodist preacher, b. (d. 1933)
George K. Rusden, Catholic priest, d. (b. 1786)
Thomas George Tucker, scholar and author, b. (d. 1946)
Gilbert White, Church of England bishop, artist, b. (d. 1933)

1859

E
Sport

During 1859
Geelong Australian Rules Football Club estb. at Geelong, Vic.
Melbourne University Boat Club and Aust. Subscription Rowing Club estb. (Among oldest Aust. rowing clubs.)

Births & Deaths
George Giffen, cricketer, noted medium-pace bowler, b. (d. 1927)

F
Historia Dignum

Population
Estimated total white, 1,097,305.

20 Jun. *Daily Examiner* newspaper estb. in Grafton, NSW.
4 Jul. The *Queensland Times* estb. in Ipswich, Qld.
6 Aug. *Admella* wrecked near Discovery Bay, Vic., 9 lives lost.
23 Sep. *Sapphire* wrecked in Torres Strait; 17 crew killed by Aborigines on Hammond I.
26 Oct. *Royal Charter* wrecked off NSW coast; 459 lives lost.
Dec. *Blervie Castle* wrecked *en route* from England; 57 lives lost.
During 1859
There are about 42,000 Chinese in Vic.
Queenslander magazine first published.
Protestant Alliance Friendly Society estb.

Births & Deaths
Sir Edward Sheldon Cunningham, journalist, b. (d. 1957)

Communities
Colac, Vic., estb.
Condobolin, NSW, estb.
Coonabarabran, NSW, estb.
Kiandra, NSW, estb.
Leopold, Vic., estb.
Louth, NSW, estb.
Menindie, NSW, estb.
Narrabri, NSW, estb.
Tumbarumba, NSW, estb.
Walgett, NSW, estb.
Wallaroo, SA, estb.
Wentworth, NSW, estb.

A
History, Politics, Economics, Law

1860

Government
9 Mar. 1860–Jan. 1861, J. Robertson Premier NSW.
9 May 1860–Oct. 1861, T. Reynolds Premier SA.
1 Nov. 1860–Aug. 1861, W. P. Weston Premier Tas.
26 Nov. 1860–Nov. 1861, R. Heales Premier Vic.

16 Jan. John Mackay begins N Qld explorations.
During Jan. Melbourne Trades Hall Committee merges with operative's Board of Trade to estb. Trades Hall Council.
17 Mar. War between Maoris and British colonists breaks out in NZ. Aust. on alert.
22 Apr. John McDouall Stuart becomes first explorer to reach centre of continent at Central Mt Stuart. (First called Mt Sturt.)
22 May. First Qld Legislative Assembly elections held. First fully representative Qld Parlt meets on 29 May.
20 Aug. Robert O'Hara Burke and William John Wills begin journey across Aust. from Melbourne to Gulf of Carpentaria.
28 Aug. Melbourne Parlt House attacked by unruly mob of unemployed while Legislative Assembly debates controversial Land Bill.
Sep. Vic. passes Nicholson Land Act to assist agricultural expansion. Act designed to sell Crown land being leased for sheep stations, providing for auction when there is competition for land.
Dec. Anti-Chinese riots begin at Lambing Flat goldfields, near Young, NSW.
During 1860
The Herbert Act in Qld opens Crown lands for selection.
Aust. Aboriginal policy of 'Civilize and Christianize' changes to 'Pacification'.
Vic. nationalizes railways.
First Tas. Divorce Act passed.
Robert Towns harvests first significant cotton crop, near Brisbane.
Afghans begin to play an important role in Aust. inland exploration.
Nathaniel Buchanan and William Landsborough begin N Qld exploration.
Vic. Govt estb. a Board for the Protection of Aborigines.
Vic. Tariff League estb. to encourage trade protection.
Amalgamated Society of Carpenters and Joiners opens branch in Adelaide. First union in SA.
NSW coalminers begin successful two-month strike against wage cuts.
c. 1860. Consumer hire purchase system begins in Aust.

Births & Deaths
Francis Allman, soldier, public servant, d. (b. 1780)
David Bowman, Qld politician, b. (d. 1916)
Alfred Wernam Canning, surveyor, explorer, b. (d. 1936)
Sir Thomas Makdougall Brisbane, NSW Governor, d. (b. 1773)
Thomas Joseph Byrnes, Qld Premier, b. (d. 1898)
Sir Joseph Cook, Liberal Prime Minister, b. (d. 1947)
Emily Caroline Creaghe, explorer, diarist, b. (d. 1944)
Edward Smith Hall, political reformer, journalist, d. (b. 1786)
Sir John Hindmarsh, first SA Governor, d. (b. 1785)
John Adrian Louis Hope, first Governor-General of Commonwealth of Australia, b. (d. 1908)
Edmund Lockyer, WA pioneer, d. (b. 1784)
William Neil MacDonald, overlander, b. (d. 1910)
Alexander Maconochie, penal reformer, d. (b. 1787)
Sir Denison Samuel King Miller, banker, first Governor of Cwlth Bank of Aust., 1912, b. (d. 1923)
Sir Ronald Craufurd Munro-Ferguson, Governor-General, b. (d. 1934)
George Robertson, Sydney bookseller, publisher, b. (d. 1933)
Sir Macpherson Robertson, confectionery manufacturer, b. (d. 1945)
Lawrence Allen Wells, explorer, surveyor, b. (d. 1938)
Henry Luke White, NSW pastoralist, ornithologist, philatelist, b. (d. 1927)

1860

B
Science, Technology, Transport, Discovery

Jan. Gold discovered at Kiandra area of Aust. Alps, NSW.
2 Jun. NSW western train line opens to Blacktown.
Aug. Gold discovered at Lambing Flat, near Young, NSW.
Oct. First steam locomotives used in Aust. arrive in Melbourne.
Nov. Suburban railway opens in Melbourne.
Dec. Torrens Gorge water supply estb. for Adelaide water.

During 1860
Enoch Hughes estb. first pig-iron rolling mill in Melbourne.
J. A. Youl, Sir Robert Officer and the Acclimatization Society of Vic. import Scottish salmon and trout ova for experimentation in Melbourne.
There are four large coalmining companies operating in Newcastle area, NSW.
Adelaide to Kapunda, SA, railway line opens.
Walter Hughes discovers copper at Wallaroo, Yorke Peninsula, SA.

Births & Deaths
Thomas Lane Bancroft, scientist, b. (d. 1933)
Andrew Barrie, photographer, b.
Ernest Sandford Jackson, physician, b. (d. 1938)
Sir Thomas Ranken Lyle, physicist, b. (d. 1944)
Robert Hamilton Russell, surgeon, b. (d. 1933)
Sir Walter Baldwin Spencer, anthropologist, among first to use cinematography and gramophone in field work, b. (d. 1929)

C
Arts

Literature

Births & Deaths
Alfred Arthur Greenwood Hales, novelist, b. (d. 1936)
John (Jack) Moses, author, balladist, b. (d. 1945)

Music, Dance

Births & Deaths
Gustav Slapoffski, operatic conductor, b. (d. 1951)

Drama, Theatre

8 Sep. R. P. Whitworth's play *Garibaldi* becomes first major Aust. drama based on overseas current affairs.

Births & Deaths
Charles Haddon Chambers, playwright, b. (d. 1921)

Fine Arts

Births & Deaths
Curzona Frances Louise Allport, portrait and landscape painter, b. (d. 1949)
Elizabeth Caroline Armstrong, flower painter, b. (d. 1930)
James Ashton, seascape painter, b. (d. 1935)
Henry Silkstone Hopwood, painter, b. (d. 1914)
Louisa J. Swan, painter, b. (d. 1955)

Architecture

During 1860
Edward Angus Hamilton designs Treasury Building in Adelaide.
Qld 'house on stilts' first appears.

Births & Deaths
Richard George Howard Joseland, architect, artist, b. (d. 1930)

D
Religion, Learning

E
Sport

1860

During 1860
First School for the Deaf estb. in Sydney. First School for the Blind estb. in Melbourne.
Ragged School for deprived children opens in Sydney.
Nicholson Museum estb. in Sydney.
Qld Grammar Schools Act provides State aid to non-denominational schools. Introduces single education system for State schools.

Births & Deaths
Lawrence Arthur Adamson, educationist, b. (d. 1932)
Thomas Hobbes Scott, Church of England Archdeacon of NSW, 1824, d. (b. 1783)

Jun. Vic. Lawn Bowling Club estb.
5 Oct. NSW Rifle Association estb.
During 1860
Regular trotting meetings begin in Melbourne. (Regular trotting begins in SA 1880, Tas. 1884, NSW 1885, Qld 1888, WA 1910.)
Southern Hunt Club estb. in Tas.
First recorded SA Aust. Rules football game played.
First racing meeting at Randwick Racecourse in Sydney.

Births & Deaths
James Scobie, horseracing trainer, b. (d. 1940)
Harry Tarrant, motorcar sportsman, b. (d. 1949)

1860

Historia Dignum

Population
Estimated total white, 1,145,585.

Mid-Feb. Braidwood district of NSW flooded.
7 Jul. *Sydney Morning Herald* sponsors the *Sydney Mail* newspaper. (Lasts until 1938.)
3 Oct. Fire destroys Prince of Wales Theatre in Sydney, claiming three lives.

During 1860
First Qld stamps showing full-face portrait of Queen Victoria issued.
South-east Aust. suffers drought.
Aust. Chess Club estb. in Sydney.
Dost Mahomet, camel driver, probably first Afghan to arrive in Aust.
Comprehensive recording of floods in Aust. begins.

Births & Deaths
William James Chidley, eccentric psychologist noted for work on sexuality, probably b. (d. 1916)
Grace Bussel, WA heroine who rescued shipwrecked survivors of *Georgette* (on 2 Dec. 1876), b. (d. 1935)
Robert Thomas, SA publisher, d. (b. 1782)
Mary Beatrice Phillips Watson, tragic heroine at Lizard I., Qld, b. (d. 1881)

Communities
Apollo Bay, Vic., estb.
Avoca, Tas., first settled
Blackwater, Qld, estb.
Bombala, NSW, estb.
Bourke, NSW, estb.
Bridgetown, WA, estb.
Buangor, Vic., estb.
Byron Bay, NSW, estb.
Caboolture, Qld, estb.
Crookwell, NSW, estb.
Cudal, NSW, estb.
Emerald, Qld, first settled
Forbes, NSW, estb.
Kadina, SA, estb.
Kameruka, NSW, estb.
Millmerran, Qld, estb.
Mornington, Vic., estb.
Murrumburrah, NSW, estb.
Port MacDonnell, SA, estb.
Rutherglen, Vic., estb.
Tambo, Qld, estb.

A
History, Politics, Economics, Law

1861

Government

10 Jan. 1861–Oct. 1863, C. Cowper Premier NSW.
22 Jan. 1861–22 Mar. 1861, John Francis Kempt administered NSW.
22 Mar. 1861–24 Dec. 1867, Sir John Young Governor NSW.
2 Aug. 1861–Jan. 1863, T. D. Chapman Premier Tas.
8 Oct. 1861–Jul. 1863, G. M. Waterhouse Premier SA.
14 Nov. 1861–Jun. 1863, J. O'Shanassy Premier Vic.
11 Dec. 1861–16 Jun. 1862, Thomas Gore Browne administered Tas.

11 Feb.
Robert O'Hara Burke and William John Wills and party cross Aust. continent to Gulf of Carpentaria arriving on 11 Feb. All except John King perish on return trip at Cooper Creek, SA, in June.

17 Feb.–30 Jun. Large mobs of Europeans attack Chinese in Lambing Flat goldfield riots, near Young, NSW.

27 Apr. Francis T. Gregory begins expedition into north-western Aust.

17 Jun. Supreme Court estb. in WA.

26 Jun. Alfred W. Howitt begins first Burke and Wills relief expedition. Expedition rescues John King and returns Melbourne with Burke and Wills' remains.

14 Aug. William Landsborough begins Burke and Wills relief expedition. (Returns Melbourne Nov. 1862.)

16 Aug. John McKinlay and party begin Burke and Wills search expedition. On 20 Oct. discover Charles Gray's grave.

Aug. Henry Parkes and William Dalley arrive in England to lecture on emigration to NSW.

7 Sep. Frederick Walker leads Burke and Wills search expedition.

17 Oct. Aborigines kill 19 settlers in surprise attack on Cullin-la-ringo station near Emerald, Qld. Reprisals take 60 Aboriginal lives.

26 Oct. John McDouall Stuart leaves Adelaide in third attempt to cross continent from S to N.

During 1861
Area of Aust. bounded by long. 132°E and long. 129°E added to SA.
NSW Govt passes Robertson Land Act, releasing Crown land for settlement. Act provides for free selection before survey and permits homesteaders to select 40 to 300 acres at £1 per acre.
NSW Govt passes anti-Chinese restrictive legislation.
First Vic. Divorce Act passed.
WA re-organizes constabulary.

Manager of NSW Coal and Copper Co. uses sailors to fill in while miners strike.
New Zealand Bank founded in NSW, SA and Vic.
Statistical conference between colonies held in Melbourne.
Melbourne Stock Exchange properly constituted. (First properly constituted stock exchange estb. in Sydney 1871, Brisbane 1885, Hobart 1882, Adelaide 1887, Perth 1889.)
Commercial pearling begins near Nickol Bay, WA.
Agitation for economic protection spreads in Vic. The Protection and Anti-Immigration League estb. in Melbourne.
Whaling industry closes in Vic.

Births & Deaths

William Throsby Bridges, 'Father of the AIF', b. (d. 1915)
Alfred John Cotton, Qld pastoralist, b. (d. 1941)
Edith Dircksey Cowan, WA politician, social worker, b. (d. 1932)
Sir George Warburton Fuller, NSW Premier, b. (d. 1940)
Edward Jenks, legal scholar, b. (d. 1939)
William Lane, Utopian socialist, b. (d. 1917)
Sir John Hubert Plunkett Murray, Papua Administrator, b. (d. 1940)
Sir Alexander James Peacock, Vic. Premier, b. (d. 1933)
William Bispham Propsting, Tas. Premier, b. (d. 1937)
Gerald Strickland, Tas., WA and NSW Governor, b. (d. 1940)
George Swinburne, Vic. politician, b. (d. 1928)

1861

B
Science, Technology, Transport, Discovery

13 Apr. Brisbane–Ipswich telegraph line opens. First in Qld.
6 Nov. Electric telegraph links Brisbane with NSW, Vic. and SA.
21 Dec. Melbourne to Brighton private railway opens.
23 Dec. First metropolitan horse-drawn carriage service begins in Sydney.
During 1861
Eugene Dominique Nicolle patents ice-making invention.
North Shore Ferry Co. estb. in Sydney.
Copper discovered at Moonta, SA.
John Mollard discovers copper at Peak Downs in Qld.
Wallaroo copper mines open on Yorke Peninsula, SA. Copper discoveries in area revive SA economy.

Births & Deaths

George Henry Bosch, watchmaker, benefactor, b. (d. 1934)
Alfred Lynch, engineer, SA politician, b. (d. 1934)
James O'Neil, medical practitioner, philanthropist, b. (d. 1939)
Walter Edmund Roth, anthropologist, b. (d. 1933)
Sir Richard Threlfall, chemist and engineer, b. (d. 1932)

C
Arts

Literature

Births & Deaths
Mary Eliza Bakewell Gaunt, novelist, b. (d. 1942)
Walter James Jeffery, author, b. (d. 1922)

Music, Dance

1 Mar. William Saurin Lyster arrives in Aust. Launches opera *Maritana* in Melbourne on 25 Mar.
19 Aug. J. H. Flexmore, dancer, makes début in Sydney.
During 1861
Hale Marsh's opera *The Gentleman in Black* first performed.
Brisbane Philharmonic Society founded.

Births & Deaths
John Lemmoné, flautist, b. (d. 1949)
Helen Porter Mitchell, better known as Dame Nellie Melba, opera singer, b. (d. 1931)

Fine Arts

24 May. National Gallery of Vic. founded as the Melbourne Museum of Art. First public art gallery in Aust.
During 1861
SA School of Arts estb. as a school of design.
First SA public art gallery opens.

Births & Deaths
Margaret Baskerville, sculptor, b. (d. 1930)
William Delafield Cook, realist painter, b. (d. 1931)
John Cecil Gasking, cartoonist, b.
George Pitt Morison, painter, b. (d. 1942)
Jan Hendrik Scheltema, cattle and horse painter, b. (d. 1938)
Clara Southern, landscape painter, b. (d. 1940)
George Alfred John Webb, portrait painter, b.

Architecture

During 1861
Mid-Victorian period of architecture begins. (Ends *c.* 1878.)

Births & Deaths
John Verge, first Aust. exponent of Regency style of architecture, d. (b. 1782)

D
Religion, Learning

12 Mar. James Quinn becomes first Catholic bishop in Brisbane.
During 1861
Construction of St Mary's Catholic Cathedral begins in Hobart. (Opens 1878.)
St Mary's Catholic Teacher Training College estb. in Sydney.
Presbyterian Church estb. Geelong College, Vic.
Some 47 per cent of elementary school aged children can read and write.

Births & Deaths
Sir William Mitchell, philosopher, benefactor, b. (d. 1962)

E
Sport

Jan. First ocean yacht races held in Aust.
7 Nov. Archer, ridden by J. Cutts, wins first Melbourne Cup in 3 minutes 52 seconds.
24 Dec. First English cricket team arrives in Melbourne. (First match 1 Jan. 1862.)
First Kiandra (NSW) Ski Club estb. Among first in world.

Births & Deaths
Charles Brownlow, Aust. Rules footballer, b. (d. 1924)
Joe Goddard, heavyweight boxer, b. (d. 1903)

1861

F
1861
Historia Dignum

Population
Estimated total white, 1,168,149;
Estimated total Aboriginal, 170,000.

26 Apr. The newspaper *Border Watch* estb. at Mount Gambier, SA.
Jul. Newspaper *Morning Bulletin* estb. at Rockhampton, Qld.
The newspaper *Chronicle* estb. at Toowoomba, Qld.
1 Oct. Second Vic. Exhibition opens.
29 Oct. First Qld Exhibition opens.
20 Dec. *Illustrated Australian Mail* first published, in Melbourne.
During 1861
There are 38,300 Chinese in Aust. Of these, 24,732 are in Vic.
Newspaper *Ballarat Mail* estb. at Ballarat, Vic.
First printed, gummed and perforated stamps appear.
Tas. Club estb. in Hobart.
George Peacock estb. a jam-making factory in Hobart.

Births & Deaths
John (Jack)Howe, world champion shearer 1892, probably b. 26 Jul. (d. 1922)

Communities
Berwick, Vic., estb.
Bowen, Qld, estb.
Brewarrina, NSW, estb.
Bundanoon, NSW, estb.
Coffs Harbour, NSW, estb.
Cootamundra, NSW, estb.
Copperfield, Qld, estb.
Inglewood, Vic., first settled
Kianga, Qld, first settled
Lilydale, Tas., estb.
Morwell, Vic., estb.
Sawtell, NSW, first settled
Walhalla, Vic., estb.
Warren, NSW, estb.
Young, NSW, estb.

A
History, Politics, Economics, Law

1862

Government

20 Feb. 1862–27 Feb. 1862, John Bruce administered WA.

28 Feb. 1862–1 Nov. 1868, John Stephen Hampton Governor WA.

4 Mar. 1862–19 Feb. 1868, Sir Dominick Daly Governor SA.

16 Jun. 1862–20 Dec. 1868, Thomas Gore Browne Governor Tas.

18 Jun. Vic. Govt passes Duffy Act, opening up Crown land for selection.

24 Jul. John McDouall Stuart reaches Chambers Bay, NT, completing south to north crossing of continent from Adelaide on route which becomes Adelaide–Darwin telegraph line. Estb. SA claim to mandate over NT.

Oct. William Landsborough returns to Melbourne after becoming first white man to cross Aust. continent from north to south.

Nov. Sir James Cockle appointed first Chief Justice of Supreme Court in Qld. (Takes up position on 23 Feb. 1863.)

During 1862

Area of Aust. bounded by long. 141°E and long. 138°E added to Qld.

Qld Govt passes Selection Acts.

Vic. Govt passes the Real Property (Torrens) Act.

NSW abolishes primogeniture law. (Vic. 1864, SA and Qld 1867, Tas. 1874.)

First Aust. pearl shell exported from WA.

Louis Hope estb. sugar cane plantation and mill near Brisbane, beginning Qld sugar industry.

F. T. Gregory opens up grasslands in north-west of WA.

NSW Govt passes Police Regulations Act, regulating Police Force. (First Police Regulation Acts passed in SA Apr. 1838, Vic. Jan. 1853, WA 1849, Qld Jan. 1864, Tas. 1865, NT 1911.)

First cotton from north-western WA exported to England.

Henry Parkes declares his commitment to Free Trade in NSW.

Federated Shipwrights' and Ship Constructors' Association of Aust. estb.

Andrew Petrie explores Fraser I., Qld.

British Govt determines that self-governing colonies bear cost of their internal defence and contribute towards external defence costs.

Births & Deaths

William Patrick Crick, constitutional lawyer, b. (d. 1908)

Andrew Fisher, Labor Prime Minister, b. (d. 1928)

William Holmes, military commander, b. (d. 1917)

William Morris Hughes, Labor and Nationalist Prime Minister, b. (d. 1952)

James Simpson Love, Qld pastoralist, benefactor, b. (d. 1933)

George Ernest (Chinese) Morrison, China authority and journalist, b. (d. 1920)

John Norton, newspaper proprietor, journalist, b. (d. 1916)

Sir Langer Meade Loftus Owen, NSW Supreme Court Judge, b. (d. 1935)

Albert Bathurst Piddington, NSW politician, High Court Judge, b. (d. 1945)

Ernest A. Tolley, vigneron, b.

1862

B

Science, Technology, Transport, Discovery

7 Apr. William Macleay founds Entomological Society of NSW.
11 Apr. Geelong–Ballarat, Vic., railway line officially opens.
Jun. James Rutherford estb. headquarters for Cobb & Co. coach services at Bathurst, NSW.
26 Dec. Ned Stringer discovers gold at Walhalla, Vic.
During 1862
Melbourne Royal Park Zoo estb.
Albert Lormer estb. Brisbane photographic studio.
Inorganic plants for production of sulphuric and nitric acids for fertilizers estb. in Sydney and Melbourne. Beginning of chemical industry.
Copper discovered near Clermont, Qld.
Silver discovered at Moruya, NSW.

Births & Deaths

Henry Walter Barnett, photographer, b. (d. 1928)
Sir James William Barrett, surgeon, b. (d. 1945)
Sir William Henry Bragg, physicist, b. (d. 1942)
Charles Hedley, naturalist, b. (d. 1926)
Sir John Michael Higgins, metallurgist and businessman, b. (d. 1937)
Arthur Francis Basset Hull, anthropologist, philatelist, b. (d. 1945)
Sir Henry Jones, industrialist, pioneer of fruit canning industry, b. (d. 1926)
Richard Sanders Rogers, physician and botanist, b. (d. 1942)

C

Arts

Literature

During 1862
Charles Harpur publishes *A Poet's Home*.
Henry Kendall publishes *Poems and Songs*.
Roderick Flanagan publishes *History of New South Wales ... and other Australasian Settlements*, among first Aust. histories.

Births & Deaths

Francis William Lauderdale Adams, author, b. (d. 1893)
John Bernard O'Hara, poet, b. (d. 1927)

Music, Dance

15 Nov. William Lyster presents Meyerbeer's *Les Huguenots*.

Births & Deaths

George William L. Marshall-Hall, composer, b. (d. 1915)

Drama, Theatre

15 Sep. George Coppin opens Haymarket Theatre in Melbourne.

Fine Arts

During 1862
Aust. art sent to international exhibition in England.
Robert Lindsay arrives in Aust., beginning Lindsay family there.

Births & Deaths

Arthur Merric Boyd (the first), watercolourist, b. (d. 1940)
Nelson Illingworth, sculptor, b. (d. 1926)
Sir William Elliott Johnson, lithographic artist, b.
Sir John Longstaff, portrait painter, five times Archibald prize winner, b. (d. 1941)
Frank Prout Mahoney, outback subject painter, b. (d. 1917)
Josephine Muntz-Adams, painter, b. (d. 1950)
François Sicard, sculptor, b. (d. 1934)
David Henry Souter, black-and-white artist, writer, b. (d. 1935)
Tudor St George Tucker, painter, b. (d. 1906)
Amy May Vale, painter, b. (d. 1945)
Ebenezer Wenban, painter, b. (d. 1934)
James White, sculptor, b. (d. 1918)
William Blamire Young, watercolourist, designer who developed art nouveau style in Aust. art, b. (d. 1935)

D
Religion, Learning

1862

Architecture

During 1862
John James Clark designs Italianate style Treasury Building in Melbourne.
John Hall designs Brisbane Town Hall.
Charles Tiffin builds first Govt House in Brisbane.

1 Sep. Vic. Govt passes Common School Act, introducing State system of education. Replaces National and Denominational Boards with Board of Education, central education authority. Separates religious from secular instruction, making religious instruction optional.

23 Dec. George Britton Halford arrives in Melbourne to estb. first medical school in Aust. First classes in May 1863.

During 1862
Baptist Association estb. in Vic. (Baptist Associations estb. in SA 1863, NSW 1868, Qld 1877, Tas. 1884, WA 1896, NT 1970.)
Methodist New Connection group begins in Adelaide. (Vic. in 1865.)
NSW Govt abolishes State aid to religious education.

Births & Deaths

Henry Carmichael, educationist, d.
Ernest Henry Clark Oliphant, Elizabethan scholar, b. (d. 1936)
Henry Worrall, Methodist minister, b. (d. 1940)

1862

E
Sport

During 1862
Archer, ridden by J. Cutts, wins Melbourne Cup in 3 minutes 47 seconds.
Aust. Rules Football clubs develop in Vic. (Clubs develop in NSW 1864, SA 1875, Qld and Tas. 1879, WA 1883.)
First intercolonial rifle-shooting competitive, between Vic. and NSW at Sandgate, Vic.
Royal Sydney Yacht Squadron estb. as Aust. Yacht Squadron in Sydney.
First record of competitive skiing, at Kiandra, NSW.
First Vic. soccer team forms.

Births & Deaths
Steve Fairbairn, rower, b. (d. 1938)
Frank Slavin, boxer, b. (d. 1929)
Charles Thomas Biass Turner, cricketer, noted bowler, b. (d. 1944)

F
Historia Dignum

Population
Estimated total white, 1,206,918.

15 Jun. Frank Gardiner, bushranger, (born Frank Christie), leads gold escort robbery at Eugowra, near Forbes, NSW.

During 1862
Sydney City Mission estb. to assist the poor.
Vic. rainfall records begin, in Bendigo, Vic.
Drought in Qld. (Until 1869.)

Communities
Apsley, Vic., probably estb.
Blinman, SA, estb.
Boggabri, NSW, estb.
Bowral, NSW, estb.
Bright, Vic., estb.
Cunnumulla, Qld, estb.
Clermont, Qld, estb.
Eidsvold, Qld, estb.
Finley, NSW, estb.
Forster, NSW, first settled
Katherine, NT, probably estb.
Mackay, Qld, estb.
Maclean, NSW, estb.
Parkes, NSW, first settled
Roma, Qld, estb.
Stirling, SA, estb.
Tocumwal, NSW, estb.

A
History, Politics, Economics, Law

1863

Government
20 Jan. 1863–Nov. 1866, J. Whyte Premier Tas.
27 Jun. 1863–May. 1868, J. McCulloch Premier Vic.
4 Jul. 1863–15 Jul. 1863, F. S. Dutton Premier SA.
15 Jul. 1863–Aug. 1864, H. Ayers Premier SA.
11 Sep. 1863–7 May 1866, Sir Charles Henry Darling Governor Vic.
16 Oct. 1863–Feb. 1865, J. Martin Premier NSW.

21 Jan. Robert O'Hara Burke and William John Wills given heroes' State Funeral in Melbourne.
Mar.–Apr. First Intercolonial Conference held, in Melbourne. Discusses adoption of uniform tariff.
Mar. John Jardine estb. Somerset settlement as prison garrison and coaling station at Port Albany, Qld.
1 Jul. First Post Office Savings Bank in Aust. estb., in WA.
6 Jul. SA takes over responsibility of NT from NSW.
22 Jul. First WA Divorce Act passed.
14 Aug. First Kanakas arrive in Brisbane, for employment on Robert Towns' cotton plantation.
Sep. First successful manufacture of sugar, at Cleveland Bay and Moreton Bay, Qld.
Dec. 1,475 Aust. volunteers sail for NZ to assist colonists in second Maori War.

During 1863
First comprehensive Foundation Company Act passed in Qld. (In Vic. and SA 1864, Tas. 1869, NSW 1874, WA 1893.)
Acclimatization Society of Vic. imports first cashmere goats.
S. S. Bassett estb. vineyard at Roma, Qld. Produces first locally produced wines sold in Qld.
Initiation of settlement in the De Grey R. district of WA.
Henry Maxwell Lefroy first to traverse Kalgoorlie–Coolgardie area of WA.

Births & Deaths
Daisy May Bates (née O'Dwyer), outback social worker with Aborigines, b. (d. 1951)
Sir Henry Yule Braddon, businessman, author, sportsman, b. (d. 1955)
Andrew Dawson, Qld Premier, b. (d. 1910)
James Oswald Fairfax, newspaper proprietor, b. (d. 1928)
Cecil Robert Gaunt, military officer, b. (d. 1938)
Sir Neville Reginald Howse, AIF medical director and first Australian to win Victoria Cross in the Boer War, b. (d. 1930)
Sir Walter Hartwell James, WA Premier, b. (d. 1943)
Sir Adrian Knox, Chief Justice, b. (d. 1932)
James Gordon Legge, military commander and an architect of Aust. defence policy, b. (d. 1947)
Sir George John Robert Murray, SA Chief Justice, b. (d. 1942)
Sir George Edward Rich, High Court Justice, b. (d. 1956)
Sir Philip Whistler Street, NSW Lieut-Governor, b. (d. 1938)
Sir Charles Gregory Wade, NSW Premier, b. (d. 1922)

1863

B

Science, Technology, Transport, Discovery

Feb. Eugene Nicolle begins manufacturing ice with improved technique.
11 Jun. First public use of electricity in Aust., in Sydney, timed to mark the marriage of Prince of Wales.
22 Jun. First gaslights in Adelaide.
1 Jul. Sydney–Picton railway line opens.

During 1863
Melbourne Observatory estb. at Domain Park.
Thomas Chuck, portrait photographer, arrives in Aust.
Qld railway building begins in Darling Downs district.

Births & Deaths
William Ernest Cooke, astronomer who invented heliochronometer, or sun-dial to determine local time and true north, b. (d. 1947)
Ernest Macartney De Burgh, engineer, bridge and dam builder, b. (d. 1929)
James Drummond, botanist, d. (b. 1783)
Alexander McAulay, mathematician, b. (d. 1931)
John Henry Michell, mathematician, b. (d. 1940)

C

Arts

Literature

Births & Deaths
George Essex Evans, poet, b. (d. 1909)

Music, Dance

Births & Deaths
August Moritz Hermann Heinicke, violinist and conductor, b. (d. 1949)

Drama, Theatre

23 May. Prince of Wales House opens in Sydney, replacing theatre of same name.
During 1863
Madame Céline Celeste, actress, arrives in Aust. from France.

Fine Arts

During 1863
Academic period of Aust. art begins. State interest in founding art institutions, influenced by sentimental genre and historicism.
Tas. Museum and Art Gallery built in Hobart.

Births & Deaths
Robert Atkinson, painter, b. (d. 1896)
Charles Bennett, painter, b. (d. 1930)
Gladstone Eyre, portrait painter, b. (d. 1933)
Albert Henry Fullwood, painter and illustrator, b. (d. 1930)
Sir Edgar Bertram Mackennal, among first Aust. sculptors to be internationally acclaimed, b. (d. 193
Girolamo Ballatti Nerli, Marchese Nerli, painter who helped introduce impressionism into Aust., b. (d. 1926)
Charles E. S. Tindall, seascape painter, b. (d. 1951)
Edward Alexander Vidler, art writer, b. (probably d. 1941)
W. Joseph Wadham, painter, b. (d. 1950)

Architecture

During 1863
First tunnel in Aust. built, at Picton, NSW.
Wall and ceiling plastering becomes popular; use of cast iron proliferates.
Construction of Edmund William Wright's Town Hall in Adelaide begins.

D

Religion, Learning

3 Jul. United Presbyterians and Free Church unite to form Presbyterian Church of Qld.
25 Sep. Ipswich Grammar School opens in Qld.
During 1863
Foundation stone of St Mary's Catholic Cathedral in Perth laid. (Opens 1865.)
Newington College opens in Sydney.
All Hallow's Catholic School opens in Brisbane.
St Mary's Convent School opens in Ipswich, Qld.

Births & Deaths

St Clair George Alfred Donaldson, Church of England bishop in Brisbane, 1904, b. (d. 1935)
Arthur Wilberforce Jose, historian, encyclopaedist and author, b. (d. 1934)
Ronald George MacIntyre, Presbyterian clergyman, b. (d. 1954)
Frank Tate, educationist, b. (d. 1939)
Griffiths Wheeler Thatcher, Semitic and biblical scholar, b. (d. 1950)

E

Sport

During 1863
Banker, ridden by H. Chifney, wins Melbourne Cup in 3 minutes 44 seconds.
Qld Turf Club estb.
Tourist skiing becomes popular in Vic. Mt Hotham ski-fields open.
First intercolonial rowing races held, in Sydney.

Births & Deaths

John Worrall, cricketer and footballer, b. (d. 1937)

1863

F
Historia Dignum

Population
Estimated total white, 1,259,292.

7 Feb. HMS *Orpheus* wrecked near NZ; 190 lives lost.
25 Jun. James Mooril (Murrell) makes himself known to Qld stockmen after having lived with Aborigines for 17 years.

During 1863
Australian Monthly magazine published in Melbourne.
Royal Society of Vic. inaugurated.
Adelaide Club estb.
Macleay R., NSW, floods, claiming 10 lives.
Canowindra township in NSW captured by bushrangers twice.
Royal Agricultural Society of Tas. estb.
Tas. Govt passes first Aust. laws protecting scenic areas.

Births & Deaths
John James Knight, Qld newspaper editor, b. (d. 1927).

Communities
Bellingen, NSW, estb.
Donald, Vic., estb.
Hervey Bay, Qld, first settled
Hillston, NSW, estb.
Junee, NSW, estb.
Marysville, Vic., estb.
Meningie, SA, estb.
Moonta, SA, estb.
Narrandera, NSW, estb.
Oberon, NSW, estb.
Port Hedland, WA, estb.
Portland, NSW, first settled
Somerset, Qld, estb.

A

History, Politics, Economics, Law

1864

Government

1864–1866, B. T. Finniss Administrator NT under SA jurisdiction.
4 Aug. 1864–Mar. 1865, A. Blyth Premier SA.

1 Jan. D. T. Seymour appointed first Qld Police Commissioner.
26 Apr. NT founded. Boyle Travers Finniss leaves Adelaide to estb. settlement in NT at Escape Cliffs. (Settlement abandoned in 1867.)
26 Apr. Qld Hansard first published.
14 May. Frank and Alexander Jardine begin expedition overlanding cattle from Rockhampton to Cape York Peninsula, Qld. (Arrive 13 Mar. 1865.)
26 Nov. Secretary of State for the Colonies in England advises end of all transportation of convicts to Aust. within three years.
During Nov. Vic. Legislative Assembly elections return J. McCulloch as Premier with large majority.
During 1864
City of Sydney Bank estb. Colonial Bank of Australasia estb.
Large-scale commercial manufacture of sugar in Qld begins. Louis Hope operates first commercial raw sugar mill at Ormiston, Qld.

Births & Deaths

Peter Bowling, miners' leader and prominent member of Industrial Workers of the World, b. (d. 1942)
Derrimut, Aborigine who saved J. P. Fawkner and other early settlers in Vic. from massacre in 1835, d. (probably b. about 1811)
Mark Foy, merchant, businessman, b. (d. 1950)
Sir Robert Gibson, businessman, banker, b. (d. 1934)
Thomas Givens, Federal politician, b. (d. 1928)
Sir Joseph John Talbot Hobbs, World War I commander and architect, b. (d. 1938)
William Lithgow, first NSW Auditor-General, d. (b. 1784)
Sir James Whiteside McCay, lawyer, Federal politician and military commander, b. (d. 1930)
Sir Thomas Tait, Vic. Railways Commissioner, b. (d. 1940)
Robert Torrens, SA colonizer, d. (b. 1780)

B

Science, Technology, Transport, Discovery

6 Apr. Telegraphic cable line links Rockhampton, Qld, to Brisbane.
17 Sep. Bendigo–Echuca railway line estb. in Vic., opening Riverina district in NSW.
1 Dec. Blacktown–Windsor–Richmond railway line opens in NSW.
During 1864
Trigonometrical surveys begin in NSW.
Salmon and brown trout eggs successfully imported to Tas.
First iron and steel blast furnace in Aust. begins, at Mittagong, NSW.
Rich coalfield discovered at Blair Athol, Qld.
Timber bridge built over Greenough R. near Geraldton, WA. (Among oldest standing timber bridges in Aust.)
Coal discovered at Anvil Creek, NSW, in the Greta–Cessnock–Maitland field.
Silver first mined near Moruya, NSW.

Births & Deaths

Carsten Egeberg Borchgrevink, naturalist and Antarctic explorer, b. (d. 1934)
Frederick Chapman, palaeontologist, science author, b. (d. 1943)
Alister Clark, rose-growing authority, b. (d. 1949)
John Walker Gregory, geologist, b. (d. 1932)
Andrew Gibb Maitland, geologist, b. (d. 1951)
Sir Richard Rawdon Stawell, medical practitioner specializing in children's diseases, b. (d. 1935)

1864

C
Arts

Literature

Births & Deaths
Andrew Barton (Banjo) Paterson, poet and author, b. (d. 1941)
Charles Henry Souter, poet, b. (d. 1944)

Music, Dance

Jan. Nellie Stewart makes first stage appearance, at six years of age.

Fine Arts

During 1864
Charles Summers, sculptor, completes first bronze casting by colonial artist, statue Burke and Wills, in Melbourne. (Unveiled on 21 Apr. 1865.)

Births & Deaths
Aby Altson, portrait painter, b. (probably d. 1950)
Georges Hippolyte Aurousseau, botanic artist, b. (d. 1953)
Luther Bradley, Melbourne *Punch* cartoonist, probably b. (d. 1917)
Rupert Charles Wulsten Bunny, leader of modernist trend in Aust. painting, b. (d. 1947)
David Davies, painter noted for lyrical nocturnes of bush landscapes, b. (d. 1939)
Agnes Goodsir, portrait painter, b. (d. 1939)
Edward Jukes Greig, first Sydney *Punch* cartoonist, d.
Edward Atkins Hornel, artist, b. (d. 1933)
John Kauffmann, pictorial photographer, 'Father of Pictorial Movement in Aust.', b. (d. 1942)
Philip William May, black-and-white artist, b. (d. 1903)
Benjamin Edwin Minns, black-and-white artist, b. (d. 1937)

Architecture

During 1864
John Mills, architect, builds Launceston Town Hall, Tas.
Henry Hunter begins work on Town Hall in Hobart.

D
Religion, Learning

Jan. Vic. introduces 'Payment by Results' education system, with payment of bonuses to teachers. (Lasts until 1901.)
1 May. National Museum opens in Melbourne.
During 1864
First Baptist Missionary Society estb., in Adelaide. (Vic. 1865, NSW 1883.)
Presbyterians estb. Ballarat College.
Qld Board of Education gives aid to Church schools.
Synod of Eastern Aust. and Synod of NSW unite to become the General Synod of the Presbyterian Church of NSW.

Births & Deaths
Daniel Mannix, Roman Catholic archbishop, b. (d. 1963)
John Smyth, educationist, b. (d. 1927)

E
Sport

9 Mar. Vic. Horse-Racing Club formed.
Apr. Melbourne Lawn Bowling Club estb. (Lawn bowling clubs estb. in Brisbane 1878, Parramatta 1880, Perth 1895, Adelaide 1897, Canberra 1930.)
During 1864
Lantern, ridden by S. Davis, wins Melbourne Cup in 3 minutes 52 seconds.
Adelaide Cup (horserace) first run.
Carlton and Melbourne Aust. Rules Football clubs founded.
University of Sydney estb. first Aust. Rugby Union football team.
Opening of Albert Sporting Ground in Sydney gives impetus to development of athletics.

F
Historia Dignum

Population
Estimated total white, 1,325,183.

Mar.–Apr. Northern NSW and southern Qld flooded.
9 Apr. The newspaper *Moreton Bay Courier* becomes the *Brisbane Courier*.
11 Apr. Fire destroys 14 shops in Brisbane.
2 Jun. Steamer *Rainbow* wrecked in Seal Rocks Bay, NSW; 7 lives lost.
1 Oct. The *Australasian* begins publication. (Becomes *Australasian Post* in 1946.)
1 Dec. Great Fire of Brisbane destroys city area bounded by Queen, George, Elizabeth and Albert streets.
During 1864
Blumenlese auf dem Felde der Neueren Literatur becomes first foreign-language magazine in Aust. Published at Tanunda, SA.
Severe two-year drought throughout most of Aust. begins.
Vic. Govt introduces compulsory registration of charities and public hospitals.
Vic. Govt becomes first to accept responsibility for neglected children.

Births & Deaths
Philip Peter Jacob Wirth, circus entertainer, b. (d. 1937)

Communities
Cardwell, Qld, estb.
Howard, Qld, estb.
Mitchell, Qld, estb.
Northampton, WA, estb.
Roebourne, WA, estb.
Townsville, Qld, estb.
Warburton, Vic., estb.
Wilcannia, NSW, estb.

A
History, Politics, Economics, Law

1865

Government
3 Feb. 1865–Jan. 1866, C. Cowper Premier NSW.
22 Mar. 1865–Sep. 1865, F. S. Dutton Premier SA.
20 Sep. 1865–Oct. 1865, H. Ayers Premier SA.
23 Oct. 1865–Mar. 1866, J. Hart Premier SA.

25 Jan. Confederate States of America warship *Shenandoah* arrives in Port Phillip Bay for repairs and supplies.
26 Jan. British Govt officially announces total cessation of all convict transportation to Aust.
25 Mar. First Qld Divorce Act passed.
11 Dec. Bank of Adelaide opens.
19 Dec. Sam Poo, the Chinese bushranger, probably Australia's only Chinese bushranger, is hanged in NSW.

During 1865
Vic. Govt repeals £10 poll tax on Chinese entering Colony.
Vic. Govt passes James Macpherson Grant's Act, opening more land to selectors.
Shorter working week principle extended to Vic. building workers. (Qld 1858; SA 1873.)
Vic. Govt introduces first protective tariffs. Policy of protection by imposition of import duties on all manufacturing. (Legislation passed in Apr. 1866.)
NSW Govt introduces stamp duties on legal documents.
First Qld brewery opens, in Rockhampton.
Aust. Joint Stock Banks estb. in NSW and Qld.
Duncan McIntyre begins ill-fated Leichhardt search expedition.
John McKinlay commissioned to lead expedition to locate suitable site for NT capital. Expedition leaves Adelaide in Sep.
Shipment of coal sent to Japan. First recorded export to Japan.
Convicts Ben Hall and John Gilbert both fatally shot in separate incidents in NSW.
Aust. colonies empowered to estb. their own naval forces, independent of the Royal Navy.

Births & Deaths
Sir William Charles Angliss, businessman, benefactor, b. (d. 1957)
Frank (Francis George) Anstey, Vic. politician, b. (d. 1940)
Egerton Lee Batchelor, SA and Federal politician, b. (d. 1911)
William Riddell Birdwood, Baron Birdwood, World War I military commander, b. (d. 1951)
Sir Henry George Chauvel, cavalry commander, first Aust. Lieut-General, in 1917, b. (d. 1945)
Francis William Sutton Cumbrae-Stewart, Qld lawyer, b. (d. 1938)
Frederick Carlton Curr, Qld pioneer and explorer, b. (d. 1953)
John Earle, Tas. Premier, b. (d. 1932)
Sir Ernest Frederick Augustus Gaunt, naval commander, b. (d. 1940)
Thomas Griffiths, territorial administrator, b. (d. 1947)
Sir William Murray McPherson, Vic. Premier, b. (d. 1932)
Sir John Monash, military commander, engineer, b. (d. 1931)
Alfred Cecil Rowlandson, publisher, b. (d. 1922)
Sir Granville de Laune Ryrie, World War I military commander, Federal politician, b. (d. 1937)
Dame Eadith Campbell Walker, hospital benefactor, probably b. (d. 1937)

B

Science, Technology, Transport, Discovery

31 Jul. First Qld public steam railway opens, from Ipswich to Bigge's camp at Grandchester.
29 Nov. First gas lighting in Brisbane.
Nov. George W. Goyder begins journey to north SA, where he establishes Goyder rainfall line.
During 1865
Scab in sheep caused by parasitic insect threatens wool industry.
First salmon hatchery in Southern Hemisphere estb., at New Norfolk, Tas.
First kerosene manufactured, at Wollongong, NSW.
James Litchfield estb. Hazeldean merino stud based on Rambouillet ewes.
Frederick H. Litchfield discovers first gold in NT, on Finniss R.
First Qld coach service opens with Cobb & Co. Brisbane to Ipswich run.
The Rack wool press first demonstrated in Melbourne.

Births & Deaths

John Stewart Dethridge, inventor, engineer, b. (d. 1926)
Walter Frederick Gale, astronomer, b. (d. 1945)
Hugh Victor McKay, farmer, inventor, b. (d. 1926)
Charles Ernest Prell, pioneer of pasture improvement, b. (d. 1946)

C

Arts

Literature

During 1865
John Gould publishes *Handbook of the Birds of Australia*.
Catherine Spence publishes *Mr Hogarth's Will*.
Henry Kingsley publishes *The Hillyars and the Burtons* in book form. (First published as serial 1863.)

Births & Deaths

Edward George Dyson, novelist and balladist, b. (d. 1931)
William Gay, poet, philosopher, b. (d. 1897)
Dame Mary Gilmore (née Mary Jean Cameron), lyric poet, social worker, b. (d. 1962)
Henry Harbord ('Harry') Morant, 'the Breaker', balladist, horseman and soldier, b. (d. 1902)
Dowell Philip O'Reilly, author, short story writer, b. (d. 1923)
Alfred George Stephens, literary critic, editor, b. (d. 1933)

Drama, Theatre

Feb. Brisbane's first regular theatre, Victoria Theatre, opens.

Births & Deaths

Elizabeth Esther Ellen Jennings, 'Essie', actress, b. (d. 1920)
May Robson, character actress, b. (d. 1942)

Fine Arts

Feb. Abram Louis Buvelot, landscape painter, arrives in Melbourne.
During 1865
Mechanical drawing classes begin at Mechanics' School of Arts in Sydney.

Births & Deaths

John Henry Chinner, illustrator and cartoonist, b. (d. 1933)
Edith E. Cusack, painter, probably b. (probably d. 1941)
Emanuel Phillips Fox, impressionist painter, b. (d. 1915)
Grace Joel, portrait painter, b. (d. 1944)

Architecture

During 1865
Individual building blocks lead to suburbs and urban sprawl in cities as railways expand.

1865

D
Religion, Learning

29 Jun. Fire destroys St Mary's Catholic Cathedral in Sydney. (Foundation stone for new cathedral laid 8 Dec. 1868.)
Sep. General Synod, Synod of Aust. and United Presbyteries unite to form the Presbyterian Church of NSW.

During 1865
Methodist Wesley College opens in Melbourne.
Bishop Hale's School in Perth becomes Church of England Collegiate School.

Births & Deaths
Samuel John Hoban, Methodist minister, b. (d. 1931)
Stephen Henry Smith, educationist, b. (d. 1943)
George Arnold Wood, historian, b. (d. 1928)

E
Sport

During 1865
Toryboy, ridden by E. Cavanagh, wins Melbourne Cup in 3 minutes 44 seconds.
Launceston Cup (horserace) first run.
Eagle Farm horseracing track opens in Brisbane.
Sydney University Cricket Club estb.
Royal Perth Yacht Club estb.
First coursing meetings held at Naracoorte, SA.

F
Historia Dignum

1865

Population
Estimated total white, 1,390,043.

Jan. *Star of Australia* lost *en route* to Rockhampton, Qld, from Brisbane; 17 aboard disappear.
Sailors' Home opens in Sydney.
20 Jun. Adelaide Town Hall opens.
2 Sep. *Australian Journal*, newspaper magazine, first published in Melbourne to encourage colonial literature.
Dec. First fish market opens in Melbourne. (Sydney 1872.)
During 1865
Brisbane Town Hall opens.
Goldfish imported to Aust. from Japan and China, beginning aquaria.
Brisbane City Volunteer Fire Brigade estb. First fire brigade in Qld.
Hibernian-Australasian Catholic Benefit Society estb. in Sydney.
William Robert Giblin estb. Hobart Working Men's Club.
c. 1865. Sydney's city night refuge and soup kitchens estb.

Births & Deaths
Henry Ernest Boote, journalist, b. (d. 1949)

Communities estb.
Charleville, Qld
Gold Coast area, Qld, settled by selectors
Maffra, Vic.
Milton, NSW
Nerang, Qld
Rosewood, Qld
Yeppoon, Qld, first settled

Communities estb. in 1860s
Anglesea, Vic.
Bencubbin, WA
Burketown, Qld
Calliope, Qld
Junction Reefs, NSW
Legerwood, Tas.
Mullewa, WA
Nambour, Qld
Nimmitabel, NSW
Richmond, Qld
Stockwell, SA
Trafalgar, Vic.
Warragul, Vic.
Woodstock, Qld

1866

A
History, Politics, Economics, Law

Government
22 Jan. 1866–Oct. 1868, J. Martin Premier NSW.
1 Feb. 1866–Jul. 1866, A. Macalister Premier Qld.
28 Mar. 1866–May 1867, J. P. Boucaut Premier SA.
7 May 1866–15 Aug. 1866, George Jackson Carey administered Vic.
20 Jul. 1866–Aug. 1866, R. G. W. Herbert Premier Qld.
7 Aug. 1866–Aug. 1867, A. Macalister Premier Qld.
15 Aug. 1866–2 Mar. 1873, Sir John Henry Thomas Manners-Sutton Governor Vic.
24 Nov. 1866–Aug. 1869, Sir R. Dry Premier Tas.
1866–1867, J. T. Manton Govt Resident NT under SA jurisdiction.

Jan. Thomas Elder imports 122 camels from India. First major commercial importation.
Feb. Sir Charles Darling, Vic. Governor, recalled to England for favouring McCulloch Ministry in constitutional conflict between the two Houses of Vic. legislature.
Australian-made sovereign coins admitted into Britain.
During 1866
Rockhampton League, Qld, estb. to fight for separation of N Qld from Brisbane.
The Commercial Bank of Aust. incorporated.
NSW Govt introduces 5 per cent duty on all goods brought into Colony, to finance public works program.
Coal Trade Association estb. by companies on N coal fields, NSW.

Births & Deaths
John Allan, Vic. Premier, b. (d. 1936)
Matthew Charlton, Federal Labor leader, b. (d. 1948)
Henry Daglish, first Labor WA Premier, b. (d. 1920)
Robert Dawson, NSW pioneer, writer, d. (b. 1782)
Edward Eager, emancipist lawyer, d. (b. 1787)
Sir Henry William Forster, Governor-General, b. (d. 1936)
Sir Ernest Augustus Lee Steere, WA pastoralist, b. (d. 1957)
Richard Denis Meagher, lawyer, Federal politician, b. (d. 1931)
Sir James Mitchell, WA Premier and Governor, b. (d. 1951)
Sir James O'Grady, Tas. Governor, b. (d. 1934)
Edith Charlotte Onians, social worker, b. (d. 1953)
Evan Kyffin Thomas, newspaper proprietor, b. (d. 1935)
Frank Gwynne Tudor, Vic. politician, b. (d. 1922)

B
Science, Technology, Transport, Discovery

1 May. Adelaide to Melbourne railway line opens as far as Bordertown, SA.
Jul. Aust. Paper Co. opens factory at Liverpool, NSW.
12 Dec. Philosophical Society of NSW becomes Royal Society of NSW.
During 1866
'Lying in Hospital', first maternity hospital in Aust. and first training school for midwives, built in Sydney.
Goyder Line established. George W. Goyder draws imaginary east-west line across SA on 25.4 cm isohyet, separating land with rainfall suited to agricultural use from land suited only to grazing activity.
NSW shale oil first processed.
Gundagai Bridge over Murrumbidgee R., NSW, opens.
Construction of bridge over Swan R., Fremantle, WA, begins.
Joseph Ross estb. bottle factory in Sydney.

Births & Deaths
John Frederick Bailey, botanist, b. (d. 1938)
Sir Robert William Chapman, engineer, authority on timber and ocean tides, b. (d. 1942)
Sir Charles James Martin, medical scientist noted for work on snake venom, b. (d. 1955)
Elgar Ravenswood Waite, scientist, museum curator, b. (d. 1928)

Arts

Literature

During 1866
George B. Barton published *Literature in New South Wales*.

Births & Deaths
Barcroft Henry Thomas Boake, poet, balladist, b. (d. 1892)
Bernard Patrick O'Dowd, poet, lawyer, b. (d. 1953)

Music, Dance

During 1866
Civil Service Musical Society estb. in Sydney.

Births & Deaths
George Howard Clutsam, composer, b. (d. 1951)
William Adolphus Laver, musician, first Aust.-born professor of music, b. (d. 1940)

Drama, Theatre

During 1866
James Dinsdale opens the Royal Alexandra Theatre in Brisbane.
Charles E. Horsley organizes music festival for Melbourne Exhibition. Opens 24 Oct.

Fine Arts

During 1866
Aust. art sent to Intercolonial Exhibition in Chicago, USA. (In later years other exhibitions using this title were held in important centres in the USA.)

Births & Deaths
Edward Colclough, painter, b. (d. 1950)
Alexander Colquhoun, painter, art critic, b. (d. 1941)
Albert J. Hanson, seascape painter, b. (d. 1914)
Ethel Maud Nicholls, street scene painter, b. (d. 1956)
Emily Letitia Paul, painter, b. (d. 1917)
John Pick, painter, b. (d. 1949)
Alfred Wadham Sinclair, watercolourist, b. (d. 1938)
John Samuel Watkins, painter, b. (d. 1942)

Architecture

During 1866
J. H. Wilson and other architects design Sydney Town Hall. (Completed 1888.)

Births & Deaths
Harold Desbrowe-Annear, architect, among first to design functional homes in open-plan, b. (d. 1933)
Robert Joseph Haddon, architect, b. (d. 1929)

1866

D Religion, Learning

19 Mar. J. E. Tenison-Woods and Mary McKillop found new Catholic Order, The Sisters of St Joseph of the Sacred Heart, specializing in teaching of young children, at Penola, SA.

During 1866
George Higinbotham conducts Commission into Vic. education system which recommends adopting a secular system.
Henry Parkes' Public Schools Act passed in NSW. Replaces dual system of education with a single Council of Education which becomes central education authority.
Aust. Cadet Corps first introduced, at Kings School, Parramatta, NSW.
W. Rooke forms first Aust. Christadelphian group, in Sydney.
NSW Act of Parlt enables Church of England to manage its own property.

Births & Deaths

George Gilbert Aimé Murray, classical scholar, b. (d. 1957)
Henry Newton, Church of England bishop, b. (d. 1947)

E Sport

8 May. Meeting at 'Freemason's Hotel' in Swanston St, Melbourne, lays down rules for Aust. Rules football to distinguish the sport from Rugby Union. Umpires first appear.

During 1866
The Barb, ridden by W. Davis, wins Melbourne Cup in 3 minutes 43 seconds.
First Sydney and Brisbane Cups (horseracing) run.
Aboriginal cricket team estb.
Brisbane Aust. Rules Football Club estb. (Qld Football Association estb. in 1879.)

Births & Deaths

Henry Ernest Searle, 'the Clarence Comet', sculler, b. (d. 1889)

F
Historia Dignum

1866

Population
Estimated total white, 1,443,955.

11 Jan. Ship *London* wrecked *en route* to Aust.; 231 lives lost.
14 May. Ship *General Grant* lost *en route* to England; 68 lives lost.
12 Jul. Ship *Cawarra* sinks entering Newcastle Harbour; 62 lives lost.
24 Oct. Intercolonial exhibition opens in Melbourne, to stimulate trade.

During 1866
First mail steamer from Panama arrives in Sydney, beginning Pacific steamer service.
SA Commercial Travellers' Association estb. (Other Commercial Travellers' Associations estb. in Vic. 1881, NSW 1883, Qld 1884, WA 1896, Tas. 1900, Federal body 1895.)

Communities
Beltana, SA, estb.
Bundaberg, Qld, first settled
Coraki, NSW, estb.
Murray Bridge, SA, estb.
Wantabadgery, NSW, estb.

1867

A
History, Politics, Economics, Law

Government
3 May 1867–Sep. 1868, H. Ayers Premier SA.
15 Aug. 1867–Nov. 1868, R. R. Mackenzie Premier Qld.
25 Dec. 1867–7 Jan. 1868, Sir Trevor Chute administered NSW.

Mar. Meeting of Ministers of Aust. colonies in Melbourne to arrange overseas postal communications. At conference Ministers resolve to form a Federal Council to discuss subjects of common interest.
25 Jun. Thomas and John Clarke, two of the most violent Aust. bushrangers, hanged in Darlinghurst jail, NSW.
Nov. Francis Cadell discovers mouth of Roper R., NT and pastoral country in area around latitude 14°S.
During 1867
Vic. imposes protective tariff legislation.
Kanaka labourers sold to Qld sugar cane growers for £7 each.
Commercial Bank of Aust. estb. in Vic., NSW, Qld, and SA.

Births & Deaths
Sir Stanley Seymour Argyle, Vic. Premier, b. (d. 1940)
Franc Brereton Sadleir Falkiner, NSW pioneer pastoralist, politician, b. (d. 1929)
Sir Robert Randolph Garran, 'Father of Canberra', barrister, b. (d. 1957)
Sir Littleton Ernest Groom, Federal politician, b. (d. 1935)
Howard Hinton, shipping merchant, philanthropist, arts patron, b. (d. 1948)
James William Macarthur-Onslow, NSW pastoralist and politician, b. (d. 1946)
Sir William Harrison Moore, constitutional lawyer, b. (d. 1935)
Pearson William Tewksbury, businessman, probably b. (d. 1953)
William Humble Ward, Earl of Dudley, Governor-General, b. (d. 1932)
John Christian Watson, first Labor Prime Minister of Aust., b. (d. 1941)

B
Science, Technology, Transport, Discovery

12 Apr. Ipswich–Toowoomba railway line completed, linking Brisbane with Darling Downs, Qld.
1 May. Sydney and Adelaide linked by electric telegraph via Wentworth, NSW.
20 May. Ernest Henry discovers copper at Cloncurry, Qld. The Great Australian Copper Mine develops.
19 Sep. Rockhampton–Westwood railway line completed in Qld.
16 Oct. James Nash discovers gold at Gympie, Qld.
During 1867
Joseph Bancroft discovers the cause of scab in sheep.
Principle of treating open wounds with an antiseptic introduced in Parramatta, NSW, before being announced abroad.
Melbourne Meat Preserving Co. experiments with meat canning.
R. Rutter invents the floating gun battery named *Australian Ironclad*.
First continuing geological survey estb. in Qld. (Estb in Vic. 1871, NSW 1873, SA and Tas. 1882, WA 1889.)
Diamond deposits discovered at Two Mile Flat near Mudgee, NSW.

Births & Deaths
John Job Crew Bradfield, civil engineer, b. (d. 1943)
Robert Hall, ornithologist, b. (d. 1949)
William David Kerr Macgillivray, ornithologist, b. (d. 1933)

C
Arts

D
Religion, Learning

Literature

During 1867
Adam Lindsay Gordon publishes *Ashtaroth* and *Sea Spray and Smoke Drift*.
Samuel Bennett publishes *The History of Australian Discovery and Colonization*, among first Aust. histories published in Aust.

Births & Deaths
Grace Elizabeth Jennings Carmichael, poet, b. (d. 1904)
Henry Lawson, poet and short story writer, b. (d. 1922)
Edwin Greenslade Murphy, also known as 'Dryblower', bush balladist, b. (d. 1939)
Roderick Joseph Quinn, lyric poet, author, b. (d. 1949)

Music, Dance

Jan. Madame Céline Celeste, dancer, makes début in Melbourne. Hester Blake, dancer, makes début in Brisbane. Martinetti troupe makes début in Melbourne in Oct. Lehman ballet makes début in Sydney.

During 1867
Hobart Philharmonic Society estb.

Births & Deaths
Louis Lavater, composer, poet, b. (d. 1953)
William Arundel Orchard, conductor, b. (d. 1961)

Fine Arts

During 1867
Artisans' School of Art and Design estb. First public school offering art instruction in Melbourne.

Births & Deaths
William S. Austin, Qld painter, b. (d. 1945)
Florence Ada Fuller, landscape and portrait painter, b. (d. 1918)
Dora Ohlfsen, medallion sculptor, b. (d. 1948)
Sir Arthur Streeton, landscape painter, b. (d. 1943)

Architecture

29 Apr. Construction of present Melbourne Town Hall begins.

17 Apr. *Vernon*, training ship, set aside in Sydney as reformatory and training ship for boys, begins operating.

During 1867
St Stanislaus Catholic College opens in Bathurst, NSW.
Prince Alfred Methodist College estb. in Adelaide. (Opens 18 Jan. 1869.)

Births & Deaths
Sir Ernest Scott, historian, b. (d. 1939)

1867

E
Sport

During 1867
Tim Whiffler, ridden by I. Driscoll, wins Melbourne Cup in 3 mins 39 seconds.
R. W. Wardell scores first century in Aust. first-class cricket.
First organized open field greyhound coursing race meeting held, at Naracoorte, SA. (Greyhound coursing begins in Vic. 1873, NSW 1876, Tas. 1878, Qld 1888.)
Burnett Hunt Club estb., Qld; first in Qld.

Births & Deaths
David McFarlane Andy Kerr, 'the Coogee Bunyip', bookmaker, b. (d. 1955)
Hugh Trumble, all-round cricketer, b. (d. 1938)

F
Historia Dignum

Population
Estimated total white, 1,483,848.

2–3 Mar. Townsville and Bowen, Qld, wrecked by cyclone.
20 Mar. Schooner *Albion* wrecked near Port Hacking, NSW; five lives lost.
10 Jun. Newspaper *Ballarat Courier* estb. (Incorporated *Ballarat Star* in 1925.)
During Jun. Samuel Bennett launches newspaper *Evening News* in Sydney; first penny paper in NSW.
30 Oct. Alfred Duke of Edinburgh arrives in Adelaide, beginning first visit by Prince of British Royal family to Aust.
During 1867
Drought in SA and N Vic. (Until 1869.)
Curtis gold nugget, weighing 975 ounces, discovered at Gympie, Qld.
Queen Victoria creates Victoria Cross medal for Imperial armed forces in recognition of bravery and devotion to duty.

Communities
Bermagui, NSW, estb.
Derrinallum, Vic., estb.
Grenfell, NSW, estb.
Gympie, Qld, estb.
Macarthur, Vic., estb.
Maroochydore, Qld, estb.
Oakey, Qld, estb.
Roseworthy, SA, estb.

A
History, Politics, Economics, Law

1868

Government

4 Jan. 1868–14 Aug. 1868, Sir Maurice Charles O'Connell administered Qld.
8 Jan. 1868–22 Feb. 1872, Sir Somerset Richard Lowry-Corry, Earl of Belmore, Governor NSW.
20 Feb. 1868–15 Feb. 1869, Francis Gilbert Hamley administered SA.
6 May 1868–Jul. 1868, C. Sladen Premier Vic.
11 Jul. 1868–Sep. 1869, J. McCulloch Premier Vic.
14 Aug. 1868–2 Jan. 1871, Samuel Wensley Blackall Governor Qld.
24 Sep. 1868–Oct. 1868, J. Hart Premier SA.
13 Oct. 1868–Nov. 1868, H. Ayers Premier SA.
27 Oct. 1868–Jan. 1870, J. Robertson Premier NSW.
2 Nov. 1868–29 Sep. 1869, John Bruce administered WA.
3 Nov. 1868–May. 1870, H. B. T. Strangways Premier SA.
25 Nov. 1868–May. 1870, C. Lilley Premier Qld.
30 Dec. 1868–15 Jan. 1869, W. C. Trevor administered Tas.

10 Jan. Last convict ship, the *Hougomont*, arrives in WA. Grand total of all convicts sent to Aust. from 1788 to 1868 is *c.* 160,500 of which *c.* 24,700 were women.
12 Mar. Henry James O'Farrell attempts to assassinate Alfred Duke of Edinburgh at Clontarf in Sydney. O'Farrell hanged on 21 Apr.
22 May. Woollen and Cloth Manufacturing Co. estb. in Geelong, Vic., to pioneer commercial manufacture of woollen cloth.

During 1868

Qld Govt passes Polynesian Labourers Act to regulate Kanaka labour. In Mar. there are *c.* 2,107 Kanakas in Aust.
Qld estb. Native Mounted Police Force at Rockhampton.
Qld Steam Navigation Co. (formed 1861) buys Australasian Steam Navigation Co.
Adelaide Co-operative Society Ltd becomes first co-operative registered in Aust.
Maria Smith cultivates apple seedlings in garden in Tas. from which she grows first Granny Smith apples.
Pearl shell first gathered in Torres Strait.
Charles Brady and Bladen Neil estb. Sericultural Society to develop export trade in silkworm eggs.
Brisbane Chamber of Commerce estb.

Births & Deaths

William Jethro Brown, jurist, b. (d. 1930)
Frederick John Napier Thesiger, Baron Chelmsford, Qld and NSW Governor, b. (d. 1933)
William Neil Gillies, Qld Premier, b. (d. 1928)
Alice Frances Mabel Moss, social worker, b. (d. 1948)
Sir Herbert Nicholls, Tas. Chief Justice, b. (d. 1940)
Robert Falcon Scott, Antarctic explorer, b. (d. 1912)
Arthur Bryant Triggs, pastoralist and art and book collector, b. (d. 1936)

1868

B
Science, Technology, Transport, Discovery

15 Jan. First public railway in Tas. opens, from Launceston to Deloraine.
Mar. James B. Higham patents first shearing machine, called a mechanical clipper.
Lucy Osburn estb. first training school for nurses in Aust., at the Sydney Hospital Infirmary.

During 1868
William Paul Dowling, photographer, arrives in Tas.
Outbreak of rust damages WA wheat crops.
Jessop and Buchanan discover gold at Ravenswood, Qld.

Births & Deaths
Alfred Walter Campbell, neurologist, b. (d. 1937)
Arthur Mills Lea, entomologist, b. (d. 1932)
Sir Herbert Lethington Maitland, surgeon, b. (d. 1923)
Norman Thomas Mortimer Wilsmore, chemist, b. (d. 1940)

C
Arts

Literature

During 1868
Yorick Club estb. in Melbourne; first Aust. Literary Society.
Catherine Spence publishes *The Author's Daughter*.

Births & Deaths
George Randolph Bedford, author, Qld politician, b. (d. 1941)
Arthur Hoey Davis, who published under pseudonym Steele Rudd, writer, journalist, b. (d. 1935)
Mary Eliza Fullerton, author, b. (d. 1946)

Music, Dance

1 Feb. Lehman Ballet Co. begins 20-week season in Melbourne. (Longest unbroken engagement by a ballet company at any Aust. theatre in 19th century.)

Drama, Theatre

Apr. Sain Lazar opens first Theatre Royal in Adelaide. (Closes in 1892.)

During 1868
William Cooper, melodramatic playwright, stages first production of *Colonial Experience* in Sydney.

Births & Deaths
Albert Edward 'Bert' Bailey, actor, producer, b. (d. 1953)

Fine Arts

Births & Deaths
Charles Conder, lyrical painter, b. (d. 1909)
Theodora Cowan, probably first woman sculptor in NSW, probably b. (d. 1949)
Bessie Gibson, miniaturist, portrait and landscape painter, b. (d. 1961)
Paul Raphael Montford, sculptor, b. (d. 1938)
William Moore, author of first comprehensive study of Aust. art, b. (d. 1937)
Percy Frederick Seaton Spence, painter and illustrator, b. (d. 1933)
Ben Strange, goldfields artist and cartoonist, b. (d. 1930)

D Religion, Learning

Architecture

During 1868
Joseph Reed designs 'Rippon Lea' mansion in Melbourne. (Completed 1876.)
Benjamin Backhouse founds first Aust. Institute of Architecture, in NSW.
'Calendar House', country mansion at Mona Vale, Tas., completed.

30 Nov. St Andrews' Church of England Cathedral in Sydney consecrated.
During 1868
Construction of St David's Cathedral begins in Hobart. (Opens 1874.)
Tas. Govt passes Public Schools Act, creating central education authority and ending State aid to denominational schools.
Christian Brothers Catholic teaching order estb. in Melbourne.

1868

E
Sport

May–Oct. Aboriginal cricket team tours England. First overseas visit of an Aust. cricket team. Wins 14 out of 28 matches.

During 1868
Glencoe, ridden by C. Stanley, wins Melbourne Cup in 3 mins 42 seconds.
First Aust. Croquet Club estb., at Kapunda, SA. (First croquet clubs estb. in Qld 1900, NSW and Vic. 1902, WA 1905, Tas. 1908.)
First Aust. amateur sculling championships held in Melbourne.
First Public School head of the river rowing race held in Melbourne. (NSW 1893, WA 1899, Qld 1918, SA 1922, Tas. 1924.)
J. Yeomans wins first Sydney athletic cup.
Adam Lindsay Gordon becomes noted steeplechase rider.
WA Rowing Club estb.

Births & Deaths
Selwyn Francis Edge, racing car driver, b. (d. 1933)
Sol Green, bookmaker, b. (d. 1948)
Jim Hall, boxer, b. (d. 1913)

F
Historia Dignum

Population
Estimated total white, 1,539,552.

16 Jan. Ship *Light of the Age* wrecked at Port Phillip Heads; 6 lives lost.
16 Aug. Tidal wave swamps Port Jackson, NSW.

During 1868
The *Daily Advertiser* newspaper estb. at Wagga Wagga, NSW.
SA drought.
Colonial Institute estb. in England to promote interests in Aust. colonies.

Births & Deaths
Amy Alfreda Vickery, philatelist, philanthropist, b. (d. 1942)

Communities
Araluen, NSW, estb.
Beenleigh, Qld, estb.
Blackall, Qld, estb.
Gingin, WA, estb.
Jindera, NSW, estb.
Maitland, SA, estb.
Normanton, Qld, estb.
Walla Walla, NSW, estb.
Yarrawonga, Vic., estb.

A

History, Politics, Economics, Law

Government

15 Jan. 1869–28 Nov. 1874, Charles Du Cane Governor Tas.
16 Feb. 1869–18 Apr. 1873, Sir James Fergusson Governor SA.
4 Aug. 1869–Nov. 1872, J. M. Wilson Premier Tas.
20 Sep. 1869–Apr. 1870, J. A. MacPherson Premier Vic.
30 Sep. 1869–3 Jan. 1875, Frederick Aloysius Weld Governor WA.
1869–1870. G. W. Goyder Govt Resident NT under SA jurisdiction.

30 Jan. SA Govt passes Henry Strangways' Selection Act, opening Crown land for selection before survey.
5 Feb. George Woodroffe Goyder arrives at Port Darwin, NT. Surveys Port Darwin and recommends site of NT capital, naming it Palmerston. (Becomes Darwin in 1911.)
3 Mar. William Lanney, 'King Billy', last Tas. full-blood male Aborigine, dies of choleraic diarrhoea.
17 Nov. Suez Canal opens, shortening sailing time to and from Britain.
During 1869
Eight Hour Extension Committee estb. in Sydney to fight for shorter working day.
SA Chamber of Manufacturers opens; first in Aust.
John and Alexander Forrest lead unsuccessful Leichhardt search expedition.
Banking Trade Employees' Union of NSW estb.

Births & Deaths

Sir George Stephenson Beeby, judge, politician noted for work on industrial legislation, b. (d. 1942)
Herbert Raine Curlewis, NSW judge, b. (d. 1942)
Sir Guy Reginald Archer Gaunt, naval officer, b. (d. 1953)
Sir John Waters Kirwan, Federal politician, WA journalist, b. (d. 1949)
John Storey, NSW Premier, b. (d. 1921)
Evan Alexander Wisdom, WA politician, World War I military commander, New Guinea administrator, b. (d. 1945)

B

Science, Technology, Transport, Discovery

23 Mar. Francis Boardman Clapp, William McCulloch and Henry Hoyt (from America) introduce Broadway stage coaches to Melbourne; estb. Melbourne Omnibus Co.
During Mar. Foundation stone laid for Prince Alfred Hospital in Melbourne.
27 Apr. Electric telegraph submarine cable line opens from Melbourne to Tas. First message sent on 1 May.
27 May. Great Southern railway from Sydney to Goulburn, NSW, opens.
21 Jun. Electric telegraph line opens from Perth to Fremantle, WA.
Sep. Alexander Thomson and Gerard Kreft gather important fossil specimens at Wellington Caves, NSW.
18 Oct. Lithgow Zig Zag railway line across Blue Mts, NSW, completed. Acclaimed as major engineering achievement.
During 1869
Dr Goold sends eucalyptus seeds to Italy for plantation in the Pontine marshes.
Gold traces discovered at Blackmore and Charlotte rivers, NT.

Births & Deaths

Richard Porteous, photographer, b. (probably d. 1922)

1869

C
Arts

Literature

During 1869
Marcus Clarke serializes his first novel, *Long Odds*.
Henry Kendall publishes *Leaves from Australian Forests*.

Births & Deaths
Edwin James Brady, author and balladist, b. (d. 1952)
William Henry Ogilvie, poet, b. (d. 1963)
David McKee Wright, poet, journalist, b. (d. 1928)

Music, Dance

4 Dec. Duvalli sisters, dancers, make début in Melbourne.

Fine Arts

During 1869
Loan Exhibition of Aust. paintings held in Melbourne.

Births & Deaths
Christina Asquith Baker, painter, b. (d. 1960)
George James Coates, painter, b. (d. 1930)
Alfred Coffey, painter, b. (d. 1950)
Robert Henderson Croll, art organizer, writer, b. (d. 1947)
Charles Web Gilbert, sculptor, b. (d. 1925)
Alice Hambridge, watercolourist, miniaturist, b. (d. 1947)
James Walter Robert Linton, watercolourist, enameller, b. (d. 1947)
Alexander McClintock, watercolourist, b. (d. 1922)
Richard John Randall, painter, b. (d. 1906)
John Alexander Thomas Shirlow, etcher, b. (d. 1936)

D
Religion, Learning

During 1869
Foundation stone of St Peter's Church of England Cathedral in Adelaide laid. (Opens 1878.)
Vic. Technological Commission estb. to improve education of industrial classes in technological subjects.
NSW Public Library building opens as the Free Public Library, in Sydney.
Brisbane Grammar School opens.

Births & Deaths
William Lindsay McKenzie, AIF Chaplain, Salvation Army Commissioner, 'Anzac Mac', b. (d. 1947)
Florence Melian Stawell, scholar, b. (d. 1936)
John Douglas Story, educationist, b. (d. 1966)

E
Sport

During 1869

Warrior, ridden by J. Morrison, wins Melbourne Cup in 3 minutes 40 seconds.
Rules for winning Aust. Rules football match change from first side to score two goals to team with most goals in set time.
Vic. defeats SA in first intercolonial Aust. Rules football match.
Royal Boneshakers Cycling Club estb. Organizes first cycle races in Aust., in Melbourne.
Golf begins in SA with construction of nine-hole golf course in Adelaide.
Adelaide Hunting Club estb.

Births & Deaths

Albert Griffiths, 'Young Griffo', featherweight boxer, b. (d. 1927)
George Towns, sculler, b. (d. 1961)

F
Historia Dignum

Population

Estimated total white, 1,592,157.

5 Feb. John Deeson and Richard Oates discover gold nugget 'Welcome Stranger', weighing 2,284 ounces, near Dunolly, Vic.
8 Feb. *Melbourne Morning Herald* becomes *Daily Telegraph*.
3 May. Agricultural Society of NSW holds first show, in Sydney.
9 May. Brig *Burnett* wrecked in Newcastle Bight, NSW; seven lives lost.
11 Sep. *Weekly Times* first published in Melbourne.

Births & Deaths

Jane Piercy, who had longest recorded life of any Australian woman (111 years 25 days), b. (d. 1981)

Communities

Alexandra, Vic., probably estb.
Allora, Qld, probably estb.
Buderim, Qld, estb.
Cargo, NSW, estb.
Darwin, NT, estb. (as Palmerston)
Woodburn, NSW, estb.

1870

A
History, Politics, Economics, Law

Government
13 Jan. 1870–Dec. 1870, C. Cowper Premier NSW.
9 Apr. 1870–Jun. 1871, J. McCulloch Premier Vic.
3 May 1870–Jan. 1874, A. H. Palmer Premier Qld.
30 May 1870–Nov. 1871, J. Hart Premier SA.
16 Dec. 1870–May 1872, Sir J. Martin Premier NSW.
1870, J. S. Millner Acting Govt Resident NT under SA jurisdiction.
1870–1873, B. Douglas Govt Resident NT under SA jurisdiction.

30 Mar.–27 Aug. John Forrest undertakes overland expedition from Perth to Adelaide; first W to E crossing of WA by land.
1 Jun. Representative government granted to WA. Partly elected Legislative Council first meets on 5 Dec.; introduces male suffrage.
23 Aug. Last British troops leave Aust. Colonies to estb. their own military forces.
14 Sep. Vic. first Colony to initiate payment of Members of Parlt in Lower House.
Dec. Vic. Govt first to pass Act allowing married women to own personal property, including wages and dividend entitlements.

During 1870
First modern style trade unions emerge.
Intercolonial Conference held in Melbourne considers tariffs, customs, unions and mail contracts.
Aust. is largest producer of gold in world, providing 39 per cent of world production.
First bananas grown in Qld.
Colonial Sugar Refining Co. develops system of central sugar mills in Qld.
Thomas Holt begins systematic oyster cultivation near Sydney.
Vic. Govt imposes death duties.

Births & Deaths
Sir William Dixson, Co. director, benefactor, b. (d. 1952)
Edmund Dwyer-Gray, Tas. Premier, b. (d. 1945)
William Grant, leader of Light Horse charge at Beersheba, b. (d. 1939)
Donald George Mackay, explorer, b. (d. 1958)
Sir Newton James Moore, WA Premier, b. (d. 1936)
Charles Samuel Nathan, WA businessman, b. (d. 1936)
Sir George Foster Pearce, Federal politician, b. (d. 1952)
Archibald Windeyer, NSW pioneer pastoralist, d. (b. 1785)

B
Science, Technology, Transport, Discovery

11 Jan. Port Wakefield–Hoyleton, SA, railway opens; first narrow-gauge railway in SA.
12 Jul. Henry C. Russell becomes director of Sydney Observatory.
15 Sep. Construction of overland telegraph line from Adelaide to Darwin begins.

During 1870
The Kelpie sheep dog developed in NSW, almost certainly from Scottish Collie.
J. E. A. Gwynne patents sheep shearing machine which incorporates a flexible joint.
Mineral beach sands first commercially exploited, at Ballina, NSW.
Donald Etheridge discovers gold in Qld.
Copper discovered at Cobar, NSW.
Cobb & Co. services in eastern colonies cover 26,000 miles a week and harness 6,000 horses a day.
Hoffman Patent Steam Brick Co. produces first brick by fully mechanized and continuous process.
Buffalo grass introduced to north-western Aust., probably through Afghan camel harnesses.
Thomas Mort and James Peter Franki put into service first wholly Aust.-produced locomotive.

Births & Deaths
Ernest Clayton Andrews, geologist, b. (d. 1948)
John Albert Leach, ornithologist, b. (d. 1929)
Anthony George Maldon Michell, engineer, inventor, b. (d. 1959)
George Robarts Smalley, astronomer, d. (b. 1822)
Bertram Dillon Steele, scientist, b. (d. 1934)
Alfred Percy Whitelaw, Tas. portrait photographer,

C
Arts

Literature

During 1870
Marcus Clarke serializes *His Natural Life*.
Adam Lindsay Gordon publishes *Bush Ballads and Galloping Rhymes*. Suicides next day.

Births & Deaths
Christopher John Brennan, poet, critic, b. (d. 1932)
Beatrice Ethel Grimshaw, author, b. (d. 1953)
Mrs Aeneas Gunn (née Taylor) author, b. (d. 1961)
Ethel Florence Lindesay Robertson, novelist who wrote as Henry Handel Richardson, b. (d. 1946)
Lilian Irene Turner, novelist, b. (d. 1956)

Music, Dance

5 Feb. William Lyster opens his second opera company with performance in Melbourne.
During 1870
Opera attracts large audiences; many overseas artists appear.
Sydney Choral Society estb.

Births & Deaths
Alfred Francis Hill, opera composer, musician, b. (d. 1960)
Tom Leopold, ballet dancer, d.
Marie Nerelle, soprano, b. (d. 1941)

Drama, Theatre

Births & Deaths
Mark Last 'Morton' King, actor, probably d.
Charles Tait, concert manager, b. (d. 1933)

Fine Arts

10 Jan. Vic. Academy of Arts founded. Melbourne National Gallery School estb. with Eugène von Guérard as Master of painting.

Births & Deaths
J. Lawson Balfour, portrait and landscape painter, b. (d. 1966)
Lucien Dechaineux, artist, b. (d. 1957)
Clewin Simon Vernon Harcourt, portrait painter, b. (d. 1965)
Percival Charles Lindsay, landscape painter, b. (d. 1952)
William Mark, sculptor, gold and silver craftsman, b.
Claude Marquet, cartoonist, b. (d. 1920)
Ernest Moffitt, artist, among first to develop Art Nouveau style in Aust., b. (d. 1899)
Anthony Dattilo Rubbo, painter, b. (d. 1955)
Emma von Srtieglitz, Tas. artist, probably d.

1870

D
Religion, Learning

7 Sep. Industrial and Technical Museum opens in Melbourne. Includes Science Museum.
26 Oct. School of Mines opens in Ballarat, Vic. Among first technical institutions in Aust.
During 1870
Vic. Govt ends State aid to religion.
Qld Govt introduces free primary school education.
Toowoomba Grammar School opens in Qld.
Tas. Public Library estb.

Births & Deaths

Robert Brodribb Stewart Hammond, Church of England archdeacon, social reformer, b. (d. 1946)
George Cockburn Henderson, historian, b. (d. 1944)
Henry Frewen Le Fanu, Church of England Archbishop of Perth, b. (d. 1946)

E
Sport

During 1870
Nimblefoot, ridden by J. Day, wins Melbourne Cup in 3 minutes 37 seconds.
Woodchopping begins as competitive sport in Tas.

Births & Deaths

Joseph Darling, cricketer, b. (d. 1946)
Sydney Edward Gregory, cricketer noted batsman and cover point fielder, b. (d. 1929)
Lance Skuthorpe, buckjumper, athlete, bullock driver, b. (d. 1958)
Tommy Williams, lawn bowler, b. (d. 1935)

Historia Dignum

1870

Population

Estimated total white, 1,647,756.
Aust.-born population outnumbers immigrant population for first time.

8 Jan. Samuel Bennett publishes *Australian Town and Country Journal* in Sydney.
30 Jan.–20 Feb. Cyclone damages Townsville and Bowen, Qld.
26 Mar. Sydney–San Francisco mail steamer service begins.
26 Apr. Ship *Walter Hood* wrecked in Wreck Bay, NSW; 13 lives lost.
Jun. Ship *Harlech Castle* with 23 crew lost *en route* to Newcastle from Melbourne.
9 Aug. Melbourne Town Hall opens.
30 Aug. Intercolonial Exhibition opens in Sydney to celebrate centenary of Cook's discovery of eastern Aust.
24 Oct. First travelling post office estb., travelling by rail between Sydney and Goulburn.

During 1870
Viscount Canterbury gold nugget, weighing 1,114 ounces, discovered at Rheola, Vic.
Vic. wins intercolonial chess match against NSW. Match conducted by electric telegraph.
Harry Redford steals over 1,000 head of cattle from Bowen Downs station in Qld.
Widespread floods in NSW, Vic. and SE Qld.
Rainfall records begin in Darwin. (Alice Springs 1874.)

Births & Deaths

Montague MacGregor Grover, journalist, b. (d. 1943)
Helena Rubinstein, beautician, probably b. (d. 1965)

Communities

Ardrossan, SA, probably estb.
Foster, Vic., estb.
Georgetown, Qld, estb.
Gulgong, NSW, estb.
Katoomba, NSW, estb.
Millicent, SA, estb.
Proserpine, Qld, estb.
Tewantin, Qld, estb.
Tingha, NSW, estb.
Warracknabeal, Vic., estb.
Woombye, Qld, estb.
Yorketown, SA, estb.

1871

A
History, Politics, Economics, Law

Government

2 Jan. 1871–12 Aug. 1871, Sir Maurice Charles O'Connell administered Qld.
19 Jun. 1871–Jun. 1872, C. G. Duffy Premier Vic.
12 Aug. 1871–12 Nov. 1874, George Augustus Constantine Phipps, Marquess of Normanby, Governor Qld.
10 Nov. 1871–Jan. 1872, A. Blyth Premier SA.

17 Mar. John Ross explores Alice Springs area of NT.
9 Apr. HMAS *Cerberus*, warship, arrives in Melbourne from England to become Vic.'s principal naval ship.
Apr. Aust. Natives Association estb. in Melbourne as Friendly Society of Vic. Natives. Becomes powerful proponent of Federation.
25 May. Sydney Trades and Labour Council holds first meeting.
During May. John Moresby arrives in Aust. to police Act regulating blackbirding, the practice of importing cheap coloured labour (Kanakas) into Aust. from SW Pacific.
Jun. Free Trade League in WA protests against tariffs imposed on imported flour.
13 Jul. British Colonial Secretary objects to complex tariffs between Aust. colonies.
27 Sep. Delegations from NSW, Vic., SA and Tas. meet and object to imperial interference with their mutual fiscal arrangements.

During 1871
First permanent Aust. Military Force estb., in NSW.
Vic. Govt passes a No Liability Act to encourage investment by minimizing risk associated with goldmining speculation.
Annual eight-hour day celebrations begin in Sydney.
Qld produces peak 7,694,000 pounds (5,204 bales) of cotton. (Production declines rapidly after end of American Civil War brings American cotton back to world market.)
Castlemaine Brewery estb. in Qld.
Alexander Forrest explores large sections of WA, opening up pastoral land south-east of Perth and a route from north-western WA to the overland telegraph line in NT.
SA first colony to legalize marriage with deceased wife's sister. (Legalized in Vic. 1872, Tas. 1873, NSW 1875, WA and Qld 1877.)
Wool surpasses gold as top Aust. export earner.
Stockbrokers estb. a new Sydney Stock Exchange.
Arthur Orton, alias Thomas Castro, falsely claims to be Roger Tichborne, missing heir to a Hampshire baronetcy, in legal action lasting until Feb. 1872. In Mar. 1874 Orton sentenced to jail for perjury.

Births & Deaths

David Wynford Carnegie, WA desert explorer, administrator, b. (d. 1900)
Edward Rowland Huey Edkins, Qld pioneer pastoralist, b. (d. 1939)
John Simeon Colebrook Elkington, public health administrator, b. (d. 1955)
Vermont Hamersley, WA politician, b. (d. 1946)
William Arthur Holman, NSW Premier, b. (d. 1934)
Rosa Sibella Macarthur-Onslow, charity worker, b. (d. 1943)
Sir John Beverley Peden, lawyer, NSW politician, b. (d. 1946)
William Alexander Watt, Vic. Premier and acting Aust. Prime Minister, b. (d. 1946)
Eleanor Sophia Wood, Sydney University benefactor, b. (d. 1962)

B

Science, Technology, Transport, Discovery

10 Feb. Launceston–Deloraine railway line opens; first steam railway line in Tas.
9 Nov. British Telegraph Co. submarine cable reaches Darwin from Java. First telegram to Darwin from abroad sent on 20 Nov.
4 Dec. James Smith discovers tin at Mt Bischoff, Tas.
During 1871
First WA private timber railway line opens, in Lockville area.
Gold discovered at Gulgong, NSW.
Commercial tin mining begins at Inverell, NSW.
Marine Board of NSW estb. to administer ports.
W. Rutt presents aeronautical research papers.

Births & Deaths

Frank Bottril, inventor, b. (d. 1953)
John Anderson Gilruth, scientist, administrator, b. (d. 1937)
Lawrence Herschel Levi Harris, radiologist, X-ray pioneer, b. (d. 1920)
Frank Sandland Hone, physician, b. (d. 1951)
Sir Grafton Elliot Smith, anatomist and anthropologist, b. (d. 1937)

C

Arts

Literature

During 1871
Mrs Fortune, using the pseudonym W. W., publishes *The Detective's Album. Recollections of an Australian Police Officer*, first book of detective stories to appear in Aust.
James Brunton Stephens publishes the poem *Convict Once*.
Marcus Clarke publishes *Old Tales of a New Country*.
Cyrus Mason publishes *The Australian Christmas Story Book*, among first children's books illustrated in colour.

Births & Deaths

John Le Gay Brereton, poet, scholar, b. (d. 1933)
Louis Stone, novelist, playwright, b. (d. 1935)

Music, Dance

10 Apr. Signor Donato, 'the one legged dancer', makes Aust. début in Melbourne.
7 Jun. An Italian opera company opens Aust. tour in Melbourne.

Births & Deaths

Bessie Campbell, virtuoso banjo player, 'The Banjo Queen', b. (d. 1964)
Ada Jemima Crossley, oratorio singer, b. (d. 1929)
Ernest Hutcheson, pianist, composer, b. (d. 1951)

Drama, Theatre, Film

Births & Deaths

John Stanger Heiss Oscar Asche, actor-manager, b. (d. 1936)
John Henry Tait, theatrical entrepreneur, film producer, b. (d. 1955)
Hugh Joseph Ward, actor, dancer, b. (d. 1941)
Florence Young, actress, singer, b. (d. 1920)

Fine Arts

25 Apr. NSW Academy of Arts estb. to promote fine arts.
During 1871
Sydney Art Gallery founded. (Facilities built 1885.)

Births & Deaths

Myer Blashki, 'Miles Evergood', painter, b. (d. 1939)
Henry Harrison, black- and-white cartoonist, b. (d. 1949)
Lewis J. Harvey, pioneer art teacher, b. (d. 1948)

1871

1871

Mabel Hookey, painter, b. (d. 1953)
Sydney Long, painter, etcher, b. (d. 1955)
Edward Cairns Officer, landscape painter, b. (d. 1921)
James Peter Quinn, portrait painter, b. (d. 1951)
Percival Serle, art biographer, b. (d. 1951)

Architecture

During 1871
NSW Institute of Architects estb.

D Religion, Learning

Mar. First Synagogue in Adelaide opens.
4 Aug. WA Govt passes Elementary Education Act, estb. central education authority and compulsory primary education system.

During 1871
Andrew Fisher, 'Nunawading Messiah', declares himself the Messiah, successfully gaining about 100 disciples in Vic.
Rockhampton and Maryborough Grammar Schools open in Qld.
St Francis Xavier Catholic Secondary School estb. in Adelaide.
NSW and Vic. first to admit girls to public and university matriculation exams.
William Adam Dixon begins teaching chemistry at School of Arts in Sydney.

Births & Deaths

James Sykes Battye, librarian, WA historian, b. (d. 1954)
Frank William Boreham, Baptist clergyman, author, (d. 1959)
Sir James Duhig, Qld Roman Catholic Archbishop, 1917 b. (d. 1965)

E
Sport

During 1871
The Pearl, ridden by J. Cavanagh, wins Melbourne Cup in 3 minutes 39 seconds.
Brisbane Cup first run, at Eagle Farm.
Tas. Turf Club estb.
SA Cricket Association estb.
John Allen and Thomas Gale make hot air balloon ascents over Sydney.

Births & Deaths
Charles Cavill, swimmer, b. (d. 1897)
John Wren, sporting promoter and financier, b. (d. 1953)

F
Historia Dignum

Population
Estimated total white, 1,700,888.

8 Aug. Weld Club for men estb. in Perth.
13 Oct. Germans at Tanunda, SA, celebrate German victories in Franco-German War with the Great German Peace Festival.
During 1871
The newspaper *Northern Daily Leader* estb. in Tamworth, NSW.
Royal Society for the Prevention of Cruelty to Animals (RSPCA) launched in Melbourne.
SA Govt estb. first forestry policy in Aust. NSW Govt estb. first timber reserves.
c. 1871. World's first sheepdog trials held, at Forbes, NSW.

Births & Deaths
Eleanor Mackinnon, founder of Junior Red Cross Society in 1914, b. (d. 1936)

Communities
Cobar, NSW, estb.
Condamine, Qld, estb.
Edithburg, SA, estb.
Evans Head, NSW, estb.
Gladstone, SA, estb.
Jamestown, SA, estb.
Lorne, Vic., estb.
Natimuk, Vic., estb.
Pine Creek, NT, estb.
Port Broughton, SA, estb.
Waratah, Tas., estb.

1872

A History, Politics, Economics, Law

Government

22 Jan. 1872–Jul. 1873, Sir H. Ayers Premier SA.
23 Feb. 1872–2 Jun. 1872, Sir Alfred Stephen administered NSW.
14 May 1872–Feb. 1875, H. Parkes Premier NSW.
3 Jun. 1872–19 Mar. 1879, Sir Hercules George Robert Robinson Governor NSW.
10 Jun. 1872–Jul. 1874, J. G. Francis Premier Vic.
4 Nov. 1872–Aug. 1873, F. M. Innes Premier Tas.
7 Dec. 1872–8 Jun. 1873, Sir Richard Davies Hanson administered SA.
Feb. Union of Miners estb. at Sandhurst (Bendigo), Vic., to improve working conditions in goldmines.
13 Apr. First gold escort run from Etheridge goldfields, Qld, begins.
3 Jun. Qld National Bank opens.
12 Jun. Royal Mint opens in Melbourne.
15 Aug. Land S of Goyder's line of rainfall opened to sale.
Aug.–Nov. Ernest Giles leads expedition to investigate central Aust.
21 Sep. P. Egerton Warburton leaves Adelaide to begin east–west Aust. crossing.
Oct.–Nov. Prince Philip and Prince Augustus of Saxe-Coburg visit Aust.
During 1872
Premiers and Colonial Secretaries of all colonies meet in Sydney.
British Govt passes Pacific Islanders Protection Act (generally known as Kidnapping Act) to regulate the indenting of Kanaka labour.
Seamen's Union of Aust. estb.
Wentworth D'Arcy Uhr first to overland cattle from Charters Towers, Qld, to Darwin.
Charters Towers goldfield in Qld proclaimed.
Goldrush to Pine Creek, NT.
William Hann explores north Qld coastal region as far as fourteenth parallel.
W. W. Mills discovers the Alice Springs, NT. (Settlement named Stuart until 1933.)
Parkland for King's Park, Perth, dedicated for public use.
South British Insurance Co. Ltd. estb.
Northern Coal Sales Association, The Vend, estb. in NSW.

Births & Deaths

William Lygon, Earl of Beauchamp, NSW Governor, b. (d. 1901)
Donald Charles Cameron, Qld pioneer pastoralist, d.
Frank Arthur Cooper, Qld Premier, b. (d. 1949)
Ada Emily Evans, first woman law graduate in Aust., b. (d. 1947)
Sir John Gellibrand, soldier, administrator, b. (d. 1945)
Lyndhurst Falkiner Giblin, economist, b. (d, 1951)
Alexander Gore Arkwright Hore-Ruthven, Earl of Gowrie, SA and NSW Governor, Governor-General, b. (d. 1955)
John Barkell Holman, WA politician, b. (d. 1925)
James Milson, pioneer settler, Sydney yachtsman, d. (b. 1783)

B

Science, Technology, Transport, Discovery

12 Jan. Tin discovered at Tenterfield, NSW, and Stanthorpe, Qld.
During Jan. H. Mosman and G. E. Clarke discover gold at Charters Towers, Qld.
13 Mar. Institute for Deaf, Dumb and Blind opens in Sydney.
22 Aug. Adelaide to Port Darwin overland telegraph line completed. Submarine cable from Java to Port Darwin joined to overland telegraph line. First cable message from Sydney to London via Adelaide and Port Darwin sent on 22 Oct.
During 1872
James Harrison demonstrates process of making cheap ice at Melbourne Exhibition.
Frederick York Wolseley evolves first working model of successful shearing machine.
Boophilus microplus cattle tick introduced to Aust. from Java in Zebu cattle.
Gold discovered at Pine Creek, NT.
First recorded precious opal discovered, near Avadale, Qld.
Some English cattle introduce last case to date of foot-and-mouth disease in Aust.
Glass first made commercially in Melbourne.

Births & Deaths
Alfred James Ewart, botanist, b. (d. 1937)
Inigo Owen Jones, meteorologist, b. (d. 1954)
Roberta Henrietta Margaritta Jull, first woman doctor in Perth, b. (d. 1961)
Charles MacLaurin, physician, b. (d. 1925)
John Pomeroy, inventor explosive bullet, b. (d. 1950)
Edward Edgar Prescott, horticulturist, botanist, b. (d. 1954)
Herman Montague Rucker Rupp, orchard researcher, clergyman, b. (d. 1956)
George Augustine Taylor, inventor, aviation and radio pioneer, b. (d. 1928)

C

Arts

Literature

Births & Deaths
Arthur Henry Adams, journalist and author, b. (d. 1936)
Helena Mabel Checkley Forrest, author, b. (d. 1935)
John Shaw Neilson, 'the Keats of Australia', lyric poet, b. (d. 1942)
Bertram Stevens, literary and art critic, b. (d. 1922)
Ethel Sibyl Turner, novelist and children's writer, b. (d. 1958)

Music, Dance

24 Aug. Henry Hoyt's Prince of Wales Opera House opens in Melbourne.
During 1872
Simonsen Opera Co. first performs at Royal Victoria Theatre.

Drama, Theatre, Film

5 Nov. Coppin's new Theatre Royal in Melbourne opens. Old Theatre Royal gutted by fire on 20 Mar.

Fine Arts

During 1872
Art Union of Vic. estb. to assist impoverished artists. (Closes 1876.)
Port Adelaide Art Gallery estb. (Becomes nautical museum in 1932.)

Births & Deaths
Amy Bosworth, painter, b.
Joseph Luke Fleury, religious painter, b.
Douglas Fry, animal painter, b. (d. 1911)
Robert Edward Taylor Ghee, painter, b. (d. 1951)
Millicent Hambridge, watercolourist, portrait painter, b. (d. 1938)
Norman MacGeorge, painter, critic, b. (d. 1952)
Charles Nuttall, black-and-white artist, b. (probably d. 1934)
Bruce Robertson, painter, etcher, b.
Violet Helen Evangeline Teague, painter, murals designer, b. (d. 1951)
John William Tristram, painter, architect, b. (d. 1938)
Marie Tuck, portrait, figure painter, b. (d. 1947)
Joseph Wolinski, portrait painter, b.

1872

1872

D
Religion, Learning

2 Feb. Roman Catholic Cathedral opens in Armidale, NSW. Cathedral in Goulburn, NSW, opens 17 Nov.
Sep. Vic. Govt passes Secular Education Act; estb. first comprehensive system of State education in Aust., introducing compulsory primary education. Creates Dept of Education in Public Service. (Similar legislation passed in SA and Qld 1875, NSW 1880, Tas. 1885, WA 1893.)
3 Oct. General Synod of the Church of England estb. in Sydney.
During 1872
John Dunmore Lang appointed Moderator of Presbyterian Church.
Sacred Heart Catholic College opens in Maitland, NSW.
Marist Brothers' Catholic Teaching Order estb. in Sydney.

Births & Deaths
George Lyndon Carpenter, Salvation Army officer, b. (d. 1948)
Francis Xavier Gsell, First Roman Catholic Bishop of Darwin, 1938, b. (d. 1960)

E
Sport

During 1872
The Quack, ridden by W. Enderson, wins Melbourne Cup in 3 minutes 39 seconds.
Sydney Amateur Athletic Club estb. First Aust. athletic organization.
Sydney Amateur Sailing Club estb.
c. 1872. First intercolonial handball matches played.
First Organized golf in SA begins. (Adelaide Golf Club estb. in 1892.)

F
Historia Dignum

1872

Population
Estimated total white, 1,742,847.

25 Feb. Ship *Maria* wrecked off north Qld coast; 39 lives lost.
Apr. John Strachan estb. Good Templar Temperance Society in Tas.
6 May. Adelaide GPO opens. Brisbane GPO opens on 28 Sep.
3 Jul. *Sydney Morning Herald* receives first direct news cable from London.
1 Oct. The *Telegraph* estb. as broadsheet in Brisbane.
1 Oct. The *Standard* newspaper estb. in Warrnambool, Vic.
19 Oct. Bernard Otto Holtermann discovers mass of reef gold known as Holtermann's nugget, weighing 630 pounds, at Hill End, NSW.
Nov. River steamer *Providence* explodes on Darling R. near Kinchega, NSW; five lives lost.
During 1872
Grasshoppers devastate large areas of NSW and SA.
Severe earthquake shock at Braidwood, NSW.
Intercolonial Exhibition opens in Melbourne.
Young Women's Christian Association, (YWCA) first begins in Aust., at Geelong, Vic.

Communities
Aramac, Qld, estb.
Barrow Creek, NT, estb.
Charters Towers, Qld, estb.
Daly Waters, NT, estb.
Laura, SA, estb.
Murwillumbah, NSW, estb.
Rum Jungle, NT, estb.
Stanthorpe, Qld, estb.

A
History, Politics, Economics, Law

1873

Government
3 Mar. 1873–30 Jul. 1873, Sir George Ferguson Bowen administered Vic.
9 Jun. 1873–29 Jan. 1877, Sir Anthony Musgrave Governor SA.
22 Jul. 1873–Jun. 1875, A. Blyth, Premier SA.
30 Jul. 1873–22 Feb. 1879, Sir George Ferguson Bowen Governor Vic.
4 Aug. 1873–Jul. 1876, A. Kennerley Premier Tas.
1873, J. S. Millner Acting Govt Resident NT under SA jurisdiction.
1873–1876, G. B. Scott Govt Resident NT under SA jurisdiction.

15 Apr. Peter Egerton Warburton begins exploring country between Alice Springs and Roebourne, WA. Crosses western desert to overland telegraph line in NT. (Arrives Roebourne 26 Jan. 1874.)
23 Apr. William Christie Gosse begins unsuccessful expedition to estb. route from Alice Springs to Perth. Discovers Ayers Rock, NT, on 18 Jul.
28 Apr. Duke of Genoa visits Melbourne on board Italian war vessel.
Jun. Vic. Govt passes first Workrooms and Factories Act, regulating employment of females in factories and workrooms. (Factory Acts passed in NSW 1896, Qld 1896 and 1900, SA 1894 and 1900, WA 1904, Vic. again in 1896.)
4 Aug. Ernest Giles begins expedition from Alberga R. SA; travels 700 miles; discovers extensive pastoral country.
1 Sep. SA Govt introduces eight-hour working day.
19 Nov. Sir James Martin appointed NSW Chief Justice.

During 1873
Intercolonial Conference held in Sydney.
First NSW Divorce Act passed.
NSW becomes a free trade colony; Vic. remains protectionist as British Govt grants colonies right to impose intercolonial trade preferences.
Salmon fishing industry begins in Tas.
Melbourne Glass Bottle Works estb. Aust. Consolidated Industries Ltd.
Mort's Dock and Engineering Co. in Sydney is first Aust. company to engage in profit sharing.
Palmer R. goldfields, Qld, proclaimed.
Capt. John Moresby names Port Moresby in New Guinea.
Truganini is probably last full-blooded surviving Tas. Aboriginal.
Fremantle Chamber of Commerce estb. in WA.
Master Coachmakers' Association of Vic. estb.
Iron Trades Employers' Association estb. in NSW.

Chinese workers used to break miners' strike at Clunes, Vic., Riots follow.

Births & Deaths
Alexander Berry, merchant, d. (b. 1781)
Phillip Collier, WA Premier, b. (d. 1948)
John Saumarez Dumaresq, naval officer, inventor, designer, b. (d. 1922)

B

Science, Technology, Transport, Discovery

Jun. James Venture Mulligan discovers payable gold at Palmer R., Qld.
2 Aug. Adelaide–Glenelg, SA, railway opens.
19 Nov. Melbourne–Wodonga, Vic., railway line opens.

During 1873
James Harrison invents process of freezing meat; attempts unsuccessfully to ship to England.
Thomas Mort builds first meat chilling works, at Lithgow, NSW.
Microscopical Society of Vic. estb.
WA nationalizes all railways except Midlands Railway Co. Ltd.
David Ryan discovers brown coal at Morwell, Vic.

Births & Deaths
Henry James Burrell, naturalist, platypus authority, b. (d. 945)
Walter Reginald Hume, engineer, inventor, b. (d. 1943)
Sir George Alfred Julius, engineer, inventor, b. (d. 1946)
Sir Frederick Duncan McMaster, pastoralist noted for work on soil erosion prevention and pasture improvement, b. (d. 1954)
William Alexander Osborne, physician, b. (d. 1967)

C

Arts

Literature

During 1873
Edward William Cole opens first book arcade in Melbourne.

Births & Deaths
Matilda Ann Aston, author and teacher, b. (d. 1947)
Mary Theodora Joyce Wilcox, poet, b. (d. 1953)

Music, Dance

Births & Deaths
Fanny Osborne, dancer, d.
Henry Tate, musician, poet, b. (d. 1926)
Henri Verbrugghen, conductor, b. (d. 1934)

Drama, Theatre, Film

During 1873
Garnet Walch's *Laughing Jackass* pantomime produced.

Fine Arts

During 1873
Australian Sketcher magazine published.

Births & Deaths
Florence Turner Blake (née Greaves), painter, b. (d. 1959)
Gerald Fitzgerald, painter, b. (d. 1935)
Naylor Gill, bush life painter, b. (probably d. 1945)
Florence Thorne Lake, painter, b.
George Washington Thomas Lambert, sculptor, sketcher, painter, b. (d. 1930)
Harold Parker, sculptor, b. (d. 1962)
John Salvana, painter, b. (d. 1956)
Lawrence B. Taylor, artist, b.
Hal Thorpe (also known as John Hall), newspaper artist, b. (d. 1947)

1873

1873

D
Religion, Learning

16 Dec. Roger William Bede Vaughan, Roman Catholic prelate, arrives in Sydney.

During 1873
School of Mines opens in Bendigo, Vic.
Sydney Mechanics' School of Arts estb.
Sisters' of Mercy open Convent School at Toowoomba, Qld.

E
Sport

During 1873
Don Juan, ridden by W. Wilson, wins Melbourne Cup in 3 minutes 36 seconds.
Vic. Coursing Club estb. Determines regular coursing rules.
Essendon, Hawthorn and St Kilda Aust. Rules Football Clubs estb. in Melbourne.

Births & Deaths

Montague Alfred Noble, cricketer, all-rounder, b. (d. 1940)
Albert Edwin Trott, cricketer, noted batsman, b. (d. 1914)

F
Historia Dignum

1873

Population
Estimated total white, 1,794,520.

29 Jan. Fire destroys nine shops in George St, Sydney.
3 Apr. Sir Hercules Robinson opens Intercolonial Exhibition in Sydney.
Spanish ship deliberately rams the *Northfleet* vessel *en route* from London to Hobart claiming 300 lives.
28 Apr. First Aust. mustard factory estb., in SA.
7 Nov. *Northern Territory Times* published; first NT newspaper.
Dec. *Sun Foe* becomes first mail steamer to pass through Torres Strait.
During 1873
Cutty Sark, clipper, begins carrying wool to England and coal to Asia. (Until 1895.)
Ostriches imported to SA for plumes to decorate women's clothing.
SA Govt introduces first Aust. re-afforestation program.

Births & Deaths
Robert Samuel Ross, socialist journalist, b. (d. 1931)

Communities
Beaudesert, Qld, estb.
Birdsville, Qld, estb.
Cooktown, Qld, estb.
Ingham, Qld, estb.
Minlaton, SA, estb.
Mundaring, WA, estb.

1874

A History, Politics, Economics, Law

Government

8 Jan. 1874–Jun. 1876, A. Macalister Premier Qld.
31 Jul. 1874–Aug. 1875, G. B. Kerferd Premier Vic.
12 Nov. 1874–23 Jan. 1875, Sir Maurice Charles O'Connell administered Qld.
30 Nov. 1874–13 Jan. 1875, Sir Francis Smith administered Tas.

6 Feb. NSW Govt introduces triennial Parlts.
18 Mar. John and Alexander Forrest begin expedition from Perth to Adelaide via Geraldton and Peak Hill, WA. Arrive in Adelaide 3 Nov., becoming first to cross through centre of Aust. from west to east through the Gibson Desert.
2 Apr. Some 2,300 miners at Moonta copper mines in SA strike for over a week when management announces reduction in wages.
Jun. Angus Cameron becomes first Labor member of Parlt in NSW.
William Guthrie Spence estb. Amalgamated Miners' Union at Sandhurst (Bendigo), Vic.
10 Oct. NSW Govt formally accepts sovereignty of Fiji Islands.
6 Nov. SA Govt opens all land below lat. 26°S to selection.

During 1874
Intercolonial Conference held in Sydney.
Sir Henry Parkes unsuccessfully proposes to estb. a British colony in New Guinea.
Vic. Govt includes eight-hour day clauses in all govt contracts.
NSW coalminers receive ten-hour working day.
John Lewis crosses from east of telegraph line, NT, tracing Cooper Creek to Lake Eyre, SA.
Maloga Mission estb. in NSW for surviving NSW Aborigines.
NSW first exports wool to Japan.
Brisbane Permanent Benefit and Investment Society estb. (Becomes Bank of Qld Ltd in 1970.)
The United Tradesmen's Society estb. in SA.

Births & Deaths

John Lawrence Baird, Viscount Stonehaven, Governor-General, b. (d. 1941)
Sir Thomas Rainsford Bavin, NSW Premier and judge, b. (d. 1941)
Thomas Denman, Baron Denman, Governor-General, b. (d. 1954)
Otway Rothwell Falkiner, NSW pastoralist, b. (d. 1961)
Sir Norman William Kater, NSW politician, grazier, businessman, doctor, b. (d. 1965)
Sir Walter Massy-Greene, Federal politician, WA businessman, b. (d. 1952)
Harry Lyon Moss, financier, investor, b. (d. 1960)
Sir Ernest Henry Shackleton, Antarctic explorer, b. (d. 1922)
Crawford Vaughan, SA Premier, b. (d. 1947)

B

Science, Technology, Transport, Discovery

22 Nov. First sod of first WA Govt railway turned.
9 Dec. Transit of Venus observed from Sydney Observatory.

During 1874
Adelaide Observatory estb.
Linnean Society of NSW estb.
Louis Brennan invents a torpedo.
David Browne invents renewable blades for sheep shears.
Robert Scott opens Aust. Explosives and Chemical Co. in Sydney to manufacture explosives for deep quartz goldmining.

Births & Deaths

Sir Charles Bickerton Blackburn, physician, b. (d. 1972)
Abercrombie Anstruther Lawson, botanist, b. (d. 1927)
Sir Robert Blakeway Wade, surgeon, b. (d. 1954)

C

Arts

Literature

During 1874
Marcus Clarke publishes *His Natural Life* in book form. (After Clarke's death title changed to *For the Term of His Natural Life*.)

Births & Deaths

John Henry Macartney Abbot, author, b. (d. 1953)
Sir Frank Ignatius Fox, author and journalist, b. (d. 1960)
Edith Joan Lyttleton, novelist who wrote under pseudonym G. B. Lancaster, b. (d. 1945)
Marie Louise Mack, author, journalist, b. (d. 1935)
Sir Walter Logie Forbes Murdoch, among first major Aust. essayists, b. (d. 1970)

Music, Dance

Births & Deaths

Joseph Chambers, dancer, d. (b. 1837)
Fritz Bennicke Hart, composer, b. (d. 1949)
Lalla Miranda, soprano, b. (d. 1940)
Alberto Zelman, violinist, conductor, b. (d. 1927)

Drama, Theatre, Film

Apr. Morton Tavares opens Qld Theatre in Brisbane.
1 Aug. J. C. Williamson and Maggie Moore open at Coppin's Theatre Royal in Melbourne with *Struck Oil*.

Births & Deaths

Gregan McMahon, actor, producer, b. (d. 1941)

Fine Arts

Births & Deaths

Walter Armiger Bowring, illustrator and portrait painter, b. (d. 1931)
Joseph Thomas Connor, watercolourist, b. (d. 1954)
Charles Hamilton, art critic, b. (d. 1967)
Arthur James Hingston, painter and cartoonist, b. (d. 1912)
Sir Lionel Arthur Lindsay, graphic artist, b. (d. 1961)
Francis John McComas, painter, b. (d. 1938)
Matthew James MacNally, watercolourist, b. (d. 1943)
Ashton Murphy, black-and-white artist, b.
Albert A. Pedvin, painter, b. (d. 1900)
Alfred Vincent, newspaper artist, b. (d. 1915)

1874

1874

Architecture

15 Jun. First Victoria Bridge opens in Brisbane; first permanent bridge in Brisbane.

Births & Deaths

Harry John Weston, architect, cartoonist, b.

D

Religion, Learning

5 Feb. Bishop Short consecrates St David's Church of England Cathedral in Hobart.

4 May. James Alipius Goold becomes first Catholic Archbishop of Melbourne.

17 May. St Stephen's Catholic Cathedral opens in Brisbane.

Oct. Church of England Defence Association estb. to oppose a national education system.

Sep. James Greenwood of Baptist Church estb. NSW Public School League to promote national education system.

During 1874

Scots Church in Melbourne completed.

Sisters of Mercy open convent school at Warwick, Qld.

University of Melbourne becomes first Aust. university to admit women.

William Wilkins recommends that teachers be examined and classified and that school inspectors be appointed in NSW.

Presbytery of VDL becomes the Presbyterian Church of Tas.

E
Sport

During 1874
Haricot, ridden by P. Piggott, wins Melbourne Cup in 3 minutes 37½ seconds.
Tas. Horse Racing Club estb. Hobart.
Southern Rugby Union Football, first Aust. Rugby Union control board, estb. in Sydney. (Becomes NSW Rugby Union in 1892.)
South Melbourne and North Melbourne Victorian Football League Clubs estb.
William Miller becomes first Aust. wrestling star.
Lacrosse first played in Aust.
First women's cricket match played, at Bendigo, Vic. (Women's cricket estb. in Sydney in 1886.)
Derwent Sailing Boat Club estb. in Hobart. (Disbanded in 1886, re-established in 1910 as Royal Yacht Club of Tas.)
First Aust. woodchopping contests held in Tas. (First tournament 1891.)

Births & Deaths
Edwin Flack, athlete, b. (d. 1935)

F
Historia Dignum

1874

Population
Estimated total white, 1,849,392.

23 May. Ship *British Admiral* wrecked off King I.; 79 lives lost.
1 Sep. New General Post Office building in Sydney opens.
18 Nov. Ship *Cospatrick* burns *en route* from London to NZ; 475 lives lost.
During Nov. Measles epidemic in Vic. Vic. Govt requires all children to be vaccinated against smallpox within six months of birth.
23 Dec. Fire destroys 45 houses at Windsor, NSW.
During 1874
Royal Humane Society of Australasia estb. in Melbourne. (Becomes Vic. Humane Society in 1882.)

Communities
Tatura, Vic., estb.

1875

A
History, Politics, Economics, Law

Government
4 Jan. 1875–10 Jan. 1875, E. D. Harvest administered WA.
11 Jan. 1875–6 Sep. 1877, William Cleaver Francis Robinson Governor WA.
13 Jan. 1875–5 Apr. 1880, Frederick Aloysius Weld Governor Tas.
23 Jan. 1875–14 Mar. 1877, William Wellington Cairns Governor Qld.
9 Feb. 1875–Mar. 1877, J. Robertson Premier NSW.
3 Jun. 1875–Jun. 1876, J. P. Boucaut Premier SA.
7 Aug. 1875–Oct. 1875, G. Berry Premier Vic.
20 Oct. 1875–May 1877, Sir J. McCulloch Premier Vic.

26 Feb. SA Govt holds one of first plebiscites in Aust., on routing of suburban railways in Adelaide.
6 May. Ernest Giles begins expedition from Beltana, SA, through Aust. interior to Perth, arriving on 10 Nov. Discovers Gibson Desert and crosses Nullarbor Plain.
28 Nov. First Aust.-made champagne exhibited in Sydney.
During 1875
Western Pacific High Commission estb. to control British subjects in the Western Pacific.
Qld Govt introduces £10 poll tax on Chinese entering the colony.
First ostrich farm in Aust. estb. near Swan Hill, Vic.
William Oswald Hodgkinson explores head of Cloncurry and Leichhardt rivers, Qld; follows Diamentina R. into SA, connecting with Lake Eyre.
Wool first exported to China.
Melbourne building unions estb. the Associated Building Trades.
Vic. Master Builders' Association estb.

Births & Deaths
Sir John Lavington Bonython, company director, b. (d. 1960)
William Henry Donald, China expert, journalist, b. (d. 1946)
Sir Frederick William Eggleston, diplomat, author, b. (d. 1954)
William Hilton Hovell, explorer, d. (b. 1786)
Sir Harry Sutherland Wightman Lawson, solicitor, politician, company director, b. (d. 1952)
George Macleay Macarthur-Onslow, soldier, NSW pastoralist, b. (d. 1931)
Sir Charles Rosenthal, soldier, administrator and architect, b. (d. 1954)
James Robert Tyrrell, bookseller, publisher, author, b. (d. 1961)

B
Science, Technology, Transport, Discovery

16 Dec. Eskbank iron works estb. at Lithgow, NSW beginning rapid development of Aust. iron and steel industry.
During 1875
Hobart Hospital estb. nursing school.
First large-scale discovery of silver-lead ore, at Thackaringa Station, near Broken Hill, NSW.
Construction of iron bridge across Murray R. begins. (Completed 1878.)
Royal National Agricultural and Industrial Association of Qld estb.
Adelaide Steamship Co. estb. Begins regular Adelaide–Melbourne steamship service.

Births & Deaths
Sir Harold Winthrop Clapp, railway engineer, transport authority, b. (d. 1952)
Sir Colin Fraser, metallurgist, company director, b. (d. 1944)
Walter Rosenhain, glass and metals physicist, b. (d. 1934)
Carl Adolph von de Heyde Sussmilch, geologist, educationist, b. (d. 1946)
Georgina Sweet, scientist, social worker benefactor, (d. 1946)
Hubert Edwin Whitfeld, mining engineer, b. (d. 1939)
John Cadell Windeyer, obstetrician, gynaecologist, b. (d. 1951)

C

Arts

1875

Literature

Births & Deaths
William Gosse Hay, novelist, b. (d. 1945)

Drama, Theatre, Film

11 Dec. New Theatre Royal in Sydney opens on site of burnt-out Prince of Wales Theatre.
During 1875
Adelaide Ristori, tragic actress from Italy, visits Aust.

Births & Deaths
David Burn, among first playwrights in Aust., d. (probably b. 1799)
Sir Benjamin John Fuller, theatrical entrepreneur, b. (d. 1952)

Fine Arts

24 May. Public Library opens Picture Gallery in Melbourne.
During 1875
Aust. art sent to Intercolonial Exhibition in Philadelphia, USA.
SA Institute starts SA National Art collection.
Chevalier Jules Lefebvre paints *Chloe* in Paris.
NSW Govt estb. Art Gallery in Sydney.
Achille Simonetti becomes first instructor of modelling for sculpture at NSW Academy Of Arts in Sydney.
William Ford paints *Picnic Party at Hanging Rock near Mount Macedon*.
c. 1875. Edward Carlton Booth publishes two art volumes entitled *Australia*.

Births & Deaths
Norman St Clair Carter, portrait painter, b. (d. 1963)
Gordon Coutts, painter, b. (d. 1937)
William Paul Dowling, convict engraver, d.
James Ferries, painter, b. (d. 1951)
Joseph Christian Goodhart, etcher, b. (d. 1954)
Samuel Jackson, cycloramic artist, Melbourne's first practising architect, d.
Duncan Max Meldrum, portrait painter who developed theory of naturalism based on tone, b. (d. 1955)
Ada May Plante, lyrical landscape painter, b. (d. 1950)
Margaret Rose Preston, née McPherson, post-impressionist landscape painter, b. (d. 1963)
Ernest Short, art writer, b. (d. 1959)

Architecture

During 1875
Edmund William Wright and Lloyd Taylor design ANZ Bank in Adelaide.
Horbury Hunt, architect, designs Church of England Cathedral in Armidale, NSW.

1875

D
Religion, Learning

Feb. Presbyterian Ladies College opens in Melbourne; first academic college for girls in Aust.

9 Nov. Sydney Orangemen and other Protestants hold a 10,000-strong march 'defending Protestant faith'.

15 Dec. Matthew B. Hale becomes Church of England Bishop of Brisbane.

During 1875
SA secular primary education system made compulsory.
Qld free education system becomes secular and falls under ministerial control.
St Patrick's Catholic College opens in Goulburn, NSW.
St Joseph's Catholic College founded in Brisbane.
St Stephen's Catholic Secondary School for boys founded in Brisbane.
Girls admitted to Brisbane Grammar School.
Mining and Geological Museum estb. in Sydney.

Births & Deaths
Charles Henry Bertie, historian, author, b. (d. 1952)
George Merrick Long, Church of England bishop, educationist, b. (d. 1930)

E
Sport

During 1875
Wollomai, ridden by R. Batty, wins Melbourne Cup in 3 minutes 38 seconds.
Vic. Amateur Turf Club estb.
Hobart Cup (horseracing) first run.
First recorded game of polo played in Melbourne.
Aust. Rules football estb. in Tas.

Births & Deaths
Percy Cavill, swimmer, b. (d. 1940)
James Scott, golfer, b. (d. 1901)

F
Historia Dignum

1875

Population
Estimated total white, 1,898,223.

24 Feb. Steamer *Gothenburg* wrecked on Great Barrier Reef; 102 lives lost.
6 Apr. Intercolonial Exhibition opens in Sydney.
1 May. The *Echo* newspaper first published in Sydney.
1 Jul. Sydney Town Hall opens.
2 Sep. Exhibition in Melbourne opens, previewing items for the Philadelphia Exhibition in USA.
24 Dec. Storm destroys pearling fleet in Exmouth Gulf, WA, claiming 59 lives.
Dec. First Aust. postcard issued, in Sydney.
During 1875
Ship *Strathmore* wrecked while carrying emigrants from London; 362 lives lost.
Severe drought begins in eastern Aust.
Widespread floods on NSW coast.
The Aust. Health Society founded in Melbourne.
NSW Fresh Food and Ice Co. estb. (Delivers first milk from Bowral, NSW, to Sydney in 1876.)

Communities
Crow's Nest, Qld, estb.
Numurkah, Vic., estb.
Terowie, SA, probably estb.

1876

A
History, Politics, Economics, Law

Government
5 Jun. 1876–Mar. 1877, G. Thorn Premier Qld.
6 Jun. 1876–Oct. 1877, J. Colton Premier SA.
20 Jul. 1876–Aug. 1877, T. Reibey Premier Tas.
1876–1833, E. W. Price Govt Resident NT under SA jurisdiction.

13 Jan. Ernest Giles begins return journey to SA from Perth, becoming first European to cross western half of Aust. in both directions.
During 1876
SA Govt first to legalize Trade Unions. SA Trade Union Act provides for registration of trade unions and protection of funds.
NSW Govt grants legislative protection to Trade Unions.
NSW Coal Mines Act regulates hours of work for youths, and forbids employment in mines of children under 13 years of age.
Coniferous timber planting begins in Aust. Radiata pines first planted in SA.
West End Brewery estb. in Adelaide.

Births & Deaths
Sir Charles Frederic Belcher, jurist, ornithologist, b. (d. 1970)
George Alan Bond, manufacturer, b. (d. 1950)
Hermann Paul Leopold Buring, vigneron, b. (d. 1961)
Dame 'Annie' Florence Gillies Cardell-Oliver, first woman in Aust. to become member of Cabinet, b. (d. 1965)
Martin Richard 'Mark' Freney, prospector, adventurer, b. (d. 1963)
Sir Philip Woolcott Game, NSW Governor, b. (d. 1961)
Sir Thomas William Glasgow, Qld politician, b. (d. 1955)
Sir Samuel Hordern, businessman, b. (d. 1956)
John Thomas Lang, politician, NSW Premier, 'The Big Fellow', b. (d. 1975)
Hugh Donald McIntosh, theatre, sport and business entrepreneur, b. (d. 1942)
Eugene Patrick O'Neill, trade union leader, b. (d. 1953)
William Sydney Robinson, industrialist, b. (d. 1963)
Thomas Joseph Ryan, Qld Premier, b. (d. 1921)
John Scaddan, WA Premier, b. (d. 1934)
James Henry Scullin, Labor Prime Minister, b. (d. 1953)
Albert Edgar Solomon, Tas. Premier, b. (d. 1914)
Sir Cyril Brudenell Bingham White, first Aust. General, b. (d. 1940)
Jeanne Forster Young, welfare worker, social reformer, b. (d. 1955)

B
Science, Technology, Transport, Discovery

20 Feb. First message sent on newly completed Sydney to Wellington, NZ, submarine telegraphic cable.
Mar. Hobart–Evandale railway line opens in Tas.
4 Apr. Great Western Railway from Sydney reaches Bathurst, NSW, completing link across the Blue Mts.
Jun. Robert Bowyer Smith invents stumpjump plough, made to leap over objects in ground. First exhibited on 9 Nov.
5 Jul. Railway line from Ipswich, Qld, to Brisbane opens.
Deniliquin–Moama railway line in NSW opens Riverina district.
During 1876
First coke manufactured in Wollongong, NSW.
Eugene Nicolle experiments with refrigeration device based on liquefaction of ammonia gases.
Joseph Bancroft discovers filarial parasite which causes the condition elephantiasis. Among first medical researches of world importance conducted in Aust.
George Lansell introduces diamond drill for deep lead-mining.
First steel rolling mills begin, at Lithgow, NSW.
Tas. Govt takes over privately owned Hobart–Launceston railway line.

Births & Deaths
Charles Anderson, mineralogist, b. (d. 1944)
Louis Charles Bernacchi, scientist and Antarctic explorer, b. (d. 1942)
Sir Thomas Peel Dunhill, surgeon, b. (d. 1957)
Gregory Macalister Mathews, ornithologist, artist, b. (d. 1949)
Sir Alfred Edward Rowden White, physician, b. (d. 1963)
Walter George Woolnough, geologist, b. (d. 1958)

C
Arts

Literature

During 1876
Cole's Funny Picture book published.

Births & Deaths
Clarence Michael James (C. J.) Dennis, author, poet, 'The Laureate of the Larrikin', b. (d. 1938)
Winifred Llewellyn James, author, b. (d. 1941)
William (Will) Lawson, poet, author, b. (d. 1957)
Hugh Raymond McCrae, poet, artist, b. (d. 1958)
Sir Archibald Thomas Strong, poet and scholar, b. (d. 1930)

Music, Dance

18 Nov. Emila Pasta and Alfredo Borzini, dancers, make début in Sydney.
During 1876
First Italian opera season opens at Theatre Royal in Sydney.

Births & Deaths
Florrie Forde, vaudeville singer, b. (d. 1940)
Horace Ernest Stevens, opera singer, b. (d. 1950)

Drama, Theatre, Film

5 Nov. Academy of Music Theatre opens in Melbourne. (Becomes Bijou Theatre in 1880)
During 1876
Scott Siddons, actress, tours Aust.
Bland Holt, 'King of Melodrama', makes first Aust. professional appearance in Sydney.

Births & Deaths
James Nevin Tait, theatrical entrepreneur, b. (d. 1961)

Fine Arts

Births & Deaths
Alice Marion Ellen Bale, oil painter, b. (d. 1955)
Ethel Barnes, painter, b. (d. 1980)
Victor Emanuel Cobb, etcher, b. (d. 1945)
Ambrose Dyson, cartoonist, illustrator, b. (d. 1913)
Ethel Carrick Fox, painter, probably b. (d. 1952)
Herbert Samuel Gilkes, keeper of prints, b. (probably d. 1952)
William Gregory Grant, painter, b. (d. 1951)
Laurence Hotham Howie, painter and sculptor, b. (d. 1963)
Richard Haley Lever, painter, b. (d. 1958)
Benjamin Sheppard, sculptor, b. (d. 1910)

Architecture

During 1876
James Barnet, architect, designs Lands Department Building in Sydney.

Births and Deaths
Walter Burley Griffin, architect, b. (d. 1937)

1876

1876

D
Religion, Learning

25 Apr. University of Adelaide opens.
Jun. Adelaide Teacher Training College opens.

Births & Deaths

James Noble, Aboriginal Church of England preacher, b. (d. 1941)
Frederick William Norwood, Congregational clergyman, b. (d. 1958)

E
Sport

27 Jun. Edward Trickett becomes world's first sculling champion and first Aust. to win a world championship in any sport.
During 1876
Briseis, ridden by P. St Albans, wins Melbourne Cup in 3 minutes $36\frac{1}{2}$ seconds.
Coursing estb. in NSW.
First Intercolonial School sporting competitions held between Sydney and Melbourne.
Qld Cricket Association estb.

Births & Deaths

William Tindall, 'Betting Billy Tindall', jockey, punter, b. (d. 1953)

F
Historia Dignum

1876

Population
Estimated total white, 1,958,679.

Feb. Cyclone sweeps through Bowen, Qld.
21 Mar. Steamship *Banshee* wrecked at Cape Sandwich Qld; 17 lives lost.
17 Apr. Six Fenian (Irish Republican Brotherhood) convicts escape from WA in American whaling ship *Catalpa*.
20 May. Vic. Humane Society estb.
Jul. Barque *Giltwood* wrecked near Rivoli Bay, SA; 27 lives lost.
6 Aug. Two constables accidently shoot Rev William Healy, Catholic priest, mistaking him for a bushranger.
12 Aug. The ship *Great Queensland* disappears *en route* to Melbourne from London; 70 lives lost.
20 Aug. Intercolonial Exhibition opens in Qld.
10 Sep. The Ship *Dandenong* founders near Jervis Bay, NSW, claiming 40 lives.
2 Dec. Grace Bussel rescues crew and 48 passengers of coastal steamer wrecked off WA coast.

During 1876
Newspaper *North Queensland Register* published in Townsville, Qld.
Biggest picnic racing Carnival in Aust. begins at Onkaparinga, SA; thenceforth held annually.
The Italian bee introduced into Aust.
Rainfall records begin in Perth.

Communities
Boulia, Qld, estb.
Cairns, Qld, estb.
Cloncurry, Qld, estb.
Jeparit, Vic., estb.
Kilcoy, Qld, estb.
Port Douglas, Qld, estb.
Werris Creek, NSW, estb.
Winton, Qld, estb.

1877

A
History, Politics, Economics, Law

Government
29 Jan. 1877–24 Mar. 1877, S. J. Way administered SA.
8 Mar. 1877–Jan. 1879, J. Douglas Premier Qld.
14 Mar. 1877–10 Apr. 1877, Sir Maurice Charles O'Connell administered Qld.
22 Mar. 1877–Aug. 1877, H. Parkes Premier NSW.
24 Mar. 1877–17 May 1877, Sir W. W. Cairns administered SA.
11 Apr. 1877–20 Jul. 1877, Sir Arthur Edward Kennedy administered Qld.
17 May 1877–2 Oct. 1877, S. J. Way administered SA.
21 May 1877–Mar. 1880, G. Berry Premier Vic.
20 Jul. 1877–2 May 1883, Sir Arthur Edward Kennedy Governor Qld.
9 Aug. 1877–Mar. 1878, P. O. Fysh Premier Tas.
17 Aug. 1877–Dec. 1877, Sir J. Robertson Premier NSW.
7 Sep. 1877–11 Nov. 1877, E. D. Harvest administered WA.
2 Oct. 1877–9 Jan. 1883, Sir William Francis Drummond Jervois Governor SA.
26 Oct. 1877–Sept. 1878, J. P. Boucaut Premier SA.
12 Nov. 1877–29 Jan. 1878, Sir Harry St George Ord Lieut-Governor WA.
18 Dec. 1877–Dec. 1878, J. S. Farnell Premier NSW.

May. Last convicts removed from Port Arthur to Hobart jail. Port Arthur closed.
16 Aug. Vote by secret ballot approved for WA Legislative Council.

During 1877
Sir William Jervois and Peter H. Scratchley arrive in Aust. to report on system of defence.
Somerset settlement at Port Albany, Qld, transferred to Thursday I.
Qld Govt passes Chinese Restriction Act to prevent Chinese working on goldfields.
Sir Samuel Wilson introduces Californian salmon to Vic.
Vic. Govt imposes land taxes and charges heavy duty on livestock shipped on Murray R.
Vic. Chamber of Manufactures estb.

Births & Deaths
Macartney Abbott, NSW politician, b. (d. 1960)
Sir Henry Newman Barwell, SA Premier, b. (d. 1959)
Edmund Albert Brooks, SA and WA pastoralist, b. (d. 1964)
Sir Winston Joseph Dugan, SA and Vic. Governor, b. (d. 1951)
John Frost, Chartist, d. (b. 1784)
Sir George Francis Hyde, naval officer, b. (d. 1937)
Sir John Greig Latham, Chief Justice, b. (d. 1964)
Sir Henry Edward Manning, NSW politician, b. (d. 1963)
Arnold Wienholt, Qld pastoralist, politician, b. (probably d. 1941)

B

Science, Technology, Transport, Discovery

19 Feb. Registration of stumpjump plough patent in SA.
Feb. NSW estb. first daily weather charts, incorporating meteorological information from each colony.
28 Mar. Robert Savage and Frederick York Wolseley patent wool shearing machines.
8 Nov. Henry King first detects phylloxera insect at Geelong, Vic.
1 Dec. Adelaide–Perth telegraph line opens. Perth linked to London on 8 Dec.

During 1877
Melbourne Harbour Trust appointed to deepen Yarra R., Melbourne.
Messrs Anderson & Co. estb. Orient Steam Navigation Co.; significant in development of steam communication.
NSW Govt abolishes road tolls.
First stages of Gippsland railway line, Vic., open.
SA first to join International Telegraph Union. (Now International Telecommunication Union.)
William Branwhite Clarke awarded Murchison Medal of Geological Society of London for identifying Permian stratigraphy of NSW coal deposits.

Births & Deaths
R. S. Falkiner, inventor, b.
Sir William Colin MacKenzie, anatomist, b. (d. 1938).
David George Stead, naturalist, b. (d. 1957).
Gustavus Athol Waterhouse, entomologist, b. (d. 1950).

C

Arts

Literature

During 1877
Marcus Clarke publishes *Four Stories High*.
James Brunton Stephen publishes poem 'The Dominion of Australia'.

Births & Deaths
Amy Eleanor Mack, author, journalist, probably b. (d. 1939).
Mary Elizabeth Osborn, author, b. (d. 1971).
Mary Louisa Skinner, usually known as Mollie Skinner, author, nurse, b. (d. 1955).

Music, Dance

During 1877
Sydney Musical Union estb.

Births & Deaths
Alfred Ernest Floyd, musician, b. (d. 1974).

Drama, Theatre, Film

Births & Deaths
Arthur Tauchert, film actor, b. (d. 1933).

Fine Arts

Births & Deaths
Julian Howard Ashton, landscape painter, b. (d. 1964).
Henry Glede Garlick, animal painter, b. (d. 1910).
Hans Heysen, watercolourist, landscape painter, b. (d. 1968).
Ambrose McCarthy Patterson, portrait, landscape painter, b. (d. 1967).
Emily Harriet Pelloe, botanical artist, b. (d. 1941).
Hugh Ramsay, oil portrait painter, b. (d. 1906).
Isabel Hunter Tweddle, portrait, landscape, flower painter, b. (d. 1945).
Victor Zelman, landscape painter, b. (d. 1960).

Architecture

During 1877
M. McMullen designs terrace house precinct in North Terrace, Adelaide.

1877

1877

D
Religion, Learning

16 Mar. Roger W. B. Vaughan becomes Catholic Archbishop of Sydney.
8 Jun. W. F. Schwartz and A. H. Kempe estb. Hermannsburg Lutheran mission near Alice Springs, NT.
During 1877
The New Synagogue opens in Melbourne.
St Columba's Convent School opens in Dalby, Qld.

Births & Deaths
William Herber Ifould, librarian, b. (d. 1969)
Sir Walter Ramsay McNicoll, educationist, b. (d. 1947)

E
Sport

15–17 Mar. First cricket Test match held between England and Aust., in Melbourne.
During 1877
Chester, ridden by P. Piggott, wins Melbourne Cup in 3 minutes $33\frac{1}{2}$ seconds.
Jem Mace King opens Boxing Academy in Sydney.
Vic. Football Association estb. to administer Aust. Rules football.
Vic. Rowing Association estb.
Wimbledon tennis championships begin.

Births & Deaths
Sir Norman Everard Brookes, tennis player, b. (d. 1968)
Arthur Cavill, swimmer credited with popularizing Australian Crawl swimming stroke, b. (d. 1947)
Clement Hill, cricketer, noted left-handed batsman, b. (d. 1945)
Freddy Lane, swimmer, b. (d. 1969)
Victor Thomas Trumper, cricketer, noted batsman, b. (d. 1915)

F

Historia Dignum

1877

Population
Estimated total white, 2,031,130.

28 Feb. *Figaro* journal printed in SA. (Until 15 Dec.)
Apr. W. L'Estrange walks across tight rope 340 feet above Middle Harbour in Sydney.
11 May. Unusual tidal disturbances on E coast of Aust.
During 1877
Freemasons Grand Lodge of NSW estb. (Tas. 1875, Vic. 1883, SA 1884, WA 1900, WA 1904.)
Scottish Highland Society of NSW estb.
Severe drought in Qld, WA and western Vic. retards pastoral progress.

Births & Deaths
Joseph Forbes, 'Timor Joe', seaman, d.

Communities
Drouin, Vic., estb.
Hughenden, Qld, estb.
Lockhart, NSW, estb.
Miles, Qld, estb.
Mossman, Qld, estb.
Thursday I., Qld, estb.

1878

A
History, Politics, Economics, Law

Government
30 Jan. 1878–9 Apr. 1880, Sir Harry St George Ord Governor WA.
5 Mar. 1878–Dec. 1878, W. R. Giblin Premier Tas.
27 Sep. 1878–Jun. 1881, W. Morgan Premier SA.
20 Dec. 1878–Oct. 1879, W. L. Crowther Premier Tas.
21 Dec. 1878–Jan. 1883, Sir H. Parkes Premier NSW.

9 Jan. 'Black Wednesday'. Vic. Premier Graham Berry dismisses more than 200 public servants after Legislative Assembly rejects Appropriation Bill, leaving no money legally available for payment of salaries. On **28 Mar.** Legislative Council passes a Payment of Members Bill, re-appointing sacked public servants.
Jul. Stephen Henry Parker estb. Reform League in WA to fight for responsible government.
26 Oct. Ned Kelly shoots and kills three police at Stringybark Creek, Vic.
18 Nov. Seamen in Vic., NSW and Qld strike against number of Chinese employed on coastal vessels.
Dec. Graham Berry and Professor C. H. Pearson take 'Victorian Embassy' to London in effort to get British Govt to legislate in disputes between Vic. Legislative Assembly and Legislative Council.

During 1878
Nathaniel Buchanan blazes trail for world's longest stock route, from Aramac, Qld, to Daly R., NT.
Steamship Owners' Association of Aust. estb.
The SA Conspiracy Act outlaws strikes as a breach of contract.
Judicature system estb. in SA.
City of Melbourne Bank estb.

Births & Deaths
James Dooley, NSW Premier, b. (d. 1950)
Harold Edward Elliott, World War I commander, b. (d. 1931)
Sir Henry Somer Gullett, politician, journalist, b. (d. 1940)
Sir Charles Lloyd Jones, company director, b. (d. 1958)
Sir Redmond Lionel Leane, AIF commander, b. (d. 1962)
Sir John Cameron McPhee, Tas. Premier, b. (d. 1952)
John McTaggart, SA pioneer settler, b. (d. 1907)
Sidney Baevski Myer, born Simcha Baevski, businessman, retailer, b. (d. 1934)
Sir William Lennon Raws, Melbourne businessman, b. (d. 1958)
Oswald Julian Syme, newspaper proprietor, b. (d. 1967)
Walter Oswald Watt, World War I Flying Corps commander, b. (d. 1921)

B
Science, Technology, Transport, Discovery

9 Jan. Railway line to Portland, Vic., opens.
1 Feb. Burnie–Waratah railway line opens in Tas.
10 Jun. Privately owned horse tramways begin running in Adelaide.
25 Jun. Vic. Govt purchases Hobson Bay Private Railway Co., completing the nationalization of all railways in colony.
Jul. Ernest Favenc begins exploring route for proposed Brisbane–Darwin railway.
3 Sep. Great Southern Railway reaches Wagga Wagga, NSW, from Sydney. On **15 Oct.** Great Northern Railway reaches Tamworth, NSW, from Sydney.

During 1878
First flowing man-made water bore sunk, at Killara station, near Bourke, NSW.
Henry Sutton presents aeronautical research papers.
Melbourne builds first telephone exchange in Aust. (Opens in 1880.)
First telephone services operate in Melbourne. Long-distance telephone calls first demonstrated in SA, between Semaphore and Port Augusta.
First steam or dry process brickworks estb. in Sydney
Royal Zoological Society of SA estb. as Acclimatization Society. (Name changes in 1883.)
Lawrence Hargrave begins research into movement of birds, fish and insects.
Cumming, Smith and Co. begin production of superphosphate at Yarraville, Vic.

Births & Deaths
Isaac Herbert Boas, scientist, pioneer of Aust. paper making industry, b. (d. 1955)
Sir John Burton Cleland, scientist, naturalist, b. (d. 1971)
Sir Hugh Berchmans Devine, surgeon, b. (d. 1959)
James Frederick William Watson, medical superintendant, author, b. (d. 1945)

C
Arts

Literature

Births & Deaths

Mary Grant Bruce, writer, b. (d. 1958)
Patrick Joseph Hartigan, priest and author who used pseudonym John O'Brien, b. (d. 1952)

Music, Dance

30 Nov. Peter Dodds McCormick's song 'Advance Australia Fair' first performed, at a St Andrew's Day ceremony in Sydney.

Births & Deaths

Horace Gleeson, song writer, b.

Drama, Theatre, Film

Mar. Theatre Royal in Adelaide opens.

During 1878
Political satire drama, *Clay*, produced at Theatre Royal in Melbourne.

Births & Deaths

Thomas Louis Buvelot Esson, 'Founder of Australian Drama', b. (d. 1943)
Raymond Hollis Longford, actor, pioneer producer of silent films, b. (d. 1959)
Edward Joseph Tait, theatrical entrepreneur, b. (d. 1947)

Fine Arts

Births & Deaths

Gustave Adrian Barnes, designer, modeller, painter, b. (d. 1921)
George Henry Frederick Bell, 'Father of Modern Art in Australia', b. (d. 1966)
Harold Cazneaux, 'Doyen of Australian Pictorials', photographer, b. (d. 1953)
Joseph Fowles, marine painter, d.
Harley Griffiths, painter, b. (d. 1951)
Harry Bromilow Harrison, painter, b. (d. 1948)
Frederick Leist, painter, illustrator, b. (d. 1946)
James Stuart MacDonald, painter, art organizer, b. (d. 1952)
Harold Septimus Power, horse painter, b. (d. 1951)
Bess Norris Tait, miniaturist, b. (d. 1939)

D
Religion, Learning

1 Mar. Perth High School opens. First State-subsidized non-denominational high school in Perth.
Aug. Rev. J. H. Smith appointed Officiator of Unitarian Church in NSW.

During 1878
St Xavier Catholic College estb. in Melbourne.
St Peter's Church of England Cathedral built in Adelaide.
First Teachers' Union estb. in Vic.
The Working Men's College estb. in Sydney.

Births & Deaths

Sir Francis William Rolland, Presbyterian minister and teacher, b. (d. 1965)

1878

E
Sport

May–Sep. First representative Aust. cricket team tours England.
Aug. Melbourne Bicycle Club estb. (Sydney 1879, Hobart 1880, Adelaide and Brisbane 1881.)
Sep. Brisbane Lawn Bowling Club estb.
11 Nov. About 8,000 spectators attend intercolonial athletics festival in Adelaide.
During 1878
Calamia, ridden by T. Brown, wins Melbourne Cup in 3 minutes $35\frac{1}{4}$ seconds.
National Coursing Club of Tas. estb.
Charles Bannerman is first Aust. cricketer to score a century in England.
First Aust. versus USA-Canada cricket match held in USA.
First official tennis match in Aust. played on asphalt court at Melbourne Cricket Ground.
Sydney Lawn Tennis Club estb. as the Association Ground Lawn Tennis Club. First in Aust.
First Stawell Gift foot race run in Vic.
H. Thompson wins first Sheffield athletic handicap in NSW.
Emanuel Jackson makes successful hot air balloon flight in Vic.
Melbourne wins first intercolonial rowing competitions, held in Melbourne.
c. 1878. Harry Boyle creates cricket fielding position 'silly mid-on'.

Births & Deaths
Freda Maud Cavill, swimmer, diver, b. (d. 1961)
Harry 'Jersey' Flegg, Rugby League administrator, b. (d. 1960)
S. H. 'Yabba' Gascoigne, cricket barracker, b. (d. 1942)
Charles W. Gregory, cricketer, b. (d. 1910)
Bobby Lewis, jockey, b. (d. 1947)
Horrie Rice, tennis player, b. (d. 1947)
Michael Scott, yachtsman, b. (d. 1959)

F
Historia Dignum

Population
Estimated total white, 2,092,164.

14 Jan. Cyclone damages Darwin. On 8 Mar. a cyclone damages Cairns, Qld.
30 Jan. Head-on train collision at Emu Plains, NSW, claims five lives.
31 May. Ship *Loch Ard* wrecked off Vic. coast; 50 lives lost.
23 Jul. Ship *James Service* wrecked *en route* to Melbourne from Calcutta; 24 lives lost.
During Jul. N. N. Mikluho-Maklai, one of first Russians to settle in Aust., first visits Sydney.
During 1878
Qld *Punch* magazine first published.
NSW Govt passes first Lunacy Act.

Births & Deaths
Claude McKay, journalist, b. (d. 1972)

Communities
Beachport, SA, estb.
Crystal Brook, SA, estb.
Joadja, NSW, estb.
Kingaroy, Qld, estb.
Kooweerup, Vic., estb.
Morgan, SA, estb.
Port Germein, SA, estb.
Quorn, SA, estb.
Snowtown, SA, estb.
Tamborine Mountain, Qld, estb.

A

History, Politics, Economics, Law

Government

21 Jan. 1879–Nov. 1883, T. McIlwraith Premier Qld.
27 Feb. 1879–29 Apr. 1879, George Augustus Constantine Phipps, Marquess of Normanby, administered Vic.
20 Mar. 1879–3 Aug. 1879, Sir Alfred Stephen administered NSW.
29 Apr. 1879–18 Apr. 1884, George Augustus Constantine Phipps, Marquess of Normanby, Governor Vic.
4 Aug. 1879–9 Nov. 1885, Lord Augustus William Frederick Spencer Loftus Governor NSW.
30 Oct. 1879–Aug. 1884, W. R. Giblin Premier Tas.

8 Feb.–26 Mar. Employees of Agricultural Implement Manufacturing Co. of Gawler, SA, strike when management attempts to impose a nine-hour instead of eight-hour day. General strike almost follows. Employees granted eight-hour day.
10 Feb. Ned Kelly and gang hold up Jerilderie Post Office, NSW.
Feb.–Oct. Alexander Forrest leads expedition opening up Kimberley district, WA. Discovers Fitzroy pastoral country. Discovers Ord R. on 24 Jul.
May Provincial and Suburban Bank in Melbourne closes. Aust. and European Bank closes in Jun.
11 Aug. Sir Charles Windeyer appointed a temporary (later permanent) judge of Supreme Court of NSW.
Oct. First Intercolonial Trade Union Congress held under auspices of Sydney Trades and Labour Council in Sydney. Passes eight-hour day resolution.

During 1879
First commercial wheat in Qld harvested, at Dalby.
George Shead estb. Qld branch of the Society of Carpenters and Joiners.

Births & Deaths

Sir Francis Grenville Clarke, Vic. politician businessman, b. (d. 1955)
Thomas John Ley, NSW politician, criminal. b. (d. 1947)
Joseph Aloysius Lyons, UAP and UAP–Country coalition Prime Minister, b. (d. 1939)
William McCormack, Qld Premier, b. (d. 1947)
Sir Fergus McMaster, airline pioneer and grazier, b. (d. 1950)
Edmund Resch, brewer, b. (d. 1963)
John Collings Willcock, WA Premier, b. (d. 1956)

B

Science, Technology, Transport, Discovery

24 Mar. Zoological Society of NSW estb.
26 Mar. Wrought iron bridge opens at Murray Bridge, SA.
26 Jul. First WA Govt railway, linking Geraldton to Northhampton, opens.
28 Sep. Sydney estb. steam trams for inner city street transport.
Nov. First successful shipment of meat using Bell Coleman cold air machine leaves for England.

During 1879
Aust. branch of British Medical Association founded in Adelaide. (Other branches estb. in NSW and Vic. 1880, Qld 1894, WA 1898, Tas. 1911.)
Copper discovered at Herberton, Qld.
Gold discovered at Temora, NSW.
First non-mechanical lift exhibited at Sydney Exhibition.
First section of Central Aust. Railway, from Port Augusta to Quorn, SA, opens. (Alice Springs linked with Adelaide on 2 Aug. 1929.)
Horace Lamb publishes *A Treatise on the Motion of Fluids* (later published as *Hydrodynamics*).

Births & Deaths

Dame Constance Elizabeth D'Arcy, gynaecologist, b. (d. 1950)
Walter Geoffrey Duffield, astronomer, astrophysics pioneer, b. (d. 1929)
Sir Wilfrid Russell Grimwade, manufacturer, industrial chemist, druggist, b. (d. 1955)
Margaret Hilda Harper, physician, child care authority, b. (d. 1964)
Frederic Wood Jones, anatomist, zoologist, b. (d. 1954)

1879

C

Arts

Literature

During 1879
Richard Birnie publishes *Essays: Social, Moral, and Political.* Among first Aust. essays.
NSW Copyright Act passed. (SA 1878, Qld 1887, Vic. 1890, WA 1895, Tas. 1943.)

Births & Deaths
Charles Leslie Barrett, author, naturalist, b. (d. 1959)
Charles Edwin Woodrow Bean, author, historian, Official World War I correspondent, b. (d. 1968)
(Stella Maria Sarah) Miles Franklin, author, b. (d. 1954)

Music, Dance

Jul. J. C. Williamson returns permanently to Aust. Produces first light operas, including Gilbert and Sullivan.

Drama, Theatre, Film

During 1879
St George's Hall Theatre opens in Perth.

Births & Deaths
Otto Peter Heggie, actor, b. (d. 1936)

Fine Arts

25 Feb. Thomas Woolner's Captain Cook Statue unveiled at Hyde Park in Sydney.

During 1879
The new Art Gallery opens in Sydney.
First display of contemporary European art exhibited in Melbourne and Sydney.

Births & Deaths
James Muir Auld, painter, illustrator, b. (d. 1942)
Arthur James Wetherall Burgess, marine painter, b. (d. 1957)
Bessie Davidson, painter, b. (d. 1965)
Thomas Freidensen, etcher, b. (d. 1931)
Thomas Balfour Garrett, monotype painter, b. (d. 1952)
Percy Stanhope Hobday, graphic artist, b. (d. 1951)
Norman Lindsay, artist, author, b. (d. 1969)
Will Longstaff, mystic allegory painter, b. (d. 1953)
Alethea Mary Proctor, modern artist, watercolourist, b. (d. 1966)
James Fraser Scott, war artist, b. (d. 1932)

J. A. Turner, oil painter, probably b. (d. 1907)
Leslie Andrew Wilkie, portrait painter, b. (d. 1935)

Architecture

During 1879
E. J. Woods, architect, builds Mitchell Building at Adelaide University.
c. 1879. High Victorian period of architecture begins. (Ends *c.* 1892.)

Births & Deaths
Florence Mary Taylor, first Aust. woman architect, engineer and town planner, b. (d. 1969)

D
Religion, Learning

Oct. David Shearer begins regular Presbyterian Church services in Perth. Founds St Andrew's Presbyterian church.

The Advanced State Secondary School for Girls opens in Adelaide.

During 1879
Hermannsburg Aboriginal Mission School estb. in NT.

First Aust.-born professor appointed at Sydney University, to Chair of Applied Sciences.

Births & Deaths
Francis de Witt Batty, Church of England bishop, Newcastle, NSW, b. (d. 1961)

Percival Richard Cole, educationist, b. (d. 1948)

E
Sport

28 Apr. Coburg Football Association team in Melbourne makes record score in Aust. Rules football history: 64 goals, 28 points (412).

6 Aug. First Aust. Rules football night game held in Melbourne.

During 1879
Darriwell, ridden by S. Cracknell, wins Melbourne Cup in 3 minutes 30¼ seconds.

First Caulfield Cup (horseracing) run in Melbourne.

Jem Mace teaches first glove boxing in Melbourne.

First Lacrosse clubs founded in Melbourne.

First lawn tennis court laid in Melbourne.

First intercolonial Aust. Rules football match played, between Vic. and SA in Melbourne.

The Southern Tas. Football Association founded in Hobart.

F. R. 'Demon' Spofforth takes first hat-trick in Test cricket, against England in Melbourne.

Births & Deaths
Warwick Windridge Armstrong, all-round cricketer, b. (d. 1947)

1879

F
Historia Dignum

1879

Population
Estimated total white, 2,162,343.

Jan. Qld Club founded. (Now oldest Qld club for men.)
28 Apr. Sutherland National Park, near Sydney, dedicated. First reserve in world to be named a National Park. (Becomes Royal National Park in 1954.)
1 Jul. The *Daily Telegraph* newspaper estb. as *Daily Pictorial* in Sydney.
17 Sep. First Aust. International Exhibition begins in Sydney.
25 Oct. SA Govt approves use of totalizator at race meetings. (Qld 1889, Tas. 1891, WA 1893, NSW 1916, and Vic. 1930.)

During 1879
NSW Stamp Collector's Magazine published; first philatelic magazine in Aust.
The *Walgett Mail* first published, in NSW.
Snowfalls recorded in Melbourne.

Births & Deaths
Arthur Henry Wickham Cunningham, founder of Scartwater Trust, which provided loans from cattle property profits for north Qld ex-servicemen, b. (d. 1942)
Grace Emily Munro, founder of Country Women's Association, b. (d. 1964)
Leslie 'Squizzy' Taylor, Melbourne gangster, b. (d. 1927)

Communities
Beaconsfield, Tas., estb.
Cleve, SA, estb.
Corryong, Vic., estb.
Lake Cargelligo, NSW, estb.
Moe, Vic., estb.
Nathalia, Vic., estb.

A
History, Politics, Economics, Law

B
Science, Technology, Transport, Discovery

Government
5 Mar. 1880–Aug. 1880, J. Service Premier Vic.
6 Apr. 1880–21 Oct. 1880, Sir Francis Smith administered Tas.
10 Apr. 1880–13 Feb. 1883, Sir William Cleaver Francis Robinson Governor WA.
3 Aug. 1880–Jul. 1881, G. Berry Premier Vic.
21 Oct. 1880–6 Dec. 1881, Sir John Henry Lefroy administered Tas.

2 Feb. World's first successful cargo of frozen meat from Aust. arrives in England. Aust. Frozen Meat Export Co. estb. beginning meat export industry.
7 Sep. Judicature system estb. in WA.
8 Sep. George Shenton becomes first Mayor of Perth.
11 Nov. Edward 'Ned' Kelly, bushranger, hanged at Melbourne jail. Kelly was wounded and captured at Glenrowan, Vic., on 29 Jun.

During 1880
Vic. makes salary payments to Members of Parlt permanent.
Federal Conferences held in Melbourne and Sydney.
Peter Lalor, Eureka Stockade miners' leader, appointed Speaker of Vic. Legislative Assembly.
SA formally adopts Aboriginal Protection policy.
Isaac Alfred Isaacs graduates, beginning notable career in constitutional law.
British Govt grants full responsibility for immigrants to colonial govts.
Sir Henry Parkes calls for intercolonial conference to discuss 'Chinese problem'.
Industrial unrest increases; reflects declining economic conditions in eastern Aust.
George Hall Peppin's sheep strain widely recognized and in demand.
Comptoir National d'Escompte de Paris, French Banking House, opens branch in Melbourne to assist French wool buyers finance their purchases. First continental bank in Aust.
John Lysaght Aust. Ltd founded in Melbourne as Vic. Galvanized Iron and Wire Co.
Macpherson Robertson estb. MacRobertson's, confectionery manufacturers.
Temora, NSW, goldrush begins.
Capt. R. Pennefather explores Cape York Peninsula, Qld.
Aust. Typographic Union estb. (Lasts until 1915.)
NSW Govt estb. rates for handling goods on wharves.
Angus cattle introduced to Aust.

Births & Deaths
Lewis Hubert Lasseter, later known as Harold Bell Lasseter, prospector, b. (d. 1931)
Sir Earle Christmas Grafton Page, Country-UAP coalition Prime Minister, b. (d. 1961)

1 Mar. Foundation stone for new lighthouse at South Head, Sydney, laid.
Apr. John Newell discovers tin at Herberton, Qld.
Aug. Adrian Charles Mountain introduces wooden paving blocks for use in Sydney streets.
Henry Byron Moore opens (privately owned) telephone exchange in Melbourne.
Oct. Central telephone exchange opens at GPO Brisbane.

During 1880
Rabbits cross Murray R. into NSW, damaging good grazing land.
Field Naturalists' Club of Vic. founded in Melbourne.
Dry plates for photography first available in Aust.
George Hooley and Alfred Richardson discover opals at White Cliffs, NSW.
There are 4,000 miles of railway tracks in Aust., mostly in Vic. and NSW.
Royal Society of SA estb.

Births & Deaths
Archibald George Campbell, ornithologist, b. (d. 1954)
John Howard Lidgett Cumpston, first Director-General of Cwlth Dept of Health, 1921, b. (d. 1954)
Launcelot Harrison, zoologist, b. (d. 1928)
Tom Iredale, zoologist, b. (d. 1972)
Thomas Howell Laby, physicist, co-designer of first anti-gas respirator, b. (d. 1946)
Anthony George Maldon-Mitchell, engineer, inventor, b. (d. 1959)
Thomas Griffith Taylor, geologist, geographer and Antarctic explorer, b. (d. 1963)

C

1880

Arts

Literature

During 1880
Henry Kendall publishes *Songs from the Mountains*.
Alexander Forrest publishes *Journal of an Expedition from De Grey to Port Darwin*.
Alfred William Howitt and Lorimer Fison publish *Kamilaroi and Kurnai*, first scientific study of Aboriginal tribal unit.

Births & Deaths
Noel Fulford Learmonth, author, Vic. historian, b. (d. 1970)

Music, Dance

During 1880
Operetta becomes popular.

Births & Deaths
Edgar Leslie Bainton, composer, conductor, b. (d. 1956)
Rosina Buckman, soprano, probably b. (d. 1948)
Amy Eliza Castles, soprano, b. (d. 1951)

Drama, Theatre, Film

22 Jul. Royal Victoria Theatre in Sydney destroyed by fire.
During 1880
Nellie Stewart makes first starring performance, in *Sinbad the Sailor*, at Theatre Royal in Melbourne.

Fine Arts

During 1880
Cyrus Mason estb. Buonarotti Sketch and Music Club in Melbourne.
Louis Buvelot, Swiss painter, inspires new School of Art.
Edward Roper paints *Kangaroo Hunt* at Mt Zero in the Grampians, Vic.
Sydney Art Gallery becomes Art Gallery of NSW.
Art criticism becomes regular feature of Aust. art environment.
Royal Art Society of NSW founded.
Norman Young buys Chevalier Jules Lefebvre's painting *Chloe* to hang in bar of Young and Jackson's Hotel in Melbourne.
c. 1880. W. H. Traill active in estb. standard black-and-white cartoon work in Aust.

Births & Deaths
Cyril Dillon, etcher, probably b.
William Henry Dyson, caricaturist, cartoonist, b. (d. 1938)
William Dunn Knox, painter, b. (d. 1945)
Frances Vida Lahey, post impressionist painter, b. (d. 1968)
Mildred E. Lovett, painter, sculptor, b. (d. 1955)
Margit Pogany, painter, b. (d. 1964)
Frederick George Reynolds, portrait, landscape painter, b. (d. 1972)
William Montague Whitney, painter, probably b.

Architecture

During 1880
David Mitchell builds Exhibition Building in Melbourne.

Births and Deaths
Louis Laybourne-Smith, architect, b. (d. 1965)

D
Religion, Learning

E
Sport

16 Apr. NSW Govt passes Public Instruction Act, introducing compulsory and secular primary education. State aid to denominational schools ends unless Church schools comply with Govt teaching standards and use Govt school textbooks. Children between ages of 6 and 14 not attending voluntary Church schools are obliged to attend State schools.

5 Sep. John Gore and Edward Saunders hold first official Salvation Army meeting, in Botanic Park, Adelaide.

During 1880

Period of free, compulsory and secular education begins. Catholic education expands; examinations begin; secondary schools and colleges develop; humanist curricula emerge. Humanist utilitarian or humanist realist tradition emphasizes moral and character development, not just intellectual disciplines. (Period lasts until c. 1904.)

Construction of St George's Church of England Cathedral begins in Perth. (Completed 1888.)

Foundation stone of St Paul's Cathedral in Melbourne laid. (Opens 1891.)

Museum of Applied Sciences founded in Sydney as Sydney Technological Museum.

Young Women's Christian Association (YWCA) estb. in Sydney.

University of Melbourne admits women, but not to study medicine.

St Ignatius Catholic school founded in Sydney.

Births & Deaths

John Flynn, Presbyterian minister and missionary, b. (d. 1951)

6 May. Rose Hill Lawn Bowling Club estb. First in NSW.

22 May. NSW Lawn Bowling Association estb. First in Aust. (Associations form in Vic. on 23 Jul. 1880, WA 1898, Tas. 1901, SA 1902, Qld 1903.)

During 1880

Grand Flaneur, ridden by T. Hales, wins Melbourne Cup in 3 minutes $34\frac{1}{4}$ seconds.

J. W. Fletcher introduces Soccer at Parramatta, NSW. First Soccer club, The Wanderers, forms in Aug. (Soccer introduced Melbourne 1883, Brisbane 1884.)

Aust. Rules football umpires wear all-white uniforms.

Aust. Rules football begins in NSW.

Melbourne Gun Club estb.

First golf played in Qld.

White Aust. cricket team plays first Test match held in England.

Intercolonial lawn bowls competition begin.

Vic. Tennis Championship, first major tennis tournament in Aust., played in Melbourne.

c. 1880. Aust. wrestling becomes professional.

Births & Deaths

Norrie Claxton, all-round sportsman, b. (d. 1951)
Eric Connolly, turf gambler, b. (d. 1944)

Historia Dignum

1880

Population
Estimated total white, 2,231,531.

31 Jan. J. F. Archibald and John Haynes launch the *Bulletin* in Sydney to provide writers with wider market and to encourage an aggressive pro-Australian attitude.

1 Oct. Melbourne Intercolonial Exhibition opens.

8 Oct. Five people connected with the Montreal gold-diggings disappear in what becomes known as the Bermagui Mystery, at Bermagui, NSW.

Oct. Solomon I. natives loot Qld schooner *Borealis*, killing most of crew.

During 1880
Qld Coastal and Torres Strait Marine Pilot Service estb. (Becomes most extended marine pilot service in the world.)

Fortnightly mail service between Melbourne and London estb.

First telephone directory in Aust., listing 44 subscribers, issued in Melbourne.

Serious smallpox epidemic in NSW. (Ends 1882.)

A severe national drought begins. (Ends in 1886.)

Communities
Babinda, Qld, estb.
Boonah, Qld, estb.
Derby, WA, estb.
Dorrigo, NSW, estb.
Fifield, NSW, estb.
Harden, NSW, estb.
Innisfail, Qld, estb.
Kaniva, Vic., estb.
Korumburra, Vic., estb.
Mareeba, Qld, estb.
Medlow Bath, NSW, first settled
Mungindi, NSW, estb.
Narromine, NSW, estb.
Nhill, Vic., estb.
Nyngan, NSW, estb.
Peterborough, SA, estb.
Sarina, Qld, estb.
Silverton, NSW, estb.
Temora, NSW, estb.

A

History, Politics, Economics, Law

Government
24 Jun. 1881–Jun. 1884, J. C. Bray Premier SA.
9 Jul. 1881–Mar. 1883, Sir B. O'Loghlen Premier Vic.
7 Dec. 1881–28 Oct. 1886, Sir George Cumine Strahan Governor Tas.

Jan. Intercolonial Conference recommends against large-scale introduction of Chinese into Aust.
15 May. HRH Prince George of Wales (later King George V) arrives in Aust.
Nov. Vic. Govt successfully exports butter to London.
Dec. NSW Govt legalizes trade unions.
During 1881
Vic. Legislative Council Constitution reformed.
There are 43,706 Chinese in Aust., 12,128 in Vic.
Vic., NSW, and Qld impose further Chinese restriction measures.
Henry Parkes calls for a council to examine a Federal Constitution for an independent Federal Parlt. (Council meets 1883.)
Name Hobart Town officially shortened to Hobart.
New Italy settlement estb. near Woodburn, NSW. (Lasts 10 years.)
Aust. Institute of Marine Engineers estb.
NSW Tinsmiths' and Sheet Metal Workers' Union estb.

Births & Deaths
William Chapman, NSW grazier, b. (d. 1969)
Sir John Alexander Ferguson, judge, bibliographer, b. (d. 1949)
Lionel Laughton Hill, SA Premier, b. (d. 1963)
Peter Imlay, NSW pioneer, d. (b. 1787)
Sir Frederick Richard Jordan, NSW Lieut-Governor and Chief Justice, b. (d. 1949)
Sir Anthony Langlois Lefroy, WA pastoralist, b. (d. 1958)
Thomas William McCawley, Qld Chief Justice, b. (d. 1925)
Hugh Denis Macrossan, Qld Chief Justice, b. (d. 1940)
Marion Phillips, economics and politics administrator, b. (d. 1932)
Thomas Alison Scott, NSW pioneer sugar grower, d. (probably b. 1777)

B

Science, Technology Transport, Discovery

3 Feb. Sydney–Albury, NSW, railway line completed.
1 Mar. Fremantle–Perth–Guildford, WA, railway line opens.
6 Aug. Maryborough–Gympie, Qld, railway line opens.
During 1881
First passenger lifts using Otis principle of suspended cable installed in Sydney.
SA develops practice of scrub-rolling—clearing land for ploughing.
Sydney Infirmary and Dispensary becomes Sydney Hospital.
First drilling for oil begins, at Salt Creek, SA.
Robert Watson surveys proposed railway line from Roma, Qld, to Gulf of Carpentaria.
SA Govt estb. Roseworthy Experimental Farm.
Iron suspension bridge constructed over Fitzroy R. at Rockhampton, Qld.
Baron von Mueller introduces paspalum grass into Vic. for cattle.
J. D. Custance experiments with superphosphate as fertilizer for cereal crops, at Roseworthy, SA.
John Tebbutt discovers the great comet of 1881.
Adam Johns and Philip Saunders discover gold in Kimberley district, WA.

Births & Deaths
Herbert Basedow, scientist and explorer, b. (d. 1933)
Samuel Henry Harris, surgeon, b. (d. 1936)
Thomas Harvey Johnston, biologist, zoologist, world authority on parasites, b. (d. 1951)
Essington Lewis, industrialist, mining engineer, b. (d. 1961)
Stanley Robert Mitchell, metallurgist, anthropologist, b. (d. 1963).
Walter Ernest Isaac Simmons, medical researcher noted for work on miners' pthisis, b. (d. 1970)
Robin (Robert) John Tillyard, entomologist, b. (d. 1937)

C

Arts

Literature

During 1881
Mrs Campbell Praed (née Rosa Caroline Murray Prior) publishes *Policy and Passion, A Novel of Australian Life*; later published under title *Longleat of Kooralbyn*.

Births & Deaths
Percy Neville Barnett, author, authority on book plates, b. (d. 1953)
Henry Mackenzie Green, author, pioneer in study of Aust. literature, b. (d. 1962)
Frank Leslie Thompson Wilmot, poet who wrote mainly as Furnley Maurice, b. (d. 1942)

Music, Dance

Births & Deaths
Madame Elsa Stralia, dramatic soprano whose real name was Elsa Fischer, b. (d. 1945)
Edgar Ford, musician, b. (d. 1961)

Drama, Theatre, Film

Births & Deaths
Leon Errol, comedian, b. (d. 1951)

Fine Arts

18 Jun. National Art Gallery of SA opens.
During 1881
M. Phillips becomes first instructor at Sydney School of Arts.

Births & Deaths
Sir John William (Will) Ashton, landscape and seascape oil painter, b. (d. 1963)
Meyer Daniel Alston, portrait painter, b. (d. 1965)
Henry Edgecombe, painter, b.
Jesse Jewhurst Hilder, watercolourist, b. (d. 1916)
John Joseph Wardell Power, painter, b. (d. 1943)
Florence Rodway, portrait painter, b. (d. 1971)
Jessie Constance Alicia Traill, first to exhibit paintings in Central Aust., 1928, b. (d. 1967)
Ernest Ewart Unwin, watercolourist, b. (d. 1944)
Henry B. van Raalte, etcher, b. (d. 1929)
Charles Arthur Wheeler, painter, b. (d. 1977)
William Hardy Wilson, architect, watercolourist, writer, b. (d. 1955)

Architecture

During 1881
William Farmer's drapery store in Sydney is first to install plate-glass windows.

D
Religion, Learning

E
Sport

During 1881
Capt. and Mrs T. Sutherland hold regular Salvation Army Corps meetings in Adelaide. (Salvation Army estb. in NSW 1882, Tas. and Vic. 1883, Qld 1885, WA 1891.)
David Blair writes *Cyclopaedia of Australasia*, first Aust. encyclopaedia.
Royal Melbourne Institute of Technology founded as Working Mens' College.
University of Sydney first admits women students.

Births & Deaths
Samuel Angus, New Testament theologian at Sydney University 1914–1943, b. (d. 1943)
Sir Reginald Charles Halse, Church of England Bishop of Brisbane, b. (d. 1962)
Terence Bernard McGuire, Roman Catholic Archbishop, b. (d. 1957)
Frederick Edward Hulton Sams, Church of England bush clergyman, b. (d. 1915)

During 1881
Zulu, ridden by J. Gough, wins Melbourne Cup in 3 minutes $32\frac{1}{2}$ seconds.
Six-day cycle races begin at Melbourne Exhibition track.
First women's lawn bowls match held, at Stawell, Vic.

Births & Deaths
Carnegie Clark, golfer, b. (d. 1959)
Frederick Septimus Kelly, sculler, b. (d. 1916)

1881

F
Historia Dignum

Population
Estimated total white, 2,250,194.

3 Apr. First Aust.-wide simultaneous census taken.
Jun.–Jan. 1882. Smallpox outbreak in Sydney effects 154, claiming 40 lives.
30 Aug. Train derailment at Jolimont, Vic., claims four lives.
Oct. Steamship *Balclutha* disappears off southern NSW; 22 lives lost.

During 1881
Charlotte Adams first white women to climb summit of Mt Kosciusko, NSW.
Robert Joel Cooper, 'King of Melville I.', arrives Melville I., NT.
First Adelaide and Perth International Exhibition opens.
George Adams runs first public Tattersall's sweep, on horserace Sydney Cup.
Royal Caledonian Scottish Society of SA estb.
Society of St Vincent de Paul estb. in Sydney.

Communities
Collinsvale, Tas., estb.
Coolamon, NSW, estb.
Ravenshoe, Qld, estb.
Tibooburra, NSW, estb.

A

History, Politics, Economics, Law

Nov. About 1,000 Sydney wharf labourers successfully strike for increased hourly rates of pay.
10 Dec. Female employees working for a Melbourne clothing manufacturer successfully strike when piece-work rates are reduced. First large-scale organized strike by body of female employees.
15 Dec. Tailoress's Union estb. First all-female Union.

During 1882
Amalgamated Miners' Association estb.
Franc Falkiner estb. F. S. Falkiner and Sons. (Becomes world's largest merino stud organization.)
William MacDonald begins world's longest droving run, from Goulburn, NSW, to Fossil Downs, SA. (Takes three years.)
Ernest Giles surveys country west of Peak Downs, Qld, into NT.
Hobart Stock Exchange opens.
Isaac Alfred Isaacs called to Bar. (Not fully established as successful barrister until 1890.)

Births & Deaths
Francis Edwin Birtles, overlander, b. (d. 1941)
Sir Michael Frederick Bruxner, NSW politician, b. (d. 1970)
Charles Price Conigrave, explorer, b. (d. 1960)
Sir Alfred Charles Davidson, banker, b. (d. 1952)
Sir Charles Leonard Gavan Duffy, judge, b. (d. 1961)
Sir Albert Arthur Dunstan, Vic. Premier, b. (d. 1950)
Sir Iven Giffard Mackay, military commander, educationist, diplomat, b. (d. 1966)
Sir Walter Thomas Merriman, NSW pastoralist, b. (d. 1972)
William John Smith, industrialist, b. (d. 1971)
Emil Robert Voigt, commercial radio pioneer, b. (d. 1973)
Maurice Wilder-Neligan, World War I military commander, b. (d. 1923)

B

Science, Technology, Transport, Discovery

1882

22 Mar. Telephone exchange estb. at Sydney GPO.
Jun. Aust. Electric Co. exhibits first electric lamps in Aust. in Melbourne. By Nov. electric lights illuminate Spencer Street railway station.
Jul. Thomas and Edwin Morgan peg claim to gold discovered at Mt Morgan, Qld.
4 Dec. Townsville–Charters Towers, Qld, railway begins operating.

During 1882
Prince Alfred Hospital opens in Melbourne.
Gold discovered near Cossack, WA.
Telephone exchange opens at Maryborough, Qld.
First country exchange in Aust.
James Richmond estb. Haddon Rig sheep stud near Warren, NSW.
Henry Corbett estb. first Aust. Corriedale sheep stud.

Births & Deaths
Sir Constantine Trent Champion de Crespigny, SA medical practitioner, b. (d. 1952)
Frank Debenham, geographer, Antarctic explorer, b. (d. 1965)
Norman C. Deck, photographer, b.
John Robertson Duigan, pioneer aviator, b. (d. 1951)
Sir Douglas Mawson, geologist, Antarctic explorer, b. (d. 1958)
Geoffrey H. Vernon, medical practitioner, b. (d. 1946)

1882

C
Arts

Literature

1 Jul. Thomas A. Browne, under pseudonym Rolf Boldrewood, begins publishing *Robbery Under Arms* in serial form.

Births & Deaths

Frederic Manning, novelist and poet, b. (d. 1935)
Alan Durward Mickle, author, artist, b. (d. 1969)

Music, Dance

Births & Deaths

Peter Dawson, baritone, b. (d. 1961)
George Percy Grainger, pianist, composer, who took professional name Percy Aldridge Grainger, b. (d. 1961)
Cyril Monk, violinist, b. (d. 1970)

Drama, Theatre, Film

During 1882
James C. Williamson estb. theatrical business with Arthur Garner and George Musgrove. First major performance at Theatre Royal Melbourne on 1 Jul.

Fine Arts

Births & Deaths

Alfred T. Clint, watercolourist, b. (d. 1936)
John Barclay Godson, painter and etcher, b. (d. 1957)
Elioth Gruner, artist, b. (d. 1939)
Hubert Jarvis, painter, b.
Mary Cockburn Mercer, painter, b. (d. 1963)
Albert Sherman, flower painter, b.
Marshall Wood, sculptor, d.

Architecture

During 1882
John Young builds The Abbey, Gothic style house at Annandale, Sydney.

Births and Deaths

Leslie Wilkinson, architect, b. (d. 1973)

D
Religion, Learning

During 1882
University of Adelaide opens.
Methodist Ladies College estb. in Melbourne.

Births & Deaths

George Mackaness, educationist, historian and autho b. (d. 1968)
Thomas Craike Rentoul, Methodist clergyman, b. (d. 1945)

E
Sport

Apr. NSW Soccer Association estb.
Jun. Robert Sievier, also known as Bob Sutton, becomes first bookmaker on an Aust. horseracing track, at Morphettville, SA.
12 Aug. NSW wins (28 to 4) first intercolonial Rugby football match, against Qld.
During 1882
The Assyrian, ridden by C. Hutchins, wins Melbourne Cup in 3 minutes 40 seconds.
Clay target shooting begins in Aust.
The Aust. Golf Club estb. in Sydney; first Aust. Golf Club. (First Golf Club estb. in Qld 1890, Vic. 1891, SA 1893, WA 1895.)
Aust. Cricket Team defeats England, becoming first team to bring back 'the Ashes' of English cricket. Begins Ashes trophy.
NSW Rugby Union football team visits NZ. First overseas visit by an Aust. Rugby Union side.
South British Football Soccer Association estb. First Aust. controlling body.
Water polo first played in Aust.
First Vic. Lacrosse championships held.

Births & Deaths

Peter McLaren, axeman, b.
Rufus Theodore Naylor, 'The Mastermind of The Turf', sport promoter, gambler, b. (d. 1939)
Arthur B. Postle, sprinter, b. (d. 1965)
Dan Souter, golf course designer, b. (d. 1937)
Clarence Weber, athlete, b. (d. 1930)

F
Historia Dignum

1882

Population
Estimated total white, 2,388,082.

16–17 Jan. Severe cyclone damages Darwin.
1 Mar. NSW Govt estb. Forestry Conservation Branch.
26 Jul. The *Daily News* becomes Perth's first daily newspaper.
22 Sep. Garden Palace in Sydney burns down.
11 Nov. Orient Liner *Austral* sinks in Neutral Bay, Sydney, while loading coal; five lives lost.
2 Dec. Train collision at Burnley, Vic., claims seven lives.
12 Dec. Goldmine near Creswick, Vic., floods, claiming 22 lives.
During 1882
The newspaper *Cairns Post* first published, Qld.
First Aust. Women's Christian Temperance Union estb. in Sydney.
Ferntree Gully, Vic., reserved as a scenic park; among first areas in Vic. so reserved.
Smallpox epidemic in Vic.
SA Firebrigades Board estb.

Communities

Ayr, Qld, estb.
Mt Morgan, Qld, estb.
Mourilyan, Qld, estb.

1883

A
History, Politics, Economics, Law

Government

5 Jan. 1883–Oct. 1885, A. Stuart Premier NSW.
9 Jan. 1883–19 Feb. 1883, S. J. Way administered SA.
14 Feb. 1883–1 Jun. 1883, Henry (later Sir Henry) Thomas Wrenfordsley administered WA.
19 Feb. 1883–5 Mar. 1889, Sir William Cleaver Francis Robinson Governor SA.
8 Mar. 1883–Feb. 1886, J. Service Premier Vic.
2 May 1883–6 Nov. 1883, Sir Arthur Hunter Palmer administered Qld.
2 Jun. 1883–20 Dec. 1889, Sir Frederick Napier Broome Governor WA.
6 Nov. 1883–9 Oct. 1888, Sir Anthony Musgrave Governor Qld.
13 Nov. 1883–Jun. 1888, S. W. Griffith Premier Qld.
1883–1884, G. R. McMinn Acting Govt Resident NT under SA jurisdiction.

4 Apr. Qld Premier Sir Thomas McIlwraith instructs Henry Majoribanks Chester, resident police magistrate on Thursday I., to raise British flag at Port Moresby, taking possession of eastern New Guinea. British Govt repudiates action.
During Apr. James Burns and Robert Philp estb. Burns, Philp & Co. Ltd. This trading company's interests spread throughout the Pacific.
28 May. Ernest Favenc sets out to explore country along the south-western coast of Gulf of Carpentaria, NT.
2 Jun. David Lindsay begins exploring Arnhem Land and Roper R., finding grazing lands.
Aug. Vic. becomes first colonial govt to estb. a Public Service Board. (NSW 1884, Qld 1889.)
28 Nov.–9 Dec. Intercolonial Conference held in Sydney. On 6 Dec. conference recommends annexation of New Guinea. On 7 Dec. conference recommends formation of a Federal Council of Australasia to legislate on matters of common concern.

During 1883
Graham Berry introduces Mallee Lands Act, opening land to farmers in Mallee district, Vic.
Gradual formation begins of Aust. fleet and army.
Beche-de-mer licences issued. (Discontinued from 1905.)
Sydney Scott imports first typewriters to Aust.
The NSW Aborigines Protection Board estb.
Vic. Govt authorizes formation of irrigation trusts.
Trades and Labor Councils estb. at Hobart and Brisbane.
Judicature system estb. in Vic.

Births & Deaths

Fred Blakeley, Lasseter's Reef expedition leader, b. (d. 1962)
Stanley Melbourne Bruce, Nationalist–Country coalition Prime Minister, b. (d. 1967)
Sir Reginald Marcus Clark, businessman, b. (d. 1953)
Edmond John Hogan, Vic. Premier, b. (d. 1958)
John Campbell Miles, prospector, b. (d. 1965)
John Joseph Simons, newspaper proprietor, b. (d. 1948)

1883

B
Science, Technology, Transport, Discovery

Feb. Coalmining complex opens at Port Kembla, NSW.
13 Apr. Phoenix Foundry Co. at Ballarat, Vic., manufactures its one-hundredth engine.
23 May. Adelaide Zoo estb.
14 Jun. Rail junction made between Wodonga, Vic., and Albury, NSW, completing direct Sydney–Melbourne railway line. First inter-capital train trip on 20 Aug.
During Jun. Bridge over Murray R. opens at Albury.
5 Sep. Charles Rasp discovers silver-lead-zinc deposits, which he mistakenly believes to be tin, at Broken Hill, NSW.
During 1883
Adelaide, Hobart and Launceston Telephone Exchanges open. NSW Govt acquires Royal Telephone Exchange in Sydney.
William Tuttle, Sydney photographer, opens for business.
Field Naturalists' Section of the Royal Society of SA estb. in Adelaide.
Copper discovered at Mt Lyell, Tas.
Coal discovered at Collie, WA. (Mining starts 1897.)
Portland Cement Co. Pty Ltd (so named in 1910) estb. as the Cullen Bullen Lime and Cement Co., in NSW.
Charles Todd uses time signals sent from Greenwich to determine Aust. longitudes.
Robert Christison's pastoral company estb. first export frozen meat works in Qld. (Devastated by cyclone 30 Jan. 1884.)

Births & Deaths
Leo Arthur Cotton, scientist, b. (d. 1963)
William John Dakin, zoologist, whaling authority, b. (d. 1950)
Sir John Robert Kemp, Qld engineer, b. (d. 1955)
Stanley David Porteus, psychologist, b. (d. 1972)
Arnold Edwin Victor Richardson, agricultural scientist, b. (d. 1949)
Roy Lister Robinson, Baron Robinson, forestry expert, b. (d. 1952)
Sir Herbert Henry Schlink, gynaecologist, developed international system of post-cancer checks, b. (d. 1962)
Headlie Shepherd Taylor, engineer and inventor, b. (d. 1957)
Hubert Massey Whittell, ornithologist, b. (d. 1954)

C
Arts

Literature

Births & Deaths
Ethel Louisa Anderson, poet, author, b. (d. 1958)
Charles William Blocksidge, who adopted the name William Baylebridge, philosopher and poet, b. (d. 1942)
Thomas Charles Dunbabin, author, journalist, b. (d. 1973)
Katharine Susannah Prichard, novelist, short story writer, b. (d. 1969)

Music, Dance

During 1883
Immanuel G. Reimann founds first Aust. College of Music, in Adelaide.

Births & Deaths
William Richard Cade, musician, conductor, b. (d. 1957)
Alda Frances, soprano, b. (d. 1952)

Drama, Theatre, Film

During 1883
George Darrell writes and produces *The Sunny South*, melodrama.

Births & Deaths
Nat Phillips, 'Stiffy', comedian, b. (d. 1932)
Frank Samuel Tait, theatrical entrepreneur, b. (d. 1965)
Francis (Frank) William Thring, pioneer film producer, theatrical entrepreneur, b. (d. 1936)

Fine Arts

During 1883
Publication of *Picturesque Atlas of Australia* begins. Attracts best local artists and engravers to Sydney.
Art Gallery of NSW premises built. Becomes National Gallery of NSW.
Tomaso Sani carves figures on spandrels of facade of GPO Sydney.

Births & Deaths
John Banks, ship and seascape painter, b. (d. 1945)
Leslie Board, painter, scenic artist, b. (d. 1935)
Doris Boyd (née Gough), painter, probably b. (d. 1960)

1883

Charles David Jones Bryant, marine painter, b. (d. 1937)
Samuel Byrne, naïve painter, b. (d. 1978)
Albert Collins, painter, commercial artist, b. (d. 1951)
Frank R. Crozier, painter, illustrator, b. (d. 1948)
Janet Agnes Cumbrae-Stewart, painter, b. (d. 1960)
Polly Hurry (real name Mary Farmer), painter, b. (d. 1963)
Dora Lynell Wilson, street scene painter, b. (d. 1946)

Architecture

During 1883
Charles Webb begins work on Windsor Hotel in Melbourne. (Then called Grand Hotel.)

D Religion, Learning

6 Mar. Protestants meet in Sydney to protest against Irish National League's fund-raising tour of Aust.
May. Melbourne National Gallery opens on Sundays but opposition from Lord's Day Observance Society forces Parlt to close it. (Opens again on Sundays in 1904.)
Jun. Servants' Training Institution estb. in Melbourne.
1 Aug. NSW Govt estb. State system of technical education. NSW Board of Education takes over Sydney Technical College.
Dec. Bella Guerin graduates with BA from Melbourne University, becoming first women to graduate from an Aust. University.

During 1883
Vic. first to introduce competitive Public Service examinations.
NSW opens State high schools for girls.
First medical school opens in Sydney.
Six high schools estb. in NSW.

Births & Deaths

James Jervis, educationist, historian, b. (d. 1963)
Garnet Vere Portus, educationist, b. (d. 1954)
Eleanor Rivett, Christian educationist, b. (d. 1972)
David Stewart, pioneer of adult education, b. (d. 1954)

E
Sport

During 1883
Martini Henry, ridden by J. Williamson, wins Melbourne Cup in 3 minutes 30½ seconds.
Moonee Valley Cup (horseracing) first run in Melbourne.
Footscray Australian Rules Football Club estb. in Melbourne.
The Rangers, first Qld soccer Club, estb.
First intercolonial soccer matches played in NSW and Vic.
First trotting championships held in Melbourne.
Kiandra Snow Shoe Ski Club estb., NSW.
NSW Cyclists' Union estb.

Births & Deaths
Warren Bardsley, cricketer, noted batsman, b. (d. 1954)
Albert 'Tibbie' Cotter, cricketer, noted fast bowler, b. (d. 1917)
Chris McKivat, Rugby Union footballer, b. (d. 1941)
Herbert Henry 'Dally' Messenger, Rugby League footballer, b. (d. 1959)

F
Historia Dignum

Population
Estimated total white, 2,505,736.

17 Nov. Newspaper *Tasmanian News* first published. (Ceases publication 1911.)

During 1883
The Southern Cross, a unique pearl-compound formation in the shape of a crucifix, discovered near Broome, WA.

Communities
Bridport, Tas., estb.
Broken Hill, NSW, estb.
Broome, WA, estb.
Carnarvon, WA, estb.
Marree, SA, estb.
Narooma, NSW, estb.
Onslow, WA, estb.
Urangan, Qld, estb.

1884

A
History, Politics, Economics, Law

Government
18 Apr. 1884–15 Jul. 1884, Sir William Foster Stawell administered Vic.
16 Jun. 1884–Jun. 1885, J. Colton Premier SA.
15 Jul. 1884–15 Nov. 1889, Sir Henry Broughman Loch Governor Vic.
15 Aug. 1884–Mar. 1886, A. Douglas Premier Tas.
1884–1890, J. L. Parsons Govt Resident NT under SA jurisdiction.

31 Jan. SA Trades and Labor Council estb.
During Jan. Charles Winnecke completes explorative mapping expedition from Warburton R., SA, to Qld.
Feb. Amalgamated Society of Carpenters and Joiners estb. in Fremantle. First permanent union in WA.
Apr. Construction of Largs Bay Fort, SA, completed and ready for defence operation. Warship *Protector* arrives from England in Aug. to begin SA Navy.
May. First cargo of frozen meat sent from Brisbane to London.
3 Nov. North-east New Guinea, Bismarck Archipelago and adjoining islands proclaimed a German Protectorate. On 6 Nov. Commodore Erskine proclaims south-west New Guinea and adjoining Is a British Protectorate under name of British New Guinea. Germany formally annexes north-western New Guinea on 16 Nov.
Nov. Vic., Tas., and Qld accept Federation scheme. NSW opposes. On 11 Dec. British Govt defers further consideration of scheme.
Dec. Several colonies protest against German annexations in New Guinea.

During 1884
SA Govt introduces first land and income taxes. (Vic. 1890 and 1895, NSW 1895, WA 1907, Tas. 1894 and 1910, Qld 1915.)
Tas. passes Factory Act to protect workers from exploitation.
Second Intercolonial Trades Union Congress held in Melbourne. Recommends estb. of a federation of Aust. Trade Unions.
Vic. Govt attempts to legalize Trade Unions, but not fully successful until Act amended in 1886.
First Industrial Life Insurance Companies estb. in Sydney and Brisbane.
The Perpetual Executors and Trustees Association of Aust. Ltd incorporated.
First commercial cargo of Tas. apples exported to London.
Nathaniel Buchanan overlands first cattle from Qld to Kimberley district, WA.
First systematic Crown land legislation introduced in NSW.

Births & Deaths
Frank Horton Berryman, soldier, probably b.
Sir Thomas Albert Blamey, World War II military commander, b. (d. 1951)
Sir Robert Cosgrove, Tas. Premier, b. (d. 1969)
John King Davis, Antarctic navigator, explorer, b. (d. 1967)
Clement John De Garis, financier, pioneer of dried fruit industry who pioneered sky writing as commercial offshoot of aviation, b. (d. 1926)
Edmund Alfred Drake-Brockman, Federal politician, judge, b. (d. 1949)
Sir Geoffrey George Knox, diplomat, b. (d. 1958)
Henry William Murray, military commander, b. (d. 1975)
Edward Owen Giblin Shann, economist, b. (d. 1935)
Edward Granville Theodore, 'Red Ted', Qld and Federal politician, businessman, b. (d. 1950)

B

Science, Technology, Transport, Discovery

Feb. Hugh V. McKay demonstrates Stripper Harvester to clean, thresh and winnow grain while harvesting.
Nov. William and Michael McDonough and Steven Karlson discover gold at Mt Lyell, Tas.
During 1884
Royal Society of Qld founded.
Shearing machines with cog gear and universal joint manufactured.
Royal Commission estb. to examine methods of irrigation in Vic.
Zoological Gardens at Moore Park in Sydney open to public.
Sydney's first cable trams estb.
Trinder, Aderson and Co. begin Fremantle–Singapore steamer service.
Edward Chippendale discovers pearls in Darwin Harbour.
Opals discovered at White Cliffs, NSW.
Tas. Govt passes first Dental Act in Aust., to regulate dentistry.
Lawrence Hargrave presents paper, 'Trochoided plane', expounding his nature-based theories of flight, to Royal Society of NSW.

Births & Deaths

William Rowan Browne, geologist, b. (d. 1975)
George Nicholas, chemist, b. (d. 1960)
Henry Caselli Richards, geologist, b. (d. 1947)
Thorburn Brailsford Robertson, physiologist, biochemist, b. (d. 1930)

C

Arts

Literature

During 1884
Nathaniel Gould, always known as Nat Gould, writer, arrives in Aust. (Stays for 11 years.)

Music, Dance

During 1884
Joshua Ives appointed first Professor of Music in Aust., at Adelaide University. (Arrives 1885.)

Drama, Theatre, Film

Births & Deaths

Claude Flemming, actor, singer and film producer, b. (d. 1952)

Fine Arts

During 1884
Louisa J. Swan founds Art Society of Tas. as Art Association.
Ballarat Fine Arts Gallery founded. Vic.'s first provincial Art Gallery.

Births & Deaths

Isaac Michael Cohen, portrait painter, b. (d. 1951)
Henry Thomas Gibbons, painter, b. (d. 1972)
E. Hilda Rix Nicholas, painter, b. (d. 1961)
Desiderius Orban, painter, b.
Ruth Sutherland, painter, writer, b. (d. 1948)
Maria Teresa Vigano, painter, b. (d. 1969)

Architecture

During 1884
Lloyd Taylor, architect, builds Kamesburgh House in Vic.

1884

1884

D
Religion, Learning

1 Jan. Alfred Barry consecrated Church of England Bishop of Sydney and Primate of Aust.
21 Mar. Patrick Francis Moran becomes first Roman Catholic archbishop to reside in Aust. (In Aust. for 27 years.)
Jul. First Young Men's Christian Association building opens, in Adelaide.
During 1884
First Central Methodist Mission estb. in Sydney. (Melbourne 1893.)
Qld School of Arts estb. Brisbane Technical College.
SA Public Library estb. (Becomes State Library of SA in Apr. 1967.)
Roseworthy Agricultural College, SA, officially opens for enrolment. First Agricultural College in Aust. (Classes begin on 3 Feb. 1885.)
Sydney University conducts first evening classes.

Births & Deaths
Charles Albert Edward Fenner, educationist, geographer, b. (d. 1955)
John Stoward Moyes, Church of England bishop, b. (d. 1972)

E
Sport

26 Jul. First heavyweight boxing championship with gloves held, between Bill Farnan and Peter Jackson in Melbourne.
During 1884
Malua, ridden by A. Robertson, wins Melbourne Cup in 3 minutes $31\frac{1}{4}$ seconds.
Australian Rules football umpires first signal goals with white flags.
Fitzroy Australian Rules Football Club estb. in Melbourne.
NZ Rugby Union football team makes first tour of Aust.
First organized soccer in Vic. begins. Anglo-Aust. Soccer Association estb.
Minmi Range Soccer Club estb. in Newcastle NSW.
Bare-knuckle boxing ruled illegal after death of Alex Edgar at Randwick, NSW.
Bobby McDonald, athlete, first uses crouch start technique.
Lacrosse Clubs estb. in Sydney. (SA 1885, Qld 1886, WA 1890, Tas. 1895.)

Births & Deaths
Reginald Leslie 'Snowy' Baker, all round sportsman, b. (d. 1953)
Nigel Barker, first athlete to hold recognized world athletic record, b. (d. 1949)
A. J. Hunting, speedway organizer, b. (d. 1962)
R. W. Skelton, 'The Baron', punter, b. (d. 1957)
Legh Winser, golfer, b.

Historia Dignum

1884

Population
Estimated total white, 2,605,725.

7 Jan. Fire destroys Academy of Music Theatre in Adelaide.
30 Jan. Cyclone damages Bowen, Qld.
2 Apr. Two trains collide at Little River, Vic., claiming three lives.
May. A. Edwards among first to ride a bicycle from Sydney to Melbourne.

During 1884
Fire Brigades Board of Sydney estb.
Tot Flood and James Barden initiate crouched-seat style of horse-riding.
Severe two-year drought damages Qld.
Asiatic mongoose imported to northern Qld.
Smallpox epidemic in Vic. and Tas.

Communities
Camooweal, Qld, estb.
Canungra, Qld, estb.
Iluka, NSW, estb.

1885

A History, Politics, Economics, Law

Government

16 Jun. 1885–Jun. 1887, J. W. Downer Premier SA.
7 Oct. 1885–Dec. 1885, G. R. Dibbs Premier NSW.
10 Nov. 1885–11 Dec. 1885, Sir Alfred Stephen administered NSW.
12 Dec. 1885–3 Nov. 1890, Charles Robert Wynn-Carrington, Lord Carrington, Governor NSW.
22 Dec. 1885–Feb. 1886, (Sir) J. Robertson Premier NSW.

15 Feb. British Govt accepts offer by NSW to send contingent of troops to Sudan. On 3 Mar. 818 men depart, returning on 23 Jun. six killed. First armed force dispatched overseas by a British Colony and first Aust. expeditionary force.
13 Mar. Vic. Employers' Union estb.
Apr. North Qld Separation League agitates for a separate colony.
15 May. Melbourne Waterside Workers estb. union.
10 Aug. Charles Rasp and associates estb. Broken Hill Pty Ltd, mining company with 16,000 shares at £20 each. (Becomes largest nationwide mining and industrial consortium.)
14 Aug. British Govt passes Federal Council of Australasia Act, giving Federal Council statutory status. (Council first meets in Hobart 1886.)
9 Oct. First direct shipment of sugar from Brisbane to London.
During Oct. Third Intercolonial Trades Union Congress, held in Sydney, discusses proposal to form an Aust. Federation of Labour. (Estb. 1927.)

During 1885
NSW Chamber of Manufactures estb.
Colonial branches of Imperial Federation League estb.
Vic. Govt passes Factory Act to improve working conditions.
Royal Commission appointed to examine activities of six ships engaged in 'blackbirding', kidnapping of South Sea Islanders for work on cotton and sugar plantations.
Qld Govt passes Act prohibiting indenture of Kanaka labour after 1890.
Royal Bank of Qld estb.
New Oriental Bank estb. in NSW and Vic.
First Aust. Institute of Accountants estb., in Adelaide, as Aust. Society of Accountants.
Durack family reaches Ord R., WA, after overland journey from Qld lasting two years and four months.
Brisbane Stock Exchange opens.

Births & Deaths

Sir Richard Layton Butler, SA Premier, b. (d. 1966)
Joseph Benedict Chifley, Labor Prime Minister, b. (d. 1951)
Sir George James Coles, businessman, b. (d. 1977)
John Joseph Curtin, Labor Prime Minister, b. (d. 1945)
Harold Gordon Darling, industrialist, b. (d. 1950)
Sir Walter Gordon Duncan, SA politician, member of Legislative Council for 44 years, b. (d. 1963)
John Gunn, SA Premier, b. (d. 1959)
Sir Edward Wheewall Holden, car manufacturer, b. (d. 1947)
James Francis Frank Hurley, explorer, photographer, probably b. (d. 1962)
Sir John Dudley Lavarack, Qld Governor, military commander, b. (d. 1957)
Arthur Murray Longmore, pioneer naval pilot, b. (d. 1970)

B

Science, Technology, Transport, Discovery

1885

12 Aug. Brisbane horse-drawn tramway system begins.
During Aug. Charles Hall and Jack Slattery discover payable gold in Kimberley district, WA. Halls Creek goldrush follows.
3 Sep. Sydney–Bourke, NSW, railway line opens.
11 Nov. Francis Clapp estb. cable trams in Melbourne. (Last until 1940.)
2 Dec. Lawrence Hargrave flies model aeroplane, using rubber bands for propulsion.
During 1885
Lead and zinc mines first worked at Broken Hill, NSW.
G. Dagmar Berne first woman medical student in Aust., at Sydney.
First load of silver ore (165 bags) sent from Silverton, NSW, to Port Pirie, SA.
Silver-lead discovered at Mt Zeehan, Tas.
Prospectors discover gold on the Margaret and Ord rivers in Kimberley district, WA.
Gasworks Bridge built over Parramatta R. at Parramatta, NSW.
Mechanical dentistry course estb. at Sydney Technical College.
Hugh Victor McKay patents his Sunshine Harvester.
c. 1885. The phonograph imported to Aust.
James Alston introduces the Aust. water pumping windmill.

Births & Deaths
Sir John Henry Butters, engineer, b. (d. 1969)
John Clark, entomologist, Aust. ant expert, b. (d. 1956)
James Davidson, entomologist, b. (d. 1945)
Rupert Major Downes, surgeon, b. (d. 1945)
Albert Cecil Fewtrell, railway engineer, b. (d. 1950)
William Ewart Hart, pioneer aviator, b. (d. 1943)
Andrew Keith Jack, physicist, Antarctic explorer, b. (d. 1966)
Charles Edward Lane-Poole, forestry officer, b. (d. 1970)
Charles Robert Montague Luke, photographer, b.
Allan Riverstone McCulloch, zoologist, b. (d. 1925)
Herbert Michael Morgan, physician, author, b. (d. 1945)
William Henry Nicholls, orchidologist, b. (d. 1951)
Sir (Albert Cherbury) David Rivett, chemist, b. (d. 1961)

C

Arts

Literature

During 1885
Harry Emmet publishes *Our Own Authors and their Productions*, among first listings of Aust. authors.
Marcus Clarke's *His Natural Life* retitled *For the Term of His Natural Life*.

Births & Deaths
Henry George Lamond, author, b. (d. 1967)
Dorothea Isobel Marion Mackellar, lyrical poet, novelist, b. (d. 1968)
(Edward) Vance Palmer, novelist and short story writer, b. (d. 1959)
Janet Gertrude Nettie Palmer, always known as Nettie Palmer, author, poet, critic and promoter of Aust. literature, b. (d. 1964)

Music, Dance

Apr. Reconstituted Sydney Philharmonic Society estb. First concert on 1 Oct.

Births & Deaths
Mary Hannah (May) Brake, song composer, b. (d. 1957)
Percy Brier, composer, b. (d. 1970)
Frederick Collier, bass baritone, b. (d. 1964)
Gustav Massartic, ballet dancer, d.
Nelson Oliver, violin maker, b.

Drama, Theatre, Film
During 1885
Brough-Boucicault Comedy Theatre Company estb. in Melbourne.

Births & Deaths
Frank Harvey, actor and playwright, b. (d. 1965)
George Sorlie, drama producer, 'King of the Road', b. (d. 1948)

Fine Arts

24 Dec. National Art Gallery of NSW building opens in Sydney.
During 1885
Impressionist Art period in Aust. begins. Influenced by French impressionism and reaction away from English aesthetic tradition; *plein-air* painting; growth of aesthetic influence of English decadence, neo-romanticism, tonal and academic impressionism.

1885

Tom Roberts, Frederick McCubbin and Louis Abrahams estb. artists' camp at Box Hill, Vic. Becomes Heidelberg School and introduces distinctive style of Aust. landscape painting based on impressionistic and *plein-air* techniques.
Buxton Art Gallery estb. in Melbourne.
Royal Art Society begins holding art classes.
Norwood Art School estb. in Adelaide. (Closes 1895.)
SA Academy of Art estb.
Etching introduced to Aust.

Births & Deaths

William Leslie Bowles, sculptor, b. (d. 1954)
Horace Brodzky, painter graphic artist, b. (d. 1919)
May Grigg, painter, b. (d. 1969)
Gordon Holdsworth, ecclesiastical sculptor, b. (d. 1965)
Harry Julius, theatre caricaturist, b.
Henry Lamb, painter, b. (d. 1960)
Derwent Lees, painter, b. (d. 1931)
Gerrard Gayfield Shaw, etcher and engraver, b.
Evelyn W. Syme, painter, b. (d. 1961)

Architecture

During 1885
Ernest Wunderlich imports first stamped and pressed zinc windows.
Cavity walls first used in building.
James Barnet, architect, builds Customs House at Circular Quay, Sydney.
First 10-storey building erected in Melbourne.

D

Religion, Learning

9 Jun. First Seventh-Day Adventists arrive in Sydney.
27 Jul. Archbishop Patrick Francis Moran becomes first Cardinal appointed in Aust.
Nov. First Plenary council of 18 Catholic bishops, archbishops and advisors held in Sydney.
Charles Strong founds Aust. Church in Melbourne, advocating promotion and practice of Christianity a a spirit of life rather than as a theological creed.

During 1885
St Andrews Cathedral Choir founded in Sydney. Becomes largest Church of England Choir School outside England.
Methodist Ladies College opens in Sydney.
Abbotsleigh Church of England School for Girls opens in Sydney.
Catholic Ladies College estb. in Melbourne.
Tas. introduces compulsory and secular primary school education system, ending State aid to denominational schools.
State School Teachers' Union of Vic. estb.
Brisbane Synagogue opens.

Births & Deaths

Ernest Henry Burgmann, Church of England bishop, b. (d. 1967)
Philip Thomas Byard Clayton, clergyman, b. (d. 1972)
Kinglsey Ogilvie Fairbridge, social worker, b. (d. 1924)

E
Sport

8 May. First WA Aust. Rules football played. WA Football Association estb. (Becomes WA National Football League in 1980.)
6 Jun. First Soccer Cup final held in Sydney. Rainsford trophy inaugurated.
During 1885
Sheet Anchor, ridden by M. O'Brien, wins Melbourne Cup in 3 minutes 29½ seconds.
Richmond Aust. Rules Football Club estb. in Melbourne.
Baseball first played in Aust. Becomes popular in Vic.
Brisbane Amateur Sailing Club estb. (Becomes Qld Yacht Club in 1894; receives Royal warrant in 1902.)
c. 1885. Professional wrestling matches become popular.

Births & Deaths
Francis Bullock, jockey, b. (d. 1958)
Albert Rosenfeld, Rugby League footballer, b. (d. 1970)

F
Historia Dignum

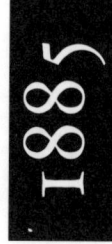

Population
Estimated total white, 2,694,518.

25 Jan. Cootamundra, NSW, train falls into wash-out gap. Seven lives lost.
Mar. Newcastle Benevolent Society opens to aid the poor.
10 Jun. SS *Cahors* wrecked off Evans Head, NSW.
Sep. First philatelic society estb. in Sydney.
15 Nov. William H. L. Bailey estb. *Sunday Times* newspaper in Sydney. First Sunday paper in NSW.
19 Dec. The *Western Mail* published in Perth.
During 1885
Maurice Brodzky founds *Table Talk*, weekly magazine, in Melbourne.
National Chess championships begin.
English journalist George Augustus Sala gives a booming Melbourne the title 'Marvellous Melbourne'.
NSW Sudan contingent ex-service organization estb. in Sydney.
First postal notes sold in Vic.
c. 1885. Colonel Tom Price originates Aust. military slouch hat.

Communities
Adaminaby, NSW, estb.
Atherton, Qld, first settled
Bedowrie, Qld, estb.
Borroloola, NT, estb.
Childers, Qld, estb.
Coolangatta, Qld, estb.
Croydon, Qld, estb.
Dwellingup, WA, estb.
Eucla, WA, estb.
Guyra, NSW, estb.
Keith, SA, estb.
Merriwa, NSW, estb.
Nambucca Heads, NSW, estb.
Orbost, Vic., estb.
Rylstone, NSW, estb.
Terrigal, NSW, probably estb.

1886

A
History, Politics, Economics, Law

Government
18 Feb. 1886–Nov. 1890, D. Gillies Premier Vic.
26 Feb. 1886–Jan. 1887, (Sir) P. A. Jennings Premier NSW.
8 Mar. 1886–Mar. 1887, J. W. Agnew Premier Tas.
29 Oct. 1886–18 Nov. 1886, W. R. Giblin administered Tas.
18 Nov. 1886–11 Mar. 1887, Sir William Dobson administered Tas.

25 Jan. Formal opening of Federal Council of Australasia, in Hobart.
During Jan. Wharf labourers strike in Melbourne over wages and working conditions on coastal ships. First strike to be settled by arbitrators.
George Robertson and David Angus open their first bookshop in Sydney, Angus & Robertson. (Now oldest Aust. publishing house.)
12 Jun. William Guthrie Spence estb. Amalgamated Shearers' Union of Australasia in Ballarat, Vic. to fight pastoralists' wage-cutting practices. Branches estb. in NSW and SA.
16 Sep. Qld Govt introduces payment of salaries to Members of Parlt. Govt legalizes trade unions.
During Sep. Fourth Intercolonial Trade Union Congress meets in Adelaide. Recommends direct representation of Labour in Parlt.
Dec. James P. Garvan estb. Citizens' Life Assurance Co. Ltd in Sydney. (Becomes Mutual Life and Citizens' Assurance Co. in 1898.)
The Reform Association replaces the Reform League in WA.

During 1886
Vic. Govt passes second Factory Act to improve working conditions.
WA formally adopts Aboriginal Protection policy. Estb. Protection Board.
Commercial Bank of SA collapses.
Aust. has contributed *c*. £324 million in gold to world bullion reserves.
David Lindsay crosses Aust. from Spencer Gulf, SA to Gulf of Carpentaria; explores country between Qld and SA.
Julian Edmund Tenison-Woods explores NT.
WA Govt restricts Chinese immigration.
Goldrush to Kimberley district, WA, begins.
Vic. Govt estb. Wages Board system to fix wages and conditions in trades.
Alfred Deakin inaugurates the Murray Valley Irrigation Scheme.
William Bede Dalley becomes first Aust. to be appointed to Privy Council.

Births & Deaths
Charles Lydiard Aubrey Abbott, NT Administrator, b. (d. 1975)
Sir Owen Dixon, High Court Chief Justice, b. (d. 1972)
Edward Clarence Evelyn Dyason, economist, stockbroker, engineer, b. (d. 1949)
Alfred William Foster, judge, b. (d. 1962)
Sir Edward John Lees Hallstrom, businessman, benefactor, b. (d. 1970)
Margaret Edgeworth McIntyre, first woman elected to Tas. Parlt, b. (d. 1948)
Richard Charles Mills, economist, b. (d. 1952)
Sir Keith Arthur Murdoch, newspaper proprietor, journalist and arts promoter, b. (d. 1952)

B

Science, Technology, Transport, Discovery

Feb. George Chaffey arrives in Vic. to pioneer Riverina irrigation. Signs agreement with Vic. Govt on 21 Oct. to begin irrigation scheme at Mildura.
6 May. Broken Hill Proprietary Co. Ltd smelters open at Broken Hill, NSW.
22 May. North Sydney cable tram service opens. First in Sydney.
3 Aug. Sir T. W. Edgeworth David discovers coal at Greta, NSW.
Dec. River steamer *Jane Eliza* completes 3½-year journey on Darling R. to Bourke, NSW. Longest single river trade voyage recorded.

During 1886
Iron smelting works at Mittagong, NSW, close.
Rabbits reach Qld–NSW border.
Aboriginal cranium 'Talgai Skull' discovered at Talgai Station, Qld. Skull between 14,000 and 16,000 years old.
W. J. Farrer begins wheat-breeding experiments at Lambrigg, on Murrumbidgee R., near site of Canberra.
Aust. and NZ Association for the Advancement of Science (ANZAAS) estb.
Gold discovered at Mt Lyell, Tas. (Copper discovered there in 1891.)
Coal discovered at St Marys, Tas.
Construction of Central Aust. Railway from Adelaide to Alice Springs, NT, begins.
Ungamulla water bore at Cunnamulla, Qld, sunk. Among first.
WA Steam Navigation Co. estb.
Adelaide–Port Adelaide telephone trunk line opens. First trunk line in Aust.
Royal Meteorological Society of Aust. estb.

Births & Deaths
Robert Marshall Allan, obstetrician, b. (d. 1946)
Sir Ernest Thomas Fisk, radio pioneer, b. (d. 1965)
Sister Elizabeth Kenny, nurse and innovator, poliomyelitis therapist, b. (d. 1952)
Morton Henry Moyes, engineer, meteorologist, Antarctic explorer, b. (d. 1981)
Sir Raymond Edward Priestley, geologist, Antarctic explorer, university administrator, b. (d. 1974)
Samuel White Sweet, SA and NT photographer, d. (b. 1825)

C

Arts

Literature

During 1886
Edward Curr publishes first vols of *The Australian Race: its Origins, Languages, Customs*.
Fergus Hume publishes *The Mystery of a Hansom Cab*.
Francis William I. Adams publishes *Australian Essays*.

Births & Deaths
Mervyn Garnham Skipper, author, journalist, b. (d. 1959)

Music, Dance

Births & Deaths
Harold Brewster Jones, composer, b. (d. 1949)

Drama, Theatre, Film

May. Alfred Dampier, actor, opens Royal Standard Theatre in Sydney. In June adapts novel *For The Term of His Natural Life* for stage.
1 Oct. Alexandra Theatre opens in Melbourne.
18 Dec. Remodelled Princess Theatre opens in Melbourne.
26 Dec. Criterion Theatre opens in Sydney.

Fine Arts

During 1886
Aust. Artists' Association estb. in Vic.
Julian Ashton becomes President of Art Society of NSW.
Heidelberg School named at Box Hill, Vic.
National Gallery of Vic. Travelling Scholarship first awarded.

Births & Deaths
George C. Benson, watercolourist, b. (d. 1960)
Neville William Cayley, ornithological artist, b. (d. 1950)
Marjorie Gwynne, painter, b. (d. 1958)
Ambrose Lance Hallen, painter, b. (d. 1943)
James Ranalph Jackson, painter, b. (d. 1975)
Charles Henry Lancaster, painter, b.
Ian McKinnon, watercolourist, b. (d. 1960)
James Squire Morgan, artist, etcher, b. (d. 1974)
Kathleen O'Connor, painter, b. (d. 1968)
Gordon Lyall Trindall, portrait painter, b.

1886

1886

Architecture

During 1886
First Marseilles terracotta tiles imported from France.
Charles H. E. Blackman and John Sulman, architects, build Bank of NSW in Sydney.
SA Institute of Architects estb.

D
Religion, Learning

Jan. S. N. Haskell, J. O. Corliss and M. C. Israel estb. first Seventh-Day Adventist church in Aust., in Melbourne.

During 1886
Methodist Ladies College opens in Hobart.
Federated Union of Churches holds first meeting in Sydney.
Sydney University first to conduct adult education courses.
Dookie Agricultural College opens in Vic.

Births & Deaths
Frederic Morely Cutlack, World War I historian and journalist, b. (d. 1967)
Joseph Benedict Serra, pioneer Roman Catholic prelate, d. (b. 1810)

E
Sport

Arsenal, ridden by E. English, wins Melbourne Cup in 3 minutes 31 seconds.

Births & Deaths
Walter Addison, SA marksman, b. (d. 1956)
John (Jack) Donaldson, athlete and sprinter, b. (d. 1933)
Barney Bede Kieran, swimmer, b. (d. 1905)
Charles George (Charlie) Macartney, cricketer, noted batsman, b. (d. 1958)
Judy Masters, soccer player (male), b.
Alick Wickham, diver and swimmer, b.
Leonora Wray, women's golf pioneer, b. (d. 1979)

F
Historia Dignum

Population
Estimated total white, 2,788,050.

1 Jan. Serious bushfires between Warrnambool and Port Phillip district, Vic.
30 May. The ship *Ly-ee-Moon* wrecked; 76 lives lost.
9 Sep. Mary Jane Hicks, 16 years old, pack-raped in Sydney; 11 men charged. (Four hanged on 7 Jan. 1887.)
8 Dec. Ship *Helen Nicol* collides with *Keilawarra* off North Solitary I., claiming 36 lives.
24 Dec. Fire destroys Academy of Music Theatre in Adelaide, claiming two lives.
During 1886
Jubilee International Exhibition opens in Adelaide.
Over past 51 years 23 vessels wrecked around King I., Tas., claiming aggregate 805 lives.
Drought, fluctuations in overseas capital investments, public works policies, contribute to serious unemployment in and around Sydney. In Dec. Govt estb. Carrington relief depot.
Typhoid outbreak in Sydney.

Communities
Barcaldine, Qld, estb.
Kyabram, Vic., estb.
Mt Nicholas, Tas., estb.
Nevertire, NSW, area first settled
Wyndham, WA, estb.

1887

A
History, Politics, Economics, Law

Government
20 Jan. 1887–Jan. 1889, (Sir) H. Parkes Premier NSW.
11 Mar. 1887–30 Nov. 1892, Sir Robert George Crookshank Hamilton Governor Tas.
29 Mar. 1887–Aug. 1892, P. O. Fysh Premier Tas.
11 Jun. 1887–Jun. 1889, T. Playford Premier SA.

Feb. Vic. and NSW Premiers appeal for political federation of Aust. colonies.
4 Apr.–9 May. First Colonial Conference in London, held between British Prime Minister, Secretary of State for Colonies and Premiers of Aust. colonies, to discuss matters of mutual interest.
3 May. Monster meeting held in Sydney to protest against an influx of Chinese. Further anti-Chinese rally held on 2 Jun.
Jun. The Reform Association in WA sponsors first formal party organization in WA Legislative Council.
16 Nov. SA introduces payment of Members of Parlt.

During 1887
Commissioners appointed by Chinese Govt, Wong Yung Ho and U Tsing, arrive to inquire into conditions of Chinese living in Aust.
NSW revokes assisted immigration policy.
Qld granted responsibility for administering British New Guinea (later Papua), with financial assistance from NSW and Vic.
Swan Brewery Co. estb. in Perth.
Thomas Hardy and Sons Wine Co. estb.
Edward A. Petherick estb. Colonial Booksellers Agency.
SA Govt imposes protective tariff to stimulate local manufacturing.
Adelaide Stock Exchange opens.
Qld Labour League estb.
SA Employers' Union estb.
Vic. Board of Conciliation estb. NSW and Qld each debate conciliation procedures.

Births & Deaths
Sir Adolph Basser, businessman, benefactor, b. (d. 1964)
Henry Gordon Bennett, military commander, b. (d. 1962)
John Cain, Vic. Premier, b. (d. 1957)
Edward Michael Hanlon, Qld Premier, b. (d. 1952)
Sir Edward Henry Bruce Lefroy, WA politician and pastoralist, b. (d. 1966)
Sir Leslie James McConnan, banker, b. (d. 1954)
Elsie Rivett, social worker, b. (d. 1964)
William Forgan Smith, Qld Premier, b. (d. 1953)
Sir William Flood Webb, High Court Judge, b. (d. 1972)

B
Science, Technology, Transport, Discovery

1 Jan. Clement Wragge appointed Qld Govt meteorologist. Introduces practice of naming cyclones to arouse public interest in weather bureau.
19 Jan. Melbourne–Adelaide railway linked at Serviceton, Vic.
4 Feb. Brisbane–Wallangarra, Qld, railway line completed.
13 Apr. Robert Etheridge becomes first trained palaeontologist to follow profession in NSW.
14 Jun. Port Pirie–Cockburn, SA, railway line open.
Jul. Naturalists' Society of NSW estb. as the Natural History Association of NSW.
Aug.–Sep. First intercolonial Medical Conference held, in Adelaide.
9 Oct. Townsville–Hughenden, Qld, railway line opens.

During 1887
William Chaffey joins his brother George in Vic. to pioneer Riverina Irrigation Scheme.
Perth telephone exchange opens.
Qld electric trams begin running.
Irrigation scheme estb. at Renmark, SA.
Vic. Govt buys Melbourne Telephone Exchange Co. setting Aust. pattern of govt-owned telephone services.
Silver discovered in mountains south-west of Bathurst, NSW.
Gold discovered at Yilgarn and Southern Cross, WA.
Black opals discovered at Lightning Ridge, NSW.
The Australasian United Steam Navigation Co. estb.
c. 1887. Low-wheeled safety bicycles introduced. (Pneumatic tyres introduced by 1890.)

Births & Deaths
Henry Richard Busteed, pioneer of naval aviation, b. (d. 1965)
Sir William Edward Lodewyk Hamilton Crowther, medical practitioner, b. (d. 1981)
George Harris Sarjeant Dovers, surveyor, cartographer, Antarctic explorer, b. (d. 1971)
Sir Hibbert Alan Stephen Newton, surgeon, b. (d. 1949)

C
Arts

Literature

1 Oct. Henry Lawson publishes his first poem, 'Song of the Republic', in the *Bulletin*.
During 1887
John Farrell publishes *How He Died and Other Poems*.

Births & Deaths
Frederick Thomas Bennett Macartney, poet and critic, b.
Jack McLaren, author, b. (d. 1954)

Music, Dance

2 May. Francis Ormond sponsors Chair of Music at Melbourne University.
During 1887
Dame Nellie Melba makes operatic début in Brussels in opera *Rigoletto*.
Electric light first used in Aust. theatres.

Births & Deaths
Robert Dalley-Scarlett, musician, b. (d. 1959)

Drama, Theatre, Film

10 Sep. Her Majesty's Theatre opens in Sydney.

Fine Arts

During 1887
Qld Art Society founded. (Granted Royal charter 1927.)
Tom Roberts paints *Sunny South*, probably first nude study in an Aust. landscape setting.
Art Society of NSW estb.
The Tas. Museum and Art Gallery formally opens.
John Longstaff wins first Vic. travelling scholarship for art.

Births & Deaths
Clarice Beckett, oil painter, b. (d. 1935)
George Garden Colville, impressionist, landscape painter, b. (d. 1970)
Ruby Lindsay, black-and-white artist, b. (d. 1919)
Reginald Russom, painter, b. (d. 1952)
Sydney Ure Smith, artist, publisher, art promoter, b. (d. 1949)
Roland Shakespeare Wakelin, among first painters to introduce neo-impressionism into Aust., b. (d. 1971)
Archibald Bertram Webb, watercolourist, graphic artist, b. (d. 1914)
Tina Wentcher, sculptor, b. (d. 1974)

Architecture

During 1887
William Pitt, architect, designs for Princess Theatre, Melbourne, world's first opening roof and ceiling.
F. D. G. Stanley, architect, builds Qld National Bank in Brisbane.

Births & Deaths
Alexander Stewart Jolly, architect, b. (d. 1957)

1887

D
Religion, Learning

31 Jan. Hobart Quakers open co-educational boarding school.
6 May. Working Men's Technical College estb. in Melbourne. (Later renamed Royal Melbourne Institute of Technology.)
14 Nov. Gordon Technical College opens at Geelong, Vic. (Later renamed Deakin University.)
During 1887
Public Library of WA estb.
Building of Queen Victoria Museum commenced in Launceston.

E
Sport

20 Apr. NSW Amateur Athletics Association estb.
Dec. Aust. begins the six-ball cricket over in bowling (Britain follows in 1900.)
During 1887
Dunlop, ridden by T. Sanders, wins Melbourne Cup in 3 minutes $28\frac{1}{2}$ seconds.
Up to 10,000 spectators attend the Sheffield athletics handicaps in Sydney.
First Austral Wheel bicycle race held, in Melbourne.
Wallsend Rovers Soccer Club estb. in NSW.
Henry Alcock, Melbourne billiard table manufacturer stimulates interest in billiards and snooker.

Births & Deaths

Harold Baker, athlete, all-round sportsman, b. (d. 1962)
Bernard 'Brownie' Carslake, jockey, b. (d. 1946)
Annette Maria Sarah Kellerman, swimmer, probably b. (d. 1975)
David McNamara, Aust. Rules footballer, b. (d. 1967)
Reginald McNamara, cyclist, b. (d. 1971)
Arthur Alfred Mailey, cricketer, slow bowler, b. (d. 1967)
Fred Popplewell, golfer, b.

F
Historia Dignum

1887

Population
Estimated total white, 2,881,362.

20 Mar. Ship *Derry Castle* wrecked *en route* to England from Geelong, Vic.; about 15 lives lost.
23 Mar. Gas explosion at Bulli, NSW, colliery claims 83 lives.
22 Apr. Storm destroys pearling fleet at Eighty Mile Beach, WA, wrecking 22 boats and claiming 140 lives.
11 May. Steam tram collision at Prahran, Melbourne, claims six lives.
21 Jun. Peat's Ferry train collision in NSW claims six lives.
During Jun. Adelaide Exhibition opens to celebrate Queen Victoria's Fiftieth Jubilee.
Jul. First meeting of St John's Ambulance Association held in Melbourne.
13 Aug. Alexander Forrest publishes first *Possum* magazine.
19 Nov. The *Boomerang*, radical labour periodical, estb.
Dec. The newspaper *Australian Star* estb. in Sydney.
During 1887
Severe floods in Qld and Vic.
The National Fire Brigade Association of Vic. estb.
Smallpox epidemic in Tas.

Communities
Beerwah, Qld, first settled
Birchip, Vic., estb.
Cobram, Vic., estb.
Longreach, Qld, estb.
Mildura, Vic., estb.
Morisset, NSW, estb.
Ocean Grove, Vic., estb.
Renmark, SA, estb.
Southern Cross, WA, estb.
Tailem Bend, SA, estb.

1888

A
History, Politics, Economics, Law

Government
13 Jun. 1888–Nov. 1888, (Sir) T. McIlwraith Premier Qld.
9 Oct. 1888–1 May. 1889, Sir Arthur Hunter Palmer administered Qld.
30 Nov. 1888–Aug. 1890, B. D. Morehead Premier Qld.

16–19 Jan. Federal Council of Australasia holds second meeting, in Hobart.
Apr. Vic. Rangers Defence Corps estb.
Mar. Fifth Intercolonial Trade Union Congress held, in Brisbane; resolves to urge abolition of State-aided immigration.
12–14 Jun. Intercolonial Conference held in Sydney to consider public anti-Chinese sentiments. Conference recommends uniform legislation restricting Chinese immigration.
13 Aug. British Govt passes Imperial Defence Act to effect agreement stationing British naval forces in Aust.
Aug. Newcastle, NSW, coalminers begin 13-week strike over wage reductions. Near riots on 18 Sep. cause Govt to send in troops.
4 Sep. British New Guinea (Papua) Protectorate becomes a Crown Colony administered by Qld and Great Britain. William Macgregor appointed first Administrator.

During 1888
All Aust. colonies increase poll tax on Chinese immigrants to £100.
Britain formally annexes Christmas I., in Indian Ocean.
Phrase 'White Australia Policy' first appears, in the *Boomerang* magazine in Qld.
SA Govt Agriculture Bureau estb.
Bank of North Qld estb.
SA Brewing Co. estb. in Adelaide.
W. M. Foster brews beer in Melbourne. (First Foster's Lager produced in 1889.)
Chaffey Bros begin Mildara Wine Co.
Tooth and Co. Ltd brewery incorporated in Sydney.
Goldsbrough and Co. amalgamates with Mort and Co. to form agricultural company (Now Elder Smith Goldsbrough Mort.)
Estimated total value of Aust. exports £57,605,472.
Stuart, NT (later Alice Springs), surveyed. (Becomes Alice Springs in 1933.)
SA Govt estb. marketing standard for wheat. (Vic. 1891, NSW 1899, WA 1905.)
Aust. tobacco production peaks at 3,175 tons.
Qld Labourers' Union estb.
NSW Employers' Union estb.

Births & Deaths
Francis Edward De Groot, soldier and New Guard member, b. (d. 1969)
Sir George Hubert Wilkins, explorer and pioneer of polar aviation, b. (d. 1958)

B

Science, Technology, Transport, Discovery

12 Jan. Adelaide–Broken Hill, NSW, railway connected.
16 Jan. NSW and Qld railway systems connected at Wallangarra, Qld.
1 Jun. Sydney experiments with battery-run trams. Concept unsuccessful.
27 Aug. Australasian Association for the Advancement of Science first meets in Sydney.
3 Oct. Sydney–Kiama, NSW, railway line opens.
9 Nov. Tamworth, NSW, becomes first country town in Aust. lit by electricity.
During 1888
First large-scale sheep shearing machine demonstrated when all sheep on Dunlop station, NSW, are shorn with mechanical shears. First complete machine shearing in the world.
Royal Commission estb. to examine effects on human life of propagating diseases natural to rabbits.
Perth to Derby, WA, telegraphic line opens.
Brisbane–Charleville, Qld, railway completed.
First trout released in NSW. (SA 1910, WA 1930.)
Coal discovered at Leigh Creek, SA.
c. 1888. Cream separator device, separating cream from skimmed milk, invented.

Births & Deaths

Reginald Duigan, pioneer aviator, b.
Una Lucy Fielding, neuro-anatomist, b. (d. 1969)
John George Hunter, pioneer of organized medicine, b. (d. 1964)
Sir Thomas Ernest Victor Hurley, surgeon, air force commander, b. (d. 1958)
William Wilson Ingram, physician, medical scientist, b.
Frederick Arthur Maguire, anatomist, gynaecologist, b. (d. 1953)
Theodore Cleveland Roughley, zoologist, Great Barrier Reef expert, b. (d. 1961)
Frank I. Stillwell, geologist and Antarctic explorer, b. (d. 1963)
Arthur Mitchel Wilson, obstetrician, b. (d. 1947)

C

Arts

Literature

22 Dec. Henry Lawson publishes his first short story in the *Bulletin*, 'His Father's Mate'.
During 1888
Oceanic Publishing Co. publishes *The History of Capital and Labour in All Lands and Ages*.
Angus & Robertson publish their first book, H. Peden Steel's *A Crown of Wattle*.
Douglas Sladen publishes *A Century of Australian Song*.
Thomas Alexander Browne, using pseudonym Rolf Boldrewood, publishes *Robbery Under Arms*.
Edmund Finn publishes *Chronicles of Early Melbourne*.
Archibald Liversidge publishes *The Minerals of New South Wales*.

Births & Deaths

A. R. Chisholm, author, scholar, authority on French literature, b. (d. 1981)
Arthur William Upfield, author, b. (d. 1964)

Music, Dance

During 1888
The Frederick Cowan Orchestra estb. in Melbourne. First sizeable professional orchestra in Aust.
J. C. Williamson founds Royal Comic Opera Co.
Royal Ballerinas make début in Melbourne. First troupe of Aust.-trained dancers, directed by Marie Reddall.

Births & Deaths

William David Murdoch, pianist, b. (d. 1942)

Drama, Theatre, Film

During 1888
Brisbane's first large-capacity theatre, Her Majesty's Opera House, opens.

Fine Arts

Jan. Magazine *Australian Art* first published, by George Collingridge. (Ceases after three issues.)
Oct. Charles Conder, impressionist artist, arrives in Melbourne. Estb. artists' camp at Eaglemont, Melbourne, with Arthur Streeton.
During 1888
Vic. Academy of Arts and Aust. Artists' Association unite to form Vic. Artists' Society.
Warrnambool Art Gallery, Vic., estb.

1888

Births & Deaths

W. Wallace Anderson, sculptor. b. (d. 1975)
David Barker, cartoonist, illustrator, b.
William Merric Boyd, pioneer ceramic artist, potter, b. (d. 1959)
Stan Cross, cartoonist, b.
Harold Frederick Neville (Hal) Gye, black-and-white illustrator, painter, b. (d. 1967)
John Drummond Moore, painter, architect, b. (d. 1958)
Frank Waldo Potts, painter, b.
Geoffrey Keith Townshend, black-and-white artist, b. (d. 1969)
Julius Wentcher, painter, probably b. (d. 1962)

Architecture

Nov. Great Hall of Sydney Town Hall completed. Contains first metal ceiling in Aust.
During 1888
Highly modelled and decorative plasterwork influences architecture.
William Pitt, architect, builds Federal Hotel in Melbourne.
Qld Institute of Architects estb.
c. 1888. Strathroy House built near Launceston.

D
Religion, Learning

Feb. Christian Endeavour Movement, Protestant interdenominational movement, begins in Aust.
During 1888
Macleay Natural History Museum estb. in Sydney.
Technical Schools open in Hobart and Launceston.
Christian Brothers Catholic School estb. at Maryborough, Qld.
SA School of Mines estb. in Adelaide.
Presbyterian Ladies College estb. in Sydney.
Melbourne Teachers' College opens.
Kyneton School of Mines estb. in Vic.
Fanny E. Hunt becomes first woman to graduate in science in Aust., taking a Bachelor of Science at Sydney University.

Births & Deaths

Alexander Clifford Vernon, historian, b. (d. 1942)

E
Sport

27 Oct. Henry Searle defeats Peter Kemp for world sculling championship.
8 Dec. J. T. Williams makes first parachute jump from a balloon in Aust., over Sydney.
During 1888
Mentor, ridden by M. O'Brien, wins Melbourne Cup in 3 minutes 30½ seconds.
Federal Council of Rifle Associations of Australasia estb.
First State athletics title staged in Sydney.
Charles Samuels, first notable Aboriginal sprinter, runs 130 yards in 12½ seconds.
Dot Morrell wins world's first cycle race for women, at Ashfield, NSW.
First national cycling championships held, in Adelaide.
Gardiner Soccer Cup inaugurated. (Awarded until 1928.)
First intercolonial lacrosse match, between Vic. and SA.
First English Rugby Union footabll team visits Aust.
Ernest Cavill sets world swimming record for 100 yards.
Qld Lawn Tennis Association estb. (SA 1889, NSW 1890, Vic. 1892.)
c. 1888. Water polo first played in Aust.

Births & Deaths

Leonard Brown, rugby league footballer, b.
Frederick William Lindrum, billiards pioneer, b. (d. 1958)
Joe Wallis, boxing referee, b. (d. 1952)

F
Historia Dignum

Population
Estimated total white, 2,981,677.

2 Jan. Newspaper *Torres Strait Daily Pilot* estb. Initially world's smallest newspaper, with only three columns. (Ceases publication in 1940.)
3 Jan. *Illustrated London News: Australasian Edition* published in Melbourne. (Until 1891.)
8 Feb. Newspaper *Barrier Miner* published in Broken Hill, NSW.
17 Feb. Cyclone damages Mackay, Qld.
15 May. Louisa Lawson publishes suffragette newspaper, *Dawn: A Journal for Australian Women*, in Sydney. (Until 1905.)
Aug. Second Melbourne Intercolonial Exhibition opens.
5 Nov. Broken Hill, NSW township, destroyed by fire.
Nov. A Quaker conference in Sydney begins a peace movement in Aust.
During 1888
NSW issues Centenary stamps, these being among world's first commemorative postage stamps.
Severe drought widespread throughout Aust.
Fortnightly mail service to England begins.
Vic. bushfires spread from Warrnambool to Gippsland.
Draughts, or checkers, game first organized nationally.
State Lodges (Freemason), organize into United Grand Lodges. United Grand Lodge of NSW estb. on 16 Aug.
There are *c.* 50,000 Chinese in Aust.

Communities

Berrigan, NSW, estb.
Captains Flat, NSW, estb.
Chillago, Qld, estb.
Devonport, Tas., estb.
Gilgandra, NSW, estb.
Goondiwindi, Qld, estb.
Mullumbimby, NSW, estb.
Woolgoolga, NSW, estb.

1889

A
History, Politics, Economics, Law

Government
17 Jan. 1889–Mar. 1889, G. R. Dibbs Premier NSW.
6 Mar. 1889–11 Apr. 1889, S. J. Way administered SA.
8 Mar. 1889–Oct. 1891, Sir H. Parkes Premier NSW.
11 Apr. 1889–10 Apr. 1895, Algernon Hawkins Thomond Keith-Falconer, Earl of Kintore, Governor SA.
1 May 1889–31 Dec. 1895, Sir Henry Wylie Norman Governor Qld.
27 Jun. 1889–Aug. 1890, J. A. Cockburn Premier SA.
16 Nov. 1889–27 Nov. 1889, Sir William Cleaver Francis Robinson administered Vic.
28 Nov. 1889–12 Jul. 1895, John Adrian Louis Hope, Earl of Hopetoun, Governor Vic.
21 Dec. 1889–19 Oct. 1890, Sir Malcolm Fraser administered WA.

29 Jan.–4 Feb. Federal Council of Australasia meets in Melbourne.
Feb. Sixth Intercolonial Trades and Labour Union Congress, held in Hobart, discusses direct representation of Labor in Parlt.
May. Free Trade and Liberal Association of NSW estb.
11 Jun. Aust. Labour Federation estb. in Brisbane. First Aust. party with direct participation by trade unions, hence first Labor Party.
Aug. Aust. workers contribute £24,000 to striking dock labourers in London.
21 Sep. NSW introduces payment of Members of Parlt.
Oct. Henry Parkes delivers Federation speech at Tenterfield, NSW, advocating a central Parlt and Executive.
25 Nov. Warship *Persia* launched.
During 1889
New Constitution framed in WA.
Tas. legalizes trade unions.
J. Bevan Edwards of British Army advises colonies on their defences; recommends federation of defence forces, which influences argument for Federation of Aust. colonies.
Beginning of economic depression in eastern colonies.
Royal Commission into sugar industry recommends that use of Kanakas or Polynesian labour in Aust. continue.
Unilever Aust. Pty Ltd estb.
Total estimated value of Aust. exports £62,585,856.
John Caruthers marks out E border of NT to Gulf of Carpentaria. Engaged in triangular surveying in Musgrave and Mann Ranges S of Ayers Rock, NT.
WA Govt estb. 'Agricultural Areas' to encourage farming.

Perth Stock Exchange opens.
Early Closing Associations form in Fremantle, WA, and Brisbane; encourage shops to close early.
Criminal Law Amendment Act in Tas. prohibits strikes.

Births & Deaths
Ronald Fife Angas, company director, b.
Clive Latham Baillieu, company director, b. (d. 1967)
Sir Edward Ritchie Knox, company director, b. (d. 1973)
Neal William Macrossan, Qld Chief Justice, b. (d. 1955)
Sir Leslie James Morshead, World War II military commander, b. (d. 1959)
Jack Keith Murray, administrator, agriculturist, b.
Sir Frank Keith Officer, diplomat, b. (d. 1969)
Sir Bertram Sydney Barnsdale Stevens, NSW Premier, b. (d. 1973)
Jessie Mary Grey Street (née Lillingston), known later as Lady Jessica Street, Federal politician, prominent women's rights campaigner, b. (d. 1970)

B

Science, Technology, Transport, Discovery

9 Apr. Cable from Roebuck Bay, NT, to Batavia (now Jakarta) opens.
May. Hawkesbury R. railway bridge opens. Links northern with southern and western railway lines.
1 Jun. Albany–Beverley, WA, railway line opens.
Jul. Hydraulic lifts introduced in Melbourne. (Sydney 1891.)
Milk pasteurization begins.
10 Oct. NT's first railway, Darwin–Pine Creek, opens.

During 1889
Melbourne–Adelaide and Sydney–Brisbane railway lines open for service.
Lawrence Hargrave discovers principle of rotary engine. Develops model of flying machine powered by compressed air engine.
Electric trams run in Melbourne and Perth.
Pneumatic tyres improve bicycle riding.
First gaslights in Perth.
Henry R. Hancock invents percussion drill used for deep mining. Calls drill a 'Bob Ridley'.
Lead smelting works estb. at Port Pirie, SA, to process Broken Hill ore.
John Mathew acclaimed for work on Aboriginal anthropology.
The Great Morwell Coal Mining Co. begins mining at Morwell, Vic. First briquettes made.

Births & Deaths

Henry John (Harry) Butler, pioneer aviator, b. (d. 1924)
Jack Cato, Tas. photographer, b.
Harry George Hawker, aviator, b. (d. 1921)
Sir Cecil Harold Hoskins, steel industry pioneer, b. (d. 1971)
Charles Halliley Kellaway, noted for work on snake venom, b. (d. 1952)
Cecil Thomas Madigan, geologist, explorer, b. (d. 1947)
Thomas Haynes Upton, engineer, b. (d. 1956)

C

Arts

Literature

During 1889
Women's Literary Society estb. in Sydney.
Andrew Barton (Banjo) Paterson publishes 'Clancy of the Overflow' in the *Bulletin*.

Music, Dance

During 1889
James C. Williamson estb. first professional ballet company, in Melbourne.
c. 1889. Luscombe Searelle, composer, active.

Drama, Theatre, Film

During 1889
Alfred Dampier writes *Marvellous Melbourne*, urban melodrama.

Fine Arts

17 Aug. Heidelberg School holds *Nine by Five* impressionist art exhibition in Melbourne.
During 1889
Arthur Streeton paints *Golden Summer*.
Tom Roberts paints *Shearing the Rams*.

Births & Deaths

James Charles Bancks, cartoonist, b. (d. 1952)
Frederick Christian Britton, painter, etcher, b. (d. 1931)
William Gilbert Collins, painter, b. (d. 1957)
J. V. Duhig, art critic, b. (d. 1963)
Percival Alexander Leason, painter and illustrator, b. (d. 1959)
Matilda Lister, naive painter, probably b. (d. 1965)
Rose Lowcay, painter, b. (d. 1968)
Richard Matthew McCann, landscape painter, probably b.
William Beckwith McInnes, portrait painter, b. (d. 1939)
Max Martin, painter, b.
Gladys Mary Owen, painter, b. (d. 1960)
Harry Rosengrave, graphic artist, painter, b.
Clive Travers Stephen, sculptor, b. (d. 1957)
John Christie Wright, sculptor, b. (d. 1917)

Architecture

27 Nov. Great Hall of Sydney Town Hall opens.
During 1889
The Australian Building completed in Melbourne. (Then tallest office building in the world.)
E. J. Woods completes classical Parlt House in Adelaide.
John Horbury Hunt begins building shingle-style houses with steep gables, tall chimneys and deep recessed verandas.

D
Religion, Learning

Jun. Victoria Public Library opens in Perth. (Becomes Public Library of WA in 1904.)
During 1889
Qld Teachers' Union estb.
Hobart Technical College estb.
Longerenong Agricultural College opens, Vic.
Melbourne Teachers' College estb.
St Patrick's College (Catholic Institute of Sydney) estb. at Manly, Sydney.
SA School of Mines and Industries estb. (SA Institute of Technology in 1965.)
SA Govt estb. monthly school paper, *The Childrens Hour*.

Births & Deaths

Leib Aisack Falk, Jewish rabbi, b. (d. 1957)
James Robert Beattie Love, Presbyterian missionary, b. (d. 1947)

E
Sport

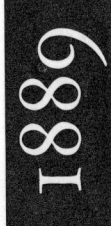

During 1889
Bravo, ridden by J. Anwin, wins Melbourne Cup in 3 minutes 32¼ seconds.
Grace Park Lawn Tennis Club estb. in Melbourne. First tennis club in Vic.
Rugby Union football estb. in Vic.

Births & Deaths

Herbert L. Collins, cricketer, noted batsman, b. (d. 1959)
Harold Hardwick, swimmer, boxer, b. (d. 1959)
W. H. (Midge) McLachlan, jockey, b.
John (Jack) Ryder, cricketer, noted batsman, b.

F
Historia Dignum

Population
Estimated total white, 3,062,477.

16 Jan. Record shade temperature of 127.5°F (53.1°C) at Cloncurry, Qld.
22 Apr. Fire destroys the Bijou Theatre in Melbourne, claiming two lives.
Jun. SA estb. annual Arbor Day for primary schools.
13 Sep. Fire destroys George & George Dept store in Melbourne, claiming three lives.
28 Dec. SA celebrates jubilee with International Exhibition in Adelaide.
During 1889
Vic. prohibits sale of Sunday papers. (Effective until 1949.)
There are 36,332 officers and men in Aust. land forces.
Typhoid fever epidemic in Melbourne claims over 400 lives.
Floods in Vic. and WA.

Communities

Alice Springs (named 1933), NT, estb. as Stuart
Nullagine, WA, estb.
Peak Hill, NSW, estb.
Pingelly, WA, estb.
Wallangarra, Qld, estb.

A
History, Politics, Economics, Law

1890

Government

12 Aug. 1890–Mar. 1893, Sir S. W. Griffith Premier Qld.
19 Aug. 1890–Jun. 1892, T. Playford Premier SA.
20 Oct. 1890–17 Mar. 1895, Sir William Cleaver Francis Robinson Governor WA.
3 Nov. 1890–15 Jan. 1891, Sir Alfred Stephen administered NSW.
5 Nov. 1890–Feb. 1892, J. Munro Premier Vic.
29 Dec. 1890–Feb. 1901, Sir J. Forrest Premier WA.
1890–1892, J. G. Knight Govt Resident NT under SA jurisdiction.

6–14 Feb. Conference of delegates from all Aust. colonies to consider Federation and defence policy held in Melbourne. Duncan Gillies elected chief representative. On 13 Feb. colonies unanimously adopt Sir Henry Parkes' motion for union of colonies under one govt. National Australasian Convention to consider Federation estb. on 14 Feb.
10 Feb. H. C. L. Anderson appointed first Director of Agriculture in NSW.
May. Henry George, American political economist, lectures in Aust. on the importance of tax in removing social inequalities.
25 Jul. Act passed conferring Constitution of WA. Responsible govt proclaimed on 21 Oct. Legislative Council nominated but to be elected after six years or when population reached 60,000. Legislative Assembly elected on restricted franchise. First representative parlt met on 30 Dec.
1 Aug. Aust. Labour Federation active in Brisbane to unify trade union movement. William Lane drafts platform for federated political action. (Qld. Labor Party estb. by 1 May 1891.)
16 Aug.–17 Oct. Maritime strike over victimization causes industrial chaos. On 30 Aug. great labour demonstrations in Sydney; on 19 Sep. Govt reads Riot Act; on 6 Oct. eight-hour demonstrations; on 18 Oct. 10,000 men join in sympathy demonstration in Adelaide. Strike is first major clash between employers and trade union movement in Aust.
29 Sep. Qld introduces triennial parlts.
Oct. Aust. branch of US secret society, the Knights of Labor, estb.
28 Nov. Tas. introduces payment of Members of Parlt.
Dec. Premier Permanent Building Land and Investment Association (founded by James Mirans in 1874) collapses. Several directors charged with conspiracy to defraud.
SA Labour Disputes Settlement Bill estb. Boards of Conciliation.

During 1890

SA confers part franchise on NT. Two NT members elected to Legislative Assembly in Adelaide.
A NSW Royal Commission appointed to examine causes and cures of strikes. (Recommends a Board Conciliation and Arbitration in May 1891.)
Sir Samuel Griffith first propounds basic wage doctrine.
Shearing shed hands estb. union. In May waterside unionists refuse to handle wool shorn by men not belonging to Shearers' Union.
Declining economic conditions force Govt to abolish assisted immigration.
Indenturing of Kanakas labourers prohibited.
Estimated total value of Aust. exports £62,594,163.
United Graziers Association estb. in Qld.
Falling wool prices contribute to declining economic climate.
Qld Govt imposes first income tax on companies. (C individuals in 1902.)
The Master Builders' Federation of Aust. estb. First national employers' organization.

Births & Deaths

Sir Norman Brearley, air service pioneer, b.
Richard Gardiner Casey, Baron Casey, Governor-General noted for projecting concern for Asia's emerging nations and for strengthening bonds with USA and UK, b. (d. 1976)
Sir Adolph Alexander Fitzgerald, public accountant, b. (d. 1965)
Francis Michael Forde, Labor Prime Minister, b. (d. 1983)
Irvine Owen Gaze, Antarctic explorer, farmer and businessman, b. (d. 1978)
Donald McLennan Grant, IWW member and NSW Senator, b. (d. 1970)
Robert James Heffron, NSW Premier, b. (d. 1978)
James William Herd, marine surveyor, b. (d. 1956)
James McGirr, NSW Premier, b. (d. 1957)
Sir John Northcott, World War II military commander, NSW Governor, b. (d. 1966)
Sir Stanley George Savige, World War II military commander, businessman, b. (d. 1954)
Sir Kenneth Whistler Street, NSW Supreme Court Judge, b. (d. 1972)
Sir Richard Williams, RAAF commander, b. (d. 1980)
Gordon Leslie Wood, economist, b. (d. 1953)

B

Science, Technology, Transport, Discovery

1 Jan. North Shore railway line opens in Sydney.
7 Feb. Emma Constance Stone first woman doctor registered by an Aust. Medical Board, in Melbourne.
Jul. J. F. Connolly reports gold in Murchison district, Qld.

During 1890
Rabbits spread in Qld.
The Aust. blue-speckle cattle dog, Aust. Heeler or Qld Heeler, estb. as a pure breed.
First locomotive built in SA, at Gawler.
Aust. scientists develop an anthrax vaccine.
First intercolonial Rust-in-Wheat Conference held.
Commercial manufacture of preserved and concentrated milk begins at Bacchus Marsh, Vic.
First Aust. cotton mill built, at Ipswich, Qld.
Aust. astronomers begin work on the international Astrographic Program to compile Great Star Catalogue.

Births & Deaths
Sir William Lawrence Bragg, physicist, b. (d. 1971)
Robert Hall Chapman, engineer, b. (d. 1953)
Alexander Hugh Chisholm, ornithologist, encyclopaedist and author, b. (d. 1977)
Frank Stanley Cotton, physiologist, inventor, b. (d. 1955)
Donald Harkness, car designer, b. (d. 1972)
A. L. Kennedy, mining engineer, Antarctic explorer, b. (d. 1973)
Arthur Vincent Meehan, orthopaedic surgeon, b. (d. 1955)
Charles Pearcy Mountford, anthropologist, author, film director, b. (d. 1976)
Sir Keith Macpherson Smith, aviator, b. (d. 1955)
Cyril Tenison White, botanist, b. (d. 1950)

C

Arts

Literature

26 Apr. Andrew Barton (Banjo) Paterson first publishes 'The Man From Snowy River' in the *Bulletin*.

Births & Deaths
Dame Mabel Balcombe Brookes, author, social worker expert on Napoleon, b. (d. 1975)
Zora Bernice May Cross, poet, author, actress, b. (d. 1964)
Mary Elizabeth Kathleen Dulcie Deamer, 'Queen of Bohemia', writer, b. (d. 1972)
James Devaney, author noted for Aboriginal lore and natural history, b. (d. 1976)
Malcolm Henry Ellis, author, historian, b. (d. 1969)
Ion Llewellyn Idriess, author b. (d. 1979)

Music, Dance

During 1890
Sydney Town Hall organ completed.

Births & Deaths
Gertrud Bodenwieser, dancer, choreographer, b. (d. 1959)
Clara Serena, contralto, b. (d. 1972)

Drama, Theatre, Film

During 1890
Garrick Theatre opens in Sydney.
First pantomime performed at Her Majesty's Theatre in Sydney.

Fine Arts

Oct. Monthly magazine *Australasian Critic* first published. (Lasts until 1891.)

During 1890
Tom Roberts and Arthur Streeton estb. 'Curlew Camp' at Mosman in Sydney.
Ballarat Ladies' Art Association, Vic. estb. First women's art society in Aust.
Bendigo Art Gallery, Vic., estb.
Charterisville Mansion at Heidelberg, Vic., becomes artists' colony.
Wilgie Art Club estb. in Perth to unite landscape painters.

Births & Deaths
Henry Allport, Tas. art expert, b. (d. 1965)
Ralph Balson, oil abstract painter, b. (d. 1964)

1890

Theodore Penleigh Boyd, landscape painter, etcher, b. (d. 1923)
Alfred Coleman, landscape painter, probably b. (d. 1952)
Aileen Rose Dent, portrait, still life painter, b. (d. 1979)
Orlando Dutton, sculptor, probably b. (d. 1962)
William Frater, post-impressionist painter, b. (d. 1974)
Herbert Gallop, painter, commercial artist, b. (d. 1958)
Inez Hutchison, painter, b. (d. 1970)
Robert Johnson, landscape painter, b. (d. 1964)
Joe Jonsson, cartoonist, illustrator, b. (d. 1963)
Adrian Lawlor, painter, critic, b. (d. 1969)
Sir Daryl Lindsay, painter, illustrator, b. (d. 1976)
Louis McCubbin, painter, b. (d. 1952)
Charles M. Meere, painter, illustrator, b. (d. 1961)
Herbert Rose, landscape painter, etcher, b. (d. 1937)
Ethel L. Spowers, painter, b. (d. 1947)
Reginald Ward Sturgess, watercolourist, b. (d. 1932)

Architecture

During 1890
Ernest Wunderlich begins pressing metal sheets, beginning structural use of steel in buildings.
Anketell Henderson alters Bank of Australasia at Port Fairy, Vic. (Built 1856.)
Customs House at Rockhampton, Qld, completed.
Depression ends high Victorian expenditure on public buildings.
Queen Anne Revival houses popular in Sydney.

Births & Deaths
Arthur George Stephenson, architect, b. (d. 1967)

D Religion, Learning

30 Jun. Adelaide Public Library opens.

During 1890
First Christian Science meetings held.
University of Tas. opens, in Hobart.

Births & Deaths
Charles Herbert Currey, historian, b. (d. 1970)
Howard West Kilvinton Mowll, Church of England primate, b. (d. 1958)

E
Sport

During 1890
Carbine, ridden by R. Ramage, wins Melbourne Cup in 3 minutes 28¼ seconds.
Albert Griffiths wins World Featherweight Boxing title. First Aust. world title fight.
First intercolonial women's cricket match played in Sydney. Rosalie Dean scores two centuries.

Births & Deaths
Sir Harry Alderson, rowing administrator, b.
Charlie East, racing car driver, b. (d. 1960)
Bill Foulsham, jockey, b. (d. 1979)
Howard Hallett, Rugby League footballer, b. (d. 1970)
Norman Smith, 'Wizard', motorcar sportsman, b. (d. 1958)

F
Historia Dignum

Population
Estimated total white, 3,151,355.

20 Feb. Ship *Quetta* wrecked near Thursday I., claiming 134 lives.
1 Mar. The newspaper *Worker* published in Brisbane.
6 Mar. Ship *Eliza Mary* wrecked near New Hebrides (Vanuatu), claiming 37 lives.
During Mar. Brisbane R., Qld, floods. Darling R., NSW, floods.
25 Apr. Train collision at Bathurst, NSW, claims four lives.
3 Aug. John Norton publishes newspaper Sydney *Truth*. (Runs until 1958.)
27 Aug. Perth GPO officially opens.
1 Oct. The newspaper *Advocate* published in Launceston, Tas.
2 Oct. Fire destroys centre of Sydney's commercial quarter.
During 1890
Royal Agricultural Society of Vic. estb.
c. 1890. First canned fruit appears.

Communities
Cockburn, SA, estb.
Coolah, NSW, estb.
Gascoyne Junction, WA, estb.
Oodnadatta, SA, estb.
Rainbow, Vic., estb.
White Cliffs, NSW, estb.

1891

A
History, Politics, Economics, Law

Government
15 Jan. 1891–2 Mar. 1893, Victor Albert George Child-Villiers, Earl of Jersey, Governor NSW.
23 Oct. 1891–Aug. 1894, G. R. Dibbs Premier NSW.

7 Jan. United Trades and Labor Council in Adelaide estb. the United Labor Party. On 9 May, 3 ULP candidates win seats in SA Legislative Council, becoming first Labor Party candidates elected to SA Parlt.

20–24 Jan. Federal Council meets in Hobart Vic., Qld and Tas. represented.

Jan.–Jun. Qld and NSW shearers strike over wage reductions and freedom of contract; 1,000 striking shearers estb. quasi-military camp at Barcaldine, Qld. In May 12 unionists are convicted for conspiracy after angry rioting.

2 Mar.–9 Apr. The National Australasian Convention, the first Federal Convention, meets in Sydney. Sir Henry Parkes elected president on 2 Mar. Convention adopts title 'Commonwealth of Australia' on 1 Apr. First draft Federal Constitution to estb. Federal Parlt as Govt for Cwlth of Aust. completed on 9 Apr.

30 Apr. Tas. introduces triennial parlts.

2 May. David Lindsay begins 11 months exploration from Warrina, SA, to W coast of Aust. Arrives Esperance Bay, WA, 14 Oct.

30 May–2 Jun. Progressive Political League of Vic. estb. to unite Labor in Vic.

13 Jun. Sir Henry Parkes addresses large crowd on Federation at the Gaiety Theatre in Sydney. When Parkes retires Edmund Barton accepts leadership for the movement but plans temporarily halted.

17 Jun. Labor Electoral League, estb. in Apr., wins 22 per cent of vote at NSW elections. In first notable Labor victory, 37 members sit in NSW Legislative Assembly in Jul.

3 Aug. Bank of Van Diemen's Land collapses. Oct. British Bank of Aust. and Anglo-Aust. Bank collapse.

27 Aug. First Brisbane wool sales.

5 Sep. British Royal Navy's Aust.-Auxiliary Squadron (seven ships) arrives in Sydney to form nucleus of a united Aust. navy.

1 Oct. Aust. enters the Universal Postal Union, world-wide postal federation.

During 1891
Vic. Govt introduces voluntary arbitration system to resolve industrial disputes. (NSW 1892.)
Qld Govt rejects Bill to divide colony into southern, central and northern districts for legislative and administrative functions.
NSW Govt terminates assisted immigration policy.
Rose Scott begins campaigning for Female Suffrage.
George Clunies-Rose and John Murray granted 99 year lease of Christmas I.
WA Trade and Labor Council estb.
The Pastoralists' Federal Council (Aust. Woolgrowers and Graziers' Council) estb.
First Mildura, Vic., fruit for drying harvested.

Births & Deaths
Joseph Palmer Abbott, pastoralist, NSW politician, b. (d. 1965)
Sir Richard James Fildes Boyer, pastoralist, ABC chairman, b. (d. 1961)
John Joseph Cahill, railway fitter who became NSW Premier, instrumental in planning estb. of Sydney Opera House, b. (d. 1959)
Roderic Stanley Dallas, World War I fighter pilot, b. (d. 1918)
Sir Frederick Lloyd Dumas, company director, editor b. (d. 1973)
Stanley James Goble, RAAF commander, b. (d. 1948)
Sir William John McKell, Governor-General, NSW Premier, b. (d. 1985)
Albert George Ogilvie, Tas. Premier, b. (d. 1939)
Sir William Joseph Slim, Governor-General, b. (d. 1970)

B

Science, Technology, Transport, Discovery

During 1891
George Chaffey installs pumping plant, pioneering use of direct-action triple expansion engines to drive centrifugal pumps.
Lawrence Hargrave creates model flying machine powered by a three-cylinder engine.
Record value ambergris discovered in Aust. waters in whale at Port Davey, Tas.
Charles O'Conner designs and supervises construction of Fremantle Harbour, WA.
Clara Stone first of two women to graduate in medicine from an Aust. University.
Adelaide–Oodnadatta section of transcontinental railway line completed.
Brisbane–Bundaberg, Qld, railway line opens.
Gold discovered at Cue and on Murchison R., WA.
Cyanide process of gold extraction first used, at Ravenswood, Qld.
Sir Henry Jones begins canning fruit in Hobart (IXL label).
Edward Lascelles demonstrates (in Vic.) benefits of irrigation.

Births & Deaths
Sir Harold Robert Dew, surgeon, b. (d. 1962)
Adolphus Peter Elkin, anthropologist, leading authority on Aboriginals, b. (d. 1979)
Sir Neil Hamilton Fairley, physician, expert on malaria and tropical diseases, b. (d. 1966)
Arthur Sidney Hoskins, iron and steel entrepreneur, b. (d. 1959)
James Roy Kinghorn, naturalist specializing in study of snakes and birdlife, b.

C

Arts

Literature

During 1891
Edward Kinglake publishes *The Australian at Home*.

Births & Deaths
Edwin Field Gerald, war balladist who used pseudonym Gerardy, b. (d. 1965)
Arthur Walter Osborne, author, b. (d. 1976)
Percival Charles Rodda, author, journalist, b.

Music, Dance

Jun. Grand National Eisteddfod of Australasia estb.
During 1891
G. W. L. Marshall-Hall, music professor, arrives in Melbourne.
South Street Music Competitions inaugurated in Ballarat, Vic.

Drama, Theatre, Film

During 1891
Theatre in Aust. prospers.
Sarah Bernhardt performs in Sydney and Melbourne.

Births & Deaths
Lottie Lyell, silent film actress, among first Aust. film stars, b. (d. 1925)

Fine Arts

29 Apr. Queen Victoria Museum and Art Gallery opened in Launceston, Tas.
Launceston Art Society estb.

Births & Deaths
Dorrit Black, oil landscape cubist painter, b. (d. 1951)
Ian Fairweather, abstract figurative painter, b. (d. 1974)
Rah Fizelle, modernist painter, b. (d. 1964)
Carlyle Jackson, watercolourist, b. (d. 1940)
Sir David Alexander Cecil Low, political cartoonist, b. (d. 1963)
Albert Ernest Newbury, landscape and portrait painter, b. (d. 1941)
Adelaide Perry, painter, probably b. (d. 1973)
George Whinnen, painter, b. (d. 1950)

Architecture

Mutual Life Assurance building in Sydney completed.
Yarralumla House built in Canberra. (Bought by Govt in 1913 for Governor-General's residence.)
J. B. Spencer's Strand Arcade built in Sydney.

1891

D
Religion, Learning

During 1891
Christian Science organization estb. in Aust.
Theosophical Society estb. in Aust.
First Baptist Theological College estb., in Vic. (NSW 1916, Qld 1931, SA 1952, WA 1964.)
Church of England Aust. College of Theology founded.
St Joseph's Catholic College estb. in Qld.
Hawkesbury Agricultural College estb. in NSW.
Ballarat School of Mines founded as Academy and School of Design, Vic.
Burnley Horticultural College estb. (Only college providing horticultural instruction until 1956.)
W. Catton Grasby publishes *Teaching in Three Continents* to reform Aust. education.

Births & Deaths
Sir John Dudley Gibbs Medley, educationist, university administrator, b. (d. 1962)

E
Sport

18 Jun. United Australasian Axemen's Association estb. First woodchopping competitions held.
4 Jul. Caulfield Golf Club estb. in Melbourne; introduces caddies.

During 1891
Malvolio, ridden by G. Redfearn, wins Melbourne Cup in 3 minutes $29\frac{1}{4}$ second.
J. M. Bruce estb. Royal Melbourne Golf Club.
Vic. Amateur Athletic Association estb. (Qld 1895, Tas. 1902, SA & WA 1905.)
Aust. Rules football boundary umpires introduced.
Last penny-farthing bicycle used in the Austral Wheelrace.

Births & Deaths
Sir Francis Joseph Edmund (Frank) Beaurepaire, swimmer, businessman, b. (d. 1956)
Clarence V. (Clarrie) Grimmett, cricketer, noted slow bowler, b. (d. 1980)
Patrick O'Harawood, tennis player, b.

F
Historia Dignum

1891

Population
Estimated total white (5 Apr.), 3,240,985.
There are *c.* 38,077 Chinese and *c.* 60,000 Aborigines in Aust.

1 Jan. Mr Goschen's plan for universal uniform colonial 2½ penny postage stamp accepted by all colonies.
Jul. The Australia Hotel opens in Sydney. Largest hotel in Southern Hemisphere.
Serious floods in Melbourne.
6 Sep. Barque *Fiji* wrecked near Moonlight Head, Vic., 12 lives lost.
8–9 Oct. Thieves steal mace from Vic. Parlt House.
During 1891
Dutch impound Aust. whaling ship *Costa Rica Packet*, causing international incident.
International Exhibition opens in Launceston, Tas.
Murrumbidgee R. floods in NSW.
Belair Park, SA, reserved; among first parks reserved in SA.
Greeks and Italians introduce lobster pots to NSW.

Births & Deaths
Samuel Emanuel Jervis, 'Sammy Cox', among first white men to live with Aborigines, possibly among longest-living Aust. males (118 yrs), d. (probably b. 1773)
Lady Vera White (née Deakin), Red Cross worker, b.

Communities
Lightning Ridge, NSW, first settled
Merredin, WA, estb.
Mingenew, WA, estb.
Murchison, Vic., estb.
Rosebery, Tas., estb.

1892

A
History, Politics, Economics, Law

Government

16 Feb. 1892–Jan 1893, W. Shiels Premier Vic.
21 Jun. 1892–Oct. 1892, F. W. Holder Premier SA.
17 Aug. 1892–Apr. 1894, H. Dobson Premier Tas.
15 Oct. 1892–Jun. 1893, Sir J. W. Downer Premier SA.
30 Nov. 1892–8 Aug. 1893, Sir William Dobson administered Tas.
1892–1905, C. J. Dashwood Govt Resident NT under SA jurisdiction.

Apr. Shortage of manpower in sugar industry leads Qld Govt to officially re-introduce indenture of Kanakas. (Until 1901.)
4 Jul. At Broken Hill, NSW, 6,000 miners begin 18-week strike over freedom of contract.
5 Jul. Qld becomes first Govt to introduce preferential voting system.
Aug. First Labor-in-Politics Convention meets in Brisbane.
During 1892
Amalgamated Workers' Union form Women's Division.
Aust. economic affairs, particularly financial institutions in Vic., deteriorate.
NSW Govt estb. a Labour Bureau (employment service).

Births & Deaths

Cyril Albert Clowes, military commander, b. (d. 1968)
Sir Arthur William Coles, businessman, politician, b. (d. 1982)
Sir Eric John Harrison, Federal politician, b. (d. 1974)
Sir Edmund Francis Herring, military commander, jurist, administrator, b. (d. 1982)
John Simpson Kirkpatrick, 'Man with the Donkey', Gallipoli field ambulance hero, b. (d. 1915)
Lawrence Dominic McCarthy, World War I soldier, b. (d. 1976)
Samuel McCaughey, pastoralist, b. (d. 1955)
Sir Daniel McVey, public servant and industrialist, b. (d. 1972)
Henry Neilson Wrigley, air force officer, b.

B
Science, Technology, Transport, Discovery

4 Feb. Strahan–Zeehan railway opens in Tas.
Jul. William Ford and Arthur Bayley discover gold a Coolgardie, WA.
During 1892
Complete skeleton of prehistoric Diprotodon discovered at Lake Callabonna, SA.
Dental College opens in Melbourne.
Wagga Agricultural Farm estb. as experimental farm, NSW.
First drilling for oil at Salt Creek in Coorong area of SA.
Babcock test to measure butterfat content in milk estb. in Gisborne, Vic., from USA.
Rockhampton–Longreach, Qld, railway opens.
First milking machine imported to NSW from Scotland by the Bodalla Co.

Births & Deaths

Vere Gordon Childe, archaeologist, b. (d. 1957)
Sir Norman McAlister Gregg, ophthalmologist, b. (d. 1966)
Sir Cedric Stanton Hicks, physiologist and pharmacologist, b.
Herbert John Louis Hinkler, always known as Bert Hinkler, pioneer aviator, 'The Lone Eagle', b. (d. 1933)
Sir Ross Macpherson Smith, aviator, b. (d. 1922)
Sir Harry Wyatt Wunderly, physician, medical administrator, b. (d. 1971)

C
Arts

1892

Literature

During 1892
William Astley, using the pseudonym Price Warung, publishes collection of stories, *Tales of the Convict System*.
William Lane, using pseudonym John Miller, publishes *The Workingman's Paradise: An Australian Labour Novel*.

Births & Deaths
Leon Maxwell Gellert, author, journalist, b. (d. 1966)

Music, Dance

Births & Deaths
Mirrie Irma Hill, composer, b.
Francis Hutchens, pianist, composer, b. (d. 1965)
Horace Stanley Keats, composer, b. (d. 1945)
Gladys Moncrieff, singer, actress, b. (d. 1976)
Isabel Varney Desmond Monk, composer, b. (d. 1967)

Drama, Theatre, Film

17 Jun. Fire destroys Theatre Royal in Sydney.

Births & Deaths
Roy Rene, born Henry van der Sluice and better known as 'Mo', b. (d. 1954)

Fine Arts

c. 1892. Cannibal Art Club estb. in Melbourne.
Ishmael Artists Club active in Melbourne.

Births & Deaths
Ethel Alicia Bishop, painter, b. (d. 1958)
Edouard Joseph Goerg, painter and etcher, b.
Ola (Carola) Cohn, sculptor, b. (d. 1964)
John Roy Eldershaw, landscape watercolourist, b. (d. 1973)
Harry L. Fern, watercolourist, b. (d. 1945)
Harold Brocklebank Herbert, watercolourist, b. (d. 1945)
Cyril George Lander, painter, b.
Frank Medworth, tropical painter, etcher, b. (d. 1947)
Esther Paterson, portrait artist, b. (d. 1971)
Grace Cossington Smith, post-impressionist painter, b. (d. 1984)
Vivian Phillip Webb, painter, b.

Architecture

c. 1892. Stonnington House in Malvern, Melbourne completed.
First 12-storey buildings built in Melbourne and Sydney.

1892

D
Religion, Learning

29 Jan. Institute of Bankers estb. in Sydney to train banking staff.
During 1892
Compulsory and secular primary education system in SA becomes free.
First WA kindergarten estb.
WA Museum opens.

Births & Deaths
Sir Archibald Grenfell Price, educationist, historian, geographer, b. (d. 1977)
Dorothy Ross, educationist, b. (d. 1982)

E
Sport

During 1892
Glenloth, ridden by G. Robson, wins Melbourne Cup in 3 minutes $36\frac{1}{4}$ seconds.
Vic. wins first Sheffield Shield cricket match.
Collingwood Australian Rules Football Club estb. in Melbourne.
The Austral Professional Bicycle Club estb. in Sydney.
Mark Foy founds Sydney Flying Squad Sailing Club.
NSW Amateur Swimming Association estb. in Sydney.
First athletics championships held in Melbourne. Bill McPherson first Aust. athlete to run 100 yards inside 10 seconds (9.9).

Births & Deaths
Cecil Blinkhorn, Rugby League footballer, b. (d. 1977)
Johnny Hoskins, speedway motorcyclist, b.
Alban George Johnnie Moyes, cricketer, commentator, b. (d. 1963)
Jimmy Pike, jockey, b. (d. 1969)
Ivo Whitton, golfer, b. (d. 1967)

F
Historia Dignum

1892

Population
Estimated total white, 3,305,753.

27 Apr. Train derailment at Tarana, NSW, claims eight lives.

During 1892
Le Courrier Australien, foreign-language newspaper, estb.
Antipodean magazine published.
John (Jack) Howe estb. world shearing record, 321 sheep in 8 hours 40 minutes at Blackall, Qld. (Holds record for 58 years.)
John Makin, Sydney baby murderer, hanged.
Sydney fire authority imports horse-drawn steam fire engine 'Big Ben'. (Among biggest of kind in world.)

Communities
Callide, Qld, probably first settled
Coolgardie, WA, estb.
Cue, WA, estb.

A
History, Politics, Economics, Law

Government
23 Jan. 1893–Sep. 1894, J. B. Patterson Premier Vic.
3 Mar. 1893–29 May 1893, Sir Frederick Darley administered NSW.
27 Mar. 1893–Oct. 1893, Sir T. McIlwraith Premier Qld.
29 May 1893–15 Mar. 1895, Sir Robert William Duff Governor NSW.
16 Jun. 1893–Dec. 1899, C. C. Kingston Premier SA.
8 Aug. 1893–14 Aug. 1900, Jenico William Joseph Preston, Viscount Gormanston, Governor Tas.
27 Oct. 1893–Apr. 1898, H. M. Nelson Premier Qld.

26 Jan. Federal Council meets in Hobart. Approves Cwlth Bill on 29 Jan.
28 Jan. Federal Bank of Aust. closes in Melbourne, beginning bank crash. On 14 Apr. Commercial Bank of Aust. suspends operations, and 14 other Banks suspend payments during monetary crisis. Special Premiers Conference called in Melbourne on 27 May. By Jul. most suspended banks re-open.
29 Apr. Coat of Arms of Qld granted. (Arms of NSW 11 Oct. 1908, Vic. 6 Jun. 1910, Tas. 21 May 1917, SA 20 Nov. 1936, WA 17 Mar. 1969.)
13 Jun. NSW abolishes plural voting for Legislative Assemblies.
31 Jul. The Aust. Federation Conference opens in Sydney.
During Jul. Seamen strike over wage reductions. Aust. Federation League estb. Holds conference at Corowa, NSW.
Oct. William Lane estb. Utopian settlement called New Australia in Paraguay. First group of 209 pioneers leave Sydney for Paraguay on 16 Jul. Second group of 212 leave Adelaide on 31 Dec. In 1894, because New Australia did not conform to his Utopian ideals, Lane estb. new settlement called Cosmé.
Nov. William Arthur Holman introduces 'the Pledge' into NSW Labor Party to ensure that all party representatives vote uniformly.
During 1893
WA Govt abolishes primogeniture law. On 13 Oct. Govt abolishes property qualifications for members of Legislative Assembly.
Goldrush to Kalgoorlie, WA.

Births & Deaths
William Shepherd Morrison, Viscount Dunrossil, Governor-General, b. (d. 1961)
Mary Alice Holman, known as May Holman, WA politician b. (d. 1939)
Albert Jacka, first Aust. to win the Victoria Cross in World War I, b. (d. 1932)
Robert Harold Nimmo, World War I military commander, b. (d. 1966)
Sir George Frederick Wootten, World War II commander, b. (d. 1970)

B

Science, Technology, Transport, Discovery

8 Mar. First public telephone in NSW estb., at Sydney GPO.
14 Jun. Patrick Hannan and friends discover gold at Kalgoorlie, WA, in area which becomes known as the Golden Mile.
20 Sep. Electric tram services begin running from North Sydney to Mosman.
23 Sep. Electric traction tramway begins in Hobart; first in Southern Hemisphere.

During 1893
First hydro-electricity scheme begins, at Thargomindah, Qld.
Billy Elliot imports first car to Aust., a De Dion Voiturette.
District nursing services begin in Tas.
John Hartnett and David Robinson patent milking machine using pulsating vacuum and double-chambered teat cups. Estb. principle of modern milking machine.
Timber and iron bridge opens over Lachlan R. at Cowra, NSW.
Aust. Institute of Mining Engineers estb. First professional association of mining men.
William Sutherland presents paper on gaseous viscosities which includes Sutherland's constant equation.

Births & Deaths

Thomas Noel Burke-Gaffney, seismologist, astronomer, b. (d. 1958)
Sir Ralph West Cilento, medical administrator, tropical disease expert, b. (d. 1985)
Sir Victor Marcus Coppleson, surgeon, world authority on shark attacks, b. (d. 1965)
Raymond Arthur Dart, doctor, anthropologist, b.
Raymond Trewolla Littlejohns, naturalist, b. (d. 1961)
Florence Violet McKenzie, electrical engineer who influenced estb. of women's RAN service, b.
Dame Ida Caroline Mann, eye disease specialist, b.
Horace Clive Miller, pioneer aviator, b.
Ellis Le Geyt Troughton, zoologist, expert on mammals, b. (d. 1974)
Francis Edgar Williams, anthropologist, b. (d. 1943)

C

Arts

Literature

During 1893
F. W. L. Adams publishes *The Australians*.

Births & Deaths
Martin à Beckett Boyd, novelist, b. (d. 1972)
Francis Patrick (Frank) Clune, author, b. (d. 1971)
Frank Dalby Davison, novelist, b. (d. 1970)

Music, Dance

9 Sep. Rosalie Phillipini's *Turquoisette: A Study in Blue* becomes first original ballet entirely conceived, created and performed in Aust.

During 1893
Octavius Beale estb. piano factory at Annandale, Sydney.

Births & Deaths
Roy Ewing Agnew, composer, pianist, b. (d. 1944)
Arthur Leslie Benjamin, composer, conductor, b. (d. 1960)
Sir Eugene Goossens, composer, conductor noted for raising Aust. orchestral standards to international level, b. (d. 1962)
Daisy Kennedy, violinist, b.
Harold Williams, baritone, b. (d. 1976)

Drama, Theatre, Film

During 1893
Bland Holt produces *The Breaking of the Drought*, melodrama.
'Harry Rickards' (Henry B. Leete) starts Tivoli Variety circuit.

Births & Deaths
Diane Cicely Courtneidge, actress, comedian, b.

Fine Arts

During 1893
Emanuel Fox opens the modernist Melbourne School of Art. (Closes 1899.)

Births & Deaths
Mary Cecil Allen, avant-garde painter, b. (d. 1962)
Reginald Ernest Rex Battarbee, Central Aust. watercolourist, noted for encouraging Aboriginal art, b. (d. 1973)
William Rubery Bennett, harbour scene and landscape painter, b.

1893

1893

Stella Esther Gwendolyn Bowen, painter, b. (d. 1947)
John W. Elischer, sculptor, b. (d. 1966)
Harold Frederick Weaver Hawkins, painter graphic artist, sculptor, b. (d. 1977)
Ludwig Hirschfeld-Mack, painter, b. (d. 1964)
Harold R. Hughan, ceramic artist, among first to make stoneware, b. (d. 1975)
Justus Jorgensen, painter, b. (d. 1975)
Godfrey Clive Miller, abstract painter, b. (d. 1964)

Architecture

During 1893
Late Victorian Period of architecture begins. (Ends *c.* 1900.)
George McRae, architect, designs Queen Victoria Building in Sydney.

D
Religion, Learning

During 1893
WA introduces compulsory primary education system ending State aid to denominational schools.
Vic. Teachers' Training College closes in depression. (Reopens 1900.)

Births & Deaths
John Anderson, philosopher and controversialist, b. (d. 1962)

E
Sport

During 1893
Tarcoola, ridden by H. Cripps, wins Melbourne Cup in 3 minutes 30½ seconds.
Bicycle League of Professional Wheelmen estb. in NSW.
Royal Sydney Golf Club estb.
First Aust. walking championships held.

Births & Deaths
Roy Cazaly, Aust. Rules footballer noted for high marking ability, b. (d. 1963)
Joseph Wakefield Kent, known as Mick King, middleweight boxer, b. (d. 1948)
Robert Spears, cyclist, b. (d. 1950)
Tommy Uren, boxer, b. (d. 1954)
Frank Wootton, horseracing trainer, b. (d. 1940)

F
Historia Dignum

Population
Estimated total white, 3,361,895.

30 Jan.–18 Feb. Three cyclones damage south-eastern Qld and northern NSW, claiming 11 lives.
3 Feb. Highest recorded rainfall (until 1979) in Aust. over 24-hour period, at Crohamhurst Observatory, Qld.
During Feb. Brisbane R. rises twice in 22 days, causing severe flooding.
During 1893
The 'Tantanoola tiger', a wild dog resembling a Syrian wolf, is assumed to have killed many sheep around Tantanoola, SA. The term 'Tantanoola tiger' becomes a catch-phrase indicating something mythical.
Great Drought begins. (Lasts until 1902.)
First voluntary Ambulance Service estb. in Brisbane, (NSW 1895.)
NSW Govt arms police.
Smallpox epidemic in Perth. (Ends in 1894.)

Communities
Armadale, WA, estb.
Esperance, WA, estb.
Gordonvale, Qld, estb.
Marble Bar, WA, estb.
West Wyalong, NSW, estb.
Yarram, Vic., estb.

A
History, Politics, Economics, Law

Government

14 Apr. 1894–Oct. 1899, Sir E. Braddon Premier Tas.
3 Aug. 1894–Sep. 1899, G. H. Reid Premier NSW.
27 Sep. 1894–Dec. 1899, G. Turner Premier Vic.

Feb. Intercolonial conference of shearers resolves to amalgamate bush unions in NSW, Vic., SA and Qld. Amalgamated Shearers' Union joins with other unions to form Aust. Workers' Union.

Jul.–Sep. Qld and northern NSW shearers strike in last and most violent of large industrial confrontations in the period.

Oct. Military commandants hold conference in Sydney to examine mobilization of a united defence scheme.

21 Dec. SA Govt first in Aust. and among first in world to grant female suffrage. (WA 1899, NSW and Cwlth 1902, Tas. 1903, Qld 1905, Vic. 1908.)

SA Govt first in Aust. to give women full political rights to sit in Parlt. (Cwlth 1902, Qld 1915, NSW 1918, WA 1920, Tas. 1921, Vic. 1923.)

SA Govt first to provide for limited compulsory conciliation and arbitration in industrial disputes and for estb. of tribunals. (Vic. 1896, WA 1900, NSW 1901, Qld 1908, Tas. 1910.)

During 1894

Second Colonial Conference held in England.

SA Govt passes Factory Act to protect workers from exploitation.

William Morris Hughes enters NSW Parlt.

Period of experiment and reform in land settlement begins. Large estates resumed and subdivided for closer settlement.

Striking shearers set fire to paddle-steamer *Rodney* on the Murray R.

Vic. first to provide rural credit in long-term loans. WA estb. first Agricultural Bank for this purpose. (SA 1895, Qld 1902, Tas. 1907.)

Births & Deaths

Arthur Samuel Allen, soldier and accountant, b. (d. 1959)
Sir Douglas Berry Copland, economist, diplomat, administrator, b. (d. 1971)
Arthur Henry Cobby, RAAF commander, b. (d. 1955)
Sir Peter Roy Maxwell Drummond, RAAF commander, b. (d. 1945)
Herbert Vere Evatt, Labor politician, judge, b. (d. 1965)
Charles Allen Seymour Hawker, SA politician and pastoralist, b. (d. 1938)
Frank Hubert McNamara, RAAF commander, b. (d. 1961)
Sir Robert Gordon Menzies, Liberal-Country coalition Prime Minister, b. (d. 1978)
Sir Horace Clement Hugh Robertson, infantry commander, b. (d. 1960)
Sir Sydney Fairbairn Rowell, World War II military commander, b. (d. 1975)
Geoffrey Austin Street, Federal politician, military commander, b. (d. 1940)

B

Science, Technology, Transport, Discovery

Jan. First plate sheet iron, steel sheet rolling and galvanizing and corrugating plant opens at Esbank, near Lithgow, NSW.
8 Mar. Electric lighting installed in Melbourne central business district.
May. Horn Scientific Expedition to central Aust. begins. (Returns in Aust. 1896.)
19 Sep. King Street, Sydney, electric tram service opens.
12 Nov. A train of four box kites lifts Lawrence Hargrave 16 feet above ground at Stanwell Park, NSW, pioneering aeronautical experiments in Aust.

During 1894
Charles Highland builds a three-wheeled vehicle with Daimler petrol engine in Sydney. Probably first car built in Aust.
The Shearer car built in SA; among first built in Aust. (The Pioneer Vic. 1897, the Thompson 1898, the Ziegler 1898, the Sutton auto car 1900, Australis 1901, Tarrant 1901–1903.)
New Sydney Hospital opens.
Operating Theatres estb. in hospitals.
Rainbow trout introduced into NSW from NZ.
Standard Time Zones legislated for by Parlts of all Aust. Colonies. 150th degree E of longitude standard mean time for Qld, NSW, Vic. and Tas.; 135th degree for SA; 120th degree for WA. Begins operating 1895.

Births & Deaths

Sir John Victor Hall Best, dental surgeon, b. (d. 1972)
Lady Phyllis Dorothy Cilento (née McGlew), medical worker, b.
Sidney Cotton, aviator, b. (d. 1969)
Leonard Bell Cox, neurologist, b. (d. 1976)
Raymond John Paul Parer, pioneer aviator, b. (d. 1967)
Mervyn Victor Richardson, inventor, b.

C

Arts

Literature

During 1894
George Lewin Becke publishes *By Reef and Palm*.
'Red Page' feature of the *Bulletin* begins as 'Books of the Day'. (Becomes 'Red Page' in 1896.)
Henry Lawson publishes *Short Stories in Prose and Verse*.
Ethel Sibyl Turner publishes *Seven Little Australians*.

Births & Deaths

Paul Langton Grano, poet, b. (d. 1975)
Eric Honeywood Partridge, author, philologist, b.

Music, Dance

During 1894
Conservatorium estb. in Adelaide. First permanent musical training centre in Aust.
Alice Mason Beatty estb. School of Dancing. (Now among oldest surviving dance schools in Aust.)

Births & Deaths

Florence Austral (real name Florence Wilson), dramatic soprano, b. (d. 1968)
Sir Bernard Thomas Heinze, conductor, b. (d. 1982)
Gertrude Emily Johnson, opera singer, b. (d. 1973)

Drama, Theatre, Film

During 1894
Alfred Dampier produces *Robbery Under Arms* as play in London.

Births & Deaths

George Stevenson Wallace, comedian, b. (d. 1960)

Fine Arts

During 1894
Emanuel Fox paints *The Art Students*, one of earliest impressionistic works painted in Aust.

Births & Deaths

William Bustard, stained-glass designer, b. (d. 1973)
Archibald Douglas Colquhoun, portrait, landscape painter, b.
Leroy Leveson Laurent Joseph (Roy) de Maistre, modern art pioneer, among first to introduce post-impressionism and cubism, b. (d. 1968)
Adrian Feint, painter of decorative surrealistic flower pieces, b. (d. 1971)
John Richard Flanagan, illustrator, b. (d. 1964)

1894

1894

Cecil L. Hartt, cartoonist, probably b. (d. 1930)
George Rayner Hoff, sculptor, b. (d. 1937)
Elizabeth Deans Paterson, portrait and watercolour painter, b. (d. 1970)
John Thomas Nightingale Rowell, landscape painter, b. (d. 1973)
Mervyn Napier Waller, stained-glass window designer, muralist, b. (d. 1972)
Cyril Leyshon White, artist, probably b. (d. 1962)
Rhys Williams, engraver, painter, b.
Margery Pitt Withers, painter, b. (d. 1966)

Architecture

During 1894
Houses built on stumps, and with wide verandas, become popular in Qld.

D
Religion, Learning

During 1894
Matilda Ann (Tilly) Aston estb. Library of the Vic. Association of Braille writers.
Agnes Lloyd Bennett becomes first woman science graduate from Sydney University.

E
Sport

Aug. First Aust. women's amateur golf championship held at Geelong, Vic. First Aust. men's golf championship held in Melbourne on 9 Nov.
During 1894
Patron, ridden by H. W. Dawes, wins Melbourne Cup in 3 minutes 31 seconds.
First Aust. national swimming championships for men held.
NSW controlling baseball body estb.
Sydney Harbour Life Saving Society begins lifesaving activity in Aust.

Births & Deaths
Tommy Corrigan, jockey, b.
Fanny Durack, swimmer, b. (d. 1960)
Harold Horder, Rugby League footballer, b. (d. 1978)
William Albert Stanley (Bert) Oldfield, cricketer, b. (d. 1976)
Harry Plant, racehorse trainer, b. (d. 1978)
Victor York Richardson, all-round sportsman and commentator, b. (d. 1969)
A. W. (Nick) Winter, athlete, triple jumper, b.
Stanley Wootton, jockey trainer, b.

F
Historia Dignum

Population
Estimated total white, 3,426,760.

15 Jan. Francis Knorr hanged in Melbourne for murdering unwanted babies.
28 Apr. First annual Saturday hospital collection taken, in Sydney. Method rapidly spreads through Aust.
1 Jul. First letter cards sold at Sydney GPO.
3 Sep. Ship *Cambus Wallace* wrecked on Stradbroke I., Qld, claiming five lives.
13 Oct. Train collision at Redfern, Sydney, claims 13 lives.
22 Oct. Martha Needle, arsenic murderer, hanged in Melbourne.
28 Oct. SS *Wairapa* wrecked, claiming 125 lives.
During 1894
Melbourne Bush Walking and Touring Club estb.

Communities
Lyrup Village, SA, estb.
Menzies, WA, estb.
Waikerie, SA, estb.
Wickepin, WA, first settled

A

History, Politics, Economics, Law

Government
17 Jan. 1895–29 Oct. 1895, S. J. Way administered SA.
16 Mar. 1895–22 Nov. 1895, Sir Frederick Darley administered NSW.
18 Mar. 1895–22 Dec. 1895, Sir Alexander Campbell Onslow administered WA.
27 Mar. 1895–24 Oct. 1895, Sir John Madden administered Vic.
25 Oct. 1895–31 Mar. 1900, Thomas Brassey, Lord Brassey, Governor Vic.
29 Oct. 1895–29 Mar. 1899, Sir Thomas Fowell Buxton Governor SA.
15 Nov. 1895–9 Apr. 1896, Sir Arthur Hunter Palmer administered Qld.
22 Nov. 1895–5 Mar. 1899, Henry Robert Brand, Viscount Hampden, Governor NSW.
23 Dec. 1895–29 Jun. 1900, Sir Gerard Smith Governor WA.

23 Jan. The Australasian Federation League meets in Melbourne to discuss federation of colonies.
24 Jan. Carsten Egeberg Borchgrevink, Norwegian settler, takes part in the first landing on Antarctic mainland, from Norwegian whaler *Antarctic*.
30 Jan. Premiers Conference in Hobart decides that a convention of 10 delegates from each colony frame a Federal Constitution to be submitted to the Queen after approval by the colonies.
May. Labour Electoral League and Aust. Labor Federation merge to form the Political Labour League, uniting Labour movement.

During 1895
Closer Settlement Act in NSW makes land available to farmers on easy terms. (Vic. 1898.)
Aust. Paper Mills Pty Ltd estb.
H. C. Sleigh Ltd, shipowners, petroleum marketers, exporters and merchants, estb.
Vic. Govt introduces minimum wage concept.
James Cuthbert Brown estb. first commercial fishery in WA, at Fremantle.

Births & Deaths
Sir Harry Graham Alderman, lawyer, b. (d. 1962)
Sir Harold Leslie Boyce, Lord Mayor of London, b. (d. 1955)
Archie Galbraith Cameron, Federal politician, b. (d. 1956)
Arthur William Fadden, Country-UAP coalition Prime Minister, b. (d. 1973)
Stanley Fowler, fisheries exploration pioneer, b. (d. 1961)
Sir Wilfred Selwyn Kent Hughes, politician and sportsman, b. (d. 1970)
Sir David Fletcher Jones, businessman, b. (d. 1977)
Robert Alexander Little, World War I fighter pilot, b. (d. 1918)
Sir George Francis Reuben Nicklin, Qld Premier, b. (d. 1978)
Sir Andrew Bruce Small, businessman, land developer, b. (d. 1980)
George Alan Vasey, military commander, b. (d. 1945)
John de Vere Loder, Baron Wakehurst, NSW Governor, b. (d. 1970)

B

Science, Technology, Transport, Discovery

During 1895
Duck Reach Hydro-electric Station on South Esk R., near Launceston, Tas., estb.
American-based Vacuum Oil Co. becomes first oil company in Aust.
Hampden Bridge opens over Murrumbidgee R. at Wagga Wagga, NSW.
G. J. Berthond estb. Hamel State Farm near Waroona, WA.

Births & Deaths
Sir Albert Ernest Coates, surgeon, b. (d. 1977)
Hedley Herbert Finlayson, scientist noted for work on chemistry of plant life, b.
Sir Wilmot Hudson Fysh, pioneer aviator, b. (d. 1974)
Sir Lionel Alfred George Hooke, radio pioneer noted for work on electronic communications, b. (d. 1974)
Alexander John Nicholson, biologist, b. (d. 1969)
Annie Moriah Sage, nurse, b. (d. 1969)
Alfred Hermann Traeger, electrical engineer, b.

C

Arts

Literature

During 1895
Angus & Robertson publish Banjo Paterson's first volume of poetry *The Man From Snowy River and Other Verses*. Begins large-scale commercial book publishing in Aust.

Births & Deaths
William Edward Harney (Billarney), poet, author, drover, bushman, b. (d. 1962)
Leonard Mann, poet, novelist, b.
Edward Vivian Timms, novelist, b. (d. 1960)

Music, Dance

28 Feb. George Williams and Marshall Hall estb. Conservatorium of Music in Melbourne.
During 1895
Brass Band Association of NSW estb. (Organizes first national band contest in 1896.)
A. B. Banjo Paterson composes lyrics for 'Waltzing Matilda'. First sung at Winton, Qld, in May.

Births & Deaths
Harry Lindley Evans, pianist, composer, b.
Margherita Grandi, dramatic soprano, probably b.
William Garnet James, composer, pianist, b. (d. 1977)

Drama, Theatre, Film

During 1895
The Kinetoscope introduced to Aust. It enabled one person at a time to watch moving pictures on a loop of running film.

Fine Arts

31 Jul. WA Art Gallery in Perth estb. Qld Art Gallery in Brisbane opens on 29 Mar. Launceston Art Gallery, Tas., estb.
During 1895
James Ashton estb. SA Academy of Arts. (Closes 1927.)
Mary Ann Bailey begins painting Murray R. Aborigines.
Bowral Art Prize estb., NSW.
NSW Society of Artists estb. in Sydney.
Tom Roberts paints *The Hold-Up*, better known as *Bailed Up*.

1895

1895

Births & Deaths

Arthur d'Auvergne Boxall, painter and architect, b. (d. 1943)
Donald Samuel Cohen, watercolourist, b. (d. 1924)
George Edmond Finey, caricaturist, painter, b.
Francis Maude (Madge) Freeman, urban scene painter, b. (d. 1977)
Guy Ennis (Frank) Lynch, sculptor, landscape painter, b. (d. 1967)
Lloyd Frederic Rees, oil painter, b.
Vincent Sheldon, etcher, commercial artist, b. (d. 1945)
Nora Cassen Simpson, painter, b. (d. 1974)
Christian Waller, painter, b. (d. 1956)

Architecture

During 1895
First re-inforced concrete structures built in Sydney, first in Aust.
Aust.-designed cavity walls become popular overseas.

D

Religion, Learning

Jul. WA abolishes State aid to religion. Compulsory primary education system becomes secular.
Nov. Catholic archbishops and bishops meet in Sydney for second Plenary Council.

During 1895
First Baptist church in WA estb., in Perth.
Brisbane Public Library estb. (Becomes Public Library of Qld in 1898 and State Library of Qld in 1971.)
Grafton Smith first student to graduate Doctor of Medicine in Sydney.
NSW Teachers' Institute estb.
The Christian Brothers' College estb. in Perth

Births & Deaths

George Hermon Gill, naval historian, b. (d. 1973)
Eris O'Brien, Catholic prelate, historian, b. (d. 1974)

E
Sport

During 1895
Auraria, ridden by J. Stevenson, wins Melbourne Cup in 3 minutes 29 seconds.
First WA lawn bowling green opens in Perth.
Warrnambool–Melbourne road cycling race first contested. (Among world's oldest cycling events.)
Perth Golf Club founded.

Births & Deaths
James O. Anderson, tennis player, b. (d. 1960)
Percy Wells Cerutty, athlete, b. (d. 1975)
James Leslie Darcy, boxer, b. (d. 1917)
Jack Morrison Gregory, cricketer, noted fast bowler, b. (d. 1973)
Hunter I. (Stork) Hendry, cricketer, b.
Gerald Leighton Patterson, tennis player, b. (d. 1967)
Duncan Thompson, Rugby League footballer, b.

F
Historia Dignum

Population
Estimated total white, 3,491,621.

10 Jul. Mining disaster at Eldorado in Vic. claims six lives.
18 Jul. Mining disaster at Broken Hill, NSW, claims nine lives.
8 Aug. SS *Catterthun* wrecked, claiming at least 31 lives.

During 1895
Matilda Ann (Tilly) Aston estb. Association for Advancement of the Blind.
Seven-year national drought begins, hampering recovery from economic depression. Reduces sheep number by 50 per cent, cattle by 40 per cent.
Annual Sydney Sheep Show begins. Among largest of its type in world.

Communities
Brookton, WA, estb.
Cobden, Vic., estb.
Cunderdin, WA, estb.
Home Hill, Qld, probably estb.
Kalgoorlie, WA, estb.
Mandurah, WA, estb.
Moora, WA, estb.
Narrogin, WA, estb.
Norseman, WA, estb.
Sea Lake, Vic., estb.

1896

A
History, Politics, Economics, Law

Government
9 Apr. 1896–31 Dec. 1900, Charles Wallace Alexander Napier Cochrane Baillie, Lord Lamington, Governor Qld.

Mar. Intercolonial conference in Sydney resolves that provisions of Chinese Restriction Acts should be extended to all coloured races.
May. New Labor organization, the United Labor Party, estb. in Vic.
25 May. Women exercise the right to vote for first time in SA.
Jun. Vic. Govt estb. special board to fix wages; sets minimum wages for Vic. Govt employees.
Newcastle coalminers begin 11-week strike over reduction in wages.
17–21 Nov. Australasian Federation League holds unofficial Peoples' Convention in Bathurst, NSW, to discuss federation.

During 1896
NSW Govt passes Coloured Races Restriction and Regulation Act.
National Council of Women of Aust. estb. to promote advancement of women.
Trading and manufacturing improve with commercial revival.
Lawrence Allen Wells leads expedition across Great Sandy Desert, WA.
James Sinclair appointed first Vic. Govt commercial agent in London.
WA Govt first in Aust. to approve adoption by law.

Births & Deaths
Sir Reginald Alexander Dallas Brooks, Vic. Governor, b. (d. 1966)
Arthur Augustus Calwell, politician, b. (d. 1973)
Sir Kenneth Frank Coles, company director, b.
Sir Gordon Stewart McArthur, Vic. pastoralist, politician, b. (d. 1965)
Sir Edwin McCarthy, diplomat, b.
Joseph Maxwell, World War I soldier, b. (d. 1967)
Sir Thomas Playford, SA Premier, longest-serving Premier in Aust., 27 years, b. (d. 1981)
Sir Hamilton Morton Howard Sleigh, oil developer, b.
Kathleen Alice Syme, newspaper proprietor, b. (d. 1977)
Mary Cecil Tenison-Woods, lawyer, b. (d. 1971)
Sir William Gaston Walkley, oil exploration pioneer, b. (d. 1976)
Jack Watson, stockman, NT station manager, 'The Gulf Hero', d.

B
Science, Technology, Transport, Discovery

23 Mar. Perth–Coolgardie, WA, railway opens.
May. Female doctors Aldreda Hilda Gamble and Janet Lindsay Greig appointed medical and surgical officers at Melbourne Hospital.
Dec. Tarrant Motor Co. imports petrol-driven self-propelled four-wheeled car, a $4\frac{1}{2}$ horsepower Benz.

During 1896
Sir William Henry Bragg pioneers Aust. use of X-ray. Later, with son, Sir William Lawrence Bragg, pioneers X-ray spectre and the elucidation of the structure of crystals.
J. H. Maiden estb. Sydney Herbarium.
Perth Observatory estb.
Herbert Thomson builds first steam car in Aust., a steam-powered motor phaeton, at Armadale, Vic.
There are 2,650 medical doctors operating in Aust. and NZ, of whom 2,480 are engaged in private practice.
C. H. Packham produces first Packham Triumph pears, near Molong, NSW.
Queen Victoria Memorial Hospital for Women and Children estb. in Melbourne.
John Ashburton Thompson acclaimed for research on leprosy.

Births & Deaths
Sir Hugh William Bell Cairns, brain surgeon, b. (d. 1952)
Charles Austin Gardner, botanist, b. (d. 1970)
Sir Ivan Nello Holyman, civil aviation pioneer, b. (d. 1957)
Cliff Howard, inventor, b. (d. 1971)
Sir William Hudson, hydro-electric engineer, b. (d. 1978)
Paul J. McGinness, aviator, b. (d. 1952)
Oscar Adolf Mendelsohn, scientist, author, composer, b.
Noel Monkman, naturalist, film producer, musician, b.
Sir John Stanley Storey, industrialist, b. (d. 1955)
Sir Patrick Gordon Taylor, pioneer aviator, b. (d. 1966)
Sir Lawrence James Wackett, pioneer aircraft designer, b. (d. 1982)

C
Arts

1896

Literature

29 Aug. Alfred George Stephens estb. 'Red Page' segment of the *Bulletin* to encourage self confidence in national literature.

During 1896
Henry Lawson publishes *While the Billy Boils* (short stories), and *In the Days When the World was Wide* (verse).

Births & Deaths
Edward Philip Harrington, poet, balladist, b. (d. 1966)
Cecil McDonald Mann, author, journalist, b. (d. 1967)

Music, Dance

6 Apr. Jennie Brenan, dancer, makes début in Melbourne. Bessie Clayton, dancer, makes début in Sydney on 27 Jun.

During 1896
John Dunne produces opera, *The Mandarin*.

Births & Deaths
Edwin Clement Hosking, folk singer, b.
Evelyn Scotney, soprano, b. (d. 1967)

Drama, Theatre, Film

3 Jul. Brough Comedy Co. stages first production in Brisbane.
22 Aug. Carl Hertz holds first screening of moving pictures in Aust., in Melbourne. Opens first public film season at Tivoli Theatre in Sydney on 19 Sep.
28 Sep. Marius Sestier opens Salon Lumière, first cinema in Aust., in Sydney. Shoots first Aust. films around Sydney Harbour.
During Sep. Joseph McMahon holds first private cinematograph screenings in Sydney.
5 Nov. Marius Sestier films Melbourne Cup carnival and part of the race. Premiers in Melbourne on 19 Nov.

During 1896
George Adams opens the Palace Theatre for vaudeville in Sydney.
Alfred Dampier produces melodrama *To The West*.

Births & Deaths
Dorothy Brunton, musical comedy actress, b. (d. 1976)
Louise Carbrasse, actress, b.

Fine Arts

During 1896
WA Society of Arts and Crafts founded in Perth.
Julian Rossi Ashton founds Academy Julian in Sydney. (Becomes Sydney Art School in 1907 and Julian Ashton Art School in 1935.)
Geelong Art Gallery founded.

Births & Deaths
Henri Bastin, oil landscape painter, b. (d. 1979)
Grace Adela Williams Crowley, oil abstract painter, probably b. (d. 1979)
Maximilian Feuerring, painter, b.
Arthur Fleischman, sculptor, b.
Harry Garnet Kelly, landscape painter, b.
Gino Nibbi, art critic, b. (d. 1969)
Francis Roy Thompson, painter, b. (d. 1967)

Architecture

During 1896
First diplomas in architecture issued in Sydney.
John Horbury Hunt designs Chapel of the Sacred Heart Convent at Rose Bay, Sydney.
Royal Institute of Architects of WA estb.

1896

D
Religion, Learning

During 1896
Kindergarten Union of NSW estb.
Library Association of Australasia estb.
Mary Gilmore reaches Cosmé, Aust. Utopian Settlement in Paraguay. Later teaches at Patagonia, Paraguay.
Archimandrite Dorotheos, first Greek Orthodox priest, arrives in Aust.

Births & Deaths
Matthew Beovich, Catholic prelate, b.
Sir Norman Thomas Gilroy, first Aust.-born Catholic Cardinal, Archbishop of Sydney 1940–1971, b. (d. 1977)

E
Sport

Apr. Edwin H. Flack, athlete, wins first Aust. gold medals at inauguration of modern Olympic Games in Athens.
20 Sep. Charles Cavill becomes first man to swim the Golden Gate in USA.

During 1896
Newhaven, ridden by H. Gardiner, wins Melbourne Cup in 3 minutes $28\frac{1}{2}$ seconds.
Eight Australian Rules football clubs break away from the Vic. Football Association (VFA) and form the Vic. Football League (VFL).
Don Walker reaches world standard in cycling.
Newlands Golf Club estb. in Tas.
E. Walker becomes first Australian to break rifle shooting world record.
WA Hunt Club (named 1905) estb. as Fremantle Hunt Club.

Births & Deaths
Frank Burge, Rugby League footballer, b. (d. 1958)
David Smith, boxer, b. (d. 1945)

F
Historia Dignum

1896

Population
Estimated total white, 3,553,098.

26–27 Jan. Cyclone Sigma moves from Townsville to Brisbane, claiming 18 lives.
3 Feb. Ferry boat *Pearl* wrecked on Brisbane R., claiming 30 lives.
During 1896
Lance Skuthorpe repeats Adam Lindsay Gordon's leap over fence at Blue Lake, Mt Gambier, SA.

Communities
Boulder, WA, estb.
Ceduna, SA, estb.
Leonora, WA, estb.
Meekatharra, WA, estb.
Mt Garnet, Qld, estb.
Mt Lyell, Tas., estb.

1897

A
History, Politics, Economics, Law

15 Jan. Administration of Norfolk I. vested in NSW.
26 Jan. Aust. Federal Council meets in Hobart; Sir John Forrest elected President. Premiers Conference in Hobart on 2–4 Feb.
30 Jan. Tas. holds first Aust. election under system of proportional voting, the Hare-Clark system.
23 Mar.–23 Apr. The Second Federal Convention on Aust. Federal Constitution meets in Adelaide; C. C. Kingston elected President. Constitutional, finance and judiciary committees appointed on 31 Mar. Edmund Barton presents draft Constitutional Bill on 12 Apr. Convention meets in Sydney on 2 Sep.
Jul. Third Colonial Conference held in London.
28 Sep. Edmund James Banfield leases and settles on Dunk I., Qld.

During 1897
Robert Garran appointed Secretary to the Drafting Committee of the Federal Convention.
Qld adopts formal Aboriginal Protection policy. Govt passes Aboriginal Protection Act. (Later imitated by other Govts.) In Nov. control of Aboriginal reserves transferred from missions to Govt.
All colonies introduce death duties.
Whites shoot 20 Aborigines in King Leopold Ranges Massacre, WA.
Sir Samuel Way, SA Chief Justice, first Aust. judge to be appointed to the Judicial Committee of the Privy Council.

Births & Deaths
Charles Groves Wright Anderson, only Aust. to win a Victoria Cross in World War II Malayan campaign, b. (d. 1975)
Sir Frederick Galleghan, 'Black Jack Galleghan', military commander, b. (d. 1971)
Dame Enid Muriel Lyons, Federal politician, b. (d. 1981)
Sandamara, also known as Pigeon, Aboriginal who planned and attempted to drive whites away from Aust., shot dead.
Sir Percy Claude Spender, jurist, diplomat, b. (d. 1985)

B
Science, Technology, Transport, Discovery

1 Jan. Perth to Kalgoorlie, WA, goldfields railway opens.
21 Jun. Electric tramways begin operating in Brisbane. (Until 1969.)
During Jun. Engineering and Electrical Exhibition opens in Sydney.
1 Aug. Universal Morse Code system introduced in Aust.

During 1897
BHP smelting works estb. at Port Pirie, SA.
Mueller Botanic Society of WA estb. (Becomes WA Natural History and Science Society in 1909.)
Harold Bell Lasseter claims discovery of rich gold in Petermann Ranges, NT.
H. G. Smith and R. T. Baker begin research on volatile plant oils.
c. 1897. Local anaesthetics introduced.

Births & Deaths
Maude Rose Bonney, first woman aviator to fly around Aust., b.
Edgar Wikner Percival, aircraft designer and builder, b.
Sir Charles Edward Kingsford Smith, aviator, b. (d. 1935)

C
Arts

1897

Literature

During 1897
Barcroft Boake's work collected, and published under title *Where the Dead Men Lie, and other Poems*

Births & Deaths
Marjorie Faith Barnard, author and historian noted for her treatment of character and mood, b.
Dale Collins, author and journalist, b. (d. 1956)
Flora Sydney Patricia Eldershaw, author, historian, b. (d. 1956)
Richard Sydney Porteous, author, b. (d. 1963)
Helen de Guerry Simpson, novelist, b. (d. 1940)

Music, Dance

Apr. Minnie Everett appears as *première danseuse* at Bijou Theatre in Melbourne.
During 1897
J. C. Williamson opens free ballet Dancing School in Melbourne. Minnie Everett first teacher of organized ballet in Aust.
SA Conservatorium of Music founded as Elder Conservatorium, at Adelaide University.

Births & Deaths
Margaret Ada Sutherland, composer, pianist, b. (d. 1984)

Drama, Theatre, Film

Aug. Joseph Perry begins production of a series of films on the Salvation Army.
3 Nov. Sydney Polytechnic holds film exhibition.
During 1897
T. G. Molloy builds the Theatre Royal in Perth. Opens with *The Silver King*.
Edward Duggan's *Eureka Stockade* premières at Theatre Royal in Adelaide.

Births & Deaths
Mae Busch, actress, b. (d. 1946)
Charles Edward Chauvel, among first independent film makers of sound film industry, b. (d. 1959)
Doris Alice Fitton, actress, theatre director, b.

Fine Arts

During 1897
Richard Wynne estb. the Wynne Art Prize for landscape painting in Sydney; one of first art prizes in Aust.
Sydney Long, artist, paints *The Spirit of the Plains*.
Datillo Rubbo opens Art School in Sydney.

Births & Deaths
Harry Buckie, painter, b.
Ernest Buckmaster, landscape painter, b. (d. 1968)
Basil Burdett, art organizer, b. (d. 1942)
Colin Colahan, painter, b.
Lillian Mayo Daphine, sculptor, b.
Gordon Esling, landscape painter, b.
John MacCormack Farmer, painter, b.
Marion Jones, painter, probably b. (d. 1977)
Norman Lloyd, landscape painter, b.
Kenneth MacQueen, painter, b. (d. 1960)
Sydney Nicholls, cartoonist, b. (d. 1977)
Jules Henry Roy Rousel, painter, b.
Arnold Joseph Victor Shore, artist noted for sensitive portrayal of Aust. bush, b. (d. 1963)
Imre Szigeti, draughtsman, b. (d. 1975)

Architecture

During 1897
Queen Anne style of architecture becomes popular.

1897

D
Religion, Learning

30 Jun. Gatton Agricultural College, Qld, opens for enrolments.
14 Sep. Nathaniel Dawes estb. Church of England Bush Brotherhood organization to provide Church contact with outback. George Dowglass Halford first Bush Brother.

During 1897
Greek Orthodox Church introduced in Aust. (First church built in Sydney in 1898.)
Avondale College Estate, Seventh-Day Adventist Tertiary Training College, estb. at Cooranbong, NSW.
Swan R. Mechanics' Institute (estb. 1860) and Geological Museum of Fremantle (estb. 1881) merge to form the WA Museum.
WA technical education begins in Perth.
First Kindergarten Teachers' Training College in Aust. opens, in Sydney.
Cyril Jackson begins reforming WA education system.

Births & Deaths
Clarence Irving Benson, Methodist minister, b.

E
Sport

Oct. Amateur Athletics Association of Australasia estb. in Sydney.

During 1897
Gaulus, ridden by S. Callinan, wins Melbourne Cup 3 minutes 31 seconds.
Essendon Football Team wins first VFL Premiership in Melbourne.
'Behinds' added to Aust. Rules football, making goal worth six points and behinds one point.
First rodeo event in Aust. held, at Gayndah, Qld.
Percy Cavill becomes first Aust. world champion swimmer.
Alick Wickham's swimming style, popularized by Arthur Cavill, named the Australian Crawl.
Adelaide Lawn Bowling Club estb.
National Coursing Association of SA estb. (Associations estb. in Vic. 1877, Tas. 1878, NSW 1881, Qld 1901.)
c. 1897. Table Tennis introduced to Aust.

Births & Deaths
Sydney Godfrey, boxer, b.
Alan Falconer Kippax, cricketer, noted batsman, b. (d. 1972)
Sir Thomas Chester Manifold, father of Vic. horse-racing, Vic. politician, b. (d. 1979)
Ivor Warne-Smith, VFL footballer, b. (d. 1960)
William Falconer 'Bill' Woodfull, cricketer, noted batsman, b. (d. 1965)

F
Historia Dignum

1897

Population
Estimated total white, 3,617,783.

6 Jan. Cyclone devastates Palmerston (Darwin), claiming 38 lives.
19 Jan. V. C. B. Vosper estb. Perth newspaper *Sunday Times*.
Feb. NSW Post Office first officially uses bicycles to deliver mail.
15 Mar. George Morrison takes up duty as permanent Peking correspondent.
22 Jun. Governor Phillip's statue in Sydney Botanical Gardens unveiled.
21 Nov. Fire destroys a Melbourne softgoods warehouse, putting 2,000 employees out of work.
Dec. Bushfires in Tas. claim six lives.
During 1897
Kerry Holden and party make first winter ascent of Mt Kosciusko, NSW.

Communities
Collie, WA, estb.
Kambalda, WA, estb.
Kellerberrin, WA, estb.
Leadville, NSW, estb.
Queenstown, Tas., estb.

A

History, Politics, Economics, Law

Government
13 Apr. 1898–Oct. 1898, T. J. Byrnes Premier Qld.
30 Sep. 1898–10 Apr. 1899, S. J. Way administered SA.
1 Oct. 1898–Dec. 1899, J. R. Dickson Premier Qld.

19 Jan.–16 Mar. The third Federal Convention on Aust. Federal Constitution meets in Melbourne.
27 Jan. Constitution Convention accepts motion that conciliation and arbitration powers be included in Constitution.
During Jan. Sir John Forrest, WA Premier, mobbed by angry goldminers over regulations disallowing sinking of shafts beyond 10 feet.
3–4 Jun. Draft Federal Constitution Bill submitted to electors at referendums in NSW, Vic., Tas., and SA. Requisite statutory number of votes obtained in Vic., Tas. and SA. NSW rejects the Bill. No referendums held in WA and Qld.
Jul. Queen Victoria Market opens in Sydney.
During 1898
Eighth Intercolonial Trades and Labour Union Congress held in Adelaide. Urges minimum or basic wage for all Aust.

Births & Deaths
Persia Campbell, economist who contributed to World War II breakthrough in consumer protection, b.
Sir Charles Gairdner, WA and Tas. Governor, b.
Charles Hardy, NSW politician, b. (d. 1941)
Sir David Roy McCaughey, NSW pastoralist, b. (d. 1971)
Sir Norman Baevski Myer, company chairman, b. (d. 1956)

B

Science, Technology, Transport, Discovery

During 1898
John Hackett estb. zoological gardens in south Perth
Carbolic (antisepsis) in Aust. hospitals begins to be replaced by steam and rubber gloves (asepsis).
Lewis F. East invents automatic lid for jugs.
Aust. Illawarra Shorthorn cattle breed developed in NSW.
SA amends the standard time provision accepted in 1894 and adopts the mean solar time of the longitu 142°30′E (9.5 hours ahead of GMT).

Births & Deaths
Raymond Cottam Allsop, radio pioneer who developed and patented method of recording soun on film, b. (d. 1972)
Thomas Foster Chuck, portrait photographer, d.
Edward Holbrook Derrick, medical scientist, expert on fevers, discoverer of Q fever, b. (d. 1976)
Sir Howard Walter Florey, Baron of Adelaide and Marston, scientist, co-discoverer of penicillin, b. (d. 1968)
Sir Claude Gibb, engineer and industrialist, b. (d. 1959)
Sir Laurence John Hartnett, engineer, b.
John Irvine Hunter, anatomist, b. (d. 1924)
John Alexander Hughes McGeorge, psychiatrist, forensic medicine pioneer, b.
Charles Thomas Philippe Ulm, pioneer aviator, b. (d. 1934)

C
Arts

Literature

During 1898
Victor Daley publishes *At Dawn and Dusk* (poetry).
Edward Dyson publishes *Below and On Top* (stories).
Edward E. Morris publishes *Austral English: a Dictionary of Australasian Words, Phrases and Usages.*
A. C. Rowlandson begins paperback novel industry. Becomes chief pioneer publisher of Aust. fiction.

Music, Dance

Births & Deaths
Lauri Kennedy, cellist, b.
John Francis O'Hagan, composer, b.

Drama, Theatre, Film

May. Salvation Army film, *Our Social Triumphs*, premièrs in Melbourne.
During 1898
Alfred Cord Haddon begins expedition to Torres Strait; films some of first footage of Aboriginal life.

Births & Deaths
Dame Judith Anderson (originally Francis Margaret Anderson), dramatic actress, b.

Fine Arts

During 1898
Julian Rossi Ashton organizes Grafton Gallery Exhibition in London. Among first Aust. exhibitions sent overseas.
Bill Barak, known as King Billy, Aboriginal painter working in European style, active in Vic.
C. D. Richardson founds Yarra Sculptors' Society in Melbourne. First Society of sculptors estb. in Aust.

Births & Deaths
John Charles Goodchild, painter, etcher, b. (d. 1980)
Alastair Cameron Gray, watercolourist, b. (d. 1972)
Sali Herman, street scene painter, b. (d. 1937)
Colin Hunt, landscape painter, b. (d. 1952)
Sir Eric Langker, marine and landscape painter, b. (d. 1982)
William Nicholas Rowell, portrait and landscape painter, b. (d. 1946)
Eric Scott, etcher, probably b.
Ronald Hewison Steuart, painter, commercial artist, b.
J. Alan Stubbs, watercolourist, b.

Architecture

During 1898
Alfred Barton Brady begins work on Customs House in Rockhampton, Qld.

1898

D
Religion, Learning

29 May. Greeks and Lebanese build Orthodox church in Sydney dedicated to the Holy Trinity. First in Aust.

During 1898
First Christian Science services in Aust. held, in Melbourne. (Sydney 1900.)
Interest in Froebelian kindergarten methods revived.
Union of Methodist Church groups in Qld.
State School Teachers' Union of WA estb.
Mosque estb. in Adelaide. (Perth 1905.)

Births & Deaths
Sir William Keith Hancock, historian, b.

E
Sport

During 1898
The Grafter, ridden by J. Gough, wins Melbourne Cup in 3 minutes $29\frac{1}{4}$ seconds.
Fitzroy football team wins VFL Premiership in Melbourne.
First SA Aust. Rules football Magarey Medal awarded for best and fairest player.
First table tennis championships played in Adelaide.
Aust. Golf Union estb.
Rainsford Bowling Club estb. in Melbourne. First women's Bowling Club in Aust.

Births & Deaths
Don Athaldo, strongman, b. (d. 1965)
George Cook, boxer, b. (d. 1943)
Eugene St Clair (Hughie) Dwyer, boxer, b.
Walter Albert Lindrum, billiards player, b. (d. 1960)

F
Historia Dignum

1898

Population
Estimated total white, 3,664,715.

Jan.–Feb. Bushfires sweep through western and southern Gippsland, Vic.
4 Feb. Cyclone damages Mackay, Qld.
21 Mar. Gas explosion at Dudley mines, Stockton, NSW, claims 15 lives.
6 May. Ship *Maitland* wrecked near Broken Bay, NSW, in gale, claiming 27 lives.
10 Sep. *Barrier Truth* newspaper published at Broken Hill, NSW.

During 1898
The *Recorder* newspaper estb. at Port Pirie SA.
Hannah Maclurcan publishes popular cook book.
The Kookaburra or laughing jackass introduced into WA. (Tas. 1905.)
Floods in Brisbane.
During year 24 vessels wrecked off NSW coast, claiming 79 lives.
NSW Govt publishes first statistics on childbirth and infant mortality.
WA Fire Brigades Board estb.

Communities
Katanning, WA, estb.
Laverton, WA, estb.
Luina, Tas., estb.
Wagin, WA, estb.
Zeehan, Tas., estb.

A
History, Politics, Economics, Law

Government

5 Mar. 1899–18 May 1899, Sir Frederick Darley administered NSW.
10 Apr. 1899–31 Dec. 1900, Hallam Tennyson, Lord Tennyson, Governor SA.
18 May 1899–31 Dec. 1900, William Lygon, Earl Beauchamp, Governor NSW.
14 Sep. 1899–Mar. 1901, W. J. Lyne Protectionist Premier NSW.
12 Oct. 1899–Apr. 1903, N. E. Lewis Conservative Premier Tas.
1 Dec. 1899–Dec. 1899, A. Dawson Labor Premier Qld.
1 Dec. 1899–Dec. 1899, V. L. Solomon Conservative Premier SA.
5 Dec. 1899–Nov. 1900, A. McLean Liberal Premier Vic.
7 Dec. 1899–Sep. 1903, R. Philp Conservative Premier Qld.
8 Dec. 1899–May 1901, F. W. Holder Liberal Premier SA.

25 Jan. Federal demonstration in Melbourne on the eve of the anniversary of the first European settlement in Aust.
28 Jan.–3 Feb. Premiers Conference in Melbourne to consider amendments to Draft Constitution.
May–Sep. Second referendum on the Constitution in all colonies except WA. Draft Constitution Bill accepted.
20 Jun. Royal Mint opens in Perth.
During Jun. Australasian Steamship Owners' Federation estb.
11 Jul. Qld Govt offers assistance of 250 mounted infantrymen in event of hostilities breaking out in South Africa. Other colonies follow. On 11 Oct. war between Britain and Transvaal (Boer War) begins. On 31 Oct. Aust. contingent leaves for South Africa.
30 Aug. Vic. Govt abolishes plural voting for Legislative Assembly.
During Aug. Aust. naval conference favours creation of a naval reserve force in Melbourne.
Sep. Address to the Queen from all legislatures except WA praying for the adoption of the Cwlth Bill and the granting of a Federal Constitution.
1 Dec. First Labor Govt in Aust. forms in Qld. (Lasts six days.)
16 Dec. WA Govt introduces female suffrage and adopts Factory Act to protect workers from exploitation.
During 1899
First WA Trades Union and Labour Congress, at Coolgardie, founds a Labor Party.
Tas. Police Regulation Act centralizes Police Force and appoints a Police Commissioner.
Daisy May Bates commissioned to investigate charge of ill treatment of WA Aborigines.
WA Govt introduces company taxes.

Births & Deaths

Rudolph Bierwirth, military commander, b.
Sir Edgar Barton Coles, managing director of G. J. Coles Pty Ltd for 27 years, b. (d. 1981)
Sir John Augustus Collins, naval officer, b.
Harold Bruce Farncomb, naval officer, b. (d. 1971)
Harold James Mortimer, pastoralist, b.
Sir William Francis Langer Owen, High Court Judge b. (d. 1972)
Elliot Price, SA Pastoralist, b. (d. 1969)
Harold de Vahl Rubin, grazier, philanthropist, b. (d. 1964)
Sir John Armstrong Spicer, judge and politician, b. (d. 1978)
Michael Terry, explorer and author, b.
Edward John Ward, Federal politician, b. (d. 1963)
Sir Eric Winslow Woodward, soldier and NSW Governor, b. (d. 1967)

B

Science, Technology, Transport, Discovery

14 Jan. L. Dhiel demonstrates bromo-cyanide process for faster extraction of gold from ores.
Mar. SA Ornithological Association estb.
8 Dec. Electric tram services begin in Sydney central business district.
During 1899
International Mining and Industrial Exhibition held at Coolgardie, WA.
Ceramic product manufacturing begins in NSW.
Broken Hill Proprietary Co. Ltd gains control of iron ore deposits at Iron Knob, near Whyalla, SA.
Australasian Trained Nurses Association estb. in Sydney.
Harley Tarrant and Howard Lewis build the first entirely Aust.-made petrol-driven vehicle.
Horse and steam tram services begin in Perth.
Hamel State Farm in WA conducts tests on safflower.

Births & Deaths

Keith Anderson, pioneer aviator, probably b. (d. 1929)
Alwyn James Arnott, dentist, b. (d. 1973)
Sir Ian Clunies Ross, scientist, b. (d. 1959)
Sir (Frank) Macfarlane Burnet, biologist, b. (d. 1985)
James Norman Kirkby, industrialist, b. (d. 1971)
Ivor Ewing McIntyre, pioneer RAAF seaplane pilot, b. (d. 1928)
John Laird Somerville, chemist, noted for work on pulping eucalypt wood, b.

C

Arts

Literature

Jun. The Aust. Literature Society estb.
During 1899
Walter Baldwin Spencer and Francis Gillen publish *The Native Tribes of Central Australia*.
Arthur Hoey Davis, using pseudonym Steele Rudd, publishes *On Our Selection*. (Published by the *Bulletin*.)
Ethel Pedley publishes *Dot and the Kangaroo*, children's story.

Births & Deaths

Chester Francis Cobb, novelist, first Aust. to use stream of consciousness technique, b. (d. 1943)
Ernestine Hill, author, journalist, b. (d. 1972)
Nevil Shute Norway, author who wrote as Nevil Shute, b. (d. 1960)

Music, Dance

26 Dec. Newsky family, Russian folk dancers, arrive in Sydney.
During 1899
Wax cylinder recordings made of Aborigines singing.

Births & Deaths

Dudley Glass, composer, author, b.
William Lovelock, composer, b.

Drama, Theatre, Film

12 Sep. Tivoli Theatre in Sydney burns down.
Dec. Salvation Army completes feature film about early Christian martyrs.

Births & Deaths

Cyril Trimnell Ritchard, actor, producer, b. (d. 1977)

Fine Arts

Mar. *Australasian Art Review* first published. (Published until Sep. 1901.)
During 1899
George W. Lambert paints *Across the Blacksoil Plains*.
Bertha Merfield pioneers mural painting in Melbourne.

Births & Deaths

Herbert Edward Badham, painter and writer, b. (d. 1961)
Robert Emerson Curtis, painter, illustrator, b.
Sir William Dobell, painter, b. (d. 1970)
Frederick Millward Grey, painter, b. (d. 1957)

1899

Ian Hassall, painter, sculptor, illustrator b.
Edith Lilla Holmes, oil painter, b. (d. 1973)
Sir Rex de Charambac Nan Kivell, art dealer, collector, b. (d. 1977)
Reginald Henry Jerrold Nathan, portrait painter, b. (d. 1979)
Theo Scharf, painter, b.
Horace Hurtle Trenerry, painter, b. (d. 1958)
Danila Vassilieff, painter, sculptor, b. (d. 1958)

D
Religion, Learning

During 1899
WA. Public Library estb.
Aust. Subscription Library becomes Public Library of NSW.

Births & Deaths
Sir James Ralph Darling, educationist, b.
Edward John Davidson, NSW Church of England Bishop, b. (d. 1958)
Sir Philip Nigel Warrington Strong, Church of England primate, b.

E
Sport

During 1899
Merriwee, ridden by V. Turner, wins Melbourne Cup in 3 minutes 36¼ seconds.
Fitzroy football team wins VFL Premiership in Melbourne.
Victor Trumper first plays cricket for Aust.
Northern Challenge Polo Cup estb. NSW. Oldest polo cup in Aust.
Competitive baseball begins in NSW; first interstate games held.
First Aust.-England rugby union football Test game played, in Sydney.
Albert Park Ladies Bowling Club estb. in Melbourne. (First women's Clubs estb. NSW 1901, Qld 1922, SA and WA 1926.)

Births & Deaths
Glyn de Villiers Bosisto, lawn bowls player, b.
Frank Dempsey, jockey, b.
James Sydney Wallace Eve, sport administrator, b.
Arthur 'Pony' Halloway, rugby league pioneer, b.
Joseph H. Kirkwood, golfer, b. (d. 1970)
George Mendies, flyweight boxer, b. (d. 1924)

F
Historia Dignum

Population
Estimated total white, 3,715,988.

Jan. A. G. Stephens founds *Bookfellow* magazine in Sydney.
4–5 Mar. Cyclone Bahina devastates Cooktown area, Qld. Destroys pearling fleet in Bathurst Bay, claiming 307 lives.
13 Jul. Barque *Carlisle Castle* wrecked near Rockingham, WA, claiming 11 lives.
8 Oct. John Norton coins word 'wowser' to describe puritanical fanatics.

During 1899
Many phonographs installed in Aust. homes.
Vic. bushfires claim three lives.

Communities
Coonawarra, SA, estb.
Gloucester, NSW, estb.
Mt Barker, WA, estb.
Waroona, WA, estb.

A
History, Politics, Economics, Law

1900

Government
15 Jan. 1900–2 Jan. 1901, Sir John Madden administered Vic.
30 Jun. 1900–3 Mar. 1901, Sir Alexander Campbell Onslow administered WA.
14 Aug. 1900–8 Nov. 1901, Sir John Dodds administered Tas.
1 Nov. 1900–27 May 1902, Sir Frederick Darley administered NSW.
19 Nov. 1900–Feb. 1901, Sir G. Turner Liberal Premier Vic.

24 Jan. and 19 Apr. Premiers Conference on proposed amendments to Federation Bill held in Sydney.

24–25 Jan. Intercolonial conference on the formation of a Federal Labor Party held in Sydney.

28 Jan. Tas. Govt introduces manhood suffrage and abolishes plural voting for Legislative Assembly. On 14 Sep. Govt abolishes property qualifications for Members of Legislative Assembly.

During Jan. Second Aust. contingent leaves for South Africa to fight in Boer War. First contingent returns in May to heroes' welcome. George Griffin first Aust. to die in Boer War, on 16 Jan.

Feb. Intercolonial conference of free-traders held in Sydney. Protectionists hold conference in Sydney on 18–19 Apr.

27 Mar. Federal delegates received by Queen at Windsor in England. Cwlth Bill introduced to House of Commons on 14 May. On 9 Jul. Commonwealth of Australia Constitution Act, uniting the six colonies, given Royal assent. Proclamation of Cwlth signed on 17 Sep.

2 Jul. First Aust. naval contingent sent to China to assist British in suppressing Boxer Rebellion; 572 Aust. men serve in campaign.

14 Jul. Lord Hopetoun appointed Governor-General of Aust. (Arrives in Aust. on 15 Dec.). On 30 Dec. first Federal Ministers announced. (Sworn in on 1 Jan. 1901.)

24 Jul. Captain Neville Reginald Howse becomes first Aust. to win Victoria Cross for action in Boer War.
Combined total of colonies military forces reaches 27,353.

31 Jul. Cwlth Bill adopted by WA after referendum. This ensures all six colonies federate.

5 Dec. WA Govt introduces triennial parlts and payment of Members of Parlt.

During 1900
WA legalizes trade unions, but prohibits strikes.
Sidney Myer opens his first drapery shop, at Bendigo, Vic.

NSW Govt provides for modest workers' compensation scheme in mining industry.
First public housing in Aust. provided—by NSW Govt, in Sydney, for waterside workers.

Births & Deaths
Sir John Keith Angas, administrator, b. (d. 1977)
William Lionel Buckland, Vic. businessman, b. (d. 1964)
Marie Beuzeville Byles, lawyer, author, b.
Albert Redvers George Hawke, WA Premier, b.
Byron Hugh MacLachlan, pastoralist, b.
Sir John McEwen, Liberal-Country coalition Prime Minister, b. (d. 1980)
Albert Ernst Monk, union leader, b. (d. 1975)
Sir Charles Joseph Alfred Moses, broadcasting administrator, b.
Margery Merlyn Baillieu Myer, social administrator, b.
Hugh Stevenson Robertson, politician, author, b.
Kenneth Eyre Inverell Wallace-Crabbe, air force officer, author, designer, b.
Hector MacDonald Laws Waller, World War II RAN officer, b. (d. 1942)
Sir William John Victor Windeyer, High Court Judge, b.

B

Science, Technology, Transport, Discovery

During 1900
First Aust. steel-making furnace opens at Eskbank works, Lithgow, NSW.
Rabbits spread throughout WA.
First tin dredge operates at Tingha, NSW.
James Trackson builds steam car in Brisbane.
Vivian Lewis builds single-cylinder petrol-driven car in Adelaide.
Aust. has about 11,200 miles of railway line.
Natural gas first discovered, at Roma, Qld.
Gold discovered at Tennant Creek, NT.
The Bureau of Sugar Experiment Stations estb. in Qld.
c. 1900. Charles Vincent Potter discovers method of extracting zinc from ore.

Births & Deaths
Sir Lorimer Fenton Dods, paediatrician, b. (d. 1981)
Cecil Ernest Eddy, nuclear radiation physicist, b. (d. 1956)
Harold Arthur Lindsay, naturalist, expert on Aboriginal life in semi-desert conditions, b. (d. 1969)
Sir Leslie Harold Martin, physicist, b.
Harold George Raggatt, govt geologist, b. (d. 1968)
Norman Barnett Tindale, anthropologist, b.

C

Arts

Literature

During 1900
Henry Lawson publishes three works, *On the Track* and *Over the Sliprails*, both short stories, and *Verses, Popular and Humorous*.

Births & Deaths
Nancen Beryl Chauncy, childrens' book author, b. (d. 1970)
Jack Lindsay, poet, author, historian whose autobiographical trilogy set a new pattern in Aust. writing, b.
Frances Margaret McGuire, author, b.

Music, Dance

During 1900
Fritz Hart, conductor, arrives in Aust.

Births & Deaths
John Donald Mackenzie Brownlee, baritone, b. (d. 1969)

Drama, Theatre, Film

Apr. New Tivoli Theatre in Sydney replaces burnt-out Tivoli.
13 Sep. Salvation Army screens feature film *Soldiers of the Cross*, four hours of film, sermons and music. (Probably first short story film ever screened.)

Births & Deaths
Madge Elliott, musical comedy actress, b. (d. 1955)

Fine Arts

During 1900
NSW Society of Artists' Travelling Scholarship first awarded.
Art Gallery of SA erected under sponsorship of Sir Thomas Elder.

Births & Deaths
George Allen, sculptor, b. (d. 1972)
Howard Barron, portrait painter, b.
Douglas Roberts Dundas, painter, b. (d. 1981)
Percy Eagles, painter, cartoonist, b.
Victor Greenhalgh, sculptor, b. (d. 1983)
Melville Haysom, landscape painter, b. (d. 1976)
Andor Meszaros, medallion sculptor, b. (d. 1972)
Douglas Fieldew Pratt, etcher, painter, b. (d. 1972)
Alison Baily Rehfisch, painter, b. (d. 1975)

1900

Raymond Wallis, painter, b. (d. 1963)
Cecil (Unk) White, artist, b.

Architecture

During 1900
Hand-crafted building industry by now replaced by machine technology.
Jefferson Jackson, architect, introduces the Californian bungalow style house in Sydney.

Births and Deaths
W. Wray, architect, d.

D
Religion, Learning

Jan. Adelaide University assumes responsibility for teacher training in SA.
Feb. Vic Teachers' Training College reopens.
First United Conference of Methodism in SA held, in Adelaide.
Oct. First conference of Library Association of Australasia held, in Adelaide.

During 1900
Qld free and secular education system made compulsory.
Perth Technical College estb. as Perth Technical School.
Sydney Kindergarten Teachers' College estb.
Of all elementary school-aged children in Aust., 90 per cent can read and write.

Births & Deaths
Redmond Prendiville, Catholic Archbishop, b. (d. 1965)
Frederick Joyce Schonell, educationist, b. (d. 1969)

E
Sport

During 1900
Clean Sweep, ridden by R. Richardson, wins Melbourne Cup in 3 minutes 29 seconds.
Melbourne football team wins VFL Premiership in Melbourne.
First Aust. tennis championships played.
Dwight F. Davis, American tennis player, donates trophy, beginning Davis Cup tennis world team competitions.
Frederick Lane wins first Aust. gold medal for swimming at Paris Olympics.
Aust. wins two gold medals at Paris Olympics.
Badminton first played in Perth. (Clubs estb. in Vic. 1920, Tas. 1925, SA 1930, NSW 1936, Qld 1950, ACT 1974.)
Basketball first played in SA.
First Aust. men's hockey plays in SA. (NSW 1905, Vic. 1906.)
Aust. Bowling Council estb.
Bocce variation of bowls first played as sport.
Competitive motor cycle racing begins.
Sydney Rugby Union football premiership competition estb.
Royal SA Yacht Squadron forms. First SA Sailing Club.
Herbert Thomson and Edward Holmes attempt first long-distance drive in Aust., Bathurst, NSW, to Melbourne.
The Gun Clubs Association of Vic. estb.
Trotting in Tas. begins, in Hobart.
c. 1900. Organized racing of homing pigeons begins.

Births & Deaths
Sydney Coventry, VFL footballer, b. (d. 1976)
Billy Duncan, jockey, b.
Bob Marshall, billiards player, b.
William Harold Ponsford, cricketer, noted batsman, b.
Tom Sulman, racing car driver, b. (d. 1970)
Gladys Sutcliffe, lawn bowler, b.
Benny Wearing, Rugby League footballer, b.

F
Historia Dignum

Population
Estimated total white, 3,760,482.

19 Jan.–Aug. Bubonic plague breaks out in Adelaide and NSW, mostly in Sydney. Of 303 cases reported, 103 are fatal.
During 1900
Donald Mackay cycles around Aust. in 240 days.
Aborigines Jimmy and Joe Governor kill seven white people in NSW.

Communities
Batlow, NSW, estb.
Rapid Bay, SA, estb.
Widgiemooltha, WA, estb.
Wondai, Qld, estb.

1901

A
History, Politics, Economics, Law

Government

1 Jan. 1901–9 Jan. 1903, John Adrian Louis Hope, Earl of Hopetoun, Governor-General Cwlth of Aust.

1 Jan. 1901–24 Sep. 1903, First Cwlth Ministry, Edmund Barton Protectionist Prime Minister Aust.

1 Jan. 1901–30 Apr. 1901, William Lygon, Earl Beauchamp, Governor NSW.

1 Jan. 1901–19 Dec. 1901, Charles Wallace Alexander Napier Cochrane Baillie, Lord Lamington, Governor Qld.

1 Jan. 1901–17 Jul. 1902, Hallam Tennyson, Lord Tennyson, Governor SA.

2 Jan. 1901–10 Dec. 1901, Sir John Madden administered Vic.

12 Feb. 1901–Jun. 1902, A. J. Peacock Liberal Premier Vic.

15 Feb. 1901–May 1901, G. Throssell Premier WA.

4 Mar. 1901–30 Apr. 1901, Edward Albert Stone administered WA.

28 Mar. 1901–Jun. 1904, J. See Premier NSW.

1 May 1901–13 Aug. 1902, Sir Arthur Lawley Governor WA.

15 May 1901–Mar. 1905, J. G. Jenkins Liberal-Conservative Premier SA.

27 May 1901–Nov. 1901, G. Leake Premier WA.

21 Jun. 1901–24 Mar. 1902, Sir Samuel Griffith administered Qld.

1 Nov. 1900–27 May 1902, Sir Frederick Darley administered NSW in absence of Earl Beauchamp.

8 Nov. 1901–16 Apr. 1904, Sir Arthur Elibank Havelock Governor Tas.

21 Nov. 1901–Dec. 1901, A. E. Morgans Premier WA.

10 Dec. 1901–24 Nov. 1903, Sir George Sydenham Clarke Governor Vic.

23 Dec. 1901–Jul. 1902, G. Leake Premier WA.

1 Jan. Governor-General, Earl of Hopetoun, at Centennial Park in Sydney, proclaims Federal Constitution. Aust. colonies federated as the Commonwealth of Australia and the designation 'Colonies' officially changed to 'States'.

Interstate free trade estb.

1 Mar. Cwlth Govt assumes control of all postal and telegraph services. Passes Pacific Islands Labourers Act to end indenture of Kanaka labour by 1904. Takes control of all military forces.

29–30 Mar. National election held for the first Cwlth Parlt. F. W. Holder, ex SA Premier, elected first speaker of House of Representatives on 9 May.

25 Apr. China Field Force returns after assisting British in Boxer Rebellion. (Six Aust. casualties.)

During Apr. John Christian Watson elected leader of Federal Labor Party at first caucus meeting.

9 May. Frederick Slade Drake-Brockman begins expedition which explores area between King Sound and Cambridge Gulf, WA.

Prince George, Duke of York (later King George V), opens the first Cwlth Parlt in Melbourne. Govt consists of Governor-General, representing the British Monarch, a Senate or Upper House composed of six senators from each of the six States and a House of Representatives composed of 75 members. First Federal Parlt includes three parties Free Trade, Labor, and Protectionist, none with absolute majority. (Dissolution first Parlt 23 Nov. 1903.)

9 May. Federal Parlt meets in Exhibition Building, Melbourne.

3 Sep. Aust. national flag flown for the first time, over dome of Exhibition Building in Melbourne.

8 Oct. Sir George Turner introduces Federal budget which includes high tariffs with new duties fixed on tea, sugar, alcohol and tobacco.

Nov. Federal Govt introduces Immigration Restriction Act, which becomes known as White Australia Policy. Dictation test used to exclude from Aust. unwanted immigrants. (Dictation tests abolished 1958.)

Plans made for administration of British New Guinea to be transferred to Cwlth of Aust., but not formally accepted by Aust. until 1906. (Then officially called Papua.)

During 1901

Public Service Act estb. conditions of new Cwlth Public Service.

Andrew Fisher, William Morris Hughes, John Forrest, Joseph Cook, George Reid and John Watson enter Federal Parlt.

NSW and Vic. Govts introduce old age pensions. (Qld 1908.)

First Premiers Conference under Federation held.

Robert Falcon Scott pioneers route through McMurdo Sound on to Ross ice shelf in Antarctica.

NSW Industrial Arbitration Act provides for registration of unions and estb. Arbitration Court with one judge.

The Vic. Employers' Federation estb.

The Criminal Code of Qld, compiled by Sir Samuel Walker Griffith 1896–1899, comes into force. First Criminal Code in Aust.

George Houston Reid becomes Free Trade leader of the Federal Opposition (until 1904.)

B

Science, Technology, Transport, Discovery

1901

Births & Deaths

Sir Donald McKinnon Cleland, PNG administrator, b. (d. 1975)
Sir Adrian Herbert Curlewis, judge and founder of Outward Bound adventure group, b. (d. 1985)
Edward Alfred Daly, air force commander, b.
Sir Roy Russel Dowling, naval commander, b. (d. 1969)
Sir Warwick Oswald Fairfax, businessman, b.
Vincent Clair Gair, Qld Premier, 42 years in State and Federal politics, b. (d. 1980)
Sir Warren D'Arcy McDonald, banker, industrialist, b. (d. 1965)
Lloyd Maxwell Ross, academic, union official, and author, b.
Sir Alan Russell Taylor, High Court Judge, b. (d. 1969)

18 May. First wireless transmission in Aust. made from Queenscliff, Vic., as Duke and Duchess of York sail through Port Phillip Heads in Royal yacht.
Nov. Australasian Ornithologists' Union estb. (Becomes 'Royal' in 1910.)

During 1901

There are *c.* 33,000 telephones in use.
Brown trout introduced to SA.
First university Dental School estb., in Sydney.
William Farrer names his drought-resistant wheat 'Federation'. Wheat released to farmers.

Births & Deaths

Sir Mark Marcus Laurence Elwin Oliphant, atomic scientist, b.
Harold Clayton Owen, pioneer aviator, b.

1901

C

Arts

Literature

During 1901
The *Bulletin* employs Norman Lindsay.
Miles Franklin publishes *My Brilliant Career* (written c. 1899).
Henry Lawson publishes *Joe Wilson and His Mates*.
Matilda Ann (Tilly) Aston publishes *Maiden Verses*.
Victor Daley, using pseudonym Creeve Roe, publishes 'A Ballad of Eureka'.
Power to prohibit imports of blasphemous or indecent literature transferred from States to Cwlth.

Births & Deaths
Eleanor Dark (née O'Reilly), author, poet, b. (d. 1985)
Henrietta Francis York Drake-Brockman (née Jull), author, b. (d. 1968)
Maysie Coucher Greig, who also wrote as Jennifer Ames, author who published c. 200 novels, b. (d. 1971)
Alfred Francis Xavier Herbert, author, b. (d. 1984)
Tom Inglis Moore, critic, poet, b. (d. 1978)
Kenneth Adolph Slessor, poet, b. (d. 1971)
Percy Reginald Stephensen, author, b. (d. 1965)

Music, Dance

During 1901
George Musgrove and J. C. Williamson introduce opera seasons.
Nellie Stewart becomes first performing artist officially recognized by the Cwlth when she sings 'Australia' at opening of Federal Parlt.
W. H. Wale estb. Sydney Conservatorium.

Births & Deaths
Sir William Neil McKie, organist, b.
Arnold Matters, baritone, b.
Horace James Perkins, composer, b.

Drama, Theatre, Film

16 Mar. John Fuller's Minstrel and Variety Co. opens in Sydney.
18 May. 'Harry Rickards' (Henry B. Leete) opens new Opera House in Melbourne.
During 1901
Walter Baldwin Spencer begins filming Aboriginal tribes in Central Aust.

Births & Deaths
Kenneth George Hall, film producer, among first to develop sound potential, b.
Evelyn 'Queenie' Paul, actress, producer, b.

Fine Arts

During 1901
Tom Roberts commissioned to paint opening of Federal Parlt.

Births & Deaths
Alison M. Ashby, botanical artist, b.
Hatton Beck, ceramic artist, b.
Thomas Henry Bone, watercolourist, b. (d. 1953)
Vincent Brown, painter, b.
Sybil Craig, impressionist flower painter, b.
Aubrey Hickes Lawson Gibson, art patron, b. (d. 1975)
Henry Aloysius Hanke, artist, b.
George Feather Lawrence, impressionist painter, b. (d. 1981)
Roy Phillip Parkinson, watercolourist, b. (d. 1945)
Maxwell Richard Christopher Ragless, landscape painter, b. (d. 1981)
John Reed, art organizer, b. (d. 1981)
Gert Sellheim, graphic artist, industrial designer, b.

Architecture

During 1901
Edwardian period of architecture begins. (Ends c. 1916.)

D
Religion, Learning

Jan. Federal Education Conference held in Melbourne.
24 Jul. State Presbyterian Churches form federal union called the Presbyterian Church of Australia.
12 Aug. Report of Vic. Royal Commission into Technical Education recommends new type of technical secondary school.

During 1901
Commonwealth Parliamentary Library founded. (National Library of Aust. separated from Cwlth Parlt. Library 1960.)
David Mitchell donates 60,000 books to the Library of NSW, (Collection becomes Mitchell library in 1910.)
WA compulsory secular primary education system becomes free.
Claremont Teachers' Training College opens, WA.
Foundation stone laid for St John's Church of England Cathedral in Brisbane.
Travelling Schools estb. in Qld.

Births & Deaths
Gavin Merrick Long, historian and journalist, b. (d. 1968)
Sir Stephen Henry Roberts, historian and university administrator, b. (d. 1971)

E
Sport

1 Jan. First motor vehicle race held in Sydney.
During 1901
Revenue, ridden by F. Dunn, wins Melbourne Cup in 3 minutes $30\frac{1}{2}$ seconds.
Essendon football team wins VFL Premiership in Melbourne.
First women's hockey games begin in NSW, SA and Tas.
Women's rowing begins in Melbourne.
Aust. Federal Cycling Council estb.
National Rifle Association of Aust. (named 1971) estb. as Common Council of Rifle Associations of Aust.

Births & Deaths
E. W. 'Slip' Carr, athlete, b.
Maurice Froomes 'Moss' Christie, swimmer, b. (d. 1978)
Gordon Coventry, VFL footballer, b. (d. 1968)
Ernie McQuillan, boxing trainer, b.

1901

F

Historia Dignum

Population
Estimated total white, 3,773,801.
Estimated Aboriginal, 95,000.

15 Feb. Train derailment at Sydenham, NSW, claims nine lives.
15 Mar. State Historical Society estb. in NSW. (Estb. Vic. on 21 May 1909, Qld 1913, WA Sep. 1926, Tas. Oct. 1951, ACT 10 Dec. 1953, SA 1974.)
21 Mar. Ship *Federal* sinks in Bass Strait, claiming 21 lives.
1 Jul. Fire destroys Anthony Hordern store in Sydney, claiming five lives.
Sep. Cwlth receives 30,000 entries in a national flag competition.
During 1901
Australian flag first flown.

Births & Deaths
Harry Redford, cattle duffer, 'King of the Cattle-Duffers', d.

Communities
Dumbleyung, WA, estb.

A

History, Politics, Economics, Law

1902

Government

24 Mar. 1902–10 Oct. 1904, Sir Herbert Charles Chermside Governor Qld.
27 May 1902–24 Mar. 1909, Sir Harry Holdsworth Rawson Governor NSW.
10 Jun. 1902–Feb. 1904, W. H. Irvine Reform Premier Vic.
1 Jul. 1902–Aug. 1904, Sir W. H. James Liberal Premier WA.
17 Jul. 1902–9 Jan. 1903, Hallam Tennyson, Lord Tennyson, Acting Governor-General.
17 Jul. 1902–1 Jul. 1903, Sir Samuel Way administered SA.
14 Aug. 1902–23 Mar. 1903, Sir Edward Stone administered WA.

27 Feb. H. H. 'Breaker' Morant and P. J. Handcock executed for murdering Boer prisoners in South Africa.
9 Mar. Federal Govt takes over administrative control of British New Guinea from Qld.
During Mar. National Council of Women of Vic. estb. to campaign for welfare reform.
9 Apr. Federal Electoral Act grants universal adult suffrage. Act enfranchises women for Federal elections. (Aust. second country in world to enfranchise women.)
15–16 May. Conference of State Premiers held in Melbourne.
31 May. Boer War in South Africa ends. Of 16,175 Aust. soldiers involved, 251 killed in action, 267 died of disease and 882 wounded.
27 Aug. NSW Govt grants female suffrage. (Women permitted to sit in Parlt in 1918.)
9 Sep. Cwlth Tariff Bill passed by the Senate. Balance between Vic. protectionist policy advocating high tariffs and NSW free-trade policy advocating low tariffs.
18 Dec. Title of Lord Mayor conferred in Sydney and Melbourne.
During Dec. First Federal Labor Party conference officially estb. Aust. Labor Party.
During 1902
Fourth Colonial Conference in England discusses trade and defence problems and seeks to raise revenue for State and Federal Govts.
Cwlth Govt unites colonial military forces into one army.
WA first State to introduce legislation for workers compensation. (Qld 1905, NSW and Tas. 1910, SA 1911, Vic. 1914.)
Ada Emily Evans becomes first woman in Aust. to qualify in law.
High Court of Aust. estb. to define and determine Cwlth and State powers and validity of legislation flowing from them.
WA Govt estb. minimum wage principle.
William Morris Hughes registers the Waterside Workers' Federation with NSW Arbitration Court.
The Criminal Code of WA comes into force.

Births & Deaths

Sir Walter Russel Crocker, diplomat, b.
Tom Nicholson Pearce Dougherty, politician, union leader, b. (d. 1972)
Leslie Clement Haylen, Federal politician and author, b. (d. 1977)
Sir Leslie James Herron, jurist, b. (d. 1973)
Frank Rutledge Louat, lawyer, b. (d. 1963)
Sir Leslie Galfried Melville, economist, b.
Sir Reginald Richard Sholl, judge, b.
John Trezise Tonkin, WA Premier, b.

1902

B
Science, Technology, Transport, Discovery

3 Nov. Pacific submarine telegraphic cable from Southport, Qld, to Vancouver, Canada, opens. Estb. trans-Pacific cable communications.

During 1902
John Pomeroy invents first exploding bullet, in NZ.
Thomas Lane Bancroft, noted for work on Qld lungfish, demonstrates how hookworm enters the human body.
Black opals discovered at Lightning Ridge, NSW.
First interstate telephone trunk line in Aust. opens, between Mt Gambier, SA, and Nelson, Vic.

Births & Deaths
Cecil Arthur Butler, aviator, b.
John Edward Cummins, scientist, b.
Sir Edward Ford, physician, b.
Sir Leonard Holden Huxley, scientist, noted for work on gaseous electrons in upper atmosphere, b.

C
Arts

Literature

Barbara Baynton publishes *Bush Studies*, collection of stories.
Henry Lawson publishes *Children of the Bush*, verse and prose.

Births & Deaths
Ellen Dymphna Cusack, novelist, playwright, possibly b.
Robert David Fitzgerald, poet, b.
Alan Marshall, author, b. (d. 1984)
Christina Ellen Stead, novelist b. (d. 1983)

Music, Dance

14 Sep. Nellie Melba gives recital in Brisbane after returning from Europe.

Births & Deaths
Edouard Borovansky, ballet dancer, b. (d. 1959)
Richard Charles Watson, bass singer, b. (d. 1968)

Drama, Theatre, Film

15 Feb. *Sweet Nell of Old Drury*, starring Nellie Stewart, becomes stage success at Princess Theatre in Melbourne.
23 Mar. Her Majesty's Theatre in Sydney burnt down.

Fine Arts

During 1902
Vic. Women's Art Club estb. in Melbourne.
Charles Piguenit paints *Mt Kosciusko*.

Births & Deaths
Neville Mirvane Bunning, sculptor, potter, b.
Robert Richmond Campbell, watercolourist noted for oil paintings of Sydney Harbour, b. (d. 1972)
Karl Duldig, sculptor, b.
Harry den Hartog, painter, b.
Emile Mercier, cartoonist, b.
Arthur James Murch, war painter, sculptor, b.
Albert Namatjira, painter, first widely acclaimed Aboriginal painter, b. (d. 1959)
Ralph Malcolm Warner, watercolourist, b. (d. 1966)
Frank Weitzell, sculptor, probably b. (d. 1932)

D

Religion, Learning

1902

Architecture

During 1902
Robert Haddon, architect, develops Art Nouveau style which soon dominates decoration.
Brewery-built hotels in Sydney demonstrate Art Nouveau style.
House planning revolutionized by principle of orientating to northern exposure and utilizing sun.

During 1902
Prime Minister Edmund Barton receives medal from Pope in Rome. Protestants protest with petition to Parlt.
Melbourne University introduces a diploma course in Education.
c. 1902. South Brisbane Technical College estb.

Births & Deaths
Christopher Carroll, teacher with continuous career of 55 years 7 months, b. (d. 1975)

1902

E Sport

Jun. NSW Trotting Club estb. in Sydney. First meeting on 19 Nov. First trotting organization in Aust.

2 Nov. W. H. Gocher challenges law prohibiting daylight swimming by swimming in surf at Manly, Sydney. Gocher arrested but not prosecuted. (Law changed to permit daylight swimming in Sydney 1906.)

During 1902
The Victory, ridden by R. Lewis, wins Melbourne Cup in 3 minutes 29 seconds.
Collingwood football team wins VFL Premiership in Melbourne.
Aust. National Football League estb. in Sydney.
The SA British Football Association estb. in SA. First SA soccer clubs estb.
Aust. wins cricket Test match in Manchester, England.
Victor Trumper becomes first batsman to score 100 runs before lunch.
First Test Cricket series between Aust. and South Africa played, in South Africa.
First motor car race meetings held in Perth.
Arthur Cavill first to use the Australian Crawl swimming stroke in official competitions.
Freddy Lane first to swim 100 yards in 1 minute flat.
Annette Kellerman first Aust. champion woman swimmer.
NSW Table Tennis Association estb.
Jim Brennan opens National Sporting Club in Sydney for boxing.
c. 1902. Bronte Surf Club estb., Sydney.

Births & Deaths
George Oswald (Gubby) Allen, cricketer, noted fast bodyline bowler, b.
Billy Grime, boxer, b. (d. 1952)
Arthur 'Snowy' Justice, Rugby League footballer, b. (d. 1977)
Percy Paver, rifle shooter, b.
Jack Toohey, jockey, b.
Merv Williams, boxer, b.

F Historia Dignum

Population
Estimated total white population 3,875,318.

Jan. Finger-printing introduced in Sydney; known as the Bertillon system of identification.
31 Jul. Mt Kembla, NSW, mining disaster. Miner's lamp ignites coal gas; explosion claims 95 lives.
1 Aug. *New Idea*, women's magazine, first published.
9 Nov. SS *Elingamite* wrecked on King I., claiming 43 lives.
11 Nov. Uniform rates for postage of newspapers and transmission of telegrams estb.

During 1902
Herald and Weekly Times Ltd estb., Vic.
Eighth year of Great Drought, sheep numbers fall by 36,000,000. Sep. 7 declared day of humiliation and prayer for rain. (Drought probably worst recorded in Aust. history.)
Royal Humane Society of Sydney instituted as the National Shipwreck Relief Society of NSW.
Melbourne Distributing Kitchen Co. estb. to deliver home meals to the needy.
c. 1902. Gas coppers begin to replace wood fuel coppers. Gas water heaters replace kerosene water heaters in bathrooms and gas stoves replace iron wood-burning stoves in kitchens.

Communities
Kurri Kurri, NSW, estb.

A
History, Politics, Economics, Law

1903

Government

9 Jan. 1903–21 Jan. 1904, Hallam Tennyson, Lord Tennyson, Governor-General Aust.
24 Mar. 1903–22 Apr. 1909, Sir Frederick George Denham Bedford Governor WA.
9 Apr. 1903–Jul. 1904, W. B. Propsting Liberal-Democrat Premier Tas.
1 Jul. 1903–18 Feb. 1909, Sir George Ruthven Le Hunte Governor SA.
17 Sep. 1903–Jan. 1906, A. Morgan Premier Qld.
24 Sep. 1903–27 Apr. 1904, Second Cwlth Ministry, Alfred Deakin Protectionist Prime Minister Aust.
24 Nov. 1903–25 Apr. 1904, Sir John Madden administered Vic.

15 Apr. Premiers' Conference held in Sydney.
8–15 May. Vic. railway engine drivers' and firemens' strike begins. First large-scale disruption of Govt public utility.
24 May. Proclamation of Empire Day.
Jul. Federal Govt Sugar Bounties Act provides rebate on excise duty on all sugar grown in Aust. by whites. (To discourage continued use of Kanaka labour.)
25 Aug. Senate passes Naval Agreement Bill, determining yearly payment to Imperial navy for next 10 years.
High Court of Aust. constituted. On 24 Sep. Sir Samuel Griffith appointed Federal Chief Justice (until 17 Oct 1919), with Sir Edmund Barton (until 1920) and Richard Edward O'Connor (until 1912) appointed justices. First sitting of the High Court held in Banco Court of Supreme Court Building in Melbourne on 6 Oct.
23 Nov. Dissolution of First Federal Parlt. Elections for new Parlt on 16 Dec.
10 Dec. Tas. Govt introduces female suffrage. (Women permitted to sit in Parlt in 1921.)
16 Dec. Women vote for first time in Federal elections.

During 1903
First Federal Naturalization Act passed.
Defence Act estb. principle of conscription for home service during wartime.
Federal Govt attempts unsuccessfully to buy western New Guinea from Holland.
Vic. becomes first State to admit women to practise law. (Tas. 1904, Qld 1905, SA 1911, NSW 1918, WA 1923.)
Tas. Labor Party founded as Tas. Workers' Political League.
Tas. scallop industry begins.
Pearling industry in Broome, WA, involves 300 vessels.
WA Govt commissions Frank Hann to open stock route across the Great Victoria Desert, SA.
Associated Chambers of Manufactures of Aust. estb. as The Federal Council of the Chamber of Manufactures.
The Employers' Federation of NSW estb.

Births & Deaths

Sir Garfield Edward John Barwick, High Court Chief Justice, b.
Edward Waterfield Hayward, businessman, b.
Sir Leslie Joseph Hooker, real estate company director, b. (d. 1976)
Sir Frank Walters Kitto, jurist, b.
Dominic Paul McGuire, diplomat, author, b.
Sir Reginald George Pollard, military commander, b. (d. 1978)
Hugh Randall Syme, pioneer of mine disposal operations, newspaper proprietor, b. (d. 1965)

1903

B

Science, Technology, Transport, Discovery

24 Jan. WA Goldfields Water Supply Scheme, designed and largely constructed by Charles Y. O'Connor, completed. Links Kalgoorlie to Perth with 30-inch water pipeline. First major water supply pipeline in Aust.
3 Feb. Nepean R. Bridge at Maldon, NSW, opens.
14 Feb. Steam tram line opens from Manly Pier to Curl Curl, Sydney.
During 1903
Dunlop Pneumatic Tyre Co. of Aust. Ltd manufactures first pneumatic tyres in Aust.
Herman Everingham develops aeronautical research in Aust.
Brisbane–Rockhampton, Qld, railway line completed.
First Prior barley seeds available in SA.

Births & Deaths

Sir John Carew Eccles, neuro-physiologist, b.
Harold Charles Gatty, pioneer air navigator, b. (d. 1957)
Edward Graem Robertson, neurologist and architectural historian, b. (d. 1975)

C

Arts

Literature

During 1903
Joseph Furphy, using pseudonym Tom Collins, publishes *Such is Life*.
Arthur Hoey Davis, using pseudonym Steele Rudd, publishes *Our New Selection*.

Births & Deaths

Lennie Waldemar Lower, author, b. (d. 1947)
Alfonso Bernard O'Reilly, author, bushman, b. (d. 1975)
Robert Shaw Close author, b. (d. 1984)
Alan John Villiers, author, sailor, b. (d. 1982)

Music, Dance

During 1903
Ada Crossley and Percy Grainger tour Aust.

Births & Deaths

John Bishop, music professor, b. (d. 1964)
Frank Coughlan, jazz, player of trombone, trumpet,
Clive Martin Douglas, composer, conductor, b. (d. 1977)

Drama, Theatre, Film

1 Aug. Rebuilt Her Majesty's Theatre in Sydney opens.

Fine Arts

During 1903
James White finishes memorial to Queen Victoria in Melbourne.
Hans Heysen returns to Adelaide after studying art in Europe. Begins large no. of works; specializes in landscape and gum tree scenes.

Births & Deaths

Douglas Annand, painter, graphic advertising artist, b. (d. 1976)
Enid Helen Gray Cambridge, watercolourist, b. (d. 1976)
Irwin Crowe, painter, b.
Vaughan Murray Griffin, painter, graphic artist, b.
Percy Ivor Hunt, watercolourist, b. (d. 1971)
John S. Loxton, watercolourist, art critic, b. (d. 1971)
Raymond McGrath, painter, architect, b. (d. 1977)
Pixie O'Harris, born Rhona Olive Harris, artist, author, noted for children's drawings, b.
Henry Hewitt Rainer, etcher, b. (d. 1957)

D

Religion, Learning

During 1903
G. H. Knibbs and J. W. Turner report on NSW education system.
The WA School of Mines estb. at Kalgoorlie, WA.

E

Sport

During 1903
Lord Cardigan, ridden by N. Godby, wins Melbourne Cup in 3 minutes 29¼ seconds.
Collingwood football team wins VFL Premiership in Melbourne.
First Aust. v. NZ Rugby Union football Test Match in Sydney.
David Cavill wins all men's freestyle events in Aust. swimming championships.
Hugh Trumble takes his second hat trick in English cricket Test in Melbourne.
First car races held at Maribyrnong, Vic.
First Motor Cycle Racing Club estb. in NSW. (WA and Vic 1904.)
SA Mens' Hockey Association estb. in Adelaide. (Vic and NSW Associations estb. 1906, WA 1908, Qld 1921, Tas. 1934.)
First Aust. Women's Hockey Club estb., in Sydney.
Amos Murrell becomes woodchopping star.
Australasian Amateur Boxing Association estb.
c. 1903. Manly Surf Club estb. in Sydney.

Births & Deaths
Daphne Akhurst, tennis player, b. (d. 1933)
Dick Eve, swimmer, diver, b.
Ray Stehr, Rugby League player, b.

1903

F *Historia Dignum*

Population
Estimated total white, 3,916,592.

9 Mar. Cyclone Leonta damages Townsville, Qld, claiming eight lives.
20 Mar. Automobile Club of Aust. estb. in Sydney to provide facilities for motorists and to defend against repressive road legislation. (Becomes Royal in 1930.)
26 May. Ship *Oakland* wrecked off Port Stephens, NSW, claiming 11 lives.
1 Jul. *Sunday Sun* first published in Sydney.
3 Oct. Newspaper *Brisbane Daily Mail* first published.
24 Oct. Newspaper *Border Morning Mail* first published, in Albury, NSW.
28 Nov. *People's Daily*, labour newspaper, first published, in Melbourne.
9 Dec. Royal Automobile Club of Vic. estb. SA Club estb. on 30 Sep.
During 1903
First crematorium in Aust. opens, in Adelaide.
Mixed bathing legalized on many Aust. beaches.
  (Legalized on Sydney beaches in 1906.)
The blowfly becomes serious pest for sheep.

Communities
Gormanston, Tas., estb.
Weston, NSW, estb.

A

History, Politics, Economics, Law

1904

Government

21 Jan. 1904–9 Sep. 1908, Henry Stafford Northcote, Lord Northcote, Governor-General Aust.
16 Feb. 1904–Jan. 1909, T. Bent Reform Premier Vic.
16 Apr. 1904–28 Oct. 1904, Sir John Dodds administered Tas.
25 Apr. 1904–6 Jul. 1908, Sir Reginald Arthur James Talbot Governor Vic.
27 Apr. 1904–17 Aug. 1904, Third Cwlth Ministry, John Christian Watson Labor Prime Minister Aust.
15 Jun. 1904–Aug. 1904, T. Waddell Protectionist Premier NSW.
11 Jul. 1904–Jun. 1909, J. W. Evans Liberal Premier Tas.
10 Aug. 1904–Aug. 1905, H. Daglish Labor Premier WA.
18 Aug. 1904–5 Jul. 1905, Fourth Cwlth Ministry, George Houston Reid Free Trade–Protectionist coalition Prime Minister Aust.
29 Aug. 1904–Oct. 1907, J. H. Carruthers Liberal Reform Premier NSW.
10 Oct. 1904–30 Nov. 1905, Sir Hugh Muir Nelson administered Qld.
28 Oct. 1904–20 May 1909, Sir Gerald Strickland Governor Tas.

5 Feb. Conference between Federal and State Treasurers opens. Discusses proposed transfer of State debts to Cwlth and best method of encouraging immigration.
During Feb. Govt concern at declining birth rate. Proposals for encouraging immigration from Britain considered. NSW Govt estb. Royal Commission into contraception and declining birth rate. (First such inquiry in English-speaking world.)
Council of Employers' Federation of Aust. estb.
1 Mar. Cwlth Defence Act comes into force. Federal Govt assumes control of navy from States; William Creswell appointed director of naval forces in Dec.
2 Mar. Second Federal Parlt opens. (Dissolution 5 Nov. 1906.)
9 Aug. Federal Parliament selects Dalgety in Bombala district of NSW for site of Federal Capital. NSW Parlt disagrees, and the dispute ends in 1908 when Canberra is chosen.
18 Aug. John Christian Watson Labor leader of the Federal Opposition. (Until 1905.)
25 Nov. Scheme of national defence providing for Council of Defence to include members with consultative powers for supervision of Naval and Military Boards passed in the House of Representatives.
15 Dec. Commonwealth Conciliation and Arbitration Act assented. Court of Conciliation and Arbitration estb. Recognizes equal standing of employers and unions in disputes.

During 1904
Recruiting of Kanakas ceases. (Since 1847 *c.* 57,000 Kanakas have worked in Aust.)
Arthur Arnott founds biscuit company.
Amatil Ltd (so-named 1977) estb. Becomes one of largest Aust. companies and oldest tobacco manufacturer.
Cherbourg Aboriginal community estb. near Gympie, Qld.
Federal Govt estb. first Tariff Commission.
c. 1904. Wheat becomes major Aust. export.

Births & Deaths

Henry Mackay Burrell, naval commander, b.
Ulrich Ruegg Ellis, New State campaigner, author, b.
Edward Joseph Frederick Holman, WA politician, b. (d. 1951)
Sir Richard Clarence Kirby, judge, industrial arbitrator, b.
Sir Denzil Macarthur-Onslow, military commander, pastoralist, b.
Sir Frederick Rudolph William Scherger, air force commander, b.
Bernard Sugerman, jurist, b. (d. 1976)
Sir Roland Wilson, economist, company director, b.

1904

B

Science, Technology, Transport, Discovery

8 Jul. Sydney City Council introduces scheme providing household power and electric street lighting.

During 1904
Balloon above Sydney takes first significant aerial photographs in Aust.
Tas. Field Naturalists' Club estb. in Hobart.
Broken Hill Proprietary Co. produces zinc concentrate by flotation process.
Wireless telegraphy installed between Queenscliff, Vic., and Devonport, Tas.
WA passes Motor Car Act, requiring owners to carry registration discs.
Rabbit-proof fence erected between Port Hedland and Esperance Bay, WA.
Tom Farrell discovers tungsten ore, scheelite, on King I.

Births & Deaths
Sir Eric Ashby, botanist, educationist, b.
William Alan Stewart Butement, scientist, b.
Keith Alfred Hindwood, ornithologist, b. (d. 1971)
Herbert Ian Priestley Hogbin, anthropologist, b.
David Victor Isaacs, engineer, b.
Amy Johnson, pioneer aviatrix, first woman to qualify as ground engineer, b. (d. 1940)
Sir Maurice Alan Edgar Mawbey, mining engineer, b. (d. 1977)
Karl Eric Oom, hydrographer, b. (d. 1972)
Francis Noble Ratcliffe, naturalist, b. (d. 1970)
Donald Munro Shand, agriculturist, b. (d. 1976)
William Alan Stewart, scientist, b.
Geoffrey Neville Wikner, light aircraft designer, manufacturer, b.
Brian Wellington Windeyer, radiologist, b.

C

Arts

Literature

During 1904
Walter Baldwin Spencer and Francis Gillen publish *The Northern Tribes of Central Australia*.
Arthur Hoey Davis, using pseudonym Steele Rudd, publishes *Steele Rudd's Magazine* (runs until 1930).
Alfred William Howitt publishes *The Native Tribes of South-East Australia*.

Births & Deaths
John Keith Ewers, author, b.
John Alexander Ross Mackellar, poet, b. (d. 1932)
John Gordon Morrison, novelist, b.
Brian Con Penton, author, journalist, b. (d. 1951)

Music, Dance

26 Nov. The Peschoff Russian dancers perform in Melbourne.
During 1904
Jan Paderewski, pianist, tours Aust.
Peter Dawson, singer, makes first of 3,500 records.
Nellie Melba makes first records.
Alfred Hill's *Tapu* Maori operetta performed in Sydney.

Births & Deaths
John Henry Antill, composer, b.
Alan Eddy, singer, b.

Drama, Theatre, Film

During 1904
Leon Brodzky estb. Aust. Theatre Society Repertory Co., in Melbourne.
Her Majesty's Theatre opens in Perth.
S. Fitzgerald makes feature film, *John Vane, Bushranger*

Births & Deaths
George Landen Dann, playwright, draughtsman, b.
John Villiers Farrow, film director, author, b. (d. 1963)
Wilfrid Coad Thomas, producer, media personality,

Fine Arts

During 1904
Broken Hill Art Gallery and Art Prize estb., NSW.
Art and Architecture magazine published. (Becomes the *Salon* in 1911.)
New Art Society estb. in Qld.
Alfred Felton bequest starts National Gallery of Vic

Melbourne is last city in British Empire to permit Art Galleries, Museums and Public Libraries to open on Sundays.

Norman Lindsay's *Pollice Verso*, showing naked Romans and their women making gestures at a crucified Christ, causes public outcry.

Births & Deaths
James Cook, painter, war artist, b. (d. 1960)
George Bernard Duncan, painter, b. (d. 1974)
Aeneas John Lindsay, art collector, b. (d. 1963)
Raymond Lindsay, painter, b. (d. 1960)
John Richard Passmore, abstract painter, b. (d. 1985)
Mervyn Ashmore Smith, watercolourist, architect, b.
Eric Anchor Thake, surrealist painter, b. (d. 1982)

Architecture

During 1904
William Wolff architect completes 'His Majesty's', hotel and theatre, in Perth.

Births & Deaths
Sydney Ancher, architect, b.

D

Religion, Learning

During 1904
First Jehovah's Witnesses (known until 1931 as Watchtower Bible and Tract Society) office opens in Melbourne.

W. A. Barton selected first Aust. Rhodes Scholar.

Educational Ladder period begins. (Ends *c.* 1938.) Reforms estb. greater educational opportunity, emphasis on career, professional vocations; liberal-humanist curriculum includes history, literature and science.

United Methodists under George Lane conduct first General Conference, in Melbourne.

1904

E Sport

Mar. First Henley-on-Yarra annual rowing regatta held in Melbourne.

During 1904
Acrasia, ridden by T. Clayton, wins Melbourne Cup in 3 minutes 28¼ seconds.
Fitzroy football team wins VFL Premiership in Melbourne.
Aust. has only one competitor in third Olympic Games, held at St Louisa, USA. (No medals won.)
Michael Scott wins first Aust. open golf championship at Botany, NSW.
Lawn Tennis Association of Australasia estb.
First car race held, at Sandown in Melbourne.
First Aust. soccer team visits NZ.

Births & Deaths
Edward Greeves, VFL footballer, b.
Alan Hopkins, VFL footballer, b.
Maurice McCarten, jockey, b.
Sir Hubert Opperman, cyclist, Federal politician, b.
Bob Pearce, sculler, b.
Cyril Towers, Rugby Union footballer, b.
Timothy Wall, cricketer, noted fast bowler, b.

F Historia Dignum

Population
Estimated total white, 3,974,150.

Mar.–Sep. Twelve cases of bubonic plague reported in Sydney; six deaths.
Apr. First motorized fire-fighting vehicle, imported from England, arrives in Sydney.
25 May. Goldmine accident at east Coolgardie, WA, claims five lives.
14 Oct. Charters Towers, Qld, goldmine fire claims five lives.

During 1904
John Henderson introduces first flood warning system.
Cyclone devastates Broome, WA.
First Aust. cigarette cards appear.
Aust. birth rate declines due to spread of contraception devices and introduction of family planning.
Charles Nuttall publishes comic strip *Peter Wayback Visits the Melbourne Cup*.
First maternal and infant welfare services estb., in Sydney.

Communities
Merbein, Vic., estb.
Ouyen, Vic., estb.
Wongan Hills, WA, estb.

A
History, Politics, Economics, Law

1905

Government

1 Mar. 1905–Jul. 1905, R. Butler Conservative Premier SA.
5 Jul. 1905–13 Nov. 1908, Fifth Cwlth Ministry, Alfred Deakin Protectionist Prime Minister Aust.
26 Jul. 1905–Jun. 1909, T. Price Labor-Liberal coalition Premier SA.
25 Aug. 1905–May 1906, Sir C. H. Rason Liberal Premier WA.
20 Nov. 1905–26 May. 1909, Frederic John Napier Thesiger, Lord Chelmsford, Governor Qld.
1905–1910, C. E. Herbert Government Resident NT under SA jurisdiction.

12 Jan. Fed. Govt estb. Naval Board to organize an Aust. naval fleet.
25 Jan. Qld Govt abolishes plural voting for Legislative Assembly; introduces female suffrage. (Women allowed to sit in Parlt in 1915.)
17 Feb. Conference of Federal and State Ministers in Hobart ends. States resolve that Cwlth take over State debts.
5 Jul. Sir George Houston Reid Free Trade leader of Federal Opposition. (Until 1908.)
8 Nov. Court of Conciliation and Arbitration first sits.
10 Nov. NSW re-introduces assisted immigration. (Some 390,000 Britons arrive during next nine years.)
23 Nov. First Federal Trade Marks legislation passed. (Effective from 2 Jul. 1906.)

During 1905
'Yellow Peril' fear prevails throughout Aust.
Dictation test in Cwlth Immigration Restriction Act extended to use of test in any language.
Federal Govt passes Papua Act, providing for government of former British New Guinea.
Interstate conferences estb. Federal Labor platform.
The WA Aborigines Act estb. reserves and 'protectors'.
Cwlth Steamship Owners' Association estb.
SA Association of Clerks estb. First office workers' union organization in Aust.
A Labour-in-Politics Convention officially adopts name Qld Labor Party.

Births & Deaths

John Langdon Bonython, lawyer, company director, b.
Colin Grant Clarke, economist, b.
Edward Rowland Edkins, Qld pioneer pastoralist, d. (b. 1840)
Sir Paul Meernaa Caedwalla Hasluck, Aust. Governor-General, historian, politician, b.
Francis Patrick McManus, DLP politician, b. (d. 1983)
James Cairns Morrow, naval commander, b. (d. 1963)
John Riddoch Rymill, polar explorer, b. (d. 1968)
Everest Reginald York Seymour, NSW businessman and benefactor, b. (d. 1966)

1905

B
Science, Technology, Transport, Discovery

18 Oct. Experimental radio communication regulated by Wireless Telegraphy Act.
During 1905
First official radio transmitting station built, at Point Lonsdale, near Queenscliff, Vic., by Marconi Co. for demonstration.
Anthony G. M. Michell patents first thrust block, enabling propulsion of large ships.
Motor cars become numerous.
Vic. railway inaugurates Malvern–Prahran steam omnibus service in Melbourne.
First motor buses begin running in Sydney.
Radios first fitted in Aust. ships.
Massey, Harris Co. invents the header harvester.
Cwlth Oil Corporation begins oil shale mining operations at Newnes, near Lithgow, NSW.
Thomas Lane Bancroft demonstrates that mosquitoes carry organism dengue fever.

Births & Deaths

Sir John Philip Baxter, engineer noted for work on nuclear projects, including Hiroshima bomb, b.
T. Griffiths, scientist noted for work on tropical pastures, b. (d. 1969)
Norman Joseph King, sugar industry technologist, b.
Gilbert Edward Phillips, neurosurgeon, b. (d.1952)

C
Arts

Literature

During 1905
Mrs Aeneas Gunn publishes *The Little Black Princess*.
Henry Lawson publishes collection of verse, *When I was King*.

Births & Deaths

Donald Herbert Edwards, author, teacher, b. (d. 1963)
Brian Charles Fitzpatrick, writer, historian, b. (d. 1965)

Music, Dance

During 1905
Arundel Orchard writes opera *Coquette*.

Births & Deaths

Albert Arlen, composer, author, b.
Stanley Leigh Clarkson, opera singer, b. (d. 1961)
John Dudley, singer, b.

Drama, Theatre, Film

1 Jul. Charles Cozens Spencer begins film exhibition in Sydney.
During 1905
The Tait Brothers make film *The Story of the Kelly Gang*, claimed to be world's first full-length feature film.

Births & Deaths

Alexander Mervyn Archdale, actor, b.
Leslie Rees, drama authority, author, b.

Fine Arts

During 1905
Govt House in Hobart holds *Exhibition of Living Pictures*.
Melbourne Gallery buys its first French impressionist painting.

Births & Deaths

John Brackenreg, painter, b.
Bernard Hesling, cartoonist, b.
Louis Kahan, portrait painter, illustrator, stage designer, b.
Gerald Francis Lewers, sculptor, b. (d. 1962)
Rosamond Anne Veitch McCulloch, painter, b. (d. 1971)

Anton David Riebe, landscape painter, b.
James Campbell Sharp, painter, graphic artist, b.
William Joshua Smith, artist, b.

Architecture

c. 1905. Concrete widely used as a structural building material.

Births & Deaths

Sir Roy Burman Grounds, architect, b. (d. 1981)

D
Religion, Learning

1 Jan. W. L. Neale appointed Director of Education in Tas. Reforms education system.
8 Feb. Peter Board appointed Director of Education in Sydney.
Feb. Melbourne Continuation School for teacher training opens. Effectively first high school in Vic.
Dec. Vic. reforms education system; re-inforces compulsory attendance, enforces registration of teachers and schools.

During 1905
Sydney Teachers' College opens.
Sydney Day Nursery and Nursery Schools Association estb.
Kindergarten Union of SA estb.
Tas. Teachers' Federation estb.

Births & Deaths

Sir Harold Leslie White, parliamentary librarian, first national librarian, b.

1905

E
Sport

During 1905
Blue Spec, ridden by F. Bullock, wins Melbourne Cup in 3 minutes 27½ seconds.
Fitzroy football team wins VFL Premiership in Melbourne.
R. W. Heath wins first Aust. open men's tennis championship.
First Aust. tennis challenge for Davis Cup.
Aust. Board of Control replaces Aust. Cricket Council.
First surf rescue boats appear on Sydney beaches.
Annette Kellermann swims 4 miles in Yarra R., Melbourne, in 1 hour 48 minutes. Attracts much publicity.
First Aust. open golf title played.
Fremantle Golf Club estb. WA.
Roller skating begins in Aust., in Adelaide. (Sydney 1907.)
Nigel Barker's athletic record among first Aust. records accepted internationally.
Power boating competitions begin in Sydney. Motor Boat Club estb.
First motor racing reliability trials held. Mrs Ben Thompson first woman competitor.
c. 1905. Netball first played in Aust.

Births & Deaths
Bill Henneberry, boxing referee, b.
Rae 'Togo' Johnstone, jockey, b. (d. 1964)
Jim Munro, jockey, b. (d. 1974)
Len Nettlefold, golfer, b. (d. 1971)
Sir William Herbert Northam, yachtsman, businessman, b.
William Joseph 'Bill' O'Reilly, cricketer, noted spin-bowler, b.
Margaret Elizabeth Maynard Peden, cricketer, founder of Aust. Womens' Cricket Council, b.
George Ryder, turf club administrator, b.
Clifford Ewing Sproule, tennis player, b.
Tommy Woodcock, horserace trainer, Phar Lap's strapper, b. (d. 1985)
William John Young, cyclist, sport administrator, b.

F
Historia Dignum

Population
Estimated total white, 4,032,977.

Feb. Premiers' Conference declares Queen Victoria's birthday a public holiday.
During 1905
Annette Kellermann displays one-piece bathing costume.
Vic. first State to enact food regulations with Pure Food Act.
Automobile Clubs estb. in Qld, WA and Tas.
Melbourne Esperanto Club estb.
John Joseph Symons founds Young Aust. League, a non-denominational youth welfare organization, in WA.
Hobart Baby Show held; first of kind recorded in Aust.
Largest recorded diamond discovered, near Mt Werong, NSW.
The Bird Observers' Club of Vic. estb. in Melbourne

Communities
Arrino, WA, estb.
Nornalup, WA, area probably first estb.
Pinnaroo, SA, estb.

A

History, Politics, Economics, Law

1906

Government

19 Jan. 1906–Nov. 1907, W. Kidston Premier Qld.
7 May 1906–Sep. 1910, (Sir) N. J. Moore Liberal Premier WA.

15 Jan. Record wool clip of more than 11,000,000 bales.
18 Jan. First commercial sale of clover seeds.
Mar. Report of Federal Navigation Commission favours preferential treatment of British ships if carrying British goods or manned by British sailors. On 25 Sep. Federal Govt passes resolution supporting preference to British goods brought to Aust. by British ships manned by white labour.
5 Apr. Premiers' Conference in Sydney resolves to promote immigration. (WA not represented.)
21 May. Japanese naval squadron visits Aust.
During May. Alfred Canning leads expedition in WA. Estb. longest stock route in Aust., from Kimberleys to Wiluna.
1 Sep. Papua Act officially proclaimed. British New Guinea becomes Aust. Territory of Papua.
13 Sep. Federal Govt approves preferential tariff with NZ. On 9 Oct. passes South African Preference Treaty.
12 Oct. Sir Isaac Alfred Isaacs appointed Justice of the High Court of Aust. (Until 1930.)
13 Oct. Henry Bournes Higgins appointed Justice of the High Court of Aust. (until 1929) and in 1907 appointed President of Court of Conciliation and Arbitration (until 1922).
22 Oct. Sydney traders protest that the New Hebrides Convention estb. French predominance in strategically important places in Pacific, thus endangering British trade route between America and Aust.
23 Nov. Repatriation of Kanakas to SW Pacific Islands.
12 Dec. Federal Legislative elections held. Alfred Deakin re-elected Protectionist Prime Minister of Aust. on 12 Dec.
12 Dec. First Cwlth referendum taken in all States, on Senators' election terms, carried.
During 1906
Cwlth estb. Bureau of Census and Statistics.
Cwlth prohibits States from borrowing overseas money.
High Court of Aust. increased to five Justices, being a Chief Justice and four Justices.
The Australian Industries Protection Act formalizes New Protection policy. Links tariffs with living wages, thus forcing companies to pay fair and reasonable wages.
Kiwi Shoe Polish Co. estb.
Night-shift work in coal mines abolished.
NSW Govt authorizes Murrumbidgee R. Irrigation Scheme.
The Australasian Meat Industry Employees' Union estb.

Births & Deaths

Herbert Cole (Nugget) Coombs, economist, administrator, b.
Thomas Tuke Hollway, Vic. Premier who modernized railways and was responsible for electoral reform, b. (d. 1971)
Sir Douglas Ralph Nicholls, SA Governor, first Aboriginal Governor, b.
Sir Douglas Frank Hewson Packer, media proprietor, b. (d. 1974)

1906

B
Science, Technology, Transport, Discovery

1 Jan. Cwlth Govt prohibits importation of opium except for medical purposes.
5 May. St Kilda–Brighton Melbourne electric street tramway service opens. Electric tram service begins in Adelaide.
12 Jul. Marconi Co. officially inaugurates wireless telegraphy between Queenscliff, Vic., and Devonport, Tas.
4 Aug. Central Railway Station opens in Sydney.
Dec. Burrinjuck Dam, NSW, scheme launched. (Completed 1937.)
During 1906
Qld Naturalists' Club estb. in Brisbane.
SA first records Paterson's Curse plant.
Natural gas first exported commercially from Roma, Qld.
A. J. Smith discovers Radium Hill, SA.
Frank Bottrill invents the Dreadnought road wheel for vehicles and travelling machines.
C. P. Bartholomew erects experimental wireless station in Sydney.

Births & Deaths

Keith Edward Bullen, mathematician, scientist, b. (d. 1976)
David Forbes Martyn, geophysicist, b. (d. 1970)

C
Arts

Literature

During 1906
A. B. 'Banjo' Paterson publishes *An Outback Marriage*
Arthur Hoey Davis, using pseudonym Steele Rudd, publishes *Back at Our Selection*.
Edward Dyson publishes *Fact'ry 'ands*.
C. J. Dennis and A. E. Martin found the *Gadfly*, a satirical magazine, in Adelaide.

Births & Deaths

Cyril Alston, author, journalist, b.
Robert Guy Howarth, author, academic, b. (d. 1974)
James Picot, poet, short story writer, b. (d. 1944)
Stanley Clive Perry Turnbull, author, journalist, b. (d. 1975)

Music, Dance

During 1906
Alberto Zelman estb. Melbourne Symphony Orchestra, first permanent Aust. symphony orchestra.
Alfred Hill's opera *A Moorish Maid* performed in Sydney.

Births & Deaths

Joseph Mozart Post, musician, conductor, b. (d. 197

Drama, Theatre, Film

Mar. T. J. West holds film exhibitions in Sydney.
26 Dec. S. Fitzgerald's *The Story of the Kelly Gang*, fu length feature film, first screened, at Athenaeum Theatre in Melbourne. Made by Millard Johnson and William Gibson.

Fine Arts

During 1906
Sydney Ure Smith and H. Julius estb. commercial ar studio.
Society of Arts and Crafts of NSW estb. in Sydney.

Births & Deaths

Harold Frederick Abbott, painter, b.
Leonard Lloyd Annois, watercolourist, mural painte b. (d. 1966)
William Henry Archibald Constable, theatre designe commercial artist, b.
Olive Mary Finnin, artist, poet, b.
James Flett, painter, graphic artist, b.

Francis Henry Critchley Hinder, painter, stage designer, b.
Margel Ina Harris Hinder, sculptor, b.
Richard Haughton James, painter, industrial designer, b.
Herbert McClintock, painter, b.
Harold 'Hal' Missingham, artist, photographer, author, b.
Eileen Palmer, lino-cut printer, b. (d. 1958)
Ivor Pengelly, painter, b.
Ernest Sidney Philpot, painter, critic, b.
Constance Stokes, artist (modernist specializing in female nude), b.
Harald Vike, painter, illustrator, theatre designer, b.

D

Religion, Learning

1 Apr. Teachers' Training College opens in Hobart.
During 1906
NSW secular and compulsory primary education system becomes free.
Creche and Kindergarten Association of Qld estb.
First private SA Kindergarten opens.
Newcastle High School opens. First new State High School in NSW for 20 years.
Broken Hill Library becomes first free library in NSW.
De La Salle Brothers Catholic teaching order estb. in Aust.

Births & Deaths

Raymond Maxwell Crawford, historian, b.
Francis Stanislaus Flynn, Catholic priest, author, b.
Norman Denholm Harper, historian, b.

1906

E
Sport

6 Feb. Bondi Bathers' Lifesaving Club founded in Sydney.
23 Dec. Lifesaving reels first used at Bondi beach Sydney; devised by Lyster Ormsby.
During 1906
Poseidon, ridden by T. Clayton, wins Melbourne Cup in 3 minutes $31\frac{1}{2}$ seconds.
Carlton football team wins VFL Premiership in Melbourne.
Walter Biddell builds first Aust. lifesavers' rescue boat in Sydney.
City rodeos first appear in Sydney. Lance Skuthorpe widely acclaimed for controlling 'Buck-Jumper Bobs', a horse tossing 800 previous riders.
Aspendale speedway near Melbourne opens; first professional motor racing circuit in Aust.
First Aust. Rules Football Council estb. (Becomes Aust. National Football Council.)

Births & Deaths

Cyril Angles, radio sportscaster, b. (d. 1962)
Arthur Hardwick (Jack) Carroll, middleweight boxer, b. (d. 1976)
Henry Christian (Harry) Hopman, tennis player, coach, b.
Sutton McMillan, trotter driver, b.
Vic Meyer, yachtsman, b.

F
Historia Dignum

Population
Estimated total white, 4,091,485.

28 Jan. Cyclone damages Cairns, Qld.
4 Mar. Cyclone damages Croydon, Qld.
19 Nov. Submarine earthquake reading 7.75 recorded near Monte Bello Is.
During 1906
State Govts enforce regulations to control impure food problem.
First Parent and Citizen Association estb. in NSW.
Widespread river floods effect NSW, Vic., Qld and SA.
Drought conditions in NT.
NSW councils empowered to estb. bushfire brigades.

Births & Deaths

Cecil John Seddon Purdy, international chess master, b. (d. 1979)
Archer Kyffin Thomas, newspaper administrator, b. (d. 1978)

Communities

Buladelah, NSW, estb.
Murgon, Qld, estb.
Tully, Qld, estb.

A

History, Politics, Economics, Law

1907

Government

2 Oct. 1907–Oct. 1910, C. G. Wade Liberal Premier NSW.

19 Nov. 1907–Feb. 1908, R. Philp Premier Qld.

15 Feb. Qld Premier allows immigration of Italians into Qld to replace Kanaka labourers on North Qld sugar plantations. Kanakas return to Pacific Is.

20 Feb. Third Federal Parlt opens. (Dissolution 19 Feb 1910.)

25 Apr. Electoral Act comes into force in Tas. introducing Hare-Clark system of proportional representation of single transferable vote.

During Apr. Fifth Colonial Conference held in England. Name changed to Imperial Conference.

26 May. Premiers' Conference held to discuss States' debts.

Aug. Members of Cwlth Parlt vote themselves a 50 per cent pay increase.

Oct. Industrial Workers of the World organization, also known as 'the Wobblies', spreads to Aust. from USA. Supports one single union for all workers.

8 Nov. Justice Henry B. Higgins hands down Harvester Judgment, thus introducing basic or minimum wage concept. Initially 7 shillings per day for a six-day working week.

20 Dec. Federal Parlt passes Bill authorizing transfer of control of NT from SA to the Cwlth. (Not effective until 1911.)

20 Dec. WA Govt introduces manhood suffrage and abolishes plural voting for Legislative Assembly.

During 1907
NZ becomes an independent Dominion.
NSW Govt first to institute invalid pensions.
Second Cwlth tariff increases rates up to 12 per cent.
Carlton and United Breweries Ltd estb. in Melbourne.
The Aust. Sugar Producers' Association estb.
WA Govt imposes income taxes.

Births & Deaths

Helen Elizabeth (Betty) Archdale, educationist, lawyer, b.
Norman Cameron Coles, company director, b.
Stanley Darling, naval commander, b. (d. 1961)
Sir Ivan Noel Dougherty, military commander, b.
George Brereton Sadleir Falkiner, pastoralist, b. (d. 1961)
Galfry George Ormond, naval commander, b.
Robert William Rankin, naval commander, b. (d. 1942)
Julius Stone, jurist, b. (d. 1985)
Sir Edward Ronald Walker, economist, diplomat, b.
William Charles Wentworth, Federal politician, b.
Sir Kenneth Clinton Wheare, political scientist, university administrator, b. (d. 1979)

B

Science, Technology, Transport, Discovery

1 Jan. Cwlth Bureau of Meteorology estb. with Henry Ambrose Hunt first director.

10 Jul. Telephone trunk line between Sydney and Melbourne opens.

During 1907
Cwlth Parlt allocates funds for survey of trans-Aust. railway.
O. U. von Miller, scientist, publishes work on photoconductivity of amorphous selenium used in xerox copying machines.
Octavius C. Beale publishes critical report on patent medicines in Aust.
First electric stoves imported from USA.
Murrumbidgee Irrigation Scheme, NSW, begins.
Harley Tarrant imports first Ford motor cars.
Felix Caldwell builds first four-wheel drive truck in Aust.
George Julius develops automatic totalizator invention in Sydney.
L. J. R. Jones conducts aeronautical research using steam turbine engines.
Rabbit-proof fence 1,138 miles long constructed in WA.
Coal discovered at Leigh Creek, SA.
The Lumiere autochrome process brings first commercially successful colour photographs to Aust.

Births & Deaths

David Howells Fleay, zoologist, world authority on platypus and marsupials, b.

431

1907

C
Arts

Literature

Births & Deaths

Gavin Stodart Casey, novelist, short story writer, b. (d. 1964)
John Aikman Hetherington, novelist, journalist, b. (d. 1974)
Alec Derwent Hope, poet and critic, b.
John O'Grady, author who wrote as Nino Culotta, b.
Thomas Matthew Ronan, author, b. (d. 1976)
John Joseph Meagher Thompson, author, b. (d. 1968)

Music, Dance

During 1907
Nellie Melba begins second Aust. concert tour.

Drama, Theatre, Film

During 1907
Adelaide Amateur Repertory Co. founded.
James C. Williamson's Proprietary Co. dominates Aust. theatrical life.

Births & Deaths

John Gordon Buchanan Alden, Shakespearian actor, b. (d. 1962)
Charles Walter 'Dick' Bentley, actor noted for musical comedy, b.
Gwenyth Valmai Meredith, radio playwright, b.

Fine Arts

During 1907
Academy Julian becomes Sydney Art School.
Aust. Exhibition of Women's Art held in Melbourne.

Births & Deaths

Alfred Herbert Cook, watercolourist, etcher, b. (d. 1970)
Edmund Arthur Harvey, painter, b.
Allan Lowe, ceramic artist, b.
Alan McLeod McCulloch, painter, critic, b.
Eileen McGrath, sculptor, b.

Architecture

Births & Deaths

Henry Ingham Ashworth, architect noted for contribution to Sydney Opera House, b.

D
Religion, Learning

During 1907
Mitchell Library founded in Sydney. (Opens 1910.)
First SA State High School opens.
First Vic. State Kindergarten opens.
Adelaide Kindergarten Teachers' Training College estb. as the Kindergarten College. (Brisbane 1911, Perth 1912, Melbourne 1916.)

Births & Deaths

Sir James Darcy Freeman, Catholic Cardinal, b.
Israel Porush, Rabbi, scholar, b.
Sir Frank Woods, Anglican Archbishop of Melbourne 1957–77, b.

E
Sport

May. Melbourne Trotting Club holds first meeting.
Sep. Vic. Ladies' Bowling Association estb. First in world.
Oct. Surf-Bathing Association of NSW founded. Lifesaving reel first used.

During 1907
Apologue, ridden by W. Evans, wins Melbourne Cup in 3 minutes $27\frac{1}{2}$ seconds.
Carlton football team wins VFL Premiership in Melbourne.
Rugby League professional football begins in Sydney when players break away from Rugby Union football after dispute over expenses. First interstate matches played between NSW and Qld. First match against NZ played in Sydney.
Record crowd of 52,000 attends Rugby Union match in Sydney.
Norman Brookes known as 'The Fox', first Aust. and first non-British player to win Wimbledon tennis championship.
Byron Bay Surf Club estb., NSW.
First Women's Rowing Clubs estb. in Sydney and Melbourne.
First Women's State Hockey Association estb. in NSW.
Chris Webb becomes noted Aust. sailing champion.
NSW bans bookmaking outside athletic race tracks.

Births & Deaths

Frank Arthur, speedway cyclist, b. (d. 1973)
Bill Buckley, Rugby League player, b. (d. 1973)
Andrew Murray 'Boy' Charlton, swimmer, b. (d. 1975)
Harry Collier, VFL footballer, b.
Edgar (Dunc) Gray, cyclist, b.
Jack Haines, middleweight boxer, b.
Reg Hickey, VFL footballer, b. (d. 1973)
Victor Huxley, speedway sportsman, b.
Ron Johnson, pioneer speedway rider, b.
Bill Mohr, VFL footballer, b.
Keith Oliver, cyclist, b. (d. 1978)
John O'Sherwood, motor sportsman, b.
Alf Quill, soccer player, b.

F
Historia Dignum

Population
Estimated total white, 4,161,722.

16 Jan. Exhibition of Aust. products opens in Melbourne.
19 Jan. Cyclone damages Cooktown, Qld.
22 Apr. Barque *Ardencraig* runs down and sinks barque *Norma* in Port Adelaide.
May. John Archibald publishes *The Lone Hand*, general and cultural magazine. (Lasts until 1931.)
15 Sep. Fire destroys many buildings in Murwillumbah, NSW.

During 1907
Annette Kellermann arrested for swimming in a revealing one-piece bathing costume.
The Aquarium Society of NSW estb.

Births & Deaths
Gregory Koshnitsky, chess master, b.

Communities
Loxton, SA, estb.

1908

A
History, Politics, Economics, Law

Government

18 Feb. 1908–Feb. 1911, W. Kidston Premier Qld.
6 Jul. 1908–26 Jul. 1908, Sir John Madden administered Vic.
27 Jul. 1908–19 May 1911, Sir Thomas David Gibson Carmichael Governor Vic.
9 Sep. 1908–31 Jul. 1911, William Humble Ward, Earl of Dudley, Governor-General Aust.
13 Nov. 1908–2 Jun. 1909, Sixth Cwlth Ministry, Andrew Fisher Labor Prime Minister Aust.

31 Mar. Vic. Govt introduced female suffrage. (Women permitted to sit in Parlt in 1923.)
28 Apr. Premiers' Conference in Melbourne.
7 May. King Edward VII grants Aust. Cwlth Coat of Arms featuring kangaroo and emu.
10 Jun. Cwlth Govt passes old age pension Bill, paying £26 per year. (Effective from 1 Jul. 1909.)
25–30 Jul. Sydney tramway strike over dismissal of an employee.
8 Aug. Govt inaugurates national policy of Tariff Protection; provides for five per cent margin of preference to British made goods.
20 Aug.–Sep. 'The Great White Fleet', US Pacific Fleet, visits Aust. Alfred Deakin arranges visit without approval of Colonial Office in London.
14 Nov. Cwlth rejects Dalgety, NSW, as site for Federal capital. Canberra district accepted.
Nov. Joseph Cook Free Trade leader of Federal Opposition. (Until 1909.)
31 Dec. Broken Hill, NSW, miners begin six-months strike over wage reductions. (Strike collapses on 23 May 1909.)

During 1908
John Murray appointed Lieut-Governor of Papua. (Holds position for 32 years.)
Cwlth Conference declares 'Labor' as official spelling of the political party.
Douglas Mawson's British Antarctic Expedition (1907–1908), which includes Sir T. W. Edgeworth David and A. F. Mackay, climbs Mt Erebus, Antarctica.
Aboriginal stockman, Major, with two friends spear two white men in Kimberley district, WA.
Aust. Kodak Co. Ltd estb.
A Federal Quarantine Act replaces State Acts.
Harold Dannevig appointed first Cwlth Director of Fisheries.
Qld Govt estb. Wages Boards.
Federated Clerks' Union estb. in Vic.

Births & Deaths

John Ignatius Armstrong, politician, b. (d. 1977)
Otto Humphrey Becher, naval commander, b. (d. 1977)
Sir Henry Edward Bolte, Vic. Premier, b.
Alan Watson West Cilento, banker, b.
Harold Edward Holt, Liberal-Country Coalition Prime Minister, b. (d. 1967)
Sir William McMahon, Liberal-Country Coalition Prime Minister, b.
Sir Alan Wedel Ramsay McNicoll, naval commander, b.
Dame Annabelle Jane Mary Rankin, politician, first woman to enter Federal Parlt, b.
Reginald John David Turnbull, Tas. and Federal politician, b.
Sir Henry Arthur Winneke, jurist, Vic. Governor, b.

B

Science, Technology, Transport, Discovery

During 1908
Electrolytic refining and smelting works estb. at Port Kembla, NSW.
NSW Govt estb. Bureau of Microbiology to study dengue fever. First medical research organization in Aust.
Electric trams and motor buses begin running in Adelaide.
G. and C. Hoskins Ltd estb. steel works at Lithgow, NSW. (Becomes Aust. Iron and Steel Co.)
Townsville–Cloncurry, Qld, railway line opens.

Births & Deaths
Sir Harrie Stewart Wilson Massey, physicist, b.
William Saville-Kent, naturalist, Great Barrier Reef expert, b.
Alexander John Maum Sinclair, psychologist, b.
Sir Kenneth William Starr, surgeon, b. (d. 1976)

C

Arts

Literature

31 Mar. First Cwlth Year Book published.
During 1908
Henry Handel Richardson publishes her first novel, *Maurice Guest*.
Mrs Aeneas Gunn publishes *We of the Never Never*.
Cwlth Literary Fund estb. to assist poor authors.
Arthur Hoey Davis, using pseudonym Steele Rudd, publishes *Dad in Politics*.
James Banfield publishes *Confessions of a Beachcomber*, which draws worldwide attention to the Great Barrier Reef.
Dorothea Mackellar publishes poem 'My Country' in England. Poem later becomes one of Australia's best-known.

Births & Deaths
Eve Langley, novelist, b. (d. 1974)
Douglas Henry Pike, general editor of first five volumes of *Australian Dictionary of Biography*, b. (d. 1974)
Colin Simpson, author, journalist, b.

Music, Dance

During 1908
Sydney Symphony Orchestra inaugurated.

Births & Deaths
Marjorie Florence Lawrence, dramatic soprano, probably b. (d. 1979)

Drama, Theatre, Film

During 1908
Adelaide Repertory Theatre Society estb. as Adelaide Literary Theatre. (Repertory Theatre begins in Melbourne 1911, Sydney 1918, Perth 1919, Brisbane 1925.)
King's Theatre in Melbourne opens.

Births & Deaths
Colin Sandergrove Ballantyne, theatre producer, b.
John F. Sheridan, actor, d.

Fine Arts

25 Jun. Perth Art Gallery opens.
During 1908
Arts and Crafts Society of Vic. founded.
Vic. Arts Society Journal published. (Until 1918.)

W. Lister Lister and Penleigh Boyd win Canberra Art competition estb. to commemorate founding of Federal Capital.
Modern Society of Portrait Painters estb.

Births & Deaths
Normand H. Baker, portrait painter, b. (d. 1955)
Lyndon Dadswell, modern sculptor, b.
Charles Doutney, romantic realist painter, b. (d. 1957)
Moya Dyring, among first women cubist painters, b. (d. 1967)
Harley Cameron Griffiths, painter, b. (d. 1981)
Geoffrey Jones, painter, b.
Vernon Samuel Charles Jones, painter, sculptor, b.
Roger Kemp, symbolic expressionist, b.
Rudy Komon, among first to promote contemporary Aust. painters and sculptors, b. (d. 1982)
Margo Lewers, painter, fabric designer, potter, b. (d. 1978)
Ludmilla Meilerts, impressionist painter, b.
Edgar Ritchard, watercolourist, graphic artist, b.
Jack Carrington Smith, painter, b. (d. 1972)

Architecture

During 1908
R. J. Haddon publishes *Australian Architecture*.
First cantilevered awnings appear.

Births & Deaths
Arthur Denis Winston, town planner, b. (d. 1980)

D

Religion, Learning

During 1908
Tas. secular and compulsory primary education system becomes free.
Brisbane Technical College estb.
The Free Kindergarten Union of Vic. estb.
Swinburne Technical College estb. in Melbourne as the Eastern Suburbs Technical College.
Tas. infant schools begin.
Adelaide High School estb. from amalgamation of Continuation School for Boys and Advanced School for Girls. (High School is first free State high school in Aust.)
The Christian Brothers estb. Mount St Mary College of Education at Strathfield, Sydney.

Births & Deaths
Peter Anthony Vasquez Russo, scholar, writer, b.

E
Sport

During 1908
Lord Nolan, ridden by J. R. Flynn, wins Melbourne Cup in 3 minutes 28¼ seconds.
Carlton football team wins VFL Premiership in Melbourne.
South Sydney Rugby League football team wins first Premiership in Sydney.
First Rugby League football clubs form in Sydney, Newtown, South Sydney, Balmain, Eastern Suburbs, Western Suburbs and North Sydney.
First Australian Rugby League Team, the Kangaroos, and Rugby Union Team, the Wallabies, estb. Tour England and win gold medal at London Olympics.
Vic. wins first interstate Aust. Rules Football competition.
Aust. wins one gold, two silver and three bronze medals at London Olympics.
Ice hockey first played in Aust., in Sydney.
First interstate men's hockey matches played, in Sydney.
Mrs Jack London first woman admitted to a boxing fight in Aust.
Jack Johnson defeats Tommy Burns for world heavyweight boxing championship in Sydney.
First Aust. Surf Carnival held, at Manly, NSW. Bondi Surf Lifesaving Association stages march past demonstrating drill which leads to lifesaving and efficiency competitions.
Organized car and motorcycle meetings held in Sydney.
Tas. Croquet Association estb. (Vic. 1914, SA 1916, NSW 1918, WA 1928.)
Women's singles tennis championships begin.
Diabolo becomes a fashionable game.

Births & Deaths
Harold Badger, jockey, b.
Sir Donald Bradman, cricketer, noted batsman who holds record batting averages for Shield, Test and First Class cricket, b.
Joe 'Chimpy' Busch, Rugby League player, b.
Jimmy Charlton, athlete, b.
John Herbert (Jack) Crawford, tennis player, b.
John Henry Webb (Jack) Fingleton, cricketer, noted opening batsman, b.
Peter Heard, golfer, b.
Frank Kleinig, racing car driver b. (d. 1976)
Leslie Walter Lock, rifle shooter, b.
Bill McConnel, boxing trainer, b. (d. 1970)
Lionel van Praag, speedway rider, b.
Jack Titus, VFL footballer, b. (d. 1978)

F
Historia Dignum

Population
Estimated total white, 4,232,278.

20 Apr. Train collision at Sunshine, near Melbourne, claims 44 lives.
27 Apr. Storm destroys pearling fleet at Eighty Mile Beach, WA, claiming 50 lives.

During 1908
The Reason Why published as first Aust. advertising magazine.
Scouting movement estb. in Aust. 1st Mosman Kangaroos in Sydney is first registered patrol.
Soft-fronted shirts begin to replace stiff starched-front shirts.
South African Soldiers' Association estb.
Witches Fall on Tamborine Mt, Qld, declared first National Park in first legislation in Aust. to provide specifically for setting aside of National Parks State wide. (First State legislation Tas. 1916; Vic. 1956, SA 1966, NSW 1967, WA 1976, NT 1977.)
Claude Marquet's *Vumps*, comic paper, published.
Mary Gilmore begins writing and editing women's page of the *Australian Worker*. (Continues until 1931.)
Fraser I., Qld declared a forestry reserve.

Communities
Gnowangerup, WA, estb.
Roper River mission and village, NT, estb.
Sheffield, Tas., estb.

437

1909

A
History, Politics, Economics, Law

Government

2 Jan. 1909–29 Mar. 1909, Sir Samuel Way administered SA.
8 Jan. 1909–May 1912, J. Murray Liberal Premier Vic.
24 Mar. 1909–27 May 1909, Sir George Bowen Simpson administered NSW.
29 Mar. 1909–22 Mar. 1914, Sir Day Hort Bosanquet Governor SA.
23 Apr. 1909–30 May 1909, Sir Edward Stone administered WA.
21 May 1909–29 Sep. 1909, Sir John Dodds administered Tas.
27 May 1909–2 Dec. 1909, Sir Arthur Morgan administered Qld.
28 May 1909–11 Mar. 1909, 1913. Frederic John Napier Thesiger, Lord Chelmsford, Governor NSW.
31 May 1909–3 Mar. 1913, Sir Gerald Strickland Governor WA.
2 Jun. 1909–28 Apr. 1910, Seventh Cwlth Ministry, Alfred Deakin, Fusion Liberal (Free Traders and ex-Protectionists) Prime Minister Aust.
5 Jun. 1909–Jun. 1910, A. H. Peake Liberal Premier SA.
19 Jun. 1909–Oct. 1909, Sir N. E. Lewis Liberal Fusion Premier Tas.
29 Sep. 1909–10 Mar. 1913, Sir Harry Barron Governor Tas.
20 Oct. 1909–Oct. 1909, J. Earle Labor Premier Tas.
27 Oct. 1909–Jun. 1912, Sir N. E. Lewis Liberal Premier Tas.

16 Jan. Sir Tannatt William Edgeworth David, Douglas Mawson and A. F. Mackay reach and fix exact site of South Magnetic Pole, Antarctica. (British Antarctic Expedition 1907–1909.)
5 Feb. Cwlth Govt orders three new torpedo boat destroyers from England.
5–12 Mar. Premiers' Conference in Hobart discusses Cwlth and State finances.
Jun. Andrew Fisher Labor Leader of Federal Opposition. (Until 1910.)
Alfred Deakin estb. first Federal Liberal Party from union of Free Traders and Protectionists, beginning bi-party political system in Aust. politics. Party at first known as Fusion Liberals.
Imperial Defence Conference in London. In Nov. Cwlth Govt approves scheme of defence adopted at Conference. Australian Defence Act provides for compulsory military training for those of ages 12–26.
12 Aug. Community land at the colony of Cosmé in Paraguay (estb. by William Lane in 1894) sold to private owners, thus ending Lane's Utopian experiment.
18 Oct. NSW Govt passes the Seat of Government Surrender Act, transferring territory to Cwlth for Aust. Capital Territory.
6 Nov. NSW coalminers begin five-months strike over wide range of grievances. Peter Bowling jailed for inciting strike.
Dec. Sir George Reid appointed to London as first Aust. High Commissioner. First Aust. diplomatic appointment abroad. (Effective from 26 Feb. 1910.)

During 1909
Lord Herbert Horatio Kitchener arrives in Aust. to advise on defence requirements.
NSW formally adopts Aboriginal Protection policy.
Federal quarantine system introduced. All ships medically inspected and special protection against plague introduced.

Births & Deaths
Sir Reginald Myles Ansett, aviator, company director, b. (d. 1981)
Sir Robert, Robin William Askin, NSW Premier, b. (d. 1981)
Sir Stanley Charles Burbury, Tas. Governor, b.
William Philip Sidney, Viscount De L'Isle, Governor General, b.
Sir Vincent Charles Fairfax, company director, b.
Otway McLaurin Falkiner, NSW pastoralist, politician, b.
William Douglas Forsyth, diplomat, author, b.
Leon Verdi Goldsworthy, naval officer noted for disarming German mines, b.
Sir Ian Munro McLennan, company director, b.
Dame Elizabeth Joy Murdoch, Life Governor of Royal Women's Hospital, b.
Eric Elliott Reece, Tas. Premier, b.
Mrs Seymour, one of last surviving Tas. Aborigines, d.

B

Science, Technology, Transport, Discovery

Jul. First large-scale mining of coal begins at Wonthaggi, Vic.

5 Dec. George Augustine Taylor and Florence Taylor make first free-flight in Aust., in a Voisin-type glider heavier-than-air machine, an engineless bi-plane steered by body balance, at Narrabeen, NSW. Taylor estb. first aircraft factory in Southern Hemisphere and founds Aerial League of Aust. on 28 Apr.

9 Dec. Colin Defries attempts first powered flight in Aust. at Victoria Park racecourse, Sydney, in a Wilbur Wright bi-plane.

During 1909

Aust. Institute of Tropical Medicine estb., in Townsville, Qld.

A. J. Smith estb. first radium mine in Aust., at Radium Hill, SA.

NSW Govt enforces first Motor Traffic Act.

Motorized taxis first appear in Sydney, Melbourne and Adelaide.

First veterinary school in Aust. estb., in Vic.

H. V. McKay builds disc-cultivator; among first.

Births & Deaths

Langley George Hancock, mining industrialist, b.
Sir Leslie Charles Thiess, industrialist, b.
Keith Allison Virtue, aviation pioneer, b.

C

Arts

Literature

During 1909

Hugh McCrae publishes *Satyrs and Sunlight: Silvarum Libri*.

Arthur Hoey Davis, using pseudonym Steele Rudd, publishes *From Selection to City*.

Births & Deaths

Ronald Cecil Hamlyn McKie, author, journalist, b.

Music, Dance

During 1909

Sydney Philharmonic Society becomes Royal Philharmonic Society of Sydney.

Nellie Melba makes third concert tour of Aust.

Births & Deaths

Sir Robert Murray Helpmann, dancer, choreographer, actor, b.
Donald Richard Peart, musicologist and composer, b.

Drama, Theatre, Film

During 1909

Franklyn Barrett produces *A Message From Mars*, first science fiction film.

William Moore organizes first playwrights' theatre, with Aust. Drama Nights in Melbourne. Increases interest in Aust. theatre.

Katherine Susannah Prichard's play *The Burglar* produced in Melbourne.

J. D. Williams opens first continuously running cinema in Aust.

Births & Deaths

John Coffage, better known as Chips Rafferty, actor, film producer, b. (d. 1971)
Errol Leslie Flynn, actor, b. (d. 1959)

Fine Arts

During 1909

Sir E. Bertram Mackennal first Australian elected member of the Royal Academy.

Melbourne Society of Women Painters and Sculptors estb. (Revitalized in 1975 as Women's Exposé.)

Births & Deaths

Lina Bryans, portrait and landscape painter, b.
Elaine Alys Haxton, painter, decor designer, b.
Bim Vernon Arthur Hilder, sculptor, painter, b.

1909

Vernon Hodgman, painter, b.
Ursula Hoff, art historian, b.
Bernard John Lawson, painter, b.
William Edwin Pidgeon (WEP), portrait artist, cartoonist, b. (d. 1981)
Carl Olaf Plate, artist, b. (d. 1977)
James Newton Russell, cartoonist, b.

Architecture

During 1909
Architects influenced by a Japanese-designed pre-fabricated house displayed in Brisbane.
Donald Esplin builds one of first flat-roofed houses in Sydney.

Births & Deaths
Edward Herbert Farmer, architect specializing in hospital and school designs, b.

D

Religion, Learning

During 1909
Charles Bertie appointed first Sydney Municipal City Librarian. (Holds position for 21 years.)
Yanco Agriculture College estb. to advise on Murrumbidgee Irrigation project.

Births & Deaths
David Arthur Garnsey, Church of England minister b.
Sir Arthur Dale Trendall, university administrator, classicist, b.

E
Sport

Apr. First power boat reliability trials held, between Sydney and Newcastle, NSW.
During 1909
Prince Foote, ridden by W. H. McLachlan, wins Melbourne Cup in 3 minutes 27½ seconds.
South Melbourne football team wins VFL Premiership in Melbourne.
South Sydney football team wins Rugby League Premiership in Sydney.
First Anglo-Aust. Rugby League football test played in England.
Amateur Swimming Union of Aust. estb.
Mt Kosciusko Ski Club estb.

Births & Deaths
Jean Gardner Batten, aviator, b.
James Carlton, athlete and runner, b. (d. 1951)
Albert Collier, VFL footballer, b.
Archie A. Jackson, cricketer, noted batsman, b. (d. 1973)
Billy Lamont, motorcyclist, b.
Bob Pratt, VFL footballer, b.
Norman Smith, VFL football coach, b.

F
Historia Dignum

Population
Estimated total white, 4,323,960.

5 Jun. First Imperial Press Conference held in London.
18 Jun. Barque *Errol* wrecked on Middleton Reef, claiming 17 lives.
Jul. Steamship *Waratah* disappears *en route* to South Africa, with 211 on board.
During 1909
Dan Cooper, using shearing machine, shears 316 sheep in one day.
Mt Kosciusko Hotel becomes first ski resort in NSW.
Wildlife Preservation Society of Aust. estb.
Tradition of throwing streamers from departing ship to friends on pier begins in Sydney.
The Gould League of Bird Lovers estb. in Vic.
Trouser cuffs become fashionable.
Vic. Govt grants half-holiday on Saturdays in metropolitan Melbourne. Shopowners compensated with late-night shopping on Fridays.
Widespread flooding in north-western NSW, south-eastern Qld and south-western SA.

Births & Deaths
Robert Neal (Bob) Dyer, radio and television personality, b. (d. 1984)

Communities
Dunedoo, NSW, estb.
Wonthaggi, Vic., estb.

A
History, Politics, Economics, Law

1910

Government

29 Apr. 1910–24 Jun. 1913, Eighth Cwlth Ministry, Andrew Fisher Labor Prime Minister Aust.
3 Jun. 1910–Feb. 1912, J. Verran Labor Premier SA.
16 Sep. 1910–Oct. 1911, F. Wilson Liberal Premier WA.
21 Oct. 1910–Jun. 1913, J. S. T. McGowan Labor Premier NSW.
1910, S. J. Mitchell Govt Resident NT under SA jurisdiction.

9 Feb. Destroyer *Parramatta* launched as first ship of Aust. navy. The *Yarra* launched on 9 Apr. Both reached Aust. Sep.
18 Feb. Herbert Horatio Kitchener issues report to Aust. Govt on defences. Recommends citizen army of 80,000.
11 Mar. Newcastle, NSW, coalminers' strike ends. Peter Bowling, miners' leader, released from jail on 14 Oct.
13 Apr. For first time in Aust. politics, one Party, Labor, wins absolute majority in national elections.
Referendum on Cwlth takeover of State debts carried. Referendum on allocation of customs and excise revenue between Cwlth and States rejected.
Apr. Alfred Deakin Liberal Leader of Federal Opposition. (Until 1913.)
1 Jul. Fourth Federal Parlt opens. (Dissolution 23 Apr. 1913.)
Aug. Cwlth legislation passed for introduction of uniform Aust. currency. First Aust. Cwlth coins and notes issued.
17 Nov. Federal Govt introduces Land Tax Act to break up large property holdings. First Cwlth attempt to introduce a direct tax. (Abandoned in 1952 to States.)
25 Nov. Aust. Navy created. (Becomes Royal Aust. Navy 10 Jul. 1911.)
5 Dec. Proclamation issued vesting the ACT in the Cwlth on and from 1 Jan. 1911.

During 1910
Sir Reginald Anderson visits Aust. to advise on naval defences.
Cwlth Govt buys Duntroon Station from Campbell family in Canberra district to estb. a Military College.
James Scullin enters Federal Parlt.
Cwlth introduces invalid pensions.
NSW Agriculture Bureau estb.
Charles Price Conigrave leads expedition to explore the Kimberleys, WA.
Herbert Schlink leads first ski party across Mt Kosciusko, NSW.
Tas. Govt estb. Wage Boards.
NSW Govt introduces workers' compensation.
c. 1910. State Govts introduce housing loans.

Births & Deaths

Donald Clifford Tyndall Bennett, air force commander, b.
Clive Robertson Caldwell, fighter pilot, b.
Sir John Grenfell Crawford, economist, b.
Sir Alexander Russel Downer, politician, diplomat, (d. 1981)
Sir John Wallace Dunlop, businessman, b. (d. 1983)
John William Galbally, Member of Vic. Legislative Council who introduced more private Members' Bills than any other politician in Aust., b.
Sir Douglas Anthony Kendrew, WA Governor, b.
Sir Wallace Hart Kyle, WA Governor, b.
John Stuart Mould, pioneer of underwater mine clearing in World War II, b. (d. 1957)
Sir Charles Chambers Fowell Spry, Director-General Aust. Security Intelligence Organization 1950–1969 b.
Sir John Gordon Noel Wilton, military commander b. (d. 1981)

B

Science, Technology, Transport, Discovery

17 Mar. F. Custance claims to have made first successful powered flight in Aust. in a Bleriot monoplane at Bolivar, SA. Claim dubious.
18 Mar. Ehrich Weiss, better known as Harry Houdini, makes first proven controlled powered flight above 100 feet, in a Voisin, at Diggers Rest, Vic.
19 May. W. E. Raymond photographs Halley's Comet on its transit of the Sun.
16 Jul. J. R. Duigan flies in first Aust.-made aeroplane, a Farman type monoplane, at Botany, NSW.
19 Nov. P. Woodward makes first sustained flight in Aust. in a home-made Aust.-built aircraft, a Bleriot type, in Perth.
During 1910
G. A. Taylor founds the Wireless Institute of Aust. First organization of radio experimenters in British Empire.
Walter Hume invents centrifugal spun-concrete pipe.
John Dethridge invents direct measuring water meter.
Mt Stromlo Observatory built in ACT.
F. J. Lister develops commercial process of extracting zinc and silver-lead selectively, at Broken Hill, NSW.
c. 1910. Lady Dudley founds Bush Nursing Service.

Births & Deaths

Harry Frank (Jim) Broadbent, aviator, b. (d. 1958)
Sir Sydney Sunderland, anatomist, neurologist, b.
Freda Thompson, aviator, first woman in Aust. to get instructor's rating, b.
Sir James Vernon, industrialist, b.

C

Arts

Literature

During 1910
Mary Gilmore publishes *Marri'd and Other Verses*.
Mary Grant Bruce publishes *A Little Bush Maid*.
Henry Handel Richardson publishes *The Getting of Wisdom*.
Mungo MacCallum publishes *Shakespeare's Roman Plays and their Background*.
C. E. W. Bean publishes *On the Wooltrack*.

Births & Deaths

Brian Robinson Elliott, author, teacher, b.
Alan McCrae Moorehead, author, b.
Paul Hamilton Hume White, author, doctor, b.

Music, Dance

24 Sep. Ivy Schilling begins dancing career in production of *Our Miss Gibbs* in Sydney.
During 1910
Touring American vaudeville artists introduce ragtime jazz in Aust.

Births & Deaths

Dame Margaret (Peggy) van Praagh, ballet dancer, b.

Drama, Theatre, Film

12 Mar. Cozens Spencer's narrative film, *The Life and Adventures of John Vane, the Notorious Australian Bushranger*, premières in Melbourne.
During 1910
J. H. Perry directs film, *Heroes of the Cross*.
William Moore's play, *The Tea Room Girl*, produced in Melbourne.
King's Theatre Sydney built; first theatre designed solely for screening films.

Births & Deaths

John Andrew (Jack) Davey, radio and television entertainer, b. (d. 1959)

Fine Arts

During 1910
Cubism begins to influence Aust. art.
Society of Women Painters of NSW estb.
Patrick Sullivan, black-and-white artist, creator of 'Felix the Cat', active.

1910

443

1910

Births & Deaths
G. F. Bissietta, painter, b.
Arthur Sharland Boothroyd, illustrator, b.
Sue Edna May Buckley, painter, printmaker, b.
Roy Frederick Leslie Dalgarno, painter, graphic artist, b.
Ambrose Dyson, social realist, cartoonist, probably b. (probably d. 1950)
Strom Gould, painter, illustrator, b.
Alan Robert Colquhoun Grieve, painter, b.
James Grove, convict artist, d.
Michael Kmit, oil painter, b. (d. 1981)
John Knight, ceramic artist, b.
Frank Lumb, sculptor, b.
Wilfred Arthur McCulloch, painter, b. (d. 1942)
Karlis Mednis, city-scape painter, b.
Vaclovas Ratas, graphic artist, printmaker, b.
Alan Reeve, caricaturist, b. (d. 1962)
Leo Skivers, painter, b.
Margarita Anna Stipnieks, oil painter, b.
Dorothy Thornhill, painter, b.
Karlis Trumpis, painter, b.

Architecture

During 1910
G. D. Payne, architect, completes St Andrew's Presbyterian church in Brisbane.
First concepts of modern architecture arrive in Aust. from USA.
First successful production of Plaster of Paris made, in SA.
Louis Spear Robertson designs Nelson House in Sydney; first fully steel framed building in Aust.

Births & Deaths
George Molnar, architect, cartoonist, b.

D

Religion, Learning

8 Mar. Mitchell Library, named after David Scott Mitchell, first major collector of Australiana, opens in Sydney.
Dec. NSW reorganizes State secondary education system.
During 1910
Dr Wright, Archbishop of Sydney, appointed Anglican Primate of Aust.
Vic. Education Act authorizes State to provide secondary and technical education. Provides for estb of Technical Preparatory Trade, Higher Elementary and District High Schools.
Kindergarten Union of Tas. estb.
Perth Modern School estb.

E
Sport

Sep. Trotting sire, Globe Derby, foaled in Bathurst, NSW.

During 1910
Comedy King, ridden by W. H. McLachlan, wins Melbourne Cup in 3 minutes $27\frac{3}{4}$ seconds.
Collingwood football team wins VFL Premiership in Melbourne.
Newtown football team wins Rugby League Premiership in Sydney.
First Rugby League football Test in Aust., against England, held in Sydney.
Frank Beaurepaire becomes noted swimmer in Europe.
Jack Donaldson sets 100 yards record in South Africa ($9\frac{3}{8}$ seconds; stands until 1948.)
South African Test cricket team first tours Aust.
All Aust. Women's Hockey Association estb.
First woman lifesaver appears at Manly, Sydney.
Mt Buffalo Ski Resort estb. Vic.
Royal Yacht Club of Tas. estb.

Births & Deaths
Ted Bartle, jockey, b.
Bill Bolger, golfer, b.
Bill Cerutty, Rugby Union player, b. (d. 1965)
Kenneth William George Farmer, Aust. Rules footballer, b.
Leslie O'Brien Fleetwood-Smith, cricketer, noted bowler, b. (d. 1971)
Jack Green, all round sportsman, b. (d. 1972)
Nell Hopman, tennis player, b. (d. 1968)
Ken Howard, horserace commentator, b. (d. 1976)
Lewis Huxton, rower, sportsman, b.
Jimmy Kelso, boxer, b.
Stanley Joseph McCabe, cricketer, b. (d. 1968)
Jack Murray, motor sportsman, b.
Laurie Nash, VFL footballer, cricketer, b.
Ronald Richards, boxer, b. (d. 1967)

F
Historia Dignum

1910

Population
Estimated total white, 4,425,083.

7 Mar. *Daily Herald* newspaper estb. in Adelaide. (Until 1924.)
1 Jul. The *Sun* newspaper in Sydney begins.
18 Jul. Train collision at Richmond, Vic., claims nine lives.
23 Jul. Aust.-wide penny postage estb. Postage on letters to any destination costs 1 penny. (Adopted by all States on 1 May 1911.)
Nov. Cyclone at Broome, WA, claims 90 lives.

During 1910
Aust. Journalists Association estb.
NSW first State to introduce motor driving test.
Australasian Pioneers Club estb. to foster friendship among descendants of pioneers.
Girl Guiding movement begins in Aust. (Estb. in all States by 1921.)
First electric washing machines appear on the market.
Women begin to wear Canadian costume, woollen knickerbockers and tunic.
Toppers and plumes headwear popular among upper classes.
Possibly largest blue whale in world (97 feet long) killed at Twofold Bay, NSW.

Communities
Berri, SA, estb.
Brandon, Qld, estb.
Craboon, NSW, estb.
Manjimup, WA, estb.
Mundubbera, Qld, estb.

A
1911
History, Politics, Economics, Law

Government

7 Feb. 1911–Jun. 1915, D. F. Denham Liberal Premier Qld.

19 May 1911–24 May 1914, Sir John Madden administered Vic.

24 May 1911–31 Jan. 1914, Sir John Michael Fleetwood Fuller Governor Vic.

31 Jul. 1911–18 May 1914, Thomas Denman, Lord Denman, Governor-General Aust.

7 Oct. 1911–Jul. 1916, J. Scaddan Labor Premier WA.

1911–1912, S. J. Mitchell Acting Administrator NT under Cwlth jurisdiction.

1 Jan. Cwlth creates and controls Australian Capital Territory (ACT).

1–2 Jan. Cwlth takes over from SA the administration of NT in accordance with Agreement of 7 Dec. 1907. Name Palmerston changed to Darwin.

4 Apr. *Warrego*, first warship (destroyer) built in Aust., launched in Sydney.

26 Apr. Referendum to extend powers of the Cwlth defeated in rejections of amendments to Constitution in respect of trade and commerce, control of corporations, labor and employment, control of monopolies.

27 Jun. Sir William Throsby Bridges opens Royal Military College, Duntroon, in ACT; 41 cadets enrol.

1 Jul. Compulsory naval and military training inaugurated.

6 Oct. Enrolment on national electoral rolls made compulsory.

11 Oct. Royal Aust Navy officially estb. Named on 10 Jul.

2 Dec. Douglas Mawson begins Australasian Antarctic Expedition. (Lasts three years.)

22 Dec. Federal Govt estb. Cwlth Bank. (Opens 1912.)

During 1911

NT formally adopts Aboriginal Protection Policy.

Vic. Govt adopts preferential voting system.

Cwlth Parliamentary Association estb. as Empire Parliamentary Association.

Sixth Imperial Conference held in London.

First air base estb. at Pt Cook, Vic. (Air Force created 1921.)

Federated Ironworkers' Association of Aust. estb.

Sidney Myer buys Melbourne drapery business.

Births & Deaths

Sir Johannes Bjelke-Peterson, Qld Premier, b.

Sir Charles Walker Michael Court, WA Premier, b.

Sir John Grey Gorton, Liberal-Country coalition Prime Minister, b.

Sir Robert Gillman Allen Jackson, United Nations administrator, b.

Dudley McCarthy, diplomat, b.

Roderick William Miller, shipping trader, b. (d. 197

Jack Charles Allan Pizzey, Qld Premier, b. (d. 1968)

Dame Dorothy Margaret Tangney, Federal politicia b.

B

Science, Technology, Transport, Discovery

1 Jan. Cwlth Govt takes over the Northern and Central Aust. Railways from SA.
9 Jan. J. J. Hammond makes first significant powered aircraft flight in Aust. Flies 45 minutes in Bristol Boxkite aircraft at Perth. Makes first passenger-carrying flight on 23 Feb.
25 Apr. A. M. Longmore becomes first Aust. awarded an internationally recognized aviation certificate.
5 Dec. William E. Hart takes out first Aust. air pilot's licence and makes first cross-country flight, from Penrith to Parramatta, NSW.

During 1911
Observation from Mt Stromlo Observatory in ACT begins.
First Aust. airport opens, at Penrith, near Sydney.
Radio station in the Domain, Sydney, estb. for transmission of commercial messages.
Construction of first Cwlth Wireless Station begins.
Opals discovered and mined at Coober Pedy, SA.
Silk Culture Society of NSW estb. in Sydney.
Vic. Bush Nursing Association estb.

Births & Deaths

John Allan Dulhunty, geologist, b.
Alan John (Jock) Marshall, naturalist, biologist, writer, b. (d. 1967)

C

Arts

Literature

During 1911
Louis Stone publishes *Jonah*.
Henry Lawson publishes *Mateship*.
Edward Dyson publishes *Benno and Some of the Push*.
Arthur Hoey Davis, using pseudonym Steele Rudd, publishes *The Book of Dan*.

Births & Deaths

George Michell Farwell, author, b. (d. 1976)
Ian Mayelston Mudie, poet, author, b. (d. 1976)
Peter 'Hal' Porter, short story writer, b. (d. 1984)
Colin Roderick, author, b.
Olaf Ruhen, author, journalist, b.
Dallas George 'Dal' Stivens, author, b.
Judah Waten, novelist short story writer, b. (d. 1985)
Reginald William Winchester Wilmot, World War II author, broadcaster, b. (d. 1954)

Drama, Theatre, Film

4 Mar. Amalgamated Pictures Ltd Film Co. estb.
24 Apr. Raymond Longford produces his first feature film, *A Fatal Wedding*. First of 30 films.
6 Dec. James Pinkerton Campbell appointed first Cwlth cinematographer.

During 1911
Louis Esson's drama *Dead Timber* produced in Melbourne.
Adelphi Theatre opens in Sydney.
James Williamson registers J. C. Williamson Ltd.
Gregan McMahon estb. Melbourne Repertory Theatre for production of Aust. plays. (Ceases 1918, revived 1929.)

Births & Deaths

Neva Carr Glyn, actress, b. (d. 1975)
Merle Oberon, film actress, probably b.

Fine Arts

Dec. Aust. national art collection begins in ACT.
During 1911
William Merric Boyd estb. Art Pottery Studios at Murrumbeena, Vic. Among first.
Julian Rossi Ashton estb. Fine Arts Gallery in Sydney.
Cwlth Art Advisory Board estb. to advise on suitable artists to paint portraits.

1911

1911

Births & Deaths

Valerie Albiston, painter, b.
Francis Charles Andrew, painter advertising artist, b.
Jean Appleton, still life and seascape painter, b.
Sam Atyeo, abstract painter, b.
James Cant, surrealist painter, noted for reproductions of Aboriginal cave paintings, b. (d. 1983)
Frank Charvat, abstract expressionist painter, b.
Neil Douglas, potter painter, b.
John Flexmore, painter, b.
Hector Beaumont Gilliland, watercolourist, b.
Allen Adolph Peter Hansen, painter, b.
Nora Heysen, still life painter, portrait painter, b.
Brett Hilder, painter, sea captain, b.
Roy Cecil Hodgkinson, illustrator and cartoonist, b.
Jean de Courtenay Isherwood, portrait painter, graphic artist, watercolourist, b.
Leonard H. Long, painter, b.
Alastair Ardoch Morrison, painter, industrial designer, b.
Robert Pulleine, painter, b.
Arthur Evan Read, painter noted for canefield landscapes, b. (d. 1978)
Alan Robert Melbourne Sumner, painter, silk screen printer and glass stainer, b.
Gordon Andrew Thompson, gallery administrator, b.
Geoffrey Tyson, watercolourist, commercial artist, b.
Eric Wilson, painter, b. (d. 1947)

Architecture

During 1911
First Pasadena-type American bungalows built in Melbourne. Bungalow houses popular.

D

Religion, Learning

14 Mar. Qld University opens.

During Mar. University of WA estb. First free university in British Empire. (Opens 1913.)

During 1911
Sydney, Melbourne and Adelaide universities become affiliated with English Workers' Educational Association.
Branch of the Order of the Star in the East founded in Sydney.
Compulsory cadet drill estb. in some schools.
Vic. introduces Qualifying Certificate exam as a requirement for post-primary study.
Perth Modern Teacher Training School opens.
Sydney Teachers' College introduces education diploma.
F. X. Gsell estb. Aboriginal mission on Bathurst I.
Brisbane Kindergarten Teachers' College estb.
Nicholas Shehadie estb. first Lebanese Orthodox parish in Sydney.

Births & Deaths

Sir Marcus Lawrence Loane, Anglican prelate, author, b.
Alexander George Mitchell, linguist, b.
Gordon George Powell, Presbyterian minister, b.
Alan Walker, Uniting Methodist minister, b.

E
Sport

During 1911
The Parisian, ridden by R. Cameron, wins Melbourne Cup in 3 minutes 27¾ seconds.
Essendon football team wins VFL Premiership in Melbourne.
Eastern Suburbs football team wins Rugby League Premiership in Sydney.
VFL players permitted to receive payment.
Sydney Cricket Ground first used for Rugby League football.
Second Kangaroo Rugby League team tours England. Wins Ashes.
All States adopt uniform registration of horses.
NSW Trotting Club buys Harold Park from Metropolitan Rugby Union. Course known as Epping until 1929.
Aust. Lawn Bowling Council estb.
First official Aust. lawn bowling championship held, in Melbourne.
Canoeing becomes popular.
Australasian Professional Golf Association estb.
Festival of Empire Games held in England.

Births & Deaths
Percy Beames, VFL football player, cricketer, b.
Billy Briscoe, jockey, b.
Cyril (Pluto) Brown, boxer, b. (d. 1979)
Haydn Bunton, Aust. Rules footballer, b. (d. 1956)
Fred Henneberry, milddleweight boxer, b.
Harry Hinton, motorcyclist, b. (d. 1978)
Ambrose Palmer, boxer, b.
Jack Rennie, boxer trainer, b.
Andrew (Bluey) Wilkinson, speedway rider, b. (d. 1940)

F
Historia Dignum

Population
Estimated total white, 3 Apr., 4,573,786.
First Cwlth census estimates white population at 4,455,005.

16 Mar. Storm damages Cairns–Innisfail area, Qld.
23–24 Mar. Ship *Yongala* sinks near Cape Bowling Green, Qld, claiming 120 lives. (Declared historic wreck 1981.)
During 1911
Cwlth estb. Historical Memorials Committee.
Five-year drought begins; affects most of Aust.
Sir James Burns estb. foster care programme for children at Burnside Homes in Sydney.
Hobble skirts in fashion.

Communities
Iron Knob, SA, estb.
Julia Creek, Qld, estb.
Karoonda, SA, estb.
Pemberton, WA, estb.

1911

1912

A
History, Politics, Economics, Law

Government
17 Feb. 1912–Apr. 1915, A. H. Peake Liberal Premier SA.
18 May 1912–Dec. 1913, W. A. Watt Liberal Premier Vic.
14 Jun. 1912–Apr. 1914, A. E. Solomon Liberal Premier Tas.
1912–1919, J. A. Gilruth Administrator NT under Cwlth jurisdiction.

31. Jan.–6 Mar. General strike in Brisbane develops from tramway strike over refusal of tramway authorities to allow union members to wear badges.
13 Jun. WA Farmers and Settlers' Association estb.
3 Jul. Cwlth Govt orders first military aircraft, from England.
15 Jul. Cwlth Bank opens for business as savings bank. (Opens as trading bank on 20 Jan 1913.)
9 Oct. Federal Govt introduces maternity allowance or 'Baby Bonus'; maximum £5 for every child of white parents born in Aust.

During 1912
Federal Water Conservation and Irrigation Commission estb.
Aust. Freedom League estb. to oppose implementation of Defence Act.
Transport Workers Union (TWU) estb.
High Court of Aust. increased to seven Justices, a Chief Justice and six Justices.
Francis Ernest Osborn, vigneron, begins McLaren Vale wineries.
WA State Shipping Service estb.
Retail Price Index, indicating inflation rate, first published.
Federated Storemen and Packers' Union estb.

Births & Deaths
David Brand, WA Premier, b. (d. 1979)
Sir Bede Bertrand Callaghan, banker, b.
Charles Douglas Candy, air force commander, b.
Owen Lennox Davis, diplomat, b.
Allan James Eastman, diplomat, b.
Sir James William Harrison, SA Governor, b. (d. 1971)
Sir Asher Alexander Joel, politician, cultural organizer, b.
Ernest Henry Lee-Steere, WA pastoralist, b.
Lionel Colin Matthews, military commander, b. (d. 1944)
George Radford Warfe, World War II commander, noted for use of jungle warfare tactics, b. (d. 1977)

B
Science, Technology, Transport, Discovery

3 Jan. W. E. Hart officially begins flying training school at Penrith NSW.
May. Federal Committee of the British Medical Association meets.
6 Jul. First automatic telephone exchange opens, at Geelong, Vic.
During Jul. First water from Murrumbidgee Irrigation Scheme, NSW, supplied.
6 Aug. H. A. Petrie appointed first Aust. military aviator.
19 Aug. Radio Station opens near Pennant Hills Sydney; among first.
14 Sep. Construction of East–West Transcontinental railway line begins at Port Augusta, SA. (Completed 1917.)
24 Oct. Harry G. Hawker sets British aeronautical endurance and altitude records.

During 1912
Solar research begins at Mt Stromlo Observatory, ACT.
Richmond, NSW, aerodrome opens.
Thomas H. Johnston begins work on finding way to eradicate prickly pear.
F. J. Lister discovers method of selective zinc concentration by flotation.
Lance de Mole, engineer, submits tank invention to War Office in London. (Originally rejected, later used in field 1916.)
Hedlie Taylor invents header (harvester).
John Job Crew Bradfield designs bridge to cross Sydney Harbour. Proposals accepted in 1913. Work not commenced until after World War I.
Electric street lights installed in Perth.
Francis E. Birtles and S. R. Ferguson drive Brush car from Fremantle, WA, to Sydney, pioneering overland driving and becoming first to cross west to east by car.
Construction of Taronga Park Zoo begins in Sydney.
Qld Govt estb. first nurse registration system in Aust.
George Hubert Wilkins suggests use of polar observation posts to predict world weather patterns.
Gypsum first mined in SA.

Births & Deaths
Phillip Garth Law, scientist, Antarctic explorer, b.
Susan Watkins, WA photographer, b.

C Arts

1912

Literature

During 1912
Walter Baldwin Spencer and Francis Gillen publish *Across Australia*.
Cwlth Copyright Act begins operating.

Births & Deaths
John Sidney Baker, author, linguist, b. (d. 1976)
George Henry Johnston, novelist, b. (d. 1970)
Joan Margaret Philipson, author of children's books, b.
Roland Edward Robinson, poet, author, b.
Katherine (Kylie) Tennant, author, b.
Patrick White, novelist, short story writer, playwright, b.

Music, Dance

During 1912
Quinlan Opera Co. introduces many first performances.

Births & Deaths
Sylvia Gwendoline Victoria Fisher, operatic soprano, b.
Peggy Glanville-Hicks, composer, critic, b.
Dame Joan Hammond, dramatic soprano, golfer, b.
Robert Hughes, classical music composer, b.
Eileen Joyce, concert pianist, b.
Henry Joseph Krips, conductor, composer, probably b.

Drama, Theatre, Film

11 Jan. Newly renovated Theatre Royal in Hobart opens.
During 1912
Albert Edward (Bert) Bailey and Arthur Hoey Davis (Steele Rudd) write play version of *On Our Selection*. Adaptation popular, first performance on 4 May.
Govt film-making begins.
Raymond Longford makes film *The Midnight Wedding*.
Bert Bailey and Julius Grant form Bert Bailey Dramatic Society.
Amalgamated Pictures opens the Majestic Theatre in Melbourne; first luxury cinema in Aust.
NSW Govt bans bushranger films.
Cozens Spencer builds Australasian Film Studio, in Sydney.

Births & Deaths
Damien Parer, film-maker, photographer, b. (d. 1944)

Fine Arts

During 1912
Australian Art Association founded in Melbourne.
The *Salon*, monthly journal of art and architecture, published.

Births & Deaths
Peter Richard Bellew, art critic, b.
Bernard Boles, painter, b.
George Wilson Cooper, watercolourist, cartoonist, b.
Sir William Alexander Dargie, portrait painter, winner of eight Archibald Prizes, b.
Sir Russell George Drysdale, painter of Aust. outback, noted for elongated figures whose style breaks with local impressionistic tradition, b. (d. 1981)
Tasman Julius August Fehlberg, landscape painter, b.
Ambrose Sylvester Griffin, painter, b.
Edward Heffernan, painter, b.
Ivor Henry Thomas Hele, oil painter who wins five Archibald Prizes, b.
Adam Kriegel, painter, musician, b.
John Lunghi, painter, b.
Mary McCartney MacQueen, painter and graphic artist, b.
Geoffry Richard Mainwaring, painter, b.
Ralph T. Walker, sculptor, b.
Noel Wood, painter, b.

Architecture

During 1912
Construction of first Aust. sky-scraper, Culwulla Chambers, begins in Sydney.
Walter Burley Griffin wins first prize in international competition for design of Canberra.
First sheets of fibrous plaster imported to Melbourne from NZ.

Births & Deaths
Walter Ralston Bunning, architect, town planner, specialized in camouflage in World War II, b. (d. 1977)

1912

D
Religion, Learning

Jan. W. J. Elliot appointed first Inspector of NSW Secondary Schools.
26 Sep. Rev. John Flynn estb. Presbyterian Aust. Inland Mission to serve outback Aust.

During 1912
Kingsley Ogilvie Fairbridge estb. Fairbridge Society Farm School at Pinjarra, WA, for outback migrant children from deprived English families.
Daniel Mannix appointed Roman Catholic Coadjutor Archbishop of Melbourne. Arrives March 1913. Becomes full Archbishop in May 1917 and holds position until his death in 1963.
First Progressive Education movement begins. Lasts until World War II.
First Branch of the Workers' Educational Association (WEA) estb. NSW.
First Qld State high school opens.
Kindergarten Association of WA estb.
Sydney Municipal Library opens first Public Children's Library in Aust.
First Aust. New Apostolic Church services held, in Qld.

Births & Deaths

William Alfred Beatty, Australiana expert, musician, b.
Rudolph Brasch, Rabbi, author, pioneer of inter-faith work, b.
Ian Francis McLaren, historian, author, Vic. politician, b.

E
Sport

29 Jun. William Hart wins first air race in Aust., between Botany Bay and Parramatta and return.
12 Nov. First common rules for all Aust. horseracing enforced.

During 1912
Piastre, ridden by A. Shanahan, wins Melbourne Cup in 3 minutes $27\frac{3}{4}$ seconds.
Essendon football team wins VFL Premiership in Melbourne.
Eastern Suburbs football team wins Rugby League Premiership in Sydney.
Albert Rosenfeld sets world Rugby League try-setting record with 78 tries. (Record unbroken.)
Aust. wins two gold, two silver and two bronze medals at Stockholm Olympics.
Fanny Durack becomes first woman to win gold medal at Olympic in any sport. Wins freestyle swimming race.
The Vic. Canoe Club estb. (NSW 1930s, Qld 1947, S 1948.)
T. J. Matthews takes two hat-tricks in one test match against South Africa. (Never repeated.)
Electric timer first used in Aust. sport.
Sydney Fencing Club estb. (Renamed Sydney Sword Club in 1913.) Fencing officially organized.
Aust. loses Davis Cup (tennis) to British Isles after three successes against USA.
Rupert Jeffkins becomes first motor racing hero in Aust.
Sydney Rowing Club wins first international rowing competition.

Births & Deaths

Fred Best, jockey, horse-trainer, b.
W. A. 'Billy' Brown, cricketer, noted opening batsman, b.
Perce Hall, trotting driver, b.
Horace Lindrum, snooker and billiards player, b. (d. 1974)
Herb Narvo, boxer, Rugby League player, b. (d. 1957)
Jack Regan, VFL footballer, b.
Ray Revell, racing-car driver, b. (d. 1967)
Alan Waterson, golfer, b.

F
Historia Dignum

1912

Population
Estimated total white, 4,746,589.

21 Mar. Liner *Koombana* sinks on WA coast, claiming 138 lives.
12 Oct. Fire breaks out at Mt Lyell copper mine, Tas., claiming 42 lives.
10 Dec. The newspaper *Daily Standard* published in Brisbane. (Until 1936.)

During 1912
Institute of Admen estb. in Melbourne. First advertising agency.
Adelaide passes by-law preventing women from wearing unprotected hat pins on trams.
First domestic refrigerators introduced.
First Estonian Club in Aust. estb. in Sydney. (Melbourne in 1914.)
Liquor licensing authorities estb. in NSW and Qld. (Tas. 1932, SA 1967, Vic. 1968, WA 1970.)

Communities
Griffith, NSW, estb.
Leeton, NSW, estb.
Morawa, WA, estb.
Wyalkatchem, WA, estb.

1913

A History, Politics, Economics, Law

Government

4 Mar. 1913–16 Mar. 1913, Sir Edward Stone administered WA.
10 Mar. 1913–4 Jun. 1913, Sir John Dodds administered Tas.
11 Mar. 1913–14 Mar. 1913, Sir William Cullen administered NSW.
14 Mar. 1913–27 Oct. 1917, Sir Gerald Strickland Governor NSW.
17 Mar. 1913–26 Feb. 1917, Sir Harry Barron Governor WA.
4 Jun. 1913–31 Mar. 1917, Sir William Grey Ellison-Macartney Governor Tas.
24 Jun. 1913–17 Sep. 1914, Ninth Cwlth Ministry, Joseph Cook Liberal Prime Minister Aust.
30 Jun. 1913–12 Nov. 1916, W. A. Holman Labor Premier NSW.
28 Aug. 1913–23 Feb. 1914, Sir John Madden administered Vic.
9 Dec. 1913–22 Dec. 1913, G. A. Elmslie Labor Premier Vic.
22 Dec. 1913–18 Jun. 1914, W. A. Watt Liberal Premier Vic.

11 Feb. Sir Frank Gavan Duffy appointed a Justice of High Court of Aust. (until 1931); Sir Charles Powers on 5 Mar. (until 1929); Albert Bathurst Piddington on 6 Mar. (until later in year); Sir George Rich (until 1950).
1 Mar. Royal Aust Naval College estb., temporarily at Geelong, Vic. (Estb. at Jervis Bay in 1915.)
9 Mar. WA Farmers' and Settlers' Association estb. the WA Country Party.
12 Mar. Canberra named capital city of Aust. Foundation stone laid.
31 May. National election. Referendum on amendments to the Constitution again defeated.
May. First Aust. Cwlth banknotes printed.
Jun. Point Cook Aviation School estb. (First courses start on 17 Aug. 1914.)
9 Jul. Fifth Federal Parlt opens. (Double dissolution 30 July 1914.)
24 Jul. Foundation stone of Australia House, Australian headquarters in London, laid by the King.
4 Oct. First ships of RAN arrive from England to form Aust. Fleet. HMAS *Australia* first Aust. capital ship commissioned.

During 1913
Joseph Cook Liberal Leader of Federal Opposition until 24 Jun. Andrew Fisher then becomes Labor Leader of Federal Opposition until 1914.
Cwlth Arbitration Court fixes first minimum wage at 7 shillings per day for man with wife and three children.
J. T. Lang enters NSW Parlt.
Administration and Clerical Officers' Association (ACOA) estb.
Cwlth Govt passes Norfolk Islands Act. Norfolk I. becomes territory of Aust. Jurisdiction transferred from NSW to Cwlth in 1914.
Cwlth Govt begins first official statistical collation of strikes.
The Overseas Shipping Representatives' Association estb. in Sydney.
First successful banana crops grown, at Coffs Harbour, NSW.
The Grand Federal Labor Council estb. at Interstate Union Congress in Adelaide.
WA Employers' Federation estb.

Births & Deaths

Thomas Daly, military commander in Korean War, b.
Sir Cecil Thomas Looker, businessman, b.
Roma Flinders Mitchell, SA Justice, b.
Una Gailey Prentice, lawyer, first woman law graduate admitted to Qld Bar, b.
Sir Victor Alfred Trumper Smith, RAN commander, b.

B

Science, Technology, Transport, Discovery

May. H. Hawker, aviator, estb. altitude record of 11,450 feet. (Also sets world air speed record 82 mph.)
Jul. New Melbourne Hospital opens.
During 1913
Hedlie Taylor patents his Sunshine Header.
Broken Hill Pty Co. Ltd estb. Port Kembla iron and steel works.
George Julius' Automatic Totalizator invention is first used on racecourses in NZ.
Marconi and Aust. Wireless Co. unite to form Amalgamated Wireless (Australasia) Ltd (AWA).
Sydney Hospital uses radium treatment.
Vic. Country Road Board forms. First State road regulatory body. (Qld 1920, NSW and WA 1925, SA 1926, Tas. 1939.)

Births & Deaths

Victor David Hopper, scientist, b.
Sir Rutherford Ness Robertson, plant physiologist, biochemist, b.

C

Arts

Literature

During 1913
C. J. Dennis publishes *Backblock Verses and Other Verses*.
Norman Lindsay publishes *A Curate in Bohemia*.

Births & Deaths

John Bligh, poet, b.
Dame Mary Durack, author specializing in pioneering and Aboriginal subjects, b.
Jack Lawson Glassop, author, journalist, b. (d. 1966)
Reginald Rex Charles Ingamells, poet, b. (d. 1955)
Kenneth MacKenzie, who wrote as Seaforth MacKenzie, poet and novelist, b. (d. 1955)
Sibyl Elyne Keith Mitchell, author, b.
Douglas Alexander Stewart, poet, critic, playwright, b. (d. 1984)

Music, Dance

21 Jun. Adeline Genée begins 16 week Aust. tour with Imperial Russian Ballet Co.
8 Jul. Imperial Russian ballet makes Aust. début in Melbourne.

Births & Deaths

Neville Amadio, flautist, b.
Hector William Crawford, musician, director, b.
Raymond Charles Hanson, composer, b. (d. 1976)
Dulcie Sybil Holland, composer, pianist, b.
Miriam Beatrice Hyde, composer, pianist, b.

Drama, Theatre, Film

6 Jan. Australasian Films Ltd and Union Theatres Ltd estb.
During 1913
Hugh Buckler estb. The Little Theatre in Sydney.
Frank Hurley makes *Home of the Blizzard*, documentary film on Antarctica.

Births & Deaths

Coral Edith Browne, actress, b.
Robert Krasker, motion picture cameraman, b.

Fine Arts

During 1913
Castlemaine Art Gallery and Historical Museum founded, Vic.
NSW Education Dept Art Gallery estb. in Sydney.

1913

1913

New Modern Movement in Aust. art begins, influenced by post-impressionism, aestheticism in criticism, cubism, constructivism, surrealism, abstract art.
Nora Simpson, painter, brings illustrations of impressionism and cubism to Aust.
Max Meldrum estb. his school of painting in Melbourne.

Births & Deaths
Edgar Eduard Aavik, sculptor, b.
Christine Gray Aldor, graphic artist, b. (d. 1969)
Julian Richard Ashton, seascape painter, b.
Joseph Terence Anthony Burke, fine arts professor, b.
Ronald A. Center, still life painter, b.
Margaret Agnes Coen, flower and landscape painter, b.
Noel Jack Counihan, social realist painter, cartoonist, b.
Peter Ingram Cox, painter, b.
Francis Kenneth de Silva, painter, b.
Tom Green, painter, geographic artist, b.
Gordon Stuart McAustan, sculptor, painter, potter, b.
Alan Lester McIntyre, painter, art critic, b.
Peter Charles Roderick Purves-Smith, painter, b. (d. 1949)
Stanislaus Ivan Rapotec, oil painter, probably b.
Lance Vaiben Solomon, landscape painter, b.
Hayward Veal, painter, b. (d. 1968)
James Douglas Watson, painter, graphic and commercial artist, b.

Architecture

Births & Deaths
Sir John Wallace Overall, architect, b.
Frederick Romberg, architect, b.

D
Religion, Learning

Jan. First Tas. high schools open, in Hobart and Launceston.
13 Feb. University of WA opens.
Nov. Melbourne Public Library opens.
During 1913
Workers' Education Association of NSW estb. to promote Aust. intellectual life.
Frensham School for Girls founded at Mittagong, NSW.
State Baptist Societies unite to form Aust. Baptist Missionary Society.
Minimum school leaving age in Tas. raised from 13 to 14.
Southport Boys School estb. Qld.
Warrnambool Technical School estb. in Vic.
St Joseph's Training School estb. in Sydney. (Becomes Catholic Teachers' College of Sydney in 1960.)

Births & Deaths
Gordon Greenwood, historian, social scientist, b.

E
Sport

20 Mar. L. B. Nott passes first surf lifesaving exam. Becomes first official lifesaving instructor.
Jul. First squash court completed at Melbourne Club.
3 Oct. Standard set of weights for all boxing divisions and conditions for boxing championships estb.
During 1913
Posinatus, ridden by A. Shanahan, wins Melbourne Cup in 3 minutes 31 seconds.
Fitzroy football team wins VFL Premiership in Melbourne.
Eastern Suburbs football team wins Rugby League Premiership in Sydney.
First WA trotting meeting held, in Perth.
Jerry Jerome becomes first Aboriginal national middleweight boxing champion.
Bill Lonworth wins all NSW and Aust. swimming titles.

Births & Deaths
Edgar Britt, jockey, b.
David Michael Brown, Rugby League player, b. (d. 1974)
Jack Dyer, VFL footballer, b.
Lindsay Hassett, cricketer, noted batsman, b.
Victor Hey, Rugby League footballer, b.
Aub Lawson, motorcyclist, b. (d. 1977)
Herbert Matthews, VFL footballer, b.
Jim Metcalfe, athlete, jumper, b.
David Hugh (Darby) Munro, jockey, b. (d. 1966)
Adrian Karl Quist, tennis player, b.

F
Historia Dignum

1913

Population
Estimated total white, 4,893,741.

20 Jan–4 Feb. Floods in Cairns–Innisfail area, Qld.
30 Jan. Train collision at Murphy Creek, Qld, claims six lives.
Jan. First Cwlth stamp, kangaroo on map of Aust., issued.
12 Mar. Lady Denman, wife of Governor-General, is responsible for pronounciation of 'Canberra' with stress on first syllable.
During 1913
Smallpox outbreak in NSW.
Bryant and May estb. Federal Match Co. First match Co. in Aust.
The Aust. Friends' Peace Board estb.

Communities
Whyalla, SA, estb.

1914

A

History, Politics, Economics, Law

Government

2 Feb. 1914–18 Apr. 1914, Sir Samuel Way administered SA.
23 Feb. 1914–30 Jan. 1920, Sir Arthur Lyulph Stanley Governor Vic.
6 Apr. 1914–Apr. 1916, J. Earle Labor Premier Tas.
18 Apr. 1914–30 Apr. 1920, Sir Henry Lionel Galway Governor SA.
18 May 1914–6 Oct. 1920, Sir Ronald Craufurd Munro-Ferguson Governor-General Aust.
18 Jun. 1914–Nov. 1917, Sir A. J. Peacock, Liberal Premier Vic.
16 Jul. 1914–15 Mar. 1915, Sir Arthur Morgan administered Qld.
17 Sep. 1914–27 Oct. 1915, Tenth Cwlth Ministry, Andrew Fisher, Labor Prime Minister Aust.

16 Feb. NSW Govt introduces basic wage.
30 Mar. Norfolk I. transferred to Cwlth.
15 May. WA Country Party is first Country Party to win seats in any Aust. Parlt.
5 Sep. National election. Joseph Cook Liberal Leader of Federal Opposition. (Until 1916.)
8 Oct. Sixth Federal Parlt opens. (Dissolution 26 Mar. 1917.)
Nov. Qld first State to introduce compulsory enrolment and voting at State elections.
During 1914
First Cwlth Crimes Act passed and assented to.
Cwlth Govt introduces Probate Tax.
George J. Coles opens first Coles Store in Collingwood, Melbourne. Store sold in 1916 when Coles enlists. New Coles store opened 1919.

World War I

4 Aug. Great Britain declares war on Germany. Aust. Prime Minister Joseph Cook officially announces situation on 5 Aug. On declaration of war Aust. fires first shot from Queenscliff, Vic., at German vessel *Pfalz*.
6 and 10 Aug. Exports of certain articles prohibited, including copper and tin.
8 Aug. Sir William Thomas Bridges names the Aust. Imperial Force (AIF), which begins enlistment.
10 Aug. Aust. navy placed at disposal of British Admiralty.
11 Aug. Cwlth Govt imposes censorship.
17 Aug. Aust. Flying Corps estb. at Point Cook, Vic. First military flying courses run.
19 Aug. Aust. force leaves Sydney to seize German wireless station and occupy German territory in the Pacific. Arrive New Britain 11 Sep.
11 Sep. First Aust. war victims fall when six die while storming a German radio post at Rabaul.
14 Sep. Aust. loses first submarine, *AE1*, off coast of New Britain.
13 Sep. German New Guinea surrenders to Aust.
23 Oct. Cwlth Govt passes Act prohibiting trade with enemy.
29 Oct. War Precautions Act gives Cwlth Govt authority to control commerce during war.
1 Nov. First of over 20,000 Aust. and NZ troops (ANZACS) leave Albany, WA, for Britain, but are disembarked at Alexandria, Egypt, on 3 Dec.
6 Nov. Aust. occupies German I. of Nauru.
9 Nov. HMAS *Sydney* destroys German cruiser *Emden* off Cocos I.
21 Dec. War Pensions Act passed.
During 1914
Sir Ian Hamilton arrives in Aust. to report on defence scheme.
William Riddell Birdwood estb. Aust. and NZ Army Corps (ANZAC) and is appointed Commanding Officer.

Births & Deaths

James Ford Cairns, politician, author, b.
Thomas Currie Derrick, soldier, b. (d. 1945)
John Hurst Edmondson, first Aust. to win Victoria Cross in World War II, b. (d. 1941)
Sir Hughie Idwal Edwards, WA Governor, b.
Sir Gordon Freeth, Federal politician, diplomat, b.
Sir William Archer Gunn, grazier, company director b.
Sir Colin Thomas Hannah, Qld Governor, b. (d. 1978)
Paul Gotthard Henschke, pioneer vigneron, d.
Sir John Robert Kerr, Governor-General, b.
Sir Arthur Harold Tange, public servant, b.
Sir John Keith Waller, diplomat, b.

B

Science, Technology, Transport, Discovery

1 Mar. Lieuts Harrison and Petre fly first military aircraft in Aust., at Point Cook, Vic.
25 May. Canberra–Queanbeyan, NSW, railway opens.
6 Jun. Automatic telephone exchange opens at Newtown, Sydney. First automatic exchange opens in Melbourne this year.
16–18 Jul. Maurice Guillaux becomes first pilot in Aust. to use aircraft for commercial purposes.
During Jul. *Medical Journal of Australia* founded.
During 1914
A. Delfoise Badgery builds Gaudron bi-plane in Sydney. First flight on 8 Jul.
George Nicholas makes the Aust. Aspro (Patented in 1917.)
WA Natural History and Science Society becomes Royal Society of WA.
Melbourne–Adelaide telephone trunk line opens.
British Association for the Advancement of Science holds 84th meeting, in Sydney.

Births & Deaths

Irvine Armstrong Watson, agriculturist, scientist, noted for work on disease resistant varieties of crop plants, b.
Sydney Edward Wright, pharmacist, b. (d. 1966)

C

Arts

1914

Literature

During 1914
Walter Baldwin Spencer publishes *The Native Tribes of the Northern Territory of Australia*.
Christopher J. Brennan publishes *Poems 1913*.

Births & Deaths

Peter Walkinshaw Cowan, author, b.

Music, Dance

During 1914
Maud Allen, dancer and choreographer, tours Aust. Introduces barefoot free dance style.
NSW Conservatorium of Music estb. (Opens on 6 May 1915.)
Henri Verbrugghen develops Sydney orchestral tradition. Estb. Sydney Conservatorium orchestra.
The Tango dance from Argentina becomes popular in Melbourne and Sydney.
Alfred Hill and Fritz Hart estb. Aust. Opera League.
Nat Phillips, 'Stiffy', and Roy Rene, 'Mo', form vaudeville team.
c. 1914. William G. James, song writer, active.

Births & Deaths

Graeme Emerson Bell, jazz musician, composer, b.
David Frederick (Dave) Dallwitz, jazz musician, b.
Ronald Down, operatic singer, tenor, b.

Drama, Theatre, Film

13 Jun. Raymond Longford produces film *The Silence of Dean Maitland*.
16 Nov. Film *A Long Way to Tipperary* released.
23 Nov. Film *The Day* released.
During 1914
Revue *Come Over Here*, produced. Among first of kind in Aust.

Fine Arts

During 1914
Aust. art sent to Panama Pacific Exhibition in San Francisco, USA.
Middle Period of modern Aust. art begins, marking decline of Aust. impressionism and emphasizing pictorial aspects of landscape painting. (Ends *c.* 1939.)
Aust. Natives Association Art Competition for landscape painting held.

1914

Births & Deaths

Denis Adams, marine painter, b.
Max Rupert Angas, Tas. painter, b.
Alan Douglas Baker, portrait painter, b.
Dorothy Baker, painter, b.
Ian Bow, painter, sculptor, b.
Francis J. Broadhurst, illustrator, commercial artist, b.
Rosa Garlick, semi-abstract painter, b.
Harold Greenhill, painter, b.
Paul Haefliger, painter art critic, b. (d. 1982)
Stanley S. Hammond, sculptor, b.
Newton Samuel Hedstrom, portrait painter, b.
Roger Paton James, painter, b.
Jack Louis Koskie, painter, b.
Henry Reginald McDonald, painter, b.
Colin MacInnes, art critic, writer, b. (d. 1976)
Laurence Scott Pendlebury, painter, b.
Edward Shaw, ceramic artist, b.
Gordon Arthur Speary, painter, b.
Ruth Tuck, watercolourist, b.
Albert Lee Tucker, pioneer of modern expressionist and surrealist painting, b.
Laurence Oliphant Campbell White, painter, b.

D

Religion, Learning

28 Nov. Richard Williams first graduate from Point Cook Aviation School, Vic.

During 1914

Montessori education methods, emphasizing individual and intellectual freedom, introduced into NSW schools.
Ida Stanley first Alice Springs, NT, school teacher, estb. school for half-caste children.
First Aust. Correspondence School estb., in Vic.
Eastern Goldfields High School opens. Among first high schools in WA.
WA Govt removes fees from all State education institutions.
Brisbane Teacher Training College estb.
Church of England Grammar School estb. in Brisbane.
Narrogin Agricultural College estb. in WA.

Births & Deaths

Margaret Loch Kiddle, historian and author, b. (d. 1958)
James Robert Knox, Catholic Archbishop of Melbourne 1967, b. (d. 1983)

E
Sport

During 1914
Kingsburgh, ridden by G. Meddick, wins Melbourne Cup in 3 minutes 26 seconds.
Carlton football team wins VFL Premiership in Melbourne.
South Sydney football team wins Rugby League Premiership in Sydney.
Aust. Aero Club estb.
Night trotting estb. in Perth.
Norman Brookes first Aust. to win Wimbledon tennis title.
L. H. Kelly, athlete, first Aust. to jump over six feet.

Births & Deaths
William Ackland-Horman, SA golfer, b.
Arthur Edward (Scobie) Breasley, jockey, b.
Eric James Cremin, golfer, b. (d. 1973)
Richard E. Garrard, wrestler who wins 516 out of 525 bouts, b.
Ron Masters, diver and swimmer, b.
Norman Guy von Nida, golfer, b.
Decima Norman, athlete, b.
James William George (Bill) Roycroft, equestrian champion, b.
Kevin Ryan, racing handicapper, b.
Ernie Toshock, cricketer, b.

F
Historia Dignum

1914

Population
Estimated total white, 4,971,778.

16 Mar. Railway collision at Temora, NSW, claims 14 lives.
27 Mar. Ship *St Paul* wrecked at Cape Moreton, Qld, claiming 18 lives.
16–18 Jul. French pilot Maurice Guillaux makes first official air mail delivery from Melbourne to Sydney. First inter-capital flight. Delivers 1,785 letters.

During 1914
Australian Red Cross Society estb. as branch of British Red Cross.
Severe nation-wide drought reduces wheat harvest. Affects over 90 per cent of continent.
First lettergram service estb., in Sydney.

Communities
Merrygoen, NSW, estb.

1915

A
History, Politics, Economics, Law

Government
15 Mar. 1915–3 Feb. 1920, Sir Hamilton John Goold-Adams Governor Qld.
3 Apr. 1915–Jul. 1917, C. Vaughan Labor Premier SA.
1 Jun. 1915–Oct. 1919, T. J. Ryan Labor Premier Qld.
27 Oct. 1915–14 Nov. 1916, Eleventh Cwlth Ministry, William Morris Hughes Labor Prime Minister Aust.

1 Jan. Two Turks attack train carrying picnickers near Broken Hill, NSW, killing four.
4 Sep. NSW Govt transfers land at Jervis Bay, NSW, to Cwlth for use as port for ACT.
13 Sep. Cwlth first imposes income tax, as a wartime measure.
During Sep. Universal Service League estb. to promote compulsory military service.
12 Nov. Qld Govt introduces the Constitution Act Amendment Bill to abolish Legislative Council. Rejected in Dec.
1 Dec. NSW and SA Women Police Branch estb. First in British Empire. (First women police WA 1917, Vic. 1924, Qld 1931.)
14 Dec. Farmers' and Settlers' Association estb. in SA.
During 1915
Qld enforces compulsory voting at Legislative Assembly elections. (Cwlth 1924, Vic. 1926, NSW and Tas. 1928, WA 1936, SA 1942.)
Qld Branch of National Country Party estb.
Counter Espionage Bureau estb. First secret intelligence service in Aust.; becomes Special Intelligence Bureau in 1917.
Cwlth Wheat Marketing Scheme introduced.
Soya bean industry begins in NSW.
Deepwater fish trawling begins in Aust.
Forestry operations begin at Mt Stromlo, ACT.
Ship Painters and Dockers Union and Federated Miscellaneous Workers' Union estb.

World War I
Jan. Code name ANZAC officially adopted for Aust. and NZ Army Corps in Egypt.
10 Feb. RAN College transferred to Jervis Bay, NSW, Named HMAS *Creswell*. (Transferred to Flinders Naval Depot in 1930; returned to Jervis Bay in 1957.)
17 Feb. HMAS *Australia* joins the Grand Fleet.
20 Apr. Small unit of Aust. Flying Corps leaves for Mesopotamia.
25 Apr. Aust. loses second submarine, in Dardanelles. ANZAC Forces land at Gallipoli. Aust. attacks Lone Pine in unsuccessful Battle of Sari Bair on 6 Aug.
19 May. Private John Simpson Kirkpatrick, 'the Man with the Donkey', killed while carrying wounded soldiers to safety.
19–20 May. Corporal Albert Jacka at Gallipoli displays bravery which earns him a Victoria Cross. (First Aust. to win a Victoria Cross in World War I.)
8–20 Dec. Evacuation of Gallipoli. Total Gallipoli casualties c. 8,587 killed and 19,367 wounded.

Births & Deaths
Richard Ivan Downing, economist administrator, b. (d. 1975)
Bartholomew Augustine Santamaria, publicist, organizer of Catholic-based political movement, b.
Francis Phillip Serong, authority on counter-insurgency operations, b.

B

Science, Technology, Transport, Discovery

Mar. Broken Hill Proprietary Co. Ltd opens steelworks at Newcastle, NSW, beginning large-scale steel production.
Jun. First lock on the Murray R. opens, at Blanchetown, SA.

During 1915
Alf Hannaford invents wheat pickler for cleaning wheat.
Lance-Corporal Beech invents periscope rifle at Gallipoli.
River Murray Commission estb. to control river flow and irrigation.
Sir William Lawrence Bragg and Sir Henry William Bragg win Nobel Prize for research in X-ray spectra and the structure of crystals.
NSW State Dockyard, at Newcastle, opens.
Darnell Smith uses copper carbonate to control bunt disease in cereals.

Births & Deaths
Charlotte Anderson, medical researcher, noted for work on coeliac disease, b.
Vivian Bullwinkel, World War II nursing matron, b.
Evelyn Ernest Owen, inventor, b. (d. 1949)

C

Arts

Literature

During 1915
Monthly literary periodical *Triad* first published, in Sydney.
Katherine S. Prichard publishes *The Pioneers*.
C. J. Dennis publishes *Songs of a Sentimental Bloke*.
Vance Palmer publishes short story, 'The World of Man'.
Douglas Mawson publishes *The Home of The Blizzard*, polar classic.

Births & Deaths
David Watt Ian Campbell, poet, author, b. (d. 1979)
Thomas Arthur Guy Hungerford, author, journalist, b.
John Streeter Manifold, poet, b.
David Martin, novelist, poet, b.
Judith Arundel Wright, poet noted for ability to combine local themes with modern sophisticated techniques, b.

Music, Dance

During 1915
Nellie Melba estb. singing school in Melbourne.

Births & Deaths
Dorian Leon Marlois Le Gallienne, composer, b. (d. 1963)
Ernest Victor Llewellyn, conductor, violinist, b.

Drama, Theatre, Film

During 1915
Alan Wilkie forms Shakespearian Acting Company.
Hippodrome Theatre opens in Sydney. (Becomes Capitol in 1927.)
First American film exchange opens in Aust.

Fine Arts

During 1915
Grace Cossington Smith and Roland Wakelin exhibit first post-impressionist paintings in Aust.
Margaret Holden produces *Greyhound*, sculpture.

Births & Deaths
John Simeon Ashworth, painter, b. (d. 1979)
Dorra Cecil Chapman, painter, b.
Jack Courier, painter, b.
John Stuart Dowie, sculptor, painter, b.
Phyl Dunn, ceramic artist, b.

1915

1915

Ivan Oscar Englund, potter, b.
Harold Emanuel Freeman, illustrator, graphic artist, b.
Donald Stuart Leslie Friend, artist noted for draughtmanship and evocation of Eastern culture, b.
James Timothy Gleeson, surrealist artist, b.
Nornie Gude, watercolourist, b.
Grahame King, painter, industrial designer, b.
Garrett Kingsley, portrait painter, b.
Hans Knorr, sculptor, b.
Ron Lilburne, painter, b. (d. 1962)
Alan Moore, painter, b.
James Grainger Phillips, painter and illustrator, b.
Joe Rose, painter, b.
Rachel Roxburgh, ceramics artist, b.
Roderick Malcolm Shaw, painter, illustrator, b.
Leonard Shillam, sculptor, potter, b.
Lawrence Nicholas Barrett Thomas, art organizer, critic, b. (d. 1974)
Wallace Keogh Thornton, painter, art critic, b.
Adolphas Vaicaitis, graphic artist, b.
Eric Ernest Westbrook, art administrator, b.

Architecture

Births & Deaths

Stuart Burrell Hall Game, architect, b.

D
Religion, Learning

During 1915

Centre Technical College estb. in Brisbane.
Footscray Institute of Technology estb. as Footscray Technical College, in Melbourne.
Beatrice Ensor estb. the Fraternity in Education group of progressive teachers.
Teaching of German in Lutheran schools prohibited.

Births & Deaths

Charles Manning Hope Clark, historian, b.

E
Sport

Feb. Duke Kahanamoku introduces surfboard riding to Aust.
9 Apr. Aust. Aero Club first meets in Melbourne. (Branches estb. in NSW, Qld, SA and Tas. in 1919.)
27 Dec. James Darey wins world middleweight boxing title in Sydney.

During 1915
Patrobus, ridden by R. Lewis, wins Melbourne Cup in 3 minutes 28½ seconds.
Carlton football team wins VFL Premiership in Melbourne.
Balmain football team wins Rugby League Premiership in Sydney.
NSW Rugby Union suspended because of war. (Rugby League continues.)
First NSW Surf lifesaving championship held, at Bondi, Sydney.
Claude West first notable surfer in Aust.

Births & Deaths
Reginald Dale, soccer player, b.
Victor Duggan, speedway rider, b.
James Ferrier, golfer, b.
Sir Arthur George, soccer organizer, b.
Jack Iverson, cricketer, b. (d. 1973)
Jack Meuller, VFL footballer, b.
Richard Reynolds, VFL footballer, b.
John Alexander Sturrock, yachtsman, b.
Ron Todd, VFL footballer, b.
Doug Whiteford, motorcyclist, car racer, b. (d. 1979)
Harry Williams, golfer, b. (d. 1961)

F
Historia Dignum

1915

Population
Estimated total white, 4,969,457.

Jan. Bushfires burn in Huon R. area, Tas.
20 Sep. The Returned Soldiers' Association of NSW estb.

During 1915
First Wolf Cub packs estb. in Sydney.
Aust.-wide drought continues.
Tuberculosis claims *c.* 4,000 lives.
Joe Dempsey becomes 'Two-up King' of the army.
Top hat and cutaway jacket in fashion.
Letter carriers become known as postmen.

Communities
Coober Pedy, SA, estb.
Kandos, NSW, estb.
Kyancutta, SA, district settled

1916

A
History, Politics, Economics, Law

Government
15 Apr. 1916–Aug. 1922, Sir W. Lee Liberal/Nationalist Premier Tas.
27 Jul. 1916–Jun. 1917, F. Wilson Liberal Premier WA.
14 Nov. 1916–17 Feb. 1917, Twelfth Cwlth Ministry, William Morris Hughes National Labor Prime Minister Aust.

12 Apr. NSW passes Eight-Hour Act.
Jun. Cwlth Govt purchases 15 British steamships and forms Commonwealth Government Line.
14 Sep. Restrictions imposed on franchise of German citizens.
30 Sep. Aust. Farmers' Federal Organization estb. in Melbourne. (First Council meeting on 17 Apr. 1917.)
28 Oct. National referendum defeats first proposal for compulsory overseas military service. (51.61 per cent vote against 48.39 per cent vote for.)
Oct.–Dec. NSW coalminers strike over wages and conditions.
14 Nov. Labor Party splits on conscription issue. William Hughes (pro-conscription) expelled from Labor Party but retains office as Prime Minister supported by his own National Labor Party and by Liberals.
12 Dec. Twelve members of the Wobblies, Industrial Workers of the World, convicted of arson and sedition and jailed.

During 1916
Renmano wines estb. First co-operative winery in Aust.
Record wheat harvest for the year of 180,000,000 bushels.
High Court determines extent of legal limitations of Cwlth Govt power in order to manage war effort in Bread Case.
The Broken Hill Trades and Labor Council estb.

World War I
14 Feb. 5,000 AIF troops in camp near Liverpool, England, rebel after refusing to undergo new training syllabus.
16 Mar. No. 1 Squadron Aust. Flying Corps sails for Egypt. First complete flying squadron sent abroad by any Dominion.
21 Mar. First Aust. Corps begins landing in France. Second on 7 Jun.; Third on 22 Nov.
Apr. Aust. and NZ Mounted troops join Sinai and Palestine campaign.
1 Jul. Aust. infantry begins action in France at Somme offensive. Campaign claims nearly 7,000 Aust. lives by end of Sep.
7 Aug. Heavy German attack repulsed by Aust. Division at Pozières in France.
6 Oct. HMAS *Melbourne* joins Grand Fleet. HMAS *Sydney* joins on 31 Oct.

Births & Deaths
Thomas Kingston Critchley, diplomat, b.
Sir Arthur Roden Cutler, diplomat, NSW Governor, b.
Robert Henry Maxwell Gibbes, World War II air force commander, b.
Sir Rupert James (Dick) Hamer, Vic. Premier, b.
Rawdon Hume Middleton, World War II air force commander, b. (d. 1942)
Russel Prowse, banker, b. (d. 1982)
Sir James Maxwell Ramsay, Qld Governor, b.
Keith William (Bluey) Truscott, World War II fighter pilot, b. (d. 1943)
Edward Gough Whitlam, Labor Prime Minister, b.
John Lloyd Waddy, air force commander, politician, b.

B

Science, Technology, Transport, Discovery

May. The Walter and Eliza Hall Institute of Medical Research estb. in Melbourne.
Nov. Taronga Park Zoo officially opens in Sydney.

During 1916
Cwlth Serum Laboratories (so-named in 1921) estb. to supply essential biological products for national health.
Great Lake hydro electric power system connected to Hobart.
Sidney Cotton devises the Sidcot Flying Suit.
Gloucester Park racecourse in Perth installs first tote (automatic totalizator).
Newcastle–Stockton, NSW, ferry service begins.
R. A. Squire invents Spring Tyne Drill Cultivator combining cultivation and sowing.

Births & Deaths
Sir Ernest William Titterton, nuclear scientist, b.

C

Arts

Literature

During 1916
Arthur Hoey Davis, using pseudonym Steele Rudd, publishes *Grandpa's Selection*.
C. J. Dennis publishes *The Moods of Ginger Mick*.
Ernest Scott publishes *A Short History of Australia*.
Literary magazine *Birth* first published, in Melbourne.

Births & Deaths
Paul Chester Jerome Brickhill, author, journalist, b.
Shawn Hamilton O'Leary, poet and author, b.
Harold Frederick Stewart, poet, b.
Morris Langley West, novelist, b.

Music, Dance

During 1916
Mosman Musical Society Ballet estb. in Sydney.
Henri Verbrugghen appointed first director of NSW Conservatorium of Music.
The Gonzales Opera Co. tours Aust.

Births & Deaths
Alan Light, bass singer, b.
Laurel Martyn, dancer, choreographer, b.

Drama, Theatre, Film

8 Jul. Harry van der Sluys, known as Roy Rene or Mo, first appears at Princess Theatre in Sydney.
During 1916
Oscar Asche's play *Chu Chin Chow* opens in London. (Runs for record five years.)
NSW Govt estb. a State Film Censorship Board. (SA 1917, Tas. 1920.)

Births & Deaths
Peter George Frederick Ingle Finch, actor, b. (d. 1977)
John Whiteford Heyer, documentary film producer, b.

Fine Arts

During 1916
Sydney Ure Smith publishes magazine *Art in Australia*, giving Aust. artists first serious recognition at home and abroad.
Post Gallery Students Society estb. in Melbourne.

1916

Births & Deaths
Joyce L. Allen, painter, b.
Sir Thomas Dwyer Bass, sculptor, b.
Clifford William Bayliss, painter, b.
Reschid Bey, painter, b.
Lucy Boyd, ceramic artist, b.
Jo Caddy, painter, b.
Elizabeth Durack, painter and illustrator, b.
Ella Fry, WA painter, b.
Guy Edward Grey-Smith, painter, graphic artist, potter, b. (d. 1981)
Helen Grey-Smith, textile designer, graphic artist, potter, b.
Robert Keith Reeve Haines, art director, b.
Dermont James John Hellier, landscape painter, b.
Francis Lymburner, painter and draughtsman, b. (d. 1972)
Frank McNamara, watercolourist, b.
Vlades Meskenas, portrait painter, b.
Graham Hinton Moore, painter, b.
Michael Nicholson, painter, sculptor, graphic artist, b.
Charles Frank Norton, marine painter, b.
Wilfred John Piesley, painter, b.
Reginald Wilfred Whiting Rowed, landscape painter, AIF war artist, b.
Kathleen Shillam, sculptor, potter, b.
Bernard Smith, art historian, b.
Lawrence Rex Veale, painter, b. (d. 1942)

Architecture

During 1916
SA passes first Town Planning and Housing Bill in Aust.
John Cyril Hawes, architect, builds St Francis Xavier Cathedral at Geraldton, WA.

D

Religion, Learning

Jul. Aust. Directors of Education first meet, in Adelaide.
28 Aug. NSW Govt Aviation School opens at Richmond, NSW.
During 1916
The United Church of North Aust. estb. Aboriginal mission at Goulburn I., NT.

Births & Deaths
Alan George Lewers Shaw, historian, b.
Sir Guilford Clyde Young, Catholic prelate, b.

E
Sport

During 1916
Sasanof, ridden by F. Foley, wins Melbourne Cup in 3 minutes 27¼ seconds.
Fitzroy football team wins VFL Premiership in Melbourne.
Balmain football team wins Rugby League Premiership in Sydney.
Les Darcy becomes heavyweight boxing champion.
First Gliding Club estb., at Granville, NSW.

Births & Deaths
Alan Barnes, cricket administrator, b.
Mick Bartley, known as 'Melbourne Mick', gambler, b.
Claire Dennis, swimmer, b.
Frank Lewis, racehorse trainer, b.
Vivian Bede McGrath, one of first tennis players to perfect double-handed hold style, b. (d. 1978)
Garney Nobel, lawn bowler, b.
Jock O'Sullivan, jockey, b.
Donald Tallon, cricketer, noted wicket-keeper, b.
Alan Westbury, boxer, b. (d. 1968)

F
Historia Dignum

Population
Estimated total white, 4,917,949.

15 Feb. Train derailment at Campania, Tas., claims four lives.
25 Apr. ANZAC day first celebrated.
10 Jun. NSW, Vic. and Tas. introduce six o'clock hotel closing.
During Jun. Returned Sailors' and Soldiers' Imperial League of Aust. estb. in Melbourne. (Becomes Returned Services League of Aust. in 1965.)
27–29 Dec. Floods at Clermont, Qld, claim 67 lives. Widespread river floods throughout Aust.
During 1916
Tas. becomes first State to introduce daylight saving.
Golden Casket lottery begins in Qld.
Mt Field, Tas., reserved. Among first scenic reserves in Tas.

1917

A
History, Politics, Economics, Law

Government

17 Feb. 1917–10 Jan. 1918, Thirteenth Cwlth Ministry, William Morris Hughes Nationalist Prime Minister Aust. (National War Govt.)
27 Feb. 1917–8 Apr. 1917, Sir Edward Stone administered WA.
31 Mar. 1917–6 Jul. 1917, Sir Herbert Nicholls administered Tas.
9 Apr. 1917–8 Apr. 1920, Sir William Grey Ellison-Macartney Governor WA.
28 Jun. 1917–Apr. 1919, (Sir) H. B. Lefroy Liberal Premier WA.
6 Jul. 1917–9 Feb. 1920, Sir Francis Alexander Newdigate Newdegate Governor Tas.
14 Jul. 1917–Apr. 1920, A. H. Peake Liberal-National coalition Premier SA.
28 Oct. 1917–17 Feb. 1918, Sir William Cullen administered NSW.
29 Nov. 1917–Mar. 1918, J. Bowser National Premier Vic.

7 Feb. The Nationalist Party formed out of the Liberal Party under Joseph Cook and the group led by William Morris Hughes which split from the Labor Party in 1916. W. M. Hughes leader.
16 Feb. Cwlth Shipping Board estb.
17 Feb. Aust. National War Govt takes office.
5 May. National election. Frank Gwynne Tudor Labor Opposition leader. (Until 1922.)
14 Jun. Seventh Federal Parlt opens. (Dissolution 3 Nov. 1919.)
22 Jul. War Profiteering Act passed. Introduced to ensure that profiteers contribute to war effort.
2 Aug.–9 Sep. NSW railway and tramway employees strike against new system of recording work performed. Grows into general strike involving 70,000 workers. Twenty-four NSW unions deregistered.
12 Dec. A Cwlth Police Force estb. after The Warwick Egg incident at Warwick, Qld on 29 Nov. when Prime Minister Hughes was hit by an egg while addressing a meeting. The Qld Labor Govt refused action by Qld police, so Hughes estb. a Cwlth force.
20 Dec. Second referendum on proposal for compulsory overseas military service defeated. (53.79 per cent vote against; 46.21 per cent vote for.)

During 1917
Vic. Country Party estb. (SA 1918, NSW 1920, Tas. 1922.)
Surfers Paradise opened as holiday resort under name of Umbigumbi.
Mary Tennison-Woods becomes first woman called to SA Bar.

World War I

Imperial War Conference held in England.
19 Apr. Second Battle of Gaza, Palestine; heavy casualties. Turks evacuate Gaza on 6 Nov. after Third Battle.
11 Apr. 4th Division attacks Hindenberg Line near Bullecourt, France; 3,000 Aust. casualties. Second attack on 3 May; 7,000 Aust. casualties.
7 Jun. Attack on Messines Ridge begins; nearly 7,000 Aust. casualties.
31 Jul. Ypres offensives begin; 38,000 Aust. casualties.
31 Oct. Aust. takes part in cavalry charge against Turks at Beersheba, Palestine; leads to third Battle Gaza.

Births & Deaths

Donald George Anderson, airline administrator, b. (d. 1975)
Donald Cochrane, economist, b. (d. 1983)
David St Alban Dexter, diplomat, World War I historian, b.
Sir David Eric Fairbairn, Federal politician, b.
Sir Donald Hibberd, mining and economics expert, (d. 1983)
Charles Learmonth, World War II pilot, b. (d. 1944)
Sir James Plimsoll, diplomat, b.

B

Science, Technology, Transport, Discovery

4 Apr. Electric tram service begins in Adelaide.
17 Oct. Trans-Aust. Railway, linking eastern and western Aust., completed; opens on 22 Oct.
12 Nov. W. J. Strutt in Curtiss bi-plane makes first inter-capital Melbourne–Sydney flight, in 1 day 7 hours 13 mins.
20 Nov. Clifford Peel suggests scheme involving aircraft for Aust. Inland Mission to cover outback areas.

During 1917
Timber-cutters discover Hastings Caves in Tas., containing some of largest stalactites in world.
Holden Co. at Woodville, Adelaide, switches from making horse-drawn coaches to making motor car bodies.
Buttons moulded from imported phenolformaldehyde. Beginning of plastics industry.
Vic. Govt appoints Brown Coal Advisory Board to examine feasibility of generating electricity from Latrobe Valley coal.
Skeleton weed first identified, at Wagga Wagga, NSW.
The Electrolytic Zinc Co. of Australasia Ltd (estb. in 1916) produces first zinc at Risdon, Tas.

Births & Deaths

Sir John Warcup Cornforth, scientist noted for work on organic chemistry, b.
Derek Randal Cumming, RAAF test pilot, pioneered jet flying in Aust., b.
Sir Ronald Sydney Nyholm, chemist, b. (d. 1971)
George Anthony Morgan Taylor, geologist, vulcanologist, b. (d. 1972)
Peter Clive Thonemann, physicist, leader of team developing Zeta machine for nuclear energy experiments, b.

C

Arts

Literature

During 1917
Henry Handel Richardson (real name Ethel Richardson) publishes *Australia Felix*, first volume of trilogy, *The Fortunes of Richard Mahony*.
A. B. 'Banjo' Paterson publishes *Saltbush Bill, JP., and Other Verses*.
C. J. Dennis publishes *Doreen* and *The Glugs of Gosh*.

Births & Deaths

Nancy Fotheringham Cato, author, b.
Jon Stephen Cleary, author, b.
Sumner Locke Elliott, author, b.
Frank (Francis Joseph) Hardy, novelist, short story writer, b.
Barbara Tarlton Jefferis, author, b.
James Edmond MacDonnell, author of naval stories, b.
James Phillip McAuley, poet and critic noted for neo-classic verse forms, b. (d. 1976)
D'Arcy Francis Niland, author, journalist, b. (d. 1967)
Dennis Ashton Warner, author, journalist, b.

Music, Dance

During 1917
Henry Tate publishes *Australian Musical Resources*.

Births & Deaths

Adrian 'Ade' Monsbourgh, jazz musician, b.
Albert James Penberthy, composer, conductor, b.

Drama, Theatre, Film

19 Mar. Beaumont Smith's film *Our Friends the Hayseeds* premières in Sydney.
During 1917
Majestic Theatre in Sydney becomes Elizabethan Theatre.

Births & Deaths

Cecil Robert Burnet, theatre manager, stage director, b.
'Googie' (Georgette Lizett) Withers, actress, b.

Fine Arts

During 1917
'Twenty Melbourne Painters' art group estb.

1917

471

1917

Births & Deaths
Paul Beadle, sculptor, b.
Alfred Calkoen, painter, b. (d. 1951)
J. Wolfgang Cardamatis, painter, decor designer, b.
Raymond Boultwood Ewers, sculptor, b.
Wanda Garnsey, ceramic artist, b.
Peter Glass, landscape painter, b.
Elwyn Augustus Lynn, painter, b.
William M. Montgomery, stained glass designer, b.
Sidney Robert Nolan, painter, b.
Rosaleen Norton, illustrator and painter, b.
Justin Maurice O'Brien, painter noted for religious art, b.
Reginald Preston ceramic artist, b.
William Smith, painter, b.
Charles Swain, ceramic artist, b.
Phyllis Paulina Waterhouse, portrait and landscape painter, b.

Architecture

During 1917
First national conference of town planners held in Adelaide.
A transition period of Aust. architecture begins. Ends c. 1929.

Births & Deaths
Robert Andrew Gilling, architect, b.

Religion, Learning

During 1917
SA bans teaching of German language in schools.
Daniel Mannix appointed Catholic Archbishop of Melbourne. (Until 1963.)
Qld estb. high schools closely associated with technical colleges.

Births & Deaths
Peter Morton Moyes, educationist, b.

E
Sport

During 1917
Westcourt, ridden by W. H. McLachlan, wins Melbourne Cup in 3 minutes $26\frac{3}{4}$ seconds.
Collingwood football team wins VFL Premiership in Melbourne.
Balmain football team wins Rugby League Premiership in Sydney.
Govt restricts number of sporting fixtures to boost war effort.
Tote (automatic totalizator) first used at Randwick racecourse in Sydney.
Annette Kellermann sets a world record for a dive by a woman.

Births & Deaths
Hockey Bennell, boxer, b.
Nancye Meredith Bolton, tennis player, b.
Eddie Miller, boxer, b.
Julius (Judy) Patching, athlete, b.
Horace H. A. (Ossie) Pickworth, golfer, b. (d. 1969)
Mervyn Thomas Wood, sculler, b.

F
Historia Dignum

1917

Population
Estimated total white 4,982,063.

Apr. Cyclone damages Darwin.
May. Mice plague affects Melbourne wheat stores.
Jun. Frank Hurley appointed official war photographer.
24 Sep. Herbert Henry Klingberg first to pass driving test for motor car licence.

During 1917
Star of the West pearl discovered near Broome. (Most notable pearl found in Aust.)
SA passes Nomenclature Act. German names of 42 towns changed.
Mosquitoes transmit the viral disease Aust. Arbo-Encephalitis (Murray Valley Encephalitis) in NSW and Qld claiming 94 lives. Other outbreaks in 1922, 1925–1926, 1951 (19 deaths) and 1974 (10 deaths).

Births & Deaths
Rohan Deakin Rivett, journalist, b. (d. 1977)

Communities
Quilpie, Qld, estb.

A
History, Politics, Economics, Law

1918

Government

10 Jan. 1918–9 Feb. 1923, Fourteenth Cwlth Ministry, William Morris Hughes Nationalist Prime Minister Aust. (Second National War Govt.)

18 Feb. 1918–16 Sep. 1923, Sir Walter Edward Davidson Governor NSW.

21 Mar. 1918–Apr. 1924, H. S. W. Lawson National Party Premier Vic.

Apr. Cwlth Board of Trade estb. to advise Govt on trade and industry.

Sep. First Aust. Trade Commissioner appointed (to USA), Henry Yule Braddon.

13 Nov. Townsville, Qld, meatworkers strike over efforts by management to bring union under State jurisdiction.

21 Nov. Cwlth Electoral Act consolidates common roll for State and Federal elections and amends election laws. Preferential voting system for Federal elections introduced.

13 Dec. Federal Trade and Customs Minister, Jens Jensen, dismissed by Governor-General.

14 Dec. W. G. Gibson wins Corangamite, Vic., by-election, becoming first Country Party (then called Farmers' Union Party) member to enter Federal Parlt.

During 1918
Title Australian Labor Party (ALP) adopted uniformly throughout Aust.
Stanley Melbourne Bruce enters Federal Parlt.
Rose Scott influential in establishing Childrens' Courts and in formulating Women's Status Act.
Women permitted to practise law in Aust. Cwlth.
Seppelt family buys vineyards at Great Western, Vic.
Qld Govt estb. Aboriginal mission on Palm I.
NT Aboriginals Ordinance prohibits Aborigines from drinking alcohol. Among many other restrictions.
Tom Barker, leader of the Wobblies (IWW), deported to Chile.

World War I

19 Feb. ANZAC Mounted Corps captures Jericho in Middle East.

13 Mar. Lieut Frank Pogson Bethune issues famous battle orders at Passchendaele in France.

21 Mar. Great German offensive commences in France. ANZAC forces stop German attack on Amiens and counter other critical attacks.

4 Apr. Infantry recaptures Villers Bretonneux. German Somme offensive ends.

May. Aust. troops in France form into an Army Corps led by Lieut-General Sir William Birdwood as commander of AIF in Europe.

4 Jul. Aust. Forces capture Hamel in France.

18 Sep. Attack on Hindenberg Line on Western Front. On 2 Sep. Aust. captures Mont St Quentin, which dominates approaches to Somme R. crossing

30 Sep. AIF (Light Horse) in Palestine captures 4,00 of Turkish army near Damascus. Almost ends campaign in Palestine. Turkey surrenders on 30 Oc

11 Nov. Armistice with Germany signed. World Wa I ends. Of a total Aust. force of 417,000; 329,000 served overseas, 166,819 wounded, 59,342 killed. 6 Australians awarded the Victoria Cross.

During 1918
Cwlth Repatriation Committee estb.

Births & Deaths

Sir Edward John Bunting, public servant, diplomat, b.
Harry Chan, first elected president of NT Legislative Council 15 Dec 1965, b. (d. 1969).
Francis George Hassett, Chief of Defence Force staff b.
Sir Harold Brownlow Martin, air force commander, b.
Maxwell Henry Shean, submarine officer, b.

B
Science, Technology, Transport, Discovery

22 Sep. Ernest Fisk receives first direct overseas radio telephone transmission from England, at Wahroonga, Sydney.
6 Oct. First electric suburban railway in Aust. runs, between Newmarket and Flemington in Melbourne (Essendon–Sandringham line opens on 28 May 1919.)
During 1918
Professors Payne in Melbourne and W. Warren in Sydney conduct aeronautical research into suitable timber for aircraft.

C
Arts

Literature

During 1918
Sir Timothy Augustine Coghlan publishes *Labor and Industry in Australia 1788–1901*; among first accepted serious social and economic histories of Aust.
May Gibbs publishes *Snugglepot and Cuddlepie*.
Norman Lindsay publishes *The Magic Pudding*.
C. J. Dennis publishes *Digger Smith*.

Births & Deaths
Douglas Wright Lockwood, author and journalist, b. (d. 1983)

Music, Dance

During 1918
Nellie Melba made Dame Commander of the British Empire.
Billy Romaine leads first Aust. ragtime jazz band.
Sydney Conservatorium of Music High School founded. (Opens in Apr. 1919.)
The Aust. Music Examination Board estb.

Births & Deaths
Tex Morton, country and western singer, b. (d. 1983)

Drama, Theatre, Film

11 Mar. Film, *The Enemy Within*, starring Reg L. 'Snowy' Baker, premières.

Births & Deaths
Margaret Annette McCrie Johnston, actress, b.
John Neil McCallum, actor producer, b.
Ronald Egan Randell, stage and film actor, b.
Adrian Consett Stephen, playwright, d.

Fine Arts

During 1918
William Frater and Arnold Shore begin Impressionist art movement in Melbourne.
Aust. War Art sent to Grafton Galleries for Exhibition in London.
c. 1918. Fine Arts Society Gallery opens in Melbourne. (Closes in 1940.)

Births & Deaths
Margaret Ruth Adams, sculptor, b.
Leo Jack Little Bainbridge, painter, b.
May Barrie, sculptor, b.
Frederic Bates, painter, b.

1918

Ronald Charles Bell, painter, b.
George Browning, painter, cycloramic artist, b.
Wladyslaw Dutkiewicz, abstract impressionist painter, b.
Gilda Gude, painter, probably b.
Peter Christian Kaiser, painter, b.
Inge King, sculptor, b.
Clifford Last, sculptor, wood carver, b.
Victor G. O'Connor, painter, b.
Louise B. Riggall, painter, b.
Loudon Sainthill, stage designer, b. (d. 1969)
Margaret E. Sinclair, sculptor, b.
James Wigley, painter draughtsman, b.
Reinis Zusters, painter draughtsman, b.

Architecture

During 1918
Spanish style bungalows introduced in WA.
Leslie Wilkinson estb. first School of Architecture at Sydney University.

Births & Deaths
Joern Utzon, architect, b.

E

Sport

During 1918
Night Watch, ridden by W. Duncan, wins Melbourne Cup in record time of 3 minutes $25\frac{3}{4}$ seconds.
South Melbourne football team wins VFL Premiership in Melbourne.
South Sydney football team wins Rugby League Premiership in Sydney.
Aqua-planing introduced as forerunner to water skiing.
The cricket over increased from six to eight balls.

Births & Deaths
Sidney G. Barnes, cricketer, b. (d. 1973)
John Edward Bromwich, tennis player, b.
Ian William Johnson, cricketer, b.
Thelma Long, tennis player, b.
Keith Pix, golfer, b.
Douglas Ring, cricketer, b.

F
Historia Dignum

1918

Population
Estimated total white, 5,080,912.
Cwlth census on 30 Jun. estimated 4,980,565, not including an estimated 75,000–100,000 Aborigines.

20–22 Jan. Cyclone and tidal wave at Mackay, Qld, claim 30 lives.
2 Feb. Tornado damages Brighton, Melbourne.
9–10 Mar. Cyclone damages Innisfail, Qld, and many areas in northern Qld, claiming 17 lives.
23 Mar. Newspaper *Newcastle Sun* estb.
20 Sep. Ship *Undola* sinks near Wollongong, NSW; all on board lost.

During 1918
First Aust. Advertising Convention held, in Brisbane.
Widespread national drought begins. (Ends in 1920.)
The Flame Queen opal discovered at Lightning Ridge, NSW.
Pneumonic influenza epidemic breaks out, claiming 848 lives in Aust.
Sale or possession of ostrich feathers banned.
c. 1918. The brassiere becomes popular with Aust. women. Soon becomes a moral 'must' for all 'decent' women.

1919

A
History, Politics, Economics, Law

Government
17 Apr. 1919–May 1919, Sir H. P. Colebatch Liberal Premier WA.
17 May 1919–Apr. 1924, Sir J. Mitchell National/Country coalition Premier WA.
22 Oct. 1919–Feb. 1925, E. G. Theodore Labor Premier Qld.
1919, H. E. Carey Director NT under Cwlth jurisdiction.
1919–1921, M. S. C. Smith Acting Administrator NT under Cwlth jurisdiction.

Jan. Interstate Trade Union Conference discusses combining all trade unions into One Big Union.
26 Feb. H. E. Jones becomes first director of Cwlth Investigation Branch, incorporating Special Intelligence Branch (estb. in 1916).
24 Mar. Riots in Brisbane result from confrontation between trade unionists demonstrating against the continuance of the War Precautions Act and a large mob led by returned soldiers; 19 men injured before order restored.
Apr. Migration scheme for British exservicemen begins.
9 May–26 Aug. Seamen's strike in Melbourne and Sydney halts most shipping services around Aust.
15 May. AWU publishes manifesto condemning the Workers' Industrial Union as imitation of the American IWW.
During May. Riots at Fremantle, WA, when non-unionists attempt to perform work of striking lumber unionists.
May–Sep. Aust. army joins British units in attempt to defeat Russian Revolution at Archangel.
28 Jun. Peace Treaty signed at Versailles. William Morris Hughes represents Aust. Aust. ratifies the Treaty of Versailles on 10 Sep.
2 Jul. Agreement signed with Britain and NZ for the administration of Nauru. Nauru Island Agreement Act approved on 28 Oct.
During Jul. Commercial Activities Act provides for continuation of war regulations as to dairy products, sugar, wool, flax etc.
15 Oct. Cwlth adopts preferential voting system.
18 Oct. Sir Adrian Knox appointed Chief Justice of the High Court. (Until 31 Mar. 1930.)
8 Dec. Townsville Meat Workers' strike ends after violent rioting on 29 Jun.
13 Dec. William Morris Hughes returned as Nationalist Prime Minister at Federal elections. Referendums held on Constitutional extension of Cwlth powers in wartime legislation and the nationalization of monopolies. Both proposals defeated.

During 1919
King O'Malley retires from politics after election defeat.
Aust. granted C Grade mandate over former Pacific territories, including New Guinea, at Versailles Peace Conference.
Earle Page enters Federal Parlt as member for Cowper, NSW.
E. P. (Paddy) O'Neill leads unsuccessful Broken Hill miners' strike (lasting 18 months) over wages and conditions.
Working days lost because of strikes to now number 6,308,226.
Coastwatchers estb. to detect and report on enemy movements in wartime along N and NW coast of Aust. (Expanded during World War II.)
Wage rate payable to females set at 54 per cent of male Cwlth basic wage.
The Repatriation Commission estb. (Dept of Repatriation opens in 1920, becomes Dept of Veteran Affairs in 1976.)

Births & Deaths
Lance Herbert Barnard, Labor politician, b.
Sir Zelman Cowen, Governor-General, b.
William Ellis Newton, World War II pilot, b. (d. 1943).

B

Science, Technology, Transport, Discovery

13 Aug. Ernest Fisk gives first public demonstration of wireless telephony in Sydney.
21 Aug. Aust. National Research Council estb.
13 Oct. Aust. signs the Convention for the Regulation of Aerial Navigation, in Paris.
During Oct. Aust. Aircraft and Engineering Co. Ltd estb. to promote and sell Aust. aircraft.
12 Nov.–10 Dec. Prize of £10,000 offered by Aust. Govt on 10 Mar. for first aeroplane flight from England to Aust. within minimum time won by Ross and Keith Smith, who flew England to Port Darwin in 27 days 20 hours 20 minutes. About 11,500 miles.
16 Nov. Henry Neilson Wrigley and A. W. Murphy make first south-north aerial crossing of Aust. from Melbourne to Darwin.
16 Dec. A. L. Long makes first aerial crossing of Bass Strait, from Stanley, Tas., to Melbourne.

During 1919
Sir Ross McPherson Smith, aged 26, becomes youngest Aust. to be appointed KBE.
Walter and Eliza Hall Institute Laboratory opens, initially to study snake and other venoms.
Airport at Mascot near Sydney named Kingsford-Smith.
Aust. Institute of Engineers estb.
Oil traces in water lead to first oil drilling in the Canning Basin, WA.
Cliff Howard invents rotary hoe.
Electrocardiography begins at Sydney Hospital.
First Kikuyu grass seeds planted in NSW. First Wimmera rye grass recorded in Vic.

C

Arts

Literature

During 1919
Willam Gosse Hay publishes *The Escape of the Notorious Sir William Heans*.
John Shaw Neilson publishes collection of poems, *Heart of Spring*.

Births & Deaths
Ruth Park, author, journalist. b.

Music, Dance

During 1919
Henri Verbrugghen estb. all-year-round NSW State Orchestra. (Disbanded in 1922.)

Births & Deaths
Raymond Nilsson, tenor, b.
Robert Trumble, composer, b.

Drama, Theatre, Film

During 1919
Films screened in 750 cinemas and theatres throughout Aust.
George Wallace, comedian, joins comedy team 'Dinks and Onkus'.
Raymond Longford produces film *The Sentimental Bloke*; among first Aust. film classics.
Frank Hurley, documentary photographer, makes film, *In the Grip of the Polar Ice*.
Perth Repertory Club stages first performance.

Fine Arts

During 1919
Julian Ashton criticizes post-impressionist painting.
Elioth Gruner paints beach scene, *Tamarama*.
Aust. Arts Club estb. Holds only two exhibitions.
c. 1919. Leroy (Roy) De Maistre, Roland Wakelin and Verbrugghen devise scheme of harmonizing colour with sound, painting first abstracts.
Aust. soldier artists estb. Earl's Court art group in London.

Births & Deaths
Warwick Armstrong, painter, theatre designer, b.
Charles Bannon, painter noted for use of triangular shapes, b.
Jean Mary Bellette, still life figure artist, b.
Charles William Bush, artist, probably b.
Lindsay Edward, painter, mosaic artist, b.

1919

Owen John Garde, portrait painter, b.
Stanislav Halpern, painter, ceramic artist, b.
Francis George Hodgkinson, abstract painter, b.
Irvine Homer, naïve painter, b.
Murray Hugh Latimer, painter, b.
Ivan McMeekin, ceramic artist, b.
Thomas Maxwell Newton, painter and commercial artist, b.
George Olszanski, painter, b.
Betty Pauline Quelhurst, painter, b.
Oliffe Richmond, sculptor, b. (d. 1977)
Douglas Roberts, painter, b.
Eric John Smith, painter, noted for religious themes, b.
Gray Smith, painter, b.
David Edgar Strachan, painter, b. (d. 1970)
Alan Edwin Warren, painter, b.

Architecture

During 1919
The Californian Bungalow popular in post World War I Service Homes Scheme.

Births & Deaths
Robin Gerard Penleigh Boyd, architect, author, b. (d. 1971)

Religion, Learning

During 1919
Bush Church Aid Society founded in Sydney.
Presbyterian Scotch College estb. in Adelaide.
NSW Teachers' Federation estb.
The Aust. College of Physical Education estb. as The Sword Club in Sydney.
First Armenians arrive in Melbourne. Arthur Aginian estb. Armenian church.

E
Sport

During 1919
Artilleryman, ridden by R. Lewis, wins Melbourne Cup in 3 minutes 24½ seconds.
Collingwood football team wins VFL Premiership in Melbourne.
Balmain football team wins Rugby League Premiership in Sydney.
Vigoro first played in Aust.
Aust. Imperial Force Rowing Eight wins trophy which becomes King's Cup.
Fitz Lough becomes first Aust. surf belt champion.

Births & Deaths
Bill Alley, cricketer, b.
Gilbert Roche Andrew Langley, cricketer, noted wicket-keeper, b.
David Henry Lewis, sailor, scientist, author, b.
Keith Ross Miller, cricketer, b.
Raymond Walker Mitchell, international boxing referee, sports commentator, b.
Bob Newbiggen, surf swimmer, b.
Clem Sands, boxer, b.

F
Historia Dignum

Population
Estimated total white, 5,303,574.

13 Jan. Widespread Vic. bushfires begin; claim three lives.
Feb.–Jul. Pneumonic influenza epidemic death rate in Aust. rises to 11,552.
1 Mar. Sir James Joynston Smith estb. *Smith's Weekly* as a broadsheet in Sydney.
1 Jul. Monthly magazine *Aircraft* first published, in Sydney.

During 1919
Six o'clock hotel closing made permanent.
War Service Home Scheme begins, encouraging population to spread into suburbs.
Ribbons and veils become essence of femininity in fashion.
Over 1,000,000 koalas killed in open shooting season.
Stan Cross creates comic strip *The Potts* under title of *You and Me*.

Communities
Ooldea, SA, settled.
Red Cliffs, Vic., estb.

1920

A
History, Politics, Economics, Law

Government
31 Jan. 1920–24 Feb. 1921, Sir William Hill Irvine administered Vic.
3 Feb. 1920–3 Dec. 1920, William Lennon administered Qld.
9 Feb. 1920–16 Apr. 1920, Sir Herbert Nicholls administered Tas.
10 Feb. 1920–9 Jun. 1920, Sir George Murray administered SA.
8 Apr. 1920–Apr. 1924, H. N. Barwell Liberal Premier SA.
9 Apr. 1920–16 Jun. 1924, Sir Francis Alexander Newdigate Newdegate Governor WA.
12 Apr. 1920–Oct. 1921, J. Storey Labor Premier NSW.
16 Apr. 1920–27 Jan. 1922, Sir William Lamond Allardyce Governor Tas.
9 Jun. 1920–30 May. 1922, Sir William Ernest George Archibald Weigall Governor SA.
6 Oct. 1920–8 Oct. 1925, Henry William Forster, Lord Forster, Governor-General Aust.
3 Dec. 1920–27 Oct. 1925, Sir Matthew Nathan Governor Qld.

10 Jan. Aust. becomes original member of the League of Nations.
20 Jan. Aust. Air Corps estb. Replaces Aust. Flying Corps, disbanded in 1919.
22–23 Jan. Country Party founded on a national level. (State branches founded in WA 1914, Qld 1915 and Vic. 1917.)
26 Feb. Eighth Federal Parlt opens. (Dissolution 6 Nov. 1922.)
25 Mar. Tariff resolution adopted to increase duties on goods which could be manufactured in Aust.
19 May. Federal Act makes provision for repatriation of Aust. soldiers.
26 May. Prince of Wales visits Aust.
During May. King George V approves the Aust. Naval Board Flag.
8 Jul. NSW Police Association estb.
10–31 Jul. WA civil servants and teachers strike over salaries. First teachers' strike in Aust.
13 Sep. Industrial Peace Act signed. Amended on 2 Dec.
30 Oct. Communist Party of Aust. founded in Sydney.
11 Nov. Hugh Mahon expelled from Cwlth Parlt for describing the British Empire as 'This Bloody and Accursed Empire'. First and only member expelled from Parlt for expressing anti-British sentiments.
2 Dec. Aliens Registration Act passed.
20 Dec. Mandate of Aust. for German New Guinea, the Bismarck Archipelago, part of Solomon I. and other former German South Pacific islands confirmed and defined by the Council of the League of Nations.

During 1920
Imperial Statistical Conference held in London.
William Henry Donald estb. Chinese Bureau of Economic Information.
Sir Hayden Starke appointed a Justice of the High Court. (Until 1950.)
Royal Commission on basic wage recommends higher rates and automatic wage adjustments.
Groote Eylandt in Gulf of Carpentaria, NT, declared an Aboriginal Reserve.
Hours of work reduced to a 44-hour week in many industries throughout Aust.

Births & Deaths
Hugh Reskymer (Kym) Bonython, company director, jazz musician, speed car driver, b.
Sir Keith Douglas Seaman, SA Governor, b.

B

Science, Technology, Transport, Discovery

8 Jan. Raymond Parer first flies single-engine aircraft from England to Aust. Arrives in Darwin on 2 Aug.
4 Apr. J. Gibson first Sydney to Melbourne paying aircraft passenger.
Jun. Radio telephony transmission and reception demonstrated in Melbourne.
Sep. Act of Parlt estb. Institute of Science and Industry.
16 Nov. Hudson Fysh and P. J. McGinness found Qld and NT Aerial Services Ltd (Qantas in 1934) at Winton, Qld. (Now oldest airline in English-speaking world.)
30 Nov. First east-west transcontinental flight from Melbourne to Perth. F. S. Briggs arrives in Perth on 2 Dec.

During 1920
Prickly pear infests 50 million acres. Cwlth Prickly Pear Board estb.
William Wege invents valveless petrol engine.
'The Australian Six' motor car launched. Assembled at Ashfield, NSW from 75 per cent Aust.-made components. Production stops 1924.
H. G. Hawker Engineering Co. estb.
Subsurface agricultural tile drains used at Mildura, Vic., to cope with salinity problems of Murray R.
Bulk handling of wheat from farms begins in NSW.
A. C. Howard demonstrates his rotary hoe at Gilgandra, NSW.

Births & Deaths

Robert Kerford Morton, biochemist, world authority on enzymes as cause and cure of cancer, b. (d. 1963)

C

Arts

Literature

During 1920
Norman Lindsay publishes *Creative Effort*.
Meredith Atkinson edits *Australia Economic and Political Studies*.
Furnley Maurice (pseudonym of F. L. T. Wilmot) publishes *Ways and Means*.
Hugh McCrae publishes *Colombine*.
William Hardy Wilson publishes *The Cow Pasture Road*.

Births & Deaths

Rosemary de Brissac Dobson, poet and author, b.
Gwen Harwood, poet, b.
Colin Milton Thiele, author noted for children's books, b.
Kathleen (Kath) Walker, Aboriginal poet, b.

Music, Dance

13 Oct. L. Walker sings on demonstration radio in Melbourne; first singer on radio.

Drama, Theatre, Film

21 Feb. Harry Southwell's film, *The Kelly Gang*, released.
19 Jun. Franklyn Barrett's film *The Breaking of the Drought* opens in Melbourne.
24 Jul. Raymond Longford releases first film version of *On Our Selection*.

During 1920
J. C. Williamson Theatres merge with Tait Brothers Co.
Duncan and Pakie Macdougall start Playbox Theatre in Sydney.
Feature film industry thrives. Over 150 films made in Aust. by this time. (Disastrous effect on Aust. theatre.)
Actors Equity of Aust. estb. as The Aust. Federation of Actors.
Wilfred Lucas and Bess Meredith, American filmmakers make three outback western films in Sydney.

Births & Deaths

Hayes Gordon, actor, director, producer, b.
Harold Francis (Hal) Lashwood, actor, comedian television writer and producer, b.
Leo Reginald McKern, actor, b.
Michael Pate, actor, b.

1920

1920

Fine Arts

During 1920
Elioth Gruner paints *The Sovereign River Tenterfield*.
Gayfield Shaw founds Aust. Painters'-Etchers' Society. (Holds first exhibition in Sydney in 1921.)
Bendigo Art Society estb. in Vic.
Raymond Wallis begins Decoration Galleries in Melbourne.
Exhibition of Aust. Art at Burlington House in London.
Michael O'Connell, fabric designer, arrives in Aust.
Western Institute of Art founded in Perth. (Closes after one exhibition.)
c. 1920. Perth School of Art founded.

Births & Deaths
Ronald George Appleyard, SA gallery director, b.
Geoffrey Barwell, graphic artist, probably b.
Josl Bergner, abstract social realist painter, b.
Arthur Merric Bloomfield Boyd, potter, painter, ceramic sculptor, b.
Cecil John Brack, figures and landscape painter, b.
Judy Cassab, portrait painter, b.
Hazen Kenneth Cook, painter, antique restorer, b.
Leonard Gordon Crawford, abstract painter, b.
Mollie Douglas, ceramic artist, b.
Cedric Flower, painter, stage designer, b.
Jack Freeman, social realist painter, b.
Joy Hester, painter, graphic artist, b. (d. 1960)
Jacqueline Hick, painter, b.
Herman Hohaus, sculptor, b.
Alan Ingham, sculptor, b.
Louis Robert James abstract painter, b.
Frederick Jessup, painter, b.
Ronald Hugh Kirk, painter, b.
Robert Klippel, sculptor, b.
David W. J. Lawrence, painter, art organizer, b.
Vane Lindesay, black-and-white artist, b.
George Luke, sculptor, b.
Dawson McDonald, painter, b.
Jean McManus, painter, b.
Charles A. Miller, sculptor, b.
George W. Neville, decorative artist, probably b. (d. 1969)
Keith Nichol, decorative artist, probably b.
Jan Nigro, painter, b.
Lorna Muir Nimmo, painter, graphic artist, b.
William Peascod, painter, b.
Wesley Penberthy, painter, b.
Dick Roughsey, artist, probably b.
Peter Rushforth, ceramic artist, b.
Edwin Tanner Russell, painter, b.
Frederick Schonbach, graphic artist and illustrator, b.
Elsie Margaret Stones, botanical painter, b.
Ernest von Hattum, painter, b.
George Voudouris, painter, commercial artist, b.
Edward Albert Douglas Watson, war artist, b. (d. 1972)

Architecture

During 1920
Melbourne University Architectural Atelier founded.
Florence Taylor becomes first woman architect student in Aust.
c. 1920. Motor car garages estb. in homes.

Births & Deaths
Robin Dods, architect noted for awareness of potential of climate and environment on buildings, b.

D

Religion, Learning

18 Apr. Bahai Faith estb. in Aust., in Sydney.
24 May. First Orthodox Lebanese church consecrated, in Sydney.
7 Nov. Some 10,000 people demonstrate in Melbourne against British decision preventing Archbishop Daniel Mannix from visiting Ireland.

During 1920
State Archive institution estb. in SA. (WA 1923, NSW 1953, Tas. 1956, Qld 1959, Vic. 1973.)
Cwlth Govt estb. Soldiers' Children Education Scheme.

E

Sport

During 1920
Poitrel, ridden by K. Bracken, wins Melbourne Cup in 3 minutes $25\frac{3}{4}$ seconds.
Richmond football team wins VFL Premiership in Melbourne.
Balmain football team wins Rugby League Premiership in Sydney.
Aust. wins two silver and one bronze medal at Antwerp Olympics.
St George Rugby League Football Club estb. in Sydney.
First official handball championships held, in Melbourne.
Ski Club of Aust. estb.
Arch Smith sets world speed motorcycling record.
White water and river canoeing popular.
Robert Spears wins world sprint cycling championship to become first Aust. world professional cycling champion.
Jim Brown, ice hockey player, becomes active.
Squash begins in Qld.

Births & Deaths
Bill Emmerton, long-distance runner, b.
Helen Firth, athlete and high jumper, b.
Desmond Fothergill, VFL footballer, b.
Stan Jones, racing car driver, b. (d. 1973).
Billy Lapin, jockey, b. (d. 1940)
Kelvin David George (Kel) Nagle, golfer, b.
Vic Patrick, boxer, b.
Warwick Selvey, athlete in shot put and discus, b.
Billy Sidwell, tennis player, b.
Tommy Smith, jockey, b.
Arthur Ward, jockey, b.

1920

F

Historia Dignum

Population
Estimated total white, 5,411,297.

2 Feb. Cyclone damages Atherton Tableland, Qld.
3 Aug. Train accident at Hurstville, NSW, claims five lives.
Sep. Barque *Southern Cross* disappears in Bass Strait, claiming 11 lives.
2 Oct. Newspaper *Sunraysia Daily* published at Mildura, Vic.
6 Nov. Timber train crashes near Wokalup, WA, claiming nine lives.

During 1920
Magazine *The Home* first published.
First ski chalet built at Mt Buffalo, Vic.
Stanley Savige estb. Legacy Club to care for children of killed or disabled servicemen.
Aust. Federal Council of Boy Scouts' Association estb.
First kerbside petrol pumps in Aust. installed, in Melbourne.
Some 21,722 cars are registered in Aust.
SA holds one of first Aust. automotive shows, in Adelaide.
Bushfires devastate north-west Tas.
National Roads and Motorists' Association (NRMA) estb. in NSW as branch of National Roads Association. (Becomes NRMA in 1923.)

Births & Deaths
John Frederick Moyes, journalist, b.

Communities
Monto, Qld, probably estb.
Northcliffe, WA, estb.

A
History, Politics, Economics, Law

1921

Government

24 Feb. 1921–7 Apr. 1926, George Edward John Mowbray Rous, Earl of Stradbroke, Governor Vic.
10 Oct. 1921–20 Dec. 1921, J. Dooley Labor Premier NSW.
20 Dec. 1921, Sir G. W. Fuller Nationalist-Progressive Premier NSW. Held office for one day only.
20 Dec. 1921–Apr. 1922, J. Dooley Labor Premier NSW.
1921, E. T. Leane Acting Administrator NT under Cwlth jurisdiction.
1921–1926, F. C. Urquhart Administrator NT under Cwlth jurisdiction.

Jan. The British-Aust. Wool Realization Association estb. to sell Aust. wool.
7 Mar. Cwlth Department of Health estb.
22 Mar. Percy Brookfield, member for Broken Hill in NSW Legislative Assembly, shot dead by maniac.
31 Mar. Richard Williams founds Royal Aust. Air Force (RAAF).
Mar. WA Govt inaugurates first group settlement scheme, in south-western WA, to develop dairy industry.
9 May. Civil administration estb. in New Guinea and other islands under mandate.
27 Oct. Qld Legislative Council votes itself out of existence. (Qld becomes only State without an Upper House in 1922.)
Oct. Labor Party endorses policy of socialization of industry, production, distribution and exchange.
15 Dec. Tariff Board estb. to curb overseas competition with protective tariffs and to assist local manufacturing industries. Designed to protect producers against foreign dumping of cheap goods by providing for preference to goods shipped from UK to Aust. and for reciprocal tariff agreements with other countries.
16 Dec. Arbitration Court adopts principle of adjusting wages in accordance with fluctuations in the cost of living as shown by the statistician's quarterly index numbers.

During 1921
Edith Cowan, Nationalist, elected to Legislative Assembly of WA, becoming first woman member of any Aust. Parlt.
First State Electricity Commission estb., in Vic. (Tas. 1929, Qld 1938, WA and NSW 1945 and SA 1946.)
Imperial Conference held in England.
Commercial production of sandalwood oil begins in WA.
Amalgamated Printing Trades Employees' Union estb. (Becomes Federal Union in 1944.)
Martin Richard Mark Freney founds Kimberley Oil Co., among earliest oil search development groups.
Horwitz Group Books, publishers, estb.
Manufacturing employees out-number those in primary production for first time.
Surge of Italian migration to Aust. begins.
The Australasian Transport Officers' Federation estb.

Births & Deaths

Kenneth Baillieu Myer, company chairman, b.
Sir Edward Stratten Williams, judge, b.

1921

B
Science, Technology, Transport, Discovery

Jul. Springleigh bore in Qld completed. (Deepest water bore in Aust.)
7 Aug. First circumnavigation of Aust. by air.
22 Sep. A Royal Commission recommends a uniform Aust. railway gauge (4 feet 8½ inches).
Oct. AWA begins weekly wireless concerts in Melbourne.
5 Dec. Norman Brearley issued with first post-war commercial pilots licence in Aust. Starts MacRobertson-Miller aviation line (WA Airways) at Wyndham, WA, beginning first successful commercial air mail service in British Cwlth. Inaugural flight Geraldton to Carnarvon, WA.

During 1921
Longreach, Qld, becomes first aircraft production centre in Aust.
Walter Bassel estb. first aeronautical laboratory, at Melbourne University.
Essendon airport estb. in Melbourne.
Rice first cultivated at Yanco Experimental Farm, NSW.
Navigation Act passed, enforcing compulsory radio transmitters for all vessels over 1,600 tons.
Hydraulic lifts begin to replace mechanical varieties.
Sugar-cane harvester patented.
Melbourne Gas Co. constructs first all-welded gasometer in world.
John Lysaght estb. rolling steel mill at Newcastle, NSW.
Cwlth Govt shipping line begins passenger services between England and Aust.
The Ford Motor Co. begins assembling cars in Aust.

C
Arts

Literature

During 1921
C. E. W. Bean publishes first two volumes of *The Official History of Australia in the War of 1914–1918*.
C. J. Dennis publishes *A Book for Kids*.
K. S. Prichard publishes *Black Opal*.
Patrick J. Hartigan (John O'Brien) publishes *Around the Boree Log*.

Births & Deaths
Russell Reading Braddon, author, b.
Maxwell Hemby Harris, author, art critic, journalist, b.
Donald Richmond Horne, author, editor, political scientist, b.
Joyce Nicholson, author, b.
Ivan Francis Southall, author, children's writer, b.

Music, Dance

22 Jan. Gladys Moncreiff first sings in musical, *The Maid of the Mountain*, in Melbourne.

Births & Deaths
Raymond Edward Price, musician, b.

Drama, Theatre, Film

3 Dec. Frank Hurley's documentary film *Pearls and Savages* opens in Sydney.
During 1921
Greghan McMahon estb. the Sydney Repertory Co.
Ray Allsop shoots first synchronized sound film in Aust.

Fine Arts

During 1921
W. B. McInnes wins first Archibald Prize for *Desbrow Annear*.
Edward A. Vidler founds Australian Institute of Arts and Literature in Melbourne.
Ella Lilian Pedersen, painter and designer, arrives in Aust.
Qld Authors' and Artists Society founded.
School of Fine Arts founded in Adelaide.
Aust. Society of Painters–Etchers holds first exhibition.

Births & Deaths
William Allen Baker, painter, b.
Lindsay Sorel Churchland, painter, b.

Ludwig Dutkiewicz, abstract painter, b.
Roy George Herbert Fluke, painter, b.
Douglas A. Green, painter, b.
Paul Jones, flower painter, b.
Julius Kane, sculptor, b. (d. 1962)
Henri Le Grande, potter, b.
Peter Fletcher Miller, realist painter, b.
Ailsa O'Connor, sculptor, b.
Jeffrey Smart, realist painter, b.
John Anthony Tuckson, art organizer, b. (d. 1973)
Margaret Tuckson, ceramic artist, b.
Guy Wilkie Warren, painter, b.

Architecture

Births & Deaths

Harold Bryce Mortlock, architect, b.

Religion, Learning

During 1921
The United Evangelical Lutheran Church of Aust. estb. (Renamed Lutheran Church of Aust. in 1966.)

1921

E
Sport

During 1921

Sister Olive, ridden by E. O'Sullivan, wins Melbourne Cup in 3 minutes 27¾ seconds.
Richmond football team wins VFL Premiership in Melbourne.
North Sydney football team wins Rugby League Premiership in Sydney.
First national diving championships held.
First speedway motorcycles race held, on one-mile dirt track at Penrith, NSW.
The Goodall Cup for ice hockey estb.
First WA Aust. Rules Football Sandover Medal awarded for best and fairest player.

Births & Deaths

Forbes Carlile, swimming coach, b.
Clarence Edgar Mick Harvey, cricket umpire, b.
Raymond Russell Lindwall, cricketer and noted fast bowler, b.
Merv McIntosh, WA Aust. Rules footballer, b.
Dinny Pails, tennis player, b.
Jack Purtell, jockey, b.
Jack Thompson, jockey, b.
Colin Windon, Rugby Union footballer, b.

F
Historia Dignum

Population

Estimated total white population 5,510,944.
Second Cwlth census on 4 Apr. estimates white population at 5,435,734 and full-blooded Aboriginal population at 60,000.

13 Jan. Fire destroys over 10 buildings in Perth.
21 Jan. Cyclone moves from Roebourne, WA, to Geraldton, WA, causing widespread damage.
25 Jun. Ship *Our Jack* sinks off Manning R., NSW, claiming five lives.
26 Jun. Ship *Fitzroy* sinks in gale off Manning R., NSW, claiming 30 lives.
19 Sep. Mining disaster at Mt Mulligan, Qld. Coal dust explosion claims 76 lives.
5 Dec. First regular internal Aust. air mail service estb., between Geraldton and Derby, WA.
6 Dec. Goldmine accident at Kalgoorlie, WA, claims six lives.
13 Dec. Fire destroys Kirribilli Wool Stores in Sydney.

During 1921

James Charles Bancks, cartoonist, creates Ginger Meggs character. First published in colour supplement of Sydney's *Sunday Sun*.
SA Motor Association raises speed limit for cars to 2 miles per hour in cities.
The first 'Golden Gate' soda fountain opens in Sydney.
The Eton cut; bobbed hair comes into fashion.
Bubonic plague outbreak begins in Sydney. (1921–1922, 161 cases, 73 deaths.)
First Aust. Rotary Clubs estb., in Sydney and Melbourne.
Number of horses in Aust. reaches estimated peak of 2.5 million.
Barnardo's Homes for underprivileged children begun in Sydney.
Bushfires devastate north-east Tas.
Widespread floods affect north-east NSW, north Vic. southern Qld, and northern SA.
First direct radio press message received from England.

Communities

Barmera, SA, estb.
Margaret River, WA, estb.
Tea Tree Well, NT, estb.

A

History, Politics, Economics, Law

1922

Government

28 Jan. 1922–22 Dec. 1924, Sir Herbert Nicholls and, during his illness, Mr Justice Ewing administered Tas.

13 Apr. 1922–Jun. 1925, Sir G. W. Fuller Nationalist-Progressive Premier NSW.

24 Apr. 1922–4 Dec. 1922, Sir George Murray administered SA.

12 Aug. 1922–Aug. 1923, J. B. Hayes Nationalist-Country coalition Premier Tas.

4 Dec. 1922–4 Dec. 1927, Sir George Tom Molesworth Bridges Governor SA.

9 Feb. Aust.'s only battle-cruiser, HMAS *Australia*, placed on reserve as result of Washington Conference Agreement. Crew of 450 dismissed.

14 Feb. Tas. women become eligible for election to State Parlt.

22 Feb. Economic Conference of representatives of capital and labour in Sydney fails to reach agreement.

23 Mar. Qld Legislative Council ceases to exist, Qld thus becoming only Aust. State with one House of Parlt.

3 Jul. 'New Staters' group meets in Albury, NSW, to discuss subdividing four of the existing States into smaller ones.

1 Sep. Reciprocal tariff agreement between Aust. and NZ comes into effect.

25 Sep. The Empire Settlement Act comes into force. Encourages assisted immigration for British migrants to Aust.

During Sep. NT first represented in Federal Parlt. Has member in House of Representatives without voting rights.

10 Dec. William Morris Hughes returned as Nationalist Prime Minister at Federal elections. Matthew Charlton Labor Opposition leader. (Until 1928.)

During 1922

Qld first State to abolish capital punishment.

Michael Francis Forde enters Federal Parlt.

G. F. Pearce represents Aust. on British delegation at Washington at Four Powers Pacific Treaties Conference.

Aust. Consolidated Industries Ltd incorporated.

Francis J. E. Beaurepaire starts Beaurepaire Tyre Service in Melbourne.

Melbourne University Press estb. (Other University Presses estb. Qld 1948, WA 1953, Sydney 1964 and ANU 1966.)

Cwlth Arbitration Court awards payment of sick leave. Initially six days per year.

Aust. rice industry founded at Leeton, in Murrumbidgee Irrigation Area, NSW.

Births & Deaths

Alan George Moyes, company director, b.

Lionel Keith Murphy, High Court Justice, Federal politician, b.

Alan Bishop Stretton, military commander, lawyer, b.

Neville Thomas Bonner, Aboriginal Senator, b.

1922

B
Science, Technology, Transport, Discovery

13 Mar. First Aust.-built airliner, the *AAEC BI*, demonstrated at Mascot in Sydney.
6 Apr. First air route estb. between Derby and Geraldton, WA.
Apr. Broken Hill Proprietary Co. closes steel works in NSW for 13 months.
21 Sep. Solar eclipse across Aust. lasts 6.1 minutes.
Dec. Qantas, as Qld and NT Aerial Services Ltd, begins first regular service, between Charleville and Cloncurry, Qld.

During 1922
Tractors begin to take over work of horses.
Michael Terry first to cross Aust. by car—from Winton, Qld, to Broome, WA.
Lou Benjamin pioneers making paper from eucalyptus.
Standards Association of Aust. founded as Cwlth Engineering Standards Association.
The Murray Multiplex telegraphic system first used, between Sydney and Melbourne.

Births & Deaths
Harry Messel, physicist, b.
Leo Port, engineer, b. (d. 1978)

C
Arts

Literature

During 1922
Who's Who in Australia first published, in Melbourne.

Births & Deaths
Clement Byrne, author and editor, b.
Geoffrey Piers Henry Dutton, author, biographer, b.

Music, Dance

During 1922
John Francis (Jack) O'Hagan writes song 'Along the Road to Gundagai'.

Births & Deaths
Leonard Bruce Hungerford, pianist, b. (d. 1977)
Donald Smith, tenor, b.
Felix Werder, composer, b.

Drama, Theatre, Film

May. Raymond Longford and Lottie Lyell form film company Longford–Lyell Aust. Productions.
During 1922
Vance Palmer, Louis Esson and Stewart Macky estb. The Pioneer Players in Melbourne.
Doris Fitton founds Independent Theatre Co. in Sydney.

Births & Deaths
Gordon Chater, actor noted for revue type shows, b.
Raymond Evenor Lawler, playwright, b.
Leonard Teale, actor, b.
Ric Prichard Throssell, playwright and diplomat, b.

Fine Arts

During 1922
W. B. McInnes wins Archibald Prize for *Harrison Moore*.
Bertram MacKennal, sculptor, becomes member of Royal Academy.
Collectors and Connoisseurs' Society of NSW estb. (Disbanded in 1925.)

Births & Deaths
Tate Adams, painter, graphic artist, b.
Owen Broughton, sculptor, b.
Mitty Lee Brown, painter, b.
William Coleman, painter, b.
Ray Austin Crooke, landscape painter, b.
Max Dimmack, painter, b.

D

Religion, Learning

Patricia Enalund, potter, b.
Paul Desmond Fitzgerald, portrait painter, b.
Klaus Friederberger, graphic artist, painter, b.
Samuel Sydney Fullbrook, painter, b.
Roger Johnson, painter, architect, b.
Vincas Jomantis, sculptor, b.
Gunars Jurjans, painter, television designer, b.
Max Middleton, portrait and landscape painter, b.
Ronald Millen, painter, b.
Joseph Stanislaw Ostoja-Kotkowski, painter, industrial designer, b.
Margaret Priest, sculptor, b.
John Thomas Rigby, painter, b.
Kenneth Rowell, stage designer, painter, b.
Richard Edric Scarvell, painter, b.
Milan Vojsk, sculptor, b.
Frank Werther, landscape painter, b.
Teisutis Zikaras, sculptor, b.

During 1922
Melbourne Kindergarten Teachers' College opens.
Methodist William Powell Home for Discharged Prisoners opens in Brisbane.
Aust. Association of Psychology and Philosophy estb.
Aust. Teachers' Federation estb.
Caulfield Technical School (now Caulfield Institute of Technology) opens in Melbourne.

1922

E
Sport

During 1922
King Ingoda, ridden by A. Wilson, wins Melbourne Cup in 3 minutes 28¼ seconds.
Fitzroy football team wins VFL Premiership in Melbourne.
North Sydney football team wins Rugby League Premiership in Sydney.
First Aust. soccer Test matches played in NZ.
First interstate water polo matches played for the Regal Cup.
Alfred Goullet becomes noted all-round cyclist.
J. M. Gregory scores fastest ever Test cricket century, in 70 minutes, against South Africa.
Surf Life Saving Association of Aust. estb.
Swimmer Frank Beaurepaire sets 14 world records; has won over 200 titles.

Births & Deaths
Fred Atkins, wrestler, b.
Douglas Bachli, golfer, b.
Cyril Burke, Rugby Union player, b.
Don Cordner, VFL footballer, b.
Magnus Halvorsen, yachtsman, b.
Jack Hoobin, road cyclist, b.
William Arras Bill Johnston, cricketer, noted fast medium bowler, b.
Tony McAlpine, motorcyclist, b.
Noel McGrowdie, jockey, b. (d. 1962)
Arthur Robert Morris, cricketer, noted left-hand batsman, b.
Geoffrey Murphy, better known as Tommy Burns, welterweight boxer, b.
Percy (Ritchie) Sands, boxer, b.

F
Historia Dignum

Population
Estimated total white, 5,637,286.
Estimated Aboriginal, c. 72,000.

6 Jan. Newspaper *Labor Daily* (so-named on 23 Jan. 1924) published as the Sydney *Daily Mail*.
13 Apr. Sir Ross Smith and J. M. Bennett, airmen, killed at Brooklands, Qld, while testing an aircraft.
24 Apr. Colin Campbell Ross hanged in Melbourne for the 'Gun Alley Murder'. (Committed in Dec. 1921.)
11 Sep. Newspaper *Sun News Pictorial* estb. in Melbourne.

During 1922
Aust. Chess Federation estb.
Women begin to smoke cigarettes in public.
Bobbed and shingled women's hair styles popular; cloche hats fashionable.
Straight tubular dresses showing no bust, waist or hipline popular.
Smith Family Welfare Organization estb. in Sydney.
Jack Chalmers and Frank Beaurepaire receive first two Meritorious Awards, for rescuing a swimmer at Coogee, NSW. Beaurepaire estb. car tyre business with reward of £500 for the rescue.
Florence Gordon, Grace Emily Munro and Richard Arthur estb. first Aust. Country Women's Association, to help women and children in country areas NSW.
Drought affecting many parts of Aust. begins. (Ends in 1929.)

Communities
Mukinbudin, WA, estb.
Yallourn, Vic., estb.

A

History, Politics, Economics, Law

Government

9 Feb. 1923–22 Oct. 1929, Fifteenth Cwlth Ministry, Stanley Melbourne Bruce Nationalist-Country coalition Prime Minister Aust.

14 Aug. 1923–Oct. 1923, Sir W. H. Lee Nationalist Premier Tas.

16 Sep. 1923–27 Feb. 1924, Sir William Cullen administered NSW.

25 Oct. 1923–Jun. 1928, J. A. Lyons Labor Premier Tas.

28 Feb. Ninth Federal Parlt opens. (Dissolution 3 Oct. 1925.)

23 Mar. Special Federal Tribunal in Sydney rejects demands of NSW, Vic., Qld and Tas. coal operators for reduction of miners' wages by one-third.

May.–Jun. Premiers' Conference agrees to estb. Loans Council to rationalize competition for funds on the Aust. and London money markets and to co-ordinate borrowings by Federal and State Govts. (Becomes statutory body in 1928.)

Jun. NSW ALP agrees to include Communists in its membership. Motion rescinded in Oct. because of adverse reaction from parliamentarians.

Aug. Work commences on site of Federal Parlt House in Canberra.

1 Sep. Air Force Act estb. regulations for organization of Royal Aust. Air Force.

31 Oct. Melbourne police strike for five days against principle of plain-clothes officers supervising constables. Rioting and looting break out in Melbourne; streets terrorized by mobs.

During 1923

Qld Govt introduces first unemployment benefits scheme.

State branches of Women's Council form a National Council to promote reform.

Imperial Conference in London decides to estb. a naval base at Singapore. Seen as fundamental to Empire defence.

George A. Bond estb. cotton manufacturing in Sydney, beginning modern cotton industry in Aust. Federal Govt increases cotton growing acreage and guarantees minimum price.

Marie Beuzeville Byles becomes one of first women solicitors admitted to practise in NSW. Noted for work on conservation.

Aust. begins exporting sugar.

Births & Deaths

Frank Knopfelmacher, social scientist, commentator, b.

Sir Ninian Martin Stephen, Governor-General Aust., b.

B

Science, Technology, Transport, Discovery

1923

Jan. George A. Taylor estb. the Association for the Development of Wireless in Aust. NZ and Fiji.

Mar. John Campbell Miles discovers silver and lead at Mt Isa, Qld.

28 Jul. Preparations for the construction of Sydney Harbour Bridge begin. John Bradfield appointed supervisor.

30 Oct. (to 20 Apr. 1924) temperatures at Marble Bar, WA, exceed 100°F. (37.8°C.) for 161 consecutive days. (Longest recorded consecutive period of temperatures above 100°F.)

23 Nov. At 8.00 pm regular radio broadcasting using sealed-set system officially begins with 2SB (later 2BL) radio station transmitting a concert from studios of Sydney Broadcasters Ltd.

1 Dec. Townsville–Mt Isa, Qld, railway opens.

During 1923

Inigo Jones makes first significant long-range weather forecasts.

First electric lifts installed in Melbourne.

Walter Hume invents method of curving sheet metal to make pipes and tubular products.

National Museum of Aust. Zoology estb.

First meeting of Aust. Medical Congress.

Frederick Walker first produces vegemite.

Aust. Nursing Federation estb.

Cwlth agrees to provide aid for construction of State roads.

Edward Holden estb. factory to manufacture motorcar bodies in Adelaide.

Last horse-drawn trams run in Melbourne.

Construction of Maylands Aerodrome in Perth begins.

Sydney–Brisbane telephone trunk line opens.

WA wheat variety Nabawa found to be resistant to flag smut disease.

Cwlth Serum Laboratories in Melbourne begin producing insulin.

1923 C

Arts

Literature

May. Literary quarterly *Vision* first published, in Sydney.
During 1923
Ex-Libris Society founded in Sydney.
Jack Lindsay and Kenneth Slessor publish *Poetry in Australia*.
John (Jack) Moses publishes poem 'Nine Miles from Gundagai' in collection for verse and short stories, *Beyond the City Gates*
D. H. Lawrence writes *Kangaroo* while living at Thirroul, NSW.
A Sydney branch of the English Association estb. to facilitate study of Aust. literature.

Births & Deaths
Charmian Clift, author, journalist, b. (d. 1969)
Gerald Marcus Glaskin, author, playwright, b.
Dorothy Hewett, poet, playwright, b.
Nancy Keesing, poet and writer, b.
W. N. (Bill) Scott, poet, b.

Music, Dance

During 1923
Essie Ackland becomes noted vocalist.
Arundel Orchard becomes director of NSW Conservatorium

Births & Deaths
Donald Oscar Banks, composer, lecturer, b. (d. 1980)
Elizabeth Fretwell, soprano, b.
John Lanchbery, conductor, composer, b.
Noel Newton-Wood, pianist, b. (d. 1953)

Drama, Theatre, Film

Births & Deaths
Robin Casper Lovejoy, stage actor, producer, b.
Eleanor Witcombe, playwright noted for children's theatre, b.

Fine Arts

During 1923
W. B. McInnes wins Archibald Prize for *Portrait of a Lady*.
Aust. art exhibition at Royal Academy in London.
Cwlth Govt conducts ANZAC Memorial sculpture competition for an equestrian work in commemoration of ANZAC light horse cavalry achievements in Palestine during World War I.
European Contemporary Pictures Exhibition tours Aust.
United Arts Club estb. in Adelaide.
G. Rayner Hoff, modernist sculptor, arrives in Sydney.

Births & Deaths
Uldis Abolins, watercolourist, b.
David Edward Armfield, painter, b.
Ian Armstrong, painter, b.
Guy Martin Boyd, sculptor, b.
Rex Bramleigh, painter, b.
Marc Clark, sculptor, painter, b.
Herbert Flugelman, abstract painter, sculptor, b.
Quentin Hole, painter, theatre designer, b.
Graeme Inson, painter, b.
Aina Regina Jaugietis, sculptor, b.
Ronald Lambert, contemporary painter, b.
Bryant McDiven, painter, sculptor, b.
Alan Martin, portrait painter, b.
Joe Mason, sculptor, b.
Gael Elton Mayo, artist, writer, b.
Jon Molvig, expressionist painter, b. (d. 1970)
Margaret Hannah Olley, portrait painter, b.
Geoff O'Loughlin, painter, commercial artist, b.
Robert Parr, sculptor, b.
John Perceval, painter potter, ceramic sculptor, b.
Ieva Pocius, sculptor, b.
Richard Murray Scales, painter, b.
Anthony Underhill, painter, b.
Bronwyn J. D. Yeates, painter, b.
John Yule, painter, b.

Architecture

During 1923
John Murdoch, architect, draws up plans for temporary Parlt House in Canberra.

Births & Deaths
Harry Seidler, contemporary architect noted for using modern materials, b.

D
Religion, Learning

During 1923
First religious radio broadcasting begins.

E
Sport

1923

Oct. Aust. Soccer Association founded. (Becomes Aust. Soccer Federation in 1963.)
15 Dec. Maitland motorcycle speed racing track estb. in NSW.
During 1923
Bitalli, ridden by A. Wilson, wins Melbourne Cup in 3 minutes $24\frac{1}{4}$ seconds.
Essendon football team wins VFL Premiership in Melbourne.
Eastern Suburbs football team wins Rugby League Premiership in Sydney.
Crowd of 47,000 at China–Aust. soccer match in Sydney.
SA and Qld Table Tennis Associations estb. (Vic. 1925, NSW 1930.)
Doomben racecourse opens in Brisbane.
Warwick Farm racecourse purchased for horseracing in Sydney.
Brisbane Amateur Turf Club estb.
Vic. Women's Cricket Association estb. (NSW 1927, SA 1930, WA 1931.)
Johnny Hoskins promotes speedway motorcycle racing as popular sport.

Births & Deaths

Harry Berwick, golfer, b.
Garnet Bougoure, jockey, b.
Lionel Cooper, Rugby League footballer, b.
Bill Hutchison, VFL footballer, b.
Len Luckey, racing car driver, b.
George Moore, jockey, b.
Athol George Mulley, jockey, b.
Frank Parsons, soccer player, b.
Lou Richards, VFL footballer and sports commentator, b.
Neville Sellwood, jockey, b.
Bill Williamson, jockey, b. (d. 1979)

1923

F

Historia Dignum

Population
Estimated total white, 5,755,986.

23 Mar.–9 Apr. Cyclone damages area surrounding Gulf of Carpentaria.

Mar. Sir John Gellibrand estb. Legacy Club in Hobart as the Remembrance Club. Melbourne Legacy Club estb. in Sep.

Apr. Henry McEwan arrested in Vic. Becomes first convicted drug trafficker in Aust.

2 Jul. The newspaper *Daily Guardian* published in Sydney.

24 Jul. The newspaper *News* begins publication in Adelaide.

1 Sep. Mine explosion at Bellbird Colliery, near Cessnock, NSW, claims 21 lives.

During 1923
Waist line on dresses drops.
The Wattle Park Palais de Danse at St Kilda, Melbourne, claims to have largest soda fountain in Southern Hemisphere.
Eskimo Pie icecream reaches Aust.
Farmer and Co. Ltd receive first Aust. Govt broadcasting licence in Aust.
Vic. police first in world to use a two-way radio communication system, between headquarters and patrolling vehicles.

Communities
Mt Isa, Qld, first settled
Surfers Paradise, Qld, estb.

A
History, Politics, Economics, Law

1924

Government
28 Feb. 1924–8 Apr. 1930, Sir Dudley Rawson Stratford De Chair Governor NSW.
16 Apr. 1924–Aug. 1926, J. Gunn Labor Premier SA.
16 Apr. 1924–Apr. 1930, P. Collier Labor Premier WA.
28 Apr. 1924–Jul. 1924, Sir A. J. Peacock National Premier Vic.
17 Jun. 1924–27 Oct. 1924, Sir Robert Furse McMillan administered WA.
18 Jul. 1924–Nov. 1924, G. M. Prendergast Labor Premier Vic.
28 Oct. 1924–8 Jun. 1931, Sir William Robert Campion Governor WA.
18 Nov. 1924–May. 1927, J. Allan Country-National Premier Vic.
23 Dec. 1924–23 Dec. 1930, Sir James O'Grady Governor Tas.

Feb. Loans Council estb. to co-ordinate Federal, State and Local Govt loans.
13 Mar. Aust. Govt disappointed at British decision not to proceed with naval base at Singapore. Aust. supported naval base as a defence against Japanese.
Mar. The Barrier Industrial and Political Council estb. in Broken Hill to unite Broken Hill Trades and Labor Council with local ALP.
4 Apr. Criminal Code of Tas. enacted.
12 Apr. HMAS *Australia* sunk in accordance with provisions of Washington Naval Treaty.
25 Jul. Cwlth Govt introduces compulsory voting at Federal elections. (Compulsory voting at State elections introduced in Vic. 1926, NSW and Tas. 1928.)
Aug. Directorate of Commonwealth Bank appointed. Bank becomes more independent of the Federal Govt.

During 1924
Richard Gardiner Casey appointed first Aust. Liaison Officer in England.
Federal Capital Commission appointed to manage construction of Canberra. (Commission abolished in 1930.)
First land leases sold in Canberra.
Qld Govt introduces a 44-hour week (NSW 1925, WA 1927.)
Export trade in sugar estb.
First commercial production of rice at Yanco experimental farm, near Leeton, NSW.
Aust. has exported two million koala pelts from eastern States, resulting in near extinction of koalas in Vic. and NSW.
Aust. Dairy Corporation (so named 1975) estb., as Aust. Dairy Produce Board.

Woolworths Ltd founded and incorporated in Sydney.
Wine bounty increases exports.
Peanut Marketing Board estb. in Kingaroy, Qld.
Advertising introduced into radio broadcasting.
Mt Isa Mines Ltd Estb.

Births & Deaths
Horace William Madden, military officer, b. (d. 1951)

1924

B
Science, Technology, Transport, Discovery

10 Jan. Sydney radio station 2 FC officially opens. In Melbourne 3 AR opens on 26 Jan; 6 WF Perth opens on 4 Jun.
During Jan. RAAF Aeronautical Research Station estb. at Randwick, Sydney.
24 Mar. Dorman Long and Co. appointed to build Sydney Harbour Bridge.
6 Apr.–19 May. Stanley J. Goble and Ivor McIntyre make first flight around Aust., in an RAAF Fairey III D seaplane, in 44 days.
Apr. George Taylor proposes to estb. *A* class radio stations (financed by listener fees) and *B* class radio stations (financed by advertising). On 7 Nov. 2 BL Sydney opens as first *B*-class licensed station.
15 Jun. Electricity from Yallourn, Vic., power station first reaches Melbourne.
25 Jul. First oil discovery in Aust. made, at Lake Bunga, Vic.
7–29 Aug. H. C. Brinsmead, E. J. Jones and R. Buchanan make first landplane flight around Aust., in a DH50A.
Aug. Last Cobb & Co. coaches run in Qld, on Yeulba–Surat link.
Oct. Farmer and Co. estb. the Broadcasting Co. of Aust. (3LO Melbourne).
Dec. Qld's coastal railway to Cairns completed.
During 1924
Qantas flies first cabin aircraft.
WA Naturalists' Club estb. in Perth.
Radio broadcasting rapidly expands.
Crystal radio sets become popular.
Car radios introduced.
Hedlic Taylor invents first fully self propelled auto header (harvester).
Direct telephone operator dialling estb. on some trunk routes in Vic.
Waite Agricultural Research Institute estb. in Adelaide.
D. Davis begins manufacturing gramophone records, using Brunswick label.

Births & Deaths

Stephen Spurling, Tas. photographer, d.
Eric Worrell, herpetologist noted for work on snake venom, b.

C
Arts

Literature

During 1924
Kenneth Slessor publishes 'Thief of the Moon'.
Nettie Palmer publishes *Modern Australian Literature 1900–23*.
Associated Booksellers of Aust. and NZ estb. (Now Australian Booksellers Association.)

Births & Deaths

David Harold Rowbotham, poet, author, journalist, b.

Music, Dance

During 1924
Evelyn Scotney and Elsa Stralia, singers, tour Aust.
Nellie Melba's Aust. farewell appearance broadcast.
The Melbourne Sun Aria (Royal South Street Competition) singing competitions estb.
Henry Tate publishes monograph *Australian Musical Possibilities*.

Births & Deaths

Harold Blair, tenor, first Aboriginal to gain diploma in USA, b. (d. 1976)
Elsie Jean Morrison, soprano, b.

Drama, Theatre, Film

During 1924
Vance Palmer produces *The Black House and Other Plays*.
Picture theatres Wintergarten in Brisbane, Prince Edward in Sydney and Capital in Melbourne open.

Births & Deaths

Bobby Limb, stage radio and television entertainer, b.
John Hackman Sumner, stage director, b.

Fine Arts

25 Mar. Aust. Watercolour Institute founded in Sydney.
During 1924
W. B. McInnes wins Archibald Prize for *Miss Collins*
Tom Alban, Russian-born painter and illustrator, arrives in Aust.
Aust. Society of Black-and-White Artists founded in Sydney.
Exhibition of Aust. paintings and sculpture in Faculty of Arts Gallery in London.

Adrian Feint estb. Grosvenor Art Gallery in Sydney. (Closes 1928.)
Miguel McKinley, artist, exhibits in London.
Art magazine *Undergrowth* published in Sydney. (Until 1930.)
Manly Art Gallery and Art Prizes founded in Sydney.
NSW Society of Artists' Medal first awarded.
Younger Group of Aust. artists estb. in Sydney.

Births & Deaths

Geoffrey Allen, painter, b.
Ojars A. Bisenieks, painter, b.
David Boyd, potter and painter, b.
Raymond Coles, graphic artist, b.
Arch F. Cuthbertson, painter, b.
Stan de Teliga, abstract painter, b.
Robert Henry Dickerson, figurative painter, b.
Stephen Astley Earle, oil painter, b.
Max Grierson, graphic artist, b.
Robert Henderson Grieve, watercolourist, graphic artist, b.
Kenneth William David Jack, painter, graphic artist, b.
Dzems Krivs, painter, graphic artist, b.
Lenton Parr, sculptor, b.
Clifton Ernest Pugh, portrait and landscape painter, b.
William Rutledge, painter, musician, b.
Eve Sandor, graphic artist, illustrator, b.

Architecture

During 1924
William Hardy Wilson publishes *Old Colonial Architecture in NSW and Tasmania*. Revives interest in Aust. Georgian and Colonial architecture.
J. F. W. Ballantyne builds Dixon House, Vic.

Births & Deaths

Peter Burns, architect, designer, typographic painter, b.

D Religion, Learning

7 Mar. The Greek Orthodox Holy Metropolis of Aust. and NZ estb. On 8 Jul. Christophoros Knetes arrives in Aust. as first Metropolitan.

During 1924
University of Melbourne estb. a School of Commerce to train people for business.
Mungo MacCallum becomes first full-time Vice-Chancellor in Aust., at Sydney University.
School radio broadcasts begin in Sydney.
Order of the Star of the East estb. an amphitheatre at Balmoral in Sydney to view Second Coming of Christ. (Seats cost between £5 and £100 each.)
Pembroke Baptist and Congregational School estb. in Adelaide.
Vic. and SA Presbyterian Churches unite.

1924

E
Sport

3 Oct. Amateur Boxing and Wrestling Union of Aust. estb.

During 1924
Blackwood, ridden by P. Brown, wins Melbourne Cup in 3 minutes 26½ seconds.
Essendon football team wins VFL Premiership in Melbourne.
Balmain football team wins Rugby League Premiership in Sydney.
Aust. Rules Football Brownlow Medal first awarded, to Best and Fairest VFL player. First won by E. (Cargie) Greeves of Geelong team.
Aust. wins three gold, one silver and two bronze medals at the Paris Olympics.
Dick Eve becomes only Aust. Olympic diving medal winner.
Andrew (Boy) Charlton wins gold medal in Paris for freestyle swimming (1,500 m event).
James Eve introduces lanes to competition swimming in Aust.
NSW and Qld estb. Aust. Rugby League Board of Control.
Aust. challenges for Davis Cup for first time without NZ representation.
First interstate netball games held.
Canadian Soccer Team first visits Aust. (England 1925.)
Athlete Union of Australasia becomes Amateur Athletic Union of Aust and NZ.

Births & Deaths
Harry Bath, Rugby League player, b.
Geoffrey Brown, tennis player, b.
Arthur Clues, Rugby League footballer, b.
Dennis Cordner, VFL footballer, b.
Lex Davison, racing car driver, b. (d. 1965)
Trygve Halvorsen, yachtsman, b.
Bob Hank, SA Aust. Rules footballer, b.
Colin Hayes, horseracing trainer, b.
Ken Kearney, Rugby Union and League player, b.
George Sands, boxer, b.
John Arthur Winter, athlete, high jumper, b.

F
Historia Dignum

Population
Estimated total white, 5,882,002.

Feb. Vic. bushfires claim 31 lives.
26 Apr. Fire destroys SS *City of Singapore* in Port Adelaide, claiming three lives.
4 Jun. Direct regular airmail services between Adelaide, Sydney and Melbourne begin.

During 1924
Aust. Automobile Association (AAA) estb.
Yellow Cab taxis estb. in Sydney.
Stanley Gillick Drummond estb. Royal Far West Children's Health Scheme, caring for children from western districts of NSW.
Tubular look begins to replace breast and waist coat in men's fashions.
Women's fashions expose ankles for first time.
Some 171,680 cars are registered in Aust.
Royal Aust. Nursing Federation estb.

Births & Deaths
Frank John Partridge, quiz champion, b. (d. 1964)

A

History, Politics, Economics, Law

Government
26 Feb. 1925–Oct. 1925, W. N. Gillies Labor Premier Qld.
17 Jun. 1925–Oct. 1927, J. T. Lang Labor Premier NSW.
8 Oct. 1925–2 Oct. 1930, Sir John Lawrence Baird, Lord Stonehaven, Governor-General Aust.
22 Oct. 1925–May 1929, W. McCormack Labor Premier Qld.
27 Oct. 1925–13 Jun 1927, William Lennon administered Qld.

12 Jan. Riots in Sydney over activities of Shipping Labour Bureau (SLB) to protect strike-breakers during shipping strike. SLB abolished on 28 Feb. as demanded by trade unions.
3 Apr. May Holman becomes first woman Labor member of WA Parlt and of any Aust. Parlt.
6 Apr. Prohibition referendum in WA defeated 64,377 against to 35,806 for.
8 Apr. British and Aust. Govts sign £34 million Agreement for Empire Land Settlement Scheme; to provide loans to State Govts for increasing numbers of assisted immigrants.
30 May. Millicent Preston-Stanley becomes first woman member of NSW Legislative Assembly.
Jun. Aust. Guarantee Corporation estb. to provide finance for purchase of cars.
23 Sep. Cwlth Govt amends Immigration Act to empower deportation of alien agitators causing industrial trouble.
14 Nov. Stanley Melbourne Bruce returned as Nationalist-Country coalition Prime Minister.
3 Dec. Cwlth Govt announces removal of ban against immigration from Germany, Austria, Hungary, Bulgaria and Turkey.
During 1925
NSW Govt passes Acts introducing 44-hour week and widows' pensions.
Rural Credits section of Cwlth Bank estb. to aid primary producers.
Employers in some industries are required to allow apprentices time off during working hours to attend technical classes.
Aust. signs tariff preferences agreement with NZ.

Births & Deaths
Leonard G. Casley, WA pastoralist, b.
Donald Leslie Chipp, Federal politician, b.
William Arthur Neilson, Tas. Premier, b.

B

Science, Technology, Transport, Discovery

1925

26 Jan. First commercial radio station, radio 2UE, opens at Maroubra, NSW.
During Jan. Brisbane–Grafton, NSW, railway, linking Brisbane to Sydney linked with uniform gauge line, completed.
May. Prickly pear infects 26 million hectares. Prickly Pear Board imports *Cactoblastis cactorum* moth from Argentina. (The plant almost eradicated by 1940.)
During 1925
Ford Motor Co. of Aust. Pty Ltd estb. in Vic. to produce Model T Fords.
First coal briquettes made at Yallourn, Vic.
Frank Debenham, becomes founder and first director of Scott Polar Research Institute (UK).
Tas. Hydro Electricity Commission estb.
Electrical microphone recording process reaches Aust.
Five-valve set radio introduced in Aust.
R. S. Falkiner invents sugar-cane harvester.
Petrol-driven buses begin service in Brisbane.
Aboriginal fossil Cohuna skull discovered in Vic.
Vere Gordon Childe publishes *The Dawn of European Civilization*, making new departure in pre-history and archaeology.
An inland wireless system estb.
Automatic telephone exchange opens in Brisbane. (Hobart 1929.)
NSW Dept of Agriculture identifies Bunchy Top disease affecting bananas.

Births & Deaths
Robert Lennox Walker, meteorologist, noted for long-range weather forecasting, b.

1925 C

Arts

Literature

During 1925
Chester Cobb publishes *Mr. Moffat*.
Vol. 1 of First Edition of *The Australian Encyclopaedia* published. Edited by A. W. Jose and H. J. Carter. (Second and final volume published 1926.)
c. 1925. Jack Lindsay and Percy R. Stephenson estb. Fanfrolico Press in Sydney to publish Aust. literature; high standards of typography and binding.

Births & Deaths
Thea Beatrice Astley, author, b.
Leonie Judith Kramer, author, academic, b.
John Russell Rowland, poet and diplomat, b.
Francis Charles Webb, poet, b. (d. 1973)

Music, Dance

During 1925
Sun Aria singing competitions in Geelong and Bendigo, Vic., first held.
Bernard Heinze founds the Melbourne String Quartet.
Frank Coughlan's *Milenburg Joys* becomes first professional jazz record made in Aust. First acoustic jazz recordings made in Melbourne.
NSW Conservatorium estb. an Opera School.

Births & Deaths
Tristram Carey, composer, b.
Alfred Bruce Clarke, musician, composer, pioneer of electronic music in Aust. b.
Albert Lance, tenor, b.
Raymond McDonald, tenor, b.
Sir Alan Charles MacLaurin Mackerras, conductor, b.
Ray Powell, dancer, choreographer, b.

Drama, Theatre, Film

During 1925
There are more than 1,200 cinemas in Aust.
More than 60 films produced in Aust. this year.
Capitol Theatre opens in Melbourne.
Melbourne radio station 3LO broadcasts *The Barbarous Barber*, first radio play in Aust.
Brisbane Repertory Theatre estb.
Cwlth Film Laboratories Ltd (Colorfilm) estb. in Sydney.

Fine Arts

Apr. Aust. War Memorial founded. (Building completed 1941.)
8 Nov. C. Web Gilbert's *Matthew Flinders* bronze memorial unveiled in Melbourne.
During 1925
John Longstaff wins Archibald Prize for *Maurice Moscovitch*.
Aust. Art Exhibition held at Spring Gardens Gallery in London.
Macquarie Art Galleries estb. in Sydney.
United Arts Club estb. in Adelaide.
George H. F. Bell becomes major influence in estb. modern art in Aust.

Births & Deaths
Evelyn Baxter, flower painter, b.
John Coburn, painter, designer, b.
Brian Finemore, art organizer, b. (d. 1975)
Thomas Gleghorn, abstract expressionist landscape painter, b.
Peter Graham, abstract painter, b.
Anne Graham, painter, graphic artist, b.
Gerald Havekes, painter, sculptor, illustrator, b.
Malcolm Horsley, painter, b.
Ena Elizabeth Joyce, painter, b.
David Newbury, painter, b.
John Ogburn, painter, b.
Henry Salkauskas, painter, graphic artist, b.
Tom Sanders, ceramic artist, b.
Max Sherlock, painter, b.
Geoffrey James Spruzen, painter, b.

Architecture

During 1925
Spanish mission-style architecture reaches Aust.

D
Religion, Learning

During 1925
Aust. Forestry School estb. in Adelaide. (Transferred to Canberra in 1927.)
Philip Thomas Byard Clayton estb. Toc H Aust. Inc., an Inter-denominational Christian organization devoted to community service.
Church of England Church Missionary Society estb. Aboriginal Mission at Oenpelli, NT.
Roman Catholics and Protestants united in opposition to attempt by NSW Govt to reform Marriage Act.

E
Sport

May. Amateur Rowing Council estb.
During 1925
Windbag, ridden by J. Munro, wins Melbourne Cup in record time 3 minutes $22\frac{3}{4}$ seconds.
Geelong football team wins VFL Premiership in Melbourne.
South Sydney football team wins Rugby League Premiership in Sydney.
Colin Watson of St Kilda VFL team awarded Brownlow Medal.
Aust. Gold Cup for polo introduced.
Maroubra racing track opens in Sydney.
Aust. Hockey Association estb.
French open tennis championships are opened to non-French countries.

Births & Deaths
Reginald Arnold, cyclist, b.
Brian Bevan, Rugby League player, b.
Victor Bulgin, Rugby League player, golfer, b.
Len (Chic) Cowie, Rugby League player, b.
Charlie Eastes, Rugby Union player, b.
Ken Grieves, soccer player, cricketer, b.
Duncan Hall, Rugby League player, b.
Robert Howe, tennis player, b.
Des Hoysted, race caller, b.
Ken Le Breton, motorcyclist, b. (d. 1951)
Ken MacKay, cricketer, b.
Joe Marston, soccer player, b.
F. (Tiger) Moore, jockey, b.
Shirley Strickland, sprinter and hurdler, b.
Jack Young, speedway rider, b.

1925

F

1925

Historia Dignum

Population

Estimated total white, 6,003,027.

24 Mar. Sydney radio station 2FC broadcasts a parliamentary debate. Possibly first broadcast of kind in the world.
Mar. Cyclone damages Port Hedland, WA.
9 Jun. Train derailment at Traveston, Qld, claims 10 lives.
22 Jul. First regular Sydney–Melbourne airmail service estb.
25 Aug.–30 Dec. Neville Reid Westwood and G. L. Davies first to drive around Aust., in 127 days.
During Nov. The 'Great White Train', travelling exhibition of Aust. made goods, begins year-long tour of NSW to promote 'Buy Australian Made' concept.
During 1925
Richard Linton founds Big Brother Movement to encourage migration of boys from England to Aust.
Murrumbidgee R., NSW, floods.
Short skirts exposing knees cause public controversy.
The Peace Officer Guard estb. to protect Cwlth property.

Births & Deaths

Ronald Ryan, Vic. criminal, b. (d. 1967)

A

History, Politics, Economics, Law

Government

8 Apr. 1926–27 Jun. 1926, Sir William Hill Irvine administered Vic.
28 Jun. 1926–23 Jun. 1931, Arthur Herbert Tennyson Somers Cocks, Lord Somers, Governor Vic.
28 Aug. 1926–Apr. 1927, L. L. Hill Labor Premier SA.
1926–1927, E. C. Playford Acting Administrator NT under Cwlth jurisdiction.

13 Jan. Tenth Federal Parlt opens (Dissolution 9 Oct. 1928.)
Feb. NSW adopts preferential voting system.
16 Mar. Federal Govt amends Cwlth Crimes Act to deal with Communists and others alleged to be subverting peace.
1 Jul. J. McCallum Smith begins secessionist campaign in WA. Secessionist League estb. on 2 Aug.
4 Sep. Referendum on Constitutional amendments to give the Cwlth power to regulate industry and commerce and to carry on public services in event of interruption or threat of interruption defeated.
30 Sep. The Aust. Country Party Association estb. to organize Country Party at Federal level.
19 Oct.–23 Nov. Imperial Conference in London defines Dominion status. All dominions to be equal.

During 1926
North Australia Act divides NT into North Aust., north of 20th parallel, and Central Aust. (Reverts to NT in 1931.)
Development and Migration Commission estb. to examine relationship of industry and labour to migration.
Sidney Myer estb. Myer Emporium in Melbourne.
High Court of Aust. estb. principle that Cwlth awards should take precedence over State awards.

Births & Deaths

Donald Allan Dunstan, SA Premier, b.
Albert Jaime Grassby, politician, b.
Colin Victor James Mason, politician, journalist, author, b.
Sir Billy Mackie Snedden, politician, b.
Neville Kenneth Wran, NSW Premier, b.

B

Science, Technology, Transport, Discovery

1926

1 Mar. First regular electric train services begin in Sydney. Suburban railway system electrified. First section of Sydney underground railway opens on 20 Dec.
May. Council for Scientific and Industrial Research (CSIR) replaces the Institute of Science and Industry.
30 Jun. A. Cobham begins first Aust.–England–Aust. return flight.

During 1926
Alf Traeger and John Flynn estb. tele-radio communications, pedal wireless, at Hermannsburg Aboriginal School in NT. Traeger manufactures pedal wireless used later for Flying Doctor Service.
Inner city electric tram services begin in Melbourne.
Rapid expansion of electrical services changes suburban life.
Five-valve radio with horn speaker introduced.
Sterilization of water supplies begins at Swan Hill, Vic.
Baker Medical Research Institute estb. at Prince Alfred Hospital in Melbourne.
Eggs of *Cactoblastis cactorum* moth released to eradicate prickly pear.
Cwlth Solar Observatory begins observing solar radiation, in ACT.

Births & Deaths

Stuart Thomas Butler, physicist, b.

1926

C

Arts

Literature

During 1926
Arthur Hoey Davis publishes *The Rudd Family*.
Kenneth Slessor publishes *Earth-visitors*.
Katherine S. Prichard publishes *Working Bullocks*.
Chester Cobb publishes *Days of Disillusion*.

Music, Dance

During 1926
Policy of setting up Symphony Orchestras in each State estb.
Columbia makes first electric recording in Aust.
Alexis Dolinoff opens ballet school in Sydney.
Dame Nellie Melba makes her last overseas performance, at Covent Garden.
Anna R. Pavlova, ballerina, tours Aust., giving impetus to status of ballet as an art. Makes Melbourne début on 13 Mar.

Births & Deaths
Bryan Ashbridge, dancer, director, b.
Eric Gross, composer, b.
Dame Joan Sutherland, soprano, b.

Drama, Theatre, Film

25 Jan. Charles Chauvel's first feature film, *The Moth of Moonbi*, premières in Brisbane.
22 Nov. Paulette, Phyllis and Isobel McDonagh make their first film, *Those Who Love*.
During 1926
Australasian Performing Rights Association estb.
St James Theatre opens in Sydney.
Marcus Clarke's *For The Term of His Natural Life* made into film. (Premières on 20 June 1927.)
Hoyts Theatres Ltd estb. under the elder F. W. Thring.

Births & Deaths
Francis William (Frank) Thring, actor, b.

Fine Arts

25 Nov. First Exhibition of Aust. Modern Art, at Grosvenor Gallery in Sydney.
During 1926
W. B. McInnes wins Archibald Prize for *Silk and Lace*.
The 'Contemporary Group' of artists forms in Sydney.
Devon Downs Aboriginal carvings discovered near Swan Reach on Murray R., SA.
Aust. Art Society founded.

Births & Deaths
Mary Boyd, painter, ceramic decorator, b.
Geoffrey Brown, painter, graphic artist, b.
Maurice Cantlon, painter, b.
Mervyn Cassidy, painter, b
Allen David, painter, b.
Erwin A. Guth, ecclesiastic sculptor, b.
George Henry Johnson, painter, b.
Franz Kempf, painter, b.
Jean Langley, graphic artist, painter, b.
Peter Phillip Laverty, painter, b.
Carl McConnell, ceramic artist, b.
Erica Margaret McGilchrist, painter, textile designer, graphic artist, b.
Brian McKay, painter, b.
Milton Moon, ceramic artist, b.
Verdon Longford Morcom, painter, graphic artist, b.
Bernar Sahm, ceramic artist, b.
Gunars Salins, painter b.
Ian Sime, abstract expressionist painter, b.
Ronald Weddell, painter, b.
Kenneth Ronald Whisson, painter, draughtsman, b.

Architecture

During 1926
Terracotta tiles in a variety of baked or ceramic colours shaped and moulded to order become available.

D
Religion, Learning

During 1926
Muresk Agricultural College opens in WA.
Baptist Union of Aust. estb.
Vic. Teachers' Union estb.
Ballarat and Bendigo Teachers' Colleges estb. in Vic.
Dominican Sisters estb. teachers' training at Signadou College of Education in Maitland, NSW.

Births & Deaths
Theodore Delwin (Ted) Noffs, Methodist minister, reformer, b.

E
Sport

During 1926
Spearfelt, ridden by H. Cairns, wins Melbourne Cup in 3 minutes 22¾ seconds before a record crowd of 118,877.
Melbourne football team wins VFL Premiership in Melbourne.
South Sydney football team wins Rugby League Premiership in Sydney.
Ivor Warne-Smith of Melbourne VFL team awarded Brownlow Medal.
First NSW Aust. Rules Football Phelan Medal awarded to best and fairest player in Sydney.
All Aust. Women's Basketball Association estb. to control netball. (Becomes Aust. Netball Association in 1970.)
Trugo game invented at Newport, Sydney.
Squash estb. in Sydney.
Sydney Showgrounds speedway opens.
The Vic. Amateur Canoe Association estb.
Regular motorcycle dirt track racing begins in Sydney.
First organized women's athletic meeting staged in Sydney.

Births & Deaths
Elliott (Elley) Bennett, Aboriginal boxer, b.
Pat Borthwick, golfer, b.
Sir John Arthur (Jack) Brabham, racing car driver, b.
Tom Brooks, Test cricket umpire, b.
Graeme French, cyclist, b.
Harry Gallagher, swimmer, b.
Jack Hassen, boxer, b.
Gordon Ingate, yachtsman, b.
George Maxwell O'Connell, cricket umpire, b.
David Ritchie Sands, Aboriginal boxer, b. (d. 1952)
Jack Sheedy, WA Aust. Rules footballer, b.

1926

1926

Historia Dignum

Population
Estimated total white, 6,124,020.

Jan. Bushfires in NSW burn area between Dubbo and Albury.
Feb. Bushfires in Vic. claim 31 lives.
10 Jun. Train accident at Aberdeen, NSW, claims five lives. Train collision at Murulla, NSW, claims 27 lives on 13 Sep. Train collision at Caulfield, Vic., claims three lives on 29 May.
3 Sep. The *Canberra Times* begins publication in Canberra.
Nov. Mining explosion at Bankstown, NSW, claims three lives.

During 1926
Sydney Guardian organizes first Miss Aust. quest competition. Won by Beryl Mills.
Girl Guides Association of Aust. estb.
Two detectives shot by thieves in WA goldfield murders.
Women begin wearing long pants.
The *Bulletin* publishes *Australian Woman's Mirror* in Sydney. (Lasts until 1961.)
First Sydney Legacy Club estb.
Vegemite first developed commercially, in Melbourne.
The Alice Springs Nursing Home opens.

A

History, Politics, Economics, Law

Government

8 Apr. 1927–Apr. 1930, R. L. Butler Liberal-Country coalition Premier SA.

20 May 1927–Nov. 1928, E. J. Hogan Labor Premier Vic.

13 Jun. 1927–7 Apr. 1932, Sir Thomas Herbert John Chapman Goodwin Governor Qld.

18 Oct. 1927–Nov. 1930, T. R. Bavin Nationalist-Country coalition Premier NSW.

6 Dec. 1927–13 May 1928, Sir George Murray administered SA.

1927–1929, C. A. Cawood Govt Resident Central Aust. (NT) under Cwlth jurisdiction.

1927–1931, R. H. Weddell Govt Resident North Aust. (NT) under Cwlth jurisdiction.

Feb. NSW Govt introduces first child endowment scheme in Aust. (Federal Govt 1941.)

22 Mar. Sir Granville Ryrie appointed to succeed Sir Joseph Cook as Aust. High Commissioner in London.

3 May. Australian Council of Trade Unions (present name 1943) estb. in Melbourne as Australasian Council of Trade Unions. Formed to govern organized trade union movement.

9 May. Transfer of seat of Federal Govt from Melbourne to Canberra. HRH Duke of York opens new Parlt House.

May–12 Sep. Sugar workers at South Johnstone mill in Qld strike over preference of jobs issue.

1–10 Sep. Railway workers strike in Qld. Railway Commissioner dismisses all workers because of union hostility but they are reinstated after signing agreement to obey regulations.

21 Nov.–7 Dec. Dock workers strike in dispute between Waterside Workers Federation and employers. Complete tie up of shipping.

During 1927

ACT Police Force estb.

RAAF takes over Richmond air base.

Emil Voigt becomes founding President of Aust. Federation of Broadcasting Stations.

Aust. Loan Council becomes permanent.

The National Advisory Committee of Employers (later the Interstate Conference of Employers) estb. to campaign against compulsory arbitration.

B

Science, Technology, Transport, Discovery

5 Feb. First Council of the College of Surgeons of Australasia (Royal Australasian College) elected.

8 Apr. High-frequency radio-beam wireless service opens for business. First public Aust.–England overseas radio-telegraph service.

During 1927

Horace Miller estb. MacRobertson-Miller Aviation Co. Ltd in Adelaide. (Taken over by ANA in 1963.)

Cecil Madigan begins geological investigation of last unexplored regions in central Aust.

First power-alcohol distillery in Aust. estb., at Sarina, Qld.

Albert Coates becomes first neurosurgeon in Aust.

All States have Nursing Registration Boards. Nursing officially recognized as a profession.

Pharmacy Guild of Aust. estb.

Lone Pine Koala Sanctuary estb. near Brisbane.

Burrinjuck Dam on Murrumbidgee R., near Yass, NSW, completed. (Enlarged in 1957.)

Rev. John Flynn, backed by Aust. Inland Mission of Presbyterian Church, founds Royal Flying Doctor Service at Cloncurry, Qld. (World's first aerial medical service.) Flynn saw the service as spreading 'a mantle of safety' over the outback. First official flying doctor trip make by Dr George Simpson on 2 Aug. from Cloncurry to Mt Isa, Qld, to treat a miner.

Births & Deaths

William Griffith McBride, gynaecologist, b.

James Joseph Thompson, nuclear engineer, b.

1927

1927 C

Arts

Literature

During 1927
Baldwin Spencer publishes *The Arunta: a Story of a Stone Age People*.
P. Serle edits *An Australian Anthology*, historical collection of verse.
Jack McLaren publishes *My Crowded Solitude*.
Cyril Goode, diarist, begins writing.
Robert D. Fitzgerald publishes *The Greater Apollo*.
Ion Idriess publishes first of some 50 books, *Madman's Island*.

Births & Deaths
Vincent Buckley, poet, critic, b.
David Ireland, novelist, b.
Charles Thomas Osborne, poet, author, b.
Gerald Alfred Wilkes, author, academic, b.

Music, Dance

Births & Deaths
Robert Allman, baritone, b.
John Raymond Hopkins, conductor, b.
Leslie Keith Humble, composer, conductor, b.
Dawn Lake, band singer, b.
Martin Mather, composer, b.

Drama, Theatre, Film

May. A Royal Commission into Aust. Film Industry appointed.
9 Jun. Tal Ordell's *The Kidstakes*, comedy film, premières in Brisbane.
During 1927
Empire Theatre in Sydney becomes Her Majesty's Theatre.

Births & Deaths
Ian Dunlop, film director noted for ethnographic documentary work, b.
Alan Seymour, playwright, author, b.
Dinah Hilary Shearing, actress, b.

Fine Arts

During 1927
George W. Lambert wins Archibald Prize for *Mrs Murdoch*.
Crouch Art Prize estb. in Ballarat. (Now oldest annual art prize in Vic.)
Joshua McClelland Print Room Private Gallery estb. in Melbourne.
State Theatre Art quest conducted in Sydney.
Canberra Arts Society holds first Art Exhibition.
G. Rayner Hoff opens modern school of sculpture in Sydney.

Births & Deaths
Earle Backen, painter, graphic artist, b.
Harold John Baily, painter, b.
William Boissevain, portrait painter, b.
Donald James Gray Cameron, painter, b.
Donald Roderick Clarke, painter, b.
Lawrence Daws, painter, b.
William J. Gleeson, surrealist painter, b.
Edward Hill, painter, b.
Helen Maudsley, painter, b.
Ronald Grenville Millar, painter, b.
Kenneth William Scarlett, sculptor, b.
Karin Schepers, graphic artist, b.
Udo Sellbach, painter, printmaker, b.
Michael Shannon, painter, b.
Douglas Stubbs, painter, b.
Stephen Walker, sculptor, b.
Lorraine Whiting, sculptor, painter, b.
Frederick Ronald Williams, landscape painter, graphic artist, b. (d. 1982)
Geoffrey Ronald Wilson, watercolourist, b.
Ian Charles Wroth, painter, b.

Architecture

Jun. First International Architecture Exhibition opens in Sydney.

Births & Deaths
Peter Robert McIntyre, architect, b.

D
Religion, Learning

During 1927
Pentecostal Assemblies estb. in Melbourne.
John Anderson becomes Professor of Philosophy at Sydney University. (Holds Chair until 1958.)

E
Sport

28 May. Night-time greyhound track racing meetings begin at Harold Park, Sydney. Day-time meetings begin on 6 Jun.
1 Dec. Mascot greyhound racing track opens in Sydney.
During 1927
Trivalve, ridden by R. Lewis, wins Melbourne Cup in 3 minutes 24 seconds.
Collingwood football team wins VFL Premiership in Melbourne.
South Sydney football team wins Rugby League Premiership in Sydney.
Sydney Coventry of Collingwood VFL team awarded Brownlow Medal.
Nobel Clay Target Club estb. in Melbourne. First clay target shooting club in Aust.
First uniform netball rule book estb.
Aust. Power Boat Association estb.
NSW Rugby Union team, the Waratahs, tours Britain.
George Aalberg becomes first prominent ski instructor at Mt Kosciusko, NSW.
Herbert Schlink leads first major ski cross-country run, from Kiandra to Mt Kosciusko, NSW.
Greyhound racing track built at Epping, Sydney. First meeting using electric hare for dog racing.
First Aust. motorcycle speedway championships held, in Brisbane.
Rufe Naylor builds Sydney Sports Arena. First multi-purpose indoor sports palace in Aust.

Births & Deaths
Trevor Allan, Rugby Union player, b.
George Barnes, boxer, b.
Clive Churchill, Rugby League player, b.
Jimmy Deane, SA Aust. Rules footballer, b. (d. 1985)
Frank Flannery, boxer, b.
Arnold Glass, motor sportsman, b.
Pat Glennon, jockey, b.
Arthur Theodore Wallace (Wally) Grout, cricketer, noted wicket-keeper, b. (d. 1968)
Tommy Hill, jockey, b.
Ron Hutchison, jockey, b.
Sidney Phillip Patterson, cyclist, b.
Desmond Robert (Des) Renford, marathon swimmer, b.
Francis Allan (Frank) Sedgman, tennis player, b.
Sir Nicholas Shehadie, Rugby Union forward, b.
Bernie Smith, VFL footballer, b.
Mickey Tollis, boxer, b.
Bill Wigzell, motor sportsman, b.

1927

1927

F

Historia Dignum

Population
Estimated total white, 6,251,016.

9 Feb. Cyclone damages Cairns, Qld.
Steam collier *Galava* sinks off Terrigal, NSW, claiming seven lives.
During Feb. Bushfires devastate south-east Tas.
27 Oct. Melbourne gangster Joseph Theodore Leslie (Squizzy) Taylor shot dead.
Oct. Late-night shopping begins in Canberra.
3 Nov. Liner *Tahiti* rams Sydney harbour ferry *Greycliffe*, claiming 40 lives.
During 1927
Aust. Red Cross Society becomes independent of British Society.
Francis Birtles begins pioneering overland route from England to Aust. by car.
Severe 9- to 12-month drought begins in western NSW.
Frederick Ward introduces modern furniture in Aust.
Time-payment method of buying goods by lay-by or hire-purchase becomes popular.
Last open koala shooting season kills over half a million koalas.
First Aust. commemorative stamp issued, to mark opening of Parlt House in Canberra.
c. 1927. Red Cab taxis appear in Sydney.

A

History, Politics, Economics, Law

Government
14 May 1928–26 Apr. 1934, Sir Alexander Gore Arkwright Hore-Ruthven Governor SA.
15 Jun. 1928–Mar. 1934, J. C. McPhee Nationalist Premier Tas.
22 Nov. 1928–Dec. 1929, Sir W. M. McPherson National Premier Vic.

12 Feb. Prime Minister calls Industrial Peace Conference.
Mar. Visit of British Economic Mission to report on development of Aust. resources.
15 May. Ships' cooks strike, tying up 13 vessels.
1 Sep. Compulsory referendum vote in NSW and Federal Territory defeats prohibition.
17 Nov. Stanley Melbourne Bruce returned as Nationalist Country coalition Prime Minister with reduced majority. James Henry Scullin Labor Opposition leader (until 1929).
States' debts financial agreement referendum carried. Financial Agreement of Cwlth and States Loan Council reconstituted, and States' debts taken over.
Dec. NSW divided into three electoral zones; Sydney, Newcastle and country areas.

During 1928
John Joseph Curtin and Joseph Benedict Chifley enter Federal Parlt.
Sir George Francis Hyde, Aust. Admiral, appointed Honorary ADC to the King.
Unemployment among registered trade unionists reaches 11 per cent.
Federal Govt takes control of technical services of Class A radio stations, providing programmes for the Australian Broadcasting Company.
Leslie Hooker begins L. J. Hooker real estate business in Sydney.
Thirty-two NT Aborigines shot in retaliation for Aborigines killing a dingo shooter.

Births & Deaths
Sir (James) Keith Campbell, businessman, b. (d. 1983).
Raymond Steele Hall, SA Premier and Federal politician, b.

B

Science, Technology, Transport, Discovery

1928

7–22 Feb. Bert Hinkler pilots first successful and record solo England–Aust. flight; 12,000 miles in 15 days $2\frac{1}{4}$ hours.
19 Mar. Mrs K. Miller arrives in Darwin, becoming first woman to fly from England to Aust.
15 Apr. (Sir) George Hubert Wilkins and C. B. Eilson begin first transpolar flight. (Longest journey attempted in Arctic region.)
9 May. Qantas begins first daily air service in Aust., between Brisbane and Toowoomba, Qld.
15 May. The Aust. Inland Mission Aerial Service inaugurated, first flying doctor service in world. Dr Kenyon St Vincent Welch first full-time doctor in Royal Flying Doctor Service. Stationed at Cloncurry, Qld, with Qantas pilot Arthur Affleck.
31 May–9 Jun. Charles Kingsford Smith and C. T. P. Ulm in monoplane *Southern Cross* make first trans-Pacific flight from California to Brisbane, 7,435 miles in 83 hours 11 mins. Begin first non-stop flight across Aust. from Perth to Point Cook, Vic., on 8 Aug. Make first crossing of Tasman sea in 14 hours 25 mins on 10–11 Sep.
During May. Monsanto-Southern Cross Chemical Co. estb. in Melbourne. Pioneers drug production in Aust. (Imperial Chemical Industries Ltd incorporated.)
Aug. Eskbank steelmaking works transferred from Lithgow to Port Kembla. Becomes Aust. Iron and Steel Ltd.

During 1928
Royal Aust. College of Surgeons estb.
The Model A Ford first produced.
De Havilland Aircraft Co. Ltd opens in Melbourne. First overseas aircraft manufacturer to open branch in Aust.
First traffic lights in Aust. installed, on corner of Collins and Swanston Streets in Melbourne.
Telefunken radio introduced.
Aust. Dental Association estb.
Waite Agricultural Research Institute discovers that manganese deficiency causes grey speck disease in oats.

1928

C

Arts

Literature

During 1928
Baldwin Spencer publishes *Wanderings in Wild Australia*.
The *Bulletin* literary prize created.
Miles Franklin, using pseudonym Brent of Bin Bin, publishes *Up the Country*.
Martyn Boyd publishes *The Montforts*.
Mary Gilmore forms the Fellowship of Aust. Writers.

Births & Deaths
Bruce Beaver, poet, b.
Elizabeth Harrower, novelist, b.

Music, Dance

During 1928
Fritz Hart stages opera *Deirdre in Exile*.
First carillon in Aust. opens, at Sydney University.
Nellie Melba begins her third and last opera season.

Births & Deaths
Donald Vernon Burrows, jazz musician, b.
Marie Elizabeth Collier, dramatic soprano, probably b. (d. 1971)
George Dreyfus, composer, b.
David Gordon Kilpatrick, better known as Slim Dusty, country singer, b.
Rex Reid, ballet dancer, choreographer, b.
John Grant Sangster, jazz musician, composer, b.
Peter Tahourdin, musician, b.

Drama, Theatre, Film

During 1928
Paulette McDonagh produces film *The Far Paradise*.
First 'talkies' films screened for Aust. public.
American features, *The Jazz Singer*, world's first talking film, and *The Red Dance* shown in Sydney.

Births & Deaths
Richard Beynon, actor, playwright probably b.
Keith Michell, actor, b.

Fine Arts

During 1928
John Longstaff wins Archibald Prize for *Dr Alexander Leeper*.
Aust.–South Africa Etchings Exhibition in South Africa.
Aust. Artists' Exhibition at Imperial Gallery of Art, Imperial Institute, in London.
Perth University Art Club estb.

Births & Deaths
Vincent Mark Arnall, sculptor, b.
Charles Raymond Blackman, figurative painter, b.
Kathleen Boyle, painter, b.
Shay Docking, painter, b.
Margaret Dredge, painter, b.
William Drew, painter, theatre designer, b.
Gerard Ebeli, painter, b.
Leonard William French, artist, muralist, b.
Marea Gazzard, ceramic artist, b.
Tom Gibbons, painter, critic, b.
Kevin Charles (Pro) Hart, painter and sculptor, b.
Kenneth Edwin Hood, painter, b.
Laurence Hope, painter, b.
Mirka Madeleine Mora, painter, graphic artist, b.
Adrian Officer, painter and commercial artist, b.
John Olsen, abstract Aust. scenery artist, tapestry designer, b.
Norma Redpath, sculptor, b.
John R. N. Rogers, painter, b.
Roy Roggenkamp, watercolourist, b.
William Arthur Salmon, painter, b.
Brian Seidel, painter and graphic artist, b.
Ernest Smith, painter, b.
Gerard van Putten, sculptor, b.

D
Religion, Learning

9 Mar. Armidale Teachers' College opens in NSW.
During 1928
Aust. Library Association estb.
H. T. Lovell, psychologist appointed first Professor of Psychology in Aust., at Sydney University.

E
Sport

During 1928
Statesman, ridden by J. Munro, wins Melbourne Cup in 3 minutes $23\frac{1}{2}$ seconds.
Collingwood football team wins VFL Premiership in Melbourne.
South Sydney football team wins Rugby League Premiership in Sydney.
Ivor Warne-Smith of Melbourne VFL team awarded Brownlow Medal.
Aust. wins one gold, two silver and one bronze medals at Amsterdam Olympics.
Aust. Rugby League team first wear green and gold colours.
Aust. Council of Judo estb.
Autocycle Council of Aust. estb to control motor-cycle racing.
First Aust. Grand Prix motor race held, at Phillip I., Vic.
Donald George Bradman plays his first Test cricket match.
E. F. Robinson first Aust. woman athlete sent overseas.
Ken Gulliver, basketball player and coach, begins a 40-year career.

Births & Deaths
Maxine Bishop, golfer, b.
Ron Clegg, VFL footballer, b.
James Bartholomew (Bart) Cummings, racehorse trainer, b.
Joan Fletcher, golfer, b.
R. Neil Harvey, cricketer, b.
Bob Jane, track cyclist and racing-car driver, b.
Frank Matich, racing-car driver, b.
Russell Mockridge, cyclist, b. (d. 1958)
Bob Rose, VFL footballer, b.
Norman B. Rydge, yachtsman, b.
Ron Toombs, motorcyclist, b. (d. 1979)
John Treloar, sprinter, b.
Graham Warren, racing-car driver, b.

1928

1928

F
Historia Dignum

Population
Estimated total white, 6,355,770.

Nov. Rural Youth Club founded as Junior Farmers' Club, at Glen Innes, NSW. (Vic. and Qld 1947, SA and WA 1952, Tas. 1950.)
During 1928
NSW introduces first bottled milk.
First airmail service from Aust. to NZ.
Eton crop hair style for women replaces bobbed curls.
National Safety Council of Aust. estb. in Melbourne.
Diphtheria epidemic claims lives of 12 children in Bundaberg, Qld.
The Vic. Bush Fire Brigades Association estb.
Bert Appleroth first makes Aeroplane Jelly, made famous by its singing commercial.

A

History, Politics, Economics, Law

1929

Government

21 May 1929–Jun. 1932, A. E. Moore Country-National-Progressive coalition Premier Qld.
22 Oct. 1929–6 Jan. 1932, Sixteenth Cwlth Ministry, James Henry Scullin Labor Prime Minister Aust.
12 Dec. 1929–May. 1932, E. J. Hogan Labor Premier Vic.
1929–1931, V. G. Carrington Govt Resident Central Aust (NT) under Cwlth jurisdiction.

Jan. Timber workers launch 10-month strike over decision to increase working hours.
4 Feb. Sir Owen Dixon appointed Justice of High Court of Aust. (Justice until 1952.)
6 Feb. Eleventh Federal Parlt opens. (Dissolution 16 Sep.)
2 Mar. Coalminers strike against wage reductions in northern NSW. (Strike lasts until Jun. 1930.)
11 May. Irene Longman becomes first woman member of Qld Parlt.
31 May. Royal Commission appointed to investigate coal strike.
Jun. NSW Govt attempts to open coalmine using non-union labour with armed police protection. On 16–17 Dec 8,000 miners attack strike-breakers in mine at Rothbury coalfields in Maitland–Cessnock region of NSW. Police fire on unionists in 'Battle of Rothbury', killing one and wounding nine.
10 Sep. Bruce Govt defeated on proposal to abolish Federal system of compulsory industrial arbitration and to transfer arbitration powers to the States.
12 Oct. Labor victory at national election. John Greig Latham Nationalist Opposition leader (until 1931).
1 Nov. Abolition of peace-time compulsory military training in favour of a voluntary system.
20 Nov. Twelfth Federal Parlt opens. (Dissolution 27 Nov. 1931.)
During Nov. Export prices begin to fall. Cwlth Bank authorized to mobilize gold reserve. Aust. depression begins in earnest Sep.–Oct.

During 1929
Joseph Aloysius Lyons enters Federal Parlt.
'Scullin Tariff' increases duty on many Aust. imports to protect Aust. industry.
SA adopts preferential voting system.
Development and Migration Commission abolished, ending assisted immigration.
Bleakley Commission examines Aboriginal conditions in NT. Recommends that Aborigines should be assimilated where in contact with white society.
The Aust. Wine Board estb. as the Wine Overseas Marketing Board.
Export of merino sheep prohibited except with Ministerial approval.
Perth Hospital and Bellingen Hospital, NSW, estb. first hospital insurance funds.

Births & Deaths

John Douglas Anthony, Federal politician, b.
Gordon Page Barton, businessman, politician, b.
Robert James Lee Hawke, Labor Prime Minister, b.
John Owen Stone, public servant, b.

519

1929

B
Science, Technology, Transport, Discovery

10 Jan. Gilbert Miles makes first TV broadcast in Aust., using mechanical scanning system from 3UZ radio station in Melbourne. First public demonstration.
25 Jun.–10 Jul. Charles Kingsford Smith and Charles Ulm make first multi-engine aircraft flight Aust.–England in *Southern Cross*. Take 12 days 21 hours 8 mins.
9 Sep. Sydney–Melbourne picturegram service begins.
During 1929
Charles Ulm and Charles Kingsford Smith launch (the first) Australian National Airways.
Lawrence Wackett begins designing and building Widgeon Amphibian and Warrigal Trainer aircraft.
Over 500,000 telephones operate in Aust.
Adelaide–Alice Springs railway opens.
Aust. Radiation Laboratory estb. as Cwlth Radium Laboratory. (Becomes X-ray and Radium Laboratory in 1935.)
Aust. Illawarra Shorthorn cattle breed officially recognized.
Aust. Broadcasting Co. estb.
First eucalyptus paper mill in Aust. opens, at Kermandie, Tas.
Noel Hunt estb. air-conditioning in Aust.
Aust. Inland Mission installs its first pedal wireless, at Cloncurry, Qld.

C
Arts

Literature

Apr. James Joyce's novel *Ulysses* banned in Aust.
During 1929
Katharine S. Prichard publishes *Coonardoo*.
'M. Barnard Eldershaw' publishes *A House is Built*.
Arthur Upfield publishes *The Barrackee Mystery*.
Frederic Manning publishes *The Middle Parts of Fortune*.
Henry Handel Richardson's trilogy, *The Fortunes of Richard Mahony*, completed.

Births & Deaths

Raymond Frank Mathews, poet, playwright, b.
Peter Porter, poet, composer, b.
Ronald Albert Simpson, poet, artist, b.

Music, Dance

9 Apr. Anna Pavlova, ballet dancer, begins second Aust. tour. Last performance in Aust. on 20 Jun. in Perth.
During 1929
First radio broadcast of an orchestral concert.
Mischa Burlakov and Louise Lightfoot estb. first Aust. Ballet Co., in Sydney.
Dame Nellie Melba gives final performance in Aust., at Geelong, Vic.
c. 1929. Percy Code, conductor, becomes active.

Births & Deaths

Robert Edward Allman, baritone singer, b.
June Mary Cough, who sang as June Mary Bronhill, opera soprano, b.
Peter Joshua Sculthorpe, composer, b.

Drama, Theatre, Film

During 1929
Doris Fitton estb. Independent Theatre in Sydney. (Opens on 30 May 1930.)
Fox Movietone News in Sydney makes first 'talkie' interview in Aust. First Movietone News on 2 Nov.
Sydney State Theatre opens. Regent Theatre in Melbourne built.
First commercial film sound shorts made in Aust.
Carrie Tennant estb. Aust. Community Theatre in Sydney.
Gregan McMahon estb. The Gregan McMahon Players Co. in Sydney.

Births & Deaths

Tim Burstall, film producer, director, b.

Gloria Dawn, actress, musicial comedienne, b. (d. 1978)
Ronald Norman Haddrick, actor, b.

Fine Arts

21 Oct. William Dixson Art Gallery of Mitchell Library opens in Sydney.
During 1929
John Longstaff wins Archibald Prize for *W. A. Holman*.
Farmers' Blaxland Art Gallery estb. in Sydney.
Alexander Melrose awards first art prize and endorsements.
c. 1929. Rusconi, sculptor, carves *Dog on the Tucker Box* at Gundagai, NSW.

Births & Deaths

Ann Church, theatre designer, b.
Pam Hallandal, sculptor, b.
John Haywood, painter, sculptor, b.
John George Henshaw, painter, b.
Robert Litchfield Juniper, painter, sculptor, potter, b.
Robert Langley, sculptor, ceramic artist, b.
Richard Larter, pop art painter, b.
Clement Meadmore, sculptor, b.
Bruce Leslie Petty, cartoonist, b.
Peter Travis, ceramics designer, b.

D
Religion, Learning

During 1929
Canberra University College estb. as affiliate of University of Melbourne.
Jehovah's Witnesses estb. headquarters in Sydney.
First Russian Orthodox church in Aust. built, in Brisbane.
The Apostolic Church (Australia) estb.
Development of education slows down because of early stages of economic crisis.

1929

E
Sport

29 Sep. Jack L. Bowers and Frank Smith complete earliest motorcycle and side car circuit in Sydney.
30 Sep.–5 Oct. Hereward de Havilland wins Sydney–Perth Transcontinental Air Race.

During 1929
Nightmarch, ridden by R. Reed, wins Melbourne Cup in 3 minutes 26½ seconds.
Collingwood football team wins VFL Premiership in Melbourne.
South Sydney football team wins Rugby League Premiership in Sydney.
Albert Collier of Collingwood VFL team awarded Brownlow Medal.
James Eve founds Empire Games movement in Aust.
Ski Council of NSW estb.
Walter Lindrum wins world snooker championship title. (Retains for 20 years.)
Ivor Burge standardizes basketball rules.
Gliding Club of Vic. estb.
Aust. wins Davis Cup tennis without NZ help.
Brisbane Rugby Union competitions begin.
Lawn Tennis Association of Aust. estb.
Women's Amateur Athletic Association of Vic. estb. (Qld 1931, NSW and SA 1932, Tas. and WA 1937.)
The *Sporting Weekly* first published in Sydney. (Until 1971.)

Births & Deaths
Dave Brockhoff, Rugby Union coach, b.
James William Carruthers, boxer, b.
Edward Charlton, snooker player, b.
John Coleman, Aust. Rules footballer, b. (d. 1973)
Alan Keith Davidson, cricketer, noted bowler, b.
John Davies, swimmer, b.
Les Favell, cricketer, b.
Rex Hartwig, tennis player, b.
Keith Victor Holman, Rugby League footballer, b.
Jim Johnson, jockey, b.
Ken McGregor, tennis player, b.
Tony Miller, Rugby Union footballer, b.
David Power, athlete, runner, b.
Alfie Sands, boxer, b.
Bob Stevens, golfer, b.
Peter William Thomson, golfer, b.
Roy Wright, VFL footballer, b.

F
Historia Dignum

Population
Estimated total white, 6,436,213.

Jan. Bushfires damage many areas in NSW.
4 Apr. Derby, Tas., tin-mine disaster when dam bursts flooding mine. Claims 14 lives.
20 May. First airmail stamp issued. Costs threepence.

During 1929
Journal *Australian Quarterly* first published, in Sydney.
Standards Association of Aust. estb.
Weekly Adelaide–Perth airmail service begins.
F. A. B. Peters launches Peters' Icecream in Melbourne, using slogan 'The Health Food of a Nation'.

A

History, Politics, Economics, Law

1930

Government

9 Apr. 1930–28 May 1930, Sir William Cullen administered NSW.

17 Apr. 1930–Feb. 1933, L. L. Hill Labor Premier SA.

24 Apr. 1930–Apr. 1933, Sir J. Mitchell National-Country coalition Premier WA.

29 May 1930–15 Jan. 1935, Sir Philip Woolcott Game Governor NSW.

3 Oct. 1930–22 Jan. 1931, Arthur Herbert Tennyson Somers Cocks, Lord Somers, Governor-General Aust.

4 Nov. 1930–May 1932, J. T. Lang Labor Premier NSW.

23 Dec. 1930–4 Aug. 1933, Sir Herbert Nicholls administered Tas.

17 Jan. Agreement signed with Germany regarding liquidation of German property.

Feb. Export prices fall dramatically. Govt ceases overseas loans, and introduces tariff embargo and rationing of imports. Introduces first sales tax to meet decline in customs duties and other receipts.

1 Apr. Douglas Mawsons's Antarctic expedition reaches Adelaide from the Antarctic.

2 Apr. Sir Isaac Alfred Isaacs appointed Chief Justice of High Court of Aust. (Until 21 Jan 1931). On 2 Dec. appointed first Aust.-born Governor-General.

5 May. The Dominion League of WA estb. to lobby for WA secession.

28 May. Senate rejects three bills to increase powers of Cwlth Parlt.

21 Jul. Lewis Harold Bell Lasseter begins expedition to alleged rich goldfield on WA–NT border. Lasseter disappears; gold reef never located.

During Jul. Report of Royal Commission on purchase of Mungana mines finds Cwlth treasurer E. G. Theodore and three others guilty of fraud. E. G. Theodore resigns from Cabinet on 9 Jul.

Aug. Premiers' Conference resolves to tighten budgets.

Sep. Sir Otto Niemeyer of Bank of England visits Aust. to discuss financial questions; advises heavy deflation programme.

Oct. Unemployment exceeds 20 per cent; 125,000 unemployed in Sydney.

19 Dec. Herbert Vere Evatt, aged 36, youngest man ever to sit on the Bench of the High Court of Aust., appointed. (Justice of High Court until 1940.)

20 Dec. Sir Edward McTiernan appointed Justice of High Court of Aust. (Until 1976.)

During 1930
Trade union movement outraged by Cwlth Court of Conciliation and Arbitration decision reducing basic wage and awards in its jurisdiction by 10 per cent. Decision accepted by 15 Aug.

Aust. Aboriginal policy of 'Protection' changes to 'Assimilation'.

Fred Blakeley leads expedition to search for Lasseter's reef in NT.

The Aborigines Progressive Association estb. branches in NSW to oppose the NSW Aborigines Protection Board.

The ACT Advisory Council estb.

Births & Deaths

John Malcolm Fraser, Liberal Prime Minister, b.

1930

B
Science, Technology, Transport, Discovery

1 Jan. (First) Aust. National Airways begins Sydney–Brisbane air service. Melbourne–Sydney air service begins on 1 Jun.
30 Apr. First commercial radio telephone service between Aust. and England begins.
5 May–24 May. Amy Johnson becomes first aviatrix to fly solo from England to Aust.
23 Jun.–4 Jul. Charles Kingsford Smith makes first London–New York flight, crossing the Atlantic.
Jul. Telephone trunk line service opens between Perth and Adelaide, linking up all mainland States by telephone.

During 1930
Royal Society of Canberra founded.
Cecil Arthur Butler designs builds and tests the first all-metal aircraft, *ABA 1*, in Aust.
Rare meteorite weighing 55 lbs falls near Karoonda, SA.
The Aust. Hen or Australorp chicken officially declared a distinct Aust. breed.
Sam Brooks and Roy Shepherd discover opals at Andamooka, SA.
School of Public Health and Tropical Medicine estb. at University of Sydney.
Cwlth Forestry Bureau (Forestry and Timber Bureau in 1946) estb.
The Association of Physicians of Australasia and NZ estb. (Royal Australasian College of Physicians in 1938.)
NSW Agriculture Department begins research into copper deficiency in soils.

Births & Deaths
Alfred Edward Ringwood, scientist, b.
Philip Jon Stephenson, geologist, b.

C
Arts

Literature

During 1930
Vance Palmer publishes *The Passage*.
Lennie W. Lower publishes *Here's Luck*.
Norman Lindsay publishes *Redheap*. (Published in England; banned in Aust.)
Frank Clune publishes his first book, *Try Anything Once*.
W. K. Hancock publishes *Australia*.

Births & Deaths
Bruce Dawe, poet, b.

Music, Dance

Births & Deaths
Harold Badger, composer, b.
Richard Bonynge, conductor, b.
Elaine Fifield, ballet dancer, b.
Clifford Scantlebury Grant, opera singer, bass, b.
Rolf Harris, song writer, entertainer, b.
David Tunley, composer, b.

Drama, Theatre, Film

During 1930
Aust. sound feature film *The Cheaters* made.

Births & Deaths
Peter Kenna, actor and playwright, b.
Rod Taylor, film actor, b.
Doreen Warburton, actress, b.

Fine Arts

During 1930
W. B. McInnes wins Archibald Prize for *Drum Major Harry McClelland*.
Exhibition of Aust. art in New York.
Perth Centenary Art Prize awarded.
Qld Art Fund estb.
Turramurra Wall painters active in Sydney.
Aust. Sculptors' Society estb.
Bruce Dellit designs Anzac Memorial in Sydney.

Births & Deaths
Roy Bizley, painter, probably b.
Marr Grounds, sculptor, b.
Daryl Hill, sculptor, painter, b.
Ursula Airlie Laverty, painter, b.
Desmond Norman, painter, b.

William Rose, painter, b.
Matcham Skipper, sculptor, b.

Architecture

Aug. Royal Aust. Institute of Architects estb.
During 1930
Early modern period of architecture begins. (Ends c. 1944.)
Sydney Edward Ancher, architect, registers in Sydney. Noted for influencing Aust. architecture with modern European movement; also noted for developing use of colonial verandas.

D
Religion, Learning

1930

During 1930
Rev. G. K. Tucker founds Brotherhood of St Laurence, Church of England welfare organization, in Melbourne.
The Aust. Council for Educational Research estb.
First Roman Catholic bishops trained in Aust. appointed. James O'Collins to Geraldton, WA, and Terence McGuire to Townsville, Qld.
The Temple Beth Israel Jewish congregation estb. in Melbourne.
William Keith Hancock publishes in London his historical work *Australia*. Book becomes widely read and influential.

Births & Deaths
Geoffrey Norman Blainey, economic and social historian, b.

1930

E
Sport

6 Jan. Don Bradman breaks first class cricket record in NSW *v.* Qld match at Sydney Cricket Ground. Scores 452 not out in 415 mins. In Jul. makes highest individual Test cricket score of 334 runs, against England at Leeds.

During 1930
Phar Lap, ridden by J. E. Pike, wins Melbourne Cup in 3 minutes 27¾ seconds.
Collingwood football team wins VFL Premiership in Melbourne.
Western Suburbs football team wins Rugby League Premiership in Sydney.
Stan Judkins of Richmond VFL team awarded Brownlow Medal.
Aust. wins first Test cricket series against West Indies in Aust.
National Skiing championship formally regulated.
First roughriding competition with clearly estb. rules staged at Warwick, Qld.
Sydney Metropolitan Gliding Club estb.
Greta Mott becomes first Aust. woman diving champion.
National swimming championships for women begin.
Miniature golf courses become popular.
First Cwlth Games, called British Empire Games, held in Canada. (Held every four years.)
Amateur Basketball Association of Vic. estb. (SA 1937, NSW 1938.)

Births & Deaths
Richard (Richie) Benaud, cricketer, journalist, b.
Len Fitzgerald, SA Aust. Rules footballer, b.
Kevin Humphreys, Rugby League organizer, b.
Don (Bronco) Johnson, boxer, b.
Trevor King, featherweight boxer, b.
John Landy, runner, b.
Ron Lord, soccer player, b.
Anthony Madigan, boxer, b.
Ray Selkrig, jockey, b.
Eddie Stapleton, Rugby Union footballer, b.
John Thornett, Rugby Union footballer, b.
Peter Toogood, golfer, b.
Frank Treen, jockey, b.

F
Historia Dignum

Population
Estimated total white, 6,500,751.

1 Jan. Sydney–Brisbane airmail service begins.
During 1930
Clarence and Norman Burt estb. first milk bar in Aust., in Sydney. (Probably first in world.)
J. T. Lang introduces Lottery Bill, setting up State lottery in NSW. (First lottery draw on 20 Aug. 1931.)
Tweed suit made in record time in Sydney, from sheep's back to finished product in 1 hour 50 minutes.
Some 144,596 cars are registered in Aust.
Flora Protection Act passed in Qld. (Vic. 1971, NSW and SA 1972, WA 1935.)
National Parks Association estb. in Qld; first in Aust.

Communities
Andamooka, SA, estb.

A
History, Politics, Economics, Law

1931

Government

22 Jan. 1931–22 Jan. 1936, Sir Isaac Alfred Isaacs Governor-General Aust.
9 Jun. 1931–29 Jun. 1932 Sir John Alfred Northmore administered WA.
24 Jun. 1931–13 May 1934, Sir William Hill Irvine administered Vic.
1931–1937, R. H. Weddell Administrator NT under Cwlth jurisdiction.

22 Jan. Sir Frank Gavan Duffy appointed Chief Justice of High Court of Aust. (Until 1 Oct. 1935.)
1 Feb. Ten per cent cut in basic wage as measure to combat worsening depression.
18 Feb. Eric Campbell (Colonel, AIF), solicitor, forms the right-wing New Guard with membership mostly of ex-servicemen. Organized on paramilitary lines to fight communism. (Lasts four years.)
During Feb. 'All for Aust. League' estb. in Sydney to oppose measures adopted by State Govt to fight depression.
26 Mar. J. T. Lang, NSW Premier, defaults on interest payments on NSW Govt bonds held in London. On 22 Apr. NSW Savings Bank suspends payments; absorbed by Cwlth Bank in Dec.
Mar. Some 10,000 people meet at Wagga Wagga, NSW, to discuss proposals to estb. new State called Riverina.
5 May. After leaving ALP over financial crisis, Joseph Aloysius Lyons forms United Australia Party (UAP), founded as United Australia Movement. (UAP exists until 1944.)
25 May. Sir Douglas Copland heads committee to study Aust. economic situation. In June 'Premiers' Plan' adopted as basis for economic policy to combat depression.
19 Jun. Police evict unemployed people from a house in Newtown, Sydney, after a two-hours battle on 'Bloody Friday'.
19 Dec. James Henry Scullin returned as Labor Prime Minister at national elections. Joseph Aloysius Lyons UAP Leader of Federal Opposition (until 1932.)
During 1931
North Australia Act repealed. Replaced by NT Administration Act providing for administration under Cwlth jurisdiction of all NT by an Administrator residing in Darwin.
British Govt passes Statute of Westminster, formally declaring cessation of British control over self-governing colonies. (Not adopted by Aust. Govt until 1939.)
Association for the Protection of Native Races estb.
Richard Casey enters Federal Parlt.
Arthur Calwell elected president of Vic. Labor Party.
Catherine Green appointed to NSW Legislative Council, becoming first woman member of an Aust. Upper House.
NSW introduces road transport tax for revenue to bolster railways.
Cwlth Bank Act amended to provide for temporary lower reserve against notes. Cwlth Bank assumes control of exchange rate and devalues currency.
Hermann Buring estb. wine company in Sydney.
Commercial production of Aust. liqueurs begins.
Donald Mackay begins aerial survey of central Aust.
The Aust. Federation of Commercial Broadcasting Stations estb.
First hops grown, at Pemberton, WA.

Births & Deaths

David Lloyd Jones, company director, businessman, b. (d. 1961)
Keith Rupert Murdoch, newspaper and television proprietor, b.

527

1931

B
Science, Technology, Transport, Discovery

19 Jan. Aust. National Airways begins Melbourne–Hobart air service. Canberra Airport opens.

During 1931
National Museum of Aust. Zoology becomes Aust. Institute of Anatomy, in Canberra.
Radio first extensively used in political campaigns.
Reginald Myles Ansett begins road passenger transport with a second-hand Studebaker car.
Holden Motor Body builders amalgamate with General Motors to form General Motors-Holdens Ltd, first to mass-produce completely Aust.-made cars.
Argentine ants enter Aust.
First trout successfully introduced to WA.
Kolling Medical Research Institute estb. at Royal North Shore Hospital in Sydney.
Cecil Arthur Butler clips two hours off England–Aust. record; flight of 23 hours in a diminutive Comper Swift monoplane.
First hospital speech therapy clinic estb., at the Royal Alexandra Hospital for Children in Sydney.

Births & Deaths
Sir Gustav Joseph Victor Nossal, medical scientist, b.

C
Arts

Literature

During 1931
Ion Idriess publishes *Lasseter's Last Ride*.
Neville William Caley publishes *What Bird is That?*
Frank Dalby Davison publishes *Man Shy*.
Manuscripts: A Miscellany of Art and Letters published in Geelong, Vic.

Births & Deaths
Shirley Hazzard, novelist, b.
Peter Mathers, novelist, short story writer, b.
Barry Oakley, novelist, playwright, b.

Music, Dance

4 Nov. Mischa Burlakov and Louise Lightfoot estb. one of first Aust. ballet organizations, The First Aust. Ballet, at Savoy Theatre in Sydney, staging *Coppelia*.
During 1931
Dorothy Gladstone founds Vic. Society of Teachers of Dancing.

Births & Deaths
Roger David Covell, musicologist, b.
Gregory John Dempsey, tenor, b.
Lauris Margaret Elms, opera singer, contralto b.
Richard Joseph (Dick) Hughes, jazz pianist, b.
David Lumsdaine, composer, b.
Barry Edmund Tuckwell, French horn player, b.
Malcolm Benjamin Graham Christopher Williamson, composer, b.

Drama, Theatre, Film

26 Sep. A. R. Harwood releases first Aust. full talkie films, *Spur of the Moment* and *Isle of Intrigue*.
7 Nov. *Cinesound Review*, first fully Aust. newsreel, premières.
Dec. Norman Dawn's first local all-talkie film, *Showgirl's Luck*, released.
During 1931
Ken Hall estb. Cinesound studios in Sydney. Makes first cinesound feature film, *On Our Selection*.
Kathleen Robinson founds Minerva Theatre, The Little Theatre, later St Martins Theatre in Melbourne.
Jack Davey, radio announcer, arrives in Aust. from NZ.

Births & Deaths
George Ogilvie, actor, b.

Fine Arts

Mar. Ola Cohn holds first exhibition of modern sculpture in Melbourne.
During 1931
Sir John Longstaff wins Archibald Prize for *Sir John Sulman*.
Stream, monthly review, first published in Melbourne.

Births & Deaths

Hermia Boyd (née Lloyd-Jones), ceramic artist, b.
Stuart Leslie Devlin, sculptor, industrial designer, b.
Leonard Hessing, abstract artist, architect, b.
John Richard Howley, abstract expressionist painter, probably b.
Donald Laycock, oil abstract expressionist painter, b.
Mary Talbot, painter and illustrator, b.
Daniel Rhys Thomas, art critic, b.
Ken Unsworth, sculptor, b.

D
Religion, Learning

During 1931
Conference of headmasters of independent schools of Aust. estb.
Title 'Jehovah's Witnesses' officially adopted by members of the Watchtower Bible and Tract Society.

1931

E
Sport

During 1931
White Nose, ridden by N. Percival, wins Melbourne Cup in 3 minutes 26 seconds.
Geelong football team wins VFL Premiership in Melbourne.
South Sydney football team wins Rugby League Premiership in Sydney.
Haydn Bunton (the elder) of Fitzroy team awarded Brownlow Medal.
Shots fired at champion horse Phar Lap in week before Melbourne Cup.
Aust. Women's Cricket Council estb.
Light Car Club of NSW estb.
Aust. ice and figure skating competitions begin.
First interstate ski races held.
First Aust. squash championships held.
First interstate vigoro matches played, in NSW and Qld.
Ivo Whitton becomes open golf champion for fifth time.

Births & Deaths
Leo Baumgartner, soccer player, b.
Neville Begg, horse trainer, b.
Jim Burke, cricketer, noted batsman, b. (d. 1979)
Keith Campbell, motorcycle racer, b. (d. 1958)
Patrick Ford, boxer, b.
Frank Gardner, all-round sportsman, b.
Hector Dennis Hogan, sprinter, b. (d. 1960)
Marjorie Jackson, runner, b.
John Marshall, freestyle swimmer, probably b. (d. 1957)
Guy Wolstenholme, golfer, b.

F
Historia Dignum

Population
Estimated total white, 6,552,606.

Jan. Golden Eagle, gold nugget weighing 1,135 ounces, discovered in Widgiemooltha area, WA.
1–8 Feb. Floods from Innisfail, Qld, to Brisbane.
20 Feb. Coalmine explosion at Wonthaggi, Vic., claims four lives.
21 Mar. Aircraft *Southern Cloud*, flagship of Aust. National Airways, crashes in Snowy Mountains killing eight. (Wreck discovered on 26 Oct. 1958.)
25 Apr. Kingsford Smith and Charles Ulm bring first airmail from England to Aust., picking it up in Timor. First official Melbourne–London airmail delivery taking 26 days, leaves Melbourne on 23 Apr., with Kingsford Smith picking it up in Darwin on 27 Apr.

During 1931
Ewan Laird, John Buchanan and Langham Proud begin Apex Club, in Geelong, Vic.
c. 1931. Household savouries become popular.

A

History, Politics, Economics, Law

Government

6 Jan. 1932–7 Nov. 1938, Seventeenth Cwlth Ministry, Joseph Aloysius Lyons United Australia Party Prime Minister Aust.
8 Apr. 1932–1 Jun. 1932, Sir James William Blair administered Qld.
16 May 1932–Aug. 1939, B. S. B. Stevens UAP-Country coalition Premier NSW.
19 May 1932–Apr. 1935, Sir S. S. Argyle UAP-Country coalition Premier Vic.
13 Jun. 1932–16 May 1937, Sir Leslie Orme Wilson Governor Qld.
17 Jun. 1932–Sep. 1942, W. Forgan Smith Labor Premier Qld.
30 Jun. 1932–10 Jul. 1933, Sir John Alfred Northmore administered WA.

17 Feb. Thirteenth Federal Parlt opens. (Dissolution 7 Aug. 1934.)
James Henry Scullin Labor Leader of Opposition (until 1935).
19 Mar. Francis Edward De Groot, member of New Guard, cuts ribbon at opening of Sydney Harbour Bridge, forestalling NSW Premier Jack Lang.
13 May. NSW Governor dismisses Premier J. T. Lang for refusing to pay interest on overseas loans and refusing to pay revenues due to Cwlth Govt. Federal Govt pays overseas bond holders and then passes Financial Agreement Enforcement Act to recoup moneys by appropriating funds of NSW Govt.
During May. Aust. Broadcasting Commission (ABC) estb. Opens on 1 Jul.
Jul.–Aug. Imperial economic conference held in Ottawa, Canada. Estb. principle of Empire preference in trade.
During 1932
Aust. Institute of Political Science (AIPS) estb. in Sydney.
Unemployment reaches 30 per cent.
Department of Interior assumes control of ACT.
First commercial development of mineral sands in Aust. begins, at Byron Bay, NSW.
Cwlth Govt begins subsidizing application of superphosphate.

Births & Deaths

Hedley Norman Bull, political scientist, b.
Jack Mundey, union leader, instigator of green ban strikes in 1971, b.

B

Science, Technology, Transport, Discovery

19 Mar. Sydney Harbour Bridge opens.
18 May. First electric trolley bus service estb. in Adelaide.
15 Aug.–27 Sep. Maude Bonney first woman to fly around Aust.
During 1932
First Ford V8 motor car produced.
Altwater-Kent six-valve radio set introduced.
(First) Aust. National Airways collapses.
Aust. Window Glass Co. produces first drawn sheet glass in Aust.
Gold discovered at Cracow, Qld.

1932

1932

C

Arts

Literature

During 1932
Kenneth Slessor publishes *Cuckooz Contrey*.
Norman Lindsay publishes *The Cautious Amorist*.
Mary Gilmore publishes *Under the Wilgas*.
Leonard Mann publishes *Flesh in Armour*.
Vance Palmer publishes *Daybreak*.

Music, Dance

During 1932
Irene Vera Young teaches first modern dance in Aust., in Sydney.

Births & Deaths
Kathleen Gorham, ballet dancer, b.
Richard Graham Meale, composer, among first to use Asian traditions in Aust. music, b.
Patrick Alan Thomas, conductor, b.

Drama, Theatre, Film

26 Mar. Film *The Sentimental Bloke* released in Melbourne.
During 1932
George Wallace stars in film, *His Royal Highness*, first Aust. musical film.
Bert Bailey stars in film *On Our Selection*, released on 6 Aug.

Births & Deaths
Walter John Cherry, playwright, b.

Fine Arts

Feb. George Bell and Arnold Shore estb. Bell–Shore modern art school in Melbourne, and with William Frater and Daryl Lindsay form Contemporary Group of painters in Melbourne.
Jul. The Sculptors' Society of Aust. estb.
During 1932
Grace Crowley and Rah Fizelle open art school in Sydney.
Ernest Buckmaster wins Archibald Prize for *Sir William Irvine*.
Quarterly *Manuscripts* published in Vic.

Births & Deaths
Kevin Connor, expressionist painter, b.
Marlene Creaser, sculptor, b.
David Clyde Dridan, oil landscape painter, b.
William Hannan, art critic, b.
Robin Hill, bird painter, b.
Alexander J. K. Leckie, sculptor, potter, b.
Ross Morrow, painter, b.
Dawn Sime, abstract mural design painter, b.
Joseph Szabo, oil painter, b.
Peter Upward, painter, b.
Dawn Frances Westbrook, painter, b.

D
Religion, Learning

During 1932
Nursery School Teachers' College estb. in Sydney. (Absorbed into Sydney College of Advanced Education in 1980.)
NSW Commission of Inquiry into Technical Education appointed.

Births & Deaths
Barry Owen Jones, teacher, author and Federal politician, b.

E
Sport

5 Apr. Champion horse Phar Lap dies of colic, from suspected poisoning, at Menlo Park, California, USA. (In racing career Phar Lap won 37 out of 41 starts.)

During 1932
Peter Pan, ridden by W. Duncan, wins Melbourne Cup in 3 minutes $23\frac{1}{4}$ seconds.
Richmond football team wins VFL Premiership in Melbourne.
South Sydney football team wins Rugby League Premiership in Sydney.
Haydn Bunton (the elder) of Fitzroy VFL team awarded Brownlow Medal.
Aust. wins three gold, one silver and one bronze medals at Los Angeles Olympics.
Aust. National Ski Federation estb. (Becomes Aust. Ski Federation in 1973.)
Dunlop Aust. Ltd pioneers manufacture of golf balls.
Walter Lindrum sets world billiards record with break of 4,137 in 2 hours 55 mins.
James Carlton runs world record 220 yards in 20.6 seconds, but disallowed by referee Laurie Drake, who ruled there was too much wind assistance.
NSW Fencing Association estb.
English cricket bowlers develop fast bowling 'bodyline' method.
First all-Aust. Aboriginal Rugby League match played, in Brisbane.
Aust. Women's Amateur Athletic Union estb.

Births & Deaths
Kevin Bacon, show jumper, b.
Peter Burge, cricketer, noted batsman, b.
James Hardy, yachtsman, b.
Ian Moir, Rugby League player, b.
William Thomas John (Bill) Moyes, kite flyer, b.
Frank Phillips, golfer, b.
Norm Provan, Rugby League player, b.
Jim Schrader, jockey, b.

1932

1932

F

Historia Dignum

Population
Estimated total white, 6,603,785.

4 Feb. Bushfires in Grampians, Vic., claim nine lives.
10 Jul. Ship *Casino* wrecked in Apollo Bay, Vic., claiming nine lives.
During 1932
Far West Children's Health Scheme begins world's first Aerial Baby Clinic.
Last officially sighted Tas. tiger shot.
Dog on Tucker Box monument unveiled near Gundagai, NSW.
Society of Aust. Genealogists estb. in Sydney. (Vic. 1941.)
First inter-city contract bridge competition held. Among first of kind in world. (First interstate competitions played in 1933.)

A

History, Politics, Economics, Law

Government

13 Feb. 1933–Apr. 1933, R. S. Richards Labor Premier SA.
18 Apr. 1933–Nov. 1938, R. L. Butler Liberal Country League Premier SA.
24 Apr. 1933–Aug. 1936, P. Collier Labor Premier WA.
11 Jul. 1933–4 Oct. 1948, Sir James Mitchell administered WA.
4 Aug. 1933–4 Aug. 1945, Sir Ernest Clark Governor Tas.

7 Feb. British Order in Council declares Antarctic Territories area, bounded by longitude 45°E to 160°E and extending to latitude 60°S, excluding Adelie Land, Aust. Territory. Aust. Antarctic Territory Acceptance Act drawn up. (Ratified on 24 Aug. 1936.)
Mar. World economic conference in London. World disarmament conference at Geneva in Jun.
8 Apr. WA votes in referendum to secede from Aust. and form separate nation, 138,653 for and 70,706 against. (British Govt rejects petition in 1935 and plan collapses.)
30 Jun. Unemployment reaches 500,000, or 24.4 per cent of work force.
2 Aug. Judicature system introduced in Tas.
18 Oct. Royal Commission in NSW into New States first meets.
11 Nov. Millie Peacock first woman to enter Vic. Parlt.

During 1933

Cwlth Grants Commission estb. to control granting of funds to States.
Aust. Institute of International Affairs estb.
Law Council of Aust. estb.
High Court of Aust. reduced to six Justices.
Woolworths opens first store in Melbourne.
Goldrush at Tennant Creek, NT, begins.
Olympic Consolidated Industries Ltd estb. as Olympic Tyre and Rubber Co. Ltd.
First Santa Gertrudis bull introduced to Qld.
Aust. signs trade agreement with Belgium.

Births & Deaths

Elizabeth Andreas Evatt, judge, b.
William George Hayden, Federal politician, b.
Sir Phillip Reginald Lynch, Federal politician, b. (d. 1984)

B

Science, Technology, Transport, Discovery

14 Apr.–21 Jun. Maude Bonney becomes first woman to fly solo Aust. to England.
15 May. Federal Committee of British Medical Association becomes incorporated body named Federal Council of the BMA in Aust.

During 1933

Following work begun at the Walter and Eliza Hall Institute in Melbourne, Macfarlane Burnet isolates an influenza virus at Britain's National Institute of Medical Research.
Broken Hill Proprietary Co. Ltd takes over steel works at Port Kembla, NSW, from Aust. Iron and Steel Ltd.
Inigo Jones predicts drought in Riverina district during 1976.
Last Tas. tiger in captivity dies.
First all-Aust.-made car, the Buckingham, launched, but not mass-produced.
Kanematsu Memorial Institute of Pathology founded at Sydney Hospital.
Leslie Thiess estb. Thiess Bros. Among largest civil engineering and contracting companies in Aust.
Private teleprinter services estb.
Elizabeth Kenny opens poliomyelitis clinic in Townsville, Qld.
Arthur Turner isolates V5 strain of pleuropneumonia. Becomes vaccine against the disease in cattle.

1933 C

Arts

Literature

Jul. Book Censorship Advisory Committee estb. to advise Govt. (Replaced by Literature Censorship Board in 1937.)
During 1933
Norman Lindsay publishes *Saturdee*.
Thomas Wood publishes *Cobbers*.

Music, Dance

During 1933
Sun Aria (City of Sydney Eisteddfod) singing competition launched.
Louise Lightfoot's *Roskanda* presented in Sydney. First complete individual ballet score commissioned from an Aust. composer.
Robert Helpmann joins Sadlers Wells Ballet Co.
Gladys Moncrieff stars in musicial *Collitt's Inn*.
Jim Davidson's recording of '42nd Street' and 'Shuffle off to Buffalo' sells 30,000 copies. Big achievement in jazz.

Births & Deaths
Robert Graeme Barnard, jazz, trumpeter, b.
Brian Brown, modern jazz musician, composer, b.
Colin Brumby, composer, b.
John Exton, musician, b.
Donald Kay, composer, b.

Drama, Theatre, Film

Nov. Depression closes Theatre Royal in Melbourne.
During 1933
Charles Chauvel directs film *In the Wake of the Bounty*.
Errol Flynn makes first film appearance.
Raymond Longford produces film *The Hayseeds*.
Ken Hall produces *The Squatter's Daughter*, sound feature film.

Births & Deaths
Zoe Caldwell, actress noted for Shakespearian roles, b.
Elizabeth Diane Cilento, actress, b.
Jill Perryman, actress, b.

Fine Arts

During 1933
Charles Wheeler wins Archibald Prize for *Ambrose Pratt*.
British Contemporary Art Exhibition tours Aust.
New Melbourne Art Club estb.
Godfrey Rivers bequest prize estb.
Paul Raphael Montford completes statue of Adam Lindsay Gordon.

Births & Deaths
Shirley J. Andrew, painter, b.
John Hamilton Andrews, architect, b.
Sydney Ball, abstract painter, b.
John Leo Borrack, watercolourist, landscape painter, b.
Colin Levy, ceramic artist, b.
Andrew Sibley, artist, b.
Michael Franklin Taylor, oil abstract painter, b.

D
Religion, Learning

During 1933
Provision for university graduates to be admitted into Cwlth public service estb.

E
Sport

During 1933
Hall Mark, ridden by J. O'Sullivan, wins Melbourne Cup in 3 minutes 27¼ seconds.
South Melbourne football team wins VFL Premiership in Melbourne.
Newtown football team wins Rugby League Premiership in Sydney.
W. (Chicken) Smallhorn of Fitzroy VFL team awarded Brownlow Medal.
England v. Aust. Test cricket bodyline bowling controversy begins. England accused of aiming at batsman as well as wicket.
Game fishing becomes popular sport in Aust. In Feb. Roy Smith lands first big game fish in Aust. waters, a 262-pound black marlin.
Norrie Claxton donates Claxton Shield for baseball. Aust. Baseball Council estb.
First Aust.–S. African Rugby Union Test held, in S. Africa.
Aust. Table Tennis Board of Control estb. First championships held in Melbourne.
Karl Atkinson begins water skiing in Aust., on Sydney Harbour.
Frank Donellan makes longest recorded boomerang throw (140 yards).
Jack Crawford first Aust. to win French tennis singles championship.

Births & Deaths
Ron Archer, cricketer, b.
Tony Boskovic, football referee, b.
Jack Clark, VFL footballer, b.
Neale Andrew Fraser, tennis player, b.
Neil Kerley, SA Aust. Rules footballer, b.
Alan Lawrence, long-distance runner, b.
Merv Lincoln, athlete, b.
Ronnie Moore, motorcyclist, b.
Ray Neville, jockey, b.
Rale Rasic, soccer coach, b.
Mervyn Rose, tennis player, b.
Edward Whitten, Aust. Rules footballer, b.

1933

F
Historia Dignum

1933

Population
Estimated total white, 6,656,695.
Third Cwlth census estimates total white population at 6,629,982, with estimated Aboriginal population at 67,000.

24 Jun. Ship *Christina Fraser* vanishes off Gabo I., Vic., with 17 on board.
28 Aug. The *Courier-Mail* newspaper published in Brisbane following merger of *Daily Mail* and *Brisbane Courier*.

During 1933
The *Australian Women's Weekly* begins publication in Sydney.
Milk bars estb. in Sydney, Melbourne and Brisbane.
Archibald Memorial Fountain built in Hyde Park, Sydney, to commemorate Aust.-French relations in World War I.
Steel tube chair made in Aust.
First Aust. Jaycees Chapters estb. in Perth as Junior Chamber of Commerce group.
Handset telephones introduced.
c. 1933. Women's fashion highlights femininity. Bodices shaped around padded shoulders emphasizing bustline, waists tighten and skirts curved out to hips and posterior then back into narrow hems. Gloves in vogue.

Communities
Tennant Creek, NT, estb.

A
History, Politics, Economics, Law

Government

15 Mar. 1934–Jun. 1934, Sir W. Lee Nationalist Premier Tas.

27 Apr. 1934–27 Jul. 1934, Sir George Murray administered SA.

14 May 1934–4 Apr. 1939, William Charles Arcedeckne Vanneck, Lord Huntingfield, Governor Vic.

22 Jun. 1934–Jun. 1939, A. G. Ogilvie Labor Premier Tas.

28 Jul. 1934–23 Feb. 1939, Sir Winston Joseph Dugan Governor SA.

29–30 Jan. Australians at Kalgoorlie, WA, attack Italians, Greeks and other immigrants over movement of large numbers of southern Europeans into State. Racial prejudice rages.

Jun. The Douglas Credit Plan, enunciated by C. H. Douglas in Canada, proposed in Sydney to combat depression.

15 Sep. Joseph Aloysius Lyons returned as UAP Prime Minister of Aust. at Federal elections.

During Sep. J. G. Latham leads Aust. goodwill mission to the East.

23 Oct. Fourteenth Federal Parlt opens. (Dissolution 21 Sep. 1937.)

During Oct. Visit of HRH Duke of Gloucester to open Vic. centenary celebrations.

9 Nov. Country Party forms coalition with United Australia Party.

During Nov. Dictation test used to bar left-wing Czech Jewish writer Egon Kisch from entering Aust. Kisch arrives in Aust on 16 Nov. 1934; deported on 11 Mar. 1935.

During 1934

Robert Gordon Menzies and John McEwen enter Federal Parlt.

Aust. Agricultural Council estb.

External Affairs separated from Prime Minister's Department to become separate Department. (Effective 1935.)

Ashmore and Cartier Islands added to Australian Antarctic territories.

Economic recovery begins with rise in export prices of primary products and expansion of secondary industry. Basic wage restored and increased.

B
Science, Technology, Transport, Discovery

1934

18 Jan. Qld and NT Aerial Services Ltd become Qantas Airways, with Hudson Fysh as first director. First Qantas passenger air service to England leaves Brisbane on 20 Apr.

22 Jan. Electric trolley buses estb. in Sydney.

24 Sep. First delivery of a commercial airliner by air from England to Aust.

28 Sep. Freda Thompson becomes first Aust.-born woman to fly solo from England to Aust.

17 Oct. England–Aust. radio-picturegram service opens.

21 Oct.–4 Nov. Sir Charles Kingsford Smith makes first north bound Brisbane–San Francisco air crossing.

During 1934

Jean Gardner Batten becomes first woman to make return England–Aust. flight.

Stanley Gable and Ivor McIntyre fly around Aust. in 44 days.

Aust. and NZ Association of Radiology estb.

Conference of State Road Authorities Association estb. Becomes National Association of Aust. and State Road Authorities (NAASRA) in 1959.

Goat Breeders Society of Aust. estb.

Val McDowall makes first successful experimental television transmissions, from old Brisbane Observatory; earliest cathode ray transmissions. On 6 May first regular, but experimental, television transmissions begin from Brisbane.

World's first production line Ford coupe style utility vehicle designed and made in Geelong, Vic.

Port Pirie, SA, lead smelter becomes largest of type in world.

Ted Lines discovers cure for coast disease in sheep, using cobalt nitrate.

1934

C

Arts

Literature

During 1934
Angela Thirkell, using pseudonym Leslie Parker, publishes *Trooper to the Southern Cross*.
Frank Wilmot publishes *Melbourne Odes*.
Christina Stead publishes *Salzburg Tales*.
John Harcourt publishes *Upsurge*.
Brian Penton publishes *Landtakers*.
Vance Palmer publishes *Sea and Spinifex*.
Eleanor Dark publishes *Prelude to Christopher*.
Bust of Adam Lindsay Gordon placed in Westminster Abbey's Poets Corner. (Only Aust. with this honour.)
Pamela Travers publishes *Mary Poppins*.

Births & Deaths
Chris Wallace Crabbe, poet and critic, b.
David Malouf, poet, b.

Music, Dance

10 Oct. Dandré-Levitoff Russian Ballet, makes Aust. début in Brisbane.
During 1934
The Westralian Modern Music Club estb. Among first jazz societies in Aust.

Births & Deaths
Peter Maxwell Davies, composer, b.
Donald Hollier, composer, b.
Larry Sitsky, composer, b.

Drama, Theatre, Film

1 Jun. Raymond Longford's film *The Man They Could Not Hang* opens in Sydney.
During 1934
'Mo' makes film *Strike Me Lucky*.
Bijou Theatre in Melbourne closes.

Births & Deaths
John Barry Humphries, actor, entertainer, author, b.
Graham Cyril Kennedy, actor, media personality, b.
John Meillon, actor, b.
Harry Maurice Miller, theatrical producer, b.

Fine Arts

During 1934
Henry Hanke wins Archibald Prize for *Self Portrait*.
William Moore publishes first major historical survey of Aust. art, *The Story of Australian Art*.
Margel I. Hinder, sculptor, arrives in Australia from Boston, USA.
Melbourne Centenary Art Prizes awarded.
NSW Travelling Art Scholarship first awarded.
Shepparton Art Gallery estb. Vic.

Architecture

During 1934
Early modern style of architecture dominates building.
John Sulman Award for Architecture created.

Births & Deaths
Gil Jamieson, painter, abstract cartoonist, b.
Hertha Kluge-Pott, graphic artist, b.
Rodney A. Milgate, abstract oil painter, b.

D

Religion, Learning

During 1934
Hobart Activity School estb. for bright students.

E

Sport

2 Aug. W. Franks swings pair of clubs through 17,280 revolutions, breaking world record.
20 Oct. Charles Scott and Campbell Black win Melbourne Centenary England–to–Melbourne air race in record-breaking time of 71 hours.

During 1934
Peter Pan, ridden by D. Munro, wins Melbourne Cup in 3 minutes $40\frac{1}{2}$ seconds.
Richmond football team wins VFL Premiership in Melbourne.
Western Suburbs football team wins Rugby League Premiership in Sydney.
Dick Reynolds of Essendon VFL team awarded Brownlow Medal.
Drag racing begins in Sydney.
Don Bradman and W. H. Ponsford make record second wicket score of 415 runs against England.
Unofficial Aust. cricket team first plays in India.
First officially recorded women's cricket match played, in Brisbane. (Sydney and Melbourne in 1935.)
Cwlth Games held in London.

Births & Deaths
Philip Billings, golfer, b.
Brian (Pop) Clay, Rugby League footballer, b.
Kevin Hartley, golfer, b.
Lewis Alan Hoad, tennis player, b.
John James, VFL footballer, b.
Marjorie McQuade, swimmer, b.
Margaret Masters, golfer, b.
Marlene Willard-Matthews, athlete, b.
Johnny Miller, jockey, b.
Bruce Morrow, soccer player, b.
Kevin Newman, trotting driver, b.
Rod Phelps, Rugby Union player, b.
Billy Pyers, jockey, b.
Kenneth Robert Rosewall, tennis player, b.
Don Talbot, swimming coach, b.
Ian Walsh, Rugby League player, b.
Rhonda Watson, golfer, b.

1934

1934

F
Historia Dignum

Population
Estimated total white, 6,707,247.

Feb. Bushfires devastate north-west and western Tas.
11–13 Mar. Cyclone in north Qld destroys pearling vessels, claiming 75 lives.
28–29 Mar. Cyclone damages Onslow, WA.
19 Oct. Bass Strait air disaster claims 11 lives.
Nov. Book Censorship Abolition League estb. Later merges with other organizations to form Aust. Council of Civil Liberties.
10 Dec. Qantas Empire Airways, with Imperial Airways, begins first airmail service to Britain, via Singapore.
During 1934
Walkabout magazine launched in Melbourne. (Until 1974.)
Shrine of Remembrance opens in Melbourne.
ANZAC Memorial unveiled in Sydney.
First Monday after 26 Jan. agreed to be observed as official Australia Day.
Construction of Toorak village shopping centre in Melbourne begins.
Captain Cook's Cottage (really the home of Cook's parents) shipped from England to Melbourne.
Vic. floods in Gippsland area claim 35 lives.

Communities
Tarraleah, Tas., estb.
Yirrkala, NT, estb.

A

History, Politics, Economics, Law

1935

Government

15 Jan. 1935–20 Feb. 1935, Sir Philip Whistler Street administered NSW.
21 Feb. 1935–22 Jan. 1936, Sir Alexander Gore Arkwright Hore-Ruthven, Lord Gowrie, Governor NSW.
2 Apr. 1935–Sep. 1943, A. A. Dunstan Country Party Premier Vic.

Jan. Royal Commission reports NSW could suitably be divided into three States.
24 May. Britain officially refuses WA petition seeking to secede from Cwlth.
Aug. Japanese good-will mission to Aust.
Sep. John Curtin Labor Leader of Federal Opposition (until 1941).
11 Oct. Sir John Latham appointed Chief Justice of High Court of Aust. (Holds position until 17 Apr. 1952.)
During Oct. Producers and General Finance Corporation Ltd estb. (Now Lombard Aust. Ltd.).
5 Nov. Charles Moses becomes general manager of Aust. Broadcasting Commission. (Holds position for 30 years.)

During 1935
Aust. attends Imperial Statistical Conference in Ottawa.
Aust. imposes sanctions against Italy; sends HMAS *Sydney* to serve in international force at Gibraltar.
Harold Holt enters Federal Parlt.
NSW first State to estb. a Council of Social Services to co-ordinate social welfare.

B

Science, Technology, Transport, Discovery

Jan. Reginald Ansett estb. Hamilton-Melbourne air service.

During 1935
Broken Hill Proprietary Ltd absorbs Aust. Iron and Steel Ltd, acquiring steel producing monopoly.
Cwlth Industrial Gases Ltd registers in NSW as manufacturer of industrial and medical gas.
Macfarlane Burnet engaged in work on psittacosis, a disease transmitted by birds.
Edgar Percival first to fly England to Africa and return in one day.
Giant toad *bufo marinus* introduced to Qld to control the grey-backed beetle.
First re-inforced concrete bow-string arch span bridge in Aust. built, over Shark Creek near Maclean, NSW.
Cambridge airport estb. near Hobart.

1935

Arts

Literature

During 1935
Kylie Tennant publishes first novel, *Tiburon*.
Leonard Mann publishes *Human Drift*.
Patrick White publishes *The Ploughman and Other Poems*.
Christina Stead publishes *Seven Poor Men of Sydney*.
Matilda Ann (Tilly) Aston publishes *Songs of Light*.

Births & Deaths
Rodney Hall, poet, b.
Thomas Michael Keneally, author, b.
Thomas William Shapcott, author, b.
Julian Randolph Stow, author, b.

Music, Dance

During 1935
Felix Demery introduces Royal Academy of Dancing to Aust. Influences ballet education.
Gertrude Johnson founds National Theatre Movement of Aust. to promote operatic performance.
Louis Lavater founds the Guild of Aust. Composers.
May Brahe composes song 'Bless This House'.
The Dame Nellie Melba Bequest Scholarship first awarded for singing.
Jim Davidson's ABC Dance Band popular in Sydney.

Births & Deaths
Nigel Henry Butterley, composer and pianist, b.
Helen Margaret Gifford, composer, b.
John Michael O'Keefe, popular singer, b. (d. 1978)
Robert Stigwood, musicals producer, b.

Drama, Theatre, Film

Mar. Charles Chauvel's second talkie film, *Heritage*, wins Cwlth film competition.
During 1935
Dymphna Cusack writes her first play, *Red Sky at Morning*.

Fine Arts

During 1935
Sir John Longstaff wins Archibald Prize for *A. B. (Banjo) Paterson*.

Births & Deaths
David Aspden, op-hard edge painter, b.
Peter Clarke, acrylic oil painter, b.
Romola Clifton, painter, b.
Janet Dawson, graphic artist, painter, gallery director, b.
Gareth Jones-Roberts, painter, b.
Colin Jordon, op art painter, abstract sculptor, b.
Maxwell W. Lyle, sculptor, b.

Architecture

During 1935
Manchester Unity building, based on a Chicago building, constructed in Melbourne.

D

Religion, Learning

During 1935
ABC starts school radio broadcasts.
Stanley Gillick Drummond estb. Royal Far West Children's Health Scheme in NSW.
Methodist Overseas Mission estb. Yirrkala Aboriginal Mission on Gove Peninsula, NT.
R. Docherty estb. Catholic Aboriginal Mission at Port Keats, NT.
Librarians draw attention to need for more public libraries to supplement Aust. education systems.
To ease unemployment in longer term, post-primary education slanted more toward technical training.
NSW Commission of Inquiry into Technical Education tables report urging greater allocation of funds to specialized technical education at college level.

E

Sport

During 1935
Marabou, ridden by K. Voitre, wins Melbourne Cup in 3 minutes $23\frac{3}{4}$ seconds.
Collingwood football team wins VFL Premiership in Melbourne.
Eastern Suburbs football team wins Rugby League Premiership in Sydney.
Haydn Bunton (the elder) of Fitzroy VFL team awarded Brownlow Medal.
Canterbury-Bankstown Rugby League team founded in Sydney.
J. Turner invents cricko.
G. Lamble and E. Skardarasy estb. Kosciusko Ski School.
Aust. Badminton Association estb. Championships begin.
Melbourne Cricket Club prohibits bodyline bowling, claiming it to be direct-attack bowling endangering batsman.
Jack Metcalfe sets world triple-jump record.
Ken Kennedy, ice hockey player, wins ice speed titles in England.

Births & Deaths
Malcolm Anderson, tennis player, b.
Allen Aylett, VFL footballer and administrator, b.
Keith Barnes, Rugby League footballer, b.
George Bracken, boxer, b.
Ian Craig, cricketer, b.
Bruce Sidney Crampton, golfer, b.
Brian Dixon, VFL footballer, b.
Graham Polly Farmer, VFL footballer, b.
Ross Hazelton, surfing long board rider, b.
Lindsay Hubert Head, SA Aust. Rules footballer, b.
Jon Henricks, swimmer, b.
Tom Phillis, motorcyclist, b. (d. 1962)
Max Stewart, motor sportsman, b (d. 1977)
Albert Thomas, runner, b.

1935

1935

F
Historia Dignum

Population
Estimated total white, 6,755,662.

25–27 Mar. Pearling fleet anchored at Lacepede Bay, SA, hit by cyclone; 142 lives lost.
1 Jul. Australian Associated Press (AAP) estb. links with international Reuters organization.
2 Oct. A DH86 aircraft crash on Flinders I. claims five lives.
During 1935
Hugh Donald McIntosh opens first milk bar in England.
Bert Sachse invents the Pavlova dish in Perth. (Named after Anna Pavlova, ballet dancer.)
Fergus McMaster becomes first regular passenger to make Aust.–England flight.
Nancy Walton becomes youngest woman in British Cwlth to acquire a commercial pilot's licence.
First Jacaranda Festival held at Grafton, NSW. First flower festival in Aust.
Padded look in fashion highlighting wide square shoulders and minimized waists becomes popular in men's fashions.
Coloured leather shoes, open-toed sandals and rayon stockings introduced into women's fashions.
Aust. Bridge Federation estb. as Aust. Bridge Council.
Hemlines plunge from knee-length to below calf.
Shark arm murder mystery unfolds in Sydney.

A

History, Politics, Economics, Law

Government

22 Jan. 1936–6 Aug. 1936, Sir Philip Whistler Street administered NSW.

23 Jan. 1936–30 Jan. 1945, Alexander Gore Arkwright Hore-Ruthven, Lord Gowrie, Governor-General Aust.

6 Aug. 1936–29 Oct. 1936, Sir David Murray Anderson Governor NSW.

20 Aug. 1936–Jul. 1945, J. C. Willcock Labor Premier WA.

29 Oct. 1936–8 Apr. 1937, Sir Philip Whistler Street administered NSW.

Apr. Aust. imposes protective duties on Japanese rayon and cotton, beginning trade war with Japan.

Jun.–Dec. Trade diversion policy restricts imports from USA and Japan, but is abandoned after extensive protest.

27 Aug. ACTU declares a two-minute national strike in support of a 40-hour week.

Nov. WA Govt introduces compulsory voting.

31 Dec. Commercial printers are first in Aust. to receive one week's paid annual leave in a Federal award.

During 1936

Stanley Bruce appointed President of League of Nations.

Arthur William Fadden enters Federal Parlt.

UK first country to have officially recognized diplomatic representation in Aust. (Canada 1939, USA 1940, China 1941.)

Dame Florence Gillies Cardell-Oliver, who becomes first woman member of State cabinet in 1951, elected member of WA Legislative Assembly.

Joint Cwlth and State Marketing Schemes invalidated by decision of Privy Council in the James case.

William Walkley estb. Ampol Petroleum Ltd, only fully Aust.-owned oil company.

Aust. Wool Board estb. to supervise orderly disposal of wool.

Births & Deaths

Charles Nelson Perkins, Aboriginal spokesman, public servant, b.

B

Science, Technology, Transport, Discovery

Feb. Reginald Myles Ansett forms Ansett Airways Pty Ltd.

Apr. Civil Aviation Board estb.

14 May. Holyman Airways, Adelaide Airways and West Australian Airways merge to form (the 2nd) Australian National Airways.

Nov. Hume Dam, Vic., completed. (Largest public works project in Aust. at that time.)

During 1936

Cwlth Aircraft Corporation Ltd estb. to make military aircraft suited to Aust. conditions.

Geoffrey Winkler builds the Wicko FWI, England's first motor car-engined aircraft.

National Health and Medical Research Council estb.

Tas.–mainland telephone service opens.

1936

1936 C Arts

Literature

During 1936
National Library first publishes the *Annual Catalogue of Australian Publications*.
A. B. (Banjo) Paterson publishes novel *The Shearer's Colt*.
Miles Franklin publishes *All that Swagger*.
Brian Penton publishes *The Inheritors*.
Ellen Dymphna Cusack publishes first novel, *Jungfrau*.
Eleanor Dark publishes *Return to Coolami*.
Jean Devanny publishes *Sugar Heaven*.
P. R. Stephensen publishes critical essay, *The Foundations of Culture in Aust.*

Music, Dance

13 Oct. Monte Carlo Russian Ballet begins Aust. tour in Adelaide.
During 1936
ABC estb. permanent studio orchestras in all capitals; introduces subscription concerts.
Graeme Bell forms jazz band, *Gay's Swing Gang*.
Joseph Post becomes conductor ABC Melbourne Symphony Orchestra. (Until 1946.) Clive Douglas becomes conductor ABC Tas. Symphony Orchestra. (Until 1939.)

Births & Deaths
Margreta Elkins, mezzo soprano, b.
Bryan Lawrence, ballet dancer, b.
Garth de Burgh Welch, ballet dancer, choreographer, b.

Drama, Theatre, Film

22 Jul. Police attempt to stop performance of anti-Nazi play *Till the Day I Die* at Savoy Theatre in Sydney.
During 1936
Dad and Dave radio serial begins. (Runs for 15 years.)
Sydney Tomholt produces *Bleak Downs and Other Plays*.

Fine Arts

During 1936
W. B. McInnes wins Archibald Prize for *Dr Julian Smith*.
The Sir John Sulman Prize for subject painting or mural decoration first awarded.
Ivor Hele wins SA Centennial Art Prize.
Danila Vassilieff paintings encourage development of expressionism and social realism.
Rex Battarbee gives Albert Namatjira lessons in watercolour materials.
International Art Exhibition held in Sydney.
Perth Society of Artists founded.
Reeves Art Prize awarded in Sydney.
Leslie Bowles completes sculpture *Diana* in Melbourne.

Architecture

During 1936
London Court in Perth designed.

Births & Deaths
Asher Bilu, space picture painter, b.
Gunter Christmann, colour field optical painter, b.
William Delafield Cook, photorealist painter, b.
John Davis, sculptor, b.
Robert R. Ingpen, painter, industrial designer, b.
Ken Reinhard, painter, b.
Max Robinson, industrial designer, painter, probably b.
David Rose, painter, graphic artist, b.
John Truscott, theatre designer, b.
Max Watters, painter, b.

D
Religion, Learning

Mar. Interstate conference on technical education, held in Melbourne, estb. Aust. Educational Council. Aim is to promote Federal funding for technical education.

During 1936
Aust. Union of Students (AUS) estb.
Aust. Education Council estb.
In Tas., Area Schools opened to consolidate smaller schools. (Become District Schools in 1973.)

E
Sport

28 Aug. Horse Solid Gold sets world steeplechasing record by jumping 36 feet over water at Wagga Wagga, NSW.

During 1936
Wotan, ridden by O. Philips, wins Melbourne Cup in 3 minutes $21\frac{1}{4}$ seconds.
Collingwood football team wins VFL Premiership in Melbourne.
Eastern Suburbs football team wins Rugby League Premiership in Sydney.
Dinny Ryan of Fitzroy VFL team awarded Brownlow Medal.
Aust. wins one bronze medal at Berlin Olympics.
Inter-Dominion Pacing Championship begins; biggest trotting event in Aust.
J. C. Pollock estb. Melbourne Fencing Club.
Lionel Van Praag wins first world motorcycle speedway championship in London.
The Aust. Clay Pigeon Trap Shooting Association estb. First Aust. championships held.
The Game Fishing Association of Aust. estb. American Zane Grey makes series of record fish catches off eastern Aust. coast.
Water skiing becomes popular in Darwin.

Births & Deaths
Graham Arthur, VFL footballer, b.
Reg Austin, athlete, b.
Ronald Dale Barassi, Aust. Rules footballer, b.
Haydn Bunton (the younger), WA and SA Aust. Rules footballer, b.
Neil Campton, jockey, b.
Ashley Cooper, tennis player, b.
Roy Emerson, tennis player, b.
Leo Geoghegan, racing car driver, b.
Charles Porter, athlete, high jumper, b.
Roy Quinton, jockey, b.
Warren Scarfe, cyclist, b. (d. 1964)
Robert Baddeley (Bobby) Simpson, cricketer, b.
Johnny Stewart, speedway driver, b.
Arthur Summons, Rugby Union player, b.
Norma Thrower, hurdler, b.
Ian Tomlinson, jumper, b.
Murray Weideman, VFL footballer, b.

1936

1936

F
Historia Dignum

Population
Estimated total white, 6,810,413.

1 Jan. Vessel *Paringa* sinks in Bass Strait, claiming 31 lives.
During Jan. B. A. Santamaria issues first *Catholic Worker*, monthly journal.
13 Mar. Greatest rainfall recorded in Aust. in one hour; 12.99 inches, at Deeral, Qld.
1 Jun. Arnold Karl Sodeman hanged in Melbourne for multiple murders.
Oct.–Nov. Fire damages Casino district and Blue Mts in NSW.
During 1936
NSW Govt introduces shark meshing on some coastal beaches.
Settlers at Boonarga in south-western Qld erect the Cactoblastic Memorial Hall in memory of caterpillar which destroyed the prickly pear. (Possibly only memorial erected anywhere in world to honour an insect.)
Man magazine first published. First print run sold out within week.

Communities
Moura, Qld, estb.

A

History, Politics, Economics, Law

Government

8 Apr. 1937–6 Jun. 1945, John de Vere Loder, Lord Wakehurst, Governor NSW.

17 May 1937–21 Nov. 1937, Sir James William Blair administered Qld.

22 Nov. 1937–23 Apr. 1946, Sir Leslie Orme Wilson Governor Qld.

1937–1946, C. L. A. Abbott Administrator NT under Cwlth jurisdiction.

6 Mar. Proposals at referendum to increase Federal Govt powers in respect of marketing and aviation rejected.

May. Coronation of King George VI in London.

23 Oct. Joseph Aloysius Lyons returned as UAP Prime Minister at national elections.

30 Nov. Fifteenth Federal Parlt opens. (Dissolution 27 Aug. 1940.)

During 1937

Arbitration Court adds six shillings prosperity allowance to basic wage.

Last formal Imperial Conference held, in London.

Sir Frank Keith Officer appointed Aust. Counsellor to British Embassy in Washington. (First Aust. diplomatic representation to a Cwlth Embassy.)

Royal Commission Report on Monetary and Banking systems in Aust. favours change to decimal currency.

Aust. Associated Stock Exchanges estb.

Modern Aust. tuna fishing industry begins.

Harold Bruce Farncomb becomes first RAN College graduate appointed captain.

At Federal Govt conference assimilation for some Aborigines adopted as official policy.

Births & Deaths

Kevin Arthur Wheatley, first of four Aust. soldiers in Vietnam to win VC, b. (d. 1965)

B

Science, Technology, Transport, Discovery

Nov. First air-conditioned train, the *Spirit of Progress*, begins Melbourne–Albury, Vic., run. Built by Harold Clapp.

During 1937

MacFarlane Burnet isolates and identifies the causal agent of *Q* fever, an infectious disease affecting people associated with cattle.

Institute of Medical and Veterinary Science estb. in Adelaide.

Refrigerators now widely used.

Westinghouse radio introduced. One million radio licences issued to date.

Modern-scale fish canning begins.

First open-cut mining of coal in Aust. begins, at Blair Athol, Qld.

Whyalla, SA, pig-iron blast furnace planned. (Operational by 1941.)

Les Vaughan invents snail killer.

1937

1937

Arts

Literature

During 1937
K. S. Prichard publishes *Intimate Strangers*.
Ernestine Hill publishes *The Great Australian Loneliness*.
Kenneth (Seaforth) McKenzie publishes *The Young Desire It*.

Births & Deaths
Colleen Margaretta McCullough, author, b.

Music, Dance

During 1937
Edouard Espinosa opens Aust. branch of British Ballet Organization, influencing Aust. ballet education.
Arthur Benjamin composes *Jamaican Rumba*.
Hélène Kirsova, dancer and choreographer, settles in Sydney.
Gordon Hamilton, ballet dancer, makes début.
Les Ballets Contemporains Co. estb. in Adelaide.
Phyllis Danaher estb. Ballet Theatre of Qld.

Drama, Theatre, Film

During 1937
Ken Hall makes sound feature film *Tall Timbers*.

Births & Deaths
Anthony Buckley, film producer, b.

Fine Arts

May. Royal British Colonial Society of Artists exhibits Aust. art.
During 1937
Norman Baker wins Archibald Prize for *Self Portrait*.
Adrian Lawler compiles *Arquebus*, book about Melbourne contemporary art movement.
Frank Hinder holds constructivist painting exhibition in Sydney.
Aust. Academy of Art estb. in Canberra.
Frances Burke becomes first registered textile screen printer in Aust.
NSW Sesqui-Centenary art prize awarded.

Births & Deaths
Janet Alderson, abstract painter, b.
Bruce Fletcher, first official Vietnam War artist, b.
Dale Hickey, painter, b.
Alun Leach-Jones, painter, graphic artist, b.
Mervyn Gregory Moriarty, painter, commercial artist, b.
Rollin Schlight, abstract painter, b.
Murray Walker, impressionist painter, graphic artist, b.
Richard J. Watkins, abstract painter, b.

Architecture

During 1937
Harry Tompkins, architect, builds Myer Emporium Melbourne.

D
Religion, Learning

E
Sport

1937

During 1937
Branches of International New Education Fellowship founded in Melbourne and Geelong, Vic. Holds conferences Australia-wide to discuss progressive education.
Aust. Institute of Librarians estb. to improve standard of Aust. librarianship.
Kingsley Fairbridge estb. Fairbridge Society farm schools at Bacchus Marsh, Vic., and Molong, NSW, to care for children of British immigrants.
Presbyterian Aboriginal Mission Ernabella estb. in Musgrave Ranges, SA. Among first successful mission schools for Aborigines.
Preston Technical School (now Preston Institute of Technology) estb. in Melbourne.
Improving economic conditions lead to revival of interest in educational reform.

During 1937
The Trump, ridden by A. Reed, wins Melbourne Cup in 3 minutes $21\frac{1}{2}$ seconds.
Geelong football team wins VFL Premiership in Melbourne.
Eastern Suburbs football team wins Rugby League Premiership in Sydney.
Dick Reynolds of Essendon VFL team awarded Brownlow Medal.
Greyhound Racing Control Council estb.
B. Peden leads first team of Aust. women cricketers on England tour.
Hazel Pritchard best batswoman in Aust. women's cricket.
Vic. Amateur Gymnastic Association organizes first gymnastic competitions.
First S. African Rugby Union Springboks team tours Aust.
Polo team from Goulburn, NSW, wins England's Premier polo trophy.
Aust. Table Tennis Association estb.

Births & Deaths
Robin Bailhache, cricket umpire, b.
Ronald William Clarke, athlete runner who breaks 17 world records, b.
Judy Dalton, tennis player, b.
John Devitt, swimmer, b.
Bruce William Devlin, golfer, b.
Laurie Dwyer, VFL footballer, b.
Dawn Fraser, swimmer, b.
William Morris Lawry, cricketer, noted batsman, b.
Billy McDonnell, boxer, b.
Stuart McKenzie, sculler, b.
Norman O'Neill, cricketer, b.
Barry Phillips-Moore, SA tennis player, b.
Russel Sands, boxer, b. (d. 1977)
Mel Schumacher, jockey, b.
Clive Stewart, boxer, b.
Judy Tegart, tennis player, b.
Ken Thornett, Rugby player, b.

F

Historia Dignum

1937

Population

Estimated total white, 6,871,492.

9 Feb. Cyclone damages Cairns, Qld. On 11 Mar. a cyclone damages Darwin, claiming five lives.
15 Feb. Explosion at Wonthaggi, Vic., coalmine claims 13 lives.
19 Feb. Stinson aircraft crashes in McPherson Ranges, Qld, claiming five lives.
1 Apr. Police Boys Club movement begins in Sydney.
Jun. Infantile paralysis epidemic in Vic.
During 1937
Tas. changes hotel closing time from 6 o'clock to 10 o'clock.
Fred and Maggie Everybody becomes one of first radio programmes to be recorded.

A
History, Politics, Economics, Law

1938

Government
5 Nov. 1938–Mar. 1965, (Sir) T. Playford Liberal Country League Premier SA.
7 Nov. 1938–7 Apr. 1939, Eighteenth Cwlth Ministry, Joseph Aloysius Lyons UAP-Country coalition Prime Minister Aust.

4 Mar. Assisted passages for nominated emigrants from Britain resume.
Jul. In effort to protect domestic iron industry, and to remove Japanese Nippon Mining Co. from Kimberley region in WA, Cwlth Govt bans export of iron ore.
Aug. Police Constable Murray shoots about 30 Aborigines in Dala and Coniston massacres in NT.
Nov. Waterside workers at Port Kembla, NSW, refuse to load pig iron bound for Japan. R. G. Menzies, Cwlth Attorney-General, threatens to invoke 'Dog Collar' Transport Workers Act against the unions, thereby earning the sobriquet 'Pig Iron Bob'.
Dec. New Defence programme involves expenditure of £63 million over three years and raises militia forces to 70,000.

During 1938
Amendment to Seat of Government Acceptances Act changes name Federal Capital Territory to Australian Capital Territory.
Pearce RAAF pilot training base estb. in WA.
Aust. purchases cruisers HMAS *Hobart* and HMAS *Perth* from Britain.
New Trade Agreement with Japan and USA signed.
Coca-Cola first made in Aust.
T. F. Elliot appointed first Agent-General for Emigration in London.
Walkerville (Southwark) Brewery estb. in Adelaide.
Aust. agrees to accept refugees from Nazi Germany.

Births & Deaths
Alan Bond, businessman, yachtsman, b.

B
Science, Technology, Transport, Discovery

Dec. Direct telephone links estb. between Canberra and Washington.

During 1938
Donald Clifford Tyndall Bennett establishes world long-distance seaplane record from, Scotland to S. Africa (9,650 kilometres in 42 hours).
Qantas launches flying boat service.
Associated Pulp and Paper Mills Ltd becomes first company to produce fine papers from Aust. hardwoods, in Burnie, Tas.
Charles Bickerton Blackburn becomes first President of Royal Aust. College of Physicians.
William Alan Stewart plans and develops first beamed radar.
National Measurement Laboratory, CSIR, estb. as National Standards Laboratory.
Melbourne Hospital appoints first dietitian.
Dept of Civil Aviation estb.
Aust. Red Cross Blood Transfusion Service estb. First of kind in world.
Lang Hancock discovers asbestos near Wittenoom, WA.
Air traffic control system begins in Aust.
The Soil Conservation Service of NSW estb.

Births & Deaths
Ralph Sarich, engineer, inventor, b.

555

1938

Arts

Literature

During 1938
Reginald (Rex) Ingamells estb. Jindyworobak group to develop Australianism in Literature.
Daisy Bates publishes *The Passing of the Aborigines*.
Xavier Herbert publishes *Capricornia*.
Robert D. FitzGerald publishes *Moonlight Acre*.
Kenneth MacKenzie publishes *Chosen People*.

Births & Deaths
Morris Lurie, author, b.
Frank Moorhouse, short story writer, b.
Leslie Allan Murray, poet, b.

Music, Dance

28 Sep. Covent Garden Russian Ballet opens Aust. tour in Melbourne.
30 Dec. Lichine's Ballet *The Prodigal Son* has world première in Sydney. First world première in Aust. by international company.

During 1938
Ida Beeby founds Patch School of Drama and Dance in Perth.

Births & Deaths
Lucette Aldous, ballet dancer, b.
Bruce James Smeaton, composer, b.

Drama, Theatre, Film

During 1938
Peter Finch makes film début in *Dad and Dave Come to Town*.
Charles Chauvel makes film *Moth of Moombi*.
Ken Hall makes film *Let George Do It*, starring George Wallace.
Playwrights Advisory Board estb. to encourage creation of Aust. drama.

Births & Deaths
Phillip Andrew Adams, film producer, actor, b.
Richard David Bradshaw, puppeteer, b.
Kenneth Gregory Horler, theatrical director, b.
Reg Livermore, entertainer, b.
Albert Watson (Bert) Newton, television entertainer and compere, b.

Fine Arts

13 Jul. George Bell estb. Contemporary Art Society in Melbourne to oppose conservative views of Academy of Art. (Branches open in NSW 1939, SA 1943, Qld and Tas. 1963, WA 1966.)
5 Dec. Albert Namatjira holds first exhibition, in Melbourne. (Sells all 41 paintings.)

During 1938
Second phase of Modern Movement of Aust. art begins, influenced by reaction against aestheticism in criticism and abstract art, growth of contemporary realism, development of writer interest in art.
Nora Heysen becomes first woman to win the Archibald Prize, for *Mme Elink Schuurman*.
First Academy of Art National Exhibition held in Sydney.
Australian Commercial and Industrial Artists Association founded.
Bendigo Art Gallery Prize founded.
One Hundred and Fifty Years of Aust. Art Exhibition held in Sydney.
Geelong Art Gallery Prize estb., Vic.
Tas. group of painters founded to encourage young painters.

Architecture

During 1938
'Waterfall Front' houses with streamlined horizontal lines evoking a 'cascading' effect become popular.

Births & Deaths
Michael Challis Brown, realist painter, b.
Frederick Cress, abstract painter, b. (d. 1961)
Brian James Dunlop, painter, b.
George Haynes, abstract painter, b.
Robert Studley Forrest Hughes, painter, cartoonist, b.
Michael Johnson, watercolourist, b.
Wendy Paramor, sculptor, b. (d. 1977)
Emmanuel Raft, painter, jewellery designer, b.
Robin Wallace-Crabbe, abstract painter, b.

D
Religion, Learning

Apr. New England University at Armidale, NSW, estb. as College of Sydney University.

During 1938
Period of transition begins in education. (Ends c. 1967.) Comprehensive schools popular.
Education Reform Association estb. to fight for free education for all and for reduction in size of classes.
New Education Fellowship Branches estb. in all States to push for educational reform.
Tas. first to reform examination system (NSW 1938–1942, SA 1942–1944, Vic. 1947. No significant changes in Qld and WA.)
School curriculums begin to change, with tendency to relax intensity of study and defer acquisition of special skills until later stages in the school.
Preston Technical College in Melbourne first Aust. school to introduce Social Studies.
Aust. Pre-School Association estb.
Francis Xavier Gsell consecrated first Roman Catholic Bishop of Darwin.
Bush Church Aid Society Flying Medical Service estb.
Cwlth Govt estb. the Lady Gowrie Child Centres for child care.

Births & Deaths
Stephen Arthur Fitzgerald, academic, diplomat, author, b.

E
Sport

Feb. Empire Games (now Cwlth Games) held in Aust. for first time, in Sydney. Aust. wins 24 out of 70 medals.
Dec. Tom Jemison first to reach 100 mph, on a 25cc motorcycle.

During 1938
Catalogue, ridden by F. Shean, wins Melbourne Cup in 3 minutes 26¼ seconds.
Carlton football team wins VFL Premiership in Melbourne.
Canterbury-Bankstown football team wins Rugby League Premiership in Sydney.
Dick Reynolds of Essendon VFL team awarded Brownlow Medal.
England Test cricket team scores record number of runs against Aust. in England, 7–903.
First Aust. women's lacrosse begins.
Edward Hirst introduces polocrosse in Aust.
Bluey Wilkinson wins world motorcycle speedway championship.
Mount Panorama speed racing circuit at Bathurst, NSW, completed.
NSW Govt bans publicans from having handball courts in or about their hotels.
Decima Norman becomes noted international athlete.
Lance Skuthorpe becomes world famous roughrider.
Aust. hard-court tennis championships begin.
First Franco–Aust. Rugby League Test match played in France.
First interstate squash games played, in Sydney.
The Archery Society of WA estb., in Perth.

Births & Deaths
Darrel Baldock, VFL footballer, b.
Richard Cavill, swimmer, d.
Gary Chapman, swimmer, b. (d. 1978)
Lorraine Crapp, swimmer, b.
Terry Curley, Rugby Union player, b.
Elizabeth (Betty) Cuthbert, sprinter, b.
Billy Dunk, golfer, b.
Herbert James (Herb) Elliott, middle-distance runner, b.
Ken Eustice, SA Aust. Rules footballer, b.
Noel Freeman, walker, b.
Roy Higgins, jockey, b.
Ken Hiscoe, squash player, b.
Bob Holmes, yachtsman, b.
Peter Johnson, Rugby Union player, b.
Colin King, sky diver, b.
Rodney George Laver, tennis player, b.
Jim Leneham, Rugby Union footballer, b.
John Nicholls, VFL footballer, b.
Doug Robson, speedway sidecar motorcyclist, b.
Barry Shepard, cricketer, b.
Frederick Sidney Stolle, tennis player, b.
David Thiele, swimmer, b.

1938

F
Historia Dignum

Population
Estimated total white, 6,935,909.

10 Jan. The *Hospital Hour* radio programme begins. Becomes longest-running radio show in Aust.

6 Feb. 'Black Sunday', day of greatest mass rescue in history of surfing, at Bondi, Sydney, when about 70 lifesavers rescue 180 swimmers of 300 swept off sand bank; 5 drown.

13 Feb. Ferry *Rodney* capsizes on Sydney Harbour; 19 lives lost.

Apr. Aboriginal newspaper *The Australian Abo Call* first published, in Sydney.

25 Oct. DC3 aircraft crashes at Mt Dandenong, Vic., claiming 18 lives. DH84 aircraft crashes at Innisfail, Qld, on 29 Aug. claiming five lives.

10 Dec. Serious NSW bushfires on 'Black Saturday'.

During 1938
The Working Men's Club built at Mildura, Vic. Contains longest bar in world.

Melbourne men officially permitted to be topless on beaches.

Silks in vogue.

The Aust. Jewish Welfare Society estb. to assist immigrants.

A
History, Politics, Economics, Law

Government

24 Feb. 1939–11 Aug. 1939, Sir George Murray administered SA.

5 Apr. 1939–16 Jul. 1939, Sir Frederick Wollaston Mann administered Vic.

7 Apr. 1939–26 Apr. 1939, Nineteenth Cwlth Ministry, Sir Earle Page Country–UAP coalition Prime Minister Aust.

26 Apr. 1939–14 Mar. 1940, Twentieth Cwlth Ministry, Robert Gordon Menzies UAP Prime Minister Aust.

11 Jun. 1939–Dec. 1939, E. Dwyer-Gray Labor Premier Tas.

17 Jul. 1939–20 Feb. 1949, Sir Winston Joseph Dugan Governor Vic.

5 Aug. 1939–May 1941, A. Mair UAP Premier NSW.

12 Aug. 1939–26 Apr. 1944, Sir Charles Malcolm Barclay-Harvey Governor SA.

18 Dec. 1939–Dec. 1947, R. Cosgrove Labor Premier Tas.

Aug. Arbitration Court introduces standard 44-hour working week into Aust. industry.

During 1939
Sydney Ure Smith founds Ure Smith Publishing Co.
Cecil Madigan leads first expedition across Simpson Desert, NT. First to cross centre of Simpson Desert.
Aust. Wheat Board estb. to control prices and marketing. Aust. Barley Board also estb.

World War II

Aug. Cwlth Govt introduces national register of manpower to meet any emergency arising from tense European situation. Registers all males aged between 18 and 64.

3 Sep. Aust. announces declaration of war on Germany. Navy placed at Britain's disposal.

Sir Thomas Blamey appointed commander of Second Aust. Imperial Force (AIF).

Press accepts censorship. Price controls commence.

Govt introduces National Security Regulations, effectively becoming a unitary government.

15 Sep. War Cabinet constituted. First of 354 meetings on 27 Sep. (Dissolved in Jan. 1946.)

Advance party leaves for Middle East.

11 Oct. Aust. announces its participation in Empire Defence Scheme, with RAF to train air force staff.

20 Oct. Menzies re-instates compulsory military training for home defence. Special volunteer force of 20,000 men enlist and train for overseas service.

Nov. Citizen Military Forces recruit 75,000 men.

Births & Deaths

Andrew Sharp Peacock, Federal politician, b.

B
Science, Technology, Transport, Discovery

27 Mar. First Aust.-built military aeroplane, Wirraway No. 1, makes test run in Melbourne.

During Mar. Govt Aircraft Factories estb. to build military aircraft.

Jul. Ready Mix Concrete Co. estb. in Sydney. Begins first pre-mix concrete business in world.

1 Oct. Sydney buses begin taking over from trams.

During 1939
William Alan Stewart Butement proposes use of guided anti-aircraft weapon, which is adopted by British War Office.

Evelyn Owen submits Owen machine gun invention to Aust. army.

Argentine ant first found in Melbourne.

Large-scale lead, copper and zinc mining begins at Captains Flat, NSW. (Exhausted by 1962.)

Ernest Fisk registers patents for sound-proof windows and ventilators.

George Shepherd invents furniture castors.

Aeronautical and Engine research test laboratory estb. in Melbourne.

BHP leaves Broken Hill, NSW, after 54 years mining.

Aust. production of textiles from rayon begins, in Sydney.

1939

C

Arts

Literature

During 1939
Patrick White publishes his first novel, *Happy Valley*.
Kenneth Slessor publishes collection of poems, *Five Bells*.
Kylie Tennant publishes *Foveaux*.

Births & Deaths
Germaine Greer, feminist writer, b.

Music, Dance

May. Edouard Borovansky opens ballet school in Melbourne from which grows the Borovansky Ballet and eventually the Aust. Ballet.
During 1939
Music for *Jacaranda Dance* composed. One of few indigenous dances developed by settlers in Aust.
National Theatre Movement in Melbourne presents its first operas.

Drama, Theatre, Film

18 May. Minerva Theatre opens in Sydney.
During 1939
Gertrude Johnson estb. National Theatre Movement in Vic.
Ken Hall produces film, *Mr Chedworth Steps Out*.

Fine Arts

16 Oct. Basil Burdett's exhibition of modern art in Melbourne is first full-scale exhibition of modern European art shown in Aust.
During 1939
Max Meldrum wins Archibald Prize for *G. J. Bell*.
The Melbourne Herald Exhibition of contemporary European art gives impetus to school of Aust. modernists.
Modern period of Aust. painting flourishes. Displaces Heidelberg School and variants with styles emanating from Europe and later USA.
Peter Richard Bellew estb. Contemporary Arts Society in Sydney. Society also estb. in Melbourne.
Desiderius Orban arrives in Aust. Influences neo-Romantic painting.

Births & Deaths
George Baldessin, sculptor, draughtsman and graphic artist, b. (d. 1978)
Kevin Mortensen, sculptor, b.
Ti Parks, sculptor, b.
Gareth Laurence Sansom, abstract oil painter, b.
Jan Senbergs, abstract painter, b.
Brett Whiteley, semi-abstract painter, b.

D
Religion, Learning

During 1939
Matthew Beovich appointed Catholic Archbishop of Adelaide.
United Church of Northern Aust. estb.
George Lyndon Carpenter elected world commander of Salvation Army.
NSW and SA Govts pass Library Acts. (Tas. and Qld 1943, Vic. 1946, WA 1951.)
Dorothy Ross becomes headmistress of Melbourne Church of England Girls' Grammar School (until 1955). Introduces progressive educational changes, including options in choice of subjects and student self-government.

E
Sport

1939

During 1939
Rivette, ridden by E. Preston, wins Melbourne Cup in 3 minutes 27 seconds. Also wins Caulfield Cup.
Melbourne football team wins VFL Premiership.
Balmain football team wins Rugby League Premiership in Sydney.
Marcus Whelan of Collingwood VFL team awarded Brownlow Medal.
National Fitness Movement founded.
First polocrosse demonstration game played, near Sydney. Ingleburn Polocrosse Club estb. in NSW.
First casting tournaments held.
Amateur Basketball Union of Aust. estb. (Becomes Aust. Basketball Federation in 1979.)
A. K. Quist and J. Bromwich win Davis Cup.
Last grain clipper race to England held.
Norman (Wizard) Smith drives around Aust. in 45 days without stopping for repairs.

Births & Deaths
Ted Ball, golfer, b.
Ken Catchpole, Rugby Union footballer, b.
Greg Davis, Rugby League footballer, b. (d. 1979)
David Forbes, yachtsman, b.
Reginald Gasnier, Rugby League footballer, b.
Ian (Pete) Geoghegan, racing car driver, b.
Pam Kilborn, athlete, b.
Geoff Lane, jockey, b.
Kevin Murray, VFL footballer, b.
John Raper, Rugby League footballer, b.
Murray Rose, swimmer, b.
Bobby Sinn, boxer, b.
Bob Skilton, VFL footballer, b.
George Tatnell, racing car driver, b.
Wally Taylor, boxer, b.
Kenneth Warby, speedboat racer, b.

1939

F

Historia Dignum

Population
Estimated total white, 7,004,912.

Jan. Vic. bushfires claim 71 lives. Bushfires burn 180,000 acres in NSW and 24,000 acres in Tas.
Mar. Cyclone damages Port Hedland, WA.
6 Nov. Two light aircraft collide at Mascot in Sydney, claiming six lives.
19 Nov. *Sunday Telegraph* newspaper first published in Sydney.
20 Dec. Radio Aust., overseas broadcasting service of ABC, begins.
During 1939
Youth Hostels Association of Aust. estb.
Southerly quarterly review published.
Outbreak of Argentine ant in Melbourne. (Perth 1941, Sydney 1949, Tas. 1952.)
Seven-year drought begins in many parts of Aust., affecting cereal growing.
Harry Gough introduces sliced bread in Sydney.
c. 1939. Euchre becomes most popular card game.

A
History, Politics, Economics, Law

Government
14 Mar. 1940–28 Oct. 1940, Twenty-first Cwlth Ministry, Robert Gordon Menzies UAP-Country coalition Prime Minister Aust.
28 Oct. 1940–29 Aug. 1941, Twenty-second Cwlth Ministry, Robert Gordon Menzies UAP-Country coalition Prime Minister Aust.

8 Jan. Richard Gardiner Casey appointed Aust. diplomat in USA, marking Aust. entry into direct diplomatic representation with countries other than UK.
11 Mar.–16 May. Coalminers strike for higher wages and shorter hours.
8 Jun. Sir Keith Murdoch appointed head of information department.
21 Sep. R. G. Menzies returned as Prime Minister in Federal election.
20 Nov. Sixteenth Federal Parlt opens. (Dissolution 7 Jul. 1943.)
During 1940
Sir Dudley Williams appointed Justice of High Court of Aust. (Until 1958.)
Arthur Augustus Calwell enters Federal Parlt.
Herbert Vere Evatt resigns from judiciary to join Labor Opposition in Federal Parlt.

World War II
10 Jan. First contingent of Second AIF (6th Division), comprising 20,000 men, leaves Sydney for Egypt.
May. Essington Lewis, Managing Director of BHP, appointed Director-General of Munitions.
15 Jun. Govt bans Communist and Fascist politicial parties in Aust.
During Jun. Cwlth Govt given increased powers to meet Nazi threat.
1 Jul.–31 Oct. RAAF pilots serve in the Battle of Britain.
11 Jul. Petrol rationing introduced. Motorists limited to 2,000 miles per year.
Sep. The George Cross award created to recognize courage by civilians.
28 Oct. The War Council estb. (Abolished 31 Aug. 1945.)
During 1940
RSL estb. voluntary defence corps; 50,000 men join in six months.
AIF age limit raised from 35 to 40 years.
Aust. in actions in Libya. Aust. cruiser *Sydney* cripples Italian cruiser *Bartolomeo Colleoni*.
Bass Strait closed after British ship mined.

B
Science, Technology, Transport, Discovery

30 Apr. Tasman Empire Airways Ltd estb.
May. Construction of Capt. Cook Graving Dock at Garden I., Sydney, begins.
6 Jul. Storey Bridge in Brisbane opens.
During 1940
Frank Stanley Cotton invents the Cotton Aerodynamic Anti-Gravity Suit to prevent pilots from blacking out during high-speed turns or dives.
Keilor Skull, ancient Aboriginal cranium dated at about 12,900 years, discovered at Keilor, Vic.
Last Melbourne cable cars run.
Sir Howard Walter Florey and Dr E. Chain successfully experiment with penicillin as an antibiotic.

1940

563

1940

C Arts

Literature

Dec. Clement Byrne Christesen founds and edits literary journal *Meanjin* in Brisbane.
During 1940
Max Harris edits first *Angry Penguins*.
Matilda Ann (Tilly) Aston publishes *The Inner Garden*.
Christina Stead publishes *The Man Who Loved Children*.

Births & Deaths
Geoffrey John Lehmann, poet, b.

Music, Dance

1 Mar. World première of Lichine's ballet *Graduation Ball* in Sydney. World première of Nina Verchinina's *Etude* in Sydney on 25 Jul. World première of Igor Schwezoff's *Etudes Symphoniques Lutte Eternelle* in Sydney on 29 Jul.
During 1940
Hélène Kirsova forms classical ballet co. in Sydney. One of first professional ballet companies in Aust.
Laurel Martyn becomes first prima ballerina of Borovansky Ballet in Melbourne.

Births & Deaths
Athol Guy, singer from 'Seekers' group, b.
Helen Quach, musician, b.

Drama, Theatre, Film

Feb. Damien Parer, first Aust. combat cameraman, leaves for Palestine.
During 1940
Charles Chauvel makes film *Forty Thousand Horsemen*, starring Chips Rafferty.

Births & Deaths
John Anthony Bell, actor, director, b.
John (Jack) Hibberd, playwright, b.
Paul Hogan, television entertainer, b.
John Payne, stage name Jack Thompson, actor, b.
Richard Wherrett, actor, b.

Fine Arts

During 1940
Max Meldrum wins Archibald Prize for *Dr J. Forbes McKenzie*.
Council for the Advancement of Aust. Art estb.
Modern Art Centre and Exhibition Gallery estb. in Sydney.
Half Dozen Art Group estb. in Qld.
Russell Drysdale begins his outback paintings.
William Dobell paints *The Cypriot*.
Sidney Nolan holds his first exhibition (unsuccessful).
Independent Group of Artists estb. in Melbourne.

Births & Deaths
Tony Bishop, sculptor, b.
Peter Booth, oil abstract painter, b.
Silver Ley Collings, sculptor, b.
Basil Hadley, painter, b.
Noel Hutchison, sculptor, b.
Michael Digby Kitching, painter, industrial designer, b.
Keith Looby, painter, b.
Tony Woods, painter, b.

Architecture

During 1940
Roy Grounds, architect, designs one of first fan-shaped block of flats, in Melbourne.

D

Religion, Learning

14 Apr. Catholic Church declares third Sunday after Easter Social Justice Sunday.

Oct. SA Govt amends Education Act to allow ministers of religion to give instruction to pupils of their own denominations in State schools. (Attempts to introduce religious instruction had previously failed in 1921, 1924 and 1934.)

During 1940
Cardinal Norman Gilroy becomes first Aust.-born archbishop in Roman Catholic Church.
Oslo school lunch trials begin in Melbourne to raise nutrition level of school lunches.
NSW raises minimum school leaving age from 14 to 15 years.

E

Sport

During 1940
Old Rowley, ridden by A. Knox, wins Melbourne Cup in 3 minutes 26 seconds.
Melbourne football team wins VFL Premiership.
Eastern Suburbs football team wins Rugby League Premiership in Sydney.
Desmond Fothergill of Collingwood and Herbert Matthews of South Melbourne VFL teams awarded the Brownlow Medal.
Billy Cook, jockey, rides 126 winners in one season.
Vic. Trugo Association estb.
Horace Lindrum wins world snooker championship.

Births & Deaths

Kevin Bartlett, racing car driver, b.
Michael Cleary, all-round sportsman, b.
Ron Corry, soccer player, b.
Peter Crittle, Rugby Union player, b.
Ken Fletcher, tennis player, b.
Tony Gresham, golfer, b.
Jules Guerassimoff, Rugby Union footballer, b.
Ken Irvine, Rugby League footballer, b.
Edward (Mick) Mallyon, jockey, b.
Allan Moffat, racing car driver, b.
Alan Murray, golfer, b.
Ingo Renner, glider, b.
Keith Stackpole, cricketer, b.
Brian Taber, cricketer, b.
Dick Thornett, water polo and rugby union player, b.
Bill Vojtek, soccer player, b.

1940

F

Historia Dignum

Population
Estimated total white, 7,077,586.

18 Feb. Cyclone damages north Qld coast.
Mar. Bushfires damage King I. and Derwent Valley, Tas.
13 Aug. RAAF aircraft crashes near Canberra, claiming ten lives, including three senior Federal Govt Ministers and Chief of the General Staff of Army.
During Nov. ABC appoints Margaret Doyle, its first woman announcer.
During 1940
The *Whyalla News* estb. at Whyalla, SA.
George Korody introduces natural-coloured wood into Aust. furniture.

A
History, Politics, Economics, Law

Government
16 May 1941–Feb. 1947, W. J. McKell Labor Premier NSW.
29 Aug. 1941–7 Oct. 1941, Twenty-third Cwlth Ministry, Arthur William Fadden, Country-UAP coalition, Prime Minister Aust.
7 Oct. 1941–21 Sep. 1943, Twenty-fourth Cwlth Ministry, John Curtin Labor Prime Minister Aust.

16 Jan. Cwlth Govt introduces nation-wide child endowment scheme, 5 shillings for each child under 16 after the first. (Becomes Family Allowance in 1976.) Financed by system of collecting payroll tax by instalments.
Oct. Arthur William Fadden Country-UAP coalition Opposition leader. (Until 1943.)
Aust. First Movement, ultra nationalistic wartime organization, estb. in Sydney to support defence of Aust. (Between Mar. and May 1942 leading members interned.)
During 1941
Fed. Govt introduces gift duties to prevent avoidance of estate duty by making gifts prior to death.
Aust. newsprint industry estb.

World War II
3 Jan. The Second AIF sees first action when 6th Division attacks Bardia in Libya.
Mar. Part of 6th Division arrives in Greece. (German invasion on 6 Apr.)
10 Apr.–10 Dec. Aust. 9th Division ('Rats of Tobruk') in siege of Tobruk.
8 Jun.–12 Jul. Aust. 7th Division provides spearhead for Syrian invasion.
19 Nov. HMAS *Sydney* sunk by German raider *Kormoran*.
7 Dec. Japan attacks Pearl Harbour and lands troops in Malaya.
8 Dec. Aust. declares war on Japan.
27 Dec. Prime Minister Curtin makes 'Aust. looks to America speech'. First American troops arrive in Brisbane on 22 Dec.
During 1941
Women's Auxiliary Aust. Air Force estb. First women's service other than nursing.

B
Science, Technology, Transport, Discovery

During 1941
Elizabeth Kenny supported in work on poliomyelitis by the medical committee of the US National Foundation for Infantile Paralysis.
Norman Gregg's discovery of the relationship between German measles (rubella) and congenital defects, such as blindness in the child, is announced.
Aust. Advisory Committee on Aeronautics estb.
Evelyn Ernest Owen's machine gun patented.
Adelaide–Darwin telephone link opens.
Broken Hill Pty Co. Ltd estb. iron smelting works at Whyalla, SA.
Steam engine 'Heavy Harry' built. Most powerful in Aust.

Births & Deaths
Robin Eve Miller, nurse with Flying Doctor Service who was to administer anti-polio vaccine in outback, b. (d. 1975)
James Nangle, astronomer, d.

1941

1941

C Arts

Literature

During 1941
Aust. *Poetry Annual* first issued.
Max Harris founds *Angry Penguins* school of Aust. poets.
Kylie Tennant publishes *The Battlers*.
Eleanor Dark publishes *The Timeless Land*.
J. A. Ferguson publishes first volume of seven-volume *Bibliography of Australia*.

Music, Dance

8 Jul. Kirsova Ballet premières in Sydney.
During 1941
SA Ballet Club estb.

Births & Deaths

Ian Farr, composer, b.
Moya Patricia Henderson, composer, b.
John Williams, guitarist, b.

Drama, Theatre, Film

During 1941
Noel Monkman produces film *The Power and the Glory*.

Births & Deaths

Michael Thornhill, film director, producer, b.

Fine Arts

During 1941
William Dargie wins Archibald Prize for *Sir James Elder*.
Orban Art School founded in Sydney.
Russell Drysdale noted for his drought and country life paintings.
Ralph Balson holds first non-figurative one-man exhibition in Aust. All abstract paintings.

Births & Deaths

Elwyn Dennis, sculptor, b.
Margaret Dodd, sculptor, b.
Lesley Dumbrell, abstract colour painter, b.
Barrie Goddard, contemporary painter, b.
Ron Robertson-Swann, sculptor, painter, b.

D Religion Learning

Jan. Jehovah's Witnesses organization declared illegal.
Mar. Army Education Service estb.
Sep. Army education journal *Salt* first published.
During 1941
National Fitness Councils estb. in all States.

E
Sport

During 1941
Skipton, ridden by W. Cook, wins Melbourne Cup in 3 minutes 23¾ seconds.
Melbourne football team wins VFL Premiership.
St George football team wins Rugby League Premiership in Sydney.
Norman Ware of Footscray VFL team awarded Brownlow Medal.
Walter Lindrum scores 100 billiard points in 46 seconds.
Arthur Dunstan wins a bicycle race riding backwards.

Births & Deaths
Lionel Cox, cyclist, b.
Rocco (Rocky) Gattellari, boxer, b.
Pat Hyland, jockey, b.
Heather Pamela McKay, squash player, b.
Graham McKenzie, cricketer, noted fast bowler, b.
Sid Prior, boxer, b.
Roy Prosser, Rugby Union player, b.
Doug Wade, VFL footballer, record goal kicker with 1,060 goals, b.
Ron Wanless, all-round sportsman, speedcar driver, b.
John Watkiss, soccer player, b.

F
Historia Dignum

Population
Estimated total white, 7,143,598.

Jan. First ABC Argonauts Club estb.
7 Feb. Govt revokes Jehovah's Witnesses radio station, fearing the group would obstruct war effort.
Feb. Alex Gurney's typical digger cartoon characters 'Bluey' and 'Curley' first appear.
13 Mar. Wilfred Thomas Dinner Show begins. Becomes longest-running compered radio show in Aust.
12 May. Sydney newspaper *Daily Mirror* begins publication.
11 Nov. Aust. War Memorial in Canberra officially opens.

During 1941
News print rationed to 55 per cent of pre-war level.
Petrol further rationed.
Bob Dyer first heard on Aust. radio.

Communities
Boys Town, WA, estb.
Leigh Creek, SA, estb.

1941

1942

A
History, Politics, Economics, Law

Government
16 Sep. 1942–Mar. 1946, F. A. Cooper Labor Premier Qld.

31 Jan. Cwlth Govt mobilizes entire Aust. workforce; implements manpower regulations.
21 Mar. Aust. and New Guinea Administration Unit estb. to control Papua and New Guinea during war.
14 May. Cwlth introduces pensions for widows.
Jun. Labour movement adopts compulsory unionism as official policy.
27 Aug. SA Govt introduces compulsory voting at State elections.
18 Dec. Labor Govt lifts ban on Communist Party of Aust. (Imposed in Jun. 1940.)
Dec. Dept of Post-War Construction estb.
During 1942
Large mobs of cattle driven inland in case of invasion.
B. A. Santamaria founds The Movement, a secret political organization and Catholic social studies movement, to fight Communist influence in trade union movement.
Cwlth Govt introduces uniform taxation to cope with war expenditure. Becomes sole income tax levying authority.
Broadcasting and Television Act regulates radio operations.
First Federal subsidy to dairy industry.
E. J. (Eddie) Ward, Minister for Labor and National Service, states that in early days of World War II Aust. Govt intended to abandon northern Aust. to enemy in event of an invasion. This begins 'The Brisbane Line' controversy.
Aust. signs a Mutual Aid Agreement with the USA with the aim of reducing protection and discrimination in world trade.
Stevedoring Industry Commission introduces practice of gang hiring on the waterfront.
Building Workers' Industrial Union (BWIU) of Aust. estb.
Aust. adopts the Statute of Westminster.

World War II
23 Jan. Japanese invade New Britain; capture Rabaul.
15 Feb. Malaya falls to Japanese, who capture Singapore, imprisoning 15,384 Aust. troops of 8th Division. Commander of 8th Division, Lieut-Gen. Henry Gordon Bennett, later criticized for escaping and leaving troops.
19 Feb. Army nurses massacred by Japanese at Banka I. Beach.
128 Japanese aircraft bomb Darwin, killing 233 and wounding 250.
8 Mar. Japanese occupy Lae and Salamaua in NG and bomb Port Moresby. On 12 Mar. Java surrenders to Japanese.
17 Mar. Gen. Douglas MacArthur arrives in Aust. Sets up headquarters for SW Pacific Command in Melbourne on 18 Apr.
During Mar. Sir Thomas Albert Blamey appointed Commander-in-chief of Aust. Military Forces.
Air Vice-Marshall Donald Clifford Tyndall Bennett founds and commands RAF pathfinder force, bomber command.
4–8 May. Allied and Japanese air and naval forces engage in Coral Sea Battle. First Pacific defeat suffered by Japanese.
31 May. Three Japanese midget submarines enter Sydney Harbour. Torpedo ferry boat *Kuttabul*, used as naval depot, killing 19.
15 Jul. Volunteer Defence Corps (Home Guard) estb.
25 Aug.–6 Sep. Aust. forces inflict first land defeat o Japanese, at Milne Bay, NG.
Sep.–Oct. Main Aust. offensive on Kokoda Trail in NG begins. Aust. wins Battle of Kokoda on 2 Nov.
23 Oct. In N. Africa Aust. 9th Division fights at El Alamein.
During 1942
Aust. Volunteer Defence Corps reaches 100,000.

Births & Deaths
Douglas Ackley Lowe, Tas. Premier, b.
Ian Lindsay Tuxworth, NT Chief Minister, b.

B

Science, Technology, Transport, Discovery

During 1942
Aust. has 1,035 Tiger Moth aircraft in service. More than any other type of aircraft.
Inigo Jones recommends estb. long-range weather forecasting trust.
National Acoustics Laboratory estb.

C

Arts

Literature

During 1942
Leonard Mann publishes *The Go-Getter*.
Eve Langley publishes *The Pea Pickers*.
John Villers Farrow publishes *Pageant of the Popes*.
Leslie Rees publishes children's book *Digit Dick on the Barrier Reef*.

Births & Deaths
Michael Wilding, short story writer, novelist, critic, b.

Music, Dance

During 1942
A. E. Floyd begins concert presentation on ABC radio.
Kenneth Murison Bourn appointed conductor of Tas. Symphony Orchestra (until 1962).

Births & Deaths
Ian Bonighton, composer, b.
Helen Reddy, singer, b.
Bruce Woodley, singer from 'Seekers' group, b.
Roger Woodward, pianist, b.

Drama, Theatre, Film

During 1942
Douglas Stewart wins two ABC play competitions with *Ned Kelly* and *The Golden Lover*.

Births & Deaths
Ronald Hugh Blair, playwright, b.
David Keith Williamson, playwright, b.

Fine Arts

During 1942
William Dargie wins Archibald Prize for *Corporal Jim Gordon*.
Contemporary Art Society holds exhibition of anti-Fascist art in Melbourne and Adelaide.

Births & Deaths
Robert Boynes, artist, b.
Tony Coleing, painter, sculptor, printmaker, b.
Carl Hampel, painter, d.
Clive White Murray, sculptor, b.
Larry Pickering, cartoonist, b.
Peter Powditch, painter, b.
Martin Ritchie Sharp, artist, b.
Guy Stuart, sculptor, b.

1942

1942

D
Religion, Learning

4 Nov. Cwlth Govt estb. University Commission to begin scholarship scheme for needy students.
During 1942
United Church of N. Aust. estb. Aboriginal mission at Elcho I., NT.
War brings major upheavals to schools. Some schools taken over by army.
Committee on Educational Extension appointed in Tas. Recommends emphasis on cultural and vocational education.
Uniform Commonwealth taxation reduces resources of States and leads to increased demand for Federal funding.

E
Sport

During 1942
Colonus, ridden by H. McCloud, wins Melbourne Cup in 3 minutes $33\frac{1}{4}$ seconds.
Essendon football team wins VFL Premiership in Melbourne.
Canterbury-Bankstown football team wins Rugby League Premiership in Sydney.
VFL Brownlow Medal suspended until 1946.
Horse and greyhound racing subject to wartime restrictions. No mid-week racing and no racing on first Saturday of each month.
Softball introduced to Aust.

Births & Deaths

Colin Bond, car racer, b.
Leslie Bowrey, tennis player, b.
Deric Clayton, athlete, b.
Margaret Court, tennis player who wins Aust. title 11 times in 14 seasons, b.
Ross Edwards, cricketer, b.
Jeff Freeman, speedway driver, b. (d. 1965)
Les Johns, Rugby League footballer, b.
Sue Knight, driver and swimmer, b.
Jon Konrads, swimmer, b.
Graeme Langlands, Rugby League footballer, b.
John McCormack, racing car driver, b.
Dick Marks, Rugby Union footballer, b.
Vern Schuppan, racing car driver, b.
Billy Smith, Rugby Union player, b.
Tony Sneazewell, high jumper, b.
Dixie Willis, runner, b.

F
Historia Dignum

1942

Population
Estimated total white, 7,201,096.

1 Jan. Daylight saving begins. Clocks advanced one hour as a wartime measure to conserve fuel and electricity.
12 Jan. Fire destroys army warehouse in Brisbane, claiming three lives.
20 Feb. DH86 aircraft crashes at Belmont, Qld, claiming nine lives. On 28 Feb. Empire Flying Boat disappears in Indian Ocean with 20 on board. On 21 Apr. a Lockheed 14 aircraft crashes at Annaburroo Station, NT, claiming 12 lives.
15 Mar. Australians required to carry identity cards.
30 Mar. Food rationing introduced for tea, sugar and butter. (Tea: one half-pound per person for five weeks; sugar: one pound per person per week; butter: one half-pound per person per week.)
9 Nov. Edward Joseph Leonski executed for multiple murders.

During 1942
NSW Police Force founds first cliff rescue squad in world.
Kindergarten of the Air begins in Perth. First radio programme of kind in world.
Cwlth introduces 'Dedman' or 'Victory' suit, restricting garment to a one-style single-breasted two-button coat with no buttons on sleeves and cuffless trousers.
ABC radio launches programme *The Village Glee Club*. (Ends Mar. 1971.)

Communities
Learmonth, WA, estb.

1943

A
History, Politics, Economics, Law

Government

14 Sep. 1943–Sep. 1943, J. Cain (the elder) Labor Premier Vic.
18 Sep. 1943–Oct. 1945, A. A. Dunstan Country-UAP coalition Premier Vic.
21 Sep. 1943–6 Jul. 1945, Twenty-fifth Cwlth Ministry, John Curtin Labor Prime Minister Aust.

4 Jan. Cwlth Govt introduces conscription for limited military service outside Aust.
Feb. Cwlth Govt introduces national welfare scheme to increase number and variety of social services. Estb. funeral benefit allowance and special benefit to unmarried mothers for limited 12-week period.
Feb. Cwlth Govt estb. Housing Commission to study and report on housing conditions. Estb. National Works Council. Price stabilization scheme fixes prices of all goods and services at ruling levels. Govt also introduces pay as you earn taxation system.
21 Aug. John Curtin returned as Labor Prime Minister at Federal elections. Robert Gordon Menzies UAP Opposition leader until 1944, and then Liberal Opposition leader until 1949.
Dorothy Margaret Tangney from WA elected to Senate and Enid Lyons from Tas. elected to Federal House of Representatives. First women elected to Federal Parlt.
23 Sep. Seventeenth Federal Parlt opens. (Dissolution 16 Aug. 1946.)
During 1943
Aust. and Soviet Union exchange diplomatic representatives.
J. T. Lang expelled from Labor Party.
Arthur Calwell appointed first Aust. Minister for Immigration.
Aust. and US soldiers riot in 'Battle of Brisbane'.
Mortgage Bank dept of Cwlth Bank opens.
Record wool clip this year.
First free medical service in Aust. introduced at Scottsdale, Tas.
Three weeks' annual leave granted to Broken Hill mine employees.

World War II

23 Jan. 8th Army occupies Tripoli.
1 Feb. Aust. 9th Division begins return voyage to Aust.
14 May. Hospital ship *Centaur* sunk by Japanese off Qld coast; 300 lives lost.
During May. Japanese bomb installations at Exmouth Gulf, WA; most southerly point of air attack in Aust.
26 Sep. Fishing boat *Krait* carries Z Force commandos on successful raid against Japanese in Singapore.
***c.* 1943.** Darwin has been bombed by Japanese 64 times since 1942.
During 1943
Some 790,000 Australians in fighting services.
Aust. forces combine with American forces to recapture much of New Guinea.

Births & Deaths

Paul Anthony Edward Everingham, NT Chief Minister and Federal politician, b.

B

Science, Technology, Transport, Discovery

31 Mar. Last Sydney suburban steam train runs.

During 1943
Marcus Oliphant works with American scientists on project which develops the atomic bomb.
David Fleay breeds first platypus bred in captivity, at Healesville, Vic.
Howard Florey discovers how to extract penicillin from mould. Cwlth Serum Laboratories first produce penicillin in commercial quantities. Successfully used in treatment of chronic diseases.
Vic. Govt develops strain 19 vaccine to control brucellosis in cattle.
Open-cut coalmining begins at Leigh Creek, SA.
C. Swan associates deafness in children with rubella in pregnancy.

C

Arts

Literature

During 1943
Marjorie Barnard publishes *The Persimmon Tree*.
Max Harris publishes *The Vegetative Eye*.
Kylie Tennant publishes *Ride on Stranger* and *Time Enough Later*.
Hal Porter publishes his first collection of short stories.
Douglas Stewart publishes verse drama, *Ned Kelly*.

Music, Dance

During 1943
Graeme Bell estb. Dixieland Jazz Band.

Births & Deaths

Judith Durham, singer from 'Seekers' group, b.
Ross Edwards, composer, teacher, b.
Graham Hair, composer, b.

Drama, Theatre, Film

During 1943
Theatre staff in Melbourne and Sydney strike for three weeks.
Damien Parer becomes first Aust. film-maker to win an Academy Award, for *Kokoda Front Line*.
Gwen Meredith's *Blue Hills* first broadcast by ABC. (Runs for 33 years.)

Fine Arts

During 1943
William Dobell wins Archibald Prize for *Joshua Smith*.
Sidney Nolan exhibits *Dimboola*.

Births & Deaths

Theo Bolschuyver, sculptor, b.
John Firth-Smith, abstract oil painter, b.
John Hopkins, painter, b.
Patrick McCaughey, art critic, b.
Jeffrey Makin, painter, b.
Paul Partos, abstract oil painter, b.

1943

D
Religion, Learning

During 1943
HMAS *Watson* estb. in Sydney as navigation school.
Vic. and WA legislate to raise minimum school leaving age to 15.
Whyalla Technical High School opens. First multi-purpose school in SA.
Tas. Public Library becomes State Library of Tas.
Gowrie Scholarship Memorial Trust Fund created.
Cwlth Financial Assistance Scheme provides for payment of university fees and living allowances for eligible students.

E
Sport

During 1943
Dark Felt, ridden by V. Hartney, wins Melbourne Cup in 3 minutes $23\frac{1}{4}$ seconds.
Richmond football team wins VFL Premiership in Melbourne.
Newtown football team wins Rugby League Premiership in Sydney.

Births & Deaths
Bill Bowrey, tennis player, b.
Stewart Boyce, Rugby Union player, b.
Barry Cable, Australian Rules footballer, b.
Ian Chappell, cricketer, b.
Gail Corry, golfer, b.
Alfredo Costanzo, racing car driver, b.
Owen Davidson, tennis coach, b.
John Letts, jockey, b.
Jim Read, drag racing car driver, b.
Ross Smith, VFL footballer, b.
Ian Stewart, VFL footballer, b.
Des Tuddenham, VFL footballer, b.
Johnny Warren, soccer player, b.

F
Historia Dignum

1943

Population
Estimated total white, 7,269,658.

8 May. Bus collides with a train at Wodonga, Vic., claiming 25 lives.
May. ABC radio launches *Guest of Honour* programme. (Runs until 1980.)
26 Nov. Aust. Lockheed Lodestar aircraft crashes at Port Moresby, claiming 15 lives.
During 1943
Vic. bushfires begin.

Births & Deaths
Prudence Leigh Acton, fashion designer, b.

Communities
Wundowie, WA, estb.

1944

A
History, Politics, Economics, Law

Government
5 Sep. 1944–30 Jan. 1945, Sir Winston Joseph Dugan administered Aust.
19 Dec. 1944–18 Jun. 1952, Sir Charles Willoughby Moke Norrie Governor SA.

21 Jan. Aust. and NZ sign Welfare Agreement. First Aust. bilateral welfare treaty.
26 Jan. Sydney and Newcastle tram and bus employees strike in protest against Govt's refusal to release more men from army to improve transport conditions.
14 Feb.–15 Mar. Coalminers in NSW strike, nearly bringing industry to halt.
Mar. Cwlth Govt introduces unemployment and sickness benefits.
19 Aug. Referendum on Fourteen Powers, regarding extent of post-war Govt reconstruction powers, not carried.
13–16 Oct. Under sponsorship of Robert Menzies, representatives of 18 political groups estb. the Liberal Party of Aust. The UAP dissolves. (Liberal Party formally inaugurated on 28 Aug. 1945.)

During 1944
Italian prisoners-of-war develop rice-growing area at Wakool, NSW.
Reginald W. Saunders commissioned. First Aboriginal army officer.
Cwlth–States Housing Agreement signed.
Hospital Benefits scheme inaugurated.
Modern crayfishery industry estb. in WA.
Cwlth Govt estb. Aust. Aluminium Production Commission.

World War II
Jan. Aust. advances in NG.
Aust. takes over from USA in Solomon Is and NG.
6 Jun. Allied forces begin invasion of France.
5 Aug. 1,100 Japanese prisoners-of-war armed with improvised weapons attempt to escape from Cowra, NSW, POW camp. Four Australians and 234 Japanese killed.
Jun. 1942–Dec. 1944 Japanese submarines sink 29 allied merchant ships off Aust. coast, claiming 577 lives.

Births & Deaths
Tom Hughes, WA bushranger, d.

B
Science, Technology, Transport, Discovery

During 1944
P. A. Yeoman begins the Keyline Plan increasing pastoral production by use of contour farming and water conservation.
Cwlth Govt legislates for introduction of free medicines.
Professional Photographers Association of Aust. estb. (becomes Institute of Aust. Photography in 1963.)
Perth airport moved from Maylands to Guildford.
Large-scale uranium exploration begins.

C

Arts

1944

Literature

During 1944
'Ern Malley hoax' perpetrated. James McAuley and Harold Stewart write nonsense poetry using fictitious name 'Ern Malley'. Unaware of its true authors, Max Harris publishes the poetry, hailing it as great example of Aust. verse.
Alan Marshall publishes *These are My People*, his first book, and *About Turkey*.
Lawson Glassop publishes *We Were The Rats*. Prosecuted for indecent language in book.
Kenneth Slessor publishes *One Hundred Poems*.
Christina Stead publishes *For Love Alone*.

Births & Deaths
Robert Adamson, poet, b.

Music, Dance

During 1944
Dorothy Helmrich forms NSW committee of what becomes the Arts Council of Australia (later Australia Council) to promote music and the arts.
Eugene Ormandy arrives in Aust. to report on Aust. music.
ABC launches annual Concerto and Vocal competition.

Births & Deaths
Alison Bauld, composer, b.
Barry Conyngham, composer, b.

Drama, Theatre, Film

During 1944
Charles Chauvel produces film *Rats of Tobruk*.

Births & Deaths
Alexander John Buzo, playwright, b.
Peter Lindsay Weir, film director, writer, b.

Fine Arts

During 1944
Joshua Smith wins Archibald Prize for *S. Rosevear*.
Supreme Court of NSW upholds Archibald Prize award to William Dobell for *Joshua Smith* portrait.
David Jones Art Gallery estb. in Sydney.
Ferntree Gully Art Society estb. in Melbourne.

Births & Deaths
Bob Jenyns, sculptor, b.
Nigel Lendon, sculptor, b.
Jeffrey Shaw, sculptor, b.
Ethel Anna Stephens, painter, b.
David Voight, acrylics painter, b.

1944

D
Religion, Learning

1 Jan. SA Govt abolishes Qualifying Certificate exam at conclusion of primary schooling.
Feb. Cwlth Repatriation Training Scheme estb. to provide ex-service personnel with technical, rural or university training.

During 1944
Home Missionary Sisters of Our Lady estb. in Tas.
Executive Council of Aust. Jewry estb.

E
Sport

During 1944
Sirius, ridden by D. Munro, wins Melbourne Cup in 3 minutes 24½ seconds.
Fitzroy football team wins VFL Premiership in Melbourne.
Balmain football team wins Rugby League Premiership in Sydney.
Greyhound Chief Havoc breaks five records in one night at Harold Park in Sydney.
Aust. Roughriding Association estb.

Births & Deaths
Jim Airey, speedway rider, b.
Kel Carruthers, motorcyclist, b.
Garry Cooper, racing car designer, b.
Kerry Wayne Devlin, boxer, b.
Bernard (Midget) Farrelly, surfer, b.
John Goss, racing car driver, b.
Phil Hawthorne, Rugby footballer, b.
John Inverarity, cricketer, b.
Ilsa Konrads, swimmer, b.
Graham Marsh, golfer, b.
Phil May, long jumper, b.
John Newcombe, tennis player, b.
Manfred Schaefer, soccer player, b.
Eric Simms, Rugby League player, b.
Harry White, jockey, b.
Robert Windle, swimmer, b.

F
Historia Dignum

1944

Population
Estimated total white, 7,347,024.

14 Jan. Bushfires in Beaumaris, Yallourn and Gippsland areas, Vic., claim 51 lives. Bushfires devastate Tas. forests.
17 Jan. Meat rationing imposed.
20 Jan. Level-crossing accident at Hawkesbury R., NSW, claims 17 lives.
20 Jul. DH89 aircraft crashes at Mt Kitchener, SA, claiming seven lives.
11 Sep. First Aust. aerograms issued.
Nov.–Dec. NSW bushfires damage Blue Mts.

During 1944
Radio serial *The Lawsons* begins.
SW Aust. struck by worst dust storms on record.
Mt Kosciusko National Park proclaimed in NSW.
Police solve mystery of identity of the 'Pyjama Girl' case, the murder of Linda Agostini, after 10 years inquiry, when Agostini's husband confesses to the murder.
The Aust. Legion of Ex-Servicemen and Women estb.
Qld Golden Casket lottery becomes first in Aust. to be completely Govt-controlled and operated.

A
History, Politics, Economics, Law

1945

Government
30 Jan. 1945–11 Mar. 1947, HRH Prince Henry William Frederick Albert, Duke of Gloucester, Governor-General Aust.
6 Jun. 1945–1 Aug. 1946, Sir Frederick Jordan administered NSW.
6 Jul. 1945–13 Jul. 1945, Twenty-sixth Cwlth Ministry, Francis Michael Forde Labor Prime Minister Aust.
13 Jul. 1945–1 Nov. 1946, Twenty-seventh Cwlth Ministry, Joseph Benedict Chifley Labor Prime Minister Aust.
31 Jul. 1945–Apr. 1947, F. J. S. Wise Labor Premier WA.
4 Aug. 1945–24 Dec. 1945, Sir John Morris administered Tas.
2 Oct. 1945–Nov. 1945, I. Macfarlan Liberal Premier Vic.
21 Nov. 1945–Nov. 1947, J. Cain (the elder) Labor Premier Vic.
24 Dec. 1945–8 May 1951, Sir Hugh Binney Governor Tas.

1 Jan. In NSW all employees not covered by a Federal Award are granted two weeks' paid annual leave.
Mar. Cwlth Govt signs an agreement with British Govt beginning free and assisted passage scheme for British emigrants to Aust.
Apr.–Jun. Aust. contributes to drawing up United Nations (UN) charter in San Francisco. UN Organization estb. on 24 Oct.
13 Jul. As Minister for Immigration, Arthur Calwell announces broad objective of raising Aust. population to 20 million.
21 Aug. Cwlth Govt passes Banking Act to protect currency and public credit and to regulate banking. Govt extends control over private trading banks.
22 Aug. War Service Land Settlement Agreement Act implemented. Federal and State Govts combine to make land available to returned servicemen. (Effective until 1970.)
28 Aug. Liberal Party of Aust. formally inaugurated.
23 Sep.–12 Dec. Steel and coal workers strike over internal trade union disputes.
15 Oct. Cwlth Govt cancels all native labour contracts in Papua and NG.
During 1945
Federal sickness, unemployment and special benefits allowance operative. Cwlth Govt introduces a social service contribution in income tax.
Re-Establishment and Employment Act passed to assist returned servicemen.

Cwlth Investigation Branch (CIB) created. Wartime Security Service closed down. (CIB responsible for internal security until creation of ASIO in 1949.)
Post-war economic boom begins in Aust.
The Cwlth and State Housing Agreement providing funds for low-rental housing comes into force.

World War II
7–8 May. Cessation of hostilities in Europe. Germany surrenders.
1–4 Jul. Aust. captures the large oil-refining centre of Balikpapan, Dutch Borneo, in last large-scale seaborne landing of World War II.
6 Aug. First atomic bomb dropped, on Hiroshima. More than 70,000 Japanese die. Second bomb dropped on Nagasaki on 9 Aug.
15 Aug. Japanese Govt surrenders, ending World War II.
Frank Horton Berryman is official Aust. representative at Japanese surrender ceremony in Tokyo Bay.
Aust. War casualties: Of total 993,000 Australians who served *c.* 33,826 killed and 180,864 wounded. Of those killed 21,558 army. 10,264 air force, 2,004 navy.

B

Science, Technology, Transport, Discovery

31 May. Qantas Empire Airways begins a weekly Sydney–England service jointly with BOAC, using Avro Lancastrians.

14 Jul. Lowest recorded temperature in Aust. Temperature of −8°F. recorded at Charlotte Pass, NSW. (Also recorded in Aug. 1947.)

16 Aug. Aust. National Airlines Commission estb. when Aust. Govt, seeking to nationalize airline industry, passes Aust. National Airlines Act. (Trans-Australia Airlines (TAA) estb. by Commission on 12 Feb. 1946.)

During 1945

Captain Cook Graving Dock opens in Sydney. Among world's largest graving docks.

Howard Florey shares Nobel Prize for development of penicillin.

National Mapping Council estb.

Joseph L. Pawsey begins radio astronomy in Aust., using wartime radar equipment to measure radio waves from the sun.

Athol Smith and B. A. Pearl become pioneers of photo-finish mechanism used on race courses, perfecting 'the magic eye' in photography.

Kimberley Research Station estb. on Ord R., WA, to investigate area's agricultural potential.

Lance Hill invents rotary clothes hoist.

W. L. Waterhouse's Gabo wheat variety becomes available.

The Aust. Institute of Hospital Administrators estb. (Becomes Aust. College of Health Service Administrators.)

C

Arts

Literature

During 1945

Morris West, using pseudonym Julian Morris, publishes first book, *Moon in My Pocket*.

Norman Lindsay publishes *The Cousin from Fiji*.

Robert Shaw Close, publishes first novel, *Love me Sailor*. (Provokes law suit in 1948 in which Close is jailed for obscene libel.)

John Sidney Baker publishes *Dictionary of Australian Slang*.

The Aust. Book Council (National Book Council) estb. in Sydney to promote book industry.

Music, Dance

Dec. Richard Goldner estb. Sydney Musica Viva (now part of Musica Viva Australia), among biggest chamber music societies in world.

Births & Deaths

Ian Robert Cugley, composer, percussionist, b.
Horace Ketas, composer, d.
Jeannie Lewis, folk, jazz and blues musician, rock singer, b.
Malcolm McEachern, basso cantante, d.
Martin Wesley-Smith, composer, b.

Drama, Theatre, Film

26 Apr. Aust. National Film Board and Cwlth Film Unit estb.

Births & Deaths

Graeme Blundell, actor, director, b.
Rex Cramphorn, actor and director, noted for Jacobean drama, b.
John Romeril, playwright, b.
Jim Sharman, producer, director, b.

Fine Arts

13–27 Feb. Aust. Present Day Art Exhibition held in Melbourne.

During 1945

William Dargie wins Archibald Prize for *Lieut-Gen Edmund Herring*.

Australia At War Art Exhibition tours Aust.

George Art Gallery opens in Melbourne.

King George V Memorial Prize for Sculpture awarded.

Merioola Group of Artists estb. in Sydney.

1945

1945

Studio of Realist Art opens in Sydney. (Closes in 1948.)
Sydney Group, art group of contemporary artists working in neo-Romantic style, forms.
Tye's Art Gallery estb. in Melbourne. (Lasts until 1954.)

Architecture

During 1945
An austerity period of architecture begins. (End c. 1954.)
Cumberland County Council constituted to administer Sydney. First metropolitan regional planning authority in Aust.

Births & Deaths
William Brown, acrylic artist, b.
Jock Clutterbuck, sculptor, b.
Richard Havyatt, modern semi-abstract painter, b.
Alan Oldfield, painter, b.
Michael Young, sculptor, b.

D

Religion, Learning

During 1945
Cwlth Office of Education estb., showing increased Federal commitment to special education problems.
Civilian adult education activities increase.

E
Sport

15 Dec. Photo-finish camera first used for horse-racing, in Sydney.
26 Dec. Sydney to Hobart yacht race estb. Yacht *Rani* wins first race.

During 1945
Rainbird, ridden by W. Cook, wins Melbourne Cup in 3 minutes 24¼ seconds.
Carlton football team wins VFL Premiership in Melbourne.
Eastern Suburbs football team wins Rugby League Premiership in Sydney.
Tas. Aust. Rules football Leitch Medal first awarded. (To best and fairest player.)
WA Aust. Rules football Simpson Medal first awarded. (To best interstate or grand final player.)
Judo becomes popular in Aust.
Aust. Roughriding championships first held. Roughriders Association standardizes championship saddles.
Aust. weight-lifting championships begin.

Births & Deaths
Kevin Barry, swimmer, b.
Arthur Beetson, Rugby League footballer, b.
Kevin Berry, sports photographer, b.
John Boulger, speedway driver, b.
Sydney Cavill, swimmer, d.
John Cole, Rugby Union footballer, b.
Ron Coote, Rugby League footballer, b.
Bob Dunlop, boxer, b.
John Famechon, boxer, b.
Johnny Fenton, speedcar driver, b.
Syd Guillford, Qld Aust. Rules footballer, b.
Alex Jesaulenko, VFL footballer, b.
Gordon Johnson, cyclist, b.
Bob McCarthy, Rugby League footballer, b.
Arthur McGill, Rugby Union footballer, b.
Linda McGill, long-distance swimmer, b.
Allan Marnoch, Rugby footballer, b.
Bob Morris, racing car driver, b.
Cam Nancarrow, squash player, b.
Phyllis O'Donnell, surfrider, b.
Marea Parsons, golfer, b.
Anthony D. Roche, tennis player, b.
John Sattler, Rugby League fooballer, b.
Randall Vines, golfer, b.
Doug Walters, cricketer, b.

F
Historia Dignum

Population
Estimated total white population 7,430,197.

17 Jan. Fire damages Fremantle harbour, WA.
31 Jan. Stinson aircraft crashes at Redesdale, Vic., claiming 10 lives.
5 May. Douglas DC3 aircraft crashes at Horn I., Qld, claiming six lives.
24 Jun. DH86 aircraft crashes at Geraldton, WA, claiming 10 lives.
30 Jun. Train derailment at Rocky Ponds, NSW, claims four lives.

During 1945
Radio serial *Biggles* begins.
First National Trust estb. in NSW. (SA 1955, Vic. 1956, WA 1959, Tas. 1960, Qld 1963, NT 1952.)
Alcoholics Anonymous estb. in Aust.
Two-year drought ends. An estimated two million sheep lost during this drought.
Cyclone destroys RAAF base at North West Cape, WA.

A
History, Politics, Economics, Law

1946

Government

7 Mar. 1946–Jan. 1952, E. M. Hanlon Labor Premier Qld.

24 Apr. 1946–30 Sep. 1946, Frank Arthur Cooper administered Qld.

1 Aug. 1946–31 Jul. 1957, Sir John Northcott Governor NSW.

1 Oct. 1946–4 Dec. 1957, Sir John Dudley Lavarack Governor Qld.

1 Nov. 1946–19 Dec. 1949, Twenty-eighth Cwlth Ministry, Joseph Benedict Chifley Labor Prime Minister Aust.

1946–1951, A. R. Driver Administrator NT under Cwlth jurisdiction.

1946, L. H. A. Giles Acting Administrator NT under Cwlth jurisdiction.

Feb. Cwlth committee on immigration announces drive for non-British as well as British immigrants. Mass immigration of Europeans planned.

Jun. Some members of ALP launch Industrial Groups to fight against Communist Party influence in trade unions.

28 Sep. Joseph Benedict Chifley returned as Labor Prime Minister at Federal elections.

Social Service powers granted to Cwlth Govt at referendum. Cwlth control of marketing primary products and industrial employment rejected.

During Sep. Resumption of wool sales boosts the Aust. economy.

6 Nov. Eighteenth Federal Parlt opens. (Dissolution 31 Oct. 1949.)

14 Nov. Engineers' strike over wages and working hours begins. (Ends May 1947.)

13 Dec. United Nations Organization grants Aust. trusteeship over Papua and NG.

During 1946

High Court of Aust. restored to seven Justices, a Chief Justice and six Justices. Sir William Webb appointed a Justice. (Until 1958.)

Security Council of United Nations Organization holds first meeting, with N. J. O. Makin (Aust.) as first president.

Sir Raphael Cilento becomes director of UN Organization for refugees and displaced persons.

Aust. mission in USA elevated to Embassy status.

Wartime manpower control ends. National security regulations abolished. Cwlth Employment Service (CES) estb.

Overseas Telecommunications Commission estb. Nationalizes international telecommunications and places overseas telephone, telegraph and cable services under Govt control.

Cwlth Govt approves broadcasting of Parliamentary proceedings. First broadcast on 10 Jul. Debates in national Parlt, hitherto known as *Parliamentary Debates* now officially known as *Parliamentary Debates (Hansard)*.

Aust. League of Rights, extreme right-wing, anti-semitic political organization, estb. in Adelaide. (Becomes national in 1960.)

Annabelle Rankin elected to Federal Parlt.

Aborigines in Pilbara region of WA form co-operative settlements.

Federal–States Housing Agreement established. To employ 130,000 over 10 years.

Cwlth Bureau of Agricultural Economics estb.

B

Science, Technology, Transport, Discovery

Jun. Derek Cumming flies first jet in Aust., a Gloster Meteor F4.
Sep. Arthur William Coles organizes Government-owned Trans-Aust. Airlines (TAA). First daily Sydney–Melbourne flight starts on 9 Sep.
Nov. William Alan Stewart Butement estb. joint Aust.–UK guided missile range project at Woomera, SA.
23 Dec. East-West Airlines Ltd estb.
During 1946
Fisk radiola introduced in Aust.
Keith Edward Bullen advances theory that earth's core is solid, not molten. (Theory proved in 1970s.)
First radio telescope in Aust. operates, near Sydney.
Frank Cotton invents ergometer which uses a stationary bicycle or rowing boat with adjustable tensions to test the potential of sportsmen.
Federal Govt estb. Bureau of Mineral Resources, Geology and Geophysics in Canberra.
The Association of Professional Engineers (APEA) estb.
Qld Institute of Medical Research estb. in Brisbane.
Herbert Schlink estb. Aust. Hospitals Association.
Aust. Transport Advisory Council estb.
John Cowley introduces electron diffraction to Aust.
R. G. Giovanelli presents a theory of solar flares.

C

Arts

1946

Literature

During 1946
Arts Council of Aust. formed.
James McAuley publishes first book of poetry, *Under Aldebaran*.
K. S. Prichard publishes *The Roaring Nineties*.
Judith Wright publishes first book of poetry, *The Moving Image*.
Martin Boyd publishes *Lucinda Brayford*.
Frank D. Davidson publishes *Dusty*.
Georgian House, publishers, prosecuted for publishing *Love Me Sailor*.
Children's Book of the Year award inaugurated.

Music, Dance

Jan. The Sydney Symphony Orchestra estb. permanently from ABC orchestra in Sydney. (Other permanent symphony orchestras estb. from ABC orchestras, Qld 1947, Tas. 1948, SA and Vic. 1949, WA 1950.)
9 May. Kathleen Gorham makes début with the Borovansky Ballet Co.
19 Aug. John Antill receives world recognition for composition, *Corroboree*, inspired by Aboriginal music.
5 Nov. Melbourne Ballet Club (Ballet Victoria) launched.
Dec. Annual jazz convention begins in Melbourne. First major Aust. jazz convention.
During 1946
Musica Viva Society promotes chamber music in Sydney.
Slim Dusty first sings 'When the Rain Tumbles Down in July'.
Laurel Martyn founds Vic. Ballet Guild in Melbourne.

Births & Deaths

Anne Elizabeth Boyd, composer influenced by Asian music, b.
Kevin Coe, ballet dancer, b.
Marilyn Rowe, ballet dancer, b.
Gailene Stock, ballet dancer, b.

Drama, Theatre, Film

27 Sep. Film *The Overlanders*, starring Chips Rafferty, released.
During 1946
Radio drama *When a Girl Marries* begins. (Runs until 1965, with 3,290 episodes.)
Ken Hall makes film *Smithy*.

587

1946

Fine Arts

During 1946
William Dargie wins Archibald Prize for *L. C. Robson*.
Sidney Nolan begins his *Ned Kelly* series of paintings.
Kogarah Arts Festival prize first awarded in NSW.
Rupert Charles Wolsten Bunny Loan Exhibition held in National Gallery, Melbourne.
The Australian Artist, quarterly art magazine, founded. (First two numbers published under name *Genre*.)
Council for the Encouragement of Music and the Arts (CEMA) holds first Exhibition in Sydney.

Births & Deaths
Peter Cole, sculptor, b.
Alan Mitelman, abstract oil painter, b.
Stelos Stelara, performance sculptor, b.
David Rankin, abstract painter, b.

D

Religion, Learning

Feb. Aust. Council of Churches estb., in Sydney.
Jun. Aust. National University (ANU) estb. in Canberra for postgraduate courses. (Undergraduates precluded until 1961, when ANU absorbs the Canberra University College.)
Jul. Fulbright student Aust.–Aust. interchange scheme introduced.
During 1946
Aust. Staff College estb. at Queenscliff, Vic., to train army officers.
Balmain Teachers College opens in Sydney. Many teachers colleges open as result of primary school teacher shortages in NSW and elsewhere.
Tas. raises minimum school leaving age to 16 years, SA to 15 years.
Melbourne University becomes first in Aust. to estb. Doctorates of Philosophy (PhDs) for postgraduate research.

E
Sport

During 1946

Russia, ridden by D. Munro, wins Melbourne Cup in 3 minutes 21¼ seconds.

Essendon football team wins VFL Premiership in Melbourne.

Balmain football team wins Rugby League Premiership in Sydney.

Don P. Cordner of Melbourne VFL team awarded Brownlow Medal.

Qld Aust. Rules Football Grogan Medal first awarded. To best and fairest player.

Aust. Polocrosse Association forms.

R. Johnson popularizes organized water skiing in Aust., at Sackville, NSW.

Marching girl teams hold first national championships.

First Aust. basketball championships held, in Sydney.

Aust. wins first cricket Test match against NZ (in NZ).

Manly–Warringah and Parramatta Rugby League Football Clubs estb. in Sydney.

Christina wins Sydney to Hobart yacht race.

Births & Deaths

Attila Abonyi, soccer player, b.
Peter Brock, touring car champion, b.
Mal Brown, WA Aust. Rules footballer, b.
Carl Ditterich, VFL footballer, b.
Ralph Doubell, athlete, b.
David Graham, golfer, b.
Peter Hudson, VFL footballer, b.
Kevin Langby, jockey, b.
John Maclean, cricketer, b.
Richard McCosker, cricketer, b.
Keith Oliver, cyclist, b.
Bob Stanton, golfer, b.

F
Historia Dignum

Population

Estimated total white, 7,517,981.

26 Jan. First celebration of Australia Day. Previously celebrated as Foundation Day or Proclamation Day.

10 Mar. DC3 aircraft crashes in Hobart, claiming 25 lives. On 23 March Lancastrian aircraft disappears over Indian Ocean with 10 on board.

During 1946

Eight-year drought throughout Aust. ends, but many areas of Qld, NSW, NT and WA affected by less severe drought until 1949.

Aust. Association of Advertising Agencies estb.

Tas. Caverneering Club estb. First Speleological Society in Aust.

Communities

Mt Beauty, Vic., estb.
Robinvale, Vic. estb.

A
History, Politics, Economics, Law

1947

Government

19 Jan. 1947–11 Mar. 1947, Sir Winston Joseph Dugan administered Aust.

6 Feb. 1947–Apr. 1952, J. McGirr Labor Premier NSW.

11 Mar. 1947–8 May 1953, Sir William John McKell Governor-General Aust.

1 Apr. 1947–Feb. 1953, Sir D. R. McLarty Liberal-Country League/Country coalition Premier WA.

20 Nov. 1947–Jun. 1950, T. T. Hollway Liberal-Country Premier Vic.

18 Dec. 1947–Feb. 1948, E. Brooker Labor Premier Tas.

Jan. Stock Exchanges freed from Govt control.
31 Mar. Cwlth Arbitration Court estb. principle of penalty rates for weekend work.
Mar. Govt streamlines Federal arbitration and conciliation system; appoints laymen as Conciliation Commissioners, leaving Arbitration Court to determine policy issues.
14 May. NT granted partly elected and partly nominated Legislative Council.
26 May. Aust. and Britain conclude bilateral assisted passage agreement under which approved migrants over 19 years of age are paid £10 for passage to Aust. (Between Mar. this year and Feb. 1955 1 million Britons migrate to Aust.)
During May. Cwlth Govt buys entire Qantas Empire Airways shareholding, thus nationalizing Qantas. (Effective 1 Jul.)
16 Aug. Fed. Cabinet organizes preparation of legislation for nationalization of banking other than State and savings banks. Bill empowering Cwlth Bank to take over the business of private banks introduced into Federal Parlt on 15 Oct. Nation-wide campaign to remove Labor from office follows.
During Aug. Arthur Calwell's immigration drive begins. First 'displaced persons' arrive from Europe. (During next 13 years 1.68 million new settlers arrive in Aust.)
8 Sep. Arbitration Court reduces working hours to a 40-hour week. (Effective from 1 Jan. 1948.)
30 Nov. Post World War II Aust. Regular Army formed.
During Nov. Aust. co-operates in General Agreement on Tariffs and Trade (GATT).
26 Dec. Heard and MacDonald Is in Antarctica transferred from British to Aust. administration.
During 1947
Last Aust. World War II troops demobilized.
Aust. joins World health Organization (WHO).
H. V. Evatt appointed chairman of UN Commission on Palestine.
Aust. recognizes Indonesian Republic following revolt against Dutch occupation. Co-sponsors Indonesia into UNO.
Economic Commission for Asia and Far East (ECAFE) estb.
Social Services Act transfers most benefit responsibility from State Govts to Federal Govt.
Stanley M. Bruce becomes first Aust. to enter British House of Lords. Made Viscount for his role in War Cabinet.
Johannes Bjelke-Petersen enters Qld Parlt.
Henry Edward Bolte enters Vic. Parlt.
Aust. Cane Growers' Association estb.
Aboriginal Pastoralists Association estb. in NT.
Deep-sea prawning industry begins.
The Royal Aust. Air Force College estb. at Point Cook, Vic.
Pacific oysters from Japan first introduced into Aust.
NSW coalminers' granted three weeks' annual leave.

B

Science, Technology, Transport, Discovery

5 Feb. First successful rain-making experiment in NSW. World's first man-made rainstorm bursts near Bathurst, NSW.
12 Aug. Air navigation charges first imposed.
Nov. Australind Express train begins running between Perth and Bunbury, WA.
During 1947
Aust. National Antarctic Research Expedition (ANARE) departs to estb. scientific research station at Heard I., Antarctica.
Donald Shand introduces aerial seeding and fertilizing to Aust.
Bread Institute of Aust. estb. in Sydney to provide technical services to bakers.
Sir Robert Robinson wins Nobel Prize for chemistry.
Privately owned VHF land and harbour mobile radio-telephones introduced.
Commercial linseed production begins in Vic.
Federal Govt estb. first Cwlth Acoustics Laboratory.
Cwlth Bureau of Dental Standards estb.

C

Arts

Literature

During 1947
M. Barnard Eldershaw (pen-name of M. F. Barnard and F. Eldershaw) publishes *Tomorrow and Tommorrow*.
Henrietta Drake-Brockman publishes *The Fatal Days*.

Music, Dance

22 May. Bernard Heinz starts ABC youth orchestral subscription concerts in Sydney.
During 1947
Qld Symphony Orchestra estb. John Farnsworth Hall appointed conductor. (Until 1954.)
Albert Penberthy founds National Theatre Ballet.

Births & Deaths
David Anthony Ahern, composer, b.
Timotheos Arvanitakis, musician, b.
Themos Mexis, musician, b.

Drama, Theatre, Film

During 1947
Patrick White writes play *The Ham Funeral*.
Ralph Smart's film *Bush Christmas* produced.

Births & Deaths
Jacki Weaver, actress, b.

Fine Arts

During 1947
William Dargie wins Archibald Prize for *Sir Marcus Clarke*.
Sidney Nolan exhibits *Ned Kelly* series of paintings.
Albury Art Prize, NSW, estb.
Minnie Crouch Watercolour Prize estb. in Ballarat, Vic.
Hotchin Art Gallery estb., WA, (First Art Prizes 1948.)
Mosman Art Prize first awarded, in Sydney.
National Roads and Motorists Association of NSW Art Prize awarded.
Henry Moore modern sculpture exhibition tours Aust.

Births & Deaths
Domenico De Clario, sculptor, b.
Ivan Durrant, acrylic realist painter, b.
David Wilson, sculptor, b.

1947

1947

Architecture

During 1947
Harry Seidler, architect, arrives in Aust.
Pre-fabricated houses proliferate because of shortage of building materials.

D Religion, Learning

Sep. Under the Cwlth Repatriation Training Scheme (CRTS) there are by this time 209,643 students receiving technical training, 5,235 rural training, and 12,401 university training.

During 1947
Council of Adult Education CAE estb in Vic.
Wagga Teachers College, NSW, opens.
WA Govt allows State schools to begin day with religious observance.
Technical education by now well established in most States.

E
Sport

Aug. Aust. Women's Bowling Council estb.

During 1947

Hiraji, ridden by J. Purtell, wins Melbourne Cup in 3 minutes 28 seconds.

Carlton football team wins VFL Premiership in Melbourne.

Balmain football team wins Rugby League Premiership in Sydney.

Bert Deacon of Carlton VFL team awarded Brownlow Medal.

Aust. Jockey Club opens Sydney laboratory for testing horse blood for doping.

John Arthur (Jack) Brabham begins racing midget cars.

The Queensland Canoe Club estb.

Aust. Casting Association estb. (First national championships in 1951.)

Aust. wins first Test cricket match played against India.

Russell Jones, ice hockey player, begins 20-year career.

Aust. pistol shooting begins in Tas. and SA.

Richard S. Charles, 'Father of Aust. skindiving' estb. Underwater Spear Fishermen's Association. (Becomes Aust. Underwater Federation.)

First Aust. softball controlling body estb., in Brisbane. First interstate games held in Qld, NSW and Vic.

Jim Ferrier wins first Aust. major overseas golf championship in USA.

Westward wins Sydney to Hobart yacht race.

Births & Deaths

Ray Baartz, soccer player, b.
Kevin Bartlett, athlete, VFL footballer, b.
Francis Bourke, VFL footballer, b.
John Brass, Rugby footballer, b.
Robert Fulton, Rugby League footballer, b.
Alan Jones, racing car driver, b.
Ian O'Brien, swimmer, b.
Kerry Reid, tennis player, b.
Barrie Robran, SA Aust. Rules footballer, b.
Peter Wilson, soccer player, b.

F
Historia Dignum

Population

Estimated total white, 7,637,963.

Fourth Cwlth census and first since 1933 estimates white population at 7,579,000 and Aboriginal population at 70,000.

23 Jan. and 12–14 Feb. Cyclones damage south-east Qld and north-east NSW.

5 May. Train derailment at Camp Mountain, Qld, claims 16 lives. On 18 Oct. train collision at Tamaree, Qld, claims eight lives.

24 May. Newspaper the *Centralian Advocate* first published as weekly in Alice Springs, NT.

Jun. Aust. Road Safety Council estb.

7 Aug. Fire destroys freighter *Mahia*, claiming 10 lives.

During 1947

Adrian Olsson Ashton appointed first president of the National Trust of Aust.

Barossa Valley vintage festival estb. (First festival Mar.–Apr. 1948.)

First Lions Club in Aust. chartered, in Lismore, NSW.

Grant Featherston begins making body-fitting chairs out of curved plywood.

Communities

Wittenoom, WA, estb.
Woomera, SA, estb.

1947

1948

A
History, Politics, Economics, Law

Government

25 Feb. 1948–Aug. 1958, R. Cosgrove Labor Premier Tas.

5 Oct. 1948–30 Jun. 1951, Sir James Mitchell Governor WA.

1 Jan. Forty-hour working week becomes effective throughout Aust.

During Jan. Tramway employees strike in Melbourne. Vic. Govt passes an Essential Services Act.

4 Feb.–2 Apr. Qld railway employees strike for increased marginal rates. Qld Govt declares State of Emergency.

8 May. Margaret Edgeworth McIntyre becomes first woman elected to Tas. Parlt.

29 May. Referendum on whether national control over rent and prices, including charges, should become permanent, rejected.

Jun. Malayan Emergency declared. (Ends 31 Jul. 1960.)

Sep. Dr H. V. Evatt, Aust. Minister for External Affairs, elected President of UN General Assembly.

6 Oct.–8 Nov. NSW coalminers strike over jurisdictional dispute with AWU.

16 Dec. HMAS *Sydney*, RAN's first aircraft carrier, commissioned.

During 1948

High Court of Aust. declares sections of 1947 Bank Nationalization Act unconstitutional.

ANZAM Agreement for military planning and consultation between Britain, Aust. and NZ estb.

Nationality and Citizen Act creates status of Australian Citizen. Becomes operative 26 Jan. 1949. (Until then Australians simply British Subjects.)

Aust. Broadcasting Control Board. estb. to ensure provision of broadcasting services (including television) in accordance with Govt policy. (Effective Mar. 1949.)

Qld–British Food Corporation estb. to grow sorghum for British consumption.

Large-scale prawning in ocean waters begins near Stockton Beach, NSW.

Electoral legislation enlarges Federal Senate from 36 to 60 members and the House of Representatives from 75 to 121 members. ACT gains representation. Cwlth Rehabilitation Service estb.

B
Science, Technology, Transport, Discovery

Oct. Cwlth Govt launches anti-tuberculosis campaign.

29 Nov. General Motors-Holden Ltd launches the Holden 48/125, first mass-produced car in Aust. Laurence Hartnett becomes 'Father of the Holden'.

During 1948

Road cattle trains first used between Alice Springs and Darwin in NT.

Woomera rocket range begins operating in SA.

Stuart Campbell estb. meteorological and scientific research station on Macquarie I.

John Curtin School of Medical Research estb. in Canberra.

CSIR invents Distance Measuring Equipment, transmitting radar pulse. Fitted to all Aust. commercial aircraft.

The Drover aircraft introduced. First Aust.-designed commercial air transport.

TAA operates first pressurized aircraft in Aust.

Manufacturing of I. B. Flemming-designed Jindivik pilotless jet-propelled radio-controlled target aircraft begins. First completely Aust. designed and built jet aircraft and first remote controlled jet aircraft built in British Cwlth.

Harvey Reservoir in south-west WA completed.

Aust. Post-Graduate Federation in Medicine founded.

Arts

1948

Literature

During 1948
Jon S. Cleary publishes *You Can't See Round Corners*.
Ruth Park publishes *The Harp in the South*.
Patrick White publishes *The Aunt's Story*.
Eleanor Dark publishes *Storm of Time*.
Francis Webb, poet, publishes *A Drum for Ben Boyd*.
K. S. Prichard publishes *Golden Miles*.
Mary Gilmore publishes *Selected Verse*.

Music, Dance

During 1948
Sir Eugene Goossens appointed first permanent conductor of Sydney Symphony Orchestra. (Until 1956.)
John Bishop organizes first National Music Camp.
An Aust. Opera Co, combining NSW and Vic. Opera companies, tours Aust.
C. T. Lorenz estb. NSW National Opera Co.
Ballet Rambert is first English ballet company to tour Aust.

Births & Deaths
Roger Donald Frampton, jazz musician, b.
Olivia Newton-John, singer, b.

Drama, Theatre, Film

21 Oct. Sumner Lock Elliott's play *Rusty Bugles* premières in Sydney.

During 1948
(Francis Margaret) Judith Anderson, actress, wins American Award for the most distinguished actress in American Theatre.
John Gordon Buchanan Alden estb. first permanent Shakespearian company in Aust.

Births & Deaths
Garry MacDonald, television actor, b.

Fine Arts

During 1948
William Dobell wins Archibald Prize for *Margaret Olley*.
Bunbury Art Gallery, WA, estb.
Eric Smith and Ola Cohn win Catholic Centenary Prize in Melbourne.
Society of Designers for Industry estb.
Vic. Sculptors' Society founded in Melbourne.

Architecture

During 1948
Harry Seidler introduces Aust. to 'International' style architecture.
First Chair of Town Planning estb. at Sydney University.

Births & Deaths
John Armstrong, sculptor, b.
James Boyd, painter, b.
Peter Cripps, sculptor, b.
Annis Laeublis, sculptor, b.
Vlase Nicoleski, sculptor, b.

1948

D
Religion, Learning

Nov. Bishop Fyodor Rafalsky arrives in Aust. as first Hierarch of the Russian Orthodox Church in Australasia.

During 1948
Douglas Copland appointed first Vice-Chancellor of Aust. National University, in Canberra.
Nuffield Travel and Study Awards estb.
Vic. Secondary Teachers Association estb.
Rising school enrolments in most States lead to shortage of teachers. Many new teacher training centres set up.

E
Sport

During 1948
Rimfire, ridden by R. Neville, wins Melbourne Cup in 3 minutes 21 seconds.
Melbourne football team wins VFL Premiership.
Western Suburbs football team wins Rugby League Premiership in Sydney.
First tied Aust. Rules football VFL grand final occurs between Melbourne and Essendon.
William Morris of Richmond VFL team awarded Brownlow Medal.
Wallabies Rugby Union team tours France for first time.
Donald Bradman retires from Test cricket after 20 years during which he scored 28,067 runs, averaging 95, and making 117 centuries.
Aust. cricket team scores world record in one day against Essex, 721 runs.
Aust. wins two gold, six silver and five bronze medals at London Olympics.
The SA Canoe Club estb.
Aust. water polo championships begin.
The Archery Association of Aust. estb.
Shirley Strickland first female athlete to win Olympic medals.
Aust. Amateur Fencing Federation estb.
Aust. Gymnastic Union estb. in Melbourne. (Holds first national gymnastics championship in 1950.)
Percy Pavey becomes noted marksman.
First Olympic yachting teams participate.
Westward wins Sydney to Hobart yacht race.

Births & Deaths
Adrian Alston, soccer player, b.
Jill Bamborough, weight lifter, b.
Gregory Stephen Chappell, cricketer, b.
Gail Couper, surfer, b.
Terry Gale, golfer, b.
Bryan Hindle, motorcyclist, b. (d. 1978)
John Hipwell, Rugby Union footballer, b.
Geoffrey Brian Hunt, squash player, b.
Malcolm Milne, skier, b.
Henry Nissen, boxer, b.
Ron Riley, hockey player, b.
Lionel Edmund Rose, boxer, b.
Bob Shearer, golfer, b.
Ian Stanley, golfer, b.
Len Thompson, VFL footballer, b.
Max Walker, cricketer, b.

F
Historia Dignum

1948

Population
Estimated total white, 7,792,465.

18 Apr. Lockhead Hudson aircraft crashes in Lae, claiming 37 lives. DC3 crashes at Quirindi, NSW, claiming 13 lives on 2 Sep. Catalina aircraft crashes on Lord Howe I., claiming seven lives on 28 Sep.
23 Aug. *Home* magazine launched in Sydney.
27 Oct. Fire destroys Covent Garden restaurant in Adelaide, claiming five lives.

During 1948
First Aust. Marriage Guidance Council estb., in Sydney.
Longest recorded snake in Aust. killed, near Cairns, Qld—a 25-foot python.
Roger McKay makes first cone-shaped plywood chair.
Bushfires in SA.

Communities
Warragamba, NSW, estb.

1949

A
History, Politics, Economics, Law

Government

21 Feb. 1949–17 Oct. 1949, Sir Edmund Francis Herring administered Vic.

18 oct. 1949–7 Jul. 1953, Sir Reginald Alexander Dallas Brooks Governor Vic.

19 Dec. 1949–11 May 1951, Twenty-ninth Cwlth Ministry, Robert Gordon Menzies Liberal-Country coalition Prime Minister Aust.

Feb. Act of Parlt unites Territories of Papua and New Guinea and estb. Legislative Council. (First sitting 1951.)

Cwlth Govt estb. Aust. Shipping Board to provide for setting up Aust. shipping line.

16 Mar. Justice G. S. Reed appointed Director-General of Security. Briefed to estb. a security service. Aust. Security Intelligence Organization (ASIO) estb.

During Mar. Cwlth Govt extends right to vote in Federal elections to some Aborigines.

May. Aust. Whaling Commission estb.

27 Jun.–15 Aug. National coal strike results from struggle between Labor Govt and some Communist-controlled unions. Chifley calls in troops to work open-cut mines and break strike.

Sep. Aust. currency devalued.

10 Dec. Joseph Benedict Chifley, Labor Prime Minister, defeated at national elections, partly because of attempts to nationalize banks. Becomes Opposition leader (until 1951).

20 Jun. Communist Party Chairman Lawrence Louis Sharkey convicted of breach of the Cwlth Crimes Act by uttering seditious words. On 17 Oct. Sharkey sentenced to three years jail for sedition.

During 1949

John Grey Gorton and William McMahon enter Federal Parlt.

Albert Ernest Monk becomes first full-time president of ACTU. (Holds position for 20 years.)

NT Broadcasting Board estb.

Aust. linseed oil first produced in quantity.

Asian immigration strictly controlled.

B
Science, Technology, Transport, Discovery

During 1949

Royal Australian College of Radiologists (so named 1972) estb. as College of Radiologists of Australasia.

Some ten million telephones operate in Aust.

G. Withnall invents Red Robin infra-red brooder for raising chickens.

Sir William Hudson becomes Commissioner of the Snowy Mountain Hydro Electric Authority. (Holds position for 18 years.) Hydroelectric scheme begins on 17 Oct.

Council for Scientific and Industrial Research renamed Cwlth Scientific and Industrial Research Organization (CSIRO). Ian Clunies Ross appointed first Director.

Vic. introduces law enforcing pasteurization of milk.

John White discovers uranium near Rum Jungle, NT (Conzinc Riotinto later develops mine.)

College of Nursing of Aust. estb.

Nancy Walton estb. Aust. Women's Pilots Association.

High-grade bauxite deposits discovered north of Gove Peninsula, NT.

Cwlth Institute of Child Health estb.

C

Arts

Literature

During 1949
Aust. Book Publishers' Association estb.
Judith Wright publishes *Woman to Man*.
David Campbell publishes *Speak with the Sun*.

Music, Dance

9 Jun. The National Theatre Ballet estb. in Melbourne.
During 1949
Mobil singing quest launched. (Continues until 1957.)
Henry Krips appointed conductor of Adelaide Symphony Orchestra. (Until 1972.)

Drama, Theatre, Film

16 Dec. Charles Chauvel's film *Sons of Matthew* released in Sydney.

Fine Arts

Nov. Vic. Sculptors' Society holds its first exhibition, in Melbourne.
During 1949
Arthur Murch wins Archibald Prize for *Bonar Dunlop*.
Geraldton Art Gallery estb. in WA.
Strathfield South Art Prize awarded in Sydney.

Births & Deaths
Tim Storrier, painter, b.
Erna Vilks, painter, fashion designer, b.

Architecture

During 1949
Cumberland County Council master plan for development of Sydney authorized.

D

Religion, Learning

During 1949
Newcastle Teachers' College, NSW, opens.
Aust.-American Fulbright Scholarships (education foundation) grants estb.
Wagga Wagga Agricultural College, NSW, opens.
Aust. Institute of Librarians reconstituted as Library Association of Aust. (Royal charter in 1963.)
Mount Scopus Memorial College opens in Melbourne.
Newcastle Teachers' College estb. (Now Newcastle College of Advanced Education.)
NSW University of Technology estb. in Sydney, becomes University of NSW in 1958.
Aust.-American Education Foundation estb. as the United States Educational Foundation in Aust.
Education Schemes for ex-service personnel and growing prosperity leads to increased numbers of students entering universities. Period of expansion of universities begins.
Federal Govt estb. permanent Cwlth Scholarship Scheme at university level.

1949

E
Sport

During 1949
Foxzami, ridden by W. Fellows, wins Melbourne Cup in 3 minutes 28½ seconds.
Essendon football team wins VFL Premiership in Melbourne.
St George football team wins Rugby League Premiership in Sydney.
Ronald Clegg of South Melbourne VFL team awarded Brownlow Medal.
Aust. Canoe Federation estb.
Aust. Softball Federation estb.
Aust. Women's Softball Council estb.
Aust. Croquet Council estb.
Donald Bradman knighted.
David Sands wins Empire middle-weight boxing title in England.
Sid Patterson wins world amateur sprint cycling championship.
Betty Wilson acclaimed as best all-rounder woman cricketer.
Equestrian Federation of Aust. estb.
First Aust. women's bowling championships held, in Sydney.
First Aust. pistol shooting competitions begin, in SA.
First national polocrosse championships held.
Trade Winds wins Sydney to Hobart yacht race.

Births & Deaths
Barry Davis, VFL footballer, b.
Gary Dempsey, VFL footballer, b.
Dennis Keith Lillee, cricketer, noted fast bowler, b.
Jim Lynch, ice skater, b.
Kerry O'Keefe, cricketer, b.
D. K. (Fred) Phillis, SA Aust. Rules footballer, b.
Hector Thompson, boxer, b.
Judy Trim, pistol shooter, b.

F
Historia Dignum

Population
Estimated total white, 8,045,570.

21 Jan. The *Sunday Herald* first published, in Sydney.
Feb.–Mar. Most of Cooktown, Qld, destroyed by cyclone.
10 Mar. Lockheed aircraft crashes at Coolangatta, Qld, claiming 21 lives. DC3 crashes at Guildford, WA, on 2 Jul., claiming 18 lives.

During 1949
The 'new look' in fashion popular. Hemline drops to near ankle-length.
Strapless swim suits and bikinis introduced.
Qld bushfires begin; Some 25,000 acres burnt in 56 outbreaks. Bushfires in WA burn many acres in 527 outbreaks.
Floods in NSW, Vic. and central interior Qld.

Births & Deaths
'Dollar' Anderson, riverboat skipper, character, d.

A

History, Politics, Economics, Law

Government

27 Jun. 1950–Oct. 1952, J. G. B. McDonald Country Party Premier Vic.

Jan. Sir Percy Spender, Minister for External Affairs, proposes Colombo Plan to aid developing countries in S. and S.E. Asia. Programme finalized in Sep.
8 Feb. Petrol rationing ends. By Jul. all World War II regulations rationing consumer goods have ended.
22 Feb. Nineteenth Federal Parlt opens. (Dissolution 19 Mar. 1951.)
Mar. Prime Minister R. G. Menzies proclaims Section 30s of Crimes Act to end Brisbane waterside workers' strike.
Apr. R. G. Menzies proposes to dissolve the Communist Party.
25 Jun. N. Korea invades S. Korea, beginning Korean War. First Aust. forces sent to Korea in Jun.–Jul.
Sep. Sir Thomas Blamey appointed first Aust. Field Marshal.
16 Oct.–8 Dec. Vic. railwaymen strike over abolition of passive time and payment for daily overtime.
Nov. R. G. Menzies re-introduces conscription. Three months compulsory military training for all 18 year olds. (Becomes selective in 1957; abolished in 1959.)
9 Dec. WA plebiscite, last of kind in Aust., rejects prohibition.

During 1950
RAAF assists British forces in anti-Communist Malaysia campaign.
Female basic wage rises from 54 per cent to 75 per cent of male rate. In Oct. basic wage increased by £1.
Sir Wilfred Fullager (until 1961) and Sir Frank Kitto (until 1970) appointed Justices of High Court of Aust.

B

Science, Technology, Transport, Discovery

1950

May. Myxomatosis virus disease to control rabbit population released at Gunbower in Murray Valley.
Oct. The GAF Pike (forerunner of the Jindivik), first jet aircraft designed and built in Aust., makes first test flight.

During 1950
UTAH American Development Co. comes to Aust. as one of largest heavy construction and mining companies.
Mobile radio telephone exchange service first introduced for commercial use.
Penicillin introduced to control mastitis in cattle.
Insecticides such as DDT are widely used as replacement for arsenic.
c. 1950. Commercial breeding of dairy cattle using artificial insemination begins in Aust.
Cultivation of subterranean clover to replace nitrogen in soil becomes widespread.

1950 C

Arts

Literature

During 1950
Frank Hardy publishes *Power Without Glory*.
Nevil Shute publishes *A Town Like Alice*.
K. S. Prichard publishes *Winged Seeds*.
Ivan Southall publishes *Meet Simon Black*.

Music, Dance

3 Jul. John Henry Antill's *Corroboree* made into ballet. Premières in Sydney.
During 1950
Cwlth ABC vocal competitions launched.
Donald Peart founds Sydney Pro Musica Society.
Joan Sutherland wins Mobil Quest.
Rudolf Pekarek appointed conductor of WA Symphony Orchestra. (Remains until 1954.) Alceo Galliera appointed conductor Melbourne Symphony Orchestra, (Remains until 1951.)

Births & Deaths
John Meehan, dancer and choreographer, b.
Graeme Lloyd Murphy, dancer and choreographer, b.

Drama, Theatre, Film

Births & Deaths
Phillip Roger Noyce, film director, b.
O. C. Perrie, motion picture photographer, b.

Fine Arts

During 1950
William Dargie wins Archibald Prize for *Sir Leslie McConnan*.
Russell Drysdale and Sidney Nolan hold their first exhibition in London.
Albany Art Gallery estb., WA.
Aust. War Memorial Art competition estb. in Canberra.
Berrima District Art Society estb., NSW.
Coastal Art Group active in Tas.
John Eldershaw wins Cwlth Centenary Prize for Art.
Dunlop Art Prizes first awarded. (Until 1955.)
Aust. Art Exhibition in Karachi, Pakistan.
Fellowship of Aust. Artists estb. in Melbourne.
Hahndorf Private Art Gallery founded, SA.
Johnstone Art Gallery estb. in Brisbane.

Births & Deaths
Alexsander Danko, sculptor, b.
Kenneth Wilkinson, art and drama critic, d.

Architecture

During 1950
Car garages become essential part of house design.
Ranch-style homes become popular.

D
Religion, Learning

E
Sport

Jul. Cwlth Govt finances distribution of free milk to all school children under 10 years of age.
During 1950
Dorothy Ross, educationist, active in promoting progressive education principles.
Cwlth Govt estb. four schools for Aborigines in NT. First serious NT attempt at Aboriginal education.
Under the Colombo Plan, Aust. educates Asian students.
Temple Society of Aust. estb.
In Vic. the Adult Education Association estb. to replace the Vic. Workers' Educational Association.
The Resettlement Department of the Australian Council of Churches opens in Melbourne as the Refugee Resettlement Office.

During 1950
Comic Court, ridden by P. Glennon, wins Melbourne Cup in 3 minutes $19\frac{1}{2}$ seconds.
Cwlth Games held in Auckland, NZ.
Essendon football team wins VFL Premiership in Melbourne.
South Sydney football team wins Rugby League Premiership in Sydney.
Alan Ruthven of Fitzroy VFL team awarded Brownlow Medal.
Nerida wins Sydney to Hobart yacht race.
First Aust. judo championships held.
Aust. Water-Ski Association estb. First controlling body.
Rae (Togo) Johnstone wins four classic English horseraces in one season.
Walter Lindrum retires from billiards with 57 world records.
Gliding Federation of Aust. estb. (First Aust. championships in 1956.)
Aust. Rugby League team wins Ashes for first time in 30 years, in Sydney.
W. E. Rieck machine shears 326 merinos in 7 hours 48 minutes, setting record.

Births & Deaths
Charky Ramon, real name David Ballard, boxer, b.
Malcolm Blight, SA Aust. Rules footballer, b.
Peter Cook, jockey, b.
Bobby Dunne, boxer, b.
Paul Ferreri, boxer, b.
Lucky Gattellari, boxer, b.
Stewart Ginn, golfer, b.
Jim Higgs, cricketer, b.
Alan Hurst, cricketer, b.
Dennis Rich-Katuna, lawn bowls player, b.
Joe Meissner, karate sportsman, b.
Jack Newton, golfer, b.
Len Pascoe, cricketer, b.
Mark Read, Vic. bookmaker, b.
Tom Roudonikis, Rugby League footballer, b.
Remo Sansonetti, cyclist, b.
Jeffrey Robert Thomson, cricketer, noted fast bowler, b.
Donald Wagstaff, diver and swimmer, b.
Jeff White, boxer, b.
Harry Williams, soccer player, b.
Robert (Nat) Young, surfer, b.

1950

F
Historia Dignum

Population
Estimated total white, 8,307,481.

18–19 Jan. Cyclone damages northern NSW, claiming seven lives.
25 Jan. Tank landing craft *Tarakan* explodes at Garden I., Sydney, claiming eight lives.
26 Jun. ANA DC4 aircraft crashes at York, WA, claiming 29 lives.
During Jun. NSW floods devastate wheat crops and stock, claiming 26 lives.
During 1950
Bushfires near Charleville, Qld, burn 60,000 acres.
Good Neighbour Councils estb. to assist migrants to Aust.

Communities
Elizabeth, SA, construction begins.

A

History, Politics, Economics, Law

1951

Government

11 May 1951–11 Jan. 1956, Thirtieth Cwlth Ministry, Robert Gordon Menzies Liberal-Country coalition Prime Minister of Aust.

1 Jul. 1951–6 Aug. 1951, Sir John Patrick Dwyer administered WA.

7 Aug. 1951–27 Aug. 1951, Albert Asher Wolff administered WA.

23 Aug. 1951–4 Jun. 1958, Sir Ronald Hibbert Cross Governor Tas.

28 Aug. 1951–5 Nov. 1951, Sir John Patrick Dwyer administered WA.

6 Nov. 1951–26 Jun. 1963, Sir Charles Henry Gairdner Governor WA.

1951–1956, F. J. S. Wise Administrator NT under Cwlth jurisdiction.

Feb. Cwlth Govt introduces modified free medical care scheme for pensioners.

9 Mar. High Court of Aust. declares Communist Party Dissolution Act invalid.

28 Apr. National elections after double dissolution of Cwlth Parlt resulting from Senate blocking Bank denationalization legislation. Second in history of Cwlth (first 1914). R. G. Menzies returned as Liberal-Country coalition Prime Minister. Herbert Vere Evatt Labor Opposition leader. (Until 1960.)

12 Jun. Twentieth Federal Parlt opens. (Dissolution 21 Apr. 1954.)

1 Jul. NSW Govt first to introduce long-service leave and paid sick leave.

1 Sep. Aust., NZ and USA sign ANZUS Pact. Aust.'s first defence treaty with foreign country.

22 Sep. Referendum on proposal to empower Cwlth Govt to ban the Communist Party rejected.

Nov. PNG Legislative Council opens. Cwlth Govt estb. Dept of Territories.

WA Aborigines holding citizen certificates given the vote.

During 1951

Third Conference of Cwlth Govt statisticians held in Canberra.

Conference of Cwlth and State Ministers committed Govts to policy of assimilation of Aborigines.

Aust. Council for Native Welfare estb.

Dame Florence Gillies Cardell-Oliver becomes first Aust. woman to become member of State Cabinet, in WA.

Wool comprises over half total rural earnings and reaches record price of £1 per pound weight.

American re-equipment programme in Korean War boosts demand for Aust. wool.

The Union Bank merges with the Bank of Australasia to become the Aust. and NZ Bank.

Portsea Officer Cadet School estb., Vic.

Harry Graham Alderman internationalizes the Aust. Legal Convention.

Aust. becomes foundation member of Intergovernmental Committee for European Migration.

1951

B
Science, Technology, Transport, Discovery

14–27 Mar. Patrick Gordon Taylor begins first Aust.–S. America flight, Sydney to Chile.
Jun. CSIRO extends myxomatosis war on rabbits.
During 1951
First shipment of iron ore from Yampi Sound, WA, to Port Kembla, NSW, stimulates steel industry.
Colonial Sugar Refining Co. (CSR) produces first Aust.-made cellulose acetate, synthetic fibre.
Melbourne GPO introduces first mechanical letter sorters.
Leonard Bell Cox becomes first president and foundation member of Aust. Association of Neurologists.
Most serious outbreak of poliomyelitis in Aust. begins. (Lasts until 1954, affecting 4,735 people.)
Mervyn Victor Richardson invents modern lawn mower.
Brisbane trolley buses begin operating.
AMPOL launched in SA. Introduces first electric petrol pumps.
Geological Society of Aust. incorporated. Estb. to advance geological sciences.
First Aust. nurse-aide training school estb., in Melbourne.

Births & Deaths
Edith Coleman, naturalist, expert on plant pollination, d.

C
Arts

Literature

During 1951
Dal Stivens publishes *Jimmy Brockett*.
Dymphna Cusack and Florence James publish *Come in Spinner*.
Colin Simpson publishes *Adam in Ochre*.
Kenneth Mackenzie publishes *Dead Man Rising*.
T. C. Roughley publishes *Fish and Fisheries of Australia*.
Paul Chester Jerome Brickhill publishes *The Dam Busters*.

Music, Dance

During 1951
National Opera Co. of NSW estb. in Sydney.
Qld National Opera Co. estb.
Walter Stiansy helps Hobart Theatre Royal Opera Co

Births & Deaths
Gary Norman, ballet dancer, b.

Fine Arts

Nov. First Aust. outdoor sculpture exhibition held, in Sydney.
During 1951
Ivor Hele wins Archibald Prize for *Laurie Thomas*.
Society of Sculptors and Associates estb. in NSW.
Justin O'Brien wins first Blake Prize for Religious Art.
Russell Drysdale influenced by Aboriginal art.
Inge King, sculptor, arrives in Aust.
Cwlth Jubilee Art Competition and Exhibition held.
Grafton Textile Prize first awarded, NSW.
Italian Art Prizes and Scholarships estb. to enable Aust. artists to study in Italy.
Katanning Art Gallery founded, WA.
Kuring-gai Art Prize estb., NSW.
Henry Caselli Richards Art Prize estb. in Brisbane.
Wagga Wagga Art Prize estb., NSW.

Births & Deaths
L. W. Appleby, pictorial photographer, d.

Architecture

During 1951
Aust. Planning Institute estb. First professional planning association in Aust.

D
Religion, Learning

During 1951

Stanley Melbourne Bruce becomes first Chancellor of Aust. National University.

Free tertiary education for Asians introduced.

'School of the Air' broadcasts begin from Flying Doctor Base at Alice Springs, NT. Molly Ferguson becomes first full-time teacher broadcasting to children in remote areas.

Newcastle University estb. as College of NSW University of Technology (later University of NSW).

Bathurst Teachers' College opens, NSW.

SA Institute of Teachers estb.

State College of Vic. estb.

Technical Teachers' College estb. at Hawthorn, Melbourne.

E
Sport

During 1951

Delta, ridden by N. Sellwood, wins Melbourne Cup in 3 minutes $24\frac{1}{4}$ seconds.

Geelong football team wins VFL Premiership in Melbourne.

South Sydney football team wins Rugby Union Premiership in Sydney.

Bernie Smith of Geelong VFL team awarded Brownlow Medal.

Frank Sedgman is ABC Sportsman of the Year.

First Aust. canoeing championships held, in Melbourne. (First women's championship held in 1953.)

Allie Duncan first noted woman angler.

Frank Sedgman first Aust. to win US tennis singles title. Wins doubles Grand Slam with Ken McGregor.

French Rugby League team begins first Aust. tour.

World's fastest boxing match, lasting seven seconds, held in Brisbane.

Jack Young wins world motorcycle speedway championship.

Struen Marie wins Sydney to Hobart yacht race.

Births & Deaths

John Alexander, tennis player, b.
Raelene Boyle, sprinter, b.
Warwick Brown, racing car driver, b.
Maureen Caird, athlete, b.
Ross Case, tennis player, b.
Evonne Fay Cawley (née Goolagong), tennis player, b.
Peter Drouyn, surf rider, b.
Gary Gilmour, cricketer, b.
Keith Greig, VFL footballer, b.
Rodney Hogg, cricketer, b.
Lynn McClements, swimmer, b.
Laurie Monaghan, Rugby Union footballer, b.
Graham Moss, VFL footballer, b.
Tony Mundine, boxer, b.
Paul Pinkewich, table tennis player, b.
Clyde Sefton, cyclist, b.
John Titman, racing car driver, b.
Michael Wenden, swimmer, b.

1951

1951

F

Historia Dignum

Population
Estimated total white, 8,527,907.

19 Feb. Jean Lee, Robert Clayton and Norman Andrews hanged in Melbourne for murder. Jean Lee is last woman in Aust. hanged.
24 Feb. Level crossing accident at Horsham, Vic., claims 11 lives.
16 Aug. The *Australian Financial Review* begins publication in Sydney as weekly. (Daily from Oct. 1963.)
15 Oct. Dover aircraft crashes at Lake Kurrawang, WA, claiming seven lives.

During 1951
Number of 'displaced persons' who have migrated to Aust. reaches 170,000.
Long jackets and thick crepe soled shoes fashionable for young men.
Bamboo hula-hoops invented in Aust.
Guide dogs for the blind movement begins in WA.
J. W. Thwaites and E. L. Field win first Aust. world contract bridge championship.
Jubilee Celebration marks 50 years of Federation.
Riverina bushfires, NSW, claim six lives. Vic.
Bushfires claim 10 lives. Bushfires in SA, Tas. Qld, WA and NT.
Extensive river floods in NSW and Vic.
Widespread national drought begins.

Communities
Kwinana, WA, planned

A

History, Politics, Economics, Law

Government

17 Jan. 1952–Aug. 1957, V. C. Gair Labor Premier Qld.

3 Apr. 1952–Oct. 1959, J. J. Cahill Labor Premier NSW.

27 Oct. 1952–30 Oct. 1952, T. T. Hollway Electoral Reform Premier Vic.

31 Oct. 1952–Dec. 1952, J. G. B. McDonald Country Party Premier Vic.

17 Dec. 1952–Jun. 1955, J. Cain (the elder) Labor Premier Vic.

6 Feb. Queen Elizabeth II succeeds as monarch her father King George VI.

Mar. Severe import restrictions imposed to cope with acute balance of payments problem.

18 Apr. Sir Owen Dixon appointed Chief Justice of High Court of Aust. (Until 13 Apr. 1964.) Sir Alan Taylor appointed a Justice of High Court of Aust. (Until 1969.)

28 Jul. RAAF personnel sent to Malta for Middle East peace-keeping operations.

Aug. Cwlth Govt reduces assisted immigration programme to cope with rising unemployment among unskilled workers.

Oct. Govt introduces two-airlines policy to maintain competition between ANA and TAA.

29 Nov. Edward Gough Whitlam enters Federal Parlt.

During 1952

Second Battalion of Aust. troops leave for Korea.

Ambassadors to W. Germany and Japan appointed.

Aborigines Benefits Trust Fund estb.

Aust. Secret Intelligence Service, ASIS, overseas espionage service, estb.

Jacaranda book publishers estb.

Cwlth Hospital Benefit scheme begins.

B

Science, Technology, Transport, Discovery

1952

Jan. Construction of first oil refineries begins at Kwinana, WA, and Kurnell, NSW.

Mar. Alan Walsh of CSIRO invents the absorption spectrophotometer.

Aug. International Scientific Radio Union Assembly held in Sydney.

3 Oct. Britain's first H-Bomb detonated in tests at Monte Bello I., off WA coast.

During 1952

Aust.-designed and built Rotolactor, automatic rotary milking machine, begins operating near Menangle, NSW.

Uranium discovered at Rum Jungle, NT, and at Radium Hill, SA.

Ken Metcalfe and Robert Wright develop system of liquid rather than dry developers for xerographic process.

Derwent Power Development Hydro-electric Scheme in Tas. begins. (Completed in 1968.)

Nuclear experiments begin at Aust. National University in Canberra.

Santa Gertrudis cattle introduced.

Lang Hancock first recognizes iron ore in the Hamersley Ranges, WA.

Social Science Research Council estb.

With development of land transport, east coast intrastate shipping services begin to decline rapidly.

1952

C
Arts

Literature

During 1952
Jon Cleary publishes *The Sundowners*.
T. A. Hungerford publishes *The Ridge and the River*.
Martin Boyd publishes *The Cardboard Crown*.
Nevil Shute publishes *The Far Country*.
Eric Lambert publishes *The Twenty Thousand Thieves*.
Judah Waten publishes *Alien Son*.
The Aust. Book Society estb. to provide wider market for Aust. writers.
Russell Reading Braddon publishes *The Naked Island*.

Music, Dance

During 1952
NSW National Opera Co. registered as National Opera of Aust.
Joan Sutherland makes début in *The Magic Flute* in London.
Kira Bousloff founds the WA Ballet Co.
Juan José Castro appointed conductor Melbourne Symphony Orchestra. (Until 1953.)

Drama, Theatre, Film

Jan. Documentary film *Mike and Stefani* premières.
During 1952
Film *Kangaroo* made.

Fine Arts

During 1952
William Dargie wins Archibald Prize for *Essington Lewis*.
Robin Boyd publishes *Australia's Home*.
Aust. sends art to Carnegie Exhibition, USA.
Indian Art Exhibition visits Aust.
Architecture and Arts published, in Melbourne.
Daub, Melbourne National Gallery students' magazine, published. (Until 1961.)
Metro-Goldwyn-Mayer Art Prize estb. in Sydney.
Northam Art Gallery estb., WA.
c. 1952. Margaret Bembina, Italian painter, arrives in Aust.

Births & Deaths
Geoffrey Bartlett, sculptor, b.

Architecture

During 1952
Pergolas become popular feature of Melbourne architecture.

D
Religion, Learning

25 Oct. Buddhist Society of NSW holds first meeting, in Sydney.
During 1952
James Stirling becomes first fully qualified Aboriginal teacher.
First selective comprehensive high schools open in Tas.
Cavendish High School founded in Qld. (First new high school in Qld since 1924.)
Libertarian Society, intellectual social movement, estb. in Sydney.
Taxpayers permitted to deduct school fees of up to £50 per annum from their incomes before paying tax.

E
Sport

During 1952
Dalray, ridden by W. Williamson, wins Melbourne Cup in 3 minutes 23¾ seconds.
Geelong football team wins VFL Premiership in Melbourne.
Western Suburbs football team wins Rugby League Premiership in Sydney.
Roy Wright of Richmond VFL team awarded Brownlow Medal.
Marjorie Jackson is ABC Sportswoman of the Year.
Aust. wins six gold, two silver and three bronze medals at Helsinki Olympics.
First Fiji-Aust. Rugby Union match played, in Sydney.
Organized volleyball competitions begin in Aust.
First Aust. waterpolo championships held.
First Aust. water ski championships held, at Penrith, NSW.
Cronulla-Sutherland Rugby League Club estb. in Sydney.
James William (Jimmy) Carruthers wins world bantam weight boxing title in South Africa.
Marjorie Jackson, sprinter, becomes first Aust. woman gold medallist in Olympic athletics.
Jack Young wins world speedway motorcycle championship for second time.
Ian Craig, aged 17 years and 8 months, is youngest cricketer to play for Aust. in Test match.
Ingrid wins Sydney to Hobart yacht race.

Births & Deaths
Danny Clark, cyclist, b.
Michael Cronin, Rugby League footballer, b.
Phillip Crump, speedway rider, b.
Steve Finnance, Rugby Union footballer, b.
Gregory Hansford, motorcyclist, b.
Jim Hindmarsh, Rugby Union player, b.
Wayne Lynch, surfer, b.
Darby McCarthy, jockey, b.
Gary Moore, jockey, b.
Ray Price, Rugby footballer, b.
Terry Randall, Rugby footballer, b.
Jan Stephenson, golfer, b.
Wendy Turnbull, tennis player, b.
Graham Yallop, cricketer, b.

F
Historia Dignum

Population
Estimated total white, 8,739,569.

Jan.–Mar. Extensive bushfires in Vic. and NSW. Vic. fires claim 10 lives.
8 Feb. The *Northern Territory News* first published, in Darwin.
7 May. Train collision at Berala, NSW, claims 10 lives.
1 Jun. Level-crossing accident at Boronia, near Melbourne, claims nine lives.
During Jun. one of worst recorded floods in Aust. history in southern NSW. Heavy rural losses. Also floods in Tas.
10 Sep. Ship *Awahou* disappears while *en route* from Sydney to Lord Howe I.; 12 lost.
During 1952
Unidentified flying objects sighted frequently from this year onwards.
Aust. National Council for the Blind estb.

Communities
Batchelor, NT, estb.

1953

A
History, Politics, Economics, Law

Government
23 Feb. 1953–7 Mar. 1960, Sir Robert Allingham George Governor SA.
23 Feb. 1953–Apr. 1959, A. R. G. Hawke Labor Premier WA.
8 May 1953–2 Feb. 1960, Sir William Joseph Slim Governor-General Aust.
8 Jul. 1953–23 Nov. 1953, Sir Charles Lowe administered Vic.
24 Nov. 1953–7 May 1963, Sir Reginald Alexander Dallas Brooks Governor Vic.

Jan. Japanese Embassy opens in Canberra. Haruhiko Nishi arrives as first Ambassador.
Cwlth Govt estb. full citizenship rights for NT Aboriginal half-castes.
USA becomes large-scale purchaser of Aust. uranium.
Feb. Aust. and International Insurances Ltd incorporated. (FAI Insurances Ltd.)
27 Jul. Korean War ends. Aust. dead in war 287 soldiers and 42 RAAF pilots.
12 Sep. Court of Conciliation and Arbitration abandons system of automatic adjustments of the basic wage in accordance with price index numbers.
During 1953
National Health Act passed. Consolidates pharmaceutical, medical and hospital benefits and a pensioner medical service. Cwlth medical benefits scheme starts in Jul.
Britain and Aust. sign agreement for reciprocity of Social Service benefits.
Cwlth Govt claims sovereignty over Aust. Continental Shelf by passing Pearl Fisheries Act.
Aust. and Japan refer fishing and pearling disputes to the International Court.
Cwlth Govt introduces first Television Bill to supervise introduction of television.
NSW control of Lord Howe I. formalized by Lord Howe Island Act.
Wool prices drop as four-year wool boom ends.
Premiers' Conference meets to consider transferring income tax powers from Cwlth to States.
Aust. ends use of pidgin English in PNG.
Donald Allan Dunstan enters SA Parlt.
Atomic Energy Act empowers Cwlth Govt to control nuclear energy.
The National Employers' Policy and Consultative Committee estb.
NT Aborigines classified as wards of the State. (Until 1960.)

B
Science, Technology, Transport, Discovery

15 Apr. Aust. Atomic Energy Commission estb. to promote discovery, production and research of uranium and atomic energy.
2 Jun. Bruce Walpole discovers uranium at El Sherana, on Alligator R., NT.
4 Dec. Oil discovered at Rough Range, on Exmouth Gulf, WA.
During 1953
Water fluoridation first introduced, at Beaconsfield, Tas.
TAA introduces first Viscount prop-jets.
Adelaide tramways begin to close.
FJ Holden car launched.
Bauxite discovered at Weipa, Qld.
B. Y. Mills of CSIRO develops the Mills Cross radiotelescope.

C
Arts

Literature

During 1953
Eleanor Dark publishes *No Barrier*.

Drama, Theatre, Film

Jan. Cecil Holmes produces film *Captain Thunderbolt*.
4 Jun. Lee Robinson produces film *The Phantom Stockman*.
Aug. John Sumner estb. Union Theatre Repertory Co. in Melbourne. First professional company producing classic, contemporary and Aust. plays.
During 1953
Dick Diamond's *Reedy River*, folk musical, premières in Sydney.

Births & Deaths
David Gulpilil, Aboriginal actor and dancer, b.

Fine Arts

During 1953
Ivor Hele wins Archibald Prize for *Sir Henry Simpson Newland*.
Art Gallery Society of NSW estb.
Latvian Artists in Aust. estb Blue Brush Exhibitions (until 1963).
Eileen Mayo, English graphic artist and illustrator, arrives in Aust.
Narrogin Art Gallery estb, WA.
Six Directors Art Group estb. in Sydney.
Yorick Art Club and Prize estb. in Melbourne.
French Painting Today Exhibition encourages abstract expressionism.
Ivan McMeekin estb. Sturt Pottery, at Mittagong, NSW.
Herald newspaper outdoor art show estb. in Melbourne.
Leroy-Alcorso prizes for textile designers first awarded.
Lismore Art Prize estb., NSW.

Architecture

During 1953
Roy Grounds completes geometrical circular house in Toorak, Melbourne.

D
Religion, Learning

18 Apr. Leonard Bullen estb. Buddhist Society of Vic.
During 1953
Burwood Teachers' College founded in Melbourne.
Methodist Church launches national evangelist campaign, Mission to the Nation.
In NSW the Committee to Survey Secondary Education, under the chairmanship of H. S. Wyndham, is appointed to investigate declining standards in schools.

1953

1953

E Sport

26 Jan. First greyhound handicap race held at Wentworth Park in Sydney.
Feb. Confederation of Aust. Motor Sport estb.
During 1953
Wodalla, ridden by J. Purtell, wins Melbourne Cup in 3 minutes $23\frac{3}{4}$ seconds.
Collingwood football team wins VFL Premiership in Melbourne.
South Sydney football team wins Rugby League Premiership in Sydney.
William Hutchison of Essendon VFL team awarded Brownlow Medal.
Jimmy Carruthers is ABC Sportsman of the Year.
SA Power Boating Council estb.
American Allstars Rugby League Team visits Aust.
Record crowd of 32,500 at boxing tournament in Sydney.
Redex road trials begin.
Live game Bow Hunters Club estb. in Vic.
Ken Rosewall, at 19 years, becomes youngest Aust. tennis champion.
Russell Mockridge wins open cycling Grand Prix in Paris.
Ronald Dale Barassi plays first senior game of Aust. Rules football, in Melbourne.
George Barnes is first boxer in world to complete a father–son double.
Sydney Cavill's butterfly swimming stroke recognized as distinctive swimming stroke.
Ripple wins Sydney to Hobart Yacht race.

Births & Deaths

Paddy Batch, Rugby Union footballer, b.
Ric Charlesworth, cricketer, hockey player, b.
Gary Cosier, cricketer, b.
Rocco (Rocky) Mattiolo, boxer, b.
Kevin Wright, cricketer, b.

F Historia Dignum

Population
Estimated total white, 8,902,686.

29 Oct. Aust. DC6 aircraft crashes in San Francisco, killing 18.
19 Dec. Train collision at Sydenham, NSW, claims five lives.
During 1953
Women's Weekly special Queen Elizabeth II Coronation issue sells 960,000 copies.
Perth Festival begins.
Aust. Folk Lore Society founded in Sydney.
First Queen Elizabeth II stamps issued.

Births & Deaths

'Gympie' Howard, shearers' cook, d.

Communities

Abergowrie, Qld, estb.
Moline, NT, area first settled.

A

History, Politics, Economics, Law

3 Feb.–1 Apr. Queen Elizabeth II becomes first reigning monarch to visit Aust.

14 Apr. R. G. Menzies announces that Soviet diplomat Vladimir Mikhailovich Petrov has defected to Aust. authorities. Aust. and Soviet Union break diplomatic relations for five years. Royal Commission estb. to investigate Soviet espionage in Aust.

29 May. R. G. Menzies, Liberal-Country coalition Prime Minister, returned at national elections.

4 Aug. Twenty-first Federal Parlt opens. (Dissolution on 4 Nov. 1955.)

8 Sep. Aust. becomes a signatory to South-East Asian Treaty Organization (SEATO).

Sep.–Oct. Cwlth Govt imposes further import restrictions to cope with balance of payments problem.

Oct. Opposition leader H. V. Evatt attacks right-wing members of the Vic. Labor Party for supporting Industrial Groups in fight against Communism.

Nov. Arbitration Court grants marginal wage increases.

During 1954

Aust. Agriculture Council estb. the Central Tobacco Advisory Committee.

Proportion of Aust. workforce unionized reaches a record 62 per cent.

Aust. Committee for Cultural Freedom estb. Becomes Aust. Association for Cultural Freedom in 1957.

B

Science, Technology, Transport, Discovery

16 Feb. Royal Aust. Academy of Science estb. to promote the natural sciences.

12 May. Nuclear Research Foundation estb. as part of Sydney University. (Becomes Science Foundation for Physics in 1966.)

Jul. Clem Walton and Norman McConachy discover uranium at Mary Kathleen, Qld.

During 1954

First major Aust. uranium treatment project begins, at Rum Jungle, NT.

Alan Walsh builds proto-type atomic absorption spectrophotometer.

Phillip Garth Law leads Aust. National Antarctic Research Expedition (ANARE) to estb. Mawson base on 13 Feb. First permanent Aust. research station in Antarctica.

Electric typewriters first used in Aust.

The first Mills Cross radio telescope built, at St Marys, NSW.

Teleprinter Exchange (TELEX) service introduced in Aust.

A. G. L. Rees publishes *The Chemistry of The Defect Solid State*.

1954

1954

C

Arts

Literature

During 1954
A. A. Phillips publishes *The Australian Tradition*.
Mary Gilmore publishes *Fourteen Men*.
Judah Waten publishes *The Unbending*.
Patricia Wrightson publishes *The Crooked Snake*.
Vance Palmer publishes *The Legend of the Nineties*.

Music, Dance

During 1954
Lee Gordon, rock and roll promoter, begins to revolutionize popular music in Aust.
Peter Sculthorpe produces *Sonatina*.
Walter Susskind appointed conductor of Melbourne Symphony Orchestra. (Until 1955.)
Aust. Elizabethan Theatre Trust founded: establishes Aust. Opera, Aust. Ballet and the Marionette Theatre of Aust., and gives financial and technical assistance to theatre groups.

Drama, Theatre, Film

Nov. Union Theatre of Melbourne first presents Ray Lawler's play, *Summer of the Seventeenth Doll*.
During 1954
John Heyer wins major international film award, the Prix Assoluto, for *The Back of Beyond*.
Hayes Gordon estb. Ensemble Studios Acting School.
Jedda, co-starring Aboriginal actors Robert Tudawali and Ngarla Kunoth, possibly first full-length colour feature film made in Aust., produced. (Released in 1955.)
Phillip Street Theatre estb. in Sydney.

Fine Arts

During 1954
Ivor Hele wins Archibald Prize for *R. G. Menzies*.
R. Dickerson wins Clint Art Prize in Sydney.
Collie Art Gallery estb., WA.
May Day Art Prize first awarded in Melbourne. (Until 1958.)
Overland quarterly review founded.
Perth Prize for Contemporary Painting estb.
Taree Art Prize first awarded, NSW.
Tas. Sesqui-Centenary Art Prize awarded.

Architecture

During 1954
Morton Herman publishes *The Early Australian Architects and Their Work*.
Arthur Stephenson becomes first Aust. to win British Architects Royal Gold Medal.

D
Religion, Learning

29 Oct. In an open letter to the Premier, Professor Sydney Sparkes Orr and 35 colleagues from University of Tas. request Tas. Govt to investigate work conditions at the university. Royal Commission appointed.

During Oct. Dr H. V. Evatt, leader of the ALP, criticizes Catholic Social Movement for its over-involvement in politics. Arouses much controversy.

During 1954

College of the University of Sydney at Armidale, NSW, becomes University of New England.

Walford Church of England Girls' Grammar School estb. in Adelaide.

Donations to private school building funds made tax deductable.

Glen Bogue estb. United Pentecostal Church in Sydney.

Increasing prosperity, population growth and the expansion of white-collar occupations account for a rapid increase in university enrolments from this time.

E
Sport

21 Jun. John Landy, 'The Geelong Galloper', becomes first Aust. and second man in world to break the four-minute mile barrier, in Finland.

During 1954

Cwlth Games held in Vancouver, Canada.

Rising Fast, ridden by J. Purtell, wins Melbourne Cup in 3 minutes 23 seconds.

Footscray football team wins VFL Premiership in Melbourne.

South Sydney football team wins Rugby League Premiership in Sydney.

Roy Wright of Richmond VFL team awarded Brownlow Medal.

John Landy is ABC Sportsman of the Year.

Jimmy Carruthers, becomes first boxer in world to retire undefeated.

Amateur Modern Pentathlon Union of Aust. estb.

Aust.–England Rugby League match abandoned because of brawl.

Peter Thomson and Ken Nagle win Canada Golf Cup for first time.

George Barnes first Aust. boxer to win British Empire boxing welterweight title.

Solveig wins Sydney to Hobart yacht race.

Births & Deaths

Bruce Allison, motor racer, b.

Joanne Barnes, swimmer, youngest person ever to represent Aust. in any sport (14 years old at 1968 Mexico Olympics), b.

Ian Cairns, surfer, b.

Graham Eadie, Rugby League footballer, b.

Kim Hughes, cricketer, b.

Lyn Jackeno, athlete, b.

Jane Lock, golfer, b.

Karen Moras, swimmer, b.

John Nicholson, cyclist, b.

Pam O'Neill, jockey, b.

George Peponis, Rugby League footballer, b.

Mike Peterson, surf rider, b.

Peter Toohey, cricketer, b.

1954

F

Historia Dignum

Population
Estimated total white, 9,989,936.
Cwlth census shows total white population at 8,986,350 and Aboriginal population at 76,000.

20–22 Feb. Flooding of northern NSW rivers claim 26 lives. Floods at Rockhampton, Qld, claim 10 lives.
1 Mar. Earthquake damages Adelaide area.
13 Oct. Coalmine gas in accident at Collinsville, Qld, claims seven lives.
Nov. WA legalizes off-course SP betting.
Dec. NSW State-wide poll favours 10 o'clock closing of hotel bars rather than 6 o'clock.
During 1954
Moomba Festival planned in Melbourne.
Hula-hoop craze spreads.
Seamless stockings arrive in Aust.
Aust. Cerebral Palsy Association Inc. conducts national Miss Aust. Quest.
Bushfires in Mt Lofty Ranges, SA.
WA Bushfires Board estb.

Communities
Humpty Doo, NT, estb.

A
History, Politics, Economics, Law

1955

Government
8 Jun. 1955–Aug. 1972 H. E. Bolte Liberal Premier Vic.

Jan. Aust. Broadcasting Control Board opens hearings which estb. first television station licences. (TCN-9 and ATN-7 in Sydney, GTV-9 and HSV-7 in Melbourne.)

Mar. Split occurs in ALP following controversy at Federal Conference in Hobart over Communism in trade unions. Attack on Industrial Groups and right-wing leadership in Victoria leads to estb. of an 'Anti-Communist Labor Party', with Frank McManus as secretary.

Death penalty for murder abolished in NSW.

Mar. and Sep. Govt imposes substantial import restrictions to correct trade deficit due to falling exports and rising imports.

Apr. Cwlth Govt sends army, air force and naval forces to Malaya to assist British in their campaign against Communist guerrillas in Emergency.

11 Jun. House of Representatives finds free-lance journalist Frank Courtney Browne and newspaper proprietor Raymond Edward Fitzpatrick guilty of breaching Parliamentary Privilege by publishing intimidating articles. (Sentenced to three months jail.)

Sep. The Petrov Commission's report tabled in Parlt.

28 Oct. HMAS *Melbourne*, RAN's second aircraft carrier, commissioned.

23 Nov. Cocos Is cease to be part of British Colony of Singapore. Becomes part of Cwlth of Aust. known as Territory of Cocos (Keeling) Is.

10 Dec. R. G. Menzies returned as Liberal-Country coalition Prime Minister at national elections.

During 1955
Two NT graziers jailed for flogging Aborigines with stock whips.

John Malcolm Fraser enters Federal Parlt.

Commercial safflower production begins in Qld.

Mabel Miller and Amelia Best, Liberals, become first women to enter Tas. Parlt.

B
Science, Technology, Transport, Discovery

Jan. Large anchorage and harbour opened at Cockburn Sound, south of Fremantle, WA.

Feb. Aust. Aluminium Production Commission produces first aluminium in Aust., at Bell Bay, Tas. Becomes site of first aluminium production unit in southern hemisphere.

Apr. Govt decides to mass-produce the anti-poliomyelitis Salk vaccine to end polio epidemics. Vaccine recently discovered by Dr Salk in USA.

Jul. Harry Evans discovers bauxite at Weipa, Qld.

Aug. Hot strip steel mill opens at Port Kembla, NSW.

2 Dec. First civil jet aircraft visits Aust.

During 1955
First Snowy Mountains hydroelectric power fed into NSW electricity system.

Kwinana Oil Refinery opens in WA.

World's largest piece of pitchblende, primary uranium ore, mined at El Sherana, NT, weight 1,874 lbs.

Adelaide airport opens.

1955

C

Arts

Literature

During 1955
John Morrison publishes *Black Cargo*.
Martin Boyd publishes *A Difficult Young Man*.
Mary Durack publishes *Keep Him My Country*.
Patrick White publishes *The Tree of Man*.
D'Arcy Niland publishes *The Shiralee*.
Alan Marshall publishes *I Can Jump Puddles*.
A. D. Hope publishes first book of verse, *The Wandering Islands*.
Colin Johnson, Aboriginal author, publishes *Wild Cat Falling*.

Music, Dance

Feb. Margaret Barr estb. Dance Drama Group in Sydney.
During 1955
Aust. Jazz Quartet estb.
Aust. National Eisteddfod (Shell Aria) singing competitions launched in Canberra.
Dandenong Festival of Music and Art for Youth estb., Vic.
J. C. Williamson estb. International Grand Opera Co.
Rudolf Pekarek appointed conductor Qld Symphony Orchestra. (Until 1967.) John Farnsworth Hall appointed conductor WA Symphony Orchestra. (Until 1964.)

Drama, Theatre, Film

27 Jul. Elizabethan Theatre Trust stages *The Sleeping Prince*.
Oct. Elizabethan Trust season opens with Judith Anderson and Clement McCallin playing in *Medea*.
During 1955
Cecil Quentin and Tom Brown estb. National Institute of Dramatic Art.
Barry Humphries' Edna Everage impersonation makes first appearance, in *Return Fare*, a Christmas review produced by Union Theatre Co. in Melbourne.
There are 1,644 picture theatres in Aust. (Only 974 by 1970.)

Fine Arts

During 1955
Ivor Hele wins Archibald Prize for *Robert Campbell*.
John Brackenreg founds Artlovers' Gallery in Sydney.
Carillon City Festival Art Prize estb. at Bathurst, NSW.
Art Gallery of NSW estb. John le Gay Brereton prize for drawings.
Brummels Art Gallery opens in Melbourne. (Later destroyed by fire.)
Newcastle War Memorial competition conducted for sculpture, NSW.
Rockdale Art competition estb., NSW.
South Melbourne Centenary Prize estb.
Women's Weekly Portrait Prize estb. in Sydney.
Adelaide Advertiser Art Prize estb. in Adelaide.
Geoffrey Collings among first to adopt modern idioms in advertising art.
American abstract art influences Sydney painters, particularly John Olsen.
Michael Kmit wins Critics' Prize for Contemporary Art in Sydney.
Kalgoorlie Art Gallery estb., WA.

Architecture

During 1955
Mid-twentieth century period of architecture begins. (Ends *c.* 1967.)
First ever exhibition of Aust. Architecture in England held.

D
Religion, Learning

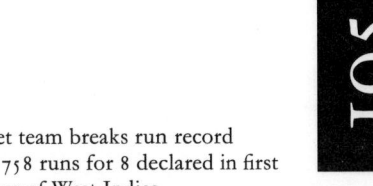

1955

May. Catholic archbishops and bishops issue joint Pastoral dealing with problems of Communism. Catholic Church criticized for interfering in Labor affairs.

During 1955
WA Public Library renamed State Library of WA.
Earle Page becomes first Chancellor of University of New England, NSW.
Sisters of Mercy estb. McAuley College in Brisbane.
The Aust. Administrative Staff College estb. at Mt Eliza, Vic.
Breakaway Methodist group forms the Aust. People's Church in Melbourne.

E
Sport

Jun. Aust. Test cricket team breaks run record against West Indies: 758 runs for 8 declared in first Aust. Test cricket tour of West Indies.

During 1955
Toparoa, ridden by N. Sellwood, wins Melbourne Cup in 3 minutes $28\frac{1}{4}$ seconds.
Melbourne football team wins VFL Premiership in Melbourne.
South Sydney football team wins Rugby League Premiership in Sydney.
Fred Goldsmith of S. Melbourne VFL team awarded Brownlow Medal.
Peter Thomson is ABC Sportsman of the Year.
Aust. wins Davis Cup tennis against USA.
'Scobie' Breasley, jockey, creates record by riding 100 winners each season, mostly in England.
Dennis Green begins canoeing career.
Aust. spearfishing championships begin.
Moonbi wins Sydney to Hobart yacht race.

Births & Deaths
Alan Border, cricketer, noted batsman b.
David Hookes, cricketer, b.
Graham Hughes, Rugby League footballer, cricketer, b.
Mark Loane, Rugby footballer, b.
Greg Norman, golfer, b.
Steve Rogers, Rugby League footballer, b.
Billy Sanders, racing car driver, b.
Graham Teasdale, VFL footballer, b.

1955

F
Historia Dignum

Population
Estimated total white, 9,311,825.

2 Jan. Bushfires ravage Adelaide area.
25 Feb. Floods at Maitland, NSW, destroy many houses, claiming 22 lives.
During Feb. NSW Govt introduces 10 o'clock hotel closing time.
7 Mar. Lugger sinks in cyclone on north Qld coast, claiming eight lives.
During Mar. Lake Pedder area, Tas., declared a National Park.
First Melbourne Moomba Festival begins.
1 Apr. Hobart becomes first Aust. city to introduce parking metres.
10 Apr. Auster aircraft crashes at Forbes, NSW, claiming five lives.
11 Jul. Newspaper *Darling Downs Star* estb. in Toowoomba, Qld.
31 Dec. Newspapers *Sunday Mail* first published, in Adelaide.
During 1955
The millionth post World War II immigrant arrives in Aust.
Mary Quant fashion look popular. Dior's A line look introduced.
National Marriage Guidance Council estb.
John Purdey, aged 19 years, becomes youngest Aust. chess champion.
National road toll 2,084.
c. 1955. First motel in Aust. opens, in Canberra.

Births & Deaths
Barney Worth, heaviest recorded Aust. male, 588 lb, d. (b. 1916)

A

History, Politics, Economics, Law

1956

Government

11 Jan. 1956–10 Dec. 1958, Thirty-first Cwlth Ministry, Robert Gordon Menzies Liberal-Country coalition Prime Minister of Aust.

1956–1961, J. C. Archer Administrator NT under Cwlth jurisdiction.

Jan. Waterside workers begin strike over work practices. Qld shearers begin six-month strike over reduction of wages.

Bank of NSW first private trading bank to estb. separate savings bank. On 19 Jan. Aust. and NZ Commercial Savings Bank opens.

15 Feb. Twenty-second Federal Parlt opens. (Dissolution 14 Oct. 1958.)

Mar. Cwlth Govt imposes supplementary budget to deal with nation's credit squeeze.

29 Sep. Democratic Labor Party (DLP) estb. in Vic. from ALP (Anti-Communist) members and other former ALP members.

8 Nov. Aust. supports Anglo-French military intervention in Middle East following Egyptian nationalization of Suez Canal on 26 Jul. R. G. Menzies appointed Chairman of Suez Canal Committee.

10 Nov.–14 Dec. Prince Philip, Duke of Edinburgh, visits Aust.

During Nov. Aust. agrees to accept displaced Hungarian refugees following Soviet intervention in Hungary.

During 1956

Amendment to Conciliation and Arbitration Act alters structure of arbitration machinery by separating judicial functions from conciliation and arbitration functions. Industrial court estb. separate from award-setting Commission.

Aust. and USA sign Bilateral Agreement for peaceful use of atomic energy.

Aust. and UK agree on comprehensive trade pact to replace 24-year-old Ottawa Agreement.

Aust. Political Studies Association (APSA) estb.

EZ Industries Ltd estb. to take over Electrolytic Zinc Co. of Aust.

Successful production of cultured pearls begins at Kuri Bay, WA.

Federal Govt estb. Department of Trade.

The Export Payment Insurance Corporation estb. to protect exporters.

B

Science, Technology, Transport, Discovery

Apr. First stainless steel railway carriages in Aust. operate in Qld.

May–Jun. British atomic bomb tests continue at Monte Bello Is, off WA coast.

Jun. First Salk vaccine for polio administered in Aust. CSIRO laboratories manufacture large quantities of the vaccine.

16 Sep. TCN-9 launches first regular television service in Sydney.

27 Sep. Melbourne commercial television station GTV 9 launches surprise transmission. Regular transmissions by ABC and commercial stations begin on 4 Nov.

During 1956

Aust. Shipping Commission estb. as the Australian Coastal Shipping Commission. Aust. National Line (ANL) Merchant Shipping Service estb.

First automatic electronic computer in Aust., SILLIAC, installed at Sydney University.

Sydney–Melbourne daylight railway express begins.

Ken Gaunt develops mechanical sugar-cane harvester.

Hobart airport opens.

CSIRO begins producing the Aust. Milking Zebu, tropical breed of dairy cattle.

Stan Hilditch discovers iron ore near Mt Newman, WA.

1956

Arts

Literature

During 1956
James McAuley publishes *A Vision of Ceremony*.
Hal Porter publishes collection of verse, *The Hexagon*.
Alan Moorehead publishes *Gallipoli*.
James McAuley founds *Quadrant* magazine.

Music, Dance

During 1956
First rock and roll music imported into Aust.
Johnny O'Keefe, 'King' of Rock'n' Roll in Aust., comperes first 'rock' show, *Six O'Clock Rock*.
Aust. Opera Co. begins first season.
Donald Peart re-establishes Aust. section of International Society for Contemporary Music.
Elizabethan Trust Opera Co. replaces National Theatre Movement and National Opera.
Qld Conservatorium of Music estb.
Kurt Woess appointed conductor Melbourne Symphony Orchestra. (Until 1960.)

Drama, Theatre, Film

Jan. Ray Lawler's *Summer of the Seventeenth Doll* applauded as major event in history of Aust. drama.
During 1956
Cecil Holmes, produces film, *Three in One*.
The new Playhouse opens in Perth.
Richard Beynon writes play *The Shifting Heart*.

Fine Arts

Apr. Direction 1 Exhibition signals turning point in abstract painting in Sydney. Exhibits paintings by Passmore, Olsen, Rose and Eric Smith.
During 1956
William Dargie wins Archibald Prize for *Albert Namatijira*.
David Boyd's non-utilitarian ceramics give impetus to Melbourne pottery.
Tom and Anne Purves estb. Australian Galleries, private gallery in Melbourne.
Brisbane Public Library Art Prize awarded to Lindsay Edward for mosaic.
F. Bates wins Concord Council Art Prize.
Orcades Travelling Art Exhibition begins.
Italian Art of the Twentieth Century Art Exhibition tours Aust.
Recent German Graphic Art Exhibition tours Aust.
French Tapestries Exhibition, first exhibition of modern tapestries, shown in Aust.
John Reed founds Gallery of Contemporary Art in Melbourne. (Becomes the Museum of Modern Art in Aust. 1958.)
Hunters Hill Art Competitions estb., NSW.
The John McCaughey Art Prize inaugurated in Melbourne.
Mildura Arts Centre estb., Vic.
Robin Hood Art competition estb.
Warringah Art Prizes estb., NSW.
Wollongong Art Prize founded, NSW.

Architecture

During 1956
Joern Utzon designs Sydney Opera House.
ICI House first building to break the 40m barrier in Melbourne.

Births & Deaths
John Cyril Haines, Spanish-style architect, d.

D
Religion, Learning

16 Mar. Professor Sydney Sparkes Orr, head of Department of Philosophy, controversially dismissed from University of Tas. for misconduct.
Jul. Cwlth Govt subsidizes Church schools in the ACT by paying the interest on loans raised by the Churches for new school buildings. Resumes system of State Aid to Church schools.
26 Sep. H. S. Wyndham opens Museum of Education in Armidale, NSW.

During 1956
Scientology (The Church of the New Faith), religious cult, becomes active in Aust.
The United Church of N. Aust. estb.
Church of God radio broadcasts begin.
British and Foreign Bible Society translates the New Testament into Aranda language.
Gordon Powell conducts first televised Church services in Aust.

E
Sport

1956

1 Jan. Vic. legalizes mechanical hare racing.
Sep. Qld Rugby League referees strike over lenient treatment of players ordered off field.
22 Nov. Sixteenth Olympic Games held in Melbourne. First time Games held in southern hemisphere and first time televised. Aust. wins thirteen gold, eight silver and four bronze medals.

During 1956
Evening Pearl, ridden by G. Podmore, wins Melbourne Cup in 3 minutes $19\frac{1}{2}$ seconds.
Melbourne football team wins VFL Premiership in Melbourne.
St George football team wins Rugby League Premiership in Sydney.
Peter Box of Footscray VFL team awarded Brownlow Medal.
Betty Cuthbert is ABC Sportswoman of the Year.
Betty Cuthbert, sprinter, first person to win Olympic gold medal on Aust. soil.
Squash booms in Aust.
In training, Lorraine Crapp breaks 18 swimming records.
First International Surf Carnival held, at Torquay, Vic.
First all Aust. Wimbledon tennis victory since 1919.
First Aust. and Pakistan Test cricket match in Pakistan.
W. C. McClelland, VFL president for 30 years, retires.
Neville Sayers becomes first Aust. pentathlon champion.
Amateur Pistol Shooting Union of Aust. estb.
Record 90,000 crowd at soccer match in Melbourne.
Trampolining begins as sport in Aust.
Solo wins Sydney to Hobart yacht race.

Births & Deaths
Gerard Barrett, athlete, b.
Suzanne Hendy, judo champion, b.
Andrew Hilditch, cricketer, b.
Graeme Wood, cricketer, b.

1956

F
Historia Dignum

Population
Estimated total white, 9,530,871.

4 Feb. Avro Anson aircraft crashes at Hawkestone Peak, WA, claiming five lives.
Mar. Cyclone Agnes damages N. Qld.
Sep. Poker machines first legalized in NSW for use in registered clubs.
1 Oct. Certified mail system estb. in Aust.
1 Dec. Train collision at Wallumbilla, Qld, claims five lives.
24 Dec. Magazine *Woman's Day* first published.
During 1956
Aust. Speleological Federation estb.
Aust. Council of Social Service (ACOSS) estb. to assist individuals and community groups achieve welfare objectives.
Flooding throughout much of Aust.
First parking meters installed in Sydney.
Outward Bound Memorial Foundation estb.
Faith Bandler and Pearl Gibbs found Aust.-Aboriginal Friendship Society in Sydney to lobby for Aboriginal equality.
Large opal named Olympic Australis discovered at Coober Pedy, SA.
National road toll 2,165.
c. 1956. First drive-in bottle department opens, in Adelaide.

A
History, Politics, Economics, Law

Government
1 Aug. 1957–31 Jul. 1965, Sir Eric Winslow Woodward Governor NSW.
12 Aug. 1957–Jan. 1968, G. F. R. Nicklin Country-Liberal coalition Premier Qld.
4 Dec. 1957–18 Mar. 1958, Sir Alan Mansfield administered Qld.

Apr. Arbitration Court increases basic wage by 10 shillings a week.
May. Cwlth Govt reduces number of national service trainees by introducing selection ballot based on date of birth.
6 Jul. Aust. signs trade agreement with Japan, eliminating trade discrimination.
Aug. Democratic Labor Party established nationally from State anti-Communist Labor breakaway groups. (Qld Labor Party joins DLP in 1962.)

During 1957
Non-Labor Govt elected in Qld for first time in 23 years. (Still in office in 1985.)
Bartholomew Santamaria elected President of National Civic Council.
National Capital Development Commission (NCDC) estb. to co-ordinate building expansion in ACT.
Cwlth Govt meets with private trading banks in Canberra to discuss changes in banking system.
Cwlth Public Servants granted long-service leave.
First significant crop of cultured pearls produced, at Brecknock, WA.
'Madman's Track', 800-mile cattle road from south of Broome, WA, to Meekatharra, WA, pioneered.
Federal Council for the Advancement of Aboriginals and Torres Strait Islanders estb. (Becomes National Aboriginal and Islander Liberation Movement in 1978).
ACTU Congress adopts 35-hour week policy and replaces compulsory unionism policy with preference for unionists.

B
Science, Technology, Transport, Discovery

Jan. Aust. National Antarctic Expedition estb. Davis, second permanent Aust. research station, on Princess Elizabeth Land, Antarctica.
Jun. Gates closed at Adaminaby Dam NSW, designed to become central storage of Snowy Mountains Hydroelectricity Scheme.
Jul. Aust. participates in International Geophysical Year.
Aug. Ansett Transport Industries buys out Aust. National Airways Pty Ltd.
Oct. Britain completes atomic bomb tests at Maralinga, SA.

During 1957
First Volkswagen car assembled in Aust.
Walter and Eliza Hall Institute produces first vaccine for Asian flu.
FE Holden car launched. First Holden to be made as station wagon.
CSIRO Division of Textile Industry invents Si-ro-set method of permanently pressing clothes.
ABC conducts experimental FM broadcasts.
Broken Hill Pty Ltd begins producing tinplate at Port Kembla, NSW.
Cobalt pellets (trace elements) given to sheep and cattle to prevent dietary deficiencies.
A satellite tracking station estb. near Woomera, SA.

1957 C Arts

Literature

During 1957
Nevil Shute publishes *On The Beach*.
Martin Boyd publishes *Outbreak of Love*.
Patrick White publishes *Voss*.
John O'Grady, under pseudonym Nino Culotta, publishes *They're A Weird Mob*.
Miles Franklin Award inaugurated.

Music, Dance

During 1957
Slim Dusty's song 'The Pub With No Beer' becomes first Aust. gold record.
Ray Price forms jazz trio.
Nikolai Malko appointed conductor of Melbourne Symphony Orchestra. (Until 1961.)

Drama, Theatre, Film

28 Jan. *Disneyland* begins on Aust. TV.
During 1957
Richard Beynon's play *The Shifting Heart* produced in Sydney.

Fine Arts

During 1957
Ivor Hele wins Archibald Prize for *Self Portrait*.
Sidney Nolan holds successful retrospective exhibition in London.
Albert Namatjira granted equal citizenship rights with white Australians.
Aust. Art in Canada Exhibition begins.
Contemporary Canadian Painters Exhibition visits Aust.
Goulburn Lilac time art prizes estb., NSW.
Journalists' Club Art Prize first awarded in Sydney.
Maitland Art Prize estb., NSW.
National Bank of Australasia Art Calendar first published.
Newcastle City Art Gallery founded, NSW.
Redcliffe Art Contest founded, Qld.
Regional Galleries Association of Vic. estb. as Vic. Public Galleries Group.
Royal Adelaide Exhibition conducted.
Terry Clune Art Gallery estb. in Sydney.
Vizard-Wholohan art prizes estb. in Adelaide.
John Olsen and Thomas Gleghorn become prominent abstract impressionist painters.

Architecture

During 1957
Joern Utzon wins first prize for world-wide Opera House design competition.
Bates, Smart and McCutcheson, Sydney architects, build MLC building in N. Sydney. Largest office building in Aust., noted for curtain wall concept which dominates architecture of the period.
Heights and Buildings Committees in Sydney and Melbourne allow buildings to exceed old height ceilings, beginning high-rise development in Aust. AMP building in Sydney among first examples.

D
Religion, Learning

Sep. The Murray Committee presents report on Aust. education. Opens period of educational expansion.
10 Oct. Bishop Derenik Poladian consecrates first Armenian church in Aust., at Surry Hills, NSW.
Nov. Aust. Universities to receive more Federal aid.

During 1957
Wyndham Report on NSW secondary school education completed. Under Wyndham Scheme education system overhauled.
First fully comprehensive high schools offer multilateral courses in Tas.
Wattle Park Teachers' College opens in Adelaide.
Co-educational Catholic schools first appear in Aust.
Van Diemen's Land Memorial Folk Museum estb. in Tas.
John Passmore publishes *A Hundred Years of Philosophy*.

E
Sport

During 1957
Straight Draw, ridden by N. McGrowdie, wins Melbourne Cup in 3 minutes 24½ seconds.
Melbourne football team wins VFL Premiership in Melbourne.
St George football team wins Rugby League Premiership in Sydney.
Brian Gleeson of St Kilda VFL team awarded Brownlow Medal.
Stuart MacKenzie is ABC Sportsman of the Year.
Aust. wins Rugby League World Cup.
Lew Hoad wins Wimbledon men's singles tennis title in 52 minutes.
Richard (Richie) Benaud estb. cricket reputation as world's best leg-spin bowler.
First Golden Slipper Stakes horserace held in Sydney.
First Aust. world road racing motorcycle championship won by Keith Campbell.
Aust. Soccer Federation estb.
Anitra V wins Sydney to Hobart yacht race.

Births & Deaths

Wayne Bartholomew, surf rider, b.
Colleen Bolton, cross-country runner, b.
Robyn Burley, ice skater, b.
Rick Darling, cricketer, b.
Shane Elizabeth Gould, swimmer, b.
Malcolm Johnston, jockey, b.

1957

1957

F
Historia Dignum

Population
Estimated total white, 9,744,087.

24 Jul. Lockheed Hudson aircraft crashes at Horn I., Qld, claiming six lives.
Oct. Automatic telephone weather service estb. in Melbourne.
Dec. Devastating bushfires in Blue Mts, NSW, claim five lives.
During 1957
Sydney Opera House Lottery begins.
Deep-frozen foods appear on Aust. market.
National Parks Association of NSW estb.
Cardin Bubble look becomes popular in fashion. Long dresses with many layers of stiff petticoats popular.
Eastern States experience severe drought. Coincides with down-turn in overseas prices for primary products.
Bob Dyer's *Pick-a-Box* radio quiz show (estb. 1947) goes on television.
National road toll 2,088.

Births & Deaths
Denis O'Duffy, tallest recorded Aust. man, 7 feet 4 inches, d. (b. 1905)

Communities
Eaton, WA, estb.
Mary Kathleen, Qld, estb.
Weipa, Qld, planned.

A

History, Politics, Economics, Law

Government

18 Mar. 1958–20 Mar. 1966, Sir Henry Abel Smith Governor Qld.

4 Jun. 1958–21 Oct. 1959, Sir Stanley Charles Burbury administered Tas.

26 Aug. 1958–May 1969, E. E. Reece Labor Premier Tas.

10 Dec. 1958–18 Dec. 1963, Thirty-second Cwlth Ministry, Robert Gordon Menzies Liberal-Country coalition Prime Minister Aust.

20 Jan. Royal Aust. Naval College moved from Flinders Naval Depot, Vic., commissioned at Jervis Bay, ACT, as HMAS *Creswell*.

14 Feb.–7 Mar. Queen Elizabeth and Queen Mother visit Aust.

May. Entry permit replaces the 57-year-old dictation test as means of controlling immigration. (Effective 1959.)

1 Oct. Christmas I. (Indian Ocean) transferred from British to Australian administration.

Oct. NSW Govt legislates for three weeks annual leave for all workers under State industrial awards. (Effective 1959.)

22 Nov. R. G. Menzies returned as Liberal-Country coalition Prime Minister at national elections.

Democratic Labor Party contests Federal election for first time.

Nov. NSW Govt codifies law of defamation prohibiting defamation of ancestors whether living or dead.

During Nov. Air pilots' dispute leads to pilots' strike over wages claims hearing. First strike among highly paid white-collar workers.

31 Dec. NSW Govt legislates for equal pay for equal work, providing for equal pay for male and female workers performing similar tasks. (SA 1967, Tas. 1966, WA 1968.)

During 1958

Integration of Cwlth and State statistical services completed.

Aust. participates in the SEATO aid programme to South Vietnam.

Aust. Council of Salaried and Professional Associations (ACSPA) estb.

Sir Douglas Menzies (until 1974) and Sir Victor Windeyer (until 1972) appointed Justices of High Court of Aust.

Robert Hawke joins ACTU as research officer.

William Gunn appointed chairman of Aust. Wool Board. Advances industry significantly during 14 years in the position.

Sir Percy Spender first Aust. Judge of International Court in The Hague, Holland.

USA replaces Britain as Australia's main beef export market.

B

Science, Technology, Transport, Discovery

15 Jan. Qantas inaugurates first commercial round-world air service.

Mar. First section of Cahill motor expressway opens in Sydney. (Completed in 1962.)

18 Apr. First nuclear reactor in Aust., High Flux Australian Reactor (HIFAR), begins operating at Lucas Heights, near Sydney.

Jul. Perth tramways close.

Oct. Overseas telex services to Britain, Canada and USA open.

During 1958

Industrial Design Council of Aust. estb.

Aust. Institute of Nuclear Science and Engineering (AINSE) estb.

National Biological Standards Laboratory estb.

FC Holden car launched.

Desmond Norman wins Aust. Industries Fair competition in Melbourne.

Adaminaby Dam in Snowy Mountains Hydroelectric Scheme completed. Contains one of largest earth and rock walls in world.

Largest artificial stock breeding centre in southern hemisphere opens, at Berry, NSW.

Spotted king prawn and humped back prawn discovered in Capricorn Bunker Group islands, Qld.

Lorimer Fenton Dods estb. Children's Medical Research Foundation.

Langley Hancock discovers large iron ore deposits in the Pilbara region of WA.

Tinaroo Dam, N. Qld, completed.

Organophosphate diazinon first used to control blowfly in sheep.

Arts

1958

Literature

Apr. Govt issues revised list of banned books.
During 1958
Second edition of *The Australian Encyclopaedia* published in 10 volumes. Editor-in-Chief Alexander Hugh Chisholm.
Thea Astley publishes *Girl with a Monkey*.
Hal Porter publishes first novel, *A Handful of Pennies*.
Randolph Stow publishes *To The Islands*.
Cyril Pearl publishes *Wild Men of Sydney*.
Russell Ward publishes *The Australian Legend*.
Colin Thiele publishes *Sun on the Stubble*.

Music, Dance

Mar. Sydney radio station 2UE presents first recognized Aust. Top 40 chart.
During 1958
Patrick Thomas founds the Patrick Thomas Singers in Brisbane.
Elizabethan Theatre Trust presents musical *Lola Montez*.
Johnny O'Keefe noted as first Aust. rock singer.
Brian Henderson's *Bandstand* television programme begins.

Births & Deaths
Danilo Radojevic, ballet dancer b.

Drama, Theatre, Film

During 1958
ABC estb. National Institute of Dramatic Art in Sydney.
Barry Humphries develops Edna Everage character impersonation.
The Aust. Film Institute estb., in Sydney.
Best Aust. Film Awards inaugurated.

Fine Arts

Apr. Arthur Boyd first exhibits the *Half-Caste Bride* series of paintings in Sydney.
Oct. Albert Namatjira sentenced to three months jail for supplying liquor to another full-blood Aboriginal.
During 1958
William Pidgeon wins Archibald Prize for *Ray Walker*.
National Gallery of NSW becomes Art Gallery of NSW.
Cessnock Art Prize estb., NSW.
Contemporary Japanese Art Exhibition tours Aust.
Hunter Valley Art Prize first awarded, NSW.
Murdoch Art Prize first awarded, in Perth.
Museum of Modern Art and Design estb. in Melbourne. (Discontinued 1966.)
Muswellbrook Art Prize estb., NSW.
Royal Agricultural Society of NSW Easter Show Art Prize estb.
Helena Rubinstein Travelling Scholarship estb.
Rudy Komon Art Gallery estb. in Sydney.
Skinner Art Galleries estb. in Perth.
Tumut Art Prize first awarded, NSW.

Architecture

During 1958
G. J. Dusseldorp, building entrepreneur, begins Aust Square project in Sydney. Project influences modern town planning.

D
Religion, Learning

Oct. NSW University of Technology becomes University of NSW.
During 1958
Francis Rolland becomes first Aust. minister of religion to be knighted.
Alexander Mackie College of Advanced Education estb. in Sydney.
Tas., WA and NSW Govts encourage growth of comprehensive high schools, offering distinctive courses in academic, commercial, technical and other disciplines.

E
Sport

During 1958
Baystone, ridden by M. Schumacher, wins Melbourne Cup in 3 minutes $21\frac{1}{4}$ seconds.
Cwlth Games held in Cardiff, Wales.
Collingwood football team wins VFL Premiership in Melbourne.
St George football team wins Rugby League Premiership in Sydney.
Neil Roberts of St Kilda VFL team awarded Brownlow Medal.
Herb Elliott is ABC Sportsman of the Year.
Parachuting begins as sport.
Aust. wins first Eisenhower world golf championship cup.
Rolly Tasker first Aust. to win world sailing championship.
First Aust. pistol shooting championship held, in Tas.
Sailor's Guide first horse to win £200,000 prize money.
Suza Javor becomes national table tennis champion.
Tony Madigan boxer wins International diamond belt award.
Marlene Mathews, athlete, sets world 90 and 200 metres running records.
Siandra wins Sydney to Hobart yacht race.

Births & Deaths

Larry Corowa, Rugby League footballer, b.
Bradley Drewett, tennis player, b.
Stephen Holland, swimmer, b.
Ian Murray, yachtsman, b.
Christian O'Neill, tennis player, b.
Mark Richards, surfer, b.

1958

1958

F

Historia Dignum

Population
Estimated total white, 9,947,358.

5 Apr. Bushfires in Wandilo district, SA, claim eight lives.
During Apr. Cyclone damages Bowen, Qld.
10 Jul. Railway accident at Lidcombe, NSW, claims four lives.
26 Sep. Newspaper *Nation* begins publication. (Becomes *Nation Review* on 22 Jul. 1972.)
Oct. Vic. first State to officially recognize a floral emblem. Chooses common pink heath. (Later NSW adopts waratah; SA, Sturt's desert pea; Tas., southern blue gum; Qld, Cooktown orchid; WA, red-and-green kangaroo paw; NT, Sturt's desert rose.)

During 1958
National Scouting Association estb. as the Boy Scouts Association. (Becomes the Scout Association of Aust. in 1972.)
Major national drought affecting many parts of Aust. begins. (Lasts 10 years.)
TV News (*TV Times*) first published. Later becomes *TV News-Times*, then *TV Times*.
TV Week first published.
Vic. becomes first State to introduce air pollution control legislation.
Periodical *Observer*, edited by Donald Horne, first published.
National road toll 2,215.

A

History, Politics, Economics, Law

Government

2 Apr. 1959–Mar. 1971, (Sir) D. Brand Liberal-Country League/Country coalition Premier WA.

21 Oct. 1959–25 Mar. 1963, Thomas Godfrey Polson Corbett, Lord Rowallan, Governor Tas.

28 Oct. 1959–Apr. 1964, R. J. Heffron Labor Premier NSW.

17 Feb. Twenty-third Federal Parlt opens. (Dissolution 2 Nov. 1961.)

Apr. At Premiers' Conference, Cwlth Govt proposes new system of road finance.

May. Uniform divorce law adopted for all Aust. (Operative 1961.)

Jul. SA politics dominated by Rupert Max Stuart case. Stuart, an Aborigine was found guilty of murder. Successive appeals to various courts were rejected, but when new evidence was discovered, a Royal Commission was appointed. It exposed underhand behaviour by members of the Adelaide establishment and Stuart was spared from the death penalty.

Nov. Conciliation and Arbitration Court grants 28 per cent wage margin increase to 250,000 metal trades employees.

1 Dec. Aust. signs Antarctic Treaty, reserving area S of 60°S latitude for peaceful purposes.

During 1959

Aust. Diplomatic mission in South Vietnam raised to Embassy status.

Aust. diplomatic relations with Egypt and USSR restored.

Most Aborigines become eligible for pensions and other allowances.

British Cwlth Defence Conference held in Canberra.

International Antarctic Analysis Centre estb. in Melbourne, within Cwlth Bureau of Meteorology.

Immigration Reform Group estb. in Melbourne to reform immigration policy.

B

Science, Technology, Transport, Discovery

1959

During 1959

Aust. takes over Wilkes Antarctic Station from USA.

Tumut power station, first major station in Snowy Mountains Scheme, begins operating. Fourteen-mile, £19 million, Eucumbene–Tumut tunnel in Snowy Mountains completed.

TAA introduces first Lockheed Electra prop-jets in Aust.

Aust. anti-tank missile, the *Malkara*, successfully tested at Woomera, SA.

Construction of radio telescope at Parkes, NSW, begins.

Qantas takes delivery of first Boeing aircraft.

Aust. Biochemical Society estb.

First commercial computers arrive in Aust.

Flying Surgeon Service in Qld estb. Services hospitals throughout Qld. First of kind in world.

Kwinana freeway in Perth opens to traffic. First Aust. high-speed freeway.

Ferry *Princess of Tasmania* begins running between Melbourne and Launceston.

First broadband telecommunication trunk system estb., between Melbourne and Bendigo, Vic.

1959

Arts

Literature

During 1959
Xavier Herbert publishes *Seven Emus*.
Alan Moorehead publishes *No Room in the Ark*.
Mary Durack publishes *Kings in Grass Castles*.
Dorothy Hewett publishes *Bobbin Up*.
Morris West publishes *The Devil's Advocate*.
Marjorie Faith Barnard publishes *A History of Australia*.

Music, Dance

24 Jan. Musical *My Fair Lady* opens in Melbourne.
11 Dec. Marilyn Jones makes ballet début in Sydney.
During 1959
Czech Philharmonic Orchestra becomes first overseas orchestra to visit Aust.
ABC begins *6 O'clock Rock* television programme. (Runs until 1962.)
Joan Sutherland internationally acclaimed for performance of Donizetti's *Lucia di Lammermoor*.
Col. Joye first tops the Top 40 chart.
First Soviet group of dancers from the Bolshoi Theatre visit Aust.

Drama, Theatre, Film

During 1959
The National Institute of Dramatic Art founded, in NSW.
Stanley Kramer produces film *On The Beach*.
Peter Kenna's play *The Slaughter on St Teresa's Day* produced in Sydney.
Grampians Wonderland coins Best Film of the Year award.

Fine Arts

Feb. Antipodean group of artists forms in Melbourne to oppose growing use of abstract expressionism. Group includes Arthur and David Boyd, John Perceval, Clifton Pugh, John Brack, Charles Blackman.
Jul. Private Gallery A estb. in Melbourne.
During 1959
William Dobell wins Archibald Prize for *Dr Edward McMahon*.
Carl Plate is first Aust. artist to take a non-figurative exhibition to London.
Margel Hinder wins ANZAC House Sculpture competition.
Brisbane Centennial Prize awarded to John Rigby.
Brisbane Eisteddfod Centenary Art Prize awarded to Arthur Evan Read.
Bunbury Art Prize estb., WA.
Adelaide University Art Prize awarded.
Toowoomba Art Gallery estb., Qld.
Aust. contributes to Matson Line Art Exhibition in USA.
Seven British Artists Exhibition visits Aust.
Modern Art News published.
National Gallery of Vic. Art Prizes first awarded.
Qld Centenary Art Prize awarded.
Rowney Drawing Prize conducted in Melbourne.
Ryde Municipal Art Society and Art Prize estb., NSW.
Centre 5 group of sculptors form in Melbourne.

Architecture

May. Construction of Sydney Opera House begins. (Completed 1973.)
13 Nov. Narrows Bridge opens across Swan R. Perth.
During 1959
Sir Roy Grounds, architect, completes Academy of Science Building in Canberra.
Sidney Myer Music Bowl in Melbourne completed.

D
Religion, Learning

May. Aust. Universities Commission constituted.
First Billy Graham Crusade in Aust.
Aust. College of Education estb., becomes a Fellowship of Teachers.
1 Sep. Greek Orthodox Metropolis of Aust. and NZ becomes an Archdiocese. (NZ separated from Aust. Archdiocese in Jan. 1970.)
During 1959
Regular School of the Air opens at Meekatharra, WA.
Frankston and Coburg Teachers' Colleges estb. in Vic.
Cwlth Fellowship Scheme estb. (First course in scheme 1961.)
Charles Knight forms Buddhist Federation of Aust.

E
Sport

Apr. Alf Dean breaks International Game Fishing Association record with 2,663 lb white pointer shark, caught at Ceduna, SA.
Oct. Aust. stages first world surf casting championship, in NSW.
During 1959
Macdougal, ridden by P. Glennon, wins Melbourne Cup in 3 minutes 23 seconds.
Melbourne football team wins VFL Premiership in Melbourne.
St George football team wins Rugby League Premiership in Sydney.
Bob Skilton of South Melbourne VFL team awarded Brownlow Medal.
John Arthur (Jack) Brabham is ABC Sportsman of the Year. Becomes first Aust. to win World Grand Prix drivers' championship.
Jon Konrads wins all men's freestyle events at Aust. swimming championships.
Aust. suspended for four years from World Soccer for poaching European players.
Cherana wins Sydney to Hobart yacht race.

Births & Deaths
Steve Foley, athlete, b.
Edwina Kennedy, golfer, b.

1959

F

Historia Dignum

Population
Estimated total white, 10,160,968.

21 Jan. Floods damage southern Qld and northern NSW.
16 Feb. Cyclone Connie damages Bowen, Qld.
May. Women admitted to 'Men Only' stand at Melbourne Cricket Ground for first time, to attend a Billy Graham evangelical crusade.
Sep. Advisory road speed signs erected on Hume Highway, NSW.
During 1959
The Aust. Consumers' Association (ACA) estb.
Hire purchase finance system booms.
National road toll 2,321.

Communities
Beauty Point, Tas., estb.

A

History, Politics, Economics, Law

1960

Government

2 Feb. 1960–3 Feb. 1961, William Shepherd Morrison, Viscount Dunrossil, Governor-General Aust.

14 Jan. Commonwealth Banks Act and Reserve Bank Act proclaimed. Estb. separate Cwlth Development Bank, Cwlth Trading Bank and Reserve Bank of Aust.

15 Feb. H. V. Evatt appointed Chief Justice of NSW. Appointment arouses much controversy.

During Feb. Goods comprising 90 per cent of Aust. imports exempted from licensing provisions.

7 Mar. Arthur Augustus Calwell Labor Opposition leader. (Until 1967.)

Mar.–May. Attempt to abolish the NSW Legislative Council fails.

24 Apr. Aust. joins International Development Association as foundation member.

27 Apr. Cwlth Police formed from amalgamation of Cwlth Investigation Service and Peace Officer Guard.

30 Jun. Cwlth Govt ends national service. Aust. military forces organized into Regular Army and Citizen Military Forces.

31 Jul. Malayan Emergency officially ends after 12 years. (Aust. garrison continues to serve until Dec. 1973.)

Sep. Cwlth Govt reduces official majority in PNG Legislative Council, increases proportion of elected members and provides for election of native members by native people.

Oct. Federation of Aust. Commercial Television Stations. (FACTS) estb.

15 Nov. Cwlth Govt imposes credit restrictions, sales tax on motor vehicles, and restriction of bank and higher purchase credit, to counterbalance payments inflationary trend following the lifting of import restrictions and fall in export earnings.

2 Dec. Govt lifts embargo on export of iron ore to Japan, facilitating huge expansion of industry in WA.

During 1960

Provision made to pay Social Service benefits to Aborigines.

Cwlth Prime Ministers' Conference takes place in London.

Telephonic Communications (Interception) Act passed. Prohibits any interception of telephone messages except in interests of national security.

Joint Intelligence Organization (JIO) estb. to analyse intelligence.

Federal House of Representatives unanimously favours report of Committee on Decimal Currency.

NSW Govt introduces Company Law Amendment Bill, the first designed to provide uniform company law throughout Aust.

Aust. League of Rights (estb. in SA in 1946) becomes a national body with Eric Butler as director.

Donald Leslie Chipp enters Federal Parlt.

R. G. Casey made a life Peer in England.

First Aust. Ambassador appointed to European Economic Community (EEC). (Estb. on 20 Mar. 1957.)

Aust. and Canada sign new agreement giving tariff preference.

Sir Douglas Berry Copland estb. Committee for Economic Development of Aust. (CEDA).

Minerals begin to replace agricultural products as principle exports.

Comalco Industries estb. to mine bauxite in Qld.

1960

B
Science, Technology, Transport, Discovery

Sep. Falcon XL car launched. Holden's first serious competitor.
14 Oct. Warragamba Dam completed, NSW. Holds four times amount of water in Sydney Harbour.
During Oct. Sir Macfarlane Burnet shares Nobel Prize for discovery of immunological tolerance. Wins first Australian of the Year Award.
Nov. Integrated iron and steel industry estb. at Kwinana, near Perth, under agreement between WA Govt and Broken Hill Pty Ltd.
20 Dec. First commercial heliport in Aust. opens, in Melbourne.

During 1960
Approval granted for 13 country areas to have national and commercial television stations.
Merredin Shire Council, WA, becomes first in Aust. to treat sewage effluent and use it for watering recreation grounds.
Eric Worrell estb. Aust Reptile Park, at Gosford, NSW.
Hobart tramways closed.
Crown of Thorns starfish begins ravaging the Great Barrier Reef.
FB Holden car launched.
Aust. Road Research Board estb.
Aboriginal fossils, Tartanga relics 6,020 years old, discovered.
Howard Florey appointed first Aust. President of the Royal Society.
Townsville copper refinery, Qld, begins production.
First Bell-Siro Cheesemaker machine commercially produced.
The Aust. Balloon Launching Station estb. at Mildura, Vic.

C
Arts

Literature

During 1960
Alan Moorehead publishes *The White Nile*.
Robin Boyd publishes *The Australian Ugliness*.

Music, Dance

Feb. Dame Margaret (Peggy) van Praagh appointed to lead the Borovansky Ballet.
Dec. Valrene Tweedie's 'Ballet Australia' gives first performance.

During 1960
Kathleen Gorman becomes prima ballerina of Aust. Ballet.
Rolf Harris makes record *Tie Me Kangaroo Down Sport*.
Adelaide Festival of Arts estb.
Charles Lisner forms the Lisner Ballet. (Becomes Qld Ballet in 1962.)

Drama, Theatre, Film

During 1960
Alan Seymour's play *The One Day of the Year* written and produced in Adelaide.
Frank Zinnemann produces film *The Sundowners*.
Anzac wins Best Film of the Year award.

Fine Arts

May. First Aboriginal rock wall paintings near Laura, Qld, discovered.
Jun.–Aug. Aust. Aboriginal Art Exhibition held.

During 1960
Judy Cassab wins Archibald Prize for *Stanislaus Rapotec*.
Argus Gallery estb. in Melbourne.
Barry Stern Modern Art Gallery estb. in Sydney.
Schmuel Gorr of Jewish Art Society conducts Ben Uri Galleries.
Kym Bonython estb. Bonython Art Gallery in Adelaide.
Chadstone Sculpture Prizes first awarded in Melbourne.
Manjimup Art Gallery estb., WA.
Melbourne Prints, known also as Melbourne Graphic Arts and Melbourne Printmakers, estb.
Myrniong Art Exhibitor Group active in Melbourne.
Qantas Airlines exhibitions and films on Aust. art begin.
Tamworth Art Society and Gallery estb., NSW.
Walkley Art awards begin in Sydney.
W. D. and H. O. Wills Art Prize estb. in Sydney.

Charles Blackman paints *Suite V*.
Fremantle Art Gallery Prize estb., WA.
Gold Coast group of painters active, Qld.
Henry Lawson Festival Art Prizes estb. at Grenfell, NSW.
Gundagai Golden Corroboree Prize first awarded, NSW.
Large exhibition of Aust. art tours Aust.

D
Religion, Learning

1960

Feb. Aust. Council of Churches holds first National Church Conference, at the Melbourne Cricket Ground.

During 1960
Vic. Public Library becomes State Library of Vic.
Aust. Association of Adult Education estb.
National Library of Aust. estb.
Canberra University College incorporated with ANU as School of General Studies.
University College of Townsville, Qld, estb., affiliated with Qld University. (Becomes James Cook University of N. Qld in 1970.)
Social pluralist tradition in education begins, characterized by development of several ideologies and neo-progressive ideas.
University of NSW estb. first university School of Librarianship.

1960

E
Sport

May. Tenpin Bowling begins in Aust., first commercial centre opens at Glenelg SA.
Oct. First fully automatic Tenpin Bowling centre opens at Hurstville in Sydney.
During 1960
Hi Jinx, ridden by W. A. Smith, wins Melbourne Cup in 3 minutes $23\frac{3}{4}$ seconds.
Melbourne football team wins VFL Premiership in Melbourne.
St George football team wins Rugby League Premiership in Sydney.
John Schultz of Footscray VFL team awarded Brownlow Medal.
Herb Elliott is ABC Sportsman of the Year.
Aust. wins eight gold, eight silver and six bronze medals at Rome Olympics.
Aust. plays West Indies in first cricket Test ever tied.
Twelve world records broken in three nights at Aust. swimming championships.
John Arthur (Jack) Brabham wins World Grand Prix for second time.
Aust. launches Diamond International Softball tournament.
Mick Bartley, gambler, backs 36 winning horses in succession.
First Aust. scuba diving championships held, at Bicheno, Tas.
Siandra wins Sydney to Hobart yacht race.

Births & Deaths
Katrina Gibbs, athlete, high jumper, b.
Wayne Harris, jockey, b.
Craig Johnston, soccer player, b.
Max Metzer, swimmer, b.
Jennifer Turrall, swimmer, b.

F
Historia Dignum

Population
Estimated total white, 10,391,920.

20 Feb. Train accident at Bogantungan, Qld, claims seven lives.
26 Mar. Cyclone damages Carnarvon, WA.
Apr. Severe floods in Derwent Valley, Tas.
May. Vic Govt authorizes estb. of Totalizator Agency Board (Tote) to provide for off-course betting for horse and trotting races. (WA 1960, Qld 1962, ACT and NSW 1964, SA 1967, Tas. 1975.)
10 Jun. Fokker Friendship crashes at Mackay, Qld, claiming 29 lives.
7 Jul. Stephen L. Bradley kidnaps and murders Graeme Thorne ($8\frac{1}{2}$ years old). First Aust. case of child kidnap for ransom.
25 Jul. Train collision at Rawlinna, WA, claims four lives.
Aug. Sydney Humanist Group estb. Becomes NSW Humanist Society. (Estb. in Vic. 1961, SA 1962.)
During 1960
Only 12 of 701 full-time parliamentarians in Aust. are women.
First Festival of Arts held in Adelaide. John Bishop guiding force behind the Festival, held biennially.
Mouth-to-mouth resuscitation officially replaces Holger-Nielsen method of livesaving.
Aust. Care for Refugees (named AUSTCARE in 1967) Organization estb.
National road toll 2,605.

Communities
Koolyanobbing, WA, estb.
Muchea, WA, estb.

A

History, Politics, Economics, Law

Government
4 Feb. 1961–3 Aug. 1961, Sir Reginald Alexander Dallas Brooks administered Aust.

5 Apr. 1961–1 Jun. 1968, Sir Edric Montague Bastyan Governor SA.

3 Aug. 1961–22 Sep. 1965, William Philip Sidney, Viscount De L'Isle, Governor-General Aust.

1961–1964, R. B. Nott Administrator NT under Cwlth jurisdiction.

7 Feb. The National Employers' Association formally constituted.

29 Apr. Referendum on abolition of NSW Legislative Council rejected.

May. First Aust. wheat, barley and flour sold to Communist China.

4 Jul. Basic wage increased by 12 shillings per week.

Nov. Significant increase of Aust. aid to South Vietnam.

9 Dec. R. G. Menzies, Liberal-Country coalition Prime Minister, returned at Federal elections with majority reduced from 32 to 2.

During 1961
Antarctic Treaty countries first meet in Canberra.

Antarctic Treaty comes into force on 23 Jun.

Diplomatic missions in United Arab Republic, Argentina, Korea and Switzerland raised to Embassy status.

NSW Govt introduces legislation providing for five-day working week for banks.

Cwlth Govt announces tax concessions to exporters for promotional expenses in developing overseas export markets.

C. Series Retail Price Index abandoned after being used for 40 years.

WA announces plans for £10 million iron industry to produce iron for export.

Sir William Owen appointed a Justice of High Court of Aust. (Until 1972.)

Successful cotton growing begins in Namoi Valley, NSW.

Unemployment reaches 3.5 per cent during credit squeeze.

State of Emergency declared in Qld when Mount Isa miners strike over bonus payments.

B

Science, Technology, Transport, Discovery

1961

8 Feb. David Henshaw of CSIRO discovers method of making a new self-twisting yarn.

Feb. Sydney tramways close. (WA and Adelaide 1958 except Glenelg line, Tas. 1960, Brisbane 1969.)

25 Oct. Aust. Medical Association registered in Canberra. (Members had previously formed part of the British Medical Association.)

Oct.–Nov. Large-scale iron ore deposits discovered at Pilbara and in Hamersley Ranges, WA.

During Oct. Second-largest radio telescope in world opens at Parkes, NSW, for tracking space probes and radio astronomy research.

3 Dec. First commercially proven oilfield in Aust. discovered, at Moonie, Qld.

During 1961
National Heart Foundation estb.

Natural gas first used in Aust. to generate electricity, at Roma, Qld.

First Aust. guided missile base opens, at Williamstown, NSW.

William Griffith McBride discovers link between the drug thalidomide and deformities in new-born babies.

EK Holden car launched.

RAF Vulcan jet bomber makes first non-stop flight from England to Richmond, NSW, in 20 hours.

Qantas inaugurates Aust.-Johannesburg flights.

Moving footways estb. in Sydney.

Vic. Govt opens petro-chemical complex at Altona, Vic.

P. & O. ship *Canberra* arrives in Aust. Largest ship ever to visit Aust. on regular basis.

The Maltby Bypass opens; first Vic. freeway.

1961

C

Arts

Literature

During 1961
Hal Porter publishes *The Tilted Cross*.
Xavier Herbert publishes *Soldiers' Women*.
Patrick White publishes *Riders in the Chariot*.
Australian Book Review, monthly, first published.
Australian National Bibliography begins publication.

Music, Dance

During 1961
Joan Sutherland wins Australian of the Year Award.
Albert Arlen's *The Sentimental Bloke* becomes first Aust. musical to be exported.
Robert Hughes composes *The Forbidden Rite*, first Aust. television ballet.
SA National Ballet estb.
Dance Co. of NSW estb.
Georges Tzipine appointed conductor Melbourne Symphony Orchestra. (Until 1964.)
Ballet Workshop estb. in WA. (Becomes Perth City Ballet in 1972.)

Drama, Theatre, Film

During 1961
Leningrad Theatre Co. tours Aust.
Tim Burstall film, *The Prize*, wins medal at Venice film festival.
New Union Theatre at Sydney University opens.

Fine Arts

Jun.–Jul. Aust. art sent to Whitechapel Exhibition in London.
During 1961
William Pidgeon wins Archibald Prize for *Rabbi Dr I. Porush*.
Sydney abstract painters estb. Sydney Nine Group.
The Critic, monthly review of art affairs, estb. in Perth.
Dutch painting exhibition visits Aust.
Jacaranda Art Exhibition estb. at Grafton, NSW.
Mildura Prize for Sculpture estb., Vic.
Mount Gambier Art Competition begins, SA.
Johnsonian Club Art Prize estb. in Brisbane.
Mirror–Waratah Festival Art Competition estb. in Sydney.
Rex de Charembac Nan Kivell art collection donated to National Library in Canberra.
Banjo Paterson Art competition estb. at Orange, NSW.
Newcastle Civic Foundation Art Competition conducted, NSW.
Portland Art Society, Prize and Gallery estb., Vic.
South Yarra Art Galleries estb. in Melbourne.
Royal National Agricultural and Industrial Association of Qld Art Prizes estb.
Rubinstein Portrait Prize first awarded, WA.
Society of Sculptors and Associates estb. in Sydney.
Transfield Co. Art Prize estb. in Sydney.
Woodward and Taranto's El Alamein fountain in Sydney acclaimed as sculptural achievement.

Architecture

During 1961
Walter Ralston Bunning principal architect of the National Library of Aust.

D
Religion, Learning

E
Sport

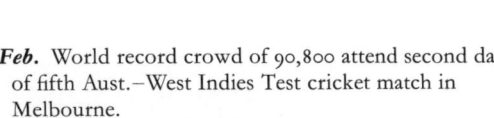
1961

16 Sep. Baha'i House of Worship at Mona Vale, near Sydney, dedicated. First in southern hemisphere.
Dec. Aust. Institute of Aboriginal Studies estb. in Canberra.

During 1961

NSW approves Wyndham Report. Secondary school education course increased to six years from 1962.

Monash University opens in Melbourne.

There are about 30 Aboriginal mission stations in WA, 16 in NSW, 14 in NT, 11 in Qld and 7 in SA.

National Library of Aust. separated from Parliamentary Library.

Clarence High School in Hobart becomes first State school in Aust. to teach driving as part of school curriculum.

Adelaide University opens branch at Bedford Park, SA. (Becomes Flinders University in 1966.)

Aust. Unitarian Association estb.

J. J. Cahill Memorial High School opens in Sydney. Among first NSW State schools to experiment with 'progressive' concepts such as no corporal punishment.

Feb. World record crowd of 90,800 attend second day of fifth Aust.–West Indies Test cricket match in Melbourne.
22 Dec. Fred A. Beck officially launches sphairee game, an abbreviated form of tennis.

During 1961

Lord Fury, ridden by R. Selkrig, wins Melbourne Cup in 3 minutes $19\frac{1}{2}$ seconds.

Hawthorn football team wins VFL Premiership in Melbourne.

St George football team wins Rugby League Premiership in Sydney.

John James of Carlton VFL team awarded Brownlow Medal.

Richie Benaud is ABC Sportsman of the Year.

Aust. Parachute Federation estb.

John Diamond, 'Mister Hundred Grand', punter, begins betting career.

Wally Grout breaks Aust. record of 23 dismissals in Test against West Indies as wicket-keeper.

Heather McKay is national squash champion. Second of 14 times.

Aust. Soccer Federation takes control of all Aust. soccer.

Rival wins Sydney to Hobart yacht race.

Births & Deaths

Paul Narracott, sprinter, b.

645

1961

F

Historia Dignum

Population
Estimated total white, 10,642,654.
Cwlth census assesses white population as 10,548,267 and Aboriginal population as 86,000.

Jan.–Mar. WA bushfires destroy timber areas. Bushfires near Melbourne claim eight lives and destroy 600 homes.
Mar. Totalizator Agency Board (TAB) estb. in Aust.
12 May. Beech aircraft crashes at Longreach, Qld, claiming five lives.
7 Jul. King Street Bridge in Melbourne collapses.
30 Nov. Vickers Viscount aircraft crashes at Botany Bay, NSW, claiming 15 lives.

During 1961
Contraceptive pill widely used.
Consolidated Press takes over the *Bulletin* magazine.
John Battista pioneers the pizza in Aust. Opens first pizza shop in Sydney.
Leo Williams breaks world record for drinking beer—2.6 pints in 7.9 seconds.
Beatnik fashion image popular.
Paula Stafford, fashion designer, pioneers the bikini costume in Aust.
Residents flee from Carnarvon, WA, to escape from flood.
Earth tremors cause extensive damage in eastern NSW.
ABC current affairs television programme *Four Corners* begins.
National road toll 2,479.

Births & Deaths
James Hull ends longest recorded male life, 109 years 139 days (b. 1852).

Communities
Kununurra, WA, estb.

A
History, Politics, Economics, Law

1962

Jan. Aust. accepts Indonesia's claim to western New Guinea (formerly a Dutch colony).

20 Feb. Twenty-fourth Federal Parlt opens. (Dissolution on 1 Nov. 1963.)

Mar. Right to vote in Cwlth elections extended to all Aborigines in Qld, NT and WA.

24 May. Aust. sends 30 military advisers to Vietnam. They join US team in training South Vietnamese troops in Jul.

1 Jul. NSW, Vic., Qld, and ACT implement Companies Acts, modernizing Aust. company legislation. (WA on 5 Oct. 1962, Tas. 1 Jan. 1963, NT 1 Jul. 1963.)

27 Jul. L. H. E. Bury, Minister for Air and Minister assisting Treasurer, dismissed because of public differences with Prime Minister on likely impact of British membership of Common Market.

3–4 Nov. Vince Gair's Qld Labor Party affiliates with Democratic Labor Party.

20 Nov.–2 Dec. Prince Philip visits Aust.

During 1962

RAAF squadron leaves for service in Thailand.

United Nations Trusteeship mission visits Canberra for talks on Nauru and PNG.

Aust. Legation in Laos raised to Embassy status.

Aust. troops transferred from Malaya for service in N. Borneo.

Five-day week for banks introduced into all States except Vic.

Redistribution of electoral boundaries as result of census count results in reduction of one seat in NSW, Qld and WA and an increase of one seat in Vic.

First major International Labor Office Conference held in Aust. opens in Melbourne.

Conzinc Riotinto of Aust. Ltd (CRA), holding and investment company, estb.

Commercial prawning begins in WA.

WA Govt signs agreement with US companies for 21-year lease to extract and export up to 15 million tons of iron ore from Pilbara deposits.

Roma Mitchell becomes first Aust. woman admitted as Queen's Counsel (QC), in Adelaide.

B
Science, Technology, Transport, Discovery

2 Jan. Uniform railway guage of 4 feet 8½ inches links Melbourne and Sydney. First express freight through train from Sydney to Melbourne leaves on 2 Jan. First passenger train, the *Southern Aurora*, departs Sydney on 13 Apr.

During 1962

First discovery of high-grade rock phosphate deposits at Rum Jungle, NT.

Co-axial telephone link between Melbourne, Canberra and Sydney opens. Subscriber trunk dialling (STD) service estb. between Canberra and Sydney.

Iron ore discovered at Mt Tom Price, in Pilbara region, WA.

Siding Springs Astronomy Station estb. near Coonabarabran, NSW.

EJ Holden car launched. One millionth Holden produced in Aust. on 25 Oct.

Chrysler Valiant car released.

Cwlth Serum Laboratory develops polyvalent snake bite antivenene.

First stage of Sydney–Auckland Trans–Pacific Cwlth Cable link opens.

First communication between space traveller and Aust. takes place at Murchea Station, WA. Message from US astronauts aboard *Friendship 7* spacecraft.

Aust. Photographic Society estb.

P. J. Adams, largest ship built in Aust. up to that date, launched at Whyalla, SA.

Aeronautical scientists from Cwlth countries meet in Melbourne to discuss aeronautical research.

First production of bauxite from Weipa deposits, Qld. (Full-scale production by April 1963.)

NSW Govt passes legislation allowing foreign doctors to register without further examination.

First automatic mail-sorting equipment in Aust. installed, at Melbourne Mail Exchange.

Births & Deaths

H. S. Spigal, astronomer, d.

C
1962

Arts

Literature

During 1962
David Martin publishes *The Young Wife*.
Alan Moorehead publishes *The Blue Nile*.
Manning Clark publishes *History of Australia*, volume 1.
First chair of Aust. Literature estb., in University of Sydney.

Music, Dance

Sep. Frank Ifield's song 'I Remember You' becomes first Aust. record on the US charts.
During 1962
Dame Margaret (Peggy) van Praagh estb. The Australian Ballet Co. Opens with *Swan Lake* on 2 Nov.
WA and Qld Ballet companies estb.
Garth de Burgh Welch is première danseur of Aust. Ballet Co.
Ray Powell appointed ballet master of Aust. Ballet Co.
Twist dance craze in Aust.
Thomas Matthews appointed conductor Tas. Symphony Orchestra. (Until 1968.)

Drama, Theatre, Film

During 1962
Andrew Steane makes children's film, *They Found a Cave*.
Frank Thring founds Arrow Theatre and Wal Cherry estb. Emerald Hill Theatre in Melbourne.
Barry Humphries' *A Nice Night's Entertainment* tours Aust.
A Report on the Political Development in the Territory of Papua New Guinea wins Best Film of the Year award.

Fine Arts

Feb. Michael Brown, Ross Crothall and Colin Lanceley, painters, exhibit in Melbourne as Annandale Imitation Realists.
Apr. John Joseph Wardell Power bequest of about £1 million to University of Sydney for acquisition and study of contemporary art implemented. Largest private gift made to a university.
Nov. *Westerly*, quarterly review, first published, in Perth.
During 1962
Louis Kahan wins Archibald Prize for *Patrick White*.
Bernard Smith publishes *Australian Painting*.
Carl Plate becomes first Aust. artist to take one-man exhibition to New York.
Von Bertouch Art Galleries in Newcastle, NSW, estb.
Contract signed for construction of new National Gallery and Cultural Centre in Melbourne.
Blue Mts Art Prize competition estb. at Katoomba, NSW.
Busselton Art Gallery estb., WA.
Margel Hinder wins Cwlth Reserve Bank Art Prize.
Cwlth Games Art Prize awarded in Perth.
Hungry House Art Gallery estb. in Sydney.
Sutherland Shire Council Art Competition held in Sydney.
Leeton Irrigana Golden Jubilee Festival Art Prize awarded, NSW.
Campbelltown Festival of Fisher's Ghost Art Competition estb., NSW.
Aust. sends art to Tate Gallery Exhibition in London. (Exhibition opens in Feb. 1963.)
Drummoyne Art Prize estb., NSW.
Sydney Printmakers estb.
Devonport Art Prize estb., Tas.
Tully Art Festive Prizes awarded, Qld.
Leveson Street Private Gallery estb. in Melbourne.
Newcastle Hotel Art Prize estb., NSW.
Wellington Tourist Festival Art Prize estb., NSW.
Young Cherry Festival Art Prize estb., NSW.

Architecture

During 1962
AMP building, (383 ft) is first to break 150 ft. height limit in Sydney.
Robin Boyd builds Domain Park Flats in Melbourne, first multi-storeyed home units in Vic.

D
Religion, Learning

1 Jan. Church of England of Australia, under new constitution becomes official title of Church of England in Aust.
During 1962
Roman Catholic deputation to NSW Premier requests extensive State aid for Catholic education.
Western Teachers' College estb. in Adelaide.
Wollongong University estb. as College of University of NSW.
NSW Govt administers Wyndham Scheme of comprehensive secondary schools.
Qld Govt approves raising school leaving age and extension of secondary school course to five years.
The Sephardi Synagogue opens in Sydney.

E
Sport

Nov.–Dec. Cwlth Games held in Perth. Aust. wins 38 gold, 36 silver and 31 bronze medals.
During 1962
Even Stevens, ridden by L. Coles, wins Melbourne Cup in 3 minutes 21.4 seconds.
Essendon football team wins VFL Premiership in Melbourne.
St George football team wins Rugby League Premiership in Sydney.
Alistair Lord of Geelong VFL team awarded Brownlow Medal.
Dawn Fraser is ABC Sportswoman of the Year.
John Sturrock, yachtsman, wins Australian of the Year Award.
Gretel competes in first Aust. challenge for America's Cup. Records first Aust. win in second round of sailing challenge. (Aust. fourth nation in 111 years to challenge the Cup. Other challenges 1967, 1970, 1974, 1977, 1980, and in 1983 the challenge was successful.)
Dawn Fraser becomes first woman swimmer to break 60 seconds for 100 m freestyle event.
Bob Pike wins Peru International surfboard riders championship.
First Aust. Volleyball championships held.
First Aust. Cup for soccer played. (Until 1968.)
Rod Laver becomes first Aust. to win the Grand Slam of major tennis titles, French, Wimbledon, American and Aust.
Aust. Tenpin Bowling Congress estb. First Aust. championships held.
Solo wins Sydney to Hobart yacht race.

Births & Deaths

Michelle Ford, swimmer, b.
Tracey Wickham, swimmer, b.

1962

F

Historia Dignum

Population
Estimated total white, 10,846,059.

Jan.–Feb. Fires damage Dandenong Ranges east of Melbourne, claiming nine lives.

During 1962
Annual Tunarama Festival begins at Port Lincoln, SA.
Tania Verstak becomes Miss International Beauty Queen.
Duke of Edinburgh Award Scheme inaugurated.
Cyclone on NSW coast causes widespread floods and severe property damage.
National road toll 2,535.

A

History, Politics, Economics, Law

1963

Government

26 Mar. 1963–24 Sep. 1963, Sir Stanley Charles Burbury administered Tas.

8 May 1963–31 May 1974, Sir Rohan Delacombe Governor Vic.

26 Jun. 1963–25 Oct. 1963, Sir John Patrick Dwyer administered WA.

24 Sep. 1963–11 Jul. 1968, Sir Charles Henry Gairdner Governor Tas.

25 Oct. 1963–28 Aug. 1973, Sir Douglas Anthony Kendrew Governor WA.

18 Dec. 1963–26 Jan. 1966, Thirty-third Cwlth Ministry, Sir Robert Gordon Menzies Liberal-Country coalition Prime Minister Aust.

18 Feb.–27 Mar. Queen Elizabeth II makes second Royal Tour of Aust. Attends jubilee celebrations of founding of Canberra.

Mar. RAAF accepts first Mirage aircraft in Paris.

17 May. Cwlth Govt approves estb. of US Naval Communications base at North-West Cape, WA.

During May. Aust. Parlt passes legislation to replace PNG Legislative Council with an elected House of Assembly.

5 Aug. Aust. signs new trade agreement with Japan.

Sep. Cwlth Govt announces decision to introduce decimal currency in Feb. 1966.

Cwlth Govt pledges Aust. military assistance to defend Malaysia against aggression. Pledge prompted by Indonesia's Confrontation Policy, which began in Jan.

Oct. Cwlth Govt announces decision to purchase two squadrons of the American F111 reconnaissance bomber aircraft. Govt orders 4 Oberon class submarines from Britain and a third guided-missile destroyer from USA.

Report on the grievances of Yirrkala Aborigines at Gove, NT, tabled in Parlt.

30 Nov. Sir R. G. Menzies returned as Liberal-Country coalition Prime Minister of Aust.

During 1963

Construction of Canberra mint begins. (Opens in Feb. 1965.)

Aust. signs Nuclear Test Ban Agreement.

Aust. Water Resources Council estb.

International Whaling Commission protects humpback whales.

Aust. Consulate-General estb. in Madrid, Spain.

First trade mission from Israel arrives in Aust.

One of world's largest and longest cattle shifts: 1,000 Hereford cattle transported by train 2,500 miles from Armidale, NSW, to Esperance, WA.

The Aust. Wool Board estb.

Three weeks annual leave becomes Federal standard.

Commercial abalone fishing industry begins.

B

Science, Technology, Transport, Discovery

Apr. First cotton gin opens in Narrabri, NSW.

Jul. First phase of Ord R. irrigation project opens at Kununurra, WA. (First stage completed in 1965.)

Hamersley Iron Ltd begins mining operation in Pilbara region, WA.

2 Dec. Cwlth Pacific Coaxial Cable (COMPAC) opens.

During 1963

Canberra hosts International Astronomical Symposium.

Sir John Eccles shares Nobel Prize for work in neurophysiology. Wins Australian of the Year award.

USA builds communications base at North-West Cape, WA, and space tracking station at Tidbinbilla, ACT.

Natural gas fields discovered at Cooper Basin, SA.

Mersey-Forth Power Development Scheme begins in Tas. (Completed in 1973.)

Petroleum Refineries (Aust.) Pty Ltd open at Port Stanvac, SA.

First shipment of Weipa, Qld, bauxite shipped to refinery at Bell Bay, Tas.

CSIRO discovers that heavy rain is more likely to fall during first and third weeks of lunar month.

Large deposits of chrysoprase discovered near Rockhampton, Qld.

CSIRO estb. Computing Research Station.

EH Holden car launched.

Large underground water supplies discovered near Alice Springs, capable of irrigating large areas of farmland.

First data transmission service opens between Melbourne and Sydney.

Teletronics develops first pacemaker for heart patients.

1963

1963

C Arts

Literature

During 1963
Geoffrey Blainey publishes *The Rush That Never Ended*.
Hal Porter publishes *The Watcher on the Cast Iron Balcony*.
K. S. Prichard publishes *Child of the Hurricane*.
C. M. Thiele publishes *Storm Boy*.
Alan Moorehead publishes *Coopers Creek*.
Martin Boyd publishes *When Blackbirds Sing*.
Morris West publishes *Shoes of the Fisherman*.
Alan Marshall publishes *In Mine Own Heart*.
Xavier Herbert publishes *Disturbing Element*.
Aust. Society of Authors estb.
Frank Hardy publishes *The Hard Way*.

Music, Dance

During 1963
Donald Peart and others found Musicological Society of Aust.
Shirley McKechnie estb. the Aust. Contemporary Dance Theatre, in Melbourne.
Margaret Lasica estb. the Modern Dance Ensemble, in Melbourne.

Births & Deaths
Lawrence Power, tenor, d.

Drama, Theatre, Film

During 1963
Robin Lovejoy, Robert Quentin and Tom Brown found Old Tote Theatre Co.
A Hole in the Ground wins Best Film of the Year award.

Fine Arts

May. *Art and Australia*, quarterly magazine edited by Mervyn Horton, first issued.
Apr. Dick Watkins exhibits painting *Moscow* in Sydney.
During 1963
J. Carington Smith wins Archibald Prize for *Professor James McAuley*.
Albany Art Gallery Art Prize estb., WA.
Armidale Art Society Competition estb., NSW.
S. Ostoja-Kotkowski wins British Petroleum Co. Prize for mural in Melbourne.
Art Teachers' Association of Vic. estb. Mary Cecil Allen Memorial Lectures.
Darwin Arts Society estb.
Aust. Painting Today exhibition tours Europe.
Recent British sculpture exhibition tours Aust.
Export Development Council and Aust. Bankers' Association poster competition held.
Finney Centenary Art Prize awarded, Qld.
Georges Invitation Art Prize estb. in Melbourne.
Aust. division of International Association of Art critics estb.
Kanyana Art Prize estb., Vic.
Kempsey Festival of Spring Annual Art Competition estb., NSW.
Mary White School of Art estb. in Sydney.
Rex and Thea Rienits publish *Early Artists of Australia*.
Northside Arts Festival estb. in Sydney.
Namatjira Memorial Art Prize estb. in Adelaide.
Osborne Art Gallery estb. in Adelaide.

Architecture

During 1963
Cwlth Bridge, Canberra, completed.
Cumberland County Council replaced by State Planning Authority of NSW. First of kind in Aust.
IBM building in Sydney becomes first glass-wall office built in Aust. (Completed 1964.)

D
Religion, Learning

Apr. SA school leaving age raised to 15 years.
May. Aust. Society for Education through the Arts (ASEA) estb. in Canberra.
Sep. NSW Govt introduces State aid to non-State schools by providing scholarships.
Nov. At the Federal election the Menzies Govt's promise to provide State aid for private schools is an important issue.

During 1963
Much public discussion takes place as to whether State Govts had previously minimized their allocations for primary and secondary education.
Rapid changes in social values disrupt traditional teaching methods.
Increase in school-going population brings about a crisis. Existing facilities in all States unable to cope with increased numbers.

E
Sport

During 1963
Gatum Gatum, ridden by J. Johnson, wins Melbourne Cup in 3 minutes 21.1 seconds.
Geelong football team wins VFL Premiership in Melbourne.
St George football team wins Rugby League Premiership in Sydney.
Bob Skilton of South Melbourne VFL team awarded Brownlow Medal.
Margaret Smith is ABC Sportswoman of the Year.
Aust. Volleyball Federation estb.
Geoffrey Nichols first in world to complete bare-foot water ski jump at world's first contest, at Manly, Sydney.
Aust. Surfriders' Association estb.
Bernard Farrelly first Aust. to win international surfriding championship, at Hawaii.
Phyllis O'Donnell first Aust. woman surfriding champion.
South African Rugby League team makes visit to Aust.
Nell Hopman begins Federation Tennis Cup, women's equivalent of Davis Cup.
Margaret Court becomes first Aust. woman to win Wimbledon women's tennis singles.
Aust. wins first netball championship, in England.
First all-Aust. women's sculling championship held.
Ken Hiscoe wins four major world squash titles.
David Mayfield wins world live bird shooting title.
Kevin Sarre becomes first world champion shearer.
Aust. wins first world women's basketball title.
George Foster sets world woodchopping record, in Tas.
Freya wins Sydney to Hobart yacht race.

Births & Deaths
Jenny Donnett, diver, b.

1963

F

Historia Dignum

Population

Estimated total white, 11,055,482.

1 Jan. Cyclone Annie damages area north of Brisbane.

26 Jan. Stephen John Lyttle is heaviest recorded new-born baby 16 lb 5 oz (7.4 kg). Born at Kempsey Hospital.

Apr. Satirical magazine *Oz* first published. (Until Oct. 1965.)

May. Townsville bulk sugar terminal destroyed by fire; £15 million damage.

Oct. *Australian Financial Review* becomes daily newspaper.

During 1963

Dr Gilbert Bogle and Margaret Chandler mysteriously found dead in Sydney.

Kristian Frederikson arrives in Aust. from NZ to design costumes for Aust. Ballet Co.

Wildlife Preservation Society of Qld estb.

Widespread floods throughout much of Aust. Severe floods in NSW and Qld.

First Redphones and Easiphones appear.

Alan Walker of Central Methodist Mission estb. Lifeline, telephone counselling service, in Sydney.

National road toll 2,598.

Communities

Exmouth, WA, estb.

A
History, Politics, Economics, Law

1964

Government

30 Apr. 1964–may 1965, J. B. Renshaw Labor Premier NSW.

1964–1970, R. L. Dean Administrator NT under Cwlth jurisdiction.

25 Feb. Twenty-fifth Federal Parlt opens. (Dissolution 31 Oct. 1966.)

Feb. First general election from common roll in PNG; 64-member House of Assembly meets in Jul.

Mar. Cwlth Govt announces £3 million military aid grant to Malaya. Sends forces for service in Apr. Arrangements for training Malaysian army personnel in Aust. announced.

27 Apr. Sir Garfield Edward John Barwick appointed Chief Justice of High Court of Aust. (Until 11 Feb. 1981.)

May. NT Legislative Council passes legislation removing some discrimination against Aborigines. Cwlth Govt expands social family benefits and introduces home ownership benefits scheme. First applications lodged for Cwlth Home Savings Grants in Jul.

Jun. Aust. Communists divide into pro-Soviet Union (CPA) and pro-China (CPA-ML) groups.

25 Aug. Members of Aust. Workers Union at Mt Isa, Qld, begin seven-months strike over wages. Qld Govt declares state of emergency.

15 Sep. Federal Govt embarrassed by Naval Board report into sinking of HMAS *Voyager*.

Oct. Aust. military forces active in Malacca during Confrontation operations.

Nov. Prime Minister announces expansion of defence provisions, including additional defence expenditure, resumption of National Service Training and estb. of Special Reserve Forces. Conscription re-introduced using birthdate ballot to select 20-year-olds.

22 Dec. Vic. Govt passes Consumers' Protection Act, pioneering protective legislation. (Similar legislation passed in NSW 1969, Qld, SA and Tas. in 1970, WA 1971, NT and ACT 1974.)

During 1964

Aust. Govt provides financial aid to help stabilize the Laotian economy.

Aust. mission in Greece raised to Embassy status. Aust. Embassy opens in Vienna; Soviet Trade Mission estb. in Sydney in May.

NSW Govt employees granted four-weeks annual leave.

Aust. represented as full regional member of Economic Commission for Asia and the Far East (ECAFE) for first time at twentieth conference in Teheran.

Malaysia–Australia Air Services Agreement signed in Kuala Lumpur.

Lake Burley Griffin completed in Canberra.

Aust. Wool Board offers technical aid to mainland China.

Basic wage increased by £1.

1964

B
Science, Technology, Transport, Discovery

Jan. Agreement concluded with USA on estb. of meteorological research station at Pearce, WA, RAAF base.
Mar. NSW Govt opens oil refinery at Kurnell.
Aust. School of Nuclear Technology estb. at Lucas Heights, near Sydney.
8 Apr. Moonie-to-Brisbane oil pipeline opens, beginning production on first commercial oilfield in Aust.
Jul. Oil discovered at Barrow I., WA. (Starts flowing in 1967.)
20 Aug. Aust. joins 18 other members of International Telecommunications Union in setting up an international communications satellite system (Intelsat).
Dec. Barracouta oil field discovered off Gippsland coast, Vic. (Yields first gas and oil on 18 Feb. 1965.)

During 1964
Air pollution controls estb. for industry in NSW.
Cwlth Govt announces estb. of new Space Tracking and Data Acquisition Station in Orroral Valley, ACT.
Tasman Bridge across Derwent R., Hobart, opens.
Sydney and Cornell (USA) universities combine to estb. Astronomy Centre, largest of kind in world.
Construction of Tullamarine Airport near Melbourne begins.
Jet aircraft first used in Aust. domestic air services: first Boeing 727s arrive in Sydney on 16 Oct.
CSIRO estb. Radioheliograph at Culgoora, near Narrabri, NSW.
Wild Life Preservation Society of Aust. estb.
Mills Cross telescope begins operating at Hoskinstown, near Canberra.
Blue Streak rocket first launched, from Woomera, SA.
Large bauxite deposits discovered at Gove, NT.
Aust. Forestry Council estb.

C
Arts

Literature

During 1964
Thomas Keneally publishes first novel, *The Place at Whitton*.
Donald Horne publishes *The Lucky Country*.
George Johnston publishes *My Brother Jack*.
Kath Walker publishes *We Are Going*.
James McAuley publishes *Captain Quiros*.
H. F. Brinsmead publishes *Pastures of the Blue Crane*.

Music, Dance

14 Mar. Robert Helpmann's ballet *The Display* premières in Adelaide.
Jun. Beatles pop group tours Aust. 'Beatlemania' spreads.

During 1964
Dean Dixon appointed conductor of Sydney Symphony Orchestra. (Until 1967.)
Jimmy Little produces song 'Radio Telephone'.
Lionel Long, traditional Aust. folk singer, popular.
Aust. Ballet School estb. in Melbourne.
Nigel Henry Butterley composes *Laudes*. Is acclaimed as a leading composer of new generation.
Elaine Fifield becomes prima ballerina of Aust. Ballet Co.
Tas. Conservatorium of Music and Canberra School of Music estb.

Births & Deaths

Beatrice Miranda, dramatic soprano, d.

Drama, Theatre, Film

During 1964
New Fortune Theatre built in WA. Among world's few practical reconstructions of Elizabethan theatres.
The Mavis Bramston Show begins on television.
Transfiguration wins Best Film of the Year award.

Fine Arts

During 1964
Archibald Prize not awarded this year.
Goya Art Awards estb. nationally.
Launceston Art Trophy estb., Tas.
Britannica Aust. Awards estb. for art, education, literature, medicine and science contributions.
Cairns Art Society Prize estb., Qld.
White Studio Gallery of Modern Art estb. in Adelaide.
Sale Regional Arts Centre estb., Vic.

Lithuanian Arts Festival held in Melbourne.
Rural Bank Art Prize held in Sydney.
Maryborough Art Gallery estb., Vic.
Toorak Art Gallery estb. in Melbourne.
Scone Art Prize estb., NSW.
Traralgon Library and Art Gallery estb., Vic.
Fred Williams paints *Trees on Hillside*.

Architecture

2 Oct. Gladesville Bridge in Sydney completed. Concrete arch among longest of type in world.
During 1964
John Hamilton Andrews, architect, designs University of Toronto, Canada. Known as 'the Megastructure', first of kind built.

D
Religion, Learning

Mar. Cwlth Govt announces programme of assistance for teaching of science.
May. Cwlth Govt extends State aid to private schools outside ACT. State aid to private schools re-introduced after lapse of nearly 100 years.
Jun. English first used in Roman Catholic Church services.
Aug. USA and Aust. Govts agree to estb. joint educational foundation to succeed Fulbright Scheme.
During 1964
Rev. Theodore Delwin Noffs estb. Wayside Chapel in Sydney. First in world to use coffee house drop-in concept.
Swan Hill Folk Museum and Art Gallery estb., Vic.
Wagga Wagga Museum and Art Gallery estb., NSW.
Charles Perkins becomes first Aboriginal to graduate from an Aust. university.

1964

E
Sport

17 Jul. Donald Campbell sets world land speed record on Lake Eyre, SA, 648.6 kmh.
31 Dec. Donald Campbell sets world water speed record 444.6 kmh.
During 1964
Polo Prince, ridden by R. Taylor, wins Melbourne Cup in 3 minutes 19.6 seconds.
Melbourne football team wins VFL Premiership in Melbourne.
St George football team wins Rugby League Premiership in Sydney.
Gordon Collis of Carlton VFL team awarded Brownlow Medal.
Dawn Fraser wins Australian of the Year award and is elected ABC Sportswoman of the Year.
Aust. wins six gold, two silver and ten bronze medals at Tokyo Olympics.
Bernard 'Midget' Farrelly becomes first Aust. to win world surfboard championship. Held at Manly, Sydney.
World's first hover vehicle race held, on Lake Burley Griffin, Canberra.
Bill Northam wins first Aust. gold medal for yachting; is world's oldest person to win a gold medal.
David Lewis begins circumnavigating world in a multihull craft. First circumnavigation of its type.
Pakistan Test cricket team makes first tour of Aust.
Aust. women's tennis team wins Federation Cup for first time.
Skateboard riding begins in Aust.
First Aust. trampoline championships held.
Katherine Troutt breaks women's world scuba diving depth record in Sydney (320 feet).
Freya wins Sydney to Hobart yacht race.

Births & Deaths
Megan Harrod, water skier, b.

F
Historia Dignum

Population
Estimated total white, 11,280,429.

13–14 Jan. Cyclone Audrey damages south-western Qld and northern NSW.
10 Feb. RAN destroyer *Voyager* sinks after collision with HMAS *Melbourne* off Jervis Bay, ACT. 81 lives lost.
15 Jul. The *Australian*, first national daily newspaper begins publication in Canberra.
During Jul. Melbourne records lowest barometric pressure for 100 years.
27 Oct. Eric Edgar Cooke, 'Moonstruck Murderer', hanged in Perth for multiple murders.
During 1964
WA first State to introduce mass finger-printing.
Tanami Desert Sanctuary, NT, proclaimed. Largest in Aust.
Folk Lore Council of Aust. estb.
Two-year drought begins. Particularly severe in NSW and Qld. Reduces sheep by 13.5 per cent and cattle by 24 per cent.
Aust. has 9,000 full-time and 3,000 part-time shearers.
National road toll 2,966.

Communities
Moonie, Qld, estb.

A
History, Politics, Economics, Law

1965

Government

10 Mar. 1965–Jun. 1967, F. H. Walsh Labor Premier SA.

7 May 1965–22 Sep. 1965, Sir Henry Abel Smith administered Aust.

13 May 1965–Jan. 1975, (Sir) R. W. Askin Liberal-Country coalition Premier NSW.

3 Aug. 1965–20 Jan. 1966, Sir Kenneth Whistler Street administered NSW.

22 Sep. 1965–30 Apr. 1969, Richard Gardiner Casey, Lord Casey, Governor-General Aust.

Jan. First Aust. Ambassador appointed to Ireland. To Greece in Feb. Diplomatic recognition of Singapore in Aug.

Feb. Aust. signs major defence agreement to buy aircraft and other military equipment from Britain and USA over next three years.

Full High Court Judgment on intrastate airlines case determines that intrastate services need to hold both State and Cwlth licences.

Mar. First ballot for National Service call-up held.

Sir Thomas Playford defeated as Premier in SA elections after record term of office of 26 years and 226 days.

28 Apr. Aust. commits combat troops to Vietnam. First Infantry Batallion flies into Vietnam in May.

Jun. Aust. passes Nauru Act, setting up Legislative Council in Nauru.

19 Jul. At 26 years of age Andrew Peacock elected State president of Vic. Liberal Party.

During Jul. First RAAF squadron equipped with Mirage jet fighters formed.

Aug. NZ–Australia Free Trade Agreement (NAFTA) negotiated.

Sep. Roma Flinders Mitchell appointed first woman judge in SA, and first in Aust.

Sir James Vernon Committee report on Aust. economy tabled in Parlt. Principal recommendations rejected. (Committee appointed 1962.)

Oct. Sir Robert Menzies appointed by Queen to post of Lord Warden of the Cinque Ports. (Invested in Jul. 1966.)

First Aust.–USSR Trade Agreement signed, in Moscow.

Dec. Aust. wool-growers reject wool reserve price marketing plan to estb. reserve price at auction.

During 1965

Aust. Govt applies economic sanctions against Smith regime in Rhodesia (now Zimbabwe).

Aust. enters into formal assisted-passage agreement with Netherlands.

Sidney James Cook becomes first Aboriginal union organizer, in NT.

Aust. has 334 registered trade unions with about 2,116,000 members.

Capital Punishment abolished in NSW.

Third Cwlth and Empire Law Conference held in Sydney.

Aust. Council for Overseas Trade (ACFOT) estb.

Commercial prawning in Gulf of Carpentaria begins.

1965

B

Science, Technology, Transport, Discovery

7 Jan. Manly hydrofoil begins service. First hydrofoil in Sydney.
During Jan. *The Empress of Australia*, passenger-, cargo-, and vehicular-carrier, begins running between Sydney and Tas.
8 Mar. First non-stop aerial crossing between Aust. and USA made by Qantas. First such crossing by commercial airliner.
During Mar. Ford Falcon XM car launched.
Apr. Aust. changes to metric system for dispensing medicines.
May. New Whyalla, SA, steelworks open.
Jul. Cwlth Govt announces estb. of a US radio research base at Amberley Air Force Base in Qld.
Nov. ANU and British Atomic Energy Authority begin to estb. one of world's largest seismological installations, in NT.
Dec. Hawkesbury to Mount White, NSW, tollway opens.
During 1965
Largest Aust.-built ship of time, 49,000 ton bulk ore carrier *Darling River*, launched.
Observatory begins operating at Siding Springs Mt, near Coonabarabran, NSW.
Ampol opens first Aust.-owned oil refinery, at Lytton, Qld.
Jack Grant invents aircraft slide inflatable raft.
ED Holden car launched.
Aboriginal fossil Green Gully skeleton discovered near Keilor, Vic. Dated at 6,460 years.
WA Botanic Gardens open in Perth.
Royal Aust. College of Dental Surgeons estb.
Dept of Radiology estb. at Melbourne University. First in Aust.
Construction of Westgate Bridge begins in Melbourne.
Gas discovered at Palm Valley, NT, and Gin Gin, Qld.

C

Arts

Literature

During 1965
Morris West publishes *The Ambassadors*.
A. D. Hope publishes collection of essays, *The Cave and the Spring*.
Thea Astley publishes *The Slow Natives*.
Graham McInnes publishes *The Road to Gundagai*.

Music, Dance

Jan. Popular song by the Seekers group, 'I'll Never Find Another You', becomes first Aust. record to sell one million copies.
17 Jun. Joan Sutherland returns to Aust. from Europe.
Sep.–Oct. Sydney Symphony Orchestra on overseas tour.
1 Oct. The Aust. Ballet begins first international tour to Europe and USA.
During 1965
Sydney Dance Co. estb.
Elizabeth Dalman estb. The Australian Dance Theatre in Adelaide.
Monash and Qld University Chairs of Music estb.
Sir Robert Helpmann wins Australian of the Year award.
The Sutherland/Williamson Opera Co. tours Aust.
Canberra School of Music estb.
John Hopkins estb. Prom concerts in Sydney.
Peter Sculthorpe composes *Sun Music I*, introduced at London Cwlth Festival of Arts.
Thomas Mayer appointed conductor of WA Symphony Orchestra. (Until 1970.) Clive Douglas appointed conductor Melbourne Symphony Orchestra.

Drama, Theatre, Film

During 1965
The SA Theatre Co. estb.
Ian Dunlop's film *Desert People* internationally acclaimed.
Faces in the Sun wins Best Film of the year award.

Fine Arts

Feb. Darlinghurst Art Gallery opens in Sydney.
Oct. First Aust. op art exhibition held, in Melbourne.
During 1965
Clifton Pugh wins Archibald Prize for *R. A. Henderson*.
Louis James wins first Corio Art Prize in Geelong.

D
Religion, Learning
1965

Eltham Art Award estb. (near Melbourne).
Gallaher Prize for portraits estb. in Sydney.
Art Gallery Association of Aust. estb., in Sydney.
Parramatta Art Prize first awarded, NSW.
Perth Festival Invitation Art Prize founded as T. E. Wardle Invitation Art Prize.
Perth Prize becomes Perth Prize for Drawing.
Sydney Trade Fair Art Award presented.
Portia Geach Memorial Award estb.
State Savings Bank of Vic. Art Prize estb.
Springbrook Art Prize estb., Qld.
Potter's Cottage Prize estb. at Warrandyte, Vic.
Watters Art Gallery estb. in Sydney.

Mar. Sir Leslie Martin Committee on tertiary education tables first report, which recommends estb. of Colleges of Advanced Education and other tertiary colleges. Cwlth agrees to provide grants subject to matching grants by States, rising from $5 million to $50 million over six-year period, for development of technical education at tertiary level.

2 Jul. Vic. Secondary Teachers' Association strikes against salary levels. Period of militancy among school teachers begins.

Sep. Vic. Board of Inquiry into Scientology movement recommends abolition of Scientology in that State on grounds that it poses serious threat to mental health of community. For a time Scientology was prohibited in Vic. though it subsequently re-appeared as a registered church.

Nov. Winston Churchill Memorial Trust announces award of first 48 Churchill Fellowships.

During 1965
University of Newcastle becomes autonomous (previously part of University of NSW). Flinders University becomes autonomous (previously part of University of Adelaide).
Hobart Matriculation College opens. Among first of kind.
NSW, WA and SA Govts implement State aid to private schools.
There are 10,065 schools in Aust. of which 7,844 are Govt. schools.
Museums and Art Gallery Board of NT estb.
The Technical Teachers' Association of Aust. estb.
NSW and Qld Institutes of Technology estb.
The Aust. Research Grants Committee estb.
Roman Catholic Church in Aust. adopts changes recommended by Second Vatican Council, including involvement of laity in Church affairs, simpler liturgy and better relations with non-Catholics.

1965

E
Sport

Aug. Linda McGill becomes first Aust. to swim English Channel.
During 1965
Light Fingers, ridden by R. Higgins, wins Melbourne Cup in 3 minutes 21.1 seconds.
Essendon football team wins VFL Premiership in Melbourne.
St George football team wins Rugby League Premiership in Sydney.
Ian Stewart of St Kilda VFL team awarded Brownlow Medal.
Ron Clarke is ABC Sportsman of the Year. During year breaks 11 world records in 16 races.
Geoffrey Hunt, aged 17, becomes national squash champion.
Aust. makes first appearance in World Cup soccer competitions.
William Nance sails around Cape Horn in a 7.6 m yacht.
Aust. first participates in world archery championship, in Sweden.
First national drag racing titles held.
Aust. first challenges for Admiral's Cup in sailing.
Record crowd of 78,056 attend Rugby League game in Sydney.
Freya wins Sydney to Hobart yacht race.

F
Historia Dignum

Population
Estimated total white, 11,505,408.

Jan.–Mar. Bushfires in NSW and Vic. claim 11 lives.
Feb. Aust. Council of National Trusts estb.
9 Nov. Explosion at Bulli Colliery, NSW, claims four lives.
Nov. Dust storm sweeps across Qld, suffocating sheep and cattle.
25 Dec.–2 Jan. 1966. Cyclone Amanda damages much of NT.
During 1965
Jean Shrimpton causes controversey at Flemington race course by wearing an above knee dress without stockings.
Aust. Conservation Foundation estb. to promote the understanding and practice of conservation.
Tas. introduces provisional drivers' licences.
Vic. fodder transported to NSW to relieve stock affected by drought.
Kevin Sarre shears 346 merinos in 7 hours 40 minute at Penshurst, Vic., breaking world record.
Women attempt to liberate public bars by staging sit-ins at Civic Hotel in Canberra and at Regatta Hotel in Brisbane.
Council of Aust. Humanist Societies estb.
National road toll 3,164.

Communities
Dampier, WA, estb.

A

History, Politics, Economics, Law

1966

Government

20 Jan. 1966–1981, Sir Arthur Roden Cutler Governor NSW.

26 Jan. 1966–14 Dec. 1966, Thirty-fourth Cwlth Ministry, Harold Edward Holt Liberal-Country coalition Prime Minister Aust.

21 Mar. 1966–20 Mar. 1972, Sir Alan Mansfield Governor Qld.

14 Dec. 1966–19 Dec. 1967, Thirty-fifth Cwlth Ministry, Harold Edward Holt Liberal-Country coalition Prime Minister Aust.

26 Jan. Sir Robert Gordon Menzies retires after record term as Prime Minister (1939–1941 and 1949–1966; Opposition Leader 1943–1949).

Dame Annabelle Rankin becomes first woman to administer a Federal Govt Department in Aust.

During Jan. NSW Law Reform Commission estb. on full-time basis.

Reserve Bank offers paid leave to female employees having babies. First maternity leave in Aust.

14 Feb. Cwlth Govt introduces decimal currency.

9 Mar. Full voting rights given to Member for ACT in Cwlth Parlt.

22 Mar.–7 Apr. Queen Elizabeth II and Queen Mother visit Aust.

During Mar. Immigration laws relaxed to allow entry of non-European races.

Cwlth Arbitration Commission hands down decision granting white rates of pay and working conditions to NT Aboriginal stockmen by Dec. 1968.

Printing and Kindred Industries Union (PKIU) estb.

Aust. and Mexico agree to exchange Ambassadors. Diplomatic relations with Malta estb. in Dec.

21 Jun. Peter Kocan unsuccessfully attempts to assassinate Opposition Leader Arthur Calwell.

During Jun. Aust. joins eight Asian and Pacific countries in forming Asian and Pacific Co-operation Council (ASPAC).

Jul. Justice Eggleton appointed first President of Trade Practices Tribunal.

Aug. Gurindji Aborigines on Wave Hill Station, NT, strike in protest against low wages and poor conditions.

26 Nov. Harold Holt returned as Liberal-Country coalition Prime Minister at national elections.

During Nov. Gordon Page Barton estb. Liberal Reform Group to oppose Aust. involvement in Vietnam War.

Nov.–Dec. Some 440 Qantas pilots strike for 27 days over pay and conditions and operational issues.

During 1966
Cwlth proclaims permanent employment for married women.

SA Govt sponsors Prohibition of Discrimination Act, prohibiting discrimination in any service industry. First in Aust.

NT Aboriginals estb. Council for Aboriginal Rights.

World's largest cattle station, Alexandria, Qld, subdivided.

Japan replaces Britain as Aust.'s best customer for exports.

First Aust. Guided Missile destroyer, HMAS *Perth*, begins service.

Courage breweries estb. (Taken over by Tooth & Co. in 1978.)

The SA Aboriginal Lands Trust Act, giving dispossessed Aborigines land ownership, passed. First of kind in Aust.

Vietnam War

Mar. Cwlth Govt decides to treble Aust. involvement in Vietnam War. Aust. Army battalion to be replaced by Task Force of two battalions and support units.

5 May. First Aust. National Servicemen arrive at Vietnam battle zone.

24 May. Private Errol Wayne Noack first conscript killed in Vietnam. First overseas national serviceman killed in action on overseas military duty when Aust. not officially at war.

Jun.–Jul. Prime Minister Holt visits USA. Promises President Johnson Aust. support for USA in escalation of Vietnam War. Coins phrase 'All the Way with LBJ'.

18 Aug. Battle of Long Tan.

Oct. President Johnson of USA visits Aust. for talks on Vietnam.

Aust. delegation attends Vietnam peace talks in Manila.

Nov. Aust. voters endorse Govt policy on Vietnam at national elections.

1966

B
Science, Technology, Transport, Discovery

28 Jan. Western Mining Corporation makes first significant nickel discovery, at Kambalda, WA, beginning nickel mining industry in Aust.
Jun. World's largest solar still, and first to be used for town water supply in Aust., estb. at Coober Pedy, SA.
Jul. Cwlth Govt estb. Motor Vehicle Design Committee to report on car safety.
24 Nov. First television programmes interchanged directly between Britain and Aust., by orbiting satellite Intelsat 2.

During 1966
Astronomical Society of Aust. estb.
Largest Aust. meteorite discovered, near Forrest, WA.
Large-scale manganese mining begins at Groote Eylandt, Gulf of Carpentaria, NT.
First nylon manufactured in Aust.
Aboriginal fossils at Broadbeach, near Qld–NSW border, dated 1,500 years, discovered.
Nickel mining operations begin at Mt Tom Price, WA.
Barrow I., WA, declared a commercial oilfield.
Automatic telex introduced in Aust.
Dongara gasfield north of Perth, and Moomba gasfield, SA, discovered.
Phosphate discovered near Duchess, Qld.
Leases for sand mining on Fraser I. granted.

C
Arts

Literature

During 1966
Peter Mathers publishes *Trap*.
Douglas Stewart publishes *The Seven Rivers*.
Alan Moorehead publishes *The Fatal Impact*.
Patrick White publishes *The Solid Mandala*.
First volume of *The Australian Dictionary of Biography* published.
Geoffrey Blainey publishes *The Tyranny of Distance*.

Music, Dance

Jan. Sydney String Quartet estb.
During 1966
Marilyn Jones becomes prima ballerina of Aust. Ballet Co.
Music Foundation estb. to offer Federal assistance to new works.
Gladys Moncrieff Club formed in Sydney.
Sir Malcolm Sargent appointed conductor Melbourne Symphony Orchestra.
The Easybeats group voted top band in Aust.
Hoadley's National Battle of the Sounds competition launched.

Drama, Theatre, Film

12 Apr. The Sydney Filmmakers Co-operative estb.
19 Aug. Film *They're a Weird Mob*, based on John O'Grady's novel, premières.
During 1966
Civic Theatre opens in Canberra.
The Admiral's Cup wins Best Film of the year award.

Fine Arts

Apr. Group of artists influenced by new theory of art to succeed abstract expressionism estb. Central Street Gallery in Sydney.
During 1966
Jon Molvig wins Archibald Prize for *Charles Blackman*.
Beaumaris Art group in Melbourne introduces Inez Hutchison Art Award.
Charles Billich estb. St Kilda Gallery in Melbourne.
Tate Adams estb. Crossley Print Gallery in Melbourne.
Australian Sculpture Centre opens in Canberra.
Alcorso-Sekers travelling scholarship award for sculpture estb.
Two Decades of American Painting exhibition visits Aust.

D Religion, Learning

1966

Alois Svihla estb. Gallery 99 in Melbourne.
International Co-Operation Art award estb.
Peace through Prayer Art Contest conducted in Qld.
Mertz collection of Aust. contemporary paintings completed.
Lake Kippax Sculpture Competition estb., NSW.
Print Council of Aust. estb.
Strines Art Gallery estb. in Melbourne.

Jan. Charles, Prince of Wales, arrives in Aust. for a period of schooling at Timbertop School, Vic.

19–31 Jun. The Church and Life Movement study encourages Christians of different denominations to communicate more effectively and hence unite.

During 1966

Bedford Park Teachers' College (later Sturt College of Advanced Education) founded, SA.

Cwlth Department of Education and Science estb.

Masada College, a progressive Jewish primary school, estb. in Sydney.

The Yeshivah Gedolah Rabbinical Academy estb. in Melbourne.

The Council for the Defence of Government Schools (DOGS) estb. in Melbourne to oppose aid to private schools.

Tas. School of Dental Nursing estb.

United Evangelical Lutheran Church of Aust. and Evangelical Lutheran Church in Aust. merge to form Lutheran Church of Aust.

1966

E
Sport

During 1966
Galilee, ridden by J. Miller, wins Melbourne Cup in 3 minutes 21.9 seconds.
St Kilda football team wins VFL Premiership in Melbourne.
St George football team wins Rugby League Premiership in Sydney.
Ian Stewart of St Kilda VFL team awarded Brownlow Medal.
John Arthur (Jack) Brabham wins Australian of the Year award and is elected ABC Sportsman of the Year.
John Arthur (Jack) Brabham wins his third Grand Prix title. First to win championship in car of own design.
Aust. wins first world lawn bowls championship, held at Kyeemagh, Sydney.
Gloria Vause becomes first Aust. woman pistol-shooting champion.
Cwlth Games held in Kingston, Jamaica.
The roller game popular.
Robert (Nat) Young wins world surfboard riding championship.
Cadence wins Sydney to Hobart yacht race.

F
Historia Dignum

Population
Estimated total white, 11,704,843.
Cwlth census calculates total Aboriginal population as 102,000.
Estimates that one-seventh of total Aust. population were born overseas (larger migrant element in population than any country except Israel).

1 Jan. Cessna aircraft crashes near Canopus Homestead, SA, claiming five lives.
26 Jan. Three Beaumont family children disappear without trace from an Adelaide beach.
Feb. Vic. Govt introduces 10 o'clock hotel closing time.
13 Aug. Fire destroys convalescent home for men in Melbourne, claiming 30 lives.
During Aug. Most drastic water restrictions in history of Murrumbidgee Irrigation Areas announced. Burrinjuck Reservoir only one-third full.
22 Sep. Vickers Viscount aircraft crashes at Winton, Qld, claiming 24 lives.
28 Sep. Lockheed Hudson aircraft crashes at Tennant Creek, NT, claiming six lives.
21 Oct. Coalmine accident at Wyee, NSW, claims five lives.
During 1966
Meter maids used to police parking on Gold Coast, Qld.
There are 647 aerodromes in Aust. and its Territories.
Use of table margarine strongly recommended by leading members of medical profession.
Two-year drought in areas of Qld, SA, WA, NSW and NT breaks.
Seven large cyclones damage part of eastern Aust.
Crown-of-Thorns starfish threaten coral around Green I., Qld.
National road toll 3,242.

Communities
Goldsworthy, WA, estb.

A
History, Politics, Economics, Law

1967

Government

1 Jun. 1967–Apr. 1968, D. A. Dunstan Labor Premier SA.
19 Dec. 1967–10 Jan. 1968, Thirty-sixth Cwlth Ministry, John McEwen Liberal-Country coalition Prime Minister Aust.

Jan. Aust. Workers Union joins ACTU.
8 Feb. Edward Gough Whitlam replaces Arthur Calwell as Labor Opposition leader. (Until 1972.)
21 Feb. Twenty-sixth Federal Parlt opens (Dissolution 29 Sep. 1969.)
Mar. Gurindji Aborigines occupy part of Wave Hill Station, NT, in attempt to retrieve tribal lands. Aboriginal Rights Council unsuccessfully appeals to United Nations.
29 Apr. Referendum in northern NSW concerning proposed estb. of new State of New England rejected.
27 May. Cwlth Referendum granting Aborigines full citizen rights and empowering Cwlth to make laws and plans for Aborigines and to include them in national census carried. Referendum proposing to abolish link between the size of Senate and House of Representatives rejected.
May–Jun. Prince Philip visits Aust.
Jun. Conciliation and Arbitration Commission replaces basic wage-plus-margins system of determining wages with a total-wage concept.
Aug. Association of South-East Asian Nations (ASEAN) estb. to accelerate economic growth, economic progress and cultural development in South-East Asia.
During Sep. Cwlth Govt limits appeals from High Court of Aust. to Privy Council in London as first step towards making High Court the final Court of Appeal for Aust. (Operative Sep. 1968.)
Cwlth Govt announces estb. of Office of Aboriginal Affairs to co-ordinate policy and provide machinery for consultation with States.
Trade Practices Act 1965–1967, designed to preserve competition in Aust. trade and commerce, takes effect.
Public controversy breaks out over Govt use of VIP jets.
NSW Govt proposes to reform Sydney City Council.
15 Nov. Vic. Trades Hall Council suspends 27 of its 83 affiliated unions for not paying affiliation fees.
Nov. Liberal Reform Group changes name to Aust. Reform Movement. (Later becomes Australia Party.)
Aust. Resources Development Bank estb. to finance Aust. participation in projects of national importance.
Nov. Legislation for control of off-shore oil and gas leases given Royal Assent.
17 Dec. Harold Holt, Liberal-Country coalition Prime Minister, disappears without trace at Portsea, Vic., while swimming.
During Dec. Senate Select Committee recommends that Aust. convert to metric system of weights and measures. (Recommendation accepted.)
During 1967
Aust. enters into formal bilateral assisted-passage migration agreement with Federal Republic of Germany, Italy and Turkey.
Cwlth Govt estb. Twelve-mile fishing zone around Aust.
HMAS *Platypus* submarine base in Sydney commissioned. First RAN submarine base.

Vietnam War

Jan. Anti-War Activists' conference held in Sydney to estb. a 'blueprint' for future protest action.
Feb. First George Medal in war awarded to Sgt. G. Butriss.
Royal Aust. Navy divers attached to US naval forces operating in enemy waters.
Mar. Navy takes over Vietnam-bound freighters when Seamen's Union places ban on cargo.
HMAS *Hobart* takes up duties with US Seventh Fleet in S. China Sea and Gulf of Tonkin. HMAS *Perth* relieves in Sep.
Apr. Australian Canberra bombers make first operational flights in Vietnam.
Aug. Aust. Govt announces approval of leave-in-Australia scheme for Aust. and US troops.
9 Sep. Brisbane police and marchers clash violently during protests against proposed changes to the laws governing demonstrations.
Oct. Eight navy helicopters join the US 135th Aviation Co.
Prime Minister announces that Aust. forces in Vietnam are to be increased by more than 1,700.
27 Dec. A third Infantry Battalion arrives in Vietnam: Aust. commitment to war now exceeds 8,000 men.
During 1967
Aust. Task Force concentrates on National Liberation Front forces, both guerrillas and cadres in the villages.

1967

B
Science, Technology, Transport, Discovery

31 Mar. SEACOM communications cable, linking Aust. with South-East Asia, opens.
Apr. UNO World Symposium on man-made forests held in Canberra.
CSIRO releases dung beetle in northern Aust. to control buffalo fly.
Jul. *Ocean Digger*, first Aust.-built off-shore drilling rig, launched at Whyalla, SA.
1 Aug. Qantas Empire Airways Ltd becomes Qantas Airways Ltd.
During Aug. CSIRO radioheliograph at Culgoora, NSW, receives radio waves from the sun for first time.
Sep. Tas. Govt approves proposals for Gordon R. Power Development Scheme.
19 Nov. First Aust.-designed WRESAT satellite launched at Woomera, SA.
During Nov. Cwlth Govt finances second stage of Ord R. scheme in WA.
Subscriber trunk dialling (STD) system extended to link most cities in eastern Aust.
During 1967
Aust. and USA top-secret joint Space Facility estb. at Pine Gap, near Alice Springs, NT.
Robert H. Burgess invents speed packer method of collecting garbage.
Aboriginal fossils discovered at Chowilla Dam, dated from 4,000–6,000 years.
Aust. Academy of Science estb.

C
Arts

Literature

During 1967
Donald Horne publishes *The Education of Young Donald*.
Dymphna Cusack publishes *The Sun Is Not Enough*.
Thomas Keneally publishes *Bring Larks and Heroes*.
Cwlth and State Govts adopt uniform censorship agreement.
National Literature Board of Review estb. to advise Govt on book censorship.

Music, Dance

Jun. Margaret Walker estb. folkloric Dance Concert group.
Nov. Johnny Farnham's song, 'Sadie, The Cleaning Lady' released.
During 1967
The Seekers group wins Australian of the Year award.
Richard Meale composes *Images*.
Record-breaking crowd, about 200,000, gather at Myer Music Bowl in Melbourne to hear the Seekers.
Willem van Otterloo appointed conductor Melbourne Symphony Orchestra. (Until 1979.)
TV Week King of Pop awards launched.
Aust. Elizabethan Theatre Trust estb. permanent orchestra in Sydney.
ABC estb. National Training Orchestra in Sydney.

Drama, Theatre, Film

During 1967
Jack Hibberd writes play *White With Wire Wheels*.
This Day Tonight, current affairs television programme begins.
Interaction: Moving and Painting wins Best Film of the Year award.

Births & Deaths
Dave Meekin, showman, d.

Fine Arts

Jan. Royal Aeronautical Society Aust. Division Centenary Art Prize awarded.
Jun.–Aug. Aspects of New British Art and Two Decades of American Painting exhibitions influences development of contemporary art movement in Aust.
During 1967
Judy Cassab wins Archibald Prize for *Margo Lewers*.
Comalco Invitation award for sculpture estb.

D
Religion, Learning

1967

Flotta Lauro Shipping Co. estb. prizes for painting and sculpture.
National Gallery of SA becomes Art Gallery of SA.
Latrobe Valley Art Centre, Morwell, Vic., receives Govt aid.
Townsville Art Award estb., Qld.
Shoalhaven Art Prize awarded, NSW.

Architecture

During 1967
Aust. Square Tower completed in Sydney. Harry Seidler and Associates architects.
Robin Boyd designs Aust. displays at *Expo* in Montreal, Canada.

Mar. La Trobe University opens in Melbourne.
During 1967
Neo-progressive education curriculum begins to replace the humanist realist curriculum.
New period of education begins. Cwlth involved in growth of education.
Vic. Tas. and Qld Govts implement State aid to private schools.
Vic. abolishes external Intermediate Certificate Examination held at end of Form 4.
First NSW secondary school Higher School Certificate exams held at end of 6th form (year 12).
Launceston Matriculation College opens.
Macquarie University opens in Sydney.
SA Public Library becomes State Library of SA.
Cwlth aid for secondary schools expands.
Technical Teachers' Association of Aust. estb. in Vic.
Qld Institute of Technology (Later Capricornia College of Advanced Education) opens at Capricornia, north of Rockhampton, Qld.
WA Secondary Teachers' College (Later Nedlands College of Advanced Education) estb. at Nedlands, WA.
Aust. Council of Churches and Roman Catholic Church agree to examine matters on which they differ.

1967

E Sport

Jan. Francis Chichester arrives in Aust. at end of outward leg of around-the-world solo yacht voyage.

During 1967
Red Handed, ridden by R. Higgins, wins Melbourne Cup in 3 minutes 20.4 seconds.
Richmond football team wins VFL Premiership in Melbourne.
South Sydney football team wins Rugby League Premiership in Sydney.
Ross Smith of St Kilda VFL team awarded Brownlow Medal.
Heather McKay is ABC Sportswoman of the Year.
First Miracle Mile trotting race held in Sydney.
Aust. Boxing Federation estb.
Linda McGill sets women's record for English Channel swim, 9 hours 59 minutes.
William Moyes first to exceed 1,000 ft in man-carrying kite. World record.
Warick Selvey, athlete, wins Aust. discus title for sixth successive year.
Dick Leffler, athlete, wins hammer throwing title for ninth successive year.
Brian Griffin becomes highly acclaimed Lacrosse player.
First Aust. biathlon and triathlon competitions held.
Rainbow II wins Sydney to Hobart yacht race.
Dame Pattie challenges for the America's Cup. (America wins 4–0.)

Births & Deaths
Noel Ryan, swimmer, d.

F Historia Dignum

Population
Estimated total white, 11,912,253.

7 Feb. Ronald Ryan executed by hanging for murder at Pentridge jail in Melbourne despite public demonstrations against the hanging.
Bushfires break out in south-eastern Tas., claiming 51 lives.
Apr. Trial system of oral customs declaration by travellers begins.
Committee on the Development of south-west Tas. recommends that Lake Pedder be made a larger reserve.
Jul. Aust. postcode system introduced.
Sep. Melbourne Italians hold Roman Carnival to welcome Italy's President Saragat on Aust. visit.
Oct. Progressive water restrictions imposed in Melbourne area during increasingly severe drought.
Oct. Daylight saving becomes effective in Tas.
29 Dec. Cessna aircraft crashes at Daly Waters, NT, claiming six lives.
31 Dec. First quintuplets in Aust. born, in Brisbane.

During 1967
SA introduces 10 o'clock hotel closing time.
Australians smoke 21 billion cigarettes a year, sixth highest in world's list of cigarette smokers.
Open-line radio programmes begin.
NSW National Parks and Wildlife Act estb. first separate National Parks administration.
National road toll 3,166.

Communities
Mt Newman, WA, estb.

A

History, Politics, Economics, Law

1968

Government

10 Jan. 1968–28 Feb. 1968, Thirty-seventh Cwlth Ministry, John Grey Gorton Liberal-Country coalition Prime Minister Aust.

17 Jan. 1968–Aug. 1968, J. C. A. Pizzey Country-Liberal Premier Qld.

28 Feb. 1968–12 Nov. 1969, Thirty-eighth Cwlth Ministry, John Grey Gorton Liberal-Country coalition Prime Minister Aust.

17 Apr. 1968–Jun. 1970, R. S. Hall Liberal-Country League Premier SA.

1 Jun. 1968–4 Dec. 1968, Sir John Mellis Napier administered SA.

12 Jul. 1968–1 Dec. 1968, Sir Stanley Charles Burbury, administered Tas.

1 Aug. 1968–Aug. 1968, G. W. W. Chalk Country-Liberal Premier Qld.

8 Aug. 1968– (Sir) J. Bjelke-Petersen Country-Liberal (Later National) Premier Qld.

2 Dec. 1968–1 Dec. 1973, Sir Edric Montague Bastyan Governor Tas.

4 Dec. 1968–15 Sep. 1971, Sir James William Harrison Governor SA.

30 Jan. Twelve-mile fishing limit around Aust. becomes effective.

31 Jan. Nauru becomes independent of Aust.

During Jan. Uniform Cwlth–State censorship laws take effect.

Aust. mail services halt for 11 days during strike over accumulated grievances. Strike begins in Sydney.

1–10 Mar. Prince Philip visits Aust.

1 Apr. Joint Cwlth–State petroleum legislation takes effect.

May. Full voting rights given to NT Member in House of Representatives.

Jul. Aust. signs the Treaty on the Non-Proliferation of Nuclear Weapons.

Oct. NT Legislative Council elections held. New council to have elected majority for first time.

Dec. Tas abolishes capital punishment.

During 1968

Aust. stock exchanges flourish as share prices soar in mineral boom.

Cwlth Govt announces five-year thousand million dollar development plan for PNG.

Cwlth Office of Aboriginal Affairs operative. (Becomes Dept of Aboriginal Affairs in 1972).

Commercial pecan nut growing begins near Moree, NSW.

Increased wheat production in Asia results in international wheat crisis.

Aust. woodchip industry begins at Eden, NSW.

Vietnam War

Jan. Conference of Radical organizations, including protest bodies, to organize protest movement held in Brisbane.

25 Feb. First Aust. tanks arrive, 15 Centurion tanks.

Feb. Twenty Australians killed and eighty wounded in Tet offensive. Following Tet offensive many Aust. Citizens begin opposing the war because all the suffering it inflicts does not appear to be providing results.

13 May. Eleven Australians killed and twenty-five wounded when North Vietnamese attack Aust. Fire Support Base.

May. Aust. sends envoy to Vietnam peace talks in Paris.

May. National Service Bill increasing penalities for evasion of national service passed by House of Representatives after being amended by Senate.

Jun. Vietnam Medal For Aust. Armed Forces created and instituted by the Queen.

After one court-martial and three civil court cases, a special magistrate rules that conscientious objections to military service by Simon Townsend are valid.

4 Jul. Two thousand anti-Vietnam War demonstrators protest outside American Consulate in Melbourne. Violent riots occur when protestors burn the American flag.

1968

B
Science, Technology, Transport, Discovery

Feb. Cwlth and State authorities estb. measures to be adopted to cope with hazards arising from oil tanker operations.
Mar. First liver transplant operation in Aust. performed, in Sydney.
May. Qld Govt rejects application to mine lime from Great Barrier Reef.
Jun. Melbourne becomes one of three vital links in World Weather Watch. (Other two Washington and Moscow.)
Jul. New safety design standards for motor cars adopted by all States. To be introduced on all cars registered from 1 Jan. 1970.
Sep. First map coverage of all Aust. with topographic information completed by Division of National Mapping.
23 Oct. Sydney surgeons under Harry Windsor complete first heart transplant in Aust. and sixty-fourth in the world.
1 Nov. Ansett-ANA becomes Ansett Airlines of Aust.
During Nov. Aust. Minerals Council estb.
During 1968
Mills Cross radio telescope discovers two pulsars in Milky Way.
Swiss-Aust. Nabalco Pty Ltd begins bauxite mining at Gove Peninsula, NT.
Leo Port's Port-El Lift Control system operative.
Aboriginal fossil bones discovered at Lake Mungo, NSW, dated 25,000 years. Kow Swamp, Vic., excavations discover skeletons dated 9,000 years.
General Practitioners Society of Aust. estb.
Motor vehicle industry begins to feel opposition from Japanese producers.
First section of Tullamarine Freeway opens in Melbourne. First section of Warringah Freeway opens in Sydney.
Coal discovered at Goonyella, Qld.
CSIRO scientists discover the reaction bonding process, improving bonding of metals to ceramics, (Patented in 1970.)

C
Arts

Literature

Jun. Ten-member Aust. Council for the Arts estb. to advise Govt and finance the Arts.
During 1968
Morris West publishes *The Tower of Babel*.
Thomas Keneally publishes *Three Cheers for the Paraclete*.
National Literature Board of Review estb.

Music, Dance

Apr. Ruth Galene estb. the New Dance Theatre.
16 Aug. Aust. Ballet Co. performs world première of *Threshold*.
During 1968
David Anthony Ahern composes *Ned Kelly Music*. Ahern becomes leader of the avant-garde of Aust. music.
Kevin Coe appointed Principal of Aust. Ballet Co.
Stanford Robinson appointed conductor Qld Symphony Orchestra. (Until 1969.)
Rolf Harris becomes international performer.

Drama, Theatre, Film

During 1968
Alexander Buzo writes play *Norm and Ahmed*.
Film *Age of Consent* released.
Alexander Mervyn Archdale forms community Theatre Killara in Sydney.
The Union Theatre Repertory Co. becomes the Melbourne Theatre Co.
Tim Burstall's first feature film, *2000 weeks*, produced. Premières in Melbourne on 27 Mar. 1969.
The Drover's Wife wins Best Film of the Year award.

Fine Arts

20 Aug. First stage of Vic. Arts Centre opens in Melbourne. The National Gallery of Vic. opens.
During 1968
William Pidgeon wins Archibald Prize for *Lloyd Rees*.
The Field Exhibition of hard-edge paintings held in Melbourne.
Horsham Art Gallery estb., Vic.

D
Religion, Learning

Aug. Cwlth, NSW, Vic. and Tas. Govts agree to reduce unnecessary differences in State education curricula.
28 Oct. Canberra College of Advanced Education estb.
Nov. Cwlth Govt announces tertiary education study grants for Aborigines, beginning in 1969. Up to $1,000 per annum for single persons plus allowances for wives and children where applicable.

During 1968
National Library of Aust. opens in Canberra. Becomes co-ordinating and biographic centre for all major Aust. libraries.
Salisbury Teachers' College estb., SA.
First open space education system appears. Open space or area schools first estb. in Qld. (SA 1969, Tas. and WA 1970, ACT 1971, Vic. 1972.)
Council for Aboriginal Affairs estb. study grants for Aborigines at all education levels.
Gippsland Institute of Advanced Education estb. in Vic.
Methodist Church permits women to train for ministry.

E
Sport

3 Jan. Linda McGill becomes first to swim 40 km across Port Phillip Bay, Vic.
Aug. Bill Moyes makes world's longest unassisted kite hang gliding flight in NSW.
24 Nov.–17 Dec. London–to–Sydney car marathon takes place.

During 1968
Rain Lover, ridden by J. Johnson, wins Melbourne Cup in 3 minutes 21.5 seconds.
Carlton football team wins VFL Premiership in Melbourne.
South Sydney football team wins Rugby League Premiership in Sydney.
Bob Skilton of S. Melbourne VFL team awarded Brownlow Medal.
Lionel Rose wins Australian of the Year award and is elected ABC Sportsman of the Year. Wins world bantamweight boxing title in Tokyo.
Aust. wins five gold, seven silver and five bronze medals at Mexico Olympics.
During past five years Ron Clarke has set 17 world and 25 Aust. athletics records.
Hang gliding begins as sport in Aust.
Ken Rosewall first to win an open tennis tournament, in England.
Rod Laver wins Wimbledon tennis tournament.
Colin King, Aust. parachuting champion, wins Australia's first parachuting medal.
Koomooloo wins Sydney to Hobart yacht race.

F
Historia Dignum

1968

Population
Estimated total white, 12,145,582.

Jan. Tas. Govt permits shops to remain open 24 hours a day seven days a week.

Sep. Fire damages Katherine and Victoria R. areas, NT.

14 Oct. Earthquake devastates Meckering, WA. Largest instrumentally measured earthquake in Aust. (6.8).

28 Oct. Twice daily suburban mail deliveries abolished.

Oct.–Nov. Bushfires at Wollongong, NSW, and in Blue Mts claim 13 lives.

8 Dec. RSL wins 'the Battle of the Elms' in Melbourne against conservationists when City Council removes seven 80-year-old elm trees close to Shrine of Remembrance.

14 Dec. Referendum in Tas. approves estb. of gambling casino.

31 Dec. Viscount aircraft crashes at Port Hedland, WA, claiming 26 lives.

Between 1947 and 1968, 2,335,000 immigrants arrive in Aust.

National road toll 3,382.

During 1968
Kentucky Fried Chicken fast food outlet first estb. in Aust., at Guildford, NSW.

A

History, Politics, Economics, Law

1969

Government

30 Apr. 1969–11 Jul. 1974, Sir Paul Meernaa Caedwalla Hasluck Governor-General Aust.

26 May 1969–May 1972, W. A. Bethune Liberal-Centre Premier Tas.

12 Nov. 1969–10 Mar. 1971, Thirty-ninth Cwlth Ministry, John Grey Gorton Liberal-Country coalition Prime Minister Aust.

Jan. Stoppages of work by railway workers in most States in support of claim for increased wages.

Feb. Three Aborigines to be appointed as liaison officers for Cwlth Office of Aboriginal Affairs.

Apr. Second annual meeting of the Board of Governors of the Asian Development Bank held in Sydney.

May. Liberal-Centre Party wins office in Tas. elections after 35 years of Labor Govt of State.

Clarrie O'Shea, Vic. tramways union leader, jailed for refusing to pay union fines. Aust.-wide stoppages over operation of the penal provisions of the Commonwealth Conciliation and Arbitration Act.

The Copyright Act 1968 operative. Aust. becomes party to Universal Copyright Convention.

Jun. Arbitration Commission grants equal pay to women for equal work. Increases to be phased in over three years.

Cwlth Govt announces programme to encourage employers to employ Aborigines for long-term job training by offering subsidy of 30 per cent of the applicable award rate and by paying living-away-from-home allowances to young Aborigines.

20 Jul. Aust. Reform Movement becomes the Australia Party.

Aug. High Court of Aust. rules that States have no rights or jurisdiction over territorial waters adjacent to their coastlines or over sea-beds.

25 Oct. John Grey Gorton returned as Liberal-Country coalition Prime Minister at national elections.

Oct. National Farmers' Union and Aust. Primary Producers' Union amalgamate to form the Australian Farmers' Federation. (Lasts until Jul. 1979.)

25 Nov. Twenty-seventh Federal Parlt opens. (Dissolution 2 Nov. 1972.)

During 1969

Cwlth Govt declares Coral Sea Islands Aust. territory.

Lord Casey, Governor-General, wins Australian of the Year award.

Federal Narcotics Bureau estb.

Czechoslovak Consul-General in Sydney defects in Aust.

R. J. Hawke elected President of ACTU.

Aust. and NZ Banking Group Ltd estb. from merging of Aust. and NZ Bank Ltd and Scottish and Aust. Bank Ltd.

Sir Cyril Walsh appointed a Justice of High Court of Aust. (Until 1973.)

Aboriginal delegation presents United Nations Secretary-General with statement on conditions of Aust. Aborigines.

Cwlth Govt begins subsidizing Aboriginal welfare organizations.

Vietnam War

Dec. First Aust. parachute operation in Vietnam takes place in Phuoc Tuy Province.

By this month all nine battalions of the Royal Aust. Regiment have served in Vietnam, 41,000 army men and 6,000 navy and air force men.

During 1969

HMAS *Brisbane* and *Vendetta* carry out duties with the US Seventh Fleet.

Helicopter squadron introduces heavily armed helicopter gunships to support and protect its own utility helicopters operating on troop movements and medical evacuations.

Aust. Forces gradually shift operations away from combating mainforce enemy units outside Phuoc Tuy to restricting guerrilla and political activities within the Province.

Last of four Victoria Crosses awarded to Aust. servicemen issued this year.

1969

B
Science, Technology, Transport, Discovery

Mar. First Aust. natural gas pipeline, from Roma, Qld, to Brisbane, opens. Natural gas first piped to metropolitan Melbourne.

21 Jul. Parkes radio telescope relays to the world first television pictures of *Apollo XI* first moon landing.

Sep. Poseidon NL, Adelaide mining company, discovers nickel at Windarra, WA, beginning nickel boom. Shares rise from 50 cents to $280 in six months.

29 Nov. Standard gauge railway line between Sydney and Fremantle, WA, completed.

During 1969
Casey scientific and meteorological research station opens at Vincennes Bay, Antarctica.
Bass Strait submarine oil first piped to Vic. shores.
Brisbane tramways close.
Rabbit Flea *Spilopsyllus cuniculi* used to aid transmission of myxomatosis.
Aboriginal fossil skeleton discovered at Lake Nitchie, NSW; dated, 6,820 years.
Phillip I. Bridge, Vic., opens.
Natural gas discovered at Roseneath and Petrel, NT.

C
Arts

Literature

During 1969
James McAuley publishes *Surprise of the Sun*.
Frank Moorhouse publishes collection of stories, *Futility and Other Animals*.
Dymphna Cusack publishes *The Half Burnt Tree*.

Music, Dance

Jun. Harry M. Miller presents rock-musical *Hair* in Sydney.
Jul. Aust. Opera Co. forms in Sydney. (First performance in 1973.)
North Qld Ballet and Dance Society estb. in Townsville.

During 1969
Sherbert pop group forms.
Robert Helpmann returns to dance in Aust. after 10 years abroad.
Anne Elizabeth Boyd co-founds first Aust. contemporary music magazine, *Music Now*.
Society of Dance Art estb. in Sydney.
Ronald Sharp begins building biggest organ in Aust. for Sydney Opera House. (Completed 30 May 1979.)
Moshe Atzmon appointed conductor Sydney Symphony Orchestra. (Until 1971.) Verdon Williams appointed conductor Tas. Symphony Orchestra. (Until 1970.)

Drama, Theatre, Film

During 1969
Albie Thoms produces film *Marinetti*.
Jack Hibberd writes *Dimboola*. (Play not performed until 1973.)
Qld Theatre Co. estb.
Jack and Jill: a Postscript wins Best Film of the Year award.

Fine Arts

During 1969
Ray Crooke wins Archibald Prize for *George Johnston*.
The Association of Sculptors of Vic. estb.

D

Religion, Learning

Jan. SA Govt appoints Peter Karmel to examine most effective use of educational resources. (Submits first report 1971.)
12 Feb. Townsville Teachers' College Qld opens. (Becomes Townsville College of Advanced Education in 1975.)
25 Jun. Aust. Academy of the Humanities estb.
Sep. Wiltshire Committee of Inquiry into Colleges of Advanced Education tables report. Recommends awarding degrees and advanced diplomas in colleges.

During 1969
H. W. Dettman Committee inquiry into WA education recommends abolishing external school exams.
Methodist-Congregational Parkin-Wesley Theological College estb. in Adelaide.
Grand Freemason Lodge temple completed in Perth. (Melbourne 1970, Sydney foundation stone laid in 1976.)
Mount Gravatt Teachers' College opens in Qld. (Becomes Mount Gravatt College of Advanced Education in 1972.)
Union Church in Adelaide estb.
Aust. Science Education Project estb. to develop instructional science materials for secondary schools.

E

Sport

21 Jan. John Famechon wins world featherweight boxing championship.
Mar. Boules, French form of bowls, played on rough ground with metal balls, becomes popular in Sydney.

During 1969
Rain Lover, ridden by J. Johnson, wins Melbourne Cup in 3 minutes 21.5 seconds.
Richmond football team wins VFL Premiership in Melbourne.
Balmain football team wins Rugby League Premiership in Sydney.
Kevin Murray of Fitzroy VFL team awarded Brownlow Medal.
Rod Laver is ABC Sportsman of the Year. Becomes first man ever to win two Grand Slams.
Rod Laver beats Tony Roche in longest recorded tennis singles match, 4 hours 35 minutes; 90 games in 5 sets.
Margaret Court wins US singles tennis title for fourth time.
Bruce Cockburn first Aust. to win world water skiing title, in Denmark.
Lee Jones and Peter Dickens make longest Aust. balloon flight, in WA; takes $28\frac{1}{4}$ hours.
Last Test cricket series played between Aust. and South Africa.
Darwin greyhound racing track opens.
First Aust. Pentathlon Academy opens in Sydney.
Canal jumping introduced in Aust.
Orienteering introduced in Aust.
Cwlth Govt estb. National Aboriginal Sports Foundation.
Morning Cloud wins Sydney to Hobart yacht race.

1969

1969

F
Historia Dignum

Population

Estimated total white, 12,407,217.
Aboriginal population estimated at 50,000 full bloods, and 90,000 half-castes.

Jan. Bushfires at Lara, near Geelong, Vic., claim 18 lives.
Cannons from James Cook's ship the *Endeavour* discovered in northern Qld waters.
7 Feb. Sydney–Melbourne express train *Southern Aurora* collides with goods train at Violet Town, Vic., claiming nine lives.
8 Feb. Cessna crashes at Kyancutta, SA, claiming six lives.
May–Jun. Floods at Launceston, Tas.
May. Conservationists begin successful campaign to save the Little Desert in north-west Vic. from development.
3 Jun. HMAS *Melbourne* collides with and sinks USA destroyer *Frank E. Evans*, claiming 74 lives.
17 Jul. Cessna crashes at Mt Buangor, Vic., claiming five lives.
25 Aug. Freighter *Noongah* sinks off NSW coast, claiming 21 lives.
12 Nov. *Canberra News* newspaper first published.
22 Dec. Cessna crashes at Gove, NT, claiming five lives.
During Dec. Bushfires damage western NSW.
During 1969
First Aust. Red Barn food dispensary estb. There are *c.* 3,468 take-away food outlets in Aust.
Desert Flame opal discovered at Andamooka, SA.
Vic. police corruption racket exposes high ranking police officers. (Found guilty 9 Apr. 1971.)
Silver 50 cent piece replaced by the 12 sided nickel piece because of high price of silver.
Cwlth Govt estb. Drought Bond Scheme to assist primary producers in droughts.
Widespread drought effects WA, NT and Qld. (Ends 1970.)
National road toll 3,502.

Communities

Karratha, WA, estb.
Moranbah, Qld, estb.
Strathgordon, Tas., estb.

A

History, Politics, Economics, Law

1970

Government

2 Jun. 1970–Feb. 1979, D. A. Dunstan Labor Premier SA.

1970–1973, F. C. Chaney Administrator NT under Cwlth jurisdiction.

5 Mar. Nuclear Non-Proliferation Treaty in force.

30 Mar. Royal visit begins.

21 Apr. Leonard George Casley, WA farmer, declares his property a Sovereign State, Hutt River Province.

During Apr. The Continental Shelf (Living Natural Resources) Act 1968 comes into force. Implements Aust. sovereignty over living resources of the continental shelf.

During May. Labor wins SA elections. Becomes only State Labor Govt in office at this time.

4 Aug. Sir Harry Talbot Gibbs appointed a Justice of High Court of Aust. (Until 1981.)

16 Oct. Four weeks' annual leave granted to oil industry employees.

During Oct. Aust. wool prices drop to lowest for 20 years. Cwlth Govt estb. the Aust. Wool Commission in Oct. and introduces a flexible reserve price scheme for wool sold at auction in NSW.

Nov. Department of External Affairs becomes Department of Foreign Affairs.

Dec. Cwlth Govt announces intention to buy all freehold land within the ACT.

Vic. Govt assents to the Environment Protection Act, providing for estb. of an environment protection authority.

During 1970

Metric Conversion Board estb. to change imperial system of weights and measures to metric.

Aust. enters into formal bilateral assisted-passage agreement with Malta and Yugoslavia.

NSW, SA and WA reduce voting age to 18 years.

SA first State to legalize abortion in certain circumstances.

Exclusive land leasing rights for specific purposes, covering 250,000 sq km of NT Aboriginal reserves, given to Aborigines.

Health Insurance Scheme based on the common fee concept introduced.

Mt Isa Mines Holdings Ltd estb. to co-ordinate interests of a group of companies.

Production quotas on Aust. wheat imposed to cope with slump in world prices.

Vietnam War

28 Feb. Nine Australians killed and twenty-nine wounded in incidents in the Long Hai hills.

8 May. Vietnam Moratorium Day. Thousands march in all State capitals to protest against Aust. participation in Vietnam War. (70,000 led by Jim Cairns march in Melbourne.)

4 Sep. Federal Govt prevents US comedian Dick Gregory from visiting Aust. to speak in Vietnam Moratorium campaigns.

Nov. Prime Minister Gorton announces reduction of Aust. forces in Vietnam by one battalion.

1970

B
Science, Technology, Transport, Discovery

Feb. Tullamarine Freeway from Melbourne to Tullamarine Airport opens. Airport officially open in Jul.
Mar. Indian-Pacific standard-gauge railway service from Sydney to Perth opens. Includes world's longest stretch of straight track, 478 km.
3 May. International terminal at Kingsford Smith Airport in Sydney opens.
Jun. The Snowy Mountains Engineering Corporation estb. to replace the Snowy Mountains Authority.
Microwave trunk system linking WA with eastern states by STD opens.
Discovery of Ranger uranium deposits near Nabarlek, east of Darwin, announced. Koongarra deposits also revealed 1970 and Jabiluka 1971.
Aug. Vera Ramaciotti estb. Clive and Vera Ramaciotti Foundation for medical education and research.
Oct. First Boeing 747 (Jumbo) aircraft to arrive in Aust. lands in Sydney. (Maiden flight on 16 Aug. 1971.)

During 1970
Cwlth Govt investigates Crown of Thorn starfish on Great Barrier Reef.
Ralph Sarich begins developing his orbital engine in Perth.
David Henshaw's Repco self-twist yarn spinning machine influences world textile industry; wins Prince Philip prize for industrial design.
World's first laser beam lighthouse operates, from Point Danger, NSW.
Bill Kerruish develops CSIRO tree harvester.
National Botanic Gardens of Aust. open in Canberra.
Sir Bernard Katz shares Nobel Prize for physiology and medicine.
Iron ore discovered at Dampier, WA.
Natural gas discovered at Palm Valley, NT.
Hospital and Allied Services Advisory Council estb.
Gippsland, Vic., Bass Strait oil and gas fields begin commercial production.

C
Arts

Literature

During 1970
Dal Stivens publishes *A Horse of Air*.
Kathleen Walker publishes collection of verse, *My People*.
A. D. Hope publishes *Dunciad Minor* (verse) and *A Midsummer Eve's Dream* (criticism).
Germaine Greer publishes *The Female Eunuch*.
Humphrey McQueen publishes *A New Britannia*.

Music, Dance

11 Jun. Bolshoi Ballet visits Aust.
During 1970
The Elizabethan Trust Opera Co. officially becomes The Australian Opera.
Marilyn Rowe becomes Principal of Aust. Ballet.
Rolf Harris' version of song 'Two Little Boys' becomes record-breaking selling song in Aust.
Peggy Glanville Hicks' opera *The Transposed Head* staged.
Peter Sculthorpe composes *Music for Japan*.
Canberra Carillon opens.
Ezra Rachlin appointed conductor of Qld Symphony Orchestra. (Until 1972.)
Liv Maesson's song, 'Knock Knock Who's There' popular.
Eva Segal estb. the Kolobok folkloric Dance Co. in Melbourne.
Qld Opera Co. estb.

Drama, Theatre, Film

During 1970
Aust. Film Development Corporation estb. to encourage locally made feature films.
Film censorship restrictions eased.
Michael Boddy and Bob Ellis produce play *The Legend of King O'Malley*.
John Anthony Bell and Ken Horler found Nimrod Street Theatre.
Films *The Naked Bunyip* and *Ned Kelly* released.
The Hoopla Theatre Foundation estb. in Melbourne.
Aust. Performing Group estb. at Melbourne Pram Factory.
Three to Go: Michael wins Best Film of the Year award.

Fine Arts

During 1970
Eric Smith wins Archibald Prize for *Neville Gruzman*.

Conceptual and lyrical abstraction art influential.
Robin Boyd designs displays at *Expo* in Japan.

Architecture

During 1970
John Andrews' King George Tower in Sydney built.

D
Religion, Learning

Jan. Federal Secondary Scholarship Scheme estb. for Aborigines beyond school leaving age.
20 Apr. James Cook University of N. Qld separates from University of Qld.
Jul. Radford Report on Qld education recommends abolition of external exams.
Nov. Bishop Gibran Ramlaoui arrives in Aust. as first Orthodox Lebanese Hierarch.
1 Dec. National Union of Aust. Students becomes Aust. Union of Students.
20 Dec. First Romanian Orthodox parishes estb. in Melbourne.
During Dec. Pope Paul VI visits Sydney. First papal visit.
During 1970
Darwin Museum and Art Gallery opens.
Cardinal Sir Norman Gilroy wins Australian of the Year award.
WA abolishes assessment of primary teachers by inspectors. (Vic. 1972, NSW 1973.)
WA Board of Secondary Education estb.
Elizabeth Matriculation College estb. in Hobart.
Karmel Report of the Committee of Inquiry into SA education recommends development of equal opportunity in education.
Goulburn Teachers' College NSW estb. (Becomes Goulburn College of Advanced Education in 1973.)
Mount Lawley Teachers' College estb. in Perth. (Becomes College of Advanced Education in 1973.)
Mitchell College of Advanced Education estb. at Bathurst, NSW.
ACTU appoints education officer.
Number of small 'alternative' schools begins to grow.

1970

E
Sport

Jan. A 14,000-mile England to Aust. air race finishes at Bankstown, NSW. (Began on 18 Dec. 1969.)
18 Apr. VFL Park football ground opens in Melbourne.
During 1970
Baghdad Note, ridden by E. Didham, wins Melbourne Cup in 3 minutes 19.7 seconds.
Carlton football team wins VFL Premiership in Melbourne in front of record crowd of 121,696.
South Sydney football team wins Rugby League Premiership in Sydney.
Peter Bedford of South Melbourne VFL team awarded Brownlow Medal.
Margaret Court is ABC Sportswoman of the Year. Becomes second woman ever to win Grand Slam women's tennis singles.
Evonne Goolagong plays first tennis overseas.
Aust. Axemen's Association estb.
Bill Youd sets world record for woodchopping.
Harry Williams becomes first Aboriginal to play soccer for Aust.
Horace Lindrum becomes first snooker player in world to make 1,000 snooker centuries.
Susan Martin sets world out-and-return gliding record.
First Aust. Bocce championship held in Melbourne.
Pedro Sidoti brings bullfighting to Aust. at Bowen Mt, near Richmond, NSW.
Orienteering Federation of Aust. estb.
Judy Trim becomes first Aust. world pistol-shooting champion.
Hans Tholstrup sets around-Aust. power boat record of 76 days. Becomes first man to circumnavigate Aust. or any continent in open runabout.
Pacha wins Sydney to Hobart yacht race.
Gretel II challenges for America's Cup. (America wins 4–1.)
Cwlth Games held in Edinburgh, Scotland.

F
Historia Dignum

Population
Estimated total white, 12,663,469.

17–18 Jan. Cyclone Ada on Qld coast claims 13 lives.
During Jan. Wrecked ship discovered off WA coast found to be the *Tryal*, which ran aground in 1622. (Earliest recorded wreck on Aust. coast.)
Feb. Oil rig boat *Sedco Helen* sinks in Joseph Bonaparte Gulf, 150 miles west of Darwin, claiming nine lives.
15 Oct. Westgate Bridge collapses in Melbourne, claiming 35 lives.
26 Oct. First padded post bags released for sale.
28 Oct. Train collision at Heathcote, NSW, claims three lives.
Dec. Floods damage Vic., NSW and Qld coasts.
During 1970
Bob Dyer's television show *Pick a Box* becomes longest running peak-hour programme.
National Parks Wildlife Foundation NSW estb. to provide additional finance for purchase of lands for National Parks.
Eating out becomes popular. Restaurant business booms.
Watermelon seed spitting competition held in Sydney
Aust. celebrates two-hundredth anniversary of James Cook's arrival at Botany Bay.
R. F. Henderson Poverty Report published.
Priority-paid mail service between capital cities introduced.
National road toll 3,798.

Communities
Paraburdoo, WA, planned.

A
History, Politics, Economics, Law

1971

Government

3 Mar. 1971–Apr. 1974, J. T. Tonkin Labor Premier WA.

10 Mar. 1971–5 Dec. 1972, Fortieth Cwlth Ministry, William McMahon Liberal-Country coalition Prime Minister Aust.

15 Sep. 1971–1 Dec. 1971, Sir John Mellis Napier administered SA.

1 Dec. 1971–30 Nov. 1976, Sir Mark (Marcus Laurence Elwin) Oliphant Governor SA.

Jan. Ownership of reserves at Lake Tyers and Framlingham granted to Vic. Aborigines.

Cwlth Govt announces that Aust. is to sign UNO Treaty banning use of nuclear weapons under the sea.

2 Feb. John Douglas Anthony appointed Leader of Federal Country Party, replacing Sir John McEwen. Transforms Country Party from farmers' party to a more broadly based national party.

5 Feb. Mineral Securities of Aust. crashes, marking end of mining share boom.

During Feb. Trade union ban on export of merino rams broken by a charter aircraft using RAAF facilities.

17 Mar.–3 Apr. Prince Philip visits Aust.

During Mar. Dame Annabelle Rankin appointed High Commissioner to NZ. First Aust. woman High Commissioner.

Apr. Programme announced for internal self-govt for PNG over period 1972–1976.

The Yirrkala Aborigines legal challenge for land rights at Gove dismissed. Aboriginal land titles in NT ruled invalid by NT Supreme Court.

Senate Select Committee's Reports on Health and Welfare and Drug Trafficking and Drug Abuse tabled.

May. Neville Bonner becomes first Aboriginal to enter Federal Parlt. Becomes Qld Senator.

New Cwlth Departments of the Environment, Aborigines and Arts estb.

Jun. ALP delegation led by Gough Whitlam visits People's Republic of China.

Jul. State of Emergency declared in Qld over anti-apartheid demonstrations against visiting South African Springbok Rugby League team.

During 1971

Five-Power Defence Agreement signed between Aust., NZ, Singapore, Malaysia and Britain.

Socialist Party of Aust. forms from Pro-Soviet Communist Party splinter group.

First Aust. Ombudsman created in WA. (SA 1972, Vic. 1973, NSW 1974, Qld 1977.)

SA reduces age of adulthood to 18.

Aust. joins Organization for Economic Co-operation and Development (OECD) to promote international co-operation in cultural, technical and scientific fields.

First Aust. wool sale held in Canberra, where buyers see only sample core tests.

Aust. Industry Development Corporation (AIDC) replaces Tariff Board. (Operative in Dec. 1973.)

NSW Aboriginal Legal Service estb.

Vietnam War

18 Aug. Prime Minister William McMahon announces that Aust. forces would be withdrawn from Vietnam, marking the beginning of the end of combat role.

During Aug. National Service reduced from two years to eighteen months.

Sep. HMAS *Brisbane*, last Aust. warship assigned to the US Seventh Fleet, returns to Aust.

Nov. Operational role of Aust. Task Force ends.

1971

B
Science, Technology, Transport, Discovery

Feb. Largest ship in Aust. to that date, *Amanda Miller*, 62,000-tonne tanker, launched.
Mar. ANU begins installing a unique tandem accelerator with guaranteed terminal of 14 million volts.
Report tabled in Cwlth Parlt indicates that Crown of Thorns starfish does not constitute a threat to the Great Barrier Reef, Qld. Further research promised.
Jun. Construction of underground railway in Melbourne begins.
Nov. *The Prospector* train begins running between Perth and Kalgoorlie, WA.
During 1971
Large deposits of natural gas discovered on North-West Shelf, 1,200 km north of Perth.
Burt Terry invents row car for handicapped children.
Ralph Sarich completes first prototype two-stroke orbital internal combustion engine.
Woodside Petroleum Ltd (so named in 1977) incorporated as Norlen Explorations.
Howard Florey Institute of Experimental Physiology estb. in Melbourne.
Scheelite mining on King I. in Bass Strait begins.

C
Arts

Literature

During 1971
James McAuley publishes *Collected Poems 1936–1970*.
Bruce Dawe publishes *Condolences of the Season*.
Thomas Keneally publishes *A Dutiful Daughter*.
Judith Wright publishes *Collected Poems 1942–1970*.
Angus & Robertson, booksellers, fined for selling Phillip Roth's *Portnoy's Complaint*.
Dymphna Cusack publishes *A Bough in Hell*.
Hal Porter publishes *The Right Thing*.

Music, Dance

3 May. The Sydney Festival Ballet estb.
Jul. First Cwlth Govt fellowships for Aust. composers awarded.
During 1971
Melbourne Ballet Guild becomes Vic. Ballet. Among first regional ballet companies in Aust.
Lucette Aldous becomes senior ballerina with Aust. Ballet Co.
Reginald Lindsay, country folk singer, popular.
Tibor Paul appointed conductor of WA Symphony Orchestra, (Until 1973.) Thomas Mayer appointed conductor Tas. Symphony Orchestra. (Until 1973.)
Johnny Young estb. *Young Talent Time* television show.
Qld Modern and Contemporary Dance Co. estb.

Drama, Theatre, Film

Mar. Aust. Film Development Corporation operative.
Nov. New film censorship certification operative. R film certificate becomes legally enforceable.
27 Dec. Tim Burstall produces film *Stork*.
During 1971
Film *Wake in Fright* released.
David Williamson finishes writing play *Don's Party*.
Homesdale wins Best Film of the Year award.

Fine Arts

During 1971
Clifton Pugh wins Archibald Prize for *Sir John McEwen*.
James Mollison appointed Director of Aust. National Gallery.
McClelland Gallery, near Frankston, Vic., completed.

D
Religion, Learning

Jul. Social Science Research Council of Aust. becomes Academy of the Social Sciences in Aust.
Dec. Aust. Commission on Advanced Education estb. Cwlth Govt announces expenditure of $30 million during next 18 months as emergency grants for non-Government schools.
During 1971
Public Library of Qld becomes State Library of Qld.
The Aust. Council on Awards in Advanced Education estb.
Tas. becomes first State to include drama as subject in secondary school syllabus.
Education Reform Association organizes the progressive school era in Vic.
Tas. Govt estb. TANSET, State-wide computerized network for educational use.

E
Sport

Apr. Aust. table tennis team visits mainland China.
5 May. First registered Sunday trotting meetings in Canberra.
During May. Greyhound racing begins in SA.
Jun. Springbok Rugby team begins Aust. tour. Anti-apartheid demonstrations in all centres where matches played.
Sep. South African cricket tour of Aust. cancelled.
During 1971
Silver Knight, ridden by R. Marsh, wins Melbourne Cup in 3 minutes 19.5 seconds.
Hawthorn football team wins VFL Premiership in Melbourne.
South Sydney football team wins Rugby League Premiership in Sydney.
Ian Stewart of Richmond VFL team awarded Brownlow Medal.
Evonne Cawley (Goolagong) wins Australian of the Year award; wins French open singles tennis championship.
Shane Gould is ABC Sportswoman of the Year.
Wayne Jones becomes first Aust. to water ski over 100 mph (161 kmh).
Orienteering and hang gliding popular.
Bill Moyes breaks world kite flight altitude record, 1447.8 metres, in NZ.
Pathfinder wins Sydney to Hobart yacht race.

1971

1971

F
Historia Dignum

Population

Estimated total white 13,198,400.
Cwlth census calculate total Aust. population at 12,755,638, including Aborigines.
Census first to include Aboriginal population (115,953). Aust. population is 85 per cent urban and 15 per cent rural.

Jan. Vic. introduces compulsory wearing of seatbelts in cars.
7 Feb. *National Times* newspaper first published weekly.
28 Feb. *Sunday Australian* newspaper first published.
Mar. Torrential rains break drought in south-west Qld and north-east SA.
May. Cigarette advertisements banned from radio and commercial television during children's peak viewing times.
Qantas pays bomb-hoaxer half a million dollars.
13 Jun. World's only known certain nonuplets born in Sydney.
Nov. Late-night shopping introduced in Vic. and NSW.
Green ban imposed by NSW Builders' Labourers Federation to prevent commercial development of the Rocks area in Sydney.
24 Dec. Cyclone Althea devastates Townsville, Qld.
During 1971
Population of WA reaches 1,000,000.
Daylight Saving introduced to all States except WA and NT.
'Hot pants' popular in fashion.
Aboriginal magazine *Identity* first published.
Pizza Hut, Wimpy Hamburger and McDonald's Burger Huts first appear.
Jeans become uniform of the young.
Nationwide rubella (German measles) immunization campaign begins.
The Lake Pedder Action Committee in Tas. attempts to stop flooding of Lake Pedder as part of the Gordon R Power Development Scheme. (Flooding begins in 1972.)
National road toll 3,590.

Communities

Shay Gap, WA, estb.
Wickham, WA, estb.

A

History, Politics, Economics, Law

1972

Government

21 Mar. 1972–20 Mar. 1977, Sir Colin Hannah Governor Qld.
3 May 1972–Mar. 1975 E. E. Reece Labor Premier Tas.
23 Aug. 1972–1981, R. J. Hamer Liberal Premier Vic.
5 Dec. 1972–19 Dec. 1972, Forty-first Cwlth Ministry, Edward Gough Whitlam Labor Prime Minister Aust.
19 Dec. 1972–11 Nov. 1975, Forty-second Cwlth Ministry, Edward Gough Whitlam Labor Prime Minister Aust.

Jan. Female employees (about 1,300,000) become entitled to equal pay.
Amalgamated Metal Workers' Union estb. from merging of three unions. Appeals to Arbitration Commission against merger rejected.
Feb. Aust. and Japan sign Nuclear Co-operation Treaty.
1 Mar. Sir Ninian Stephen (until 1982) and Sir Anthony Mason appointed Justices of High Court of Aust.
28 Mar. Liberal Movement political party estb. in SA.
Apr. Cwlth and States recommend that a judicial inquiry be held into operations of organizations which store information about people.
12 May. Women's Electoral Lobby, feminist non-party political group, forms in Melbourne.
During May. Cwlth Govt protests against continued French nuclear testing in the Pacific. ACTU black bans French shipping and aircraft in Aust.
Jun. Sir Douglas Ralph Nicholls becomes first Aboriginal to be knighted.
Oil industry maintenance workers dispute over log-of-claims lead to series of nationwide stoppages and a petrol and oil crisis. (Settled in Aug.)
Jul. Cwlth Govt removes makeshift 'Aboriginal Embassy' on grounds of Parlt House. Embassy estb. in Jan. to demonstrate for land rights.
Aug. Sir Henry Bolte retires from Vic. politics.
Oct. Aust. Wool Board and Wool Commission amalgamate to form Aust. Wool Corporation.
Indonesia signs Agreement fixing seabed boundary between Aust. and Indonesian Timor.
2 Dec. E. G. Whitlam elected Labor Prime Minister at National elections. First Labor victory for 23 years. Billy Mackie Snedden Liberal Opposition Leader. (Until 1975.)
22 Dec. Aust. estb. diplomatic relations with People's Republic of China and German Democratic Republic. Aust. envoy to Taiwan recalled.
27 Dec. Cwlth Govt ends all foreign aid to South Vietnam, withdraws last Aust. troops, ends call up of National Servicemen and releases National Service Act offenders. Of 63,740 conscripted 15,542 served in Vietnam, *c.* 423 killed and 2,398 wounded. (Of those serving, 43 per cent were National Servicemen.)
During Dec. Ministry for Aboriginal Affairs operative.
Justice A. E. Woodward appointed Commissioner to conduct judicial inquiry into the legal recognition of Aboriginal rights to land.
Elizabeth Evatt becomes first woman Presidential Member of the Conciliation and Arbitration Commission.

During 1972
Cwlth Govt protests against continued US bombing of North Vietnam.
Federal Labor Govt ends Imperial Honours List.
Arbitration reforms separate Arbitration and Conciliation Commissioners' functions and enable secret ballots to be used at strikes.
Japan replaces Europe as major buyer of Aust. wool and wheat.
South Pacific Forum estb.
Aust. dollar appreciated 7.05 per cent.
Foreign Takeovers Act empowers the Government to freeze takeovers of Aust. companies by foreign corporations.
David Lewis undertakes first solo voyage to Aust. Antarctica, in *Ice Bird*.
NSW Bureau of Crime Statistics and Research estb.

1972

B
Science, Technology, Transport, Discovery

Feb. Qantas introduces cheap excursion flights to Europe.
May. Aust. radio astronomers discover large cloud of organic molecules near centre of our galaxy, 30,000 light years from Earth.
30 Jun. Ord R. Dam, WA, officially opened.
During Jun. Aust. Institute of Marine Science estb. in Townsville, Qld.
Sep. Celsius temperature scale replaces Fahrenheit.
During 1972
Radiophysics Division of CSIRO invents Interscan aviation system enabling aircraft to approach runway at steeper angle. (Adopted for world-wide use in Apr. 1978.)
Yeelirrie uranium deposits discovered near Wiluna, WA.
Lincoln Institute of Health Sciences estb. in Melbourne.

C
Arts

Literature

During 1972
David Malouf publishes *Johnno*.
Michael Wilding publishes collection of stories, *Aspects of the Dying Process*.
T. M. Keneally publishes *The Chant of Jimmy Blacksmith*.
Kathleen Walker publishes *Stradbroke Dreamtime*.
Frank Moorhouse publishes *The Americans' Baby*.

Music, Dance

Jan. Sunbury Pop Festival held.
4 May. Rock opera *Jesus Christ Superstar* opens in Sydney.
During 1972
George Dreyfus' opera *Garni Sands* performed by University of NSW Opera. First full-length Australian opera performed for more than half a century.
Little Pattie promotes the stomp dance.
North Qld Conservatorium of music opens at Innisfail.
Richard Clapton, guitarist, song writer, is popular.
Netherlands Dance Theatre Dancing Co. visits Aust.
Helen Reddy records song 'I am a Woman'.
Perth Concert Hall opens.

Drama, Theatre, Film

23 Mar. Brian Kavanagh's film *A City's Child* released.
27 Oct. National Black Theatre premières in Sydney with *Basically Black*.
During 1972
David Williamson writes play *The Removalists*. His play *Don's Party* is staged in Sydney.
Colin Sandergrove Ballantyne estb. SA Theatre Co.
Bruce Beresford's film *The Adventures of Barry McKenzie* released.
Jim Sharman's film *Shirley Thompson Versus the Aliens* released.
La Boite Theatre opens in Brisbane.
Stork wins Best Film of the Year award.

Fine Arts

During 1972
Clifton Pugh wins Archibald Prize for *E. G. Whitlam*

D
Religion, Learning

Jan. Eric Liao estb. the Chinese Buddhist Society of Aust.
Feb. Senate Report on Education, Science and Arts, relating to Cwlth role in Teacher Education, tabled.
Apr. *The Little Red School Book* first published in Aust.
12 Jul. Creation of Darwin Community College approved.
Aug. Cwlth Govt announces large increase of expenditure on universities and colleges of advanced education.
Dec. Cwlth Govt appoints Peter Karmel Chairman of an Interim Committee for Aust. Schools Commission.
Last Qld Senior School exams held. Senior grades hereafter organized into four semesters.

During 1972
Aust. Film and Television School estb. in Sydney.
The Vic. College of Arts estb. in Melbourne.
State College of Vic. (Rusden) estb.
Churchlands Teachers' College (later College of Advanced Education) estb. near Perth.
Riverina College of Advanced Education opens in Wagga Wagga, NSW.
Newman College of Advanced Education estb. in Launceston, Tas.
Aust. Council of Churches and Roman Catholic Church jointly sponsor 'Action for World Development' to study world poverty.

E
Sport

Feb. Aust. high altitude and free fall record of 32,250 feet estb. in Vic.
6 Apr. Night greyhound racing begins in Brisbane.
During 1972
Melbourne Cup becomes metric and is run over 3,200 metres.
Piping Lane, ridden by J. Letts, wins Melbourne Cup in 3 minutes 19.3 seconds.
Carlton football team wins VFL Premiership in Melbourne.
Manly-Warringah football team wins Rugby League Premiership in Sydney.
Len Thompson of Collingwood VFL team awarded Brownlow Medal.
Shane Gould wins Australian of the Year award. Elected ABC Sportswoman of the Year. Is only woman ever to hold all world freestyle records simultaneously.
Aust. wins eight gold, seven silver and two bronze medals at Munich Olympics.
South African sporting tours banned.
Joe Meissner first non-Japanese to win world Karate championship.
Martial arts become popular.
Sinclair Hill first Aust. to reach top world polo rating of 10 goals.
Brian Morrison shears 410 sheep in 8 hours, breaking record.
Bocce Federation of Aust. estb.
Rod Dominish becomes first Aust. to complete world orienteering competitions.
Eddie Palubinskas becomes first Aust. world-class basketballer.
American Eagle wins Sydney to Hobart yacht race.

1972

Historia Dignum

Population

Estimated total Aust., 13,409,400.

20 Jan. Beech aircraft crashes at Alice Springs, claiming seven lives.

Feb. Serious floods in Melbourne.

Mar. Total Environment Centre in Sydney becomes first full-time environment centre in Aust.

2 Apr. Cessna aircraft crashes at Wilcurra homestead, NSW, claiming six lives.

13 Jul. Piper Navajo aircraft crashes in Adelaide, claiming eight lives.

31 Jul. Underground mining explosion at Box Flat, Qld, claims 17 lives.

16 Sep. Fifteen hurt in two Sydney bomb blasts attributed to Croatian extremists.

Nov. Outbreak of cholera occurs among airline passengers arriving from overseas.

Nov. *Cleo*, women's magazine, first published.

Dec. Bushfires at Mt Kosciusko National Park. Tas bushfires burn 140,900 hectares.

Cwlth Govt estb. Dept of the Media.

During 1972

Wearing of seatbelts in cars compulsory throughout Aust.

Rothmans uses Paul Hogan to promote cigarettes.

First Balloon Festival in Aust. held, at Berwick, Vic.

McDonald Hamburger Co. takes over Red Barn.

About one-third of Aust. affected by drought.

Aborigines Harold Thomas and Gary Foley design Aboriginal flag.

Marine Operations Centre estb. in Canberra to co-ordinate marine search and rescue.

A boulder opal weighing almost 16 kg discovered near Quilpie, Qld.

National road toll 3,422.

Communities

Nhulumbuy, NT, estb.

A

History, Politics, Economics, Law

1973

Government

28 Aug. 1973–7 Jan. 1974, Sir Albert Asher Wolff administered WA.
30 Nov. 1973–4 Dec. 1973, Guy Stephen Montague Green administered Tas.
5 Dec. 1973–1982, Sir Stanley Charles Burbury Governor Tas.
1973, T. A. O'Brien Acting Administrator NT under Cwlth Administration.
1973–1975, J. N. Nelson Administrator NT under Cwlth Administration.

Jan. Cwlth Govt grants an extra week's annual leave to 250,000 Cwlth public servants.
Aust. agrees to ratify Nuclear Non-proliferation Treaty and the Seabed Arms Control Treaty.
27 Feb. Twenty-eighth Federal Parlt opens. (Dissolution 11 Apr. 1974.)
28 Feb. Voting age for Federal elections lowered to 18 years. Qld and Vic. lower voting age for State elections in Mar.
During Feb. Environment impact statement becomes compulsory for all development projects having significant environmental consequences where Aust. Govt funds and/or Federal constitutional power is involved.
Britain enters EEC, ending preferential tariff arrangements with Aust.
16 Mar. Without Govt knowledge, Cwlth Attorney-General Lionel Murphy uses Cwlth police to take over ASIO headquarters in Melbourne to search for information on Croation terrorist activities in Aust.
During Mar. Aust. ratifies ILO Conventions, Freedom of Association and Rights to Organize Collective Bargaining.
Export ban on kangaroo products effective.
18 May. Ford employees in Melbourne begin violent strike for higher wages and more holiday pay.
During May. Aust.-wide ban placed on French goods, ships, aircraft and communications in response to forthcoming French nuclear tests in Pacific. Following application by Aust., International Court of Justice orders France to halt nuclear tests in atmosphere over Pacific Ocean in Jun. HMAS *Supply* enters French nuclear zone as last resort gesture against French nuclear tests. (Withdrawn in Aug.)
Minimum wage increased by $9 per week.
Jun. Cwlth Govt grants women employees in Aust. public service 12 weeks' maternity leave on full pay. Male employees eligible for one week's leave on full pay at time of birth of child.
Federal Govt Prices Justification Tribunal empowered to order cuts as well as rule against price rises.

8 Jul. Bob Hawke becomes president of the Aust. Labor Party. (Until Jul. 1978.)
18 Jul. Cwlth Govt cuts all tariffs by 25 per cent. Announces assistance for firms affected by tariff cuts.
During Jul. Cwlth Govt introduces the Supporting Mothers Benefit.
Three-year Trade Agreement between Aust. and People's Republic of China signed.
Elizabeth Reid appointed adviser to the Govt on women's affairs. First such position in world.
Sep. Cwlth and State leaders meet in Sydney for first national constitution convention since Federation.
Death Penalty abolished in ACT and NT.
Aust. dollar appreciated by 5 per cent as anti-inflation measure.
17–22 Oct. Queen Elizabeth and Prince Philip visit Aust.
During Oct. Albury–Wodonga Development Agreement signed.
$50 banknote released.
1 Dec. PNG attains self-government.
8 Dec. Referendums to empower Federal Govt to control prices and incomes rejected.
During Dec. Departments of Navy, Army and Air abolished and amalgamated into Dept of Defence.
During 1973
Aust. Workers' Party estb.
Law Reform Commission estb.
Francis James, journalist, released after three years in Chinese prison.
National Aboriginal Consultative Committee (NACC) and Aboriginal Land Rights Commission estb.
Vic. Govt adopts decentralization of industry policy.
The Aust. Institute of Criminology and the Criminology Research Council estb.
Cwlth Dept of Environment estb.
Cwlth Govt appoints Social Welfare Commission to advise on expansion of welfare policy.

1973

B

Science, Technology, Transport, Discovery

1 Jul. The NSW College of Paramedical Studies estb. (Becomes Cumberland College of Health Sciences in 1975.)
Aug. Aust.–China satellite telecommunications system operative.
During 1973
Department of Transport estb. Absorbs Civil Aviation, Shipping and Transport Departments.
Peter Whiteside invents compostumbler compost maker.
International Astronomical Union holds triennial Assembly in Sydney. First time in southern hemisphere.
Mike Debenham invents Presto can and push-button can.
Paddle-boat *The Murray River Queen* launched at Goolwa, SA.
Federal Govt estb. Ministry of Science.

C

Arts

Literature

26 Jan. Cwlth Literary Fund estb. Replaced by the Literature Board of the Aust. Council in Mar.
Aug. The Literature Board of the Aust. Council for the Arts introduces guaranteed income for selected Aust. writers.
During 1973
Patrick White awarded Nobel Prize for Literature and wins Australian of the Year award. Publishes *Eye of the Storm*.
Dick Roughsey publishes *The Giant Devil-Dingo*.

Music, Dance

Feb. Rolling Stones pop group tours Aust.
15 Jul. Leningrad Kirov Ballet begins Aust. tour in Sydney.
Jul. Marilyn Rowe and Kevin Coe win silver medals at International Ballet Competition in Moscow.
20 Oct. Sydney Opera House officially opens.
During 1973
NSW Conservatorium of Music estb. jazz courses to promote development of jazz in Aust.
Skyhooks pop group estb.
Willem van Otterloo appointed conductor Sydney Symphony Orchestra. (Until 1978.) Patrick Thomas appointed conductor Qld Symphony Orchestra. (Until 1977.)
Aust. Country Music Awards inaugurated in Tamworth, NSW. First country music festival held.

Drama, Theatre, Film

Jan. The Aust. Film and Television School opens in Sydney.
Feb. The Tas. Theatre Co. estb. formally.
2 Jun. Festival Theatre opens in Adelaide.
During 1973
ABC produces *Seven Little Australians*.
Bruce Beresford's films *Alvin Purple* and *Libido* released.
Film Radio and Television Board estb.
Tim Burstall's film *Libido: The Child* wins Best Film of the Year award.

Fine Arts

May. Aboriginal Arts Board estb.
During 1973
Janet Dawson wins Archibald Prize for *Michael Boddy*

Aust. pays $1.3 million for Jackson Pollock's *Blue Poles*.
Evenstructure Sculpture Research Group active.

Architecture

During 1973
Federal Govt estb. Department of Urban and Regional Development (DURD).

D

Religion, Learning

1973

Feb. The Fortieth International Eucharistic Congress held in Melbourne.
19 Mar. The College of Aboriginal Education estb. in Adelaide. (Becomes the Aboriginal Community College in 1975.)
During Mar. University fees abolished from 1 Jan. 1974.
May. Peter Karmel submits report of Interim Committee for Aust. Schools Commission recommending programme for Cwlth expenditure on education.
Jun. Aust. Festival of Light formally launched.
Nov. Interim Committee for Pre-School Commission recommends one year of sessional pre-school education for children before starting school.
Dec. Cwlth Govt passes legislation granting $700 million in aid to Govt and non-Govt schools over next 2 years.
During 1973
Aust. School of Pacific Administration becomes International Training Institute, providing courses for students from developing countries.
External examinations at end of Year 10 in NSW end.
There are about 240 Brethren assemblies or congregations in Aust.
The Northern Rivers College of Advanced Education estb. in NSW.
Orange Agricultural College opens in NSW.
Melbourne State College estb.
The Nepean College of Advanced Education estb.
The Serbian Orthodox Diocese of Aust. estb.
Phillip Hughes submits report recommending re-organization of education in ACT.

1973

E Sport

During 1973
Gala Supreme, ridden by F. Reys, wins Melbourne Cup in 3 minutes 19.5 seconds.
Richmond football team wins VFL Premiership in Melbourne.
Manly–Warringah football team wins Rugby League Premiership in Sydney.
Keith Greig of North Melbourne VFL team awarded Brownlow Medal.
Stephen Holland is ABC Sportsman of the Year.
Margaret Court wins her fifth US tennis singles championship.
Heather McKay wins her fourteenth Aust. women's squash title.
George Perdon runs from Fremantle to Sydney in 47 days.
First NSW air race held.
Ceil III wins Sydney to Hobart yacht race.

F Historia Dignum

Population
Estimated total Aust., 13,614,300.

8 Mar. Fire destroys 'Whiskey a Go Go' night club in Brisbane, claiming 15 lives.
May. Women's magazine *Cosmopolitan* first published.
Jun. A Federal Committee of Inquiry into Lake Pedder, Tas., recommends a moratorium on further flooding.
Jul. Melba Community Health Centre opens in Canberra.
Sep. Bus disaster near Cabramurra, NSW, claims 18 lives.
1 Oct. Postal service first uses metric weights and measures.
13 Oct. Ship *Blythe Star* wrecked off Tas. coast, claiming three lives.
During Oct. Non-union demolitionists unsuccessfully attempt to begin work on development of the Rocks area in Sydney. (Green ban lifted after residents and authorities reach compromise on development.)
4 Nov. Tornado damages Brisbane.
17–21 Nov. Cyclone Innes damages Bonaparte Gulf, WA.

During 1973
Wrest Point Hotel–Casino opens in Hobart. First legal casino in Aust.
Wine casks popular.
Institute of Ambulance Officers of Aust. estb.
Competition for Aust. National Anthem held.
Widespread floods throughout much of Aust.
National road toll 3,679.

Communities
Dysart, Qld, estb.

A
History, Politics, Economics, Law

1974

Government

7 Jan. 1974–3 Apr. 1975, Sir Hughie Idwal Edwards Governor WA.

8 Apr. 1974–Jan. 1982, Sir C. W. M. Court Liberal-Country (later Liberal-National Country) coalition Premier WA.

24 May 1974–2 Jun. 1974, Sir Henry Winneke administered Vic.

3 Jun. 1974–1 Mar. 1982, Sir Henry Winneke Governor Vic.

11 Jul. 1974–8 Dec. 1977, Sir John Robert Kerr Governor-General Aust.

Feb. Royal visit.

9 Mar. Country Party renamed National Country Party of Aust. On 6 Apr. the Qld Country Party renamed National Party of Aust., Qld.

14 Mar. Vincent Clair Gair appointed Aust. Ambassador to Irish Republic.

During Mar. First Aboriginal Special Magistrate sworn in Canberra's Supreme court. Given Jervis Bay, ACT, area of jurisdiction.

Ruth Dobson, first woman Ambassador, posted to Denmark.

4 Apr. Opposition announces intention to defer Supply. Following Senate's failure to pass a number of Bills, Governor-General proclaims simultaneous dissolution of Senate and House of Representatives on 11 Apr. under Section 57 of Constitution.

During Apr. Aust. Family Action Movement estb. as electoral arm of the Festival of Light.

Apr. The Aust. Legal Aid Office opens. (Legal Aid Commissions estb. in WA 1976, ACT and SA 1977, Qld 1978, NSW 1979, Vic. 1981.)

18 May. National elections see ALP returned to Govt with working majority, but without majority in Senate (ALP 29, Liberal-National Country 29, Independent 2.)

Referendums on simultaneous elections of both Houses of Parlt, direct access of local govt authorities to Loan Council and Cwlth grants, mode of altering Constitution, and equal electorates for Cwlth and State elections, all rejected.

During May. National Wage case increases minimum wage for adult male by $8 a week and extends minimum wage for females. To be phased in three steps so that all receive minimum wage by 30 Jun. 1975.

Jun. Cwlth Govt accepts major recommendations of Woodward Report on land rights for NT Aborigines. Report recommends that Aborigines should receive title to lands for social and economic regeneration.

9 Jul. Twenty-ninth Federal Parlt opens. (Dissolution 11 Nov. 1975.)

6–7 Aug. First joint sitting of National Parlt. Sitting first time as single legislature it approves legislation for electoral redistribution and also Health Insurance Bill.

1 Sep. Television and radio licence fees abolished.

28 Sep. NT and ACT estb. fully elected Legislative Assemblies. Allocated two places each in Senate.

1 Oct. Trade Practices Commission estb. to monitor misleading advertising.

14 Dec. Loans Affair begins when Executive Council authorizes Rex Connor, Minister for Minerals and Energy, to raise $4,000 million loan through Tirath Khemlani, a London based commodities broker.

During Dec. Jim Cairns strongly criticized for appointing Juni Morosi to his staff as office co-ordinator.

During 1974

National Employment and Training, (NEAT) Scheme to retrain workers introduced.

Langley George Hancock estb. WA Secessionist Movement to protect WA's economic and political interests.

Aust. dollar devalued by 13.6 per cent.

Gross value of wheat exceeds value of wool for first time.

Bankcard credit system introduced.

Sir Kenneth Jacobs appointed a Justice of High Court of Aust. (Until 1979.)

Aboriginal Land Fund Commission estb. to purchase land for Aboriginal groups.

Aboriginal Eric Deeral elected to Qld National Party seat of Cook.

A Floor Price, guaranteed minimum price for wool, introduced to protect wool growers.

Cambridge Credit Corp. Ltd falls into receivership.

Industrial Court deregisters the Builders' Labourers Federation. (Re-registered on 7 Oct. 1976.)

Regional Employment Development, (RED) Scheme introduced to improve employment.

Aust. ratifies World Heritage Commission agreement.

1974

B
Science, Technology, Transport, Discovery

Jun. The Distilleries Co., makers of thalidomide, announces that 17 children born with deformities caused by the drug will receive a $1.7 million settlement.
19 Oct. ABC makes first colour television test transmissions, in Melbourne.
During 1974
First official FM radio broadcasts made.
Anglo-Aust. Optical telescope opens at Siding Springs, NSW.
Mel Thompson's and Doug Lampard's work on improving methods of setting standards of measurements place Aust. as leader in field.
Liddell Thermal Power Station in Hunter Valley, NSW, completed. Largest in Aust.
Stirling Bridge over Swan R., Fremantle, opens.
North-West Coastal Highway opens in WA.
Cwlth Govt takes over Tas. railways.
Len Webb of CSIRO advises on ecology of tropical and monsoonal rainforest in eastern Aust.

C
Arts

Literature

During 1974
Thomas Keneally publishes *Blood Red, Sister Rose*.
Frank Moorhouse publishes collection of stories, *The Electrical Experience*.
Michael Wilding publishes *Living Together*.
A. D. Hope publishes *Native Companions*.
The *Age* Book Award inaugurated.

Music, Dance

Jan. Janet Mead releases song 'The Lord's Prayer'.
Apr. 'Advance Australia Fair' becomes national anthem.
Sep. Skyhooks group release record *Living in the Seventies*.
21 Oct. Stuttgart Ballet begins Aust. tour.
During 1974
Sir Bernard Heinze wins Australian of the Year award.
Peter Sculthorpe writes opera *Rites of Passage*.
Larry Sitzky stages opera *Lenz*.
Hiroyuki Iwaki appointed conductor Melbourne Symphony Orchestra. Vanco Cavdarski appointed conductor Tas. Symphony Orchestra. (Until 1977.) David Measham conductor and co-conductor WA Symphony Orchestra. (Until 1981.)
ABC begins *Countdown* television programme, hosted by 'Molly' Meldrum.
Olivia Newton-John wins two Grammy awards.

Drama, Theatre, Film

25 Jul. Esben Storms's film *27A* released.
Oct. Peter Weir releases film *The Cars that Ate Paris*.
Oct. The Seymour Theatre Centre opens in Sydney.
During 1974
Michael Thornhill's film *Between the Wars* released.
Sunday Too Far Away wins Best Film of the Year award.

Fine Arts

During 1974
Sam Fullbrook wins Archibald Prize for *Norman Stephens*.
The Aust. Centre of Photography opens gallery in Sydney.
About 120,000 people in Sydney view *Blue Poles*.
Pro Hart begins work on *Trafalgar* series of paintings

D
Religion, Learning

Architecture

During 1974
Construction of Aust. National Art Gallery begins.
NSW Planning and Environmental Commission replaces State Planning Authority of NSW.

1 Jan. Federal Govt takes over from States financial responsibility for tertiary education.
During Jan. Ken McKinnon appointed Chairman of Schools Commission.
Apr. Kangan Report on Technical Education recommends increased Govt aid for technical education.
1 Nov. The Kuring-gai College of Advanced Education in Sydney incorporated.
15 Nov. Milperra College of Advanced Education estb. in Sydney.
During 1974
Deakin University estb. at Geelong, Vic.
SA abolishes external leaving certificate school examination.
Majority of Congregational Methodist and Presbyterian Churches vote for unification.
Institute of Catholic Education estb. in Vic.
Sex education courses introduced in NSW schools.

1974

E
Sport

11 Jan. Fourteenth World Gliding Championships held at Waikerie, SA.
12 Dec. Cannington Central greyhound racing track opens in Perth.
During 1974
Think Big, ridden by H. White, wins Melbourne Cup in 3 minutes 23.2 seconds.
Richmond football team wins VFL Premiership in Melbourne.
Eastern Suburbs football team wins Rugby League Premiership in Sydney.
Keith Greig of North Melbourne VFL team awarded Brownlow Medal.
Raelene Boyle is ABC Sportswoman of the Year.
Aust. Sports Council estb.
Aust. qualifies for World Cup soccer finals for first time.
Desmond Renford swims 90 km from Sydney to north Wollongong in $27\frac{1}{2}$ hours.
Margaret Buck wins Aust. women's canoeing titles.
Trifecta first introduced to horseracing, in Melbourne.
Bart Cummings becomes first horse trainer to win over $1 million in one season.
South Africa's Gary Player wins record seventh Aust. golf championship.
Love and War wins Sydney to Hobart yacht race.
Southern Cross challenges for America's Cup. (America wins 4–0.)
Cwlth Games held in Christchurch, NZ.
Businessman Alan Bond makes unsuccessful challenge for Amercia's Cup.

F
Historia Dignum

Population
Estimated total Aust., 13,832,000.

25–29 Jan. Brisbane devastated by flood; 13 lives lost.
Jan.–Apr. North-east of Aust. subject to flooding caused by rains from monsoon troughs. Cattle losses in Qld estimated at $100 million.
23 Feb. Saturday mail deliveries abolished. Most post offices closed on Saturday mornings.
Oct. Hilton Hotel opens in Sydney as largest in Aust.
25 Dec. Darwin devastated by cyclone Tracy. Some 50 lives lost and 16 missing.
Dec. Bushfires ravage W NSW for 2 weeks. Extend into SA on edge of Great Victorian Desert.
During 1974
Television cigarette advertising banned.
Road signs metricated.
Adelaide Festival of Arts Centre completed.
Charges relating to marijuana offences laid against 7,176 people.
Natural Disasters Organization estb.
National civil defence structure estb.
Aust. Advertising Standards Authority (AASA) estb.
Fires damage area near Kalgoorlie, WA.
National road toll 3,572.

A
History, Politics, Economics, Law

1975

Government

3 Jan. 1975–Jan. 1976, T. L. Lewis Liberal Premier NSW.
31 Mar. 1975–Dec. 1977, W. A. Neilson Labor Premier Tas.
3 Apr. 1975–24 Nov. 1975, James Maxwell Ramsay administered WA.
11 Nov. 1975–22 Dec. 1975, Forty-third Cwlth Ministry, John Malcolm Fraser Liberal-National Country coalition Prime Minister Aust.
24 Nov. 1975–24 Nov. 1980, Sir Wallace Hart Kyle Governor WA.
22 Dec. 1975–20 Dec. 1977, Forty-fourth Cwlth Ministry, John Malcolm Fraser Liberal-National Country coalition Prime Minister Aust.
1975–1976, E. F. Dwyer Acting Administrator NT under Cwlth jurisdiction.

26 Jan. Right wing anti-Communist organization the Workers' Party estb. in Sydney. (Becomes Progress Party in 1977.)
14 Feb. Lionel Keith Murphy resigns from Senate and is appointed a Justice of High Court of Aust.
21 Mar. John Malcolm Fraser replaces Billy Mackie Snedden as Liberal-National Country coalition Opposition Leader. (Until 11 Nov.)
8 Apr. Capital punishment abolished in Vic.
23 Apr.–6 May. Princess Anne and Mark Phillips visit Aust.
25 Apr. Aust. withdraws diplomatic presence from Saigon. Anti-Communist Govts in Cambodia and Vietnam collapse, ending Indo-China War.
30 Apr. Arbitration Commission introduces wage indexation to restore cost of living adjustments so that wages will be regularly adjusted according to movements in the Consumer Price Index. Increase of 3.6 per cent in May and 3.5 per cent in Sep.
11 Jun. Cwlth Govt passes Racial Discrimination Act. Enables Commissioner for Community Relations to investigate complaints of racial discrimination.
1 Jul. Medibank Health Scheme begins.
Aust. Post Office divided into the Aust. Postal Commission (Australia Post) and the Aust. Telecommunications Commission (Telecom).
8 Jul. Appeals from Aust. High Court to Privy Council in England abolished in most, but not all, circumstances.
6 Sep. PNG becomes independent country.
Sep. Defence Force Reorganization Act abolishes Naval, Military and Air Boards placing Minister of Defence in charge of the Defence Force. Control of Defence administered by Navy, Army and Air Force Chiefs of Staff through a Chief of the Defence Force Staff.
Oct. Aust. Heritage Commission estb.
8 Dec. Fraser caretaker Govt condemns Indonesian invasion of E. Timor. Five Aust. journalists killed in E. Timor.
13 Dec. Liberal-NCP coalition wins landslide victory at national elections (record 55 seats). Edward Gough Whitlam ALP Opposition Leader. (Until 1978.)
Family Law Act reforms divorce law. Irretrievable breakdown of marriage becomes sole grounds for divorce.

During 1975

Export Finance and Insurance Corporation estb.
Communist League merges with Socialist Workers Party. (Both Trotskyist organizations.)
Unemployment passes 300,000, or 5.2 per cent of workforce.
Cwlth Govt hands over land lease to Gurindji tribe representatives in NT. First legal return of Aboriginal lands.
National Aboriginal and Islander Health Organization. (NAIHO) estb.
Aust. Population and Immigration Council estb. to advise the Minister on immigration.
ACTU estb. SOLO discount petrol stations.
Vic. Country Party becomes National Party.
Aust. National Parks and Wildlife Service estb.

Loans Affair

28 Jan. Executive Council reduces limit of petro dollar loan to $2000 million. Authority to raise any loan revoked on 20 May
2 Jul. Prime Minister Whitlam dismisses Treasurer Jim Cairns for allegedly misleading the House of Representatives over loans negotiations.
15 Oct. Rex Francis Connor, Minister for Minerals and Energy, resigns after being found to have continued dealings seeking loans after Executive Council revoked loan approval.

Constitutional Crisis

15 Oct. Opposition announces intention to block Appropriation Bills in Liberal-NCP-controlled Senate. Funds begin drying up. Crisis mounts with Opposition unyielding in Senate and Govt determined not to hold an election.
10 Nov. Chief Justice Sir Garfield Barwick advises Governor-General on crisis.
11 Nov. Governor-General dismisses Prime Minister Whitlam, dissolves both Houses of Parlt, and appoints Malcolm Fraser as caretaker Prime Minister until election to resolve the deadlock. Intense controversy aroused by Governor-General's actions.

1975

B
Science, Technology, Transport, discovery

1 Mar. Television broadcasting in full colour begins. Ethnic radio begins operating.
During Mar. Closed-circuit television conference facility opens between Melbourne and Sydney.
1 Jul. Cwlth Railways becomes Aust. National Railways.
Jul. Cwlth Govt commissions Ranger Uranium Environmental Inquiry into effects of mining and export of uranium.
Sep. Plan for National Trachoma and Eye Health Programme completed.
1 Nov. Maritime Telex service estb.
During Nov. Bureau of Meteorology begins giving male as well as female names to cyclones.
During 1975
CSIRO and Repco spinning machine influences world textile industry. Wins Prince Philip prize for industrial design.
Sir John Warcup Cornforth shares Nobel Prize for Chemistry. Wins Australian of the Year award.
SA (non-urban) railway system transferred to Cwlth.
Peter Bartolin invents pedalless bicycle in Sydney. Relies on up and down motion of saddle for propulsion.
Jade first mined in Aust., at Cowell, SA.
Aboriginal male skeleton discovered at Lake Mungo, north of Mildura, Vic. Dated at 35,000 years.
Bilateral agreements on scientific and technical co-operation signed with India and USSR.

C
Arts

Literature

During 1975
The Aust. Council for the Arts becomes statutory body known as Australia Council.
Thomas Keneally publishes *Whispers in the Forest*.
Frank Hardy publishes *But the Dead are Many*.
Xavier Herbert publishes *Poor Fellow My Country* (among longest novels written in English language).
Michael Cannon publishes *Life in the Cities*.

Music, Dance

Mar. AC/DC rock band releases album *High Voltage*.
Jun. Aust. Music Centre estb. as national music resource centre.
London Festival Ballet opens Aust. tour in Sydney.
During 1975
Rex Reid founds Aust. Dance Theatre School in Adelaide.
Little River Band pop group forms.
Aust. Elizabethan Theatre Trust estb. Aust. Chamber Orchestra.
Elyakum Shappira appointed conductor of Adelaide Symphony Orchestra. (Until 1979.) Peter Eros appointed co-conductor WA Symphony Orchestra.
Malcolm Williamson appointed Master of the Queen's Musick.
A new Sydney String Quartet estb.

Drama, Theatre, Film

Mar. All Aust. Govt film aid comes under control of Aust. Film Commission.
8 Aug. Peter Weir's film *Picnic at Hanging Rock* premières.
During 1975
Tim Burstall's film *Alvin Rides Again* produced.
Reg Livermore's *Betty Block Buster Follies* opens in Sydney.
Icon Theatre Co. estb. in Adelaide.
Hunter Valley Theatre Co. estb. in NSW.

Fine Arts

Mar. The Visual Arts Board of the Aust. Council estb.
During 1975
Kevin Connor wins Archibald Prize for *Sir Frank Kitto*.
Modern Masters: Manet to Matisse exhibition held in Aust.

D
Religion, Learning

1 Jan. University of Wollongong, NSW, becomes autonomous.
May. Patrick Dobson becomes first Roman Catholic Aboriginal priest ordained.
25 Jul. Sydney College of the Arts estb.
During 1975
Murdoch University, WA, opens.
Griffith University, Qld, opens.
National Curriculum Development Centre estb.
NSW Board of Senior School Studies introduces system of alternative studies for Forms 5 and 6.
United Theological College estb. in NSW to serve Methodist, Presbyterian and Congregational students.
Cwlth Labor Govt abolishes 100-year-old School Cadet Corps system.
ACTU estb. National Council for Trade Union Training.

E
Sport

During 1975
Think Big, ridden by H. White, wins Melbourne Cup in 3 minutes 29.6 seconds.
North Melbourne football team wins VFL Premiership in Melbourne.
Eastern Suburbs football team wins Rugby League Premiership in Sydney.
Gary Dempsey of Footscray VFL team awarded Brownlow Medal.
Bart Cummings is ABC Sportsman of the Year.
First ever cricket World Cup played in England.
Helen Smith becomes fencing champion.
Skateboard riding popular. Aust. Skateboard Association estb. in Nov.
Rampage wins Sydney to Hobart yacht race.

1975

1975

Historia Dignum

Population
Estimated total Aust., 13,968,900.

5 Jan. Freighter *Lake Illawarra* rams and destroys span on Hobart's Tasman Bridge. Ship sinks. Twelve lives lost.

14 Feb. Order of Aust. Award estb. Conferred on citizens for outstanding public service.

Highest recorded wind surface speed recorded, at Onslow, WA, 264 kmh.

Mar. Sydney has worst cloud burst on record, 130 mm in two hours.

May. The Cwlth Great Barrier Reef Marine Park Act passed.

Aug. Fraser I. Environmental Inquiry begins.

21 Sep. Coalmine gas explosion at Mt Kianga–Moura, Qld, claims 13 lives.

23 Oct. Heron aircraft crashes at Cairns, Qld, claiming 11 lives.

Oct.–Nov. Widespread floods throughout Aust.

Nov. National Press Council estb. to consider complaints about conduct of press.

25 Dec. Fire destroys Savoy Hotel in Sydney, claiming 15 lives.

During 1975

Canberra launches *Australia 75* Festival.

Aust. breaks world lightning speed chess record in Sydney.

Koninderie black matrix opal, weighing 65 kg, discovered at Andamooka, SA.

Gold nugget weighing 566 kg discovered in Vic. Biggest nugget discovered in twentieth century.

Campaign to save native forests estb. in WA to fight the Manjimup woodchip project.

Colour of classified telephone directories changes from pink to yellow.

Kay Priestly gives birth to first successfully separated Siamese twins in Aust.

National road toll 3,694.

A
History, Politics, Economics, Law

1976

Government

23 Jan. 1976–May 1976, (Sir) E. A. Willis Liberal Premier NSW.
14 May 1976– , N. K. Wran Labor Premier NSW.
1 Dec. 1976–30 Apr. 1977, Sir Douglas Ralph Nicholls Governor SA (first Aboriginal Governor).
1976–1978, J. A. England Administrator NT under Cwlth jurisdiction.

5 Jan. Family Law Courts begin operating.
9 Feb. Naval Board abolished. Chief of Naval Staff responsible for Navy.
17 Feb. Thirtieth Federal Parlt opens. (Dissolution 8 Nov. 1977.)
8 May. Skeleton of Truganini, which had been displayed in Tas. Museum from 1904 to 1951, is cremated. (Truganini, who died in 1876, was one of last full-blood Tas. Aborigines.)
Jun. Prime Minister Malcolm Fraser visits People's Republic of China. Uses anti-Sovietism as the centrepiece of foreign policy.
Treaty of friendship and co-operation signed with Japan.
28 Oct. First Fox Report on the Ranger Uranium Environmental Inquiry tabled. Controversy over mining and export of uranium.
10 Nov. Liberal Govt reverses previous Labor Govt's decision to permit American-owned company to mine sand on Fraser I., Qld.
During Nov. Aust. dollar devalued by 17.5 per cent.
1 Dec. The Amalgamated Metal Workers' and Shipwrights' Union estb.
9 Dec. The Federal Court of Aust. estb.
During 1976
Demonstrations throughout year against Sir John Kerr over management of Constitutional Crisis.
Liberal Govt modifies Medibank. On 12 Jul. ACTU calls 24-hour national stoppage over alteration to Medibank. First general strike in Aust.
Cwlth Govt reduces Federal public service by 10,000.
Registered unemployed now 327,534, or 5.45 per cent of workforce.
Cwlth Govt introduces income tax indexation.
Uranium Producers' Forum estb. to counter effects of public agitation against mining and export of uranium.
Position of Federal Ombudsman estb.
Flexitime approved for Federal public servants.
Nabarlek uranium field, NT, becomes Aboriginal land under Aboriginal Land Rights Act.
Aborigines receive some land under traditional principles of land tenure.
Aust. Broadcasting Tribunal replaces Aust. Broadcasting Control Board.
Aust. produces 28 per cent of world's wool.
ANZ Group Holdings Ltd estb.
First ASEAN Summit meeting held, in Bali, to give impetus to economic proposals.
Sir Keith Aickin appointed a Justice of High Court of Aust. (Until 1982.)
State Premiers adopt policy of income tax sharing to replace financial assistance grants from Federal Govt.
Under wage indexation, four wage increases granted; 6.4 per cent in Feb.; 3 per cent in May; 2.5 per cent in Aug.; 2.2 per cent in Nov.

1976

B
Science, Technology, Transport, Discovery

1 Apr. First International Subscriber Dialling service (ISD) in Aust. estb., in Sydney.
26 Sep. Sealed road across Nullarbor Plain completed.
23 Oct. Total eclipse telecast.
During 1976
Sir Edward Dunlop, surgeon, wins Australian of the Year Award.
J. Russell Gay invents Rowin table.
James Lance awarded British Migraine Association gold medal for work on association between blood serotonin and cerebral circulation.
Aust. becomes largest producer of bauxite and alumina.
Aust. has more than 40,000 km of railway line.
Uranium mining at Mary Kathleen, Qld, recommences.
Siding Springs Observatory, NSW, discovers faintest-ever measured optical star, Vela (mag. 24).
Brisbane's south and north side railway systems joined by tunnel. (Cross river link completed in Nov. 1978.)
Scientific exchange programme estb. with China.

C
Arts

Literature

During 1976
Patrick White publishes *A Fringe of Leaves*.
Robert Drewe publishes *The Savage Crows*.

Music, Dance

During 1976
Leslie Humble estb. the Aust. Contemporary Music Ensemble.
Nanette Hassall and Russell Dumas estb. Dance Exchange, modern dance group.
Kai Tai Chan estb. 'One Extra Dance Theatre' in Sydney.

Drama, Theatre, Film

23 Jan. New Theatre Royal opens in Sydney.
9 Apr. Donald Crombie's film *Caddie* opens. First Aust. film to run over a year on first release.
12 Aug. Riverina Trucking Co. community theatre estb. in Wagga Wagga, NSW.
During 1976
Films *The Devil's Playground* and *Don's Party* released. *The Devil's Playground* wins Best Film of the Year award.

Fine Arts

During 1976
Brett Whiteley wins Archibald Prize for *Self Portrait*.

Architecture

During 1976
Restoration of Elizabeth Bay House in Sydney completed.

D

Religion, Learning

During 1976
National Library purchases William Bligh's notebook for $73,000.
ACT education system separates from NSW.
There are 22,311 adherents of Islam in Aust. Mosques built at Lakemba, Sydney, and at Preston, Melbourne.
ACTU estb. Clyde Cameron College at Albury-Wodonga, NSW/Vic.

E

Sport

25 Jan. Tom Hayllar completes 12,000 km around Aust. walk begun in Mar. 1975.
Apr. Bert Flood breaks Aust. motorcycle speed record with 243.9 kmh.
Clive Green lands world's heaviest fish caught by rod and reel, at Albany, WA, a 1536.8 kg white pointer shark.
23 May. Linda McGill swims 48 km around Hong Kong.
Jul.–Aug. Hans Tholstrup is first person to drive solo across central Aust.
20–23 Oct. First Perth to Sydney air race held.
During 1976
Van Der Hum, ridden by R. Skelton, wins Melbourne Cup in 3 minutes 34.1 seconds.
Hawthorn football team wins VFL Premiership in Melbourne.
Manly-Warringah football team wins Rugby League Premiership in Sydney.
Graham Moss of Essendon VFL team awarded Brownlow Medal.
Greg Chappell is ABC Sportsman of the Year.
Aust. wins one silver and four bronze medals at Montreal Olympics.
Chris Wardlan wins San Francisco Bay to Breakers footrace.
Heather McKay wins first women's world squash championship.
Peter Townsend wins world professional surf board championship.
Leo Meier breaks Aust. boomerang distance record.
Ingo Renner wins first Aust. world gliding title, in Finland.
First Aust. hang-gliding championships held in NSW.
First skateboard park built, at Albany, WA.
Brett Austine becomes trampoline champion.
Windsurfing begins in Aust.
Piccolo wins Sydney to Hobart yacht race.

1976

1976

F

Historia Dignum

Population
Estimated total Aust., 14,109,900.
Cwlth census calculates population at 13,548,472.

Mar. Floods damage eastern and southern Qld and areas of NSW coast.
1 Sep. Cigarette tobacco advertising on television and radio banned.
4 Dec. Graham John Trent burns down hangar at HMAS *Albatross*, Nowra, NSW, destroying six aircraft.

During 1976
Backgammon popular.
Citizens' Band radio becomes popular.
Tas. Wilderness Society estb. to save the Franklin R.
Nude bathing first legalized, on two Sydney beaches.
Police break up hippy community at Cedar Bay, Qld.
Drought in Vic., WA and NSW. (Ends in 1978.)
National road toll 3,583.

A

History, Politics, Economics, Law

1977

Government

21 Mar. 1977–21 Apr. 1977, Sir Mostyn Hanger administered Qld.

22 Apr. 1977– , Sir James Maxwell Ramsay Governor Qld.

30 Apr. 1977–1 Sep. 1977, Walter R. Crocker administered SA.

1 Sep. 1977–Apr. 1982, Sir Keith Douglas Seaman Governor SA.

1 Dec. 1977–Nov. 1981 D. A. Lowe Labor Premier Tas. (Youngest Aust. State Premier to that date, 35 years.)

8 Dec. 1977–29 Jul. 1982, Sir Zelman Cowen Governor-General Aust.

20 Dec. 1977–5 Mar. 1983, Forty-fifth Cwlth Ministry, Second Fraser Ministry, John Malcolm Fraser Liberal-National Country coalition Prime Minister of Aust.

1 Jan. Abolition of death duties in Qld effective.

7–30 Mar. Royal visit as part of Queen Elizabeth's Jubilee celebrations.

24 Mar. Don Chipp resigns from Liberal Party to estb. political party Aust. Democrats.

13 Apr. Cwlth Govt persuades Premiers to support voluntary wage-price freeze for three months.

17 May. Second report of the Ranger Uranium Environmental Inquiry presented.

21 May. Referendum held proposing changes to Constitution: to ensure a casual vacancy in Senate is filled by member of same party; to allow electors in Territories vote at referendums; to provide for retiring ages for judges. All carried, but further proposal to ensure that Senate elections are held at same time as House of Representatives elections rejected.

24 May–Aug. Cwlth Govt announces Nuclear Safeguards Policy. Permits Ranger project to begin and authorizes uranium exports.

During May. National Aboriginal Conference, consultative body, estb.

Jun. Cwlth Industrial Relations Bureau estb.

9 Aug. Inquiry into Vic. Housing Commission estb. Exposes land scandal, with Commission guilty of malpractice.

5 Sep. Qld Govt bans protest street marches.

During Sep. Attorney-General Bob Ellicott leaves Cwlth Govt after being refused permission to investigate alleged loans conspiracy against Gough Whitlam and other Labor Ministers.

Federal Govt estb. Health Services Advisory Committee to advise on policy.

Oct. Cwlth Govt announces legislation to broaden penal clauses against unions breaking industrial law.

18 Nov. Federal Treasurer Phillip Lynch resigns from Cabinet while a family company is investigated. Returns to Cabinet after exoneration.

1 Dec. Confederation of Aust. Industry (CAI) estb.

10 Dec. John Malcolm Fraser returned as Prime Minister at national elections with 48 seat majority. Second-biggest land-slide in Aust. history. On 22 Dec. William George (Bill) Hayden elected ALP Opposition leader.

During 1977

Unemployment rises to over 400,000.

Office of National Assessments (ONA) estb.

Aboriginal Land Rights NT Act 1966 becomes operative. Gives Aboriginals inalienable freehold title to Aboriginal reserves totalling 20 per cent of NT.

Aboriginal Neville Perkins elected ALP member for Macdonnell in NT Legislative Assembly.

Under wage indexation four wage increases awarded: $5.70 in Mar., 1.9 per cent in May; 2 per cent in Aug.; 1.5 per cent in Dec.

Four weeks' annual leave becomes NSW standard.

Vic. power workers hold 9-week strike in demand for indexation of over-award payments. State of Emergency declared.

1977

B
Science, Technology, Transport, Discovery

Feb. Western Plains Zoo at Dubbo, NSW, opens. First Aust. open-range zoo (300 ha.).
Mar. The spotted alfalfa aphid pest begins ruining livestock fodder in eastern Aust.
Scientist at Aust. National University develop world's first large-scale solar storage system.
19 Apr. Aust. Science and Technology Council (ASTEC) estb.
May. The newspaper *Canberra Times* becomes first in Aust. to adopt computer typesetting.
Jun. Citizen Band (CB) radio legalized in Aust.
Nov. CSIRO produces biodegradable insect killer harmless to mammals and people.
Dec. Scientists confirm oldest rocks in Aust. as being 3,500 million years old. (Rocks near Marble Bar, WA.)
During 1977
Aust. has 860,000 km of roads.
Diamonds discovered in Kimberley Ranges, WA.
Rough sapphire field discovered in central Qld.
Aust. signs Convention establishing the International Satellite System (INMARSAT), becoming an original member and part-owner.
Natural gas pipeline connecting Moomba, SA, with NSW centres officially opened at Young, NSW.
CSIRO develops Sirotem instrument used in geological mapping.
Western Mining Corporation announces existence of uranium at Roxby Downs, SA.

C
Arts

Literature

May. Third edition of *The Australian Encyclopaedia* published in six volumes. Editor-in-Chief Bruce W. Pratt.
During 1977
Colleen McCullough publishes *The Thorn Birds*.
Association for the Study of Aust. literature estb.

Music, Dance

Mar. Vic. State Opera Co. begins first season.
Apr. Little River Band launches album *Diamantina Cocktail*.
26 May. Greg Smith and Marion Alleyne become first Australians to win a world Amateur Ballroom dancing championship in England.
Jul. Peter Allen releases song 'I Go To Rio'.
Danilo Radojevic wins gold medal at International Ballet Competition in Moscow.
3 Aug. First Sydney international piano competition held.
Oct. NSW Govt sponsors *Carnivale 77*, celebration of ethnic music.
During 1977
Referendum accepts 'Advance Australia Fair' as national song.

Drama, Theatre, Film

9 Sep. The Ensemble-at-the-Stables Theatre opens in Sydney.
During 1977
Gary Kildea's film *Trobriand Cricket* wins Prix Georges Sedoul.
Aust. cartoon film *Leisure* wins Australia's second Acadamý Award.
Patrick White publishes play *Big Toys*.
Peter Weir's film *The Last Wave* released.
Henri Safran's film *Storm Boy* released.
Film *The Picture Show Man* released. Wins Best Film of the Year award.
The Sullivans television drama sold to England.
Bruce Beresford's film *The Getting of Wisdom* released.

Fine Arts

Jan.–Jun. Chinese Archaeological Exhibition tours Aust.
During 1977
Kevin Connor wins Archibald Prize for *Robert Klippel*.

D Religion, Learning

1977

Architecture

During 1977
King George Tower, designed by John Hamilton Andrews, completed in Sydney.
Sydney Square completed.
Harry Seidler's MLC Tower completed in Sydney. (Among tallest concrete towers in world.)

22 Jun. Uniting Church of Aust. officially inaugurated from amalgamation of the Methodist Church with most Presbyterian and Congregational Churches in Aust.
During Jun. Technical and Further Education Council estb.
Jul. Education Programme for Unemployed Youth (EPUY) estb.
During 1977
Cwlth Govt estb. Schools Commission to advise on allocation of funds to schools.
Tertiary Education Commission estb.
Qld Itinerant Teacher Service estb. for children in remote areas.

1977

E
Sport

Apr. National Soccer League of Aust. estb.
Sep. Graham Forlonge creates round Aust. motor-cycle record of 9 days 23 hours 30 minutes.
20 Nov. Kenneth Warby breaks world speed boat record with 464.44 kmh.
17 Dec. Bruce Parry breaks world record for Eskimo rolling in a kayak.

During 1977
Gold and Black, ridden by J. Duggan, wins Melbourne Cup in 3 minutes 18.4 seconds.
North Melbourne football team wins VFL Premiership in Melbourne.
St George football team wins Rugby League Premiership in Sydney.
Graham Teasdale of South Melbourne VFL team awarded Brownlow Medal.
First Aust. windsurfing championships held.
Graham Marsh is ABC Sportsman of the Year.
Kerry Packer enlists Aust., UK and West Indies cricketers in $2.5 million deal, starting World Cricket Series.
Bobby Simpson recalled to be captain of Aust. cricket team against Indians.
Aust. wins Centenary Test cricket match against England in Melbourne by 45 runs.
First night cricket played in Aust.
Geoffrey Hunt wins world open squash championship.
Rocco (Rocky) Mattiolo wins world junior middleweight boxing championship.
First world champion archery competitions held in southern hemisphere, in Canberra.
Ingo Renner wins world's longest seaplane race, in USA.
Mitch Jones, ice hockey player, widely acclaimed in Canada.
Aust. open polo championships first held.
St George and Parammatta Rugby League Teams draw first grand final in Sydney competition.
Lyndall Coxon wins first woman's world laser class sailing championship.
Maori's Idol becomes fastest trotting horse in Aust. Breaks 2 minute barrier.
Kialoa wins Sydney to Hobart yacht race.
Australia challenges for America's Cup. (America wins 4–0.)

F
Historia Dignum

Population
Estimated total Aust., 14,280,800.

18 Jan. Bold Street Bridge at Granville, NSW, collapses after being struck by train. Crushes train, claiming 83 lives.
Feb. Bushfires in western district of Vic. claim five lives.
Feb.–Mar. Widespread floods throughout much of Aust.
27 Apr. Mining accident at Agnew nickel project in WA claims five lives.
15 Jul. Donald Mackay, anti-drug campaigner, disappears from Griffith, NSW.
16 Dec. Bushfires in Blue Mts, NSW.

During 1977
Raigh Lee, Country Women's Association worker, wins Australian of the Year award.
First Festival of Sydney held.
Smoking banned on most public transport in Sydney.
Australians consume an average of 104.6 kg of meat per person per year, compared with USA 87.8, Britain 57.5 and West Germany 70.3.
Aust. branch of Greenpeace, international environmentalist group, estb.
National road toll 3,578.

A

History, Politics, Economics, Law

1978

17 Jan. SA Police Commissioner Harold H. Salisbury dismissed for misleading SA Govt over files kept by the Special Branch.
During Jan. Livestock and Grain Producers Association of NSW estb.
9 Feb. Sir John Kerr appointed Aust. Ambassador to UNESCO. Resigns three weeks later as a result of extreme controversy. Kerr publishes *Matters for Judgement*.
21 Feb. Thirty-First Federal Parlt opens. (Dissolution 19 Sep. 1980.)
Feb. Cwlth Heads of Govt Regional Meeting (CHOGM) held in Sydney. Three die in a terrorist blast at Hilton Hotel; State of Emergency declared. Sir Robert Mark arrives in Aust. from Britain to advise on combatting terrorism.
15 Mar. Meat Industry Employees' Union imposes ban on live-sheep exports.
18–19 May. Prince Charles visits Melbourne to attend Sir Robert Menzies' funeral. (Menzies died on 15 May.)
17 Jun. NSW referendum to make NSW Legislative Council a directly elected body carried.
30 Jun. National Employers' Association abolished.
1 Jul. NT granted self-govt as step towards Statehood. Paul Everingham elected Country-Liberal Chief Minister.
During Jul. SA Govt announces that Aboriginal tribe Pitjantjatjara would be granted full rights to area of traditional land in north-west SA.
7 Aug. Federal Govt dismisses Senate Leader R. Withers after Commission found he improperly sought to influence electoral commissioners in Qld regarding the naming of an electorate.
22 Nov. Parlt approves the construction of a new Parlt House on Capital Hill, Canberra.
25 Nov. At referendum ACT electors reject proposal for self-government.
Dec. Charges against Gough Whitlam, Jim Cairns and Lionel Murphy for conspiracy in Loans Affair dropped.
During 1978
South-East Asian refugees begin entering Aust. illegally. By end of year 47 craft carrying Vietnamese have arrived in Darwin.
Democratic Labor Party (DLP) officially dissolved.
National Women's Advisory Council estb.
National Front of Aust., extremist right-wing racist organization campaigning for White Aust., estb.
Medibank dismantled. Private schemes remain.
A $10 airport departure tax introduced.
Federal Govt informally recognizes Indonesian takeover of Timor.
Federal Govt reaches agreement with Aboriginal Northern Lands Council. Signs uranium mining agreement and opens way for further mining of uranium in NT.
Galarrwuy Yunupingu, Aboriginal Land Rights leader, wins Australian of the Year award.
ACTU membership reaches 133 unions.
There are 160 Trade Commissions representing Aust. in 46 countries.
Aust. becomes largest meat exporter in world.
Decision made that whaling station near Albany, WA, last in Aust., be closed.
Unemployment exceeds 400,000.
Fifteen Aboriginal Land Trusts in NT granted land titles.
Coastal Surveillance Centre estb. to watch area between Geraldton, WA, and Cairns, Qld.
Under wage indexation three wage increases awarded; 1.5 per cent in Feb.; 1.3 per cent in Jun.; 4 per cent in Dec.

1978

B
Science, Technology, Transport, Discovery

Feb. The National Energy Advisory Committee estb. permanently.
May. National Energy Development and Demonstration Council estb. to advise on development of energy.
28 Jul. Last passenger rail service in Tas., The Tasman Ltd, closes.
15 Sep. The Aviation Industry Advisory Council first meets.
15 Nov. Westgate Bridge in Melbourne opens. Longest in Aust.
Dec. Committee of Inquiry into Technological Change estb.
During 1978
Alfred Ringwood, leading ANU team, claims to have found safe method for disposal of nuclear waste by storing inside synthetic rock (SYNROC).
Micro fossil remains of blue green algae dated 3,500 million years discovered at Marble Bar, WA.
Oil discovered at Strzelecki 3 well in SA.
Aust. hosts quadrennial congress of International Union of Geodesy and Geophysics.
Aust. Govt. requests British Govt. to remove 500 tons of plutonium buried at Maralinga, SA, which had been used during British weapons tests in 1950s and 1960s.

C
Arts

Literature

During 1978
Sumner Locke Elliott publishes *Water Under the Bridge*.
Colleen McCullough's *The Thorn Birds* sets Aust. record for hardback sales: 100,000 copies.

Music, Dance

12 Apr. Graeme Murphy's dance work *Poppy* premières in Sydney. First full-length contemporary dance work created in Aust.
27 Jun. Stars of World Ballet opens Aust. tour in Sydney.
During 1978
William van Otterloo, conductor, killed in motor accident.
Vanco Cavdarski appointed conductor Qld Symphony Orchestra. (Until 1981.)
Aboriginal and Islander Dance Theatre estb. in Sydney.

Drama, Theatre, Film

May. Fred Schepisi's film *The Chant of Jimmy Blacksmith* released.
28 Jul. Phillip Noyce's film *Newsfront* released. Wins Best Film of the Year award.
During 1978
Steve J. Spears writes play *The Elocution of Benjamin Franklin*.

Fine Arts

During 1978
Brett Whiteley wins Archibald Prize for *Self Portrait*.
First national ceramic conference held, in Sydney.
The El Dorado exhibition of gold objects from Colombia tours Aust.

Architecture

During 1978
Federal Parlt commissions new Parlt House. (Proposed to be completed by 1988.)

D
Religion, Learning

11 May. Deakin University at Geelong, Vic., officially opens.
During 1978
Sir Marcus Loane is first Aust.-born prelate to become primate of Church of England in Aust.
Five main education curricula traditions current in Aust. education: humanist realist, structure of discipline, technical vocational, neo-progressive and recreational entertainment.
Pat O'Shane becomes first Aboriginal law graduate and barrister.
Aust. Maritime College estb. at Launceston, Tas.

E
Sport

Jun. Margaret Frost becomes first woman to drive trotters against men, at Harold Park, in Sydney.
8 Oct. Kenneth Warby breaks 500 kmh world speed boat water record with 514.39 kmh.
During 1978
Arwon, ridden by H. White, wins Melbourne Cup in 3 minutes 24.3 seconds.
Hawthorn football team wins VFL Premiership in Melbourne.
Manly-Warringah football team wins Rugby League Premiership in Sydney.
Malcolm Blight of North Melbourne VFL team awarded Brownlow Medal.
Tracey Wickham is ABC Sportswoman of the Year.
Vic. legalizes boxing contests between women.
Mount Hagen, colt, becomes first yearling to fetch one million dollars at Aust. horse sales.
Patricia Harrington attains highest rank in Ju Jitsu, unarmed combat, achieved by an Aust. woman.
George Perdon runs Sydney to Melbourne in 9 days 5 hours.
Edwina Kennedy (aged 19) wins British women's amateur golf championship.
Some 20,930 runners enter the Sydney City-to-Surf foot race.
B. Laging breaks aero modelling world record for duration with 28 hours 0 minutes 28 seconds.
Jim Lynch wins ice speed-skating championship in England.
Aust. hosts world barefoot water skiing championships in Canberra.
Jill Bamborough becomes first Aust. woman to set world power lifting record.
Wayne Bartholomew wins world surfriding championship.
Love and War wins Sydney to Hobart yacht race.
Cwlth Games held in Edmonton, Canada.

F

Historia Dignum

1978

Population
Estimated total Aust., 14,429,400.

Feb. Widespread floods in WA. In Apr. cyclone Alby damages south-western WA, claiming five lives.
Mar. Margaret Throsby becomes first woman to read the ABC television 7 pm news.
Jun. Floods in Vic. and Tas.
10 Jul. Partavia aircraft crashes at Essendon, Vic., killing six occupants of a house.
22 Nov. Thieves rob Bank of NSW at Murwillumbah, NSW, of $1.7 million. Biggest bank robbery in Aust. to that date.
Nov.–Dec. Vera Randall wins the Bulletin–Veuve Clicquot Business Woman of the Year award.

During 1978
World Wildlife Fund Aust. estb.
Over one million yo-yos sold in Sydney.
National road toll 3,705.

A

History, Politics, Economics, Law

1979

Government

15 Feb. 1979–15 Sep. 1979, J. D. Corcoran Labor Premier SA.
15 Sep. 1979–6 Nov. 1982, D. O. Tonkin Liberal Premier SA.

Feb. Aust. cuts all aid to and cultural ties with Vietnam as protest against Vietnam's military takeover of Kampuchea.

Associated Securities Ltd Finance Co. collapses.

8 Mar.–1 Apr. Prince Charles visits Aust. 25–30 Sep. Prince Philip visits WA. In Jul. Princess Anne and Mark Phillips visit Aust.

9 Mar. Cwlth Arbitration Commission grants up to 12 months unpaid maternity leave to working women.

20 Apr. Qld Govt demolishes Brisbane's historic Belle Vue Hotel, causing intense controversy.

21 May. Sir Ronald Wilson appointed a Justice of High Court of Aust.

During May. National Farmer's Federation estb. to represent all farmers in Aust. excepting members of Cattlemen's Union.

21 Jun. ACTU calls general strike, second in Aust., to protest against arrest of union officials in WA.

During Jun. Aust. has taken in 22,000 Indo-Chinese refugees by this date. On 11 Jul. Cwlth Govt agrees to accept 14,000 more.

Under six monthly wage indexation, a 3.2 per cent wage increase granted.

Aug. Aust. Prime Minister Malcolm Fraser plays key role in Zambia in organizing negotiations to end Rhodesian conflict. In Nov. Aust. agrees to send military observers to Zimbabwe-Rhodesia to monitor ceasefire and new elections.

27 Sep. Ian Sinclair, Federal Primary Industry Minister, resigns from Cabinet after accusations of forgery and other offences in respect of family companies. (Exonerated on 14 Aug. 1980.)

Aust. abolishes traditional trade preferences with Britain.

During Sep. A Sydney architect awarded $480,000 damages in defamation verdict involving three newspapers. Probably largest award in history of defamation law in Aust. to that date.

7 Oct. The Aust. Refugee Advisory Council estb.

19 Oct. Cwlth and ACT police merge to form the Aust. Federal Police.

During Oct. David Armstrong appointed general manager of the Aust. Bicentennial Authority. (Resigns 1985.)

1 Nov. Cwlth Govt. proclaims fishing rights over 200 nautical mile zone around Aust.

19 Nov. Tas. Crown Advocate issues summonses against 75 State MPs and election candidates for failing to lodge election campaign spending returns. (Fifty-two fined on 19 Nov.)

During Nov. EZ Industries Ltd and Peko Wallsend Ltd secure contract to export Ranger uranium to S. Korea.

During 1979

Brambles Industries Ltd and Acmil Ltd announce one of biggest industrial mergers in Aust. history.

Norfolk I. Legislative Assembly estb.

NSW Govt permits weekend trading for small retail shops.

WA Govt agrees to grant freehold title and mineral rights to Pitjantjatjara Aborigines.

Gary Foley and Bruce McGuinness estb. Aboriginal Information Centre in London and support committees in seven other European countries.

Aurukun and Mornington I. Shire Councils in Qld become first all-Aboriginal shire councils in Aust.

1979

B
Science, Technology, Transport, Discovery

26 Jan. Harry Butler, naturalist, wins Australian of the Year award.
During Jan. Britain agrees to take back recoverable plutonium waste from the Maralinga bomb test site in SA.
Feb. Antarctic Research Policy Advisory Committee estb.
Iron ore discovered at Yandicoogina Creek, WA.
Construction work begins on the Ranger uranium project, NT.
Mar. First international solar energy conference in Aust. opens in Melbourne.
23 Jun. Eastern suburbs railway system opens in Sydney.
16 Jul. International Maritime Satellite Organization (INMARSAT), estb. to co-ordinate maritime satellite communications, becomes operational.
17 Jul. Melbourne scientists develop bionic ear invention, enabling some deaf to hear.
17 Nov. First stage of suburban railway electrification scheme opens in Brisbane.
During 1979
Oil discovered at Dullingari North I., SA.
Houghton Bridge replaces Hornibrook Bridge in Qld. Among longest road bridges in Aust.
First solar powered broadbend microwave telecommunications link estb., between Tennant Creek and Alice Springs, NT.
L. W. Davies and M. A. Green develop a new high efficiency solar cell.
Stripe rust discovered in Wimmera crops, Vic.
Aust. signs scientific and technological co-operation treaty with China.
One of three world Global Weather Experiment meteorological stations estb. in Aust.

C
Arts

Music, Dance

During 1979
Louis Fremaux appointed conductor Sydney Symphony Orchestra. (Until 1981.)
Aboriginal dancer Roslyn Watson joins the Aust. Dance Theatre.
The Kinetikos Dance Theatre estb. in Perth.

Drama, Theatre, Film

Jan. The Sydney Theatre Co. estb.
Feb. The Film and Television Production Association estb.
Apr. George Miller's film *Mad Max* released.
17 Aug. Gillian Armstrong's film *My Brilliant Career* released. Wins Best Film of the Year award.

Fine Arts

Jan. Joseph Brown private art collection, valued at $750,000 stolen from his Melbourne home. Biggest art theft in Aust. to that date.
During 1979
Wes Walters wins Archibald Prize for *Portrait of Philip Adams*.
The new Art Gallery of WA opens.

Architecture

During 1979
New Qld Parliament House opens in Brisbane.

D
Religion, Learning

1 Jan. Hartley College of Advanced Education estb.
During Jan. The Adelaide College of the Arts and Education estb.
Apr.–May. Evangelist Billy Graham visits Aust.
1 Jul. The Community College of Central Aust. estb.
Council of NT education transferred from Federal to NT Govt control.
22 Sep. The Standing Conference of Canonical Orthodox Churches in Aust. estb.
During 1979
Katherine Rural Education College, NT, opens.
The WA Academy of Performing Arts estb.
Tas. Aboriginal Education Consultative Committee estb.
Aust. Committee of Inquiry into Education and Training, chaired by Bruce R. Williams, submits three reports *Education*, *Training* and *Employment*. First comprehensive inquiry in Aust. on transition from school to workforce.

E
Sport

28 Jan. Canberra Greyhound Racing Club stages first meeting.
Feb. Jeff Thomson timed as world's fastest cricket bowler (147.9 kmh = 91.8 mph).
Mar. Women jockeys permitted to compete against men. Pam O'Neill becomes first woman jockey to ride against men. In Apr. Linda Jones becomes first registered woman jockey to win against men, at Rosehill, NSW.
Aug. For first time in 34 years Aust. Rugby Union football team defeats NZ All Blacks (25 to 11), in Sydney.
Fitzroy VFL Aust. Rules football team makes record score against Melbourne team (36 goals 22 points).
World fencing championships held in Melbourne. First time in southern hemisphere.
Oct. Alan Jones wins fourth Grand Prix car race in a row, in Canada.
During 1979
Hyperno, ridden by H. White, wins Melbourne Cup in 3 minutes 21.8 seconds.
Record $1 million paid for stallion Yallah Native.
David Graham becomes ABC Sportsman of the Year.
Carlton football team wins VFL Premiership in Melbourne.
St George football team wins Rugby League Premiership in Sydney.
Peter Moore of Collingwood VFL team awarded Brownlow Medal.
Peter Farmer makes record Aust. hammer throw in France, 68.00 metres.
Wayne Martin makes record Aust. discus throw, 65.08 metres.
Aust. Football Championships Pty Ltd estb. to run national Aust. Rules Football championships.
National Basketball League estb.
World Series Cricket and the Aust. Cricket Board unite after two-year cricket war.
Melbourne hosts World Bocce Title.
First Aust. skateboard championships held, in Albany, WA.
Robyn Burley becomes first Aust. to win an individual world ice and figure skating title, in Spain.
Bumblebee IV wins Sydney to Hobart yacht race.

1979

1979

Historia Dignum

Population
Estimated total Aust., 14,516,500.

4 Jan. Highest recorded rainfall in Aust. over 24 hours measured, at Bellenden Ker, Qld (1,140 mm). Also record rainfall for this year (11,250 mm).

12 Jan. Australian *Playboy* magazine launched, in Sydney.

During Jan. Czech migrant commits suicide outside Hobart GPO in protest against staging of 1980 Olympic Games in Moscow.

Mar. Cyclone Hazel damages WA coast and destroys fishing fleet off Carnarvon, claiming 15 lives.

Cyclone Kerry damages northern Qld coast.

Lotto begins in NSW.

May. Bodies of seven young women discovered near Truro, SA. (James William Miller convicted of six murders in Mar. 1980.)

9 Jun. Fire at Luna Park in Sydney claims seven lives.

During Jun. Great Barrier Reef Marine Park agreement signed by Cwlth Govt. Bans oil exploration on or around the park.

29 Jul. Coalmining disaster at Appin, NSW, claims 14 lives.

23 Aug. David James Ryan breaks eight-hour sheep shearing record with 500.

30 Aug. Cessna aircraft crashes at Shepparton, Vic., claiming six lives.

During Aug. Nine people suffering from cholera hospitalized.

'Life be in it' cartoons appear as part of *Project Aust.*, launched to arouse national pride.

Mike Walsh signs a $4 million television contract with Channel 9 in Melbourne, becoming highest-paid entertainer in Aust.

Oct. Australian *Penthouse* magazine launched.

Nov. Thunderstorms damage Barossa Valley, SA.

Elizabeth Manley wins the Bulletin–Veuve Clicquot Business Woman of the Year award.

During 1979

Widespread drought in many parts of Aust. begins. (Ends 1982.)

Bushfires burn country areas near Sydney.

National road toll 3,508.

A
History, Politics, Economics, Law

1980

Government

28 May 1980–7 Aug. 1980, Sir Francis Theodore Page Burt administered WA.

8 Aug. 1980–9 Nov. 1980, John Martin Lavan administered WA.

18 Oct. 1980–5 Mar. 1983, forty-sixth Cwlth Ministry, John Malcolm Fraser Liberal-National Country coalition Prime Minister Aust.

25 Nov. 1980– , Sir Richard Trowbridge Governor WA.

Jan. Under wage indexation a 4.5 per cent increase awarded and a further 4.2 per cent in Jul.

Vietnam War veterans believed to be suffering from effects of Agent Orange begin campaigning for a full investigation.

Aust. supports USA moves to cut wheat sales to USSR as protest against Soviet invasion of Afghanistan.

Mar. NSW and Vic. woolstore workers return to work after an 11-week strike over wages.

Apr. State of Emergency declared in Qld when power workers strike for three days.

Office of National Assessment loses sensitive document, *The Threat to the Internal Security of Australia.*

May. Former Federal Minister Ian Sinclair committed for trial on charges relating to making false statements on company returns. Cleared of all nine charges in Aug.

Chinese Vice-Premier Li Xiannian visits Aust. Highest ranking Chinese official to visit Aust. to that date.

Jun. Cwlth Govt announces Indo-Chinese refugee intake of 19,500 for 1980–1981.

Barbara Weise elected president of the SA Labor Party. First woman to become a State Branch president of the ALP.

17 Aug. Journalist Laurie Oakes reveals much of the Federal Budget two days before official release.

During Aug. Robert James Lee Hawke enters Federal Parlt.

SA Industrial Commission estb. independent wage-fixing system separate from Federal system.

25 Nov. Thirty-second Federal Parlt opens. (Dissolution 16 Dec. 1982.)

15 Dec. The Hill Samuel Cash Management Trust estb. Marks beginning of rapid development of Cash Management Trusts.

During Dec. Federal Govt announces deregulation of interest rates offered by banks on customer deposits.

During 1980

Aboriginal Land Fund Commission taken over by the Aboriginal Development Commission. Charles Perkins appointed president.

State Legislative powers extended to include control of coastal waters.

Aust. split on whether to send team to Moscow Olympics. In Jun. 52 per cent favour boycott in protest against USSR invasion of Afghanistan.

1980

B
Science, Technology, Transport, Discovery

22 Jan. Debbie Wardley becomes first commercial airline woman pilot, for Ansett Airlines.
24 Jan. First section of Melbourne underground rail loop opens.
5 May. Black Mt telecommunications tower opens in Canberra.
May. Aust. branch of Earthwatch launched in Sydney.
22 Jun. Aust.'s first and world's fourth test tube baby born, in Melbourne.
Jul. Energy Resources of Aust. Ltd estb. to buy Govt-controlled interests in Ranger uranium project in NT.
NSW Govt approves scheme to introduce lead-free petrol to reduce air pollution.
Aug. CSIRO scientists discover anti-venene for funnel web spider.
Oct. Largest tantalum mineral reserves in world discovered, in south-western WA.
Nov. John Ward wins Guthrie Medal awarded by London Institute of Physics. (Awarded 1981.)
Dec. Aust. produces first twins in world conceived through in vitro fertilization and embryo transfer test tube baby process.

During 1980
Oil and gas discovered in Cooper Basin, SA, and in Canning Basin, WA.
Production of yellow cake from uranium ore begins at Nabarlek, NT.
Construction of Brisbane International Airport redevelopment project begins.
World's oldest fossil fish found near Alice Springs, NT.

C
Arts

Literature

During 1980
Thomas Keneally publishes *The Cut-Rate Kingdom*.
David Malouf publishes *Fly Away Peter Venus*.
Gabrielle Lord publishes *Fortress*.
Murray Ball publishes *Homesickness*.

Music, Dance

During 1980
Jose Serebrier appointed conductor Adelaide Symphony Orchestra. (Until 1982.) Barry Tuckwell appointed conductor Tas. Symphony Orchestra.
Jo Dolce's 'Shaddup you face', Aust. record-breaking single, released.
Kim Hemsley conducts longest recorded Aust. disco dancing marathon in Tas., 132 hours 30 minutes.
Human Veins Dance Theatre estb., based in Canberra.

Drama, Theatre, Film

May. Bruce Beresford's film *Breaker Morant* released. Wins Best Film of the Year award.
Robert Stigwood launches stage show *Evita* in Adelaide.

Fine Arts

May. Ron Robertson-Swann's plate steel sculpture, *The Vault* erected in Melbourne City Square. (Removed in Jul. 1981 after intense public objection.)
During 1980
Archibald Prize not awarded.

Architecture

26 Mar. New High Court of Aust. building opens in Canberra.
26 Jun. Melbourne-born Richard Thorp, of the American firm Mitchell, Giurgola and Thorp, wins design competition for new Parlt House in Canberra. Work begins 1981.

D
Religion, Learning

E
Sport

26 Jan. Manning Clark wins Australian of the Year award.
Jan. Full Bench of High Court listed to hear a challenge to the validity of State aid to non-Govt schools.
1 Mar. Polding College estb. in Sydney.
May. The World Council of Churches' Mission and Evangelism Conference held in Melbourne.
During 1980
Sydney College of Advanced Education estb.
The Aust. Inland Mission comes under control of the Uniting Church and is re-named the Uniting Church National Mission Frontier Services.
The Aust. Maritime College opens in Launceston, Tas.
Federal Govt endorses policy to strengthen technical education.

12 Apr. Australian Rules Football, VFL, first televised in USA.
Apr. Despite Govt boycott of Moscow Olympic Games, the Aust. Olympic Federation announces a team of 204 athletes and 69 officials.
Aust. wins two gold, two silver and five bronze medals at Moscow Olympics.
1 Jul. Women allowed to join surf clubs.
Oct. Alan Jones becomes World Drivers' Champion. Elected ABC Sportsman of the Year.
During 1980
Beldale Ball, ridden by J. Letts, wins Melbourne Cup in 3 minutes 19.8 seconds.
Richmond football team wins VFL Premiership in Melbourne.
Canterbury-Bankstown football team wins Rugby League Premiership in Sydney.
Mark Ella becomes first Aboriginal to play international Rugby Union.
NSW bans women from boxing.
National Ice Hockey League competitions begin.
Grant Long becomes first Aust. world windsurf champion.
Kelvin Templeton of Footscray VFL team awarded Brownlow Medal.
Some 23,016 people run in Sydney City-to-Surf footrace.
Yacht *New Zealand* wins Sydney to Hobart yacht race.
Yacht *Australia* challenges for America's Cup. (America wins 4–1.)

1980

F
Historia Dignum

Population
Estimated total Aust., 14,697,700.
Aboriginal population estimated to be 150,000.

Jan. Records reveal that Aust. has highest per capita rate of meat consumption and second-highest rate of sugar consumption in world.
Cyclone Amy damages Goldsworthy, WA.
21 Feb. Aircraft disaster at Sydney airport claims 13 lives when a Beechcraft crashes.
During Feb. Cyclone Dean causes flooding in Pilbara region, WA; damages Port Hedland and Goldsworthy.
Bushfires burn in Adelaide Hills.
Cyclone Enid damages mining town Shay Gap, WA.
Apr. Aust. Atomic Veterans Association calls for Federal inquiry into long-term effects of atomic bomb tests in Maralinga.
Aborigines estb. the Central Aust. Aboriginal Media Association, in Alice Springs.
May. Floods damage Queenstown, Tas.
Jul. Tas. Govt declares Franklin R. part of a Wild River National Park.
Aug. Magazine *Sydney City Monthly* first published.
About two tonnes of yellow cake, a uranium oxide, stolen from Mary Kathleen mine in Qld.
24 Oct. Ethnic television stations launched in Sydney (Channel O/28) and in Melbourne (Channel O).
During Oct. Bushfires burn in east Gippsland, Vic.
Hand of Faith gold nugget discovered at Wedderburn, Vic. (Valued at $1 million.)
Mining explosion at Cobar, NSW, claims three lives.
1 Nov. Fires south of Sydney claim five lives.
15 Dec. First inquest into death of nine-week old Azaria Chamberlain begins at Alice Springs, NT.
17 Dec. Turkish Consul-General and bodyguard shot dead by two terrorists in Sydney.
24 Dec. Bomb explodes in Woolworth's Sydney Town Hall store. (Gregory Norman McHardie and Larry Burton Danielson convicted on 27 Apr. 1982.)
31 Dec. About 350 people arrested during New Year celebrations in capital cities.
During Dec. Storm damages Brisbane.
During 1980
Commercial FM radio stations estb. in Sydney, Melbourne, Brisbane, Adelaide and Perth.
Wyndham, WA, recorded as hottest place in Aust. since turn of century, with average maximum temperature of 35.7°C.
Tully, Qld, recorded as wettest place in Aust. since 1924 with 4,272 mm mean annual rainfall.
Mulka, SA, recorded as driest place in Aust. since 1923 with 119 mm mean annual rainfall.
Carla Zampatti wins Bulletin–Qantas Business Woman of the Year award.
World records show Aust. has highest per capita incidence of reported rape and second-highest incidence of juvenile crime.
National road toll 3,274.

A

History, Politics, Economics, Law

1981

Government

20 Jan. 1981– , Sir James A. Rowland Governor NSW.
28 May 1981–3 Apr. 1982, L. H. S. Thompson Liberal Premier Vic.
19 Jul. 1981–1 Aug. 1981, Sir Francis Theodore Page Burt administered WA.
25 Jul. 1981–5 Aug. 1981, Sir Guy Stephen Montague Green administered Tas.
11 Nov. 1981–26 Mar. 1982, H. N. Holgate, Labor Premier Tas.

19 Jan. Australian Consolidated Industries Ltd makes $240 million bid for Acmil Ltd. Among largest bids in Aust. history to that date.
11 Feb. Sir Harry Talbot Gibbs appointed Chief Justice of High Court of Aust. Sir Gerard Brennan appointed a Justice of the High Court on 12 Feb.
1 Mar. RAAF begins ferrying stranded passengers to and from NZ during airline strike.
9 Mar. About 30,000 people take part in anti-strike demonstrations in Sydney and Brisbane. Similar numbers in Melbourne on 11 Mar.
During Mar. Shirley McKerrow elected National Country Party Federal president. First woman president of major national political party.
11 Apr. Andrew Peacock resigns from Cabinet following the dismissal of his private secretary by Prime Minister Malcolm Fraser.
22–28 Apr. Prince Charles visits Aust.
30 Apr. Final report of the Ministerial Review of Govt by what became known as the 'Razor Gang' released. Recommends cuts in Govt spending.
14 May. The Bank of NSW launches biggest takeover bid in Aust., bidding $699 million for the Commercial Bank of Aust.
During May. User-Pays principle of health insurance replaces universal medical cover.
16 Jul. Arbitration Commission empowered to order a secret ballot of union members over industrial action.
17 Jul. Some 50,000 truck drivers begin two-week stoppage. Vic. and Qld Govts declare a state of emergency.
31 Jul. Cwlth Arbitration Commission abandons wage indexation after a 3.7 per cent wage increase in Jan. and a 3.6 per cent increase in Jul.
25 Sep. Federal Govt begins formal deregistration proceedings against the Builders' Labourers Federation.
26 Sep.–12 Oct. Queen Elizabeth and Prince Philip visit Aust.
30 Sep.–7 Oct. Cwlth Heads of Govt meeting, CHOGM, held in Melbourne and Canberra.
During Sep. NSW Court awards $2.6 million to victim of a motorcycle accident, a record amount in Aust. to that date.
Alan Bond makes largest takeover bid by an individual in Aust. history, offering $150 million for Swan Brewery Ltd in Perth.
A record $79,000 paid for a merino stud ram in Adelaide.
The Australian Bank Ltd opens in Melbourne and Sydney.
12 Oct. Prime Minister conditionally commits Aust. to a 200–300 strong contingent as part of UN–Sinai peace-keeping force.
19 Oct. Federal Govt decides to replace RAAF Mirage fighters with the McDonnell Douglas F-18 Hornet fighter aircraft.
During Oct. The National Commercial Banking Corporation of Australasia estb.
4 Nov. SA Govt grants land rights to the Pitjantjatjara Aborigines in SA.
17 Nov. Report prepared by Keith Campbell, the Campbell Report into Aust. financial systems, tabled. Recommends deregulation of the financial system and entry of foreign banks into Aust.
8 Dec. ACTU reverses two-year old ban on export of uranium.
27 Dec. Illegal immigrants numbering 127 deported. Cwlth Govt revises immigration policy. Ends traditional encouragement of migrants.
During Dec. Tas. Govt holds referendum on alternative sites for dams for hydroelectric power to break deadlock in Parlt over Franklin R. power scheme.
During 1981
Aust. Govt tests detect horse meat in samples of Profreeze export of boneless beef to USA, beginning meat scandal.
Coal becomes biggest Aust. export earner.
National Aboriginal Council holds World Council of Indigenous People conference in Canberra.
Aboriginal lawyer Pat O'Shane becomes first woman to head a NSW Govt department, Aboriginal Affairs.
Sir John Grenfell Crawford wins Australian of the Year award.

1981

B
Science, Technology, Transport, Discovery

3 Feb. Astronomers at Mt Stromlo Observatory discover the first proto star outside the Milky Way.
10 Feb. International airport opens at Townsville, Qld.
28 Apr.–1 May. Sixth International Congress of the International Microsurgical Society meets in Sydney.
13 Jul. TAA acquires its first Airbus.
During Jul. Peter Rogers and David Tribe discover new process for producing ethanol.
1 Oct. Portaprinter telephone typewriter service estb.
During 1981
NSW Govt releases feasibility study for a second Sydney harbour bridge or tunnel.
RAN's Laser airborne depth sounder to estb. sea-level datum and sounding becomes operational.
CSIRO imports weevils from Brazil to eradicate salvinia waterfern in Qld. Lake Moondarra, Qld, cleared during Nov.–Dec.

C
Arts

Literature

During 1981
Archie Weller publishes *The Day of the Dog*.
Macquarie Dictionary published.
Patrick White publishes *Flaws in the Glass: A Self Portrait*.
Colleen McCullough publishes *An Indecent Obsession*.
A. B. Facey publishes *A Fortunate Life*.
The Oxford History of Australian Literature, edited by Leonie Kramer, published.

Music, Dance

Feb. Charles Mackerras appointed conductor of Sydney Symphony Orchestra.
During 1981
Pop group Air Supply successful in USA.
Men at Work group release song 'Who Can It Be Now?'
Tas. Dance Co. estb.

Drama, Theatre, Film

7 Aug. Peter Weir's film *Gallipoli* released. Wins Best Film of the Year award.
Dec. George Miller's film *Mad Max 2* released.
During 1981
Bruce Beresford's film *Puberty Blues* released.

Fine Arts

Mar. Aboriginal Art Exhibition opens in Melbourne
During 1981
E. Smith awarded Archibald Prize for *Rudy Komon*.

Architecture

During 1981
Centrepoint Tower opens in Sydney.

D
Religion, Learning

10 Feb. Vic. Defence of Govt Schools (DOGS) loses court case challenging the principle of State aid to Church schools.

15 Jun.–3 Jul. World Council of Churches delegation visits Aust. to investigate Aboriginal life. Releases report on 10 Aug. critical of Aboriginal living conditions.

24 Aug. Title of Church of England in Aust. officially changes to Anglican Church of Australia.

Sep. The Sixth General Synod of the Anglican Church approves constitutional amendments opening way for ordination of women. (Resolution facilitating constitutional amendments still to be accepted by Aust. Synod.)

E
Sport

Jan. Aust. Institute of Sport estb. in Canberra.

1 Feb. Greg Chappell, Aust. cricket captain, causes one of the greatest furores in cricket history when he orders his brother Trevor Chappell to bowl underarm to a NZ batsman in last ball of match.

22 Jun. David Graham becomes first Aust. golfer to win the USA Open tournament.

Jul. South Melbourne Swans VFL football team apply to have their games played in Sydney. VFL accepts application in Aug.

Aug. Robert de Castella, marathon runner, wins Sydney's City-to-Surf fun run in record time. In Sep. wins 'marathon of history and pace' in Rome. In Dec., wins Fukuoka International Marathon in Japan.

During 1981

Just a Dash, ridden by P. Cook, wins Melbourne Cup in 3 minutes 21.2 seconds.

Carlton football team wins VFL Premiership in Melbourne.

Parramatta football team wins Rugby League Premiership in Sydney.

Bernie Quinlan and Barry Round, of Fitzroy and South Melbourne VFL teams respectively, awarded Brownlow Medal.

Geoff Hunt elected ABC Sportsman of the Year.

Glen, Mark and Gary Ella, Aboriginal brothers, all placed in the Aust. Rugby Union football team. First time three brothers all picked for a touring side.

Zeus II wins Sydney to Hobart yacht race.

1981

F

Historia Dignum

Population

Estimated total Aust., 14,929,100.
Aboriginal population estimated at 160,915. Cwlth census calculates population as 14,576,330.

29 Jan. Larry Burton Danielson charged with attempted robbery and extortion in respect of the Sydney Woolworth bomb scares.
During Jan. Storms damage Geelong, Vic.
Floods in northern Qld. In Feb. floods damage south-eastern Qld.
20 Feb. Coroner determines that Azaria Chamberlain was killed by a dingo. In Sep. new evidence leads to re-opening of the case and Lindy and Michael Chamberlain committed for trial. Second Azaria inquest formally opens in Darwin on 30 Nov.
During Feb. Fires burn in Zeehan, Tas.
29 Apr. Fire destroys nursing home at Sylvania, NSW, claiming 16 lives.
1 Jul. Aust. Post Express replaces the Aust. Post Courier Service.
9 Aug. Cessna aircraft with five on board disappears near Barrington Tops, NSW.
23 Aug. In Thailand Australians Paul Hayward sentenced to 20 years jail and Warren Fellows to 33 years for attempted heroin smuggling.
25 Aug. Fire destroys apartments in Kings Cross Sydney, claiming nine lives.
During Aug. About 130 people in NSW suffer from salmonella food poisoning after consuming tainted salami.
Worst drought in NSW this century officially declared over.
21 Sep. Cessna aircraft crashes at Charleville, Qld, claiming seven lives.
Nov. Federal Govt announces that 36,000 square km of Cairns section of the Great Barrier Reef will be declared a Marine Park. World Heritage Committee lists the Great Barrier Reef on World Heritage Commission Register of the National Estate.
Dec. An estimated $3 million worth of precious stones stolen from Darlington Commodities in Sydney. Biggest robbery in Aust. to that date.
During 1981
Aust. Heritage Commission and the Macmillan Co. of Aust. co-publish a register of items of the National Estate, *The Heritage of Australia*.
Joint Federal–NSW Govt Royal Commission into drug trafficking estb. to investigate Terence John Clark, alias Alexander Sinclair, in the 'Mr Asia' case.
Eve Mahlab wins Bulletin–Qantas Business Woman of the Year award.
National road toll 3,321.

A
History, Politics, Economics, Law

1982

Government

25 Jan. 1982–19 Feb. 1983, R. J. O'Connor Liberal-National Country coalition Premier WA.

1 Mar. 1982–3 Oct. 1985, Sir Brian Murray Governor Vic.

30 Mar. 1982–1 Oct. 1982, Sir Guy Stephen Montague Green administered Tas.

3 Apr. 1982– , J. Cain (the younger) Labor Premier Vic.

23 Apr. 1982– , Sir Donald Dunstan Governor SA.

15 May 1982– , R. T. Gray Liberal Premier Tas.

29 Jul. 1982– , Sir Ninian Stephen Governor-General Aust.

1 Oct. 1982– , Sir James Plimsoll Governor Tas.

6 Nov. 1982– , J. C. Bannon Labor Premier SA.

During Jan. First shipment of yellow cake marketed from Ranger uranium mine loaded in Darwin. First shipment of uranium ore leaves for USA in Aug.

Vic. police refuse to patrol in cars without air-conditioning.

13 Feb. First Indo-Chinese refugees under the Community Refugee Settlement Scheme arrive and settle at Whyalla, SA.

18 Feb. First Aust. contingent of United Nations Peacekeeping Force in the Sinai leaves Brisbane.

25 Feb. Federal Govt announces decision to purchase HMS *Invincible* from England. (Decision to purchase dropped after the Falklands War in 1983.)

Mar. Qld Govt approves proposal to transfer title of Qld Aboriginal reserves to elected Aboriginal councils, enabling Aborigines to lease the land but not to sub-divide or control mineral rights.

Federal Govt approves a $600 million development of uranium at Jabiluka, NT. On 29 Jun. Aboriginal Northern Land Council authorizes Pan-Continental Mining Co. to mine.

8 Apr. Andrew Peacock unsuccessfully challenges Malcolm Fraser for Liberal Party leadership. Peacock returns to Cabinet in Oct. as Minister for Industry and Commerce.

19 Apr. Federal Govt begins a migrant selection scheme to re-unite families.

Federal ministers Michael MacKellar and John Moore resign in controversy over MacKellar making false customs declaration in relation to a coloured television set when returning from overseas in Oct. 1981.

May. Norm Gallagher, Secretary of Builders' Labourers Federation, found guilty of contempt of court.

25 Jun. State and Cwlth Govts virtually abolish right of appeal from State Supreme Courts to the Privy Council, making the High Court of Aust. the final court of appeal.

During Jun. Local Courts replace Courts of Petty Sessions in NSW.

NSW Country Party re-named NSW National Party in line with Qld and Vic. On 16 Oct. the Federal National Country Party drops word 'Country' from title.

16 Jul. Bob Hawke unsuccessfully challenges Bill Hayden for ALP leadership.

27 Jul. International Whaling Commission phases out commercial whaling.

27 Jul. Sir William Deane appointed a Justice of the High Court of Aust. Sir Daryl Michael Dawson appointed a Justice on 16 Aug.

29 Jul. Value of Aust. dollar against the US dollar falls below parity for first time.

During Jul. Federal Govt announces that the Aust. Broadcasting Commission (ABC) is to be replaced by the Aust. Broadcasting Corporation, with a nine-member board and no longer under control of the Public Service.

15 Aug. Qld Govt workers strike for shorter hours.

24 Aug. Fourth interim report of Costigan Royal Commission into activities of Federated Ship Painters and Dockers Union reveals organized crime rackets and ignites controversy about tax avoidance by 'bottom of the harbour' company tax schemes.

25 Aug. Union ban on export of live sheep to Middle East lifted.

During Aug. Aust. Broadcasting Tribunal recommends introduction of subscription and cable television.

27 Sep.–13 Oct. Prince Philip, joined by Queen Elizabeth on 5 Oct., visits Aust.

1 Oct. The Westpac Banking Corporation estb. from merger of the Bank of NSW and the Commercial Bank of Aust. Ltd.

14–29 Oct. Miners strike on five NSW coalfields over BHP retrenchments.

During Oct. During Cwlth Games in Brisbane Aborigines strike for land rights.

Federal Govt decides to estb. a National Crimes Commission.

Nov. Federal Govt calls for a national public and private sector 12-months wage freeze.

During 1982

The 38-hour week awarded to many industries.

Recession in iron and steel industry forces Broken Hill Proprietory Ltd to cut production facilities and reduce workforce.

Sir Edward Stratten Williams, Qld Chief Justice, wins Australian of the Year award.

1982

National ALP conference reverses uranium policy, allowing for continuation of existing uranium mining projects.

Cwlth Govt announces a 10 cents tax on trading bank cheques and other account debits. (Introduced on 1 Jan. 1983.)

B

Science, Technology, Transport, Discovery

26 Jan. The Aust. Shipping Register Office opens in Canberra, ending British registration of Aust. ships.

8 Apr. NSW high speed XPT passenger train makes first run, to Dubbo, NSW.

11 Apr. Dick Smith makes record solo helicopter flight from Sydney to Bundaberg, Qld. Begins first stage of round-world helicopter flight, leaving Texas, USA, on 6 Aug.

Jun. After much controversy, SA Govt authorizes uranium mining at Roxby Downs.

Aust. takes delivery of tanker *Mobile Flinders*, largest Aust.-owned ship (149,235 tonnes) to that date.

Sep. Omega Navigation Station opens in Vic.

Oct. Ansett and TAA end city-airport bus services.

Dec. Oil discovered south of Barrow I., WA.

During 1982

The Best Linear Unbiased Prediction procedure introduced to cattle industry to analyse livestock.

Moomba–Stony Point liquids pipeline in SA operational.

C
Arts

Literature

During 1982
Thomas Keneally publishes *Schindler's Ark*.
Ian Moffit publishes *The Retreat of Radiance*.
Peter Carey publishes *Bliss*.

Music, Dance

31 Jul. The Lyric Opera of Qld estb.
During 1982
Werner Andreas Albert appointed conductor Qld Symphony Orchestra. Sir Charles Mackerras appointed conductor Sydney Symphony Orchestra.
Victorian Arts Centre Concert Hall opens.

Drama, Theatre, Film

20 Mar. Film *The Man from Snowy River* released.
May. Aust. films well received at the Cannes Film Festival in France.
28 Oct. Film *We of the Never Never* premières in Canberra.
During 1982
Aust. Aboriginal Theatre enters *The Cakeman* as Aust. entry in World Theatre Festival in USA.
Lonely Hearts wins Best Film of the Year award.

Fine Arts

21 Jun. Qld Art Gallery opens in Brisbane.
Oct. Aust. National Gallery opens in Canberra.
During 1982
E. Smith awarded Archibald Prize for *Peter Sculthorpe*.

D
Religion, Learning

Jan. Catholic and Anglican Churches call for pause in test tube baby programme until ethical problems are debated.
Jul. Vic. Govt abolishes use of corporal punishment in State schools.
Federal Govt increases aid to private schools by 7.7 per cent and to Govt schools by 2.0 per cent.

1982

E
Sport

Jan. The Lawn Tennis Association of Aust. offers nearly $1 million prize money for men's and women's open championships.
Feb. Graham Marsh wins first major golf tournaments in Aust.
Apr. South Melbourne VFL team start first season as the Sydney Swans.
Oct. Cwlth Games held in Brisbane. Aust. wins 39 gold medals.
During 1982
Gurner's Lane, ridden by L. Dittman, wins Melbourne Cup in 3 minutes 21.1 seconds.
Rugby League football game adopts a number of changes, including the increase of value of a try to 4 points.
Carlton football team wins VFL Premiership in Melbourne.
Parramatta football team wins Rugby League Premiership in Sydney.
Brian Wilson of Melbourne VFL team awarded Brownlow Medal.
Robert de Castella elected ABC Sportsman of the Year.
Scallywag wins Sydney to Hobart yacht race.

F
Historia Dignum

Population
Estimated total Aust., 15,174,500.

5 Jan. Cessna aircraft crashes at Archerfield, Qld, claiming five lives.
7 Jan. A Bell 206 B Jet Ranger helicopter, carrying television news crew, crashes near Melbourne, claiming five lives.
During Jan. Floods devastate south-western WA. Among worst in WA this century.
Feb. Tas. Govt declares state of emergency when bushfires first break out in country surrounding Hobart.
Apr. Bernard Lewis, Sydney property developer, pays a record $5.25 million for a house at Point Piper, Sydney.
Customs and police officers seize over two tonnes of Lebanese hashish, estimated value $100 million. Among biggest drug hauls in Aust. to that date.
7 May. Harry M. Miller sentenced to three years gaol for aiding and abetting fraudulent misappropriation.
During May. Thomas and Alexander Barton committed for trial in Sydney on charges of conspiracy and perjury arising out of alleged events concerning Bounty Oil.
2 Aug. Newspaper *Daily Sun* first published in Brisbane.
30 Sep. Cessna aircraft disappears en route Atherton to Mt Isa, Qld; five lives lost.
Sep.–Oct. Many environmentalists arrested during successful anti-rainforest logging protests at Nightcap Range, NSW.
Merredin Senior High School mini-bus crashes near Perth, claiming nine lives.
The Azaria Chamberlain murder trial opens in Darwin. On 29 Oct. Lindy Chamberlain sentenced to life imprisonment for murdering Azaria. (Full Bench appeals begin in Feb. 1983 but quashed on 29 Apr. 1983.)
During 1982
Video cassette recorder industry booms.
Rising hemlines and exposed body popular in women's fashion.
Aust. launches national greening programme.
Aust. hosts World Heritage Convention committee meeting. Great Barrier Reef, Qld, Willandra Lakes, NSW, Kakadu National Park, NT, and Gordon-Franklin Rivers area, Tas., recorded on World Heritage List.
Patricia Lovell wins Bulletin–Qantas Business Woman of the Year.
National road toll 3,252.

1982

Gordon–Below–Franklin Dam controversy

Feb. Tas. Govt announces that Franklin R. would be dammed in 1985 as part of State's hydroelectric scheme.

15 Jun. Tas. environmentalists begin High Court action to stop damming of Gordon and Franklin Rivers.

16 Jun. Tas. Govt passes Act for construction of dam of the Gordon R.

15 Dec. Conservationists blockade preliminary work on the dam.

Dec. SW Tas. put on World Heritage list, but Federal Govt refuses to influence Tas. Govt's determination to proceed with work on dam.

1 Jul. 1983. High Court of Aust. rules against proceeding with dam.

1983

A History, Politics, Economics, Law

Government

11 Feb. Brian Thomas Burke Labor Premier WA.

5 Mar. Forty-seventh Cwlth. Ministry, Robert James Lee (Bob) Hawke, Labor Prime Minister Aust.

Jan. Federal Govt announces decision to allow 10 foreign banks to compete in Aust.

3 Feb. Bob Hawke replaces Bill Hayden as Leader of the Aust. Labor Party and on same day Prime Minister Malcolm Fraser announces a double dissolution of Federal Parlt.

5 Mar. Thirty-third Federal Parlt. opens.

11 Mar. Andrew Peacock becomes Federal Leader of the Liberal Party.

During Mar. Prince Charles, Princess Diana and Prince William begin Aust. Royal tour.

Unemployment rises to 10.7 per cent, highest rate since Great Depression.

11–14 Apr. National Economic Summit held in Canberra. Supports return to centralized system of wage fixing and consensus approach to economic problems.

During Apr. Builders' Labourers Federation national secretary, Norm Gallagher, released from jail after serving 52 days for contempt of court.

Tas. Premier criticizes Federal Govt for using an RAAF Mirage jet to photograph work at Franklin Dam, Tas. (Photographs allegedly taken for use in High Court challenge to the dam.)

Senior cadets at Royal Military College Duntroon charged following investigation into allegations of bastardization.

Federal Govt expels Soviet Embassy First Secretary Valeriy Ivanov for spying. In May former Aust. Labor Party national secretary David Combe is barred from having professional contact with Cabinet Ministers following controversy relating to the nature of his contacts with Ivanov.

Arbitration Commission sets precedent by granting a four-day working week to about 200,000 motor trade employees.

National Constitution Conference in Adelaide opposes proposals for a fixed term of Federal Parlt, but agrees with the principle of four-year terms for Federal members with simultaneous Upper and Lower House elections.

10 May. NSW Premier Neville Wran steps aside following allegations by *Four Corners* television programme on 30 Apr. that he sought to influence a magistrate hearing charges relating to misappropriation of funds against a former Rugby League administrator Kevin Humphreys. Royal Commission appointed opening in Jun. Wran exonerated and resumes office on 28 Jul.

During May. Prime Minister announces Royal Commission to examine security services and events behind the expulsion of Valeriy Ivanov and his links with lobbyist David Combe. (Report tabled in Dec.)

Royal Commission appointed to investigate use of chemical agents, including Agent Orange, during Vietnam War.

Jun. Unions throughout Aust. criticize Federal Govt decision to impose a 30 per cent tax on superannuation lump sum payments.

Federal Govt announces introduction of Medicare Health Scheme to be financed by a 1 per cent levy on income tax. (Effective from 1 Feb. 1984.)

Aust.–French diplomatic relations deteriorate following Govt criticism of continued French nuclear tests on Mururoa Atoll. Federal Govt announces plans to stop uranium exports to France.

Vic. Govt passes legislation providing for automatic jail sentences for arsonists. Also introduces new legislation preventing jailing of people for possessing or growing up to 50 grams of marijuana.

Broken Hill Proprietary Ltd makes a $98.77 million share placement, largest undertaken by an Aust. company.

Stewart Royal Commission into drug trafficking finds evidence of widespread corruption and malpractice among police forces and in the defunct Federal Narcotics Bureau.

Ken Myer appointed first chairman of Aust. Broadcasting Corporation.

1 Jul. High Court decision supports Federal Govt right to block construction of Gordon-below-Franklin Dam, Tas.

14 Jul. Special Minister for State Mick Young resigns from Cabinet over allegations that he spoke outside his portfolio, improperly exposing the Ivanov affair. (Re-instated on 20 Jan. 1984.)

1 Aug. Former NSW Chief Stipendiary magistrate Murray Farquhar charged with perverting course of justice in the 1977 committal proceedings against former NSW Rugby League administrator, Kevin Humphreys. Humphreys found guilty on 10 of 11 charges of fraud and stealing on 18 Oct.

4 Aug. Following a debate in Qld Parlt on forming a public accounts committee, Liberal Welfare Services Minister Terry White is sacked from National-Liberal Ministry for breaching party loyalty by voting with Opposition.

31 Aug. Vic. Minister for Industrial Affairs, Bill Landeryou, is forced to resign from ministry over a conflict of interest involving union loans.

Sep. Jennie George of Aust. Council of Salaried and Professional Associations becomes first woman elected to Aust. Council of Trade Unions Executive.

B

Science, Technology, Transport, Discovery

1983

Oct. Arbitration Commission hands down a 4.3 per cent wage increase to apply from 6 Oct.
Federal Govt introduces legislation which approves divorce by mail. Consenting partners no longer required to attend court hearings or send legal representation.
Nov. Federal Caucus votes 55 to 46 in favour of mining uranium, defeating left wing of Aust. Labor Party.
Federal Govt agrees to hand over ownership of Uluru National Park, NT, including Ayers Rock, to Aborigines.
In an Aust. Secret Intelligence Service training exercise which went wrong, at the Sheraton Hotel in Melbourne, operatives smash a door, brandish firearms and grapple with hotel staff before being captured by Vic. police.
Dec. When captain of the HMS *Invincible* refuses to say whether his ship carries nuclear weapons, Defence Minister Gordon Scholes disallows access to dry-dock facilities.
During 1983
By this year Aborigines hold freehold title to more than 500,000, square kilometres throughout Aust.

Jan. Shell Aust. Ltd announces discovery of rich coalfields in south-western Tas.
The Aust. Medical Association's Report *Advances in Medicine* submits that through improved methods of diagnosis such as computerised scanning, ultrasound, arteriography and advances in endoscopy, more people are living longer.
Mar. Cooper Basin partners ship first barrels of crude oil from Strzelecki fields, SA (discovered in 1978), to Kwinana refinery in WA.
Apr. Coal development boom in Qld and NSW collapses. Interest in Kalgoorlie goldfields, WA, revives.
May. The disease, Acquired Immune Deficiency Syndrome (AIDS), first identified in USA in 1981, is found in Sydney. (First Aust. death reported in Melbourne in Jul.)
Monash University in-vitro fertilization team achieves a pregnancy following the successful freezing and thawing of human embryo in Melbourne.
Jul. Federal Govt confirms decision to launch the national communications satellite AUSSAT.
17 Oct. Broken Hill Proprietary Ltd announces significant oil finds in the Timor Sea.
During 1983
Struan Sutherland of CSIRO publishes *Australian Animal Toxins*.

1983

Arts

Literature

During 1983
Clive James publishes *Brilliant Creatures*.
Morris West publishes *The World is Made of Glass*.
Ian Moffit publishes *The Colour Man*.
Singer of the Bush, complete works of 'Banjo' Paterson 1885–1900, and *Song of The Pen*, complete works 1901–1941, published.
Fourth edition of *The Australian Encyclopaedia* published in 12 volumes. Editor-in-Chief Richard Appleton.

Music, Dance

30 Jan. Opera singers Joan Sutherland and Luciano Pavarotti (Italian) perform at Sydney Opera House in nationally televised concert.
Mar. Soviet violinist Nelli Shnolnikova defects to Aust.
May. Sydney Entertainment Centre opens.
Jul. Aust. Dancing Society calls for ballroom dancing to be introduced in schools.
Aug. Andrew Lloyd Webber's *Song and Dance* opens in Sydney.

Drama, Theatre, Film

6–9 Mar. *The Dismissal*, dramatized television film depicting events leading to the fall of the Whitlam Govt in 1975, first screened.
May–Jun. *For The Term of His Natural Life* screened on television; among most expensive Aust. television productions to that date.
14 Jun. Film *Cattle King* premières in Sydney.
Aug. Film *Phar Lap* premières in Sydney.
Sep. Film *Careful He Might Hear You* premières in Sydney. Wins 8 out of 14 awards from the Aust. Film Institute in Oct., including Best Film of the Year award.
Oct. Dramatized television film *Scales of Justice*, depicting police corruption in an unnamed Aust. State, arouses protest in police circles throughout Aust.
10 Dec. Eight-hour performance drama, *The Life and Adventures of Nicholas Nickleby*, opens in Sydney.
During 1983
Reg Livermore opens show *Firing Squad* in Melbourne.

Fine Arts

26 Mar. New England Regional Art Museum opens at Armidale, NSW.
During 1983
Nigel Thomson awarded Archibald Prize for *Chandler Coventry*.

Architecture

During 1983
Neville Gruzman's Twenty-five Small Buildings exhibition tours Aust.

D
Religion, Learning

E
Sport

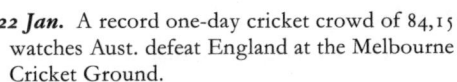

Jan. Aust. Catholic Relief Fund advises that Philippines aid money may have been passed to the outlawed Philippines Communist Party.

Teacher Unions intensify campaigns against Govt assistance to non-Govt schools.

Public controversy aroused when some members of the political wing of the Uniting Church allegedly advocate 'liberation theology', professing that capitalism is the cause of worldly injustice.

Feb. Progressive and conservative education forces argue over whether school curricula should be standardized on traditional disciplines or be more flexible.

Mar. Archbishop Edward Clancy replaces Cardinal Sir James Freeman as Catholic Archbishop of Sydney, most senior Catholic position in Aust.

SA Govt approves plans to estb. a boarding school solely for Asian secondary school students.

Aust. Catholic priest Brian Gore is charged in the Philippines for possession of explosives, incitement to rebellion and complicity in multiple murder. (Returns to Aust. on 22 Jul. 1984 after exoneration).

May. There is public disapproval at the number of overseas students gaining places in Aust. universities at the expense of young Australians.

Jul. Churches unite in expressing concern at the decline in the numbers attending church services.

Aug. Vic. Govt announces cuts in State Govt aid to 'wealthy' non-Govt schools.

27 Oct. High Court rules that Church of Scientology is a religion, thereby over-ruling a decision of the Full Bench of the Vic. Supreme Court which ruled that the Church was not a religion and was thus liable to pay Vic. payroll tax.

During Oct. Vic. Govt ends supply of free milk to pre-school kindergartens and child minding centres.

Nov. Teacher unions begin movement to introduce 'peace studies' into school curricula.

During 1983

By this year public schools offer a wide range of personal development and human relations courses.

22 Jan. A record one-day cricket crowd of 84,153 watches Aust. defeat England at the Melbourne Cricket Ground.

Mar. Cricketer Graham Yallop sets record for the most runs scored in a Sheffield season, 1254.

Apr. Peter Hadfield wins his seventh Aust. decathlon championship.

May. Potato farmer Cliff Young, aged 61, becomes a national hero after winning the first Sydney to Melbourne marathon.

Jun. Aust. youth soccer team moves to top of its group in world youth soccer championships.

2 Jul. Elisabeth Hayes becomes first woman formally admitted into Melbourne Cricket Ground Long Room.

26 Sep. *Australia II*, equipped with a revolutionary new winged keel designed by Ben Lexcen, defeats USA to win the America's Cup. First time ever Cup won by non-American yacht.

31 Oct. Ron Grant completes a round Aust. marathon run, 13,393 km, in Brisbane.

During Oct. Hawthorn football team wins VFL Premiership in Melbourne by a record 83 point margin.

Parramatta football team wins Rugby League Premiership in Sydney.

Ross Glendinning of N. Melbourne VFL team wins Brownlow medal.

Greg Norman wins the World Match Play golf championship in England (also won title in 1980).

Nov. Aust. wins women's world teams squash championship in Perth.

Dec. Jeanette Baker retains World Cup ten-pin bowling title.

During 1983

Kiwi, ridden by J. Cassidy, wins Melbourne Cup in 3 minutes 18.9 seconds.

Windsurfing now fastest-growing sport in Aust.

Condor wins Sydney to Hobart yacht race.

Pat Cash, 18 years old, becomes youngest member of an Aust. Davis Cup team since John Alexander in 1968.

Robert de Castella wins Australian of the Year award. During year wins ABC Sportsman of the Year award. In Apr. wins Rotterdam marathon in Holland. In Aug. wins gold medal at world athletics championship in Helsinki.

Historia Dignum

1983

Population
Estimated total Aust. 15,349,500.

Jan. Bushfires devastate NSW and Vic. bushland, claiming four lives.

16 Feb. The 'Ash Wednesday' bushfires begin; devastate large areas of Vic. and SA, claiming 72 lives.

During Feb. Melbourne experiences worst-ever dust storm and its highest recorded Feb. temperatures.

Mar. Drought-breaking rains begin falling. Flash floods in SA following bushfires destroy many homes. Todd R. near Alice Springs, NT, floods claiming three lives.

Evidence of the consumption of dogs in some Asian communities in Aust. rouses public outcry.

Apr. About 3,000 motor bike riders fight a pitched battle with police at the Easter race meeting at Bathurst, NSW.

3 May. Qld declared a disaster area following flooding of nine river systems.

During May. NSW police express concern at rapidly increasing number of car thefts.

Federal Govt introduces The World Heritage Conservation Bill designed to block construction of the Franklin Dam in Tas. On 1 Jul. High Court rules against building of the dam.

The Quiros Troupe perform 'The World's Greatest Circus Spectacular' at Sydney Entertainment Centre.

Jun. Police resume searching for body of anti-drugs campaigner Donald Mackay who disappeared in 1977.

30 Jul. Four prisoners escape from Jika Jika (renamed Division K in 1984), Pentridge jail's maximum security wing in Melbourne. (Two escapees recaptured in Oct.)

During Jul. Federal police seize 40 kilograms of heroin in Sydney in Australia's biggest heroin drug bust.

Epidemic of arson breaks out in Sydney.

Aug. Five people killed and 20 injured when a roadtrain driven by Douglas Edwin Crabbe ploughed into a motel at Ayers Rock, NT. Crabbe found guilty of murder in Mar. 1984.)

During Sep. Beechcraft Super King aircraft crashes in Qld, claiming 12 lives.

About 300 anti-nuclear demonstrators arrive at Roxby Downs, SA, to blockade uranium mine.

13 Nov. Police arrest 111 women demonstrators, protesting against USA bases in Aust., at Pine Gap, NT.

During Nov. About 80 police confront 350 Aborigines during night-time riots at Redfern, Sydney.

Hinke Haisma wins Bulletin–Qantas Business Woman of the Year award.

NSW police dept recommends that prostitution be legalized in commercial areas of Sydney.

During 1983
National Epilepsy Association of Aust. estb.
Mindit Beach Casino opens in Darwin.
Baggy outfits, exaggerated shapes and cropped pants now fashionable.
National road toll 2,738.

A

History, Politics, Economics, Law

1984

Government

Oct. Ian Tuxworth Country-Liberal Chief Minister NT.

1 Dec. 1984– , Forty-eighth Cwlth Ministry, R. J. Hawke Labor Prime Minister Aust.

Jan. National sharemarkets soar to record levels with the All Industrials Index breaking the 1,000-point mark for first time.

1 Feb. Medicare Health Scheme introduced. On 9 Apr. doctors call national strike over disputes arising from the scheme. In June NSW Govt passes legislation banning for seven years doctors who resign in protest against the scheme. (Legislation repealed in Aug.)

During Feb. A new Centre-Left faction of the ALP forms in Adelaide to address the imbalance between left-wing idealists and right-wing pragmatists. New faction led by W. G. Hayden.

Mar. Justice Lionel Murphy of the High Court, among others, is named as allegedly involved with questionable conduct as revealed in NSW police tapes.

Historian Geoffrey Blainey begins public controversy when he questions current immigration policies on migration from Asia. In May the balance of immigrants from Europe and Asia is debated in Federal Parlt.

Apr. Full Bench of Arbitration Commission grants 4.1 per cent rise in national wage.

More than 200,000 people take part in anti-nuclear marches throughout Aust. Biggest turn-out to that date.

Qld Aborigines seek to contest State legislation which disenfranchises them in local govt elections.

5 Jun. Federal Govt launches 'affirmative action' programme, a 12-month pilot project designed to lay basis for systematic improvement in position of women in Aust. labour force.

During Jun. Final version of pensions assets test sets a $100,000 threshold for couples assets and a $70,000 cut-off level for singles assets. Family homes exempted.

Federal Govt announces plans to revamp car industry by cutting the number of manufacturers from five to three.

Justice Donald Stewart named as chairman of the National Crime Authority scheduled to take over investigations from the Costigan Royal Commission.

Legislation to recover $270 million from 'bottom-of-the-harbour' tax evaders is blocked in Senate when Govt fails to win majority.

Aust. and NZ Banking Group announces a $280 million take-over of Grindlay's Bank of London in a move which places half ANZ's assets outside Aust.

9–13 Jul. ALP National Conference held in Canberra. Left-wing of the party suffers defeat on a number of policy issues, including uranium and E. Timor.

During Jul. Aust. dollar falls to 81.3 US cents, an all-time low against US currency to that date.

Special Minister of State Mick Young acknowledges making a false customs declaration on goods found in bags belonging to his wife on 5 Jul. This begins the 'Paddington Bear Affair.' Young reinstated in Cabinet in Sep. following inquiry.

1 Aug. Federal and State anti-discrimination laws proclaimed.

21 Aug. Federal Budget speech televised live from Parlt House, Canberra for first time.

27 Aug. Retiring head of Federal Treasury, John Stone, delivers a controversial lecture in Perth criticizing various bodies and institutions, including the Govt, for economic shortcomings.

During Aug. Aust. Arbitration Commission hands down decision giving greater job security to workers including more favourable severance payments.

Aust. Building societies lend a record $3,370 million for housing in the 1983/1984 financial year.

Aust. Broadcasting Corporation grants homosexual partners same work benefits as heterosexual partners.

G. J. Coles and Co. Ltd sets national sales record of $5,443 million in financial year.

Rock singer Peter Garrett joins former ALP Senator Jean Melzer and others to form Nuclear Disarmament Party.

24 Sep. Secret papers on the Petrov Affair released to public for first time.

During Sep. Royal Commission into the British atomic tests conducted in Aust. between 1952 and 1963 opens in Sydney.

Federal Opposition leader Andrew Peacock faces public backlash over his allegations that the Prime Minister is a 'crook' who associates with criminals.

26 Nov. PM Hawke and Opposition Leader Peacock participate in first nationally televised election campaign debate.

Nov. Australia elected to UN Security Council for two-year term.

1984

B

Science, Technology, Transport, Discovery

Mar. National heart transplant programme recommences.
Sydney doctors successfully apply the cochlear implant, an electrical ear implant device for the deaf.
6 Jun. First F-18 Hornet fighter jets arrive in Aust. as part of an RAAF order for 75 of the fighter planes.
14 Jun. Telecom opens national public videotex system, Viatel, a public information service operating via television.
During Jun. Qld Premier opens the Jackson oilfield and 800-kilometre pipeline from the field to Brisbane.
Aust. Science Technology Council recommends continued mining and export of uranium, backing Govt decision to allow Roxby Downs mine, SA, to develop.
Scientists discover important fossils of animals not previously recorded at Riversleigh, near Gregory R., in Gulf country of Qld. Among most important deposits of Aust. fossils discovered.
Jul. A new gold boom in goldfields begins at Kalgoorlie, WA.
20 Aug. General Motors-Holden launches the Holden Astra motor car.
During Aug. A survey conducted at Royal Prince Alfred Hospital in Sydney demonstrates that smoking can reduce a man's sperm count by half.
Sep. Tas. Govt prepares legislation to hand over to Aborigines ancient sub-fossil Aboriginal remains and human skeletal material from museum holdings. The remains are of important international scientific significance.
First direct Aust.–China air service begins.
Medical researchers Robin Warren and Barry Marshall uncover possible causes of ulcers and gastritis, arousing world-wide interest among scientists.
Nov. Environment Protection Authority rates Melbourne as 'smog capital' of Australia and fourth-worst affected city in world. (After Los Angeles, Tokyo and Mexico City.)
Dec. Telephone cable linking Aust. with NZ, Fiji, Hawaii and Canada completed.
Federal Govt sets up Advisory Committee on problems associated with disease AIDS.
During 1984
Aust.-born oceanographer Paul Scully-Power selected to participate as crew member of USA space shuttle *Challenger* to be launched later in the year.

C

Arts

Literature

During 1984
Germaine Greer publishes *Sex and Destiny*.
Richard Broome publishes *The Victorians Arriving*.
Tony Dingle publishes *The Victorians Settling*.
Susan Priestley publishes *The Victorians Making Their Mark*.
A Campfire Yarn, complete works of Henry Lawson 1885–1900, and *A Fantasy of Man*, complete works 1901–1922, published.

Music, Dance

May. Rap or 'break' dancing becomes popular.
29 Jul. Aust. Youth Orchestra begins first European tour.
Aug. First national recorder festival held in Melbourne.
During 1984
Vic. State Opera and Elizabethan Theatre Trust stage *The Pirates of Penzance* in Melbourne and Sydney.

Drama, Theatre, Film

Mar. Television drama *Waterfront* premières.
Apr. Television drama *Eureka Stockade* premières.
Jun. WA Govt bans X-rated videotapes. On 28 Aug. NSW Govt bans same.
Jul. Television drama *Bodyline* premières.
Aug. Television drama *Singles* premières.
Sep. Film *Street Hero* premières.
Strikebound premières in Wonthaggi, Vic.
Nov. National Film and Sound Archives opened in Canberra.
Dec. Film *Coolangatta Gold* premières.
During 1984
Boom in the video movie industry forces many drive-ins and picture theatres throughout Aust. to close.
Annie's Coming Out wins Best Film of the Year award.

Fine Arts

May. Vic. National Gallery announces that two of its masterpieces had been revealed by infra-red tests to be fake.
Jun. The Courtauld Collection of French impressionist and post-impressionist paintings exhibited at Aust. National Gallery, Canberra.
29 Oct. The three-section Victorian Arts Centre officially opened.

During 1984
Keith Looby wins the Archibald Prize for *Max Gillies*.

Architecture

Sep. 'Concrete cancer', caused by rusting reinforcement rods, threatens some modern high-rise buildings.

D
Religion, Learning

1984

Feb. Sydney police arrest for fraud members of a group called the Aust. Uniting Life Church. The group allegedly collected up to $3 million falsely claiming it to be for handicapped groups.

Federal Govt announces intention to implement a computer education programme in Aust. schools.

Apr. The Cwlth. Schools Commission submits report 'Commonwealth Standards for Australian Schools', a long-term education blueprint pushing for substantial increases in Cwlth Govt expenditure.

Jun. Melbourne's Anglican Diocese elects David Penman as archbishop.

Ken McKinnon and Doug Swan release report 'Future Directions of Secondary Education', on the planning and development of secondary education in Aust.

15 Aug. Federal Govt ends uncertainty over future funding to private schools by announcing it will continue funding to both Govt and non-Govt schools for at least the next eight years.

During Aug. Many PhD and Master graduates leave Aust. in search of work overseas.

Aust. Council for Adult Literacy estimates that over one million Australians have literacy problems.

Sep. Aust. Bureau of Statistics states that 60 per cent of Aust. population over 15 years of age have no post-school qualifications.

During 1984
Federal Govt commits $74 million to the Participation and Equity Programme designed to change senior high school education by making courses more attractive, relevant and useful, thus encouraging more students to stay at school longer.

1984

E
Sport

Feb. Greg Norman wins Aust. Masters Golf Tournament.
15 Aug. Carol Tucker becomes among first women jockeys in Melbourne to win a race against male jockeys.
18 Aug. Following doubts about the identity of a horse which raced in Brisbane as Fine Cotton, but was believed to be a better-class sprinter named Bold Personality, stewards declare the race void.
During Aug. Aust. wins four gold, eight silver, and twelve bronze medals at the Los Angeles Olympics.
9 Sep. Vic. introduces Sunday VFL games.
During Sep. Essendon football team wins VFL Premiership in Melbourne.
Peter Moore of Melbourne VFL team wins Brownlow Medal.
Canterbury-Bankstown football team wins Rugby League premiership in Sydney.
3 Oct. Tim Macartney-Snape and Greg Mortimer become first Australians to climb Mount Everest and first in world to climb north face without oxygen.
During 1984
John Sieben wins ABC Sportsman of the Year award.
Black Knight, ridden by Peter Cook, wins Melbourne Cup in 3 minutes 18.9 seconds.

F
Historia Dignum

Population
Estimated total Aust. 15,450,000.

Jan. The magazine *Star Enquirer* first published.
Heavy rains destroy about 30 per cent of Vic. and NSW wheat crops. Torrential rain and severe storms in NSW, Qld and SA cause flooding.
Vic. Govt announces plans to introduce plastic card drivers' licences, including photograph of holder, to facilitate computerized on-the-spot police checks within seconds. (Effective from 1 Nov.)
Feb. Bank robber Hakki Atahan shot dead in Sydney after leading hostages through a dramatic procession in a commandeered car.
An opal dealer, John Alexander Hay, who allegedly threatened to blow up the Hyatt Kingsgate Hotel in Sydney, surrenders after a siege lasting nearly 10 hours.
26 Mar. First $100 notes circulated.
During Mar. High Court votes three to two to reject Lindy Chamberlain's appeal against conviction for murdering her baby Azaria in 1980 at Ayers Rock, NT.
Cyclone Chloe devastates Roebourne, WA.
19 Apr. Tune of *Advance Australia Fair* proclaimed Aust. National Anthem. *God Save the Queen* becomes Royal Anthem, to be used only when member of Royal Family present.
14 May. A 14-sided one dollar coin with a kangaroo design issued to replace the dollar note.
During May. A small aircraft crashes into houses in Goulburn, NSW, killing four.
Jun. Denis Bartell takes 23 days to cross Simpson Desert unaided.
19 Jul. Television magazine *Look and Listen* first published.
During Jul. Aust. edition of *Newsweek* magazine incorporated into *The Bulletin*.
Cold weather in Vic., NSW and parts of Qld; snowfalls in many areas.
Vic. Govt announces intention to declare national park in Vic. Alps from Mansfield to NSW border despite objections from 16 municipalities. On 4 Sep. about 300 cattlemen ride on horseback through Melbourne to protest against plans to estb. the park.
Institute of Family Studies announces that almost one in five Australians live below the poverty line. On 23 Sep. the Council launches 'Fair Share' campaign to help low-income people.
Vic. State Health Commission recommends that graves more than 75 years old should be re-used after the old remains have been unearthed and reburied.

1984

Aug. Conservationists attempt to blockade the construction of a road from Daintree to Cape Tribulation, Qld, through north Qld rainforest.

2 Sep. Six men and a 14-year-old girl are killed in a shoot-out between rival motor bike gangs, the Bandinos and Commancheros, in Sydney in the 'Father's Day Massacre'.

During Sep. A survey released by the Institute of Family Studies reveals that about 40 per cent of Aust. marriages break down.

Vic. Police arrest a 20-year-old apprentice electrician over threats to poison Geelong's water supply.

During 1984

In an attempt to curb a dramatic rise in home burglaries, Vic. police introduce the Neighbourhood Watch programme which organizes citizens to play a preventative role.

Beverley Hancock, retail fashion executive, wins Bulletin–Qantas Business Woman of the Year award.

Lois O'Donaghue, Aboriginal activist, wins Australian of the Year award.

National road toll 2,822.

Index

A

Aalberg, George, 1927 E
Aavik, Edgar E. 1913 C
Abalone, 1963 A
A. B. (Banjo) Paterson (painting), 1934 C
Abbey, 1882 C
Abbot, Charles L. A. 1886 A, 1937 A
Abbot, John H. M. 1874 C
Abbott, Edward, 1807 A, 1832 A
Abbott, Harold F. 1906 C
Abbott, Jacob, 1836 D
Abbott, Joseph P. (b. 1842) 1842 A
Abbott, Joseph P. (b. 1891) 1891 A
Abbott, Macartney, 1877 A
Abbott, William E. 1844 A
Abbotsleigh Church of England School, Sydney, 1885 D
à Beckett, Edward, 1844 C
à Beckett, Thomas, 1836 A
à Beckett, Thomas T. 1808 A
à Beckett, William, 1806 A, 1852 A
Aberdeen, NSW, 1838 F, 1926 F
Abergowrie, Qld, 1953 F
Abolins, Uldis, 1923 C
Abonyi, Attila, 1946 E
Aborigines:
    Aboriginal affairs, Cwlth Office/Dept of, 1967 A, 1968 A, 1969 A, 1972 A
    alcohol, 1918 A
    annual meeting, 1816 A
    artists, *see individual entries*
    art exhibitions, 1960 C, 1981 C, *refer also to individual entries*
    Arts Board, 1973 C
    assimilation policy, 1929 A, 1930 A, 1937 A, 1951 A *see* Assimilation
    baptism, 1822 D
    Batman Treaty, 1835 A, 1837 A
    Benefit Trust Fund, 1952 A
    Broken Bay tribe, NSW, 1815 A
    Central Aust. Media Association, 1980 F
    Cherbourg, Qld, 1904 A
    citizenship, 1856 D, 1951 A, 1953 A, 1967 A
    Community College, Adelaide, 1973 D
    conditions of, 1969 A, 1981 D
    conflict with, *see individual entries*
    - NSW, 1788 A, 1799 A, 1824 A, 1838 A, 1900 F
    - NT, 1928 A, 1938 A, 1955 A, 1963 A, 1964 A
    - Qld, 1857 A, 1859 F, 1861 A
    - Tas, 1804 A
    - Vic, 1838 A
    - WA, 1834 A, 1897 A, 1908 A
    corroborees, 1833 C
    cricket, 1866 E, 1868 E
    dancers, 1978 C, 1979 C
    Development Commission, 1980 A
    disease, 1788 B, 1789 F, 1849 A
    education, 1815 D, 1968 D, 1970 D, 1973 D, 1979 D
    Education Consultative Committee, Tas, 1979 D
    Embassy, Canberra, 1972 A
    employment of, 1969 A
    equality, 1956 F
    evidence in courts, 1844 A
    farms, NSW, 1814 A
    flag, 1972 F
    fossils, 1925 B, 1960 B, 1965 B, 1966 B, 1967 B, 1968 B, 1969 B
    genocide, 1837 A
    Govt policy towards, 1860 A *see also* Assimilation, Protection
    Gurindji, NT, 1966 A, 1967 A
    individuals, *see individual names in main index*
    Information Centre, London, 1979 A
    Islander Dance Theatre, Sydney, 1978 C
    Land Fund Commission, 1974 A, 1980 A
    land rights, ownership,
    - NT, 1967 A, 1970 A, 1971 A, 1972 A, 1974 A, 1975 A, 1976 A, 1977 A, 1983 A
    - Qld, 1982 A
    - SA, 1966 A, 1978 A, 1981 A
    - Vic, 1971 A
    - WA, 1979 A
    Aboriginal Land Rights Act NT, 1976 A, 1977 A
    Land Rights Commission, 1973 A
    land trusts, NT, 1978 A
    lawyers, 1978 D
    Legal Service, NSW, 1971 A
    local government, 1979 A, 1984 A
    massacred, 1838 A, 1897 A, 1938 A
    mineral rights, 1979 A
    missions, *see individual entries*
    - Aust. wide, 1961 D
    - NSW, 1795 D, 1825 D, 1874 D
    - NT, 1879 D, 1911 D, 1916 D, 1925 D, 1935 D, 1942 D
    - Qld, 1918 A
    - SA, 1937 D
    music, 1823 C, *see section C and individual entries*
    National Aboriginal Council, 1981 A
    National Conference, 1977 A
    National Consultative Committee, 1973 A
    newspapers, 1938 F
    Northern Land Council, 1978 A, 1982 A
    NT, 1953 A, 1966 A
    Pastoralists Association, NT, 1947 A
    pensions, 1959 A
    Pitjantjatjara, 1978 A, 1979 A, 1981 A
    population, 1861 F, *refer to section F*
    priests, 1975 D
    Progressive Association, NSW, 1930 A
    protection, NSW, 1883 A, 1909 A, 1930 A
    - NT, 1911 A, 1964 A
    - Qld, 1897 A
    - SA, 1880 A
    - Tas, 1835 A
    - Vic, 1860 A
    - WA, 1886 A, 1905 A
    Aboriginal Protection Act, Qld, 1897 A
    Protection Board, 1886 A
    remains, 1984 B
    reserves,
    - NT, 1920 A, 1964 A, 1977 A
    - Qld, 1897 A, 1982 A
    restrictions, NT, 1918 A
    resistance, *see* conflict with
    Rights Council, 1967 A
    rock paintings, 1837 C, 1960 C
    schools,
    - NSW, 1815 D
    - NT, 1950 D
    - Vic, 1836 D
    settlements, WA, 1946 A
    Social Service benefits, 1960 A
    song, recordings, 1899 C
    Special Magistrate, 1974 A
    sport, *refer to section F*
    Tas, 1804 A, 1830 A, 1834 F, 1835 A, 1842 A, 1847 A, 1849 A, 1854 A, 1869 A, 1873 A, 1979 D
    teachers, 1952 D
    theatre, 1982 C
    tribal lands, 1967 A
    Truganini, 1976 A, *see individual entry*
    United Nations Organisation, delegation to, 1969 A
    voting rights, 1949 A, 1951 A, 1962 A
    WA, 1899 A
    WA Aborigines Act, 1905 A
    wages, 1966 A
    wards, NT, 1953 A
    welfare organisations, 1969 A
    Yirrkala, NT, 1963 A
Abortion, SA, 1970 A
About Turkey, 1944 C
Abrahams, Charles, 1845 C
Abrahams, Louis, 1852 C, 1885 C
Absorption spectrophotometer, 1952 B, 1954 B
Abstract art, 1919 C, 1953 C, 1955 C, 1957 C
Academy of Art, 1938 C
Academy of Art National Exhibition, Sydney, 1938 C
Academy Awards, 1943 C, 1976 C
Academy of Dancing, Sydney, 1833 C
Academy Julian, Sydney, 1896 C, 1907 C
Academy of Music Theatre, Adelaide, 1884 F, 1886 F, Melbourne, 1876 C
Academy of Performing Arts, WA, 1979 D
Academy (school), Sydney, 1803 D
Academy and School of Design, Ballarat, 1891 D
Academy of Science Building, Canberra, 1959 C
Academy of the Social Sciences, 1971 D
Accident, record court award, 1981 A
Acclimatization Society of Vic, 1857 B, 1860 B, 1863 A
SA, 1878 B
Account of the English Colony in NSW, An, 1798 C, 1803 C
AC/DC, 1975 C
Acids, 1862 B
Ackland, Essie, 1923 C
Ackland-Horman, William, 1914 E

743

Acmil Ltd, 1979 A, 1981 A
Acoustics, 1947 B
Acquired Immune Deficiency Syndrome, (AIDS), 1983 B
 Advisory Committee, 1984 B
Acrasia, 1904 E
Across Australia, 1912 C
Across the Blacksoil Plains, 1899 C
ACT, *see* Australian Capital Territory
Acton, Prudence L. 1943 F
Actors, *see under individual entries section C*
Actors Equity, 1920 C
Adam, John S. 1935 C
Adam in Ochre, 1951 C
Adam Lindsay Gordon (statue), 1933 C
Adaminaby, NSW, 1885 F, 1957 B, 1958 B
Adams, Arthur H. 1872 C
Adams, Charlotte, 1881 F
Adams, Denis, 1914 C
Adams, Francis W. L. 1862 C, 1886 C, 1893 C
Adams, George, 1839 A, 1881 F, 1896 C
Adams, John, 1829 A
Adams, Margaret R. 1918 C
Adams, Phillip A. 1938 C
Adams, P. J. (ship), 1962 B
Adams, Tate, 1922 C, 1966 C
Adams, Walter, 1830 A
Adamson, Lawrence A. 1860 D
Adamson, Robert, 1944 C
Addison, George H. M. 1858 C
Addison, Walter, 1886 E
Adelaide, 1836 A, F, 1837 A, B, 1839 A, 1866 B, 1867 B, 1870 A, B, 1873 B, 1874 A, 1875 B, 1877 B, 1881 F, 1886 B, 1888 B, 1891 B, 1897 A, 1898 A, D, 1900 D, F, 1906 B, 1908 B, 1912 F, 1916 D, 1917 B, 1924 B, 1925 D, 1929 F, 1936 C, 1941 B, 1953 B, 1954 D, F, 1955 F, 1957 D, 1962 D, 1969 D
Adelaide Advertiser, Art Prize, 1955 C
Adelaide airport, 1955 B
Adelaide Airways, 1936 B
Adelaide Amateur Repertory Co., 1907 C
Adelaide Botanical Gardens, 1855 B
Adelaide Chamber of Commerce, 1839 A
Adelaide Club, 1863 F
Adelaide College of the Arts and Education, 1979 D
Adelaide Co-operative Society Ltd, 1868 A
Adelaide Cup (horse-race), 1864 E
Adelaide Exhibition, 1887 F
Adelaide Festival of Arts, 1960 C, F
Adelaide Festival of Arts Centre, 1974 F
Adelaide Golf Club, 1872 E
Adelaide High School, 1908 D
Adelaide Hills, 1980 F
Adelaide Hunting Club, 1869 E
Adelaide jetty, 1838 A
Adelaide Kindergarten Teachers' Training College, 1907 D
Adelaide land sales, 1837 A
Adelaide Lawn Bowling Club, 1897 E
Adelaide Literary Theatre, 1908 C
Adelaide Mechanics' Institute, 1838 D
Adelaide Municipal Corporation, 1840 A
Adelaide Observatory, 1874 B
Adelaide Observer, 1843 F
Adelaide Philosophical Society, 1853 B
Adelaide Public Library, 1890 D
Adelaide Repertory Theatre Society, 1908 C
Adelaide Sovereigns, 1852 A
Adelaide Steamship Co., 1875 B
Adelaide Stock Exchange, 1887 A

Adelaide Symphony Orchestra, 1949 C, 1975 C, 1980 C
Adelaide Teacher Training College, 1876 D
Adelaide Town Hall, 1863 C, 1865 F
Adelaide University, *see* University of Adelaide
Adelaide University Art Prize, 1959 C
Adelaide water supply, 1860 B
Adelaide Zoo, 1883 B
Adélie Land (French territory, Antarctica), 1933 A
Adelong, NSW, 1856 F
Adelphi Theatre, Sydney, 1911 C
Admella, 1859 F
Administrative and Clerical Officers' Association, (ACOA), 1913 A
Administration Unit, Aust. and NG, 1942 A
Admiral's Cup, 1965 E, 1966 E, 1983 E
Adoption, WA, 1896 A
Adult Education Association, 1950 D
Adult education, Sydney, 1886 D, 1945 D
Adulthood, age of, SA, 1971 A
Advance Australia Fair, 1878 C, 1974 C, 1977 C, 1984 F
Advanced School for Girls, Adelaide, 1908 D
Advanced State Secondary School for Girls, Adelaide, 1879 D
Advances in Medicine, 1983 B
Adventure Bay, Tas., 1788 F
Adventures of Barry McKenzie, The, 1972 C
Advertiser, SA, 1858 F
Advertising, 1800 F, 1804 F, 1824 F, 1837 F, 1908 F, 1912 F, 1918 F, 1924 A, 1946 F, 1955 C, 1971 F, 1974 A, F, 1976 F
Advisory road speed signs, NSW, 1959 F
Advocate, Launceston, 1890 F
AEI (submarine), 1914 A
Aerial Baby Clinic, 1932 F
Aerial fertilising, 1947 B
Aerial League of Aust., 1909 B
Aerial navigation, 1919 B
Aerial photography, 1904 B
Aerial seeding, 1947 B
Aerial survey, Central Aust., 1931 A
Aero Clubs, 1915 E
Aero modelling, 1978 E
Aerodromes, 1966 F, *see also* Airports
Aerograms, 1944 F
Aeronautical and Engine research test laboratory, Melbourne, 1939 B
Aeronautical laboratory, Melbourne, 1921 B
Aeronautical research, 1918 B, 1924 B, 1962 B
Aeronautics, 1871 B, 1878 B, 1889 B, 1891 B, 1894 B, 1903 B, 1907 B, 1909 B, 1910 B, *see* Aviation *from 1911*
Aeroplane Jelly, 1928 C
Affirmative Action, 1984 A
Affleck, Arthur, 1928 B
Afghanistan, USSR invasion of, 1980 A
Afghans, 1860 A, F, 1870 B
Age, The (newspaper), Melbourne, 1854 F, 1856 A, F
Age Book Award, *The*, 1974 C
Age of Consent, 1968 C
Agent Orange, 1980 A, 1983 A
Aginian, Arthur, 1919 D
Agnew, James W., 1815 A, 1886 A
Agnew, Roy E., 1893 C
Agnew, WA, 1977 F
Agostini, Linda, 1944 F
'Agricultural Areas', WA, 1889 A

Agricultural Banks, 1894 A
Agricultural Colleges, *see individual entries*
Agricultural Depot, NSW, 1823 A
Agricultural expansion, Vic, 1860 A
Agricultural Implement Manufacturing Co., SA, 1879 A
Agricultural settlement, Tas, 1858 A
Agricultural Society of Berwick, Vic., 1848 F
Agricultural Society of NSW, 1869 F
Ahern, David A. 1947 C, 1968 C
A Hole in the Ground (film), 1963 C
Aickin, Keith, 1976 A
Aid, to Vietnam, 1958 A, 1961 A, 1979 A
AIDS *see* Acquired Immune Deficiency Syndrome.
AIF *see* Aust. Imperial Forces
Air disasters,
 ACT, 1940 F
 NSW, 1931 F, 1939 F, 1948 F, 1955 F, 1961 F, 1972 F, 1980 F, 1984 F
 NT, 1942 F, 1966 F, 1967 F, 1969 F, 1972 F
 Qld, 1922 F, 1937 F, 1938 F, 1942 F, 1945 F, 1949 F, 1957 F, 1960 F, 1961 F, 1966 F, 1975 F, 1981 F, 1982 F, 1983 F
 SA, 1944 F, 1966 F, 1969 F, 1972 F
 Tas, 1935 F, 1946 F, 1981 F
 Vic, 1934 F, 1938 F, 1945 F, 1969 F, 1978 F, 1979 F, 1982 F
 WA, 1942 F, 1945 F, 1946 A, 1949 F, 1950 F, 1951 F, 1956 F, 1968 F
Air Force, 1911 A, *see* Royal Aust. Air Force, RAAF
Air Force Act, 1923 A
Air navigation, 1947 B
Air pollution, NSW, 1964 B, Vic, 1958 F
Air raids, 1942 A
Air races, 1912 E, 1929 E, 1934 E, 1970 E, 1973 E, 1976 E, 1977 E
Air services, 1928 B, 1930 B, 1931 B, 1934 B, 1935 B, 1938 B, 1945 B, 1965 A, 1984 B
Air Supply (pop. group), 1981 C
Air traffic control, 1938 B
Airbus, 1981 B
Air-conditioning, 1929 B, 1934 B, 1982 A
Aircraft,
 AAEC BI, 1922 B
 ABA I, 1930 B
 Airbus, 1981 B
 Boeing 727, 1964 B
 Boeing 747, 1959 B, 1970 B
 DH 50 A, 1924 B
 DH 86, 1934 F, 1942 F
 Drover, 1948 B
 F-one-eleven, 1963 A
 Factories, 1939 B
 Fairey 111 D seaplane, 1924 B
 Gloster Meteor F4 jet, 1946 B
 Jets, 1955 B, 1961 B
 Jindivik, 1948 B
 Lockheed Electra prop jets, 1959 B
 Lockheed Lodestar, 1943 F
 Military, 1912 A, 1914 B, 1939 B
 Mirage, 1963 A, 1965 A, 1981 B
 McDonnell Douglas F-18 Hornet, 1981 A
 Pressurized, 1948 B
 Tiger Moth, 1942 B
 Viscount prop-jets, 1953 B
 Vulcan jet bomber, 1961 B
 Wicko FW1, 1936 B
 see also Aeronautics, Aviation *and individual entries*
Aircraft monthly magazine, 1919 F
Airey, Jim, 1944 E
Aireys Inlet, Vic, 1846 F

744

Airlines,
  commercial, 1934 B
  intrastate, 1965 A
Airlines strike, 1981 A
Airmail, 1914 F, 1921 B, 1924 F, 1925 F, 1928 F, 1929 F, 1930 F, 1931 F, 1934 F
Airmail stamps, 1929 F
Airport departure tax, 1978 A
Airports, *see individual entries*
Aitken, John, 1836 A
Akhurst, Daphne, 1903 E
Alan, Charles, 1931 F
Aland, John, 1937 C
Alban, Tom, 1924 C
Albany, WA, 1791 A, 1819 A, 1826 A, F, 1833 A, 1835 D, 1841 A, 1848 D, 1889 B, 1914 A, 1976 E, 1978 A, 1979 E
Albany Art Gallery, WA, 1950 C, 1963 C
Albatross, HMAS, NSW, 1976 F
Alberga R., SA, 1873 A
Albert, Werner A. 1982 C
Albert Namatjira, 1956 C
Albert Park Ladies Bowling Club, 1899 E
Albert Sporting Ground, Sydney, 1864 E
Albion, 1867 F
Albion Park, NSW, 1840 F
Albiston, Valerie, 1911 C
Albury, 1859 A
Albury, NSW, 1839 F, 1855 A, 1881 B, 1883 B, 1903 F, 1922 A, 1926 F
Albury Art Prize, NSW, 1947 C
Albury-Wodonga, 1976 D
Albury-Wodonga Development Agreement, 1973 A
Alcock, Henry U. 1853 E, 1887 E
Alcohol,
  imports, 1800 A
  liqueurs, 1931 A
  taxes, 1901 A
Alcoholics Anonymous, 1945 F
Alcorso-Sekers travelling scholarship, 1966 C
Alden, John G. B. 1907 C, 1948 C
Alderman, Harry G. 1895 A, 1951 A
Alderson, Harry, 1890 E
Alderson, Janet, 1937 C
Aldor, Christine G. 1913 C
Aldous, Lucette, 1938 C, 1971 C
Alexander, John, 1951 E
Alexander, Samuel, 1859 D
Alexander Mackie College of Advanced Education, Sydney, 1958 D
Alexandra, Vic, 1869 F
Alexandra Theatre, Melbourne, 1886 C
Alexandria cattle station, Qld, 1966 A
Alfred, Duke of Edinburgh, 1867 F, 1868 A
Alice Springs, NT, 1871 A, 1872 A, 1873 A, 1877 D, 1888 A, 1889 F, 1914 D, 1947 F, 1948 B, 1951 D, 1963 B, 1967 B, 1972 F, 1979 B, 1980 F
Alice Springs Nursing Home, 1926 F
Alien Son, 1952 C
Aliens Registration Act, Federal, 1920 A
A-line fashion, 1955 F
All for Aust. League, 1931 A
All Hallows' Catholic School, Brisbane, 1863 D
All that Swagger, 1936 C
'All the Way with LBJ', 1966 A
Allan, J. 1866 A, 1924 E
Allan, Robert M. 1886 B
Allan, Trevor, 1927 E
Allardyce, William L. 1920 E
Allen, Arthur S. 1894 A
Allen, Geoffrey, 1924 C

Allen, George, (1) 1800 A, 1822 A
Allen, George, (2), 1900 C
Allen, George O. ('Gubby'), 1902 E
Allen, George W. 1824 A
Allen, Harry B. 1854 B
Allen, John, 1871 E
Allen, Joyce L. 1916 C
Allen, Mary C. 1893 C, 1963 C
Allen, Maud, 1914 C
Allen, Peter, 1977 C
Alley, Bill, 1919 E
Alleyne, Marion, 1977 C
Alligator R., NT, 1953 B
Allison, Bruce, 1954 E
Allman, Francis, 1821 A, 1860 A
Allman, Robert E. 1927 C, 1929 C
Allora, Qld, 1869 F
Allport, Curzona F. L. 1860 C
Allport, Henry, 1890 C
Allport, Henry C. 1788 C
Allport, Mary M. 1806 C
Allport, Morton, 1830 B
Allsop, Raymond C. 1898 B, 1921 C
Almorah, 1825 A
'Along the Road to Gundagai', 1922 C
Alps, 1824 A, 1839 A, 1849 B
Alston, Adrian, 1948 E
Alston, Cyril, 1906 C
Alston, James, 1885 B
Alston, Meyer D., 1881 C
Alt, Augustus T. H. 1788 B, 1801 A, 1815 A
'Alternative' schools, 1970 D
Altona, Vic, 1961 B
Altson, Aby, 1864 C
Altwater-Kent radio, 1932 B
Alumina, production, 1976 B
Aluminium, Production Commission 1944 A
Aluminium, Tas, 1955 B
Alvin Purple, 1973 C
Alvin Rides Again, 1975 C
Amadio, Neville, 1913 C
Amalgamated Engineering Union, Sydney, 1852 A
Amalgamated Metal Workers' and Shipwrights' Union, 1976 A
Amalgamated Metal Workers' Union, 1972 A
Amalgamated Miners' Association, 1882 A
Amalgamated Miners' Union, Vic, 1874 A
Amalgamated Pictures Ltd, 1911 C, 1912 C
Amalgamated Printing Trades Employees' Union, 1921 A
Amalgamated Shearers' Union, 1894 A
Amalgamated Shearers' Union of Australasia, 1886 A
Amalgamated Society of Carpenters and Joiners, SA, 1860 A, WA, 1884 A
Amalgamated Wireless (Australasia) Ltd, AWA, 1913 B, 1921 B
Amalgamated Workers' Union, women, 1892 A
Amanda Miller, 1971 B
Amateur Athletic Associations, 1891 E
Amateur Athletic Union of Aust. and N.Z., 1924 E
Amateur Athletics Association of Australasia, 1897 E
Amateur Basketball Associations, 1930 E
Amateur Basketball Union of Aust., 1939 E
Amateur Boxing and Wrestling Union of Aust., 1924 E
Amateur Modern Pentathlon Union of Aust., 1954 E

Amateur Pistol Shooting Union of Aust., 1956 E
Amateur Rowing Council, 1925 E
Amateur Swimming Union of Aust., 1909 E
Amatil Ltd, 1904 A
Ambassadors The, 1965 C
Ambergris, 1891 B
Amberley Airforce Base, Qld, 1965 B
Ambrose Pratt, 1933 C
Ambulance, 1973 F
Ambulance services, Qld, NSW, 1893 F
America, 1845 F
America, war on Britain, 1812 A, 1814 A
America's Cup, 1962 E, 1967 E, 1970 E, 1974 E, 1977 E, 1980 E
American Allstars, 1953 E
American Eagle, 1972 E
American film exchange, 1915 E
American naval presence, 1839 A
American sealers, 1800 A, 1804 A
American troops, Brisbane, 1941 A, Paupa-New Guinea, 1943 A
Americans' Baby, The, 1972 C
Ames, Jennifer, *see* Greig, Maysie C.
Amherst, J. 1821 C
Amiens, 1918 A
Amity Point, Qld, 1847 F
Ammonia gases, 1876 B
Amphitrite, 1833 F
Ampol Petroleum Ltd, 1936 A, 1951 B, 1965 B
Amputations, first, 1788 B
Amsterdam Olympics, 1928 E
Anaesthetics, 1847 B, 1897 B
Ancher, Sydney E. 1904 C, 1930 C
Andamooka, SA, 1930 B, F, 1969 F, 1975 F
Anderson, Charles, (b. 1876) 1876 B
Anderson, Charles G. W. 1897 A
Anderson, Charlotte, 1915 B
Anderson, David M. 1936 A
Anderson, Donald G. 1917 A
Anderson, 'Dollar', 1949 F
Anderson, Ethel L. 1883 C
Anderson, Francis, 1858 D
Anderson, Francis M. (Judith), 1898 C, 1948 C, 1955 C
Anderson, H. C. L. 1890 A
Anderson, James O. 1895 E
Anderson, John, 1893 D, 1927 D
Anderson, Joseph, 1790 A
Anderson, Keith, 1899 B
Anderson, Malcolm, 1935 E
Anderson, Maybanke S. 1845 A
Anderson, Reginal, 1910 A
Anderson, Thomas P. 1856 B
Anderson, W. W. 1888 C
Anderson and Co., 1877 B
Andrew, Francis C. 1911 C
Andrew, Shirley J. 1933 C
Andrews, Ernest C. 1870 B
Andrews, E. W. 1812 F
Andrews, John H. 1933 C, 1964 C, 1970 C, 1977 C
Andrews, Norman, 1951 F
Andrews, William, 1840 C
(Andy) Kerr, 1867 E
Angas, George F. (1) 1789 A, 1835 A, 1836 A
Angas, George F. (2) 1822 C
Angas, John H. 1923 A
Angas, John K. 1900 A
Angas, Max R. 1914 C
Angas, Ronald F. 1889 A
Angaston, SA, 1841 F, 1849 B
Angles, Cyril, 1906 E
Anglesea, Vic, 1865 F

745

Anglican Church of Aust., 1981 D, 1982 D
Angling, 1951 E, see also Fishing, Casting
Angliss, William C. 1865 A
Anglo-Aust. Bank, 1891 A
Anglo-Aust. Soccer Association, 1884 E
Angora goats, 1832 A
Angry Penguins, 1940 C, 1941 C
Angus, David, 1886 A
Angus, Samuel, 1881 D
Angus cattle, 1880 A
Angus and Robertson, 1886 A, 1888 C, 1895 C, 1971 C
Anitra V, 1957 E
Anivitti, Guilo, 1850 C
Ankles, 1924 F
Anlaby stud, 1856 B
Ann Jamieson, 1833 F
Annaburoo Station, NT, 1942 F
Annand, Douglas, 1903 C
Annand Smith and Co., 1849 A
Annandale, Sydney, 1882 C, 1893 C
Annandale Imitation Realists, 1962 C
Annie's Coming Out (film), 1984 C
Annois, Leonard L. 1906 C
Annual Leave, 1936 A, 1943 A, 1945 A, 1947 A, 1958 A, 1963 A, 1964 A, 1970 A, 1973 A, 1977 A
Ansett, airport bus services, 1982 B
Ansett Airlines of Aust, 1952 A, 1968 B, 1980 B
Ansett Airways Pty Ltd, 1936 B
Ansett, Reginald M. 1909 A, 1931 B, 1935 B, 1936 B
Ansett road transport, 1931 B
Ansett Transport Industries, 1957 B
Anstey, Frank, 1865 A
Anstey, George, 1843 A
Anstey, Thomas Edward, 1851 A
Antarctic, 1831 A, 1895 A, 1908 A, 1909 A, 1930 A, 1933 A, 1934 A, 1947 A, B, 1954 B, 1957 B, 1972 A
Antarctic, 1895 A
Antarctic Research Policy Advisory Committee, 1979 B
Antarctic Treaty, 1959 A, 1961 A
Anthem, 1826 F
Anthill, Henry C. 1852 A
Anthony, J. Douglas 1929 A, 1971 A
Anthony Hordern stores, Sydney, 1901 F
Anthrax, disease, 1847 A
Anthrax, vaccine, 1890 B
Anthropology, 1889 B
Anti-aircraft weapon, 1939 B
Anti-apartheid demonstrations, Qld, 1971 A, E
Antibiotics, 1940 B
Anti-Chinese restrictive legislation, see Chinese
Anti-Communist Labor Party, 1955 A
Anti-Discrimination Law, 1984 A
Anti-Gold Licence Association, Vic, 1853 A
Antill, John H., 1904 C, 1946 C, 1950 C
Anti-nuclear marches, 1984 A
Antipodean, 1892 F
Antipodean group of artists, Melbourne, 1959 C
Antisepsis, 1898 B
Antiseptic, 1867 B
Anti-strike demonstrations, 1981 A
Anti-tank missile, 1959 B
Anti-Transportation Leagues, 1835 A, 1851 A
Anti-transportation movement, 1852 A
Ants, Argentine, 1931 B, 1939 B, F
Antwerp Olympics, 1920 E
Anvil Creek, NSW, 1864 B

Anwin, J. 1889 E
ANZ Bank, Adelaide, 1875 C
ANZ Group Holdings Ltd., 1976 A
ANZAAS, 1886 B
ANZAC (film), 1960 C
ANZAC day, 1916 F
ANZAC Forces, France, 1918 A
ANZAC House Sculpture competition, 1959 C
ANZAC Memorial Sculpture competition, 1923 C
ANZAC Memorial, Sydney, 1930 C, 1934 F
ANZAC Mounted Corps, Jericho, 1918 A
ANZAM Agreement, 1948 A
ANZUS Pact, 1951 A
Apex Club, 1931 F
Apollo Bay, Vic, 1860 F, 1932 F
Apollo XI, 1969 B
Apologue, 1907 E
'Apostle of the Blacks', 1788 A
Apostolic Church (Australia), 1929 D
Appin, NSW, 1814 F, 1979 F
Appleby, L. W. 1951 C
Apples, 1788 A, 1828 A, 1834 A, 1868 A, 1884 A
Appleroth, Bert, 1928 F
Appleton, Jean, 1911 C
Appleton, Richard, 1983 C
Appleyard, Ronald G. 1920 C
Apprentices, 1925 A
Appropriation Bills, 1878 A, 1975 A
Apsley, Vic, 1862 F
Aqua-planing, 1918 E
Aquaria, 1865 F
Aquarium Society of NSW, 1907 F
Arago, Jacques E. 1790 C
Araluen, NSW, 1868 F
Aramac, Qld, 1872 F, 1878 A
Ararat, Vic, 1854 F, 1857 A
Arbitration, compulsory, 1927 A, 1929 A
Arbitration commission, 1979 A, 1981 A, 1983 A, 1984 A
Arbitration and Conciliation, 1947 A, 1972 A
Arbitration Court, 1921 A, 1922 A, 1947 A
Arbitration reforms, 1972 A
Arbitration system, Vic, NSW, 1891 A see also Cwlth Conciliation and Arbitration Act, Conciliation, Court of Conciliation and Arbitration
Arbo-encephalitis, 1917 F
Arbor day, SA, 1889 F
Archaeological exhibition, 1977 C
Archdale, Alexander M. 1905 C, 1968 C
Archdale, H. Elizabeth (Betty) 1907 A
Archer, 1861 E, 1862 E
Archer, Archibald, 1820 A
Archer, Charles, 1813 A
Archer, Colin, 1832 A
Archer, David, 1816 A
Archer, John, 1814 A
Archer, John L. 1791 B, 1827 C
Archer, J. C. 1956 A
Archer, Ron, 1933 E
Archer, Thomas, 1823 A
Archer, William, (b. 1818) 1818 A
Archer, William, (b. 1820) 1820 B, 1854 B
Archerfield, Qld, 1982 F
Archery, 1840 E, 1856 E, 1965 E, 1977 E
Archery Association of Aust., 1948 E
Archery Society of WA, 1938 E
Archibald, John F. (also known as Jules F.), 1856 F, 1880 F, 1907 F
Archibald Memorial Fountain, Sydney, 1933 F

Archibald Prize, see each year after 1921 C, 1944 C, 1964 C, 1980 C
Architecture, see section C and individual entries
Architecture and Arts, 1952 C
Architecture diplomas, Sydney, 1896 C
Architecture, first modern, 1910 C
Architecture periods,
 austerity, 1945 C
 classical, 1830 C
 colonial Regency, 1830 C
 early modern, 1930 C, 1934 C
 Edwardian, 1901 C
 Georgian and colonial revival, 1924 C
 'International' Style, 1948 C
 primitive, 1788 C
 Queen Anne Style, 1897 C
 Spanish mission Style, 1925 C
 transition, 1917 C
 Twentieth century, mid-, 1955 C
 Victorian, early-, 1851 C
 Victorian, high-, 1879 C
 Victorian, late-, 1893 C
 Victorian, mid-, 1861 C
Arden, George, 1820 A, 1838 F, 1840 C
Ardencraig, 1907 F
Ardrossan, SA, 1870 F
Argentine ants, 1931 B, 1939 B, F
Argonauts Club, 1941 F
Argus, Melbourne, 1846 F
Argus Gallery, Melbourne, 1960 C
Argyle, Stanley S. 1867 A, 1932 A
Arlen, Albert, 1905 C, 1961 C
Armadale, Melbourne, 1896 B
Armadale, WA, 1893 F
Armenian church, 1919 D, 1957 D
Armfield, David E. 1923 C
Armidale, NSW, 1839 F, 1872 D, 1875 C, 1938 D, 1954 D, 1956 D, 1963 A, 1983 C
Armidale Art Society, NSW, 1963 C
Armidale Express (newspaper), NSW, 1856 F
Armidale Teachers' College, NSW, 1928 D
Armistice, World War I, 1918 A
Arms of states, 1893 A
Armstrong, David, 1979 A
Armstrong, Elizabeth C. 1860 C
Armstrong, Gillian, 1979 C
Armstrong, Ian, 1923 C
Armstrong, John, 1948 C
Armstrong, John I. 1908 A
Armstrong, Warwick, 1919 C
Armstrong, Warwick W. 1879 E
Army, 1902 A, 1910 A, 1919 A, 1941 D, 1943 A, 1947 A, 1960 A, see also Aust. Forces, Defence, Military, AIF
Army nurses, massacre of, 1942 A
Armytage, J. C. 1820 C
Arnall, Vincent M. 1928 C
Arndell, Thomas, 1821 B
Arnhem Land, NT, 1883 A
Arnold, Reginald, 1925 E
Arnott, Alwyn J. 1899 B
Arnott, Arthur, 1904 A
Arnott, William, 1827 A
Arnott biscuits, 1904 A
Around the Boree Log, 1921 C
Arquebus, 1937 C
Arrino, WA, 1905 F
Arrival of the First Gold Escort Melbourne June, 1852, 1852 C
Arrow Theatre, 1962 C
Arsenal, 1886 E
Arsenic, 1950 B
Arson, 1983 A
Art, conceptual and lyrical abstraction, 1970 C

746

Art, contemporary European exhibition, 1879 C
Art, criticism, 1880 C
Art, New Modern Movement, 1913 C
Art and Architecture, 1904 C
Art Association, Tas, 1884 C
Art in Australia, 1916 C
Art and Australia, 1963 C
Art Exhibition, New York, 1930 C
Art exhibitions, *see individual entries and section C*
Art Exhibitions, overseas, 1855 C, 1866 C, 1875 C, *see also individual entries*
Art Galleries, *see individual entries*
Art Gallery, Sydney, 1875 C
Art Gallery Association of Aust, Sydney, 1965 C
Art Gallery of NSW, 1880 C, 1883 C, 1953 C, 1955 C, 1958 C
Art Gallery of SA, 1900 C, 1967 C
Art Gallery Society of NSW, 1953 C
Art Gallery of WA, 1979 C
Art instruction, Melbourne, 1867 C
Artlovers' Gallery, Sydney, 1955 C
Art Nouveau, 1902 C
Art Periods,
 academic, 1863 C
 colonial, 1809 C
 early Aust., 1851 C
 early colonial, 1788 C
 impressionist, 1885 C
 late colonial, 1851 C
 modern, middle of, 1914 C
 modern movement, second phase, 1938 C, 1939 C
 romantic, 1835 C
Art Pottery Studios, Vic, 1911 C
Art School, Sydney, 1897 C
Art Society of NSW, 1886 C, 1887 C
Art Society of Tas, 1884 C
Art Students, The, 1894 C
Art Teachers' Association of Vic, 1963 C
Art Union of Vic, 1872 C
Artemesia (ship), 1848 A
Arthur, Frank, 1907 E
Arthur, George, 1824 A, 1830 A, 1833 A, 1835 A, 1854 A
Arthur, Graham, 1936 E
Arthur, John, 1846 B
Arthur, Richard, 1922 F
Artificial breeding, dairy cattle, 1950 A
Artilleryman, 1919 E
Artisans' School of Art and Design, Melbourne, 1867 C
Artists, French, 1800 C
Artists' camp, Box Hill, 1885 C
Artists' camp, Eaglemont, 1888 C
'An Artists Exhibition', Adelaide, 1847 C
Arts, *see section C*
Arts Centre Concert Hall, Melbourne, 1982 C
Arts Council, Sydney, 1944 C, 1946 C
Arts Council of Aust., 1946 C
Arts and Crafts Society of Vic, 1908 C
Arunta: a Story of a Stone Age People, The, 1927 C
Arvanitakis, Timotheos, 1947 C
Arwon, 1978 E
Asbestos, 1938 B
Asche, John S. H. O. 1871 C
Asche, Oscar, 1916 C
Asepsis, 1898 B
Ash Wednesday, 1983 F
Ashbourne, SA, 1845 F
Ashbridge, Bryan, 1926 C
Ashby, Alison M. 1901 C
Ashby, Eric, 1904 B
Ashes Trophy, 1882 E

Ashfield, NSW, 1888 E, 1920 B
Ashmore, I., Antarctic, 1934 A
Ashtaroth, 1867 C
Ashton, Adrian O. 1947 F
Ashton, George R. 1857 C
Ashton, James, 1860 C, 1895 C
Ashton, John W. ('Will'), 1881 C
Ashton, Julian H. 1877 C
Ashton, Julian Rossi, 1851 C, 1886 C, 1896 C, 1898 C, 1911 C, 1919 C
Ashton, Julian Richard, 1913 C
Ashworth, Henry I. 1907 C
Ashworth, John S. 1915 C
Asian Development Bank, 1969 A
Asian Flu, 1957 B
Asian immigration, 1949 A
Asian and Pacific Co-operation Council, ASPAC, 1966 A
Asians, tertiary education, 1950 D, 1951 D
Asiatic cholera, 1841 F
Asiatic Mongoose, 1884 F
Askin, Robert W. 1909 A, 1965 A
Aspden, David, 1935 C
Aspects of the Dying Process, 1972 C
Aspects of New British Art, Exhibition, 1967 C
Aspendale speedway, Melbourne, 1906 E
Asphalt tennis courts, 1878 E
'Aspro', 1914 B
Assets Test, 1984 E
Assignment Board, 1826 A, 1834 A
Assignment system, 1789 A, 1800 A, 1838 A, 1839 A
Assimilation policy, Aboriginals, 1929 A, 1930 A, 1937 A, 1951 A
Assisted immigration, 1831 A, 1832 A, 1835 A, 1843 A, 1845 A, 1887 A, 1890 A, 1891 A, 1905 A, 1922 A, 1925 A, 1929 A, 1938 A, 1945 A, 1947 A, 1952 A, 1965 A, 1967 A, 1970 A, *refer also to* immigration
Assisted Passage Agreement, Britain, 1947 A, Netherlands, 1965 A
Associated Booksellers of Aust. and N.Z., 1924 C
Associated Building Trades, Melbourne, 1875 A
Associated Chambers of Manufacturers of Aust., 1903 A
Associated Pulp and Paper Mills Ltd, Tas, 1938 B
Associated Securities Ltd Finance Co., 1979 A
Association for Advancement of the Blind, 1895 F
Association for the Development of Wireless, 1923 B
Association Ground Lawn Tennis Club, 1878 E
Association for the introduction of labourers from India, 1842 A
Association of Physicians of Australasia and N.Z, 1930 B
Association of Professional Engineers, APEA, 1946 B
Association for the Protection of Native Races, 1931 A
Association of Sculptors of Vic, 1969 C
Association of Southeast Asian Nations, ASEAN, 1967 A, 1976 A
Association for the Study of Aust. literature, 1977 C
Associations, *see individual entries*
Assyrian, The, 1882 E
Astley, Thea B. 1925 C, 1958 C, 1965 C
Astley, William, 1855 C, 1892 C
Astley's Amphitheatre, Melbourne, 1854 C

Aston, Matilda A. (Tilly), 1873 C, 1894 D, 1895 F, 1901 C, 1935 C, 1940 C
Astrographic Programme, 1890 B
Astrolabe, 1788 A, 1826 A
Astronomical Society of Aust., 1966 B
Astronomy, 1788 B, 1822 B, 1827 B, 1831 B, 1854 B, 1890 B, 1964 B, 1973 B, 1981 B
Asylum, mental, 1838 B
Asylum for destitute children, Sydney, 1858 D
At Dawn and Dusk, 1898 C
Atahan, Hakki, 1884 F
Athaldo, Don, 1898 E
Athenaeum Theatre, Melbourne, 1906 C
Atherton, John, 1837 A
Atherton, Qld, 1885 F
Atherton Tableland, Qld, 1920 F
Athletes Union of Aust., 1924 E
Athletics, 1850 E, 1858 E, 1864 E, 1868 E, 1878 E, 1884 E, 1887 E, 1888 E, 1892 E, 1905 E, 1910 E, 1914 E, 1926 E, 1928 E, 1929 E, 1932 E, 1935 E, 1938 E, 1948 E, 1952 E, 1954 E, 1956 E, 1958 E, 1967 E, 1968 E, 1979 E
Atkins, Fred, 1922 E
Atkins, Richard, 1800 A, 1820 A
Atkinson, Charles, 1837 C
Atkinson, James, 1795 A
Atkinson, Karl, 1933 E
Atkinson, Meredith, 1920 C
Atkinson, Robert, 1863 C
Atlas (magazine) Sydney, 1844 F, 1848 F
'Atomic Ship', 1850 B, 1851 B
Atomic bomb, 1943 B, 1945 A, 1952 B, 1956 B, 1957 B
Atomic Energy, 1953 B, 1956 A
Atomic Energy Act, Federal, 1953 A
Atomic tests, SA, 1957 B, 1980 F, 1984 A
Atrevida, 1793 B
Attorneys, 1824 A
Atyeo, Sam, 1911 C
Atzmon, Moshe, 1969 C
Aubrey, Terence, 1810 A
Auctions, land sale, 1831 A
Augusta, WA, 1830 F
Augustus, Prince of Saxe-Coburg, 1872 A
Auld, James M. 1879 C
Aunt's Story, The, 1948 C
Auraria, 1895 E
Aurora Australis, 1826 F
Aurousseau, George H. 1864 C
Aurukun I. Shire Council, Qld, 1979 A
AUSSAT, 1983 B
Austin, James, 1810 A
Austin, Reg, 1936 E
Austin, Robert, 1854 A
Austin, Thomas, 1815 A, 1859 B
Austin, William, 1852 C
Austin, William S. 1867 C
Austine, Brest, 1976 E
Austral, 1882 F
Austral, Florence, *see* Wilson, Florence
Austral English: a ... Phrases and Usages, 1898 C
Austral Professional Bicycle Club, Sydney, 1892 E
Austral Wheel bicycle race, 1887 E, 1891 E
'Australasia', (poem), 1823 C
Australasian, 1864 F
Australasian Amateur Boxing Association, 1903 E
Australasian Antarctic Expedition, 1911 A
Australasian Anti-transportation League, 1850 A

747

Australasian Art Review, 1899 C
Australasian Association for the Advancement of Science, 1888 B
Australasian Council of Trade Unions, 1927 A
Australasian Critic, 1890 C
Australasian Federation League, 1893 A, 1895 A, 1896 A
Australasian Film Studio, Sydney, 1912 C
Australasian Films Ltd, 1912 C, 1913 C
Australasian Meat Industry Employees' Union, 1906 A
Australasian Performing Rights Association, 1926 C
Australasian Pioneers Club, 1910 F
Australasian Post, 1864 F
Australasian Professional Golf Association, 1911 E
Australasian Steam Navigation Co., 1840 A, 1851 A, 1868 A
Australasian Steamship Owners' Federation, 1899 A
Australasian Trained Nurses Association, 1899 B
Australasian Transport Officers' Federation, 1921 A
Australasian United Steam Navigation Co., 1887 B
Australia (art book), 1875 C
Australia (history book), 1930 C
'Australia' (name), 1794 A, 1803 A, 1814 A, 1817 A, 1824 A
'Australia' (song), 1901 C
Australia (yacht), 1977 E, 1980 E
Australia II (yacht), 1983 E
'Australia At War', Art Exhibition, 1945 C
Australia Club, 1838 F
Australia Council, 1975 C
Australia Day, 1946 F
Australia Felix, 1836 A, 1838 A, 1839 A, 1844 F
Australia Felix (book), 1917 C
Australia First Movement, 1941 A
Australia, HMAS, 1913 A, 1915 A, 1922 A, 1924 A
Australia House, London, 1913 A
'Australia Looks to America' speech, 1941 A
Australia Party, 1967 A, 1969 A
Australia Seventy-five Festival, Canberra, 1975 F
Australia Square, Sydney, 1958 C, Tower, 1967 C
Australian, The (newspaper), 1824 F, 1826 F, 1848 F
Australian, The (newspaper), Canberra, 1964 F
Australian Abo Call, Sydney, 1938 F
Aust. Aboriginal Art Exhibition, 1960 C
Aust.-Aboriginal Friendship Society, 1956 F
Aust. Aboriginal Theatre, 1982 C
Aust. Academy of Art, Canberra, 1937 C
Aust. Academy of the Humanities, 1969 D
Aust. Academy of Science, 1967 B
Aust. Administrative Staff College, Vic, 1955 D
Aust. Advertising Standards Authority, AASA, 1974 F
Aust. Advisory Committee on Aeronautics, 1941 B
Aust. Aero Club, 1914 E, 1915 E
Aust. Agricultural Co., 1824 A, 1829 A, 1831 A, 1850 A, 1851 A, 1852 A
Aust. Agricultural Council, 1934 A, 1954 A

Aust. Air Corps, 1920 A
Aust. Aircraft and Engineering Co. Ltd, 1919 B
Aust. Alps, named 1824 A
Aust. Aluminium Production Commission, 1944 A, 1955 B
Aust. Amateur Fencing Federation, 1948 E
Aust.-American Education Foundation, 1949 D
Aust. Animal Toxins, 1983 B
Australian Antarctic Territory Acceptance Act, 1933 A
Australian Anthology, An, 1927 C
Aust. Arbo-Encephalitis, 1917 F
Australian Architecture, 1908 C
Aust. Architecture Exhibition, England, 1955 C
Australian Art, 1888 C
Aust. Art Association, Melbourne, 1912 C
Aust. Artists' Association, Vic, 1886 C, 1888 C
Aust. Art in Canada Exhibition, 1957 C
Aust. Art Exhibition, Karachi, 1950 C
Aust. Art Exhibitions, New York, 1930 C, London, 1923 C, 1924 C, 1925 C
Aust. Art Society, 1926 C
Australian Artist, The (quarterly), 1946 C
Aust. Artists' Exhibition, London, 1928 C
Aust. Arts Club, 1919 C
Australian Associated Press, AAP, 1935 F
Aust. Associated Stock Exchanges, 1937 A
Aust. Association of Adult Education, 1960 D
Aust. Association of Advertising Agencies, 1946 F
Aust. Association for Cultural Freedom, 1954 C
Aust. Association of Neurologists, 1951 B
Aust. Association of Psychology and Philosophy, 1922 D
Aust. Atomic Energy Commission, 1953 B
Aust. Atomic Veterans Association, 1980 F
Aust. Authors and Artistic Soc., Qld, 1921 C
Aust. Automobile Association, AAA, 1924 C
Aust. Auxiliary Squadron, navy, 1891 A
Aust. Axemen's Association, 1970 E
Aust. Badminton Association, 1935 E
Aust. Ballet, 1939 C, 1965 C, 1969 C
Aust. Ballet Co., 1929 C, 1954 C, 1960 C, 1962 C, 1963 C, 1964 C, 1966 C, 1968 C, 1971 C
Aust. Ballet School, Melbourne, 1964 C
Aust. Balloon Launching Station, Vic, 1960 B
Aust. Bank Ltd, Melbourne, Sydney, 1981 A
Aust. Baptist Missionary Society, 1913 D
Aust. Barley Board, 1939 A
Aust. Baseball Council, 1933 E
Aust. Basketball Federation, 1939 E
Aust. Bicentennial Authority, 1979 A
Aust. Biochemical Society, 1959 B
Aust. Board of Control, cricket, 1905 E
Aust. Board of Missions, 1850 D
Aust. Book Council, Sydney, 1945 C
Aust. Book Publishers Association, 1949 C

Australian Book Review, 1961 C
Aust. Book Society, 1952 C
Australian Booksellers' Association, 1924 C
Aust. Bowling Council, 1900 E
Aust. Boxing Federation, 1967 E
Aust. Bridge Council, 1935 F
Aust. Bridge Federation, 1935 F
Australian Broadcasting Co., 1928 A, 1929 B
Aust. Broadcasting Commission, ABC, 1932 A, 1935 A, D, C, 1936 C, 1939 F, 1940 F, 1942 C, F, 1943 C, F, 1944 C, 1946 C, 1947 C, 1950 C, 1951 E, 1957 B, 1967 C, 1973 C, 1974 B, C, 1978 F, 1982 A
Aust. Broadcasting Control Board, 1948 A, 1955 A, 1976 A
Aust. Broadcasting Corporation, 1982 A, 1983 A, 1984 A
Aust. Broadcasting Tribunal, 1976 A, 1982 A
Australian Building, Melbourne, 1889 C
Aust. Bureau of Statistics, 1984 D
Aust. Cadet Corps, 1866 D
Aust. Cane Growers' Association, 1947 A
Aust. Canoe Federation, 1949 E
Australian Capital Territory, *abbreviated as* ACT
  Advisory Council, 1930 A
  control of, 1932 A
  created, 1911 A
  education, 1976 D
  expansion, 1957 A, 1966 A
  land purchases, 1970 A
  Member for, voting rights, 1966 A
  officially named, 1938 A
  Parliamentary representation, 1948 A
  police force, 1927 A, 1979 A
  self govt rejected, 1978 A
  transfer of land for, 1909 A
Aust. Care for Refugees, AUSTCARE, 1960 F
Aust. Casting Association, 1947 E
Aust. Catholic Relief Fund, 1983 D
Aust. central authority, 1846 A
Aust. Centre for Photography, Sydney, 1974 C
Aust. Cerebral Palsy Association Inc., 1954 C
Aust. Chamber Orchestra, 1975 C
Aust. Chess Club, 1840 F, 1860 F
Aust. Chess Federation, 1922 F
Australian Christmas Story Book, The, 1871 C
Aust. Church, Melbourne, 1885 D
Australian citizen, 1948 A, 1968 A
Aust. Clay Pigeon Trap Shooting Association, 1936 E
Aust. Clerks' Provident Friendly Society, 1846 F
Aust. Coastal Shipping Commission, 1956 B
Aust. College, Sydney, 1831 D, 1835 D
Aust. College of Education, 1959 D
Aust. College of Health Service Administrators, 1945 B
Aust. College of Music, Adelaide, 1883 C
Aust. College of Physical Education, 1919 D
Aust. College of Theology, 1891 D
Aust. Colonies, self government, 1849 A
Australian Colonies Government Act, 1850 A
Aust. Commercial and Industrial Artists Association, 1938 C
Aust. Commission on Advanced Education, 1971 D

Aust. Committee for Cultural Freedom, 1954 C
Aust. Community Theatre, Sydney, 1929 C
Aust. Conservation Foundation, 1965 F
Aust. Consolidated Industries Ltd, 1873 A, 1922 A, 1981 A
Aust. Consumers' Association, ACA, 1959 F
Aust. Contemporary Dance Ensemble, 1963 C
Aust. Contemporary Music Ensemble, 1976 C
Aust. Corps, France, 1916 A
Aust. Council for Adult Literacy, 1984 D
Aust. Council for the Arts, 1968 C, 1973 C, 1975 C, D, *see also* Aust. Council
Aust. Council on Awards in Advanced Education, 1971 D
Aust. Council of Churches, 1946 D, 1950 D, 1960 D, 1967 D, 1972 D
Aust. Council of Civil Liberties, 1934 F
Aust. Council for Educational Research, 1930 D
Aust. Council of Employers' Federation of Aust, 1904 A
Aust. Council of Judo, 1928 E
Aust. Council of National Trusts, 1965 F
Aust. Council for Native Welfare, 1951 A
Aust. Council for Overseas Trade, ACFOT, 1965 A
Aust. Council of Salaried and Professional Associations, ACSPA, 1958 A
Aust. Council of Social Service, ACOSS, 1956 F
Australian Council of Trade Unions, ACTU, 1927 A, 1936 A, 1949 A, 1957 A, 1958 A, 1967 A, 1969 A, 1970 D, 1972 A, 1975 A, 1976 A, D, 1978 A, 1979 A, 1981 A
Aust. Country Music Awards, 1973 C
Aust. Country Party Association, 1926 A
Australian Courts Act, 1828 A
Australian Crawl, 1877 E, 1897 E, 1902 E
Aust. Cricket Board, 1979 E
Aust. Cricket Club, 1826 E
Aust. Cricket Council, 1905 E
Aust. Croquet Council, 1949 E
Aust. Dairy Corporation, 1924 A
Aust. Dairy Produce Board, 1924 A
Aust. Dance Theatre, Adelaide, 1965 C, 1979 C
Aust. Dance Theatre School, Adelaide, 1975 C
Aust. Dancing Society, 1983 C
Aust. Day, 1934 F
Australian Defence Act, 1909 A
Aust. Democrats, 1977 A
Aust. Dental Association, 1928 B
Australian Dictionary of Biography, The, 1966 C
Aust. dollar, 1972 A, 1973 A, 1974 A, 1976 A, 1982 A, 1984 A
Aust. Drama Nights, Melbourne, 1909 C
Australia Economic and Political Studies, 1920 C
Aust. Education Council, 1936 D
Aust. Electric Co., 1882 B
Aust. Elementary School Society, NSW, 1835 D
Aust. Elizabethan Theatre Trust, *see* Elizabethan Theatre Trust
Aust. Enactment Currency Bill, 1824 A
Australian Encyclopaedia, The, 1925 C, 1958 C, 1977 C, 1983 C
Australian Essays, 1886 C

Aust. and European Bank, 1879 A
Aust. Exhibition of Women's Art, Melbourne, 1907 C
Aust. expeditionary force, Sudan, 1885 A
Aust. Explosives and Chemical Co., 1874 B
Aust. Family Action Movement, 1974 A
Aust. Farmers' Federal Organisation, Melbourne, 1916 A
Australian Farmers' Federation, 1969 A
Aust. Federal Assembly, 1849 A
Aust. Federal Council, 1897 A
Aust. Federal Council of Boy Scouts Association, 1920 F
Aust. Federal Cycling Council, 1901 E
Aust. Federal Police, 1979 A
Aust. Federation of Actors, 1920 C
Aust. Federation of Broadcasting Stations, 1927 A
Aust. Federation of Commercial Broadcasting Stations, 1931 A
Aust. Federation Conference, Sydney, 1893 A
Aust. Federation of Labour, 1885 A
Aust. Film Commission, 1975 C
Aust. Film Development Corporation, 1970 C, 1971 C
Aust. Film Institute, Sydney, 1958 C
Aust. Film and Television School, Sydney, 1972 D, 1973 C
Australian Financial Review, Sydney, 1951 F, 1963 F
Aust. Fire and Life Assurance Co., 1836 A, 1837 F
Aust. flag, 1901 F
Aust. Flying Corps, 1914 A, 1915 A, 1916 A, 1920 A
Aust. Folk Lore Society, Sydney, 1953 F
Aust. Football Championships Pty Ltd, 1979 E
Aust. Forces,
 China, 1900 A, 1901 A
 Korea, 1952 A
 Malayan campaign, 1955 A, 1960 A, 1962 A, 1964 A
 Maori wars, 1863 A
 N Borneo, 1962 A
 NSW, 1871 A
 South Africa, 1899 A, 1900 A
 Strength, 1889 F, 1900 A
 Sudan, 1885 A
 Vietnam, 1965 A, 1966 A, 1967 A, 1968 A, 1969 A, 1970 A, 1971 A, 1972 A
 World War I, 1914 A–1919 A
 World War II, 1939 A–1945 A
 see also Defence, Army, Air Force, Navy, Aust. Corps, Military, Aust. Imperial Forces, Aust. Infantry Forces
Aust. Forestry Council, 1964 B
Aust. Forestry School, Adelaide, 1925 D
Aust. Freedom League, 1912 A
Aust. Friends' Peace Board, 1913 F
Aust. Frozen Meat Export Co., 1880 A
Australian Galleries, Melbourne, 1956 C
Aust. Gas Light Co., 1836 B, 1841 B
Aust. Golf Club, 1882 E
Aust. Golf Union, 1898 E
Aust. Guarantee Corporation, 1925 A
Aust. Gymnastic Union, 1948 E
Aust. Health Society, 1875 F
Aust. Heeler, 1890 B
Aust. Hen, 1930 B
Aust. Heritage Commission, 1975 A, 1981 F
Aust. High Commission, 1909 A, 1927 A
Aust. Hockey Association, 1925 E
Australian at Home, The, 1891 C

Aust. Hospitals Association, 1946 B
Australia Hotel, Sydney, 1891 F
Aust. Ice & Figure Skating comp., 1931 E
Aust. Illawarra Shorthorn, 1898 B
Aust. Imperial Forces, 1914 A, 1918 A, 1939 A, 1940 A, 1941 A
Aust. Industries Fair, Melbourne, 1958 B
Australian Industries Protection Act, 1906 A
Aust. Industry Development Corporation, AIDC, 1971 A
Aust. Infantry Forces, AIF, 1916 A, 1918 A, 1940 A
Aust. Inland Mission, 1912 D, 1917 B, 1927 B, 1929 B, 1980 D
Aust. Institute of Aboriginal Studies, Canberra, 1961 D
Aust. Institute of Accountants, 1885 A
Aust. Institute of Anatomy, Canberra, 1931 B
Aust. Institute of Architects, 1868 C
Aust. Institute of Arts and Literature, 1921 C
Aust. Institute of Criminology, 1973 A
Aust. Institute of Engineers, 1919 B
Aust. Institute of Hospital Administrators, 1945 B
Aust. Institute of International Affairs, 1933 A
Aust. Institute of Librarians, 1837 D, 1937 D, 1949 D
Aust. Institute of Marine Engineers, 1881 A
Aust. Institute of Marine Science, 1972 B
Aust. Institute of Mining Engineers, 1893 B
Aust. Institute of Nuclear Science and Engineering, AINSE, 1958 B
Aust. Institute of Political Science, AIPS, 1932 A
Aust. Institute of Tropical Medicine, Qld, 1909 B
Aust. Institute of Sport, 1981 E
Aust. and International Insurances Ltd, 1953 A
Aust. Iron and Steel Co., 1908 B
Aust. Iron and Steel Ltd, 1928 B, 1933 B, 1935 B
Australian Ironclad, 1867 B
Aust. Jazz Quartet, 1955 C
Aust. Jewish Welfare Society, 1938 F
Aust. Jockey Club/s, 1842 E, 1947 E
Aust. Joint Stock Banks, 1865 A
Australian Journal, Melbourne, 1865 F
Aust. Journalists Association, 1910 F
Aust. Kodak Co. Ltd., 1908 A
Aust. Labour Federation, Brisbane, 1889 A, 1890 A, 1895 A
Aust. Labor Party, ALP, 1857 A, 1902 A, 1908 A, 1918 A, 1943 A, 1955 A, 1973 A, 1974 A, 1980 A, 1982 A, 1983 A, 1984 A
Aust. Lawn Bowling Council, 1911 E
Aust. League of Rights, 1946 A, 1960 A
Aust. Legal Aid Office, 1974 A
Aust. Legal Convention, 1951 A
Australian Legend, The, 1958 C
Aust. Legion of Ex-Servicemen and Women, 1944 F
Aust. Liaison Officer, 1924 A
Aust. Library Association, 1928 D
Aust. Literature, Chair of, 1962 C
Aust. Literature Society, 1899 C
Aust. Loan Council, 1927 A
Australian Magazine, 1821 F
Aust. Maritime College, Launceston, 1978 D, 1980 D

749

Aust. Marriage Guidance Council, Sydney, 1948 F
Aust. Medical Association/s, 1859 B, 1961 B, 1983 B
Aust. Medical Congress, 1923 B
Aust. Milking Zebu, cattle, 1956 B
Aust. Minerals Council, 1968 B
Australian Monthly, Melbourne, 1863 F
Aust. Museum, Sydney, 1827 D, 1836 D, 1853 D
Aust. Music Centre, 1975 C
Aust. Music Examination Board, 1918 C
Australian Musical Possibilities, 1924 C
Australian Musical Resources, 1917 C
Aust. Mutual Provident Society, 'AMP', 1848 A, 1849 A
Aust. Mutual Provident Society building, Sydney, 1957 C, 1962 C
Aust. National Airlines Commission, 1945 B
Aust. National Airways Pty Ltd, ANA, 1929 B, 1930 B, 1931 B, F, 1932 B, 1936 B, 1950 F, 1952 A, 1957 B
Aust. National Antarctic Research Expedition, ANARE, 1947 B, 1954 B, 1957 B
Aust. national art collection, ACT, 1911 C
Australian National Bibliography, 1961 C
Aust. National Council for the Blind, 1952 F
Aust. National Eisteddfod, Canberra, 1955 C
Aust. National Film Board, 1945 C
Aust. National Football Council, 1906 E
Aust. National Football League, Sydney, 1902 E
Aust. National Gallery, Canberra, 1971 C, 1974 C, 1982 C, 1984 C
Aust. National Line, ANL, 1956 B
Aust. National Parks and Wildlife Service, 1975 A
Aust. National Railways, 1975 B
Aust. National Research Council, 1919 B
Aust. National Ski Federation, 1932 E
Aust. National University, ANU, 1946 D, 1948 D, 1951 D, 1957 B, 1960 D, 1965 B, 1971 B, 1977 B, 1978 B
Aust. nationalist War Govt, 1917 A
Aust. Natives Association, 1871 A
Aust. Natives Association Art Competition, 1914 C
Aust. Naval Board Flag, 1920 A
Aust. Netball Association, 1926 E
Aust. and New Guinea Administration Unit, 1942 A
Aust. and N.Z. Army Corps, ANZAC, 1914 A, 1915 A
Aust. and N.Z. Association for the Advancement of Science, ANZAAS, 1886 B
Aust. and N.Z. Association of Radiology, 1934 B
Aust. and N.Z. Banking Group Ltd, holdings, 1969 A, 1976 A, 1984 A
Aust. and N.Z. Bank Ltd, 1835 A, 1951 A, 1969 A
Aust. and N.Z. Commercial Savings Bank, 1956 A
Aust. Nursing Federation, 1923 B
Aust. Olympic Federation, 1980 E
Australian Opera, 1970 C
Aust. Opera Co., 1948 C, 1954 C, 1956 C, 1969 C
Aust. Opera League, 1914 C
Aust. Painter-Etchers' Society, 1920 C
Australian Painting, 1962 C
Aust. Painting Today Exhibition, 1963 C
Aust. Paper Co., 1866 B

Aust. Paper Mills Pty Ltd, 1895 A
Aust. Parachute Federation, 1961 E
'Aust. Patriot, The', 1793 A
Aust. Patriotic Association, 1835 A
Aust. Pentathlon Academy, Sydney, 1969 E
Australian Penthouse, 1979 F
Aust. People's Church, Melbourne, 1955 D
Aust. Performing Group, 1970 C
Aust. Philosophical Society, 1850 B, 1855 B
Aust. Photographic Society, 1962 B
Aust. Planning Institute, 1951 C
Australian Playboy, 1979 F
Aust. Political Studies Association, APSA, 1956 A
Aust. Polocross Association, 1946 E
Aust. Population and Immigration Council, 1975 A
Aust. Post Express, 1981 F
Aust. Postal Commission, 1975 A
Aust. Postal Courier Service, 1981 F
Aust. Post-Graduate Federation, Medicine, 1948 B
Aust. Power Boat Association, 1927 E
Aust. Pre-School Association, 1938 D
Aust. Present Day Art Exhibition, Melbourne, 1945 C
Aust. Primary Producers' Union, 1969 A
Aust. Publications, Annual Catalogue of, 1936 C
Australian Quarterly, Sydney, 1929 F
Australian Race; its Origins, Languages, Customs, The, 1886 C
Aust. Racing and Jockey Club, 1828 E
Aust. radiation Laboratory, 1929 B
Aust. Red Cross Blood Transfusion Service, 1938 B
Aust. Red Cross Society, 1914 F, 1927 F
Aust. Reform Movement, 1967 A, 1969 A
Aust. Refugee Advisory Council, 1979 A
Aust. Religious Tract Society, 1823 D
Aust. Reptile Park, NSW, 1960 B
Aust. Research Grants Committee, 1965 D
Aust. Resources Development Bank, 1967 A
Aust. Road Research Board, 1960 B
Aust. Road Safety Council, 1947 F
Aust. Roughriding Association, 1944 E, 1945 C
Aust. Rugby League Board of Control, 1924 E
Aust. Rules Football, 1858 E estb.
  Aust. wide, 1862 E, 1869 E, 1879 E, 1897 E, 1908 E, 1980 E
  NSW, 1880 E, 1926 E
  Qld, 1946 E
  SA, 1860 E, 1898 E
  Tas, 1875 E, 1945 E
  Umpires, 1880 E, 1884 E, 1891 E
  Vic, 1864 E, 1866 E, 1877 E, 1879 E, 1924 E, 1948 E, 1953 E, 1979 E
  WA, 1885 E, 1921 E, 1945 E
Aust. Rules Football Council, 1906 E
Aust. School of Pacific Administration, 1973 D
Aust. School of Nuclear Technology, Sydney, 1964 B
Aust. Schools Commission, 1972 D, 1973 D, 1974 D, 1977 D, 1984 D
Aust. Science and Technology Council, ASTEC, 1977 B, 1984 B
Aust. Sculptors' Society, 1930 C
Australian Sculpture Centre, Canberra, 1966 C

Aust. Secret Intelligence Service, ASIS, 1952 A
Aust. Security Intelligence Organization, ASIO, 1949 A, 1973 A
Aust. Shipping Board, 1949 A
Aust. Shipping Commission, 1956 B
Aust. Shipping Line, 1949 A
Aust. Shipping Register Office, Canberra, 1982 B
Aust. Skateboard Association, 1975 E
Aust. 'Six' car, 1920 B
Australian Sketcher, 1873 C
Aust. Ski Federation, 1932 E
Aust. Soccer Association, 1923 E
Aust. Soccer Federation, 1923 E, 1957 E, 1961 E
Aust. Society of Accountants, 1885 A
Aust. Society of Authors, 1963 C
Aust. Society of Black and White Artists, Sydney, 1924 C
Aust. Society for Education through the Arts, ASEA, 1963 D
Aust. Society of Painters-Etchers, 1921 C
Aust. Softball Federation, 1949 E
Aust.-South Africa Etchings Exhibition, 1928 C
Aust. Speleological Federation, 1956 F
Aust. Sports Council, 1974 E
Australian Sportsman, 1849 E
Aust. Squash championship, 1931 E
Aust. Staff College, Queenscliff Vic, 1946 B
Australian Star, Sydney, 1887 F
Aust. Station of Imperial naval command, 1859 A
Aust. Steam Conveyance Co., 1833 B
Aust. Subscription Library, 1826 D, 1843 D, 1899 D
Aust. Subscription Rowing Club, 1859 E
Aust. Sugar Co., 1839 A, 1843 A, 1855 A
Aust. Sugar Producers' Association, 1907 A
Aust. Surfriders' Association, 1963 E
Aust. Table Tennis Association, 1937 E
Aust. Table Tennis Board of Control, 1933 E
Aust. Teachers' Federation, 1922 D
Aust. Telecommunications Commission, 1975 A
Aust. Ten Pin Bowling Congress, 1962 E
Aust. Theatre Society Repertory Co., Melbourne, 1904 C
Australian Town and Country Journal, Sydney, 1870 F
Aust. Trade Union Benefit Society, 1834 A
Australian Tradition, The, 1954 C, 1958 C
Aust. Transport Advisory Council, 1946 B
Aust. Transport Officers' Federation, 1921 A
Aust. troops, *see* Aust. Forces
Aust. Typographic Union, 1880 A
Australian Ugliness, The, 1960 C
Aust. Underwater Federation, 1947 E
'Aust. Uniting Life Church', 1984 D
Aust. Union of Students, AUS, 1936 D, 1970 D
Aust. Unitarian Association, 1961 D
Aust. Universities Commission, 1959 D
Aust. Volleyball championship, 1962 E
Aust. Volleyball Federation, 1963 E
Aust. Watercolour Institute, Sydney, 1924 C
Aust. Water Resources Council, 1963 A
Aust. Water-Ski Association, 1950 E
Aust. at War Art Exhibition, 1945 C

Aust. War Memorial Art Competition, 1950 C
Aust. War Memorial, Canberra, 1925 C, 1941 F
Aust. Whaling Commission, 1949 A
Aust. Wheat Board, 1939 A
Aust. Wine Board, 1929 A
Aust. Window Glass Co., 1932 B
Aust. Wireless Association, 1921 B
Aust. Wireless Co., 1913 B
Aust. Women's Amateur Athletic Union, 1932 E
Aust. Women's Basketball Association, 1926 E
Aust. Women's Bowling Council, 1947 E
Aust. Women's Cricket Council, 1931 E
Aust. Women's Hockey Association, 1910 E
Aust. Women's Hockey Club, 1903 E
Australian Woman's Mirror, Sydney, 1926 F
Aust. Women Pilots' Association, 1949 E
Aust. Women's Softball Council, 1949 E
Australian Women's Weekly, Sydney, 1933 F
Aust. Wool Board, 1936 A, 1958 A, 1963 A, 1964 A, 1972 A
Aust. Wool Commission, 1970 A, 1972 A
Aust. Wool Corporation, 1972 A
Aust. Woolgrowers and Graziers' Council, 1891 A
Australian Worker, 1908 F
Aust. Workers' Party, 1973 A
Aust. Workers' Union, AWU, 1894 A 1919 A, 1948 A, 1964 A, 1967 A
Aust. Yacht Squadron, 1862 E
Australian of the Year Awards, *see from* 1960
Aust. Youth Orchestra, 1984 C
Australian, The, (book), 1893 C
Australia's Home, 1952 C
Australind, WA, 1839 A, 1841 A
Australind Express, 1947 B
Australis car, 1894 B
Australorp chicken, 1930 B
Author's Daughter, The, 1868 C
Auto Cycle Council, 1928 E
Automobile Club of Aust., 1903 F
Automobile Clubs, 1905 F
Automotive Show, Adelaide, 1920 F
Auxiliary Bible Society of NSW, 1817 D
Avadale, Qld, 1872 B
Aviation,
  Pre 1911 *see* Aeronautics
  Post 1911 *see* section B
Aviation Industry Advisory Council, 1978 B
Avoca, Tas, 1860 F
Avoca, Vic, 1852 F
Avon Valley, WA, 1830 A
Avondale College Estate, 1897 D
AWA, *see* Amalgamated wireless of Australia
Awahou, 1952 F
Awards, Cwlth, 1926 A
Awnings, 1908 C
Ayers, Henry, 1821 A, 1863 A, 1865 A, 1867 A, 1868 A, 1872 A
Ayers Rock, NT, 1873 A, 1889 A, 1983 F
Aylett, Allen, 1935 E
Ayr, Qld, 1882 F
'Azaria inquest', second, 1981 F

B

Baartz, Ray, 1947 E
Babbage, Benjamin H. 1815 B, 1856 A, 1858 A
Babcock test, 1892 B
Babies, heaviest, 1963 F
Babinda, Qld, 1880 F
'Baby Bonus', 1912 A
Baby Clinic, aerial, 1932 F
Baby Show, Hobart, 1905 F
Bacchus Marsh, Vic, 1838 F, 1850 D, 1890 B, 1937 D
Bachli, Douglas, 1922 E
Back at Our Selection, 1906 C
Backblock Verses and Other Verses, 1913 C
Backen, Earle, 1927 C
Backgammon, 1976 F
Backhouse, Benjamin, 1829 C, 1868 C
Backhouse, James, 1794 D, 1832 A, D
Backler, Joseph, 1815 C
Back of Beyond, The, 1954 C
Bacon, Elizabeth, 1788 D
Bacon, Kevin, 1932 E
Badger, Harold, (1), 1908 E
Badger, Harold, (2), 1930 C
Badgery, A. D. 1914 B
Badham, Charles, 1813 D
Badham, Herbert E. 1899 C
Badminton, 1900 E, 1935 E
Baghdad Note, 1970 E
Bagot, Charles H. 1788 A
Bagot, Charles S. 1842 B
Bagot, Robert C. 1827 E
Bagshaw, John, 1837 B
Bahai Faith, Sydney, 1920 D
Bahai House of Worship, NSW, 1961 D
Bahina, 1899 F
Bailed Up, 1895 C
Bailey, Albert E. ('Bert'), 1868 C, 1912 C, 1932 C
Bailey, Frederick M. 1827 B
Bailey, John, 1800 B
Bailey, John F. 1866 B
Bailey, Mary A. 1895 C
Bailey, William H. L. 1885 F
Bailhache, Robin, 1937 E
Baillie, Charles W. A. N. C., Lord Lamington, 1896 A, 1901 A
Baillieu, Clive L. 1889 A
Baillieu, James G. 1832 A
Baillieu, William L. 1859 A
Baily, Edward H. 1788 C
Baily, Harold J. 1927 C
Bainbridge, Leo J. L. 1918 C
Baines, Thomas, 1822 C
Bainton, Edgar L. 1880 C
Baird, John L. 1874 A, 1925 A
Bairnsdale, Vic, 1842 F
Baker, Alan D. 1914 C
Baker, Christina A. 1869 C
Baker, Dorothy, 1914 C
Baker, Harold, 1889 C
Baker, John S. 1912 C, 1945 C
Baker, J. 1857 A
Baker, Janette, 1983 E
Baker Medical Research Institute, Melbourne, 1926 B
Baker, Norman H. 1908 C, 1937 C
Baker, Reginald L. ('Snowy'), 1884 E, 1918 C
Baker, Richard T. 1854 B, 1897 B
Baker, William A. 1921 C
Bakers, 1947 B
Bakers workers group, Sydney, 1835 A
Balaklava, SA, 1847 F

Balance of payments, 1952 A, 1954 A, 1960 A
Balclutha, 1881 F
Balcombe, Thomas T. 1810 C
Balcombe, William, 1824 A, 1829 A
Baldessin, George, 1939 C
Baldock, Darrel, 1938 E
Bale, Alice M. E. 1876 C
Balfour, T. L. 1870 C
Ball, Henry L. 1788 A, 1790 A
Ball, Murray, 1980 C
Ball, Percival, 1844 C
Ball, Sydney, 1933 C
Ball, Ted, 1939 E
'Ballad of Eureka', 1901 C
Ballan, Vic, 1838 F
Ballantyne, Colin S. 1908 C, 1972 C
Ballantyne, J. F. W. 1924 C
Ballarat, Vic, 1851 A, B, F, 1855 C, 1856 B, 1857 B, 1858 F, 1862 B, 1870 D, 1883 B, 1886 A, 1891 D, C, 1927 C, 1947 C
Ballarat (ship), 1853 B
Ballarat College, 1864 D
Ballarat Courier, 1867 F
Ballarat Fine Arts Gallery, 1884 C
Ballarat Ladies' Art Association, 1890 C
Ballarat Mail, 1861 F
Ballarat Reform League, 1854 A
Ballarat School of Mines, 1891 D
Ballarat Star, 1867 F
Ballarat Teachers' College, Vic, 1926 D
Ballard, David, 1950 E
Ballet, *see* section C
Ballet, teaching of, 1897 C, 1937 C
Ballet Aust., 1960 C
Ballet Rambert, 1948 C
Ballet School, Sydney, 1926 C
Ballet Theatre of Qld, 1937 C
Ballet Victoria, 1946 C
Ballet Workshop, WA, 1961 C
Ballina, NSW, 1856 F, 1870 B
Ballooning, 1858 B, 1871 E, 1878 E, 1904 B, 1960 B, 1969 E, 1972 E
Ballot, conscription, 1964 A, 1965 A
Ballot, secret, 1856 A, 1877 A, 1981 A
Ballroom dancing, 1977 C
Balmain, Sydney, 1855 B
Balmain, William, 1788 B, 1803 B
Balmain Rugby League Football Club/team, 1908 E, 1915 E, 1916 E, 1917 E, 1919 E, 1920 E, 1924 E, 1939 E, 1944 E, 1946 E, 1947 E, 1969 E
Balmain Teachers College, Sydney, 1946 D
Balmoral, Sydney, 1924 D
Balranald, NSW, 1837 F
Balson, Ralph, 1890 C, 1941 C
Baly, Edward H. 1841 C
Bamborough, Jill, 1948 E, 1978 E
Bananas, 1870 A, 1913 A, 1925 B
Bancks, James C. 1889 C, 1921 F
Banco Court, Melbourne, 1903 A
Bancroft, Joseph, 1836 B, 1867 B, 1876 B
Bancroft, Thomas L. 1860 B, 1902 B, 1905 B
Bandidos, 1984 F
Bandit of the Rhine, The, 1835 C
Bandler, Faith, 1956 F
Bandstand, 1958 C
Banfield, Edmund J. 1852 C, 1897 A, 1908 C
Bungalow, Californian, 1919 C
Banjo Paterson Art Competition, 1961 C
Banjo Queen, 1871 C
Bank of Adelaide, 1865 A
Bank of Australia, 1826 A, 1828 F, 1843 A

751

Bank of Australasia, 1835 A, 1857 F, 1890 C, 1951 A
Bank of England, 1930 A
Bank managers, 1830 A
Bank Nationalization Act of 1947, 1948 A
Bank of North Qld, 1888 A
Bank of NSW, 1817 A, 1832 A, 1886 C, 1956 A, 1978 F, 1981 A, 1982 A
Bank of Qld Ltd, 1874 A
Bank robberies, 1828 F, 1978 F
Bank of Van Diemen's Land, 1824 A, 1891 A
Bank of Vic, 1852 A
Bank of WA, 1837 A, 1847 A
Banka I. Beach, 1942 A
Bankcard, 1974 A
Banker, 1863 E
Banking, 1835 A, 1945 A
Banking, nationalization, 1947 A
Banking Act, Federal, 1945 A
Banking crash, 1843 A, 1893 A
Banking system, 1957 A
Banking Trade Employees' Union, 1869 A
Banks, see individual entries
Banks, Donald O. 1923 C
Banks, foreign, 1981 A, 1983 A
Banks, John, 1883 C
Banks, Joseph, 1802 B, 1820 B, 1822 F
Banks, overdraft system, 1834 A
Bankside, SA, 1853 A
Bankstown, NSW, 1926 F, 1970 E
Bannerman, Charles, 1851 E, 1878 E
Bannister, Saxe, 1790 A, 1824 A, 1826 F
Bannister, Thomas, 1831 A
Bannon, Charles, 1919 C
Bannon, J. C. 1982 A
Banshee, 1876 F
Baptist Associations, 1862 D
Baptist church,
 Aust, 1834 D, 1913 D, 1926 D
 NSW, 1831 D, 1835 D, 1874 D
 Qld, 1849 D, 1855 D
 SA, 1838 D
 Vic, 1839 D, 1842 D
 WA, 1895 D
Baptist Missionary Society, 1864 D
Baptist Theological Colleges, 1891 D
Baptist Union of Aust., 1926 D
Bar, longest, 1938 F
Barak, William, 1898 C
Barassi, Ronald D. 1936 E, 1953 E
Barb, The, 1866 E
Barbarous Barber, The (play), 1925 C
Barber of Seville, 1843 C
Barcaldine, Qld, 1886 F, 1891 A
Barclay-Harvey, Charles M. 1939 A
Barcoo R., 1846 A, 1858 A, F
Barden, James, 1884 F
Bardsley, Warren, 1883 E
Bargo, NSW, 1815 F
Barham, NSW, 1843 F
Barker, Collet, 1831 A
Barker, David, 1888 C
Barker, Frederic, 1856 D
Barker, Frederick, 1808 D, 1859 D
Barker, James, 1931 C
Barker, Nigel, 1884 E, 1905 E
Barker, Tom, 1918 A
Barkly, Henry, 1815 A, 1856 A
Barley, Aust. Barley Board, 1939 A
Barley, SA, 1903 B
Barley Mow (hotel), Sydney, 1830 F
Barmera, SA, 1921 F
Barnard, Lance H. 1919 A
Barnard, Marjorie F. 1897 C, 1943 C, 1947 C, 1959 C
Barnard, Robert G. 1933 C
Barnardo's Homes, Sydney, 1921 F

Barnes, Alan, 1916 E
Barnes, Ethel, 1876 C
Barnes, George, 1927 E, 1953 E, 1954 E
Barnes, Gustave A. 1878 C
Barnes, Joane, 1954 E
Barnes, Keith, 1935 E
Barnes, Sidney G. 1918 E
Barnes, Stephen, 1793 D
Barnet, James J. 1827 C, 1876 C, 1885 C
Barnett, Henry W. 1862 B
Barnett, Percy N. 1881 C
Barney, George, 1792 B, 1837 B, 1846 A, 1857 C
Barometric pressure, 1964 F
Baron, The, 1884 E
Barossa Valley, SA, 1847 A, 1979 F
Barossa Valley vintage festival, SA, 1947 F
Barr, Margaret, 1955 C
Barraba, NSW, 1852 F
Barrackee Mystery, The, 1929 C
Barracouta oil field, Vic, 1964 B
Barrallier, Francis L. 1802 A, 1853 A
Barrett, Charles L. 1879 C
Barrett, Franklyn, 1909 C, 1920 C
Barrett, Gerard, 1956 E
Barrett, James, 1788 F
Barrett, James W. 1862 B
Barrette, Anette P. 1929 C
Barrie, Andrew, 1860 B
Barrie, May, 1918 C
Barrier Industrial and Political Council, 1924 A
Barrier Miner, Broken Hill, 1888 F
Barrier Reef, see Great Barrier Reef
Barrier Truth, NSW, 1898 F
Barrington, 1804 C
Barrington Tops, NSW, 1981 F
Barristers, 1824 A
Barron, Harry, 1909 A, 1913 A
Barron, Howard, 1900 C
Barrow Creek, NT, 1872 F
Barrow I., WA, 1964 B, 1966 B, 1982 B
Barrow, J. H. 1858 F
Barry, Canon, 1884 D
Barry, Kevin, 1945 E
Barry, Redmond, 1813 A, 1851 A
Barry Stern Modern Art Gallery, Sydney, 1960 C
Barsby, Samuel, 1788 F
Bartell, Denis, 1984 F
Bartholomew, C. P. 1906 B
Bartholomew, Wayne, 1957 E, 1978 E
Bartle, Ted, 1910 E
Bartlett, Geoffrey, 1952 C
Bartlett, Kevin, (b. 1933), 1933 C
Bartlett, Kevin, (b. 1940), 1940 E
Bartlett, Kevin, (b. 1947), 1947 E
Bartley, Mick, 1916 E, 1960 E
Bartolin, Peter, 1975 B
Bartolomeo Colleoni, 1940 A
Barton, Alexander, 1982 F
Barton, Edmund, 1849 A, 1891 A, 1897 A, 1901 A, 1902 D, 1903 A
Barton, George B. 1866 C
Barton, Gordon P. 1929 A, 1966 A
Barton, Thomas, 1982 F
Barton, William, 1852 A
Barton, W. A. 1904 D
Barwell, Geoffrey, 1920 C
Barwell, Henry N. 1877 A, 1920 A
Barwick, Garfield E. J. 1903 A, 1964 A, 1975 A
Baseball, 1856 E, 1885 E, 1894 E, 1899 E, 1933 E
Basedow, Herbert, 1881 B
Basic Wage, 1890 A, 1898 A, see also Wages
Basically Black, 1972 C

Baskerville, Margaret, 1861 C
Basketball, 1900 E, 1928 E, 1929 E, 1946 E, 1963 E, 1972 E
Bass, George, 1795 A, 1797 A, B, 1798 A, 1799 A, 1803 A
Bass, Thomas D. 1916 C
Bass Strait, 1800 A, 1826 A, 1835 F, 1845 F, 1901 F, 1919 B, 1920 F, 1934 F, 1936 F, 1940 A, 1969 B, 1970 B, 1971 B
Bassel, Walter, 1921 B
Basser, Adolph, 1887 A
Bassett, S. S. 1863 A
Bastardization, 1983 A
Bastin, Henry, 1896 C
Bastyan, Edric M. 1961 A, 1968 A
Batch, Paddy, 1953 E
Batchelor, Egerton L. 1865 A
Batchelor, NT, 1952 F
Batemans Bay, NSW, 1821 A, 1847 F
Bates, Daisy M. 1863 A, 1899 A, 1938 C
Bates, Frederic, 1918 C, 1956 C
Bates, Smart and McCutcheson, 1957 C
Batgi Batgi, WA, 1846 D, 1847 D
Bath, Harry, 1924 E
Bathing, 1833 F, 1903 F
Bathing, nude, 1976 F
Bathing costumes, 1905 F, 1907 F, 1938 F
Bathurst, NSW, 1814 B, 1815 F, 1817 A, 1819 A, 1824 A, 1830 A, 1836 A, 1851 A, E, 1862 B, 1867 D, 1876 B, 1887 B, 1890 F, 1896 A, 1910 E, 1938 E, 1947 B, 1955 C, 1970 D
Bathurst, Henry, 1812 A
Bathurst Bay, Qld, 1819 F, 1899 F
Bathurst burr, 1840 B
Bathurst I., NT, 1911 D
Bathurst Plains, NSW, 1813 A, 1817 A, 1818 A
Bathurst Teachers College, NSW, 1951 D
Batlow, NSW, 1900 F
Batman, John, 1801 A, 1826 A, 1827 A, 1835 A, 1836 A, F, 1837 A
Batman, treaty, 1835 A
'Batmania', 1835 A
Battarbee, Reginald E. R. (Rex) 1893 C, 1936 C
Batten, Jean G. 1909 E, 1934 B
Battista, John, 1961 F
'Battle of Boyne', 1846 F
'Battle of Brisbane', 1943 A
'Battle of Britain', 1940 A
Battle Cruiser, 1922 A
Battle of the Elms, Melbourne, 1968 F
Battle of Gaza, 1916 A, 1917 A
Battle of Kokoda, 1942 A
Battle of Long Tan, 1966 A
'Battle of Pinjarra', WA, 1834 A
'Battle of Rothbury', 1929 A
Battlers, The, 1941 C
Batty, Francis de W. 1879 D
Batty, R. 1875 C
Battye, James S. 1871 D
Baudin, Nicholas, 1800 C, 1801 A, 1802 A, 1803 A
Bauer, Ferdinand, 1826 C
Bauld, Alison, 1944 C
Baumgartner, Leo, 1931 E
Bauxite, NT, 1949 B, 1953 B, 1955 B, 1960 A, 1962 B, 1963 B, 1964 B, 1968 B, 1976 B
Bavin, Thomas R. 1874 A, 1927 A
Baxter, Edward, 1841 A
Baxter, Evelyn, 1925 C
Baxter, John P. 1905 B
Baylebridge, William, see Blocksidge, Charles W.
Bayley, Arthur, 1892 B
Bayliss, Charles, 1850 B

Bayliss, Clifford W. 1916 C
Baynton, Barbara, 1902 C
Baystone, 1958 E
Beach, William, 1850 E
Beachport, SA, 1878 F
Beaconsfield, Tas, 1879 F, 1953 B
Beaconsfield, Vic, 1845 F
Beadle, Paul, 1917 C
Beagle, 1836 B, 1837 A, 1839 A
Beale, Octavius C. 1850 C, 1893 C, 1904 B
Beames, Percy, 1911 E
Beamont, John, 1789 A
Bean, Charles E. W. 1879 C, 1910 C, 1921 C
Beaney, James G. 1828 B, 1859 C
Beargrass, 1836 A, 1837 A
Beatlemania, 1964 C
'Beatles' pop group, 1964 C
Beatnik fashion, 1961 F
Beattie, John W. 1859 B
Beatty, Alice M. 1894 C
Beatty, William A. 1912 D
Beauchamp, Robert P. 1819 C
Beauchamp, Earl of, *see* Lygon, William
Beaudesert, Qld, 1873 F
Beaufort, Vic, 1840 F
Beaumaris, Vic, 1944 F
Beaumaris Art group, Melbourne, 1966 C
Beaumont, 1850 B
Beaumont, Charles, 1836 D
Beaumont, John, 1812 A
Beaumont children, Adelaide, 1966 F
Beaurepaire, Francis J. E. 1891 E, 1910 E, 1922 A, E, F
Beaurepaire Tyre Service, Melbourne, 1922 A
Beauty and the Beast, 1837 C
Beauty contests, 1962 F
Beauty Point, Tas, 1959 F
Beaver, Bruce, 1928 C
Bêche-de-mer licences, 1883 A
Becher, Otto H. 1908 A
Beck, Fred A. 1961 E
Beck, Hatton, 1901 C
Becke, George L. 1855 C, 1894 C
Becker, Ludwig, 1808 B
Beckett, Clarie, 1887 C
Bedford, Frederick G. D. 1903 A
Bedford, Peter, 1970 C
Bedford, Randolph, 1868 C
Bedford, William, 1823 D, 1852 D
Bedford Park, SA, 1961 D
Bedford Park Teachers College, Adelaide, 1966 D
Bednego Creek, Vic, 1851 B
Bedowrie, Qld, 1885 F
Beeby, George S. 1869 A
Beeby, Ida, 1938 C
Beech, Lance corporal, 1915 B
Beechworth, Vic, 1843 B, 1852 F
Beef, 1802 A, 1808 A, 1816 A, 1958 A
Beenleigh, Qld, 1868 F
Beer, 1796 A, *see* Breweries
Beer drinking, 1961 F
Beersheba, 1917 A
Beerwah, Qld, 1887 F
Bees, 1810 A, 1822 A, 1834 A, 1876 F
Beete, Picton, 1834 A
Beetson, Arthur, 1945 E
Bega, NSW, 1839 F
Begg, Neville, 1931 E
Begg, Samuel, 1854 C
'Behinds', Aust. Rules Football, 1897 E
Belair Park, SA, 1891 F
Belcher, Charles F. 1876 A
Beldale Ball, 1980 E
Belgium, 1933 A

Bell, Archibald, 1804 A, 1823 A
Bell, George H. F. 1878 C, 1925 C, 1932 C, 1938 C
Bell, Graeme, 1914 C, 1936 C, 1943 C
Bell, John, 1830 A
Bell, John A. 1940 C, 1970 C
Bell, John P. 1938 C
Bell, Ronald C. 1918 C
Bell, Thomas, 1823 C
Bell Bay, Tas, 1955 B, 1963 B
Bell Coleman cold air machine, 1879 B
Bell system of national education, 1820 D
Bellamy, Joseph, 1788 D
Bellbird Colliery, NSW, 1923 F
Belle Vue hotel, Brisbane, 1979 A
Bellette, Jean M. 1919 C
Bellenden Ker, Qld, 1979 F
Bellew, Peter R. 1912 C, 1939 C
Bellingen, NSW, 1863 F
Bellingen Hospital, NSW, 1929 A
Bellona, 1793 A
Bells, first peal of, Sydney, 1807 D
Bell's line of road, 1823 A
Bell-Shore Modern Art School, Melbourne, 1932 C
Bell-Siro cheesemaker, 1960 B
Belmont, NSW, 1825 F
Belmont, Qld, 1942 C
Belmore, Earl of, 1868 A
Below and On Top, 1898 C
Beltana, SA, 1866 F, 1875 A
Belyando R., NSW, 1846 A
Bembina, Margaret, 1952 C
Ben Uri Galleries, 1960 C
Benalla, Vic, 1846 F
Benaud, Richard, 1930 E, 1957 E, 1961 E
Bence, Ronald A. 1937 C
Bencubbin, WA, 1865 F
Bendigo, Vic, 1851 A, B, F, 1853 A, 1854 C, 1857 C, 1862 F, 1864 B, 1872 A, 1873 D, 1874 A, E, 1900 A, 1925 C, 1959 B
Bendigo Advertiser, Vic, 1853 F
Bendigo Art Gallery, 1890 C
Bendigo Art Gallery Prize, 1938 C
Bendigo Art Society, 1920 C
Bendigo pottery, 1857 C
Bendigo Teachers' College, Vic, 1926 D
Benedictines, 1843 D, 1846 D, 1849 D, 1857 D
Benedictine Institute of the Good Samaritan, 1857 D
Benefits,
 welfare,
 –funeral, 1943 A
 –home ownership, 1964 A
 –hospital, 1944 A
 –medical, 1953 A
 –sickness, 1944 A, 1945 A
 –supporting mothers, 1973 A
 –unemployment, 1944 A, 1945 A
 –unmarried mothers, 1943 A
 –widows, 1942 A
see also individual entries
Benevolent Society of NSW, 1813 F
Benjamin, Arthur L. 1893 C, 1937 C
Benjamin, Lou, 1922 B
Bennell, Hockey, 1917 E
Bennelong, 1789 A, 1792 A, 1795 A, 1813 A
Bennett, Anges L. 1894 D
Bennett, Charles, 1863 C
Bennett, Donald C. T. 1910 A, 1938 B, 1942 A
Bennett, Elliott, 1926 E
Bennett, George, 1804 B, 1832 B
Bennett, Henry G. 1887 A, 1942 A
Bennett, J. M. 1922 F

Bennett, Joseph, A. 1853 C
Bennett, Samuel, 1815 D, 1867 C, F, 1870 F
Bennett, William R. 1893 C
Benno and Some of the Push, 1911 C
Benson, George C. 1886 C
Benson, Irving, 1897 D
Bent, Andrew, 1790 A, 1816 F, 1818 C, 1825 F, 1828 F
Bent, Ellis, 1809 A, 1815 A
Bent, Jeffery H. 1814 A, 1817 A, 1852 A
Bent, Thomas, 1838 A, 1904 A
Bentham, Jeremy, 1832 A
Bentley, Charles W. ('Dick'), 1907 C
Bentley, James, 1854 A
Benz car, 1896 B
Beovich, Matthew, 1896 D, 1939 D
Berala, NSW, 1952 F
Beresford, Bruce, 1972 C, 1973 C, 1977 C, 1980 C, 1981 C
Bergner, Josl, 1920 C
Berkeley, Martha S. 1813 C
Berlin Olympics, 1936 E
Bermagui, NSW, 1867 F, 1880 F
Bermagui Mystery, 1880 F
Bernacchi, Louis C. 1876 B
Bernays, Lewis A. 1831 A
Berne, G. D. 1885 B
Bernhardt, Sarah, 1891 C
Berri, SA, 1910 F
Berrigan, NSW, 1888 F
Berrima, NSW, 1814 A, 1816 A, 1831 F, 1834 F, 1842 F, 1847 B
Berrima District Art Society, NSW, 1950 C
Berringer, John, 1814 E
Berry, Alexander, 1822 A, 1873 A
Berry, NSW, 1822 F, 1958 B
Berry, Graham, 1822 A, 1875 A, 1877 A, 1878 A, 1880 A, 1883 A
Berry, Kevin, 1945 E
Berryman, Frank H. 1884 A, 1945 A
Berthond, G. J. 1895 B
Bertie, Charles H. 1875 D, 1909 D
Bertillon system of identification, 1902 F
Bertrand, Henry L. 1840 F
Berwick, Vic, 1861 F, 1872 F, 1972 C
Berwick, Harry, 1923 C
Best, Amelia, 1955 A
Best, Fred, 1912 E
Best, John V. H. 1894 B
Best Aust. Film Awards, *see section C from* 1959
Best Linear Unbiased Prediction, 1982 B
Beetles, 1935 B
Bethany, SA, 1842 F
Bethel Union, 1822 F
Bethune, W. A. 1969 A
Bethune, Frank P. 1918 A
Betsey, 1815 C
Betting, 1832 E
Betting, S. P. WA, 1954 F
Betty Block Buster Follies, 1975 C
Between the Wars, 1974 C
Bevan, Brian, 1925 E
Bevan, Llewelyn D. 1842 D
Beverley, WA, 1831 F, 1889 B
Beveridge, Peter, 1829 A, 1850 C
Bey, Reschid, 1916 C
Beyond the City Gates (book), 1923 C
Beynon, Richard, 1928 C, 1956 C, 1957 C
Bi-centenary of Cook's arrival, 1970 F
Bianchi, Signor, 1859 C
Bianchi troupe, 1858 C
Biathlons, 1967 E
Bibb, John, 1832 C
Bibliography of Australia, 1941 C
Bicheno, James E. 1851 A
Bicheno, Tas, 1849 F, 1960 E

753

Bicycle, pedalless, 1975 B
Bicycle clubs, 1878 E
Bicycle League of Professional
    Wheelmen, 1893 E
Bicycle riding, Sydney–Melbourne,
    1884 F
Bicycles, 1846 B, 1887 B, 1889 B, 1941 E
Biddell, Walter, 1906 E
Bierwirth, Rudolph, 1899 A
'Big Ben', 1892 F
Big Brother Movement, 1925 F
Big Fellow, The, 1876 A
Big Toys, 1977 C
Bigge, John T. 1819 A, 1821 A, 1822 A,
    1824 A, 1828 A, 1843 A
Bigge Report, first, 1822 A
Bigge's camp, Qld, 1865 B
Biggles, 1945 F
Bijou Theatre, Melbourne, 1876 C,
    1889 F, 1897 C, 1934 C
Bikinis, 1949 F, 1961 F
Billarney, 1895 C
Billiards, 1836 E, 1853 E, 1887 E, 1932 E,
    1941 E, 1950 E
Billich, Charles, 1933 C, 1966 C
Billings, Philip, 1934 E
Billy can, 1850 F
Billy Graham Crusade, first, 1959 D, F
Biloela, Qld, 1852 F
Bilu, Asher, 1936 C
Bingara, NSW, 1840 F
Bingera, Qld, 1852 B
Binney, Hugh, 1945 A
Biography, 1818 C
Bionic ear, 1979 B
Biraban, John M. 1842 A
Birchip, Vic, 1887 F
Bird Observers Club, 1905 F
Birds of Australia, 1841 C
Birds of New Holland ... History, 1813 C
Birdsville, Qld, 1873 F
Birdwood, SA, 1845 F
Birdwood, William R. 1865 A, 1914 A,
    1918 A
Birkenhead, 1852 F
Birnie, Richard, 1808 A, 1879 C
Birregurra, Vic, 1837 A
Birth (magazine), Melbourne, 1916 C
Birth rate, 1904 A, G
Birtles, Francis E. 1882 A, 1912 B,
    1927 F
Biscoe, John, 1831 A
Biscuits, 1850 B, 1904 A
Bisenieks, Ojars A. 1924 C
Bishop, Anna, 1855 C
Bishop, Ethel A. 1892 C
Bishop, Henry, 1834 C
Bishop, John, 1903 C, 1948 C, 1960 F
Bishop, Maxine, 1928 E
Bishop, Tony, 1940 C
Bishop of Botany Bay, 1827 D
Bismarck Archipelago, 1920 A
Bissietta, G. F. 1910 C
Bitalli, 1923 E
Bizley, Roy, 1930 C
Bjelke-Petersen, Johannes, 1911 A,
    1947 A, 1968 A
Black, Campbell, 1934 E
Black, Dorrit, 1891 C
Black, John, 1855 C
Black, John M. 1855 B
Black Cargo, 1955 C
'Black Caesar', 1796 A
Black House, The, and Other Plays, 1924 C
'Black Jack Galleghan', 1897 A
Black Knight, 1984 E
Black Line, 1830 A
Black Mtn. Tower, Canberra, 1980 B
Black Opal, 1921 C

Black Opals, NSW, 1887 B, 1902 B
Black Saturday, NSW, 1938 F
Black Sunday, Bondi, Sydney, 1938 F
Black Thursday, Vic–SA fires, 1851 F
Black trackers, 1825 A
Black Wednesday, Vic, 1878 A
Blackall, Qld, 1868 F, 1892 F
Blackall, Samuel W. 1868 A
Blackbirding, 1871 A, 1885 A
Blackburn, Charles B. 1874 B, 1938 B
Blackburn, James, 1803 B
Blacket, Edmund T. 1817 C, 1842 C,
    1849 C, 1854 C, 1857 C
Blackman, Charles R. 1928 C, 1959 C,
    1960 C
Blackman, Charles H. E. 1886 C
Blackman, John, 1853 E
Blackmore R., NT, 1869 B
Blacktown, NSW, 1826 F, 1860 B,
    1864 B
Blackwater, Qld, 1860 F
Blackwood, 1924 E
Blackwood, Francis P. 1809 A, 1844 A
Blainey, Geoffrey N. 1930 D, 1963 C,
    1966 C, 1984 A
Blair, David, 1881 D
Blair, Harold, 1924 C
Blair, James W. 1932 A, 1937 A
Blair, Ronald H. 1942 C
Blair Athol, Qld, 1864 B, 1937 B
Blake, Florence T. 1873 C
Blake, Hester, 1867 C
Blake Prize, 1951 C
Blakeborough, Les, 1930 C
Blakeley, Fred, 1883 A, 1930 A
Blamey, Thomas A, 1884 A, 1939 A,
    1942 A, 1950 A
Blanch Barkly, 1857 F
Blanchetown, SA, 1855 F, 1915 B
Bland, William, 1789 A, 1815 B, 1819 B,
    1826 B, 1850 B, 1851 B, 1859 B
Blansjaar, Maria, 1940 C
Blashki, Myer, 1871 C
Blaxcell, Garnham, 1810 A
Blaxland, Gregory, 1813 A, 1823 A, C,
    1853 A
Blaxland, John, 1829 A, 1845 A
Blayney, NSW, 1843 F
Bleak Downs and Other Plays, 1936 C
Bleakley Commission, 1929 A
Bleriot monoplane, 1910 B
Blervie Castle, 1859 F
Bless This House, 1935 C
Bligh, John, 1913 C
Bligh, William, 1788 A, 1789 A, 1792 A,
    1796 D, 1806 A, 1807 A, 1808 A,
    1810 A, 1811 A, 1817 A, 1976 D
Blight, Malcolm, 1950 E, 1978 E
Blind, 1860 D, 1872 B, 1951 F, 1952 F
Blinkhorn, Cecil, 1892 E
Blinman, SA, 1862 F
Blocksidge, Charles W. 1883 C
Blood, 1880 B, 1976 B
Blood Red, Sister Rose, 1974 C
Blood serotonin, 1976 B
Bloodsworth, James, 1788 C, 1804 C
Bloody Friday, Sydney, 1931 A
Blowfly, 1903 F, 1958 B
Blue, Billy, 1830 B, 1834 B
Blue Brush Exhibitions, 1953 C
Blue Hills, 1943 C
Blue Lake, SA, 1896 F
Blue Mtns, NSW, 1789 A, 1793 A,
    1802 A, 1804 A, 1812 A, 1813 A,
    1818 B, 1823 A, 1832 B, C, 1869 B,
    1936 F, 1944 F, 1957 F, 1968 F, 1977 F
Blue Mtns Art Prize, NSW, 1962 C
Blue Nile, The, 1962 C
Blue Poles, 1973 C, 1974 C

Blue Spec, 1905 E
Blue Streak, rocket, 1964 B
Blue whale, 1910 F
Bluett, T. 1843 C
Bluey and Curley, 1941 F
Blumenlese auf ... Neueren Literatur, SA,
    1864 F
Blundell, Graeme, 1945 C
Blyth, Arthur, 1823 A, 1864 A, 1871 A,
    1873 A
Blythe Star, 1973 F
Boake, Barcroft C. 1838 B
Boake, Barcroft H. T. 1866 C, 1897 C
Board, Leslie, 1983 C
Board, Peter, 1858 D, 1905 D
Board of Conciliation and Arbitration,
    1890 A
Board of Education, NSW, 1883 D
Board of Education, SA, 1847 D
Board of Education, Tas, 1853 D
Board of National Education, Vic,
    1851 D
Board of Protection, Aboriginals, Vic,
    1860 A
Board of Trade, Vic, 1860 A
Boas, Abraham, T. 1842 D
Boas, Isaac H. 1878 B
Boating, power, 1905 E, 1909 E, 1927 E,
    1953 E, 1970 E
Boating, speed records, 1977 E, 1978 E
'Bob Ridley', 1889 B
Bobbed hair, 1921 F, 1922 F, 1928 F
Bobbin Up, 1959 C
Bocce, 1900 E, 1970 E, 1979 E
Bocce Federation of Aust., 1972 E
Bock, Alfred, 1834 C
Bock, Thomas, 1790 C, 1831 C
Bodalla, NSW, 1856 F
Bodalla Co., 1892 B
Boddy, Michael, 1970 C
Bodenwieser, Gertrud, 1890 C
Bodices, 1933 F
Body exposure, fashion, 1979 F, 1982 F
Bodyline, 1984 C
Bodyline bowling, 1932 E, 1933 E, 1935 E
Boeing 747, 1959 B, 1970 B
Boeing 727, 1964 A
Boer War, 1899 A, 1900 A, 1902 A
Bogan R. 1828 A
Bogantungan, Qld, 1960 F
Boggabri, NSW, 1862 F
Bogle, Gilbert, 1963 F
Bogong Bogong, NSW, 1828 E
Bogue, Glen, 1954 D
Boissevain, William, 1927 C
'Bold Jack', 1807 A
Bold Personality, 1984 E
Bold St. Bridge, Granville, NSW, 1977 F
Boldrewood, Rolf, 1826 C, 1882 C,
    1888 C
Boles, Bernard, 1912 C
Bolger, Bill, 1910 E
Bolivar, SA, 1910 B
Bolschuyver, Theo, 1943 C
Bolshoi Ballet, 1970 C
Bolshoi Theatre, 1959 C
Bolte, Henry E. 1908 A, 1947 A, 1955 A,
    1972 A
Bolton, Colleen, 1957 E
Bolton, Mr., 1795 A
Bolton, Nancye M. 1917 E
Bomb, atomic, 1943 B
Bomb blasts, Sydney, 1972 F, 1980 F
Bombala, NSW, 1860 F
Bombala district, NSW, 1904 A
Bonaparte, Napoleon, 1816 F
Bonaparte Gulf, WA, 1973 F
Bonar Dunlop, 1949 C
Bond, Alan, 1938 A, 1974 E, 1981 A

Bond, Colin, 1942 E
Bond, George A. 1876 A, 1923 A
Bondi, Sydney, 1915 E, 1938 F
Bondi Bathers' Lifesaving Club, 1906 E
Bondi Beach Sydney, 1906 E
Bondi Surf Lifesaving Association, 1908 E
Bone, Thomas H. 1901 C
Boneshakers Cycling Club, Royal, Vic, 1869 E
Bong Bong, NSW, 1819 F
Bonington, Ian, 1942 C
Bonner, Neville T. 1922 A, 1971 A
Bonney, Charles, 1813 A, 1838 A
Bonney, Maude R. 1897 B, 1932 B, 1933 B
Bonwick, James, 1817 D
Bonynge, Richard, 1930 C
Bonython, Hugh R. Kym, 1920 A, 1960 C
Bonython, John Langdon, 1848 A
Bonython, John Lavington, 1875 A
Bonython, John L. 1905 A
Bonython Art Gallery, Adelaide, 1960 C
'Boogie Woogie' dance, 1945 C
Book censorship, 1901 C, 1933 C
Book Censorship Abolition League, 1934 F
Book Censorship Advisory Committee, 1933 C
Book of Dan, The, 1911 C
Book for Kids, A, 1921 C
Books, banned, 1958 C
'Books of the Day', 1894 C
Bookfellow, Sydney, 1899 F
Bookmakers, 1882 E, 1907 E
Booksellers, 1859 A
Boom, Post-war, 1945 A
Boomerang, 1887 F, 1888 A
Boomerang throwing, 1933 E, 1976 E
Boolaroo, NSW, 1829 F
Boonah, Qld, 1880 F
Boonarga, Qld, 1936 F
Boongaree, 1814 A, 1815 A
Boophilus microplus, 1872 B
Boorowa, NSW, 1850 F
Boort, Vic, 1847 E
Boote, Henry E, 1865 F
Booth, Charles O. 1800 A, 1834 B
Booth, Edward C. 1875 C
Booth, Edwin, 1854 C
Booth, Peter, 1940 C
Boothroyd, Arthur S. 1910 C
Bootmakers workers group, Sydney, 1841 A
Borchgrevink, Carsten E. 1864 B, 1895 A
Border, Alan, 1955 E
Border duties agreement, 1857 A
Border Morning Mail, NSW, 1903 F
Border Watch, SA, 1834 F, 1861 F
Bordertown, SA, 1845 F, 1866 B
Bore water, 1878 B
Borealis, 1880 F
Boreham, Frank W. 1871 D
Bores, water, 1878 B, 1886 B, 1921 B
Borneo, 1945 A, 1962 A
Boronia, Melbourne, 1952 F
Borovansky, Edouard, 1902 C, 1939 C
Borovansky Ballet, 1939 C, 1940 C, 1946 C, 1960 C
Borrack, John L. 1933 C
Borroloola, NT, 1885 F
Borthwick, Pat, 1926 E
Borzini, Alfredo, 1876 C
Bosanquet, Day H. 1909 A
Bosch, George H. 1861 B
Bosisto, Glyn de V. 1899 E
Bosisto, Joseph, 1824 B, 1854 B
Boskovic, Tony, 1933 E

Boston, John, 1796 A, 1804 A
Bosworth, Amy, 1872 C
Botanic Park, Adelaide, 1880 D
Botanical gardens,
    Adelaide, 1839 B, 1855 B, 1880 D
    Brisbane, 1855 B
    Canberra, 1970 B
    Melbourne, 1845 B, 1846 B
    Perth, 1965 B
    Sydney, 1816 B, 1828 A, 1838 B
Botanical and Horticultural Society of VDL, 1843 B
Botany, Tas, 1854 B
Botany, NSW, 1904 E, 1910 B
'Botany Bay' (song), 1815 C
Botany Bay, NSW, 1788 A, 1795 A, 1815 A, 1822 F, 1961 F
Botany Bay or . . . day of Australia, 1859 C
'Botany Bay Rothschild', 1838 A
Bothwell, Tas, 1821 F, 1831 C
Bottled milk, 1928 F
Bottles, 1866 B
'Bottom of the Harbour', 1982 A, 1984 A
Bottrill, Frank, 1871 B, 1906 B
Boucaut, James P. 1831 A, 1866 A, 1875 A, 1877 A
Bougainville, Baron de, 1824 A
Bough in Hell, A, 1971 C
Bougoure, Garnet, 1923 E
Boulder, WA, 1896 F
Boules, Sydney, 1969 E
Boulger, John, 1945 E
Boulia, Qld, 1876 F
Boulton, E. B. 1812 C
Boundaries, 1825 A, 1861 A, 1862 A, 1972 A
Bounty, HMS, 1788 A, 1789 A
Bounty immigration scheme, 1835 A
Bounty mutineers, 1829 A, 1856 A
Bounty Oil, 1982 C
Bounty scheme, 1847 A
Bourke, NSW, 1859 A, 1860 F, 1878 B, 1885 B, 1886 B
Bourke, Francis, 1947 E
Bourke, Richard, 1831 A,F, 1833 A, 1835 A, 1836 A,D, 1837 A, 1841 C, 1842 F, 1855 A
Bourn, Kenneth M. 1942 C
Bousloff, Kira, 1952 C
Boussole, 1788 A
Bow, Ian, 1914 C
Bow Hunters' Club, 1953 E
Bowden, Thomas, 1812 D, 1834 D
Bowen, Qld, 1861 F, 1867 F, 1870 F, 1876 F, 1884 F, 1958 F, 1959 F
Bowen, George F. 1821 A, 1859 A, 1873 A
Bowen, George M. C. 1803 A
Bowen, John, 1803 A, 1827 A
Bowen, Richard, 1791 A, 1797 A
Bowen, Stella E. G. 1893 C
Bowen, William, 1803 B
Bowen Downs Station, Qld, 1870 F
Bowen Mtn., NSW, 1970 E
Bowen R., Qld. 1859 A
Bowers, Jack L. 1929 E
Bowles, Leslie, 1936 C
Bowles, William L. 1885 C
Bowling, *see* Lawn bowling
Bowling, cricket, 1832 E
Bowling, women's, 1898 E, 1899 E, 1949 E
Bowling, Peter, 1864 A, 1909 A, 1910 A
Bowman, David, 1860 A
Bowman, James, 1819 B, 1846 B
Bowral, NSW, 1862 F, 1875 F
Bowral Art Prize, 1895 C
Bowrey, Bill, 1943 E
Bowrey, Leslie, 1942 E

Bowring, Walter A. 1874 C
Bowser, J. 1856 A, 1917 A
Box, Peter, 1956 E
Box Flat, Qld, 1972 F
Box Hill, Melbourne, 1885 C, 1886 C
Boxall, Arthur d'A. 1895 C
Boxer Rebellion, 1900 A, 1901 A
Boxing, 1814 E, 1824 E, 1832 E, 1855 E, 1861 E, 1877 E, 1879 E, 1884 E, 1890 E, 1902 E, 1908 E, 1913 E, 1915 E 1916 E, 1949 E, 1951 E, 1952 E, 1953 E, 1954 E, 1958 E, 1968 E, 1969 E, 1977 E, 1978 E, 1980 E
Boxing Academy, Sydney, 1877 E
Boy Scouts Association, 1920 F, 1958 F
Boyce, Francis B. 1844 D
Boyce, Harold L. 1895 A
Boyce, Stewart, 1943 E
Boyd, Anne E. 1946 C, 1969 C
Boyd, Arthur M. 1862 C
Boyd, Arthur M. B. 1920 C, 1958 C, 1959 C
Boyd, Benjamin, 1800 A, 1803 A, 1840 A, 1843 A, 1849 A
Boyd, David, 1924 C, 1956 C, 1959 C
Boyd, Doris, 1883 C
Boyd, Guy M. 1923 C
Boyd, Hermia, 1931 C
Boyd, James, 1948 C
Boyd, Lucy, 1916 C
Boyd, Martin a'B. 1893 C, 1928 C, 1946 C, 1952 C, 1955 C, 1957 C, 1963 C
Boyd, Mary, 1926 C
Boyd, Penleigh, 1908 C
Boyd, Robin G. P. 1919 C, 1952 C, 1960 C, 1962 C, 1967 C, 1970 C
Boyd, Theodore P. 1890 C
Boyd, William M. 1888 C, 1911 C
Boydtown, NSW, 1843 F
Boyer, Richard J. F. 1891 A
Boyes, George T. W. 1853 C
Boyle, Harry, 1878 E
Boyle, Kathleen, 1928 C
Boyle, Raelene, 1951 E, 1974 E
Boynes, Robert, 1942 C
Boys Town, WA, 1941 F
Brabham, John A. 1926 E, 1947 E, 1959 E, 1960 E, 1966 E
Brack, C. John, 1920 C, 1959 C
Bracken, George, 1935 E
Bracken, K. 1920 E
Brackenreg, John, 1905 C, 1955 C
Braddon, Edward N. C. 1829 A, 1894 A
Braddon, Henry Y. 1863 A, 1918 A
Braddon, Russell R. 1921 C, 1952 C
Bradfield, John J. C. 1867 B, 1912 B, 1923 B
Bradley, Luther, 1864 C
Bradley, Stephen L. 1960 F
Bradley, William, (b. 1757), 1833 A
Bradley, William, (b. 1800), 1800 A
Bradley's Head, Sydney, 1818 E
Bradman, Donald G. 1908 E, 1928 E, 1930 E, 1934 E, 1948 E, 1949 E
Bradshaw, Richard D. 1938 C
Brady, Alfred B. 1898 C
Brady, Charles, 1868 A
Brady, Edwin J. 1869 C
Brady, John, 1800 D, 1842 D, 1844 D
Brady, Matthew, 1799 A, 1826 A
Bragg, Henry W. 1915 B
Bragg, William H. 1862 B, 1896 B
Bragg, William L. 1890 B, 1896 B, 1915 B
Brahe, Mary Hannah, 'May', 1885 C, 1935 C
Braidwood, NSW, 1837 F, 1860 F, 1872 F
Braille, 1894 D

755

Brambles Industries Ltd, 1979 A
Bramleigh, Rex, 1923 C
Brand, David, 1912 A, 1959 A
Brand, Henry R. 1895 A
Brandon, Qld, 1910 F
Branxton, NSW, 1848 F
Brasch, Rudolph, 1912 D
Brass, John, 1947 E
Brass bands, 1845 C, 1895 C
Brass Band Association of NSW, 1895 C
Brassey, Thomas, 1895 A
Brassiere, 1918 F
Bravo, 1889 E
Bray, John C. 1842 A, 1881 A
Brazier, John W. 1842 B
Bread, NSW, 1835 A
Bread Case, 1916 A
Bread Institute of Aust., Sydney, 1947 B
'Break' dancing, 1984 C
Breaker Morant (film), 1980 C
Breaking of the Drought, The, 1893 C, 1920 C
Brearley, Norman, 1890 A, 1921 B
Breasley, Arthur E. ('Scobie'), 1914 E, 1955 E
Brecknock, WA, 1957 A
Breeding, stock, artificial, 1958 B
Bremer, Gordon, 1841 C
Bremer, James G. 1824 A, 1838 A
Brenan, Jennie, 1896 C
Brennan, Christopher J. 1870 C, 1914 C
Brennan, Gerard, 1981 A
Brennan, Jim, 1902 E
Brennan, Louis, 1852 B, 1874 B
Brennan, Thomas, 1832 F
Brent of Bin Bin, (book), 1928 C
Brereton, John Le Gay, 1871 C
Brereton Prize (Robert Le Gay Brereton Prize for Drawing), 1955 C
Brethren Assemblies, 1973 D
Brewarrina, NSW, 1861 F
Brewer, Henry, 1796 C
Breweries,
  NSW, 1795 A, 1803 A, 1835 A, 1888 A, 1966 A
  Qld, 1865 A, 1871 A
  SA, 1836 A, 1876 A, 1888 A, 1938 A
  Tas, 1032 A
  Vic, 1838 A, 1907 A
  WA, 1836 A, 1887 A, 1981 A
Brewery hotels, Sydney, 1902 C
Brick veneer, 1850 C
Brickhill, Paul C. J. 1916 C, 1951 C
Brickfield Hill, Sydney, 1788 B
Brickmakers Friendly Society, 1845 F
Bricks, 1788 B, 1810 C, 1870 B, 1878 B
Bridge, card game, 1932 F, 1935 F, 1951 F
Bridges, *see individual entries*
  ACT, 1963 C
  NSW, 1788 B, 1796 B, 1811 B, 1813 B, 1832 C, 1856 B, 1857 B, 1866 B, 1875 B, 1883 B, 1885 B, 1889 B, 1893 B, 1895 B, 1903 B, 1923 B, 1932 A, B, 1935 B, 1964 C, 1974 B, 1977 F, 1981 B
  Qld, 1874 C, 1881 B, 1979 B
  SA, 1837 B, 1879 B
  Tas, 1823 C, 1825 C, 1964 B, 1975 F
  Vic, 1961 F, 1965 B, 1969 B, 1970 F, 1978 B
  WA, 1843 B, 1864 B, 1866 B, 1959 C
Bridges, George T. M. 1922 A
Bridges, William T. 1861 A, 1911 A, 1914 A
Bridgetown, WA, 1860 F
Bridport, Tas, 1883 F
Brier, Percy, 1885 C
Brierly, Oswald W. 1817 C, 1842 C

Brigand, 1843 F
Bright, Vic, 1862 F
Brighton, Melbourne, 1861 B, 1906 B, 1918 F
Briggs, F. S. 1920 B
Briggs, Henry, 1844 D
Brilliant Creatures, 1983 C
Bring back 'the ashes', 1882 E
Bring Larks and Heroes, 1967 C
Brinsmead, H. C. 1924 B
Brinsmead, H. F. 1964 C
Briquettes, 1889 B, 1925 B
Brisbane, Qld, 1823 A, 1824 A, F, 1825 A, 1839 A, 1842 A, 1844 A, 1851 A, 1854 A, 1859 A, 1864 B, F, 1867 A, 1874 C, 1878 B, 1888 A, 1889 A, 1890 F, 1896 F, 1901 D, 1903 B, 1924 C, 1928 B, 1941 A, 1942 F, 1951 B, C, E, 1955 D, 1961 C, 1963 F, 1965 F, 1967 A, 1969 B, 1973 F, 1974 F, 1979 A, B, 1980 F
  colonisation, 1838 A
Brisbane, Alan R. 1933 C
Brisbane, Thomas M. 1821 A, 1824 A, 1825 A, 1860 A
Brisbane Amateur Sailing Club, 1885 E
Brisbane Amateur Turf Club, 1923 E
Brisbane Australian Rules Football Club, 1866 E
Brisbane Botanical Gardens, 1855 B
Brisbane Centennial Prize, 1959 C
Brisbane Chamber of Commerce, 1868 A
Brisbane Choral Society, 1859 C
Brisbane City Volunteer Firebrigade, 1865 F
Brisbane Courier, 1864 F, 1933 F
Brisbane Cup (horse-race), 1866 E, 1871 E
Brisbane Daily Mail, 1903 F
Brisbane Eisteddfod Centenary Art Prize, 1959 C
Brisbane Grammar School, 1869 D, 1875 D
Brisbane, HMAS, 1969 A, 1971 A
Brisbane International airport, 1980 B
Brisbane jetty, 1846 B
Brisbane Kindergarten Teachers' College, 1911 D
Brisbane Lawn Bowling Club, 1878 E
'Brisbane Line', 1942 A
Brisbane Observatory, 1846 B, 1934 B
Brisbane Permanent Benefit and Investment Society, 1874 A
Brisbane Philharmonic Society, 1861 C
Brisbane private schools, 1843 D
Brisbane Public Library, 1895 D
Brisbane Public Library Art Prize, 1956 C
Brisbane Repertory Theatre, 1925 C
Brisbane R., Qld, 1823 A, 1825 A, 1841 F, 1890 F, 1893 F
Brisbane School of Arts, 1851 C
Brisbane Stock Exchange, 1885 A
Brisbane Synagogue, 1885 D
Brisbane Teacher Training College, 1914 D
Brisbane Technical College, 1884 D, 1908 D
Brisbane Town Hall, 1862 C, 1865 F
Briscoe, Billy, 1911 E
Briseis, 1876 E
Bristol Boxkite aircraft, 1911 B
Britannica Aust. Awards, 1964 C
British Admiral, 1874 F
British Antarctic Expedition, 1908 A, 1909 A
British Architects Royal Gold Medal, 1954 C

British Association for the Advancement of Science, 1914 B
British Atomic Energy Authority, 1965 B
British atomic tests, 1984 A
British Aust. Wool Realization Association, 1921 A
British Ballet Organization, Aust. branch, 1937 C
British Bank of Aust., 1891 A
British Cwlth Defence Conference, 1959 A
British Contemporary Art Exhibition, 1933 C
British East India Co., monopoly, 1792 A
British Economic Mission, 1928 A
British Embassy, 1937 A
British and Foreign Bible Society, 1817 D, 1956 D
British and Foreign School Society, 1835 D, 1839 D
British Medical Association, 1859 B, 1879 B, 1912 B, 1933 B, 1961 B
British Migraine Association, 1976 B
British National Institute of Medical Research, 1933 B
British New Guinea, Papua, *see also* Papua, 1887 A, 1888 A, 1901 A, 1902 A, 1906 A
British Overseas Airways Corporation, 1945 B
British Petroleum Co., Prize, Melbourne, 1963 C
British Society of Arts, 1822 A
British subjects, 1948 A
British Telegraph Co., 1871 B
British troops, 1870 A
British war office, 1939 B
Britomart, 1840 F
Britt, Edgar, 1913 E
Britton, Frederick C. 1889 C
Broad, Alfred S. 1854 C
Broad Arrow, The, 1859 C
Broadband trunk system, 1959 B
Broadbeach, Qld, 1966 B
Broadbent, Harry F. 1910 B
Broadcasting Co. of Aust., 1924 B
Broadcasting licences, 1923 F
Broadcasting and Television Act, 1942 A
Broadford, Vic, 1847 F
Broadhurst, Francis J. 1914 C
Broadway stage coaches, 1869 B
Brock, Peter, 1946 E
Brockhoff, Dave, 1929 E
Brodribb, William A. 1809 A, 1841 A
Brodzky, Horace, 1885 C
Brodzky, Leon, 1904 C
Brodzky, Maurice, 1847 F, 1885 C
Broinowski, Gracius J. 1837 B
Broken Bay, NSW, 1898 F
Broken Bay Aboriginal tribe, 1815 A
Broken Hill, NSW, 1875 B, 1883 B, F, 1885 B, 1886 B, 1888 F, 1892 B, 1895 F, 1898 F, 1906 D, 1910 B, 1915 A, 1924 A, 1939 B, 1943 A
Broken Hill Art Gallery, 1904 C
Broken Hill Library, 1906 D
Broken Hill ore, NSW, 1889 B, *see also* Broken Hill Pty Ltd
Broken Hill picnickers, NSW, 1915 A
Broken Hill, miners' strike, 1919 A
Broken Hill Pty Ltd, 1886 B, 1897 B, 1899 B, 1904 B, 1913 B, 1915 B, 1922 B, 1933 B, 1935 B, 1939 B, 1941 B, 1957 B, 1960 B, 1982 A, 1983 A
Broken Hill Pty Ltd Silver Mining Co., 1885 A

756

Broken Hill Trades and Labor Council, 1916 A, 1924 A
Broken R., Vic, 1851 B
Bromby, Charles H. 1814 D
Bromo-cyanide process, 1899 B
Bromwich, John E. 1918 E, 1939 E
Bronhill, June M. 1929 C
Bronte Surf Club, 1902 E
Brooke, Gustavus V. 1818 C, 1855 C
Brooker, E. 1947 A
Brookes, Mabel B. 1890 C
Brookes, Norman E. 1877 E, 1907 E, 1914 E
Brookfield, Percy, 1921 A
Brooklands, Qld, 1922 F
Brookman, George, 1850 A
Brooks, Edmund A. 1877 A
Brooks, R. A. Dallas, 1896 A, 1949 A, 1953 A, 1961 A
Brooks, Sam, 1930 B
Brooks, Tom, 1926 E
Brookton, WA, 1895 F
Broome, WA, 1883 F, 1903 A, 1904 F, 1910 F, 1917 F, 1922 B
Broome, Frederick N. 1842 A, 1883 A
Broome, Richard, 1984 C
Brotherhood of St Laurence, Melbourne, 1930 D
Brough-Boucicault Comedy Theatre Co., 1885 C
Brough Comedy Co., 1896 C
Broughton, Owen, 1922 C
Broughton, William G. 1788 D, 1829 D, 1836 D, 1838 D, 1847 D
Brown, Alexander, 1827 A, 1851 A
Brown, Andrew, 1858 B
Brown, Brian, 1933 C
Brown, Cyril ('Pluto'), 1911 E
Brown, David M. 1913 E
Brown, Geoffrey, (1), 1924 E
Brown, Geoffrey, (2), 1926 C
Brown, George, 1835 D
Brown, Harry, 1845 A
Brown, Henry Y. L. 1844 B
Brown, James, 1816 A, 1851 A
Brown, James C. 1895 A
Brown, Jim, 1920 E
Brown, John, 1850 A
Brown, Joseph, 1979 C
Brown, Leonard, 1888 E
Brown, Mal, 1946 E
Brown, Michael C. 1938 C, 1962 C
Brown, Mitty L. 1922 C
Brown, P. 1924 E
Brown, Robert, 1802 B, 1810 C, 1858 B
Brown, T. 1878 E
Brown, Tom, 1955 C, 1963 C
Brown, Vincent, 1901 C
Brown, Warwick, 1951 E
Brown, W. A. ('Billy'), 1912 E
Brown, William, 1945 C
Brown, William J. 1868 A
Brown coal, Vic, 1857 B, 1873 B
Brown Coal Advisory Board, Vic, 1917 B
Browne, Coral E. 1913 C
Browne, David, 1874 B
Browne, Frank C. 1955 A
Browne, Thomas A. 1826 C, 1882 C, 1888 C
Browne, Thomas G. 1861 A, 1862 A
Browne, William R. 1884 B
Browning, George, 1918 C
Brownlee, John D. M. 1900 C
Brownless, Anthony C. 1817 B
Brownlow, Charles, 1861 E
Brownlow Medal, 1924 E, 1942 E, see each year section E after 1924
Bruce, John, 1862 A, 1868 A

Bruce, Charles, 1807 C
Bruce, J. M. 1891 E
Bruce, Mary G. 1878 C, 1910 C
Bruce, Stanley M. 1883 A, 1918 A, 1923 A, 1925 A, 1928 A, 1929 A, 1936 A, 1947 A, 1951 D
Brucellosis, 1943 B
Brumby, Colin, 1933 C
Brummels Art Gallery, Melbourne, 1955 C
Brunswick label, 1924 B
Brunton, Dorothy, 1896 C
Brush car, 1912 B
Bruxner, Michael F. 1882 A
Bryans, Lina, 1909 C
Bryant, Charles D. J. 1883 C
Bryant, Mary, 1791 A, B
Bryant and May, 1913 F
Buangor, Vic, 1860 F
Bubonic plague, 1900 F, 1904 F, 1921 F
Buchanan, John, 1931 F
Buchanan, Nathaniel, 1826 A, 1860 A, 1868 B, 1878 A, 1884 A
Buchanan, R. 1924 B
Buchanan, William F. 1824 A
Buck, Margaret, 1974 E
Buck-Jumper Bobs, 1906 E
Buckie, Harry, 1897 C
Buckingham, George, 1842 C
Buckingham (car), 1933 B
Buckland, Thomas, 1848 A
Buckland, William L. 1900 A
Buckland R., Vic, 1857 A
Buckler, Hugh, 1913 C
Buckley, Anthony, 1937 C
Buckley, Bill, 1907 E
Buckley, Sue E. M. 1910 C
Buckley, Vincent, 1927 C
Buckley, William, 1803 A, 1835 A, 1856 A
Buckley and Nunn, 1851 A
Buckman, Rosina, 1880 C
Buckmaster, Ernest, 1897 C, 1932 C
Buddhism, 1972 D, *see individual entries*
Buddhist Federation of Aust, 1959 D
Buddhist Society of NSW, 1952 D
Buddhist Society of Vic, 1953 D
Buderim, Qld, 1869 F
Budget, Federal, first, 1901 A
Budget speech televised, 1984 A
Buffalo, 1824 A
Buffalo fly, 1838 B, 1967 B
Buffalo grass, 1870 B
bufo marinus, 1935 B
Bugg, R. W. 1853 C
Builders' Labourers Federation, 1971 F, 1974 A, 1981 A, 1982 A, 1983 A
Building, expenditure, 1890 C
Building Act, NSW, 1837 C
Building industry, machine technology, 1900 C
Building regulations, 1810 C, 1827 C, 1837 C, 1838 C
Building Societies, 1854 A, *see individual entries*
Building Workers' Industrial Union of Aust., 1942 A
Buildings, multi-storied, 1885 C, 1892 C, 1912 C, 1957 C
Bulahdelah, NSW, 1906 F
Bulgin, Victor, 1925 E
Bull, Hedley N. 1932 A
Bull, John W. 1804 B
Bull, Knut G. 1811 C
Bull fighting, 1970 E
Bullen, Keith E. 1906 B, 1946 B
Bullen, Leonard, 1953 D
Bulletin (magazine), 1880 F, 1888 C, 1889 C, 1890 C, 1894 C, 1896 C,

1901 C, 1926 F, 1961 F, 1984 F
Bulletin literary prize, 1928 C
Bulletin-Qantas award, 1980 F, 1981 F, 1982 F, 1983 F, 1984 F
Bulletin-Veuve Clicquot award, 1978 F, 1979 F
Bullets, 1902 B
Bulli, NSW, 1887 F
Bulli Colliery, NSW, 1965 F
Bullion, 1886 A
Bullion Act, SA, 1852 A
Bullock, Francis, 1885 E, 1905 E
Bullocks, 1795 A
Bullwinkel, Vivian, 1915 B
Bumblebee IV, 1979 E
Bunbury, WA, 1839 A, 1841 A, 1843 F, 1947 B
Bunbury Art Gallery, WA, 1948 C
Bunbury Art Prize, WA, 1959 C
Bunbury, Henry W. St P. 1812 A, 1836 A
Bunce, Daniel, 1813 B
Bunchy top disease, 1925 B
Bundaberg, Qld, 1866 F, 1928 F
Bundanoon, NSW, 1861 F
Bungalows, 1911 C, 1918 C
Bungaree, 1830 A
Bungarribee racehorse stud farm, NSW, 1830 E
Buninyong Ranges, Vic, 1851 B
Bunn, Anna M. 1838 C
Bunning, Neville M. 1902 C
Bunning, Walter R. 1912 C, 1961 C
Bunny, Rupert C. W. 1864 C, 1946 C
Bunt disease, 1915 B
Bunting, Edward J. 1918 A
Bunton, Haydn, (b. 1911), 1911 E, 1931 E, 1932 E, 1935 E
Bunton, Haydn, (b. 1936), 1936 E
'bunyip aristocracy,' 1853 A
Buonarotti Sketch and Music Club, 1880 C
Burbury, Stanley C. 1909 A, 1958 A, 1963 A, 1968 A, 1973 A
Burdekin, R., Qld, 1859 A
Burdett, Basil, 1897 C, 1939 C
Bureau of Census and Statistics, 1906 A
Bureau of Meteorology, 1975 B
Bureau of Microbiology, NSW, 1908 B
Bureau of Mineral Resources, Geology and Geophysics, 1946 B
Bureau of Sugar Experiment Stations, Qld, 1900 B
Burge, Frank, 1896 E
Burge, Ivor, 1929 E
Burge, Peter, 1932 E
Burgess, Arthur J. W. 1879 C
Burgess, Eileen, 1821 C
Burgess, Robert H. 1967 B
Burglar, The, 1909 C
Burglaries, 1984 F
Burgmann, Ernest H. 1885 D
Burial grounds, 1788 F, 1811 F, 1820 F, *see also* Cemeteries
Buring, H. P. Leopold, 1876 A, 1931 A
Burke, Brian T. 1983 A
Burke, Cyril, 1922 E
Burke, Frances, 1937 C
Burke, Jim, 1931 E
Burke, Joseph T. A. 1913 C
Burke, Robert O. 1821 A, 1860 A, 1861 A, 1863 A
Burke and Wills, 1861 A, 1864 C
Burke and Wills relief expeditions, 1861 A
Burke-Gaffney, Thomas N. 1893 B
Burketown, Qld, 1865 F
Burlakov, Mischa, 1929 C, 1931 C
Burley, Robyn, 1957 E, 1979 E

Burlington House, London, 1920 C
Burn, E. David, 1799 C, 1829 C, 1842 C, 1875 C
Burn, Henry, 1807 C
Burn, Ian L. 1939 C
Burnet, Cecil R. 1917 C
Burnet, (Frank) MacFarlane, 1899 B, 1933 B, 1935 B, 1937 B, 1960 B
Burnett, 1869 F
Burnett Hunt Club, 1867 E
Burnett R., Qld, 1852 B
Burnie, Tas, 1827 B, 1829 F, 1878 B, 1938 B
'Burning Mountain', 1828 B
Burnley, Vic, 1882 F
Burnley Horticultural College, 1891 D
Burns, James, 1846 A, 1883 A, 1911 F
Burns, Peter, 1924 C
Burns, Tommy, 1908 E, 1922 E
Burns Philp and Co. Ltd, 1883 A
Burnside Homes, Sydney, 1911 F
Burra, SA, 1845 B,F
Burra Burra copper mine, 1848 A
Burrell, Harry J. 1873 B
Burrell, Henry M. 1904 A
Burrinjuck dam, NSW, 1906 B, 1927 B, 1966 F
Burrows, Donald V. 1928 C, 1945 C
Burstall, Tim, 1929 C, 1961 C, 1968 C, 1971 C, 1975 C
Burt, Clarence, 1930 F
Burt, Francis T. P. 1980 A, 1981 A
Burt, Norman, 1930 F
Burwood Teachers' College, Melbourne, 1953 D
Bury, L. H. E. 1962 A
Busby, James, 1801 B, 1830 A,B, 1832 A
Busby, John, 1837 B, 1857 B
'Busby's Bore', 1837 B
Busch, Joe ('Chimpy'), 1908 E
Busch, Mae, 1897 C
Buses, 1846 B, 1905 B, 1908 B, 1925 B, 1934 B, 1932 B, 1939 B, 1944 A, 1951 B, 1973 F, 1982 F
Bush, Charles W. 1919 C
Bush Ballads and Galloping Rhymes, 1870 C
Bush Brotherhood, 1897 D
Bush Christmas, 1947 C
Bush Church Aid Society, Sydney, 1919 D, 1938 D
Bush Fire Brigades Association, Vic, 1928 F
Bush Hotel, Tas, 1825 F
Bush Inn, (hotel) Tas, 1815 F
Bush Nursing Service, 1910 B
Bush Studies, 1902 C
Bush unions, 1894 A
Bush walking, Vic, 1894 F
Bushelle, Eliza W. 1823 C
Bushfires,
  NSW, 1846 F, 1926 F, 1929 F, 1936 F, 1938 F, 1939 F, 1944 F, 1951 F, 1952 F, 1957 F, 1965 F, 1968 F, 1969 F, 1972 F, 1974 F, 1977 F, 1979 F, 1980 F, 1983 F
  NT, 1951 F, 1968 F
  Qld, 1949 F, 1950 F, 1951 F
  SA, 1851 F, 1948 F, 1951 F, 1954 F, 1955 F, 1958 F, 1974 F, 1980 F, 1983 F
  Tas, 1851 F, 1897 F, 1915 F, 1920 F, 1921 F, 1927 F, 1934 F, 1939 F, 1940 F, 1944 F, 1951 F, 1967 F, 1972 F, 1981 F, 1982 F
  Vic, 1851 F, 1886 F, 1888 F, 1898 F, 1899 F, 1919 F, 1924 F, 1926 F, 1932 F, 1939 F, 1940 F, 1943 F, 1944 F, 1951 F, 1952 F, 1961 F,

1962 F, 1965 F, 1969 F, 1977 F, 1980 F, 1983 F
  WA, 1949 F, 1951 F, 1961 F, 1974 F
Bushfire brigades, NSW, 1906 F
Bushfires Board, WA, 1954 F
Bushranger, 1806 F
Bushranger films, NSW, 1912 C
Bushrangers, 1813 F, 1822 A, 1826 A, 1830 A, 1839 F, 1841 A, 1853 A, 1862 F, 1863 F, 1865 A, 1867 A, 1878 A, 1879 A, 1880 A
Bushrangers, The, 1829 C
Bushrangers: The, ... and Other Poems, 1853 C
Bushrangers; The, or Norwood Vale, 1834 C
Bushrangers of VDL, The, 1846 C
Bushranging Act, NSW, 1830 A, 1834 A
Business Woman of the Year, *see each year from 1978 section* F
Bussel, Grace, 1860 F, 1876 F
Busselton, WA, 1832 F
Busselton Art Gallery, WA, 1962 C
Bustard, William, 1894 C
Busteed, Henry R. 1887 B
But the Dead are Many, 1975 C
Butement, William A. S. 1904 B, 1939 B, 1946 B
Butler, Cecil A. 1902 B, 1930 B, 1931 B
Butler, Eric, 1960 A
Butler, Harry, 1979 B
Butler, Henry J. ('Harry'), 1889 B
Butler, Richard, 1850 A, 1905 A
Butler, Richard L. 1885 A, 1927 A, 1933 A
Butler, Stuart T. 1926 B
Butter, 1881 A, 1942 F
Butterfly, swimming stroke, 1953 E
Butterley, Nigel H. 1935 C, 1964 C
Butters, John H. 1885 B
Buttons, 1917 B
Buvelot, Abram L. 1814 C, 1865 C
Buvelot, Louis, 1880 C
Buxton, Thomas F. 1895 A
Buxton Art Gallery, Melbourne, 1885 C
'Buy Australian Made', 1925 F
Buzo, Alexander J. 1944 C, 1968 C
By Reef and Palm, 1894 C
Byles, Marie B. 1900 A, 1923 A
Byrne, Clement, 1922 C
Byrne, Samuel, 1883 C
Byrnes, Thomas J. 1860 A, 1898 A
Byron Bay, NSW, 1860 F, 1907 E, 1932 A
Byron Bay Surf Club, 1907 E

C

'Cabbage-Tree-Ned', 1833 A
Cabinet makers, 1804 F
Cabinet Makers' Society, 1833 A
Cable, Barry, 1943 E
Cable television, 1982 C
Cables, submarine, 1859 B, 1872 B, 1876 B, 1902 B, 1962 B, 1963 B, 1967 B
Caboolture, Qld, 1860 F
Cabramurra, NSW, 1973 F
Cabs, horse, Melbourne, 1847 B, 1849 B
Cactoblastis cactorum, 1925 B, 1926 B
Cactoblastis Memorial Hall, 1936 F
Caddie, 1976 C
Caddy, Jo, 1916 C
Cade, William R. 1883 C

Cadell, Francis, 1822 A, 1852 A, 1853 A, 1855 B, 1867 A
Cadence, 1966 E
Cadet Corps, 1866 D, 1911 D, 1975 D
Cadman, John, 1816 C, 1848 A
Cadman's Cottage, Sydney, 1816 C, 1847 A
Caesar, John, 1796 A
Cahill, J. Joseph, 1891 A, 1952 A, 1961 D
Cahill High School, Sydney, 1961 D
Cahill motor expressway, Sydney, 1958 B
Cahors, 1885 F
Cain, John, (1) 1887 A, 1943 A, 1945 A, 1952 A
Cain, John, (2) 1982 A
Caird, Maureen, 1951 E
Caire, John N. 1837 B
Cairns, Qld, 1876 F, 1878 F, 1906 F, 1911 F, 1913 F, 1924 B, 1927 F, 1937 F, 1948 F, 1975 F, 1978 F
Cairns, H. 1926 E
Cairns, Hugh W. B. 1896 B
Cairns, Ian, 1954 E
Cairns, James F. 1914 A, 1970 A, 1974 A, 1975 A, 1978 A
Cairns, William W. 1875 A, 1877 A
Cairns Art Society Prize, Qld, 1964 C
Cairns Post, Qld, 1882 F
Cakeman, The, 1982 C
Calamia, 1878 E
Calder, James E. 1808 C
Caldwell, Clive R. 1910 A
Caldwell, Felix, 1907 B
Caldwell, Zoe, 1933 C
Caledonia Australis, 1839 A
'Calendar House', Tas, 1868 C
Calenders, National Bank, 1957 C
Caley, George, 1800 B, 1804 A, 1829 B
Caley, Neville W. 1931 C
California, USA, 1928 B
Californian bungalow, 1900 C, 1919 C
Californian gold rushes, 1849 A, F
Californian salmon, 1877 A
Calkoen, Alfred, 1917 C
Callaghan, Bede B. 1912 A
Callide, Qld, 1892 F
Callinan, S. 1897 E
Callington, SA, 1847 F
Calliope, Qld, 1865 F
Calvert, Caroline L. W. 1834 C, 1857 C
Calvert, James S. 1825 A
Calwell, Arthur A. 1896 A, 1931 A, 1940 A, 1943 A, 1945 A, 1947 A, 1960 A, 1966 A, 1967 A
Cambage, Richard H. 1859 B
Cambodia, 1975 A
Cambridge, Ada, 1844 C
Cambridge, Enid H. G. 1903 C
Cambridge airport, Tas, 1935 B
Cambridge Credit Corp, 1974 A
Cambus Wallace, 1894 F
Camden Park Estate, NSW, 1795 A, 1805 A, 1816 A, 1827 A, 1841 D
Camels, 1840 A, 1858 A, 1866 A, 1870 B
Cameron, Angus, 1847 A, 1874 A
Cameron, Archie G. 1895 A
Cameron, Donald C. 1872 A
Cameron, Donald J. G. 1927 C
Cameron, Mary J. *see* Gilmore, Mary, Dame
Cameron, R. 1911 E
Cameron, Samson, 1833 C, 1838 C
Camm, Robert, 1847 C
Camooweal, Qld, 1884 F
Camp Mountain, Qld, 1947 F
Campania, Tas, 1916 F
Campaign spending, 1979 A

Campbell, Alfred W. 1868 B
Campbell, Archibald G. 1880 B
Campbell, Archibald J. 1853 B
Campbell, Bessie, 1871 C
Campbell, David W. I. 1915 C, 1949 C
Campbell, Donald, 1964 E
Campbell, Eric, 1931 A
Campbell, J. Keith, 1928 A
Campbell, James P. 1911 C
Campbell, John, 1840 A
Campbell, John T. 1827 A, 1830 A
Campbell, Keith, (1), 1931 E, 1957 E
Campbell, Keith, (2), 1981 A
Campbell, Persia, 1898 A
Campbell, Robert, 1800 A, 1803 A,
    1805 A, 1819 A, 1824 C, 1825 A,
    1846 A
Campbell, Robert R. 1902 C
Campbell, Stuart, 1948 B
Campbell, William, 1850 B, 1851 B
Campbell family, 1910 A
Campbell Macquarie, 1812 F
Campbell Report, 1981 A
Campbell Town, Tas, 1838 F
Campbelltown, NSW, 1810 F
Campbelltown Festival of Fisher's
    Ghost Art competition, NSW, 1962 C
Camperdown, Vic, 1850 F
Campfire Yarn, A, 1984 C
Campion, William R. 1924 A
Campton, Neil, 1936 E
Canadian costume, 1910 F
Canadian exiles, 1839 A
Canadian political prisoners, 1840 A
Canadian Soccer team, 1924 E
Canal jumping, 1969 E
Canberra and area, 1823 A, F, 1825 A,
    1908 A, 1910 A, 1913 A, 1924 A,
    1941 F, 1954 C, F, 1957 A, 1959 A, C,
    1961 D, 1963 B, D, 1965 F, 1967 B,
    1970 B, 1971 A, E, 1973 F, 1974 F,
    1977 E
Canberra, name, 1838 A
Canberra, pronunciation of, 1913 F
Canberra, RAAF crash, 1940 F
Canberra, (ship), 1961 B
Canberra Airport, 1931 B
Canberra Art competition, 1908 C
Canberra Art Society, 1927 C
Canberra city, 1912 C
Canberra College of Advanced
    Education, 1968 D
Canberra Greyhound Racing Club,
    1979 E
Canberra mint, 1963 A
Canberra News, 1969 F
Canberra School of Music, 1964 C,
    1965 C
Canberra Times, 1926 F, 1977 B
Canberra University College, 1929 D,
    1960 D
Candy, Charles D. 1912 A
Canned fruit, 1890 F, 1891 B
Cannes Film Festival, France, 1982 C
Cannibal Art Club, Melbourne, 1892 C
Canning, Alfred W. 1860 A, 1906 A
Canning, fish, 1937 B
Canning, meat, 1847 A, B, 1867 B
Canning Basin, WA, 1919 B, 1980 B
Cannington Central greyhound racing
    track, Perth, 1974 E
Cannon, Michael, 1975 C
Cannons, 1969 F
Canoe Clubs, 1912 E
Canoeing, 1911 E, 1920 E, 1951 E,
    1955 E, 1974 E
Canonical Orthodox Churches, 1979 D
Canoona, Qld, 1856 F, 1858 A, B
Canopus Homestead, SA, 1966 F

Canowindra, NSW, 1849 F, 1863 F
Cant, James, 1911 C
Canterbury–Bankstown Rugby League
    team, 1935 E, 1938 E, 1942 E, 1980 E,
    1984 E
Cantieni, Grahame, 1938 C
Cantilevered awnings, 1908 C
Cantlon, Maurice, 1926 C
Canungra, Qld, 1884 F
Cape, William, 1847 D
Cape, William T. 1806 D, 1835 D
Cape Bowling Green, Qld, 1911 F
Cape Leeuwin, WA, 1812 A
Cape Moreton, Qld, 1914 F
Cape Northumberland, SA, 1800 A
Cape Otway, Vic, 1857 F, 1859 B
Cape Sandwich, Qld, 1876 F
Cape Solander, NSW, 1797 B
Cape Town, South Africa, 1788 A
Cape York Peninsula, Qld, 1864 A,
    1880 A
Capital, Federal, 1908 A
Capital, overseas, 1820 A, 1835 A,
    1906 A
Capital punishment, 1833 A, 1922 A,
    1965 A, 1968 A, 1975 A
Capitol Theatre, Melbourne, 1924 C,
    1925 C
Capitol Theatre, Sydney, 1915 C
Capricorn Bunker Is, Qld, 1958 B
Capricornia, 1938 C
Capricornia, Qld, 1967 D
Capricornia College of Advanced
    Education, Qld, 1967 D
Captain Cook's cottage, Melbourne,
    1934 F
Captain Cook Graving Dock, Sydney,
    1940 B, 1945 B
Captain Cook Statue, Sydney, 1879 C
Capt Melville, 1822 A
'*Capt Moonlight*', 1842 A
Capt Quiros, 1964 C
'Captain Thunderbolt', 1835 A
Captain Thunderbolt (film), 1953 C
Captains Flat, NSW, 1888 F, 1939 B
Car/s, see motor car and motor car racing
Carandini, Jerome, 1841 C, 1845 C
Carandini, Maria, 1826 C, 1844 C
Carbine, 1890 E
Carboni, Raffaello, 1817 C
Carbolic (in hospitals), 1898 B
Carbrasse, Louise, 1896 C
Card games, see individual entries
Cardamatis, J. W. 1917 C
Cardboard Crown, The, 1952 C
Cardell-Oliver, Florence G. ('Annie'),
    1876 A, 1936 A, 1951 A
Cardiff, NSW, 1830 F
Cardin *Bubble* look, fashion, 1957 F
Cards, letter, 1894 F
Cardwell, Qld, 1864 F
Careful, He Might Hear You, 1983 C
Carey, George J. 1866 A
Carey, H. E. 1919 A
Carey, Peter, 1982 C
Carey, Tristram, 1925 C
Cargo, NSW, 1869 F
Carillon City Festival Art Prize, 1955 C
Carillons, 1928 C, 1970 C
Carleton, Caroline, 1859 C
Carlile, Forbes, 1921 E
Carlisle Castle, 1899 F
Carlton, James, 1909 E, 1932 E
Carlton Aust. Rules Football Club/team,
    1864 E, 1906 E, 1907 E, 1908 E,
    1914 E, 1915 E, 1938 E, 1945 E,
    1947 E, 1961 E, 1964 E, 1968 E,
    1970 E, 1972 E, 1979 E, 1981 E,
    1982 E

Carlton and United Breweries Ltd,
    1907 A
Carmichael, Grace E. J. 1867 C
Carmichael, Henry, 1834 D, 1862 D
Carmichael, Thomas D. G. 1908 A
Carnarvon, WA, 1883 F, 1961 F, 1979 F
Carnegie, David W. 1871 A
Carnegie International Exhibition,
    1952 C
Carnivale 77, NSW, 1977 C
Carpenter, George L. 1872 D, 1939 D
Carpenters workers group, 1840 A
Carr, Edwin W. ('Slip'), 1901 E
Carr, Thomas J. 1839 D
Carriage services, Sydney, 1813 F, 1861 B
Carrington, Thomas, 1843 C
Carrington, V. G. 1929 A
Carrington relief depot, Sydney, 1886 F
Carroll, Arthur H. ('Jack'), 1906 E
Carroll, Christopher, 1902 D
Carron, William, 1821 B
Carruthers, Joseph H. M. 1857 A,
    1904 A
Carruthers, James W. ('Jimmy'), 1929 E,
    1952 E, 1953 E, 1954 E
Carruthers, Kel, 1944 E
Cars that Ate Paris, The, 1974 C
Carse, J. H. 1819 C
Carslake, Bernard ('Brownie'), 1887 E
Carter, Herbert J. 1858 B, 1925 C
Carter, Norman S. 1875 C
Carter, William, 1853 A
Carter's barracks, Sydney, 1822 F
Cartier I., Antarctic, 1934 A
Cartooning, 1851 C, 1941 F
Cartoonists, see *individual entries Section C*
Cartwright, Robert, 1856 D
Caruthers, John, 1889 A
Carvosso, B. 1820 D
Cascade brewery, 1832 A
Case, Dalle, 1842 C
Case, Ross, 1951 E
Casey, Gavin S. 1907 C
Casey, Richard, G. (b. 1846), 1846 A
Casey, Richard, G. (b. 1890), 1890 A
    1924 A, 1931 A, 1940 A, 1960 A,
    1965 A, 1969 A
Casey research station, Antarctica,
    1969 B
Cash, Martin, 1808 A
Cash, Patrick, 1983 E
Cash credit, 1831 A
Cash Management Trusts, 1980 A
Cashmere goats, 1863 A
Casino, 1932 F
Casino, NSW, 1855 F, 1936 F
Casino, Tas, 1968 F, 1973 F
Casley, Leonard G. 1925 A, 1970 A
Cassab, Judy, 1920 C, 1960 C, 1967 C
Cassidy, J. 1983 E
Cassidy, Mervyn, 1926 C
Cassilis, NSW, 1838 F
Cast iron, 1845 C, 1856 B, 1863 C
Casterton, Vic, 1840 F
Casting, 1939 E, 1947 E, 1959 E, see also
    Fishing, Angling
Castle Hill, NSW, 1811 B
Castle Hill Uprising, 1804 A
Castlemaine, Vic, 1851 F, 1857 F
Castlemaine Art Gallery and Historical
    Museum, Vic, 1913 C
Castlemaine Brewery, 1871 A
Castlereagh, NSW, 1810 F, 1817 D
Castlereagh R., NSW, 1818 A, 1828 A,
    1829 A, 1831 A
Castles, Amy E. 1880 C
Castors (in furniture), 1939 B
Castro, Juan J. 1952 C
Castro, Thomas, *see* Orton, Arthur

759

Casualties,
  Korean War, 1953 A
  Vietnam War, 1968 A
  World War I, 1918 A
  World War II, 1945 A
Catalogue, 1938 E
Catalpa, 1876 F
Cataract, 1819 B
Cataraqui, 1845 F
Catarrh, 1820 F
Catchpole, Ken, 1939 E
Catchpole, Margaret, 1819 A
Caterpillars, 1810 F
Cathedrals, see *individual entries*
Catherine Adamson, 1857 F
Catholic, see Roman Catholic
Catholic Centenary Prize, Melbourne, art, 1948 C
Catholic church, Sydney, 1838 D
Catholic Institute of Sydney, 1889 D
Catholic Ladies College, Melbourne, 1885 D
Catholic school, co-educational, 1957 D
Catholic Social Movement, 1954 D
Catholic Teachers' College of Sydney, 1913 D
Catholic Worker, 1936 F
Cato, 1803 F
Cato, Jack, 1889 B
Cato, Nancy F. 1917 C
Cat-o-nine-tails, 1817 F
Catterthun, 1895 F
Cattle,
  Angus, 1880 A
  anthrax, 1847 B
  Brucellosis, 1943 B
  Dairy, 1820 A, 1942 A, 1956 B
  Devon, 1820 A
  foot-and-mouth-disease, 1872 B
  Hereford, 1826 A, 1835 A
  Illawarra Shorthorn, 1898 B, 1929 B
  livestock procedure, 1982 B
  overlanding, 1837 A, 1838 A, 1840 A, 1864 A, 1872 A, 1884 A
  pleuropneumonia, 1858 B
  record shift, 1963 A
  Red Poll, 1850 A
  Santa Gertrudis, 1933 A, 1952 B
  thefts, 1870 F
  ticks, 1872 B
  trains, 1948 B
  Zebu, 1956 B
'The Cattle King,' 1857 A
Cattle King, The (film), 1983 C
Cattlemen's Union, 1979 A
Caucus, first meeting, 1901 A
Caulfield, Melbourne, 1926 F
Caulfield Golf Club, 1891 E
Caulfield Cup (horse-race), 1879 E
Caulfield Institute of Technology, Melbourne, 1922 D
Caulfield Technical College, Melbourne, 1922 D
Causeway bridge, WA, 1843 B
Cautious Armorist, The, 1932 C
Cavanagh, E. 1865 E
Cavanagh, J. 1871 E
Cavdarski, Vanco, 1974 C, 1978 C
Cave and the Spring, The, 1965 C
Cavendish High School, Qld, 1952 D
Caverneering, Tas, 1946 F
Cavill, Arthur, 1877 E, 1897 E, 1902 E
Cavill, Charles, 1871 E, 1896 E
Cavill, David, 1903 E
Cavill, Ernest, 1888 E
Cavill, Freda M. 1878 E
Cavill, Frederick, 1839 E
Cavill, Percy, 1875 E, 1897 E
Cavill, Richard, 1938 E

Cavill, Sydney, 1945 E, 1953 E
Cavity walls, 1885 C, 1895 C
Cawarra, 1866 F
Cawood, C. A. 1927 A
Cawley, Evonne F. 1951 E, 1970 E, 1971 E
Cayley, Neville H. P. 1853 C
Cayley, Neville W. 1886 C
Cazaly, Roy, 1893 E
Cazneaux, Harold, 1878 C
'CB' radio, 1976 F, 1977 B
Cedar, 1795 A, 1822 A
Cedar Bay, Qld, 1976 F
Ceduna, SA, 1896 F, 1959 E
Ceil III, 1973 E
Ceilings, metal, 1888 C
Celsius temperature scale, 1972 B
Celebrations, foundation of Colony, 1804 F
Celeste, Céline, 1863 C, 1867 C
Cemeteries, 1790 F, 1804 F, 1811 F, 1820 F, 1829 F, 1836 F, 1837 F, 1838 F
Censorship, book, 1901 C, 1933 C, 1958 C, 1967 C
Censorship, Cwlth-state, 1968 A
Censorship, film, 1970 C, 1971 C
Censorship, press, 1824 F
Censorship, voluntary, 1852 A
Censorship, wartime, 1914 A, 1939 A
Census, Aust. wide, 1881 F, 1918 F, 1921 F, 1933 F, 1947 F, 1954 F, 1966 F, 1971 F, 1976 F, 1981 F, see Population, section F
Centaur, 1943 A
Centennial Park, Sydney, 1901 A
Center, Ronald, A. 1913 C
Central Aust., survey, 1926 A, 1927 B, 1931 A
Central Aust. Aboriginal Media Association, 1980 F
Central Council of Employees of Aust., 1904 A
Central Methodist Mission, Sydney, 1884 D, 1963 F
Central Railway Station, Sydney, 1906 B
Central Street Gallery, Sydney, 1966 C
Central Tobacco Advisory Committee, 1954 A
Centralian Advocate, The, Alice Springs, 1947 F
Centre 5 group, Melbourne 1959 C
Centre Technical College, Brisbane, 1915 D
Centre-left (ALP), 1984 A
Centrepoint Tower, Sydney, 1981 C
Century of Australian Song, A, 1888 C
Ceramics, 1899 B, 1968 B, 1978 C
Cerberus, HMAS, 1871 A
Cerebral Palsy Assoc. 1954 F
Cerebral circulation, 1976 B
Certificate exam, Vic, 1911 D
Certified mail, 1956 F
Cerutty, Bill, 1910 E
Cerutty, Percy W. 1895 E
Cessnock, NSW, 1853 F, 1923 F
Cessnock Art Prize, NSW, 1958 C
Chadstone Sculpture Prizes, Melbourne, 1960 C
Chaff cutters, 1837 B
Chaffey Bros, 1888 A
Chaffey, George, 1848 B, 1886 B, 1891 B
Chaffey, William B. 1856 B, 1887 B
Chain, E. 1940 B
Chairs, 1933 F, 1947 F, 1948 F
Chalk, G. W. W. 1968 A
Chalker, Henry, 1832 E
Challenger, 1984 B
Challis, John H. 1806 A
Chalmers, Jack, 1922 F
Chalmers, James, 1841 D

Chamber music, 1822 C, 1946 C
Chamber music societies, 1945 C
Chamberlain, Azaria, 1980 F, 1981 F, 1982 F, 1984 F
Chamberlain, Lindy, 1981 F, 1982 F, 1984 F
Chamberlain, Michael, 1981 F
Chambers, Charles H. 1842 A, 1860 C
Chambers, James, 1811 A
Chambers, Joseph, 1843 C, 1858 C, 1874 C
Chambers Bay, NT, 1862 A
Chambers of Commerce, 1825 A, 1839 A
Champ, William T. N. 1808 A, 1856 A
Champagne, 1875 A
Champion de Crespigny, C. Trent, 1882 B
Chan, Harry, 1918 A
Chan, Kai T. 1976 C
Chandler, Margaret, 1963 F
Chandler Coventry, 1983 C
Chaney, F. C. 1970 A
Chant of Jimmy Blacksmith, The, 1972 C, 1978 C
Chapel, W. C. 1858 B
Chapman, Dorra C. 1915 C
Chapman, Frederick, 1864 B
Chapman, Gary, 1938 E
Chapman, Robert H. 1890 B
Chapman, Robert W. 1866 B
Chapman, Thomas, 1849 B
Chapman, Thomas D. 1815 A, 1861 A
Chapman, Thomas E. 1788 C
Chapman, William, 1881 A
Chappell, Gregory S. 1948 E, 1976 E, 1981 E
Chappell, Ian, 1943 E
Chappell, Trevor, 1981 E
Charity, 1813 F, 1864 F, 1894 F
Charles, Prince, 1966 D, 1978 A, 1979 A, 1981 A
Charles, Richard S. 1947 E
Charles Blackman, 1966 C
Charles Eaton, 1834 F
Charlesworth, Ric, 1953 E
Charleville, Qld, 1865 F, 1888 B, 1922 B, 1950 E, 1981 F
Charlotte Pass, NSW, 1945 D
Charlotte R., NT, 1869 B
Charlton, Vic, 1848 F
Charlton, Andrew M. ('Boy') 1907 E, 1924 E
Charlton, Edward, 1929 E
Charlton, Jimmy, 1908 E
Charlton, Matthew, 1866 A, 1922 A
Charrière, M. 1841 C
Charters Towers, Qld, 1872 A, B, F, 1882 B, 1904 F
Charterisville mansion, Vic, 1890 C
Charvat, Frank, 1911 C
Chater, Gordon, 1922 C
Chatham I., 1791 A
Chatterton of the South, 1828 C
Chauncy, Nancen B. 1900 C
Chauvel, Charles E. 1897 C, 1923 C, 1926 C, 1933 C, 1935 C, 1938 C, 1940 C, 1944 C, 1949 C
Chauvel, Henry G. 1865 A
Cheaters, The, 1930 C
Checkers, 1888 F
Cheesemakers, 1960 B
Chelmsford, Baron, see Thesiger, F. J. N.
Chemical industry, 1862 B
Chemistry, 1871 D
Chemistry of the Defect Solid State, The, 1954 B
Chemists, 1820 B, 1837 B, 1844 B
Cheong, Cheok H. 1853 F

Cheques, govt tax, 1982 A
Cherana, 1959 E
Cherbourg Aboriginal community, 1904 A
Chermside, Herbert C. 1902 A
Cherra Kadisha, 1817 F
Cherry, Walter J. 1932 C, 1962 C
Chess, 1840 F, 1860 F, 1870 F, 1885 F, 1955 F, 1975 F
Chester, 1877 E
Chester, Henry M. 1832 A, 1883 A
Chevalier, Nicholas, 1828 C, 1855 C
Chichester, Francis, 1967 E
Chicken Smallhorn, 1933 E, *see* Smallhorn, W.
Chickens, 1949 B
Chidley, William J. 1860 F
Chief Havoc, 1944 E
Chief Justices, *see individual entries*
Chifley, Joseph B. 1885 A, 1928 A, 1945 A, 1946 A, 1949 A
Chifney, H. 1863 A
Child care, 1938 D
Child endowment schemes, 1927 A, 1941 A
Child of the Hurricane, 1963 C
Childbirth, 1898 F
Childe, Vere G. 1892 B, 1925 B
Childers, Qld, 1885 F
Childers, Hugh C. E. 1827 D, 1851 D
Children, 1839 F
Children, first Aust. born, 1788 D
Children, neglected, 1864 F
Children of the Bush, 1902 C
Children of school age, 1788 D
Children's Book of the Year Award, 1946 C
Children's Courts, 1918 A
Children's Hour, The, SA, 1889 D
Children's Medical Research Foundation, 1958 B
Child-Villiers, V. A. G. 1845 A, 1891 A
Chillago, Qld, 1888 F
Chiltern, Vic, 1858 F
China, scientific and technical co-operation, 1976 B, 1979 B
China, technical aid to, 1964 A
China Field Force, 1901 A
Chinese, anti-Chinese restrictive legislation, 1855 A, 1857 A, 1858 A, 1861 A, 1875 A, 1877 A, 1881 A, 1886 A, 1888 A, 1896 A
Chinese, anti-Chinese riots, sentiment, 1853 A, 1860 A, 1861 A, 1873 A, 1878 A, 1880 A, 1887 A, 1888 A
Chinese, living conditions, 1887 A
Chinese Archeological Exhibition, 1977 C
Chinese Buddhist Society of Aust., 1972 D
Chinese Bureau of Economic Information, 1920 A
Chinese bushranger, 1865 A
Chinese gold miners, 1852 A, 1854 A, 1855 F, 1865 A
'Chinese' Morrison, 1862 A
Chinese population, 1857 A, 1848 A, 1854 F, 1855 F, 1859 F, 1861 F, 1881 A, 1888 F
Chinese Restriction Act, 1877 A, 1896 A
Chinese shepherds, 1848 A
Chinese Vice Premier, 1980 A
Chinner, John H. 1865 C
Chipp, Donald L. 1925 A, 1960 A, 1977 A
Chippendale, Edward, 1884 B
Chirnside, Andrew S. 1818 A
Chirnside, Thomas, 1815 A
Chisholm, Alexander H. 1890 B, 1958 C

Chisholm, Alice I. 1856 A
Chisholm, A. R. 1888 C
Chisholm, Caroline, 1808 A, 1838 A, 1841 A, 1846 A, 1849 A
Chisholm, James (b. 1806), 1806 A
Chisholm, James (b. 1772), 1837 A
Chisholm, James K. 1830 A
Chloe, 1875 C, 1880 C
Choirs, Sydney, 1885 D
Cholera, 1841 F, 1972 F, 1979 F
Choral groups, 1853 C
Choral music, 1855 C
Choreography, 1858 C, *see individual entries and section C*
Chosen People, 1938 C
Chowilla dam, 1967 B
Christ, coming of, 1924 D
Christadelphian group, 1866 D
Christesen, Clement B. 1940 C
Christian, Fletcher, 1792 A
Christian Brothers, 1868 D, 1908 D
Christian Brothers' Catholic School, Qld, 1888 D
Christian Brothers' College, Perth, 1895 D
Christian Endeavour Movement, 1888 D
Christian Israelites, 1841 D
Christian Science, 1890 D, 1891 D, 1898 D
Christian Societies, 1850 D
Christie, Frank, 1830 A, 1862 F
Christie, Maurice F. 1901 E
Christina, 1946 E
Christina Fraser, 1933 F
Christison, Robert, 1837 A, 1883 B
Christmann, Gunter, 1936 C
Christmas I., 1888 A, 1891 A, 1958 A
Christ's College, Hobart, 1841 E
Chromolithography, 1855 C
Chronicle, Qld, 1861 F
Chronicles of Early Melbourne, 1888 C
Chrysler Valiant, 1962 B
Chrysoprase, Qld, 1963 B
Chu Chin Chow, 1916 C
Chuck, Thomas B. 1863 B, 1898 B
Church, Ann, 1929 C
Church attendance, 1810 D, 1983 D
Church of Christ, 1846 D
Church of England,
 Aust. wide, 1847 D, 1854 D, 1962 D, 1978 D, 1981 D
 NSW, 1788 D, 1803 D, 1807 D, 1810 D, 1824 D, 1826 D, 1836 D, 1866 D, 1872 D, 1884 D
 Qld, 1859 D, 1875 D
 SA, 1836 D
 Tas, 1804 D, 1838 D, 1842 D, 1852 D
 Vic, 1803 D, 1830 D, 1837 D, 1838 D, 1854 D, 1984 D
 WA, 1830 D, 1848 D, 1856 D
Church of England, education, 1815 D, 1818 D
Church of England, land, 1826 D
Church of England, outback, 1897 D
Church of England of Australia, 1962 D
Church of England Aust. College of Theology, 1891 D
Church of England Cathedral, Armidale, NSW, 1875 C
Church of England Church and School Corporation, 1824 D, 1826 D, 1833 D
Church of England Church Society, Sydney, 1856 D
Church of England Collegiate School, Perth, 1865 D
Church of England conference, Sydney, 1850 D
Church of England Defence Association, 1874 D

Church of England Grammar School, Brisbane, 1914 D
Church of England School Collegiate, Adelaide, 1847 D
Church of England Teachers' Association, Sydney, 1859 D
Church of God radio broadcasts, 1956 D
Church and Life Movement study, 1966 D
Church Missionary Society, NT, 1925 D
Church of the New Faith, 1956 D
Church of Scotland Presbytery of NSW, 1837 D
Church services, first, 1788 D, 1803 D
Church services, televised, 1956 D
Churcher, Roy, 1933 C
Churches, first, 1793 D, 1794 D
Churches, unification, 1974 D
Churchill, Clive, 1927 E
Churchill Fellowships, 1965 D
Churchill I., Vic, 1801 A
Churchland, Lindsay S. 1921 C
Churchlands Teachers College, WA, 1972 D
Chusan (ship), 1852 B, F
Chute, Trevor, 1867 A
Cigarette advertising, 1971 F, 1972 F, 1974 F, 1976 F
Cigarette cards, 1904 F
Cigarette smoking, women, 1922 F
Cigarettes, 1967 F
Cilento, Alan W. W. 1908 A
Cilento, E. Diane, 1933 C
Cilento, Phyllis D. 1894 B
Cilento, Ralph W. 1893 B
Cilento, Raphael, 1946 A
Cinema, 1896 C, 1909 C, 1919 C, 1925 C, *see also individual entries*
Cinematograph, Sydney, 1896 C
Cinesound Review, 1931 C
Cinesound studios, Sydney, 1931 C
Circular Quay, Sydney, 1837 B, C, 1885 C
Circular Head, Tas, 1826 A, 1859 B
Circumnavigation of Aust. by sea, 1790 A, 1801 A, 1803 A, 1819 A, 1970 E, by air 1921 B, 1924 B, by car 1925 F, 1939 E
Circus, 1850 F
Cities, *see individual entries*
Citizen Military Forces, 1939 A, 1960 A
Citizens' Life Assurance Co. Ltd. Sydney, 1886 A
Citizenship, 1948 A
Citizenship, Aboriginals, NT, 1951 A, 1953 A
Citrus, orchards, 1800 A
City's Child, A, 1972 C
'City Father,' 1836 A
City of Melbourne Bank, 1878 A
City night refuge and soup kitchens, Sydney, 1865 F
City of Singapore, (ship), 1924 F
City Square, Melbourne, 1980 C
City-to-surf fun run, Sydney, 1978 E, 1980 E, 1981 E
City of Sydney Bank, 1864 A
City of Sydney Eisteddfod, 1933 C
Civic Hotel Canberra, 1965 F
Civic Theatre, Canberra, 1966 C
Civil Aviation Board, 1936 B
Civil Aviation, Dept of, 1938 B
'Civil Jim', 1822 A, 1851 B
Civil legal action, first, 1795 A
Civil magistrates, powers of, 1792 A
Civil servants' strike, WA, 1920 A
Civil Service Musical Society, 1866 C
'Civilize and Christianize', 1860 A
Clampe de la, M. 1799 A

761

Clancy, Edward, 1983 D
'Clancy of the Overflow', 1889 C
Clapp, Francis B. 1833 A, 1869 B, 1885 B
Clapp, Harold W. 1875 B, 1937 B
Clapton, Richard, 1972 C
Clara Morison, 1854 C
Clare, SA, 1842 F
Claremont Teachers' Training College, WA, 1901 D
'Clarence Comet', 1866 E
Clarence High School, Hobart, 1961 D
Clarence R., NSW, 1828 A
Clarendon House, Tas, 1838 C
Clari, 1834 C
Clark, Alister, 1864 B
Clark, Andrew I. 1848 A
Clark, Carnegie, 1881 E
Clark, C. Manning H., 1915 D, 1962 C, 1980 D
Clark, Danny, 1952 E
Clark, Ernest, 1933 A
Clark, Jack, 1933 E
Clark, John, 1885 B
Clark, John J. 1838 C, 1857 C, 1862 C
Clark, Marc, 1923 C
Clark, R. Marcus, 1883 A
Clark, Terence J. 1981 F
Clark, Thomas, 1814 C
Clarke, Alfred B. 1925 C
Clarke, Andrew, 1793 A, 1824 A, 1846 A
Clarke, Bill, 1824 E
Clarke, Colin G. 1905 A
Clarke, Donald R. 1927 C
Clarke, Francis G. 1879 A
Clarke, G. E. 1872 B
Clarke, George S. 1901 A
Clarke, Henry L. 1850 D
Clarke, John, 1867 A
Clarke, Joseph A. 1840 C
Clarke, Marcus A. H. 1846 C, 1869 C, 1870 C, 1871 C, 1874 C, 1877 C, 1885 C, 1926 C
Clarke, Peter, 1935 C
Clarke, Ronald W. 1937 E, 1965 E, 1968 E
Clarke, Thomas, 1867 A
Clarke, William B. 1798 B, 1841 B, 1844 B, 1849 B, 1877 B
Clarke, William J. 1831 A
Clarke, William J. T. 1805 A
Clarkson, Stanley L. 1905 C
Classical Ballet Co., 1940 C
Claxton, Marshall, 1811 C, 1850 C
Claxton, Norrie, 1880 E, 1933 E
Claxton Shield, 1933 E
Clay, 1878 C
Clay, Brian, 1934 E
Clay, Henry E. 1844 C
Clay Pigeon Trap shooting, 1936 E
Clay target shooting, 1882 E, 1927 E
Clayton, Bessie, 1896 C
Clayton, Deric, 1942 E
Clayton, Philip T. B. 1885 D, 1925 D
Clayton, Robert, 1951 F
Clayton, Samuel, 1820 F
Clayton, T. 1904 E, 1906 E
Clean Sweep, 1900 E
Cleary, Jon S. 1917 C, 1948 C, 1952 C
Cleary, Michael, 1940 E
Clegg, Ron, 1928 E, 1949 E
Cleland, Donald M. 1901 A
Cleland, John B. 1878 B
Cleo, 1972 F
Clermont, Qld, 1862 B, F, 1916 F
Cleve, SA, 1879 F
Cleveland, Qld, 1850 F
Cleveland Bay, Qld, 1863 A
Clewett, George, 1837 C
Cliff rescue squad, NSW, 1942 F

Clift, Charmian, 1923 C
Clifton, Romola, 1935 C
Clint, Alfred, 1843 C
Clint, Alfred T. 1882 C
Clint Art Prize, Sydney, 1954 C
Clipper races, 1939 E
Clisby, Harriet, 1830 F
Clive and Vera Ramaciotti Foundation for medical research, 1970 B
Cloche hats, 1922 F
Clock makers, 1815 F
Cloncurry, Qld, 1867 B, 1875 A, 1876 F, 1889 F, 1908 B, 1922 B, 1927 B, 1928 B, 1929 B
Clontarf, Sydney, 1868 A
Close, Robert S. 1903 C, 1945 C
Closed circuit television, 1975 B
Closer Settlement Act, NSW, 1895 A
Closing times, shops, 1889 A
Clothes hoist, 1945 B
Clothing employees' strike, Melbourne, 1882 A
Clothing, wartime restrictions, 1942 F
Clover seed, 1817 A, 1906 A
Clover, subterranean, 1950 B
Clow, James, 1790 D, 1837 D
Clowes, Cyril A. 1892 A
Club swinging, 1934 E
Clubbe, Charles P. B. 1854 B
Clubs, sporting and others, *see individual entries*
Clues, Arthur, 1924 E
Clune, Francis P. 1893 C, 1930 C
Clunes, Vic, 1850 B, 1851 B, F, 1873 A
Clunies Ross, Ian, 1899 B, 1949 B
Clunies Ross, George, 1891 A
Clunies Ross, John, 1827 A
Clutsam, George H. 1866 C
Clutterbuck, Jock, 1945 C
Clyde Cameron College, 1976 D
Clyde Co., 1836 A
Clyde R., NSW, 1821 A
Coach services, 1814 B, 1829 B, 1830 B, 1832 B, 1853 B, 1854 B, 1862 B, 1865 B, 1869 B, 1870 B, 1924 B
Coachmakers' Friendly Society, Sydney, 1837 F
Coal,
  NSW, 1791 B, 1796 B, 1797 B, 1799 A, 1800 B, 1801 A, B, 1829 A, 1831 A, 1850 A, 1858 B, 1864 B, 1883 B, 1886 B, 1983 B
  Qld, 1791 B, 1825 B, 1827 B, 1864 B, 1937 B, 1968 B, 1983 B
  SA, 1791 B, 1888 B, 1907 B, 1943 B
  Tas, 1791 B, 1824 B, 1843 B, 1886 B, 1983 B
  Vic, 1791 B, 1825 B, 1857 B, 1873 B, 1909 B, 1917 B, 1925 B
  WA, 1791 B, 1846 A, B, 1883 B
Coal, exports, 1799 A, 1804 A, 1850 A, 1865 A, 1873 F, 1981 A
Coal gas, Sydney, 1820 B
Coal miners, 1874 A, 1906 A, 1923 A, 1947 A
Coal miners' strikes, 1854 A, 1855 A, 1860 A, 1861 A, 1888 A, 1896 A, 1909 A, 1910 A, 1916 A, 1929 A, 1940 A, 1944 A, 1945 A, 1948 A, 1949 A, 1982 A
Coal Mines Act, NSW, 1876 A
Coal mining cos, Newcastle, 1860 B
Coal R., NSW, 1796 B, 1804 A
Coal trade, 1851 A
Coal Trade Association, NSW, 1866 A
Coast disease, 1934 B
Coastal Art Group, Tas, 1950 C
Coastal Surveillance Centre, 1978 A
Coastal waters, state powers, 1980 A

Coastwatchers, 1919 A
Coat of Arms, Aust., 1908 A
Coates, Albert E. 1895 B, 1927 B
Coates, George J. 1869 C
Co-axial telephone link, 1962 B
Cobalt, 1934 B, 1957 B
Cobar, NSW, 1870 B, 1871 F, 1980 F
Cobb, Chester F. 1899 C, 1925 C, 1926 C
Cobb, Freeman, 1830 B, 1853 B, 1854 B
Cobb, Victor E. 1876 C
Cobb and Co., 1853 B, 1854 B, 1862 B, 1865 B, 1870 B, 1924 B
Cobbers, 1933 C
Cobbet, William P. 1853 A
Cobbity, NSW, 1827 F
Cobby, Arthur H. 1894 A
Cobden, Vic, 1895 F
Cobham, A. 1926 B
Cobram, Vic, 1887 F
Coburg Peninsula, NT, 1827 A
Coburg Teachers' College, Vic, 1959 D
Coburg Vic Football Association team, 1879 E
Coburn, John, 1925 C
Coca Cola, 1938 A
Cochlear implant, 1984 B
Cochrane, Donald, 1917 A
Cock fighting, 1805 E, 1850 E
Cockatoo I., NSW, 1839 B
Cockburn, SA, 1890 F
Cockburn, Bruce, 1969 E
Cockburn, John A. 1850 A, 1889 A
Cockburn Sound, WA, 1955 B
Cockle, James, 1819 A, 1862 A
Cocks, Arthur H. T. S. 1926 A, 1930 A
Cocoa, 1799 A
Cocos Is, 1827 A, 1914 A, 1955 A
Code, Percy, 1929 C
Coe, Kevin, 1946 C, 1968 C, 1973 C
Co-educational Schools, 1957 D
Coeliac Disease, 1915 B
Coen, Margaret A. 1913 C
Coff's Harbour, NSW, 1861 F, 1913 A
Coffage, John (Chips Rafferty), 1909 C, 1946 C
Coffey, Alfred, 1869 C,
Coghlan, Timothy A. 1856 B, 1918 C
Cogoon Station, Qld, 1848 A
Cohen, Donald S. 1895 C
Cohen, George J. 1842 D
Cohen, Isaac M. 1884 C
Cohen, John J. 1859 B
Cohen, Phillip J. 1828 D
Cohn, Ola, 1892 C, 1931 C, 1948 C
Cohuna, Vic, 1835 F
Cohuna skull, Vic, 1925 B
Coins, 1829 A
Coins, Aust., 1866 A
Coins, copper, 1800 A
Coke, NSW, 1876 B
Coke, Thomas W. 1822 D
Colac, Vic, 1859 F
Colahan, Colin, 1897 C
Colbeck, James, 1800 C, 1835 C
Colclough, Edward, 1866 C
Cole, Edward W. 1832 A, 1873 C
Cole, John, 1945 E
Cole, Percival R. 1879 D
Cole, Peter, 1946 C
Colebatch, H. P. 1919 A
Colebrook, Tas, 1843 B
Coleing, Tony, 1942 C
Coleman, Alfred, 1890 C
Coleman, Edith, 1951 B
Coleman, John, 1929 E
Coleman, William, 1922 C
Coleraine, Vic, 1839 F
Coles, Arthur W. 1892 A, 1946 B
Coles, Edgar B. 1899 C

Cole's Funny Picture book, 1876 C
Coles, George J. 1885 A, 1914 A
Coles, Kenneth F. 1896 A
Coles, L. 1962 E
Coles, Norman C. 1907 A
Coles, Raymond, 1924 C
Coles, stores, Melbourne, 1914 A
Collected Poems 1942–1970, (Wright), 1971 C
Collected Poems 1936–1970, (McAuley), 1971 C
Collectors and Connoisseurs Society of NSW, 1922 C
Collective bargaining, 1973 A
College of Aboriginal Education, Adelaide, 1973 D
College of Nursing, 1949 B
College of Radiologists of Australasia, 1949 B
Colleges of Advanced Education, 1965 D, *see also individual entries*
Colleges, girls', 1875 D
Colleges, tertiary, 1965 D
Collie, WA, 1883 B, 1897 F
Collie, Alexander, 1793 A, 1829 A
Collie Art Gallery, WA, 1954 C
Collier, Albert, 1909 E, 1929 E
Collier, Frederick, 1885 C
Collier, Harry, 1907 E
Collier, Marie E. 1928 C
Collier, Philip, 1873 A, 1924 A, 1933 A
Collingridge, Arthur de T. 1853 C
Collingridge, George A. de T. 1847 C, 1888 C
Collings, Geoffrey, 1955 C
Collings, Silver L. 1940 C
Collingwood, Melbourne, 1859 A, 1914 A
Collingwood Aust. Rules Football Club, VFL team, 1892 E, 1902 E, 1903 E, 1910 E, 1917 E, 1919 E, 1927 E, 1928 E, 1929 E, 1930 E, 1935 E, 1936 E, 1939 E, 1940 E, 1953 E, 1958 E, 1972 E, 1979 E
Collins, Albert, 1883 C
Collins, Archibald, 1853 C
Collins, Dale, 1897 C
Collins, David, 1788 A, 1798 C, 1803 A, C, 1804 A, 1810 A
Collins, Herbert L. 1889 E
Collins, John A. 1899 A
Collins, Robert, 1843 A
'Collins, Tom', *see* Furphy, Joseph
Collins, William G. 1889 C
Collinsvale, Tas, 1881 F
Collinsville, Qld, 1954 F
Collis, Gordon, 1964 E
Collitt's Inn, 1933 C
Colombine, 1920 C
Colombo Plan, 1950 A, D
Colonial Advocate, Tas, 1828 F
Colonial Bank of Australasia, 1864 A
Colonial Booksellers' Agency, 1887 A
'Colonial Cobbett', The, 1826 A
Colonial Conferences, London, 1887 A, 1894 A, 1897 A, 1902 A, 1907 A
Colonial expenses, 1801 A
Colonial Experience, 1868 C
Colonial Institute, 1868 F
Colonial Land and Emigration Commissioners, 1840 A
Colonial military forces, 1870 A, 1900 A, 1902 A
Colonial Minstrel, 1831 C, 1859 C
Colonial Museum, Sydney, 1827 D
Colonial Naval Defence Act, 1856 A
Colonial Revenue Fund, 1809 A
Colonial Songster, 1857 C

Colonial Sugar Refining Co., CSR, 1855 A, 1870 A, 1951 B
Colonial Times, Tas, 1825 F, 1828 F
Colonies, states, 1901 A
Colonization, SA, 1831 A, 1833 A, 1834 A, 1835 A, *see also individual states*
Colonization, Vic, 1835 A, *see also individual states*
Colonist, 1835 F
Colonus, 1942 E
Colour Man, 1938 C
Colour photography, 1907 B
Coloured Races Restriction and Regulation Bill, NSW, 1896 A
Coloured television, 1974 B, 1975 B
Colquhoun, Alexander, 1866 C
Colquhoun, Archibald D. 1894 C
Colton, John, 1823 A, 1876 A, 1884 A
Columbia recordings, 1926 C
Colville, George G. 1887 C
Comalco Industries, Qld, 1960 A
Comalco Invitation award, 1967 C, 1968 C
Combat, unarmed, 1978 E, *see individual entries*
Combe, David, 1983 C
Combustion engine, 1971 B
Come Over Here, 1914 C
Come in Spinner, 1951 C
Comedy King, 1910 E
Comic Court, 1950 E
Comancheros, 1984 F
Commerce training, Melbourne, 1924 D
Commercial Activities Act, Federal, 1919 A
Commercial Bank of Aust., 1866 A, 1867 A, 1893 A, 1981 A, 1982 A
Commercial Bank of SA, 1886 A
Commercial Bank of Tas, 1832 A
Commercial Banking Co. of Sydney, 1834 A
Commercial Travellers' Associations, 1866 F
Commissioner of Assignment, 1834 A
Committee on the Development of SW Tas, 1967 F
Committee for Economic Development of Aust., CEDA, 1960 A
Committee of Enquiry into Technological Change, 1978 B
Committee of Inquiry into Education Training, 1979 D
Committee to Survey Secondary Education, 1953 D
Common Council of Rifle Associations of Aust., 1901 E
Common Market, 1962 A
Common School Act, Vic, 1862 D
Common Time Zones, 1894 B
Commons, Donald G. 1855 C
Commonwealth, *abbreviated as* Cwlth
Cwlth Acoustics Laboratory, 1947 B
Cwlth Aircraft Corporation Ltd. 1936 B
Cwlth Art Advisory Board, 1911 C
Commonwealth of Australia, founded, 1901 A
'Commonwealth of Australia', name adopted, 1891 A
Commonwealth of Australia Constitution Act, 1900 A
Cwlth Bank, 1911 A, 1912 A, 1924 A, 1925 A, 1929 A, 1931 A, 1943 A
Commonwealth Bank Act, 1931 A
Cwlth Bank notes, 1913 A
Commonwealth Banks Act, 1960 A
Cwlth Bill, 1893 A, 1900 A
Cwlth Board of Trade, 1918 A
Cwlth Bridge, Canberra, 1963 C

Cwlth Bureau of Agricultural Economics, 1946 A
Cwlth Bureau of Dental Standards, 1947 B
Cwlth Bureau of Meteorology, 1907 B, 1959 B
Cwlth census, *see* Census
Cwlth Centenary Prize for Art, 1950 C
Commonwealth Conciliation and Arbitration Act, 1904 A, 1969 A
Commonwealth Crimes Act, 1914 A, 1926 A, 1949 A
Cwlth Defence Act, 1904 A
Cwlth Dept of Health, 1921 A
Cwlth Development Bank, 1960 A
Cwlth Engineering Standards Association, 1922 B
Cwlth and Empire Law Conference, Sydney, 1965 A
Cwlth Employment Service, 1946 A
Cwlth Fellowship Scheme, 1959 D
Cwlth Festival of Arts, London, 1965 C
Cwlth Film Laboratories Ltd, Sydney, 1925 C
Cwlth Film Unit, 1945 C
Cwlth Forestry Bureau, 1930 B
Cwlth Games,
  Auckland, N.Z., 1950 E
  Brisbane, Aust., 1982 A, E
  Cardiff, Wales, 1958 E
  Christchurch, N.Z., 1974 E
  Edinburgh, Scotland, 1970 E
  Edmonton, Canada, 1978 E
  Festival of Empire, England, 1911 E
  Hamilton, Canada, 1930 E
  Kingston, Jamaica, 1966 E
  London, England, 1934 E
  Perth, Aust., 1962 E
  Sydney, Aust., 1938 E
  Vancouver, Canada, 1954 E
Cwlth Games Art Prize, Perth, 1962 C
Cwlth govt, wartime powers, 1940 A
Cwlth Government Line, 1916 A, 1921 B
Cwlth Grants Commission, 1933 A
Cwlth Heads of Govt, CHOGM, Sydney, 1978 A, 1981 A, Melbourne, Canberra, 1981 A
Cwlth Home Savings Grants, 1954 A
Cwlth Hospital Benefit scheme, 1952 A
Cwlth Industrial Gases Ltd, 1935 B
Cwlth Industrial Relations Bureau, 1977 A
Cwlth Institute of Child Health, 1949 B
Cwlth Investigation Branch, CIB, 1919 A, 1945 A
Cwlth Investigation Service, 1960 A
Cwlth Jubilee Art Competition, 1951 C
Cwlth Literary Fund, 1908 C, 1973 C
Cwlth Ministries, *see* Government section A
Cwlth Office of Aboriginal Affairs, 1968 A
Cwlth Office of Education, 1945 D
Cwlth Oil Corporation, 1905 B
Cwlth Pacific Coaxial cable, COMPAC, 1963 B
Cwlth Parlt, 1901 A
Cwlth Parliamentary Association, 1911 A
Cwlth Parliamentary Library, 1901 D
Cwlth Police, 1960 A, 1973 A, 1979 A
Cwlth Police Force, 1917 A
Cwlth Prickly Pear Board, 1920 B
Cwlth Prime Ministers' Conference, London, 1960 A
Cwlth Radium Laboratory, 1929 B
Cwlth Rehabilitation Service, 1948 A
Cwlth Repatriation Committee, 1918 A

763

Cwlth Repatriation Training Scheme, 1944 E, 1947 D, 1949 D
Cwlth Scholarship Scheme, 1949 D
Cwlth Scientific and Industrial Research Organisation, CSIRO, 1949 B, 1951 B, 1956 B, 1957 B, 1963 B, 1964 B, 1967 B, 1968 B, 1970 B, 1972 B, 1974 B, 1975 B, 1977 B, 1980 B, 1981 B
Cwlth Serum Laboratories, 1916 B, 1923 B, 1943 B, 1962 B
Cwlth Shipping Board, 1917 A
Cwlth Solar Observatory, ACT, 1926 B
Cwlth Steamship Owners' Association, 1905 A
Cwlth Tariff Bill, 1902 A
Cwlth Trading Bank, 1960 A
Cwlth Wheat Marketing Scheme, 1915 A
Cwlth Year Book, 1908 C
Communication, outer space, 1962 B
Communications, maritime satellite, 1977 B, 1979 B
Communications, SEACOM cable, 1967 B
Communications, US Naval, NW Cape, 1963 A, B
Communism, 1923 A, 1926 A, 1931 A, 1940 A, 1954 A, 1955 A, D, 1964 A, 1971 A, 1975 A
Communist League, 1975 A
Communist Party of Aust., 1920 A, 1942 A, 1946 A, 1949 A, 1950 A, 1951 A
Communist Party Dissolution Act, 1951 A
Communities, *see section F and individual entries*
Community College of Central Aust., 1979 D
Community Refugee Settlement Scheme, 1982 A
Como House, Melbourne, 1855 C
Companies Act, 1962 A
Company Acts, 1863 A
Company law, uniform, 1960 A
Company Law Amendment Bill, NSW, 1960 A
Company taxes, Qld, 1890 A, WA, 1899 A
Comper Swift monoplane, 1931 B
Complete Account of the Settlement of Port Jackson, A, 1793 C
Compositors, Sydney, 1829 A, 1835 A, 1840 A
Compost, 1973 B
Compostumbler, 1973 B
Comprehensive High Schools, Tas, 1938 B, 1952 D, 1957 D, 1958 D, NSW, 1958 D, WA, 1958 D
Comptoir National d'Escompte de Paris, 1880 A
Compulsory military service, 1915 A, 1916 A, *see also* Conscription
Compulsory military training, 1911 A, 1929 A, 1939 A, *see also* Conscription
Compulsory unionism, 1942 A, 1957 A
Compulsory voting, 1915 A, 1924 A, 1936 A, 1942 A, *see also* Voting
Computer typesetting, 1977 B
Computers, 1956 B, 1959 B, 1984 D
Computing Research Station, 1963 B
Conceptual and lyrical abstraction art, 1970 C
Concert Hall, Arts Centre Melbourne, 1982 C
Concerto and Vocal competition, 1944 C
Concerts, 1826 C
Concerts, Youth, 1947 C
Conciliation, industrial, 1887 A
Conciliation and Arbitration, 1890 A, 1894 A, 1898 A, 1904 A, 1905 A, *see also* Court of
Conciliation and Arbitration Act, 1956 A
Conciliation and Arbitration Commission, 1967 A, 1969 A, 1972 A
Conciliation Commissioners, 1947 A
Concord Council Art Prize, 1956 C
Concrete, 1895 C, 1905 C, 1935 B, 1939 B
'Concrete cancer', 1984 C
Condamine, Qld, 1871 F
Condell, Henry, 1842 A
Conder, Charles, 1868 C, 1888 C
Condobolin, NSW, 1859 F
Condolences of the Season, 1971 C
Condor, 1983 E
Confalonieri, Angelo, 1846 D
Confederation of Aust. Industry, CAI, 1977 A
Confederation of Aust. Motor Sport, 1953 E
Conference of State Road Authorities Association, 1934 B
Confessions of a Beachcomber, 1908 C
Congregational Church, 1798 D, 1810 D, 1830 D, 1833 D, 1837 D, 1838 D, 1842 D, 1974 D, 1977 D
Coniferous timber, 1876 A
Conigrave, Charles P. 1882 A, 1910 A
Coniston massacre, NT, 1938 A
Connolly, Eric, 1880 E
Connolly, J. F. 1890 B
Connor, Joseph T. 1874 C
Connor, Kevin, 1932 C, 1975 C, 1977 C
Connor, Rex F. X. 1974 A, 1975 A
Conolly, Philip, 1820 D, 1821 D, 1826 D, 1839 D
Conscientious objectors, 1968 A
Conscription, 1903 A, 1909 A, 1916 A, 1939 A, 1943 A, 1950 A, 1964 A, *see also* National service *and* Compulsory military service
Conservation, 1788 F, 1863 F, 1882 F, 1923 A, 1938 B, 1944 B, 1965 F, 1969 F, 1978 F, 1982 F, 1984 F
Conservatoriums, 1894 C, 1895 C, 1897 C, 1901 C
Consolidated Press, 1961 F
Conspiracy Act, SA, 1878 A
Constable, William H. A. 1906 C
Constabulary, 1796 A, 1811 A, 1861 A, *see* police
Constitution, Federal, 1881 A, 1891 A, 1895 A, 1897 A, 1898 A, 1899 A, 1901 A
Constitution Act, 1851 D
Constitution Act, WA, 1829 A
Constitution Act Amendment Bill, Qld, 1915 A
Constitution Association, 1848 A
Constitution Bill, NSW, 1853 A
Constitutional convention, Sydney, 1973 A
Constitutional crisis, 1845 A, 1866 A, 1975 A, 1976 A
Constitutions, Colonial, 1853 A, 1855 A, 1856 A, 1881 A, 1889 A, 1890 A
Constructivist painting exhibition, Sydney, 1937 C
Consumer Price Index, 1975 A
Consumer protection, 1835 A, 1964 A
Consumers' Protection Act, Vic, 1964 A
Contemporary Art Societies, 1938 C, 1939 C, 1942 C
Contemporary Canadian Painters Exhibition, 1957 C
'Contemporary Group', Sydney, 1926 C
Contemporary Group of Painters, Melbourne, 1932 C
Contemporary Japanese Art Exhibition, 1958 C
Continental Shelf, 1953 A, 1970 A
Continental Shelf (Living Natural Resources) Act, The, 1968 A, 1970 A
Continuation School for Boys, Adelaide, 1908 D
Contour farming, 1944 B
Contraception, 1904 A, F
Contraceptive pill, 1961 F
Contract bridge, 1932 F, 1951 F
Convention for the Regulation of Aerial Navigation, 1919 B
Convicts,
 arrivals, 1792 A, 1793 A, 1797 A, 1798 A, 1812 A, 1840 A, 1849 A
 assignment, 1789 A, 1800 A, 1826 A, 1838 A, 1839 A
 barracks, Sydney, 1819 A
 conditions, 1832 A
 emancipation, 1790 A, 1792 A, 1828 A
 escapes, 1791 A, F, 1803 A, 1808 F, 1813 F, 1816 F, 1822 F, 1829 F, 1876 F
 exclusion from SA, 1843 A
 farms, 1792 A
 female accommodation, 1821 A
 First Fleet, 1788 A
 floggings, 1800 F, 1817 F, 1818 F, 1833 F, 1835 F
 labour, 1823 A, 1826 A, 1834 A
 Norfolk I., 1790 A, 1805 A, 1814 A, 1825 A, 1853 A, 1856 A
 numbers, 1853 A, 1868 A
 punishment, 1822 F
 revolts, 1797 F, 1804 F, 1806 F, 1826 F, 1831 F, 1834 F, 1846 F
 Second Fleet, 1790 A
 settlement,
 – NSW, 1801 A, 1804 A, 1819 A, 1821 A, 1823 A, 1830 A, 1839 A
 – Qld, 1826 A, 1830 A, 1840 A
 – Tas, 1804 A, 1822 A, 1830 A, 1833 A, 1835 A, 1877 A
 – Vic, 1803 A, 1826 A, 1828 A
 – WA, 1826 A, 1849 A, 1850 A
 Third Fleet, 1791 A
 ticket of leave, 1790 A, 1804 A, 1822 A
 transportation, 1846 A, 1848 A, 1849 A, 1850 A, 1851 A, 1852 A, 1853 A, 1864 A, 1865 A, *see also* transportation
Convict Once, 1871 C
Convict Prevention Act, Vic, 1852 A
Convention for the Regulation of Aerial Navigation, 1919 B
Conyngham, Barry, 1944 C
Conzinc Riotinto, 1949 B
Conzinc Riotinto of Aust. Ltd, CRA, 1962 A
Coober Pedy, SA, 1911 B, 1915 F, 1956 F, 1966 B
Coogee, NSW, 1922 F
'Coogee Bunyip', 1867 E, *see* Kerr, David M.
Cook, Alfred H. 1907 C
Cook, Billy, 1940 E
Cook, E. W. 1844 C
Cook, George, 1898 E
Cook, Hazen K. 1920 C
Cook, Henry, 1854 F
Cook, James (b. 1728), 1822 F, 1969 F, 1970 F
Cook, James (b. 1904), 1904 C
Cook, Joseph, 1860 A, 1901 A, 1908 A, 1913 A, 1914 A, 1917 A, 1927 A
Cook, Peter, 1950 E, 1981 E, 1984 E
Cook, Sidney J. 1965 A
Cook, W. 1941 E, 1945 E

Cook, William D. (b. 1861), 1861 C
Cook, William D. (b. 1936), 1936 C
Cook, W. P. 1804 D
Cook's Cottage, Melbourne, 1934 F
Cooke, Eric E. 1964 F
Cooke, William E. 1863 B
Cooktown, Qld, 1873 F, 1899 F, 1907 F, 1949 F
Coola, NSW, 1890 F
Coolamon, NSW, 1881 F
Coolangatta, Qld, 1885 F, 1949 F
Coolangatta Gold, 1948 C
Coolgardie, WA, 1863 A, 1892 B, F, 1899 A, B, 1904 F
Cooma, NSW, 1849 F
Coombs, Herbert C. 1906 A
Coonabarabran, NSW, 1859 F, 1962 B, 1965 B
Coonamble, NSW, 1855 F
Coonardoo (book), 1929 C
Coonawarra, SA, 1899 F
Cooper, Ashley, 1936 E
Cooper, Dan, 1909 F
Cooper, Daniel, 1853 A
Cooper, Frank A. 1872 A, 1942 A, 1946 A
Cooper, Garry, 1944 E
Cooper, George W. 1912 C
Cooper, Lionel, 1923 E
Cooper, Robert, 1829 B, 1857 A
Cooper, Robert J. 1881 F
Cooper, William, 1868 C
Cooper Basin, SA, 1963 B, 1980 B, 1983 B
Cooper case, 1825 A
Cooper Creek, SA, 1844 A, 1845 A, 1858 A, 1861 A, 1874 A
Co-operatives, 1868 A
Coopers Creek, 1963 C
Cooranbong, NSW, 1897 D
Coorong, SA, 1892 B
Cootamundra, NSW, 1861 F, 1885 F
Coote, Ron, 1945 E
Copeland, Douglas, 1948 D
Copland, Douglas B. 1894 A, 1931 A, 1960 A
Coppelia, 1931 C
Copper,
  NSW, 1829 B, 1870 B, 1939 B
  Qld, 1861 B, 1862 B, 1867 B, 1879 B
  SA, 1842 B, 1844 B, 1845 B, 1859 B, 1860 B, 1861 B
  Tas, 1827 B, 1883 B, 1886 B
  WA, 1846 B
Copper Refinery, Townsville, 1960 B
Copperfield, Qld, 1861 F
Coppers, gas, 1902 F
Coppin, George S. 1819 C, 1843 C, 1845 C, 1855 C, 1862 C, 1872 C
Coppleson, Victor M. 1893 B
Copyright, 1879 C, 1969 A
Copyright Act, Cwlth, 1912 C
Copyright Act, NSW, 1879 C
Copyright Act, 1969 A
Coquette, 1905 C
Coraki, NSW, 1866 F
Coral Sea Battle, 1942 A
Coral Sea Is, 1969 A
Corbett, Henry, 1882 B
Corbett, Thomas G. P. 1959 A
Corcoran, J. D. 1979 A
Cordner, Dennis, 1924 E
Cordner, Don P. 1922 E, 1946 E
Corinella, Vic, 1826 A
Corio Art Prize, Geelong, 1965 C
Corio Bay, Vic, 1824 A
Corio House/Villa, Geelong, 1855 C, 1856 C
Corliss, J. O. 1886 D

Cornforth, Sir John W. 1917 B, 1975 B
Coroners, 1825 F
Corowa, Larry, 1958 E
Corowa, NSW, 1858 F, 1893 A
Corporal Jim Gordon, 1942 C
Corporal punishment, schools, NSW, 1961 D, Vic, 1982 D
Correspondence School, Vic, 1914 D
Corriedale sheep, 1882 B
Corrigan, Tommy, 1894 E
Corroboree, 1946 C, 1950 C
Corroboree at Newcastle, 1817 C
Corrugated iron, 1849 B, 1855 C, 1894 B
Corry, Gail, 1943 E
Corry, Ron, 1940 E
Corryong, Vic, 1879 F
Cosgrove, Robert, 1884 A, 1939 A, 1948 A
Cosier, Gary, 1953 E
Cosme, Paraguay, 1893 A, 1896 D, 1909 A
Cosmopolitan, 1973 F
Cospatrick, 1874 F
Cossack, WA, 1882 B
Costa Rica Packet, 1891 F
Costanzo, Alfredo, 1943 E
Costigan Royal Commission, 1982 A
Cotter, Albert, 1883 E
Cotton,
  NSW, 1799 A, 1828 A, 1856 A, 1923 A, 1961 A, 1963 B
  Qld, 1845 A, 1860 A, 1863 A, 1871 A, 1890 B
  WA, 1862 A
Cotton, Alfred J. 1861 A
Cotton, Frank S. 1890 B, 1940 B, 1946 B
Cotton, John, 1801 A
Cotton, Leo A. 1883 C
Cotton, Sidney, 1894 B, 1916 B
Cotton Aerodynamic Anti-Gravity suit, 1940 B
Cotton exports, 1854 A, 1862 A
Cough, June M. 1929 C
Coughlan, Frank, 1903 C, 1925 C
Council for Aboriginal Affairs, 1968 D
Council for Aboriginal Rights, NT, 1966 A
Council of Adult Education, CAE, Vic, 1947 D
Council for the Advancement of Aust. Art, 1940 C
Council of Aust. Humanist Societies, 1965 F
Council of the College of Surgeons of Australasia, 1927 B
Council of Defence, 1904 A
Council for the Defence of Govt Schools, DOGS, Melbourne, 1966 D
Council of Education, NSW, 1866 D
Council for the Encouragement of Music and the Arts, CEMA, 1946 C
Council of NT education, 1979 D
Council for Scientific and Industrial Research, CSIR, 1926 B, 1938 B, 1948 B, 1949 B
Council of Social Services, NSW, 1935 A
Counihan, Noel J. 1913 C
Countdown, 1974 C
Counter Espionage Bureau, 1915 A
Counties, Nineteen, *see* Nineteen Counties
Counties, Tas, limits of, 1804 A
Country Party, Aust.,
  National, 1918 A, 1920 A, 1926 A, 1934 A, 1971 A, 1974 A
  States, 1914 A, 1917 A, 1918 A, 1982 A
Country Women's Association, 1879 F, 1922 F, 1977 F
Couper, Gail, 1948 E

Courage brewery, 1966 A
Courier, Jack, 1915 C
Courier Mail, Brisbane, 1933 F
Coursing, 1865 E, 1867 E, 1873 E, 1876 E, 1897 E *see* Greyhound racing
Court, Charles W. M. 1911 A, 1974 A
Courtald Collection, 1984 C
Court, Margaret, 1942 E, 1963 E, 1969 E, 1970 E, 1973 E
Courtneidge, Diane C. 1893 C
Courts,
  Aust. wide,
  – Children's, 1918 A
  – Conciliation and Arbitration, 1904 A, 1905 A, 1906 A, 1913 A, 1930 A, 1937 A, 1939 A, 1947 A, 1953 A, 1954 A, 1957 A, 1959 A, 1967 A
  – Family Law, 1976 A
  – Federal, of Aust., 1976 A
  – High, 1902 A
  – Industrial, 1956 A, 1974 A
  – International, 1958 A
  NSW, 1788 A, 1814 A, 1823 A, 1824 A, 1825 A, 1829 A; 1858 A, 1982 A
  Qld, 1850 A, 1857 A, 1859 A
  SA, 1839 A
  Tas, 1819 A, 1821 A, 1822 A, 1824 A
  Vic, 1838 A, 1839 A, 1841 A, 1852 A
  WA, 1832 A, 1861 A
Cousin from Fiji, The, 1945 C
Coutts, Gordon, 1875 C
Couvreur, Madame, *see* Huybers, J. C.
Covell, Roger D. 1931 C
Covent Garden, 1926 C
Covent Garden restaurant, Adelaide, 1948 F
Covent Garden Russian Ballet, 1938 C
Coventry, Gordon, 1901 E
Coventry, Sydney, 1900 E, 1927 E
Cover, James F. 1798 D, 1834 D
Cow Pasture Road, The, 1920 C
Cowan, Edith D. 1861 A, 1921 A
Cowan, Frederick, 1888 C
Cowan, Peter W. 1914 C
Cowan, Theodora, 1868 C
Cowell, SA, 1975 F
Cowen, Zelman, 1919 A, 1977 A
Cowie, Len, 1925 E
Cowley, John, 1946 B
Cowpastures, NSW, 1795 A
Cowper, NSW, 1919 A
Cowper, Charles, 1807 A, 1856 A, 1857 A, 1861 A, 1865 A, 1870 A
Cowper, Henry, 1823 B
Cowper, William, 1809 D, 1818 D, 1858 D
Cowper, William M. 1810 D
Cowra, NSW, 1846 F, 1893 B, 1944 A
Cox, Henry, 1824 A
Cox, James E. 1832 B
Cox, James C. 1834 B
Cox, J. H. 1789 A
Cox, Leonard B. 1894 B, 1951 B
Cox, Lionel, 1941 E
Cox, Peter I. 1913 C
'Cox, Sammy', *see* Jervis, S. E.
Cox, William, 1797 A, 1814 A, 1815 B, 1837 A
Coxen, Charles, 1809 A
Coxen, Henry W. 1823 A
Coxon, Lynall, 1977 E
Crabbe, Chris W. 1934 C
Crabbe, Douglas E. 1983 F
Craboon, NSW, 1910 F
Cracknell, S. 1879 E
Cracow, Qld, 1932 B
Crafers, SA, 1839 F

765

Craig, Ian, 1935 E, 1952 E
Craig, Sybil, 1901 C
Cramphorn, Rex, 1945 C
Crampton, Bruce S. 1935 E
Cranbourne, Vic, 1852 F
Cranbrook, Tas, 1821 F
Crapp, Lorraine, 1938 E, 1956 E
Crawford, Hector W. 1913 C
Crawford, John G. 1910 A, 1981 A
Crawford, John H. 1908 E, 1933 E
Crawford, Leonard G. 1920 C
Crawford, Raymond M. 1906 D
Crawl, Aust., swimming stroke, 1902 E
Crayfish, WA, 1944 A
Creaghe, Emily, C. 1860 A
Cream separator, 1888 B
Creaser, Marlene, 1932 C
Creative Effort, 1920 C
Creche and Kindergarten Association of Qld, 1906 D
Credit squeeze, national, 1956 A, 1961 A
Creeve Roe, *see* Daley, Victor
Crematoriums, 1903 C
Cremin, Eric J. 1914 E
Cress, Frederick, 1938 C
Creswell, HMAS, 1915 A, 1958 A
Creswell, William R. 1852 A, 1904 A
Creswick, Vic, 1852 F, 1882 F
Cressy Co., 1826 A
Cribb, Benjamin, 1807 A
Cribb, James C. 1856 A
Cribb, Robert, 1805 A
Cribb, Thomas B. 1845 A
Crick, William P. 1862 A
Cricket,
　Aboriginals, 1866 E, 1868 E
　Ashes, 1882 E
　Aust. Board of Control, 1905 E
　Benaud, Richie, 1957 E, *see also individual entry*
　bodyline bowling, 1932 E, 1933 E, 1935 E
　Bradman, Donald, 1928 E, *see also individual entry*
　Canada, 1878 E
　Chappell controversy, 1981 E
　clubs, *see individual entries*
　early, 1803 E, 1826 E, 1830 E, 1832 E, 1835 E, 1839 E, 1846 E, 1861 E, 1878 E
　hat tricks, 1879 E, 1903 E, 1912 E
　Intercolonial matches, 1851 E, 1856 E
　night, 1977 E
　overs, 1887 E, 1918 E
　pads and gloves, 1832 E
　round arm bowling, 1843 E
　scoring, 1867 E, 1922 E, 1930 E
　Sheffield Shield, 1892 E
　silly mid-on, 1878 E
　Test, 1877 E, 1880 E, 1902 E, 1910 E, 1930 E, 1934 E, 1938 E, 1946 E, 1947 E, 1948 E, 1952 E, 1955 E, 1956 E, 1960 E, 1961 E, 1964 E, 1969 E, 1971 E, 1977 E, 1983 E
　Trumper, Victor, 1899 E, *see also individual entry*
　USA, 1878 E
　Women's, 1874 E, 1890 E, 1923 E, 1934 E, 1937 E, 1949 E
　World Cup Series, 1975 E, 1977 E, 1979 E
Cricko, 1935 E
Crighton, Richard B. 1935 C
Crime, 1844 F, 1980 F, 1982 A, *see section F*
Crime, Statistics and Research, Bureau of, NSW, 1972 A
Crimean War, 1854 A
Crimean war relief fund, 1856 F

Crimes Act, Federal, 1914 A, 1926 A, 1949 A, 1950 A
Criminal Codes, 1901 A, 1902 A, 1924 A
Criminal Law Amendment Act, Tas, 1889 A
Criminology Research Council, 1973 A
Cripps, H. 1893 E
Cripps, Peter, 1948 C
Critchley, Thomas K. 1916 A
Criterion Theatre, Sydney, 1886 C
Critic, The, Perth, 1961 C
Critics' Prize for Contemporary Art, Sydney, 1955 C
Crittle, Peter, 1940 E
Croatian extremists, 1972 F, 1973 A
Crocker, Walter R. 1902 A, 1977 A
'Croesus of the S. Hemisphere', 1805 A
Crohamhurst Observatory, Qld, 1893 F
Croke, James, 1839 A
Croll, Robert H. 1869 C
Crombie, Donald, 1976 C
Cronin, Michael, 1952 E
Cronulla-Sutherland Rugby League Club, 1952 E
Crook, William P. 1811 D, 1813 D, 1846 D
Crooke, Ray A. 1922 C, 1969 C
Crooked Snake, The, 1954 C
Crookwell, NSW, 1860 F
Croquet, 1868 E
Croquet Associations, 1908 E
Cross, Ronald H. 1951 A
Cross, Stan, 1888 C, 1919 F
Cross, Zora B. M. 1890 C
Crossley, Ada J., 1871 C, 1874 C, 1903 C
Crossley, George, 1823 A, 1932 C
Crossley Print Gallery, Melbourne, 1966 C
Crothall, Ross, 1933 C, 1962 C
Crouch, James J. 1830 F
Crouch Art Prize, Ballarat, 1927 C
Crouch start, athletics, 1884 E
Crowds, rugby union, Sydney, 1907 E
Crowe, Irwin, 1903 C
Crowley, Grace A. W. 1896 C, 1932 C
Crown Colony, NSW, 1824 A
Crown Land, 1824 A, 1829 A, 1831 A, 1839 A, 1842 A, 1847 A, 1851 A, 1853 A, 1860 A, 1861 A, 1862 A, 1869 A, 1884 A
Crown of Thorns, 1960 B, 1967 F, 1970 B, 1971 B
Crown of Wattle, A, 1888 C
Crow's Nest, Qld, 1875 F
Crowther, Edward L. 1843 B
Crowther, William, 1788 B
Crowther, William E. L. H. 1887 B
Crowther, William L. 1817 B, 1878 A
Croydon, Qld, 1885 F, 1906 F
Crozier, Frank R. 1883 C
Crump, Phillip, 1952 E
Cryer, Enid, 1930 C
Crystal Brook, SA, 1878 F
Crystal radio sets, 1924 B
Crystal (research), 1915 B
C.S. (poem), 1804 C
Cubism, 1910 C
Cubs, Wolf, 1915 F
Cuckooz Country, 1932 C
Cudal, NSW, 1860 F
Cue, WA, 1891 B, 1892 F
Cugley, Ian R. 1945 C
Culcairn, NSW, 1848 F
Culgoora, NSW, 1964 B, 1967 B
Cullen, William P. 1855 A, 1913 A, 1917 A, 1923 A, 1930 A
Cullen Bullen Lime and Cement Co., 1883 B
Cullin-la-ringo station, Qld, 1861 A

Culotta, Nino, *see* O'Grady, John
Cultivator disc, 1909 B
Cultivators, 1916 B
Culwulla Chambers, Sydney, 1912 C
Cumberland, 1797 F, 1801 A
Cumberland College of Health Sciences, 1973 B
Cumberland County Council, Sydney, 1945 C, 1949 C, 1963 C
Cumbrae-Stewart, Francis W. S. 1865 A
Cumbrae-Stewart, Janet A. 1883 C
Cumming, Derek R. 1917 B, 1946 B
Cummings, Elisabeth, 1934 C
Cummings, J. Bartholomew, 1928 E, 1974 E, 1975 E
Cumming Smith and Co., 1878 B
Cummins, John E. 1902 B
Cumpston, John H. L. 1880 B
Cunderdin, WA, 1895 F
Cunnamulla, Qld, 1862 F, 1886 B
Cunningham, Allan, 1791 A, 1812 A, 1823 A, 1825 A, 1827 A
Cunningham, A. W. H. 1879 F
Cunningham, Edward S. 1859 F
Cunningham, Richard, 1793 B
Cunningham's Gap, Qld, 1827 A
Curate in Bohemia, A, 1913 C
Curet, Joseph, 1859 C
Curl Curl, NSW, 1903 B
Curlew Camp, Sydney, 1890 C
Curlewis, Adrian H. 1901 A
Curlewis, Herbert R. 1869 A
Curley, Terry, 1938 E
Curr, Edward, 1798 A, 1826 A
Curr, Edward M. 1820 B, 1886 C
Curr, Frederick C. 1865 A
Currency, 1800 A, 1813 A, 1824 A, 1826 A, 1829 A, 1842 A, 1849 A, 1852 A, 1866 A, 1910 A, 1913 A, 1931 A, 1937 A, 1945 A, 1949 A, 1960 A, 1963 A, 1966 A, 1969 A, 1972 A, 1973 A, 1974 A, 1976 A, 1982 A, 1984 F
Currency Lad, Sydney, 1832 F
Currency lads and lasses, 1788 D
Currency Lass, The, 1844 C
Current affairs, 1860 C
Currey, Charles H. 1890 D
Curricula, education, 1938 D, 1967 D, 1968 D, 1983 D
Currie, Mark J. 1823 A, 1829 A
Curtin, John J. 1928 A, 1935 A, 1941 A, 1943 A
Curtin School of Medical Research, Canberra, 1948 B
Curtis, James W. 1839 C
Curtis, Robert E. 1899 C
Curtis, Robert L. 1929 C
Curtis gold nugget, 1867 F
Curtiss bi-plane, 1917 B
Cusack, E. Dymphna, 1902 C, 1935 C, 1936 C, 1951 C, 1967 C, 1969 C, 1971 C
Cusack, Edith E. 1865 C
Custance, F. 1910 B
Custance, John D. 1842 B, 1881 B
Customs, 1827 A, 1967 F
Customs duties, SA, 1857 A, 1984 A
Customs and excise duties, 1800 A
Customs House, Rockhampton, 1890 C, 1898 C
Customs House, Sydney, 1800 A, 1885 C
Cuthbert, Elizabeth (Betty), 1938 E, 1956 E
Cuthbertson, Arch. F. 1924 C
Cuthbertson, James L. 1851 C
Cutlack, Frederick M. 1886 D
Cutler, A. Roden, 1916 A, 1966 A
Cutolo, Cesare S. F. 1826 C
Cut-Rate Kingdom, The, 1980 C

Cutts, J. 1861 E, 1862 E
Cutty Sark, 1873 F
Cwlth, *see* Commonwealth
Cyanide, 1891 B
Cycling, 1869 E, 1881 E, 1887 E, 1888 E, 1889 E, 1891 E, 1895 E, 1896 E, 1900 F, 1920 E, 1922 E, 1949 E, 1953 E
Cyclones,
  NSW, 1893 F, 1947 F, 1950 F, 1962 F, 1964 F, 1966 F
  NT, 1878 F, 1882 F, 1897 F, 1917 F, 1923 F, 1937 F, 1965 F, 1974 F
  Qld, 1867 F, 1870 F, 1876 F, 1878 F, 1883 B, 1884 F, 1888 F, 1893 F, 1896 F, 1898 F, 1899 F, 1903 F, 1906 F, 1907 F, 1918 F, 1920 F, 1927 F, 1934 F, 1937 F, 1940 F, 1947 F, 1949 F, 1955 F, 1956 F, 1958 F, 1959 F, 1963 F, 1964 F, 1966 F, 1970 F, 1971 F, 1972 F, 1973 F, 1979 F
  SA, 1935 F
  Vic, 1918 F, 1966 F
  WA, 1904 F, 1910 F, 1921 F, 1925 F, 1934 F, 1939 F, 1945 F, 1960 F, 1973 F, 1978 F, 1979 F, 1980 F, 1984 F
Cyclones, naming of, 1887 B, 1975 B
Cyclone Tracy, 1974 F
Cyclopaedia of Australasia, 1881 D
Cygnet, Tas, 1835 F
Cypriot, The, 1940 C
Cyprus, 1829 F
Czech Philharmonic Orchestra, 1959 C
Czechoslovak Consul-General, 1969 A

D

D Notice, 1852 A
Dad and Dave, 1936 C
Dad and Dave Come to Town, 1938 C
Dad in Politics, 1908 C
Dadswell, Lyndon, 1908 C
Daglish, Henry, 1866 A, 1904 A
Daily Advertiser, NSW, 1868 F
Daily Examiner, NSW, 1859 F
Daily Guardian, Sydney, 1923 F
Daily Herald, Adelaide, 1910 F
Daily Mail, Brisbane, 1933 F
Daily Mail, Sydney, 1922 F
Daily Mirror, Sydney, 1941 F
Daily News, Vic, 1839 F
Daily News, WA, 1882 F
Daily News and Evening Chronicle, Sydney, 1848 F
Daily Pictorial, Sydney, 1879 F
Daily Standard, Brisbane, 1912 F
Daily Sun, Brisbane, 1982 F
Daily Telegraph, Sydney, 1879 F
Daily Telegraph, Melbourne, 1869 F
Daintree, 1984 F
Daintree, Richard, 1832 B, 1859 B
Dairying, 1795 A, 1800 A, 1820 A, 1942 A, *see also* Cattle
Dakin, William J. 1883 B
Dala Massacre, NT, 1938 A
Dalby, Qld, 1842 F, 1877 D, 1879 A
Dale, Robert, 1830 A
Dale, Reginald, 1915 E
Daley, Victor J. W. P. 1858 C, 1898 C, 1901 C
Dalgarno, Isabella, 1805 A
Dalgarno, Roy F. L. 1910 C

Dalgety, NSW, 1904 A, 1908 A
Dalgety, Frederick G. 1817 A, 1846 A
Dalgety and Co., 1846 A
Dalhousie (ship), 1853 F
Dallas, Roderic S. 1891 A
Dalley, William B. 1831 A, 1861 A, 1886 A
Dalley-Scarlett, Robert, 1887 C
Dallwitz, David F. 1914 C
Dallwitz, John C. 1941 C
Dalman, Elizabeth, 1965 C
Dalray, 1952 E
Dalrymple, Alexander, 1808 B
Dalrymple, George A. F. E. 1826 A, 1859 A
Dalton, Judy, 1937 E
Dalwood vineyards, NSW, 1828 A
Daly, Dominick, 1798 A, 1862 A
Daly, Edward A. 1901 A
Daly, Thomas, 1913 A
Daly R., NT, 1878 A
Daly Waters, NT, 1872 F, 1967 F
Dam Busters, The, 1951 C
Damascus, Syria, 1918 A
Dame Pattie, 1967 E
Dampier, WA, 1965 F, 1970 B
Dampier, Alfred, 1848 C, 1886 C, 1889 C, 1894 C, 1896 C
Dams, 1857 B, *see individual entries*
Dan, Barry, 1851 C
Dana, Henry E. P. 1820 A, 1842 A
Danaher, Phyllis, 1937 C
Dance, free wheeling, Tango, 1914 C, *see also individual entries*
Dance, Geoffrey, 1930 C
Dance Co. of NSW, 1961 C
Dance Drama Group, Sydney, 1955 C
Dance Exchange, 1976 C
Dandenong, 1876 F
Dandenong Festival of Music and Art for Youth, 1955 C
Dandenong Ranges, Vic, 1962 F
Dandré-Levitoff Russian Ballet, 1934 C
Dangar, Albert A. 1840 A
Dangar, Henry, 1796 A, 1847 B
Dangar, Henry C. 1830 A
Dangar, William, 1847 B
Daniell, Richard, 1833 A, 1834 A
Danielson, Larry B. 1980 F, 1981 F
Danko, Alexsander, 1950 C
Dann, George L. 1904 C
Dannevig, Harold, 1908 A
Daphine, Lillian M. 1897 C
Daplyn, Alfred J. 1844 C
D'Arcy, Constance E. 1879 B
Darcy, J. Leslie, 1895 E, 1916 E
Dardanelles, First World War, 1915 A
Darey, James, 1915 E
Dargie, William A. 1912 C, 1941 C, 1942 C, 1945 C, 1946 C, 1947 C, 1950 C, 1952 C, 1956 C
Dark, Eleanor, 1901 C, 1934 C, 1936 C, 1941 C, 1948 C, 1953 C
Dark Felt, 1943 E
Darley, Frederick, 1893 A, 1895 A, 1899 A, 1900 A, 1901 A
Darling, Charles H. 1809 A, 1863 A, 1866 A
Darling, Eliza, 1837 C
Darling, Harold G. 1885 A
Darling, Hugh, 1855 D
Darling, James R. 1899 D
Darling, John, (1), 1831 A
Darling, John, (2), 1852 A
Darling, Joseph, 1870 E
Darling, Ralph, 1825 A, 1826 A, 1827 A, 1830 A, 1858 A
Darling, Rick, 1957 E
Darling, Stanley, 1907 A

Darling Downs, Qld, 1827 A, 1840 A, 1844 A, 1848 A, 1849 A, 1852 A, 1867 B
Darling Downs Star, Qld, 1955 F
Darling R., NSW, 1828 A, 1829 A, 1835 A, 1853 B, 1859 A, 1872 F, 1886 B, 1890 F
Darling River bulk ore carrier, 1965 B
Darlinghurst, NSW, 1844 F
Darlinghurst Art Gallery, Sydney, 1965 C
Darlinghurst jail, NSW, 1867 A
Darlington Commodities, Sydney, 1981 F
Darrell, George, 1851 C, 1883 C
Darriwell, 1879 E
Dart, Raymond A. 1893 B
Darwin, NT, 1869 A, F, 1871 B, 1878 B, 1884 B, 1897 F, 1911 A, 1917 F, 1919 B, 1920 B, 1928 B, 1936 E, 1937 F, 1941 B, 1943 A, 1948 B, 1952 F, 1969 E, 1970 B, F, 1974 F, 1982 A
Darwin, Charles R. 1836 B
Darwin, Japanese bombing of, 1942 A, 1943 A
Darwin Arts Society, 1963 C
Darwin Community College, 1972 D
Darwin Museum and Art Gallery, 1970 D
Dashwood, C. J. 1892 A
Data transmission service, 1963 B
Daub (magazine), 1952 C
Davenport, Stuart, 1858 A
Davey, Edward, 1806 B
Davey, Jack, 1931 C
Davey, John A. (Jack), 1910 C
Davey, Thomas, 1813 A, 1823 A
David, Allen, 1926 C
David, T. W. Edgeworth, 1858 B, 1886 B, 1908 A, 1909 A
David Jones Art Gallery, 1944 C
David Jones stores, 1838 A
Davidson, Alan K. 1929 E
Davidson, Alfred C. 1882 A
Davidson, Bessie, 1879 C
Davidson, Edward J. 1899 D
Davidson, Frank D. 1946 C
Davidson, James, 1885 B
Davidson, Jim, 1933 C, 1935 C
Davidson, John E. 1841 A
Davidson, Maxwell, 1853 D
Davidson, Owen, 1943 E
Davidson, Walter E. 1918 A
Davies, David, 1864 C
Davies, G. L. 1925 F
Davies, H. E. 1853 C
Davies, John, (1), 1813 A
Davies, John, (2), 1929 E
Davies, L. W. 1979 B
Davies, Matthew H. 1850 A
Davies, Peter M. 1934 C
Davis (Antarctica), 1957 B
Davis, Alexander B. 1828 D
Davis, Arthur H. 1868 C, 1899 C, 1903 C, 1904 C, 1906 C, 1908 C, 1909 C, 1911 C, 1912 C, 1916 C, 1926 C
Davis, Barry, 1949 E
Davis, C. H. 1815 D
Davis, Dwight F. 1900 E
Davis, D. 1924 B
Davis, Edward, 1816 A, 1839 F
Davis, George A. D. 1930 C
Davis, Greg, 1939 E
Davis, John, 1936 C
Davis, John K. 1884 B
Davis, Owen L. 1912 A
Davis, S. 1864 E
Davis, W. 1866 E

767

Davis Cup, tennis, 1900 E, 1905 E, 1912 E, 1924 E, 1929 E, 1939 E, 1955 E, 1963 E
Davis research station, 1957 B
Davison, Frank D. 1893 C, 1931 C
Davison, Lex, 1924 E
Dawe, Bruce, 1930 C, 1971 C
Dawes, H. W. 1894 E
Dawes, Nathaniel, 1843 D, 1897 D
Dawes, William, 1788 B, 1789 A, 1790 A, 1791 A, 1836 B
Dawes Battery, Sydney, 1790 B
Dawes Point, Sydney Cove, 1788 B
Dawn, Gloria, 1929 C
Dawn, Norman, 1931 C
Dawn: A Journal for Australian Women, Sydney, 1888 F
Dawn of European Civilization, The, 1925 B
Daws, Lawrence, 1927 C
Dawson, Andrew, 1863 A, 1899 A
Dawson, Daryl M. 1982 A
Dawson, Janet, 1935 C, 1973 C
Dawson, Peter, 1882 C, 1904 C
Dawson, Richard, 1845 C
Dawson, Robert, 1824 A, 1866 A
Dawson, Robert B. 1815 A
Day, Edward D. 1801 A
Day, J. 1870 E
Day, The, 1914 C
Day of the Dog, The, 1981 C
Daybreak, 1932 C
Daylesford, Vic, 1852 F, 1857 A
Daylight saving, 1916 F, 1942 F, 1967 F, 1971 F
Days of Disillusion, 1926 C
D.D.T. (insecticide), 1950 B
De Bavay, Auguste J. F., 1856 B
De Burgh, Ernest M. 1863 B
De Castell, Cavendish, 1833 C
De Castella, Robert, 1981 E, 1982 E, 1983 E
De Chair, Dudley R. S. 1924 A
De Clario, Domenico, 1947 C
De Crespigny, *see* Champion de Crespigny
De Dion Voiturette, 1893 B
De Freycinet, Louis C. de S., 1819 A, 1842 A
De Garis, Clement J. 1884 A
De Grey R., WA, 1863 A
De Groot, Francis E. 1888 A, 1932 A
De Havilland Aircraft Co. Ltd., 1928 B
De Havilland, Hereward, 1929 E
De La Salle Brothers, 1906 D
De L'Isle, Lord, See Sidney, William P.
De Maistre, Leroy L. L. J. (Roy), 1919 C, 1924 C
De Mole, L. 1912 B
De Silva, F. K. 1913 C
De Strzelecki, Paul, *see* Strzelecki, Paul de
De Teliga, Stan, 1924 C
Deacon, Bert, 1947 E
Dead Timber, 1911 C
Dead Man Rising, 1951 C
Deaf, 1860 D, 1943 B, 1979 B
Deaf and Dumb, 1872 B
Deakin, Alfred, 1856 A, 1886 A, 1903 A, 1905 A, 1906 A, 1908 A, 1909 A, 1910 A
Deakin University, Vic, 1887 D, 1974 D, 1978 D
Deamer, M. E. K. Dulcie, 1890 C
Dean, Alf, 1959 E
Dean, Horace, *see* Haskell, William T.
Dean, Rosalie, 1890 E
Dean, R. L. 1964 A
Dean, William, 1858 B
Deane, Jimmy, 1927 E

Deane, John P. 1796 C, 1822 C, 1834 C, 1837 C
Deane, William, 1982 A
Death duties, 1870 A, 1897 A, 1977 A
Death penalty, 1955 A, 1973 A
Debenham, Frank, 1882 B, 1925 B
Debenham, Mike, 1973 B
Debit Tax, 1982 A
Decathlon, 1983 E
Decentralization of industry, Vic, 1973 A
Dechaineux, Lucien, 1870 C
Decimal currency, 1937 A, 1960 A, 1963 A, 1966 A
Deck, Norman C. 1882 B
Declaration of war on Germany, 1939 A
Decoration Galleries, Melbourne, 1920 C
Dedman suit, 1942 F
Deeds, registration of, 1800 A
Deeming, Frederick, 1853 F
Deer, 1808 F
Deeral, Eric, 1974 A
Deeral, Qld, 1936 F
Deeson, John, 1869 F
Defamation, NSW, 1958 A
Defamation law, 1979 A
Defections, 1954 A, 1969 A
Defence, 1845 A, 1854 A, 1856 A, 1857 A, 1862 A, 1877 A, 1883 A, 1884 A, 1888 A, 1889 A, 1890 A, 1894 A, 1904 A, 1909 A, 1910 A, 1914 A, 1938 A, 1939 A, 1959 A, 1963 A, 1964 A, 1965 A, 1973 A, 1975 A, *see also* Aust. Forces, Army, Air Force, Navy, *and* Military
Defence Act, Federal, 1903 A, 1904 A, 1912 A
Defence, ANZUS Pact, 1951 A
Defence, Five Power Agreement, 1971 A
Defence Corps, voluntary, 1940 A, 1942 A
Defence Force Re-organization Act, 1975 A
Defence of Govt Schools, DOGS, 1966 D, 1981 D
Defence Notice, 1852 A
Defries, Colin, 1909 B
Degan, William, 1932 C
Degraves, Peter, 1832 A, 1852 B
Deirdre in Exile (opera), 1928 C
Delacombe, Rohan, 1963 A
Delegate, NSW, 1840 F
Dellit, Bruce, 1930 C
Deloraine, Tas, 1831 F, 1868 B, 1871 B
Delprat, Guillaume D. 1856 B
Delta, 1951 E
Demery, Felix, 1935 C
Demobilization, 1947 A
Democratic Labor Party, DLP, 1956 A, 1957 A, 1958 A, 1962 A, 1978 A
Democrats, Aust., political party, 1977 A
Demonstration, Federal, 1899 A
Demonstrations, laws, Qld, 1967 A
Demonstrations, anti-strike, 1981 A
Dempsey, Frank, 1899 E
Dempsey, Gary, 1949 E, 1975 E
Dempsey, Gregory J. 1931 C
Dempsey, Joe, 1915 F
Dengue fever, 1905 B, 1908 B
Denham, Digby F. 1859 A, 1911 A
Denichy, Daniel H. 1828 C, 1853 A
Deniliquin, NSW, 1845 B, 1848 F, 1876 B
Denison, William T. 1804 A, 1847 A, 1855 A, B
Denman, Thomas, 1874 A, 1911 A
Denman, Lady, 1913 F
Denman, Lord, *see* Denman, Thomas
Denmark, WA, 1845 F
Dennis, Claire, 1916 E

Dennis, Clarence M. J. 1876 C, 1906 C, 1913 C, 1915 C, 1916 C, 1917 C, 1918 C, 1921 C
Dennis, Elwyn, 1941 C
Denominational Schools, NSW, 1840 D
Dent, Aileen R. 1890 C
Dental Act, Tas, 1884 B
Dental College, Vic, 1892 B
Dental Standards, 1947 B
Dentistry, 1830 B, 1884 B, 1885 B, 1892 B, 1901 B
Dentists, 1818 B
D'Entrecasteaux, Joseph A. R. de B. 1792 A, 1793 A
D'Entrecasteaux channel, Tas, 1802 A, 1835 F
Departments, *see also* Commonwealth
Dept of Aboriginal Affairs, 1968 A, 1972 A
Dept of Civil Aviation, 1938 B, 1973 B
Dept of Defence, 1973 A
Dept of Education and Science, 1966 D
Dept of the Environment, 1973 A
Dept of the Environment, Aborigines and Arts, 1971 A
Dept of External Affairs, 1970 A
Dept of Foreign Affairs, 1970 A
Dept of Interior, 1932 A
Dept of the Media, 1972 F
Dept of Post-War Construction, 1942 A
Dept of Repatriation, 1919 A
Dept of Science, 1973 A
Dept of Territories, 1951 A
Dept of Trade, 1956 A
Dept of Shipping and Transport, 1973 B
Dept of Urban and Regional Development, DURD, 1973 C
Dept of Veteran Affairs, 1919 A
Departure Tax, 1978 A
Depression, economic *see* Economic depression
Derby, WA, 1880 F, 1921 F, 1922 B
Derby tin mine, Tas, 1929 F
Derrick, Edward H. 1898 B
Derrick, Thomas C. 1914 A
Derrimut, 1835 A, 1864 A
Derrinallum, Vic, 1867 F
Derry Castle, 1887 F
Derwent Power Development scheme, 1952 B
Derwent R., Tas, 1789 A, 1792 A, 1793 A, 1794 A, 1803 A, 1809 F, 1813 F, 1816 B, 1827 E, 1832 C, 1843 B, 1964 B
Derwent Sailing Boat Club, 1874 E
Derwent Star and Van Diemen's Land Intelligencer, 1810 F
Derwent Valley, Tas, 1940 F, 1960 F
Desbrowe Annear, 1921 C
Desbrowe-Annear, Harold, 1866 C
Descubierta, 1793 B
Desert Flame opal, 1969 F
Desert People, 1965 C
Detective's Album ... Australian Police Officer, The, 1871 C
Dethridge, John S. 1865 B, 1910 B
Dettman, H. W. 1969 D
Dettman Committee enquiry, WA, 1969 D
Devaney, James, 1890 C
Devanny, Jean, 1936 C
Development and Migration Commission, 1926 A, 1929 A
Devil's Advocate, The, 1959 C
Devil's Coachhouse, 1838 A
Devil's Playground, The, 1976 C
Devine, Edward, 1833 A
Devine, Hugh B. 1878 B
Devitt, John, 1937 E

Devlin, Bruce W. 1937 E
Devlin, Kerry W. 1944 E
Devlin, Stuart L. 1931 C
Devon cattle, 1820 A
Devon Downs Aboriginal carvings, SA, 1926 C
Devonport, Tas, 1888 F, 1904 B, 1906 B
Devonport Art Prize, Tas, 1962 C
Dew, Harold R. 1891 B
Dexter, Caroline, 1819 A
Dexter, David St A. 1917 A
Dexter, William, 1818 C, 1855 C
Dhiel, L. 1899 B
Diabolo, 1908 E
Diamantina Cocktail, 1977 C
Diamantina R., Qld & SA, 1875 A
Diamond, Dick, 1953 C
Diamond, John, 1961 E
Diamond drill, 1876 B
Diamond International softball tournament, 1960 E
Diamonds, 1851 B, 1867 B, 1905 F, 1977 B
Diana, 1936 C
Dibbs, G. R. 1834 A, 1885 A, 1889 A, 1891 A
Dickens, Peter, 1969 E
Dickerson, Robert H. 1924 C, 1954 C
Dickinson, John N. 1806 A, 1842 A
Dickson, James A. C. 1836 C
Dickson, James R. 1832 A, 1898 A
Dictation test, 1901 A, 1905 A, 1958 A
Dictionary of Aust. Slang, 1945 C
Didham, E. 1970 E
Die Deutsche Post ... Kolonien, Adelaide, 1848 F
Dietitian, 1938 B
Dietrich, Amalie, 1821 B
Difficult Young Man, A, 1955 C
Digby, Desmond, 1933 C
Digger Smith, 1918 C
Diggers, *see* gold miners
Diggers, The, 1854 C
'Diggers Parliament', 1856 A
Diggers Rest, Vic, 1910 B
Diggles, Silvester, 1817 C
Digit Dick on the Barrier Reef, 1942 C
'Dilley Dalley', 1831 A
Dillon, Cyril, 1880 C
Dillon, Peter, 1789 A, 1826 A
Dimboola, (painting), 1943 C
Dimboola, 1969 C
Dimier, Aurelia, 1855 C
Dimmack, Max, 1922 C
Dingle, T. 1984 C
'Dinks and Onkus', 1919 C
Dinsdale, James, 1866 C
Dionysii, 1820 D
Diphtheria, 1858 F, 1928 F
Diplomatic relations/representation:
  Argentina, 1961 A
  Austria, 1964 A
  Denmark, 1974 A
  EEC, 1960 A
  Egypt, 1959 A
  England, 1909 A
  France, 1973 A
  German Democratic Republic, 1972 A
  Greece, 1964 A, 1965 A
  Ireland, 1965 A, 1974 A
  Japan, 1952 A, 1953 A
  Korea, 1961 A
  Laos, 1962 A
  Malta, 1966 A
  Mexico, 1966 A
  New Zealand, 1971 A
  People's Republic of China, 1972 A
  Singapore, 1965 A

  Soviet Union, 1943 A, 1954 A, 1959 A, 1964 A
  Spain, 1963 A
  Switzerland, 1961 A
  Taiwan, 1972 A
  UNESCO, 1978 A
  United Arab Republic, 1961 A
  USA, 1937 A, 1940 A, 1946 A
  Vietnam S. 1959 A, 1975 A
  West Germany, 1952 A
Diplomatic representation in Aust., 1936 A
Diprotodon, SA, 1892 B
Direction 1 Exhibition, Sydney, 1956 C
Directors of Education, 1916 D
Directory, telephone, Melbourne, 1880 F
Dirranbandi, Qld, 1846 F
Disc cultivator, 1909 B
Disco dancing, 1980 C
Discoveries, *see individual entries*
Discoveries in Australia, 1846 C
Discovery Bay, Vic, 1859 F
Discus, 1967 E
Diseases, animal, 1832 B, *see individual entries*
Disneyland, 1957 C
Dismissal, The, 1983 C
Displaced persons, 1946 A, 1947 A, 1951 F
Display, The, 1964 C
Dissenting Chapel, Hawkesbury district, 1808 D
Distance Measuring Equipment, 1948 B
Distillation, 1821 F
Distillation, illicit, 1796 F
Distilleries Co., 1974 B
Distillery, alcohol power, 1927 B
District Nursing services, Tas, 1893 B
Disturbing Element, 1963 C
Ditterich, Carl, 1946 E
Dittman, L. 1982 E
Diving, 1917 E, 1921 E, 1924 E, 1930 E
Division of National Mapping, 1968 B
Divorce, 1975 A, 1983 A
Divorce Acts, 1858 A, 1860 A, 1861 A, 1863 A, 1865 A, 1873 A
Divorce law, uniform, 1959 A
Dixon, Brian, 1935 E
Dixon, Dean, 1964 C
Dixon, James, 1803 D, 1840 D
Dixon, John, 1815 B
Dixon, Owen, 1886 A, 1929 A, 1952 A
Dixon, William A. 1871 D
Dixon House, Vic, 1924 C
Dixson, Hugh, 1841 A
Dixson, William, 1870 A, 1929 C
Dixson Art Gallery, Sydney, 1929 C
Dobell, William, 1899 C, 1940 C, 1943 C, 1944 C, 1948 C, 1959 C
Dobie, John, 1838 B
Dobson, Henry, 1841 A, 1892 A
Dobson, Patrick, 1975 D
Dobson, Rosemary de B. 1920 C
Dobson, Ruth, 1974 A
Dobson, William, 1886 A, 1892 A
Docherty, R. 1935 D
Dock labourers' strike London, Aust. support, 1889 A
Dock workers' strike, 1927 A
Docking, Shay, 1928 C
Docks, Sydney, 1855 B
Dockyards, 1796 B
Doctors, foreign, registration of, 1962 B
Doctors, medical, 1896 B
Doctors, women, 1890 B
Dodd, Edward, 1789 A
Dodd, Henry E. 1791 A
Dodd, Margaret, 1941 C

Dodds, John, 1900 A, 1904 A, 1909 A, 1913 A
Dods, Lorimer F. 1900 B, 1958 B
Dods, Robin, 1920 C
'Dog Collar' Act, 1938 A
Dog on the Tuckerbox monument, NSW, 1932 C
Dog on the Tucker Box, 1929 C
Dogs, 1848 E, 1870 B, 1890 B, 1983 F, *see individual entries*
Dolce, Jo, 1980 C
Dolinoff, Alexis, 1926 C
Dollar, Holey, *see* Holey dollar
'Dollar Anderson', 1949 F
Dollars, Spanish, 1804 A
Domain, Sydney, 1911 B
Domain Park, Melbourne, 1863 B
Domain Park Flats, Melbourne, 1962 C
Dominican Sisters, NSW, 1926 C
Dominion of Aust., The, 1877 C
Dominion League of WA, 1930 A
Dominion status, 1926 A
Dominish, Rod, 1972 E
Don, Charles Jardine, 1859 A
Don John of Austria, 1847 C
Don Juan, 1873 E
Don's Party, 1971 C, 1972 C, 1976 C
Donahoo, John, 1807 A
Donald, Vic, 1863 F
Donald, William H. 1875 A, 1920 A
Donaldson, St C. George A. 1863 D
Donaldson, Jack, 1910 E
Donaldson, John, 1886 E
Donaldson, Stuart A. 1812 A, 1851 F, 1856 A
Donato, Signor, 1871 C
Dongara, WA, 1852 F
Dongara gas field, WA, 1966 B
Donnellan, Frank, 1933 E
Donnett, Jenny, 1963 E
Donnybrook, WA, 1842 F
Dookie Agricultural College, Vic, 1886 D
Dooley, James, 1878 A, 1921 A
Doomben horse race course, Brisbane, 1923 E
Dore, Richard, 1798 A
Doreen, 1917 C
Dorman Long and Co., 1924 B
Dorotheos, Archimandrite, 1896 D
Dorrigo, NSW, 1880 F
Dot and the Kangaroo, 1899 C
Doubell, Ralph, 1946 E
Double dissolution, Fed. Parlt, 1914 A, 1951 A, 1974 A, 1975 A
Dougherty, Ivan N. 1907 A
Dougherty, Tom N. P. 1902 A
Douglas, Adye, 1815 A, 1884 A
Douglas, B. 1870 A
Douglas, Clive M. 1903 C, 1936 C, 1965 C
Douglas, C. H. 1934 A
Douglas, John, 1828 A, 1877 A
Douglas, Mollie, 1920 C
Douglas, Neil, 1911 C
Douglas Credit Plan, Sydney, 1934 A
Douglass, Henry G. 1790 B, 1848 B, 1850 B
Doutney, Charles, 1908 C
Dovers, George H. S. 1887 B
Dowie, John S. 1915 C
Dowling, Dick, 1810 E
Dowling, James, 1829 A, 1837 A, 1844 A
Dowling, Robert, 1827 C
Dowling, Roy R. 1901 A
Dowling, William P. 1868 B
Dowling, William P. (d. 1875), 1875 C
Down, Ronald, 1914 C
Downer, Alexander R. 1910 A

769

Downer, John W. 1844 A, 1885 A, 1892 A
Downes, Rupert, 1885 B
Downing, Richard I. 1915 A
'Doyen of Australian Pictorials', 1878 C
Doyle, Margaret, 1940 F
Dr Alexander Leeper, (painting) 1928 C
Dr. Edward McMahon, 1959 C
Dr. Julian Smith, 1936 C
Dr. J. Forbes McKenzie, 1940 C
Drag racing, Sydney, 1934 E, 1965 E, *see also* Motor racing
Drains, agricultural, Vic, 1920 B
Drake, Laurie, 1932 E
Drake-Brockman, Edmund A. 1884 A
Drake-Brockman, Frederick S. 1901 A
Drake-Brockman, Henrietta F. Y. 1901 C, 1947 C
Drama, *see section C and individual entries*
Drama, school subject, Tas, 1971 D
Draper, Daniel J. 1810 D
Daughts, 1888 F
Dreadnought road wheel, 1906 B
Dredge, Margaret, 1928 C
Dresses, fashion, 1922 F, 1923 F, 1957 F, 1965 F
Drew, William, 1928 C
Drewe, Robert, 1976 C
Drewett, Bradley, 1958 E
Dreyfus, George, 1928 C, 1972 C
Dridan, David C. 1932 C
Driest place, 1980 F
Driscoll, I. 1867 E
Drive-in bottle departments, Adelaide, 1956 F
Driver (ship), 1846 A
Driver, A. R. 1946 A
Drivers licences, provisional, Tas, 1965 F
Driving, long distance, 1900 E, 1912 B, 1922 B, 1939 E, 1976 E
Driving regulations, 1820 F
Driving tests, 1910 F, 1917 F
Drill, percussion, 1889 B
Droughts,
  Aust. wide, 1864 F, 1880 F, 1888 F, 1893 F, 1895 F, 1902 F, 1911 F, 1914 F, 1915 F, 1918 F, 1922 F, 1939 F, 1945 F, 1946 F, 1951 F, 1958 F, 1965 F, 1966 F, 1972 F, 1979 F, 1983 F, *see also* E. Aust. *below*
  East Aust., 1839 F, 1850 F, 1857 F, 1860 F, 1875 F, 1957 F, *see* Aust. wide *above*
  NSW, 1789 F, 1803 F, 1806 A, 1809 F, 1813 F, 1826 F, 1828 F, 1837 F, 1847 F, 1927 F, 1946 F, 1964 F, 1976 F, 1981 F
  NT, 1906 F, 1946 F, 1969 F
  Qld, 1858 F, 1862 F, 1877 F, 1884 F, 1946 F, 1964 F, 1969 F
  SA, 1839 F, 1851 F, 1858 F, 1867 F, 1868 F
  Tas, 1843 F
  Vic, 1854 F, 1867 F, 1877 F, 1976 F
  WA, 1838 F, 1856 F, 1877 F, 1946 F, 1969 F, 1976 F
Drought Bond Scheme, 1969 F
Drouin, Vic, 1877 F
Drouyn, Peter, 1951 E
Drover aircraft, 1948 B
Drover's Wife, The (film), 1968 C
Droving, 1836 A
Droving run, world's longest, 1882 A
Drug abuse, 1971 A
Drug haul, 1982 F
Drug trafficking, 1923 F, 1971 A, 1981 F
Drugs, production, 1928 B

Drum for Ben Boyd, A, 1948 C
Drum Major Harry McClelland, (painting), 1930 C
Drummond, James, 1863 B
Drummond, John N. 1816 A
Drummond, Peter R. M. 1894 A
Drummond, Ralph, 1792 D, 1839 D
Drummond, Stanley G. 1924 F, 1935 D
Drummoyne Art Prize, NSW, 1962 C
Dry, Richard, 1815 A, 1858 A, 1866 A
'Dryblower', 1867 C
Dry plates, photography, 1880 B
Drysdale, G. Russell 1912 C, 1940 C, 1941 C, 1950 C, 1951 C, 1958 C
Du Cane, Charles, 1825 A, 1869 A
Du Cane, Edmund F. 1830 A
Du Faur, Eccleston F. 1832 C
Dubbo, NSW, 1849 F, 1926 F, 1977 B, 1982 B
Duchess, Qld, 1966 B
Duck Reach Hydro-electric Station, 1895 B
Duck R. bridge, NSW. 1796 B
Dudley, John, 1905 C
Dudley, Earl of, *see* Ward, W. H.
Dudley, Lady, 1910 B
Dudley mines, NSW, 1898 F
Duels, 1801 F, 1826 F, 1851 F, 1891 F
Duff, Robert W. 1893 A
Duffield, Walter G. 1879 B
Duffy, Charles G. (b. 1816) 1816 A, 1842 F, 1871 A
Duffy, Charles G. (b. 1855) 1855 A
Duffy, Charles L. G. 1882 A
Duffy, Frank G. 1852 A, 1913 A, 1931 A
Duffy, John G. 1844 F
'Duffy Act', Vic, 1862 A
Dugan, Winston J. 1877 A, 1934 A, 1939 A, 1944 A, 1947 A
Duggan, Edward, 1897 C
Duggan, J. 1977 E
Duggan, Victor, 1915 E
Duhig, James, 1871 D
Duhig, J. V. 1889 C
Duigan, John R. 1882 B, 1910 B
Duigan, Reginald, 1888 B
Duke of Edinburgh Award Scheme, 1962 F
Duldig, Karl, 1902 C
Dulhunty, John A. 1911 B
Dulhunty, John, 1828 A
Dulhunty, Robert V. 1802 A
Dullingari North I., SA, 1979 B
Dumaresq, Edward, 1802 B
Dumaresq, Henry, 1792 A
Dumaresq, John S. 1873 A
Dumaresq, William J. 1793 A
Dumaresq R., Qld, 1840 A
Dumas, Frederick L. 1891 A
Dumas, Russell, 1976 C
Dumbleyung, WA, 1901 F
Dumbrell, Lesley, 1941 C
Dumont, Jules d'U. 1790 A, 1826 A
Dump, 1813 A
Dunbabin, Thomas, 1883 C
Dunbar, 1857 F
Duncan, Allie, 1951 E
Duncan, Billy, 1900 E, 1918 E, 1932 E
Duncan, George B. 1904 C
Duncan, Walter G. 1885 A
Dunciad Minor, 1970 C
Dundas, Douglas R. 1900 C
Dunedoo, NSW, 1909 F
Dung beetle, 1967 B
Dungog, NSW, 1838 F
Dunhill, Thomas P. 1876 B
Dunk, Billy, 1938 E
Dunk I., Qld, 1897 A
Dunkeld, Vic, 1851 F

Dunlop, 1887 E
Dunlop, Bob, 1945 E
Dunlop, Brian J. 1938 C
Dunlop, Edward, 1976 B
Dunlop, Ian, 1927 C, 1965 C
Dunlop, James, 1793 B, 1822 B, 1831 B
Dunlop, John, 1851 B
Dunlop, John W. 1910 A
Dunlop Art Prizes, 1950 C
Dunlop Aust. Ltd, 1932 E
Dunlop Pneumatic Tyre Co. of Aust. Ltd, 1903 B
Dunlop Station, NSW, 1888 B
Dunn, F. 1901 E
Dunn, Johnny, 1846 A
Dunn, Phyl, 1915 C
Dunne, Bobby, 1950 E
Dunne, John, 1896 C
Dunne, Robert, 1830 D
Dunnett, Frank, 1822 C
Dunolly, Vic, 1845 F, 1869 F
Dunrossil, Viscount, *see* Morrison, W. S.
Dunstan, Albert A. 1882 A, 1935 A, 1943 A
Dunstan, Arthur, 1941 E
Dunstan, Donald, Gov. S.A. 1982 A
Dunstan, Donald A. 1926 A, 1953 A, 1967 A, 1970 A
Duntroon, land grant, 1825 A
Duntroon Military College, 1911 A
Duntroon Station, Canberra district, 1910 A
Durack, Elizabeth, 1916 C
Durack, Fanny, 1894 E, 1912 E
Durack, John, 1819 A
Durack, Mary, 1913 C, 1955 C, 1959 C
Durack, Michael, 1845 A
Durack, Patrick, 1834 A
Durack family, 1885 A
Durham, Judith, 1943 C
Durrant, Ivan, 1947 C
Duryea, Townsend, 1823 B
Dusseldorp, G. J. 1958 C
Dust storm, Vic, 1983 F
Dusty, 1946 C
Dusty, Slim, *see* Slim Dusty
Duterrau, Benjamin, 1851 C
Duties, gift, estate, 1941 A
Dutiful Daughter, A, 1971 C
Dutkiewicz, Ludwig, 1921 C
Dutkiewicz, Wladyslaw, 1918 C
Dutton, Francis S. 1816 A, 1863 A, 1865 A
Dutton, Frederick H. 1812 A, 1846 B, 1856 B
Dutton, Geoffrey P. H. 1922 C
Dutton, Orlando, 1890 C
Dutton, William, 1811 A, 1829 A
Duvalli sisters, 1869 C
Dwellingup, WA, 1885 F
Dwyer, Eugene St. C. ('Hughie'), 1898 E
Dwyer, E. F. 1975 C
Dwyer, John P. 1951 A, 1963 A
Dwyer, Laurie, 1937 E
Dwyer-Gray, Edmund, 1870 A, 1939 A
Dyason, Edward C. E. 1886 A
Dyer, Jack, 1913 E
Dyer, Robert N. ('Bob'), 1909 F, 1941 F, 1957 F, 1970 F
Dyring, Moya, 1908 C
Dysart, Qld, 1973 F
Dyson, Ambrose (b. 1876), 1876 C
Dyson, Ambrose (b. 1910), 1910 C
Dyson, Edward G. 1865 C, 1898 C, 1906 C, 1911 C
Dyson, William H. 1880 C

E

Eadie, Graham, 1954 E
Eager, Edward, 1866 A
Eagle Farm, Brisbane, 1865 E, 1871 E
Eaglemont, Melbourne, 1888 C
Eagles, Percy, 1900 C
Eardley-Wilmot, John E. 1843 A, 1845 A, 1847 A
Earl Beauchamp, 1899 A, 1901 A
Earle, Augustus, 1793 C, 1825 C
Earle, John, 1865 A, 1909 A, 1914 A
Earle, Stephen A. 1924 C
Earles, Chester, 1822 C
Earl's Court Art group, London, 1919 C
Early Artists of Australia, 1963 C
Early Australian Architects and Their Work, The, 1954 C
Early Closing Associations, WA, Qld, 1889 A
Early Closing Movement, 1855 A
Earth Visitors, 1926 C
Earthquakes, tremors,
  Monte Bello Is, 1906 F
  NSW, 1788 F, 1800 F, 1806 F, 1872 F, 1961 F
  SA, 1954 F
  Tas, 1823 F
  WA, 1968 F
Earthwatch, Sydney, 1980 B
Easiphones, 1963 F
East, Charlie, 1890 E
East, Lewis F. 1898 B
East India Co., 1805 A, 1814 A, 1825 A, 1833 A
East Timor, 1975 A
Eastern Goldfields High School, Perth, 1914 D
Eastern Suburbs Railway, 1979 B
Eastern Suburbs Rugby League Football Club, team, Sydney, 1908 E, 1911 E, 1912 E, 1913 E, 1923 E, 1935 E, 1936 E, 1937 E, 1940 E, 1945 E, 1974 E, 1975 E
Eastern Suburbs Technical College, Melbourne, 1908 D
Eastes, Charlie, 1925 E
Eastman, Allan J. 1912 A
East–West Airlines Ltd, 1946 B
Easybeats, 1966 C
Eaton, WA, 1957 F
Ebden, Charles H. 1811 A, 1837 A
Ebeli, Gerard, 1928 C
Ebenezer, NSW, 1809 D, F, 1824 D
Ebenezer, SA, 1851 F
Eccles, John C. 1903 B, 1963 B
Echo (newspaper), Sydney, 1875 F
Echuca, Vic, 1845 F, 1847 F, 1852 A, 1857 A, 1864 B
Echunga, SA, 1848 F
Eclipse, 1922 B, 1976 B
Ecology, 1974 C
Economic Commission for Asia and Far East, ECAFE, 1947 A, 1964 A
Economic Conference, Sydney, 1922 A
Economic crisis, NSW, 1807 A, 1893 A
Economic depression/decline, 1840 A, 1843 A, 1844 A, 1880 A, 1889 A, 1890 A, C, 1892 A, 1929 A, 1930 A, 1931 A, 1933 C, 1934 A, 1982 A
Economic grievances, NSW, 1819 A
Economic revival, 1845 A, 1896 A, 1934 A
Economic zone, 200 mile, 1979 A
Economics, *see section A*
ED Holden, 1965 B
Eddy, Alan, 1904 C

Eddy, Cecil E. 1900 B
Eden (ship), 1840 A
Eden, NSW, 1842 F, 1968 A
Edenglassie, Qld, 1824 A
Edgar, Alex, 1884 E
Edgar, Alexander R. 1850 D
Edge, Selwyn F. 1868 E
Edgecombe, Henry, 1881 C
Edithburg, SA, 1871 F
Edkins, Edward R. 1905 A
Edkins, Edward R. H. 1871 A
Edmond, James, 1859 C
Edmondson, John H. 1914 A
Edmund, James, 1822 A
Edmund Herring, 1945 C
Edouin dancers, 1857 C
Education, *see section D*
  ACT, 1956 D, 1976 D
  Asians, 1951 D
  Bell System, 1820 D
  Board of Senior School Studies, NSW, 1975 D
  British and Foreign School Society system, 1839 D
  Church of England control, 1815 D, 1818 D
  Computers, 1984 D
  Curricula, 1938 D, 1967 D, 1968 D, 1978 D
  Diploma courses, 1902 D, 1911 D
  Directors of, 1916 D
  Examination system, 1938 D, *see also* Examinations facilities over-taxed 1963 D
  Fees, WA, 1914 D
  free, compulsory and secular,
  – NSW, 1880 D, 1906 D
  – Qld, 1870 D, 1875 D, 1900 D
  – SA, 1852 D, 1875 D, 1892 D
  – Tas, 1885 D, 1908 D
  – Vic, 1866 D, 1872 D, 1905 D
  – WA, 1871 D, 1893 D, 1895 D, 1901 D
  Govt aid to church schools
  – ACT, 1956 D
  – Cwlth, 1964 D, 1973 D, 1980 D, 1982 D, 1983 D
  – NSW, 1800 D, 1832 D, 1843 D, 1880 D, 1962 D, 1963 D
  – Qld, 1864 D
  – SA, 1843 D, 1847 D, 1851 D, 1852 D
  – Tas, 1832 D, 1847 D, 1849 D, 1853 D, 1868 D, 1885 D
  – Vic, 1981 D
  – WA, 1832 D, 1839 D, 1849 D, 1893 D
  Govt aid to non-Church schools,
  – Cwlth, 1963 A, 1967 D, 1984 D
  – NSW, 1964 D, 1965 D
  – Qld, 1860 D, 1967 D
  – SA, 1965 D
  – Tas, 1849 D, 1967 D
  – Vic, 1967 D
  – WA, 1965 D
  Govt aid to universities, 1957 D
  Asian Secondary Sch. SA, 1983 D
  Irish national system, 1836 D, 1844 D
  Karmel Report, 1969 D, 1973 D
  Methods, 1963 D
  Montessori methods, 1914 D
  Murray Committee, 1957 D
  National systems, 1847 D, 1850 D, 1874 D
  Open space system, 1968 D
  Payments by results, system of, 1864 D
  Periods, ladder, 1904 D
  – Liberal-utilitarian, 1831 D
  – Shared power, 1848 F
  – transition, 1938 D

  – *see also* free, compulsory and secular above
  Pre-school, 1973 D, *see also individual entries*
  Progressive movement, 1912 D
  Re-organization in ACT, 1973 D
  Reform, Vic, 1905 D, WA, 1897 D
  Secondary, NSW, Vic, 1910 D, 1961 D
  Science and Arts, Senate Report, 1972 D
  Science teaching, 1964 D
  Social pluralist tradition, 1960 D
  State systems, 1862 D, 1872 D
  Teacher, 1972 D, *see* Teacher training
  Technical, 1805 D, 1869 D, 1870 D, 1897 D, 1901 D, 1910 D, 1965 D, 1974 D, 1980 D, *see also* Technical education
  Tory-Anglican traditions, 1788 D
Education Act, Vic, 1910 D
Education Foundation, United States, 1949 D
Education Programme for Unemployed Youth, EPUY, 1977 D
Education Reform Association, 1938 D, 1971 D
Education of Young Donald, The, 1967 C
Edward, Lindsay, 1919 C, 1956 C
Edward Lombe, 1834 F
Edward McMahon, 1959 C
Edwards, A. 1884 C
Edwards, Donald H. 1905 C
Edwards, Hughie I. 1914 A, 1974 A
Edwards, J. B. 1889 A
Edwards, Ross, (1), 1942 E
Edwards, Ross, (2), 1943 C
E. G. Whitlam (portrait), 1972 C
Eggleston, Francis W. 1875 A
Eggleton, Justice, 1966 A
Egypt, 1914 A, 1915 A, 1916 A, 1940 A, *see also* Diplomatic relations
Eidsvold, Qld, 1862 F
Eight-Hour Act, NSW, 1916 A
Eight-Hour demonstrations, Sydney, 1890 A
Eight-Hour Extension Committee, 1869 A
Eight-Hour Labour League, Melbourne, 1856 A
Eight-Hour Movement, 1855 A
Eight-hour working day, 1855 A, 1856 A, 1859 A, 1871 A, 1873 A, 1874 A, 1879 A
Eighty Mile Beach, WA, 1887 F, 1908 F
Eilson, C. B. 1928 B
Eisenhower world golf, 1958 E
Eisteddfods, 1855 C, 1891 C, 1933 C, 1955 C
El Alamein, 1942 A
El Alamein fountain, Sydney, 1961 C
El Dorado gold exhibition, 1978 C
El Sherana, NT, 1953 B, 1955 B
Elcho I. NT, 1942 N
Elder, Alexander, 1839 A
Elder, Thomas, 1818 A, 1839 A, 1866 A, 1900 C
Elder Conservatorium, 1897 C
Elder Smith and Co. Ltd, 1839 A
Elder Smith Goldsbrough Mort, 1888 A
Eldershaw, Flora S. P. 1897 C, 1947 C
Eldershaw, John R. 1892 C, 1950 C
Eldershaw, M. Barnard 1929 C, 1947 C
Eldorado, Vic, 1895 F
Eleanor, (ship) 1831 F
Election, first national, 1901 A
Election laws, Cwlth, 1918 A
Elections, PNG, 1964 A
Electoral Act, Cwlth, 1918 A

771

Electoral boundaries, 1962 A
Electoral enrolment, compulsory, Qld, 1914 A
Electoral legislation, Federal, 1948 A
Electoral redistribution, Federal, 1974 A, Qld, 1978 A
Electoral rolls, 1911 A
Electoral zones, 1928 A
Electric hare racing, NSW, 1927 E
Electric lighting, 1882 B, 1887 C, 1888 B, 1894 B, 1904 B, 1912 B
Electric lifts, Melbourne, 1923 B
Electric stoves, 1907 B
Electric telegraph, 1854 B, 1856 B, 1857 B, 1858 B, 1861 B, 1862 B, 1864 B, 1867 B, 1869 B, 1870 B, F, 1872 B, 1876 B, 1877 B, 1888 B, 1901 A, 1902 B, *see also* Cables
Electric timer, 1912 E
Electric typewriters, 1954 B
Electric washing machines, 1910 F
Electrical Experience, The, 1974 C
Electrical services, 1926 B
Electricity, 1863 B, 1917 B, 1921 A, 1924 B, 1955 B, 1961 B
Electrocardiography, 1919 B
Electrolytic refining, NSW, 1908 B
Electrolytic Zinc Co. of Australasia Ltd, 1917 B, 1956 A
Electron diffraction, 1946 B
Elementary Education Act, WA, 1871 D
Elementary School, Hawkesbury R., 1804 D
Elephantiasis disease, 1876 B
Elingamite, 1902 F
Elink Schuurman, 1938 C
Elischer, John W. 1893 C
Eliza (ship), 1842 F
Eliza (ship), 1843 A
Eliza Mary, 1890 F
Elizabeth, SA, 1950 F
Elizabeth II, Queen, 1952 A, 1954 A, 1958 A, 1963 A, 1965 A, 1966 A, 1973 A, 1977 A, 1981 A, 1982 A
Elizabeth Bay House, Sydney, 1832 C, 1837 C, 1976 C
Elizabeth Farm House, Parramatta, 1793 A, C
Elizabeth Matriculation College, Hobart, 1970 D
Elizabethan Theatre, Sydney, 1917 C
Elizabethan Theatre Trust, 1954 C, 1955 C, 1958 C, 1975 C, 1984 C orchestra, 1967 C, Opera Co., 1956 C, 1970 C
Elkin, Adolphus P. 1891 B
Elkington, John S. C. 1871 A
Elkins, Margreta, 1936 C
Ella, Gary, 1981 E
Ella, Glen, 1981 E
Ella, Mark, 1980 E, 1981 E
Ellicott, Bob, 1977 A
Elliot, Billy, 1893 B
Elliot, Sizar, 1846 B
Elliot, Thomas F. 1808 D, 1837 D
Elliot, W. J. 1912 D
Elliott, Brian R. 1910 C
Elliott, Harold E. 1878 A
Elliott, Herbert J. 1938 E, 1958 E, 1960 E
Elliott, Madge, 1900 C
Elliott, Sumner L. 1917 C, 1948 C, 1978 C
Ellis, Bob, 1970 C
Ellis, James, 1853 B
Ellis, John, 1842 A
Ellis, Malcolm H. 1890 C
Ellis, Ulrich R. 1904 A

Ellison-Macartney, William G. 1913 A, 1917 A
Elm trees, Melbourne, 1968 F
Elms, Lauris M. 1931 C
Elmslie, G. A. 1913 A
Elocution, 1855 C
Elocution of Benjamin Franklin, The, 1978 C
Elsey, Joseph R. 1834 A
Eltham Art Award, 1965 C
Elyard, Samuel, 1817 C
Emancipists, 1821 A, 1825 A, 1828 A
Embassy, Aboriginal, 1972 A
Emblems, Vic, 1958 F
Emden, (ship) 1914 A
Emerald, Qld, 1860 F, 1861 A
Emerald Hill Theatre, Melbourne, 1962 C
Emerson, Roy, 1936 E
Emigrant Family, The, 1849 C
Emigration to Aust, 1841 A, 1843 A, 1845 A, 1847 A, 1938 A, 1945 A
Emigration Commissioners, 1831 A
Emigration to South Africa, 1902 A
Emmerton, Bill, 1920 E
Emmet, Harry, 1885 C
Empire, (newspaper) 1850 F, 1851 F
'Empire, this bloody and accursed', 1920 A
Empire Day, proclamation of, 1903 A
Empire Defence, 1923 A
Empire Defence Scheme, 1939 A
Empire Games, 1911 E, 1929 E, 1930 E, 1938 E, *see* Cwlth Games
Empire Land Settlement Scheme, 1925 A
Empire Parliamentary Association, 1911 A
Empire Preference, 1932 A
Empire Settlement Act, Federal, 1922 A
Empire Theatre, Sydney, 1927 C
Employers' Federation of NSW, 1903 A
Employment, 1974 C
Employment, Aboriginals, 1969 A
Employment, disputes, 1818 A
Employment Service, Cwlth, 1946 A
Empress of Australia, The, 1965 B
Emu Bay, Tas, 1827 B
Emu Plains, NSW, 1818 A, 1819 A, 1878 F
Enactment of Constitution Act, 1851 D
Enalund, Patricia, 1922 C
Encephalitis, 1917 F
Enchantress, 1835 F
Encke's comet, 1822 B
Encounter Bay, SA, 1802 A, 1830 A
Encyclopaedias, 1881 D
Endeavour, 1969 F
Enderby, Samuel, 1791 A
Enderson, E. 1872 E
Enemy Within, The (film), 1918 C
Energy, 1978 B
Energy Resources of Aust. Ltd, 1980 B
Engineering, 1854 B, 1857 B, *see individual entries*
Engineering and Electrical Exhibition, Sydney, 1897 B
Engineers' strike, 1946 A
Engineers workers group, Sydney, 1841 A
Engines, rotary, 1889 B, combustion, 1971 B, *see individual entries*
England and America, 1833 C
England, J. A. 1976 A
English, E. 1886 E
English, Thomas, 1851 C
English Association, Sydney, 1923 C
English Scottish and Australian Chartered Bank, 1852 A

English Workers Educational Association, 1911 D
Englund, Ivan O. 1915 C
Ensemble-at-the-Stables Theatre, Sydney, 1977 C
Ensemble Studios Acting School, 1954 C
Ensor, Beatrice, 1915 D
Entomological Society of NSW, 1862 B
The Entrance, NSW, 1836 F
Entry permit, immigration, 1958 A
Environment, Aborigines and Arts, Dept of, 1971 A
Environment, Cwlth Dept of, 1973 A
Environmental impact statement, 1973 A
Environment protection, 1970 A
Environment Protection Act, 1970 A
Environment Protection Authority, 1984 B
Environmentalists, Greenpeace, NSW, 1977 F, Tas, 1982 F
'Epping' (race track), Sydney, 1911 E, 1927 E
Equal pay, 1958 A, 1969 A, 1972 A
Equestrian Federation, 1949 E
Ergometer, 1946 B
'Ern Malley', 1944 C
'Ern Malley' Hoax, 1944 C
Ernabella Mission, SA, 1937 D
Eros, Peter, 1975 C
Errol (ship), 1909 F
Errol, Leon, 1881 C
Erskine, George, 1823 D
Erskine, James E. 1838 A
Erskine, Lieut-Col. 1817 A
Esam, Arthur, 1850 C
Escape Cliffs, NT, 1864 A
Escape of the Notorious Sir William Heans, The, 1919 C
Esk, Qld, 1850 F
Esk R., Tas, 1895 B
Eskbank iron and steel works, NSW, 1875 B, 1894 B, 1900 B, 1928 B
Eskimo Pie, 1923 F
Esling, Gordon, 1897 C
Esmond, James, 1851 B
Esperance, WA, 1893 F, 1963 A
Esperance Bay, WA, 1891 A, 1904 B
Espinosa, Edouard, 1937 C
Espionage, 1952 A, 1954 A
Esplin, Donald, 1909 C
Essays-Social, Moral and Political, 1879 C
Essendon, Melbourne, 1918 B, 1978 B
Essendon airport, Melbourne, 1921 B
Essendon Aust. Rules Football Club/team, 1873 E, 1897 E, 1901 E, 1911 E, 1912 E, 1923 E, 1924 E, 1934 E, 1937 E, 1938 E, 1942 E, 1946 E, 1948 E, 1949 E, 1950 E, 1953 E, 1962 E, 1965 E, 1976 E, 1984 E
Essential Services Act, Vic, 1948 A
'essential trade', NSW, 1812 A
Essie, 1865 C
Essington Lewis, 1952 C
Esson, Louis, 1911 C, 1922 C
Esson, Thomas L. B. 1878 C
Estate duty, 1941 A
Estonian Club, 1912 F
Etching, 1885 C
Ethanol, 1981 B
Ether, 1847 B
Etheridge, Donald, 1870 B
Etheridge, Robert, 1846 B, 1887 B
Etheridge goldfields, Qld, 1872 A
Ethnic radio, 1975 B
Ethnic schools, SA, 1839 D
Ethnic television, Sydney, Melbourne, 1980 F
Eton crop, 1928 F
Eton cut, 1921 F

Etude, 1940 C
Eucalyptus oil, 1788 A, 1843 B, 1854 B
Eucalyptus plantations, 1857 B
Eucalyptus seeds, 1869 B
Euchre, 1939 F
Eucla, WA, 1885 F
Eucumbene–Tumut tunnel, NSW, 1959 B
Eugowra, NSW, 1834 F, 1862 F
Eureka Hill, Ballarat, 1854 A
Eureka Hotel, 1854 A
Eureka Stockade, 1854 A
Eureka Stockade, 1897 C
Eureka Stockade, T.V. prog. 1984 C
Eureka trials, 1855 A
Euroa, Vic, 1850 F
European Contemporary Pictures Exhibition, 1923 C
European Economic Community, 1960 A, 1973 A
European Migration, Intergovernmental Committee, ICEM, 1951 A
Eustice, Ken, 1938 A
Evandale, Tas, 1809 F, 1876 B
Evangelical Lutheran Church in Aust., 1966 D
Evans, Ada E. 1872 A, 1902 A
Evans, George E. 1863 C
Evans, George W. 1812 A, 1813 A, 1815 A, 1852 A
Evans, Harry, 1955 B
Evans, H. Lindley, 1895 C
Evans, J. W. 1904 A
Evans, Matilda J. 1827 C
Evans, W. 1907 E
Evans Head, NSW, 1871 F, 1885 F
Evatt, Elizabeth A. 1933 A, 1972 A
Evatt, Herbert V. 1894 A, 1930 A, 1940 A, 1947 A, 1948 A, 1951 A, 1954 A, D, 1960 A
Eve, Dick, 1903 E, 1924 E
Eve, James S. W. 1899 E, 1924 E, 1929 E
Even Stevens, 1962 E
Evening News, Sydney, 1867 F
Evening Pearl, 1956 E
Evenstructure Sculpture Research Group, 1973 C
Everage, Edna, *see* Humphries, Barry
Everett, Minnie, 1897 C
Evergood, Miles, *see* Blashki, Myer
Everingham, Herman, 1903 B
Everingham, Paul A. E. 1943 A, 1978 A
Evita, 1980 C
Ewart, Alfred J. 1872 B
Ewers, John K. 1904 C
Ewers, Raymond B. 1917 C
Examination system, 1938 D
Examinations, Public Service, Vic, 1883 D
Examinations, Girls admitted to, 1871 D
Examinations, schools, 1911 D, 1967 D, 1969 D, 1970 D, 1972 D, 1973 D, 1974 D
Examiner (newspaper), 1842 F
Executions, first, 1788 F, 1821 F
Executive Councils, state, 1824 A, 1825 A, 1826 A, 1829 A, 1832 A
Executive Council of Aust. Jewry, 1944 D
Exhibitions, 1854 F, 1861 F, 1872 F, 1887 F, *see also individual entries*
Exhibition of Aust. Art, 1960 C
Exhibition of Aust. Art, London, 1920 C, 1924 C
Exhibition Building, Melbourne, 1880 C, 1901 A
Exhibition of Aust. products, Melbourne, 1907 F
Exhibition of Living Pictures, 1905 C

Exhibition of Modern Art, Melbourne, 1939 C
Exhibition of modern sculpture, Melbourne, 1931 C
'Exiles', 1844 A
Ex-Libris Society, Sydney, 1923 C
Exmouth, WA, 1963 F
Exmouth Gulf, WA, 1875 F, 1943 A, 1953 B
Experiment, 1832 B
Experiment Farm, 1798 A
Explosives, 1874 B
Expo, Japan, 1970 C
Expo, Montreal, 1967 C
Export ban, 1973 A
Exports,
apples, 1884 A
beef, 1958 A
butter, 1881 A
canned meat, 1847 A
cedar, 1795 A, 1822 A
coal, 1799 A, 1801 A, B, 1804 A, 1850 A, 1865 A, 1873 F, 1981 A
cotton, 1854 A, 1862 A
eucalyptus oil, 1788 A
fish, 1830 A
fruit, 1828 A
gold, 1853 A, 1871 A
horses, 1844 A
iron ore, 1938 A, 1960 A, 1962 A
Japan, exports to, 1966 A
markets, 1961 A
meat, 1880 A, 1884 A, 1978 A
minerals, 1960 A
pearl shell, 1862 A
prices, 1929 A, 1930 A, 1934 A
primary products, 1960 A
restrictions, 1914 A
sheep, 1929 A, 1971 A, 1978 A, 1982 A
sugar, 1885 A, 1923 A, 1924 A
tax concessions, 1961 A
uranium, 1953 A, 1976 A, 1977 A, 1979 A, 1981 A, 1982 A, 1983 A
value, 1888 A, 1889 A, 1890 A
whaling, 1883 A
wheat, 1904 A, 1972 A, 1980 A
wine, 1823 A, 1857 A
wool, 1807 A, 1811 A, 1832 A, 1833 A, 1834 A, 1835 A, 1853 A, 1871 A, 1873 A, 1874 A, 1875 A, 1972 A
Export Development Council and Aust. Bankers' Association Poster competition, 1963 C
Export Finance and Insurance Corporation, 1975 A
Export Payment Insurance Corporation, 1956 A
Exposure, body, fashion, 1979 F, 1982 F
Expressionism, 1936 C
Expressways, *see individual entries*
External Affairs, Dept of, 1934 A, 1970 A
Exton, John, 1933 C
Eye of the Storm, 1973 C
Eyre, Edward J. 1815 A, 1836 A, 1839 A, 1840 A, 1841 A
Eyre, Gladstone, 1863 C
E.Z. Industries Ltd, 1956 A, 1979 A

F

Faces in the Sun (film), 1965 C
Facey, A.B. 1981 C
Factory Acts, 1873 A, 1884 A, 1885 A, 1886 A, 1894 A, 1899 A

Fact'ry Ands, 1906 C
Faculty of Arts Gallery, London, 1924 C
Fadden, Arthur W. 1895 A, 1936 A, 1941 A
Fahrenheit temperature scale, 1972 B
FAI Insurances Ltd, 1953 A
'fair and reasonable wages', 1906 A
Fair Maid of Perth, The, 1835 C
Fairbairn, David E. 1917 A
Fairbairn, George, (b. 1816) 1816 A
Fairbairn, George, (b. 1855) 1855 A
Fairbairn, Steve, 1862 E
Fairbridge Society Farm Schools, 1912 D, 1937 D
Fairbridge, Kingsley O. 1885 D, 1912 D, 1937 D
Fairfax, James O. 1863 A
Fairfax, James R. 1834 A
Fairfax, John, 1804 A, 1831 F
Fairfax, Vincent C. 1909 A
Fairfax, Warwick O. 1901 A
Fairley, Neil H. 1891 B
Fairs, Sydney, 1813 F
Fairweather, Ian, 1891 C
Faithfull, George, 1838 A
Faithfull, William P. 1806 A, 1838 B
Faithfull Party Massacre, 1838 A
Faked Paintings, 1984 C
Falk, Leib A. 1889 D
Falkiner, Franc S. 1833 A, 1882 A
Falkiner, Franc B. S. 1867 A
Falkiner, F. S. and Sons, 1882 A
Falkiner, George B. S. 1907 A
Falkiner, Otway M. 1909 A
Falkiner, Otway R. 1874 A
Falkiner, R. S. 1877 B, 1925 B
Falmouth, Tas, 1820 F
Famechon, John, 1945 E, 1969 E
Familiar Treatise on the Diseases of the Eye, A, 1840 C
Family Allowance, 1941 A
Family Colonization Loan Society, 1849 A
Family Law Act, Federal, 1975 A
Family Law Courts, 1976 A
Family Planning, 1904 F
Famine, 1790 A
Fancy dress ball, Sydney, 1844 F
Fanfrolico Press, Sydney, 1925 C
Fantasy of Man, 1984 C
Far Country, The, 1952 C
Far Paradise, The (film), 1928 C
Far West Scheme, 1932 F
Farewell to Judge and Juries, A, 1815 C
Farman type monoplane, 1910 B
Farmer, Caroline, 1840 A
Farmer, Edward H. 1909 C
Farmer, Graham (Polly), 1935 E
Farmer, John McD., 1897 C
Farmer, Joseph, 1840 A
Farmer, Kenneth W. G. 1910 E
Farmer, Mary, *see* Hurry, Polly
Farmer, Peter, 1979 E
Farmer, William, 1832 A, 1881 C
Farmer and Co. Ltd, 1840 A, 1923 F, 1924 B
Farmers' Blaxland Art Gallery, Sydney, 1929 C
Farmers' and Settlers' Association, SA, 1915 A
Farmers' Union Party, 1918 A
Farnan, Bill, 1884 E
Farncomb, Harold B. 1899 A, 1937 A
Farnell, Charles S. 1825 A
Farnell, J. S. 1877 A
Farnham, Johnny, 1967 C
Farquhar, George, 1789 C
Farquhar, Murray, 1983 A
Farr, Ian, 1941 C

773

Farrell, John, 1851 C, 1887 C
Farrell, Tom, 1904 B
Farrelly, Bernard, (Midget) 1944 E, 1963 E, 1964 E
Farrer, William J. 1845 B, 1886 B, 1901 B
Farrow, John V. 1904 C, 1942 C
Farwell, George M. 1911 C
Fascism, 1940 A
Fashion, *see individual entries*
Fatal Days, The, 1947 C
Fatal Impact, The, 1966 C
Fatal Wedding, A, 1911 C
'Father of the AIF', 1861 A
'Father of Australian Navy', 1852 A
'Father of Australian Rules Football', 1836 E
'Father of Aust. skindiving', 1947 E
'Father of the Basic Wage', 1851 A
'Father of Canberra', 1867 A
'Father of Engineering in the North', 1841 B
'Father of the Holden', 1948 B
Father of Modern Art in Australia', 1878 C
Father of South Australian Wine Industry, 1830 A
Father of Vic. separation, 1798 A
Father's Day Massacre, 1984 F
Faulding, F. H. 1843 B
Favell, Les, 1929 E
Favenc, Ernest, 1845 A, 1878 B, 1883 A
Fawkner, John P. 1792 A, 1829 F, 1835 A, 1836 A, 1838 F
'Fawkner Inn', 1835 F
Featherston, Grant, 1947 F
Federal (ship), 1901 F
Federal Assembly, 1849 A
Federal Bank of Aust., 1832 A, 1893 A
Federal budget leak, 1980 A
Federal Capital, 1904 A, 1908 A
Federal Capital Commission, 1924 A
Federal Capital Territory, (Aust. Capital Territory, ACT), 1909 A, 1910 A, 1911 A, 1938 A
Federal Conferences, 1880 A
Federal Constitution, 1881 A, 1891 A, 1895 A, 1897 A, 1898 A, 1899 A, *see also* Constitution
Federal Conventions, 1891 A, 1897 A, 1898 A
Federal Council, proposed, 1867 A
Federal Council for the Advancement of Aboriginals and Torres Strait Islanders, 1957 A
Federal Council of Australasia, 1883 A, 1885 A, 1886 A, 1888 A, 1889 A, 1891 A, 1893 A
Federal Council of Australasia Act, 1885 A
Federal Council of British Medical Association in Aust., 1933 B
Federal Council of the Chamber of Manufacturers, 1903 A
Federal Council of Rifle Associations of Australasia, 1888 E
Federal Court of Aust., 1976 A
Federal demonstration, 1899 A
Federal Education Conference, Melbourne, 1901 D
Federal elections, *see* changes in office *in* Government *section A*.
Federal Electoral Act, 1902 A
Federal government, transfer to Canberra, 1927 A
Federal Hotel, Melbourne, 1888 C
Federal Labor Party, 1900 A, *see also* Aust. Labor Party
Federal Match Co., 1913 F

Federal Ministers, 1900 A, *see also* individuals' names
Federal Ministries, *see* Government *section A*.
Federal Narcotics Bureau, 1969 A, 1983 A
Federal Naturalization Act, 1903 A
Federal Navigation Commission, 1906 A
Federal Parlt, 1881 A, joint sitting, 1974 A, *see also* Parlt, Federal
Federal Police, 1979 A
Federal Secondary Scholarship Scheme, 1970 D
Federal Union of Aust. Colonies, 1857 A
Federal Water Conservation and Irrigation Commission, 1912 A
Federated Clerks' Union, Vic, 1908 A
Federated Ironworkers' Association of Aust., 1911 A
Federated Miscellaneous Workers' Union, 1915 A
Federated Ship Painters' and Dockers' Union, 1982 A
Federated Shipwrights' and Ship Constructors' Association of Aust., 1862 A
Federated Storemen and Packers' Union, 1912 A
Federated Union of Churches, Sydney, 1886 D
Federation of Aust., first steps, 1857 A, 1871 A, 1884 A, 1887 A, 1889 A, 1890 A, 1896 A, 1900 A, 1901 A, *see also individual entries*
Federation of Aust. Commercial Television Stations, 1960 A
Federation of Aust. Trade Unions, 1884 A
Federation Bill, 1900 A
Federation Cup, tennis, 1963 E, 1964 E
Federation of defence, 1889 A
'Federation' wheat, 1901 B
Fehlberg, Tasman J. A. 1912 C
Feint, Adrian, 1894 C, 1924 C
'Felix the Cat', 1910 C
Fellows, Warren, 1981 F
Fellows, W. 1949 E
Fellows of the Royal Society, 1854 B
Fellowship of Aust. Artists, Melbourne, 1950 C
Fellowship of Aust. Writers, 1928 C
Fellowships for Aust. composers, 1971 C
Felonry of New South Wales, The, 1837 C
Felton, Alfred, 1831 A, 1904 C
Felton Bequest, 1904 C
Female employees' strike, Melbourne, 1882 A
Female Eunuch, The, 1970 C
Female Factory, 1819 C, 1821 A
Female Immigrants' Home, 1841 A
Female orphans, NSW, 1818 D
Female suffrage, *see* Suffrage
Female Visiting Society, 1845 D
Females, *see* Women
Femininity, fashions, 1919 F, 1933 F
Fences, rabbit proof, 1904 B, 1907 B
Fencing, 1912 E, 1975 E, 1979 E
Fenian, 1876 F
Fenner, Charles A. E. 1884 D
Fenton, Johnny, 1945 E
Ferdinand-Strebinger, Therese, 1853 C
Ferguson Hume, *see* Hume, Ferguson W.
Ferguson, John, 1852 D
Ferguson, John A. 1881 A, 1941 C
Ferguson, Molly, 1951 D
Ferguson, S. R. 1912 B
Ferguson, William J. 1932 C
Fergusson, James, 1832 A, 1869 A
Fern, Harry L. 1892 C

Ferntree Gully, Vic, 1882 F
Ferntree Gully Art Society, 1944 C
Fernyhough, W. H. 1812 C
Ferrarini, Guiseppe, 1846 C
Ferreri, Paul, 1950 E
Ferrier, James, 1915 E, 1947 E
Ferries, James, 1875 C
Ferry services, 1816 B, 1830 B, 1838 B, 1842 B, 1843 B, 1844 B, 1854 B, 1861 B, 1916 B
Fertilizers, 1862 B, 1881 B
Fertilizing, aerial, 1947 B
Festival of Arts, Adelaide, 1960 F
Festival of Empire Games, 1911 E
Festival of Light, 1973 D, 1974 A
Festival of Sydney, 1977 F
Festival Theatre, Adelaide, 1973 C
Festivals, music, 1838 C, *see individual entries*
Feverring, Maximilian, 1896 C
Fewtrell, Albert C. 1885 B
Fiaschi, Thomas H. 1853 B
Field, Barron, 1817 A, 1819 A, C, 1823 C, 1846 A
Field, E. L. 1951 F
Field Exhibition, Melbourne, 1968 C
Field Naturalists' Club of Vic, 1880 B
Field Naturalists' Section, Royal Society SA, 1883 B
Fielding, Una L. 1888 B
Fifield, NSW, 1880 F
Fifield, Elaine, 1930 C, 1964 C
Figaro, SA, 1877 F
Fiji, 1874 A
Fiji, 1891 F
Filarial parasite, 1876 B
Film, *see individual entries and Section C*
Film censorship, 1916 C, 1970 C
Film Exchange, American, 1915 C
Film exhibitions, Sydney, 1897 C, 1905 C, 1906 C
Film industry, 1896 C, 1900 C, 1905 C, 1910 C, 1920 C, 1925 C, 1927 C, 1970 C
Film making, govt, 1912 C
Film Radio and Television Board, 1973 C
Film sound shorts, commercial, 1929 C
Film and Television Production Association, 1979 C
Films, awards, 1958 C
Films, screening of, 1896 C, 1900 C, 1919 C
Films, sound, 1921 C, 1928 C
Finance, Hire Purchase, 1959 F
Finances, Cwlth, state, 1909 A
Financial Agreement Enforcement Act, Federal, 1932 A
Financial assistance, grants, to States, 1976 A
Financial boom, NSW, 1820 A
Financial crisis, 1842 A, 1843 A, 1844 A, 1930 A, *see also* Depression *and* Economic decline
Financial system, deregulation, 1981 A
Finch, Peter G. F. I. 1916 C, 1938 C
Finch-Hatton, Harold H. 1856 A
Fine Arts Exhibition, Melbourne, 1853 C
Fine Arts Gallery, Sydney, 1911 C
Fine Arts Society Gallery, Melbourne, 1918 C
Fine Cotton, 1984 E
Finemore, Brian, 1925 C
Finey, George E. 1895 C
Fingal, Tas, 1852 B, 1854 F
Finger printing, 1902 F, 1964 F
Fingleton, John H. W. 1908 E
Fink, Benjamin J. 1847 A
Fink, Theodore, 1855 D

Finlayson, Hedley H. 1895 B
Finley, NSW, 1862 F
Finn, Edmund, 1819 F, 1888 C
Finnance, Steve, 1952 E
Finney Centenary Art Prize, Qld, 1963 C
Finnin, Mary, 1906 C
Finniss, Boyle T. 1807 A, 1854 A, 1856 A, 1864 A
Finniss R., NT, 1865 B
Fire Brigades, 1827 F, 1839 F, 1845 F, 1865 F
Fire Brigades' Boards, 1882 F, 1884 F, 1898 F
Fire engines, Sydney, 1892 F, 1904 F
Fire fighting, 1837 F, 1854 F
Fire fighting, pumps, 1822 F
Fires,
  NSW, 1822 F, 1840 C, 1860 F, 1873 F, 1874 F, 1882 F, 1888 F, 1890 F, 1892 C, 1899 C, 1901 F, 1902 C, 1907 F, 1921 F, 1975 F, 1979 F, 1981 F
  Qld, 1864 F, 1942 F, 1963 F, 1973 F
  SA, 1884 F, 1886 F, 1924 F, 1948 F
  Vic, 1854 F, 1872 C, 1889 F, 1897 F, 1955 C, 1966 F
  WA, 1921 F, 1945 F
  see also Bushfires
Firing Squad. 1983 C
First Aust. Ballet, 1931 C
First Fleet, 1788 A
First Fruits of Australian Poetry, 1819 C
First, Second, ... Practice of Music, The, 1846 C
First Mosman Kangaroos, Sydney, 1908 F
Firth, Helen, 1920 E
Firth-Smith, John, 1943 C
Fiscal, colonial independence, 1871 A
Fischer, Elsa, 1881 C, 1924 C
Fish canning, 1937 B
Fish and Fisheries of Australia, 1951 C
Fish Markets, Melbourne and Sydney, 1865 F
Fish R., NSW, 1823 B
Fisher, Amandus J. 1859 C
Fisher, Andrew, (b. 1862), 1862 A, 1901 A, 1908 A, 1909 A, 1910 A, 1913 A, 1914 A
Fisher, Andrew, (Nunawading Messiah), 1871 D
Fisher, Charley, 1845 A
Fisher, James H. 1790 A, 1836 A, 1840 A
Fisher, John, 1810 E
Fisher, Sylvia G. V. 1912 C
Fisher, Thomas, 1820 A
Fishing, sport, 1933 E, 1936 E, 1959 E, 1976 E, *see also* Angling, Casting
Fishing disputes, with Japan, 1953 A
Fishing industry, 1830 A, 1835 A, 1895 A, 1937 A
Fishing zone, Twelve-mile, 1967 A, 1968 A, Two hundred miles, 1979 A
Fisk, Ernest T. 1886 B, 1918 B, 1919 B, 1939 B
Fisk radiola, 1946 B
Fison, Lorimer, 1832 D, 1880 C
Fitchett, William H. 1842 D
Fitton, Doris A. 1897 C, 1922 C, 1929 C
Fitzgerald, Adolph A. 1890 A
FitzGerald, Charles, 1791 A, 1848 A
Fitzgerald, Gerald, 1873 C
Fitzgerald, John V. 1854 A
Fitzgerald, Len, 1930 E
Fitzgerald, Paul D. 1922 C
FitzGerald, Robert D. (b. 1830), 1830 B
FitzGerald, Robert D. (b. 1902), 1902 C, 1927 C, 1938 C
Fitzgerald, S. 1904 C, 1906 C
Fitzgerald, Stephen A. 1938 D

Fitzgerald, Thomas, 1807 D
Fitzgerald, Thomas H. 1824 A
FitzGerald, Thomas N. 1838 B
Fitzpatrick, Brian C. 1905 C
Fitzpatrick, Raymond E. 1955 A
Fitzroy, 1921 F
FitzRoy, Charles A. 1796 A, 1846 A, 1851 A, 1854 A
FitzRoy, Mary, 1847 F
Fitzroy Aust. Rules Football Club/team, 1884 E, 1898 E, 1899 E, 1904 E, 1905 E, 1913 E, 1916 E, 1922 E, 1931 E, 1932 E, 1933 E, 1935 E, 1936 E, 1944 E, 1950 E, 1969 E, 1979 E, 1981 E
Fitzroy Iron Works, NSW, 1848 B
Fitzroy pastoral country, WA, 1879 A
Fitzroy R., NT, 1839 A
Fitzroy R., Qld, 1881 B
Five Bells, 1939 C
Five Islands, NSW, 1826 A
Five Power Defence Agreement, 1971 A
Fiveash, Rosa C. 1854 C
Fizelle, Rah, 1891 C, 1932 C
Flack, Edwin H. 1874 E, 1896 E
Flag, Aboriginal, 1972 F
Flag, Aust., 1901 A, F
Flag, first, 1856 F
Flag, Southern Cross, 1854 A
Flag smut disease, 1923 B
Flagstaff Hill, Melbourne, 1836 F, 1847 E, 1856 B
Flame Queen, 1918 F
Flanagan, John R. 1894 C
Flanagan, Roderick, 1828 D, 1862 C
Flannery, Frank, 1927 E
Flats, Melbourne, 1940 C
Flaws in the Glass: A Self Portrait, 1981 C
Fleay, David H. 1907 B, 1943 B
Fleetwood-Smith, Leslie O. 1910 E
Flegg, Harry ('Jersey'), 1878 E
Fleischman, Arthur, 1896 C
Flemington racecourse, Vic, 1840 E, 1965 F
Flemming, Claude, 1884 C
Flemming, I. B. 1948 B
Flesh in Armour, 1932 C
Fletcher, Bruce, 1937 C
Fletcher, Joan, 1928 E
Fletcher, Joseph J. 1850 B
Fletcher, J. W. 1880 E
Fletcher, Ken, 1940 E
Flett, James, 1906 C
Fleury, Joseph L. 1872 C
Flexmore, John, 1911 C
Flexmore, J. H. 1861 C
Flexitime, Federal, 1976 A
Flies, 1838 B
Flights, first major, 1920 B, 1928 B, 1929 B, 1930 B, 1931 B, 1933 B, 1934 B, 1935 B, 1951 B, 1961 B, 1965 B
Flinders, Matthew, 1795 A, 1796 A, 1798 A, 1799 A, 1801 A, 1802 A, 1803 A, 1810 A, 1814 A, 1817 A, 1837 A
Flinders I., 1830 A, 1835 A, 1847 A, 1849 A, 1935 B
Flinders Naval Depot, 1915 A, 1958 A
Flinders University, SA, 1961 D, 1965 D
Flogging, first, 1788 F, 1818 F, *see* Convicts
Flood, Bert, 1976 E
Flood, Tot, 1884 F
Flood warning, 1904 F
Floods,
  Aust. wide, 1916 F, 1956 F, 1963 F, 1973 F, 1975 F, 1977 F
  NSW, 1799 F, 1806 F, 1808 F, 1809 F, 1811 F, 1852 F, 1860 F, 1863 F,

1864 F, 1870 F, 1875 F, 1890 F, 1891 F, 1906 F, 1909 F, 1921 F, 1925 F, 1949 F, 1950 F, 1951 F, 1952 F, 1954 F, 1955 F, 1959 F, 1963 F, 1970 F, 1976 F, 1984 F
  NT 1983 F
  Qld, 1841 F, 1864 F, 1870 F, 1887 F, 1890 F, 1893 F, 1898 F, 1906 F, 1909 F, 1913 F, 1916 F, 1921 F, 1931 F, 1949 F, 1954 F, 1959 F, 1963 F, 1970 F, 1974 F, 1976 F, 1981 F, 1984 F
  SA, 1837 F, 1906 F, 1909 F, 1921 F, 1983 F, 1984 F
  Tas, 1809 F, 1952 F, 1960 F, 1969 F, 1978 F, 1980 F
  Vic, 1839 F, 1849 F, 1870 F, 1887 F, 1889 F, 1891 F, 1906 F, 1921 F, 1934 F, 1949 F, 1951 F, 1970 F, 1972 F, 1978 F
  WA, 1830 F, 1889 F, 1961 F, 1978 F, 1982 F
Floods, recording of, 1860 F
Floor Price, wool, 1974 A
Flora Protection Acts, 1930 F
Floral emblem, Vic, 1958 F
Floral and Horticultural Society, Sydney, 1838 F
Florey, Howard W. 1898 B, 1940 B, 1943 B, 1945 B, 1960 B, 1971 B
Flotation process, 1904 B
Flotta Lauro Shipping Co. Art Prize, 1967 C
Flour, NSW, 1836 A
Flour mills, 1813 B, 1815 B, 1840 B
Flower, Cedric, 1920 C
Floyd, Alfred E. 1877 C, 1942 C
Flugelman, Herbert, 1923 C
Fluke, Roy G. H. 1921 C
Fluoridation, 1953 B
Fly away Peter Venus, 1980 C
Flying boats, 1938 B
Flying Doctor Service, 1926 B, 1928 B, 1941 B
Flying Medical Service, 1938 D
'Flying Pieman', 1807 F, 1842 E
Flying Surgeon Service, Qld, 1959 B
Flynn, Errol L. 1909 C, 1933 C
Flynn, Francis S. 1906 D
Flynn, John, 1880 D, 1912 D, 1926 B, 1927 B
Flynn, J. R. 1908 E
FM broadcasts, 1957 B
FM radio, 1974 B
FM radio stations, 1980 F
Foard, Patsy, 1935 C
Foley, F. 1916 E
Foley, Gary, 1972 F, 1979 A
Foley, Laurence, 1848 E
Foley, Steve, 1959 E
Folingsby, George F. 1828 C
Folk Lore Council of Aust., 1964 G
Folkloric Dance Concert group, 1967 C
Food, impure, 1906 F
Food inspectors, 1839 F
Food poisoning, 1981 F
Food rationing, 1789 A, 1942 F
Foot-and-mouth disease, 1872 B
Football, *see* Aust. Rules football, Rugby League, Rugby Union, Soccer
Footracing, 1850 E, *see* Athletics
Footscray Aust. Rules Football Club/team, 1883 E, 1941 E, 1954 E, 1956 E, 1960 E, 1975 E, 1980 E
Footscray Institute of Technology, Melbourne, 1915 D
Footscray Technical College, Melbourne, 1915 D
Foott, Mary H. 1846 C

775

Footways, moving, Sydney, 1961 B
For the Term of his Natural Life (book),
   1874 C, 1885 C, 1886 C, (film), 1926 C,
   (TV Series), 1983 C
Forbes, NSW, 1860 F, 1862 F, 1871 F,
   1955 F
Forbes, David, 1939 E
Forbes, Francis, 1823 A, 1824 A, 1827 A,
   1830 D, 1841 A
Forbes, James, 1813 D, 1838 D, 1845 D
Forbes, Joseph, ('Timor Joe'), 1877 F
'Forbes Act', NSW, 1834 A
Forbidden Rite, The, 1961 C
Forces, *see* Aust. Forces
Ford, Edgar, 1881 C
Ford, Edward, 1902 B
Ford, Michelle, 1962 E
Ford, Patrick, 1931 E
Ford, William, (1), 1875 C
Ford, William, (2), 1892 B
Ford employees' strike, Melbourne,
   1973 A
Ford motor cars, 1907 B, 1928 B, 1932 B,
   1934 B, 1962 B, 1965 B
Ford Motor Co., 1921 B
Ford Motor Co. of Aust. Pty Ltd, 1925 B
Forde, Florrie, 1876 C
Forde, Francis M. 1890 A, 1945 A
Forde, Michael F. 1922 C
Foreign Affairs, Dept of, 1970 A
Foreign banks, 1981 A
Foreign capital, 1835 A
Foreign policy, anti-Sovietism, 1976 A
Foreign relations, America, 1804 A
Foreign Takeovers Act, 1972 A
Forest Creek, Vic, 1853 B
Forestry, ACT, 1915 A
Forestry conservation, NSW, 1882 F
Forestry policy, SA, 1871 F
Forestry reserves, Qld, 1908 F
Forestry and Timber Bureau, 1930 B
Forests, conservation of, WA, 1975 F
Forests, man made, 1967 B
Forgers Wife, The, 1855 C
Forlong, William, 1811 A
Forlonge, Eliza, 1831 A
Forlonge, Graham, 1977 E
Forrest, Alexander, 1849 A, 1869 A,
   1871 A, 1874 A, 1879 A, 1880 C,
   1887 F
Forrest, Helena M. C. 1872 C
Forrest, John, 1847 A, 1869 A, 1870 A,
   1874 A, 1890 A, 1897 A, 1898 A,
   1901 A
Forrest, J. Haughton, 1825 C
Forrest, WA, 1966 B
Forster, Lord, *see* Forster, H. W.
Forster, Henry W. 1866 A, 1920 A
Forster, Johann R. 1798 B
Forster, NSW, 1862 F
Forster, William, 1818 A, 1859 A
Forsyth, William D. 1909 A
Fort Denison, Sydney, 1857 A, C
Fort Dundas, NT, 1824 A
Fort St Model School, Sydney, 1850 D,
   1851 D
Fort Wellington, NT, 1827 A, 1829 A
Fortieth International Eucharistic
   Congress, Melbourne, 1973 D
Fortress, 1980 C
Fortunate Life, A, 1981 C
Fortune, Mrs, 1871 C
Fortune telling, 1846 F
Fortunes of Richard Mahony, The, 1917 C,
   1929 C
'Forty Second Street', 1933 C
Forty Thousand Horsemen, 1940 C
Fossils, 1869 B, 1966 B, 1967 B, 1968 B,
   1969 B, 1978 B, 1980 B, 1984 B

Foster, Vic, 1870 F
Foster, Alfred W. 1886 A
Foster, E. J. 1837 A
Foster, George, 1963 E
Foster, John F. L. 1818 A
Foster, W. M. 1888 A
Foster's Lager, 1888 A
Fothergill, Desmond, 1920 E, 1940 E
Foulsham, Bill, 1890 E
Foundation Company Act, Qld, 1863 A
Foundation day, 1804 F
Foundation of Culture in Aust., The,
   1936 C
'Founder of Adelaide', 1839 A
'Founder of Australian Drama', 1879 C
Four Corners, 1961 F, 1983 A
Four Powers Pacific Treaties
   Conference, 1922 A
Four Stories High, 1877 C
Four-wheel drive truck, 1907 B
Fourteen Men, 1954 C
Fourteen Powers, 1944 A
Foveaux, 1939 C
Foveaux, Joseph, 1808 A, 1809 A,
   1846 A
Fowler, Stanley, 1895 A
Fowles, Joseph, 1878 C
'Fox, The', 1907 E
Fox, Emanuel P. 1865 C, 1893 D, 1894 C
Fox, Ethel, C. 1876 C
Fox, Frank, 1874 C
Fox hounds, 1848 E
Fox Movie-Tone News, 1929 C
Fox Report, 1976 A
Foxes, 1845 F
Foxzami, 1949 E
Foy, Mark, (b. 1830), 1830 A, 1859 A
Foy, Mark, (b. 1864), 1864 A, 1892 E
Foy and Gibson's, 1859 A
Framlingham, Vic, 1971 A
Frampton, Roger D. 1948 C
Franc, Maud J. *see* Evans, M. J.
France, 1914 A, 1944 A
Frances, Alda, 1883 C
Francis, 1793 B, 1805 F
Francis, G. W. 1851 A
Francis, James G. 1819 A, 1872 A
Frank E. Evans, 1969 F
Franki, James P. 1870 B
Franklin, Jane, 1791 A
Franklin, John, 1791 A, 1837 A, 1847 A
Franklin, S. M. S. Miles, 1879 C, 1901 C,
   1928 C, 1936 C
Franklin, Tas, 1804 F
Franklin House, Tas, 1838 C
Franklin R., Tas, 1976 F, 1980 F, 1982 F
Franklin R. power scheme, Tas, 1981 A
Franks, W. 1934 E
Frankston, Vic, 1971 C
Frankston Teachers College, Vic, 1959 D
Fraser, Colin, 1875 B
Fraser, Dawn, 1937 E, 1962 E, 1964 E
Fraser, John Malcolm, 1930 A, 1955 A,
   1975 A, 1976 A, 1977 A, 1979 A,
   1980 A, 1981 A, 1982 A, 1983 A
Fraser, Malcolm, 1889 A
Fraser, Neale A. 1933 E
Fraser I. Qld, 1862 A, 1908 F, 1962 A,
   1966 B, 1975 F, 1976 A
Frater, William, 1890 C, 1918 C, 1932 C
Fraternity in Education group, 1915 D
Frazer, Charles, 1788 B, 1816 B, 1828 A
Fred and Maggie Everybody, 1937 F
Frederick (ship), 1819 F
Frederick Cowan Orchestra, Melbourne,
   1888 C
Frederikson, Kristian, 1963 F
Frederickstown, WA, 1826 A
Free Church, Qld, 1863 D

Free Falling, 1972 E
Free Grants and land settlement, 1788 A
Free Kindergarten of Vic, 1908 D
Free medical service, 1943 A, 1951 A
Free milk, 1950 D
Free Public Charity Schools, Sydney and
   Parramatta, 1810 D
Free Public Library, Sydney, 1869 D
Free settlers, 1792 A, 1793 A, 1796 A,
   1815 A
Free trade, 1859 A, 1862 A, 1873 A,
   1900 A, 1901 A
Free Trade League, WA, 1871 A
Freedom of Association and Rights,
   1973 A
Freedom of contract, 1891 A, 1892 A
Freehold land, ACT, 1970 A, WA,
   1979 A
Freeman, Francis M. 1895 C
Freeman, Harold E. 1915 C
Freeman, Jack, 1920 C
Freeman, James D. 1907 D, 1983 D
Freeman, Jeff, 1942 E
Freeman, Noel, 1938 E
Freeman, Peter, 1933 C
Freeman, Samuel, 1852 A, 1853 A
Freeman, William G. 1848 B
Freemasonry, 1803 F, 1814 F, 1816 F,
   1820 F, 1828 F, 1843 F, 1877 F, 1888 F,
   1969 D
Freemasons Grand Lodge of NSW,
   1877 F
Freemasons' Hotel, Melbourne, 1866 E
Freemasons' Tavern, Tas, 1833 C
Freeth, Gordon, 1914 A
Freetrade and Liberal Association,
   NSW, 1889 A
Freeways, *see individual entries*
Freidensen, Thomas, 1879 C
Fremantle, Charles H. 1800 A, 1829 A
Fremantle, WA, 1829 F, 1830 A, 1831 C,
   1869 B, 1881 B, 1884 B, 1889 A,
   1895 A, 1912 B, 1919 A, 1955 B,
   1969 A
Fremantle Art Gallery Prize, WA,
   1960 C
Fremantle Chamber of Commerce,
   1873 A
Fremantle Golf Club, WA, 1905 E
Fremantle Harbour, WA, 1891 B, 1945 B
Fremantle Hunt Club, 1896 E
Fremantle jetty, WA, 1832 A
Fremantle Journal and General Advertiser,
   1829 F
*Fremantle Observer Perth Gazette and West
   Australian Journal*, 1830 F
Fremaux, Louis, 1979 C
French, Charles, 1842 B
French, fears of invasion, 1826 A
French, Graeme, 1926 E
French, Leonard W. 1928 C
French, Nuclear testing, Pacific, 1973 A
French, Pacific influence, 1906 A
French artists, 1800 C
French Painting Today, Exhibition, 1953 C
French Tapestries Exhibition, 1956 C
Frenchham, H. 1851 B
Freney, Martin R. M. 1876 A, 1921 A
Frensham School, NSW, 1913 D
Fretwell, Elizabeth, 1923 C
Freya, 1963 E, 1964 E, 1965 E
Freycinet, *see* de Freycinet
Friederberger, Klaus, 1922 C
Friend, Donald S. L. 1915 C
Friendly Society of Operative
   Stonemasons, NSW, 1856 A
Friendly Society of Vic Natives, 1871 A
Friendship 7 spacecraft, 1962 B
Fringe of Leaves, A, 1976 C

Froebelian Kindergarten methods, 1898 D
Froggatt, Walter W. 1858 B
From Selection to City, 1909 C
Frome, Edward C. 1802 C
Frost, John, 1877 A
Frost, Margaret, 1978 E
Frozen foods, 1957 F
Frozen meat, 1873 B, 1880 B, 1884 A
Fruit, 1792 A, 1828 A, 1891 A, *see also individual entries*
Fruit canning, 1890 F, 1891 B
Fruit, dried, 1891 A
Fry, Douglas, 1872 C
Fry, Ella, 1916 C
Fukuoka International Marathon, Japan, 1981 E
Fulbright student interchange scheme, 1946 D, 1949 D, 1964 D
Fullager, Wilfred, 1950 A
Fullbrook, Samuel S. 1922 C, 1974 C
Fuller, Benjamin J. 1875 F
Fuller, Florence A. 1867 C
Fuller, George W. 1861 A, 1921 A, 1922 A
Fuller, John, 1901 C
Fuller, John M. F. 1911 A
Fullerton, Mary E. 1868 C
Fullwood, Albert H. 1863 C
Fulton, Henry, 1814 D, 1840 D
Fulton, Robert, 1947 E
Fulton's Classical Academy, 1814 D
Funeral benefit allowance, 1943 A
Funnel web spider, anti-venene, 1980 B
Furniture, modern, 1927 F
Furniture, wood, 1940 F
Furphy, Joseph, 1843 C, 1903 C
Fusion Liberals, 1909 A
Futility and Other Animals, 1969 C
Future Directions of Secondary Education, (Report) 1984 D
Fyans, Foster, 1790 A
Fysh, Philip O. 1835 A, 1877 A, 1887 A
Fysh, W. Hudson, 1895 B, 1920 B, 1934 B

G

G. J. Bell (painting), 1939 C
Gable, Stanley, 1934 B
Gabo I., Vic, 1933 F
Gabo wheat, 1945 B
Gadfly, Adelaide, 1906 C
G. A. F. Pike, 1950 B
Gaiety Theatre, Sydney, 1891 A
Gair, Vincent C. 1901 A, 1952 A, 1962 A, 1974 A
Gairdner, Charles H. 1898 A, 1951 A, 1963 A
Gala Supreme, 1973 E
Galava, (ship), 1927 F
Galbally, John W. 1910 A
Gale, Terry, 1948 E
Gale, Thomas, 1871 E
Gale, Walter F. 1865 B
Galene, Ruth, 1968 C
Galilee, 1966 E
Gallagher, Harry, 1926 E
Gallagher, Norm, 1982 A, 1983 A
Gallaher Prize, Sydney, 1965 C
Galleghan, Frederick G. 1897 A
Gallery of Art and School of Design, Sydney, 1855 C

Gallery of Contemporary Art, Melbourne, 1956 C
Gallery 99, Melbourne, 1966 C
Galliera, Alceo, 1950 C
Gallipoli, 1915 A, B
Gallipoli, 1956 C
Gallipoli (film), 1981 C
Gallop, Herbert, 1890 C
Galmarra, Jacky J. 1854 A
Galway, Henry L. 1914 A
Gamble, Aldreda H. 1896 B
Gambling, horses, 1960 E
Gambling, Tas, 1968 F
Game, Philip W. 1876 A, 1930 A
Game, Stuart B. H. 1915 C
Game fishing, 1933 E
Game Fishing Association of Aust., 1936 E
Gang hiring, 1942 A
Gaols, 1799 F, *see individual entries, see also* Jails
Garages, domestic, 1920 C, 1950 C
Garatt, Harvey, 1803 F
Garbage collection, 1967 B
Garde, Owen J. 1919 C
Garden I., Sydney, 1940 B, 1950 F
Garden I., WA, 1829 A
Garden Palace, Sydney, 1822 F, 1882 F
Gardiner, Frank *see* Christie, Frank
Gardiner, H. 1896 E
Gardiner, John, 1798 A, 1837 A
Gardiner Soccer Cup, 1888 E
Gardner, Charles A. 1896 B
Gardner, Frank, 1931 E
Garibaldi, 1860 C
Garling, Frederick (b. 1775), 1848 A
Garling, Frederick (b. 1806), 1806 C, 1815 C
Garlick, Henry G. 1877 C
Garlick, Rosa, 1914 C
Garner, Arthur, 1882 C
Garnier, 1800 C
Garni Sands, 1972 C
Garnsey, David A. 1909 D
Garnsey, Wanda, 1917 C
Garran, Andrew, 1825 A
Garran, Robert R. 1867 A, 1897 A
Garrard, Richard E. ('Dick'), 1914 E
Garrett, Peter, 1984 A
Garrett, Thomas, 1855 F
Garrett, Thomas, B. 1879 C
Garrick Theatre Sydney, 1890 C
Garrison church, Sydney, 1844 D
Garryowen, 1819 F
Garvan, James P. 1843 A, 1886 A
Gas/natural gas, 1820 B, 1900 B, 1906 B, 1935 B, 1961 B, 1963 B, 1964 B, 1965 B, 1966 B, 1969 B, 1970 B, 1971 B, 1977 B, 1980 B
Gas, off shore legislation, 1967 A
Gas appliances, 1902 F
Gas lighting, 1826 B, 1841 B, 1857 B, 1863 B, 1865 B, 1889 B
Gascoigne, S. H. ('Yabba'), 1878 E
Gascoyne Junction, WA, 1890 F
Gascoyne R., WA, 1848 A
Gasking, John C. 1861 C
Gasnier, Reginald, 1939 E
Gasometer, 1921 B
Gastritis, 1984 B
Gasworks Bridge, Parramatta, NSW, 1885 B
'Gates of Hell, The', 1822 A
Gattellari, Lucky, 1950 E
Gattellari, Rocco, 1941 E, 1950 E
Gatton, Qld, 1855 F
Gatton Agricultural College, Qld, 1897 D
Gatty, Harold C. 1903 B

Gatum Gatum, 1963 E
Gaudron bi-plane, 1914 B
Gaulus, 1897 E
Gaunt, Cecil R. 1863 A
Gaunt, Ernest F. A. 1865 A
Gaunt, Guy R. A. 1869 A
Gaunt, William H. 1830 A
Gaunt, Ken, 1956 B
Gaunt, Mary E. B. 1861 C
Gawler, SA, 1839 F, 1879 A, 1890 B
Gawler, George, 1795 A, 1838 A
Gawler Institute of SA, 1857 D
Gay, J. R. 1976 C
Gay, William, 1865 C
Gayndah, Qld, 1848 F, 1897 E
Gay's Swing Gang, 1936 C
Gaza, Middle East, 1916 A, 1917 A
Gaze, Irvine O. 1890 A
Gazette, NSW govt, 1832 A
Gazzard, Marea, 1928 C
Geelong, Vic, 1838 A, F, 1856 B, C, 1857 B, 1862 B, 1872 B, 1877 B, 1887 D, 1912 B, 1913 A, 1931 C, F, 1934 B, 1937 D, 1965 C, 1969 F, 1974 E, 1978 C, 1981 F, 1984 F
Geelong Advertiser, 1840 F
Geelong area, Vic, 1803 A
Geelong Art Gallery, 1896 C
Geelong Art Gallery Prize, Vic, 1938 C
Geelong Aust. Rules Football Club/ team, 1859 E, 1924 E, 1925 E, 1931 E, 1937 E, 1951 E, 1952 E, 1962 E, 1963 E
Geelong Church of England Grammar School, 1857 D
Geelong Galloper, 1954 E
Geelong Post Office, 1840 F
Geelong Town Hall, 1855 F
Geeveston, Tas, 1849 F
Geils, Andrew, 1812 A
Gellert, Leon M. 1892 C
Gellibrand, John, 1872 A, 1923 F
Gellibrand, Joseph T. 1824 A, 1827 A, 1837 A
Genealogy, 1932 F
Genée, Adeline, 1913 C
General Agreement on Tariffs and Trade, GATT, 1947 A
General Boyd (ship), 1802 A
General Grant (ship), 1866 F
General Hospital, Sydney, 1845 B
General Motors, 1931 B
General Motors Holden Ltd, 1931 B, 1948 B, 1984 B
General Observations of the Smallpox, 1804 B
General Post Offices,
 Adelaide, 1872 F
 Brisbane, 1872 F
 Perth, 1890 F
 Sydney, 1874 F, 1883 C, 1893 B, 1894 F
General Practitioners' Society of Aust., 1968 B
General strikes, 1912 A, 1917 A, 1976 A, 1979 A
General Synod, 1865 D
General Synod of the Church of England, 1872 D
General Synod of the Presbyterian Church of NSW, 1864 D
Geneva, Switzerland, 1933 A
Genoa, Duke of, 1873 A
Genocide, 1837 A
Genre, 1946 C
Gentleman in Black, The, 1861 C
Geoghegan, Edward, 1844 C
Geoghegan, Ian, 1939 E
Geoghegan, Leo, 1936 E
Geoghegan, Patrick B. 1805 D, 1839 D

777

Geological mapping, 1838 B, 1839 A, 1850 B
Geological Museum of Fremantle, 1897 D
Geological Society of Aust., 1951 B
Geological survey, 1867 B
Geology, 1951 B, *see also section B and individual entries*
Geophysics, 1978 B
George III, King, 1802 A
George III, 1835 F
George V, King, 1881 A, 1901 A
George VI, King, 1937 A, 1952 A
George, Arthur, 1915 E
George, Henry, 1890 A
George, Jennie, 1983 A
George, Robert A. 1953 A
George Art Gallery, Melbourne, 1945 C
George Cross, award, 1940 A
George and George Dept store, 1889 F
George Johnston, 1969 C
George Medal, 1967 A
George Town, Tas, 1804 A, F
Georges invitation Art Prize, Melbourne, 1963 C
Georges R., NSW, 1795 A, 1796 A
Georgetown, Qld, 1870 F
Georgian and Colonial Architecture, 1924 C
Georgian House publishers, 1946 C
Gerald, Edwin F. 1891 C
Geraldton, WA, 1850 F, 1858 A, 1864 B, 1874 A, 1879 B, 1916 C, 1921 B, F, 1930 D, 1945 F, 1949 C, 1978 A
Gerardy, *see* Gerald, Edwin F.
German citizens in Aust., 1916 A, 1925 A
German Graphic Art Exhibition, 1956 C
German language, SA, 1915 D, 1917 D, teaching of, 1915 D
German measles, 1941 B, 1971 F
German names, SA, 1917 F
German New Guinea, 1884 A, 1914 A, 1920 A
German Pacific Territories, Aust. mandate, 1920 A
German property, 1930 A
German Settlers, Qld, 1838 A, SA, 1839 D
German surrender, 1945 A
Germans, First World War, 1914 A
Germany, Nazi, 1938 A
Gerringong, NSW, 1851 F
Gertrude the Emigrant, 1857 C
Getting of Wisdom, The, 1910 C, 1977 C
Ghee, Robert E. T. 1872 C
Giant Devil-Dingo, The, 1973 C
Gibb, Claude, 1898 B
Gibbes, Robert H. M. 1916 A
Gibbeting, 1837 F
Gibbons, Henry T. 1884 C
Gibbons, Tom, 1928 C
Gibbs, Harry T. 1970 A, 1981 A
Gibbs, Katrina, 1960 E
Gibbs, May, 1918 C
Gibbs, Pearl, 1956 F
Giblin, Lyndhurst F. 1872 A
Giblin, William R. 1840 A, 1865 F, 1878 A, 1879 A, 1886 A
Gibraltar, 1935 A
Gibson, Aubrey H. L. 1901 C
Gibson, Bessie, 1868 C
Gibson, George H. 1846 C
Gibson, J. 1920 B
Gibson, Robert, 1864 A
Gibson, W. G. 1918 A
Gibson, William, 1906 C
Gibson Desert, WA, 1874 A, 1875 A
Giffen, George, 1859 E

Gifford, Helen M. 1935 C
Gift duties, 1941 A
Gilbert, Charles W. 1869 C, 1925 F
Gilbert, M. Dolores E. R. 1818 C
Gilbert, John, 1810 B
Gilbert, Johnny, 1842 A, 1865 A
Gilbert, Thomas, 1837 A
Gilbert and Sullivan, 1879 C
Giles, L. H. A. 1946 A
Giles, Ernest, 1835 A, 1872 A, 1873 A, 1875 A, 1876 A, 1882 A
Gilfillan, John A. 1793 C
Gilgandra, NSW, 1888 F, 1920 B
Gilkes, Herbert S. 1876 C
Gill, George H. 1895 D
Gill, Harry P. 1855 C
Gill, Naylor, 1873 C
Gill, Samuel T. 1818 C, 1840 C, 1847 C, 1852 C
Gillen, Francis G. 1855 B, 1899 C, 1904 C, 1912 C
Gilles, Osmond, 1788 A, 1836 A
Gillies, Duncan, 1834 A, 1886 A, 1890 A
Gillies, Max, 1984 C
Gillies, William N. 1868 A, 1925 A
Gilliland, Hector B. 1911 C
Gilling, Robert A. 1917 C
Gillison, David, 1936 C
Gilmore, Hugh, 1842 D
Gilmore, Mary, 1865 C, 1896 D, 1908 F, 1910 C, 1928 C, 1932 C, 1948 C, 1954 C
Gilmour, Gary, 1951 E
Gilroy, Norman T. 1896 D, 1940 D, 1970 D
Gilruth, John A. 1871 B, 1912 A
Giltwood, 1876 F
Ginger Meggs, 1921 F
Gingin, Qld, 1965 B
Gingin, WA, 1868 F
Ginn, Henry, 1817 C
Ginn, Stewart, 1950 E
Giovanelli, R. G. 1946 B
Gipps, George, 1791 A, 1838 A, 1839 A, 1842 A
Gippsland, Vic, 1839 A, 1841 A, 1888 F, 1898 F, 1944 F, 1970 B, 1980 F
Gippsland coast, Vic, 1964 B
Gippsland Institute of Advanced Education, Vic, 1968 D
Girgarre, Vic, 1844 F
Girl Guides Association of Aust., 1926 F
Girl Guiding movement, 1910 F
Girl with a Monkey, 1958 C
Gisborne, Henry F. 1813 A
Gisborne, Vic, 1835 F, 1892 B
Givens, Thomas, 1864 A
G. J. Coles, 1984 A
Gladesville, NSW, 1838 B
Gladesville Bridge, Sydney, 1964 C
Gladstone, Qld, 1847 F
Gladstone, Dorothy, 1931 C
Gladstone, SA, 1871 F
Gladstone Colony, 1846 A, 1847 A
Gladys Moncrieff Club, Sydney, 1966 C
Glanville-Hicks, Peggy, 1912 C
Glascow, Thomas W. 1876 A
Glaskin, Gerald M. 1923 C
Glass, 1813 B, 1872 A, 1932 B
Glass, Arnold, 1927 E
Glass, Dudley, 1899 C
Glass, Peter, 1917 C
Glass-blowing, 1813 B
Glass windows, 1881 C
Glassop, Jack L. 1913 C
Glassop, Lawson, 1944 C
Glebe I., Sydney, 1857 B
Gleeson, Brian, 1957 E
Gleeson, Horace, 1878 C
Gleeson, James T. 1915 C

Gleeson, William J. 1927 C
Gleghorn, Thomas, 1925 C, 1957 C
Glen Innes, NSW, 1851 F, 1928 F
Glen Osmond, SA, 1839 B
Glencoe, 1868 E
Glendinning, Ross, 1983 E
Glenelg, SA, 1873 B, 1960 E
Glenelg R., WA, 1838 A
Glenloth, 1892 E
Glennon, Pat, 1927 E, 1950 E, 1959 E
Glenrowan, Vic, 1880 A
Gliding, 1916 E, 1929 E, 1950 E, 1970 E, 1974 E, 1976 E
Gliding Club of Vic, 1929 E
Gliding Federation of Aust., 1950 E
Globe Derby, 1910 E
Gloster Meteor F4, 1946 B
Gloucester, NSW, 1899 F
Gloucester, Duke of, 1945 A
Gloucester Park race course, Perth, 1916 B
Glover, John, 1831 C, 1849 C
Gloves, 1933 F
Glugs of Gosh, The, 1917 C
Glyn, Neva C. 1911 C
Gnowangerup, WA, 1908 F
Go-Getter, The, 1942 C
Goat Breeders Society of Aust., 1934 C
Goats, 1832 A, 1863 A, 1934 B
Goble, Stanley J. 1891 A, 1924 B
Gocher, W. H. 1902 E
Godby, N. 1903 B
Goddard, Barrie, 1941 C
Goddard, Joe, 1861 E
Godfrey, Sydney, 1897 E
Godfrey Rivers bequest prize, 1933 C
Godson, John B. 1882 C
Goerg, Edouard Joseph, 1892 C
Gold and Black, 1977 E
Gold Coast, 1865 F, 1966 F
Gold Coast group of painters, Qld, 1960 C
Gold crushing, 1847 B
Gold Cup, polo, 1925 E
Gold discoveries, rushes, fields, California, 1849 A
NSW, 1814 B, 1823 B, 1839 B, 1841 B, 1844 B, 1851 A, 1859 B, 1860 B, 1871 B, 1879 B, 1880 A
NT, 1865 B, 1869 B, 1872 A, B, 1900 B, 1933 B
Qld, 1852 B, 1858 A, B, 1867 B, 1868 B, 1870 B, 1872 B, 1873 A, B, 1882 B, 1890 B, 1932 B
Tas, 1852 B, 1884 B, 1886 B
Vic, 1844 B, 1847 B, 1849 B, 1850 B, 1851 A, B, 1857 A, 1862 B
WA, 1881 B, 1882 B, 1885 B, 1886 A, 1887 B, 1891 B, 1892 B, 1893 A, B, 1984 B
Gold escorts, 1852 A, 1862 F, 1872 A
Gold exports, 1853 A, 1871 F
Gold extraction, 1891 B, 1899 B
Gold ingots, 1852 A
Goldminers, 1856 E, 1898 A
Gold mining, Vic, 1851 A, 1853 B, 1882 F, SA, 1846 B
Gold mining licences, 1851 A, 1852 A, 1853 A, 1854 A, 1855 A
Gold mining speculation, 1871 A
Gold nuggets, *see individual entries*
Gold production, 1870 A
Gold reserve, 1929 A
Gold robberies, 1852 F
Gold world bullion reserves, 1886 A
Golden Casket Lottery, Qld, 1916 F, 1944 F
'Golden Eagle' (nugget), 1931 F
'Golden Gate', Sydney, 1921 F

Golden Gate, USA, 1896 E
Golden Lover, 1942 C
'Golden Mile', 1893 B
Golden Miles, 1948 C
Golden Slipper Stakes, Sydney, 1957 E
Golden Summer, 1889 C
Goldfield grievances, Ballarat, 1854 A
Goldfield murders, WA, 1926 F
Goldfields, riots, *see* Chinese
Goldfields watersupply scheme, 1843 B, 1903 B
Goldfish, 1865 F
Goldner, Richard, 1945 C
Goldsbrough, Richard, 1821 A, 1848 A
Goldsbrough and Co., 1888 A
Goldsbrough Mort, 1888 A
Goldsmith, Fred, 1955 E
Goldsworthy, Leon V. 1909 A
Goldsworthy, WA, 1966 F, 1980 F
Golf, 1820 E, 1847 E, 1869 E, 1872 E, 1880 E, 1894 E, 1895 E, 1904 E, 1905 E, 1931 E, 1947 E, 1954 E, 1958 E, 1974 E, 1978 E, 1981 E, 1982 E, 1983 E, 1984 E
Golf, miniature, 1930 E
Golf balls, 1932 E
Golf caddies, 1891 E
Golf clubs, 1882 E
Gonzales Opera Co., 1916 C
Good Neighbour Councils, 1950 F
Good Samaritan Sisters, Sydney, 1858 D
Good Templar Temperance Society, 1872 F
Goodall Cup, 1921 E
Goodchild, John C. 1898 C
Goode, Cyril, 1927 C
Goodhart, John C. 1875 C
Goodman, George B. 1842 B
Goodsir, Agnes, 1864 C
Goodwin, Thomas H. J. C. 1927 A
Goolagong, Evonne, *see* Cawley, E.
Goold, Dr. 1869 B
Goold, James A. 1812 D, 1847 D, 1874 D
Goold-Adams, Hamilton J. 1915 A
Goolwa, SA, 1852 F, 1854 B, 1973 B
Goondiwindi, Qld, 1888 F
Goonyella, Qld, 1968 B
Goorangai, HMAS, 1940 F
Goossens, Eugene, 1893 C, 1948 C
Gordon, Adam L. 1833 C, 1853 C, 1867 C, 1868 C, 1870 C, 1896 F, 1933 C, 1934 C
Gordon, Florence, 1922 F
Gordon, Hayes, 1920 C, 1954 C
Gordon, Lee, 1954 C
Gordon-Below-Franklin dam controversy, 1982 F, 1983 A
Gordon R., Tas, 1971 F, 1982 F
Gordon R. Power Development Scheme, Tas, 1967 B, 1971 F
Gordon Technical College, Geelong, 1887 D
Gordonvale, Qld, 1893 F
Gore, Brian, 1983 D
Gore, John, 1846 D, 1880 D
Gore, William, 1845 A
Gorham, Kathleen, 1932 C, 1946 C, 1960 C
Gormanston, Tas, 1903 F
Gormanston, Viscount, *see* Preston, J. W. J.
Gorr, Schmuel, 1960 C
Gorton, John G. 1911 A, 1949 A, 1968 A, 1969 A, 1970 A
Goschen, Mr. 1891 F
Gosford, NSW, 1839 F, 1960 B
Goss, John, 1944 E
Goss, Michael, 1942 C

Gosse, William C. 1842 A, 1873 A
Gotch, John S. 1829 A
Gothenburg, 1875 F
Gouger, Robert, 1802 A, 1833 A, 1836 A
Gough, Harry, 1939 F
Gough, J. 1881 E, 1898 E
Goulburn, NSW, 1832 B, 1833 F, 1849 B, 1869 B, 1872 D, 1875 D, 1937 E
Goulburn, Frederick, 1788 A, 1821 A
Goulburn, Henry, 1856 A
Goulburn College of Advanced Education, NSW, 1970 D
Goulburn district, NSW, 1836 E
Goulburn I., NT, 1916 D
Goulburn Lilac time Art Prizes, NSW, 1957 C
Goulburn Plains, NSW, 1818 A
Goulburn Teachers' College, NSW, 1970 D
Gould, Elizabeth, 1804 C
Gould, James A. 1847 D
Gould, John, 1804 C, 1838 B, 1841 C, 1865 C
Gould, Nathaniel ('Nat'), 1884 C
Gould, Shane E. 1957 E, 1971 E, 1972 E
Gould, Strom, 1910 C
Gould, William B. 1801 C
Gould League of Bird Lovers, Vic, 1909 F
Gouldsmith, Edward, 1852 C
Goullet, Alfred, 1922 E
Gove, NT, 1963 A, 1964 B, 1969 F, 1971 A
Gove Peninsula, NT, 1935 D, 1949 B, 1968 B
Government, *see individual entries and Section A for political appointments*
Government Gazette, NSW, 1832 A
Government Houses, 1805 A, 1845 C
Adelaide, 1839 C
Brisbane, 1862 C
Hobart, 1805 A, 1858 C, 1905 C
Parramatta, NSW, 1790 C, 1816 C
Perth, 1859 C
Sydney, 1788 B, C, 1817 C, 1845 C
Government Rules, 1788 B
Governor, Jimmy, 1900 F
Governor, Joe, 1900 F
Governor General, first Aust. born, 1930 A
Governors and Governors General, *see individual entries and Section A for appointments*
Govett, William R. 1807 A
Govt, *abbreviation for* Government
Gowrie, Earl of, *see* Hore-Ruthven, A. G. A. 1872 A
Gowrie Scholarship Memorial Trust, 1943 D
Goya Art Awards, 1964 C
Goyder, George W. 1826 A, 1865 B, 1866 B, 1869 A
'Goyder Line', 1866 B
Goyder rainfall line, 1865 B, 1866 B, 1872 A
Grace Park Lawn Tennis Club, 1889 E
Graduates, 1984 D
Graduation Ball, 1940 C
Grafter, The, 1898 E
Grafton, NSW, 1838 F, 1859 F, 1935 F, 1961 C
Grafton Galleries, London, 1918 C
Grafton Gallery Exhibition, London, 1898 C
Grafton Steam Navigation Co., 1857 A
Grafton Textile Prize, NSW, 1951 C
Graham, Anne, 1925 C
Graham, Billy, 1959 D, 1979 D
Graham, David, 1946 E, 1979 E, 1981 E

Graham, James, 1847 E
Graham, Peter, 1925 C
Grain, 1795 A, 1798 A, 1816 A, 1831 A, 1843 B, *see also* Wheat *and individual entries*
Grainger, George Percy, 1882 C, 1903 C
Grainger, Percy A. *see* Grainger, George Percy
Grammar Schools, *see individual entries*
Grammar Schools Act, Qld, 1860 D
Grammy Awards, 1974 C
Gramophone, records, 1924 B
Gramp, Johann, 1819 A, 1847 A
Grampians, Vic, 1880 C, 1932 F
Grampians Wonderland (film), 1959 C
Granary, 1797 B
Grand Federal Labor Council, Adelaide, 1913 A
Grand Flaneur, 1880 E
Grand Fleet, First World War, 1915 A, 1916 A
Grand Freemason Lodge Temples, 1969 D
Grand Hotel, 1883 C
Grand National Eisteddfod of Australasia, 1891 C
Grand Prix, Vic, 1928 E
Grand Prix Cycling, 1953 E
Grand Prix, World, 1959 E, 1960 E
Grand Slams, tennis, 1962 E, 1969 E, 1970 E
Grand Teetotal Festival, Sydney, 1845 F
Grandchester, Qld, 1865 B
'grandfather of Aust. landscape painting', 1814 C
Grandi, Margherita, 1895 C
Grandpa's Selection, 1916 C
'Granny Smith', 1800 A
Granny Smith apples, 1868 A
Grano, Paul L. 1894 C
Grant, Clifford S. 1930 C
Grant, Donald, 1942 C
Grant, Donald M. 1890 A
Grant, Jack, 1965 E
Grant, James, 1800 A, 1801 A, 1833 A
Grant, James M. 1822 A, 1855 A, 1865 A
Grant, Julius, 1912 C
Grant, R. 1983 E
Grant, William, 1870 A
Grant, William G. 1876 C
Grants Commission, Cwlth, 1933 A
Granville, NSW, 1916 E, 1977 F
Grape vines, 1791 A, 1816 A, 1836 A, *see also* Vineyards *and* Wine
Graphic Art, 1851 C
Grasby, W. C. 1891 D
Grassby, Albert J. 1926 A
Grasshoppers, 1872 F
Graves, John W. 1795 C
Graves, re-use of, 1984 F
Gray, Alastair C. 1898 C
Gray, Charles, 1861 A
Gray, Edgar ('Dunc'), 1907 E
Gray, R. T. 1982 A
Grayson, Henry J. 1856 B
Graziers, NSW, 1820 A
Grazing licences, 1826 A, 1836 A
Grazing rights, 1835 A
'Great Australian Copper Mine', Qld, 1867 B
Great Australian Loneliness, The, 1937 C
Great Barrier Beef, Qld, 1802 A, 1834 F, 1844 A, 1875 F, 1908 C, 1960 B, 1968 B, 1970 B, 1971 B, 1975 F, 1979 F, 1981 F, 1982 F
Great Barrier Reef Marine Park, 1979 F
Great Barrier Reef Marine Park Act, 1975 F
Great Britain, 1852 B

'Great comet', 1881 B
Great Dividing Range, 1813 A, 1827 A, 1854 A
'Great Drought', 1893 F, 1902 F
Great Exhibition, London, 1851 F
Great Fire of Brisbane, 1864 F
Great German Peace Festival, 1871 F
Great Hall, Sydney Town Hall, 1888 C, 1889 C
Great Hall, Sydney University, 1854 C
Great Lake hydro electric power, Tas, 1916 B
Great Morwell Coal Mining Co., 1889 B
Great North road, 1831 B
Great Northern Railway, 1878 B
Great Northern Railway, NSW, 1857 B
Great Queensland, The, 1876 F
Great Sandy Desert, WA, 1896 A
'Great Seal Case', 1845 A
Great Southern railway, NSW, 1869 B, 1878 B
Great Star Catalogue, 1890 B
Great Victoria Desert, SA, 1903 A, 1974 F
Great Western, Vic, 1853 A, F, 1918 A
Great Western Highway, NSW, 1832 B
Great Western Railway, NSW, 1876 B
Great Western Road, NSW, 1818 B
'Great White Fleet', 1908 A
'Great White Train', 1925 F
Greater Apollo, The, 1927 C
'Greatest Liar on Earth', 1847 F
Greece, 1941 A
Greek Orthodox church, 1896 D, 1897 D, 1898 D
Greek Orthodox Holy Metropolis, 1924 D, 1959 D
Greek settlers, Melbourne, 1849 F
Green, Arthur V. 1857 D
Green, Catherine, 1931 A
Green, Clive, 1976 E
Green, Dennis, 1955 E
Green, Douglas A. 1921 C
Green, Guy S. M. 1973 A, 1981 A, 1982 A
Green, Henry M. 1881 C
Green, Jack, 1910 E
Green, M. A. 1979 D
Green, Sol, 1868 E
Green, Tom, 1913 C
Green ban, 1971 F, 1973 F
Green Gully, skeleton, Vic, 1965 B
Greenaway, Ronald L. 1932 C
Greenhalgh, Victor, 1900 C
Greenhill, Harold, 1914 C
Greening programme, 1982 F
Greenough R., WA, 1864 B
Greenough R. bridge, 1864 B
Greenpeace, 1977 F
Greenway, Francis, 1815 C, 1816 C, 1817 C, 1819 C, 1820 C, 1837 C
Greenwich, England, 1883 B
Greenwood, Edward A. 1930 C
Greenwood, Gordon, 1913 D
Greenwood, James, 1874 D
Greer, Germaine, 1939 C, 1970 C, 1984 C
Greeves, Edward, 1904 E, 1924 E
Gregan McMahon Players Co., Sydney, 1929 C
Gregg, Norman M. 1892 B, 1941 B
Gregory, Augustus C. 1819 A, 1846 A, 1848 A, B, 1855 A, 1858 A
Gregory, Charles, 1850 C
Gregory, Charles W. 1878 E
Gregory, Dick, 1970 A
Gregory, Francis T. 1821 A, 1846 B, 1858 A, 1861 A, 1862 A
Gregory, Jack M. 1895 E, 1922 E
Gregory, John W. 1864 B

Gregory, Sydney E. 1870 E
Gregory R., Qld, 1984 B
Gregson, Thomas G. 1798 A, 1857 A
Greig, Edward J. 1864 C
Greig, Janet L. 1896 B
Greig, Keith, 1951 E, 1973 E, 1974 E
Greig, Mary A. 1845 C
Greig, Maysie C. 1901 C
Grenfell, NSW, 1867 F
Gresham, Tony, 1940 E
Greta, NSW, 1842 F, 1886 B
Gretel, 1962 E
Gretel II, 1970 E
Grey, Earle, 1849 A
Grey, Frederick M. 1899 C
Grey, George, 1812 A, 1837 A, C, 1838 A, 1839 A, 1841 A
Grey, Zane, 1936 E
Grey speck disease, 1928 B
Grey-backed beetle, 1935 B
Greycliffe (ferry), 1927 F
Greyhound, (sculpture), 1915 C
Greyhound racing, 1867 E, 1927 E, 1937 E, 1942 E, 1944 E, 1953 E, 1969 E, 1971 E, 1972 E, 1974 E, 1979 E, *see also* Coursing
Greyhound Racing Control Council, 1937 E
Grey-Smith, Guy E. 1916 C
Grey-Smith, Helen, 1916 C
Grien, Henry, 1847 F
Grierson, Max, 1924 C
Grieve, Alan R. C. 1910 C
Grieve, Robert H. 1924 C
Grieves, Ken, 1925 E
Griffin, Ambrose S. 1912 C
Griffin, Brian, 1967 E
Griffin, George, 1900 A
Griffin, Thomas J. A. 1832 F
Griffin, Vaughan M. 1903 C
Griffin, W. Burley, 1876 C, 1912 C
Griffith, NSW, 1912 F, 1977 F
Griffith, Samuel W. 1845 A, 1883 A, 1890 A, 1901 A, 1903 A
Griffith University, Qld, 1975 D
Griffiths, Albert, 1869 E, 1890 E
Griffiths, Harley, 1878 C
Griffiths, Harley C. 1908 C
Griffiths, John G. 1810 C, 1842 C
Griffiths, Thomas, 1865 A, 1905 B
Grigg, May, 1885 E
Grime, Billy, 1902 E
Grimes, Charles E. 1795 A, 1802 A, 1803 A, 1804 A, 1808 A, 1858 A
Grimmett, Clarence V. 1891 E
Grimshaw, Beatrice E. 1870 C
Grimstone, Mary L. 1832 C
Grimwade, Wilfrid R. 1879 B
Grin, Henry, *see* Grien, H.
Grindley's Bank of London, 1984 A
Gritten, Henry C. 1818 C
Grogan Medal, Qld, 1946 E
Groom, Littleton E. 1867 A
Groote Eylandt, NT, 1920 A, 1966 B
Grose, Francis, 1789 A, 1792 A, 1794 B, 1814 A
Gross, Eric, 1926 C
Grosvenor Art Gallery, Sydney, 1924 C, 1926 C
Grounds, Marr, 1930 C
Grounds, Roy B. 1905 C, 1940 C, 1953 C, 1959 C
Grout, Arthur T. W. (Wally), 1927 E, 1961 E
Grove, James, 1910 C
Grover, Montague M. 1870 F
Gruner, Elioth, 1882 C, 1919 C, 1920 C
Gruzman, Neville, 1983 C
Grylls, James, 1838 D

Gsell, Francis X. 1872 D, 1911 D, 1938 D
Guardian, 1789 A
Guardian, The, 1838 C
Gude, Gilda, 1918 C
Gude, Nornie, 1915 C
Guérard, J. J. E. von, *see* von Guérard
Guerassimoff, Jules, 1940 E
Guerin, Bella, 1883 D
Guest of Honour, 1943 F
Guichen Bay, SA, 1857 F
Guide dogs, blind, 1951 F
Guided missile range project, SA, 1946 B
base, 1961 B
destroyer, 1963 A, 1966 A
Guild of Aust. Composers, 1935 C
Guild of St Mary and St Joseph, 1845 F
Guildford, NSW, 1945 E, 1968 E
Guildford, WA, 1830 F, 1881 B, 1944 B, 1949 F
Guilfoyle, William R. 1840 B
Guillaux, Maurice, 1914 B, F
Gulf of Carpentaria, 1819 A, 1860 A, 1861 A, 1881 B, 1883 A, 1886 A, 1920 A, 1923 F, 1965 A, 1966 B
Gulf, St Vincent, 1802 A, 1831 A
Gulf Hero, The, 1896 A
Gulgong, NSW, 1870 F, 1871 B
Gullet, Henry S. 1878 A
Gulliver, Ken, 1928 E
Gully, John, 1819 C
Gulpilil, David, 1953 C
Gumeracha, SA, 1855 F
'Gun Alley Murder', 1922 F
Gun battery, 1867 C
Gun Clubs Association of Vic, 1900 E
Gun powder, 1814 F, 1829 B
Gunbower, Vic, 1950 B
Gundagai, NSW, 1838 F, 1852 F, 1929 C, 1932 F
Gundagai Bridge, 1866 B
Gundagai Golden Corroboree Prize, Vic, 1960 C
Gundaroo, NSW, 1824 F
Gunn, Mrs Aeneas, 1870 C, 1905 C, 1908 C
Gunn, John, 1885 A, 1924 A
Gunn, Ronald C. 1808 B, 1854 B
Gunn, William A. 1914 A, 1958 A
Gunnedah, NSW, 1856 F
Gunning, NSW, 1824 F
Gurindji Aborigines, NT, 1966 A, 1967 A, 1975 A
Gurner's Lane, 1982 E
Gurney, Alex, 1941 F
Gustavus III, 1850 C
Guth, Erwin A. 1926 C
Guthrie Medal, 1980 B
Guthrie's hotel, Adelaide, 1837 F
Guy, Athol, 1940 C
Guyong, NSW, 1851 B
Guyra, NSW, 1885 F
Gwydir R., NSW, 1831 A
Gwynne, J. E. A. 1870 B
Gwynne, Marjorie, 1886 C
Gye, Harold F. N. ('Hal'), 1888 C
Gymnastics, 1937 E, 1948 E
Gympie, Qld, 1867 B, F, 1881 B, 1904 A
Gypsum, SA, 1912 B

H

H-Bomb, 1952 B
Habbe, Nicholas F. 1827 C
Hack, John B. 1805 A, 1837 A, B
Hackett, John W. 1848 A, 1898 B
Hacking, Henry, 1831 A
Hackney carriage, 1830 B, 1847 B
Hackwood, William, 1798 C
Haddon, Alfred C. 1898 C
Haddon, Robert J. 1866 C, 1902 C, 1908 C
Haddon Rig sheep stud, NSW, 1882 B
Haddrick, Ronald N. 1929 C
Hadfield, Peter, 1983 E
Hadley, Basil, 1940 C
Hadspen, Tas, 1820 F
Haefliger, Paul, 1914 C
Hahndorf, SA, 1839 F
Hahndorf Private Art Gallery, SA, 1950 C
Haines, Jack, 1907 E
Haines, Robert K. R. 1916 C
Haines, William C. 1810 A, 1854 A, 1855 A, 1857 A
Hair, 1921 F, 1922 F, 1928 F
Hair, 1969 C
Hair, Graham, 1943 C
Haisma, Hinke, 1983 F
Haives, John C. 1956 C
Hale, Mathew B. 1811 D, 1856 D, 1858 D, 1865 D, 1875 D
Hales, Alfred A. G. 1860 C
Hales, T. 1880 E
Half Burnt Tree, The, 1969 C
Half-caste Bride (series of paintings), 1958 C
Half Dozen Art Group, Qld, 1940 C
'Half-Length' (stamps), 1850 F
Half Moon battery, Sydney, 1798 A
Halford, George B. 1824 B, 1862 D
Halford, George D. 1897 D
Hall, Benjamin, 1837 A, 1865 A
Hall, Charles, 1885 B
Hall, Duncan, 1925 E
Hall, Edward, 1930 C
Hall, Edward S. 1826 A, F, 1829 F, 1860 A
Hall, Edward Swarbreck, 1804 B
Hall, Jim, 1868 E
Hall, John, 1862 C
Hall, John F. 1947 C, 1955 C
Hall, Kenneth G. 1901 C, 1931 C, 1933 C, 1937 C, 1938 C, 1939 C, 1946 C
Hall, Lindsay B. 1859 C
Hall, Marshall, 1895 C
Hall, Perce, 1912 E
Hall, Raymond S. 1928 A
Hall, Robert, 1867 B
Hall, Rodney, 1935 C
Hall, R. S. 1968 A
Hall, Thomas S. 1858 B
Hall, Walter R. 1831 A
Hall Mark, 1933 E
Hall's creek, WA, 1885 B
Hallandal, Pam, 1929 C
Hallen, Ambrose L. 1886 C
Hallett, Howard, 1890 E
Halley's Comet, 1910 B
Halloran, Laurence H. 1820 D, 1825 D, 1831 D
Halloway, Arthur ('Pony'), 1899 E
Hallstrom, Edward J. L. 1886 A
Halpern, Stanislav, 1919 C
Halse, Reginald C. 1881 D
Halvorsen, Magnus, 1922 E
Halvorsen, Trygve, 1924 E

Ham, Thomas, 1821 C
Ham Funeral, The, 1947 C
Hambridge, Alice, 1869 C
Hambridge, Helen, 1857 C
Hambridge, Millicent, 1872 C
Hamel, France, 1918 A
Hamel State Farm, WA, 1895 B, 1899 B
Hamer, Rupert J. ('Dick'), 1916 A, 1972 A
Hamersley, Vermont, 1871 A
Hamersley Iron Ltd, 1963 B
Hamersley Ranges, WA, 1952 B, 1961 B
Hamilton, Vic, 1838 F
Hamilton, Charles, 1874 C
Hamilton, Edward A. 1860 C
Hamilton, George, 1812 A, 1837 A
Hamilton, Gordon, 1937 C
Hamilton, Henry, 1840 A
Hamilton, Ian, 1914 A
Hamilton, Richard, 1792 A
Hamilton, Robert G. C. 1836 A, 1887 A
Hamilton, William, 1858 A
Hamilton, William H. 1790 A, 1830 A
Hamley, Francis G. 1868 A
Hammer throwing, 1967 E, 1979 E
Hammond, J. J. 1911 B
Hammond, Joan, 1912 C
Hammond, Robert B. S. 1870 D
Hammond, Stanley S. 1914 C
Hammond I., Qld, 1859 F
Hampden, Viscount, *see* Brand, H. R.
Hampden Bridge, NSW, 1895 B
Hampel, Carl, 1942 C
Hampton, John S. 1809 A, 1862 A
Hancock, Beverly, 1984 F
Hancock, Henry R. 1836 B, 1889 B
Hancock, Langley G. ('Lang'), 1909 B, 1938 B, 1952 B, 1958 B, 1974 A
Hancock, William K. 1898 D, 1930 C
Hand of Faith (nugget), 1980 F
Handball, 1789 E, 1872 E, 1920 E, 1938 E
Handbook of the Birds of Australia, 1865 C
Handcock, P. J. 1902 A
Handful of Pennies, A, 1958 C
Handicapped children, 1971 B
Hang-gliding, 1968 E, 1971 E, 1976 E
Hanger, Mostyn, 1977 A
Hanging, 1826 F, 1838 F, *see individual entries*
Hank, Bob, 1924 E
Hanke, Henry A. 1901 C, 1934 C
Hanlon, Edward M. 1887 A, 1946 A
Hann, Frank H. 1846 A, 1903 A
Hann, William, 1837 A, 1872 A
Hanna, Ken, 1975 C
Hannaford, Alf, 1915 B
Hannah, Colin T. 1914 A, 1972 A
Hannan, Patrick, 1842 A, 1893 B
Hannan, William, 1932 E
Hannon, Thomas, 1827 A
Happy Valley, 1939 C
Hansard, 1856 A, 1864 A, 1946 A
Hansen, Allen A. P. 1911 C
Hansford, Gregory, 1952 E
Hansom cab, 1849 B
Hanson, Albert J. 1866 C
Hanson, Raymond C. 1913 C
Hanson, Richard D. 1805 A, 1857 A, 1872 A
Harcourt, Clewin S. V. 1870 C
Harcourt, John, 1934 C
Hard Way, The, 1961 C
Harden, NSW, 1880 F
Harding, William A. 1930 C
Hardwick, Harold, 1889 E
Hardy, Charles, 1898 A
Hardy, Francis J. 1917 C, 1950 C, 1963 C, 1975 C

Hardy, James, 1932 E
Hardy, Thomas, 1830 A, 1853 A, 1857 A
Hare, Alexander, 1827 A
Hare racing, mechanical, Vic, 1956 E
Hare-Clarke system, Tas, 1897 A, 1907 A
Hargrave, Lawrence, 1850 B, 1878 B, 1884 B, 1885 B, 1889 B, 1891 B, 1894 B
Hargraves, Edward H. 1816 A, 1851 B
Haricot, 1874 E
Harkness, Donald, 1890 B
Harlech Castle, 1870 F
Harness racing, *see* Trotting
Harnett, Laurence J. 1898 B
Harney, William E. 1895 C
Harold Park, Sydney, 1911 E, 1927 E, 1944 E, 1978 E
Harp in the South, The, 1948 C
Harper, Andrew, 1844 D
Harper, Margaret H. 1879 B
Harper, Norman D. 1906 D
Harpur, Charles, 1813 C, 1835 C, 1845 C, 1846 C, 1853 C, 1862 C
Harrex, David M. 1929 C
Harrington, 1808 F
Harrington, Edward P. 1896 C
Harrington, Patricia, 1978 E
Harris, Alexander, 1805 C, 1847 C, 1849 C
Harris, George P. R. 1810 C
Harris, John, (1), 1802 D, 1819 D
Harris, John, (2), 1803 A
Harris, John, (3), 1838 B
Harris, John, (4), 1798 A
Harris, Laurence H. L. 1871 B
Harris, Maxwell H. 1921 C, 1940 C, 1941 C, 1943 C, 1944 C
Harris, Richard D. P. 1817 D
Harris, Rolf, 1930 C, 1960 C, 1968 C, 1970 C
Harris, Samuel H. 1881 B
Harris, Wayne, 1960 E
Harrison, Eric J. 1892 A
Harrison, Harry B. 1878 C
Harrison, Harry C. A. 1836 E, 1858 E
Harrison, Henry, 1871 C
Harrison, James, 1816 B, 1850 B, 1852 B, 1856 B, 1872 B, 1873 B
Harrison, James W. 1912 A, 1968 A
Harrison, John, 1802 A
Harrison, Launcelot, 1880 B
Harrison, Lieut. 1914 A
Harrison Moore, 1922 C
Harrod, Megan, 1964 E
Harrow, Vic, 1836 F
Harrower, Elizabeth, 1928 C
Harry Seidler and Associates, 1967 C
Hart, Fritz B. 1874 C, 1900 C, 1914 C, 1928 C
Hart, John, 1809 A, 1831 A, 1865 A, 1868 A, 1870 A
Hart, Kevin C. 1928 C
Hart, Mr. 1830 B
Hart, Kevin C. (Pro), 1974 C
Hart, William, 1912 E
Hart, William E. 1885 B, 1911 B, 1912 B
Hartigan, Patrick J. 1878 C, 1921 C
Hartley, Kevin, 1934 E
Hartley, NSW, 1833 F, 1841 B
Hartley College of Advanced Education, 1979 D
Hartnett, John, 1893 B
Hartnett, Laurence J. 1898 B
Hartnett, Laurence, 1948 B
Hartney, V. 1943 E
Hartog, Harry den, 1902 C
Hartt, Cecil L. 1894 C
Hartwig, Rex, 1929 E
Harvest, E. D. 1875 A, 1877 A
Harvester Judgment, 1907 A

781

Harvesters, 1843 B, 1884 B, 1905 B, 1912 B, 1913 B, 1921 B, 1924 B, 1925 B, 1956 B, 1970 B
Harvey, Clarence E. M. 1921 E
Harvey, Edmund A. 1907 C
Harvey, Frank, 1885 C
Harvey, Hannah, 1803 F
Harvey, Lewis J. 1871 C
Harvey, R. Neil, 1928 E
Harvey Reservoir, WA, 1948 B
Harwood, A. R. 1931 C
Harwood, Gwen, 1920 C
Hashemy, 1849 A
Hashish, 1982 F
Haskell, S. N. 1886 D
Haskell, William T. 1814 B
Haslem Creek, NSW, 1857 F
Hasluck, Paul M. C. 1905 A, 1969 A
Hassal, Rowland, 1808 D
Hassall, Ian, 1899 C
Hassall, Nanette, 1976 C
Hassall, Rowland, 1820 D
Hassall, Thomas, 1794 D
Hassen, Jack, 1926 E
Hassett, Francis G. 1918 A
Hassett, Lindsay, 1913 E
Hasting Caves, Tas, 1917 B
Hastings R., NSW, 1818 A
Haswell, William A. 1854 B
Hat, cloche, 1922 F
Hat, slouch, 1885 F
Hat pins, 1912 F
Havilah merino stud, 1832 B
Havekes, Gerald, 1925 C
Havelock, Arthur E. 1901 A
Havyatt, Richard, 1945 C
Hawdon, Joseph, 1813 A, 1837 A, 1838 A, F
Hawes, John C. 1916 C
Hawk and Co, Pty Ltd, 1857 B
Hawke, Albert R. G. 1900 A, 1953 A
Hawke, Robert J. L. 1929 A, 1958 A, 1969 A, 1973 A, 1980 A, 1982 A, 1983 A, 1984 A
Hawker, Charles A. S. 1894 A
Hawker, George C. 1818 A
Hawker, Harry G. 1889 B, 1912 B, 1913 B, 1920 B
Hawker, H. G. Engineering Co., 1920 B
Hawkesbury Agricultural College, NSW, 1891 D
Hawkesbury Horse Race Club, 1832 E
Hawkesbury R., flooding, 1799 F, 1806 F, 1808 F, 1809 F, 1811 F
Hawkesbury R., NSW, 1789 A, 1794 A, 1797 F, 1799 A, 1804 D, 1810 F, 1828 A, 1844 B, 1944 F
Hawkesbury R. railway bridge, 1889 B
Hawkestone Peak, WA, 1956 F
Hawkins, Harold F. W. 1893 C
Hawthorn Aust. Rules Football Club/team, 1873 E, 1961 E, 1971 E, 1976 E, 1978 E, 1983 E
Hawthorn Teachers' College, 1951 D
Hawthorne, Phil, 1944 E
Hay, W. Gosse, 1919 C
Hay, NSW, 1858 F
Hay, J. A. 1984 B
Hay, William G. 1875 C, 1919 C
Hayden, William G. 1933 A, 1977 A, 1978 A, 1980 A, 1982 A, 1983 A, 1984 A
Hayes, Catherine, 1854 C
Hayes, Colin, 1924 E
Hayes, Elisabeth, 1983 E
Hayes, Henry B. 1803 C, F, 1832 F
Hayes, John, 1789 A, 1793 A, 1794 A, 1831 A
Hayes, J. B. 1922 A

Haylen, Leslie C. 1902 A
Hayllar, Tom, 1976 E
Haymarket Theatre, Melbourne, 1862 C
Haynes, George, 1938 C
Haynes, John, 1880 F
Hayseeds, The, 1933 C
Haysom, Melville, 1900 C
Hayter, Henry H. 1821 B
Hayward, Edward W. 1903 A
Hayward, Paul, 1981 F
Haywood, John, 1929 C
Haxton, Elaine A. 1909 C
Hazeldean merino stud, 1865 B
Hazelton, Ross, 1935 E
Hazzard, Shirley, 1931 C
Head, Lindsay H. 1935 E
Head of the river rowing races, 1868 E
Head trade, 1831 F
Headers, *see* Harvesters
Headwear, 1910 F
Heales, Richard, 1822 A, 1860 A
Healesville, Vic, 1943 B
Heally, William, 1876 F
Health, 1971 A
Health, mental, 1843 B
Health Insurance Bill, Federal, 1974 A
Health Insurance Schemes, 1970 A, 1975 A, 1978 A, 1981 A
Health Service Advisory Committee, 1977 A
Heard, Peter, 1908 E
Heard I., 1947 A, B
Hearn, William E. 1826 A
Heart of Spring, 1919 C
Heart transplant, 1968 B
Heaters, gas, 1902 F
Heath, R. W. 1905 E
Heathcote, NSW, 1970 F
Heathcote, Vic, 1852 F
Heaton, John H. 1848 A
'Heavy Harry', 1941 B
Hedley, Charles, 1862 B
Hedstrom, Newton S. 1914 C
Heeler, 1890 B
Heffernan, Edward, 1912 C
Heffron, Robert J. 1890 A, 1959 A
Heggie, Otto P. 1879 C
Heidelberg, Vic, 1890 C
Heidelberg School, 1885 C, 1886 C, 1889 C, 1939 C
Heights and Buildings Committees, Sydney and Melbourne, 1957 C
Heinicke, A. M. Hermann, 1863 C
Heinze, Bernard T. 1894 C, 1925 C, 1947 C, 1974 C
Hele, Ivor H. T. 1912 C, 1936 C, 1951 C, 1953 C, 1954 C, 1955 C, 1957 C
Helen Nicol, 1886 F
Helena Rubinstein Travelling Scholarship, 1958 C
Helicopter flights, 1982 B, squadron, 1969 A
heliochronometer, 1863 B
Heliport, Melbourne, 1960 B
Hellier, Dermont J. J. 1916 C
Hellyer, Henry, 1790 A, 1827 A
Helmrich, Dorothy, 1944 C
Helpman, Lieut. 1850 B
Helpmann, Robert M. 1909 C, 1933 C, 1964 C, 1965 C, 1969 C
Helsinki, Finland, 1952 E, 1983 E
Hely, Hovenden, 1823 A, 1852 A
Hemlines, 1935 F, 1949 F, 1982 F
Hemsley, Kim, 1980 C
Henderson, Anketell, 1890 C
Henderson, Brian, 1958 C
Henderson, George C. 1870 D
Henderson, John B. (1), 1827 C
Henderson, John B. (2), 1836 B, 1904 F

Henderson, Moya P. 1941 C, 1965 C
Henderson, R. F. 1970 F
Hendry, Hunter L. 1895 E
Hendy, Suzanne, 1956 E
Henley-on-Yarra, 1904 E
Henneberry, Bill, 1905 E
Henneberry, Fred, 1911 E
Henricks, Jon, 1935 E
Henry, Alice, 1857 A
Henry, Ernest, 1837 A, 1867 B
Henry, Lucien, 1850 C
Henry Caselli Richards Art Prize, 1951 C
Henry Lawson Festival Art Prizes, Grenfell, NSW, 1960 C
Hens, 1930 B
Henschke, Paul G. 1914 A
Henshaw, David, 1961 B, 1970 B
Henshaw, John G. 1929 C
Henty, Charles S. 1807 A
Henty, Edward, 1834 A, 1835 A
Henty, James, 1800 A
Henty, Stephen G. 1811 A
Henty, Thomas, 1834 A, 1839 A
Henty, William, 1808 A
Hepburn, John, 1837 A
Her Majesty's Opera House, Brisbane, 1888 C
Her Majesty's Theatre, Perth, 1904 C
Her Majesty's Theatre, Sydney, 1887 C, 1890 C, 1902 C, 1903 C, 1927 C
Herald, Art Show, Melbourne, 1953 C
Herald and Weekly Times Ltd, 1902 F
Herbert, A. F. Xavier, 1901 C, 1938 C, 1959 C, 1961 C, 1963 C, 1975 C
Herbert, C. E. 1905 A
Herbert, Daniel, 1797 C, 1831 C, 1835 C
Herbert, Harold B. 1892 C
Herbert, Robert G. W. 1831 A, 1859 A, 1866 A
Herbert Act, Qld, 1860 A
Herberton, Qld, 1879 B, 1880 B
Herd, James W. 1890 A
Hereditary nobility, 1853 A
Hereford cattle, 1826 A
Here's Luck, 1930 C
Heritage, 1935 C
Heritage of Australia, The, 1981 F
Heritage Commission, 1975 A
Herman, Sali, 1898 C
Hermannsburg Aboriginal School, NT, 1879 D, 1926 B
Hermannsburg Lutheran Mission, NT, 1877 D
Herman, Morton, 1954 C
Hermit of Van Diemen's Land, The, 1829 C
Hern, Charles E. 1848 C
Hero of Waterloo Hotel, NSW, 1838 F
Heroes of the Cross, 1910 C
Heroin smuggling, 1981 F, 1983 F
Herring, Edmund F. 1892 A, 1949 A
Herron, Leslie J. 1902 A
Hertz, Carl, 1896 C
Hervey Bay, Qld, 1863 F
Hesling, Bernard, 1905 C
Hessing, Leonard, 1931 C
Hester, Joy, 1920 C
Hetherington, John A. 1907 C
Hewett, Dorothy, 1923 C, 1959 C
Hey, Victor, 1913 E
Heyer, John W. 1916 C, 1954 C
Heyfield, NSW, 1858 F
Heysen, Hans, 1877 C, 1903 C
Heysen, Nora, 1911 C, 1938 C
Heywood, Vic, 1842 F
Hexagon, The, 1956 C
Hi Jinx, 1960 E
Hibberd, Donald, 1917 A
Hibberd, John, 1940 C, 1967 C, 1969 C

Hibernia, 1833 F
Hibernian–Australasian Catholic Benefit Society, 1865 F
Hick, Jacqueline, 1920 C
Hickey, Dale, 1937 C
Hickey, Reg, 1907 E
Hicks, Mary J. 1886 F
Hicks, Peggy G. 1970 C
Hicks, Stanton Cedric, 1892 B
Hickson, Robert R. P. 1842 B
Higgins, Henry B. 1851 A, 1906 A, 1907 A
Higgins, John M. 1862 B
Higgins, Mat. 1858 E
Higgins, Roy, 1938 E, 1965 E, 1967 E
Higgs, Jim, 1950 E
High Commissioner, London, 1927 A
High Court of Aust., Canberra, 1902 A, 1903 A, 1906 A, 1912 A, 1916 A, 1919 A, 1926 A, 1929 A, 1930 A, 1931 A, 1933 A, 1935 A, 1940 A, 1946 A, 1948 A, 1951 A, 1952 A, 1958 A, 1961 A, 1964 A, 1965 A, 1967 A, 1969 A, 1970 A, 1974 A, 1975 A, 1976 A, 1976 C, D, 1981 A, 1982 A, 1983 A, F, 1984 F
High Flux Australian Reactor, HIFAR, 1958 B
High rise buildings, *see* Multi-storey buildings
High rise development, 1957 C
High Schools,
  NSW, 1883 D
  Qld, 1912 D, 1917 D
  SA, 1907 D, 1908 D
  Tas, 1913 D, 1952 D, 1957 D
  Vic, 1905 D
  see individual entries
High Voltage, 1975 C
Higham, James B. 1868 B
Higher School Certificate, NSW, 1967 D
Highland, Charles, 1894 B
Highland, William, 1814 B
Highland Society of Maryborough, Vic, 1857 F
Higinbotham, George, 1826 A, 1866 D
Hilder, Bim V. A. 1909 C
Hilder, Brett, 1911 C
Hilder, Jesse J. 1881 C
Hilditch, Andrew, 1956 E
Hilditch, Stan, 1956 B
Hill, Alfred F. 1870 C, 1904 C, 1906 C, 1908 C, 1914 C
Hill, Arthur, 1826 F
Hill, Charles, 1824 C
Hill, Clement, 1877 E
Hill, Daryl, 1930 C
Hill, Edward, 1927 C
Hill, Ernestine, 1899 C, 1937 C
Hill, Fidelia S. T. 1840 C
Hill, Lance, 1945 B
Hill, Lionel L. 1881 A, 1926 A, 1930 A
Hill, Mirrie I. 1892 C
Hill, Robin, 1932 C
Hill, Rowland, 1849 F
Hill, Samuel P. 1820 C
Hill, Sinclair, 1972 E
Hill, Tommy, 1927 E
Hill End, NSW, 1851 F, 1872 F
Hill, Samuel, Cash Management Trust, 1980 A
Hillston, NSW, 1863 F
Hilly, John F. 1810 B
Hillyars and the Burtons, The, 1865 C
Hilton Hotel, Sydney, 1974 F, 1978 A
Hind, R. V. 1846 C
Hindenberg Line, France, 1917 A, 1918 A
Hinder, Francis H. C. 1906 C, 1937 C

Hinder, Margel I. H. 1906 C, 1934 C, 1959 C, 1962 C
Hindle, Bryan, 1948 E
Hindmarsh, Jim, 1952 E
Hindmarsh, John, 1836 A, B, 1860 A
Hindmarsh, Mary, 1817 C
Hindustan, 1810 A
Hindwood, Keith A. 1904 B
Hingston, Arthur J. 1874 C
Hinkler, Herbert J. L. ('Bert'), 1892 B, 1928 B
Hinton, Harry, 1911 E
Hinton, Howard, 1867 A
Hints for the Preservation of the Teeth, 1830 B
Hipkiss, Richard, 1853 A
Hippies, Qld, 1976 C
Hippodrome Theatre, Sydney, 1915 C
Hipwell, John, 1948 E
Hire Purchase, 1860 A, 1927 F
Hire Purchase, finance, 1959 F
Hiraji, 1947 E
Hiroshima, Japan, 1945 A
Hirsch, Max, 1852 A
Hirschfeld-Mack, Ludwig, 1893 C
Hirst, Edward, 1938 E
'His Father's Mate', 1888 C
His Majesty's hotel and theatre, Perth, 1904 C
His Natural Life, 1870 C, 1874 C, 1885 C
His Royal Highness, 1932 C
Hiscock, Thomas, 1851 B
Hiscoe, Ken, 1938 E, 1963 E
Historia Dignum, (Memorable events), *see Section F*
Historical Memorials Committee, 1911 F
Historical Societies, 1901 F
History, *see section A*
History of Australia, A, 1959 C
History of Australia, 1962 C
History of Australian Discovery and Colonization, 1867 C
History of Capital and Labour in All Lands and Ages, The, 1888 C
History of New South Wales ... Other Australian Settlements, 1862 C
History of Tasmania, The, 1852 C
Hitchcock, George, 1837 A
Ho, Wong Y. 1887 A
Hoad, John C. 1856 A
Hoad, Lewis A. 1934 E, 1957 E
Hoadley's National Battle of the Sounds, 1966 C
Hoban, Samuel J. 1865 D
Hobart, HMAS (1) 1938 A
Hobart, HMAS (2) 1967 A
Hobart, Tas, 1804 F, 1807 A, B, 1816 B, 1818 B, 1821 D, 1825 C, 1828 A, 1830 B, 1832 D, 1833 C, 1834 C, 1837 F, 1840 F, 1841 A, 1843 F, 1844 D, 1853 A, 1857 B, 1876 B, 1877 A, 1881 A, 1886 A, 1895 A, 1897 A, 1955 F, 1961 D, 1970 D, 1973 F, 1975 D
Hobart Activity School, 1934 D
Hobart airport, 1956 B
Hobart Free Labour Union, 1847 A
Hobart G.P.O., 1979 F
Hobart jail, 1877 A
Hobart High School, 1850 D
Hobart Cup (horse-racing), 1875 E
Hobart Hospital, 1875 B
Hobart to Launceston land route, 1807 A
Hobart Matriculation College, 1965 D
Hobart Mechanics' Institute, 1827 D
Hobart Observatory, 1840 B
Hobart Philharmonic Society, 1867 C
Hobart Stock Exchange, 1882 A

Hobart Technical College, 1889 D
Hobart Theatre Royal Opera Co. 1951 C
Hobart Town, 1804 A, 1811 A, 1881 A
Hobart Town Book Society, 1826 D
Hobart Town Cricket Club, 1832 E
Hobart Town Gazette and Southern Reporter, 1816 F, 1825 F
Hobart Town Hall, 1864 C
Hobart Town Monthly Magazine, 1833 F
Hobart Working Men's Club, 1865 F
Hobarton Mercury, 1854 F
Hobbes, Thomas, 1819 A
Hobble skirts, 1911 F
Hobbs, Joseph J. T. 1864 A
Hobday, Percy S. 1879 C
Hobson, Edward, 1841 A
Hobson, William, 1793 A, 1840 A, 1841 A
Hobson Bay Private Railway Co. Vic, 1878 B
Hockey, 1900 E, 1901 E, 1908 E, 1910 E
Hockey Association, 1903 E
Hoddle, Robert, 1794 A, 1837 A, 1838 A
Hodge, Thomas, 1841 C
Hodgkinson, Francis G. 1919 C
Hodgkinson, Roy C. 1911 C
Hodgkinson, William O. 1835 A, 1875 A
Hodgman, Vernon, 1909 C
Hoff, G. Rayner, 1894 C, 1923 C, 1927 C
Hoff, Ursula, 1909 C
Hoffman, Samuel, 1795 A
Hoffman Patent Steam Brick Co., 1870 B
Hogan, Edmond J. 1883 A, 1927 A, 1929 A
Hogan, Hector D. 1931 E
Hogan, Paul, 1940 C, 1972 F
Hogbin, Herbert I. P. 1904 B
Hogg, Rodney, 1951 E
Hohaus, Herman, 1920 C
Hoists, 1840 B
Holbrook, NSW, 1858 F
Hold-up, The, 1895 C
Holden,
  Astra, 1984 B
  ED, 1965 B
  EH, 1963 B
  EJ, 1962 B
  EK, 1961 B
  FB, 1960 B
  FC, 1958 B
  FE, 1957 B
  FJ, 1953 B
  48/125, 1948 B
Holden, Edward W. 1885 A, 1923 B
Holden, Kerry, 1897 F
Holden, Margaret, 1915 C
Holden Co., 1917 B
Holden Motor Body Builders, 1931 B
Holden station wagon, 1957 B
Holder, Frederick W. 1850 A, 1892 A, 1899 A, 1901 A
Holdsworth, Gordon, 1885 C
Hole, Quentin, 1923 C
Holey Dollar, 1813 A, 1824 A, 1842 A
Holgate, H. N. 1981 A
Holger-Neilsen, life saving, 1960 F
Holidays, public, Vic, 1909 F
Holland, Dulcie S. 1913 C
Holland, Stephen, 1958 E, 1973 E
Hollier, Donald, 1934 C
Hollway, Thomas T. 1906 A, 1947 A, 1952 A
Holman, Edward J. F. 1904 A
Holman, John B. 1872 A
Holman, Keith, 1929 E
Holman, Mary A. ('May') 1893 A, 1925 A
Holman, William A. 1871 A, 1893 A, 1913 A

783

Holmes, Bob, 1938 E
Holmes, Cecil, 1953 C, 1956 C
Holmes, Edith L. 1899 C
Holmes, Edward, 1900 E
Holmes, William, 1862 A
Holt, Harold E. 1908 A, 1935 A, 1966 A, 1967 A
Holt, Joseph, 1826 A
Holt, Joseph B. (Bland) 1853 C, 1876 C, 1893 C
Holt, Thomas, 1811 A, 1870 A
Holtermann, Bernhardt O. 1838 A, 1872 F
Holtermann's nugget, 1872 F
Holtze, Maurice W. 1840 B
Holy Willie, 1852 D
Holyman Airways, 1936 B
Holyman, Ivan N. 1896 B
Holyman, William, 1833 A
Holzner, Anton, 1935 C
Home, 1920 C
Home, Sydney, 1948 F
Home of the Blizzard (film), 1913 C
Home of the Blizzard (book), 1915 C
Home Guard, 1942 A
Home Hill, Qld, 1895 F
Home Missionary Sisters of Our Lady, Tas, 1944 D
Home ownership benefits scheme, 1964 A
Homer, Irvine, 1919 C
Homesdale (film), 1971 C
Homesickness, 1980 C
Homing pigeons, 1900 E
Hone, Frank S. 1871 B
Honey, 1822 A
Honours list, 1972 A
Hoobin, Jack, 1922 E
Hood, Kenneth E. 1928 C
Hood, Robert V. 1812 C
Hooke, Lionel A. G. 1895 B
Hooker, Joseph D. 1817 C
Hooker, Leslie J. 1903 A, 1928 A
Hookey, Mabel, 1871 C
Hookes, David, 1955 C
Hookworm, 1902 B
Hooley, George, 1880 B
Hoopla Theatre Foundation, Melbourne, 1970 C
Hope (medallion), 1798 C
Hope, Alec D. 1907 C, 1955 C, 1965 C, 1970 C, 1974 C
Hope, John A. L. 1860 A, 1889 A, 1900 A, 1901 A
Hope, Laurence, 1928 C
Hope, Louis, 1817 A, 1854 C, 1862 A, 1864 A
Hopetoun, Lord, *see* Hope, John A. L.
Hopkins, Alan, 1904 E
Hopkins, Henry, 1851 A
Hopkins, John, 1943 C
Hopkins, John R. 1927 C, 1965 C
Hopkins, Livingstone, 1846 C
Hopman, Henry C. 1906 E
Hopman, Nell, 1910 E, 1963 E
Hopper, Victor D. 1913 B
Hops, 1843 B, 1931 A
Hopwood, Henry, 1813 A, 1857 A
Hopwood, Henry S. 1860 C
Horder, Harold, 1894 E
Hordern, Anthony, 1789 A, 1819 A, 1840 A, 1901 F
Hordern, Samuel, 1876 A
Hordern Bros, 1840 A
Hordern family, 1823 A
Hore-Ruthven, Alexander G. A. 1872 A, 1928 A, 1935 A, 1936 A
Horler, Kenneth G. 1938 C, 1970 C
Horn, William A. 1841 A

Horn I., Qld, 1945 F, 1957 F
Horn Scientific Expedition, 1894 B
Horne, Donald R. 1921 C, 1958 F, 1964 C, 1967 C
Horne, Richard H. 1803 C
Hornel, Edward A. 1864 C
Hornet Bank station, Qld, 1857 A
Hornet fighter aircraft, 1981 A, 1984 B
Hornibrook bridge, Qld, 1979 B
Horrocks, John A. 1818 A
Horse of Air, A, 1970 C
Horse racing,
  Aust. wide, 1849 E, 1912 E, 1940 E, 1942 E, 1955 E, 1979 E
  England, 1950 E, 1955 E
  NSW, 1810 E, 1825 E, 1832 E, 1851 E, 1852 E, 1860 E, 1866 E, 1923 E, 1945 E, 1957 E
  Qld, 1865 E, 1866 E, 1871 E, 1923 E
  SA, 1838 E, 1864 E
  Tas, 1814 E, 1865 E, 1875 E
  Vic, 1838 E, 1840 E, 1864 E, 1879 E, 1883 E, 1972 E, 1974 E
  WA, 1833 E
Horse racing carnivals, SA, 1876 F
Horse racing clubs, *see individual entries*
Horse meat, 1981 A
Horse riding, crouched seat style, 1884 F
Horse sales, 1978 E, 1979 E
Horses, breeding, 1830 E
Horses, doping of, 1947 E
Horses, exports, 1830 A, 1844 A
Horses, numbers, 1921 F
Horses, registration, 1911 E
Horses, stallions, 1799 A
Horses, treadmill, 1832 B
Horsham, Vic, 1847 F, 1951 F
Horsham Art Gallery, 1968 C
Horsley, Charles E. 1822 C, 1866 C
Horsley, Malcolm, 1925 C
Horticulture, 1891 C
Horton, Mervyn, 1963 C
Horton, William, 1821 D, 1836 D
Horton College, Hobart, 1855 D
Horwitz Group Books, 1921 A
Hosking, Edwin C. 1896 C
Hosking, John, 1809 D, 1842 A
Hosking, Arthur S. 1891 D
Hoskins, Cecil H. 1889 B
Hoskins, Charles H. 1851 B
Hoskins, Johnny, 1892 E, 1923 E
Hoskins, Ltd, G. and C. 1908 B
Hoskinstown, ACT, 1964 B
Hospital and Allied Services Advisory Council, 1970 B
Hospital Benefits schemes, 1944 A, 1952 A
Hospital fees, 1839 B
Hospital Hour, 1938 F
Hospital insurance, 1929 A
Hospital ship, *Centaur*, 1943 A
Hospitals, 1788 B, 1811 B, 1845 B, 1864 F, 1866 B, *see also individual entries*
Hospitals, operating theatres, 1894 B
'Hot pants', 1971 F
Hotchin Art Gallery, WA, 1947 C
Hotels, *see individual entries*
Hotels, closing time, 1916 F, 1919 F, 1937 F, 1954 F, 1955 F, 1966 F, 1967 F
Hotham, Charles, 1806 A, 1854 A, 1855 A
Houdini, Ehrich W. 1910 B
Houghton bridge, Qld, 1979 B
Houghton vineyards, WA, 1859 A
Hougomont, 1868 A
Hounds, 1812 E
Hours of work, *see* Working hours
House of Assembly, New Guinea, 1963 A, 1964 A

House is Built, A, 1929 C
House of Commons, 1900 A
House of Lords, 1947 A
House of Representatives, Federal, 1901 A, 1943 A, 1948 A
House of Representatives, voting rights for NT member, 1968 A
'House on stilts', Qld, 1860 C
Household power, Sydney, 1904 B
Houses, orientation, 1902 B
Houses, prefabricated, 1804 C, 1947 C
Houses, Queen Anne Revival, 1890 C
Houses, ranch style, 1950 C
Houses, stumped, 1894 C
Housing Agreement, Cwlth and State, 1944 A, 1945 A, 1946 A
Housing Commission, 1943 A
Housing loans, 1910 A
Housing, public, 1900 A
Houten van der, Henricus L. 1801 C
Hovell, William, 1824 A, 1875 A
Hover vehicle racing, 1964 E
How He Died and Other Poems, 1887 C
Howard, A. C. 1920 B
Howard, Amos W. 1848 B
Howard, Cliff, 1896 B, 1919 B
Howard, 'Gympie', 1953 F
Howard, Henry, 1859 D
Howard, Ken, 1910 E
Howard Florey Institute of Experimental Physiology, Melbourne, 1971 B
Howard, Qld, 1864 F
Howarth, Robert G. 1906 C
Howchin, Walker, 1845 B
Howe, George, 1802 C, 1803 F, 1819 C, 1821 C
Howe, George T. 1806 F
Howe, John, (b. 1774) 1819 A, 1852 A
Howe, John, (b. 1861) 1861 F, 1892 F
Howe, Michael, 1813 F, 1818 A, C, 1821 C
Howe, Robert (1), 1795 F
Howe, Robert (2), 1925 E
Howe Bridge, NSW, 1813 B
Howie, Lawrence H. 1876 C
Howitt, Alfred W. 1830 A, 1861 A, 1880 C, 1904 C
Howitt, Godfrey, 1800 B
Howitt, Richard, 1799 C
Howitt, William, (1), 1792 C
Howitt, William, (2), 1847 C
Howley, John R. 1931 C
Howse, Neville R. 1863 A, 1900 A
Howson, F. 1841 C
Hoyleton, SA, 1870 B
Hoysted, Des, 1925 E
Hoyt, Henry, 1869 B, 1872 C
Hoyte, John B. C. 1835 C
Hoyts Theatres Ltd, 1926 C
Hubbe, Ulrich, 1805 A
Huddart, James, 1847 B
Hudson, Henry, 1836 B
Hudson, Peter, 1946 E
Hudson, William, 1896 A, 1949 B
Hughan, Harold R. 1893 C
Hughenden, Qld, 1877 F
Hughes, Enoch, 1860 B
Hughes, George, 1796 B
Hughes, Graham, 1955 E
Hughes, Kim, 1954 E
Hughes, Matthew, 1798 D
Hughes, Phillip, 1973 D
Hughes, Richard J. 1931 C
Hughes, Robert, 1912 C, 1961 C
Hughes, Robert S. F. 1938 C
Hughes, Tom, 1944 A
Hughes, Walter W. 1803 A, 1860 B
Hughes, Wilfred S. K. 1895 A

Hughes, William M. 1862 A, 1894 A, 1901 A, 1902 A, 1915 A, 1916 A, 1917 A, 1918 A, 1919 A, 1922 A
Hula-hoops, 1951 F, 1954 F
Hull, Arthur F. B. 1862 B
Hull, James, 1852 F, 1961 F
Human Drift, 1935 C
Human head trade, 1831 F
Human Veins Dance Theatre, 1980 C
Humble, Leslie K. 1927 C, 1976 C
Hume, Ferguson W. 1859 C, 1886 C
Hume, Hamilton, 1797 A, 1814 A, 1816 A, 1817 A, 1818 A, 1824 A
Hume, Walter, 1873 B, 1910 B, 1923 B
Hume Dam, Vic, 1936 B
Hume Highway, NSW, 1959 F
Hume R., 1824 A, 1830 A
Humped back prawn, 1958 B
Humphrey, Adolarius W. H. 1818 A, 1829 A
Humphrey, Thomas, 1858 C
Humphreys, Kevin, 1930 E, 1983 A
Humphries, J. Barry, 1934 C, 1955 C, 1958 C, 1962 C
Humpty Doo, NT, 1954 F
Hundred Years of Philosophy, A, 1957 C
Hungarian refugees, 1956 A
Hungerford, Leonard B. 1922 C
Hungerford, Thomas A. G. 1915 C, 1952 C
Hungry House Art Gallery, Sydney, 1962 C
Hunt, Colin, 1898 C
Hunt, Fanny E. 1888 D
Hunt, Geoffrey B. 1948 E, 1965 E, 1977 E, 1981 E
Hunt, H. A. 1907 B
Hunt, J. Horbury, 1838 C, 1875 C, 1889 C, 1896 C
Hunt, Noel, 1929 B
Hunt, Percy I. 1903 C
Hunt, Susannah, 1793 D, 1805 D
Hunter, Henry, 1832 C, 1864 C
Hunter, John, 1795 A, 1796 A, 1798 C, 1821 A
Hunter, John G. 1888 B
Hunter, John I. 1898 B
Hunter Coal Miners' Union, 1854 A
Hunter R., NSW, 1797 A, B, 1819 A, 1823 A, 1827 A, 1829 A, 1830 A
Hunter R. district, NSW, 1800 B, 1841 A
Hunter River Gazette, NSW, 1841 F
Hunter River Steam Navigation Co., 1839 B, 1841 B, 1851 A
Hunter Valley, NSW, 1825 A, 1828 A, 1832 A, 1843 A, 1856 A, 1974 B
Hunter Valley Art Prize, NSW, 1958 C
Hunter Valley Theatre Co., NSW, 1975 C
Hunters' Hill Art Competitions, NSW, 1956 C
Hunting, 1810 E, 1812 E, 1836 E, 1840 E, 1841 E, 1848 E
Hunting, A. J. 1884 E
Huntingfield, Lord, *see* Vanneck, William C. A.
Huon R., Tas, 1915 F
Huonville, Tas, 1843 F
Hurley, Frank, 1913 C, 1917 F, 1919 C, 1921 C
Hurley, James F. 1885 A
Hurley, Thomas E. V. 1888 B
Hurry, Polly, 1883 C
Hurst, Alan, 1950 E
Hurstville, NSW, 1920 F, 1960 E
Huskisson, NSW, 1827 F
Hutchens, Francis, 1892 C
Hutcheson, Ernest, 1871 C
Hutchins, C. 1882 E

Hutchins, William, 1792 D
Hutchins Grammar School, Tas, 1846 D
Hutchinson, Bill, 1923 E, 1953 E
Hutchinson, Ron, 1927 E
Hutchison, Inez, 1890 C, 1966 C
Hutchison, Noel, 1940 C
Hutchison, William, 1953 E
Hutt, John, 1795 A, 1839 A
Hutt River Province, WA, 1970 A
Hutton, Edward T. H. 1848 A
Huxley, Leonard H. 1902 B
Huxley, Thomas H. 1825 B, 1847 A
Huxley, Victor, 1917 E
Huxton, Lewis, 1910 E
Huybers, Jessie C. 'Tasma', 1848 C
Hyatt Kingsgate Hotel, 1984 F
Hydatids, 1851 B
Hyde, George F. 1877 A, 1928 A
Hyde, Miriam B. 1913 C
Hyde Park, Sydney, 1810 E, F, 1848 B, 1933 F
Hyde Park Barracks, 1819 A
Hydraulic lifts, 1889 B, 1921 B
Hydro-electricity, 1893 B, 1895 B, 1916 B, 1925 B, 1949 B, 1952 B, 1963 B, 1981 A, 1982 B
Hydro Electricity Commission, Tas, 1925 B
Hydrofoil, 1965 B
Hyland, Pat, 1941 E
Hyperno, 1979 E

I

'I am Woman', 1972 C
I Can Jump Puddles, 1955 C
'I Go To Rio', 1977 C
'I Remember You', 1962 C
IBM building, Sydney, 1963 C
Ice, 1861 B, 1863 B, 1872 B
Ice Bird, 1972 A
Icecream, 1923 F
Ice hockey, 1908 E, 1920 E, 1921 E, 1935 E, 1947 E, 1977 E, 1980 E
Ice skating, 1931 E, 1978 E, 1979 E
Ice works, Vic, 1852 B
Icely, Thomas, 1797 A
ICI House, Melbourne, 1956 C
Icon Theatre Co., Adelaide, 1975 C
Identification, finger printing, 1902 F
Identity, 1971 F
Identity cards, wartime, 1942 F
Idriess, Ion L. 1890 C, 1927 C, 1931 C
Ifield, Frank, 1962 C
Ifould, William H. 1877 D
'I'll never find another you', 1965 C
Illawarra region, NSW, 1796 A, 1797 B, 1812 A, 1817 A, 1820 A, 1822 A, 1826 A, 1834 D
Illawarra Mercury, NSW, 1855 F
Illawarra Shorthorn, cattle, 1898 B, 1929 B
Illawarra Steam Navigation Co., 1853 A
Illegal immigrants, 1981 A
Illingworth, Nelson, 1862 C
Illustrated Australian Mail, Vic, 1861 F
Illustrated Journal of Australasia, 1856 F
Illustrated London News: Australasian Edition, Melbourne, 1888 F
Iluka, NSW, 1884 F
Images, 1967 C
Imlay, Alexander, 1801 A
Imlay, George, 1795 A
Imlay, Peter, 1881 A

Immigration,
 colonies/states 1793 A, 1822 A, 1825 A, 1827 A, 1830 A, 1831 A, 1832 A, 1835 A, 1836 A, 1839 A, 1842 A, 1846 A, 1848 A, 1880 A, 1887 A, 1888 A, 1890 A, 1891 A, 1904 A, 1905 A, 1906 A
 Cwlth/Federal 1901 A, 1904 A, 1905 A, 1919 A, 1922 A, 1925 A, 1929 A, 1934 A, 1937 D, 1938 A, 1945 A, 1946 A, 1947 A, 1949 A, 1951 F, 1952 A, 1955 F, 1958 A, 1959 A, 1966 A, 1967 A, 1968 F, 1970 A, 1975 A, 1981 A, 1982 A, 1984 A
 see also Assisted immigration
Immigration Act, Federal, 1925 A
Immigration Reform Group, Melbourne, 1959 A
Immigration Restriction Act, Federal, 1901 A, 1905 A
Immunisation, rubella, 1971 F
Immunological tolerance, 1960 B
Imperial Airways, 1934 F
Imperial Chemical Industries Ltd., ICI, 1928 B
Imperial Conferences, England, 1907 A, 1911 A, 1921 A, 1923 A, 1926 A, 1937 A
Imperial Defence Act, 1888 A
Imperial Defence Conference, London, 1909 A
Imperial Economic Conference, Canada, 1932 A
Imperial Federation League, 1885 A
Imperial Forces, 1854 A
Imperial Gallery of Art, London, 1928 C
Imperial Press Conference, London, 1909 F
Imperial Russian Ballet Co., 1913 C
Imperial Statistical Conference, London, 1920 A, Ottawa, 1935 A
Imperial War conference, England, 1917 A
Import agencies, 1831 A
Import duties, 1819 A, 1828 A, 1831 A, 1839 A, 1865 A, 1866 A
Import restrictions, 1952 A, 1954 A, 1955 A
Imports, 1800 A, 1929 A, 1960 A, *see also individual entries*
Impressionist Art Movement, Melbourne, 1918 C
In the Days When the World was Wide, 1896 C
In the Grip of the Polar Ice, 1919 C
In Mine own Heart, 1963 C
In the Wake of the Bounty, 1933 C
Income tax, 1884 A, 1890 A, 1907 A, 1915 A, 1942 A, 1953 A, 1976 A
Indecent Obsession, An, 1981 C
Indefatigable, 1812 A
Independent Group of Artists, Melbourne, 1940 C
Independent Order of Oddfellows Friendly Society, 1836 F
Independent Theatre Co., Sydney, 1922 C, 1929 C
Indian Art Exhibition, 1952 C
Indian-Pacific railway, 1970 B
Indo-Chinese refugees, 1979 A, 1980 A, 1982 A
Indonesia, 1962 A, 1972 A, 1975 A, 1978 A
Indonesia, claim to W New Guinea, 1962 A
Indonesia, Confrontation Policy, 1963 A
Indonesian Republic, 1947 A

785

Industrial Arbitration Act, NSW, 1901 A
Industrial arbitrators, 1886 A
Industrial Commission, SA, 1980 A
Industrial Design Council of Aust., 1958 B
Industrial Groups, 1946 A, 1954 A, 1955 A
Industrial harbour, Cockburn Sound, WA, 1954 B
Industrial law, 1977 A
Industrial Life Insurance Co., Sydney, Brisbane, 1884 A
Industrial mergers, 1979 A
Industrial Peace Act, 1920 A
Industrial Peace Conference, 1928 A
Industrial Relations Bureau, 1977 A
Industrial and Technical Museum, Melbourne, 1870 D
Industrial unrest, 1880 A, 1919 A
Industrial Workers of the World, 1864 A, 1907 A, 1916 A, 1918 A, 1919 A
Inez Hutchison Art Award, Melbourne, 1966 C
Infant mortality, 1898 F
Infant School Societies, 1832 D
Infant schools, NSW, 1824 D, Tas, 1908 D
Infant welfare service, Sydney, 1904 F
Infantile paralysis, Vic, 1937 F, *see* Poliomyelitis
Inflation, 1912 A, 1960 A
Influenza, 1826 F, 1838 F
Influenza, pneumonic, 1919 F
Influenza virus, 1933 B
Information, organisations, 1972 A
Information Department, 1940 A
Ingamells, Reginald C. '(Rex)' 1913 C, 1938 C
Ingham, Qld, 1873 F
Ingham, Alan, 1920 C
Ingate, Gordon, 1926 E
Ingleburn Polocrosse Club, NSW, 1939 E
Inglewood, Vic, 1861 F
Ingpen, Robert R. 1936 C
Ingram, William W. 1888 B
Ingrid, 1952 E
Inheritors, The, 1936 C
Inland sea, 1813 A, 1830 A, 1844 A
Inland wireless system, 1925 B
INMASAT, *see* International Satellite System
Inner Garden, The, 1940 C
Innes, Archibald C. 1800 A
Innes, Frederick M. 1816 A, 1872 A
Innisfail, Qld, 1880 F, 1911 F, 1913 F, 1918 F, 1931 F, 1938 F, 1972 C
Innisfail area, Qld, 1913 F
Insecticides, 1950 B, 1977 B
Inson, Graeme, 1923 C
Institute of Admen, Melbourne, 1912 F
Institute of Ambulance Officers Aust., 1973 F
Institute of Architecture, Vic, 1856 C
Institute of Aust. Photography, 1944 B
Institute of Bankers, Sydney, 1892 D
Institute of Catholic Education, Vic, 1974 D
Institute for Deaf, Dumb and Blind, Sydney, 1872 B
Institute of Family Studies, 1984 F
Institute of Medical and Veterinary Science, Adelaide, 1937 B
Institute of Science and Industry, 1920 B, 1926 B
Instructions for the Constables of Country Districts, 1796 B

Insurance, hospital, 1929 A
Insurance Cos, *see individual entries*
Insulin, 1923 B
Intellectual Sciences, The, 1850 D
Intelligence organisations, 1952 A, 1960 A, 1977 A, 1980 A, *see also individual entries and* ASIO
Intelligence service, ASIS, 1952 A
Intelsat, 1964 B, 1966 B
Intemperance, 1857 F
Interaction: Moving and Painting (film), 1967 C
Interception, telephones, 1960 A
Intercolonial Conferences, 1863 A, 1870 A, 1873 A, 1874 A, 1881 A, 1883 A, 1888 A, 1896 A, 1900 A
Intercolonial Exhibitions, 1866 C, F, 1870 F, 1872 F, 1873 F, 1875 F, 1876 F, 1880 F, 1888 F
Intercolonial Medical Conference, Adelaide, 1887 B
Intercolonial school sporting competitions, 1876 E
Intercolonial trade preferences, 1873 A
Intercolonial Trade Union Congresses, 1879 A, 1884 A, 1885 A, 1886 A, 1888 A, 1889 A, 1898 A
Inter-Dominion Pacing Championships, 1936 E
Interest rates, deregulation of, 1980 A
Intergovernmental Committee for European migration, 1951 A
Interim Committee for Aust. Schools Commission, 1973 D
Interim Committee for Pre-School Commission, 1973 D
Interior, Dept of, 1932 A
Intermediate Certificate, Vic, 1967 D
International Antarctic Analysis Centre, Melbourne, 1959 A
International Architecture Exhibition, Sydney, 1927 C
International Art Exhibition, Sydney, 1936 C
International Association of Art critics, 1963 C
International Astronomical Symposium, 1963 B
International Astronomical Union, 1973 B
International Ballet Competition, Moscow, 1973 C, 1977 C
International Co-operation Art award, 1966 C
International Court, Holland, 1953 A, 1958 A, 1973 A
International Development Association, 1960 A
International Exhibitions, 1855 C, 1862 C, 1879 F, 1881 F, 1889 F, 1891 F
International Game Fishing Association, 1959 E
International Geophysical Year, 1957 B
International Grand Opera Co., 1955 C
International Labor Office Conference, Melbourne, 1962 A
International Labor Organisation, ILO, 1973 A
International Maritime Satellite Organisation, INMARSAT, 1977 B, 1979 B
International Microsurgical Society, Sydney, 1981 B
International Mining and Industrial Exhibition, WA, 1899 B
International New Education Fellowship, 1937 D
International Piano Competition, Sydney, 1977 C

International Satellite System, 1977 B
International Scientific Radio Union Assembly, Sydney, 1952 B
International Society for Contemporary Music, 1956 C
International Subscriber Dialling, 1976 B
International Surf Carnival, 1956 E
International Telecommunication Union, 1877 B, 1964 B
International Telegraph Union, 1877 B
International Training Institute, 1973 D
International Union of Geodesy and Geophysics, 1978 B
International Whaling Commission, 1963 A, 1982 A
Interscan aviation system, 1972 B
Interstate Conference of Employers, 1927 A
Interstate Trade Union Conference, 1919 A
Intimate Strangers, 1937 C
Intrastate airlines, 1965 A
Invalid pensions, 1907 A, 1910 A
Inverarity, John, 1944 E
Inverell, NSW, 1838 A, 1853 F, 1871 B
Investigator, 1804 C
Investment, 1871 A, *see also individual entries*
Invincible, HMS, 1982 A, 1983 A
In-Vitro Fertilization, 1980 B, 1982 B, 1983 B
Ipswich, Qld, 1825 B, 1827 B, F, 1859 F, 1861 B, 1863 D, 1865 B, 1867 B, 1876 B, 1890 B
Ipswich Court House, Qld, 1859 C
Ipswich Grammar School, Qld, 1863 D
Iredale, Tom, 1880 B
Ireland, David, 1927 C
Irish famine, relief fund, 1846 F
Irish Grand Lodge, 1816 F
Irish national education system, 1836 D, 1844 D, 1853 D
Irish National League, 1883 D
Irish national unity, 1842 F
Irish Republican Brotherhood, 1876 F
Iron, 1045 C, 1848 B, 1860 B, 1875 B, 1894 B, 1937 B
Iron, corrugated, 1849 B, 1855 C
Iron post boxes, 1856 B
Iron Knob, SA, 1899 A, 1911 F
Iron ore, exports, 1938 A, 1960 A, 1962 A
NSW, 1833 B, 1850 B
SA, 1899 B
WA, 1951 B, 1952 B, 1956 B, 1958 B, 1961 B, 1962 A, B, 1970 B, 1979 B
'Iron Pot', 1855 C
Iron and steel industry, 1847 B, 1848 B, 1864 B, 1875 B, 1886 B, 1913 B, 1941 B, 1960 B, 1961 A, 1982 A
Iron Trades Employers' Association, 1873 A
'Ironbark', 1846 C
Ironside, Adelaide, 1831 C
Irrigation,
NSW, 1828 A, 1906 A, 1915 B
NT, 1963 B
SA, 1887 B
Tas, 1843 B
Vic, 1880 B, 1883 A, 1884 B, 1886 B, 1887 B
WA, 1963 B
Irvine, Ken, 1940 E
Irvine, William H. 1858 A, 1902 A, 1920 A, 1926 A, 1931 A
Irving, John, 1790 A, 1795 A
Irving, Martin H. 1831 D
Irwin, Frederick C. 1832 A, 1847 A
Irwin R., WA, 1846 B

Isaacs, David V. 1904 B
Isaacs, Isaac A. 1855 A, 1880 A, 1882 A, 1906 A, 1930 A, 1931 A
Isherwood, Jean de C. 1911 C
Ishmael Artists Club, Melbourne, 1892 C
Islam, 1976 D
Isle of Intrigue, 1931 C
Israel, M. C. 1886 D
Italian Art Prizes and Scholarships, 1951 C
Italian Art of the Twentieth Century Exhibition, 1956 C
Italian opera, 1871 C, 1876 C
Italian prisoners of war, Wakool, NSW, 1944 A
Italians, 1907 A, 1921 A, 1967 F
Italy, 1935 A
Ivanov, V. 1983 A
Iverson, Jack, 1915 E
Ives, Joshua, 1884 C
Iwaki, Hiroyuki, 1974 C
IXL Label, 1891 B

J

Jabiluka, NT, 1970 B, 1982 A
Jacaranda Art Exhibition, NSW, 1961 C
Jacaranda dance, 1939 C
Jacaranda Festival, NSW, 1935 F
Jacaranda publishers, 1952 A
Jack, Andrew K. 1885 B
Jack, Kenneth W. D. 1924 C
Jack, Robert L. 1845 B
Jack Thompson, 1940 C
Jacka, Albert, 1893 A, 1915 A
Jack and Jill: A Postscript (film), 1969 C
Jackeno, Lyn, 1954 E
Jackets, 1951 F
'Jackey Jackey', 1820 A
Jackson, Archie A. 1909 E
Jackson, Carlyle, 1891 C
Jackson, Cyril, 1897 D
Jackson, Emanuel, 1878 E
Jackson, Ernest S. 1860 B
Jackson, James R. 1886 C
Jackson, Jefferson, 1900 C
Jackson, Marjorie, 1931 E, 1952 E
Jackson, Peter, (1), 1847 B
Jackson, Peter, (2), 1884 E
Jackson, Robert G. A. 1911 A
Jackson, Samuel, 1806 C, 1846 C, 1875 C
Jackson oilfield pipeline, 1984 B
Jacob Creek, SA, 1847 A
Jacobs, Kenneth, 1974 A
Jade, SA, 1975 B
Jails, *see individual entries*
Jam, 1861 F
Jamaican Rumba, 1937 C
Jamberoo, NSW, 1840 F
James, Florence, 1951 C
James, Francis, 1973 A
James, John, 1934 E, 1961 E
James, John S. 1843 C
James, Louis R. 1920 C, 1965 C
James, Richard H. 1906 C
James, Roger P. 1914 C
James, T. H. and Co. 1824 A
James, Walter H. 1863 A, 1902 A
James, William G. 1895 C, 1914 C
James, Winifred L. 1876 C
James Case, 1936 A
James Cook University of North Qld, 1960 D, 1970 D
James Service, 1878 F

Jamestown, SA, 1871 F
Jamieson, Gil, 1934 C
Jamieson, William, 1853 A
Jamison, John, 1830 A, 1835 A, 1844 A
Jamison, Thomas, 1804 B
Jane, Bob, 1928 E
Jane Eliza, 1886 B
Japan, declaration of war against, 1941 A
Japan, exports to, 1865 A, 1874 A, 1966 A, 1972 A
Japan, Treaty of friendship, 1976 A
Japanese bombings, WA, 1943 A, *see also* Darwin
Japanese Embassy, 1953 A
Japanese good will mission, 1935 A
Japanese midget submarines, Sydney, 1942 A
Japanese prisoners of war, Cowra, NSW, 1944 A
Japanese squadron, 1906 A
Japanese submarines, 1944 A
Japanese surrender, 1945 A
Jardine, Alexander W. 1843 A, 1864 A
Jardine, Francis L. 1841 A, 1864 A
Jardine, John, 1807 A, 1863 A
Jarrett, William, 1833 D
Jarvis, Hubert, 1882 C
Jaugietis, Aina R. 1923 C
Java, 1871 B, 1872 B, 1942 A
Javor, Suza, 1958 E
Jaycees, Perth, 1933 F
Jazz, 1925 C, 1933 C, 1934 C, 1936 C, 1955 C, 1957 C, 1973 C
Jazz, Dixieland, 1943 C
Jazz, ragtime, 1910 C, 1918 C
Jazz convention, Melbourne, 1946 C
Jazz Singer, The, 1928 C
Jeanneret, Henry, 1830 B
Jeans, 1971 C
Jedda, 1954 C
Jeffcott, John, 1837 A
Jefferis, Barbara T. 1917 C
Jefferis, James, 1833 D
Jeffkins, Rupert, 1912 E
Jeffery, Walter J. 1861 C
Jehovah's Witnesses, 1904 D, 1929 D, 1941 D, F
Jemison, Tom, 1938 E
Jemmy Green in Australia, 1845 C
Jenkins, J. G. 1901 A
Jenks, Edward, 1861 A
Jenner, Isaac W. 1836 C
Jennings, Elizabeth E. E. 1865 C
Jennings, Patrick A. 1831 A, 1886 A
Jenolan Caves, NSW, 1838 A
Jensen, Jens, dismissal, 1918 A
Jenyns, Bob, 1944 C
Jeparit, Vic, 1876 F
Jericho, Middle East, 1918 A
Jerilderie, NSW, 1858 F, 1879 A
Jerome, Jerry, 1913 E
Jerry's Plains, NSW, 1825 F
Jersey, Earl of, *see* Child-Villiers, V. A. G.
Jervis, James, 1883 D
Jervis, Samuel E. 1891 F
Jervis Bay, NSW, 1791 A, 1818 A, 1841 F, 1876 F, 1913 A, 1915 A, 1958 A, 1964 F, 1974 A
Jervois, William F. D. 1821 A, 1877 A
Jesaulenko, Alex, 1945 E
Jessop, 1868 B
Jessup, Frederick, 1920 C
Jesus Christ Superstar, 1972 C
Jets, 1946 B, 1964 B
Jets, VIP, 1967 C
'Jewboy', 1816 A, 1839 F
'Jewboy's Mob', 1841 A

Jewel, Richard R. 1810 C, 1859 C
Jewish Art Society, 1960 C
Jews, 1817 F, 1820 D, 1821 F, 1830 D, 1832 F, 1871 D, 1930 D, 1938 F, 1944 D, 1966 D
Jika Jika, 1983 F
Jimbour, Qld, 1841 F
Jimmy Brockett, 1951 C
Jindera, NSW, 1868 F
Jindivik, 1948 B, 1950 B
Jindyworobak group, 1938 C
Jitterbugging (dance), 1945 C
Jiu Jitsu, 1978 E
Joadja, NSW, 1878 F
Jockeys, 1810 E
Jockeys, women, 1979 E, 1984 E
Jockeys' silks, 1842 E
Jocko, the Brazilian Ape, 1851 C
Joe Wilson and His Mates, 1901 C
Joel, Asher A. 1912 A
Joel, Grace, 1865 C
John Curtin School of Medical Research, Canberra, 1948 B
John Lysaght Aust. Ltd, 1880 A
John McCaughey Art Prize, 1956 C
John Miller, 1892 C, *see* Lane, William
John Sulman, 1931 C
John Sulman Award for Architecture, 1934 C
John Vane, Bushranger, 1904 C
Johnno, 1972 C
Johns, A. 1881 B
Johns, Joseph B. 1827 A
Johns, Les, 1942 E
Johnson, Amy, 1904 B, 1930 B
Johnson, Colin, 1955 C
Johnson, Don (Bronco), 1930 E
Johnson, George H. 1926 C
Johnson, Gertrude E. 1894 C, 1935 C, 1939 C
Johnson, Gordon, 1945 E
Johnson, Graeme H. 1935 C
Johnson, Ian W. 1918 E
Johnson, Jack, 1908 E
Johnson, Jim, 1929 E, 1963 E, 1968 E, 1969 E
Johnson, L. B. 1966 A
Johnson, Mary, 1791 D
Johnson, Michael, 1938 C
Johnson, Millard, 1906 C
Johnson, Peter, 1938 E
Johnson, Richard, 1788 A, D, 1792 D, 1793 D, 1798 D, 1827 D
Johnson, Robert, 1890 C
Johnson, Roger, 1922 C
Johnson, Ron, 1907 E, 1946 E
Johnson, William E. 1862 C
Johnsonian Club Art Prize, Brisbane, 1961 C
Johnston, Craig, 1960 E
Johnston, George, 1804 A, 1808 A, 1809 A, 1811 A, 1817 A, 1823 A
Johnston, George B. 1829 A, 1855 A
Johnston, George H. 1912 C, 1964 C
Johnston, Malcolm, 1957 E
Johnston, Margaret A. M. 1918 C
Johnston, Robert, 1821 A
Johnston, Thomas H. 1881 B, 1912 B
Johnston, William A. B. 1912 E
Johnstone, Henry J. 1835 C
Johnstone, Rae, ('Togo'), 1905 E, 1950 E
Johnstone, Robert A. 1843 A
Johnstone, Art Gallery, Brisbane, 1950 C
Joiners and plumbers workers groups, Sydney, 1840 A
Joint Intelligence Organisation, JIO, 1960 A
Jolimont, Vic, 1881 F

787

Jolly, Alexander S. 1887 C
'Jolly Sailor' (hotel), 1798 F
Jomantis, Vincas, 1922 C
Jonah, 1911 C
Jones, Alan, 1947 E, 1979 E, 1980 E
Jones, Barry O. 1932 D
Jones, Brian, 1932 C
Jones, Charles L. 1878 A
Jones, Clytie L. 1929 C
Jones, David, 1793 A, 1838 A
Jones, David F. 1895 A
Jones, David L. 1931 A
Jones, E. J. 1924 B
Jones, Frederick W. 1879 B
Jones, Geoffrey, 1908 C
Jones, Harold B. 1886 C
Jones, Henry, 1862 B, 1891 B
Jones, Henry G. 1804 C
Jones, H. E. 1919 A
Jones, Inigo, 1872 B, 1923 B, 1933 B, 1942 B
Jones, Lee, 1969 E
Jones, Linda, 1979 E
Jones, L. J. R. 1907 B
Jones, Marilyn, 1959 C, 1966 C
Jones, Marion, 1897 C
Jones, Mitch, 1977 E
Jones, Paul, 1921 C
Jones, Phillip S. 1836 B
Jones, Richard ('China') 1852 A
Jones, Russel, 1947 E
Jones, Stan, 1920 E
Jones, Vernon S. C. 1908 A
Jones, Wayne, 1971 E
Jones-Roberts, Gareth, 1935 C
Jonsson, Joe, 1890 C
Jordan, Frederick, 1881 A, 1945 A
Jordon, Colin, 1935 C
Jorgensen, Jorgen, 1841 A
Jorgensen, Justus, 1893 C
Jorrocks, 1851 E
Jose, Arthur W. 1863 D, 1925 C
Joseland, Richard G. H. 1860 C
Joseph, Moses, 1832 F
Joseph Bonaparte Gulf, 1970 F
Joshua McClelland Print Room, Melbourne, 1927 C
Joshua Smith, 1943 C, 1944 C
Joubert, Jules F. de S. 1824 F
Journal of ... in New South Wales, A, 1823 C
Journal of a Voyage to New South Wales, 1790 C
Journal of an ... to Port Darwin, 1880 C
Journalists' Club Art Prize, Sydney, 1957 C
Joyce, Alfred, 1821 A
Joyce, Eileen, 1912 C, 1945 C
Joyce, Ena E. 1925 C
Joyce, James, 1929 C
Joye, Col, 1959 C
Ju-Jitsu, 1978 E
Jubilee Celebrations, 1951 F, 1963 A, 1977 A
Jubilee International Exhibition, Adelaide, 1886 F
Judicature Act, NSW, 1828 A
Judiciary, 1878 A, 1880 A, 1883 A, 1933 A
Judkins, Stan, 1930 E
Judo, 1928 E, 1945 E, 1950 E
Jugiong, NSW, 1834 F
Jukes, J. B. 1850 B
Julia Creek, Qld, 1911 F
Julian Ashton Art School, Sydney, 1896 C
Julian Morris, *see* West, Morris, 1945 C
Julius, George A. 1873 B, 1907 B, 1913 B
Julius, Harry, 1885 C, 1906 C

Jull, Roberta H. M. 1872 B
Jumbo, aircraft, 1970 B
'Junction Inn', 1845 F
Junction Reefs, NSW, 1865 F
Junee, NSW, 1863 F
Jungfrau, 1936 C
Junior Chamber of Commerce group, Perth, 1933 F
Junior Farmers' Club, NSW, 1928 F
Juniper, Robert L. 1929 C
Juno (ship), 1853 F
Juries, 1824 A, 1825 A, 1828 A, 1832 A, 1833 A, 1839 A
Jurjans, Gunars, 1922 C
Just a Dash, 1981 E
Justice, *see* Law *and individual entries*
Justice, Arthur 'Snowy', 1902 E
Justices, *see individual entries*
Justices of the Peace, 1818 A

K

Kable, Henry, 1846 A
Kable, John, 1824 E, 1832 E
Kadina, SA, 1860 F
Kahan, Louis, 1905 C, 1962 C
Kahanamoku, Duke, 1915 E
Kaiser, Peter C. 1918 C
Kakadu National Park, NT, 1982 F
Kalgoorlie, WA, 1863 A, 1893 A, B, 1895 F, 1897 B, 1903 B, D, 1921 F, 1934 A, 1971 B, 1974 F, 1983 B, 1984 B
Kalgoorlie Art Gallery, WA, 1955 C
Kambalda, WA, 1897 F, 1966 B
Kameruka, NSW, 1860 F
Kamesburgh House, Vic, 1884 C
Kamilaroi and Kurnai, 1880 C
Kampuchea, 1979 A, *see also* Cambodia
Kanakas, Kanaks, 1849 A, 1863 A, 1867 A, 1868 A, 1871 A, 1872 A, 1885 A, 1889 A, 1890 A, 1892 A, 1901 A, 1903 A, 1904 A, 1906 A, 1907 A
Kandos, NSW, 1915 F
Kane, Julius, 1921 C
Kanematsu Memorial Institute of Pathology, Sydney, 1933 B
Kangan report, education, 1974 D
Kangaroo (book), 1923 C
Kangaroo (film), 1952 C
Kangaroo Hunt, 1880 C
Kangaroo I., SA, 1803 A, 1836 A, 1837 F, 1839 A
Kangaroo products, 1973 A
Kangaroos, 1832 B, 1833 B
Kangaroos (footballers), 1908 E
Kaniva, Vic, 1880 F
Kanyana Art Prize, Vic, 1963 C
Kapunda, SA, 1842 B, F, 1844 B, 1868 E
Karachi, 1950 C
Karate, 1972 E
Karlson, Steven, 1884 B
Karmel, Peter, 1969 D, 1972 D, 1973 D
Karmel report, SA, 1970 D
Karoonda, SA, 1911 F, 1930 B
Karratha, WA, 1969 F
Katanning, WA, 1898 F
Katanning Art Gallery, WA, 1951 C
Kater, Henry E. 1841 A
Kater, Henry H. 1813 A
Kater, Norman W. 1874 A
Katherine, NT, 1862 F
Katherine R. NT, 1968 F

Katherine Rural Education College, NT, 1979 D
Katoomba, NSW, 1870 F, 1962 C
Katz, Bernard, 1970 B
Kauffmann, John, 1864 C
Kavanagh, Brian, 1972 C
Kavel, August L. C. 1798 A, 1838 A, D
Kay, Barry, 1932 C
Kay, Donald, 1933 C
Kay, William P. 1858 C
Kayaking, 1977 E
Kearney, Ken, 1924 E
Keats, Horace, 1892 C
Keats of Australia, 1872 C
Keeling Is, 1827 A, 1955 A
Keep Him My Country, 1955 C
Keese, Oliné, *see* Leakey, Caroline W.
Keesing, Nancy, 1923 C
Keilawarra, 1886 F
Keilor, Vic, 1940 B, 1965 B
Keilor Skull, 1940 B
Keith, SA, 1885 F
Keith-Falconer, Algernon H. T. 1852 A, 1889 A
Keky, Eva, 1931 C
Kellaway, Charles H. 1889 B
Kellerberrin, WA, 1897 F
Kellermann, Annette M. S. 1887 E, 1902 E, 1905 E, F, 1907 F, 1917 E
Kelly, Frederick, 1881 E
Kelly, G. Edward (Ned), 1855 A, 1878 A, 1879 A, 1880 A
Kelly, Harry G. 1896 C
Kelly, James, 1791 A, 1815 A
Kelly, L. H. 1914 E
Kelly, Michael, 1850 D
Kelly, Thomas, 1827 A
Kelly Gang, The, (film), 1920 C
Kelpie sheep dog, 1870 B
Kelso, Jimmy, 1910 E
Kemp, Charles, 1813 F, 1831 F
Kemp, John R. 1883 B
Kemp, Peter, 1888 E
Kemp, Roger, 1908 C
Kempe, A. H. 1877 D
Kempf, Franz, 1926 C
Kempsey, NSW, 1836 F, 1849 D
Kempsey Festival of Spring Annual Art Competition, NSW, 1963 C
Kempsey Hospital, Sydney, 1963 F
Kempt, John F. 1861 A
Kendall, (Thomas) Henry, 1839 C, 1862 C, 1869 C, 1880 C
Kendrew, Douglas A. 1910 A, 1963 A
Keneally, Thomas M. 1935 C, 1964 C, 1967 C, 1968 C, 1971 C, 1972 C, 1974 C, 1975 C, 1980 C, 1982 C
Kenna, Peter, 1930 C, 1959 C
Kennedy, Alexander, 1837 A
Kennedy, Arthur E. 1810 A, 1855 A, 1877 A
Kennedy, A. L. 1890 B
Kennedy, Daisy, 1893 C
Kennedy, Edmund B. C. 1818 A, 1845 A, 1847 A, 1848 A
Kennedy, Edwina, 1959 E, 1978 E
Kennedy, Graham C. 1934 C
Kennedy, Ken, 1935 E
Kennedy, Lauri, 1898 C
Kennedy, Margaret, 1851 B
Kennerley, Alfred, 1810 A, 1873 A
Kenny, Elizabeth, 1886 B, 1933 B, 1941 B
Kent, Joseph W. 1893 E
Kent, Thomas, 1819 B, 1832 B
Kent, William, 1800 A, 1812 A
Kentucky Fried Chicken, 1968 F
Kerang, Vic, 1856 F
Kerferd, George B. 1831 A, 1874 A

Kerley, Neil, 1933 E
Kermandie, Tas, 1929 B
Kernot, William C. 1845 B
Kerosene, NSW, 1865 B
Kerr, David M. 1867 E
Kerr, John R. 1914 A, 1974 A, 1975 A, 1976 A, 1978 A
Kerr and Knight, 1856 C
'Kerr Hundredweight', 1851 F
Kerruish, Bill, 1970 B
Ketas, Horace, 1945 C
Keyline Plan, 1944 B
Khemlani, Tirath, 1974 A, 1975 A
Kialoa, 1977 E
Kiama, NSW, 1838 F
Kiama Steam Navigation Co., 1853 A
Kiandra, NSW, 1859 B, F, 1862 E, 1927 E
Kiandra Ski Club, NSW, 1861 E
Kiandra Snow Shoe Ski Club, 1883 E
Kianga, Qld, 1861 F, 1975 F
Kiddle, Margaret L. 1914 D
Kidman, Sidney, 1857 A
Kidnapping, 1960 F
Kidnapping Act, 1872 A
Kidstakes, The, 1927 C
Kidston, William, 1849 A, 1906 A, 1908 A
Kieran, Barney B. 1886 E
Kikuyu grass, NSW, 1919 B
Kilborn, Pam, 1939 E
Kilburn, Douglas, 1847 B
Kilcoy, Qld, 1876 F
Kildea, Gary, 1977 C
Killara Station, NSW, 1878 B
Killara Theatre, Sydney, 1968 C
Kilmore, Vic, 1837 F
Kilpatrick, David G. 1928 C
Kimberley district, WA, 1837 C, 1879 A, 1884 A, 1885 B, 1886 A, 1906 A, 1908 A, 1910 A, 1938 A
Kimberley Oil Co., 1921 A
Kimberley Ranges, WA, 1977 B
Kimberley Research Station, WA, 1945 B
Kinchega, NSW, 1872 A
Kincumber, NSW, 1830 F
Kindergarten of the Air, Perth, 1942 F
Kindergarten Association of WA, 1912 D
Kindergarten College, Adelaide, 1907 D
Kindergarten Teachers' Training College, Sydney, 1897 D
Kindergarten Teachers' Training Colleges, 1900 D, 1907 D
Kindergarten Union, NSW, 1896 D
Kindergarten Union of SA, 1905 D
Kindergarten Union of Tas, 1910 D
Kindergartens, 1892 D, 1906 D, 1907 D
Kinetikos Dance Theatre, Perth, 1979 C
Kinetoscope, 1895 C
King, Colin, 1938 E, 1968 E
King, Grahame, 1915 C
King, Henry, 1877 B
King, Inge, 1918 C, 1951 C
King, James, 1800 A, 1832 A
King, Jem M. 1877 E
King, John, 1841 A, 1861 A
King, Mark L. ('Morton'), 1870 C
King, Mick, *see* Kent, Joseph W.
King, Norman J. 1905 B
King, Philip G. 1788 A, 1790 A, 1791 A, 1800 A, D, 1801 A, D, 1802 A, 1808 A
King, Phillip P. 1791 A, 1812 A, 1817 A, 1818 A, 1819 A, 1822 A, 1855 A
King, Trevor, 1930 E
King, William F. 1807 F, 1842 E
'King of Bass Strait', *see* Munro, James, 1845 F

'King Billy' (d. 1869), *see* Lanney, William
'King Billy' (artist), *see* Barak, Bill
'King of the Cattle-Duffers', 1901 F
'King v Cooper', 1825 A
King George, 1805 A
King George V Memorial Prize for Sculpture, 1945 C
King George Sound, WA, 1791 A, 1802 A, 1817 A, 1826 A, 1828 A, 1831 A
King George Tower, Sydney, 1970 C, 1977 C
King I., 1802 A, 1859 B, 1886 F, 1902 F, 1904 B, 1940 F, 1971 B
King Ingoda, 1922 E
King Leopold Range, WA, 1897 A
King of Melbourne Show Business, 1845 C
'King of Melodrama', 1876 C
'King of Melville Island', 1881 F
King of Pop awards, 1967 C
'King of the Ranges', 1818 A
'King of the Ring', 1838 E
'King of the Road', 1885 C
King Street Bridge, Melbourne, 1961 F
Kingaroy, Qld, 1878 F, 1924 A
Kinghorn, James R. 1891 B
Kinglake, Edward, 1891 C
Kingower, Vic, 1857 F
Kings Cross, Sydney, 1981 F
Kings Cup, rowing, 1919 E
Kings in Grass Castles, 1959 C
Kings Orphan Schools, Tas, 1828 D
Kings Park, Perth, 1872 A
King's Schools, Sydney and Parramatta, 1832 D, 1843 D, 1866 D
King's Theatre, Melbourne, 1908 C
King's Theatre, Sydney, 1910 C
King's Wharf, Sydney, 1813 B, 1833 F
Kingsburgh, 1914 E
Kingscote, SA, 1836 F, 1837 F
Kingsford Smith, Charles E. 1897 B, 1928 B, 1929 B, 1930 B, 1931 F, 1934 B
Kingsford Smith airport, Sydney, 1919 B, 1970 B
Kingsley, Garrett, 1915 C
Kingsley, Henry, 1830 C, 1859 C, 1865 C
Kingston, Charles C. 1850 A, 1893 A, 1897 A
Kingston, Norfolk I., 1788 F
Kingston, SA, 1858 F
Kingston, Tas, 1804 F
Kintore, Earl of, *see* Keith-Falconer, A. H. T.
Kippax, Alan F. 1897 E
Kirby, Joseph C. 1837 D
Kirby, Richard C. 1904 A
Kirk, Ronald H. 1920 C
Kirkby, James N. 1899 B
Kirkpatrick, John S. 1892 A, 1915 A
Kirkton, NSW, 1832 A
Kirkwood, Joseph H. 1899 E
Kirribilli Point, Sydney, 1820 A, D
Kirribilli Wool Stores, Sydney, 1921 F
Kirsova, Hélène, 1937 C, 1940 C
Kirsova Ballet, 1941 C
Kirwan, John W. 1869 A
Kisch, Egon, 1934 A
Kissing Point, Sydney, 1798 D
Kitchen, John, 1841 A, 1855 B
Kitchener, Herbert H. 1909 A, 1910 A
Kitching, Michael D. 1940 C
Kites, 1894 B, 1967 E, 1968 E, 1971 E
Kitto, Frank W. 1903 A, 1950 A
Kiwi (horse), 1983 E
Kiwi Shoe Polish Co., 1906 A
Kleinig, Frank, 1908 E
Klingberg, Herbert H. 1917 F
Klippel, Robert, 1920 C

Kluge-Pott, Hertha, 1934 C
Kmit, Michael, 1910 C, 1955 C
Knatchbull, John, 1790 A, 1844 F
Knetes, Christophoros, 1924 D
Knibbs, George H. 1858 A, 1903 D
Knickerbockers, 1910 F
Knight, Charles, 1959 D
Knight, John, 1910 C
Knight, John G. 1826 C, 1890 A
Knight, John J. 1863 F
Knight, Sue, 1942 E
Knighthood, first Aust., 1858 A
Knights of Labor, 1890 A
'Knock Knock Who's There', 1970 C
Knopfelmacher, Frank, 1923 A
Knopwood, Robert, 1803 D, 1804 D, 1838 D
Knorr, Francis, 1894 F
Knorr, Hans, 1915 C
Knox, A. 1940 E
Knox, Adrian, 1863 A, 1919 A
Knox, Edward, 1819 A
Knox, Edward R. 1889 A
Knox, Geoffrey G. 1884 A
Knox, James R. 1914 D
Knox, Robert, 1855 A
Knox, William D. 1880 C
Koalas, 1919 F, 1924 A, 1927 F
Kocan, Peter, 1966 A
Koenig Willem II, 1857 F
Kogarah Arts Festival prize, NSW, 1946 C
Kojonup, WA, 1840 F
Kokoda Front Line, 1943 C
Kokoda Trail, New Guinea, 1942 A
Kolling Medical Research Institute, 1931 B
Kolobok Folkloric Dance Co., Melbourne, 1970 C
Komon, Rudy, 1908 C, 1958 C
Koninderie opal, SA, 1975 F
Konrads, Ilsa, 1944 E
Konrads, John, 1942 E, 1959 E
Kookaburra, WA, Tas, 1898 F
Koolgardie, WA, 1863 A
Koolyanobbing, WA, 1960 F
Koombana, 1912 F
Koomooloo, 1968 E
Koongarra, WA, 1970 B
Koorda, WA, 1826 F
Kooweerup, Vic, 1878 F
Korean War, 1950 A, 1951 A, 1952 A, 1953 A
Kormoran, 1941 A
Kornhardt, Carl, 1848 F
Korody, George, 1940 F
Koroit, Vic, 1837 F
Korumburra, Vic, 1880 F
Kosciusko Ski School, 1935 E
Koshnitsky, Gregory, 1907 F
Koskie, Jack L. 1914 C
Kossatz, Les, 1943 C
Kow Swamp, Vic, 1968 B
Krait, 1943 A
Kramer, Leonie J. 1925 C, 1981 C
Kramer, Stanley, 1959 C
Krasker, Robert, 1913 C
Kreft, Gerard, 1869 B
Kriegel, Adam, 1912 C
Krips, Henry J. 1912 C, 1949 C
Krivs, Dzems, 1924 C
Kruse, Johan S. 1859 C
Kuhn, Maria, 1937 C
Kunoth, Ngarla, 1954 C
Kununurra, WA, 1961 F, 1963 B
Kuri Bay, WA, 1956 B
Kuring-gai Art Prize, NSW, 1951 C
Kuring-gai College of Advanced Education, Sydney, 1974 D

789

Kurnell, NSW, 1952 B, 1964 B
Kurri Kurri, NSW, 1902 F
Kuttabul, 1942 A
Kwinana, WA, 1951 F, 1952 B, 1955 B, 1960 B, 1983 B
Kwinana freeway, Perth, 1959 B
Kyabram, Vic, 1886 F
Kyancutta, SA, 1915 F, 1969 F
Kyeemagh, Sydney, 1966 E
Kyle, Wallace H. 1910 A, 1975 A
Kyneton, Vic, 1836 F, 1888 D
Kyneton School of Mines, Vic, 1888 D
Kyogle, NSW, 1839 F

L

La Boite Theatre, Brisbane, 1972 C
La Muette de Portics, 1845 C
La Pérouse, Jean F. de, 1788 A, 1826 A
La Somnambule, 1847 C
La Trobe, Charles J. 1801 A, 1839 A, 1845 B, 1846 A, 1851 A, 1853 A
La Trobe University, Melbourne, 1967 D
'Labor', 1908 A
Labor Daily, Sydney, 1922 F
Labor Electoral League, NSW, 1891 A
Labor and Industry in Australia, 1918 C
Labor League, Political, NSW, 1895 A
Labor-in-Politics Conventions, Brisbane, 1892 A, 1905 A
Labor Parties/politics,
 Federal, 1900 A, 1901 A, 1902 A, 1905 A, 1908 A, 1910 A, 1916 A, 1917 A, 1921 A, 1955 A
 NSW, 1874 A, 1891 A, 1893 A, 1894 A
 Qld, 1890 A, 1899 A, 1905 A, 1957 A, 1962 A
 SA, 1970 A, 1980 A
 Tas, 1903 A, 1969 A
 Vic, 1859 A, 1891 A, 1931 A, 1954 A
 WA, 1899 A
Labour Bureau (employment service), NSW, 1892 A
Labour Disputes Settlement Bill, SA, 1890 A
Labour Electoral League, NSW, 1857 A
Laby, Thomas H. 1880 B
Lacepede Bay, SA, 1935 F
Lacrosse, 1874 E, 1879 E, 1882 E, 1888 E, 1938 E, 1967 E
Lacrosse Clubs, 1884 E
Lachlan R., NSW, 1815 A, 1817 A, 1829 A, 1893 B
Lady Augusta (ship), 1853 A
Lady Bird (ship), 1857 F
Lady Gowire Child Centres, 1938 D
Lady Juliana, 1790 A
Lady Munro, 1833 F
Lady Nelson, 1800 A, 1802 A
Lady Shore, 1797 F, 1799 A
Lae, PNG, 1942 A, 1948 F
Laeublis, Annis, 1948 C
Laging, B. 1978 F
Lahey, Frances V. 1880 C
Lahiff, Trevor, 1938 C
Laird, Ewan, 1931 F
Lake, Dawn, 1927 C
Lake, Florence T. 1873 C
Lake Alexandrina, SA, 1830 A, 1852 A
Lake Bathurst, NSW, 1818 A
Lake Bunga, Vic, 1924 B
Lake Burley Griffin, Canberra, 1964 A, E
Lake Callabonna, SA, 1892 B

Lake Cargelligo, NSW, 1879 F
Lake Eyre, SA, 1874 A, 1875 A, 1964 E
Lake Framlingham, Vic, 1971 A
Lake George, NSW, 1820 A, 1824 A
Lake Illawarra, NSW, 1796 A, 1975 F
Lake Kippax Sculpture Competition, NSW, 1966 C
Lake Kurrawang, WA, 1951 F
Lake Macquarie, NSW, 1825 D
Lake Moondarra, Qld, 1981 B
Lake Mungo, NSW, 1968 B, 1975 B
Lake Nitchie, NSW, 1969 B
Lake Pedder, Tas, 1955 F, 1967 F, 1971 F, 1973 F
Lake Pedder Action Committee, Tas, 1971 F
Lake Torrens, SA, 1839 A, 1856 A
Lake Tyers, Vic, 1971 A
Lakemba, 1976 D
Lakes Entrance, Vic, 1850 F
Lal Lal, Vic, 1857 B
Lalor, Peter, 1827 A, 1854 A, 1880 A
Lamb, Henry, 1885 C
Lamb, Horace, 1849 B, 1879 B
Lambe, David, 1803 C, 1824 C
Lamber, John, 1853 B
Lambert, Eric, 1952 C
Lambert, George W. T. 1873 C, 1899 C, 1927 C
Lambert, Ronald, 1923 C
Lambing Flat, NSW, 1860 A, B, 1861 A
Lamble, G. 1935 E
Lambrigg, NSW, 1886 B
Lamington, Lord, *see* Baillie, C.W.A.N.C.
Lamond, Henry G. 1885 C
Lamont, Billy, 1909 E
Lampard, Doug, 1974 B
Lancaster, Charles H. 1886 C
Lancastrian air service, Sydney–England, 1945 B
Lancastrian education system, 1812 D
Lancastrian monitorial teaching system, 1811 D
Lance, Albert, 1925 C
Lance, James, 1976 B
Lanceley, Colin, 1938 C, 1962 C
Lancer Military Barracks, Parramatta, 1820 C
Lanchbery, John, 1923 C
Land Bill, Vic, 1860 A
 grants, 1788 A, 1789 A, 1791 A, 1792 A, 1794 A, 1827 A, 1831 A
Land,
 leases, 1797 A, 1924 A
 policy, 1840 A, 1852 A
 reform Vic, 1855 A
 rights, *see* Aboriginals
 route, Hobart to Launceston, 1807 A
 sales, Crown land, 1831 A, 1842 A
 – NSW, 1839 A
 – Qld, 1842 A
 – SA, 1835 A, 1837 A, 1872 A
 – Tas, 1828 A
 – Vic, 1837 A, 1839 A, 1860 A
 – WA, 1829 A
 scandal, Vic, 1977 A
 selection, 1861 A, 1865 A, 1869 A, 1874 A
 settlement, 1788 A, 1829 A, 1894 A, *see also* individual entries and Communities *section* F
 speed record, 1964 E
 taxes, 1877 A, 1884 E
 titles, 1800 A, 1857 A, 1858 A
 transport, growth of, 1952 B
Land Tax Act, Federal, 1910 A
Lander, Cyril G. 1892 C
Landeryou, W. 1983 A

'Landholders, Merchants ... of the Colony', 1819 A
Landowners, numbers, 1806 A
Lands Department Building, Sydney, 1876 C
Landsborough, William, 1825 A, 1860 A, 1861 A, 1862 A
Landtakers, 1934 C
Landy, John, 1930 E, 1954 E
Lane, Freddy, 1877 E, 1900 E, 1902 E
Lane, Geoff, 1939 E
Lane, George, 1904 D
Lane, William, 1861 A, 1890 A, 1892 C, 1893 A, 1909 A
Lane-Poole, Charles E. 1885 B
Lang, John D. 1799 D, 1823 D, 1824 D, 1826 F, 1831 D, 1835 F, 1837 D, 1852 A, 1872 D
Lang, John G. 1816 C, 1853 C, 1855 C, 1859 C
Lang, John T. 1876 A, 1913 A, 1925 A, 1930 A, G, 1931 A, 1932 A, 1943 A
Langby, Kevin, 1946 E
Langhorne, George, 1836 D
Langker, Eric, 1898 C
Langlands, Graeme, 1942 E
Langley, Eve, 1908 C, 1942 C
Langley, Gilbert R. A. 1919 E
Langley, Jean, 1926 C
Langley, Robert, 1929 C
Lanney, William, 1869 A
Lansell, George, 1823 A, 1876 B
Lantern, 1864 E
Laos, Aust. aid, 1964 A
Lapin, Billy, 1920 E
Lara, Vic, 1969 F
Largs Bay Fort, SA, 1884 A
Larter, Richard, 1929 C
Lascelles, Edward H. 1847 A, 1891 B
Laser beam, 1970 B
Laser depth sounder, 1981 B
Lashwood, Harold F. (Hal), 1920 C
Lasica, Margaret, 1963 C
Lasseter, Lewis H. (Harold Bell), 1880 A, 1897 B, 1930 A
Lasseter's Last Ride, 1931 C
Lasseter's Reef, central Aust., 1883 A, 1930 A
Last, Clifford, 1918 C
Last Wave, The, 1977 C
Last and Worst ... Van Diemen's Land, The, 1818 C
Late night shopping, 1909 F, 1927 F, 1971 F
Latest Information with Regard to Australia Felix, 1840 C
Latham, John G. 1877 A, 1929 A, 1934 A, 1935 A
Latimer, Murray H. 1919 C
Latrobe, Tas, 1850 F
Latrobe Valley Art Centre, Vic, 1967 C
Latrobe Valley Coal, Vic, 1917 B
Latvian Artists, 1953 C
Laudes, 1964 C
Laughing Jackass, 1873 C
Laughing jackass, 1898 F
Laughton, Annie W. 1858 C
Launceston, Tas, 1806 F, 1807 A, 1818 B, 1823 F, 1825 F, 1827 B, 1831 A, 1842 F, 1845 C, 1847 B, 1857 B, 1868 B, 1876 B, 1888 C, 1890 F, 1895 B, 1959 B, 1969 F, 1978 D
Launceston Advertiser, 1829 F
Launceston Art Gallery, Tas, 1895 C
Launceston Art Society, 1891 C
Launceston Art Trophy, Tas, 1964 C
Launceston Cricket Club, 1832 E, 1843 E
Launceston Grammar School, 1846 D
Launceston Cup, (horse-race) 1865 E

Launceston Matriculation College, 1967 D
Launceston Savings Bank, 1835 A
Launceston Theatre, Tas, 1843 C
Launceston Town Hall, 1864 C
Laura, Qld, 1960 C
Laura, SA, 1872 F
'Laureate of the Larrikin', 1876 C
Laurie Thomas (painting), 1951 C
Lavan, John M. 1980 A
Lavarack, John D. 1885 A, 1946 A
Lavater, Louis, 1867 C, 1935 C
Laver, Rodney G. 1938 E, 1962 E, 1968 E, 1969 E
Laver, William A. 1866 C
Laverton, WA, 1898 F
Laverty, Peter P. 1926 C
Laverty, Ursula A. 1930 C
Law, Benjamin, 1807 C, 1836 C
Law, first civil action, 1795 A, *see individual entries*
Law, Phillip G. 1912 B, 1954 B
Law Concil of Aust, 1933 A
Law Institute of Vic, 1859 A
Law Reform Commission, 1973 A
Lawes, William G. 1839 D
Lawler, Raymond E. 1922 C, 1954 C, 1956 C
Lawley, Arthur, 1901 A
Lawlor, Adrian, 1890 C, 1937 C
Lawn bowling, 1844 E, 1845 E, 1880 E, 1881 E, 1895 E, 1911 E, 1966 E
Lawn Bowling Association, 1880 E, *see also individual entries*
Lawn Bowling Clubs, first, 1864 E, *see also individual entries*
Lawn mower, 1951 B
Lawn tennis, Melbourne, 1879 E
Lawn Tennis Association of Aust., 1929 E, 1982 E
Lawn Tennis Association of Australasia, 1904 E
Lawn Tennis Associations, 1888 E, *see also individual entries*
Lawrence, Alan, 1933 E
Lawrence, Bryan, 1936 C
Lawrence, David H. 1923 C
Lawrence, David W. J. 1920 C
Lawrence, George F. 1901 C
Lawrence, Marjorie F. 1908 C
Lawry, William M. 1937 E
Lawson, Abercrombie A. 1874 B
Lawson, Aub, 1913 E
Lawson, Bernard J. 1909 C
Lawson, Henry S. W. 1875 A, 1918 A
Lawson, Henry, 1867 C, 1887 C, 1888 C, 1894 C, 1896 C, 1900 C, 1901 C, 1902 C, 1905 C, 1911 C, 1984 C
Lawson, Louisa, 1848 A, 1888 F
Lawson, William, (1), 1813 A, 1821 A, 1850 A
Lawson, William, (2), 1876 C
Lawsons, The, 1944 F
Lawyers, 1798 A, 1902 A, 1903 A, 1918 A
Lay-by, 1927 F
Laybourne-Smith, Louis, 1880 C
Laycock, Donald, 1931 C
Laycock, Thomas, 1807 A
Lazar, John, 1837 C, 1841 C
Lazar, Sain, 1868 C
L. C. Robson, 1946 C
Le Breton, Ken, 1925 E
Le Courrier Australien, 1892 F
Le Fanu, Henry F. 1870 D
Le Gallienne, Dorian L. M. 1915 C
Le Grande, Henri, 1917 C
Le Hunte, George R. 1903 A
Le Souef, William H. D. 1857 B
Lea, Arthur M. 1868 B

Leach, John A. 1870 B
Leach-Jones, Alun, 1937 C
Lead,
  NSW, 1875 B, 1883 B, 1885 B, 1939 B
  Qld, 1923 B
  SA, 1839 B, 1841 B, 1889 B, 1934 B
  Tas, 1885 B
  WA, 1848 B
Lead extractions, NSW, 1910 B
Lead mining, 1876 B
Lead pipes, 1854 B
Leader, Melbourne, 1856 F
Lead-free petrol, 1980 B
Leadville, NSW, 1897 F
League of Nations, 1920 A, 1936 A
Leake, George, 1856 A, 1901 A
Leakey, Caroline W. 1827 C, 1859 C
Leane, E. T. 1921 A
Leane, Redmond L. 1878 A, 1921 A
Lear, Simon, 1818 B
Learmonth, Charles, 1917 A
Learmonth, Noel F. 1880 C
Learmonth, Peter, 1871 A
Learmonth, Somerville, 1819 A
Learmonth, Thomas, 1818 A
Learmonth, WA, 1942 A
Learmonth, William, 1815 A
Learning, *see section E and* Education
Leason, Percival A. 1889 C
Leather, 1820 A
Leaves from Australian Forests, 1869 C
Lebanese Hierarch, 1970 D
Lebanese Orthodox church, Sydney, 1898 D, 1911 D, 1920 D, 1970 D
Lebrun, 1800 C
Leckie, Alexander J. K. 1932 C
Lee, George, 1834 A
Lee, Jean, 1951 F
Lee, Raigh, 1977 F
Lee, William, 1794 A
Lee, W. H. 1916 A, 1923 A, 1934 A
Lee Steere, Ernest A. 1866 A
Lee-Steere, Ernest H. 1912 A
Lee-Steere, James G. 1830 A
Leeper, Alexander, 1848 D
Lees, Derwent, 1885 C
Lees, John, 1817 D
Leete, Henry B. 1845 C, 1893 C, 1901 C
Leeton, NSW, 1912 F, 1922 A, 1924 A
Leeton Irrigana Golden Jubilee Festival Art Prize, NSW, 1962 C
Lefebvre, C. J. 1875 C, 1880 C
Leffler, Dick, 1967 E
Lefroy, Anthony L. 1881 A
Lefroy, Anthony O. 1816 A
Lefroy, Edward H. B. 1887 A
Lefroy, Gerald de C. 1819 A
Lefroy, Henry B. 1854 A, 1917 A
Lefroy, Henry M. 1818 A, 1843 A, 1863 A
Lefroy, John H. 1880 A
Left hand driving, 1820 F
Legacy Clubs, 1920 F, 1923 F, 1926 F
Legal Aid Commissions, 1974 A
Legend of King O'Malley, The, 1970 C
Legend of the Nineties, The, 1954 C
Legerwood, Tas, 1865 F
Legge, James G. 1863 A
Legge, William V. 1840 B
Legislative Assemblies/Councils,
  NSW, 1823 A, 1824 A, 1828 A, 1832 A, 1834 A, 1836 A, 1842 A, 1845 A, 1848 A, 1856 A, 1891 A, 1893 A, 1921 A, 1925 A, 1931 A, 1960 A, 1961 A, 1978 A
  Norfolk I., 1979 A
  NT, 1947 A, 1968 A, 1974 A, 1977 A
  PNG, 1949 A, 1951 A, 1960 A, 1963 A

  Qld, 1860 A, 1905 A, 1915 A, 1921 A, 1922 A
  SA, 1842 A, 1843 A, 1851 A, 1852 A, 1857 A, 1890 A
  Tas, 1828 A, 1851 A, 1852 A, 1856 A, 1900 A
  Vic, 1852 A, 1856 A, 1864 A, 1878 A, 1881 A, 1899 A
  WA, 1830 A, 1832 A, 1851 A, 1870 A, 1877 A, 1887 A, 1890 A, 1893 A, 1907 A
Lehman Ballet Co., 1867 C, 1868 C
Lehmann, Geoffrey J. 1940 C
Leichhardt, F. W. Ludwig, 1813 A, 1844 A, 1845 A, B, 1846 A, 1847 A, 1848 A, 1852 A, 1858 A
Leichhardt R., Qld, 1875 A
Leichhardt search expeditions, 1865 A, 1869 A
Leigh Creek, SA, 1841 F, 1888 B, 1907 B, 1941 F, 1943 B
Leigh, Samuel, 1815 D, 1816 D, 1817 D, 1821 D, 1852 D
Leist, Frederick, 1878 C
Leisure, 1977 C
Leitch Medal, Tas, 1945 E
Lemmone, John, 1861 C
Lempriere, Thomas J. 1796 C
Lendon, Nigel, 1944 C
Leneham, Jim, 1938 C
Leningrad Kirov Ballet, 1973 C
Leningrad Theatre Co., 1961 C
Lennon, William, 1920 A, 1925 A
Lennox, David, 1788 B, 1832 C, 1846 C, 1850 C
Lennox Bridge, NSW, 1832 C
Lenz, 1974 C
Leonora, WA, 1896 F
Leonski, Edward J. 1942 F
Leonta, 1903 F
Leopold, Tom, 1870 C
Leopold, Vic, 1859 F
Leopold dancers, 1857 C
Leprosy, 1857 F, 1896 B
Leroy-Alcorso prizes, 1953 C
Les Ballets Contemporains Co., 1937 C
Les Emigrés aux Terres Australes, 1792 C
Les Huguenots, 1862 C
Les Sylphides, 1845 C
Leslie, Patrick, 1815 A, 1840 A, 1846 C
Leslie Parker, *see* Thirkell, Angela, 1934 C
L'Estrange, W. 1877 F
Lesueur, Charles A. 1846 C
Let George Do It, 1938 C
Letter cards, 1894 F
Letter carriers, 1915 F
Letter sorters, mechanical, 1951 B
Letter from Sydney, A, 1829 A
Lettergram service, Sydney, 1914 F
Letts, John, 1943 E, 1972 E
Lever, Richard H. 1876 C
Leveson street Private Gallery, Melbourne, 1962 C
Levey, Barnett, 1798 C, 1821 C, F, 1829 C, 1833 C
Levey, G. C. 1853 B
Levey, Solomon, 1794 A
Levy, Colin, 1933 C
Lewers, Gerald F. 1905 C
Lewers, Margo, 1908 C
Lewin, John W. 1800 C, 1805 C, 1808 B, 1812 C, 1813 C, 1819 C
Lewis, Bernard, 1982 F
Lewis, Bobby, 1878 E
Lewis, David H. 1919 E, 1964 E, 1972 A
Lewis, Essington, 1881 B, 1940 A
Lewis, Frank, 1916 E
Lewis, Howard, 1899 B

791

Lewis, Jeannie, 1945 C
Lewis, John, 1842 A, 1874 A
Lewis, Mortimer W. 1796 C, 1830 C, 1835 C, 1841 D
Lewis, Neil E. 1858 A, 1899 A, 1909 A
Lewis, R. 1902 E, 1915 E, 1919 E, 1927 E
Lewis, T. L. 1975 A
Lewis, Vivian, 1900 B
Lewis Ponds, NSW, 1851 B
Lexcen, Ben, 1983 E
Ley, Thomas J. 1879 A
Leysalle, Emily, 1857 C
Lhotsky, John, 1795 B, 1834 A, C, 1839 C
Liao, Eric, 1972 D
Liardet, Wilbraham F. E. L. 1799 A, 1840 E
Libel, 1829 F, 1945 C, 1946 C
Liberal-Centre Party, Tas, 1969 A
Liberal Movement, Political party, SA, 1972 A
Liberal Party of Aust., 1944 A, 1945 A
Liberal Party, Federal, 1909 A, 1917 A
Liberal Party, Vic, 1965 A
Liberal Reform Group, 1966 A, 1967 A
Liberation Theology, 1983 D
Libertarian Society, 1952 D
Libido, 1973 C
Librarianship, 1937 D, 1960 D
Libraries, 1822 D, 1836 D, 1844 D, 1849 D, 1859 D, 1912 D
Library Act, states, 1939 D
Library Association of Aust., 1896 D, 1949 D
Library Association of Australasia, 1896 D, 1900 D
Library of NSW, 1901 D
Library of the Vic Association of Braille writers, 1894 D
Libya, 1940 A
Libya, Bardia, 1941 A
Licences,
  drivers, 1965 F, 1984 F
  goldmining, 1851 A
  hotel, 1798 F
  pilots, 1911 B, 1921 B, 1935 F
  radio, 1937 B, 1974 A
  radio stations, 1924 B
  television, 1974 A
Lichine, 1938 C, 1940 C
Lid, auto, 1898 B
Lidcombe, NSW, 1857 F, 1958 F
Liddell Thermal Power Station, NSW, 1974 B
Lieut-Gen. Edmund Herring (painting), 1945 C
Lien-on-Wool-Act, NSW, 1843 A
Life and Adventures of Nicholas Nickleby, The, 1983 C
Life be in it, 1979 F
Life in the Cities, 1975 C
Life and ... Notorious Australian Bushranger, The, 1910 C
Lifeline, 1963 F
Lifesavers rescue boat, 1906 E
Lifesaving, 1894 E, 1908 E, 1910 E, 1913 E, 1960 F
Lifesaving reels, 1906 E, 1907 E
Lifton, Charles, 1814 E
Lifts, 1855 B, 1879 B, 1881 B, 1889 B, 1921 B, 1923 B, 1968 B
Light, Alan, 1916 C
Light, William, 1836 A, 1837 A, 1839 A
Light of the Age, 1868 F
Light Car Club of NSW, 1931 E
Light Fingers, 1965 E
Light Horse, 1918 A
Lightfoot, Louise, 1929 C, 1931 C, 1933 C

Lighthouses, 1817 C, 1818 B, 1832 C, 1880 B, 1970 B
Lighting, 1826 B, 1857 B, 1865 B, 1888 B, 1889 B, 1894 B, 1904 B, 1912 B, *see also* Electric
Lightning Ridge, NSW, 1887 B, 1891 F, 1902 B, 1918 F
Likie, Jean, 1934 C
Lilburne, Ron, 1915 C
Lillee, Dennis K. 1949 E
Lilley, Charles, 1830 A, 1868 A
Lilydale, Vic, 1838 A
Lilydale, Tas, 1861 F
Limb, Bobby, 1924 C
Lime, Qld, 1968 B
Limestone Plains, 1821 A
Lincoln, Merv, 1933 E
Lincoln Institute of Health Sciences, Melbourne, 1972 B
Lindeman, Henry J. 1811 A, 1843 A
Lindesay, Patrick, 1831 A, 1839 A
Lindesay, Vane, 1920 C
Lindie Hop dance, 1945 C
Lindrum, Frederick W. 1888 E
Lindrum, Horace, 1912 E, 1940 E, 1970 E
Lindrum, Walter A. 1898 E, 1929 E, 1932 E, 1941 E, 1950 E
Lindsay, Aeneas J. 1904 C
Lindsay, Daryl, 1890 C, 1932 C
Lindsay, David, 1856 A, 1883 A, 1886 A, 1891 A
Lindsay, Harold A. 1900 B
Lindsay, Jack, 1900 C, 1923 C, 1925 C
Lindsay, Lionel A. 1874 C
Lindsay, Norman, 1879 C, 1901 C, 1904 C, 1913 C, 1918 C, 1920 C, 1930 C, 1932 C, 1933 C, 1945 C
Lindsay, Percy C. 1870 C
Lindsay, Raymond, 1904 C
Lindsay, Reginald, 1971 C
Lindsay, Robert, 1862 C
Lindsay, Ruby, 1887 C
Lindt, John W. 1845 B
Lindwall, Raymond R. 1921 E
Linen, 1801 A, 1803 A
Lines, Ted, 1934 B
Linger, Carl, 1810 C, 1859 C
Linnean Society of NSW, 1874 B
Linseed, 1947 B
Linseed oil, 1949 A
Linton, James W. R. 1869 C
Linton, Richard, 1925 F
Lions Club, NSW, 1947 F
Liqueurs, 1931 A
Liquidity crisis, 1822 A, 1827 A
Liquor licensing authorities, 1912 F
Liquor-licensing Statute, 1825 A
Lismore, NSW, 1855 F, 1947 F
Lismore, Vic, 1853 F
Lismore Art Prize, NSW, 1953 C
Lisner, Charles, 1960 C
Lisner Ballet, Qld, 1960 C
Lister, F. J. 1910 B, 1912 B
Lister, John, 1851 B
Lister, Matilda, 1889 C
Lister, William L. 1859 C, 1908 C
Litchfield, Frederick H. 1865 B
Litchfield, James, 1825 A, 1865 B
Literacy rates, 1861 D, 1900 D
Literacy News: A Review ... and Belles Lettres, 1837 C
Literary Society, Melbourne, 1868 C
Literary Society, SA, 1834 C
Literature, *see individual entries and section C*
Literature Board, 1973 C
Literature Censorshop Board, 1933 C
Literature, Chair of, Sydney, 1962 C

Literature in New South Wales, 1866 C
Lithgow, NSW, 1839 B, 1841 B, 1855 F, 1858 B, 1869 B, 1873 B, 1875 B, 1876 B, 1894 B, 1900 B, 1905 B, 1908 B, 1928 B
Lithgow, William, 1864 A
Lithographs, Arrival of ... June, 1852, 1852 C
Lithography, 1821 C, 1851 C
Lithotomy, 1819 B
Lithuanian Arts Festival, Melbourne, 1964 C
Little, Jimmy, 1964 C
Little, Robert A. 1895 A
Little Black Princess, The, 1905 C
Little Bush Maid, A, 1910 C
Little Desert, Vic, 1969 F
Little Pattie, 1972 C
Little Red School Book, The, 1972 D
Little R., Vic, 1884 F
Little River Band, 1975 C, 1977 C
Little Theatre, The, 1913 C
Little Theatre, Melbourne, 1931 C
Littlehampton, SA, 1849 F
Littlejohns, Raymond T. 1893 B
Live game Bow Hunters Club, Vic, 1953 E
Liver transplant, 1968 B
Livermore, Reg, 1938 C, 1975 C, 1983 C
Liverpool, England, 1916 A
Liverpool, NSW, 1810 F, 1814 B, 1846 F, 1857 B, 1866 B
Liverpool Plains, NSW, 1818 A, 1823 A, 1825 A, 1853 A
Liversidge, Archibald, 1847 B, 1888 C
Livestock Analysis, 1982 B
Livestock duties, Vic, 1877 A
Livestock and Grain Producers' Association of NSW, 1978 A
Living in the Seventies, 1974 C
Living Together, 1974 C
Llewellynn Ernest V. 1915 C
Lloyd, Henry G. 1830 C
Lloyd, Norman, 1897 C
Lloyd Rees, 1968 C
Loan Exhibition, Melbourne, 1869 C
Loane, Marcus L. 1911 D, 1978 D
Loane, Mark, 1955 E
Loans Affair, 1974 A, 1975 A, 1977 A, 1978 A
Loans Council, 1923 A, 1924 A
Lobethal, SA, 1842 F
Lobsters, NSW, 1891 F
Loch Ard, 1878 F
Loch, Henry B. 1884 A
Lock, Jane, 1954 E
Lock, Leslie W. 1908 E
Lockhart, NSW, 1877 F
Lockheed Electra Prop-jets, 1959 B
Lockwood, Douglas W. 1918 C
Lockyer, Edmond, 1825 A, B, 1826 A, 1860 A
Locomotives, 1854 B, 1860 B, 1870 B, 1890 B
Loder, John de V. 1895 A, 1937 A
Loftus, Augustus W. F. S. 1879 A
Logan, Patrick, 1791 A, 1826 A
Lola Montez, 1818 C, 1958 C
Lombard Aust. Ltd, 1935 A
London (ship), 1866 F
London, Mrs Jack, 1908 E
London Court, Perth, 1936 C
London Festival Ballet, 1975 C
London Institute of Physics, 1980 B
London Missionary School, NSW, 1799 D, 1802 D
London Missionary Society, 1796 D, 1798 D, 1799 D, F, 1825 D
'Lone Eagle', 1892 B

Lone Hand, The, 1907 F
Lonely Hearts (film), 1982 C
Lone Pine, 1915 A
Lone Pine Koala Sanctuary, Brisbane, 1927 B
Long, A. L. 1919 B
Long, Gavin M. 1901 D
Long, George M. 1875 D
Long, Grant, 1980 E
Long, Leonard H. 1911 C
Long, Lionel, 1964 C
Long, Sydney, 1871 C, 1897 C
Long, Thelma, 1918 E
Long distance driving, 1900 E
Long Hai hills, 1970 A
Long Odds, 1869 C
Long service leave, 1951 A, 1957 A
Long Tan, Battle of, 1966 A
Long Way to Tipperary, A, 1914 C
Longbottom, William, 1799 D
Longerenong Agricultural College, Vic, 1889 D
Longford, Raymond H. 1878 C, 1911 C, 1912 C, 1914 C, 1919 C, 1920 C, 1933 C, 1934 C
Longford, Tas, 1827 F
Longford-Lyell Aust. Productions, 1922 C
Longitudes, Aust., 1883 B
Longman, Irene, 1929 A
Longmore, Arthur M. 1885 A, 1911 B
Longreach, Qld, 1887 F, 1892 B, 1921 B, 1961 F
Longstaff, John, 1862 C, 1887 C, 1925 C, 1928 C, 1929 C, 1931 C, 1935 C
Longstaff, Will, 1879 C
Lonsdale, William, 1800 A, 1836 A
Lonworth, Bill, 1913 E
Looby, Keith, 1940 C, 1984 C
Look and Listen, 1984 F
Looker, Cecil T. 1913 A
Lord, Alistair, 1962 E
Lord, Edward, 1810 A
Lord, Gabrielle, 1980 C
Lord, Ron, 1930 E
Lord, Simeon, 1813 B, 1815 A, 1840 A
Lord Cardigan, 1903 E
Lord Fury, 1961 E
Lord Howe I., NSW, 1788 A, 1834 A, F, 1948 F, 1952 F, 1953 A
Lord Howe Island Act, 1953 A
Lord Mayors, 1840 A, 1902 A, *see also* Mayors
Lord Nolan, 1908 E
Lord Warden of the Cinque Ports, 1965 A
Lord's Day Observance Society, Melbourne, 1883 D
'Lord's Prayer, The', 1974 C
Lorenz, C. T. 1948 C
Loring, William, 1859 A
Lormer, Albert, 1862 B
Lorne, Vic, 1871 F
Lotteries, Qld, 1916 F, 1930 F, 1944 F, 1957 F, 1979 F
Lotto, NSW, 1979 F
Louat, Frank R. 1902 A
Lough, Fitz, 1919 E
Loureiro, Arthur J. de S. 1854 C
Louth, NSW, 1859 F
Love, James R. B. 1889 D
Love, James S. 1862 A
Love me Sailor, 1945 C, 1946 C
Love and War, 1974 E, 1978 E
Lovejoy, Robin C. 1923 C, 1963 C
Lovekin, Arthur, 1859 A
Lovell, H. T. 1928 D
Lovell, Patricia, 1982 F
Lovelock, William, 1899 C

Lovett, Mildred E. 1880 C
Low, David A. C. 1891 C
Lowcay, Rose, 1889 C
Lowe, Allan, 1907 C
Lowe, Charles, 1953 A
Lowe, Douglas A. 1942 A, 1977 A
Lowe, Robert, 1811 A, 1842 A, 1844 D, F
Lower, Lennie W. 1903 C, 1930 C
Lowry-Corry, Somerset R. 1868 A
Loxton, John S. 1903 C
Loxton, SA, 1907 F
Lucas, Wilfred, 1920 C
Lucas Heights, NSW, 1958 B, 1964 B
Lucinda Brayford, 1946 C
Luckey, Len, 1923 E
Lucknow, NSW, 1851 F
Lucky Country, The, 1964 C
Luina, Tas, 1898 F
Luke, Charles R. M. 1885 B
Luke, George, 1920 C
Luker, Joseph, 1803 F
Lumb, Frank, 1910 C
Lumiere process, 1907 B
Lumsdaine, David, 1931 C
Luna Park, Sydney, 1979 F
Lunacy Act, NSW, 1878 F
Lungfish, Qld, 1902 B
Lunghi, John, 1912 C
L'Uranie, 1819 A
Lurie, Morris, 1938 C
Lutheran church, 1838 D, 1921 D
Lutheran church of Aust., 1966 D
Lutheran schools, 1915 D
Lutte Eternelle, 1940 C
Lutwyche, Alfred J. P. 1810 A, 1859 A
Ly-ee-Moon, 1886 F
Lycett, Joseph, 1824 C
Lyell, Lottie, 1891 C, 1922 C
Lygon, William, 1872 A, 1899 A, 1901 A
'Lying-in Hospital', Sydney, 1866 B
Lyle, Maxwell W. 1935 C
Lyle, Thomas R. 1860 B
Lymburner, Francis, 1916 C
Lynch, Alfred, 1861 B
Lynch, Guy E. (Frank), 1895 C
Lynch, Jim, 1949 E, 1978 E
Lynch, John, 1812 A, 1842 F
Lynch, Phillip R. 1933 A, 1977 A
Lynch, Wayne, 1952 E
Lynd R., Qld, 1845 B
Lyndhurst, NSW, 1852 D
Lyndoch, SA, 1838 F
Lyne, William J. 1844 A, 1899 A
Lynn, Elwyn A. 1917 C
Lyon, A. S. 1846 F
Lyons, Enid M. 1897 A, 1943 A
Lyons, Joseph A. 1879 A, 1923 A, 1929 A, 1931 A, 1932 A, 1934 A, 1937 A, 1938 A
Lyric Opera of Qld, 1982 C
Lyrup Village, SA, 1894 F
Lysaght, John, 1880 A, 1921 B
Lyster, William S. 1828 C, 1861 C, 1862 C, 1870 C
Lyttle, Stephen J. 1963 F
Lyttleton, Edith J. 1874 C
Lytton, Qld, 1965 B

Mc/Mac

Macalister, Arthur, 1818 A, 1866 A, 1874 A
McAlpine, Tony, 1922 E
Macarthur, Archibald, 1822 D, 1823 D

McArthur, David C. 1810 A
MacArthur, Douglas, 1942 A
Macarthur, Edward, 1789 A, 1856 A
Macarthur, Elizabeth, 1850 A
Macarthur, Frances, 1836 E
Macarthur, George F. 1825 D
McArthur, Gordon S. 1896 A
Macarthur, Hannibal H. 1788 A
Macarthur, James, 1798 A, 1840 A
McArthur, John, 1790 C
Macarthur, John, 1793 A, C, 1794 A, 1795 A, 1797 A, 1801 A, F, 1802 A, 1804 A, 1805 A, 1807 A, 1808 A, 1809 A, 1811 A, 1813 A, 1816 A, 1817 A, 1820 A, 1821 A, 1822 A, 1827 A, 1834 A, 1846 B
Macarthur, Vic, 1867 F
Macarthur, William, 1800 B
Macarthur-Onslow, Annette R. 1933 C
Macarthur-Onslow, Denzil, 1904 A
Macarthur-Onslow, George M. 1875 A
Macarthur-Onslow, James W. 1867 A
Macarthur-Onslow, Rosa S. 1871 A
Macartney, Charles G. 1886 C
Macartney, Frederick T. B. 1887 C
Macartney, Hussey B. 1799 D
McAulay, Alexander, 1863 B
McAuley, James P. 1917 C, 1944 C, 1946 C, 1956 C, 1964 C, 1969 C, 1971 C
McAuley College, Brisbane, 1955 D
McAustan, Gordon S. 1913 C
McBride, William G. 1927 B, 1961 B
McBrien, James, 1823 B
McCabe, Stanley J. 1910 E
McCallin, Clement, 1955 C
McCallum, Francis M. M. 1822 A
McCallum, J. Neil, 1918 C
MacCallum, Mungo W. 1854 C, 1910 C, 1924 D
McCann, Richard M. 1889 C
McCarten, Maurice, 1904 E
McCarthy, Bob, 1945 E
McCarthy, Darby, 1952 E
McCarthy, Dudley, 1911 A
McCarthy, Edwin, 1896 A
McCarthy, Lawrence D. 1892 A
Macartney-Snape, Tim, 1984 E
McCaughey, Patrick, 1943 C
McCaughey, Roy, 1898 A
McCaughey, Samuel, (1) 1835 A
McCaughey, Samuel, (2) 1892 A
McCaughey Art Prize, 1956 C
McCawley, Thomas W. 1881 A
McCay, James W. 1864 A
McClelland, Joshua, 1927 C
McClelland, W. C. 1956 E
McClelland Gallery, Vic, 1971 C
McClements, Lynn, 1951 E
Macclesfield, SA, 1845 F
McClintock, Alexander, 1869 C
McClintock, Herbert, 1906 C
McCloud, H. 1942 E
McColl, Hugh, 1819 A
McComas, Francis J. 1874 C
McConachy, Norman, 1954 B
McConnan, Leslie J. 1887 A
McConnel, Bill, 1908 E
McConnel, Carl, 1926 C
McConnel, David C. 1818 A
MacConnell, James, 1805 D
McCormac, Andrew, 1826 C
McCormack, John, 1942 E
McCormack, William, 1879 A, 1925 A
McCormick, Peter D. 1878 C
McCosker, Richard, 1946 E
McCoy, Frederick, 1817 B
McCrae, George G. 1833 C
McCrae, Georgiana H. 1804 C
McCrae, Hugh R. 1876 C, 1909 C, 1920 C

793

McCrae, Vic, 1843 F
McCrone, Francis N. 1809 C, 1849 C
McCubbin, Charles, 1931 C
McCubbin, Frederick, 1855 C, 1885 C
McCubbin, Louis, 1890 C
McCulloch, Alan M. 1907 C
McCulloch, Alan R. 1885 B
McCulloch, James, 1819 A, 1863 A, 1864 A, 1868 A, 1870 A, 1875 A
McCulloch, Rosamond A. V. 1905 C
McCulloch, Wilfred A. 1910 C
McCulloch ministry, Vic, 1866 A
McCullogh, William, 1869 B
McCullough, Colleen M. 1937 C, 1977 C, 1978 C, 1981 C
McDiven, Bryant, 1923 C
McDonagh, Isobel, 1926 C
McDonagh, Paulette, 1926 C, 1928 C
McDonagh, Phyllis, 1926 C
McDonald, Bobby, 1884 E
McDonald, Dawson, 1920 C
Macdonald, Donald A. 1857 F
MacDonald, Garry, 1948 C
McDonald, Henry R. 1914 C
MacDonald, James S. 1878 C
MacDonald, J. G. B. 1950 A, 1952 A
Macdonald, Louisa, 1858 D
McDonald, Raymond, 1925 C
McDonald, Warren D'A. 1901 A
MacDonald, William N. 1860 A, 1882 A
McDonald Hamburger Co., 1972 F
MacDonald I., 1947 A
McDonald's Burger Huts, 1971 F
McDonnell, Billy, 1937 E
MacDonnell, James E. 1917 C
Macdonnell, (parliamentary seat) NT, 1977 A
MacDonnell, Richard G. 1814 A, 1885 A
McDonough, Michael, 1884 B
McDonough, William, 1884 B
Macdougal, 1959 E
Macdougall, Duncan, 1920 C
Macdougall, Pakie, 1920 C
McDowall, Val, 1934 B
McEacharn, Malcolm, 1852 A
McEachern, Malcolm, 1945 C
McEncroe, John, 1794 D, 1832 D
McEwen, Henry, 1923 F
McEwen, John, 1900 A, 1934 A, 1967 A, 1971 A
MacFarlan, I. 1945 A
Macfarland, John H. 1851 D
McGarvie, William, 1831 F
McGeorge, John A. H. 1898 B
MacGeorge, Norman, 1872 C
McGilchrist, Erica M. 1926 C
McGill, Arthur, 1945 E
McGill, Linda, 1945 E, 1965 E, 1967 E, 1968 E, 1976 E
Macgillivray, William D. K. 1867 B
McGinness, P. J. 1896 B, 1920 B
McGirr, James, 1890 A, 1947 A
McGowan, James S. T. 1855 A, 1910 A
McGowan, Samuel W. 1829 B, 1854 B
McGrath, Eileen, 1907 C
McGrath, Raymond, 1903 C
McGrath, Vivian B. 1916 E
McGregor, Alexander, 1821 A
McGregor, Ken, 1929 E, 1951 E
MacGregor, William, 1846 A, 1888 A, 1909 A
McGrowdie, Noel, 1922 E, 1957 E
McGuinness, Bruce, 1979 A
McGuire, Dominic P. 1903 A
McGuire, Frances M. 1900 C
McGuire, Terence B. 1881 D, 1930 D
McHardie, Gregory N. 1980 F
McIlwraith, John, 1828 A, 1855 B

McIlwraith, Thomas, 1835 A, 1879 A, 1883 A, 1893 A
MacInnes, Colin, 1914 C
McInnes, Graham, 1965 C
McInnes, William B. 1889 C, 1921 C, 1922 C, 1923 C, 1924 C, 1926 C, 1930 C, 1936 C
McIntosh, Hugh D. 1876 A, 1935 F
McIntosh, Merv, 1921 E
McIntosh, William P. 1857 C
McIntyre, Alan L. 1913 C
McIntyre, Duncan, 1831 A, 1865 A
McIntyre, Ivor E. 1899 B, 1924 B, 1934 B
McIntyre, Margaret E. 1886 A, 1948 A
McIntyre, Peter R. 1927 C
MacIntyre, Ronald G. 1863 D
McIntyre, William, 1830 D, 1855 D
McKaeg, John, 1831 D
Mackaness, George, 1882 D
Mackay, A. F. 1908 A, 1909 A
McKay, Brian, 1926 C
McKay, Claude, 1878 F
Mackay, Donald, 1977 F, 1983 F
Mackay, Donald G. 1870 A, 1900 F, 1931 A
McKay, Heather P. 1941 E, 1961 E, 1967 E, 1973 E, 1976 E
McKay, Hugh V. 1865 B, 1884 B, 1885 B, 1909 B
Mackay, Ivan G. 1882 A
Mackay, J. 1860 A
Mackay, Ken, 1925 E
Mackay, Qld, 1862 F, 1888 F, 1898 F, 1918 F, 1960 F
McKay, Roger, 1948 F
McKechnie, Shirley, 1963 C
McKell, William J. 1891 A, 1941 A, 1947 A
Mackellar, Charles K. 1844 B
MacKellar, Dorothea, 1885 C, 1908 C
MacKellar, John A. R. 1904 C
McKellar, Michael, 1982 A
MacKennal, Bertram, 1922 C
MacKennal, Edgar B. 1863 C, 1909 C
MacKennal, John S. 1834 C, 1854 C
McKenzie, Florence V. 1893 B
McKenzie, Graham, 1941 E
MacKenzie, Kenneth Seaforth, 1913 C, 1937 C, 1938 C, 1951 C
Mackenzie, Robert R. 1811 A, 1867 A
McKenzie, Stuart, 1937 E, 1957 E
MacKenzie, William C. 1877 B
MacKenzie, William D. 1869 D
McKern, Leo R. 1920 C
Mackerras, A. Charles M. 1925 C, 1981 C, 1982 C
McKerrow, Shirley, 1981 A
Mackie, Alexander, 1958 D
McKie, Ronald C. H. 1909 C
McKie, William N. 1901 C
McKillop, Mary H. 1842 D, 1866 D
McKinlay, John, 1819 A, 1861 A, 1865 A
McKinley, Miguel, 1924 C
McKinnon, Ian, 1886 C
McKinnon, Ken, 1974 D, 1984 D
Mackinnon, Eleanor, 1871 F
Mackinnon, Lauchlan, 1817 A
Mackinnon, Lauchlan C. 1848 A
McKivat, Chris, 1883 E
Macky, Stewart, 1922 C
Macky, William M. D. 1849 D
MacLachlan, Byron H. 1900 A
McLachlan, Lachlan, 1810 A, 1853 A
McLachlan, W. H. 1889 E, 1909 E, 1910 E, 1917 E
McLaren, Ian F. 1912 D
McLaren, Jack, 1887 C, 1927 C
McLaren, Peter, 1882 E
McLaren Flat, SA, 1835 F

McLaren Vale wines, 1912 A
McLarty, D. R. 1947 A
MacLaurin, Charles, 1872 B
MacLaurin, Henry N. 1835 B
McLean, Allan, 1840 A, 1899 A
Maclean, John, 1946 E
Maclean, NSW, 1862 F, 1935 B
McLeay, Alexander, 1826 A, 1836 D, 1843 A, 1848 A
Macleay, George, 1809 A
Macleay, William J. 1820 B, 1862 B
Macleay, William S. 1792 B
Macleay Natural History Museum, Sydney, 1888 D
Macleay R., NSW. 1863 F
McLennan, Ian M. 1909 A
Macleod, William, 1850 C
Maclurcan, Hannah, 1898 F
Macmillan Co. of Aust., 1981 C
McMahon, Gregan, 1874 C, 1911 C, 1921 C, 1929 C
McMahon, Joseph, 1896 C
McMahon, William, 1908 A, 1949 A, 1971 A
McManus, Francis P. 1905 A, 1955 A
McManus, Jean, 1920 C
McMaster, Fergus, 1879 A, 1935 F
McMaster, Frederick D. 1873 B
McMeekin, Ivan, 1919 C, 1953 C
McMillan, Angus, 1810 A, 1839 A
McMillan, Robert F. 1924 A
McMillan, Sutton, 1906 E
McMinn, G. R. 1883 A
McMullen, M. 1877 C
McMurdo Sound, Antarctica, 1901 A
MacNally, Mathew J. 1874 C
McNamara, David, 1887 E
McNamara, Frank, 1916 C
McNamara, Frank H. 1894 A
McNamara, Reginald, 1887 E
McNeilage, Ian, 1932 C
McNicoll, Alan W. R. 1908 A
McNicoll, Walter R. 1877 D
Maconochie, Alexander, 1840 A, 1860 A
McPhee, John C. 1878 A, 1928 A
McPherson, Alpin, 1841 A
McPherson, Billy, 1892 E
MacPherson, John A. 1833 A, 1869 A
McPherson, William M. 1828 A, 1865 A
McPherson Ranges, Qld, 1937 F
McQuade, Marjorie, 1934 E
Macquarie, Elizabeth H. 1835 A
Macquarie, Lachlan, 1809 A, 1810 A,C,D, 1811 A,B, 1813 A,D, 1815 A,D, 1817 A,D, 1818 D, 1819 A,D, 1820 A, 1821 D, 1822 A, 1824 A
Macquarie Art Galleries, Sydney, 1925 C
Macquarie Dictionary, 1981 C
Macquarie Harbour, Tas, 1822 A,F, 1827 B, 1829 F, 1833 A
Macquarie I., 1810 A, 1812 F, 1948 B
Macquarie Place, Sydney, 1826 B
Macquarie R., NSW, 1813 A, 1828 A
Macquarie University, Sydney, 1967 D
Macquarie Valley, NSW, 1841 A
McQueen, Humphrey, 1970 C
MacQueen, Kenneth, 1897 C
McQueen, Mary M. 1912 C
Macqueen, T. P. 1825 A
McQuillan, Ernie, 1901 E
McRae, George, 1893 C
MacRobertson Confectionery, 1880 A
MacRobertson-Miller aviation line, 1921 B, 1927 B
Macrossan, Hugh D. 1881 A
Macrossan, John M. 1832 A
Macrossan, Neal W. 1889 A
McTaggart, John, 1878 A

McTiernan, Edward, 1930 A
McVey, Daniel, 1892 A

M

Mace, Jem, 1879 E
Mace, Vic Parlt House, 1891 F
Machine gun, 1939 B, 1941 B
Mack, Amy E. 1877 C
Mack, Marie L. 1874 C
Mad Max, 1979 C
Mad Max 2, 1981 C
Madagascar, 1854 F
Madden, Frank, 1847 A
Madden, Horace W. 1924 A
Madden, John, (1) 1817 A
Madden, John, (2) 1844 A, 1895 A, 1900 A, 1901 A, 1903 A, 1908 A, 1911 A, 1913 A
Madden, Walter, 1848 A
Maddock, Beatrice, 1934 C
Madigan, Anthony, 1930 E, 1958 E
Madigan, Cecil T. 1889 B, 1927 B, 1939 A
Madman's Island, 1927 C
Madman's Track, WA, 1957 A
Maesson, Liv, 1970 C
Maffra, Vic, 1865 F
Magarey, Thomas, 1825 D, 1846 D
Magarey Medal, 1898 E
Magazines, 1837 F, see also individual entries
Magee, Michael, 1838 F
'magic eye', photography, 1945 B
Magic Flute, The, 1952 C
Magic Pudding, The 1918 C
Magistrates, NSW, powers of, 1792 A
Magnesia, distilling of, SA, 1843 B
Maguire, Frederick A. 1888 B
Mahia, 1947 F
Mahlab, Eve, 1981 F
Mahomet, Dost, 1860 F
Mahon, Hugh, 1858 A, 1920 A
Mahoney, Frank P. 1862 C
Maid of the Mountain, The, 1921 C
Maiden, James, 1845 F
Maiden, Joseph H. 1859 B, 1896 B
Maiden Verses, 1901 C
·Mail, 1835 F, 1839 F, 1844 F, 1852 F, 1856 B, F, 1914 F, 1970 F
Mail deliveries, 1897 F, 1968 F, 1974 F
Mail receiving boxes, 1844 F
Mail services, 1816 F, 1825 A, 1829 A, 1830 A, 1837 A, 1838 F, 1839 F, 1844 F, 1847 F, 1870 F, 1880 F, 1888 F, 1901 A, 1921 F, 1968 A, 1970 F, 1973 F
Mail sorting, Melbourne, 1962 B
Mail steamers, 1866 F, 1870 F, 1873 F
Mail strike, 1968 A
Mailey, Arthur A. 1887 E
Mainwaring, Geoffrey R. 1912 C
Mair, A. 1939 A
Maistre de, Leroy L. L. J. 1894 C
Maitland (ship), 1898 F
Maitland, NSW, 1824 F, 1829 A, 1839 D, 1841 F, 1872 D, 1923 E, 1955 F
Maitland, SA, 1868 F
Maitland, Andrew G. 1864 B
Maitland, Herbert L. 1868 B
Maitland Art Prize, NSW, 1957 C
Maitland Mechanics' Institute, 1839 D
Maitland Mercury, NSW, 1843 F
Maitland Railway Co., 1853 B
Majestic Theatre, 1912 C, 1917 C
Major, 1908 A

Makin, Jeffrey, 1943 C
Makin, John, 1892 F
Makin, N. J. O. 1946 A
Malacca, Aust. military forces, 1964 A
Malaya, 1941 A, 1942 A, 1962 A, 1964 A
Malayan Emergency, 1948 A, 1955 A, 1960 A
Malays, 1827 A
Malaysia, Aust. military assistance, 1963 A
Malaysia campaign, 1950 A
Malaysia–Australia Air Services Agreement, 1964 A
Malcolm, John, 1850 F
Maldon, NSW, 1903 B
Maldon, Vic, 1853 F
Maldon-Mitchell, Anthony G. 1880 B
Male suffrage, *see* Suffrage
Malkara, 1959 B
Malko, Nikolai, 1957 C
Mallacoota, Vic, 1841 F
Mallee district, Vic, 1883 A
Mallee Lands Act, Vic, 1883 A
Mallyon, Edward (Mick), 1940 E
Maloga Mission, NSW, 1874 A
Maloney, William R. N. 1854 A
Malouf, David, 1934 C, 1972 C, 1980 C
Malta, 1952 A, 1970 A
Maltby Bypass, Vic, 1961 B
Malua (horse), 1884 E
Malvern, Melbourne, 1892 C, 1905 B
Malvolio, 1891 E
Man (magazine), 1936 F
'Man with the Donkey', 1892 A, 1915 A
Man Shy, 1931 C
Man From Snowy River, The (poem), 1890 C
Man from Snowy River, The (film), 1982 C
Man From Snowy River and Other Verses, The, 1895 C
Man They Could Not Hang, The, 1934 C
Man Who Loved Children, The, 1940 C
Manchester Unity building, Melbourne, 1935 C
Manchester Unity Independent Order of Oddfellows, 1839 F
Mandarin, The, 1963 C
Mandurah, WA, 1895 C
Mangalore, Vic, 1838 C
Manganese, 1928 B, 1966 B
Manifold, John S. 1915 C
Manifold, Thomas, 1809 A
Manifold, Thomas C. 1897 E
Manifold, William, 1851 A
Manildra, NSW, 1830 F
Manilla, NSW, 1853 F
Manjimup, WA, 1910 F
Manjimup Art Gallery, WA, 1960 C
Manjimup woodchip project, WA, 1975 F
Manley, Elizabeth, 1979 F
Manly, Sydney, 1889 D, 1903 B, 1908 E, 1964 E
Manly Art Gallery, Sydney, 1924 C
Manly beach, Sydney,· 1902 E
Manly hydrofoil service, Sydney, 1965 B
Manly Surf Club, 1903 E
Manly-Warringah Rugby League Football Club/team, 1946 E, 1972 E, 1973 E, 1976 E, 1978 E
Mann, Cecil M. 1896 C
Mann, Frederick W. 1939 A
Mann, Ida C. 1893 B
Mann, John F. 1819 C
Mann, Leonard, 1895 C, 1932 C, 1935 C, 1942 C
Mann Ranges, NT, 1889 A
Manners-Sutton, John H. T. 1814 A, 1866 A

Manning, Frederic, 1882 C, 1929 C
Manning, Henry E. 1877 A
Manning, William M. 1811 A
Manning R., NSW, 1818 A, 1853 F, 1921 F
Mannix, Daniel, 1864 D, 1912 D, 1917 D, 1920 D
Mannum, SA, 1853 B, 1854 F
Manpower control, wartime, 1939 A, 1946 A
Manpower regulations, Cwlth, 1942 A
Mansfield, Alan, 1957 A, 1966 A
Mansfield, George A. 1834 C
Mansfield, Ralph, 1799 D
Mansfield, Vic, 1855 F
'mantle of safety', 1912 D
Manton, J. T. 1866 A
Manual of ... Wine in NSW, A, 1830 B
Manufacturing, early, 1788 B
Manufacturing, employees, 1921 A
Manuscripts, Vic, 1932 C
Manuscripts: A Miscellany of Art and Letters, 1931 C
Maori wars, 1845 A, 1860 A, 1863 A
Maori's Idol, 1977 E
Mapping, 1838 B, 1850 B, 1884 A, 1968 B, 1977 B
Marabou, 1935 E
Maralinga, SA, 1957 B, 1978 B, 1979 B, 1980 F
'marathon of history and pace', Rome, 1981 E
Marble, NSW, 1842 B
Marble Bar, WA, 1893 F, 1923 B, 1977 B, 1978 B
Marching girls, 1946 E
Marconi Co., 1905 B, 1906 B, 1913 B
Marcus, Joseph, 1820 D
Mareeba, Qld, 1880 F
Margaret Olley, 1948 C
Margaret R., WA, 1885 B, 1921 F
Margarine, 1966 F
Margarot, Maurice, 1815 A
Margo Lewers, 1967 C
Maria, (1) 1840 F
Maria, (2) 1872 F
Maribyrnong, Melbourne, 1903 E
Marijuana, 1974 F, 1983 A, see also Hashish
Marine Board of NSW, 1871 B
Marine Operations Centre, Canberra, 1972 F
Marine Park, 1981 F
Marine pilots, 1792 A
Marine pilot service, 1880 F
Marinetti, 1969 C
Marionette Theatre of Aust., 1954 C
Marist Brothers, Sydney, 1872 D
Maritana, 1844 C, 1849 C, 1861 C
Maritime disasters, 1845 F, 1955 F, see also individual entries
Maritime strike, 1890 A
Maritime Telex service, 1975 B
Mark, Robert, 1978 A
Mark, William, 1870 C
'Market Act', NSW, 1839 F
Marketing Scheme, joint Cwlth and state, 1936 A
Marketing standard, wheat, 1888 A
Markets, 1810 A, 1813 A, 1865 F, 1898 A
Marks, Dick, 1942 E
Marksmen, 1948 E
Marlin, 1933 E
Marnoch, Allan, 1945 F
Maroochydore, Qld, 1867 F
Maroubra, NSW, 1925 B
Maroubra racing track, Sydney, 1925 E
Marquess of Normanby, 1871 A, 1879 A
Marquet, Claude, 1870 C, 1908 F

795

Marree, SA, 1883 F
Marriage, 1803 F, 1871 A, 1925 D
Marriage Guidance, 1948 F
Marri'd and Other Verses, 1910 C
Married women, rights, 1870 A
Marriott-Woodhouse, Archibald, 1930 C
Marsden, Samuel, 1794 D, 1795 D, 1796 D, 1797 A, 1801 D, 1803 D, 1807 D, 1810 A, D, 1811 A, 1814 A, 1823 D, 1824 D, 1838 D
Marseilles terracotta tiles, 1886 C
Marsh, Graham, 1944 E, 1977 E, 1982 E
Marsh, Hale, 1861 C
Marsh, R. 1971 E
Marsh, Stephen H. A. 1805 C
Marshall, Alan, 1902 C, 1944 C, 1955 C, 1963 C
Marshall, Alan J. ('Jock'), 1911 B
Marshall, Barry, 1984 B
Marshall, Bob, 1900 E
Marshall, John, 1931 E
Marshall-Hall, G. W. L. 1862 C, 1891 C
Marston, Joe, 1925 E
Marsupials, 1800 B, 1831 B
Martens, Conrad, 1801 C, 1835 C
Martial arts, 1972 E, 1978 E
Martial law, 1804 A, 1824 A, 1854 A
Martin, A. E. 1906 C
Martin, Alan, 1923 C
Martin, Charles J. 1866 B
Martin, David, 1915 C, 1962 C
Martin, Harold B. 1918 A
Martin, James, 1820 A, 1863 A, 1866 A, 1870 A, 1873 A
Martin, Leslie H. 1900 B, 1965 D
Martin, Max, 1889 C
Martin, Susan, 1970 E
Martin, Wayne, 1979 E
Martinetti troupe, 1867 C
Martini Henry, 1883 E
Martyn, David F. 1906 B
Martyn, Laurel, 1916 C, 1940 C, 1946 C
'Marvellous Melbourne', 1885 F
Marvellous Melbourne melodrama, 1889 C
Mary, 1845 F
Mary Ann, 1853 B
Mary Anne, 1791 A
Mary Cecil Allen Memorial Lectures, 1963 C
Mary Kathleen, Qld, 1954 B, 1956 A, 1957 F, 1976 B, 1980 F
Mary-le-bone Cricket Club, 1832 E
Mary Poppins, 1934 C
Mary Quant fashion, 1955 F
Mary White School of Art, Sydney, 1963 C
Maryborough, Qld, 1847 F, 1881 B, 1882 B, 1888 D
Maryborough, Vic, 1849 B, 1854 F, 1855 A, 1857 F
Maryborough Art Gallery, Vic, 1964 C
Maryborough Grammar School, Qld, 1871 D
Maryborough Mutual Protection Society, Vic, 1855 A
Marysville, Vic, 1863 F
Masada College, Sydney, 1966 D
Mascot, Sydney, 1919 B, 1922 B, 1939 F
Mascot greyhound racing, Sydney, 1927 E
Mason, Anthony, 1972 A
Mason, Colin V. J. 1926 A
Mason, Cyrus, 1830 C, 1871 C, 1880 C
Mason, Joe, 1923 C
Masonic Lodge, Sydney, 1814 F
Massartic, Gustav, 1885 C
Massey, Harrie S. W. 1908 B
Massey Harris Co., 1905 B
Massina, A. H. 1834 A

Masson, David O. 1858 B
Massy-Greene, Walter, 1874 A
Master Builders' Federation of Aust., 1890 A
Master Coachmakers' Association of Vic, 1873 A
Master of Queen's Musick, 1975 C
'Mastermind of the Turf', 1882 E
Masters, Judy, 1886 E
Masters, Margaret, 1934 E
Masters, Ron, 1914 E
Masters and Servants Act, 1847 C
Mastitis, 1950 B
Matches, 1913 F
Maternal welfare service, Sydney, 1904 F
Maternity allowance, Federal, 1912 A
Maternity Hospital, Sydney, 1866 B
Maternity leave, 1966 A, 1973 A, 1979 A
Mateship, 1911 C
Mather, John, 1848 C
Mather, John B. 1853 C
Mather, Martin, 1927 C
Mathers, Peter, 1931 C, 1966 C
Mathew, Daniel D. 1813 C
Mathew, John, 1889 B
Mathews, Gregory M. 1876 B
Mathews, Marlene, see Willard-Mathews, M.
Mathews, Raymond F. 1929 C
Mathews, Robert H. 1841 B
Mathewson, Thomas, 1835 B
Matich, Frank, 1928 E
Matra, James M. 1806 A
Matriculation exams, girls admitted, 1871 D
Matson Line Art Exhibition, 1959 C
Matters, Arnold, 1901 C
Matters for Judgement, 1978 A
Matthew, John, 1788 D
Matthew Flinders (sculpture), 1925 F
Matthews, Herbert, 1913 E, 1940 E
Matthews, Julia, 1842 C, 1855 C
Matthews, Lionel C. 1912 A
Matthews, Neville, 1930 C
Matthews, Thomas, 1962 C
Matthews, T. J. 1912 E
Mattiolo, Rocco R. 1953 E, 1977 E
Maud, Jean Franc, 1827 C, see Evans, Matilda Jane.
Maudsley, Helen, 1927 C
Maudsley, Henry C. 1859 B
Mauger, Samuel, 1857 A
Maurice, Furnley, see Wilmot F. L. T.
Maurice Guest, 1908 C
Maurice Moscovitch (painting), 1925 C
Mavis Bramston Show, The, 1964 C
Mawbey, Maurice A. E. 1904 B
Mawson, Douglas, 1882 B, 1908 A, 1909 A, 1911 A, 1915 C, 1930 A
Mawson base, 1954 B
Maxwell, George A. 1859 A
Maxwell, Joseph, 1896 A
May, Phil, 1944 E
May, Philip W. 1864 C
May Day Art Prize, Melbourne, 1954 C
Mayer, Thomas, 1965 C, 1971 C
Mayfield, David, 1963 E
Maylands, WA, 1944 B
Maylands Aerodrome, Perth, 1923 B
Mayo, Eileen, 1953 C
Mayo, Gael E. 1923 C
Mayors, 1842 A, 1844 F, 1853 A, 1880 A, see also Lord Mayors
Mead, Janet, 1974 C
Meadmore, Clement, 1929 C
Meadows, SA, 1838 F
Meagher, Richard D. 1866 A
Meale, Richard G. 1932 C, 1967 C
Mealmaker, George, 1808 F

Meanjin Quarterly, Brisbane, 1940 C
Measham, David, 1974 C
Measles, 1874 F
Measurement, standards, 1974 B
Meat, horse, 1981 A
Meat canning, 1847 A, B, 1867 B
Meat consumption, 1977 F, 1980 F
Meat exports, 1847 A, 1879 B, 1880 A, 1884 A, 1978 A
Meat freezing, 1873 B
Meat Industry Employees' Union, 1978 A
Meat preservation, 1846 B
Meat rationing, 1944 F
Meat refrigeration, 1879 B, 1880 A
Meat scandal, 1981 A
Meat shortages, 1802 A
Meat workers' strike, Townsville, 1918 A, 1919 A
Meatworks, frozen, 1880 A, B
Mechanical drawing, 1865 C
mechanical clipper, 1868 B
Mechanical Hare, 1956 E
Mechanics' Institutes, 1827 D, 1839 D, 1854 D, see also individual entries
Mechanical letter sorters, 1951 B
Mechanics' School of Arts, Sydney, 1833 D, 1865 C
Meckering, WA, 1968 F
Medallions, 1798 C
Meddick, G. 1914 E
Medea, 1955 C
Medibank, 1975 A, 1976 A, 1978 A
Medical aid, Sydney, 1826 B
Medical Benefits, 1952 A, 1953 A
Medical care scheme, Cwlth, 1951 A
Medical conference, first intercolonial, 1887 B
Medical Congress, Aust., 1923 B
Medical instruments, 1819 B
Medical insurance, 1981 A
Medical Journal of Aust., 1914 B
Medical practice, 1815 B, 1838 B
Medical research, 1908 B, 1916 B, 1948 B, 1970 B
Medical schools, 1862 D, 1883 D
Medical Service, flying, 1938 D
Medical services, free, 1943 A
Medical students, women, 1885 B
Medicare, 1983 A, 1984 A
Medicine, 1846 B, 1890 B, 1891 B, 1895 D, 1944 B, 1948 B, see also individual entries
Medley, John D. G. 1891 D
Medlow Bath, NSW, 1880 F
Mednis, Karlis, 1910 C
Medworth, Frank, 1892 C
Meehan, Arthur V. 1890 B
Meehan, James, 1803 A, 1807 A, 1818 A, 1826 A
Meehan, John, 1950 C
Meekatharra, WA, 1896 F, 1957 A, 1959 D
Meekin, Dave, 1967 C
Meere, Charles M. 1890 C
Meet Simon Black, 1950 C
Megastructure, 1964 C
Mei Quong Tart, see Quong Tart
Meier, Leo, 1976 E
Meilerts, Ludmilla, 1908 C
Meillon, John, 1934 C
Mein, James, 1802 A, 1827 A
Meissner, Joe, 1950 E, 1972 E
Melba, Nellie, 1861 C, 1887 C, 1902 C, 1904 C, 1907 C, 1909 C, 1915 C, 1918 C, 1924 C, 1926 C, 1928 C, 1929 C, 1935 C
Melba Community Health Centre, Canberra, 1973 F

Melbourne, Vic, 1835 A, F, 1836 A, 1837 A, 1839 D, 1842 A, 1844 F, 1847 A, 1860 A, 1866 B, 1869 B, 1873 A, B, 1875 B, 1878 B, E, 1879 E, 1892 C, 1894 B, 1898 A, 1899 A, 1901 A, 1902 A, 1904 C, D, E, 1905 B, 1907 B, 1908 A, 1916 C, 1919 B, 1920 B, 1936 F, 1937 C, 1946 B, C, 1951 B, 1959 A, B, 1960 C, 1964 F, 1965 B, 1967 E, 1968 B, 1970 C, E, F, 1971 B, 1981 C, 1984 B
Melbourne, HMAS, 1916 A, 1955 A, 1964 F, 1969 F
Melbourne Academy, 1851 D
Melbourne Advertiser, 1838 F, 1839 F
Melbourne Athenaeum, 1839 C
Melbourne Australian Rules Football Club/team, 1858 E, 1864 E, 1900 E, 1926 E, 1928 E, 1939 E, 1940 E, 1941 E, 1946 E, 1948 E, 1955 E, 1956 E, 1957 E, 1959 E, 1960 E, 1964 E, 1979 E, 1982 E, 1984 E
Melbourne Ballet Club, 1946 C
Melbourne Ballet Guild, 1971 C
Melbourne Bicycle Club, 1878 E
Melbourne Botanical Gardens, 1845 B, 1846 B
Melbourne Brokers' Association, 1859 A
Melbourne Bush Walking and Touring Club, 1894 F
Melbourne Centenary Air Race, 1934 E
Melbourne Centenary Art Prizes, 1934 C
Melbourne Church of England Grammar School, 1858 D, E
Melbourne Club, 1838 F, 1858 C, F, 1913 E
Melbourne Continuation School, 1905 D
Melbourne Council, 1842 A, 1968 F
Melbourne Cricket Club, 1838 E, 1935 E
Melbourne Cricket Ground, 1853 E, 1878 E, 1959 F, 1960 E
Melbourne Cultural Centre, 1839 C
Melbourne Cup, 1972 E
Melbourne Cup carnival, 1896 C
Melbourne Cup horse race, *see each year from* 1861 E
Melbourne Distributing Kitchen Co., 1902 F
Melbourne Esperanto Club, 1905 F
Melbourne Exhibition, 1854 F, 1866 C, 1872 B, 1875 B
Melbourne Fencing Club, 1936 E
Melbourne Fire Prevention Society, 1845 F
Melbourne Gallery, 1905 C
Melbourne Gas Co., 1921 B
Melbourne General Post Office, 1951 B
Melbourne Glass Bottle Works, 1873 A
Melbourne Grammar School, 1858 D, E
Melbourne Graphic Arts, 1960 C
Melbourne Gun Club, 1880 E
Melbourne Harbour Trust, 1877 B
Melbourne Herald Exhibition, 1939 C
Melbourne Horse Racing Club, 1838 E
Melbourne Hospital, 1846 C, 1896 B, 1913 B, 1938 B
Melbourne Hunt Club, 1854 E
Melbourne jetty, 1840 A
Melbourne Kindergarten Teachers' College, 1922 D
Melbourne land sales, 1837 A
Melbourne Lawn Bowling Club, 1864 E
Melbourne Mail Exchange, 1962 B
Melbourne Meat Preserving Co., 1867 B
Melbourne Mechanics' Institute and School of Arts, 1839 C, 1853 C, 1854 D
Melbourne Metropolitan Police Force, 1852 A

'Melbourne Mick', *see* Bartey, Mick
Melbourne Morning Herald, 1840 F, 1869 F
Melbourne Museum of Art, 1861 C
Melbourne National Gallery, 1883 D
Melbourne National Gallery School, 1870 C, 1952 C
Melbourne Observatories, 1856 B, 1863 B
Melbourne Odes, 1934 C
Melbourne Omnibus Co., 1869 B
Melbourne Philharmonic Society, 1853 C
Melbourne Post Office, 1841 A
Melbourne Pram Factory, 1970 C
Melbourne Printmakers, 1960 C
Melbourne Prints, 1960 C
Melbourne Public Library, 1854 C, D, 1856 D, 1913 D
Melbourne Punch, 1855 C, F, 1856 F
Melbourne Repertory Theatre, 1911 C
Melbourne Royal Park Zoo, 1862 B
Melbourne School of Art, 1893 C
Melbourne Society of Women Painters and Sculptors, 1909 C
Melbourne State College, 1973 D
Melbourne Stock Exchange, 1861 A
Melbourne String Quartet, 1925 C
Melbourne Symphony Orchestra, 1906 C, 1950 C, 1952 C, 1954 C, 1956 C, 1957 C, 1961 C, 1965 C, 1966 C, 1967 C, 1974 C
Melbourne Teachers College, 1888 D, 1889 D
Melbourne Telephone Exchange Co., 1887 B
Melbourne Theatre Co., 1968 C
Melbourne Town Hall, 1854 F, 1867 C, 1870 F
Melbourne Trades Hall, 1859 A
Melbourne Trades Hall Committee, 1860 A
Melbourne Trotting Club, 1907 E
Melbourne University Architectual Atelier, 1920 C
Melbourne University Boat Club, 1859 E
Melbourne University Press, 1922 A
Meldrum, D. Max 1875 C, 1913 C, 1939 C, 1940 C
Meldrum, James M. 1931 C
Meldrum, 'Molly', 1974 C
Melrose, Alexander, 1929 C
Melton, Vic, 1845 F
Melville, Henry, 1800 A, 1834 C
Melville, Leslie G. 1902 A
Melville I., NT, 1824 A, 1827 A, 1881 F
Melwraith, T. 1888 A
Melzer, J. 1984 A
Memoirs, 1819 C
Memorials, James Cook, 1822 F
Men at Work, 1981 C
Menangle, NSW, 1952 B
Mendelsohn, Oscar A. 1896 B
Mendies, George, 1899 E
Mendooran, NSW, 1848 F
Menindie, NSW, 1859 F
Meningie, SA, 1863 F
Menlo Park, California, 1932 E
Menpes, Mortimer, 1859 C
Mental asylums, NSW, 1811 B
Mental health, NSW, 1843 B
Mentor, 1888 E
Menz, W. 1850 B
Menzies, WA, 1894 F
Menzies, Douglas, 1958 A
Menzies, Robert G. 1894 A, 1934 A, 1938 A, 1939 A, 1940 A, 1943 A, 1944 A, 1949 A, 1950 A, 1951 A, 1954 A, 1955 A, 1956 A, 1958 A, 1961 A, 1963 A, 1965 A, 1966 A, 1978 A

Merbein, Vic, 1904 F
Mercantile Bank of Aust., 1832 A
Mercer, John E. 1856 D
Mercer, Mary C. 1882 C
Mercier, Emile, 1902 C
Mercury, Tas, 1854 F
Meredith, Bess, 1920 C
Meredith, George, 1856 A
Meredith, Gwenyth V. 1907 C, 1943 C
Meredith, Louisa A. 1812 C, 1844 C
Merfield, Bertha, 1899 C
Merimbula, NSW, 1855 F
Merino rams, export of, 1929 A, 1971 A
Merino sheep, 1794 A, 1795 A, 1797 A, 1801 A, 1805 A, 1817 A, 1832 B, 1981 A
Merino stud organization, 1882 A
Merioola Group of Artists, Sydney, 1945 C
Merlin, Henry B. 1830 B
Merredin, WA, 1891 F
Merredin Senior High School, WA, 1982 F
Merredin Shire Council, WA, 1960 B
Merriman, Walter T. 1882 A
Merriwa, NSW, 1885 F
Merriwee, 1899 E
Merrygoen, NSW, 1914 F
Mersey-Forth Power Development Scheme, Tas, 1963 B
Mertz collection, 1966 C
Meryon, Charles, 1845 C
Meskenas, Vlades, 1916 C
Mesopotamia, First World War, 1915 A
Message From Mars, A, 1909 C
Messel, Harry, 1922 B
Messenger, Herbert H. ('Dally'), 1883 E
'Messiah, Nunawading', 1871 D
Messines Ridge, 1917 A
Meston, Archibald, 1851 A
Mestre De, Prosper, 1793 A
Meszaros, Andor, 1900 C
Metal ceilings, 1888 C
Metcalfe, Jack, 1935 E
Metcalfe, Jim, 1913 E
Metcalfe, Ken, 1952 B
Meteorites, 1845 B, 1930 B, 1966 B
Meteorology, 1877 B, 1948 B, 1964 B, 1975 B, 1979 B
Meter, water, 1910 B
Meter Maids, Qld, 1966 F
Methodist chapels, 1817 D, 1821 D, 1844 D
Methodist Church,
 Aust. wide, 1953 D, 1968 D, 1974 D, 1977 D
 NSW, 1812 D, 1815 D, 1816 D, 1840 D, 1844 D, 1855 D
 NT, 1935 D
 Qld, 1840 D, 1898 D
 SA, 1836 D, 1840 D, 1900 D
 Tas, 1820 D, 1821 D, 1840 D
 Vic, 1836 D, 1840 D, 1904 D, 1955 D
 WA, 1828 D
Methodist Ladies' Colleges, 1882 D, 1885 D, 1886 D
Methodist New Connection group, 1862 D
Methodist Society, Tas, 1820 D
Metric Conversion Board, 1970 A
Metric system, 1965 B, 1967 A, 1970 A, 1973 F
Metro-Goldwyn-Mayer Art Prize, Sydney, 1952 C
Metropolitan Permanent Building Society, Melbourne, 1854 A
Metzer, Max, 1960 E
Meuller, Jack, 1915 E
Meuller Botanic Society of WA, 1897 B

Mexis, Themos, 1947 C
Meyer, Vic, 1906 E
Meyerbeer, 1862 C
Meynell, Kevin, 1929 C
Mice, Melbourne, 1917 F
Michael Boddy, 1973 C
Michel, Louis, 1851 B
Michell, Anthony G. M. 1870 B, 1905 B
Michell, John H. 1863 B
Michell, Keith, 1928 C
Mickle, Alan D. 1882 C
Microphones, 1925 B
Micro wave trunk system, 1970 B
Microscopical Society of Vic, 1873 B
Microsurgical Society, Sydney, 1981 B
Middle East, 1939 A, 1956 A
Middle East, Peace Keeping, 1952 A, 1981 A, 1982 A
'Middle Garden', 1816 B
Middle Harbour, Sydney, 1877 F
Middle Head, Sydney, 1834 F
Middle Parts of Fortune, The, 1929 C
Middleton, Max, 1922 C
Middleton, Rawdon H. 1916 A
Middleton Reef, 1909 F
Midlands Agricultural Show, Tas, 1838 F
Midlands Railway Co. Ltd, 1873 B
Midnight Wedding, The, 1912 C
Midsummer Eve's Dream, A, 1970 C
Midwives, training of, 1866 B
Midwood, Tom, 1855 C
Migrant selection scheme, Federal, 1982 A
Migration, 1919 A, 1921 A, 1925 F, 1947 A, 1951 A
Migration Commission, 1926 A
Mike and Stefani, 1952 C
Mikluho-Maklai, Nikolai N. 1846 B, 1878 F
Milbert (French artist), 1800 C
Mildara Wine Co., 1888 A
Mildura, Vic, 1886 B, 1887 F, 1891 A, 1920 B, F, 1938 F, 1960 B
Mildura Arts Centre, Vic, 1956 C
Mildura Prize for Sculpture, Vic, 1961 C
Milenburg Joys, 1925 C
Miles, Gilbert, 1929 B
Miles, John C. 1883 A, 1923 B
Miles, Qld, 1877 F
Miles Evergood, 1871 C *see* Blashki, Myer
Miles Franklin Award, 1957 C
Milgate, Rodney A. 1934 C
Military advisors, Vietnam, 1962 A
Military aid, Malaya, 1964 A
Military aircraft, 1912 A, 1963 A, 1965 A
Military assistance, Malaysia, 1963 A
Military Cricket Club, Sydney, 1826 E
Military forces, 1870 A, 1871 A, 1901 A, 1964 A, *see also* Aust. Forces
Military Hospital, Sydney, 1815 B
Military medical service, NSW, 1848 B
Military night patrol, Sydney, 1810 A
Military observers, Zimbabwe-Rhodesia, 1979 A
Military service, compulsory, 1915 A
Military service/training, compulsory, 1909 A, 1911 A, 1915 A, 1916 A, 1917 A, 1929 A, 1939 A, 1950 A, *see also* Conscription.
Military volunteers, Maori wars, 1863 A
Milk, 1875 F, 1890 B, 1892 B
Milk, bottled, 1928 F
Milk, free, 1950 D, 1983 D
Milk bars, 1930 F, 1933 F, 1935 F
Milk pasteurization, 1889 B, 1949 B
Milking machines, 1892 B, 1893 B, 1952 B

Milky Way, 1968 B, 1981 B
Millar, Ronald G. 1927 C
Millen, Ronald, 1922 C
Miller, Alexander, 1842 A
Miller, Charles A. 1920 C
Miller, Denison S. K. 1860 A
Miller, Eddie, 1917 E
Miller, Edward, 1848 A
Miller, Frederick, 1830 D
Miller, George, 1979 C, 1981 C
Miller, Godfrey C. 1893 C
Miller, Harry M. 1934 C, 1969 C, 1982 F
Miller, Henry (1), 1809 A
Miller, Henry (2), 1824 A
Miller, Horace C. 1893 B, 1927 B
Miller, James W. 1979 F
Miller, John, *see* Lane, William
Miller, Johnny, 1934 E, 1966 E
Miller, Keith R. 1919 E
Miller, K. 1928 B
Miller, Mabel, 1955 A
Miller, Peter F. 1921 C
Miller, Robin E. 1941 B
Miller, Roderick W. 1911 A
Miller, Tony, 1929 E
Miller, William, 1846 E, 1874 E
Millicent, SA, 1870 F
Millmerran, Qld, 1860 F
Millner, J. S. 1870 A, 1873 A
Mills, B. Y. 1953 B
Mills, Beryl, 1926 F
Mills, John, 1864 C
Mills, Richard C. 1886 A
Mills, W. W. 1872 A
Mills Cross radiotelescope, 1953 B, 1954 B, 1964 B, 1968 B
Milne, Malcolm, 1948 E
Milne Bay, New Guinea, 1942 A
Milperra College of Advanced Education, Sydney, 1974 D
Milson, James, 1872 A
Milton, NSW, 1865 F
Mindit, 1983 C
Mineral boom, 1968 A
Mineral Resources, Bureau of, 1946 B
Mineral rights, 1979 A, 1982 A
Mineral Sands, 1932 A, 1966 D
Mineral Securities of Aust., 1971 A
Minerals exports, 1960 C
Minerals of New South Wales, The, 1888 C
Miner's Right, 1855 A
Miners' strikes,
 NSW, 1892 A, 1908 A, 1909 A, 1910 A, 1916 A, 1919 A
 Qld, 1961 A
 SA, 1848 A, 1874 A
 Vic, 1873 A
 see also coal miners' strikes
Minerva, 1838 F
Minerva Theatre, Melbourne, 1931 C
Minerva Theatre, Sydney, 1939 C
Mingaye, 1849 B
Mingenew, WA, 1891 F
Mining, *see section B and individual entries*
Mining boom, decline of, 1971 A
Mining disasters,
 NSW, 1887 F, 1895 F, 1898 F, 1902 F, 1923 F, 1926 F, 1966 F, 1979 F, 1980 F
 Qld, 1904 F, 1921 F, 1938 F, 1954 F, 1972 F, 1975 F
 Tas, 1912 F, 1929 F
 Vic, 1882 F, 1895 F, 1931 F, 1937 F
 WA, 1904 F, 1921 F, 1977 F
Mining and Geological Museum, Sydney, 1875 D
Ministries, Cwlth, *see* Government *section A*
Minlaton, SA, 1873 F

Minmi Range Soccer Club, 1884 E
Minnie Crouch Watercolour Prize, Vic, 1947 C
Minns, Benjamin E. 1864 C
Minstrel and Variety Co., 1901 C
Minstrel Waltz, The, 1836 C
Mints, 1855 A, 1872 A, 1899 A, 1963 A, *see also individual entries*
Miracle Mile, 1967 E
Mirage aircraft, 1963 A, 1965 A, 1981 A
Miranda, Francis, 1857 F
Miranda, Lalla, 1874 C
'Miranda swindle', 1857 F
Miranola, Beatrice, 1964 C
Mirans, James, 1890 A
Mirror, Sydney, 1961 C
Mirror, Waratah Festival Art Competition, 1961 C
Miscellany of Art and Letters, 1931 C
Miss Aust. quest, 1926 F, 1954 F
Miss Collins, 1924 C
Missile base, NSW, 1961 B
Missingham, Harold, H. 1906 C
Mission to the Nation, 1953 D
Missions, *see* Aboriginals *and individual entries*
Mister Hundred Grand, 1961 E
Mitchel, John, 1815 A
Mitchell, Alexander G. 1911 D
Mitchell, Captain, 1825 A
Mitchell, David, 1829 C, 1880 C
Mitchell, David S. 1836 D, 1901 D, 1910 D
Mitchell, Edward F. 1855 A
Mitchell, Helen P. 1861 C
Mitchell, James (b. 1972), 1972 B
Mitchell, James (b. 1835), 1835 B
Mitchell, James (b. 1866), 1866 A, 1919 A, 1930 A, 1933 A, 1948 A
Mitchell, John, 1805 D
Mitchell, Peter S. 1856 A
Mitchell, Qld, 1864 F
Mitchell, Raymond W. 1919 E
Mitchell, Roma F. 1913 A, 1962 A, 1965 A
Mitchell, S. J. 1910 A, 1911 A
Mitchell, Sibyl E. K. 1913 C
Mitchell, Stanley R. 1881 B
Mitchell, Thomas L. 1792 A, 1828 A, 1831 A, B, 1832 B, 1835 A, 1836 A, 1838 B, 1845 A, 1846 A, 1847 A, 1851 F
Mitchell, William (b. 1786), 1837 A
Mitchell, William (b. 1861), 1861 D
Mitchell, William H. F. 1811 A
Mitchell building, Adelaide, 1879 C
Mitchell College of Advanced Education, NSW, 1970 D
Mitchell, Giurgole and Thorpe, 1980 C
Mitchell Library, Sydney, 1901 D, 1907 D, 1910 D, 1929 C
Mitelman, Alan, 1946 C
Mittagong, NSW, 1833 B, 1841 F, 1848 B, 1850 B, 1864 B, 1886 B, 1913 D, 1953 C
Mixed bathing, 1903 F
Mme Elink Schuurman, 1938 C
'Mo', *see* Rene, Roy
Moama, NSW, 1845 F, 1876 B
Mobil singing quest, 1949 C, 1950 C
Mobile Flinders, 1982 B
Mobile radio telephone exchange service, 1950 B
Mockbridge, Russell, 1928 E, 1953 E
Model A Ford, 1928 B
Model T Fords, 1925 B
Modern Art, 1926 C
Modern Art Centre, Sydney, 1940 C
Modern Art News, 1959 C
Modern Australian Literature, 1924 C

Modern dance, 1932 C
Modern Dance Ensemble, 1963 C
Modern Masters: Manet to Matisse, 1975 C
Modern Society of Portrait painters, 1908 C
Moe, Vic, 1879 F
Moffat, Allan, 1940 E
Moffat, John, 1841 B
Moffit, Ian, 1982 C
Moffitt, Ernest, 1870 C
Mohr, Bill, 1907 E
Moir, Ian, 1932 E
Molesworth Committee, 1937 A, 1838 A
Moline, NT, 1953 F
Mollard, John, 1861 B
Mollison, James, 1971 C
Molloy, Georgiana, 1805 B
Molloy, T. G. 1897 C
Molnar, George, 1910 C
Molong, NSW, 1845 F, 1896 B, 1937 D
Molvig, John, 1923 C, 1966 C
Mona Vale, NSW, 1961 D
Mona Vale, Tas, 1868 C
Monaghan, Laurie, 1951 E
Monaro Plains, NSW, 1823 A
Monarto, SA, 1847 F
Monash, John, 1865 A
Monash University, Melbourne, 1961 D, 1965 C, 1983 B
Moncrieff, Gladys, 1892 C, 1921 C, 1933 C
Monetary confusion, 1843 A
Money lending laws, 1834 A
Mongoose, Asiatic, 1884 F
Monitor, Sydney, 1826 F, 1829 F
Monk, Albert E. 1900 A, 1949 A
Monk, Cyril, 1882 C
Monk, Isabel V. D. 1892 C
Monkman, Noel, 1896 B, 1941 C
Monsanto-Southern Cross Chemical Co., Melbourne, 1928 B
Monsbourgh, Adrian, 1917 C
Mont St Quentin, 1918 A
Montagu, John, 1797 A
Monte Bello Is, 1906 F, 1952 B, 1956 B
Monte Carlo Russian ballet, 1936 C
Montefiore, Eliezer L. 1820 C
Monterey pine, 1857 B
Montessori education, 1914 D
Montez, Lola, 1818 C, 1856 C
Montford, Paul R. 1868 C, 1933 C
Montforts, The, 1928 C
Montgomery, Henry H. 1847 D
Montgomery, William M. 1917 C
Month: A Literary and Critical Journal, The, 1857 F
Monto, Qld, 1920 F
Montreal Olympics, 1976 E
Monumental City (ship), 1853 F
Moods of Ginger Mick, The, 1916 C
Moomba, SA, 1977 B
Moomba Festival, Melbourne, 1954 F, 1955 F
Moomba gas field, SA, 1966 B
Moomba–Stony Point pipeline, SA, 1982 A
Moon, Milton, 1926 C
Moon landing, 1969 B
Moon in My Pocket, 1945 C
Moonbi, 1955 E
Moondyne Jo, *see* Johns, Joseph Bolitho
Mooney, Thomas, 1854 C
Moonee Valley Cup (horse-race), 1883 E
Moonie, Qld, 1961 B, 1964 B, F
Moonlight Acre, 1938 C
Moonlight Head, Vic, 1891 F
Moonstruck Murderer, 1964 F
Moonta, SA, 1861 B, 1863 F
Moonta copper mines, SA, 1874 A

Moora, WA, 1895 F
Moore, Alan, 1915 C
Moore, A. E. 1929 A
Moore, Charles, 1820 B
Moore, F. ('Tiger'), 1925 E
Moore, Gary, 1952 E
Moore, George, 1923 E
Moore, George F. 1798 A
Moore, Graham H. 1916 C
Moore, Henry, 1947.C
Moore, Henry B. 1880 B
Moore, John, 1982 A
Moore, John D. 1888 C
Moore, Joshua J. 1790 A, 1823 A
Moore, Maggie, 1851 C, 1874 C
Moore, Newton J. 1870 A, 1906 A
Moore, Peter, 1979 E
Moore, Ronnie, 1933 E
Moore, Thomas, 1840 A
Moore, T. Inglis, 1901 C
Moore, William, (b. 1837) 1837 C, 1909 C, 1910 C
Moore, William, (b. 1868) 1868 C, 1934 C
Moore, William H. 1815 A, 1867 A
Moore Park, Sydney, 1884 B
Moore Theological College, Sydney, 1840 F
Moorehead, Alan, 1910 C, 1956 C, 1959 C, 1960 C, 1962 C, 1963 C, 1966 C
Moorhouse, Frank, 1938 C, 1969 C, 1972 C, 1974 C
Mooril, James, 1863 F
Moorish Maid, A, 1906 C
Mora, Mirka, M. 1928 C
Moran, Patrick F. 1830 D, 1884 D, 1885 D
Moranbah, Qld, 1969 F
Morant, Henry H. (Breaker), 1865 C, 1902 A
Moras, Karen, 1954 E
Morawa, WA, 1912 F
Morcom, Verdon L. 1926 C
Moreau, Mr, 1846 F
Moree, NSW, 1851 F, 1968 A
Morehead, Boyd D. 1843 A, 1888 A
Moresby, John, 1830 A, 1871 A, 1873 A
Moreton Bay, Qld, 1823 A, 1824 A, 1825 A, 1826 A, 1827 A, 1828 D, 1830 A, 1840 A, 1842 A, 1845 A, 1851 A, 1859 A, 1863 A
Moreton Bay Courier, 1846 F, 1864 F
Moreton Bay Horse Racing Club, 1842 F
Moreton Bay Savings Bank, 1854 A
Morgan, SA, 1878 F
Morgan, Arthur, 1856 A, 1903 A, 1909 A, 1914 A
Morgan, Daniel, 1830 A
Morgan, Edwin, 1882 B
Morgan, Herbert M. 1885 B
Morgan, James, 1886 C
Morgan, Molly, 1835 A
Morgan, Thomas, 1882 B
Morgan, William 1828 A, 1878 A
Morgans, A. E. 1901 A
Moriarty, Mervyn G. 1937 C
Morison, Elsie J. 1924 C
Morison, George P. 1861 C
Morisset, NSW, 1887 F
Morisset, James T. 1852 A
Mormon church, 1851 D
Morning Bulletin, Qld, 1861 F
Morning Cloud, 1969 E
Mornington, Vic, 1860 F
Mornington I. Shire Council, Qld, 1979 A
Morosi, Juni, 1974 A
Morphesis, George, 1849 F
Morphett, John, 1809 A

Morphettville, SA, 1882 E
Morrell, Dot, 1888 E
Morris, Arthur R. 1922 E
Morris, Augustus, 1820 A
Morris, Bob, 1945 E
Morris, Edward E. 1843 D, 1898 C
Morris, John, 1945 A
Morris, Julian *see* West, M.
Morris, William, 1948 F
Morrison, Alastair A. 1911 C
Morrison, Brian, 1972 E
Morrison, George E. 1862 A, 1897 F
Morrison, John G. 1904 C, 1955 C
Morrison, J. 1869 E
Morrison, William S. 1960 A
Morrow, Bruce, 1934 E
Morrow, James C. 1905 A
Morrow, Ross, 1932 C
Morse Code, 1897 B
Morshead, Leslie J. 1889 A
Mort, Thomas S. 1816 A, 1843 A, 1845 B, 1855 B, 1870 B, 1873 B
Mort and Co.,1843 A, 1888 A
Mortensen, Kevin, 1939 C
Mortgage Bank Dept, 1943 A
Mortimer, G. 1984 E
Mortimer, Harold J. 1899 A
Mortlake, Vic, 1838 F
Mortlock, Harold B. 1921 C
Morton, Robert K. 1920 B
Morton, Tex, 1918 C
Morts Dock and Engineering Co. Ltd, 1854 B, 1873 A
Moruya, NSW, 1851 F, 1862 B, 1864 B
Morwell, Vic, 1861 F, 1873 B, 1889 B, 1967 C
Moscow, 1963 C
Moscow Olympics, 1979 F, 1980 A, E
Moses, Charles J. A. 1900 A, 1935 A
Moses, John, 1860 C, 1923 C
Mosman, Archibald, 1799 A, 1830 A
Mosman, Hugh, 1843 A, 1872 B
Mosman, Sydney, 1890 C
Mosman Art Prize, Sydney, 1947 C
Mosman Musical Society Ballet, Sydney, 1916 C
Mosques, 1898 D, 1976 D
Mosquito, 1917 F
'*Mosquito*', 1825 F
Mosquitos, 1905 B
Moss, Alice F. M. 1868 A
Moss, Graham, 1951 E, 1976 E
Moss, Harry L. 1874 A
Moss, Mr. 1838 A
Moss Vale, NSW, 1817 A, 1819 A, 1853 F
Mossman, Qld, 1877 F
Motel, 1955 F
Moth of Moonbi, The, 1926 C, 1938 C
Mother Mary of the Cross, 1842 D, *see* McKillop, Mary Helen
Mother's Offering to her Children, A, 1841 C
Motor Association, SA, 1921 F
Motor Boat Club, Sydney, 1905 E
Motor Car Act, WA, 1904 B
Motor Car industry, 1960 A, 1984 A
Motor car racing, 1901 E, 1902 E, 1903 E, 1904 E, 1905 E, 1906 E, 1908 E, 1912 E, 1928 E, 1947 E, 1959 E, 1960 E, 1979 E, 1980 E
Motor cars, *see also individual entries*,
  Aust. made, 1931 B, 1933 B, *see also individual entries*
  Chrysler, 1962 B
  First, 1893 B, 1894 B, 1896 B, 1899 B, 1900 B
  Ford, 1907 B, 1921 B, 1925 B, 1928 B, 1932 B, 1934 B, 1960 B, 1962 B, 1965 B

799

Holden, 1923 B, 1948 B, 1953 B, 1957 B, 1958 B, 1960 B, 1961 B, 1963 B, 1965 B
marathon, London–Sydney, 1968 E
numbers, 1905 F, 1930 F
radios, 1924 B
registration, 1920 F, 1924 F
safety, 1966 B, 1968 B
Six cylinder, 1920 B
trans-Aust. journey, 1922 B
Volkswagen, 1957 B
Motor cycle racing, 1900 E, 1903 E, 1908 E, 1920 E, 1921 E, 1923 E, 1926 E, 1927 E, 1928 E, 1929 E, 1936 E, 1938 E, 1951 E, 1952 E, 1957 E, 1976 E, 1977 E
Motor phaeton, 1896 B
Motor Traffic Act, NSW, 1909 B
Motor Vehicle Design Committee, 1966 B
Mott, Greta, 1930 E
Mould, John S. 1910 A
Moulton, James E. 1841 D
Mount Alexander, Vic, 1851 A, B
Mount Barker, SA, 1841 F
Mount Barker, WA, 1899 F
Mount Beauty, Vic, 1946 F
Mount Bischoff, Tas, 1871 B
Mount Buangor, Vic, 1969 F
Mount Buffalo, Vic, 1910 E
Mount Buffalo Ski chalet, Vic, 1920 F
Mount Dandenong, Vic, 1938 F
Mount Eliza, Vic, 1955 D
Mount Erebus, Antarctica, 1908 A
Mount Everest, 1984 E
Mount Field, Tas, 1916 F
Mount Gambier, SA, 1847 F, 1861 F, 1896 F, 1902 B
Mount Gambier Art competition, SA, 1961 C
Mount Garnet, WA, 1854 A
Mount Garnet, Qld, 1896 F
Mount Gravatt College of Advanced Education, Qld, 1969 D
Mount Gravatt Teachers' College, Qld, 1969 D
Mount Hagen (horse), 1978 E
Mount Hotham, Vic, 1863 E
Mount Isa, Qld, 1923 B, F, 1927 B, 1961 A, 1964 A
Mount Isa Mines Holdings Ltd, 1924 A, 1970 A
Mount Kembla, NSW, 1902 F
Mount Kianga, Qld, 1975 F
Mount Kitchener, SA, 1944 F
Mount Kosciusko, 1902 C
Mount Kosciusko, NSW, 1840 A, 1881 F, 1897 F, 1910 A, 1927 E, 1972 F
Mount Kosciusko Hotel, 1909 F
Mount Kosciusko National Park, 1944 F, 1972 F
Mount Kosciusko Ski Club, 1909 E
Mount Lawley Teachers' College Perth, 1970 D
Mount Lofty Ranges, SA, 1954 F
Mount Lyell, Tas, 1883 B, 1884 B, 1886 B, 1896 F, 1912 F
Mount Macedon, Vic, 1844 F
Mount Morgan, Qld, 1882 B, F
Mount Mulligan, Qld, 1921 F
Mount Newman, WA, 1956 B, 1967 F
Mount Nicholas, Tas, 1886 F
Mount Panorama racing circuit, NSW, 1938 E
Mount Pleasant, SA, 1842 F
Mount Scopus Memorial College, Melbourne, 1949 D
Mount St Mary College of Education, Sydney, 1908 D

Mount Stromlo, ACT, 1981 B
Mount Stromlo Observatory, ACT, 1910 B, 1911 B, 1912 B, 1981 B
Mount Stuart, NT, 1860 A
Mount Tamborine, Qld, 1908 F
Mount Tom Price, WA, 1962 B, 1966 B
Mount Victoria, NSW, 1832 F
Mount Werong, NSW, 1905 F
Mount White, NSW, 1965 B
Mount Wingen, NSW, 1828 B
Mount Zeehan, Tas, 1885 B
Mount Zero, Vic, 1880 C
Mountain, Adrian C. 1880 B
Mountain-climbing, 1984 E
Mountaineers or Love and Madness, The, 1838 C
Mountford, Charles P. 1890 B
Mountgarrett, Jacob, 1828 B
Moura, Qld, 1936 F, 1975 F
Mourilyan, Qld, 1882 F
Mouritz, John, 1842 D
Mouth to Mouth resuscitation, 1960 F
Movement, The, 1942 A
Movietone News, 1929 C
Moving Image, The, 1946 C
Moving footways, Sydney, 1961 B
Mowll, Howard W. K. 1890 D
Moyes, Alan G. 1922 A
Moyes, Alban G. J. 1892 E
Moyes, John F. 1920 F
Moyes, John S. 1884 D
Moyes, Morton H. 1886 B
Moyes, Peter M. 1917 D
Moyes, William T. J. (Bill), 1932 E 1967 E, 1968 E, 1971 E
Mr Asia case, 1981 F
Mr Chedworth Steps Out, 1939 C
Mr Hogarth's Will, 1865 C
Mr Moffat, 1925 C
Mrs Murdoch (painting), 1927 C
Muchea, WA, 1960 F
Mudgee, NSW, 1821 A, 1836 B, 1867 B
Mudie, Ian M. 1911 C
Mudie, James, 1837 C, 1852 A
Mueller, Ferdinand J. H. von, 1825 B, 1853 B, 1854 A, 1855 A, 1881 B
Mukinbudin, WA, 1922 F
Mulgoa, NSW, 1938 F
Mulgrave, Peter A. 1821 D, 1847 D
Mulka, SA, 1980 F
Mullagh, Johnny, 1843 E
Mullewa, WA, 1865 F
Mulley, Athol G. 1923 E
Mulligan, James V. 1837 A, 1873 B
Mullumbimby, NSW, 1888 F
Multi-National Peacekeeping Force, Middle East, 1982 A
Mundaring, WA, 1873 G
Mundey, Jack, 1932 A
Mundine, Tony, 1951 E
Mundubbera, Qld, 1910 F
Mungana mines, Qld, 1930 A
Mungindi, NSW, 1880 F
Munich Olympics, 1972 E
Munro, David H. 1913 E, 1934 E, 1944 E, 1946 E
Munro, Grace E. 1879 F, 1922 F
Munro, James (b. 1763), 1845 F
Munro, James (b. 1832), 1832 A, 1890 A
Munro, Jim, 1905 E, 1925 E, 1928 E
Munro-Ferguson, Ronald C. 1860 A, 1914 A
Muntz-Adams, Josephine, 1862 C
Mural painting, 1899 C, *see section C*
Murch, Arthur J. 1902 C, 1949 C
Murchea Station, WA, 1962 B
Murchison, Vic, 1891 F
Murchison district, Qld, 1890 B
Murchison Medal, 1877 B

Murchison R. WA, 1839 A, 1848 B, 1854 A, 1891 B
Murdoch, Elizabeth J. 1909 A
Murdoch, James, 1856 D
Murdoch, John, 1851 D
Murdoch, John (architect), 1923 C
Murdoch, Keith E. 1886 A, 1940 A
Murdoch, K. Rupert, 1931 A
Murdoch, Walter L. F. 1874 C
Murdoch, William D. 1888 C
Murdoch, William L. 1855 E
Murdoch Art Prize, Perth, 1958 C
Murdoch University, WA, 1975 D
Muresk Agricultural College, WA, 1926 D
Murgon, Qld, 1906 F
Murphy, Ashton, 1874 C
Murphy, A. W. 1919 B
Murphy, Edwin G. 1867 C
Murphy, Francis; 1795 D, 1844 D
Murphy, Geoffrey, 1922 E
Murphy, Graeme L. 1950 C, 1978 C
Murphy, Lionel K. 1922 A, 1973 A, 1975 A, 1978 A, 1984 C
Murphy Creek, Qld, 1913 F
Murray, Alan, 1940 E
Murray, Alexander B. 1816 A
Murray, Brian, 1982 A
Murray, Clive W. 1942 C
Murray (constable), 1938 A
Murray, David, 1829 C
Murray, Ebenezer, 1848 C
Murray, George G. A. 1866 D
Murray, George J. R. 1863 A, 1920 A, 1922 A, 1927 A, 1934 A, 1939 A
Murray, Henry W. 1884 A
Murray, Ian, 1958 E
Murray, Jack, 1910 E
Murray, Jack K. 1889 A
Murray, John (1), 1801 A, 1802 A, 1810 A
Murray, John (2), 1851 A, 1909 A
Murray, John H. P. 1861 A, 1891 A, 1908 A
Murray, Kevin, 1939 E, 1969 E
Murray, Leslie A. 1938 C
Murray, Robert W. F. L. 1850 F
Murray Bridge, SA, 1866 F, 1879 B
Murray Committee, 1957 D
Murray Multiplex telegraphic system, 1922 B
Murray-Prior, Rosa C., *see* Praed, Mrs C.
Murray-Prior, Thomas L. 1819 A
Murray R., NSW, SA, Vic, 1824 A 1830 A, 1835 A, 1841 A, 1851 A, 1852 A, 1853 A, B, 1855 A, B, 1857 A, 1875 B, 1883 B, 1915 B, 1920 B
Murray R. Aboriginals, 1895 C
Murray River Queen, The, 1973 B
Murray Valley, Vic, 1950 B
Murray Valley Encephalitis, 1917 B
Murray Valley Irrigation Scheme, 1886 A
Murrell, Amos, 1903 E
Murrell, James, 1863 F
Murringo, NSW, 1850 F
Murrumbeena, Vic, 1911 C
Murrumbidgee Irrigation, NSW, 1906 A, 1907 B, 1909 D, 1912 B, 1922 A, 1966 F
Murrumbidgee R., NSW, 1824 A, 1829 A, 1849 B, 1866 B, 1891 F, 1895 B, 1906 A, 1925 F, 1927 B
Murrumburrah, NSW, 1860 F
Murrurundi, NSW, 1839 F
Murtoa, Vic, 1845 F
Murulla, NSW, 1926 F
Mururoa Atoll, 1983 A
Murwillumbah, NSW, 1872 F, 1907 F, 1978 F

Museum of Applied Sciences, Sydney, 1880 D
Museum and Art Gallery, Tas, 1838 C
Museum of Education, NSW, 1956 D
Museum of Modern Art in Aust., 1956 C
Museum of Modern Art and Design, Melbourne, 1958 C
Museums, *see individual entries*
Museums and Art Gallery Board of NT, 1965 D
Musgrave, Anthony, 1873 A, 1883 A
Musgrave Ranges, NT, SA, 1889 A, 1937 D
Musgrove, George, 1854 C, 1882 C, 1901 C
Music, first performance, 1788 C, *see individual entries*
Music Foundation, 1966 C
Music for Japan, 1970 C
Music Now, 1969 C
Music shop, Sydney, 1824 C
Musica Viva, 1945 C, 1946 C
Musicological Society of Aust., 1963 C
Mustard, 1873 F
Muswellbrook, NSW, 1827 F
Muswellbrook Art Prize, NSW, 1958 C
Mutton, production, 1808 A
Mutual Aid Agreement, with USA, 1942 A
Mutual Life Assurance building, Sydney, 1891 C
Mutual Life and Citizens' Assurance Co., Sydney, 1886 A, building 1957 C, tower 1977 C
Mutual Protection Society, Sydney, 1843 A
My Brilliant Career, 1901 C, 1979 C
My Brother Jack, 1964 C
'My Country', 1908 C
My Crowded Solitude, 1927 C
My Fair Lady, 1959 C
My People, 1970 C
Myall Creek Massacre, 1838 A
Myer, Kenneth B. 1921 A, 1983 A
Myer, Margery M. B. 1900 A
Myer, Norman B. 1898 A
Myer, Sidney B. 1878 A, 1900 A, 1911 A, 1926 A, 1959 C
Myer Emporium, Melbourne, 1840 A, 1926 A, 1937 C
Myer Music Bowl, Melbourne, 1959 C, 1967 C
Myrniong Art Exhibitor Group, Melbourne, 1960 C
Myrtleford, Vic, 1855 F
Mystery of a Hansom Cab, The, 1886 C
Myxomatosis, 1950 B, 1951 B, 1969 B

N

Nabalco Pty Ltd, 1968 B
Nabarlek, NT, 1970 B, 1980 B
Nabarlek uranium field, NT, 1976 A
Nabawa wheat, 1923 B
Nagasaki, Japan, 1945 A
Nagle, Kelvin D. G. 1920 E, 1954 E
Naked Bunyip, The, 1970 C
Naked Island, The, 1952 C
Namatjira, Albert, 1902 C, 1936 C, 1938 C, 1957 C, 1958 C
Namatjira Memorial Art Prize, Adelaide, 1963 C
Nambour, Qld, 1865 F
Nambucca Heads, NSW, 1885 F

Namoi Valley, NSW, 1961 A
Nan Kivell, Rex de C. 1899 C, 1961 C
Nan Kivell art collection, 1961 C
Nanango, Qld, 1845 F
Nancarrow, Cam, 1945 E
Nance, William, 1965 E
Nangle, James, 1941 B
Nannup, WA, 1854 F
Napier, John M. 1968 A, 1971 A
Naracoorte, SA, 1845 F, 1865 E, 1867 E
Narcotics, 1969 A
Narellan, NSW, 1827 F
Narembeen, WA, 1836 F
Narooma, NSW, 1883 F
Narrabeen, NSW, 1909 B
Narrabri, NSW, 1859 F, 1963 B,
Narracott, Paul, 1961 E
Narrandera, NSW, 1863 F
Narrative of the Expedition to Botany Bay, 1789 C
Narrogin, WA, 1895 F
Narrogin Agricultural College, WA, 1914 D
Narrogin Art Gallery, WA, 1953 C
Narromine, NSW, 1880 F
Narrows bridge, WA, 1959 B
Narvo, Herb, 1912 E
Nash, James, 1867 B
Nash, Laurie, 1910 E
Nathalia, Vic, 1879 F
Nathan, Charles S. 1870 A
Nathan, Isaac, 1790 C, 1841 C, 1846 C, 1847 C
Nathan, Matthew, 1920 A
Nathan, Miss, 1832 F
Nathan, Reginald H. J. 1899 C
Natimuk, Vic, 1871 F
Nation, 1842 F
Nation, newspaper, 1958 F
Nation Review, 1958 F
Nation Rose Society, 1912 F
National Aboriginal and Islander Health Organization, NAIHO, 1975 A
National Aboriginal and Islander Liberation Movement, 1957 A
National Aboriginal Conference consultative body, 1977 A
National Aboriginal Consultative Committee, NACC, 1973 A
National Aboriginal Council, 1981 A
National Aboriginal Sports Foundation, 1969 E
National Acoustics Laboratory, 1942 B
National Advisory Committee of Employers, 1927 A
National Anthem, 1973 F, 1977 F, 1984 F
National Art Gallery of NSW, 1885 C
National Art Gallery of SA, 1881 C
National Art School, Sydney, 1859 C
National Association of Aust. and State Road Authorities, NAASRA, 1934 B
National Australasian Convention, 1890 A, 1891 A
National Bank of Australasia, 1858 A
National Bank of Australasia Art Calendar, 1957 C
National Bank of Vic, 1852 A
National Basketball League, 1979 E
National Biological Standards Laboratory, 1958 B
National Black Theatre, Sydney, 1972 C
National Book Council, Sydney, 1945 C
National Botanic Gardens of Aust., Canberra, 1970 B
National Capital, 1913 A
National Capital Development Commission, NCDC, 1957 A
National ceramic conference, Sydney, 1978 C

National Church Conference, 1960 D
National Civic Council, 1957 A
National civil defence, 1974 F
National Commercial Banking Corporation of Australasia, 1981 A
National Constitution Conference, 1983 A
National Council of Women of Aust., 1896 A
National Council of Women of Vic, 1902 A
National Country Party, Qld, 1915 A
National Country Party of Aust., 1974 A, 1981 A, 1982 A
National Coursing Associations, 1897 E
National Coursing Club of Tas, 1878 E
National Crime Authority, 1984 A
National Crimes Commission, 1982 A
National Curriculum Development Centre, 1975 D
National and Denominational School Boards, NSW, 1848 D
National Economic Summit, 1983 A
National Employers' Association, 1961 A, 1978 A
National Employers' Policy and Consultative Committee, 1953 A
National Employment and Training, NEAT scheme, 1974 A
National Energy Advisory Committee, 1978 B
National Energy Development and Demonstration Council, 1978 B
National Epilepsy Assoc. of Aust., 1983 F
National Estate, 1981 F
National Farmers' Federation, 1979 A
National Farmers' Union, 1969 A
National Film & Sound Archives, 1984 C
National Fire Brigade Association of Vic, 1887 F
National Fitness Councils, 1941 D
National Fitness Movement, 1939 E
National Football Council, 1906 E
National Foundation of Infantile Paralysis, 1941 B
National Front of Aust, 1978 A
National Gallery and Cultural Centre, Melbourne, 1962 C
National Gallery of NSW, 1883 C, 1958 C
National Gallery of SA, 1967 C
National Gallery of Vic, 1861 C, 1886 C, 1904 C, 1968 C
National Gallery of Vic Art Prizes, 1959 C
National Health Act, 1953 A
National Health and Medical Research Council, 1936 B
National Heart Foundation, 1961 B
National Heart Transplant programme, 1984 B
National Herbarium of Vic, 1857 B
National Ice Hockey League, 1980 E
National Institute of Dramatic Art, Sydney, 1955 C, 1958 C, 1959 C
National Institute of Medical Research, Britain, 1933 B
National Labor Party, 1916 A, *see also* Aust. Labor Party *and* Labor Party
National Library of Aust., 1901 D, 1936 C, 1960 D, 1961 C, D, 1968 D, 1976 D
National Literature Board of Review, 1967 C, 1968 C
National Mapping Council, 1945 B
National Marriage Guidance Council, 1955 F

National Measurement Laboratory, 1938 B
National Museum, Melbourne, 1864 D
National Museum of Aust. Zoology, 1923 B, 1931 B
National Museum of Vic, 1854 D
National Music Camp, 1948 C
National Opera, 1956 C
National Opera of Aust., 1952 C
National Opera Co. of NSW, 1951 C
National Parks, NSW, 1879 F, 1908 F, 1984 F, see also individual entries
National Parks, administration, NSW, 1967 F
National Parks Association, Qld, 1930 F
National Parks Association of NSW, 1957 F
National Parks Wildlife Foundation, NSW, 1970 F
National Parks and Wildlife Service, 1975 A
National Party, NSW, 1982 A
National Party of Aust. (Qld), 1974 A
National Party, Vic, 1975 A
National Press Council, 1975 F
National Rifle Association of Aust., 1901 E
National Road Tolls, see from 1955 section F
National Roads Association, 1920 F
National Roads and Motorists' Association, NRMA, NSW, 1920 F, Art Prize 1947 C
National Safety Council of Aust., 1928 F
National schools, 1834 D, 1849 D, 1850 D, 1851 D
National Scouting Association, 1958 F
National Security Regulations, wartime, 1939 A, 1946 A
National Service, 1957 A, 1960 A, 1964 A, 1965 A, 1966 A, 1968 A, 1971 A, 1972 A, see also conscription and military
National Service Act, 1972 A
National Shipwreck Relief Society of NSW, 1902 F
National Soccer League of Aust., 1977 E
National Sporting Club, Sydney, 1902 E
National Standards Laboratory, 1938 B
National strike, 1936 A
National system of schools, NSW, 1847 D
National Theatre Ballet, 1947 C, 1949 C
National Theatre Movement, 1935 C, 1939 C, 1956 C
National Times, 1971 F
National Trachoma and Eye Health Programme, 1975 B
National Trades Hall and Literary Institute, Melbourne, 1856 A
National Training Orchestra, Sydney, 1967 C
National Trust of Aust., NSW, 1947 F
National Trusts, 1945 F
National Trusts, Aust. Council of, 1965 F
National Union of Aust. Students, 1970 D
National Welfare scheme, 1943 A
National Women's Advisory Council, 1978 A
National Works Council, 1943 A
Nationalization, Banks 1947 A Qantas 1947 A
Nationalist Party, Federal, 1917 A
Nationality and Citizen Act, Federal, 1948 A
Native Companions, 1974 C
Native labour contracts, PNG, 1945 A
Native Mounted Police Force, Qld, 1848 A, 1868 A

Native Tribes of Central Australia, The, 1899 C
Native Tribes of Northern Territory of Australia, The, 1914 C
Native Tribes of South East Australia, The, 1904 C
Natural Disasters Organization, 1974 F
Natural gas, 1900 B, 1906 B, 1961 B, 1963 B, 1969 B, 1970 B, 1971 B, 1977 B, see also Gas
Natural History Association of NSW, 1887 B
Naturalization, 1825 A
Naturalization Act, Federal, 1903 A
Naturalists' Society of NSW, 1887 B
Nauru, 1914 A, 1919 A, 1962 A, 1965 A, 1968 A
Nauru Act, 1965 A
Nauru I. Agreement Act, 1919 A
Nautical Museum, Adelaide, 1872 C
Nautical zone, 200 mile, 1979 A
Naval Agreement Bill, 1903 A
Naval base, Singapore, 1924 A
Naval Board, 1905 A, 1964 A, 1976 A
Naval Defence Act, 1856 A
Navigation, aerial, 1919 B
Navigation Act, 1849 A
Navigation Act, Federal, 1921 B
Navigation School, Sydney, 1943 D
Navy, 1855 A, 1856 A, 1859 A, 1865 A, 1871 A, 1884 A, 1889 A, 1890 A, 1891 A, 1899 A, 1900 A, 1903 A, 1904 A, 1905 A, 1910 A, 1911 A, 1913 A, 1914 A, 1923 A, 1924 A, 1973 A, 1976 A
see also Royal Aust. Navy
Naylor, Rufus T. 1882 E, 1927 E
Nazi Germany, refugees, 1938 A
Neale, W. L. 1905 D
Ned Kelly series of paintings, 1946 C, 1947 C
Ned Kelly (verse play), 1942 C, 1943 C
Ned Kelly (film), 1970 C
Ned Kelly Music, 1968 C
Nedlands, WA, 1967 D
Nedlands College of Advanced Education, WA, 1967 D
Needle, Martha, 1894 F
Neglected children, Vic, 1864 F
Neighborhood Watch programme, 1984 F
Neil, Bladen, 1868 A
Neilson, John S. 1872 C, 1919 C
Neilson, William A. 1925 A, 1975 A
Nellie Melba Bequest Scholarship, 1935 C
Nelson (ship), 1852 F
Nelson, Vic, 1902 B
Nelson, Hugh M. 1835 A, 1893 A, 1904 A
Nelson, Isaac, 1798 D, 1803 D
Nelson, J. N. 1973 A
Nelson House, Sydney, 1910 C
Nepean College of Advanced Education, 1973 D
Nepean R., NSW, 1789 A, 1795 A, 1856 B
Nepean R. Bridge, 1903 B
Nerang, Qld, 1865 F
Nerelle, Marie, 1870 C
Nerida, 1950 E
Nerli, Girolamo B. (Marchese Nerli) 1863 C
Netball, 1905 E, 1924 E, 1926 E, 1927 E, 1963 E
Netherlands Dance Theatre Dancing Co., 1972 C
Nettlefold, Len, 1905 E
Neumayer, George B. von, 1826 B

Neurology, 1951 B
Neurophysiology, 1963 B
Neutral Bay, Sydney, 1882 F
Neva, 1835 F
Nevertire, NSW, 1886 F
Neville, George W. 1920 C
Neville, Ray, 1933 E, 1948 E
Neville Gruzman, 1970 C
New Apostolic Church, Qld, 1912 D
New Art Gallery, The, Sydney, 1879 C
New Art Society, Qld, 1904 C
New Australia, 1893 A
New Britain, 1914 A, 1942 A
New Britannia, A, 1970 C
New Caledonia, 1853 A
New Dance Theatre, 1968 C
New Education Fellowship, 1937 D, 1938 D
New England district, NSW, 1832 A, 1967 A
New England Regional Art Museum, 1983 C
New England University, NSW, 1938 D
New Fortune Theatre, WA, 1964 C
New Guard, 1931 A, 1932 A
New Guinea, 1873 A, 1882 A, 1883 A, 1884 A, 1903 A, 1921 A, 1942 A, 1943 A, 1944 A, 1949 A, 1962 A, see also Papua
New Hebrides, convention, 1890 F, 1906 A
New Holland, 1801 A, 1829 A
New Idea, 1902 F
New Italy settlement, NSW, 1881 A
'new look', fashion, 1949 F
New Melbourne Art Club, 1933 D
New Norcia mission, WA, 1846 D, 1847 D
New Norfolk, Tas, 1807 F, 1815 F, 1825 F, 1865 B
New Oriental Bank, 1885 A
New Protection Policy, 1906 A
New South Wales, abbreviated as NSW
 boundaries, 1825 A, 1967 A
 Crown Colony, 1824 A
 districts, 1840 A
 electoral zones, 1928 A
 jurisdiction, 1839 A
 possession of, 1788 A
 representative govt, 1842 A, 1843 A
NSW Aboriginal Legal Service, 1971 A
NSW Aborigines Protection Board, 1883 A, 1930 A
NSW Academy of Arts, 1871 C, 1875 C
NSW Advertiser, 1842 F
NSW Agricultural Bureau, 1910 A
NSW Alliance for the Supression of Intemperance, 1857 F
NSW Amateur Athletics Association, 1887 E
NSW Amateur Swimming Association, Sydney, 1892 E
NSW Board of Senior School Studies, 1975 D
NSW Bureau of Crime Statistics and Research, 1972 A
NSW Charter of Justice, 1824 A
NSW Coal and Copper Co., 1861 A
NSW College of Paramedical Studies, 1973 B
NSW Conservatorium of Music, 1914 C, 1916 C, 1923 C, 1925 C, 1973 C
NSW Constitution, 1843 A, 1853 A
NSW Corps, 1790 A, 1792 A, 1793 A, 1800 A, 1803 A, 1809 A
NSW Cyclists' Union, 1883 E
NSW Dept of Aboriginal Affairs, 1981 A
NSW Dept of Agriculture, 1925 B, 1930 B

NSW Education Board, 1856 D
NSW Education Dept Art Gallery, 1913 C
NSW Education Fellowship, 1938 D
NSW Employers' Union, 1888 A
NSW Fencing Association, 1932 E
NSW Fresh Food and Ice Co., 1875 F
New South Wales General Standing Orders: ... Governors, 1802 C
NSW Goldfields Management Act, 1852 A
NSW Govt Aviation School, 1916 D
NSW Government Gazette, 1832 A
NSW Humanist Society, 1960 F
NSW Institute of Architects, 1871 C
NSW Institute of Technology, 1965 D
New South Wales Judicature Act, 1823 A
NSW Law Reform Commission, 1966 A
NSW Lawn Bowling Association, 1880 E
NSW National Opera Co., 1948 C, 1952 C
NSW National Parks and Wildlife Act, 1967 F
NSW Planning and Environment Commission, 1974 C
NSW Police Association, 1920 A
NSW Police Force, 1942 F
NSW Public Library, 1869 D
NSW Public School League, 1874 D
NSW Rifle Association, 1860 E
NSW Rugby Union, 1874 E
NSW Savings Bank, 1819 A, 1931 A
NSW Sesqui-Centenary Art prize, 1937 C
NSW Soccer Association, 1882 E
NSW Society of Artists, 1895 C, 1900 C
NSW Society of Artists' Medal, 1924 C
NSW Society for the Relief of Destitute Children, 1851 F
New South Wales Sporting Magazine, 1848 E
NSW Stamp Collectors' Magazine, 1879 F
NSW State Orchestra, 1919 C
NSW State Dockyard, 1915 B
NSW Sudan contingent ex-service organisation, 1885 F
NSW Sunday School Institution, 1815 D
NSW Table Tennis Association, 1902 E
NSW Teachers' Federation, 1919 D
NSW Teachers' Institute, 1895 D
NSW Temperance Society, 1834 F
NSW Travelling Art Scholarship, 1934 C
NSW Trotting Club, 1902 E, 1911 E
NSW University of Technology, 1949 D, 1951 D, 1958 D
New Staters, NSW, 1922 A
New States, NSW, 1933 A
New Synagogue, Melbourne, 1877 D
New Town, Tas, 1807 B, 1828 D
New Year celebrations, 1980 F
New Zealand, 1814 A, 1831 F, 1832 A, 1839 A, 1840 A, 1841 A, 1845 A, 1860 A, 1863 A, 1876 B, 1907 A, 1971 A
New Zealand, 1980 E
New Zealand–Aust Free Trade Agreement, NAFTA, 1965 A
New Zealand Bank, 1861 A
Newbiggen, Bob, 1919 E
Newbury, Albert E. 1891 C
Newbury, David, 1925 C
Newcastle, NSW, 1801 A, F, 1804 A, 1819 B, 1821 F, 1823 A, 1831 A, 1851 A, 1854 A, 1855 A, 1858 F, 1860 B, 1884 E, 1888 A, 1896 A, 1915 B, 1921 B, 1962 C

Newcastle Benevolent Society, 1885 F
Newcastle Blight, 1869 F
Newcastle City Art Gallery, NSW, 1957 C
Newcastle Civic Foundation Art competition, NSW, 1961 C
Newcastle College of Advanced Education, 1949 D
Newcastle East Public School, 1816 D
Newcastle Harbour, NSW, 1866 F
Newcastle High School, 1906 D
Newcastle Hotel Art Prize, NSW, 1962 C
Newcastle Morning Herald and Miners' Advocate, 1858 F
Newcastle Sun, 1918 F
Newcastle Teachers College, NSW, 1949 D
Newcastle University, NSW, 1951 D
Newcastle War Memorial Sculpture competition, 1955 C
Newcombe, John, 1944 E
Newdegate, Francis A. N. 1917 A, 1920 A
Newell, John, 1880 B
Newhaven, 1896 E
Newington College, Sydney, 1863 D
Newlands Golf Club, Tas, 1896 E
Newman College of Advanced Education, Tas, 1972 D
Newman, J. H. 1830 B
Newman, Kevin, 1934 E
Newmarket, Vic, 1918 B
Newnes, NSW, 1905 B
Newport, Sydney, 1926 E
News (newspaper), Adelaide, 1923 F
News, movie, 1929 C
News cables, 1872 F
News print, 1941 A, F
Newsfront, 1978 C
Newsky family, 1899 C
Newsletter of Australasia, 1856 F
Newspaper reporters, NSW, 1838 F
Newspapers, *see individual entries*
Newsreel, 1931 C
Newstead House, Brisbane, 1846 C
Newsweek, 1984 C
Newton, Albert W. 1938 C
Newton, Henry, 1866 D
Newton, Hibbert A. S. 1887 B
Newton, Jack, 1950 E
Newton, Sydney, 1931 A
Newton, Thomas M. 1919 C
Newton, William E. 1919 A
Newton-John, Olivia, 1948 C, 1974 C
Newton-Wood, Noel, 1923 C
Newtown, NSW, 1931 A
Newtown Rugby League Football Club/team, 1908 E, 1910 E, 1933 E, 1943 E
Nhill, Vic, 1880 F
Nhulumbuy, NT, 1972 F
Nibbi, Gino, 1896 C
Nice Night's Entertainment, A, 1962 C
Nichol, Keith, 1920 C
Nichol Bay, WA, 1861 A
Nicholas, George, 1884 B, 1914 B
Nicholas, E. Hilda R. 1884 C
Nicholas, William, 1809 C
Nicholls, Douglas R. 1906 A, 1972 A, 1976 A
Nicholls, Ethel M. 1866 C
Nicholls, Herbert, 1868 A, 1917 C, 1920 A, 1922 A, 1930 A
Nicholls, John, 1938 E
Nicholls, Sydney, 1897 C
Nicholls, William H. 1885 B
Nichols, Geoffrey, 1963 E

Nichols, Isaac, 1798 F, 1809 A, 1810 A, 1819 A
Nicholson, Alexander J. 1895 B
Nicholson, Charles, 1808 A, 1850 B
Nicholson, John, 1954 E
Nicholson, John H. 1838 C
Nicholson, Joyce, 1921 C
Nicholson, Michael, 1916 C
Nicholson, W. 1859 D
Nicholson Act, Vic, 1860 A
Nicholson Museum, 1860 D
Nickel, WA, 1966 B, 1969 B
Nickel boom, 1969 B
Nicklin, Francis R. 1895 A, 1957 A
Nicoleski, Vlase, 1948 C
Nicolle, Eugene D. 1823 B, 1861 B, 1863 B, 1876 B
Niemeyer, Otto, 1930 A
Night patrol, military, 1810 A
Night refuge, Sydney, 1865 F
Night Shift, 1906 A
Night Watch, 1918 E
Nightcap Range, NSW, 1982 F
Nightmarch, 1929 E
Nightwatch, 1789 A
Nigro, Jan, 1920 C
Niland, D'Arcy F. 1917 C, 1955 C
Nilsson, Raymond, 1919 C
Nimblefoot, 1870 E
Nimmitabel, NSW, 1865 F
Nimmo, Lorna M. 1920 C
Nimmo, Robert H. 1893 A
Nimrod Street Theatre, 1970 C
'Nine by Five' art exhibition, 1889 C
'Nine Miles from Gundagai', 1923 C
Nine Mile Springs, Tas, 1852 B
Nineteen Counties, 1829 A, 1847 A
Nippon Mining Co., 1938 A
Nisbet, Hume, 1849 C
Nishi, Haruhiko, 1953 A
Nissen, Henry, 1948 E
Nitric acid, 1862 B
Nixon, Francis R. 1803 D, 1842 D
No Barrier, 1953 C
No Liability Act, Vic, 1871 A
No Room in the Ark, 1959 C
Noach, Veronica, 1941 C
Noack, Errol W. 1966 A
Noarlunga, SA, 1840 F
Nobel, Garney, 1916 E
Nobel Clay Target Club, Melbourne, 1927 E
Nobel Prize, 1915 B, 1945 B, 1947 B, 1960 B, 1963 B, 1970 B, 1973 C, 1975 B
Noble, James, 1876 D
Noble, Montague A. 1873 E
Noel, Jane, 1806 D
Noffs, Theodore D. 1926 D, 1964 D
Nolan, Sidney R. 1917 C, 1940 C, 1943 C, 1946 C, 1947 C, 1950 C, 1957 C
Nomenclature Act, SA, 1917 F
Non-Proliferation of Nuclear Weapons, 1968 A
Nonuplets, 1971 F
Nook, Tas, 1852 B
Noon, Thomas, 1827 A
Noongah, 1969 F
Norfolk, 1789 F
Norfolk I., 1788 A, 1789 F, 1790 A, 1805 A, 1807 A, 1814 A, 1825 A, 1826 F, 1834 F, 1840 A, 1842 F, 1844 A, 1846 F, 1853 A, 1858 F, 1897 A, 1913 A, 1914 A, 1979 A
Norfolk Islands Lands Act, Cwlth, 1913 A
Norlen Explorations, 1971 C
Norling, Robert C. 1940 C
Norm and Ahmed, 1968 C
Norma (opera), 1852 C

803

Norma (ship), 1907 F
Normal Institution, 1834 D
Norman, Decima, 1914 E, 1938 E
Norman, Desmond, 1930 C, 1958 B
Norman, Gary, 1951 C
Norman, Greg, 1955 E, 1983 E, 1984 E
Norman, Henry W. 1889 A
Norman Stephens, (painting), 1974 C
Normanton, Qld, 1868 F
Normanville, SA, 1849 F
Nornalup, WA, 1905 F
Norrie, Charles W. M.1944 A
Norseman, WA, 1895 F
North, Alfred, J. 1855 B
North Aust., Colonization of, 1824 A
North Australia Act, 1926 A, 1931 A
North Australia Colony, 1846 A
North Aust Expedition, 1855 A
North Coast Steam Navigation Co., NSW, 1857 A
North Melbourne Aust. Rules Football Club/team, 1874 E, 1973 E, 1974 E, 1975 E, 1977 E, 1978 E, 1983 E
North Qld, separation, 1866 A, 1885 A
North Qld Ballet and Dance Society, 1969 C
North Qld Conservatorium of Music, 1972 C
North Queensland Register, Townsville, 1876 F
North Qld Separation League, 1885 A
North Shore Ferry Co., Sydney, 1861 B
North Shore ferry service, Sydney, 1842 B
North Sydney Rugby League Football Club/team, 1908 E, 1921 E, 1922 E
North Terrace, Adelaide, 1877 C
North-West Coastal Highway, WA, 1974 B
Northam, WA, 1830 F
Northam, William H. 1905 E, 1964 E
Northam Art Gallery, WA, 1952 C
Northampton, WA, 1864 F
Northampton district, WA, 1848 B
Northcliffe, WA, 1920 F
Northcote, Henry S. 1846 A, 1904 A
Northcote, John C. 1817 C
Northcott, John, 1890 A, 1946 A
Northern Challenge Polo Cup, NSW, 1899 E
Northern Coal Sale Association, 1872 A
Northern Daily Leader, NSW, 1871 F
Northern Lands Council, 1978 A
Northern Rivers College of Advanced Education, NSW, 1973 D
Northern Territory, *abbreviated as* NT
  Administration, 1863 A, 1907 A, 1911 A, 1931 A, *see also individual entries*
  borders, boundaries, 1889 A, 1926 A
  capital, 1865 A
  foundation, 1864 A
  representation in SA Parlt 1890 A, –in Federal Parlt 1922 A, 1968 A
  self govt, 1978 A
NT Aboriginals Ordinance, 1918 A
NT Administration Act, 1931 A
NT Broadcasting Board, 1949 A
NT Legislative Council, 1947 A
Northern Territory News, Darwin, 1952 F
Northern Territory Times, 1873 F
Northern Tribes of Central Australia, The 1904 C
Northfleet, 1873 F
Northmore, John A. 1931 A, 1932 A
Northside Arts Festival, Sydney, 1963 C
North-West Cape, WA, 1817 A, 1945 F, 1963 A, B
North-West Shelf, WA, 1971 B

Norton, Charles F. 1916 C
Norton, John, 1862 A, 1890 F, 1899 F
Norton, Rosaleen, 1917 C
Norvie, James S. 1844 B
Norway, Nevil S. 1899 C
Norwegian settlers, 1895 A
Norwood, Frederick W. 1876 D
Norwood Art School, Adelaide, 1885 C
Nossal, Gustav J. V. 1931 B
Notes and Sketches of New South Wales, 1844 C
Nott, L. B. 1913 E
Nott, R. B. 1961 A
Novelists, *see individual entries*
Novels, *see individual entries*
Nowra, NSW, 1857 F, 1976 F
Noyce, Phillip R. 1950 C, 1978 C
Nuclear Co-operation Treaty, 1972 A
Nuclear Disarmament Party, 1984 A
Nuclear energy, 1953 A
Nuclear experiments, ANU, 1952 B
Nuclear Non-Proliferation Treaty, 1970 A, 1973 A
Nuclear reactor, Lucas Heights, NSW, 1958 B
Nuclear Research Foundation, Sydney, 1954 B
Nuclear Safeguards Policy, 1977 A
Nuclear Test Ban Agreement, 1963 A
Nuclear testing, French, 1972 A, 1973 A
Nuclear waste, 1978 B
Nuclear weapons, 1968 A, 1970 A, 1971 A, 1983 A
Nude bathing, 1976 F
Nuffield Travel and Study Awards, 1948 D
Nullagine, WA, 1889 F
Nullarbor Plain, WA, 1875 A, 1976 B
Numurkah, Vic, 1875 F
Nunawading Messiah, 1871 D
Nundah, Qld, 1838 F
Nuriootpa, SA, 1854 F
Nurse-aides, Melbourne, 1951 B
Nursery Schools Association, 1905 D
Nursery School Teachers' College, Sydney, 1932 D
Nurses, army, massacre of, 1942 A
Nursing, 1838 B, 1868 B, 1875 B, 1899 B, 1912 B
Nursing Home, Alice Springs, 1926 F
Nursing Registration Boards, 1927 B
Nursing services, Tas, 1893 B
Nutrition, 1940 D
Nuts, pecan, 1968 A
Nuttall, Charles, 1872 C, 1904 F
Nyholm, Ronald S. 1917 B
Nylon, 1966 B
Nyngan, NSW, 1880 F

O

Oakes, Laurie, 1980 A
Oakey, Qld, 1867 F
Oakland, (ship) 1903 F
Oakley, Barry, 1931 C
Oakwood, Tas, 1835 B
Oates, Richard, 1869 F
Oatlands, Tas, 1823 F
Oatley, James, 1815 F, 1839 B
Oats, 1928 B
Oberon, Merle, 1911 C
Oberon, NSW, 1863 F
Oberon submarines, 1963 A
O'Brien, Eris, 1895 D

O'Brien, George, 1821 C
O'Brien, Henry, 1793 A, 1843 A
O'Brien, Ian, 1947 E
'O'Brien, John', *see* Hartigan, Patrick J.
O'Brien, Justin, 1917 C, 1951 C
O'Brien, M. 1885 E, 1888 E
O'Brien, T. A. 1973 A
Observatories,
  ACT, 1910 B, 1911 B, 1926 B
  NSW, 1788 B, 1820 A, 1822 B, 1847 B, 1857 B, 1870 B, 1874 B, 1965 B
  Qld, 1829 C, 1846 B,
  SA, 1874 B
  Tas, 1840 B
  Vic, 1853 B, 1856 B, 1863 B
  WA, 1896 B
Observatory Hill, Sydney, 1795 B, 1815 B
Observer, 1958 F
Ocean Digger, 1967 B
Ocean Grove, Vic, 1887 F
Oceanic Publishing Co., 1888 C
O'Collins, James, 1930 D
O'Connell, George M. 1926 E
O'Connell, Maurice C. P. 1846 A, 1848 A
O'Connell, Maurice C. 1812 A, 1868 A, 1871 A, 1874 A, 1877 A
O'Connell, Michael, 1920 C
O'Conner, Charles, 1891 B
O'Connor, Ailsa, 1921 C
O'Connor, Charles Y. 1843 B, 1903 B
O'Connor, Kathleen, 1886 C
O'Connor, Richard E. 1851 A, 1903 A
O'Connor, R. J. 1982 A
O'Connor, Victor G. 1918 C
Octagon Church, WA, 1835 D
Oddie, James, 1824 C
O'Donaghue, Lois, 1984 F
O'Donnell, Phyllis, 1945 E, 1963 E
O'Dowd, Bernard P. 1866 C
O'Duffy, Denis, 1957 F
Oenpelli, NT, 1925 D
O'Farrell, Henry J. 1868 A
Off-course betting, WA, 1954 F
Office of Aboriginal Affairs, 1967 A
Office of National Assessments, ONA, 1977 A, 1980 A
Officer, Adrian, 1928 C
Officer, Charles M. 1827 A
Officer, Edward C. 1871 C
Officer, Frank K. 1937 A
Officer, Keith, 1889 A
Officer, Robert, 1800 B, 1860 B
Officer, Suetonius H. 1830 A
Official History of Australia in the War 1914–1918, 1921 C
O'Flynn, Jeremiah, 1817 D, 1818 D
Ogburn, John, 1925 C
Ogilvie, Albert G. 1891 A, 1934 A
Ogilvie, George, 1931 C
Ogilvie, William H. 1869 C
O'Grady, James, 1866 A, 1924 A
O'Grady, John, 1907 C, 1957 C, 1966 C
O'Hagan, John F. 1898 C, 1922 C
O'Halloran, Thomas S. 1797 A, 1840 A
O'Hara, John B. 1862 C
O'Harawood, Patrick, 1891 E
O'Harris, Pixie, 1903 C
O'Hea, Timothy, 1846 A
O'Hearne, John, 1811 B
Ohlfsen, Dora, 1867 C
Oil,
  NSW, 1866 B, 1905 B, 1964 B
  Qld, 1961 B, 1964 B
  SA, 1881 B, 1892 B, 1978 B, 1979 B, 1980 B
  Vic, 1924 B, 1964 B, 1969 B, 1970 B
  WA, 1919 B, 1953 B, 1964 B, 1966 B, 1980 B, 1982 B, 1983 B

Oil, off shore legislation, 1967 A
Oil, sea elephant, 1805 A
Oil companies, 1895 B, *see individual entries*
Oil exploration, banned, 1979 F
Oil pollution, 1968 B
Oil refineries, 1952 B, 1955 B, 1964 B, 1965 B
Oil workers strike, 1972 A
O'Keefe, John, 1796 C
O'Keefe, John M. 1935 C, 1956 C, 1958 C
O'Keefe, Kerry, 1949 E
Old age pensions, 1901 A, 1908 A
Old Colonial Architecture in NSW and Tasmania, 1924 C
'Old Commodore', 1834 B
Old Farm, WA, 1834 C
Old lags, 1826 A
Old Mill, Brisbane, 1829 C
Old Rowley, 1940 E
Old Tales of a New Country, 1871 C
Old Tote Theatre Co., 1963 C
Oldfield, Alan, 1945 C
Oldfield, William A. S. 1894 E
O'Leary, Shawn H. 1916 C
Oline Keese, *see* Leakey, Caroline Woolmer
Oliphant, Ernest, H. C. 1862 D
Oliphant, Marcus L. E. ('Mark'), 1901 B, 1943 B, 1971 A
Olive oil, 1851 A
Oliver, Keith, (b. 1907), 1907 E
Oliver, Keith, (b. 1946), 1946 E
Oliver, Nelson, 1885 C
Olives, SA, 1836 A
Olley, Margaret H. 1923 C
O'Loghlen, Bryan, 1828 A, 1881 A
O'Loughlin, Geoff, 1923 C
Olsen, John, 1928 C, 1955 C, 1956 C, 1957 C
Olszanski, George, 1919 C
Olympic Australis, 1956 F
Olympic Consolidated Industries Ltd, 1933 A
Olympic Games,
  Athens, 1896 E
  Amsterdam, 1928 E
  Antwerp, 1920 E
  Berlin, 1936 E
  Helsinki, 1952 E
  London, 1908 E, 1948 E
  Los Angeles, 1932 E, 1984 E
  Melbourne, 1956 E
  Mexico City, 1968 E
  Montreal, 1976 E
  Moscow, 1979 F, 1980 A, E
  Munich, 1972 E
  Paris, 1900 E, 1924 E
  Rome, 1960 E
  St Louis, USA, 1904 E
  Stockholm, 1912 E
  Tokyo, 1964 E
Olympic Theatre, Melbourne, 1855 C
Olympic Theatre, Sydney, 1842 C
Olympic Tyre and Rubber Co. Ltd, 1933 A
O'Malley, King, 1858 A, 1919 A
Ombudsmen, 1971 A, 1976 A
Omega Navigation Station, Vic, 1982 B
Omeo, Vic, 1835 F
On Our Selection, 1899 C, 1912 C, 1920 C, 1931 C, 1932 C
On The Beach, 1957 C, 1959 C
On the Track, 1900 C
On the Wooltrack, 1910 C
One Big Union, 1919 A
The One Day of the Year, 1960 C

One Extra Dance Theatre, Sydney, 1976 C
One Hundred and Fifty Years of Aust. Art Exhibition, Sydney, 1938 C
One Hundred Poems, 1944 C
'One legged dancer' (stamp), 1854 F, 1871 C
O'Neil, James, 1861 B
O'Neill, Christian, 1958 E
O'Neill, Eugene P. 1876 A, 1919 A
O'Neill, Norman, 1937 E
O'Neill, Pam, 1954 E, 1979 E
'One-penny black' (stamp), 1854 F
Onians, Edith C. 1866 A
Onkaparinga, SA, 1876 F
Onslow, Alexander C. 1842 A, 1895 A, 1900 A
Onslow, Arthur A. W. 1833 A
Onslow, Arthur E. 1804 A
Onslow, WA, 1883 F, 1934 F, 1975 F
Oodnadatta, SA, 1890 F, 1891 B
Ooldea, SA, 1919 F
Oom, Karl E. 1904 B
Op-art Exhibition, Melbourne, 1965 C
Opals,
  NSW, 1880 B, 1884 B, 1887 B, 1902 B, 1918 F
  Qld, 1872 B, 1972 F
  SA, 1849 B, 1911 B, 1930 B, 1956 F, 1969 F, 1975 F
Open-cut coal mining, 1937 B
Open-line radio programmes, 1967 F
Opera, 1870 C, *see individual entries*
Opera House, Melbourne, 1901 C
Opera School, NSW, 1925 C
Operating theatres, 1894 B
Operetta, 1880 C
Ophir district, NSW, 1851 B
Opium, 1906 B
Opperman, Hubert, 1904 E
Optical telescope, NSW, 1974 B
opuntia stricta, 1839 B
Orange, NSW, 1829 F
Orange Agricultural College, NSW, 1973 D
Orange Banjo Paterson Art competition, NSW, 1961 C
Orange Lodge, Melbourne, 1845 F
Orange trees, 1788 A
Orangemen, 1875 D
Orban, Desiderius, 1884 C, 1939 C
Orban Art School, Sydney, 1941 C
Orbital engine, Perth, 1970 B, 1971 B
Orbost, Vic, 1885 F
Orcades Travelling Art Exhibition, 1956 C
Orchard, Arundel, 1905 C, 1923 C
Orchard, William A. 1867 C
Orchards, citrus, 1800 A
Orchestras, ABC, 1936 C, *see also individual entries*
Orchestras, Federick Cowan, 1888 C
Ord, Harry St G. 1877 A, 1878 A
Ord R., WA, 1879 A, 1885 A, B, 1945 B
Ord R. Irrigation project, WA, 1963 B, 1967 B, 1972 B
Ordell, Tal, 1927 C
Order of Aust., award, 1975 F
Order of the Star in the East, 1911 D, 1924 D
O'Reilly, Alfonso B. 1903 C
O'Reilly, Dowell P. 1865 C
O'Reilly, John B. 1844 C
O'Reilly, William J. 1905 E
Organ, 1825 C
Organ, Sydney Opera House, 1969 C
Organ, Sydney Town Hall, 1890 C
Organization for Economic Co-operation and Development, OECD, 1971 A

Organized crime, 1982 A
Organophosphate diazinon, 1958 B
Orient Steam Navigation Co., 1877 B
Orienteering, 1969 E, 1971 E, 1972 E
Orienteering Federation of Aust, 1970 E
Original Contribution to the Practice of Conservative Surgery, 1859 C
'Orion', Horne, *see* Horne, R. H.
Ormandy, Eugene, 1944 C
Ormiston, Qld, 1864 A
Ormiston House, Brisbane, 1854 C
Ormond, Francis, 1829 A, 1887 C
Ormond, Galfry, G. 1907 A
Ormsby, Lyster, 1906 E
Ornithology, 1808 B, 1899 B, 1901 B
Orphan School, Parramatta, 1818 D
Orphan School, Sydney, 1819 D
Orphanages, 1828 D, 1834 D
Orphans, female, NSW, 1818 D
Orphans, Sydney, 1819 D
Orpheus, 1863 F
Orr, John, 1841 A
Orr, Sydney S. 1954 D, 1956 D
Orroral Valley, ACT, 1964 B
Orton, Arthur, 1834 F, 1871 A
Orton, Joseph R. 1795 D, 1836 D
Osborn, Francis E. 1912 A
Osborn, Mary E. 1877 C
Osborne, Arthur W. 1891 C
Osborne, Charles T. 1927 C
Osborne, Fanny, 1873 C
Osborne, William A. 1873 B
Osborne Art Gallery, Adelaide, 1963 C
Osburn, Lucy, 1835 B, 1868 B
O'Shanassy, John, 1818 A, 1857 A, 1858 A, 1861 A
O'Shane, Pat, 1978 D, 1981 A
O'Shea, Clarrie, 1969 A
O'Sherwood, John, 1907 E
Oslo school lunch trials, 1940 D
Ostoja-Kotkowski, Joseph S. 1922 C, 1963 C
Ostrich feathers, 1918 F
Ostriches, 1873 F, 1875 A
O'Sullivan, Edward W. 1846 A
O'Sullivan, E. 1921 E
O'Sullivan, Jack, 1916 E, 1933 E
otis principle, 1881 B
Ottawa, Canada, 1932 A
Ottawa Agreement, 1956 A
Our Friends the Hayseeds, 1917 C
Our Jack, 1921 F
Our Miss Gibbs, 1910 C
Our New Selection, 1903 C
Our Own Authors and their Predictions, 1885 C
Our Social Triumphs, 1898 C
Outback Marriage, An, 1906 C
Outbreak of Love, 1957 C
Outdoor sculpture exhibition, Sydney, 1951 C
Outward Bound, 1901 A
Outward Bound Memorial Foundation, 1956 F
Ouyen, Vic, 1904 F
Ovens, John, 1788 B, 1823 A
Ovens district, Vic, 1854 A
Ovens R., Vic, 1844 B
Over the Sliprails, 1900 C
Overall, John W. 1913 C
Overdraft system, 1834 A
Overland, 1954 C
Overland driving, 1912 B
Overland routes, 1818 A, 1831 A
Overland telegraph, Adelaide–Port Darwin, 1870 B, 1872 B
Overlanders, The, 1946 C
Overlanding cattle, 1837 A, 1838 A, 1840 A, 1864 A, 1872 A, 1884 A

805

Overseas money, 1906 A
Overseas Shipping Representatives' Association, Sydney, 1913 A
Overseas Students, 1983 D
Overseas Telecommunications Commission, 1946 A
Owen, Evelyn E. 1915 B, 1939 B, 1941 B
Owen, Gladys M. 1889 C
Owen, Harold C. 1901 B
Owen, Langer M. L. 1862 A
Owen, William, 1834 A
Owen, William F. L. 1899 A, 1961 A
Owen machine gun, 1939 B, 1941 B
Oxford History of Australian Literature, The, 1981 C
Oxley, John J. W. M. 1804 A, 1812 A, 1817 A, 1818 A, 1823 A, 1828 A
Oysters, 1870 A, 1947 A
Oz, 1963 F

P

P. & O. Shipping, 1961 B
Pacemaker, 1963 B
Pacha, 1970 E
Pacific Is, Aust. mandate, 1920 A
Pacific Island Labourers Act, Cwlth, 1901 A
Pacific Islanders Protection Act, 1872 A
Pacific oysters, 1947 A
Pacific Steamer service, 1866 F
Pacific submarine telegraphic cable, 1902 B
Pacific Territories, Aust. mandate, 1919 A
'Pacification', 1860 A
Packer, D. Frank H. 1906 A
Packer, Kerry, 1977 E
Packham, C. H. 1896 B
Packham Triumph pears, 1896 B
Padded look, fashions, 1935 F
Paddle Steamers, 1853 B
Paderewski, Jan. 1904 C
Paganini of Australia, *see* Wallace, W. V.
Page, Earle C. G. 1880 A, 1919 A, 1939 A, 1955 D
Pageant of the Popes, 1942 C
Pails, Dinny, 1921 E
Painters workers groups, 1840 A
Painting, *see section* C
  see also Art periods *and individual entries*
Pakenham, Vic, 1852 F
Palace Theatre, Sydney, 1896 C
Palaeontology, NSW, 1887 B
Palestine, 1916 A, 1918 A, 1940 C
Paling, William H. 1825 C
Palm I., Qld, 1918 A
Palm Valley, NT, 1965 B, 1970 B
Palmer, Ambrose, 1911 E
Palmer, Arthur H. 1819 A, 1870 A, 1883 A, 1888 A, 1895 A
Palmer, Eileen, 1906 C
Palmer, Janet G. ('Nettie'), 1885 C, 1921 C
Palmer, John, 1833 A
Palmer, Thomas F. 1802 D
Palmer, E. Vance, 1885 C, 1915 C, 1922 C, 1924 C, 1930 C, 1932 C, 1934 C, 1954 C
Palmer R., Qld, 1873 A, B
Palmerston, Christie, 1850 A
Palmerston, NT, 1869 A, F, 1897 F, 1911 A
Palubinskas, Eddie, 1972 E
Pan-Continental mining Co., 1982 A

Panama Pacific Exhibition, USA, 1914 C
Pandora, HMS, 1791 F
Pandora's Pass, 1823 A
Pantomimes, Sydney, 1890 C
Panton, J. A. 1853 C
Pants, 1926 F
Paper, 1820 F, 1922 B, 1929 B, 1938 B
Papermills, 1818 A
Papua, 1887 A, 1888 A, 1901 A, 1906 A, 1908 A, 1942 A, 1949 A
Papua, union with New Guinea, 1949 A
Papua Act, 1905 A, 1906 A
Papua New Guinea, PNG, 1945 A, 1946 A, 1951 A, 1953 A, 1960 A, 1963 A, 1964 A, 1971 A, 1973 A, 1975 A
Paraburdoo, WA, 1970 F
Parachuting, 1888 E, 1958 E, 1968 E, 1969 A, 1972 E
Paraguay, South America, 1893 A
Paramor, Wendy, 1938 C
Pardons, 1817 F
Parent and Citizen Association, NSW, 1906 F
Parer, Damien, 1912 C, 1940 C, 1943 C
Parer, Raymond J. P. 1894 B, 1920 B
Paringa, 1936 F
Paris Olympics, 1900 E, 1924 E
Parisian, The, 1911 E
Park, Ruth, 1919 C, 1948 C
Parker, Charles, 1859 C
Parker, Harold, 1873 C
Parker, Henry W. 1808 A, 1856 A
Parker, Langloh, *see* Stow, Catherine S.
Parker, Leslie, *see* Thirkell, A.
Parker, Stephen H. 1846 A, 1878 A
Parkes, NSW, 1862 F, 1959 B, 1961 B, 1969 B
Parkes, Henry, 1815 A, 1838 A, 1850 F, 1861 A, 1862 A, 1866 D, 1872 A, 1874 A, 1877 A, 1878 A, 1880 A, 1887 A, 1881 A, 1889 A, 1890 A, 1891 A
Parkes radio telescope, 1969 B
Parkin-Wesley Theological College, Adelaide, 1969 D
Parking meters, 1955 F, 1956 F
Parkinson, Roy P. 1901 C
Parks, Ti, 1939 C
Parlt, *abbreviation for* Parliament, Debates, 1925 F, 1946 A
  Federal, 1881 A, 1901 A, 1903 A, 1930 A, 1974 A
  Female representation,
  –Federal, 1902 A, 1943 A, 1946 A, 1960 F
  –NSW, 1894 A, 1902 A, 1925 A, 1931 A
  –Qld, 1894 A, 1905 A, 1929 A
  –SA, 1894 A
  –Tas, 1894 A, 1903 A, 1922 A, 1948 A, 1955 A
  –Vic, 1894 A, 1908 A, 1933 A
  –WA, 1894 A, 1921 A, 1925 A, 1936 A, 1951 A
  First meetings,
  –Federal, 1901 A
  –State, 1856 A, 1857 A
  Houses of, Adelaide, 1889 C
  –Brisbane, 1979 C
  –Canberra, 1923 A, C, 1927 A, 1978 A, 1978 E, 1980 C
  –Melbourne, 1856 C, 1860 A
  Labor representation, 1889 A
  Library, Federal, 1961 D
  Payment of Members,
  –Federal, 1907 A
  –NSW, 1889 A
  –Qld, 1886 A
  –SA, 1887 A

  –Tas, 1890 A
  –Vic, 1870 A, 1880 A
  –WA, 1900 A
  Privilege, 1955 A
  Proceedings broadcasted, 1946 A
  Property qualifications,
  –NSW, 1858 A
  –Tas, 1900 A
  –SA, 1856 A
  –Vic, 1857 A, 1859 A
  –WA, 1893 A
  Sittings, Federal,
    1st 1901 A 2nd 1904 A 3rd 1907 A
    4th 1910 A 5th 1913 A 6th 1914 A
    7th 1917 A 8th 1920 A 9th 1923 A
    10th 1926 A 11th 1929 A 12th 1929 A
    13th 1932 A 14th 1934 A 15th 1937 A
    16th 1940 A 17th 1943 A 18th 1946 A
    19th 1950 A 20th 1951 A 21st 1954 A
    22nd 1956 A 23rd 1959 A 24th 1962 A
    25th 1964 A 26th 1967 A 27th 1969 A
    28th 1973 A 29th 1974 A 30th 1976 A
    31st 1978 A 32nd 1980 A 33rd 1983 A
  Triennial,
  –NSW, 1874 A
  –Qld, 1890 A
  –SA, 1856 A
  –Tas, 1891 A
  –Vic, 1859 A
  –WA, 1900 A
Parnell, D. 1804 D
Parr, Lenton, 1924 C
Parr, Robert, 1923 C
Parramatta (destroyer), 1910 A
Parramatta, NSW, 1788 A, F, 1790 A, 1791 A, 1794 B, 1798 A, 1810 B, 1813 A, 1814 B, 1818 B, 1820 C, 1822 B, 1831 E, 1850 B, 1880 E, 1885 B, 1911 B
Parramatta Art Prize, NSW, 1965 C
Parramatta jail, NSW, 1801 A
Parramatta Marist High School, 1821 D
Parramatta Observatory, 1821 C, 1847 B
Parramatta Rugby League Football Club/team, 1946 E, 1977 E, 1981 E, 1982 E, 1983 E
Parry, Bruce, 1977 E
Parry, William E. 1790 A, 1829 A
Parsons, Frank, 1923 E
Parsons, J. L. 1884 A
Parsons, Marea, 1945 E
Participation and Equity Programme, 1984 D
Partos, Paul, 1943 C
Partridge, Eric H. 1894 C
Partridge, Frank J. 1924 F
Pasadena Bungalow, 1911 C
Pascoe, Len, 1950 E
Paspalum grass, Vic, 1881 B
Passage, The, 1930 C
Passchendaele, France, 1918 A
Passenger boat services, NSW, 1813 F
Passenger flight, first, 1911 B
Passing of the Aborigines, The, 1938 C
Passmore, John R. 1904 C, 1956 C
Passmore, John, 1957 C
Pasta, Emila, 1876 C
Pasteurization, milk, 1889 B, 1949 B
Pastoral Association of NSW, 1844 A
Pastoral expansion, NSW, 1820 A
'Pastoral Hotel', Melbourne, 1846 F
Pastoral production, 1944 B
Pastoral Society of 'Australia Felix', 1844 A
Pastoralists Federal Council, 1891 A
Pastures of the Blue Crane, 1964 C
Patch School of Drama and Dance, Perth, 1938 C
Patching, Julius (Judy), 1917 E

Pate, Michael, 1920 C
Paternity leave, Cwlth, 1973 A
Paterson, Andrew B. ('Banjo'), 1864 C, 1889 C, 1890 C, 1895 C, 1906 C, 1917 C, 1936 C
Paterson, Elizabeth D. 1894 C
Paterson, Esther, 1892 C
Paterson, John F. 1851 C
Paterson, William, 1794 A, 1801 A, 1804 A, 1809 A, 1810 A
Paterson's curse, SA, 1906 B
Pathfinder, 1971 E
Pathfinder Force, 1942 A
Paton, George, 1819 A
Paton, John G. 1824 D
Patrick, Vic, 1920 E
Patrick Thomas singers, Brisbane, 1958 C
Patrick White, 1962 C
Patridge, Frank J. 1924 F
'Patriotic Six', political crisis, Tas, 1845 A, 1847 A
Patrobus, 1915 E
Patron, 1894 E
Patterson, Ambrose M. 1877 C
Patterson, Gerald L. 1895 E
Patterson, James B. 1833 A, 1893 A
Patterson, Sidney P. 1927 E, 1949 E
Paul, Emily L. 1866 C
Paul, E. 'Queenie', 1901 C
Paul, Tibor, 1971 C
Pavarotti, Luciano, 1983 C
Pavey, Percy, 1902 E, 1948 E
Pavlova, 1935 F
Pavlova, Anna R. 1926 C, 1929 C, 1935 F
Pawsey, Joseph L. 1945 B
'Payment by Results' system, 1864 D
Payment of Members Bill, Vic, 1878 A
Payne, G. D. 1910 C
Payne, John, 1940 C
Payne, Professor, 1918 B
Pea Pickers, The, 1942 C
Peace Keeping Force, Middle East, 1981 A, 1982 A
Peace Movement, 1888 F
Peace Officer Guard, 1925 F, 1960 A
'Peace Studies', 1983 D
Peace through Prayer Art contest, Qld, 1966 C
Peacock, Alexander J. 1861 A, 1901 A, 1914 A, 1924 A
Peacock, Andrew S. 1939 A, 1965 A, 1981 A, 1982 A, 1983 A, 1984 A
Peacock, George, 1861 F
Peacock, George E. 1837 C
Peacock, Millie, 1933 A
Peak Downs, Qld, 1852 A, 1861 B, 1882 A
Peak Hill, NSW, 1889 F
Peak Hill, WA, 1874 A
Peake, Archibald H. 1859 A, 1909 A, 1912 A, 1917 A
Peanut Marketing Board, 1924 A
Pearce, Alexander, 1822 F
Pearce, Bob, 1904 E
Pearce, George F. 1870 A, 1922 A
Pearce, Henry John, 1851 E, 1938 A
Pearce, WA, 1964 B
Pearl, The, 1871 E
Pearl, 1896 F
Pearl, B. A. 1945 B
Pearl, Cyril, 1958 C
Pearl Fisheries Act, 1953 A
Pearl Harbour, Hawaii, 1941 A
Pearl shell, 1850 B, 1862 A, 1868 A
Pearling, 1861 A, 1875 F, 1887 F, 1903 A, 1908 F
Pearling disputes, with Japan, 1953 A

Pearls, 1883 F, 1884 B, 1917 F, 1956 A, 1957 A
Pearls and Savages (film), 1921 C
Pears, NSW, 1896 B
Pearse, Mark, 1941 C
Pearson, Charles H. 1830 D, 1878 A
Peart, Donald, 1909 C, 1950 C, 1956 C, 1963 C
Peascod, William, 1920 C
Peat, George, 1844 F
Peat's Ferry, NSW, 1887 F
Pecan nut, NSW, 1968 A
Pechell, Charles, 1810 C
Peck, John M. 1830 B, 1853 B
Pedal wireless, 1926 B, 1929 B
Pedder, John L. 1793 A, 1824 A
Peden, B. 1937 E
Peden, John B. 1871 A
Peden, Margaret E. M. 1905 E
Pedersen, Ella L. 1921 C
Pedestrian sport, 1810 E, 1842 E
Pedley, Ethel, 1899 C
Pedvin, Albert A. 1874 C
Peel, Clifford, 1917 B
Peel, Thomas, 1793 A, 1829 A
Peel R., NSW, 1818 A, 1853 A
Peel River Land and Mineral Co. Ltd, 1853 A
Pekarek, Rudolf, 1950 C, 1955 C
Peko Wallsend Ltd, 1979 A
Pelloe, Emily, H. 1877 C
Pelorus (brig), 1839 F
Pemberton, WA, 1911 F, 1931 A
Pembroke School, Adelaide, 1924 D
Penal settlements, *see* Convicts, settlement
Penalty rates, 1947 A
Penberthy, Albert J. 1917 C, 1947 C
Penberthy, Wesley, 1920 C
Pendlebury, Laurence S. 1914 C
Penfold, Christopher R. 1811 A, 1844 A
Penfold, Mary, 1818 A
Penfolds wineries, 1844 A
Pengelly, Ivor, 1906 C
Penguin, Tas, 1858 F
Penicillin, 1940 B, 1943 B, 1945 B, 1950 B
Penman, D. 1984 D
Pennant Hills, Sydney, 1912 B
Pennefather, Capt, 1880 A
Penny-farthing bicycle, 1891 E
Penny paper, NSW, 1867 F
Penny Post, 1838 F
Penny postage, 1910 F
Penola, SA, 1836 F, 1866 D
Penrith, NSW, 1856 B, 1911 B, 1912 B, 1921 E, 1952 B
Penrith airport, 1911 B
Penshurst, Vic, 1840 F, 1965 F
Pensions, *see individual entries and benefits*
Pentathlon, 1956 E, 1969 E
Pentecostal Assemblies, Melbourne, 1927 D
Penthouse, magazine, 1979 F
Penton, Brian C. 1904 C, 1934 C, 1936 C
Pentridge jail, Melbourne, 1967 F, 1983 F
People's Convention, NSW, 1896 C
People's Daily, Melbourne, 1903 F
People's Republic of China, 1971 A, 1973 A, 1976 A
Peponis, George, 1954 E
Peppin, George H. 1800 A, 1880 A
Peppin sheep, 1858 B, 1880 A
Perceval, John, 1923 C, 1959 C
Percival, Edgar W. 1897 B, 1935 B
Percival, N. 1931 E
Percussion drill, 1889 B
Perdon, George, 1973 E, 1978 E
Pergolas, 1952 C

Periodicals, *see individual entries*
Periscope rifle, 1915 B
Perkins, Charles N. 1936 A, 1964 D, 1980 A
Perkins, Horace J. 1901 C
Perkins, Neville, 1977 A
Peron, Francois, 1810 A
Perpetual Executors and Trustees Association of Aust. Ltd, 1884 A
Perpetual leases, Sydney, 1827 C
Perrie, O. C. 1950 C
Perry, Adelaide, 1891 C
Perry, Charles, 1807 D, 1847 D, 1854 D
Perry, Joseph H. 1897 C, 1910 C
Perryman, Jill, 1933 C
Persia, 1889 A
Persimmon Tree, The, 1943 C
Perth, (1), HMAS, 1938 A
Perth, (2), HMAS, 1966 A, 1967 A
Perth, Tas, 1836 F
Perth, WA, 1829 A, F, 1830 A, 1869 B, 1870 A, 1874 A, 1876 A, 1877 B, 1880 A, 1881 B, F, 1885 F, 1896 B, 1897 B, 1898 B, D, 1899 A, B, 1904 C, 1910 B, 1911 B, 1912 B, 1916 B, 1920 B, 1923 B, 1928 B, 1935 F, 1942 F, 1947 B, 1956 C, 1958 B, 1961 B, 1965 B, 1971 B, 1974 E, 1976 E
Perth airport, 1944 B
Perth Art Gallery, 1908 C
Perth Centenary Art Prize, 1930 C
Perth City Ballet, 1961 C
Perth Colonial Boys' School, 1847 D
Perth Concert Hall, 1972 C
Perth Festival, 1953 F
Perth Festival Invitation Art Prize, 1965 C
Perth Gazette and Western Australian Journal, 1833 F
Perth Golf Club, 1895 E
Perth High School, 1878 D
Perth Hospital, 1929 A
Perth Hotel, 1830 C
Perth Modern School, 1910 D
Perth Modern Teacher Training School, 1911 D
Perth Observatory, 1896 B
Perth Prize for Contemporary Painting, 1954 C
Perth Prize for Drawing, 1965 C
Perth Repertory Club, 1919 C
Perth School of Art, 1920 C
Perth Society of Artists, 1932 C, 1936 C
Perth Stock Exchange, 1889 A
Perth Technical College, 1900 D
Perth Technical School, 1900 D
Perth University Art Club, 1928 C
Peschoff Russian dancers, 1904 C
Peter Pan, 1932 E, 1934 E
Peter Sculthorpe, 1982 C
Peter Wayback Visits the Melbourne Cup, (Comicstrip), 1904 F
Peterborough, SA, 1880 F
Petermann Ranges, SA, 1897 B
Peters, F. A. B., 1929 F
Peterson, Mike, 1954 E
Petherick, Edward A. 1847 D, 1887 D
Petit, 1800 C
Petre, H. A. 1912 B, 1914 B
Petrel, NT, 1969 B
Petrie, Andrew, 1798 A, 1862 A
Petrie, John, 1859 A
Petrie, Thomas, 1831 A
Petrochemical industry, 1857 B, 1961 B
Petrol, lead-free, 1980 B
Petrol engine, 1920 B
Petrol pumps, 1920 F, 1951 B
Petrol rationing, wartime, 1940 A, 1941 F, 1950 A

807

Petroleum, legislation, 1968 A
Petroleum Refineries (Aust.) Pty Ltd, 1963 B
Petrov Affair, 1954 A
Petrov, Vladimir M. 1954 A
Petrov Commission, 1955 A
Petticoats, stiff, 1957 F
Petty, Bruce L. 1929 C
Pfalz, 1914 A
Phantom Stockman, The, 1953 C
Phar Lap, 1930 E, 1931 E, 1932 E
Phar Lap (film), 1983 C
Pharmaceutical organizations, first, 1857 B
Pharmaceutical shop, Sydney, 1820 B
Pharmaceutical Society of Vic, 1857 B
Pharmacy Acts, 1857 B
Pharmacy Guild of Aust., 1927 B
Pharmacy and Poisons Act, Tas, 1837 B
Phelan medal, 1926 E
Phelps, Rod, 1934 E
Philadelphia, 1792 B
Philatelics, 1879 F, 1885 F, *see also* Stamps
Philatelic Society, Sydney, 1885 F
Philharmonic Society, first, 1833 C, *see also individual entries*
Philip, Prince, Duke of Edinburgh, 1967 A, 1968 A, 1971 A, 1973 A, 1981 A, 1982 A
Philip, Prince, of Saxe-Coburg, 1872 A
Philips, O. 1936 E
Philipson, Joan M. 1912 C
Phillip, Arthur, 1788 A, F, 1789 A, 1790 A, 1792 A, 1814 A, 1897 F
Philip I., Vic, 1928 E
Phillip I. Bridge, Vic, 1969 B
Phillip Street Theatre, Sydney, 1954 C
Phillipini, Rosalie, 1893 C
Phillips, A. A. 1954 C
Phillips, Frank, 1932 E
Phillips, Gilbert E. 1905 B
Phillips, James G. 1915 C
Phillips, Marion, 1881 A
Phillips, M. 1881 C
Phillips, Nat ('Stiffy'), 1883 C, 1914 C
Phillips-Moore, Barry, 1937 E
Phillis, D. K. (Fred), 1949 E
Phillis, Tom, 1955 E
Philosophical Institute of Vic, 1854 B, 1859 B
Philosophical Society of Australasia, 1821 B
Philosophical Society of NSW, 1822 F, 1855 B, 1856 B, 1866 B
Philosophical Society of Qld, 1859 B
Philosophical Society of Vic, 1854 B
Philp, Robert, 1851 A, 1883 A, 1899 A, 1907 A
Philpot, Ernest S. 1906 C
Phipps, George A. C. 1871 A, 1879 A
Phoenix Foundry Co., Vic, 1883 B
Phonographs, 1885 B, 1899 F
Phosphate, 1962 B, 1966 B
Photo finish, 1945 B, E
Photoconductivity, 1907 B
Photographic Society, Sydney, 1855 B
Photographic studios, 1848 B, 1862 B
Photography,
    aerial, 1904 B
    colour, 1907 B
    dry plates, 1880 B
    first, 1841 F, 1859 B
    'magic eye', 1945 B
    wartime, 1917 F
Photography Exhibition, Sydney, 1858 B
Phuoc Tuy, Vietnam, 1969 A
Phylloxera insect, 1877 B
Physiography, SA, 1858 A
Piano, 1790 C, 1879 C, 1893 C

Piastre, 1912 E
Piccolo, 1976 E
Pick, John, 1866 C
Pick-a-Box, 1957 F, 1970 F
Pickering, Larry, 1942 C
Pickitt, 1845 B
Pickworth, Horace H. A. O. 1917 E
Picnic at Hanging Rock (film), 1975 C
Picnic Party at Hanging Rock near Mount Macedon, 1875 C
Picot, James, 1906 C
Picton, NSW, 1845 F, 1863 C
Picture Gallery, Melbourne, 1875 C
Picture Show Man, The, 1977 C
Picture theatres, 1955 C
Picturegram services, 1929 B
Picturesque Atlas of Australia, 1883 C
Piddington, Albert B. 1862 A, 1913 A
Pidgeon, William E. ('Wep'), 1909 C, 1958 C, 1961 C, 1968 C
Pidgin English, PNG, 1953 A
Piercy, Jane, 1869 F
Piesley, Wilfred J. 1916 C
Pigeon, 1897 A
Pigeon racing, 1900 E
Pigeon shooting, 1831 E
Piggott, P. 1874 E, 1877 E
Pig iron, 1860 B, 1938 A
Pig Iron Bob, 1938 A
Pigs, 1820 A
Piguenit, Charles, 1902 C
Pigeunit, William C. 1836 C
Pike, Bob, 1962 E
Pike, Douglas H. 1908 C
Pike, Jimmy E. 1892 E, 1930 E
Pilbara, WA, 1961 B, 1962 A, B, 1963 B
Pilbara region, WA, 1946 A, 1958 B, 1980 F
Pill, contraceptive, 1961 F
Pilots, marine, 1792 B, 1811 A
Pilots, women, Ansett, 1980 B
Pilots' licences, 1911 B, 1935 F
Pilots' strikes, 1958 A, 1966 A
Pine Creek, NT, 1871 C, 1872 A, B
Pine Gap, Alice Springs, 1967 B, 1983 F
Pines, 1857 B, 1876 A
Pingelly, WA, 1889 F
Pinjarra, WA, 1834 A, 1857 F, 1912 D
Pink pages, 1975 F
Pinkewich, Paul, 1951 E
Pinnaroo, SA, 1905 F
Pioneer car, 1894 B
Pioneer Players, Melbourne, 1922 C
Pioneers, The, (book), 1915 C
Piper, John, 1851 A
Pipes, concrete, 1910 B
Pipes, metal, 1923 B
Piping Lane, 1972 E
Pirates of Penzance, 1984 C
Pisé building, 1820 C
Pistol shooting, 1947 E, 1949 E, 1958 E, 1966 E, 1970 E
Pitcairn Is, 1856 A
Pitchblende, NT, 1955 B
Pitjantjatjara Aboriginals, 1978 A, 1979 A, 1981 A
Pitman, Timothy G. 1825 A
Pitt, William, 1887 C, 1888 C
Pitt Town, NSW, 1810 F
Pittsworth, Qld, 1854 F
Pix, Keith, 1918 E
Pizza, 1961 F
Pizza Hut, 1971 F
Pizzey, Jack C. A. 1911 A, 1968 A
P. J. Adams, 1962 B
Place at Whitton, The, 1964 C
Plague, 1900 F, 1909 A, 1921 F
Plant, Harry, 1894 E
Plant oils, 1897 B

Plante, Ada M. 1875 C
Plaster, 1912 E
Plaster of Paris, SA, 1910 C
Plastering, 1863 C
Plasterwork, 1888 C
Plastic industry, 1917 B
Plate, Carl O. 1909 C, 1959 C, 1962 C
Plate-glass windows, 1881 C
Platypus, 1797 F, 1943 B
Platypus HMAS, Sydney, 1967 A
Playbills, 1800 F
Playbox Theatre, Sydney, 1920 C
Playboy magazine, 1979 F
Player, Gary, 1974 E
Playford, E. C. 1926 A
Playford, Thomas (b. 1837), 1837 A, 1887 A, 1890 A
Playford, Thomas (b. 1896), 1896 A, 1938 A, 1965 A
Playhouse, first full-time, 1796 C
Playhouse, Perth, 1956 C
Plays, *see individual entries*
Plays and Fugitive Pieces in Verse, 1842 C
Playwrights' Advisory Board, 1938 C
Plebiscite, 1875 A, 1950 A
'Pledge', 1893 A
plein-air painting, 1885 C
plenary council, 1885 D, 1895 D
Pleuropneumonia, 1858 B, 1933 B
Plimsoll, James, 1917 A, 1982 A
Plough, stump-jump, 1876 B, 1877 B
Plough match, 1828 E
Ploughing, bullocks, 1795 A
Ploughman and other Poems, The, 1935 C
Plumes, 1910 F
Plunkett, John H. 1802 A, 1832 D, 1836 A
Plural voting, 1893 A, 1899 A, 1900 A, 1905 A, 1907 A
Plutonium, Maralinga SA, 1978 B, 1979 B
Pneumatic tyres, 1889 B, 1903 B
Pneumonia, 1918 F, 1919 F
PNG, *see* Papua New Guinea
Pocius, Ieva, 1923 C
Podmore, George, 1819 C
Podmore, G. 1956 E
Poems 1913, 1914 C
Poems and Recollections of the Past, 1840 C
Poems and Songs, 1862 C
Poetry, *see individual entries*
Poetry Annual, 1941 C
Poetry in Australia, 1923 C
Poets Corner, Westminster Abbey, 1934 C
Poet's Home, A, 1862 C
Pogany, Margit, 1880 C
Point Cook, Vic, 1911 A, 1914 A, B, 1928 B, 1947 A
Point Cook Air Base, Vic, 1911 A
Point Cook Aviation School, Vic, 1913 A, 1914 D
Point Danger, NSW, 1852 F, 1970 B
Point Hicks, Vic, 1797 A
Point Lonsdale, Vic, 1905 B
Point Piper, Sydney, 1982 F
Point Puer, Tas, 1835 A
Point Puer Experiment, Tas, 1834 D
Poitrel, 1920 E
Poker machines, NSW, 1956 F
Poladian, Derenik, 1957 D
Polar observation, 1912 B
Polding, John B. 1794 D, 1834 D, 1835 D, 1836 D, 1837 D, 1842 D, 1843 D
Polding College, Sydney, 1980 D
Police,
    ACT, Cwlth, Federal, 1917 A, 1927 A, 1960 A, 1979 A

NSW, 1789 A, 1809 A, 1810 A,
  1811 A, 1825 A, 1833 A, 1847 A,
  1852 A, 1862 A, 1893 F, 1942 F
  Qld, 1848 A, 1868 A
  SA, 1838 A
  Tas, 1830 A, 1899 A
  Vic, 1842 A, 1851 F, 1852 A, 1853 A,
  1923 F, 1969 F, 1982 A
  WA, 1829 A, 1861 A
Police arms, 1893 F
Police Boys' Club, Sydney, 1937 F
Police Corruption, 1983 A
Police radios, 1923 F
Police Regulation Acts, 1862 A, 1899 A
Police strike, Melbourne, 1923 A
Police women, 1915 A
Policy, 1804 A
Policy and Passion, A Novel of Australian Life, 1881 C
Polio, *see* Poliomyelitis
Poliomyelitis, 1937 F, 1941 B, 1951 B, 1955 B
Poliomyelitis clinic, Qld, 1933 B
Political Labor League, Sydney, 1895 A
Political and Social Labour League of Vic, 1859 A
Politics, *see section A and individual entries*
Pollard, Reginald G. 1903 A
Pollice Verso, 1904 C
Pollock, David, 1859 B
Pollock, Jackson, 1973 C
Pollock, John, 1859 B
Pollock, J. C. 1936 E
Pollution, air, 1964 B, 1980 B
Pollution, oil, 1968 B
Pollution control legislation, Vic, 1958 F
Polo, 1875 E, 1899 E, 1925 E, 1937 E, 1972 E, 1977 E
Polo Prince, 1964 E
Polocrosse, 1938 E, 1939 E, 1949 E
Polynesian labour, *see* Kanakas
Polynesian Labourers Act, Qld, 1868 A
Pomeroy, John, 1872 B, 1902 B
Ponsford, William H. 1900 E, 1934 E
Pons's comet, 1822 B
Pontine marshes, Italy, 1869 B
Poo, Sam, 1865 A
Poor Fellow My Country, 1975 C
Poor Soldier, The, 1796 C
Pope Paul VI, 1970 D
Popplewell, Fred, 1887 E
Poppy, 1978 C
Population, *see figures for each year in section F*
Population, Aust. born, 1870 F
Population exodus, 1849 F, 1852 A
Porpoise, 1803 F
Port, Leo, 1922 B, 1968 B
Port Adelaide, 1839 B, 1907 F, 1924 F
Port Adelaide Art Gallery, 1872 C
Port Albany, Qld, 1863 A, 1877 A
Port Arthur, Tas, 1830 A, F, 1833 A, 1834 D, 1877 A
Port Augusta, SA, 1852 B, F, 1858 A, 1912 B
Port Bowen, Qld, 1802 A
Port Broughton, SA, 1871 F
Port Curtis, Qld, 1802 A, 1846 A, 1847 A
Port Darwin, NT, 1839 A, 1869 A, 1919 B
Port Davey, Tas, 1891 B
Port Douglas, Qld, 1876 F
Port-El Lift Control, 1968 B
Port Elliot, SA, 1850 F, 1854 B
Port Essington, NT, 1838 A, 1839 F, 1844 A, 1845 A, 1846 A
Port Fairy, Vic, 1810 F, 1835 F, 1890 C
Port Germein, SA, 1878 F
Port Hacking, NSW, 1796 A, 1867 F

Port Hedland, WA, 1863 F, 1904 B, 1925 F, 1939 F, 1968 F, 1980 F
Port Jackson, Sydney, 1788 A, 1827 E, 1868 F
'Port Jackson Painter', 1788 C
Port Keats, NT, 1935 D
Port Kembla, NSW, 1826 F, 1883 B, 1908 B, 1913 B, 1928 B, 1933 B, 1938 A, 1951 B, 1955 B, 1957 B
Port King, Vic, 1802 A
Port Lincoln, SA, 1834 F, 1962 F
Port MacDonnell, SA, 1860 F
Port Macquarie, NSW, 1821 A, F, 1822 A, 1824 A, D, 1830 A
Port Melbourne, 1854 A
Port Moresby, PNG, 1873 A, 1883 A, 1942 A, 1943 F
Port Phillip Association, 1835 A
Port Phillip Bank, 1843 A
Port Phillip Bay, Vic, 1802 A, 1835 A, 1940 F, 1968 E
Port Phillip district, Vic, 1824 A, 1836 A, 1839 A, 1840 A, 1845 A, 1847 A, 1848 A, 1849 A, 1850 A, 1851 A, 1886 F
Port Phillip Farmers Society, 1848 F
Port Phillip Gazette, 1838 F
Port Phillip Heads, Vic, 1868 F, 1901 B
Port Phillip Herald, 1840 F
Port Phillip Magazine, 1843 F
Port Phillip Medical Association, 1846 B
Port Phillip Native Police, 1842 A
Port Phillip Patriot and Melbourne Advertiser, 1839 F
Port Phillip Savings Bank, 1841 A, 1843 A
Port Phillip settlement, 1836 A
Port Pirie, SA, 1848 F, 1889 B, 1897 B, 1898 F
Port Pirie lead smelter, SA, 1934 B
Port Sorell, Tas, 1834 F
Port Stanvac, SA, 1963 B
Port Stephens, NSW, 1791 B, 1795 A, 1826 F, 1903 F
Port Victoria, NT, 1838 A
Port Wakefield, SA, 1850 F, 1870 B
Portaprinter telephone typewriter service, 1981 B
Porteous, Richard, 1869 B
Porteous, Richard S. 1897 C
Porter, Charles, 1936 E
Porter, Peter, 1929 C
Porter, Peter ('Hal'), 1911 C, 1943 C, 1956 C, 1958 C, 1961 C, 1963 C, 1971 C
Porteus, Stanley D. 1883 B
Portia Geach Memorial Award, 1965 C
Portland, NSW, 1863 F
Portland, Vic, 1834 A, F, 1836 A
Portland Art Society, Vic, 1961 C
Portland Bay, Vic, 1829 A, 1831 A, 1839 F
Portland Cement Co. Pty Ltd, NSW, 1883 B
Portlock, Nathaniel, 1792 A
Portnoy's Complaint, 1971 C
Portrait painting, *see* Visual Arts section C
Portrait of a Lady, 1923 C
Portrait of Philip Adams, 1979 C
Portsea, Vic, 1842 F, 1852 F, 1967 A
Portsea Officer Cadet School, 1951 A
Portus, Garnet V. 1883 D
Porush, Israel, 1907 D
Poseidon, 1906 E
Poseidon NL, 1969 B
Posinatus, 1913 E
Possum, 1887 F
Post, Joseph M. 1906 C, 1936 C
Post bags, padded, 1970 F

Post boxes, iron bell-shaped, 1856 B
Post boxes, Melbourne, 1844 F
Post Gallery Students Society, Melbourne, 1916 C
Post mortems, first, 1788 B
Post Office Savings Bank, WA, 1863 A
Post Offices, 1809 A, 1810 A, 1870 F, *see also* General Post Offices *and individual entries*
Post-war boom, 1945 A
Post-War Construction, Dept of, 1942 A
Postage, 1838 F, 1910 F
Postage stamps, 1849 F, 1850 F, 1852 F, 1853 F, 1854 F, 1855 F, 1856 F, 1860 F, 1861 F, 1888 F, 1891 F, 1902 F, 1913 F, 1927 F, 1929 F, 1953 F
Postal Acts, 1825 A, 1829 A
Postal administration, 1975 A
Postal communications, overseas, 1867 A
Postal notes, Vic, 1885 F
Postal services, *see* Mail services
Postcards, 1875 F
Postcodes, 1967 F
Postle, Arthur B. 1882 E
Postmaster, first, 1809 A, 1812 A, 1829 A, 1837 A, 1859 A
Postmen, 1915 F
Postmistress, first, 1838 F
Potatoes, 1788 A, 1834 A
Potter, Charles V. 1900 B
Potter's Cottage prize, 1965 C
Pottery, 1788 B, 1857 C, 1956 C, *see also individual entries*
Pottinger, Frederick W. 1831 A
Potts, The, 1919 F
Potts, Frank, 1815 A
Potts, Frank W. 1888 C
Pounds, animal, 1797 F, 1811 F
Poverty, 1970 F
Powditch, Peter, 1942 C
Powell, Gordon G. 1911 D, 1956 D
Powell, Ray, 1925 C, 1962 C
Powell, Walter, 1854 F
Powell, William, 1922 D
Power, David, 1929 E
Power, Harry, 1891 A
Power, Harold S. 1878 C
Power, household, Sydney, 1904 B
Power, John J. W. 1881 C, 1962 C
Power, Lawrence, 1963 C
Power boating, 1905 E, 1909 E, 1927 E, 1953 E, 1970 E, 1977 E, 1978 E
Power and the Glory, The, 1941 C
Power Without Glory, 1950 C
Power workers' strike, Qld, 1980 A, Vic, 1977 A
Powers, Charles, 1913 A
Poverty line, 1984 F
Pozières, France, 1916 A
Praed, Mrs Campbell (Rosa C.) 1851 C, 1881 C
Prahran, Melbourne, 1887 F, 1905 B
Prahran College of Advanced Education, Melbourne, 1854 D
Pram Factory, theatre, Melbourne, 1970 C
Pratt, Bob, 1909 E
Pratt, Bruce W. 1977 C
Pratt, Douglas F. 1900 C
Prawning, 1947 A, 1948 A, 1962 A, 1965 A
Prawns, Qld, 1958 B
Pre-fabricated houses, 1853 C, 1909 C, 1947 C
Preference for unionists, 1957 A
Preferential trade, 1906 A, 1908 A
Preferential voting,
  Cwlth, 1918 A, 1919 A

809

NSW, 1926 A
Qld, 1892 A
SA, 1929 A
Vic, 1911 A
Prell, Charles E. 1865 B
Prelude to Christopher, 1934 C
Premier Permanent Building Land and Investment Association, 1890 A
Premiers conferences, 1872 A, 1893 A, 1895 A, 1897 A, 1899 A, 1900 A, 1901 A, 1902 A, 1903 A, 1905 F, 1906 A, 1907 A, 1908 A, 1909 A, 1923 A, 1930 A, 1953 A, 1959 A
Prendergast, George M. 1854 A, 1924 A
Prendiville, Redmond, 1900 D
Prentice, Una G. 1913 A
Presbyterian church,
    Aust. wide, 1974 D, 1977 D
    NSW, 1802 D, 1809 D, 1823 D, 1824 D, 1842 D, 1855 D, 1865 D, 1872 D
    Qld, 1849 D, 1863 D
    SA, 1839 D, 1924 D, 1937 D
    Tas, 1822 D, 1823 D, 1874 D
    Vic, 1837 D, 1838 D, 1861 D, 1864 D, 1924 D
    WA, 1879 D
Presbyterian Church of Australia, 1901 D
Presbyterian Church of NSW, 1865 D
Presbyterian Church of Qld, 1863 D
Presbyterian Ladies' College, Melbourne, 1875 D
Presbyterian Ladies' College, Sydney, 1888 D
Presbyterian schools, Melbourne, 1851 D
Presbyterian settlers, Sydney, 1802 A
Presbytery of NSW, 1832 D
Presbytery of VDL, 1874 D
Prescott, Edward E. 1872 B
Preservation I., Tas, 1797 F
Press, 1975 F
Press, censorship, 1824 F, 1939 A
Press licensing Act, 1828 F
Press, radio, 1921 F
Press, steam, 1853 B
Presto can, 1973 B
Preston, Vic, 1976 D
Preston, E. 1939 E
Preston, Jenico W. J. 1893 A
Preston, Lieut. 1829 A
Preston, Margaret R. 1875 C
Preston, Reginald, 1917 C
Preston, Walter, 1812 C
Preston-Stanley, Millicent, 1925 A
Preston Institute of Technology, Melbourne, 1937 D
Preston Technical School, Melbourne, 1937 D, 1938 D
Price, A. Grenfell, 1892 D
Price, Elliot, 1899 A
Price, E. W. 1876 A
Price, John G. 1808 A, 1857 F
Price, Ray, 1952 E
Price, Raymond E. 1921 C, 1957 C
Price, Thomas, 1852 A, 1885 F, 1905 A
Price controls, wartime, 1939 A
Price Index, 1953 A, 1961 A
Price stabilization scheme, 1943 A
Prices, fixing, 1943 A
Prices Justification Tribunal, 1973 A
Prichard, Katherine S. 1883 C, 1909 C, 1915 C, 1921 C, 1926 C, 1929 C, 1937 C, 1946 C, 1948 C 1950 C, 1963 C
Prickly pear, 1839 B, 1912 B, 1920 B, 1925 B, 1926 B, 1936 B
Prickly Pear Board, 1925 B
Pride of the Fancy, *see* Foley, L. L.
Priest, Margaret, 1922 C

Priestley, Raymond E. 1886 B
Priestly, Kay, 1975 F
Priestly, Susan, 1984 C
Primary production, employees, 1921 A
Prime Ministers, *see government section A and individual entries*
Prime Minister's Dept, 1934 A
Primitive Methodist church, 1840 D
Primogeniture law, 1862 A, 1893 A
Prince Albert Cricket Club, Melbourne, 1840 E
Prince Alfred Hospital, Melbourne, 1869 B, 1882 B, 1926 B
Prince Alfred Methodist College, Adelaide, 1867 D
Prince Edward Theatre, Sydney, 1924 C
Prince Foote, 1909 E
Prince George, Duke of York, 1901 A
Prince Philip Prize, 1970 B, 1975 B
Prince of Wales House, Sydney, 1863 C
Prince of Wales Opera House, Melbourne, 1872 C
Prince of Wales Theatre, Sydney, 1860 F
Princes Bridges, Melbourne, 1846 C, 1850 C
Princess Elizabeth Land, Antarctica, 1957 B
Princess of Tasmania, 1959 B
Princess Theatre, Melbourne, 1854 C, 1886 C, 1887 C, 1902 C
Princess Theatre, Sydney, 1916 C
Princess of Wales Theatre, Sydney, 1855 C
Print Council of Aust., 1966 C
Printers, 1936 A
Printers' Benefit Society, 1844 F
Printing, 1788 B, 1796 B, 1836 B, 1937 C
Printing and Kindred Industries Union, 1966 A
Prior, Sid, 1941 E
'Prior' barley seeds, 1903 B
Prison school, Tas, 1834 D
Prisoners of War, 1942 A, 1944 A
Pritchard, Hazel, 1919 E
Private Gallery A, Melbourne, 1959 C
Privy Council, 1886 A, 1897 A, 1936 A, 1967 A, 1975 A, 1982 A
Prix Assoluto, 1954 C
Prix Georges Sedoul, 1977 C
Prize, The, 1961 C
Pro Musica Society, Sydney, 1950 C
Probate tax, Cwlth, 1914 A
Proctor, Althea M. 1879 C
Prodigal Son, The, 1938 C
Prodromus Entymology ... Insects of NSW, 1805 C
Prodromus Florae Novae ... Van-Diemen, 1810 C
Producers and General Finance Corporation Ltd, 1935 A
Professional Photographers' Association of Aust., 1944 B
Professor James McAuley, 1963 C
Professors, first Aust. born, 1879 D
Profit sharing, 1873 A
Profreeze export boneless beef, 1981 A
Progress Party, 1975 A
Progressive Education Principles, 1950 D
Progressive Political League of Vic, 1891 A
Progressive schools, 1971 A
Prohibition, NSW, 1928 A, WA, 1925 A, 1950 A
Prohibition of Discrimination Act, SA, 1966 A
Project Australia, 1979 F
Prom concerts, Melbourne, 1853 C, Sydney, 1965 C
Proprietary School, WA, 1832 D

Propsting, William B. 1861 A, 1903 A
Proserpine, Qld, 1870 F
Prospector, The, 1971 B
Prosser, Roy, 1941 E
Prostitution, 1983 F
Protection,
    Aboriginals, 1860 A, 1880 A, 1886 A, 1897 A
    consumer, 1835 A, 1964 A
    tariffs, 1840 A, 1865 A, 1867 A, 1887 A, 1906 A
    trade, 1831 A, 1839 A, 1840 A, 1859 A, 1861 A, 1900 A
Protection and Anti-Immigration League, Melbourne, 1861 A
Protectionist party, 1901 A
Protector, 1884 A
Protest marches, Qld, 1977 A
Protestant Alliance Friendly Society, 1859 F
Protestants, Sydney, 1843 D, 1875 D, 1883 D
Proto Star, 1981 B
Proud, Langham, 1931 F
Prout, John S. 1806 C, 1845 C
Prout, Samuel, 1851 C
Provan, Norm, 1932 E
Providence, 1872 F
Provincial and Suburban Bank, Melbourne, 1879 A
Prowse, Russel, 1916 A
Prussia, 1838 A
Psittacosis, 1935 B
Psychology, NSW, 1928 D
Pthisis, 1881 B
Pub With No Beer, The, 1957 C
Puberty Blues, 1981 C
Public art gallery, Melbourne, 1859 C
Public bars, women, 1965 F
Public flogging, 1818 F
Public Health Act, Vic, 1855 B
Public holidays, 1905 F
Public housing, Sydney, 1900 A
Public Instruction Act, NSW, 1880 D
Public Library, Melbourne, 1875 C
Public Library of NSW, 1899 D
Public Library of Qld, 1895 D, 1971 D
Public Library of WA, 1887 D, 1889 D
Public meetings, first, 1799 F
Public railway, first, 1854 B
Public Schools Acts, 1866 D, 1868 D
Public Service, Cwlth, 1901 A, 1957 A, 1976 A
Public Service, Vic, 1853 A
Public Service Act, 1901 A
Public Service Boards, 1883 A
Public transport, smoking on, 1977 F
Publishers, 1852 A
Pugh, Clifton E. 1924 C, 1959 C, 1965 C, 1971 C, 1972 C
Pugh, William, 1847 B
Pulleine, Robert, 1911 C
Pulteney Grammar School, Adelaide, 1848 D
Pumping machinery, 1891 B
Pumps, fire fighting, 1822 F
Punch, Qld, 1878 F
Punch, Sydney, Melbourne, 1856 F
Punters, 1961 E
Purdy, Cecil J. S. 1906 F
Purdy, John, 1955 F
Pure Food Act, Vic, 1905 F
Purtell, Jack, 1921 E, 1947 E, 1953 E, 1954 E
Purves, Anne, 1956 C
Purves, Tom, 1956 C
Purves-Smith, Peter C. R. 1913 C
Pyers, Billy, 1934 E
'Pyjama Girl' mystery, 1944 F

Pyramid Hill, Vic, 1845 F
Python, 1948 F

Q

Q fever, 1898 B, 1937 B
Qantas, 1920 B, 1922 B, 1924 B, 1928 B, 1934 B, 1938 B, 1958 B, 1959 B, 1961 B, 1965 B, 1966 A, 1971 F, 1972 B
Qantas Airlines exhibitions, 1960 C
Qantas Airways Ltd, 1967 B
Qantas Empire Airways, 1934 B,F, 1945 B, 1947 A, 1967 B
Qantas Flying Boat service, 1938 B
Quach, Helen, 1940 C
Quack, The, 1872 E
Quadrant, 1956 C
Quaife Barzillai, 1850 D
Quakers, 1832 D, 1887 D, 1888 F
Qualifying certificate, 1911 D, 1944 E
Quant, Mary, 1955 F
Quarantine, 1838 F, 1909 A
Quarantine Acts, 1832 A, 1908 A
Quart pot, 1850 F
Quartz mining, 1853 B
Queanbeyan, NSW, 1838 F
Queen Anne Revival houses, Sydney, 1890 C
Queen Anne style architecture, 1897 C
Queen of Bohemia, 1890 C
Queen Victoria Market building, Sydney, 1893 C, 1898 A
Queen Victoria memorial, Melbourne, 1903 C
Queen Victoria Memorial Hospital, Melbourne, 1896 B
Queen Victoria Museum, Launceston, 1887 D, 1891 C
Queen Victoria, stamps, 1853 F
'Queen with diadem' (stamp), 1855 F
Queen's Counsel, women, 1962 A
Queen's orphan schools, Tas, 1854 D
Queen's Room picture gallery, Melbourne, 1859 F
Queen's School, Hobart, 1842 D
Queen's Theatre, Adelaide, 1841 C, Melbourne, 1845 C, 1850 C
Queenscliff, Vic, 1846 F, 1901 B, 1904 B, 1906 B, 1914 A, 1946 D
Queensland, *abbreviated as* Qld
government, politics, 1843 A, 1856 A, 1859 A
named, 1859 A
Qld administration of Papua, 1887 A, 1888 A
Qld and NT Aerial Services Ltd, 1920 B, 1922 B, 1934 B
Qld Art Fund, 1930 C
Qld Art Gallery, 1895 C, 1982 C
Qld Art Society, 1887 C
Qld Authors and Artists Society, 1921 C
Qld Ballet Co., 1960 C, 1962 C
Qld boundaries, 1862 A
Qld-British Food Corporation, 1948 A
Qld Canoe Club, 1947 E
Qld Centenary Art Prize, 1959 C
Qld Club, 1879 F
Qld Coastal and Torres Strait Marine Pilot Service, 1880 F
Qld Conservatorium of Music, 1956 C
Qld Country Party, 1974 A
Qld Cricket Association, 1876 E
Qld districts, 1891 A
Qld Football Association, 1866 E

Qld Heeler, 1890 B
Qld Institute of Architects, 1888 C
Qld Institute of Medical Research, Brisbane, 1946 B
Qld Institute of Technology, 1965 D, 1967 D
Qld Labour League, 1887 A
Qld Labor Party, 1890 A, 1905 A, 1957 A, 1962 A
Qld Labourers' Union, 1888 A
Qld Lawn Tennis Association, 1888 E
Qld Modern and Contemporary Dance Co., 1971 C
Qld Museum, 1855 D
Qld National Bank, 1872 A, 1887 C
Qld National Opera Co., 1951 C
Qld Native Police Corps, 1848 A
Qld Naturalists' Club, 1906 B
Qld Opera Co., 1970 C
Qld School of Arts, 1849 C, 1884 D
Qld State String Quartet, 1945 C
Qld Steam Navigation Co., 1868 A
Qld Symphony Orchestra, 1947 C, 1955 C, 1968 C, 1970 C, 1973 C, 1978 C, 1982 C
Qld Teachers' Union, 1889 D
Qld Theatre, Brisbane, 1874 C
Qld Theatre Co., 1969 C
Queensland Times, 1859 F
Qld Turf Club, 1863 E
Qld Yacht Club, 1885 E
Queenslander, 1859 F
Queenstown, Tas, 1897 F, 1980 F
Quelhurst, Betty P. 1919 C
Quentin, Cecil, 1955 C
Quentin, Robert, 1963 C
Quetta, 1890 F
Quick, John, 1852 A
Quill, Alf, 1907 E
Quilpie, Qld, 1917 F, 1972 F
Quinine, 1823 B
Quinlan, Bernie, 1981 E
Quinlan Opera Co., 1912 C
Quinn, James, 1819 D, 1861 D
Quinn, James P. 1871 C
Quinn, Roderic J. 1867 C
Quinton, Roy, 1936 E
Quintuplets, 1967 F
Quintus Servinton, 1830 C
Quirindi, NSW, 1856 F, 1948 F
Quiros Troupe, 1983 F
Quist, Adrian K. 1913 E, 1939 E
Quong Tart, Mei, 1850 A
Quorn, SA, 1878 F

R

R film certificate, 1971 C
RAAF, *see* Royal Aust. Air Force
Rabaul, PNG, 1914 A, 1942 A
Rabbi Dr. I. Porush, 1961 C
Rabbit Flea, 1969 B
Rabbit proof fences, WA, 1904 B, 1907 B
Rabbits, 1859 B, 1880 B, 1886 B, 1888 B, 1890 B, 1900 B, 1951 B
Rabl, Julian F. 1936 C
Race courses, *see individual entries*
Rachlin, Ezra, 1970 C
Racial Discrimination Act, Federal, 1975 A
Racial prejudice, WA, 1934 A
Rack wool press, 1865 B
Radar, 1938 B, 1945 B
Radford report, Qld, 1970 D

Radiata pines, 1876 A
R. A. Henderson, 1965 C
Radio, 1905 B, 1910 B, 1919 B, 1921 B, *see also* Wireless
advertising, 1924 A, 1976 F
Altwater-Kent, 1932 B
broadcasting, 1923 B, 1924 B, 1929 C, 1935 D
car, 1924 B
CB, 1976 F, 1977 B
five valve set, 1925 B
FM, 1974 B, 1980 F
horn speaker, 1926 B
licences, 1937 B, 1974 A
open-line programmes, 1967 F
plays, 1925 C
political campaigns, 1931 B
press messages, 1921 F
religious programmes, 1923 D
research, 1965 B
school broadcasts, 1924 D, 1935 D
shipping, 1905 B, 1921 B
six valve set, 1932 B
stations, 1911 B, 1912 B, 1923 B, 1924 B, 1925 B,C,F, 1928 A, 1929 B, 1941 F
Westinghouse, 1937 B
Radio astronomy, 1945 B, 1961 B, 1972 B
Radio Aust., service, 1939 F
Radio-picturegram services, 1934 B
Radio-telegraph, Aust.–England, 1927 B
'Radio Telephone', 1964 C
Radio telephony, 1918 B, 1919 B, 1920 B, 1930 B, 1947 B, 1950 B
Radio-telescopes, 1946 B, 1953 B, 1954 B, 1959 B, 1961 B, 1969 B
Radioheliograph, 1964 B, 1967 B
Radiola, 1946 B
Radiology, 1949 B
Radiology, Dept of, Melbourne, 1965 B
Radiophysics, 1972 B
Radium, SA, 1909 B
Radium Hill, SA, 1906 B, 1909 B, 1952 B
Radium treatment, Sydney, 1913 B
Radojevic, Danilo, 1958 C, 1977 C
Rae, John, 1813 C
Rafalsky, Fyodor, 1948 D
Rafferty, Chips, *see* Coffage, John
Raffles Bay, NT, 1827 A, 1829 A
Raft, Emmanuel, 1938 C
Rafts, inflatable, 1965 B
Raggatt, Harold G. 1900 B
Ragged School, Hobart, 1855 D, Sydney, 1860 D
Ragless, Maxwell R. C. 1901 C
Railton, Tas, 1853 F
Railways,
Cwlth, 1974 B, 1975 B
disasters,
–NSW, 1849 F, 1857 F, 1878 F, 1885 F, 1887 F, 1890 F, 1892 F, 1894 F, 1901 F, 1914 F, 1920 F, 1926 F, 1944 F, 1945 F, 1952 F, 1953 F, 1958 F, 1970 F, 1977 F
–Qld, 1913 F, 1925 F, 1947 F, 1956 F, 1960 F
–Tas, 1916 F
–Vic, 1881 F, 1882 F, 1884 F, 1908 F, 1910 F, 1926 F, 1943 F, 1951 F, 1952 F, 1969 F
–WA, 1920 F, 1960 F
gauges, 1848 B, 1852 B, 1853 B, 1870 B, 1921 B, 1925 B, 1962 B
interstate, 1866 B, 1879 B, 1883 B, 1886 B, 1887 B, 1888 B, 1889 B, 1907 B, 1911 B, 1912 B, 1914 B, 1917 B, 1925 B, 1929 B, 1935 B, 1937 B, 1956 B, 1962 B, 1969 B, 1970 B

811

intrastate,
  −NSW, 1846 B, 1849 B, 1850 B, 1853 B, 1854 B, 1855 A, B, 1856 B, 1857 B, 1860 A, B, 1863 B, 1864 B, 1869 B, 1876 B, 1878 B, 1881 B, 1885 B, 1888 B, 1890 B, 1906 B, 1926 B, 1943 B, 1979 B
  −NT, 1889 B, 1911 B
  −Qld, 1863 B, 1865 B, 1867 B, 1876 B, 1881 B, 1882 B, 1887 B, 1888 B, 1891 B, 1892 B, 1903 B, 1908 B, 1923 B, 1924 B, 1976 B, 1979 B, 1982 B
  −SA, 1856 B, 1857 B, 1860 B, 1870 B, 1873 B, 1875 A, 1878 B, 1879 B, 1887 B, 1888 B, 1891 B, 1911 B, 1975 B
  −Tas, 1835 B, 1868 B, 1871 B, 1876 B, 1892 B, 1974 B, 1978 B
  −Vic, 1857 B, 1860 A, B, 1861 B, 1862 B, 1864 B, 1873 B, 1877 B, 1878 B, 1905 B, 1918 B, 1954 B, 1971 B, 1980 B
  −WA, 1871 A, 1873 B, 1874 B, 1879 B, 1881 B, 1889 B, 1896 B, 1897 B
strikes, 1903 A, 1917 A, 1927 A 1948 A, 1950 A, 1969 A
tracks, 1880 B, 1900 B, 1976 B
trains,
  − airconditioned, 1935 B, 1937 B
  − Australind Express, 1947 B
  − Prospector, 1971 B
  − *Southern Aurora*, 1962 B
  − *Spirit of Progress*, 1937 B
  − Sydney Express, 1935 B
  − XPT, 1982 B
urban expansion of, 1865 C
Rain, 1963 B, 1975 F, 1984 F
Rain Lover, 1968 E, 1969 E
Rain making, NSW, 1947 B
Rainbird, 1945 E
Rainbow, Vic, 1890 F
Rainbow, 1864 F
Rainbow II, 1967 E
Rainbow trout, 1894 B
Raine, Thomas, 1794 A, 1818 A, 1823 A, 1836 A
Raine and Ramsay Co., 1823 A
Rainer, Henry H. 1903 C
Rainfall, records/recording of, 1839 B, 1840 B, 1841 B, 1844 F, 1862 F, 1870 F, 1876 F, 1893 F, 1936 F, 1963 B, 1979 F, 1980 F
Rainforest, 1974 B, 1982 F, 1984 F
Rainsford Bowling Club, 1898 E
Rainsford trophy, 1885 E
Ralph Rashleigh, 1845 C
Ram Head, Vic, 1837 F
Ramaciotti, Vera, 1970 B
Ramaciotti Foundation, medical, 1970 B
Ramage, R. 1890 E
Rambouillet sheep, 1856 B, 1865 B
Ramlaoui, Gibran, 1970 D
Ramon, Charky, *see* Ballard, David
Rampage, 1975 E
Rams, merino, 1981 A, *see also* Sheep
Ramsay, David, 1823 A
Ramsay, Edward P. 1842 B
Ramsay, Hugh, 1877 C
Ramsay, James M, 1916 A, 1975 A, 1977 A
RAN, *see* Royal Aust. Navy
Ranch homes, 1950 C
Randall, Richard J. 1869 C
Randall, Terry, 1952 E
Randall, Vera, 1978 F
Randell, Ronald E. 1918 C
Randell, William R. 1824 A, 1853 A, 1859 A

Randolph, 1849 A
Randwick, Sydney, 1884 E, 1924 B
Randwick race course, Sydney, 1832 E, 1860 E, 1917 E
Ranger Uranium Environmental Enquiry, 1975 B, 1976 A, 1977 A
Ranger uranium project, NT, 1970 B, 1977 A, 1979 A, B, 1980 B, 1982 A
Rangers, Qld, 1883 E
Rani (yacht), 1945 E
Rankin, Annabelle J. M. 1908 A, 1946 A, 1966 A, 1971 A
Rankin, David, 1946 C
Rankin, Robert W. 1907 A
Rap dancing, 1984 C
Rape, 1886 F, 1980 F
Raper, George, 1797 C
Raper, John, 1939 E
Rapotec, Stanislaus I. 1913 C
Rapid Bay, SA, 1900 F
Rasic, Rale, 1933 E
Rason, Cornthwaite H. 1858 A, 1905 A
Rasp, Charles, 1846 A, 1883 B, 1885 A
Ratas, Vaclovas, 1910 C
Ratcliffe, Francis N. 1904 B
Rationing, war-time, 1942 A
Rationalist Movement, 1855 D
Rats of Tobruk, 1941 A
Rats of Tobruk (film), 1944 C
Rattlesnake, 1847 A
Ravenshoe, Qld, 1881 F
Ravensthorpe, WA, 1848 F
Ravenswood, Qld, 1868 B, 1891 B
Rawlinna, WA, 1960 F
Raws, William L. 1878 A
Rawson, Harry H. 1843 A, 1902 A
Ray Walker, 1958 C
Raymond, James, 1829 A, 1838 F, 1851 A
Raymond, W. E. 1910 B
Raymond Terrace, NSW, 1832 A, 1837 F
Rayon, Sydney, 1939 B
Rayon stockings, 1935 F
'Razor Gang' Report, 1981 A
Re-afforestation, SA, 1873 F
Re-Establishment and Employment Act, 1945 A
Re-inforced concrete, Sydney, 1895 C
Reaction bonding, 1968 B
Read, Arthur E. 1911 C, 1959 C
Read, Jim, 1943 E
Read, Mark, 1950 E
Read, Richard, 1813 C, 1814 C
Ready Mix Concrete Co., 1939 B
Real Property (Torrens) Act, Vic, 1862 A
Reason Why, The, 1908 F
Recent British Sculpture Exhibition, 1963 C
Recent German Graphic Art Exhibition, 1956 C
Reciprocal Tariff Agreement, Aust.− N.Z., 1922 A
Recollections of Geoffrey Hamlyn, The, 1859 C
Recorder, SA, 1898 F
Recorders, 1984 C
Recording, 1899 C, 1925 B, C, 1926 C
Records, gramophone, 1924 B
Recruiting Officer, The, 1789 C, 1800 F
Red Barn, 1969 F, 1972 F
Red Cab taxis, 1927 F
Red Cliffs, Vic, 1919 F
Red Cross, 1927 F, 1938 B
Red Dance, The, 1928 C
Red Handed, 1967 E
'Red Page', 1894 C, 1896 C
Red phones, 1963 F
Red Poll cattle, 1850 A

'Red Robin' brooders, 1949 B
Red Sky at Morning, 1935 C
'Red Ted', 1884 A, *see* Theodore, E. G.
Redcliffe, Qld, 1824 F
Redcliffe Art Contest, Qld, 1957 C
Redcliffe Point, Qld, 1824 A
Reddall, Thomas, 1820 D, 1824 D
Reddall, Marie, 1888 C
Reddington, Charles, 1929 C
Reddy, Helen, 1942 C, 1972 C
Rede, Robert W. 1854 A
Redesdale, Vic, 1945 F
Redex road trials, 1953 E
Redfearn, G. 1891 E
Redfern, Sydney, 1849 F, 1894 F, 1983 F
Redfern, William, 1808 B, 1833 B
Redford, Harry, 1870 F, 1901 F
Redheap, 1930 C
Redpath, Norma, 1928 C
Redphones, 1963 F
Reece, Eric E. 1909 A, 1958 A, 1972 C
Reed, A. 1937 E
Reed, G. S. 1949 B
Reed, Henry, 1806 A, 1831 A
Reed, John, 1901 C, 1956 C
Reed, Joseph, 1823 C, 1854 C, 1868 C
Reed, R. 1929 E
Reedy River, 1953 C
Rees, A. G. L. 1954 B
Rees, Leslie, 1905 C, 1942 C
Rees, Lloyd F. 1895 C
Reeve, Alan, 1910 C
Reeves Art Prize, Sydney, 1936 C
Referendum,
  national, 1898 A, 1899 A, 1906 A, 1910 A, 1911 A, 1913 A, 1916 A, 1917 A, 1919 A, 1926 A, 1928 A, 1937 A, 1944 A, 1946 A, 1948 A, 1961 A, 1967 A, 1973 A, 1974 A, 1977 A
  state, 1900 A, 1925 A, 1928 A, 1933 A, 1961 A, 1968 F, 1978 A, 1981 A
Reform Association WA, 1886 A, 1887 A
Reform League, Ballarat, 1854 A, WA, 1878 A, 1886 A
Refrigeration, 1850 B, 1856 B, 1876 B, 1879 B, 1937 B, 1912 F
Refugee Resettlement Office, 1950 D
Refugees,
  Hungarian, 1956 A
  illegal, 1978 A
  Indo-Chinese, 1978 A, 1979 A, 1980 A, 1982 A
  Nazi Germany, 1938 A
  UNO, 1946 A
Regal Cup, 1922 E
Regan, Jack, 1912 E
Regatta Hotel, Brisbane, 1965 F
Regent Theatre, Melbourne, 1929 C
Regiments, colonial, 1809 A, 1810 A, 1814 A, 1816 F, 1817 A, 1823 A, 1824 A, 1829 C
Regional Employment Development (RED) Scheme, 1974 A
Regional Galleries Association of Vic, 1957 C
Register of manpower, national, 1939 A
Registered mail, 1835 F
Registration of,
  births, deaths and marriages,
  −NSW, 1856 A
  −SA, 1842 A
  −Tas, 1839 A
  −Vic, 1853 A
  −WA, 1841 A
  carriages, 1813 F
  cars/vehicles, 1904 B, 1924 F
  charities, 1864 F

horses, 1911 E
public hospitals, 1864 F
Rehfisch, Alison B. 1900 C
Reibey, Mary, 1855 A
Reibey, Thomas (d. 1811) 1811 A
Reibey, Thomas (b. 1821) 1821 A, 1876 A
Reid, D. G. 1933 C
Reid, Elizabeth, 1973 A
Reid, George H. 1845 A, 1894 A, 1901 A, 1904 A, 1905 A, 1909 A
Reid, Kerry, 1947 E
Reid, Rex, 1928 C, 1975 C
Reimann, Immanuel G. 1883 C
Reinhard, Ken, 1936 C
Religion, *see individual entries and section E*
Religion, govt aid to, 1836 D, 1840 D, 1846 D, 1851 D, 1856 D, 1862 D, 1870 D, 1895 D
Religious duties, 1813 D
Religious equality, 1836 D
Religious radio broadcasts, 1923 D
Religious Society of Friends, *see* Quaker
Remembrance Club, Hobart, 1923 F
Removalists, The, 1972 C
Rene, Roy, 1892 C, 1914 C, 1916 C, 1934 C
Renford, Desmond R. 1927 E, 1947 E
Renmano wines, 1916 A
Renmark, SA, 1887 F
Renner, Ingo, 1940 E, 1976 E, 1977 E
Rennie, Edward H. 1852 B
Rennie, Jack, 1911 E
Renshaw, J. B. 1964 A
Rentoul, John L. 1846 D
Rentoul, Thomas C. 1882 D
Renwick, Arthur, 1837 B
Repatriation, 1918 A, 1919 A, 1920 A
Repatriation Commission, Cwlth, 1919 A
Repco spinning machine, 1970 B, 1975 B
Repertory Theatre, 1908 C
Representative govt,
first, 1823 A
NSW, 1842 A, 1843 A
see individual entries
Resch, Edmund, 1879 A
Reserve Bank, 1960 A, 1966 A
Reserve Bank Act, 1960 A
Reserve Bank Art Prize, 1962 C
Responsible govt, 1830 A, 1833 A, 1855 A, 1856 A, *see also individual entries*
Restaurants, 1970 F
Resuscitation, 1960 F
Retail Price Index, 1912 A, 1961 A
Retreat of Radiance, 1982 C
Return to Coolami, 1936 C
Return Fare, 1955 C
Returned Sailors' and Soldiers' Imperial League of Aust., 1916 F
Returned Services League of Aust., RSL, 1916 F, 1940 A, 1968 F
Returned Soldiers' Association of NSW, 1915 F
Reuters, 1935 F
Reveley, Henry W. 1788 B, 1831 C
Revell, Ray, 1912 E
Revenge, The, 1795 C
Revenue, 1901 E
Reynell, John, 1809 A, 1839 A, 1843 A
Reynella, SA, 1854 F
Reynolds, Christopher A. 1834 D
Reynolds, Frederick G. 1880 C
Reynolds, Richard, 1915 E, 1934 E, 1937 E, 1938 E
Reynolds, Thomas, 1818 A, 1860 A
Reys, F. 1973 E
R. G. Menzies (portrait), 1954 C

Rheola, Vic, 1870 F
Rhodes Scholars, 1904 D
Rhodesia, 1965 A, 1979 A
Ribbons, 1919 F
Rice, Horrie, 1878 E
Rice, NSW, 1921 B, 1922 A, 1924 A, 1944 A
Rich, George E. 1863 A, 1913 A
Rich-Katuna, 1950 E
Richards, Henry C. 1884 B, 1951 C
Richards, Lou, 1923 E
Richards, Mark, 1958 E
Richards, Ronald, 1910 E, 1933 A
Richards Art Prize, Brisbane, 1951 C
Richardson, Alfred, 1880 B
Richardson, Arnold E. V. 1883 B
Richardson, Charles D. 1853 C, 1898 C
Richardson, D. K. 1929 C
Richardson, Ethel F. L. *see* Richardson, Henry H.
Richardson, Henry H. 1870 C, 1908 C, 1910 C, 1917 C, 1929 C
Richardson, Mervyn V. 1894 B, 1951 B
Richardson, R. 1900 E
Richardson, Victor Y. 1894 E
Richardson, William, 1793 D, 1798 D
Richmond, James, 1834 A, 1882 B
Richmond, Melbourne, 1910 F
Richmond, NSW, 1810 F, 1823 A, 1864 B, 1912 B, 1961 B, 1970 E
Richmond, Oliffe, 1919 C
Richmond, Qld, 1858 F, 1865 F
Richmond, Tas, 1824 F, 1836 D, 1838 D
Richmond air base, NSW, 1927 A
Richmond aerodrome, NSW, 1912 B
Richmond Aust. Rules Football Club/team, 1885 E, 1920 E, 1921 E, 1930 E, 1932 E, 1934 E, 1943 E, 1948 E, 1952 E, 1954 E, 1967 E, 1969 E, 1971 E, 1973 E, 1974 E, 1980 E
Richmond Bridge, Tas, 1823 C, 1825 C
Richmond Hill, NSW, 1806 F
Richmond R., NSW, 1828 A
Rickards, Harry, *see* Leete, Henry B.
Ride on Stranger, 1943 C
Riders in the Chariot, 1961 C
Ridge and the River, The, 1952 C
Ridley, James, 1840 A
Ridley, John, 1806 B, 1843 B
Ridley, William 1819 D
Riebe, Anton D. 1905 C
Rieck, W. E. 1950 E
Rienits, Rex and Thea, 1963 C
Rifle, periscope, Gallipoli, 1915 B
Rifle shooting, 1862 E, 1896 E, *see also* Shooting
Rigby, 1859 A
Rigby, John T. 1922 C, 1959 C
Riggall, Louise B. 1918 C
Right Thing, The, 1971 C
Rignold, George R. 1839 C
Rigoletto, 1887 C
Riley, Alexander, 1797 A, 1810 A, 1826 A, 1833 A
Riley, Charles O. L. 1854 D
Riley, Ron, 1948 E
Rimfire, 1948 E
Ring, Douglas, 1918 E
Ringwood, Alfred E. 1930 B, 1978 B
Rintel, Moses, 1823 D
Riots, industrial unrest, 1919 A, *see also individual entries*
Ripon Regulations, 1831 A
Ripple, 1953 E
Rippon Lea, Melbourne, 1868 C
Risdon, Tas, 1917 B
Risdon Cove, Tas, 1803 A, 1804 A
Rising Fast, 1954 E
Riske, Jan, 1933 C

Ristori, Adelaide, 1875 C
Ritchard, Cyril T. 1899 C
Ritchard, Edgar, 1908 C
Rites of Passage, 1974 C
Rival, 1961 E
River Murray Commission, Vic, 1915 B
River trade voyage, longest, 1886 B
River transport, 1859 B
Riverina, proposed state, 1931 A
Riverina College of Advanced Education, NSW, 1972 D
Riverina district, NSW, 1864 B, 1876 B, 1886 B, 1933 B, 1951 B
Riverina Irrigation Scheme, 1887 B
Riverina Trucking Co., 1976 C
Rivers, *see individual entries*
Rivers, Godfrey, 1933 C
Rivers, Richard G. 1859 C
Riversleigh, Qld, 1984 B
Rivett, Albert, 1854 D
Rivett, David, 1885 B
Rivett, Eleanor, 1883 D
Rivett, Elsie, 1887 A
Rivett, Rohan D. 1917 F
Rivette, 1939 E
Riviere du Nord, Tas, 1792 A
Rivoli Bay, SA, 1876 F
Rixon, Amelia, 1806 F
Road to Gundagai, The, 1965 C
Roads,
authorities, 1913 B, 1934 B
Cwlth aid, 1923 B, 1959 A
kilometres, 1977 B
national road tolls, *see from 1955 section F*
signs, metric conversion, 1974 F
states,
— NSW, 1788 B, 1794 B, 1810 B, 1814 A, B, 1815 B, 1818 B, 1823 A, 1826 B, 1831 B, 1832 B, 1835 B
— Qld, 1840 B
— SA, 1839 B, 1976 B
— Tas, 1807 B, 1818 B, 1827 B
— Vic, 1835 B
— WA, 1850 B, 1974 B, 1976 B
tolls, 1810 F, 1877 B
transport, 1931 A, B
trials, Redex, 1953 E
Roaring Nineties, The, 1946 C
Robberies, 1828 F, 1978 F, 1979 C, 1981 F, *see also individual entries*
Robbery Under Arms, 1882 C, 1888 C, 1894 C
Robbins, Charles, 1802 A, 1804 A
Robe, Frederick H. 1802 A, 1845 A
Robe, SA, 1846 F, 1857 A
Robert Campbell, 1955 C
Robert Klippel, 1977 C
Robert le Gay Brereton Prize, 1955 C
Robert Lowe Committee, 1844 D
Robert Towns and Co., 1842 A
Roberts, Alfred, 1823 B
Roberts, Douglas, 1919 C
Roberts, Neil, 1958 E
Roberts, Stephen H. 1901 D
Roberts, Thomas W. 1856 C, 1885 C, 1887 C, 1889 C, 1890 C, 1895 C, 1901 C
Roberts, William, 1814 B
Robertson, A. 1884 E
Robertson, Bruce, 1872 C
Robertson, Edward G. 1903 B
Robertson, Ethel F. L. 1870 C
Robertson, George, (1), 1825 A, 1852 A
Robertson, George, (2), 1860 A
Robertson, Horace C. H. 1894 C
Robertson, Hugh S. 1900 A
Robertson, John, 1816 A, 1860 A, 1868 A, 1875 A, 1877 A, 1885 A
Robertson, Louis S. 1910 C
Robertson, Macpherson, 1860 A, 1880 A

813

Robertson, Martin and Smith, 1854 B
Robertson, Rutherford N. 1913 B
Robertson, Thorburn B. 1884 B
Robertson-Swann, Ron, 1941 C, 1980 C
Robertson Land Act, NSW, 1861 A
Robin Hood Art competition, 1956 C
Robinson, David, 1893 B
Robinson, E. F. 1928 E
Robinson, George A. 1788 A, 1830 A, 1835 A, 1886 A
Robinson, Hercules G. R. 1824 A, 1872 A, 1873 F
Robinson, John, 1941 C
Robinson, Kathleen, 1931 C
Robinson, Lee, 1953 C
Robinson, Max, 1936 C
Robinson, Michael M. 1810 C, 1826 C
Robinson, Robert, 1947 B
Robinson, Roland E. 1912 C
Robinson, Roy L. 1883 B
Robinson, Stanford, 1968 C
Robinson, William C. F. 1875 A, 1880 A, 1883 A, 1889 A, 1890 A
Robinson, William S. 1876 A
Robinsons' Baths, Sydney, 1846 E
Robinvale, Vic, 1946 F
Robran, Barrie, 1947 E
Robson, Doug, 1938 E
Robson, G. 1892 E
Robson, May, 1865 C
Roche, Anthony D. 1945 E, 1969 E
Rochester, Vic, 1854 F
Rock phosphate, NT, 1962 B
Rock n' Roll, 1954 C, 1956 C, 1958 C, 1959 C
Rockdale Art competition, NSW, 1955 C
Rockhampton, Qld, 1855 F, 1858 B, 1861 F, 1864 A, 1865 A, 1868 A, 1881 B, 1890 C, 1892 B, 1898 C, 1903 B, 1954 F, 1963 B, 1967 D
Rockhampton Grammar School, Qld, 1871 D
Rockhampton League, 1866 A
Rockingham, WA, 1830 F, 1899 F
Rocks, oldest, 1977 B
Rocks area, Sydney, 1971 F, 1973 F
Rocky Point, Vic, 1852 B
Rocky Ponds, NSW, 1945 F
Rodda, Percival C. 1891 C
Rodeos, 1897 E, 1906 E
Roderick, Colin, 1911 C
Rodius, Charles, 1802 C
Rodney, 1894 A
Rodney, 1938 F
Rodrigues, Antonio, 1930 C
Rodway, Florence, 1881 C
Rodway, Leonard, 1853 B
Roe, Creeve, *see* Daley, V.
Roe, John S. 1797 A, 1830 A, 1848 A
Roe, Richard, 1851 A
Roebourne, WA, 1864 F, 1873 A, 1921 F
Rogers, G. H. 1842 C
Rogers, John R. N. 1928 C
Rogers, Peter, 1981 B
Rogers, Richard S. 1862 B
Rogers, Steve, 1955 E
Roggenkamp, Roy, 1928 C
Rogue's March, The, 1788 C
Rolland, Francis W. 1878 D, 1958 D
Rolland Plains, NSW, 1824 A
Roller game, 1966 E
Roller skating, 1905 E
Rolling Stones, 1973 C
Roma, Qld, 1862 F, 1863 A, 1881 B, 1900 B, 1906 B, 1961 B, 1969 B
Romaine, Billy, 1918 C
Roman Carnival, Melbourne, 1967 F
Roman Catholic church, 1820 D, 1834 D, 1885 D, 1940 D, 1955 D, 1964 D, 1965 D, 1967 D, 1972 D, 1975 D, 1982 D
NSW, 1803 D, 1818 D, 1821 D, 1829 D, 1932 D, 1933 D, 1842 D, 1843 D, 1844 D, 1845 D, 1872 D, 1873 D, 1877 D, 1884 D, 1885 D, 1895 D, 1983 D
NT, 1935 D, 1938 D
Qld, 1843 D, 1861 D, 1874 D, 1930 D
SA, 1844 D, 1866 D, 1939 D
Tas, 1821 D, 1844 D, 1861 D, 1944 D
Vic, 1839 D, 1845 D, 1847 D, 1874 D, 1912 D, 1917 D
WA, 1842 D, 1847 D, 1930 D
Roman Catholic mission, Sydney, 1803 D
Roman Catholic missionaries, 1846 D
Roman Catholic schools, 1805 D, 1822 D, 1826 D, 1844 D, 1845 D, 1846 D, 1851 D, 1957 D, *see also individual entries*
Romberg, Frederick, 1913 C
Romeril, John, 1945 C
Ronan, Thomas M. 1907 C
Roof overhangs, 1815 C, 1834 C
Roofing, 1838 C, 1909 C
Rooke, W. 1866 D
Rooney, Elizabeth U. 1929 C
Rooney, Robert, 1937 C
Roper, Edward, 1880 C
Roper R., NT, 1883 A, 1908 F
Roper R., SA, 1867 A
Rose, Bob, 1928 E
Rose, David, 1936 C, 1956 C
Rose, Herbert, 1890 C
Rose, Joe, 1915 C
Rose, Lionel E. 1948 E, 1968 E
Rose, Mervyn, 1933 E
Rose, Murray, 1939 E
Rose, Rabbi, 1835 D
Rose, William, 1930 C
Rose Hill, NSW, 1788 A, 1979 E
Rose Hill farm, 1789 A
Rose Hill Lawn Bowling Club, 1880 E
Rose Hill Packet, 1789 B
Rosebery, Tas, 1891 F
Rosenberg, Giacomo di, *see* Tucker, James
Roseneath, NT, 1969 B
Rosenfeld, Albert, 1885 E, 1912 E
Rosengrave, Harry, 1889 C
Rosenhain, Walter, 1875 B
Rosenthal, Charles, 1875 A
Rosewall, Kenneth R. 1934 E, 1953 E, 1968 E
Rosewood, Qld, 1865 F
Roseworthy, SA, 1867 F, 1881 B
Roseworthy Agricultural College, 1884 D
Roseworthy Experimental Farm, SA, 1881 B
Roskanda, 1933 C
Roslyndale, Woollahra, 1856 C
Ross, Tas, 1812 F, 1836 C
Ross, Colin C. 1922 C
Ross, Dorothy, 1892 D, 1950 D
Ross, Ian Clunies, *see* Clunies Ross, I.
Ross, John, (b. 1817) 1817 A, 1871 A
Ross, John, (b. 1833) 1833 A
Ross, Joseph, 1866 B
Ross, Lloyd M. 1901 A
Ross, Robert, 1790 A
Ross, Robert S. 1873 F
Ross Ice shelf, Antarctica, 1901 A
Rossi, Francis, 1823 A
Rossi, Francis N. 1825 A, 1851 A
Rosson, Isabella, 1789 D
Rotary clothes hoist, 1945 B
Rotary Clubs, 1921 F
Rotary engine, 1889 B
Rotary hoe, 1919 B, 1920 B
Roth, Henry L. 1855 B
Roth, Phillip, 1971 C
Roth, Walter E. 1861 B
Rothbury coalfields, NSW, 1929 A
Rothmans, 1972 F
Rotolactor, 1952 B
Rotterdam Marathon, 1983 E
Roudonikis, Tom, 1950 E
Rough Range, WA, 1953 A
Roughley, Theodore C. 1888 B, 1951 C
Roughriding, 1930 E, 1938 E, 1945 E
Roughsey, Dick, 1920 C, 1973 C
Roumanian Orthodox Parishes, Melbourne, 1970 D
Round, Barry, 1981 E
Round House gaol, WA, 1831 C
Rous, George E. J. M. 1921 A
Rous, Henry J. 1795 A, 1827 E, 1828 A
Rouse, Richard, 1852 A
Rousel, Jules H. R. 1897 C
Row car, 1971 B
Rowan, Marian Ellis, 1848 C
Rowbotham, David H. 1924 C
Rowcroft, Charles, 1843 C, 1846 C
Rowe, George, 1797 C
Rowe, Marilyn, 1946 C, 1970 C, 1973 C
Rowe, Thomas, 1829 C
Rowed, Reginald W. W. 1916 C
Rowell, John T. N. 1894 C
Rowell, Kenneth, 1922 C
Rowell, Sidney F. 1894 A
Rowell, William N. 1898 C
Rowin table, 1976 B
Rowing, 1818 E, 1827 E, 1859 E, 1863 E, 1868 E, 1878 E, 1901 E, 1904 E, 1907 E, 1912 E, 1919 E
Rowland, James A. 1981 A
Rowland, John R. 1925 C
Rowlandson, Alfred C. 1865 A
Rowney Drawing Prize, Melbourne, 1959 C
Roxburgh, Rachel, 1915 C
Roxby Downs, SA, 1977 B, 1982 B, 1983 F, 1984 B
Royal Academy, 1909 C, 1922 C
Royal Academy of Dancing, 1935 C
Royal Adelaide Exhibition, 1957 C
Royal Adelaide Theatre, 1846 C
Royal Aeronautical Society Art Prize, 1967 C
Royal Agricultural and Horticultural Society of SA, 1839 F
Royal Agricultural Society of NSW, 1822 F, Easter Show Art Prize, 1958 C
Royal Agricultural Society of Tas, 1863 F
Royal Agricultural Society of Vic, 1848 F, 1890 F
Royal Agricultural Society of WA, 1829 F
Royal Alexandra Hospital, Sydney, 1931 B
Royal Alexandria Theatre, Brisbane, 1866 C
Royal Art Society, 1885 C
Royal Art Society of NSW, 1880 C
Royal Australasian College of Dental Surgeons, 1965 B
Royal Australasian College of Physicians, 1930 B, 1938 B
Royal Australasian College of Surgeons, 1928 B
Royal Australasian Ornithologists' Union, 1901 B
Royal Aust. Academy of Science, 1954 B
Royal Aust. Air Force, RAAF, 1921 A, 1923 A, 1924 B, 1927 A, 1938 A,

1941 A, 1950 A, 1952 A, 1953 A, 1962 A, 1963 A, 1965 A, 1971 A, 1981 A, 1983 A
Royal Aust. Air Force College, Point Cook, Vic, 1947 A
Royal Aust. College of Radiologists, 1949 B
Royal Aust. Equestrian circus, 1850 F
Royal Aust. Institute of Architects, 1930 C
Royal Aust. Navy, RAN, 1910 A, 1911 A, 1913 A, 1939 A, 1967 A
Royal Aust. Naval College, NSW, 1913 A, 1915 A, 1937 A, 1958 A
Royal Aust. Nursing Federation, 1924 F
Royal Automobile Club of Aust., 1903 F
Royal Automobile Club of SA, 1903 F
Royal Automobile Club of Vic, RACV, 1903 F
Royal Ballerinas, 1888 C
Royal Bank of Aust., 1840 A, 1843 A
Royal Bank of Qld, 1885 A
Royal birthday odes, 1810 C
Royal Boneshakers Cycling Club, 1869 E
Royal British Colonial Society of Artists, 1937 C
Royal Caledonian Scottish Society of SA, 1881 F
Royal Charter, 1828 A
Royal Charter (ship), 1859 F
Royal College of Physicians, 1823 B
Royal College of Surgeons, 1823 B, 1928 B
Royal Comic Opera Co., 1888 C
Royal Exchange, Sydney, 1857 A
Royal Far West Children's Health Scheme, NSW, 1924 F, 1932 F, 1935 D
Royal Flying Doctor Service, 1927 B, 1928 B
Royal Hotel, Sydney, 1845 C
Royal Hotel theatre, Sydney, 1829 C
Royal Humane Society of Australasia, 1874 F
Royal Humane Society of Sydney, 1902 F
Royal Institute of Architects, WA, 1896 C
Royal Melbourne Golf Club, 1891 E
Royal Melbourne Institute of Technology, 1881 D, 1887 D
Royal Meteorological Society of Aust., 1886 B
Royal Military College, Duntroon, 1911 A, 1983 A
Royal Mints,
  Melbourne, 1872 A
  Perth, 1899 A
  Sydney, 1855 A
Royal National Agricultural and Industrial Association of Qld, 1875 B, Art Prizes, 1961 C
Royal National Park, 1879 F
Royal North Shore Hospital, Sydney, 1931 B
Royal Pavilion Saloon, Melbourne, 1841 C
Royal Perth Yacht Club, 1865 E
Royal Philharmonic Society of Sydney, 1909 C
Royal Qld Art Society, 1887 C
Royal Qld Yacht Club, 1885 E
Royal SA Society of Arts, 1856 C
Royal SA Yacht Squadron, 1900 E
Royal Societies in Aust., 1843 B
Royal Society, the, 1854 B, 1960 B
Royal Society of Canberra, 1930 B
Royal Society of NSW, 1821 B, 1866 B, 1884 B

Royal Society for the Prevention of Cruelty to Animals, RSPCA, 1871 F
Royal Society of Qld, 1884 B
Royal Society of SA, 1853 B, 1880 B, 1883 B
Royal Society of Tas, 1843 B
Royal Society of VDL ... Advancement of Science, 1843 B
Royal Society of Vic, 1859 B, 1863 F
Royal Society of WA, 1914 B
Royal South Street Competition, Melbourne, 1924 C
Royal Standard Theatre, Sydney, 1886 C
Royal Sydney Golf Club, 1893 E
Royal Sydney Yacht Squadron, 1862 E
Royal Theatre, Ballarat, 1859 C
Royal Victoria Cricket Club, 1839 E
Royal Victoria Theatre,
  Adelaide, 1838 C
  Hobart, 1837 C
  Sydney, 1838 C, 1840 C, 1843 C, 1880 C
Royal Victoria Yacht Club, 1856 E
Royal visits, 1829 A, 1881 A, 1920 A, 1934 A, 1954 A, 1956 A, 1958 A, 1962 A, 1963 A, 1966 A, 1967 A, 1968 A, 1970 A, 1971 A, 1973 A, 1974 A, 1975 A, 1977 A, 1978 A, 1979 A, 1981 A, 1982 A, 1983 A
Royal Yacht Club of Tas, 1874 E, 1910 E
Royal Zoological Society, SA, 1878 B
Roycroft, J. William G. ('Bill'), 1914 E
Rubber gloves, 1898 B
Rubbo, A. Datillo, 1870 C, 1897 C
Rubella, 1941 B, 1943 B, 1971 F
Rubin, Harold de V. 1899 A
Rubinstein, Helena, 1870 F, 1958 C
Rubinstein Portrait Prize, WA, 1961 C
Rubo, Anthony D. 1870 C
Rudd, Steele, *see* Davis, Arthur H.
Rudd Family, The, 1926 C
Rudy Komon, 1981 C
Rudy Komon Art Gallery, Sydney, 1958 C
Rugby League Football, 1907 E, 1908 E, 1909 E, 1910 E, 1911 E, 1912 E, 1915 E, 1928 E, 1932 E, 1938 E, 1946 E, 1950 E, 1951 E, 1953 E, 1954 E, 1956 E, 1963 E, 1965 E, 1982 E
Rugby League Premierships, Sydney, *see each year section E from 1908*
Rugby League World Cup, 1957 E
Rugby Union football, 1829 E, 1864 E, 1874 E, 1882 E, 1884 E, 1888 E, 1889 E, 1899 E, 1900 E, 1903 E, 1907 E, 1908 E, 1915 E, 1927 E, 1929 E, 1933 E, 1937 E, 1948 E, 1952 E, 1979 E, 1980 E, 1981 E
Ruhen, Olaf, 1911 C
Rules for the ... Schools in Sydney, 1818 D
Rum, (as currency), 1806 A, 1807 A
Rum Corps, 1790 A, 1806 A, 1808 A
'Rum Hospital,' Sydney, 1811 B
Rum Jungle, NT, 1872 F, 1949 B, 1952 B, 1954 B, 1962 B
'Rum Rebellion', 1808 A, 1811 A
Rumker, Charles L. 1827 B
Rümker, Christian C. L. 1788 B, 1822 B
Running, 1973 E, 1976 E, 1978 E, 1980 E, 1981 E
Rupert C. W. Bunny Loan Exhibition, Melbourne, 1946 C
'Rupert Max Stuart case', SA, 1959 A
Rupp, Herman M. R. 1872 B
Rural Bank Art Prize, Sydney, 1964 C
Rural credits, 1894 A, 1925 A
Rural Youth Clubs, 1928 F
Rusconi, 1929 C

Rusden, George K. 1859 D
Rusden, George W. 1819 D, 1849 D
Rusden College, Melbourne, 1972 D
Ruse, Elizabeth, 1792 A
Ruse, James, 1789 A, 1791 A, 1837 A
Rush That Never Ended, The, 1963 C
Rushcutters Bay, NSW, 1788 A
Rushforth, Peter, 1920 C
Rushworth, Vic, 1853 F
Russell, Arthur, 1929 C
Russell, Edwin T. 1920 C
Russell, George, 1812 A
Russell, Henry C. 1836 B, 1870 B
Russell, Henry S. 1818 A
Russell, James N. 1909 C
Russell, John, 1840 A
Russell, John P. 1859 C
Russell, Peter N. 1816 B, 1847 B
Russell, Robert, 1808 C, 1836 C
Russell, Robert H. 1860 B
Russia (horse), 1946 E
Russian Cape, 1820 A
Russian folk dancers, 1899 C
Russian invasion fears, 1854 A
Russian Orthodox church, 1820 D, 1929 D, 1948 D
Russian revolution, Archangel, 1919 A
Russo, Peter A. V. 1908 D
Russom, Reginald, 1887 C
Rust, Bernard, 1929 C
Rust, stripe, 1979 B
Rust, wheat, 1868 B, 1890 B
Rust-in-Wheat Conference, 1890 B
Rusty Bugles, 1948 C
Rutherford, James, 1827 A, 1862 B
Rutherglen, Vic, 1860 F
Ruthven, Alan, 1950 E
Rutledge, Mary A. 1838 F
Rutledge, William, 1924 C
Rutt, W. 1871 B
Rutter, R. 1867 B
Ryan, Charles S. 1853 B
Ryan, David, 1873 B
Ryan, David J. 1979 F
Ryan, Dinny, 1936 E
Ryan, Kevin, 1914 E
Ryan, Noel, 1967 E
Ryan, Ronald, 1925 F, 1967 F
Ryan, Thomas J. 1876 A, 1915 A
Ryde Municipal Art Society, NSW, 1959 C
Ryder, George, 1905 E
Ryder, John, 1889 E
Rydge, Norman B. 1928 E
Rye grass, Vic, 1919 B
Rylstone, NSW, 1885 F
Rymill, John R. 1905 A
Ryrie, Granville de L. 1865 A, 1927 A
Ryrie, William, 1838 A

#

S. Rosevear, 1944 C
Sachse, Bert, 1935 F
Sackville, NSW, 1946 E
Sacred Concerto, 1845 C
Sacred Heart Catholic College, NSW, 1872 D
Sacred Heart Convent, Rose Bay, Sydney, 1896 C
Sacred music, 1834 C
Saddleworth, SA, 1851 F
Sadie, The Cleaning Lady, 1967 C
Sadler's Wells Ballet Co., 1933 C

Safety standards, cars, 1968 B
Safflower, 1899 B, 1955 A
Safran, Henri, 1977 C
Sage, Annie M. 1895 B
Sahm, Bernar, 1926 C
Sailboarding, 1983 E
Sailing, 1827 E, 1900 E, 1907 E, 1939 E, 1958 E, 1967 E, 1977 E
Sailor's Guide, 1958 E
Sailors' Home, Sydney, 1839 F, 1865 F
St Albans, NSW, 1842 F
St Albans, P. 1876 E
St Andrew's Cathedral, Sydney, 1837 D, 1868 D
St Andrew's Cathedral Choir, Sydney, 1885 D
St Andrew's Church, Brisbane, 1910 C
St Andrew's Church, Perth, 1879 D
St Arnaud, Vic, 1842 F
St Columba's Convent School, Dalby, 1877 D
St David's Cathedral, Hobart, 1868 D, 1874 D
St David's cemetery, Tas, 1804 F
St David's Church, Hobart, 1817 D, 1822 C, 1823 D, 1825 C
St Francis' Church, Melbourne, 1841 D, 1845 D
St Francis Xavier's Cathedral, Adelaide, 1856 D
St Francis Xavier Cathedral, Geraldton, WA, 1916 C
St Francis Xavier School, Adelaide, 1871 D
St George, Qld, 1846 F
St George Rugby League Football Club/team, 1920 E, 1941 E, 1949 E, 1956 E, 1957 E, 1958 E, 1959 E, 1960 E, 1961 E, 1962 E, 1963 E, 1964 E, 1965 E, 1966 E, 1977 E, 1979 E
St George's Cathedral, Perth, 1880 D
St George's Church, Perth, 1845 C
St George's Hall Theatre, Perth, 1879 C
St Helens, Tas, 1834 F
St Ignatius School, Sydney, 1880 D
St James' Church, Sydney, 1819 D, 1820 D
St James Church of England Teacher Training School, Sydney, 1858 D
St James Theatre, Sydney, 1926 C
St John, Parish, NSW, 1802 D
St John's Ambulance Association, Melbourne, 1887 F
St John's Cathedral, Brisbane, 1901 D
St John's Cemetery, Parramatta, 1790 F
St John's Church, Albany, WA, 1848 D
St John's Church, Camden, 1841 D
St John's Church, Parramatta, 1803 D
St John's Church, Richmond, Tas, 1836 D
St Joseph's Catholic College, Qld, 1891 D
St Joseph's College, Brisbane, 1875 D
St Joseph's Training School, Sydney, 1913 D
St Julian, Charles, 1848 F
St Kilda, 1906 B, 1923 F
St Kilda Aust. Rules Football Club/team, 1873 E, 1925 E, 1957 E, 1958 E, 1965 E, 1966 E, 1967 E
St Kilda Gallery, Melbourne, 1966 C
St Luke's Church, Richmond, Tas, 1838 D
St Martin's Theatre, Melbourne, 1931 C
St Mary's, NSW, 1803 F, 1954 B
St Mary's, Tas, 1855 F, 1886 B
St Mary's Benedictine Monastery, Sydney, 1842 D

St Mary's Cathedral, Hobart, 1861 D
St Mary's Cathedral, Perth, 1863 D
St Mary's Cathedral, Sydney, 1821 D, 1829 D, 1836 D, 1838 C, 1865 D
St Mary's Catholic Teacher Training College, Sydney, 1861 D
St Mary's College, NSW, 1852 D
St Mary's Convent School, Ipswich, 1863 D
St Mary's Seminary School, Sydney, 1837 D
St Matthew's Church, Windsor, 1817 D
St Patrick's Cathedral, Melbourne, 1850 D, 1858 C
St Patrick's Church, Sydney, 1845 D
St Patrick's College, Goulburn, NSW, 1875 D
St Patrick's College, Melbourne, 1854 D
St Patrick's College, Sydney, 1889 D
St Paul (ship), 1914 F
St Paul's Cathedral, Melbourne, 1839 D, 1880 D
St Peter's Cathedral, Adelaide, 1869 D, 1878 D
St Peter's College, Adelaide, 1847 D
St Phillip's Church, Sydney, 1807 D, 1810 D
St Phillip, (parish), NSW, 1802 D
St Stanislaus' Catholic College, 1867 D
St Stephen's Cathedral, Brisbane, 1874 D
St Stephen's Catholic Secondary School, Brisbane, 1875 D
St Thomas' Church, Port Macquarie, NSW, 1824 D
St Vincent de Paul, Sydney, 1881 F
St Xavier College, Melbourne, 1878 D
Sainthill, Loudon, 1918 C
Sala, George A. 1885 F
Salami, 1981 F
Sale, Vic, 1845 F
Sale Regional Arts Centre, Vic, 1964 C
Sales tax, 1930 A, 1960 A
Salinity, Murray R., 1920 B
Salins, Gunars, 1926 C
Salisbury, Harold H. 1978 A
Salisbury College of Advanced Education, SA, 1968 D
Salisbury Teachers College, SA, 1968 D
Salk vaccine, 1955 B, 1956 B
Salkauskas, Henry, 1925 C
Salmon, 1860 B, 1864 B, 1865 B, 1873 A, 1877 A
Salmon, William A. 1928 C
Salmonella food poisoning, 1981 F
Salon, 1904 C, 1912 C
Salon Lumière, 1896 C
Salt, 1790 B, 1803 A
Salt Creek, SA, 1881 B, 1892 B
Saltbush Bill and Other Verses, 1917 C
Salter, William 1804 A
Salvado, Rosendo, 1814 D, 1846 D
Salvana, John, 1873 C
Salvation Army, 1880 D, 1881 D, 1897 C, 1898 C, 1899 C, 1900 C, 1939 D
Salvinia waterfern, Qld, 1981 B
Salzburg Tales, 1934 C
Sams, Frederick E. H. 1881 D
Samson, Lionel, 1799 A, 1829 A
Samuels, Charles, 1888 E
Samuels, Joseph, 1803 F
San Francisco, mail to, 1870 F
San Francisco Bay to Breakers footrace, 1976 E
Sand mining, NSW, 1870 B, 1932 A, Qld, 1966 B, 1976 A
Sandals, 1935 F
Sandalwood, WA, 1846 A
Sandalwood oil, WA, 1921 A
Sandamara (pigeon), 1897 A

Sanders, Billy, 1955 E
Sanders, T. 1887 E
Sanders, Tom, 1925 C
Sandford, Vic, 1837 F
Sandford, William, 1840 B
Sandgate, Vic, 1862 E
Sandhurst, Vic, 1872 A, 1874 A
Sandor, Eve, 1924 C
Sandover Medal, WA, 1921 E
Sandown, Melbourne, 1904 E
Sandringham, Vic, 1918 B
Sands, Alfie, 1929 E
Sands, Clem, 1919 E
Sands, David R. 1926 E, 1949 E
Sands, George, 1924 E
Sands, Percy, 1922 E
Sands, Russell, 1937 E
Sandstone, WA, 1854 F
Sangster, John G. 1928 C
Sani, Tomaso, 1839 C, 1883 C
Sansom, Gareth L. 1939 C
Sansonetti, Remo, 1950 E
Santa Gertrudis cattle, 1933 A, 1952 B
Santamaria, Bartholomew A. 1915 A, 1936 F, 1942 A, 1957 A
Sapphire, 1859 F
Sapphires, Qld, 1977 B
Sargent, Malcolm, 1966 C
Sari Bair, (ANZACS), 1915 A
Sarich, Ralph, 1938 B, 1970 B, 1971 B
Sarina, Qld, 1880 F, 1927 B
Sarre, Kevin, 1963 E, 1965 F
Sasanof, 1916 E
Satellite tracking station, SA, 1957 B
Satellites, WRESAT, 1967 B
Sattler, John, 1945 E
Saturday hospital collection, 1894 F
Saturday I. WA, 1850 B
Saturdee, 1933 C
Satyrs and Sunlight: Silvarum Libri, 1909 C
Saunders, Edward, 1880 D
Saunders, John, 1806 D, 1834 D, 1835 D
Saunders, P. 1881 B
Saunders, Reginald W. 1944 A
Savage, Robert, 1877 B
Savage Crows, The, 1976 C
Savery, Henry, 1791 C, 1829 C, 1830 C
Savige, Stanley, G. 1890 A, 1920 F
Saville-Kent, William, 1908 B
Savings banks, first, 1819 A
Savings Bank of NSW, 1832 A, 1956 A
Savings Bank of SA, 1847 A
Savouries, 1931 F
Savoy Hotel, Sydney, 1975 F
Savoy Theatre, Sydney, 1931 C, 1936 C
Saw-fish, 1845 B
Sawtell, NSW, 1861 F
Sawtell, Thomas, 1837 A
Saxe-Coburg, Princes of, 1872 A
Saxon merinos, 1832 B, 1856 B
Sayers, Neville, 1956 E
Scab, sheep, 1832 B, 1865 B, 1867 B
Scaddan, John, 1876 A, 1911 A
Scales, Richard M. 1923 C
Scales of Justice, 1983 C
Scallops, Tas, 1903 A
Scallywag, 1982 E
Scarfe, Warren, 1936 E
Scarlet fever, 1841 F
Scarlett, Kenneth W. 1927 C
Scarvell, Richard E. 1922 C
Scenic areas, Tas, 1863 F
Scenic Parks, Vic, 1882 F
Schaefer, Manfred, 1944 E
Schaeffer, Philip, 1790 F
Schaffer, Phillip, 1797 A
Scharf, Theo, 1899 C
Schaw, 1837 F
Scheelite, Tas, 1904 B, 1971 B

Scheltema, Jan H. 1861 C
Schepers, Karin, 1927 C
Schepisi, Fred, 1978 C
Scherger, Frederick R. W. 1904 A
Schilling, Ivy, 1910 C
Schindler's Ark, 1982 C
Schlight, Rollin, 1937 C
Schlink, Herbert H. 1883 B, 1910 A, 1927 E, 1946 B
Scholarships, 1886 C, 1887 C, 1966 C
Scholes, Gordon, 1983 A
Schomburgk, M. Richard, 1811 B
Schonbach, Frederick, 1920 C
Schonell, Frederick J. 1900 D
Schools, *see also* Education *and individual entries*
  boarding, 1804 D
  collegiate, 1831 D
  correspondence, 1914 D
  Curriculums, 1938 D
  first schools, 1789 D, 1791 D, 1792 D, 1793 D, 1797 D, 1798 D, 1804 D, 1806 D, 1835 D, 1848 D
  fees, 1952 D
  free milk, 1950 D
  govt, Perth, 1830 D
  infant, 1824 D, 1908 D, *see also* Kindergartens
  inspectors, 1874 D, 1912 D
  leaving age, 1913 D, 1940 D, 1943 D, 1946 D, 1962 D, 1963 D, 1974 D
  'national', 1834 D, 1847 D, 1849 D, 1850 D
  numbers, 1820 D, 1848 D, 1965 D
  open space, 1968 D
  orphans, 1801 D, 1819 D
  private, 1800 D, 1807 D, 1843 D, *see individual entries*
  radio broadcasts, 1924 D, 1935 D
  Roman Catholic, 1805 D, 1845 D, 1846 D, *see individual entries*
  secondary, WA, 1858 D, *see individual entries*
  sport, 1835 E, 1876 E
  travelling, 1901 D
Schools of the Air, 1951 D, 1959 D
School of Architecture, Sydney University, 1918 C
School of Arts, Sydney, 1833 D, 1871 D
Schools of dancing, Sydney, 1833 C, 1894 C
School of Dental Nursing, Tas, 1966 D
School of Design, 1827 D
School of Fine Arts, Adelaide, 1921 C
School of General Studies, ANU, 1960 D
School of Industry, 1826 D
School of Librarianship, 1960 D
School of Mines, Ballarat, 1870 D, 1891 D, Bendigo, 1873 D
School of Music, Sydney, 1836 C
School of Public Health and Tropical Medicine, 1930 B
School of Sculpture, Sydney, 1927 C
Schrader, Jim, 1932 E
Schramm, Alexander, 1814 C
Schultz, John, 1960 E
Schwartz, W. F. 1877 D
Schumacher, Mel, 1937 E, 1958 E
Schuppan, Vern, 1942 E
Schwezoff, Igor, 1940 C
Science, *see section B and individual entries*
Science Foundation for Physics, Sydney, 1954 B
Science Museum, Melbourne, 1870 D
Science teaching, 1964 D
Scientific agreements, with USSR and India, 1975 B

Scientific exchange programme, China, 1976 B
Scientific expedition, Russian, 1820 A
Scientific Society, Tas, 1829 B
Scientific and technological co-operation treaty, China, 1979 B
Scientology, 1956 D, 1965 D, 1983 D
Scobie, James, (1), 1854 A
Scobie, James, (2), 1860 E
Scone, NSW, 1837 F, 1839 B
Scone Art Prize, NSW, 1964 C
Scotch College,
  Adelaide, 1919 D
  Melbourne, 1851 D, 1858 E
Scotney, Evelyn, 1896 C, 1924 C
Scots Church,
  Adelaide, 1851 C
  Melbourne, 1874 D
  Sydney, 1824 D
Scots School, Melbourne, 1838 D
Scott, Andrew G. 1842 A
Scott, Charles, 1934 E
Scott, Clow and Prebble, 1856 B
Scott, Eric, 1898 C
Scott, Ernest, 1867 D, 1916 C
Scott, G. B. 1873 A
Scott, James (b. 1790), 1790 B
Scott, James (b. 1875), 1875 E
Scott, James F. 1879 C
Scott, Michael, 1878 E, 1904 E
Scott, Robert, 1874 B
Scott, Robert F. 1868 A, 1901 A
Scott, Rose, 1847 A, 1891 A, 1918 A
Scott, Sydney, 1883 A
Scott, Thomas A. 1823 B, 1881 A
Scott, Thomas H. 1824 D, 1825 D, 1860 D
Scott, W. N. 1923 C
Scott Polar Research Institute, 1925 B
Scottish and Aust. Bank Ltd, 1969 A
Scottish Australia Co., 1840 A
Scottish Aust. Holdings Ltd, 1840 A
Scottish Collie, 1870 B
Scottish Highland Society of NSW, 1877 F
Scottish Martyrs, 1794 A
Scottish Societies, 1857 F, *see individual entries*
Scottsdale, Tas, 1855 F, 1943 A
Scout Association of Aust., 1958 F
Scouting, 1908 F, 1920 F
Scratchley, Peter H. 1835 B, 1877 A
scrub-rolling, 1881 B
Scuba diving, 1960 E, 1964 E
Scullin, James H. 1876 A, 1910 A, 1928 A, 1929 A, 1931 A, 1932 A
Scullin Tariff, 1929 A
Sculling, 1866 E, 1868 E, 1876 E, 1888 E, 1963 E
Scully-Power, Paul, 1984 B
Sculptors' Society of Aust., 1932 C
Sculpture, *see* Visual Arts *section C and individual entries*
  early, 1798 C
  modern, 1931 C
  outdoor exhibition, Sydney, 1951 C
Sculthorpe, Peter J. 1929 C, 1954 C, 1965 C, 1970 C, 1974 C
Sea elephant oil, 1805 A
Sea Lake, Vic, 1895 F
Sea and Spinifex, 1934 C
Sea Spray and Smoke Drift, 1867 C
Seabed Arms Control Treaty, 1973 A
Seabed boundary, 1972 A
SEACOM cable, 1967 B
Seal, Territorial, 1791 A, 1817 F
Seal of Government Acceptances Act, 1938 A

Seal of Government Surrender Act, NSW, 1909 A
Seal Rocks Bay, NSW, 1864 F
Seal skins, 1805 A
Sealing, 1791 A, 1800 A, 1803 A, 1804 A, 1810 A
Seaman, Keith D. 1920 A, 1977 A
Seamen's Union of Aust., 1872 A
Seamen's bans, 1967 A
Seamen's strikes, 1893 A, 1919 A
Seaplane race, 1977 E
Searelle, Luscombe, 1889 C
Searle, Henry E. 1866 E, 1888 E
Seatbelts, 1971 F, 1972 F
Secession, WA, 1926 A, 1930 A, 1933 A, 1935 A, 1974 A
Secessionist League, WA, 1926 A
Second Advent, The, 1859 C
Second Fleet, 1790 A
Second World War, 1939 A, 1940 A, 1941 A, 1942 A, 1943 A, 1944 A, 1945 A, 1947 A, 1950 A
Secondary School Academy, Sydney, 1804 D, 1805 D
Secret ballot,
  NSW, 1858 A
  Qld, 1859 A
  SA, 1856 A
  Tas, 1858 A
  Vic, 1856 A
  WA, 1877 A
Secret ballot, industrial action, 1981 A
Secret ballots at strikes, 1972 A
Secret Intelligence Service, 1915 A
Secular Education Act, Vic, 1872 D
Security, 1980 A
Security, national regulations, wartime, 1946 A
Security Council, UNO, 1946 A
Security organizations, ASIO, 1973 A, *see also individual entries*
Security services, 1945 A, 1949 A, *see also individual entries*
Sedco, Helen, 1970 F
Sedgman, Francis A. 1927 E, 1951 E
See, John, 1844 A, 1901 A
Seeding, aerial, 1947 B
Seekers, 1965 C, 1967 C
Seffrin, Nickolaus J. 1931 C
Sefton, Clyde, 1951 E
Segal, Eva, 1970 C
'Segenhoe', Hunter Valley, NSW, 1825 A
Seidel, Brian, 1928 C
Seidler, Harry, 1923 C, 1947 C, 1948 C, 1967 C, 1977 C
Seismology, NT, 1965 B
Selected Verse, 1948 C
Selection, land, 1860 A, 1861 A, 1862 A, 1865 A, 1869 A, 1874 A
Selection Acts, 1858 A, 1862 A, 1869 A
Self government, colonial, 1825 A, 1849 A
Self Portrait, Norman Baker, 1937 C
Self Portrait, Henry Hanke, 1934 C
Self Portrait, Ivor Hele, 1957 C
Self Portrait, Brett Whiteley, 1976 C, 1978 C
Selfe, Norman, 1839 B
Selig, Sylviane, 1940 C
Selkrig, Ray, 1930 E, 1961 E
Sellbach, Udo, 1927 C
Sellheim, Gert, 1901 C
Sellwood, Neville, 1923 E, 1951 E, 1955 E
Selvey, Warick, 1920 E, 1967 E
Semaphore, SA, 1878 B
Senate, Federal, 1901 A, 1902 A, 1930 A, 1943 A, 1948 A

Senbergs, Jan, 1939 C
Senior exams, Qld, 1972 D
Sentimental Bloke, The (film), 1919 C, 1932 C, (musical), 1961 C
Separation, Tas, 1824 A
Sephardi Synagogue, Sydney, 1962 D
Seppelt, Joseph E. 1813 A, 1851 A
Seppelt family, 1918 A
Seppeltsfield, SA, 1851 A
Serbian Orthodox Diocese of Aust., 1973 D
Serebrier, Jose, 1980 C
Serena, Clara, 1890 C
Sericultural Society, 1868 A
Serle, Percival, 1871 C, 1927 C
Serong, Francis P. 1915 A
Serotonin, 1976 B
Serra, Joseph M. B. 1846 D, 1886 D
Servants, 1826 D
Servants, Training Institution, Melbourne, 1883 D
Service, James, 1823 A, 1880 A, 1883 A
Service Homes Scheme, 1919 C
Serviceton, Vic, 1887 B
Sestier, Marius, 1896 C
Settlement, land, 1788 A, 1894 A
Settlements, communities, *see each year section E and individual entries*
Settlers and Convicts, 1847 C
Seven British Artists Exhibition, 1959 C
Seven Emus, 1959 C
Seven Hill, SA, 1845 F
Seven Little Australians (book), 1894 C
Seven Little Australians (series), 1973 C
Seven Poor Men of Sydney, 1935 C
Seven Rivers, The, 1966 C
Seventh Day Adventists, 1885 D, 1886 D, 1897 D
Sewage effluent, 1960 B
Sex and Destiny, 1984 C
Seymour, Alan, 1927 C, 1960 C
Seymour, David T. 1831 A, 1864 A
Seymour, Everest R. Y. 1905 A
Seymour, Mrs, 1909 A
Seymour, Vic, 1839 F
Seymour Theatre Centre, Sydney, 1974 C
Shackleton, Ernest H. 1874 A
'Shaddup you face', 1980 C
Shakespeare's Roman Plays and their Background, 1910 C
Shakespearian Acting Co., 1915 C
Shakespearian Theatre Co., 1948 C
Shale mining, NSW, 1905 B
Shale oil, NSW, 1866 B
Shanahan, A. 1912 E, 1913 E
Shand, Donald M. 1904 B, 1947 B
Shann, Edward O. G. 1884 A
Shannon, Michael, 1927 C
Shapcott, Thomas W. 1935 C
Shappira, Elyakum, 1975 C
Share markets, 1984 A
Shark arm murder mystery, Sydney, 1935 F
Shark creek, NSW, 1935 B
Shark meshing, NSW, 1936 F
Sharkey, Lawrence L. 1949 A
Sharman, Jim, 1945 C, 1972 C
Sharp, James C. 1905 C
Sharp, Martin R. 1942 C
Sharp, Ronald, 1969 C
Shaw, Alan G. L. 1916 D
Shaw, Edward, 1914 C
Shaw, Gayfield, 1920 C
Shaw, George 1794 A
Shaw, Gerrard G. 1885 C
Shaw, Jeffrey, 1944 C
Shaw, Michael, 1937 C
Shaw, Roderick M. 1915 C

Shay Gap, WA, 1971 F, 1980 F
Shead, George, 1879 A
Shean, F. 1938 E
Shean, Maxwell H. 1918 A
Shearer, Bob, 1948 E
Shearer, David, 1879 D
Shearer car, 1894 B
Shearers, 1894 A, 1964 F
Shearer's Colt, The, 1936 C
Shearers' strikes, 1891 A, 1894 A, 1956 A
Shearers' Union, 1890 A
Shearing, 1835 A, 1874 B, 1892 F, 1909 F, 1950 E, 1963 E, 1965 F, 1972 E, 1979 F
Shearing, Dinah H. 1927 C
Shearing, records, 1892 F, 1965 F
Shearing machines, 1868 B, 1870 B, 1872 B, 1877 B, 1884 B, 1888 B
Shearing the Rams, 1889 C
Shearing, Shed Hands Union, 1890 A
Shears, sheep, 1874 B
Sheedy, Jack, 1926 E
Sheep, 1802 A, 1820 A, 1831 A, 1835 A, 1836 A, 1837 A
  anthrax, 1847 B
  'Australia Felix', 1839 A
  blowfly, 1903 F, 1958 B
  breeding, 1793 A, 1797 A, 1826 A, 1838 B
  breeds and flocks,
  – Corriedale, 1882 B
  – Haddon Rig stud, 1882 B
  – Hazeldean merino stud, 1865 B
  – Merino, 1794 A, 1795 A, 1797 A, 1981 A
  Peppin, 1858 B, 1880 A
  coast disease, 1934 B
  dog trials, 1871 F
  exports, 1929 A, 1971 A, 1978 A, 1982 C
  farming, 1805 A
  scab, 1832 B, 1865 B, 1867 B
  Sydney Show, 1895 F
Sheet Anchor, 1885 E
Sheffield, Tas, 1908 F
Sheffield Athletic Handicap, NSW, 1878 E
Sheffield athletics, Sydney, 1887 E
Sheffield Shield cricket, 1892 E, 1983 E
Shehadie, Nicholas (1), 1911 D
Shehadie, Nicholas (2), 1927 E
Sheldon, Frederick S. 1853 C
Sheldon, Vincent, 1895 C
Shell Aria, Canberra, 1955 C
Shell Aust. Ltd, 1983 B
Shellharbour, NSW, 1835 F
Shenandoah, 1865 A
Shenton, George, 1880 A
Shepard, Barry, 1938 E
Shepherd, George, 1939 B
Shepherd, Roy, 1930 B
Sheppard, Benjamin, 1876 C
Shepparton, Vic, 1843 F, 1979 F
Shepparton Art Gallery, Vic, 1934 C
Sherbert, 1969 C
Sheridan, John F. 1908 C
Sherlock, Max, 1925 C
Sherman, Albert, 1882 C
Sherratt, Thomas B. 1835 D
Sherwin, Amy, 1855 C
Sherwin, Walter, 1856 C
Sherwin, William, 1804 B, 1823 B
Shield, William, 1796 C
Shiels, William, 1848 A, 1892 A
Shifting Heart, The, 1956 C, 1957 C
Shillam, Kathleen, 1916 C
Shillam, Leonard, 1915 C
Shingle houses, 1889 C
Shingled hair, 1922 F
Ship-building, NSW, 1813 A, 1819 B

Ship Painters and Dockers' Union, 1915 A
Shipping, 1813 A, B, 1921 B
Shipping Labour Bureau, SLB, 1925 A
Shipping pilots, 1803 B
Shipping services, 1823 B, 1921 B, 1952 B
Shipping strike, Sydney, 1925 A, 1928 A
Ships, 1965 B, 1971 B
Ships, capital, 1913 A
Shipwrecks, *see individual entries and section F*
Shipwrights' Society, 1840 A
Shipwrights' United Friendly Society, 1830 A
Shiralee, The, 1955 C
Shirley Thompson Versus the Aliens, 1972 C
Shirlow, John A. 1869 C
Shirts, 1908 F
Shoalhaven R., NSW, 1797 A
Shoalhaven Art Prize, NSW, 1967 C
Shoes, 1935 F, 1951 F
Shoes of the Fisherman, 1963 C
Sholl, Lionel H. 1844 A
Sholl, Reginald, R. 1902 A
Sholl, Richard, 1836 A
Sholl, Robert J. 1819 A
Sholl, William H. 1808 B
Shooting, 1831 F, 1862 E, 1896 E, 1927 E, 1956 E, 1963 E, *see also* Pistol *and* Clay target
Shop, first, 1790 A
Shopping hours, 1813 F, 1909 F, 1927 F, 1968 F, 1971 F, 1979 A
Shore, Arnold J. V. 1897 C, 1918 C, 1932 C
Short, Augustus, 1802 D, 1847 D, 1974 D
Short, Ernest, 1875 C
Short, William, 1834 C
Short History of Australia, A, 1916 C
Short Stories in Prose and Verse, 1894 C
Shorter hour movement, 1840 A, *see also* Working hours
Shortland, John (b. 1739), 1797 A, B, 1803 A
Shortland, John (b. 1769), 1810 A
Shortland, Peter F. 1813 A
Showgirl's Luck, 1931 C
Shows, *see individual entries*
Shows, agricultural, 1838 F, *see individual entries*
Shrimpton, Jean, 1965 F
Shrine of Remembrance, Melbourne, 1934 F, 1968 F
'Shuffle off to Buffalo', 1933 C
Shute, Nevil, 1899 C, 1950 C, 1952 C, 1957 C
Si-ro-set method, 1957 B
Siamese twins, 1975 F
Siandra, 1958 E, 1960 E
Sibley, Andrew, 1933 C
Sicard, Francois, 1862 C
Sick leave, 1922 A, 1951 A
Sickness benefits, Cwlth, 1944 A, 1945 A
Sidaway, Robert, 1796 C, 1798 C, 1800 C, 1809 C
Sidcot Flying Suit, 1916 B
Siddons, Scott, 1876 C
Siding Springs, NSW, 1974 B
Siding Springs Astronomy Station, NSW, 1962 B
Siding Springs Observatory, NSW, 1965 B, 1974 B, 1976 B
Sidney, William P., Viscount de L'Isle, 1909 A, 1961 A
Sidoti, Pedro, 1970 E
Sidwell, Billy, 1920 E
Sieben, John, 1984 E
Sievier, Robert, 1882 E

Sigma, 1896 F
Sign posts, Sydney, 1810 A
Signadou College of Education, NSW, 1926 D
Silence of Dean Maitland, The, 1914 C
Silk, 1848 A, 1938 F
Silk Culture Society of NSW, 1911 B
Silk and Lace (painting), 1926 C
Silk worm, 1868 A
Silkhorne, John, 1803 F
Silks, jockey, 1842 E
SILLIAC computer, 1956 B
Silly mid-on, 1878 E
Silver, 1839 B, 1841 B, 1862 B, 1864 B, 1875 B, 1883 B, 1885 B, 1887 B, 1923 B
Silver currency, 1969 F
Silver extraction, NSW, 1910 B
Silver King, The, 1897 C
Silver Knight, 1971 E
Silverton, NSW, 1880 F, 1885 B
Sime, Dawn, 1932 C
Sime, Ian, 1926 C
Simmons, Walter E. I. 1881 B
Simms, Eric, 1944 E
Simonetti, Achille, 1840 C, 1875 C
Simons, John J. 1883 A
Simonsen Opera Co., 1872 C
Simple Rules for the Guidance of Persons in Humble Life, 1837 C
Simpson, Bobby, 1977 E
Simpson, Colin, 1908 C, 1951 C
Simpson, George, 1927 B
Simpson, George B. 1909 A
Simpson, Helen de G. 1897 C
Simpson, Nora C. 1895 C, 1913 C
Simpson, Percy, 1823 A
Simpson, Robert B. 1936 E
Simpson, Ronald A. 1929 C
Simpson Desert, NT, SA, 1845 A, 1939 A
Simpson Medal, WA, 1945 E
Simson, David D. 1842 A
Simson, Donald C. 1851 A
Simson, Hector N. 1820 A
Simson, John C. C. 1840 A
Sinai campaign, Middle East, 1916 A
Sinbad the Sailor, 1880 C
Sinclair, Alexander, 1981 F
Sinclair, Alexander J. M. 1908 B
Sinclair, Alfred W. 1866 C
Sinclair, Ian, 1979 A, 1980 A
Sinclair, James, 1896 A
Sinclair, John, 1856 A
Sinclair, Margaret E. 1918 C
Singapore, Aust. naval base, 1923 A, 1924 A
Singapore, fall of, 1942 A, raid, 1943 A, defence treaty, 1971 A
Singer of the Bush, 1983 C
Singles, 1984 C
Singleton, NSW, 1820 F, 1826 B
Sinn, Bobby, 1939 E
Sir Frank Kitto, 1975 C
Sir Henry Simpson Newland, 1953 C
Sir James Elder, 1941 C
Sir John McEwen, 1971 C
Sir John Sulman, 1931 C
Sir Leslie McConnan, 1950 C
Sir Marcus Clarke, 1947 C
Sir Richard Bourke (statue), 1841 C, 1842 F
Sir William Irvine, 1932 C
Sirius HMS, 1788 A, 1789 A, 1790 A
Sirius, 1944 E
Sirotem instrument, 1977 B
Sister Olive, 1921 E
Sisters of Mercy, 1873 D, 1874 D, 1955 D
Sisters of St Joseph of the Sacred Heart, 1866 D
Sitsky, Larry, 1934 C, 1974 C

Six Directors Art Group, Sydney, 1953 C
Sixth General Synod of Anglican Church, 1981 D
Skardarasy, E. 1935 E
Skateboard riding, 1964 E, 1975 E, 1976 E, 1979 E
Skeleton weed, NSW, 1917 B
Skelton, R. 1976 E
Skelton, R. W. 1884 E
Ski chalets, 1920 F
Ski Club of Aust., 1920 E
Ski Council of NSW, 1929 E
Ski resorts, 1909 F, 1910 E
Skiing, 1861 E, 1862 E, 1863 E, 1927 E, 1930 E, 1931 E, 1935 E
Skilton, Bob, 1939 E, 1959 E, 1963 E, 1968 E
Skindiving, 1947 E, *see also* Scuba diving
Skinner, Mary L. 1877 C
Skinner Art Galleries, Perth, 1958 C
Skipper, John M. 1815 C
Skipper, Matcham, 1930 C
Skipper, Mervyn G. 1886 C
Skipton, 1941 E
Skipton, Vic, 1852 F
Skirts, 1911 F, 1925 F, 1933 F
Skirving, Robert S. 1859 B
Skivers, Leo, 1910 C
Skulls, Talgai, 1886 B
Skuthorpe, Lance, 1870 E, 1896 F, 1906 E, 1938 E
Sky scraper, 1912 C
Skyhooks, 1973 C, 1974 C
Sladen, Charles, 1816 A, 1868 A
Sladen, Douglas B. W. 1856 C, 1888 C
Slaney, 1825 A
Slang dictionary, 1819 C
Slapoffski, Gustave, 1860 C
Slattery, Jack, 1885 B
Slaughter houses, 1834 A
Slaughter on St Teresa's Day, The, 1959 C
Slavin, Frank, 1862 E
Sleeping Prince, The, 1955 C
Sleigh, Hamilton M. H. 1896 A
Sleigh, H. C. 1895 A
Slessor, Kenneth A. 1901 C, 1923 C, 1924 C, 1926 C, 1932 C, 1939 C, 1944 C
Sliced bread, 1939 F
Slim William J. 1891 A, 1953 A
'Slim Dusty', 1928 C, 1946 C, 1957 C
'Slippery Charlie,' *see* Cowper, Sir Charles
Slouch hat, 1885 F
Slow Natives, The, 1965 C
Small, Andrew B. 1895 A
Smalley, George R. 1870 B
Smallhorn, W. ('Chicken'), 1933 E
Smallpox, 1788 B, 1789 F, 1804 B, 1874 F, 1880 F, 1881 F, 1882 F, 1884 F, 1887 F, 1893 F, 1913 F
Smart, Jeffrey, 1921 C
Smart, Ralph, 1947 C
Smart, Thomas C. 1816 B
Smeaton, Bruce J. 1938 C
Smith, A. J. 1906 B, 1909 B
Smith, Arch, 1920 E
Smith, Artie, 1945 C
Smith, Athol, 1945 B
Smith, Beaumont, 1917 C
Smith, Bernard, 1916 C, 1962 C
Smith, Bernie, 1927 E, 1951 E
Smith, Billy, 1942 E
Smith, Charles, 1830 E
Smith, Darnell, 1915 B
Smith, David, 1896 E
Smith, Dick, 1982 B
Smith, Donald, 1922 C

Smith, Eric J. 1919 C, 1948 C, 1956 C, 1970 C, 1981 C, 1982 C
Smith, Ernest, 1928 C
Smith, Frances, 1938 C
Smith, Francis V. 1819 A, 1857 A, 1874 A, 1880 A
Smith, Frank, 1929 E
Smith, Frederick C. 1819 C
Smith, Gerard, 1895 A
Smith, Grace Cossington, 1892 C, 1915 C
Smith, Grafton E. 1871 B, 1895 D
Smith, Gray, 1919 C
Smith, Greg, 1977 C
Smith, H. G. 1897 B
Smith, Helen, 1975 E
Smith, Henry A. 1958 A, 1965 A
Smith, Henry T. 1858 B
Smith, J. Carrington, 1908 C, 1963 C
Smith, J. H. 1878 D
Smith, J. M. 1926 A
Smith, James (1), 1788 A
Smith, James (2), 1820 C, 1855 F
Smith, James ('Philosopher Smith', b. 1827), 1827 B, 1871 B
Smith, James J. 1855 A, 1919 F
Smith, John, 1821 B
Smith, John McG. 1844 B
Smith, Joshua, 1944 C
Smith, Keith M. 1890 B, 1919 B
Smith, Leon, 1935 C
Smith, Louis L. 1830 B
Smith, M. S. C. 1919 A
Smith, Margaret, 1963 E
Smith, Maria A. 1800 A, 1868 A
Smith, Mervyn A. 1904 C
Smith, Norman, ('Wizard'), 1890 E, 1939 E
Smith, Norman, (b. 1909), 1909 E
Smith, Pamela J. 1937 C
Smith, Robert Barr, 1824 A
Smith, Robert Bower, 1838 B, 1876 B
Smith, Ross, 1943 E, 1967 E
Smith, Ross M. 1892 B, 1919 B, 1922 F
Smith, Roy, 1933 C
Smith, Samuel, 1812 A
Smith, Stephen H. 1865 D
Smith, Sydney Ure, 1887 C, 1906 C, 1916 C, 1939 A
Smith, Tommy, 1920 E
Smith, Victor A. T. 1913 A
Smith, William, 1917 C
Smith, William F. 1887 A, 1932 A
Smith, William H. 1813 A
Smith, William John, 1882 A
Smith, William Joshua, 1905 C
Smith, William R. 1859 B
Smith, William S. 1836 D
Smith, W. A. 1960 E
Smith, Family Welfare Organisation, Sydney, 1922 F
Smith-Hambleton case, 1847 C
Smith's Weekly, Sydney, 1919 F
Smithton, Tas, 1855 F
Smithy, 1946 C
Smog, 1984 B
Smoking, 1922 F, 1967 F, 1977 F, 1984 B
Smyth, 1844 B
Smyth, John, 1864 D
Snail killer, 1937 B
Snake bite antivenene, 1962 B
Snake venom, 1899 B, 1919 B
Snakes, 1948 F
Sneazewell, Tony, 1942 E
Snedden, Billy M. 1926 A, 1972 A, 1975 A
Smolnikova, Nelli, 1983 C
Snodgrass, Kenneth, 1836 A, 1837 A, 1853 A
Snooker, 1887 E, 1929 E, 1940 E, 1970 E   819

Snow, Melbourne, 1840 F, 1879 F
Snow, Sydney, 1836 F
Snowtown, SA, 1878 F
Snowy Mountains, NSW, Vic, 1834 A, 1931 F, 1949 B
Snowy Mountains Authority, 1970 B
Snowy Mountains Engineering Corporation, 1970 B
Snowy Mountains Hydro Electricity Scheme, 1949 B, 1955 B, 1957 B, 1958 B, 1959 B
Snowy R., 1834 A, 1839 A
Snugglepot and Cuddlepie, 1918 C
Soap, 1855 B
Soccer, 1862 E, 1880 E, 1882 E, 1883 E, 1884 E, 1885 E, 1888 E, 1902 E, 1904 E, 1922 E, 1923 E, 1924 E, 1956 E, 1959 E, 1962 E, 1965 E, 1970 E, 1974 E, 1977 E
Social grievances, NSW, 1819 A
Social Justice Sunday, 1940 D
Social and Military Virtues no. 227 (lodge), 1814 F
Social Science Research Council, 1952 B, 1971 D
Social service benefits agreement, 1953 A
Social services, Federal govt, 1943 A, 1945 A, 1946 A, 1960 A
Social Services Act, Federal, 1947 A
Social studies, 1938 D
Social Studies Research Council, 1971 D
Social welfare, NSW, 1935 A
Social Welfare Commission, 1973 A
'socialisation of industry', 1921 A
Socialist Party of Aust., 1971 A
Socialist Workers Party, 1975 A
Society of Arts and Crafts of NSW, 1906 C
Society of Aust. Genealogists, 1932 F
Society of Carpenters and Joiners, Qld, 1879 A
Society of Dance, Sydney, 1969 C
Society of Designers for Industry, 1948 C
Society of Friends, 1832 D
Society of Emigrant Mechanics, 1833 A
Society for Promoting Christian Knowledge, 1826 D
Society for the Promotion of the Fine Arts, Sydney, 1847 C, 1849 C
Society for the Propagation of the Gospel, 1797 D
Society of St Vincent de Paul, Sydney, 1881 F
Society of Sculptors and Associates, NSW, 1951 C, 1961 C
Society of Women Painters of NSW, 1910 C
Soda fountains, 1921 F, 1923 F
Sodeman, Arnold K. 1936 F
Softball, 1942 E, 1947 E, 1960 E
Soil Conservation Service of NSW, 1938 A
Soils, copper deficiency, 1930 B
Solar cell, 1979 B
Solar energy conference, Melbourne, 1979 C
Solar flares, 1946 B
Solar powered telecommunications, NT, 1979 B
Solar radiation, 1926 B
Solar research, 1912 B
Solar still, SA, 1966 B
Solar storage system, 1977 B
Solar time, SA, 1898 B
Soldiers' Children Education Scheme, 1920 D
Soldiers of the Cross, 1900 C
Soldiers' Women, 1961 C

Solicitors, 1815 A, 1822 A, 1923 A
Solid Gold, 1936 E
Solid Mandala, The, 1966 C
Solo, 1956 E, 1962 E
SOLO petrol stations, 1975 A
Solomon, Albert E. 1876 A, 1912 A
Solomon, Lance V. 1913 C
Solomon, V. L. 1899 A
Solomon Is, 1920 A, 1944 A
Solveig, 1954 E
Somens, Lord, *see* Cocks, A.H.T.S.
Somerset, Qld, 1863 A, F, 1877 A
Somerville, John L. 1899 B
Somme offensive, 1916 A
Somnambule, La, 1847 C
Sonatina, 1954 C
Song of Australia, 1859 C
Song of the Pen, 1983 C
Song of the Republic, 1887 C
'Song of the Women of the Menero Tribe', The, 1834 C
Songs of Light, 1935 C
Songs from the Mountains, 1880 C
Songs of a Sentimental Bloke, 1915 C
Sons of Matthew, 1949 C
Sophia Jane, 1831 B
Sorell, Tas, 1819 F
Sorell, William, 1817 A, 1820 A, 1822 A, 1848 A
Sorghum, 1948 A
Sorlie, George, 1885 C
Sorrento, Vic, 1803 A, F
Sound films, 1898 B, 1921 C
Souter, Charles H. 1864 C
Souter, Dan, 1882 E
Souter, David H. 1862 C
South Africa, 1899 A, 1900 A, 1971 E, 1972 E
South African Preference Treaty, 1906 A
South African Soldiers' Association, 1908 F
South Australia/n, *abbreviated as* SA
SA, representative govt, 1851 A
SA Aboriginal Lands Trust Act, 1966 A
SA Academy of Art, 1885 C
SA Academy of Arts, 1895 C
South Australian Advertiser, 1858 F
SA Agricultural Bureau, 1888 A
SA Art Gallery, 1861 C
SA Association, 1833 A, 1835 A
SA Association of Clerks, 1905 A
SA Ballet Club, 1941 C
SA border, 1839 A
SA boundaries, 1861 A
SA Brewing Co., 1888 A
SA British Football Association, 1902 E
SA Canoe Club, 1948 E
SA Centennial Art Prize, 1936 C
SA Chamber of Manufacturers, 1869 A
South Australian Colonization Act, 1834 A
SA Commercial Travellers' Association, 1866 F
SA Commissioner, 1840 A
SA Company, 1836 A, 1837 A, 1839 A
SA Conservatorium of Music, 1897 C
SA Cricket Association, 1871 E
SA Destitute Board, 1848 F
SA Education Act, 1852 D
SA Employers' Union, 1887 A
SA financial crisis, 1842 A, 1852 A
South Australian Gazette and Colonial Register, 1836 F
SA Industrial Commission, 1980 A
SA Institute, 1856 D, 1875 C
SA Institute of Architects, 1886 C
SA Institute of Teachers, 1951 D
SA Institute of Technology, 1889 D
SA Jockey Club, 1856 E

SA Land and Colonization Co., 1835 A
SA Library, 1856 D
SA Literary Society, 1834 C, 1837 D
South Australian Magazine, 1841 F
SA mandate over NT, 1862 A, 1863 A
SA Mechanics' Institute, 1856 D
SA Men's Hockey Association, 1903 E
SA Museum, 1855 D
SA National Art Collection, 1875 C
SA National Ballet, 1961 C
SA Ornithological Association, 1899 B
SA Parlt, 1855 A, *see* Government *section A and individual entries*
SA Police Commissioner, 1978 A
SA Power Boating Council, 1953 E
SA proclaimed, 1836 A
SA Public Library, 1884 D, 1967 D
South Australian Register, 1837 F
SA School of Arts, 1861 C
SA School of Mines, Adelaide, 1888 D
SA School of Mines and Industries, 1889 D
SA School Society, 1836 D, 1838 D
SA Subscription Library, 1844 D
SA Theatre Co., 1965 C, 1972 C
SA Trades and Labor Council, 1884 A
South Brisbane Technical College, 1902 D
South British Football Soccer Association, 1882 E
South British Insurance Co. Ltd, 1872 A
South Cape Bay, Tas, 1824 B
South Creek, Windsor, NSW, 1813 B
South East Asian refugees, 1978 A
South East Asian Treaty Organization, (SEATO), 1954 A, 1958 A
South Head, Sydney, 1817 C, 1818 B, 1844 F, 1857 F, 1880 B
South Johnstone mill, Qld, 1927 A
South Korea, uranium, 1979 A
South Magnetic Pole, 1909 A
South Melbourne Aust. Rules Football Club/team, 1874 E, 1909 E, 1918 E, 1933 E, 1940 E, 1949 E, 1955 E, 1959 E, 1963 E, 1968 E, 1970 E, 1977 E, 1981 E, 1982 E
South Melbourne Centenary Prize, 1955 C
South Pacific Forum, 1972 A
South Street Music Competition, Vic, 1891 C
South Sydney Rugby League Football Club/team, 1908 E, 1909 E, 1914 E, 1918 E, 1925 E, 1926 E, 1927 E, 1928 E, 1929 E, 1931 E, 1932 E, 1950 E, 1951 E, 1953 E, 1954 E, 1955 E, 1967 E, 1968 E, 1970 E, 1971 E
South Vietnam, aid to, 1958 A, *see also* Vietnam, South
South West Pacific Command, Melbourne, 1942 A
South Yarra Art Galleries, Melbourne, 1961 C
Southall, Ivan F. 1921 C, 1950 C
Southerly, 1939 F
Southern, Clara, 1861 C
Southern Aurora, 1962 B, 1969 F
Southern Cloud, 1931 F
Southern Cross, WA, 1887 B, F
Southern Cross (ship), 1920 F
Southern Cross (yacht), 1974 E
Southern Cross (aircraft), 1928 B, 1929 B
Southern Cross flag, 1854 A
Southern Cross pearls, 1883 F
Southern Hunt Club, 1860 E
Southern Rugby Union Football, 1874 E
Southern Tas Football Association, 1879 E

Southland, 1803 A
Southport Boys' School, Qld, 1913 D
Southwark Brewery, Adelaide, 1938 A
Southwell, Charles, 1855 D
Southwell, Harry, 1920 C
Sovereign (ship), 1847 F
Sovereign River Tenterfield, The, 1920 C
Sovereigns (coins), 1866 A
Soviet Trade Mission, Sydney, 1964 A
Sowden, William J. 1858 A
Soya bean industry, NSW, 1915 A
Space Tracking and Data Acquisition Station, ACT, 1963 B, 1964 B
Spalding, SA, 1855 F
Spanish Benedictines, 1846 D
Spanish dollars, 1804 A
Spanish Mission style architecture, 1918 C, 1925 C
'Spanish Prize', 1799 A
Speak with the Sun, 1949 C
Spearfelt, 1926 E
Spearfishing, 1955 E
Spears, Robert, 1893 E, 1920 E
Spears, S. J. 1978 C
Speary, Gordon A. 1914 C
Special Branch, SA, 1978 A
Special Intelligence Branch, 1919 A
Special Intelligence Bureau, 1915 A
Special Reserve Forces, 1964 A
Spectrophotometer, 1952 B, 1954 B
Speculative market collapse, 1842 A
Speech therapy, 1931 B
Speed boating, 1977 E, 1978 E
Speed limit, 1921 F
Speed signs, 1959 F
Speedways, *see* Motor cycle racing
Speers Point, NSW, 1829 E
Speleological Societies, 1946 F
Spence, Catherine H. 1825 C, 1854 C, 1865 C, 1868 C
Spence, Percy F. S. 1868 C
Spence, William G. 1846 A, 1874 A, 1886 A
Spencer, C. Cozens, 1905 C, 1910 C, 1912 C
Spencer, J. B. 1891 C
Spencer, Richard, 1833 A, 1839 A
Spencer, W. Baldwin, 1860 B, 1899 C, 1901 C, 1904 C, 1912 C, 1914 C, 1927 C, 1928 E
Spencer Gulf, SA, 1802 A, 1886 A
Spencer Street railway station, Melbourne, 1882 B
Spender, Percy C. 1897 A, 1950 A, 1958 A
Sperm count, 1984 B
Sphairee, 1961 E
Spicer, John A. 1899 A
'Spider dance', 1856 C
Spigl, H. S. 1962 B
Spilopsyllus cuniculi, 1969 B
Spirit of the Plain, The, 1897 C
Spirit of Progress, 1937 B
Spirits, imports, 1810 A
Spitfire, 1855 A
Spofforth, Frederick R. ('Demon'), 1853 E, 1879 E
Spong, William B. 1851 C
Sport, *see section E and individual entries*
Sporting Associations, *see individual entries*
Sporting Clubs, *see individual entries*
Sporting restrictions, wartime, 1917 E
Sporting Weekly, Sydney, 1929 E
Sports Arena, Sydney, 1927 E
Sportsmen/women of the Year, ABC, *see from 1951 section E*
Spotted alfalfa aphid, 1977 B
Spotted King prawn, 1958 B

Spowers, Ethel L. 1890 C
Spring Gardens Gallery, London, 1925 C
Spring Tyne Drill, cultivator, 1916 B
Springboks, 1937 E, 1971 A, E
Springbrook Art Prize, Qld, 1965 C
Springleigh bore, Qld, 1921 B
Springthorpe, John W. 1855 B
Springwood, NSW, 1815 F
Sproule, Clifford E. 1905 E
Spruzen, Geoffrey J. 1925 C
Spry, Charles C. F. 1910 A
Spur of the Moment, 1931 C
Spurling, Stephen, 1837 B, 1924 B
Squash, 1913 E, 1920 E, 1926 E, 1931 E, 1938 E, 1956 E, 1961 E, 1963 E, 1965 E, 1973 E, 1976 E, 1977 E, 1983 E
Squatters, 1826 A, 1836 A, 1839 A, 1843 A, 1844 A, 1847 A, 1849 A
Squatter's Daughter, The, 1933 C
Squire, James, 1795 A, 1822 A
Squire, R. A. 1916 B
Stackpole, Keith, 1940 E
Stafford, Paula, 1961 F
Stage coaches, 1869 B
Stalactites, Tas, 1917 B
Stallions, 1799 A, *see also* horses
Stamp covers, 1838 F
Stamp duties, NSW, 1865 A
Stamps, 1849 F, 1850 F, 1852 F, 1853 F, 1854 F, 1855 F, 1856 F, 1860 F, 1861 F, 1888 F, 1891 F, 1913 F, 1927 F, 1929 F, 1953 F, *see also* postage
Stamps, One Penny Black, 1854 F
Standard, NSW, 1872 F
Standards Association Aust., 1922 B, 1929 F
Standing Conference of Canonical Orthodox Churches in Aust., 1979 D
Stanford, William, 1837 C
Stanislaus Papotec, 1960 C
Stanley, Tas, 1826 F
Stanley, Arthur L. 1914 A
Stanley, C. 1868 E
Stanley, F. D. G. 1887 C
Stanley, G. H. 1853 D
Stanley, Ian, 1948 E
Stanley, Ida, 1914 E
Stanley, Owen, 1811 A, 1848 A
Stanthorpe, Qld, 1872 B, F
Stanton, Bob, 1946 E
Stanton, George H. 1835 D
Stanwell Park, NSW, 1894 B
Stapleton, Eddie, 1930 E
Star of Australia, 1865 F
Star of the West, 1917 C
Starfish, 1960 B, 1970 B, 1971 B
Stark, Mr. and Mrs., 1853 C
Starke, Hayden, 1920 A
Starr, Kenneth W. 1908 B
Stars of World Ballet, Sydney, 1978 C
State Archive Institutions, 1920 D
State Baptist Societies, 1913 D
State College of Vic, 1951 D, 1972 D
State debts, 1904 A, 1905 A, 1907 A
State education, 1872 D
State Electricity Commissions, 1921 A
State of Emergency,
  NSW, 1978 A
  Qld, 1948 A, 1961 A, 1964 A, 1971 A, 1980 A, 1981 A
  Tas, 1982 F
  Vic, 1977 A, 1981 A
State Film Censorship Board, 1916 C
State Hockey Association, NSW, women's, 1907 E
State Library of Qld, 1895 D, 1971 D
State Library of SA, 1884 D, 1967 D

State Library of Tas, 1943 D
State Library of Vic, 1960 D
State Library of WA, 1955 D
State Planning Authority of NSW, 1963 C, 1974 C
State Savings Bank of Vic Art Prize, 1965 C
State School Teachers' Union of Vic, 1885 D
State School Teachers' Union of WA, 1898 D
State Theatre Art Quest, Sydney, 1927 C
States, 1901 A
Statesman, 1928 E
Station wagon, 1957 B
Statistical, Historical ... of New South Wales, A, 1819 C
Statistical Conference, Melbourne, 1861 A
Statistical services, 1958 A
Statisticians, Cwlth, 1951 A
Statistics, 1935 A
Statues, Governor Phillip, Sydney, 1897 F, *see also individual entries*
Statute of Westminster, 1931 A, 1942 A
Stawell, Vic, 1853 F, 1881 E
Stawell, Florence M. 1869 D
Stawell, Richard R. 1864 B
Stawell, William F. 1815 A, 1854 D, 1884 A
Stawell Gift, Vic, 1878 E
Stead, Christina E. 1902 C, 1934 C, 1935 C, 1940 C, 1944 C
Stead, David G. 1877 B
Steam, in hospitals, 1898 B
Steam car, 1896 B
Steam engines, 1813 B, 1815 B, 1941 B, 1943 B
Steamship communication/services, 1831 B, 1833 B, 1852 B, 1875 B, 1877 B, 1884 B
Steamship Owners' Association of Aust., 1878 A
Steamships, *see individual entries*
Steane, Andrew, 1962 C
Steel, in building, 1890 C
Steel, H. P. 1888 C
Steel, Robert, 1827 D
Steel frames, 1910 C
Steel industry, 1864 B, 1876 B, 1894 B, 1900 B, 1915 B, 1921 B, 1922 B, 1933 B, 1935 B, 1951 B, 1955 B, 1965 B
Steel workers' strike, 1945 A
Steel works, NSW, 1908 B
Steele, Bertram, D. 1870 B
Steele Rudd's Magazine, Brisbane, 1904 C
Steeplechasing, 1830 E, 1868 E, 1936 E
Steere, Ernest A. 1866 A
Stehr, Ray, 1903 E
Steiglitz, Vic, 1855 F
Stein, Guenter, 1935 C
Stelara, Stelos, 1946 C
Stenhouse, Nicol D. 1806 D
Stephen, Adrian C. 1918 C
Stephen, Alfred, 1802 A, 1872 A, 1879 A, 1885 A, 1890 A
Stephen, Clive T. 1889 C
Stephen, George, 1794 A
Stephen, George M. 1812 A, 1838 A
Stephen, John, 1824 A, 1833 A
Stephen, Matthew H. 1828 A
Stephen, Ninian M. 1923 A, 1972 A, 1982 A
Stephens, Alfred G. 1865 C, 1896 C, 1899 F
Stephens, Edward, 1811 A
Stephens, Ethel A. 1944 C
Stephens, James B. 1835 C, 1871 C, 1877 C

821

Stephens, John, 1806 C, 1843 F
Stephens, Samuel, 1809 A, 1837 A
Stephens, Ward, 1831 F
Stephensen, Percy R. 1901 C, 1925 C, 1936 C
Stephenson, Arthur G. 1890 C, 1954 C
Stephenson, Jan, 1952 E
Stephenson, Philip J. 1930 B
Sterilization, water, Vic, 1926 B
Stern, Barry, 1960 C
Steuart, Ronald, H. 1898 C
Stevedoring Industry Commission, 1942 A
Stevens, Bertram, 1872 C
Stevens, Bertram S. B. 1889 A, 1932 A
Stevens, Bob, 1929 E
Stevens, Horace E. 1876 C
Stevenson, George, 1799 F, 1838 A
Stevenson, J. 1895 E
Stewart, Clive, 1937 E
Stewart, David, 1883 D
Stewart, Donald, 1984 C
Stewart, Douglas A. 1913 C, 1942 C, 1943 C, 1966 C
Stewart, Harold F. 1916 C, 1944 C
Stewart, Ian, 1943 E, 1965 E, 1966 E, 1971 E
Stewart, Johnny, 1936 E
Stewart, Max, 1935 E
Stewart, Nellie, 1858 C, 1864 C, 1880 C, 1901 C, 1902 C
Stewart, William, 1825 A
Stewart, William A. 1904 B, 1938 B
Stiansy, Walter, 1951 E
Sticht, Robert C. 1856 B
Stigwood, Robert, 1935 C, 1980 C
Still, Robert S. 1822 E, 1843 E
Stillwell, Frank L. 1888 B
Stilts, Qld houses, 1860 C
Stinson aircraft, 1937 F
Stipnieks, Margarita A. 1910 C
Stirling, Edward C. 1848 B
Stirling, James (1), 1791 A, 1827 A, 1828 A, 1829 A, 1832 A, 1834 A
Stirling, James (2), 1952 D
Stirling, SA, 1862 F
Stirling Bridge, WA, 1974 B
Stirling Castle, 1836 F
Stivens, Dallas G. 1911 C, 1951 C, 1970 C
Stock, Gailene, 1946 C
Stock Banks, 1865 A
Stock Breeding, 1958 B
Stockbrokers, 1852 A, 1871 A
Stock companies, 1840 A
Stock Exchanges, 1861 A, 1889 A, 1947 A, 1968 A
Stock routes, 1878 A, 1903 A, 1906 A, 1957 A, see also Droving
Stockings, 1935 F, 1954 F
Stockton, NSW, 1898 F, 1916 B, 1948 A
Stockton beach, NSW, 1948 A
Stockwell, SA, 1865 F
Stokes, Constance, 1906 C
Stokes, Frederick M. 1831 F
Stokes, John L. 1812 A, 1836 A, 1837 A, 1839 A, 1846 C
Stolle, Frederick S. 1938 E
Stomp dance, 1972 C
Stone, Clara, 1891 B
Stone, Edward A. 1901 A, 1902 A, 1909 A, 1913 A, 1917 A
Stone, Emma C. 1856 B, 1890 B
Stone, John O. 1929 A, 1984 A
Stone, Julius, 1907 A
Stone, Louis, 1871 C, 1911 C
Stone dwelling, first, Sydney, 1803 C
Stonehaven, Viscount, see Baird, John L.
Stonemasons, Sydney, 1855 A
Stonemasons' Society, Vic, 1850 A

Stonemasons' Union, Qld, 1858 A
Stones, Elsie M. 1920 C
Stonnington House, Melbourne, 1892 C
Storey, John, 1869 A, 1920 A
Storey, John S. 1896 B
Storey Bridge, Brisbane, 1940 B
Stork (film), 1972 C
Storm, Esben, 1974 C
Storm Boy, 1963 C, 1977 C, F
Storm of Time, 1948 C
Storms,
  NSW, 1795 F, 1798 F, 1887 F, 1984 F
  Qld, 1911 F, 1965 F, 1980 F, 1984 F
  SA, 1944 F, 1979 F, 1984 F
  Vic, 1918 F, 1981 F
  WA, 1875 F, 1908 F, see also Cyclones
Storrier, Tim, 1949 C
Story, John D. 1869 D
Story of Australian Art, The, 1934 C
Story of the Kelly Gang, The, 1905 C, 1906 C
Stoves, electric, 1907 B,
  gas, 1902 B
Stow, Catherine S. 1855 C
Stow, J. Randolph, 1935 C, 1958 C
Stow, Thomas Q. 1801 D, 1837 D
Straachan, David E. 1919 C
Strachan, John, 1872 F
Stradbroke, Earl of, see Rous, G.E.J.M.
Stradbroke Dreamtime, 1972 C
Stradbroke I., Qld, 1894 F
Strahan, George C. 1881 A
Strahan, Tas, 1822 F, 1892 B
Straight Draw, 1957 E
Straiter, James, 1822 A
Stralia, Madame Elsa, see Fischer, Elsa
Strand Arcade, Sydney, 1891 C
Strange, Ben, 1868 C
Strange, Frederick, 1807 C
Strangways, Henry B. T. 1832 A, 1868 A, 1869 A
Strathalbyn, SA, 1839 F
Strathfield, Sydney, 1796 A, 1908 D
Strathfield South Art Prize, 1949 C
Strathgordon, Tas, 1969 F
Strathmore, 1875 F
Strathroy House, Launceston, 1888 C
Stratten, Edward, 1982 A
Strawberry Hill, WA, 1834 C
Streaky Bay, SA, 1839 F, 1858 A
Stream, Melbourne, 1931 C
Street, Geoffrey A. 1894 A
Street, Jessie M. G. 1889 A
Street, John, 1853 A
Street, Kenneth W. 1890 A, 1965 A
Street, Philip W. 1863 A, 1935 A, 1936 A
Street Hero, 1984 C
Street lamps, Sydney, 1826 B, 1912 B
Street names, 1810 A
Streeter, Catherine E. 1842 C
Streeton, Arthur, 1867 C, 1888 C, 1889 C, 1890 C
Streets, Sydney, 1880 B
Stretton, Alan B. 1922 A
Strickland, Gerald, 1861 A, 1904 A, 1909 A, 1913 A
Strickland, G. K. 1839 C
Strickland, Shirley, 1925 E, 1948 E
Strike action, 1799 A, 1822 A, 1829 A, 1840 A, 1848 A, 1878 A, 1882 A, 1913 A, 1919 A, 1927 A, 1929 A, see individual entries
Strike Bound, 1984 C
Strike me Lucky, 1934 C
Strikes, NSW, Royal Commission into, 1890 A
Strines Art Gallery, Melbourne, 1966 C
String quartet, Sydney, 1837 C

Stringer, Ned, 1862 B
Stringybark Creek, Vic, 1878 A
Stripe rust, Vic, 1979 B
Stripper-Harvesters, 1843 B, 1884 B
Strode, Thomas, 1838 F .
Strong, Archibald T. 1876 C
Strong, Charles, 1844 D, 1885 D
Strong, Philip N. W. 1899 D
Stroud, NSW, 1826 F
Struck Oil, 1874 C
Struen Marie, 1951 E
Strutt, William, 1825 C
Strutt, W. J. 1917 B
Strzelecki Paul E. de, 1797 A, 1839 A, B, 1983 B, 1840 A
Strzelecki, SA, 1978 B
Stuart, Alexander, 1824 A, 1883 A
Stuart, Guy, 1942 C
Stuart, James, 1802 B
Stuart, John McD. 1815 A, 1844 A, 1858 A, 1860 A, 1861 A, 1862 A
Stuart, Rupert M. 1959 A
Stuart, NT, 1872 A, 1888 A, 1889 F, see also Alice Springs
Stubbs, Douglas, 1927 C
Stubbs, J. A. 1898 C
Stubbs, Thomas, 1836 C
Stukeley, Simon, 1829 C
Studebaker, 1931 B
Studio of Realist Art, Sydney, 1945 C
Stump-jump plough, 1838 B, 1876 B, 1877 B
Stumped houses, 1894 C
Sturgess, Reginald W. 1890 C
Sturrock, John A. 1915 E, 1962 E
Sturt, Charles, 1795 A, 1828 A, 1829 A, 1830 A, 1832 C, 1838 A, 1844 A, 1845 A, 1846 A, 1853 A
Sturt College of Advanced Education, SA, 1966 D
Sturt Pottery, NSW, 1953 C
Stutchbury, Samuel, 1850 B
Stuttgart Ballet, 1974 C
Subiaco Convent, NSW, 1849 D
Submarine cable,
  Bass Strait, 1859 B
  Darwin–Java, 1871 B
  NT, 1889 B
  Tasman, 1876 B
Submarines, 1914 A, 1915 A, 1942 A, 1944 A, 1963 A, 1967 A
Subscriber trunk dialling systems, 1962 B, 1967 B, 1970 B, 1976 B
Subscribers' School, WA, 1832 D
Subscription television, 1982 C
Suburbs, 1865 C, 1919 F
Such is Life, 1903 C
Sudan contingent, 1885 A
Sudds, Joseph, 1826 A
Sudds-Thompson case, 1826 A
Suez Canal, Middle East, 1869 A, 1956 A
Suez Canal Committee, 1956 A
Suffrage,
  male, 1856 A, 1857 A, 1858 A, 1859 A, 1870 A, 1900 A, 1907 A
  female, 1891 A, 1894 A, 1896 A, 1899 A, 1902 A, 1903 A, 1905 A, 1908 A
  universal adult, 1902 A
Sugar, 1821 A, 1822 A, 1823 B, 1824 A, 1859 A, 1862 A, 1863 A, 1864 A, 1892 A, 1901 A, 1903 A
Sugar Bounties Act, Federal, 1903 A
Sugar cane harvesters, 1921 B, 1925 B, 1956 B
Sugar consumption, 1980 F
Sugar exports, 1885 A, 1923 A, 1924 A
Sugar Heaven, 1936 C
Sugar mills, Qld, 1870 A

Sugar workers' strike, Qld, 1927 A
Sugden, Edward H. 1854 D
Sugerman, Bernard, 1904 A
Suicide, 1803 F
Suicide, Tas, 1979 F
Suite V, 1960 C
Suits, 1930 F
Sullivan, Patrick, 1910 C
Sullivans, The, 1977 C
Sullivan's Cove, Vic, 1803 A
Sulman, John, 1849 C, 1886 C, 1936 C
Sulman, Tom, 1900 E
Sulman Prize, 1936 C
Sulphuric acid, 1857 B, 1862 B
Summer of the Seventeenth Doll, 1954 C, 1956 C
Summers, Charles, 1827 C, 1853 C, 1864 C
Summers, Charles F. 1858 C
Summons, Arthur, 1936 E
Sumner, Alan R. M. 1911 C
Sumner, John H. 1924 C, 1953 C
Sun, Sydney, 1910 F
Sun Aria, Sydney, 1933 C
Sun Aria, Vic, 1924 C, 1925 C
Sun-dial, 1863 B
Sun Foe, 1873 F
Sun Is Not Enough, The, 1967 C
Sun Music I, 1965 C
Sun News Pictorial, Melbourne, 1922 F
Sunbury, Vic, 1851 F
Sunbury Pop Festival, 1972 C
Sunday Australian, 1971 F
Sunday Herald, Sydney, 1949 F
Sunday Mail, Adelaide, 1955 F
Sunday newspapers, Vic, 1889 F
Sunday opening, 1904 C
Sunday School, 1813 D, 1815 D, 1821 D
Sunday Sun, Sydney, 1903 F, 1921 F
Sunday Telegraph, Sydney, 1939 F
Sunday Times, Perth, 1897 F
Sunday Times, Sydney, 1885 F
Sunday Too Far Away (film), 1974 C
Sundays, 1813 D, F, 1883 D
Sunderland, Sydney, 1910 B
Sundowners, The, 1952 C, 1960 C
Sunny South, The, 1883 C
Sunny South, 1887 C
Sun on the Stubble (film), 1958 C
Sunraysia Daily, Mildura, 1920 F
Sunshine, Melbourne, 1908 F
Sunshine Harvester, 1885 B
Sunshine Header, 1913 B
Superannuation, 1983 A
Superphosphate, 1878 B, 1881 B, 1932 A
Supply, parliamentary blockage of, 1974 A
Supply HMAS, 1973 A
Supply, HMS, 1788 A, 1790 A
Supporting Mothers' Benefit, 1973 A
Supreme Court jury, first, 1825 A, *see also* Courts
Surat, Qld, 1849 F
Surf-Bathing Association, NSW, 1907 E
Surf board riding, *see* surfing
Surf boats, 1905 E
Surf carnival, 1908 E, 1956 E
Surf casting, 1959 E
Surf clubs, 1980 E
Surf Life Saving Association of Aust., 1922 E
Surfers Paradise, Qld, 1917 A, 1923 F
Surfing, Sydney, 1902 E, 1915 E, 1919 E, 1938 E, 1956 E, 1962 E, 1963 E, 1964 E, 1966 E, 1976 E, 1978 E
Surprise, 1831 B
Surprise of the Sun, 1969 C
Surry Hills, NSW, 1957 D
Surveillance, coastal, 1978 A

Surveying, 1827 A, 1829 C
Surveyor General Inn, NSW, 1834 F
Surveyors, geological, 1850 B, *see individual entries*
Susskind, Walter, 1954 C
Sussmilch, Carl A. von de H. 1875 B
Sutcliffe, Gladys, 1900 E
Sutherland, Alexander, 1852 C
Sutherland, Capt. and Mrs T. 1881 D
Sutherland, Jane, 1855 C
Sutherland, Joan, 1926 C, 1950 C, 1952 C, 1959 C, 1961 C, 1965 C, 1983 C
Sutherland, Margaret A. 1897 C
Sutherland, Ruth, 1884 C
Sutherland, Struan, 1983 B
Sutherland, William, 1859 B, 1893 B
Sutherland National Park, NSW, 1879 F
Sutherland Shire Council Art competition, Sydney, 1962 C
Sutherland/Williamson Opera Co., 1965 C
'Sutherland's constant', 1893 B
Sutton, Bob, *see* Sievier, R.
Sutton, auto car, 1894 B
Sutton, Henry, 1856 B, 1878 B
Suttor, Francis B. 1839 A
Suttor, George, 1800 A, 1859 A
Suttor, John B. 1809 A
Suttor, William H. (1), 1805 A
Suttor, William H. (2), 1834 A
Svihla, Alois, 1966 C
Swain, Charles, 1917 C
Swan, C. 1943 B
Swan, D. 1984 D
Swan, James, 1846 F
Swan, Louisa J. 1860 C, 1884 C
Swan Brewery Co., 1887 A, 1981 A
Swan Hill, Vic, 1846 F, 1850 C, 1875 A, 1926 B
Swan Hill Folk Museum and Art Gallery, Vic, 1964 D
Swan Lake, 1962 C
Swan Reach, SA, 1835 F, 1926 C
Swan R., WA, 1819 A, 1827 A, 1828 A, 1829 A, 1830 B, 1837 A, 1843 B, 1854 B, 1859 A, 1866 C, 1959 C, 1974 B
Swan River Guardian, WA, 1836 F
Swan R. Mechanics' Institute, 1897 D
Swans VFL team, 1981 E, *see* South Melbourne
Swansea, NSW, 1825 F
Swansea, Tas, 1827 F
Swanston, Charles, 1789 A, 1831 A, 1834 A
Swanton, James, 1853 B
Sweet, Georgina, 1875 B
Sweet, S. W. 1886 B
Sweet Nell of Old Drury, 1902 C
Swift, 1804 A
Swimming, 1846 E, 1888 E, 1894 E, 1896 E, 1897 E, 1900 E, 1902 E, 1903 E, 1905 E, 1910 E, 1912 E, 1913 E, 1924 E, 1930 E, 1953 E, 1956 E, 1959 E, 1960 E, 1962 E, 1965 E, 1967 E, 1968 E, 1972 E, 1974 E, 1976 E
Swimming, 'the crawl', 1902 E
Swimming suits, 1949 F
Swinburne, George, 1861 A
Swinburne Technical College, 1908 D
Sword Club, Sydney, 1919 D
Sydenham, NSW, 1901 F, 1953 F
Sydney, NSW, 1788 A, F, 1867 B, 1870 B, 1875 A, 1876 B, 1881 B, 1892 C, 1899 F, 1900 F, 1902 C, 1907 B, E, 1912 B, 1938 E, 1946 B, 1950 C, 1965 B, 1970 B, C, F, 1976 E
Sydney, incorporation of, 1842 A
Sydney Airport, 1919 B

Sydney Amateur Athletic Club, 1872 E
Sydney amateur concerts, 1826 C
Sydney Amateur Sailing Club, 1872 E
Sydney Archery Club, 1856 E
Sydney Art Gallery, 1871 C, 1875 C, 1880 C
Sydney Art School, 1896 C, 1907 C
Sydney Athletic Cup, 1868 E
Sydney Banking Co., 1843 A
Sydney Bethel Union, 1822 F
Sydney Botanical Gardens, 1838 B
Sydney Broadcasters Ltd, 1923 B
Sydney Chamber of Commerce, 1825 A
Sydney Choral Society, 1870 C
Sydney City Council, 1904 B, 1967 A
Sydney City Mission, 1862 F
Sydney City Monthly, 1980 F
Sydney College, 1830 D, 1835 D
Sydney College of Advanced Education, 1980 D
Sydney College of the Arts, 1975 D
Sydney Conservatorium of Music, 1901 C
  High School, 1918 C
  orchestra, 1914 C
Sydney Council chambers, 1838 F
Sydney Cove, 1788 A, 1798 A, 1818 E
Sydney Cove (ship), 1797 A, B, F
Sydney Cricket Ground, 1911 E, 1930 E
Sydney Cup (horse-race), 1866 E, 1881 F
Sydney Dance Co., 1965 C
Sydney Day Nursery and Nursery Schools Association, 1905 D
Sydney Dispensary, 1826 B, 1845 B
Sydney Entertainment Centre, 1983 C
Sydney Exchange Co., 1851 A
Sydney Female School of Industry, 1826 D
Sydney Fencing Club, 1912 E
Sydney Festival Ballet, 1971 C
Sydney Filmmakers Co-operative, 1966 C
Sydney Fire Insurance Co., 1844 F
Sydney Floral and Horticultural Society, 1838 F
Sydney Flying Squad Sailing Club, 1892 E
Sydney Free Public Grammar School, 1825 D
Sydney Gazette, 1806 F, 1810 C, 1820 F, 1824 A, 1842 F
Sydney Gazette and New South Wales Advertiser, 1803 F
Sydney General Post Office, 1874 F
Sydney Grammar School, 1830 D, 1857 D
Sydney Group, art, 1945 C
Sydney Guardian, 1926 F
Sydney Harbour, 1842 F, 1854 A, 1942 A
Sydney Harbour Bridge, 1815 C, 1923 B, 1924 B, 1932 A, B, 1981 B
Sydney Harbour Life Saving Society, 1894 E
Sydney Harmonic Vocal Society, 1859 C
Sydney Herald, 1831 F, 1837 F, 1840 F, 1842 F
Sydney Herbarium, 1896 B
Sydney, HMAS, (1), 1914 A, 1916 A, 1935 A, 1940 A, 1941 A
Sydney, HMAS, (2), 1948 A
Sydney-Hobart yacht race, *see each year section E from 1945*
Sydney Horse Racing Cup, 1866 E
Sydney Hospitals, 1816 B, 1848 B, 1868 B, 1881 B, 1894 B, 1913 B, 1919 B, 1933 B
Sydney Humanist Group, 1960 F
Sydney Hunt Club, 1811 E

823

Sydney Infirmary and Dispensary, 1845 B, 1881 B
Sydney Kindergarten Teachers' College, 1900 D
Sydney laboratory, 1947 E
Sydney Lawn Tennis Club, 1878 E
Sydney Mail, 1860 F
Sydney manufacturing centre, 1840 A
Sydney Mechanics' School of Arts, 1833 D, 1859 C, 1873 D
Sydney Metropolitan Gliding Club, 1930 E
Sydney Millwrights' and Engineers' Provident Society, 1847 F
Sydney military night patrol, 1810 A
Sydney Morning Herald, 1831 F, 1842 F, 1853 B, 1860 F, 1872 F
Sydney Municipal Council, 1842 A
Sydney Municipal Library, 1909 D, 1912 D
Sydney Musica Viva, 1945 C
Sydney Musical Union, 1877 C
Sydney Nine Group, 1961 C
Sydney Observatory, 1857 B, 1870 B, 1874 B
Sydney Opera House, 1956 C, 1957 C, 1959 C, 1973 C, 1983 C
Sydney Opera House Lottery, 1957 F
Sydney Philharmonic Society, 1854 C, 1885 C, 1909 C
Sydney police districts, 1810 A
Sydney Polytechnic, 1897 C
Sydney Printmakers, 1962 C
Sydney Pro Musica Society, 1950 C
Sydney Punch, 1856 F, 1864 C
Sydney Railway Co., 1855 A
Sydney Repertory Co., 1921 C
Sydney Rifle Club, 1842 E
Sydney Rowing Club, 1912 E
Sydney School of Arts, 1881 C
Sydney School of Arts Theatre, 1837 C
Sydney Sheep Show, 1895 F
Sydney Showgrounds speedway, 1926 E
Sydney sign posts, 1810 A
Sydney Square, 1977 C
Sydney State Theatre, 1929 C
Sydney Stock Exchange, 1857 A, 1871 A
Sydney street names, 1810 A
Sydney String Quartet, 1966 C, 1975 C
Sydney Swans, 1982 E
Sydney Swords Club, 1912 E
Sydney Symphony Orchestra, 1908 C, 1946 C, 1948 C, 1964 C, 1965 C, 1969 C, 1973 C, 1979 C, 1981 C, 1982 C
Sydney Teachers' College, 1905 D, 1911 D
Sydney Technical College, 1883 D, 1885 B
Sydney Technological Museum, 1880 D
Sydney Theatre, 1832 C
Sydney Theatre Co., 1979 C
Sydney Times, 1834 F
Sydney Topographical Society, 1851 F
Sydney Town Hall, 1866 C, 1875 F, 1888 C, 1889 C, 1890 C
Sydney Trade Fair Art Award, 1965 C
Sydney Trades and Labour Council, 1871 A, 1879 A
Sydney Tramroad and Railway Co., 1846 B
Sydney Turf Club, 1825 E
Sydney University, *see* University of Sydney.
Sydney University Cricket Club, 1865 E
'Sydney Views' (stamps), 1850 F
Sydney, Viscount, 1788 A
Sylvania, NSW, 1981 F
Syme, David, 1827 A, 1856 A
Syme, Ebenezer, 1826 A, 1856 A
Syme, Evelyn W. 1885 C
Syme, George A. 1859 B
Syme, Hugh R. 1903 A
Syme, John H. 1859 A
Syme, Joseph C. 1852 A
Syme, Kathleen A. 1896 A
Syme, Oswald J. 1878 A
Symmonds, Thomas, 1848 C
Symons, John J. 1905 F
Symon, Josiah H. 1846 A
Symphony Orchestras, 1926 C, 1946 C, *see individual entries*
Synagogues, 1830 D, 1844 D, 1885 D, 1871 D, 1877 D
Synod, Anglican, 1981 D
Synod of Aust., Presbyterian, 1842 D, 1864 D, 1865 D
Synod of NSW, Presbyterian, 1837 D
Synroc, 1978 B
Synthetic fibre, 1951 B
Syrian invasion, Middle East, 1941 A
Szabo, Joseph, 1932 C
Szigeti, Imre, 1897 C

T

T. E. Wardle Invitation Art Prize, 1965 C
Taber, Brian, 1940 E
Taber, Thomas, 1798 D
Table Margarine, 1966 F
'Table of minimum requirements', education NSW, 1856 D
Table Talk, Melbourne, 1885 F
Table Tennis, 1897 E, 1898 E, 1923 E, 1933 E, 1958 E, 1971 E
Tahiti, 1788 A
Tahiti, 1927 F
Tahourdin, Peter, 1928 C
Tailem Bend, SA, 1887 F
Tailoresses' Union, 1882 A
Tailors' strikes, 1834 A, 1840 A
Tailors' workers' group, Sydney, 1835 A
Tait, Bess N. 1878 C
Tait, Charles, 1870 C
Tait, Edward J. 1878 C
Tait, Frank S. 1883 C
Tait, James N. 1876 C
Tait, John H. 1871 C
Tait, John T. 1829 C
Tait, Thomas, 1864 A
Tait brothers, 1905 C
Tait Brothers Co., 1920 C
Take-away food, 1969 F, 1971 F
Talbot, Don, 1934 E
Talbot, Mary, 1931 C
Talbot, Reginald A. J. 1904 A
Tales of the Colonies, 1843 C
Tales of the Convict System, 1892 C
Talgai Skull, 1886 B
Talgai Station, Qld, 1886 B
'Talkie' films, 1928 C, 1929 C, 1931 C
Tall Timbers, 1937 C
Tallangatta, Vic, 1855 F
Tallon, Donald, 1916 E
Tallow, 1838 A, 1843 A
Tamar R., Tas, 1804 A
Tamarama, 1919 C
Tamaree, Qld, 1947 F
Tambo, Qld, 1860 F
Tambo R., Vic, 1839 A
Tamborine Mountain, Qld, 1878 F
Tamworth, NSW, 1839 F, 1871 F, 1878 B, 1888 B, 1973 C
Tamworth Art Society, NSW, 1960 C
Tanami Desert, NT, 1964 F
Tandem accelerator, 1971 B
Tange, Arthur H. 1914 A
Tangney, Dorothy M. 1911 A, 1943 A
Tango, 1914 C
Tank, military, 1912 B
Tank Stream, Sydney Cove, 1788 B, F
Tank Stream bridge, Sydney, 1788 B, 1811 B
Tanning materials, 1819 B
Tantalum, WA, 1980 B
Tantanoola, SA, 1893 F
Tantanoola tiger, 1893 F
Tanunda, SA, 1839 F, 1864 F, 1871 F
Tapu, 1904 C
Tara, Qld, 1848 F
Tarakan, 1950 F
Taralga, NSW, 1825 F
Tarana, NSW, 1892 F
Taranna, Tas, 1835 B
Tarcoola, 1893 E
Tarcutta, NSW, 1835 F
Taree, NSW, 1854 F
Taree Art Prize, NSW, 1954 C
Tariff Agreement, Aust.-N.Z., 1922 A
Tariff Bill, Cwlth, 1902 A
Tariff Board, 1921 A, 1971 A
Tariff Commission, Cwlth, 1904 A
Tariff League of Vic, 1859 A
Tariff preferences, N.Z., 1925 A, 1960 A
Tariff protection, 1867 A, 1887 A, 1907 A, 1908 A
Tariffs,
  cuts, 1973 A
  Cwlth, 1907 A
  intercolonial, 1871 A
  resolution, 1920 A
  Scullin, 1929 A
  uniform, 1863 A
Taronga Park Zoo, Sydney, 1912 B, 1916 B
Tarraleah, Tas, 1934 F
Tarrant, Harley, 1899 B, 1907 B
Tarrant, Harry, 1860 E
Tarrant car, 1894 B
Tarrant Motor Co., 1896 B
Tartanga relics, 1960 B
Tasker, Rolly, 1950 E
'Tasma', *see* Huybers, Jessie C.
Tasman Bridge, Tas, 1964 B, 1975 F
Tasman Empire Airways Ltd, 1940 B
Tasman Ltd, 1978 B
Tasman Sea, 1815 F, 1928 B
Tasman Peninsula, 1830 A
Tasmania/n, *abbreviated as* Tas
  abbreviation for Tasmania, 1869 B, 1965 B
  circumnavigation of, 1798 A, 1799 A, 1815 A
  independence, 1825 A
  name, 1842 D, 1846 A, 1855 A
  proclamation of as VDL, 1802 A
  representative govt, 1851 A
Tas Caverneering Club, 1946 F
Tas Club, 1861 F
Tas Conservatorium of Music, 1964 C
Tas Croquet Association, 1908 E
Tas Crown Advocate, 1979 A
Tas Dance Co., 1981 C
Tas Field Naturalists' Club, 1904 B
Tas Group of Painters, 1938 C
Tas Horse Racing Club, 1874 E
Tas Hydro Electricity Commission, 1925 B
Tas Labor Party, 1903 A
Tas Museum, 1976 A
Tas Museum and Art Gallery, 1863 C, 1887 C

Tas political crisis, 1979 A
Tas Public Library, 1849 D, 1870 D, 1943 D
Tas School of Dental Nursing, 1966 D
Tas Sesqui-Centenary Art Prize, 1954 C
Tas Society of Natural History, 1837 B, 1842 B
Tas Symphony Orchestra, 1942 C, 1962 C, 1969 C, 1971 C, 1974 C, 1980 C
Tas Teachers' Federation, 1905 D
Tas Theatre Co., 1973 C
Tas tiger, 1932 F, 1933 B
Tas Turf Club, 1871 E
Tas Workers' Political League, 1903 A
Tas Wilderness Society, 1976 F
Tasmanian, 1825 F
Tasmanian Journal of Natural Science, 1842 B
Tasmanian News, 1883 F
'Tasmanian Nightingale', 1855 C
Tate, Frank, 1863 D
Tate, Henry, 1873 C, 1917 C, 1924 C
Tate, R. 1840 B
Tate Gallery Exhibition, London, 1962 C
Tatnell, George, 1939 E
Tattersall's, Sydney, 1881 F
Tatura, Vic, 1874 F
Tauchert, Arthur, 1877 C
'Taung Skull', 1925 B
Tavares, Morton, 1874 C
Tawell, John, 1820 B, 1836 F, 1845 A, F
Tax, 1800 A, 1819 A, 1830 A, 1890 A
 airport departure, 1978 A
 avoidance, 1982 A
 cheques, 1982 A
 Chinese polltax, 1855 A, 1865 A, 1888 A
 Company, 1899 A
 gold mining, 1857 A
 income, 1884 A, 1907 A, 1915 A, 1953 A, 1976 A
 land, 1884 A, 1877 A
 pay as you earn, 1943 A
 road transport, 1931 A
 sales, 1930 A
 school donations, 1954 D
 school fees, 1952 D
 squatters, 1839 A
 uniform, 1942 A
Taxis, 1909 B, 1924 F, 1927 F
Taylor, Alan R. 1901 A, 1952 A
Taylor, Florence M. 1879 C, 1909 B, 1920 C
Taylor, George A. 1872 B, 1909 B, 1910 B, 1923 B, 1924 B
Taylor, George A. M. 1917 B
Taylor, Hedlie S. 1883 B, 1912 B, 1913 B, 1924 B
Taylor, James, 1829 C
Taylor, Joseph T. L. ('Squizzy'), 1879 F, 1927 F
Taylor, Lawrence B. 1873 C
Taylor, Lloyd, 1875 C, 1884 C
Taylor, Michael F. 1933 C
Taylor, Patrick G. 1896 B, 1951 B
Taylor, Rod, 1930 C
Taylor, R. 1964 E
Taylor, Thomas G. 1880 B
Taylor, Wally, 1939 E
Tea, 1901 A
Tea Room Girl, The, 1910 C
Tea Tree Well, NT, 1921 F
Teacher training, 1825 D, 1834 D, 1850 D, 1851 D, 1900 D, 1906 D, colleges, *see individual entries*
Teachers, 1874 D, 1914 D, 1948 D, 1970 D
Teachers' strikes, WA, 1920 A

Teachers' Union, Vic, 1878 D
Teaching, Lancastrian monitorial system, 1811 D
Teaching in Three Continents, 1891 D
Teague, Violet H. E. 1872 C
Teale, Leonard, 1922 C
Teasdale, Graham, 1955 E, 1977 E
Tebbit, Henri, 1852 C
Tebbutt, John, 1834 B, 1854 B, 1881 B
Technical education, 1883 D, 1888 D, 1897 D, 1901 D, 1947 D, 1965 D, 1974 D, 1980 D, *see also* Education *and individual entries*
Technical and Further Education Council, 1977 D
Technical Teachers' Association of Aust., 1965 D, 1967 D
Technical Teachers' College, Melbourne, 1951 D
Technical training, Sydney, 1805 D
Technology, 1978 B, *see section B*
Teetotallers, 1845 F
Tegart, Judy, 1937 E
Tegg, James, 1837 F
Telecom, 1984 B
Telecommunications, 1946 A, 1959 B, 1964 B, 1973 B, 1979 B, 1980 B
Telefunken radio, 1928 B
Telegraph, Brisbane, 1872 F
Telegraph, electric, *see* Electric telegraph
Telegraphy, 1904 B, 1922 B
Telephone directories, 1880 F, 1975 F
Telephone exchanges, 1878 B, 1880 B, 1882 B, 1883 B, 1887 B, 1912 B, 1914 B, 1925 B
Telephone lines/services, 1878 B, 1886 B, 1902 B, 1907 B, 1914 B, 1923 B, 1930 B, 1936 B, 1938 B, 1941 B, 1962 B, 1967 B, 1984 B
Telephone typewriter service, 1981 B
Telephones, 1893 B, 1901 B, 1924 B, 1929 B, 1933 F, 1949 B, 1960 A, 1963 F, 1970 B, 1976 B
Telephonic Communications (Interception) Bill, 1960 A
Teleprinter Exchange services, TELEX, 1933 B, 1954 B, 1958 B, 1966 B, 1975 B
Teleradio, 1926 B
Telescope, 1974 B
Teletronics, 1963 B
Television, 1929 B, 1934 B, 1953 B, 1955 B, 1956 B, 1966 B
 coloured, 1974 B, 1975 B
 Intelsat, 1966 B
 licences, 1974 A
 stations, 1955 A, 1956 B, 1960 B, 1980 F
 subscription and cable, 1982 A
TELEX, *see* Teleprinter exchange services
Temora, NSW, 1879 B, 1880 A, F, 1914 F
Temperance, 1834 F, 1836 F, *see also individual entries*
Temperatures,
 highest, 1889 F, 1923 B,
 lowest, 1945 B
 hottest place, 1980 F
Temple Beth Israel, Melbourne, 1930 D
'Temple of Infamy', 1846 C
Temple Society of Aust., 1950 D
Templeton, Janet, 1857 A
Templeton, Kelvin, 1980 E
Ten-hour-day, 1855 A
Tench, Watkin, 1789 A, C, 1791 A, 1793 A, 1833 C
Tenerani, Pietro, 1789 C
Tenison-Woods, Julian E. 1832 B, 1866 D, 1886 A
Tenison-Woods, Mary C. 1896 A, 1917 A

Tennant, Carrie, 1929 C
Tennant, Katherine, 'Kylie', 1912 C, 1935 C, 1939 C, 1941 C, 1943 C
Tennant Creek, NT, 1900 B, 1933 A, F, 1966 F, 1979 B
Tennis, 1877 E, 1878 E, 1880 E, 1888 E, 1889 E, 1900 E, 1905 E, 1907 E, 1908 E, 1912 E, 1914 E, 1924 E, 1925 E, 1929 E, 1933 E, 1938 E, 1939 E, 1951 E, 1953 E, 1955 E, 1956 E, 1957 E, 1962 E, 1963 E, 1964 E, 1968 E, 1969 E, 1970 E, 1971 E, 1973 E, 1982 E, *see also* Lawn tennis
Tennyson, Hallam, 1852 A, 1899 A, 1901 A, 1902 A, 1903 A
Tenpin Bowling, 1960 E, 1962 E, 1983 E
Tenterfield, NSW, 1848 F, 1872 B, 1889 A
Terang, Vic, 1850 F
Terowie, SA, 1875 F
Terra Australis, 1803 A
Terrace houses, 1840 C, 1877 C
Terracotta roof tiles, 1859 C, 1886 C, 1926 C
Terrigal, NSW, 1885 F, 1927 F
Territorial seal, 1791 A, 1817 F
Territorial waters, jurisdiction of, 1969 A
Territories, Dept of, Cwlth, 1951 A
Territory of Cocos, 1955 A
Terror of Van Diemen's Land, The, 1821 C
Terrorism, 1978 A
Terrorists, Sydney, 1980 F
Terry, Burt, 1971 B
Terry, Frederick C. 1825 C
Terry, Leonard, 1825 C, 1858 C
Terry, Michael, 1899 A, 1922 B
Terry, Samuel, 1838 A
Terry Clune Art Gallery, Sydney, 1957 C
Tertiary education, 1965 D, 1974 D, Asians, 1951 D
Tertiary Education Commission, 1977 D
Test cricket, *see* Cricket
'Test tube baby' programme, 1980 B
Tet offensive, Vietnam, 1968 A
Tewantin, Qld, 1870 F
Tewksbury, Pearson W. 1867 A
Texas, Qld, 1842 F
Textile printing, 1937 C
Textiles, 1939 B, 1970 B
Thackaringa, NSW, 1875 B
Thailand, RAAF, 1962 A
Thake, Eric P. A. 1904 C
Thalidomide, 1961 B, 1974 B
Thargomindah, Qld, 1893 B
Thatcher, Charles R. 1831 C, 1859 C
Thatcher, Griffiths W. 1863 D
Thatcher, Robert, 1857 C, 1864 C
Theatre, first performance, 1789 C, 1839 C, *see individual entries*
Theatre, first professional, 1833 C
Theatre, prosperity, 1891 C
Theatre Royal, Adelaide, 1838 C, 1868 C, 1878 C, 1897 C
 Bendigo, 1854 C
 Hobart, 1834 C, 1912 C
 Melbourne, 1855 C, 1872 C, 1874 C, 1878 C, 1880 C, 1882 C, 1933 C
 Perth, 1897 C
 Sydney, 1833 C, 1835 C, 1840 C, 1875 C, 1876 C, 1892 C, 1976 C
Theatre staff strike, Melbourne, Sydney, 1943 C
Theodore, Edward G. 1884 A, 1919 A, 1930 A
Theosophical Society, 1891 D
Thermal power, 1974 B

825

Therry, John J. 1790 D, 1820 D, 1821 D, 1834 D
Therry, Roger, 1800 A, 1841 A
These are my People, 1944 C
Thesiger, Frederic J. N. 1868 A, 1905 A, 1909 A
They Found a Cave, 1962 C
They're A Weird Mob (book), 1957 C, (film), 1966 C
Thief of the Moon, 1924 C
Thiele, Colin M. 1920 C, 1958 C, 1963 C
Thiele, David, 1938 E
Thiess, Leslie C. 1909 B, 1933 B
Thiess Bros, 1933 B
Think Big, 1974 E, 1975 E
Third Fleet, 1791 A
Thirkell, Angela, 1934 C
Thirroul, NSW, 1923 C
This Day Tonight, 1967 C
Tholstrup, Hans, 1970 E, 1976 E
Thomas, Albert, 1935 E
Thomas, Archer K. 1906 F
Thomas, Daniel R. 1931 C
Thomas, David E. L. 1937 C
Thomas, David J. 1813 B
Thomas, Edmund, 1827 C
Thomas, Evan H. 1801 C, 1835 C, 1866 A
Thomas, Harold, 1972 F
Thomas Laurie, 1839 F
Thomas, Lawrence N. B. 1915 C
Thomas, Margaret, 1840 C
Thomas, Patrick A. 1932 C, 1958 C, 1973 C
Thomas, Robert, 1860 F
Thomas, Robert G. 1820 C
Thomas, Wilfred C. 1904 C, 1941 F
Thomas, William K. 1821 A
Thomas Hardy and Sons Wine Co., 1887 C
Thompson, Andrew, 1810 A
Thompson, Mrs Ben, 1905 E
Thompson, Duncan, 1895 E
Thompson, Francis R. 1896 C
Thompson, Freda, 1910 B, 1934 B
Thompson, Gordon A. 1911 C
Thompson, Hector, 1949 E
Thompson, H. 1878 E
Thompson, Jack, 1921 E
Thompson, Jack, *see* Payne, John
Thompson, James J. 1927 B
Thompson, Joe, 1838 E
Thompson, John A. 1848 B, 1896 B
Thompson, John J. M. 1907 C
Thompson, Len, 1948 E, 1972 E
Thompson, L. H. S. 1981 A
Thompson, Mel, 1974 B
Thompson, Patrick, 1826 A
Thompson car, 1894 B
Thoms, Albie, 1969 C
Thomson, Alexander, 1869 B
Thomson, Edward D. 1800 A, 1837 A
Thomson, Herbert, 1896 B, 1900 E
Thomson, James P. 1854 B
Thomson, Jeffrey R. 1950 E, 1979 E
Thomson, N. D. 1983 C
Thomson, Peter W. 1929 E, 1954 E, 1955 E
Thomson R., SA, 1858 A
Thomson, William, 1819 B
Thonemann, Peter C. 1917 B
Thorn, George, 1838 A, 1876 A
Thorn Birds, The, 1977 C, 1978 C
Thorne, Graeme, 1960 E
Thorne, William J. H. 1803 F
Thornett, Dick, 1940 E
Thornett, John, 1930 E
Thornett, Ken, 1937 E
Thornhill, Dorothy, 1910 C

Thornhill, Michael, 1941 C, 1974 C
Thornton, Wallace K. 1915 C
Thorp, Richard, 1980 C
Thorpe, Hal, 1873 C
Those Who Love, 1926 C
Thoughts: A Series of Sonnets, 1845 C
Threat to the Internal Security of Australia, The, 1980 A
Three Bees, 1814 F
Three Cheers for the Paraclete, 1968 C
Three in One, 1956 C
Threlfall, Richard, 1861 B
Threlkeld, Lancelot E. 1788 D
Threshold, 1968 C
Thring, Francis W. (1), 1883 C
Thring, Francis W. (2), 1926 C, 1962 C
Throsby, Charles, 1817 A, 1818 A, 1819 A, 1821 A, 1828 A
Throsby, Margaret, 1978 F
Throssell, George, 1840 A, 1901 A
Throssell, Ric P. 1922 C
Thrower, Norma, 1936 E
Thrust block, 1905 B
Thursday I. Qld, 1877 A, F, 1883 A, 1890 F
Thwaites, J. W. 1951 F
Tibbie Cotter, 1883 E
Tibbits, William, 1837 C
Tibooburra, NSW, 1881 F
Tiburon, 1935 C
Tichborne, Roger, 1871 A
Ticket of Leave, 1790 A, 1804 A, 1822 A
Ticks, 1872 B
Ticonderoga (ship), 1852 F
Tidal Wave, NSW, 1868 F
Tidbinbilla, ACT, 1963 B
Tides, 1821 F, 1877 F
Tie Me Kangaroo Down Sport, 1960 C
Tietkins, William H. 1844 A
Tiffen, Charles, 1859 C, 1862 C
Tiger, Tantanoola, 1893 F
Tiger, Tas, 1932 F, 1933 B
Tiger Moth, 1942 B
Tight rope, 1877 F
Tiles, terracotta, 1886 C, 1926 C
Till the Day I Die, 1936 C
Tillyard, Robin, 1881 B
Tilted Cross, The, 1961 C
Tim Whiffler, 1867 E
Timber, 1876 A
Timber reserves, NSW, 1871 F
Timber workers' strike, 1929 A
Timbertop School, Vic, 1966 D
Time, SA, 1898 B
Time Enough Later, 1943 C
Time Zones, 1894 C
Timeless Land, The, 1941 C
Timms, Edward V. 1895 C
Timor, 1972 A, 1975 A, 1978 A, 1984 A
Timor Joe, *see* Forbes, Joseph
Tin, 1843 B, 1846 B, 1849 B, 1851 B, 1854 A, 1871 B, 1872 B, 1880 B, 1900 B
Tinaroo Dam, Qld, 1958 B
Tindale, Norman B. 1900 B
Tindall, Charles E. S. 1863 C
Tindall, William, 1876 E
Tingha, NSW, 1870 F, 1900 B
Tinned food, 1846 B
Tinplate, NSW, 1957 B
Tinsmiths' and Sheet Metal Workers' Union, NSW, 1881 A
Tipperary riots, Vic, 1855 A
Titman, John, 1951 E
Titterton, Ernest W. 1916 B
Titus, Jack, 1908 E
Tivoli Theatre Sydney, 1896 C, 1899 C, 1900 C
Tivoli Variety circuit, 1893 C
To The Islands, 1958 C

To The West, 1896 C
Toads, 1935 B
Tobacco, 1818 A, 1822 A, 1824 A, F, 1839 A, 1842 A, 1888 A, 1901 A, 1904 A, *see also* Advertising
Tobin, George, 1838 C
Tobruk, N Africa, 1941 A
Toc H Inc., 1925 D
Tocumwal, NSW, 1862 F
Todd, Charles H. 1826 B, 1883 B
Todd, Ron, 1915 E
Todt, Emil, 1854 C
Toilets, 1830 C
Tokyo Olympics, 1964 E
Toll bridges, WA, 1843 B
Tolley, Bruce, 1933 C
Tolley, David, 1936 C
Tolley, Ernest A. 1862 A
Tollis, Mickey, 1927 E
Tolls, road, 1810 F, 1877 B, *see also* Tollways
Tollways, NSW, 1965 B, *see also* Tolls
Tolmer, Alexander, 1815 A, 1852 A
Tolpuddle Martyrs, 1834 A
Tom, James, 1851 B
Tom, William, 1851 B
Tom Thumb, 1795 A
Tomholt, Sydney, 1936 C
Tomlinson, Ian, 1936 E
Tomorrow and Tomorrow, 1947 C
Tompkins, Harry, 1937 C
Tompson, Charles, 1807 C, 1826 C
Tonkin, D. O. 1979 A
Tonkin, John T. 1902 A, 1971 A
Too Clever by Half, 1853 C
Toodyay, WA, 1839 F
Toogood, Peter, 1930 E
Toohey, Jack, 1902 E
Toohey, Peter, 1954 E
Toombs, Ron, 1928 E
Toongabbie, NSW, 1792 A, 1799 D
Toorak, Melbourne, 1953 C
Toorak Art Gallery, Melbourne, 1964 C
Toorak Village, Melbourne, 1934 F
Tooth and Co. Ltd, 1888 A, 1966 A
Tooths Brewery, 1835 A
Toowoomba, Qld, 1849 F, 1861 F, 1867 B, 1873 D, 1955 F
Toowoomba Art Gallery, Qld, 1959 C
Toowoomba Grammar School, Qld, 1870 D
Top 40 chart, 1958 C, 1959 C
Top hats, 1910 F, 1915 F
Toparoa 1955 E
Topography, 1968 B
Tornados, *see* Cyclones
Toronto, NSW, 1855 F
Torpedo, 1874 B
Torquay, Vic, 1956 E
Torrens, Robert, 1864 A
Torrens, Robert R. 1814 A, 1835 A, 1857 A
Torrens Basin, SA, 1858 A
Torrens Gorge, SA, 1860 B
Torrens R., SA, 1837 A
Torrens Real Property Act, SA, 1858 A
Torrens system, 1857 A
Torrens Title, 1858 A
Torres Strait, 1791 F, 1819 A, 1845 F, 1859 F, 1868 A, 1898 C
Torres Strait Daily Pilot, 1888 F
Toryboy, 1865 E
Toshock, Ernie, 1914 E
Total Enviroment Centre, Sydney, 1972 F
Totalizator, 1879 F, 1907 B, 1913 B, 1916 B, 1917 E, 1960 F, 1961 F
Totalizator Agency Board, TAB, 1960 F, 1961 F

Tote, 1916 B, 1917 E, 1960 F, 1961 F
Tower of Babel, The, 1968 C
Tower Lighthouse, Sydney, 1817 C
Towers, Cyril, 1904 E
Town Halls, *see individual entries*
Town Like Alice, A, 1950 C
Town Planners, 1917 C
Town Planning, 1948 C, 1958 C
Town Planning and Housing Bill, SA, 1916 C
Towns, *see Communities section F and individual entries*
Towns, George, 1869 E
Towns, Robert, 1794 A, 1842 A, 1860 A, 1863 A
Townsend, Peter, 1976 E
Townsend, Simon, 1968 A
Townshend, Geoffrey K. 1888 C
Townshend, Thomas, 1788 A
Townsville, Qld, 1864 F, 1867 F, 1870 F, 1876 F, 1882 B, 1903 F, 1908 B, 1909 B, 1918 A, 1919 A, 1923 B, 1930 D, 1933 B, 1960 B, 1967 C, 1969 C, 1971 F, 1972 B, F
Townsville bulk sugar terminal, 1963 F
Townsville College of Advanced Education, 1969 D
Townsville International Airport, Qld, 1981 B
Townsville Teachers' College, Qld, 1969 D
Trachoma, 1975 B
Trackson, James, 1900 B
Tractors, 1922 B
Trade,
  Campbell business, 1800 A
  Commissioners, 1918 A, 1978 A
  Cwlth, 1918 A, 1956 A
  deficit, 1955 A
  diversion policy, 1936 A
  embargoes, 1807 A
  essential, 1812 A
  foreign, 1792 A
  –Belgium, 1933 A
  –Britain, 1849 A, 1921 A, 1956 A, 1973 A, 1979 A
  –Canada, 1956 A, 1960 A
  –China, PRC, 1961 A, 1973 A
  –India, 1811 A
  –Israel, 1963 A
  –Japan, 1865 A, 1936 A, 1938 A, 1957 A, 1963 A, 1972 A
  –New Zealand, 1965 A, *see also individual entries*
  –USA, 1807 A, 1814 A, 1918 A, 1936 A, 1938 A, 1942 A
  –USSR, 1965 A
  Free, *see* Free trade
  NSW Corps, 1792 A
  Preferences 1932 A, 1979 A, *see also individual entries*
  prohibitions, First World War, 1914 A
  protection, 1802 A, 1859 A, 1860 A, 1861 A, 1865 A, 1873 A
  routes, Pacific, 1906 A
  war, 1936 A
Trade Marks, 1905 A
Trade Practices, 1966 A, 1967 A, 1974 A
Trade Union Act, SA, 1876 A
Trade Union conference, 1919 A
Trade Unions, *see individual entries*
  compulsory membership, 1942 A
  legalisation of, 1825 A, 1881 A, 1884 A, 1886 A, 1889 A, 1900 A
  prohibited, 1799 A
  protection of, 1876 A
  membership, 1954 A
  modern, 1870 A
  numbers, 1965 A

officials, jailed 1979 A
training, 1975 D
Trade Winds, 1949 E
Trades Hall Committee, Melbourne, 1857 A
Trades Hall Council, Vic, 1860 A, 1967 A
Trades and Labor Councils, 1883 A, 1884 A, 1891 A
Trade Practices Act 1965–1967, 1967 A
Trade Practices Commission, 1974 A
Trades Union Congress, Intercolonial, 1879 A, 1884 A, 1885 A, 1886 A, 1888 A, 1889 A, 1891 A, 1898 A
Trades Union and Labor Congress, WA, 1899 A
Tradesmen's tokens, 1849 A
Trading Banks, 1945 A
Traeger, Alfred H. 1895 B, 1926 B
Trafalgar, 1974 C
Trafalgar, Vic, 1865 F
Traffic lights, Melbourne, 1928 B
'Tragedians', 1853 C, 1855 C
Tragedy of Donohoe, The, 1835 C
Traill, Jessie C. A. 1881 C
Traill, W. H. 1844 F, 1880 C
Train, George F. 1829 A
Trains, *see* Railways *and individual entries*
Tram disasters, *included in* Railway disasters
Trampolining, 1956 E, 1964 E, 1976 E
Trams,
  NSW, 1879 B, 1884 B, 1886 B, 1888 B, 1893 B, 1894 B, 1899 B, 1903 B, 1939 B, 1961 B
  Qld, 1885 B, 1887 B, 1897 B, 1912 A, 1961 B, 1969 B
  SA, 1854 B, 1878 B, 1906 B, 1908 B, 1917 B, 1953 B, 1961 B
  Tas, 1834 B, 1893 B, 1960 B, 1961 B
  Vic, 1885 B, 1889 B, 1906 B, 1923 B, 1926 B, 1940 B
  WA, 1889 B, 1899 B, 1958 B, 1961 B
Tramway strikes, 1908 A, 1917 A, 1944 A, 1948 A
Trans–Australia Airlines, TAA, 1945 B, 1946 B, 1948 B, 1952 A, 1953 B, 1959 B, 1981 B, 1982 B
Trans–Pacific cable, 1902 B, 1962 B
Trans–Pacific flights, 1928 B
Trans–polar flight, 1928 B
Transcontinental flights, 1920 B
Transfield Co. Art Prize, Sydney, 1961 C
Transit of Venus, 1874 B
Transport, *see section B and individual entries*
Transport, Cwlth Dept of, 1973 B
Transport, land, sea, 1952 B
Transport employees' strike, NSW, 1944 A
Transport Workers Act, 1938 A
Transport Workers' Union, TWU, 1912 A
Transportation of convicts, 1798 A, 1812 A, 1835 A, 1837 A, 1838 A, 1840 A, 1846 A, 1847 A, 1848 A, 1849 A, 1850 A, 1851 A, 1852 A, 1853 A, 1864 A, 1865 A, *see also* Convicts
Transposed Head, The, 1970 C
Tranthim-Fryer, John R. 1858 C
Trap, 1966 C
Traralgon, Vic, 1845 F
Traralgon Library and Art Gallery, Vic, 1964 C
Travelling art scholarships, 1886 C, 1887 C, 1900 C, 1958 C, 1966 C
Travelling libraries, 1859 D
Travelling post office, 1870 F

Travelling Schools, Qld, 1901 D
Travers, Pamela, 1934 C
Traveston, Qld, 1925 F
Travis, Peter, 1929 C
Trawling, 1915 A
Treadmill, 1822 F, 1840 A
Treasurers conferences, 1904 A, 1905 A
Treasury Buildings, 1857 C, 1860 C, 1862 C
Treatise . . . on the Motion of Fluids, A, 1879 C
Treaty of friendship, Japan, 1976 A
Treaty of Versailles, 1919 A
Tree felling, 1788 F
Tree of Man, The, 1955 C
Treen, Frank, 1930 E
Trees on Hillside, 1964 C
Treloar, John, 1928 E
Trendall, Arthur D. 1909 D
Trends in Dutch Painting Exhibition, 1961 C
Trenerry, Horace H. 1899 C
Trent, Graham J. 1976 F
Trenwith, William A. 1847 A
Trevor, W. C. 1868 A
Triabunna, Tas, 1825 F
Triad (magazine), 1915 C
Trial, 1816 F
Trial by jury, 1824 A, 1830 A, 1832 A, 1833 A
Triathlons, 1967 E
Tribal lands, 1967 A
Tribe, David, 1981 B
Trickett, Edward, 1876 E
Trifecta, 1974 E
Triggs, Authur B. 1868 A
Trigonometrical survey, 1864 B
Trim, Judy, 1949 E, 1970 E
Trindall, Gordon L. 1886 C
Trinder Aderson and Co., 1884 B
Triplets, 1806 F
Tripoli, 1943 A
Tristram, John W. 1872 C
Trivalve, 1927 E
Trobriand Cricket, 1977 C
Trocoided Plane, The, 1884 B
Trooper to the Southern Cross, 1934 C
Trotskyites, 1975 A
Trott, Albert E. 1873 E
Trotting, 1803 E, 1810 E, 1860 E, 1883 E, 1900 E, 1902 E, 1910 E, 1911 E, 1913 E, 1914 E, 1936 E, 1967 E, 1971 E, 1977 E, 1978 E
Troughton, Ellis Le G. 1893 B
Trousers, cuffs, 1909 F
Trousers, cuffless, 1942 F
Trout, 1841 A, 1860 B, 1864 B, 1888 B, 1894 B, 1901 B, 1931 B
Troutt, Katherine, 1964 E
Trowbridge, Richard, 1980 A
Truck drivers' strike, 1981 A
Trucks, 1907 B
Truganini, 1803 A, 1830 A, 1873 A, 1976 A
Trugo, 1926 E, 1940 E
Trumble, Hugh, 1867 E, 1903 E
Trumble, Robert, 1919 C
Trump, The, 1937 E
Trumper, Victor T. 1877 E, 1899 E, 1902 E
Trumpis, Karlis, 1910 C
Trunk lines, *see* Telephone lines/services
Truro, SA, 1845 F, 1979 F
Truscott, John, 1936 C
Truscott, Keith W. (Bluey), 1916 A
Truth, Sydney, 1890 F
Try Anything Once, 1930 C
Tryal, 1970 F
Tryon, George, 1832 A

827

Tryon, Henry, 1856 B
Tsing U, 1887 A
Tuberculosis, 1915 F, 1948 B
Tubular dresses, 1922 F
Tubular look, 1924 F
Tuck, Marie, 1872 C
Tuck, Ruth, 1914 C
Tucker, Albert L. 1914 C
Tucker, Carol, 1984 E
Tucker, G. K. 1930 D
Tucker, James R. 1803 C, 1845 C
Tucker, Thomas G. 1859 D
Tucker, Tudor St G. 1862 C
Tuckey, James H. 1816 A
Tuckson, John A. 1921 C
Tuckson, Margaret, 1921 C
Tuckwell, Barry E. 1931 C, 1980 C
Tudawali, Robert, 1954 C
Tuddenham, Des, 1943 E
Tudor, Frank G. 1866 A, 1917 A
Tufnell, Edward W. 1814 D, 1859 D
Tull, John, 1800 D
Tullamarine Airport, Melbourne, 1964 B, 1970 B
Tullamarine Freeway, Melbourne, 1968 B, 1970 B
Tully, Qld, 1906 F, 1980 F
Tully Art Festive Prizes, Qld, 1962 C
Tumbarumba, NSW, 1859 F
Tumut, NSW, 1824 F
Tumut Art Prize, NSW, 1958 C
Tumut power station, NSW, 1959 B
Tuna fishing industry, 1937 A
Tunarama Festival, SA, 1962 F
Tungsten, Vic, 1904 B
Tunley, David, 1930 C
Tunnels, 1863 C, 1976 B
Turkish attack, Broken Hill, NSW, 1915 A
Turkish Consul General, 1980 F
Turnbull, Reginald J. D. 1908 A
Turnbull, Stanley C. P. 1906 C
Turnbull, Wendy, 1952 E
Turner, Arthur, 1933 B
Turner, Charles T. B. 1862 E
Turner, Ethel S. 1872 C, 1894 C
Turner, George, 1851 A, 1894 A, 1900 A, 1901 A
Turner, Henry G. 1831 A
Turner, J. 1935 E
Turner, J. A. 1879 C
Turner, J. W. 1903 D
Turner, Lilian I. 1870 C
Turner, V. 1899 E
Turner, W. 1836 C
Turnpike, 1810 B
Turon R., NSW, 1851 A, F
Turquoisette: A Study in Blue (ballet), 1893 C
Turral, Jennifer, 1960 E
Turramurra Wall Painters, Sydney, 1930 C
Tuttle, William, 1883 B
Tuxworth, Ian Lindsay, 1942 A, 1984 A
TV News, 1958 F
TV Times, 1958 F
TV Week, 1958 F, 1967 C
Tweed Heads, NSW, 1850 F
Tweed R., NSW, 1828 B
Tweed suit, 1930 F
Tweedie, Valrene, 1960 C
Tweddle, Isabel H. 1877 C
Twenty-five Small Buildings, 1983 C
Twenty Melbourne Painters Group, 1917 C
Twenty-Seven A (film), 1974 C
Twenty Thousand Thieves, The, 1952 C
Twins, *in vitro* fertilization, 1980 B
Twist dance, 1962 C

Two Airline Policy, 1952 A
Two Decades of American Painting Exhibition, 1966 C, 1967 C
Two Expeditions into ... 1831 in London, 1832 C
'Two Little Boys', 1970 C
Two Mile Flat, NSW, 1867 B
Two thousand weeks, 1968 C
Two-up King of the army, 1915 F
Twofold Bay, NSW, 1910 F
Tye's Art Gallery, Melbourne, 1945 C
Tyers, Charles J. 1806 A, 1839 A
Typesetting, computer, 1977 B
Typewriters, 1883 A, 1954 B
Typhoid fever, 1838 F, 1852 F, 1886 F, 1889 F
Tyranny of Distance, The, 1966 C
Tyres, pneumatic, 1889 B, 1903 B
Tyrrel, James R. 1875 A
Tyrrell, William, 1807 D, 1847 D
Tyson, Geoffrey, 1911 C
Tyson, James, 1819 A
Tzipine, Georges, 1961 C

U

Uhr, D'Arcy W. 1845 A, 1872 A
Ulcers, 1984 B
Ulladulla, NSW, 1820 F
Ullathorne, William B. 1806 D, 1833 D, 1838 D
Ulm, Charles T. P. 1898 B, 1928 B, 1929 B
Ulverstone, Tas, 1856 F
Ulysses, 1929 C
Umbigumbi, Qld, 1917 A
Umpires, Aust. Rules Football, 1866 E, 1880 E, 1884 E
Unarmed combat, *see individual entries*
Unbending, The, 1954 C
Under Aldebaran, 1946 C
Under the Wilgas, 1932 C
Undergrowth, Sydney, 1924 C
Underhill, Anthony, 1923 C
Underwater Spear Fishermens' Association, 1947 E
Underwood, James, 1789 B, 1844 A
Underwood, Joseph, 1833 A
Undola (ship), 1918 F
Unemployment, Sydney, 1886 F, 1928 A, 1930 A, 1932 A, 1933 A, 1952 A, 1961 A, 1975 A, 1976 A, 1977 A, 1978 A, 1983 A
Unemployment benefits, 1923 A, 1944 A, 1945 A
UNESCO, 1978 A
Ungamulla water bore, Qld, 1886 B
Uniacke, John F. 1798 A
Unidentified flying objects, 1952 F
Uniform Aust. currency, 1910 A
Uniform tariff, 1863 A
Unilever Aust. Pty Ltd, 1889 A
Union Bank, 1951 A
Union Bank of Aust., 1837 A
Union Church, Adelaide, 1969 D
Union Congress, Adelaide, 1913 A
Union of Miners, Bendigo, 1872 A
Union of Students, 1970 D
Union Theatre, Sydney, 1961 C
Union Theatre of Melbourne, 1954 C, 1955 C
Union Theatre Repertory Cos, 1953 C, 1968 C
Union Theatres Ltd, 1913 C

Unions, *see* Trade Unions
Unitarian Church, 1850 D, 1853 D, 1855 D, 1878 D
United Arts Club, Adelaide, 1923 C, 1925 C
United Australia Movement, 1931 A
United Australia Party, UAP, 1931 A, 1934 A, 1937 A, 1944 A
United Australasian Axemen's Association, 1891 E
United Church, NT, 1942 D
United Church of North Aust., 1916 D, 1939 D, 1942 D, 1956 D
United Conference of Methodism, SA, 1900 D
United Evangelical Lutheran Church of Aust., 1921 D, 1966 D
United Grand Lodge of NSW, 1888 F
United Graziers' Association, Qld, 1890 A
United Labor Party,
  SA, 1891 A
  Vic, 1896 A
United Methodist Free Churches Group, 1848 D
United Methodists, Melbourne, 1904 D
United Nations, UN, charter, 1945 A
United Nations Organization, UNO, 1945 A, 1946 A, 1947 A, 1948 A, 1967 A, B, 1969 A, 1971 A, 1984 A
United Nations, Palestine Commission, 1947 A
United Nations Peacekeeping Force, 1981 A, 1982 A
United Nations, Trusteeship, 1962 A
United Operative Masons' Society, 1851 A
United Pentecostal Church, Sydney, 1954 D
United Presbyterians, 1855 D, 1863 D, 1865 D
United Secession Church of Scotland, 1822 D
United States Education Foundation in Aust., 1949 D
United States Forces, 1941 A
United Theological College, NSW, 1975 D
United Trades and Labor Council, Adelaide, 1891 A
United Tradesmen's Society, SA, 1874 A
United Waterman's Benefit Society, 1844 F
Uniting Church of Aust., 1977 D
Uniting Church National Mission Frontier Services, 1980 D
Unity (ship), 1813 F
Universal Copyright Convention, 1969 A
Universal Postal Union, 1891 A
Universal Service League, 1915 A
Universities, *see individual entries*
Universities, Federal aid, 1957 D, 1972 D
University of Adelaide, 1876 D, 1882 D, 1884 C, 1900 D, 1911 D, 1961 D, 1965 D
University College of Townsville, Qld, 1960 D
University Commission, Cwlth, 1942 D
University fees, 1973 D
University graduates, Cwlth Public service, 1933 D
  women, 1891 B, 1894 D
University of Melbourne, 1855 D, 1874 D, 1880 D, 1883 D, 1887 C, 1902 D, 1911 D, 1924 D, 1929 D, 1946 D, 1965 D
University of Melbourne Library, 1856 D

University of New England, NSW, 1954 D, 1955 D
University of Newcastle, NSW, 1951 D, 1965 D
University of NSW, 1949 D, 1958 D, 1960 D, 1962 C, 1965 D
University Presses, 1922 A
University of Queensland, 1911 D, 1960 D, 1965 D, 1970 D
University of Sydney, 1852 D, 1854 C, 1857 C, 1879 D, 1881 D, 1884 D, 1886 D, 1888 D, 1894 D, 1924 D, 1928 C, 1930 B, 1948 C, 1951 D, 1954 B, 1956 B, 1961 C, 1962 C, 1964 B
University of Sydney Rugby Union football team, 1864 E
University of Tas, 1890 D, 1954 D, 1956 D
University of WA, 1911 D, 1913 D
University of Wollongong, 1962 D, 1975 D
'unlock the lands', 1855 A, 1857 A
Unmarried mothers' allowance, 1943 A
Unsworth, Ken, 1931 C
Unwin, Ernest E. 1881 C
Up the Country, 1928 C
Upfield, Arthur W. 1888 C, 1929 C
Upsurge, 1934 C
Upton, John A. 1850 C
Upton, Ronald, 1937 C
Upton, Thomas H. 1889 B
Upward, Peter, 1932 C
Uraidla, SA, 1855 F
Uralla, NSW, 1852 F
Urangan, Qld, 1883 F
Uranium,
  ALP policy, 1982 A, 1984 A
  Atomic Energy Commission, 1953 B
  Exploration, 1944 B
  Exports, 1953 A, 1976 A, 1977 A, B, 1979 A, 1981 A, 1983 A, 1984 B
  NT, 1949 B, 1952 B, 1953 B, 1954 B, 1955 B, 1970 B, 1975 B, 1977 A, 1978 A, 1980 B, 1982 A
  Producers' Forum, 1976 A
  Qld, 1954 B, 1956 A, 1976 B, 1980 F
  Ranger, 1975 B, 1977 A
  Roxby Downs, 1977 B, 1983 F
  SA, 1952 B, 1977 B, 1982 B
  WA, 1972 B
Urban and Regional Development, Dept of, 1973 C
Urban sprawl, 1865 C
Ure Smith Publishing Co., 1939 A
Uren, Tommy, 1893 E
Urquhart, Frederick C. 1858 A, 1921 A
Urunga, NSW, 1850 F
USSR, Afghanistan, 1980 A, *see also* Russia *and* Soviet Union
UTAH American Development Co., 1950 B
Utzon, Joern, 1918 C, 1956 C, 1957 C

V

Vaccine, influenza, 1957 B, Strain, 1943 B
Vacuum Oil Co., 1895 B
Vaicaitis, Adolphas, 1915 C
Vale, Amy M. 1862 C
Vale of Clwydd, NSW, 1839 B
Valiant, 1962 B
Van Der Hum, 1976 E
van der Houten, Henricus L. 1801 C

van der Sluys, Henry, *see* Roy Rene, 1914 C
Van de Struick, Bernard, 1929 C
Van Diemen's Land, VDL, 1802 A, 1803 A, 1804 A, D, F, 1805 A, D, 1806 A, F, 1811 A, 1813 A, 1815 A, 1816 A, 1817 A, 1820 A, 1821 A, 1823 A, 1824 A, 1825 A, 1826 A, 1828 A, 1830 A, 1833 A, 1834 D, 1835 A, B, 1836 D, 1838 D, 1844 A, 1846 A, 1853 A, F, 1855 A, *see also* Tasmania, Tas
Van Diemen's Land Co., 1825 A, 1826 A, 1827 A
Van Diemen's Land Gazette and General Advertiser, 1814 F
Van Diemen's Land Memorial Folk Museum, 1957 D
Van Diemen's Land Museum, 1829 D
Van Diemen's Land Philosophical Society, 1829 B
van Otterloo, Willem, 1967 C, 1973 C, 1978 C
Van Praag, Lionel, 1908 E, 1936 E
Van Praagh, Margaret, (Peggy), 1910 C, 1960 C, 1962 C
van Putten, Gerard, 1928 C
van Raalte, Henry B. 1881 C
Vancouver, George, 1791 A
Vandenberg, Gerard, 1932 C
Vanneck, William C. A. 1934 A
Vasey, George A. 1895 A
Vassilieff, Danila, 1899 C, 1936 C
Vaucluse House, Sydney, 1803 C
Vaudeville, 1896 C
Vaughan, Crawford, 1874 A, 1915 A
Vaughan, Les, 1937 B
Vaughan, Roger W. B. 1834 D, 1873 D, 1877 D
Vault, The, 1980 C
Vause, Gloria, 1966 E
Vaux, James H. 1819 C, 1853 F
Veal, Hayward, 1913 C
Veale, Lawrence R. 1916 C
Vegemite, 1923 B, 1970 C
Vegetables, Tas, 1792 A, 1816 A
Vegetative Eye, The, 1943 C
Veilburn, Madame, 1840 C
Veils, 1919 F
Vela (star), 1976 B
Vend, 1872 A
Vendetta, HMAS, 1969 A
Venice Film Festival, 1961 C
Ventilators, 1939 B
Venus, 1874 B
Venus (ship), 1806 F
Verandas, 1815 C, 1834 C, 1838 C, 1894 C, 1930 C
Verbrugghen, Henri, 1873 C, 1914 C, 1916 C, 1919 C
Verchinina, Nina, 1940 C
Verco, Joseph, 1851 B
Verge, John, 1828 C, 1830 C, 1832 C, 1834 C, 1837 C, 1861 C
Vernon, 1867 D
Vernon, Alexander C. 1888 D
Vernon, Geoffrey H. 1882 B
Vernon, Howard, 1845 C
Vernon, James, 1910 B, 1965 A
Vernon report, 1965 A
Verran, John, 1856 A, 1910 A
Versailles, France, 1919 A
Versailles Peace Conference, 1919 A
Verstak, Tania, 1962 F
Verses, Popular and Humorous, 1900 C
Veteran Affairs, Cwlth dept of, 1919 A
Veterinary School, Vic, 1909 B
VFL, *see* Victorian Football League, *see also* Aust. Rules Football

televised USA, 1980 E
payment of players, 1911 E
VFL Park, Melbourne, 1970 F
Viatel, 1984 B
Vicars, Sir William, 1859 A
Vickery, Amy A. 1868 F
Vickery, Ebenezer, 1827 A
Victor Harbour, SA, 1837 F
Victoria/n, *abbreviated as* Vic
named, 1851 A
Vic Academy of Arts, 1870 C, 1888 C
Vic Amateur Canoe Association, 1926 E
Vic Amateur Gymnastic Association, 1937 E
Vic Amateur Turf Club, 1875 E
Vic Archery Club, 1857 E
Vic Architects' Association, 1851 C
Vic Artists' Society, 1888 C
Vic Arts Centre, Melbourne, 1968 C, 1982 C, 1984 C
Vic Arts Society Journal, 1908 C
Vic Association for the Protection of Native Industry, 1858 A
Vic Ballet, 1971 C
Vic Ballet Guild, Melbourne, 1946 C
Vic Board of Conciliation, 1887 A
Vic border, 1839 A
Vic Bush Fire Brigade Association, 1928 F
Vic Bush Nursing Association, 1911 B
Vic Canoe Club, 1912 E
Vic Chamber of Manufacturers, 1877 A
Vic College of Arts, Melbourne, 1972 D
Vic Country Party, 1975 A
Vic Country Road Board, 1913 B
Vic Coursing Club, 1873 E
Vic Employers' Federation, 1901 A
Vic Employers' Union, 1885 A
Vic Fine Arts Society, 1853 C
Vic Football Association, VFA, 1877 E, 1896 E
Vic Football League, VFL, 1896 E, 1956 E, 1970 E, 1984 E, *see also individual entries*
Vic Football League Premiers, *see each year section E from 1897 E*
Vic Galvanized Iron and Wire Co., 1880 A
Vic Horse Racing Club, 1864 E
Vic Housing Commission, 1977 A
Vic Humane Society, 1874 F, 1876 F
Vic Institute for the Advancement of Science, 1854 B
Vic Institute of Architects, 1856 C
Vic Jockey Club, 1857 E
Vic Ladies' Bowling Association, 1907 E
Vic Lawn Bowling Club, 1860 E
Vic Master Builders' Association, 1875 A
Vic Master Printers' Association, 1854 A
Vic National Gallery, 1984 C
Vic navy, 1856 A
Vic Opera Co., 1948 C
Vic police, 1969 F, 1982 A, *see also* Police
Vic Public Galleries Group, 1957 C
Vic Public Library, 1960 D
Vic Rangers' Defence Corps, 1888 A
Vic Representative govt, 1851 A
Vic Rowing Association, 1877 E
Vic Sculptors' Society, 1948 C, 1949 C
Vic Secondary Teachers' Association, 1948 D, 1965 D
Vic Society of Fine Arts, 1853 C, 1856 C
Vic Society of Fine Arts Exhibition, 1857 C
Vic Society of Teachers of Dancing, 1931 C
Vic State Opera Co., 1977 C, 1984 C
Vic State Public Library, 1853 D
Vic Tariff League, 1860 A

829

Vic Teachers' Training College, 1893 D, 1900 D
Vic Teachers' Union, 1926 D
Vic Technological Commission, 1869 D
Vic Tennis Championships, 1880 E
Vic Trugo Association, 1940 E
Vic Women's Art Club, 1902 C
Vic Workers' Educational Association, 1950 D
Vic Yacht Club, 1856 E
Victoria, Queen, 1850 A, F
Victoria (warship), 1856 A
Victoria Barracks, Melbourne, 1854 C
Victoria bridge, Brisbane, 1874 C
Victoria Cross, 1867 F, 1893 A, 1897 A, 1900 A, 1915 A, 1918 A, 1937 A, 1969 A
Victoria Pass, NSW, 1832 B
Victoria Park, Sydney, 1909 B
Victoria Public Library, Perth, 1889 D
Victoria R., NT, 1968 F
Victoria Theatre, Brisbane, 1865 C
 Melbourne, 1841 C
 Sydney, 1844 F, 1845 F, 1855 C
'Victorian Embassy', 1878 A
Victorians Arriving, The, 1984 C
Victorians Making Their Mark, The, 1984 C
Victorians Settling, The, 1984 C
Victory, The, 1902 E
'Victory' suit, 1942 F
Vidal, Mary T. 1815 C
Video cassette recorders, 1982 F
Videotapes, 1984 C
Videotext, 1984 B
Vidler, Edward A. 1863 C, 1921 C
Vietnam, Aust. aid, 1961 A, 1979 A
Vietnam, Aust. military advisors, 1962 A
Vietnam North, US bombing of, 1972 A
Vietnam Medal, 1968 C
Vietnam Moratorium day, 1970 A
Vietnam peace talks, Paris, 1968 A
Vietnam War, 1962 A, 1965 A, 1966 A, 1967 A, 1968 A, 1969 A, 1970 A, 1971 A, 1972 A, 1975 A
Vietnam war veterans, 1980 A
'View of Sydney Cove, A', 1794 C
Views of Australia, 1824 C
Vigano, Maria T. 1884 C
Vigoro, 1919 E, 1931 E
Vike, Harald, 1906 C
Vilks, Erna, 1949 C
Village Glee Club, The, 1942 F
Villers Bretonneux, 1918 A
Villiers, Alan J. 1903 C
Vincennes Bay, Antarctica, 1969 B
Vincent, Alfred, 1874 C
Vincent, John, 1828 D
Vines, 1802 A, 1816 A, 1830 A, 1837 A, 1839 A, 1840 A, 1843 A, 1847 A, 1853 A, *see also* Wines
Vines, Randall, 1945 E
Vineyards, 1832 A, 1838 A, 1851 A, 1853 A, 1859 A, 1863 A, 1918 A
 WA, 1835 A
Violet town, Vic, 1838 F, 1969 F
Virtue, Keith A. 1909 B
Virtue, Peter, 1839 E
Viscount Canterbury nugget, 1870 F
Viscount prop-jets, 1953 B
Vision (magazine), Sydney, 1923 C
Vision of Ceremony, A, 1956 C
'Vision of Melancholy, A Fragment' (poem), 1804 C
Visual arts, *see* Section C
Visual Arts Board of the Aust. Council, 1975 C
Viveash, Samuel W. 1799 B

Vizard-Wholohan Art Prizes, Adelaide, 1957 C
Vocabulary of the Flash Language, 1819 C
Voight, David, 1944 C
Voigt, Emil R. 1882 A, 1927 A
Voisin aircraft, 1909 B, 1910 B
Voitre, K. 1935 E
Vojsk, Milan, 1922 C
Vojtek, Bill, 1940 E
Volkswagen, 1957 B
Volleyball, 1952 E, 1962 E
Voluntary defence corps, 1940 A
Volunteer Defence Corps, 1942 A
von Bertouch Art Galleries, Newcastle, 1962 C
von Guerard, Eugene, 1811 C, 1870 C
von Hattum Ernest, 1920 C
von Miller, O. U. 1907 B
von Mueller, Ferdinand J. H. *see* Mueller von
von Nida, Norman G. 1914 E
von Strieglitz, Emma, 1870 C
Vosper, V. C. B. 1897 F
Voss, 1957 C
Voting,
 Aboriginals, 1949 A, 1951 A
 age, 1970 A, 1973 A
 compulsory, 1914 A, 1915 A, 1924 A, 1936 A, 1942 A
 plural, 1893 A, 1899 A, 1900 A
 preferential, 1892 A, 1911 A, 1918 A, 1919 A, 1926 A, 1929 A
 proportional, 1897 A
 see also Suffrage
Voudouris, George, 1920 C
Voyage to Terra Australis, A, 1814 A
Voyager, 1964 A, F
Vulcan jet bomber, 1961 B
Vumps, 1908 F

W

W. A. Holman (painting), 1929 C
Wuuksumheyuli, 1790 A
Wackett, Lawrence J. 1896 B, 1929 B
Waddell, Thomas, 1854 A, 1904 A
Waddy, John L. 1916 A
Wade, Charles G. 1863 A, 1907 A
Wade, Doug, 1941 E
Wade, Robert B. 1874 B
Wadell, Dr., 1824 A
Wadham, W. J. 1863 C
Wage indexation, 1975 A, 1976 A, 1977 A, 1978 A, 1979 A, 1980 A, 1981 A, 1983 A
Wage-price freeze, 1977 A
Wages, Aboriginal stockmen, NT, 1966 A
 Basic, minimum, 1895 A, 1896 A, 1898 A, 1902 A, 1907 A, 1913 A, 1914 A, 1920 A, 1930 A, 1931 A, 1934 A, 1937 A, 1950 A, 1953 A, 1957 A, 1961 A, 1964 A, 1973 A, 1974 A
 Boards, 1886 A, 1908 A, 1910 A
 fair and reasonable, 1906 A
 female, 1919 A, 1950 A, 1972 A
 fixing, 1796 A, 1886 A, 1896 A, 1980 A, 1983 A
 freeze, 1982 A
 increases, adjustments, 1921 A, 1953 A, 1954 A, 1959 A, 1984 A, *see also* Wage indexation

 payment of, 1818 A
 systems, 1967 A
Wagga Wagga, NSW, 1849 F, 1868 C, 1878 B, 1892 B, 1895 B, 1917 B, 1931 A, 1936 E, 1972 E, 1976 C
Wagga Wagga Agricultural College, NSW, 1949 E
Wagga Wagga Agricultural Farm, 1892 B
Wagga Wagga Art Prize, NSW, 1951 C
Wagga Wagga Museum and Art Gallery, NSW, 1964 D
Wagga Wagga Teachers' College, NSW, 1947 D
Wagin, WA, 1898 F
Wagstaff, Donald, 1950 E
Wahroonga, Sydney, 1918 B
Waikerie, SA, 1894 F, 1974 E
Wainewright, Thomas G. 1794 C
Wairapa, 1894 F
Waist coats, 1924 F
Waist-lines, 1923 F, 1933 F
Waitangi, Treaty of, N.Z., 1840 A
Waite, Elgar R. 1866 B
Waite, James C. 1832 C
Waite, Peter, 1834 A
Waite Agricultural Research Institute, Adelaide, 1924 B, 1928 B
Wake in Fright, 1971 C
Wakefield, Edward G. 1796 A, 1829 A, 1831 A, 1833 C, 1839 A
Wakefield Scheme, 1836 A, 1839 A
Wakehurst, Baron, *see* Loder, John de. V.
Wakelin, Roland S. 1887 C, 1915 C, 1919 C
Wakool, NSW, 1944 A
Walch, Garnet, 1843 C, 1873 C
Wale, W. H. 1901 C
Walcha, NSW, 1852 F
Walford Grammar School, Adelaide, 1954 D
Walgett, NSW, 1859 F
Walgett Mail, NSW, 1879 F
Walhalla, Vic, 1861 F, 1862 B
Walkabout, Melbourne, 1934 F
Walker, Alan, 1911 D, 1963 F
Walker, Don, 1896 E
Walker, Eadith C. 1865 A
Walker, E. 1896 E
Walker, Frederick, 1807 A, 1861 A, 1923 B
Walker, George W. 1800 D, 1832 D
Walker, James, 1843 D, 1854 B
Walker, Kathleen, 1920 C, 1964 C, 1970 C, 1972 C
Walker, L. 1920 C
Walker, Margaret, 1967 C
Walker, Max, 1948 E
Walker, Murray, 1937 C
Walker, Ralph T. 1912 C
Walker, Robert L. 1925 B
Walker, Ronald, 1907 A
Walker, Stephen, 1927 C
Walker, Teresa S. 1807 C
Walker, Thomas, 1804 A
Walker, William, 1800 D, 1822 D
Walkerville Brewery, Adelaide, 1938 A
Walking, 1893 E, 1976 E
Walkley, William G. 1896 A, 1936 A
Walkley Art Awards, Sydney, 1960 C
Wall, Timothy, 1904 E
Walla Walla, NSW, 1868 F
Wallabadah, NSW, 1852 E
Wallabadah Horse Racing Club, 1852 E
Wallabies (footballers), 1908 E, 1948 E
Wallace, George S. 1894 C, 1919 C, 1932 C, 1938 C
Wallace, William V. 1812 C, 1833 C, 1836 C, 1838 C, 1844 C, 1849 C

Wallace-Crabbe, Kenneth E. I. 1900 A
Wallace-Crabbe, Robin, 1938 C
Wallach, Rose, 1856 C
Wallangarra, Qld, 1888 B, 1889 F
Wallaroo, SA, 1859 F, 1860 B
Wallaroo copper mines, 1861 B
Waller, 1850 B
Waller, Christian, 1895 C
Waller, Hector M. L. 1900 A
Waller, John K. 1914 A
Waller, Mervyn N. 1894 C
Wallerawang, NSW, 1824 F
Wallis, Capt., 1822 A
Wallis, James, 1817 C
Wallis, Joe, 1888 B
Wallis, Raymond, 1900 C, 1920 C
Walls, cavity, 1885 C
Wallsend Rovers Soccer Club, NSW, 1887 E
Wallumbilla, Qld, 1956 F
Walpole, Bruce, 1953 B
Walsh, Alan, 1952 B, 1954 B
Walsh, Cyril, 1969 A
Walsh, Eliza, 1827 A
Walsh, F. H. 1965 A
Walsh, Ian, 1934 E
Walsh, Mike, 1979 F
Walter and Eliza Hall Institute, 1916 B, 1919 B, 1933 B, 1957 B
Walter Hood (ship), 1870 F
Walters, Doug, 1945 E
Walters, Wes, 1979 C
Walton, Clem, 1954 B
Walton, Nancy, 1935 F, 1949 B
Waltzing Matilda, 1895 C
Wandell, Charles, 1851 D
Wanderers, 1880 E
Wandering Islands, The, 1955 C
Wanderings in Wild Australia, 1928 C
Wandilo district, SA, 1958 F
Wangaratta, Vic, 1845 E
Wanless, Ron 1941 E
Wantabadgery, NSW, 1866 F
War Cabinet, 1939 A
War Council, 1940 A
War govt, 1917 A
War Memorial, Canberra, 1941 F
War Pensions Act, 1914 A
War Precautions Act, Cwlth, 1914 A, 1919 A
War Profiteering Act, 1917 A
War Service Home Scheme, 1919 F
War Service Land Settlement Agreement Act, 1945 A
Waratah, 1909 F
Waratah, Tas, 1871 F, 1878 B
Waratah Festival Art competition, Sydney, 1961 C
Waratahs (football team), 1927 E
Warburton, Vic, 1864 F
Warburton, Doreen, 1930 C
Warburton, Peter E. 1813 A, 1858 A, 1872 A, 1873 A
Warburton R., SA, 1884 A
Warby, Kenneth, 1939 F, 1977 E, 1978 E
Ward, Arthur, 1920 E
Ward, Edward J. 1899 A, 1942 A
Ward, Frederick ('Thunderbolt'), 1835 A
Ward, Frederick W. 1847 F, 1927 F
Ward, Hugh J. 1871 C
Ward, John, 1980 B
Ward, Russel, 1958 C
Ward, William H. 1867 A, 1908 A
Wardell, Robert, 1794 A, 1824 A, F, 1826 F
Wardell, R. W. 1867 E
Wardell, William W. 1823 C, 1858 C
Wardlan, Chris, 1976 E
Wardle, T. E. 1965 C

Wardley, Debbie, 1980 B
Wards of the State, NT, 1953 A
Ware, Norman, 1941 E
Warehouses, Sydney, 1803 A
Warfe, George R. 1912 A
Warialda, NSW, 1849 F
Warne-Smith, Ivor, 1897 E, 1926 E, 1928 E
Warner, Dennis A. 1917 C
Warner, Ralph M. 1902 C
Waroona, WA, 1895 B, 1899 F
Warracknabeal, Vic, 1870 F
Warragamba, NSW, 1948 F
Warragamba Dam, NSW, 1960 B
Warragul, Vic, 1865 F
Warrandyte, Vic, 1965 C
Warrego, 1911 A
Warren, NSW, 1861 F, 1882 B
Warren, Alan E. 1919 C
Warren, Graham, 1928 E
Warren, Guy W. 1921 C
Warren, John, 1836 A
Warren, Johnny, 1943 E
Warren, Robin, 1984 B
Warren, Walter H. 1852 B, 1918 B
Warrigal Trainer aircraft, 1929 B
Warringah Art Prizes, NSW, 1956 C
Warringah Freeway, Sydney, 1968 B
Warrior, 1869 E
Warrnambool, Vic, 1847 F, 1872 F, 1886 F, 1888 F
Warrnambool–Melbourne road cycling race, 1895 E
Warrnambool Art Gallery, Vic, 1888 C
Warrnambool Technical School, Vic, 1913 D
Warung, Price, *see* Astley, William
Warwick, Qld, 1848 F, 1874 D, 1917 A, 1930 E
Warwick egg incident, 1917 A
Warwick Farm horse racing course, Sydney, 1923 E
Washing machines, electric, 1910 F
Washington Naval Treaty, 1924 A
Watcher on the Cast Iron Balcony, The, 1963 C
Watchmen, 1796 A
Waten, Judah, 1911 C, 1952 C, 1954 C
Water bores, NSW, 1878 B
Water conservation, 1944 B
Water fluoridation, 1953 B
Water meter, 1910 B
Water police, Sydney, 1847 A
Water polo, 1888 E, 1922 E, 1948 E, 1952 E
Water restrictions, 1966 F, 1967 F
Water skiing, 1918 E, 1933 E, 1936 E, 1946 E, 1952 E, 1963 E, 1969 E, 1971 E, 1978 E
Water speed record, 1964 E
Water sterilization, Vic, 1926 B
Water supplies, 1837 B, 1857 B, 1860 B, 1903 B, 1948 F, 1963 B, 1966 B
Water Under the Bridge, 1978 C
'Waterfall Front' houses, 1938 C
Waterfield, William, 1795 D, 1838 D
Waterfront, 1984 C
Waterfront workers, 1942 A
Waterhouse, George M. 1824 A, 1861 A
Waterhouse, Gustav A. 1877 B
Waterhouse, Henry, 1794 A, 1795 A, 1797 A, 1812 A
Waterhouse, Phyllis P. 1917 C
Waterhouse, W. L. 1945 B
Waterloo veterans relief fund, 1816 F
Watermelon, seed spitting, 1970 F
Waterside unionists, 1890 A
Waterside workers, Sydney, 1900 A

Waterside Workers' Federation, 1902 A, 1927 A
Waterside workers' strikes, 1950 A, 1956 A
Waterside Workers' Union, Melbourne, 1885 A
Waterson, Alan, 1912 E
Watkins, John S. 1866 C
Watkins, Richard J. 1937 C, 1963 C
Watkins, Susan, 1912 B
Watkiss, John, 1941 E
Watling, Thomas, 1792 C, 1794 C, 1814 C
Watsford, John, 1820 D
Watson, Archibald A. 1849 B
Watson, Colin, 1925 E
Watson, Edward A. D. 1920 C
Waston, Irvine A. 1914 B
Watson, Jack, 1896 A
Watson, James D. 1913 C
Watson, James F. W. 1878 B
Watson, John, 1834 F
Watson, John C. 1867 A, 1901 A, 1904 A
Watson, Mary B. P. 1860 F
Watson, Rhonda, 1934 E
Watson, Richard C. 1902 C
Watson, Robert (1), 1811 A, 1819 A
Watson, Robert (2), 1881 B
Watson Roslyn, 1979 C
Watson, HMAS, 1943 D
Watt, Walter O. 1878 A
Watt, William A. 1871 A, 1912 A, 1913 A
Wattamolla, NSW, 1796 A
Watters, Max, 1936 C
Watters Art Gallery, Sydney, 1965 C
Wattle bark, 1819 B
Wattle Park Palais de Danse, Melbourne, 1923 C
Wattle Park Teachers College, Adelaide, 1957 D
Watts, Henry, 1838 A
Watts, James L. 1849 C
Watts, John, 1815 B, 1816 C
Watts, Terry, 1934 C
Watts, William, 1838 B
Wauchope, NSW, 1837 F
Waugh, Hal, 1941 C
Wave Hill Station, NT, 1966 A, 1967 A
Way, James, 1850 D
Way, Samuel J. 1836 A, 1877 A, 1883 A, 1889 A, 1895 A, 1897 A, 1898 A, 1902 A, 1909 A, 1914 A
Ways and Means, 1920 C
Wayside Chapel, Sydney, 1964 D
We are Going, 1964 C
We of the Never Never, 1908 C, 1982 C
We Were The Rats, 1944 C
Weapons, 1939 B
Wearing, Benny, 1900 E
Weather, World Watch, 1968 B, 1979 B
Weather Bureaus, 1856 B, 1887 B
Weather charts, NSW, 1877 B
Weather forecasting, 1923 B, 1942 B
Weather observation 1856 B
Weather patterns, 1912 B
Weather telephone service, Melbourne, 1957 F
Weaver, Jacki, 1947 C
Webb, Archibald B. 1887 C
Webb, Charles, 1883 C
Webb, Chris, 1907 E
Webb, Francis C. 1925 C, 1948 C
Webb, George A. J. 1861 C
Webb, Len, 1974 C
Webb, Vivian P. 1892 C
Webb, William F. 1887 A, 1946 A
Webber, Henry, 1798 C, 1826 C
Weber, Clarence, 1882 E
Webster, W. 1793 D
Weddell, Ronald, 1926 C

831

Weddell, R. H. 1927 A, 1931 A
Wedderburn, Vic, 1980 F
Wedge, John H. 1792 A, 1835 A
Wee Waa, NSW, 1854 F
Weekend trading, NSW, 1979 A
Weekly Times, Vic, 1869 F
Weevils, 1981 B
Wege, William, 1920 B
Weideman, Murray, 1936 E
Weigall, Albert B. 1840 D
Weigall, William E. G. A. 1920 A
Weight lifting, 1945 E, 1978 E
Weights and measures, metric, 1967 A
Weipa, Qld, 1953 B, 1955 B, 1957 F, 1962 B, 1963 B
Weir, Peter L. 1944 C, 1974 C, 1975 C, 1977 C, 1981 C
Weise, Barbara, 1980 A
Weitzell, Frank, 1902 C
Welch, Garth de B. 1936 C, 1962 C
Welch, Kenyon St V. 1928 B
Welch, Robert P. 1840 C
'Welcome Nugget', 1858 F
'Welcome Stranger', 1869 F
Weld, Frederick A. 1823 A, 1869 A, 1875 A
Weld Club, 1871 F
Welfare, 1969 A, 1971 A, 1973 A, *see also* Benefits *and* Social service
Welfare Agreement, Aust-N.Z., 1944 A
Weller, Archie, 1981 C
Wellington, 1826 F
Wellington, NSW, 1823 A, F
Wellington Caves, NSW, 1831 B, 1869 B
Wellington Tourist Festival Art Prize, NSW, 1962 C
Wellington Valley, NSW, 1838 B
Wells, Lawrence A. 1860 A, 1896 A
Wells, Thomas, 1818 C, 1833 A
Wells, Thomas G. 1934 C
Wenban, Ebenezer, 1862 C
Wenden, Michael, 1951 E
Wentcher, Julius, 1888 C
Wentcher, Tina, 1887 C
Wentworth, D'Arcy, 1810 A, 1819 B, 1827 B
Wentworth, NSW, 1859 F
Wentworth, SA, 1867 B
Wentworth, William C. (b. 1793), 1793 A, 1813 A, 1819 C, 1823 C, 1824 A, F, 1825 A, 1835 A, 1853 A
Wentworth, William C. (b. 1907) 1907 A
Wentworth Park, Sydney, 1953 E
'Wep', *see* Pidgeon, William Edwin, 1909 C
Werder, Felix, 1922 C
Were, Johnathan, B. 1809 A
Werner, Alice, 1859 C
Werner, Richard, 1932 C
Werris Creek, NSW, 1876 F
Werther, Frank, 1922 C
Wesley-Smith, Martin, 1945 C
Wesley College, Melbourne, 1865 D
Wesleyan Church, 1812 D, *see* Methodist church
West, Claude, 1915 E
West, John, 1809 D, 1851 A, 1852 C
West, Morris L. 1916 C, 1945 C, 1959 C, 1963 C, 1965 C, 1968 C, 1983 C
West, T. J. 1906 C
West Australian, 1833 F
West Australian Times, 1830 F
West End Brewery, 1876 A
West Maitland High School, NSW, 1855 D
West New Guinea, 1903 A
West Wyalong, NSW, 1893 F
Westall, William, 1801 C, 1804 C, 1850 C
Westbrook, Dawn F. 1932 C

Westbrook, Eric E. 1915 C
Westbury, Alan, 1916 E
Westbury, Tas, 1828 F
Westcourt, 1917 E
Westerly (quarterly), Perth, 1962 C
Western Australia/n, *abbreviated as* WA
first settlement, 1826 A
WA Academy of Performing Arts, 1979 D
WA Airways, 1921 B, 1936 B
WA Art Gallery, 1895 C, 1979 C
WA Ballet Co., 1952 C, 1962 C
WA Board of Secondary Education, 1970 D
WA Botanic Gardens, Perth, 1965 B
WA Bushfires Board, 1954 F
WA Company, 1839 A, 1841 A
WA Country Party, 1913 A, 1914 A
WA Employers' Federation, 1913 A
WA Farmers' and Settlers' Association, 1912 A, 1913 A
WA Firebrigades Board, 1898 F
WA Football Association, 1885 E
WA goldfields Water Supply Scheme, 1903 B
WA Hunt Club, 1896 E
WA Mining Co., 1846 A
Western Australian Monthly Magazine, 1843 F
WA Museum, 1892 D, 1897 D
WA named, 1829 A
WA National Football League, 1885 E
WA Natural History and Science Society, 1897 B, 1914 B
WA Naturalists' Club, 1924 B
WA Plebiscite, 1950 A
WA Public Library, 1899 D, 1955 D
WA Representative govt, 1870 A, 1890 A
WA Rowing Club, 1868 E
WA School of Mines, 1903 D
WA Secessionist Movement, 1930 A, 1933 A, 1935 A, 1974 A
WA Secondary Teachers' College, 1967 D
WA settlement, 1826 A, 1829 A
WA Society of Arts and Crafts, 1896 C
WA State Shipping Service, 1912 A
WA Steam Navigation Co., 1886 B
WA Symphony Orchestra, 1950 C, 1955 C, 1965 C, 1971 C, 1974 C, 1975 C
WA Turf Club, 1852 E
Western Institute of Art, Perth, 1920 C
Western Mail, Perth, 1885 F
Western Mining Corporation, 1966 B, 1977 B
Western Pacific High Commission, 1875 A
Western Plains Zoo, NSW, 1977 B
Western Suburbs Rugby League Football Club/team, 1908 E, 1930 E, 1934 E, 1948 E, 1952 E
Western Teachers' College, Adelaide, 1962 D
Westernport, Vic, 1797 A, 1798 A, 1801 A, 1804 A, 1826 B, 1827 A, 1828 A, 1840 A
Westgarth, William, 1815 A
Westgate Bridge, Melbourne, 1965 B, 1970 F, 1978 F
Westinghouse radio, 1937 B
Weston, Harry J. 1874 C
Weston, NSW, 1903 F
Weston, William P. 1804 A, 1857 A, 1860 A
Westpac Banking Corporation, 1982 A
Westralian Modern Music Club, 1934 C
Westward, 1947 E, 1948 E
Westwood, Neville R. 1925 F
Westwood, William, 1820 A

Wetherbys, The, 1853 C
Whalan, Charles, 1838 A
Whale, record size, 1910 F
Whale Fishery hotel, Tas, 1807 F
Whales, Humpback, 1963 A
Whaling, 1791 A, 1798 A, 1799 A, 1803 A, 1805 A, 1806 A, 1813 A, 1829 A, 1830 A, 1831 A, 1833 A, 1841 A, 1843 A, 1845 A, 1861 A, 1891 B, F, 1978 A, 1982 A
Wharf labourers' strikes, 1882 A, 1886 A
Wharves, 1803 A, 1813 B, 1880 A, *see also individual entries*
What Bird is That?, 1931 C
Wheare, Kenneth C. 1907 A
Wheat,
Aust. Wheat Board, 1939 A
breeding, 1886 B
bulk handling, 1920 B
crisis, 1968 A
exports, 1904 A, 1961 A, 1972 A, 1980 A
Federation, 1901 B
first harvests, 1789 A, 1802 A, 1879 A
Gabo, 1945 B
prices, 1806 A
production, 1793 A, 1801 A, 1820 A, 1916 A
marketing standard, 1888 A
Nabawa, 1923 B
pickler, 1915 B
quotas, 1915 A
rust, 1868 B, 1890 B
value, 1974 A
Wheat Marketing Scheme, Cwlth, 1915 A
Wheatley, Kevin A. 1937 A
Wheeler, Charles A. 1881 C, 1933 C
Whelan, Marcus, 1939 E
When Blackbirds Sing, 1963 C
When a Girl Marries, 1946 C
When I was King, 1905 C
When the Rain Tumbles Down in July (song), 1946 C
Where the Dead Men Lie and other Poems, 1897 C
Wherrett, Richard, 1940 C
While the Billy Boils, 1896 C
Whimmen, George, 1891 C
Whiskey a Go Go, Brisbane, 1973 F
Whispers in the Forest, 1975 C
Whisson, Kenneth R. 1926 C
White, Alfred E. R. 1876 B
White, Andrew, 1788 F
White, C. B. B. 1876 A
White, Cecil ('Unk'), 1900 C
White, Cyril L. 1894 C
White, Cyril T. 1890 B
White, Frederic, 1833 C
White, George, 1818 B
White, Gilbert (1), 1842 A
White, Gilbert (2), 1859 D
White, Harold L. 1905 D
White, Harry, 1944 E, 1974 E, 1975 E, 1978 E, 1979 E
White, Henry L. 1860 A
White, James (b. 1828), 1828 A
White, James (b. 1862), 1862 C, 1903 C
White, Jeff, 1950 E
White, John (1), 1788 B, 1790 C, 1832 B
White, John (2), 1854 C
White, John (3), 1949 B
White, John C. 1836 D
White, Laurence O. C. 1914 C
White, Patrick, 1912 C, 1935 C, 1939 C, 1947 C, 1948 C, 1955 C, 1957 C, 1961 C, 1966 C, 1973 C, 1976 C, 1977 C, 1981 C

White, Paul H. H. 1910 C
White, Samuel, 1835 B
White, T. 1983 A
White, Vera, 1891 F
White Aust. campaign, 1978 A
White Australia Policy, 1888 A, 1901 A
White Cliffs, NSW, 1880 B, 1890 F
White Nile, The, 1960 C
White Nose, 1931 E
White Studio Gallery of Modern Art, Adelaide, 1964 C
White With Wire Wheels, 1967 C
Whitechapel Exhibition, London, 1961 C
Whiteford, Doug, 1915 E
Whitehead, John, 1814 A
Whitelaw, Alfred P. 1870 B
Whitelegge, Thomas, 1850 B
Whiteley, Brett, 1939 C, 1976 C, 1978 C
Whiteside, Peter, 1973 B
Whitfeld, Hubert E. 1875 B
Whiting, Ada, 1858 C
Whiting, Lorraine, 1927 C
Whitlam, Edward Gough, 1916 A, 1952 A, 1967 A, 1971 A, 1972 A, 1975 A, 1977 A, 1978 A
Whitney, William M. 1880 C
Whittell, Hubert M. 1883 B
Whitten, Edward, 1933 E
Whittle, Sgt., 1803 F
Whitton, Ivo, 1892 E, 1931 E
Whitton, John, 1819 B
Whitworth, R. P. 1860 C
Who Can It Be Now, 1981 C
Who's Who in Australia, 1922 C
Whooping cough, 1828 F
Whyalla, SA, 1899 B, 1913 F, 1937 B, 1940 F, 1941 B, 1962 B, 1965 B, 1967 B, 1982 A
Whyalla News, SA, 1940 F
Whyalla pig iron blast furnace, SA, 1937 B
Whyalla steel works, SA, 1965 B
Whyalla Technical High School, SA, 1943 D
Whyte, James, 1820 A, 1863 A
Wickepin, WA, 1894 F
Wickham, Alick, 1886 E, 1897 E
Wickham, John C. 1798 A
Wickham, Tracey, 1962 E, 1978 E
Wickham, WA, 1971 F
Wicko FW1, 1936 B
Widgeon Amphibian aircraft, 1929 B
Widgiemooltha, WA, 1900 F, 1931 F
Widows' pensions benefit allowance, 1942 A
Widow's Victim, The, 1842 C
Widows' pensions, NSW, 1925 A
Wienholt, Arnold, 1877 A
Wigley, James, 1918 C
Wigzell, Bill, 1927 E
Wikner, Geoffrey N. 1904 B
Wilberforce, NSW, 1810 F
Wilbur Wright bi-plane, 1909 B
Wilcannia, NSW, 1864 F
Wilcox, Mary T. J. 1873 C
Wilcurra Homestead, NSW, 1972 F
Wild, Joseph, 1820 A, 1847 A
Wild Cat Falling, 1955 C
Wild Men of Sydney, 1958 C
Wild Notes from ... a Native Minstrel, 1826 C
Wild River National Park, Tas, 1980 F
'Wild Scotsman', *see* McPherson, Alpin, 1841 A
Wilder-Neligan, Maurice, 1882 A
Wilding, Michael, 1942 C, 1972 C, 1974 C
Wild Life Preservation Society, Qld, 1963 F

Wild Life Preservation Society of Aust., 1909 F, 1964 B
Wilfred Thomas Dinner Show, 1941 F
Wilgie Art Club, Perth, 1890 C
Wilkes, Gerald A. 1927 C
Wilkes Antarctic station, 1959 B
Wilkie, Alan, 1915 C
Wilkie, David E. 1815 B
Wilkie, Leslie A. 1879 C
Wilkins, George H. 1888 A, 1912 B, 1928 B
Wilkins, William, 1827 D, 1851 D, 1874 D
Wilkinson, Andrew ('Bluey'), 1911 E, 1938 E
Wilkinson, Kenneth, 1950 C
Wilkinson, Leslie, 1882 C, 1918 C
Willandra Lakes, NSW, 1982 F
Willard-Mathews, Marlene, 1934 E, 1958 E
Willcock, John C. 1879 A, 1936 A
Willemering, 1790 A
William Irvine, 1932 C
William Powell Home for Discharged Prisoners, Brisbane, 1922 D
Williams, Bruce R., 1979 D
Williams, Dudley, 1940 A
Williams, Edward S. 1921 A, 1982 A
Williams, Francis E. 1893 B
Williams, Frederick R. 1927 C, 1964 C
Williams, George, 1895 C
Williams, Harold, 1893 C
Williams, Harry (b. 1915), 1915 E
Williams, Harry (b. 1950), 1950 E, 1970 E
Williams, James, 1796 A, 1822 A
Williams, John, 1941 C
Williams, J. D. 1909 C
Williams, J. T. 1888 E
Williams, Leo, 1961 F
Williams, Merv, 1902 E
Williams, Mrs, 1806 D
Williams, Rhys, 1894 C
Williams, Richard, 1890 A, 1914 D, 1921 A
Williams, Thomas, 1804 F
Williams, Tommy, 1870 E
Williams, Verdon, 1969 C
Williams, WA, 1850 F
Williamson, Bill, 1923 E, 1952 E
Williamson, David K. 1942 C, 1971 C, 1972 C
Williamson, James C. 1845 C, 1874 C, 1879 C, 1882 C, 1888 C, 1889 C, 1897 C, 1901 C, 1907 C, 1911 C, 1920 C, 1955 C
Williamson, J. 1883 E
Williamson, Malcolm B. G. C. 1931 C, 1975 C
Williamstown, Melbourne, 1835 A, 1852 F, 1857 F
Williamstown Observatory, Melbourne, 1853 B
Williamtown, NSW, 1961 B
Willis, Dixie, 1942 E
Willis, E. A. 1976 A
Willis, John W. 1841 A
Willis, Matthew, 1811 C
Willoughby, Howard, 1839 F
Wills, Horatio S. H. 1811 A
Wills, H. O. 1960 C
Wills, Thomas W. 1835 E, 1858 E
Wills, William J. 1834 A, 1860 A, 1861 A, 1863 A
Wills, W. D. 1960 C
Wills Art Prize, Sydney, 1960 C
Willson, Robert W. 1794 D, 1844 D
Wilmot, Frank L. T. 1881 C, 1920 C, 1934 C

Wilmot, Reginald W. W. 1911 C
Wilsmore, Norman T. M. 1868 B
Wilson, A. 1922 E, 1923 E
Wilson, Anne, 1848 C
Wilson, Arthur M. 1888 B
Wilson, Betty, 1949 E
Wilson, Brian, 1982 E
Wilson, David, 1947 C
Wilson, Dora L. 1883 C
Wilson, Edward, 1813 F, 1857 B
Wilson, Eric, 1911 C
Wilson, Florence, 1894 C
Wilson, Frank, 1859 A, 1910 A, 1916 A
Wilson, Geoffrey R. 1927 C
Wilson, J. H. 1866 C
Wilson, James, 1839 D
Wilson, James M. 1812 A, 1869 A
Wilson, John (1), 1798 A
Wilson, John (2), 1930 C
Wilson, Leslie O. 1932 A, 1937 A
Wilson, Peter, 1947 E
Wilson, Roland, 1904 A
Wilson, Ronald, 1979 A
Wilson, Samuel, 1832 A, 1877 A
Wilson, William H. 1881 C, 1920 C, 1924 C
Wilson, W. 1873 E
Wilson's Promontory, Vic, 1798 A, 1800 A
Wilton, John G. N. 1910 A
Wiltshire, William P. 1807 C
Wiltshire Committee of Enquiry, 1969 D
Wiluna, WA, 1906 A, 1972 B
Wimbledon tennis, 1877 E, 1907 E, 1914 E, 1956 E, 1957 E, 1963 E, 1968 E
Wimmera, Vic, 1919 B, 1979 B
Wimpy hamburger, 1971 F
Winchelsea, Vic, 1837 A, 1859 B
Wind speed, record, 1975 F
Windarra, WA, 1969 B
Windbag (horse), 1925 E
Windeyer, Archibald, 1870 A
Windeyer, Brian W. 1904 B
Windeyer, Charles, 1855 A, 1879 A
Windeyer, John C. 1875 B
Windeyer, Richard, 1806 A
Windeyer, Victor, 1958 A
Windeyer, William C. 1834 A
Windeyer, William J. V. 1900 A
Windich, Tommy, 1840 A
Windle, Robert, 1944 E
Windmills, flour grinding, 1795 B
Windmills, water pumping, 1885 B
Windon, Colin, 1921 E
Windows, glass, 1881 C
Windows, sound proof, 1939 B
Windows, zinc, 1885 C
Windsor, Harry, 1968 B
Windsor, NSW, 1794 F, 1802 D, 1810 F, 1813 B, 1817 D, 1819 A, 1864 B, 1874 F
Windsor Hotel, Melbourne, 1883 C
Windsurfing, 1976 E, 1977 E, 1980 E, 1983 E
Wine, 1801 B, 1823 A, 1827 A, 1832 A, 1834 A, 1838 A, 1843 A, 1857 A, 1863 A, 1924 A, 1929 A, 1931 A, 1973 F, *see also* Vines, Vineyards
Wine, Overseas Marketing Board, 1929 A
Wineries, *see individual entries*
Winged Seeds, 1950 C
Wingham, NSW, 1843 F
Winkler, Geoffrey, 1936 B
Winnecke, Charles, 1884 A
Winneke, Henry A. 1908 A, 1974 A
Winser, Legh, 1884 E
Winstanley, Edward, 1820 C
Winstanley, Eliza, 1818 C

Winston, Arthur D. 1908 C
Winston Churchill Memorial Trust, 1965 D
Winter, A. W. 1894 E
Winter, John A. 1924 E
Winterbottom, J. 1853 C
Wintergarten theatre, Brisbane, 1924 C
Winton, Qld, 1816 F, 1876 F, 1895 C, 1920 B, 1922 B, 1966 F
Wireless, 1901 B, 1904 B, 1906 B, 1911 B, 1919 B, 1921 B, 1925 B, 1927 B, see also Pedal wireless, Radio
Wireless Institute of Aust., 1910 B
Wireless Telegraphy Act, Federal, 1905 B
Wirraway No. 1, 1939 B
Wirth, Philip P. J. 1864 F
Wisdom, Evan A. 1869 A
Wise, F. J. S. 1945 A, 1951 A
Wiseman, J. 1846 B
Wiseman, Solomon, 1838 A
Wishart, James, 1810 A
Witches Fall (park), 1908 F
Witcombe, Eleanor, 1923 C
Withers, Georgette L. 1917 C
Withers, Margery P. 1894 C
Withers, Senator, 1978 A
Withers, Walter H. 1854 C
Withnall, G. 1949 B
Withnell, Emma M. 1842 A
Wittenoom, Edward H. 1854 A
Wittenoom, John B. 1788 D, 1830 D
Wittenoom, WA, 1938 B, 1947 F
'Wobblies', 1907 A, 1916 A, 1918 A
Wodalla, 1953 E
Wodonga, Vic, 1852 F, 1873 B, 1883 B, 1943 F
Woess, Kurt, 1956 C
Wokalup, WA, 1920 F
Wolf Cubs, Sydney, 1915 F
Wolff, Albert A. 1951 A, 1973 A
Wolff, William, 1904 C
Wolinski, Joseph, 1872 C
Wollaston, John R. 1791 D
Wollomai, 1875 E
Wollombi, NSW, 1835 F
Wollongong, NSW, 1816 F, 1855 F, 1865 B, 1876 D, 1968 F
Wollongong Art Prize, NSW, 1956 C
Wollstonecraft, Edward, 1822 A, 1832 A
Wolseley, Frederick Y. 1837 B, 1872 B, 1877 B
Wolstenholme, Guy, 1931 E
Woman to Man, 1949 C
Woman's Day, 1956 F
Woman's Love, 1832 C
Women, see also individual entries
  advancement of, 1896 A
  Advisory Councils, 1923 A, 1978 A
  Air Force, 1941 A
  Amalgamated Workers' Union, 1892 A
  Business women of the year, see each year section F from 1978
  equal pay, 1969 A, 1972 A
  in law, 1902 A, 1903 A, 1918 A, 1923 A, 1962 A, 1965 A
  married, employment, 1966 A
  in ministry, 1968 D
  Parlt representation, 1894 A, see also Parlt, *individual entries*
  police, 1915 A, see also Police
  public bars, 1965 F
  rights, 1870 A, 1874 D, 1880 D, 1881 D, see also individual entries
  smoking, 1922 F
  sports, see *individual entries and section E*
  suffrage, 1894 A, see also Suffrage
  University of Melbourne, 1874 D

University graduates, 1883 D, 1894 D
wages, 1919 A, 1958 A
Women's Amateur Athletic Associations, 1929 E
Women's Auxiliary Aust. Air Force, 1941 A
Women's Christian Temperance Union, Sydney, 1882 F
Women's Council, 1923 A
Women's Electoral Lobby, Melbourne, 1972 A
Women's Exposé, 1909 C
Women's Literary Society, Sydney, 1889 C
Women's Status Act, 1918 A
Women's Weekly, 1953 F
Women's Weekly Portrait Prize, Sydney, 1955 C
Wondai, Qld, 1900 F
Wongan Hills, WA, 1904 F
Wonthaggi, Vic, 1909 B, F, 1931 F, 1937 F, 1984 C
Wood, Edward, 1805 A
Wood, Eleanor S. 1871 A
Wood, furniture, 1940 F
Wood, George A. 1865 D
Wood, Gordon L. 1890 A
Wood, Graeme, 1956 E
Wood, Isaac, 1815 D
Wood J. C. 1855 D
Wood, Marshall, 1882 C
Wood, Mervyn T. 1917 E
Wood, Noel, 1912 C
Wood, Thomas, 1933 C
Wood paving blocks, 1880 B
Woodburn, NSW, 1869 F, 1881 A
Woodbury, Walter B. 1850 B
Woodchip industry, NSW, 1968 A
Woodchopping, 1870 E, 1874 E, 1891 E, 1903 E, 1963 E, 1970 E
Woodcock, Tommy, 1905 E
Woodend, Vic, 1855 F
Woodfull, William F. 1897 E
Woodhouse, Frederick, 1820 C
Woodley, Bruce, 1942 C
Woods, E. J. 1879 C, 1889 C
Woods, Frank, 1907 D
Woods, Tony, 1940 C
Woodside, SA, 1850 F
Woodside Petroleum Ltd, 1971 B
Woodstock, Qld, 1865 F
Woodville, Adelaide, SA, 1917 B
Woodward, Albert E. 1972 A
Woodward, Bernard H. 1847 C
Woodward, Eric W. 1899 A, 1957 A
Woodward, P. 1910 B
Woodward, Roger, 1942 C
Woodward and Taranto, 1961 C
Woodward Report, 1974 A
Wool, see also Sheep
  Anlaby, 1856 B
  auctions, 1821 A, 1843 A, 1970 A
  Aust. Wool Board, 1936 A
  awards, 1822 A
  classers, 1805 A
  exports, 1800 A, 1807 A, 1811 A, 1813 A, 1832 A, 1834 A, 1853 A, 1871 A, 1874 A, 1875 A, 1972 A
  floor price, 1974 A
  import duty, 1819 A
  industry, 1801 A, 1820 A, 1832 A, 1833 A, 1835 A, 1848 A,
  presses, 1865 B
  prices, 1827 A, 1890 A, 1951 A, 1953 A, 1965 A, 1970 A
  production, 1801 A, 1906 A, 1943 A, 1976 A
  river transport, 1859 B

  sales, 1804 A, 1891 A, 1946 A, 1951 A, 1971 A
  strike, 1980 A
  value, 1974 A
Woolgoolga, NSW, 1888 F
Woollahra, Sydney, 1856 C
Woollen cloth, Vic, 1868 A
Woollen and Cloth Manufacturing Co., 1868 A
Woollen Mills, 1803 A, 1815 A
Woolley, John, 1816 D
Woolls, William, 1814 B
Woolner, Thomas, 1825 C, 1879 C
Woolnough, Walter G. 1876 B
Woolstore workers' strike, NSW, Vic, 1980 A
Woolworths Ltd, 1924 A, 1933 A, 1980 F, 1981 F
Woombye, Qld, 1870 F
Woomera, SA, 1946 B, 1947 F, 1957 B, 1959 B, 1964 B, 1967 B
Woomera rocket range, SA, 1948 B
Wootten, George F. 1893 E
Wootten, Stanley, 1894 E
Wootton, Frank, 1893 E
Worker, Brisbane, 1890 F
Workers' compensation, NSW, 1900 A, 1902 A, 1910 A
Workers' Educational Association, 1911 D, 1912 D
Workers' Industrial Union, 1919 A
Workers' Party, 1975 A
Workers' Political League, Tas, 1903 A
Workforce, 1942 A, 1954 A
Working Bullocks (book), 1926 C
Working hours, 1840 A, 1855 A, 1856 A, 1865 A, 1869 A, 1873 A, 1874 A, 1876 A, 1879 A, 1920 A, 1924 A, 1925 A, 1936 A, 1939 A, 1947 A, 1948 A, 1957 A, 1961 A, 1962 A, 1982 A
Working Men's Club, Mildura, Vic, 1938 F
Working Men's College, Sydney, 1878 D, Melbourne, 1881 D
Working Men's Technical College, Melbourne, 1887 D
Workingman's Paradise: An Australian Labour Novel, The, 1892 C
Workrooms and Factories Act, Vic, 1873 A
World champion, first Aust., 1876 E
World Council of Churches, 1980 D, 1981 D
World Council of Indigenous People, Canberra, 1981 A
World Series Cricket, 1977 E, 1979 E
World Cup, cricket, 1975 E
World Cup, soccer, 1965 E, 1974 E
World disarmament conference, Geneva, 1933 A
World economic conference, London, 1933 A
World Health Organisation, WHO, 1947 A
World Heritage Commission, 1974 A, 1981 F
World Heritage Conservation Bill, 1983 F
World Heritage Convention, 1982 F
World Heritage List, 1982 F
World Heritage: Register of the National Estate, 1981 F
World of Man, The, 1915 C
World is made of Glass, 1983 C
World Theatre Festival, USA, 1982 C
World War I, 1914 A, 1915 A, 1916 A, 1918 A
World War II, 1939 A, 1940 A, 1941 A,

1942 A, 1943 A, 1944 A, 1945 A, 1947 A, 1950 A
World Weather Watch, 1968 B, 1979 B
World Wildlife Fund Aust., 1978 F
'World's Greatest Circus Spectacular', 1983 F
Worrall, Henry, 1862 D
Worrall, John, 1863 E
Worrell, Eric, 1924 B, 1960 B
Worth, Barney, 1955 F
Wotan, 1936 E
Woureddy, 1836 C
'Wowser', 1899 F
Wragge, Clement L. 1852 B, 1887 B
Wran, Neville K. 1926 A, 1976 A, 1983 A
Wray, Leonora, 1886 E
Wray, W. 1900 C
Wreck Bay, NSW, 1870 F
Wren, John, 1871 E
Wrensford, Henry, 1816 D
Wrenfordsley, Henry T. 1883 A
WRESAT Satellite, 1967 B
Wrest Point Hotel-Casino, Hobart, 1973 F
Wrestling, 1874 E, 1880 E, 1885 E
Wright, David M. 1869 C
Wright, Dr. 1910 E
Wright, Edmund W. 1824 B, 1848 C, 1863 C, 1875 C
Wright, John C. 1889 C
Wright, Judith A. 1915 C, 1946 C, 1949 C, 1971 C
Wright, Kevin, 1953 E
Wright, Robert, 1952 B
Wright, Roy, 1929 E, 1952 E, 1954 E
Wright, Samuel, 1826 A
Wright, Sydney E. 1914 B
Wright, Thomas, 1830 C
Wrightson, Patrica, 1954 C
Wrigley, Henry N. 1892 A, 1919 B
Wroth, Ian C. 1927 C
Wunderly, Henry W. 1892 B
Wunderlich, Ernest H. C. 1859 C, 1885 C, 1890 C
Wundowie, WA, 1943 F
'WW' (Mrs Fortune), 1871 C
Wyalkatchen, WA, 1912 F
Wyatt, Joseph, 1838 C, 1855 C
Wyatt, William, 1804 B
Wyee, NSW, 1966 F
Wylde, John, 1816 A, 1859 A
Wylie, 1824 A
Wyndham, WA, 1886 F, 1921 B, 1980 F
Wyndham, George, 1828 A
Wyndham, H. S. 1956 D
Wyndham report, NSW, 1957 D, 1961 D
Wyndham Scheme, NSW, 1957 D, 1962 D
Wynn-Carrington, Charles R. 1843 A, 1885 A
Wynne, Richard, 1897 C
Wynne, Watkin, 1844 A
Wynne Art Prize, 1897 C
Wynyard, Edward B. 1788 A, 1847 A
Wynyard, Tas, 1841 F
Wyong, NSW, 1823 F
Wyselaskie, John D. 1818 A

X

X-ray, 1896 B
X-Ray and Radium Laboratory, 1929 B
X-Ray spectra, 1915 B
Xanthium spinosum, 1840 B
Xerographic process, 1907 B, 1952 B
Xiannian, Li, 1980 A
XPT passenger train, 1982 B

Y

Yachting, 1856 E, 1861 E, 1862 E, 1948 E, 1962 E, 1964 E, 1965 E, 1967 E
  Sydney to Hobart race *see each year section E from 1945 E*
Yachting, America's Cup, 1967 E, 1970 E, 1974 E, 1977 E, 1980 E
Yallah Native, 1979 E
Yallop, Graham, 1952 E, 1983 E
Yallourn, Vic, 1922 F, 1924 B, 1925 B, 1944 F
Yampi Sound, WA, 1951 B
Yan Yean dam, 1857 B
Yanco Agricultural College, NSW, 1909 D
Yanco Experimental Farm, NSW, 1921 B, 1924 A
Yandicoogina Creek, WA, 1979 B
Yankee Jack, 1842 A
Yarn, self twisting, 1961 B
Yarra, destroyer, 1910 A
Yarra Ranges, Vic, 1851 B
Yarra R., Melbourne, 1803 A, 1835 A, 1838 B, 1839 F, 1846 C, 1877 B, 1905 E
Yarra Sculptors' Society, 1898 C
Yarratribe, 1903 A
Yarralumla House, Canberra, 1891 C
Yarram, Vic, 1893 F
Yarraville, Vic, 1878 B
Yarrawonga, Vic, 1868 F
Yass, NSW, 1927 B
Yea, Vic, 1855 F
Yeates, Bronwyn J. D. 1923 C
Yeelirrie uranium, WA, 1972 B
Yellingbo, Vic, 1842 F
Yellow Cab taxis, 1924 F
Yellow cake, uranium, 1980 B, F, 1982 A
Yellow pages, 1975 F
'Yellow Peril', 1905 A
Yemmerrawannie, Aborigine, 1789 A, 1792 A, 1794 A
Yeoman, P. A. 1944 B
Yeomans, J. 1868 E
Yeppoon, Qld, 1865 F
Yeshivah Gedolah Rabbinical Academy, Melbourne, 1966 D
Yilgarn, WA, 1887 B
Yirrkala, NT, 1934 F
Yirrkala Aboriginals, NT, 1935 D, 1963 A, 1971 A
Yo yos, 1978 F
Yongala, 1911 F
Yorick Art Club and Prize, Melbourne, 1953 C
Yorick Club, Melbourne, 1868 C
York, WA, 1831 F, 1843 A, 1950 F
York, Duke of, 1927 A
Yorke Peninsula, SA, 1859 B, 1860 B, 1861 B
Yorketown, SA, 1870 F
You Can't See Round Corners, 1948 C
You and Me, 1919 F
Youd, Bill, 1970 E
Youl, James A. 1810 A, 1860 B
Young, NSW, 1860 A, B, 1861 A, F, 1977 B
Young, Charles H. F. 1819 C, 1843 C
Young, Edward, 1795 C

Young, Florence, 1871 C
Young, Guilford C. 1916 D
Young, Henry E. F. 1808 A, 1848 A, 1855 A
Young, Irene V. 1932 C
Young, Jack, 1925 E, 1951 E, 1952 E
Young, Jeanne F. 1876 A
Young, John (b. 1807), 1807 A, 1861 A
Young, John (b. 1827), 1882 C
Young, Johnny, 1971 C
Young, Michael, 1945 C
Young, Mick, 1983 C, 1984 A
Young, Norman, 1880 C
Young, Robert ('Nat'), 1950 E, 1966 E
Young, William B. 1862 C
Young, William J. 1905 E
Young Aust. League, WA, 1905 F
Young Cherry Festival Art Prize, NSW, 1962 C
Young Desire It, The, 1937 C
Young and Jackson's Hotel, Melbourne, 1880 C
Young Men's Christian Association ('YMCA'), 1850 D, 1884 D
Young Talent Time, 1971 C
Young Wife, The, 1962 C
Young Women's Christian Association ('YWCA'), 1872 F, 1880 D
Younger Group, Sydney, 1924 C
Youth Concerts, 1947 C
Youth Hostels Association of Aust., 1939 F
Youth Soccer, 1983 E
Ypres offensive, 1917 A
Yugoslavia, 1970 A
Yule, John, 1923 C
Yunupingu, Galarrwuy, 1978 A
Yuranigh, 1850 A

Z

Z Force, 1943 A
Zambia, 1979 A
Zampatti, Carla, 1980 F
Zebu, dairy cattle, 1872 B, 1956 B
Zeehan, Tas, 1892 B, 1898 F, 1981 F
Zelman, Alberto, 1874 C, 1906 C
Zelman, Victor, 1877 C
Zeus II, 1981 E
Ziegler car, 1894 B
Zig Zag railway, 1869 B
Zikaras, Teisutis, 1922 C
Zimbabwe-Rhodesia, 1979 A
Zinc, 1883 B, 1885 B, 1900 B, 1904 B, 1910 B, 1912 B, 1917 B, 1939 B
Zinc windows, 1885 C
Zinnemann, Frank, 1960 C
Zoological gardens,
  Perth, 1898 B
  Sydney, 1884 B
Zoological Society of NSW, 1879 B
Zoology, 1923 B, 1931 B
Zoos, 1848 B, 1850 B, 1853 B, 1862 B, 1883 B, 1912 B, 1916 B, 1977 B
Zulu, 1881 E
Zusters, Reinis, 1918 C